10-27	Building, $2,543,300
10-28	(a) $96,000 allocated to Land
10-29	(b) Year 2, $23,400; (c) year 2, $21,250
10-30	No key figure
10-31	19X3 depreciation, $2,220
10-32	(a) 19X3 depreciation, $4,800
10-33	(b) 19X2 reduction in tax payment, $5,130
10-27A	Land, $239,400
10-28A	(a) $36,800 allocated to Trucks
10-29A	(b) 19X3, $15,600; (c) 19X3, $13,500
10-31A	19X5 depreciation, $2,670
10-32A	(b) $27,525

Business Decision Problem No key figure

11-27	(d) Loss on sale of plant assets, $6,000
11-28	No key figure
11-29	(b) $22,000
11-30	No key figure
11-31	(b) Leasehold improv. amort. expense, $150
11-32	Total assets, $671,000
11-27A	(f) Theft loss, $4,175
11-28A	No key figure
11-29A	(c) $103,500
11-31A	No key figure
11-32A	Total assets, $1,510,000

Business Decision Problem Recommended purchase price, $2,000,000

12-24	(a) $3,500
12-25	(a) Payroll payable, $80,570
12-26	Sales tax liability, $5,040
12-27	(a) Payroll payable, $63,360
12-28	(a) Total net earnings, $1,360.73
12-24A	(a) $2,180
12-25A	(a) Payroll payable, $48,500
12-26A	Sales tax liability, $9,240
12-27A	(a) Payroll payable, $35,030
12-28A	(a) Total net earnings, $1,178.20

Business Decision Problem No key figure

13-24	No key figure
13-25	(a) Mar., $750; Apr., $3,400; May, $2,050 loss
13-26	(b)(2) 19X8, $24,000
13-27	(b)(2) 19X2, $5,800,000
13-28	Net income, $42,400
13-29	No key figure
13-30	No key figure
13-31	(a) $14,000
13-24A	No key figure
13-27A	(b)(2) 19X4, $1,750,000
13-28A	Net income, $70,575
13-29A	No key figure
13-31A	(a) $8,000

Business Decision Problem 19X1 revenue, $116,800

14-26	(a)(3) Credits to capital: Hall, $8,000; Mills, $4,000
14-27	(a)(3) Credits to capital: Moss, $3,750; Todd, $3,750; Hall, $7,500
14-28	(c) Credits to capital: Dorth, $3,000; Nunn, $3,000; Boen, $12,000
14-29	(c) Debits to capital: Victor, $40,000; Stedd, $3,000; Dobbs, $3,000
14-30	(b) Capital balances: Goss, $18,000; Carr, $12,000
14-31	Ending capital balances: Anson, $37,000; Ford, $25,000; Pratt, $0
14-32	(a) Cash distribution: Foe, $10,000; Gahn, $37,000; Hoxx, $18,000
14-33	(b)(4) Cash distribution: Boa, $39,250; Domm, $7,750

14-26A	(a)(3) Credits to capital: Barr, $7,500; Mason, $4,500
14-27A	(a)(3) Credits to capital: Maus, $18,000; Taylor, $27,000; Hamm, $9,000
14-28A	(c) Credits to capital: Davis, $5,000; Noonan, $5,000; Beecham, $28,000
14-29A	(c) Debits to capital: Stans, $8,000; Vasser, $60,000; Dubbs, $8,000
14-32A	(a) Cash distribution: Faley, $4,500; Goode, $15,500; Hill, $47,000
14-33A	(b)(4) Cash distribution: Oscar, $50,250; Poe, $29,250

Business Decision Problem Ivan should have received $110,000

15-26	(b) Total stockholders' equity, $1,448,000
15-27	(b) Dividends: Preferred, $42,000; common, $94,000
15-28	(c) Total stockholders' equity, $1,957,000
15-29	(b) $14/share
15-30	(a) Preferred stock, $103; common stock, $27.15
15-31	(c) Total stockholders' equity, $1,275,500
15-32	No key figure
15-26A	(b) Total stockholders' equity, $1,045,000
15-27A	(c) Dividends: Preferred, $55,000; common, $170,000
15-28A	(c) Total stockholders' equity, $1,799,500
15-30A	(a) Preferred stock, $52; common stock, $19.10
15-31A	(c) Total stockholders' equity, $1,682,200

Business Decision Problem (a) Total assets, $324,300

16-27	(a) Net income, $28,000
16-28	(a) $4.40
16-29	Net income, $90,000
16-30	(b) $225,400
16-31	(b) Retained earnings, Dec. 31, 19X2, $364,000
16-32	(b) Retained earnings, Dec. 31, 19X4, $495,440
16-33	(c) Total stockholders' equity, $1,951,125
16-27A	(a) Net income, $189,000
16-28A	(a) $8
16-29A	Net income, $204,000
16-31A	(b) Retained earnings, Dec. 31, 19X9, $213,500
16-32A	(b) Retained earnings, Dec. 31, 19X5, $510,450
16-33A	(c) Total stockholders' equity, $1,917,060

Business Decision Problem (b) 19X7, $46; 19X8, $41

17-24	(b) Loss on bond retirement, $2,100
17-25	(a)(4) Loss on bond retirement, $3,000
17-26	(a) Book value, end of period 2, $891,948
17-27	(a) Book value, end of period 2, $2,252,314
17-28	No key figure
17-29	No key figure
17-30	No key figure
17-31	(a) 19X3 income tax liability, $80,000; (b) 19X3 pretax accounting income, $152,000
17-24A	(b) Gain on bond retirement, $1,475
17-25A	(a)(4) Loss on bond retirement, $6,000
17-26A	(a) Book value, end of period 2, $564,998
17-27A	(a) Book value, end of period 2, $637,717
17-29A	No key figure
17-30A	No key figure
17-31A	(a) 19X2 income tax liability, $38,000; (b) 19X2 pretax accounting income, $75,000

Business Decision Problem (a) 19X3 income tax liability, $45,200; (b) 19X3 pretax accounting income, $122,000

A-1	(a)(1) $25,760; (c) $1,083.80; (e) $20,001.60
A-2	$15,972
A-3	$9,228.80

Principles
of Accounting

Third Edition

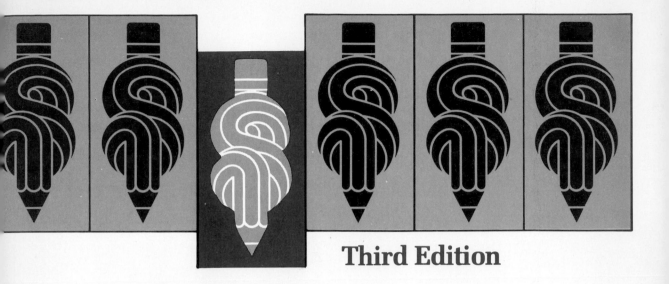

Third Edition

Principles of Accounting

Paul H. Walgenbach
The University of Wisconsin

Norman E. Dittrich
The University of Tennessee

Ernest I. Hanson
The University of Wisconsin

HARCOURT BRACE JOVANOVICH, PUBLISHERS
San Diego   New York   Chicago   Atlanta   Washington, D.C.
London   Sydney   Toronto

Illustrations by Evanelle Towne.

ISBN: 0-15-571350-7
Library of Congress Catalog Card Number: 83-81976
Printed in the United States of America

PREFACE

L ike its earlier editions, the third edition of *Principles of Accounting* provides a comprehensive first course in accounting for students planning a career in the field as well as students desiring a general understanding of the subject. Accordingly, we provide a balance of conceptual and procedural text material, straightforward exhibits and examples, a variety of interesting problems, and carefully organized study aids and ancillary materials.

This edition has been extensively revised to make the sequence of topics more natural, to clarify discussions and illustrations, to add new study aids for the student within the text itself, and to make the material more readable.

New features in this edition include the following:

■ New exhibits have been added to help students with difficult material. Examples include a matrix exhibit in Chapter 3 summarizing the various types of adjusting entries, a partnership liquidation exhibit in Chapter 14, a summary exhibit of major classes of income statement data in Chapter 16, and a worksheet exhibit for cash flow statements in Chapter 19.

■ Corporate accounting is contained in the second half of the text. Both sets of Working Papers for the text contain the basic corporation material, so these topics can be covered in either the first or second semester.

■ All of the boxed inserts (enrichment pieces) are new to this edition. These items furnish students with either additional background, extended coverage, or real-world examples of the accounting and business topics discussed in the chapter. They treat a range of subjects, such as the accountant's modern image, accounting estimates, stockholders' reports, microcomputers, deferred taxes, accounting for goodwill, updating cost accounting systems, and taxpayer compliance with tax laws.

■ Completely up-to-date discussions of FASB pronouncements are incorporated in the third edition, including the FASB conceptual framework. The text material also integrates appropriate content from the 1981 and 1982 tax reform acts.

■ The basic ideas of present values and effective interest have been integrated with text material in the chapter on bond investments and long-term liabilities (Chapter 17). A more technical treatment has been consigned to the chapter appendix.

- We have added carefully selected questions to our exhibit of a major public corporation's annual report (Whirlpool Corporation), which appears at the end of the text. These questions lead students to interesting aspects of the report that are related to major concepts discussed in the text.

- All of the questions, exercises, and problems have been thoroughly reviewed and revised. Many problems are new to this edition, corresponding to added and updated topics and changes in topic sequence. Successful problems and exercises from previous editions have been revised and edited for clarity and realism.

- The third edition retains the open, inviting design of the previous edition. Color is used constructively, and the layout of exhibits is designed to make the material accessible to students.

A number of successful features have been carried forward from previous editions, including the following:

- Demonstration Problems for Review in selected chapters aid students in understanding significant processes or ideas.

- A Business Decision Problem in each chapter applies accounting concepts to typical business decision situations.

- Alternate problems for the key ideas of each chapter permit greater depth in the study of particular concepts and more flexibility for instructors in assigning material.

- Key Points to Remember at the end of each chapter give students an inventory of the main ideas contained in the chapter.

- A Glossary at the end of the text makes it easy for students to locate the definition for any particular term at any point in their study.

- A Checklist of Key Figures on the endpapers of the text provides detail and summary figures to enable students to check their work without having the complete solution.

HIGHLIGHTS OF CHANGES AND ADDITIONS IN THE THIRD EDITION

Although the concept of depreciation is presented in Chapter 1, its use in transaction analysis is deferred to Chapter 3. This shift permits students to begin study of the content of basic financial statements without unnecessary complications. In Chapter 4, we expand the worksheet from 8 to 10 columns, adding the adjusted trial balance columns. The expanded worksheet emphasizes the role of adjustments. In Chapter 5, we simplify closing procedures and the placement of inventories in the worksheet. Students may now construct closing entries more easily from the worksheet. We combine the discussion of the voucher system with that of special journals in Chapter 6, covering all special journals in one chapter. We also reduce emphasis on computer hardware in our discussion of electronic data processing, placing more emphasis on a comparison of manual and electronic data processing.

Our discussion of short-term investments (previously treated with other investments) is now more naturally combined with cash accounting in Chapter 7. Short-term investments are current assets, and today there is a greater emphasis on cash-equivalent items, particularly in cash flow statements. We expand the treatment of inventories in Chapter 9 to emphasize perpetual inventory systems.

In previous editions, we treated plant assets, depreciation, natural resources, and intangible assets in one chapter. The third edition covers this material in two chapters that permit expanded coverage, particularly of natural resources and intangible assets accounting.

Additional material on the FASB conceptual framework appears in Chapter 13 dealing with accounting principles and inflation accounting. Discussion of interperiod tax allocation and deferred tax liabilities moves to Chapter 17, which deals with long-term liabilities. This placement is logical because most deferred tax liabilities are classified as long-term liabilities. Chapter 17 also contains a nontechnical treatment of effective interest amortization of bond discount and premium. Present value theory and the determination of bond prices are treated in an appendix to this chapter.

In Chapter 18, we combine long-term stock investments with consolidated financial statements. This combination permits the contrast of the accounting treatment of (a) noncontrolling and noninfluential stock interests, (b) influential but noncontrolling interests, and (c) controlling interests. We also reduce the emphasis on pooling of interests in this chapter, leaving a detailed treatment of this topic for advanced accounting courses.

Editorial changes in the managerial chapters (21 through 27) have clarified concepts and examples. Chapter 28, Income Taxes and Their Effect on Business Decisions, incorporates recent changes in the tax laws and also has a newly designed exhibit of the format for determining individual tax liability.

PROGRAM OF SUPPLEMENTARY AIDS

TEST BOOKLET   A class-tested Test Booklet is a part of the instructional package. For this edition, we have revised and updated the 25 multiple-choice questions and 15 other objective questions for each chapter, and we have added five or six short exercises for each chapter. The new booklet contains more than 1,250 items.

ACHIEVEMENT TESTS   Sixteen Achievement Tests—14 two-chapter tests suitable for 50-minute class periods, and two comprehensive tests, each covering 14 chapters—are available to adopters of the book. A Key to the Achievement Tests is also provided.

SOLUTIONS MANUAL   The Solutions Manual describes all the problem material and requirements and offers probable difficulty and estimated time for solution of each problem. Answers are given for all questions, exercises, and problems at the end of each chapter and appendix.

STUDY GUIDE   Prepared by Imogene A. Posey of the University of Tennessee, the Study Guide provides a comprehensive Chapter Review, a Check Your Knowledge section, and a set of exercises for each chapter and appendix. Answers to questions and solutions to exercises appear at the end of each Study Guide chapter.

WORKING PAPERS   Two sets of Working Papers are provided for the problems and alternate problems at the end of each chapter. All working papers are identified by problem number and name. When appropriate, given problem data have been entered to save time for the students. Working papers related to the two corporation chapters (15 and 16) are included in each set, so that this material may be covered in either the first or second semester.

TRANSPARENCIES   Transparencies of the problem solutions given in the Solutions Manual are available on request to departments adopting the textbook. In addition, Teaching Transparencies of text material are available from the publisher on request.

PRACTICE SETS   Five practice sets, keyed to the chapters in the book, are available with the third edition. Both Practice Set A and Practice Set A with Business Papers deal with a single proprietorship. Practice Set B deals with a corporation, and Practice Set C uses a manufacturing company. A computerized practice set, new to this edition, illustrates accounting for a corporation by using a computer. Practice Sets A and B were prepared by Joan Donen and C.R. Collins of Spokane Falls Community College. The computerized practice set was prepared by Joan Donen, C.R. Collins, and Robert Aasen, all of Spokane Falls Community College.

INSTRUCTOR'S MANUAL   New to this edition, an Instructor's Manual contains learning objectives and an outline of lecture points for each chapter and analyzes end-of-chapter problems in terms of the learning objectives covered. The Instructor's Manual was prepared by Richard W. Metcalf and Thomas E. Balke, both of the University of Nebraska, Lincoln. The solutions to the practice sets are also included in the Instructor's Manual.

COMPUTER RESOURCE GUIDE   Prepared by John W. Wanlass, De Anza College, this unique guide is new to this edition. Part 1 adapts selected end-of-chapter problems to a real-world computer system. Part 2 is a comprehensive practice set in which a new company develops from a sole proprietorship to a partnership and finally to a corporation.

We are indebted to many people for the success of the first two editions of *Principles of Accounting* and for their contributions to the third edition. We are especially grateful to James Bower, University of Wisconsin; Pauline Corn, Virginia Polytechnic Institute; Harriet Klapper, College at New Paltz, State University of New York; Bruce Lindsey, Genesee Community College; and James Skidmore, Grand Rapids Junior College, for their many valuable comments and suggestions, and to James Hamre, Informax Corporation, and C. Douglass Izard, University of Tennessee, for their contributions to this revision. We also thank Ralph Kapalczynski of Whirlpool Corporation for his kind assistance in furnishing his firm's annual report for the text, and for answering related inquiries.

Our thanks also go to editors William Knowles and Steven Dowling, who greatly assisted in planning and executing the revision. Probably our greatest debt is to Peggy Monahan, who edited all of the material and who assisted us unfailingly throughout the entire process of revision. We also acknowledge the considerable assistance of Harriet Meltzer, production editor; Eleanor Garner, permissions editor; Pat Braus, production manager; and thank Ann Smith for her attractive design work.

PAUL H. WALGENBACH
NORMAN E. DITTRICH
ERNEST I. HANSON

ACKNOWLEDGMENTS

We wish to thank the following users of the second edition who responded to detailed questionnaires relating to the third edition: Leonard Anderson, Grand Rapids Junior College; Boyd Arnold, York College of Pennsylvania; Jack Arnsparger, Community College of Denver; Lloyd Baldwin, Agricultural and Technical College; John Barbor, York College of Pennsylvania; Gregory Barnes, Clarion State College; Jack Barron, Lakewood Community College; C.A. Black, University of Wisconsin; Michael Blay, Florida Junior College; Richard Boes, Idaho State University; Verlin Boram, St. Leo College; Herbert Boswell, Central State University; Virginia Brunell, Diablo Valley College; Keith Burdick, University of Wyoming; Dave Cameron, Delta College; James Capone, Kean College; Charles Chanter, Grand Rapids Junior College; Benny Copeland, North Texas State University; Edward Corcoran, Community College of Philadelphia; Janie Council, Elon College; John Daly, Regis College; Jones Davis, Florida Junior College; G. DiLorenzo, Gloucester County College; Charles Dye, York College of Pennsylvania; Ed Fankhauser, University of Utah; Ken Ferris, Southern Methodist University; Floyd Feusse, Delta College; Kenneth Fiori, Lake Tahoe Community College; Ronald Flinn, University of Hartford; Tahirih Foroughi, University of Nevada, Reno; Dan Galvin, Diablo Valley College; Linda Garceau, University of Hartford; Frances Garrow, University of Wisconsin; Gary Giles, Southern Utah State College; M. Ginsberg, Rockland Community College; Clayton Hallett, Jackson Community College; H.C. Herring, University of Tennessee; Bill Hieber, Delta College; Jean Marie Hudson, Lamar University; Harry Hughes, University of Tennessee; Art Hyde, Grand Rapids Junior College; Don Jones, North Texas State University; Walter Kell, University of Michigan; Mike Kennedy, Hanover College; Ronald Kilgore, University of Tennessee; Harriet Klapper, SUNY at New Paltz; Dennis Knapp, University of Wisconsin; Jack Kochentiet, Columbus Technical Institute; Ralph Koorenny, Walla Walla College; Terry Lewis, State Community College; Douglas Lower, Idaho State University; Pam Melville, Kings River College; David Millman, Dowling College; Joseph Murray, Community College of

Philadelphia; Kalo Neidert, University of Nevada, Reno; Jon Nitschke, College of Great Falls; Al Pasek, Delta College; Murray Portnoy, Sacred Heart University; William Pound, Rainy River Community College; Dale Pulliani, West Texas State University; Cecily Raiborn, Texas Woman's University; Fred Richardson, Virginia Polytechnic Institute; Michael Robinson, Carroll College; Donald Rogoff, California State University, Northridge; Augusta Rolfe, Genesee Community College; Richard Roscher, SUNY at Fredonia; R. Rosenthal, Rockland Community College; Roger Sass, Cedar Crest College; Steve Senge, Principia College; Henry Smith, College of Great Falls; Elvin Sutherland, Walsh College; Randy Swad, California State University, Fullerton; Thad Tedrowe, St. Leo College; Kirk Tennant, Southern Methodist University; Clifford Toews, Pacific Union College; Anne Townsend, Southern Methodist University; R.L. Townsend, University of Tennessee; Gerald Unruh, Arapahoe Community College; Wayne Vandevere, Southern Missionary College; William Van Dongen, University of Wisconsin; Charles Wagner, Gustavus Adolphus College; Richard Wald, University of Illinois Medical Center; Thomas Warren, Florida Junior College; Pearl Washington, State Community College; Jack Waxman, Diablo Valley College; Rodney Wehtje, Walla Walla College; William Wilkinson, Valdosta State College; Michael Williamson, Pacific Union College: Marilyn Willis, University of Tennessee; Monsie Wolcott, California State University, Fullerton; James Woolley, University of Utah; and Allan Wright, Jackson Community College.

We also acknowledge the assistance of first edition users: Gerry Axel, Nassau Community College; Pauline Corn, Virginia Polytechnic Institute; John A. Dettmann, University of Minnesota; Paul Doran, Jefferson State Junior College; Milton Fink, University of Alaska; Dick Gilman, University of Hartford; John Gilmore, Rutgers University; Dick Houser, Northern Arizona University; Arthur Hirshfield, Bronx City College; Thomas Holowaty, St. Vincent College; Rita Huff, late of Sam Houston University; Stanley Katz, Rutgers University; William Kamenoff, Community College of Baltimore; Robert Landry, Massasoit Community College; Shirley Larson, Blue Mountain Community College; Robert Lewis, Kishwaukee College; Raymond Luoma, East Tennessee State University; Calvin Mercer, East Tennessee State University; William J. Newman, Jefferson State Junior College; Marcia Niles, University of Arizona; James Quinn, University of Tennessee; Richard Romanowski, Parkersburg Community College; Peggy Self, Stephen F. Austin State University; and Ed Wiener, Kingsborough Community College.

Thanks also go to users who participated in questionnaires for both the second and third editions: Sonia Brecha, Wright State University; John Burns, Genesee Community College; Mel Choate, North Seattle Community College; Walter Doehring, Genesee Community College; Bruce Lindsey, Genesee Community College; and James Skidmore, Grand Rapids Junior College.

CONTENTS

15 CORPORATIONS: ORGANIZATION AND CAPITAL STOCK 503

16 CORPORATIONS: EARNINGS DISCLOSURE, DIVIDENDS, AND RETAINED EARNINGS 535

17 LONG-TERM LIABILITIES AND BOND INVESTMENTS 569

28 INCOME TAXES AND THEIR EFFECT ON BUSINESS DECISIONS

1

Accounting: An Information System

Modern accounting is widely recognized as a basic component of business management. Accounting is the means by which managers are informed of the financial status and progress of their companies, thus contributing to the continuing processes of planning, control of operations, and decision making. Accounting provides a method of systematically recording and evaluating business activities. This is, perhaps, the fundamental reason for business managers and business students to familiarize themselves with the accounting discipline.

A large portion of the information that a business manager requires is derived from accounting data. The ability to analyze and use these data helps managers accomplish their objectives. Through your study of accounting, you will discover the types of business activities that can be accounted for usefully, the methods used to collect accounting data, and the implications of the resulting information. Furthermore—and often just as important—you will become aware of the limitations of accounting reports.

ACCOUNTING AS AN INFORMATION SYSTEM

Virtually all profit-seeking organizations and most nonprofit organizations maintain extensive accounting records. One reason is that these records are often required by law. A more basic reason is that, even in a very small organization, a manager is confronted with a multitude of complex variables. Not even the most brilliant manager can be sufficiently informed just by observing daily operations. Instead, he or she must depend on the accounting process to convert business transactions into useful statistical data that can be abstracted and summarized in accounting reports. In every sense, this process is essential to the coordinated and rational management of most organizations—regardless of their size. Thus, accounting is an *information system* necessitated by the great complexity of modern business.

In today's society, many persons and agencies outside of management are involved in the economic life of an organization. These persons frequently require financial data. For example, stockholders must have financial information in order to measure management's performance and to evaluate their own holdings. Potential investors need financial data in order to compare prospective investments. Creditors must consider the financial strength of an organization before permitting it to borrow funds. Also, labor unions, financial analysts, and economists often expect a considerable amount of reliable financial data. Finally, many laws require that extensive financial information be reported to the various levels of government. As an information system, the accounting process serves persons both inside and outside an organization.

THE ACCOUNTING PROCESS

Accounting can be defined as the process of (1) *recording*, (2) *classifying*, and (3) *reporting and interpreting* the financial data of an organization. Once an accounting system has been designed and installed, recording and classifying data may become somewhat routine and repetitive. While it is important for accountants to have a sound knowledge of this phase of the accounting process, it is often a relatively minor part of their total responsibility. Accountants direct most of their attention to the reporting and interpretation of the meaningful implications of the data.

Except in small businesses, much routine accounting work has become highly mechanized and automatic. Thus, many persons not acquainted with current accounting trends think that the profession is becoming progressively narrower. Quite the contrary is true. The emergence of mechanized and electronic data processing has freed accountants from the routine aspects of recording and classifying data, enabling them to concentrate more on the analytical and interpretive aspects of the accounting function. These are the areas most affected by the new demands for accounting information. Indeed, the number of licensed accountants in the United States has grown from a few hundred in 1900 to about 250,000 today; the number has doubled just during the past decade. The demand for better educated and more experienced accountants will undoubtedly continue to rise in the future.

Whether the accounting records for a given organization should be maintained manually, mechanically, or electronically will depend on several things, such as the size of the organization, the amount of data to be processed, the amount of information required, and the need for prompt access to stored data. At one extreme, the modest accounting requirements of a small organization would not justify the cost of an electronic computer, while on the other hand, a manually maintained accounting system would not fill the extensive requirements of a large organization.

Regardless of the method used, the underlying accounting concepts are essentially the same. Because a manually maintained system is most easily handled in the classroom and in problem situations, we use this type of system throughout this book. Where appropriate, however, we include comments relating to mechanized and electronic systems.

GOOD-BYE TO THE INK-STAINED WRETCH

Accounting has never set the popular imagination to flights of rapturous veneration. The practitioners of other professions have all taken turns waltzing in the limelight, extolled in verse or song, held up as heroes. Yet we search long and hard to find the accountant assigned any part in literature or theater, and when he is, he is usually a bloodless drudge—Dickens' Uriah Heep, for example. This nineteenth century image seems to have endured, more or less intact, into the modern era. As recently as 1960, two social scientists who conducted a government-backed survey of attitudes among 1,000 students at five unnamed but "highly selective" universities found that in the students' eyes, "The accountant is the anti-hero of the occupational world. . . . The accountant is a conformist, with a minimum of social skills. . . . He is rated as passive, weak, soft, shallow, and cold." Even accounting's most distinguished scholars have been apologetic about their profession. For instance, Henry Rand Hatfield's famous treatise on accounting, first delivered as a speech in 1923, is titled "An Historical Defense of Bookkeeping."

Things have been changing during the past two decades, and the profession is now in a full-fledged boom in terms of size, wealth, and even status. U.S. colleges and universities awarded some 53,000 undergraduate and 7,000 graduate degrees in accounting in 1979—triple the number issued a decade before. Not long ago, one business magazine quoted the chairman of the accounting department at the University of Southern California as saying, "Suddenly students see accounting as glamorous, sexy. Many of our best students, who would have gone to law school a couple of years ago, are now going into public accounting." The reasons are no mystery—plenty of job openings in accounting, and the salaries are increasingly attractive.

The ranks of certified public accountants—an appellation acquired after passing a uniform nationwide examination, and one that is necessary to become a partner in any well-regarded accounting firm—have swelled from 59,000 in the early 1960s to an estimated 250,000 today. Over the same period, the total number of accountants—certified or not, including those working for corporations, government agencies, or wherever—has increased from 496,000 to more than one million, according to the U.S. Bureau of Labor Statistics. There are about two lawyers for every CPA, but there are two general accountants for every lawyer. At the so-called Big Eight accounting firms, the thousands of partners earn an average of more than $100,000 a year. (The eight firms are Arthur Andersen; Arthur Young; Coopers & Lybrand; Deloitte, Haskins & Sells; Ernst & Whinney; Peat, Marwick, Mitchell; Price Waterhouse; and Touche Ross.) For those in top positions at the leading firms, the rewards reportedly range as high as $800,000.

The causes of the profession's ascent are many and varied. Generally speaking, accounting is being assigned an expanded role in society as greater answerability is demanded of all institutions, both public and private. This demand has undoubtedly been fueled by the breakdown of confidence in institutional authority following Vietnam, Watergate, and various revelations of corporate malfeasance. The result has been a new stream of regulatory legislation, such as the Federal Election Campaign Act Amendments of 1974 and the 1977 Foreign Corrupt Practices Act. That stream simply added to the torrent of government regulation that increased steadily through the 1960s and most of the 1970s: securities and tax laws, environmental controls, and social reforms—such as the 1974 Employee Retirement Income Security Act—that require large amounts of auditing services. Moreover, whereas the national mood now seems opposed to adding new regulatory programs, the existing legislation isn't about to be overturned.

Accounting is control, and it is being used increasingly as an instrument of social control. Thus, members of the accounting profession, it is said, should be society's tribunes, ensuring that the institutions to which power and authority have been granted are properly answerable to their constituents. It may be an exaggeration to suggest, as some have, that accountants constitute a "new elite" in America. Nonetheless, it is clear that the stereotypical image of the accountant as an ink-stained wretch wearing a green eyeshade and sitting on a three-legged stool is a relic of the past.

Steve Lohr, "Good-bye to the Ink-stained Wretch" as it appeared in *Atlantic Monthly*, August, 1980. Reprinted by permission of the author.

THE REPORTING PROCESS

The reporting process, comprising four main channels of information flow, is graphically represented in Exhibit 1–1.

Channel (1): Managerial Data and Reports

A major function of accounting is to provide management with the data needed for decision making and for efficient operation of the firm. Although management people routinely receive the financial reports, tax returns, and special reports prepared for outsiders, they also require various other information, such as the

EXHIBIT 1–1
Typical Flows of Accounting Information

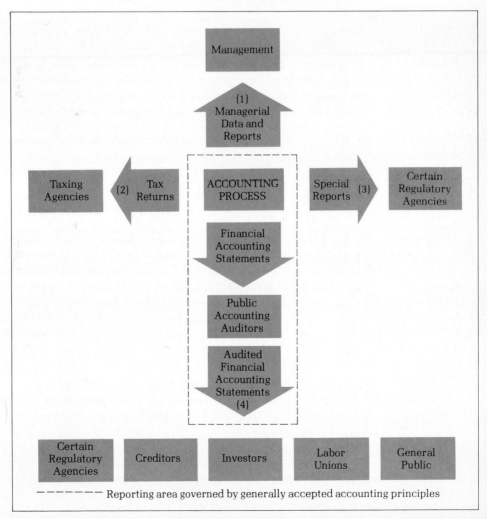

Reporting area governed by generally accepted accounting principles

unit cost of a product, estimates of the profit earned from a specific sales campaign, cost comparisons of alternative courses of action, and long-range budgets. Because of the strategic nature of some of this information, it may be available only to the firm's high-level management. The process of generating and analyzing such data is often referred to as **managerial accounting.** Emphasis on this area of accounting has increased in recent years as a result of the implementation of computers and sophisticated quantitative tools.

Channel (2): Tax Returns

Most businesses are required to file many kinds of tax returns—for example, federal, state, and municipal income taxes, excise taxes, and payroll taxes. The preparation of these returns is governed by the rulings and special reporting requirements of the taxing agencies involved. Proper compliance is generally a matter of law and can be quite complicated. Consequently, many firms, especially when preparing income tax returns, retain certified public accountants or attorneys specializing in taxation.

Channel (3): Special Reports

Some companies, by the nature of their activities, are required to report periodically to certain regulatory agencies. For example, commercial trucking companies must report to the Interstate Commerce Commission, and most public utility companies must report to a public utility commission. The regulatory agency may use the reported information to establish the rates to be charged (as in the trucking industry) or the rate of income to be earned (as in the case of public utilities). Although these reports are based primarily on accounting data, often they must be prepared in accordance with additional conditions, rules, and definitions. Some agencies, such as stock exchanges and the Securities and Exchange Commission, do require reports prepared in accordance with the generally accepted accounting principles that we shall discuss later. We have therefore shown certain regulatory agencies in both channels (3) and (4) of Exhibit 1–1.

Channel (4): Financial Accounting Statements

One of the most important functions of the accounting process is to accumulate and report accounting information that shows an organization's financial position and the results of its operations. Many businesses publish such financial statements at least annually. The subdivision of the accounting process that produces these general-purpose reports is referred to as **financial accounting.** Financial accounting is essentially retrospective, because it deals primarily with historical information, or events that have already happened. Its focus is on income determination and financial position as an aggregate financial picture of an enterprise.

Although financial accounting data are primarily historical, they are also useful for planning and control. Indeed, a considerable amount of planning must be based on what has happened in the recent past. In addition, historical financial information is inherently a control mechanism, since it can be used to measure the success of past planning. We should also emphasize that, although financial accounting is primarily historical, it is not merely a process of "filling in the numbers." As you study further, you will discover that determining the financial position and profitability of an enterprise is an exceedingly complex job that requires professional judgment.

Financial accounting statements are the main source of information for parties—other than governmental agencies—outside the business firm. Because these reports will often be used to evaluate management, their objectivity could be subject to question. To establish the validity of their financial statements, most firms have them audited by independent public accountants. The independent auditor examines the statements and suggests any changes that may be warranted. He or she then expresses a professional opinion that the financial statements are fairly stated "in accordance with generally accepted accounting principles" or indicates any reservations about the statements. Usually, outside parties have greater faith in financial statements that have been audited. Both the role of the professional public accountant and the nature of "generally accepted accounting principles" are complex. Therefore, each is treated separately in later sections of this chapter.

ACCOUNTING PRINCIPLES

To be useful, financial accounting information must be assembled and reported objectively. Those who must rely on such information have a right to be assured that the data are free from bias and inconsistency, whether deliberate or not. For this reason, financial accounting relies on certain standards or guides that have proved useful over the years in imparting economic data. These standards are called **generally accepted accounting principles.** Because accounting is more an art than a science, these principles are not immutable laws like those in the physical sciences. Instead, they are *guides to action* and may change over time. Sometimes specific principles must be altered or new principles must be formulated to fit changed economic circumstances or changes in business practices.

Because accounting principles are based on a combination of theory and practice, there has always been, and probably always will be, some controversy about their propriety. A number of organizations are concerned with the formulation of accounting principles. The most prominent among these is the Financial Accounting Standards Board (FASB). The FASB, organized in 1973, is a nongovernmental body whose pronouncements have the force of dictating authoritative rules for the general practice of financial accounting. Before the creation of the FASB, the Accounting Principles Board (APB) of the American Institute of Certified Public Accountants (AICPA) fulfilled the function of formulating accounting principles. If the *attest* function (auditing and independent reporting) of the independent certified public accountant is to be meaningful, the business enterprises of this country must generally observe substantially comparable accounting principles.

Various regulatory bodies—such as the Securities and Exchange Commission and the Internal Revenue Service—also prescribe rules to be used in financial accounting. Because these rules often touch upon accounting principles and may conflict with the rules and practices specified by other agencies, compromises sometimes have to be made in financial reporting. This has been especially true when the rules of a regulatory body have conflicted with those considered "generally accepted" by accounting practitioners.

Often, income determined by tax regulations differs from that determined by generally accepted accounting principles. When rules or methods prescribed by the Internal Revenue Service for the determination of taxable income conflict with those acceptable for business reporting, an enterprise may keep more than one set of records to satisfy both reporting requirements. Uninformed people may think that this practice is illegal or unethical; actually, there is nothing sinister or illegal about keeping separate records to fulfill separate needs, as long as all the records are subject to examination by the appropriate parties.

As Exhibit 1–1 indicates, generally accepted accounting principles are primarily relevant to financial accounting. In managerial accounting, the main objective is to assist management in making decisions and in operating effectively, and in such cases it is frequently useful to depart from concepts utilized in financial accounting. On many occasions, financial accounting data must be reassembled or altered to be most useful in solving internal business problems.

FIELDS OF ACCOUNTING ACTIVITY

Accountants perform many diverse services and are engaged in various types of employment. The three major fields of accounting activity are private accounting, public accounting, and governmental accounting. Because each of these may comprise many aspects of accounting activity, it is possible to give only a broad description for each type of accounting employment.

Private Accounting

More accountants are employed in private accounting than in any other field. Private employers of accountants include manufacturers, wholesalers, retailers, and service firms. Depending on the size and complexity of the business, the private accountant's duties may vary from routine reporting to the design and implementation of electronic accounting systems. The major objective of the private accountant, however, is to assist management in planning and controlling the firm's operations. In many large business firms, the head of the accounting department is called the **controller** and is a key executive who works closely with other management personnel.

Frequently, a large company will have an **internal auditing** staff that reports to a high-ranking management officer or to an audit committee of the board of directors. Internal auditing is an appraisal activity conducted within the business firm to determine if management's financial and operating controls are effective and are being properly utilized. An internal auditor investigates policies and procedures designed to safeguard assets, promote operational efficiency, and provide reliable information.

Public Accounting

The field of public accounting is composed of firms that render independent, expert reports on financial statements of business enterprises. Public accounting firms also perform a wide variety of accounting and managerial services, acting as consultants to their clients. Most accountants in public accounting firms are certified public accountants (CPAs), holding certificates from the particular states in which they work.[1] These certificates declare that the CPA has passed a rigorous examination and has met the requirements for education and experience set by the state to ensure high standards of performance. The CPA profession, like the older professions of law and medicine, has a comprehensive code of ethics—a set of rules of professional conduct—that governs the behavior of its practitioners in the performance of their work.

The professional responsibility of the certified public accountant is unique. While the attorney and the physician are responsible only to their clients and patients, the certified public accountant may be professionally responsible to third parties who rely on the financial statements the CPA has audited. This is true even though the third party in no way contributes to the fee paid for the audit and has no contractual relationship whatsoever with the accountant.

Governmental Accounting

A large number of accountants are employed by federal, state, and local governmental agencies. The services performed by these accountants parallel those of private and public accountants and may cover the entire spectrum of financial and managerial accounting. For example, the General Accounting Office of the federal government and the Department of Audit in the various state governments engage in auditing activities similar to those of public accountants. Audits may be conducted not only of governmental agencies but of private firms doing business with a governmental unit. Accounting personnel of the Internal Revenue Service and the corresponding state agencies conduct accounting investigations of firms and individuals in connection with their tax liabilities. Among the many other governmental agencies and regulatory bodies that employ accountants are the Securities and Exchange Commission, the Department of Defense, the Federal Power Commission, the Interstate Commerce Commission, and state utility commissions and agencies.

BASIC FINANCIAL REPORTS

As we mentioned earlier, one of the major functions of accounting is to provide periodic reports to management, owners, and outsiders. The two principal reports resulting from the process of financial accounting are the balance sheet and the income statement. Although the form of these financial statements may vary among different business firms or other economic units, their basic purpose is the same. The balance sheet portrays the financial position of the organization at a particular point in time. The income statement portrays the operating results for a period of time. These financial statements are prepared at least yearly, but quarterly or monthly reports are also customary.

[1]Most states still allow certain accountants who are not "certified" to practice public accounting.

Another basic statement, called the **statement of changes in financial position,** is generally required in reporting to outsiders. This statement will be discussed in Chapter 19.

Although the balance sheet and income statement are the end result of the process of financial accounting, we shall introduce them in simplified form here, early in our study. Having some knowledge of the ultimate objective of financial accounting will help you understand the various steps in the accounting process.

THE BALANCE SHEET

The balance sheet, sometimes called the statement of financial position, is a listing of a firm's assets, liabilities, and owners' equity on a given date (these terms are explained below). Exhibit 1–2 is a balance sheet prepared for Star Photolab, a single-owner business, showing its financial position at December 31, 19XX.

The proper heading of a balance sheet consists of (1) the name of the organization, (2) the title of the statement, and (3) the date for which the statement was prepared.

The body of the statement in Exhibit 1–2 contains three major sections: assets, liabilities, and owner's equity. With this presentation, the reader can tell at a glance that the resources of this firm total $95,000 and that these assets are being financed by two sources—$25,000 by the creditors (liabilities) and $70,000 by the owner (owner's equity). Occasionally, the right-hand portion of this state-

EXHIBIT 1–2

Star Photolab
Balance Sheet
December 31, 19XX

Assets		Liabilities		
Cash	$ 4,000	Accounts Payable	$ 2,000	
Accounts Receivable	3,000	Mortgage Payable	23,000	
Supplies on Hand	5,000			
		Total Liabilities		$25,000
Equipment (Less Accumulated Depreciation)	40,000	**Owner's Equity**		
Building (Less Accumulated Depreciation)	35,000	George Taylor, Capital		70,000
Land	8,000	Total Liabilities and Owner's		
Total Assets	$95,000	Equity		$95,000

ment is called *Equities,* with subdivisions called *Creditors' Equity* and *Owners' Equity.* The total assets always equal the sum of the creditors' and owners' equities. This balancing is sometimes described as the **accounting equation,** which dictates that all of the listed resources are attributed to claims of creditors and owners. Conversely, the claims of both creditors and owners must be balanced by total listed resources. These relationships can be diagramed as follows:

Technical terms:	**Assets**	=	**Liabilities**	+	**Owners' Equity**
Basic meanings:	Business resources	=	Outsiders' claims	+	Owners' claims
Amounts (Exhibit 1–2):	$95,000	=	$25,000	+	$70,000

We now briefly explain each of the three elements in the accounting equation.

Assets

Assets are the economic resources of the business that can usefully be expressed in monetary terms. Assets may take many forms. Some assets—such as land, buildings, and equipment—may have readily identifiable physical characteristics. Others may simply represent claims for payment or services, such as amounts due from customers (accounts receivable), or prepayments for future services (for example, prepaid insurance). As a convenience to the reader of the balance sheet, the assets are usually listed in an established order, with the most liquid assets (cash, receivables, supplies, and so on) preceding the more permanent assets (equipment, buildings, and land).

Assets are usually recorded at their acquisition price, or cost. The recorded costs of assets may be reduced for a variety of reasons. Supplies are used up, and assets such as equipment and buildings depreciate. For example, in Exhibit 1–2, Star Photolab's equipment and building have both been reduced by accumulated depreciation over the years. We shall develop the concept of depreciation in Chapter 3 and discuss it fully in Chapter 10.

Accounting principles do not permit upward valuation of assets, simply because it is often difficult or impossible to determine the *actual value* of an asset at regular intervals in a completely *objective* way. Assume, for example, that 10 years ago a firm purchased some real estate for $20,000. Today the property may well be worth considerably more, at least in "current" dollars. Assigning a current dollar value to the real estate may be helpful, but it would be difficult to accomplish unless the property were offered for sale. However, most business firms plan to *use* their long-term operating assets, not to sell them. Therefore, the accounting convention of reflecting assets in financial statements at acquisition cost has persisted, although criticism is frequently leveled at this practice.

Liabilities

Liabilities, or creditors' equity, are the obligations, or debts, that the firm must pay in money or services at some time in the future. They therefore represent creditors' claims on the firm's assets. Liabilities are listed on the balance sheet in the order that they will come due. Short-term liabilities—such as notes payable given for money borrowed for relatively short periods, accounts payable to creditors, and salaries owed employees—are usually shown first. Below the short-term liabilities, the long-term debt is presented. Long-term debt—for example, mortgages and bonds payable—will normally not be repaid in full for several years.

Although most liabilities are payable in cash, some may involve the performance of services. A magazine publisher, for example, may receive advance payments for three- or five-year subscriptions. These payments constitute a liability that the publishing company will reduce periodically by supplying the publication during the subscription period. Should the publisher be unable to fulfill this commitment, the unexpired portion of the subscription amount must be refunded.

Owners' Equity   The owners' equity in the resources, or assets, of the firm is shown below the liabilities. The owners' interest is equal to the **net assets** of the business, which is defined as the difference between the assets and the liabilities. Thus, owners' equity is a *residual claim*—a claim to the assets remaining after the debts to creditors have been discharged. Formerly, the term *net worth* was frequently used to describe owners' equity. This expression is no longer considered good terminology, because it conveys an impression of value, and as we have seen, the value, or current worth, of assets may not be portrayed in the balance sheet. We also often employ the term **capital** to describe owners' interest in a firm. (This practice is derived from legal usage of the term.) Sometimes in economic literature the assets of a business are referred to as the firm's "capital." This use of the term is avoided in accounting literature.

The owner's equity in Star Photolab amounts to $70,000. It consists of the amounts invested in the organization and the net earnings of the organization that have not been withdrawn by the owner.

FORMS OF BUSINESS ORGANIZATION

The principal forms of business organization are the **sole proprietorship,** the **partnership,** and the **corporation.** Although sole proprietorships, or single-owner businesses, are probably the most numerous, the corporate form of business is the most important in our economy. The partnership form is often used when two or more sole proprietorships merge into one business. For many years, professional people such as physicians, attorneys, and public accountants operated as partnerships because their codes of ethics or state laws prohibited incorporation. Most states now permit a special type of incorporation or association, and professional organizations have changed their codes of ethics to accommodate this change. Most professional firms, however, still operate as partnerships. For large-scale operations, the corporate form of organization has many advantages. These will be discussed in Chapter 15.

The principal differences in the balance sheets for the three types of business organizations just described appear in the owners' equity section. State corporation laws require that corporations segregate, in their balance sheets, the owners' investment (the amount paid for their stock) and any accumulated earnings. Because there are no comparable legal restrictions on sole proprietorships and partnerships, these types of businesses do not have to distinguish between amounts invested by owners and undistributed earnings.

The following illustrations demonstrate the variations in the balance sheet presentation of owners' equity for the three forms of business organization. In Chapters 14–18, we will consider in more detail the distinctive features of corporation and partnership accounting.

CASE I: SOLE PROPRIETORSHIP George Taylor originally invested $40,000 in a photography business. Subsequent earnings left in the business amounted to $30,000. The owner's equity section of the firm's balance sheet would appear as follows:

Owner's Equity

George Taylor, Capital	$70,000

CASE II: PARTNERSHIP George Taylor, Eva Williams, and John Young invested $16,000, $14,000, and $10,000, respectively, in a photography business. Each partner's share of subsequent earnings not withdrawn from the business was $10,000. The owners' equity section of this firm's balance sheet would appear as follows:

Owners' Equity

George Taylor, Capital	$26,000
Eva Williams, Capital	24,000
John Young, Capital	20,000
Total Owners' Equity	$70,000

CASE III: CORPORATION George Taylor, Eva Williams, and John Young began a corporation, investing $16,000, $14,000, and $10,000, respectively, and receiving shares of stock for those amounts. Subsequent earnings not distributed, identified as *retained earnings*, amounted to $30,000. The owners' equity section of this firm's balance sheet would appear as follows:

Stockholders' Equity

Capital Stock	$40,000
Retained Earnings	30,000
	$70,000

The owners may, from time to time, withdraw money or property from the business for personal use or for engaging in other business activities. Such withdrawals reduce both the assets and the owners' equity of the business. In sole proprietorships and partnerships, withdrawals are made quite informally at the owners' discretion; in corporations, withdrawals must be accomplished more formally. The board of directors, elected by the stockholders, must meet and "declare a dividend" before a distribution can be made to the stockholders. Declaration of dividends reduces the retained earnings portion of the owners' equity of the corporation and creates a liability called Dividends Payable. Payment of the dividend eliminates the liability and reduces assets (usually cash).

UNDERLYING ACCOUNTING CONCEPTS

Certain fundamental concepts provide a framework for recording and reporting business transactions. These concepts have been developed over time to provide general guides to making financial reports as objective and as useful as possible. Although various terms—such as **principles, standards, assumptions,** and **conventions**—are often used to describe such guides, a distinction among these terms is not essential to an understanding of the guides. At this point, a brief discussion of certain of these guides may be helpful in understanding the structure of the accounting process. A more thorough discussion is given in Chapter 13.

The Accounting Entity

Any business enterprise—whether a sole proprietorship, a partnership, or a corporation—is an individual accounting unit separate and distinct from the other economic activities and the personal affairs of the owners. Thus, in Case I of our previous example, if sole proprietor George Taylor owned other businesses or participated in other economic ventures, these activities would be accounted for separately and would not affect the accounting for the sole proprietorship photography business. A separate set of accounting records would be maintained, and a separate set of financial statements would be prepared for each enterprise. Similarly, the three partners in Case II and the three stockholders in Case III might have other business interests, but these activities would not be mingled in accounting for the partnership or corporation.

Historical Cost

We have mentioned that assets are recorded and subsequently reported at their acquisition price, or **historical cost.** Although other measurements, such as appraised values or market prices, might be used for reporting in subsequent periods, accountants have long recognized that historical cost is probably the most objective and verifiable basis for reporting assets. As you will learn, reported asset costs are often *reduced* over time to reflect expiration, and in some cases, they may be reduced to market values; upward revaluations, however, are not permitted in conventional financial statements. We explain later how certain reported *supplemental* information departs from the cost principle.

Objectivity

Because accounting data are most useful when they are objective and verifiable, the recording of transactions should be based on actual invoices, physical counts, and other relatively bias-free evidence whenever possible. Undocumented opinions of management or others do not provide a good basis for accounting determinations. Even when a certain amount of subjectivity cannot be avoided—as in estimating the useful lives of plant assets, collectibility of accounts receivable, or possible liability for product warranties—it is important that such estimates be supported by some sort of objective analysis.

Going Concern

The **going concern** concept is based on the presumption that a business will continue indefinitely and will not be sold or liquidated. This assumption permits the accountant to carry certain incurred costs such as plant assets and supplies into future periods and to reflect them as costs of operation when the items are used in operations. The concept also supports the cost principle, because it assumes that such assets will be used in operating the business rather than sold; hence, it is considered rational to use cost, rather than market price or liquidation value, as the basis for measurement.

The Measuring Unit

Accounting transactions and their results appearing in financial statements are expressed in terms of a monetary unit (the dollar in the United States). Unfortunately, the U.S. dollar (as well as the currencies of other countries) is not a stable unit of measure. The worldwide inflation of the past several years has caused all currencies to decline sharply in purchasing power. As a result, use of the cost principle has distorted the financial statements of business firms, because the amounts appearing in the statements are expressed in dollars of different vintages. Over the years, there have been many proposals to adjust the amounts in financial statements by the use of price indexes or to substitute some current value such as replacement cost or appraisal value. Currently, conventional financial statements prepared in this country are still unadjusted, cost-based statements. In 1979, however, the Financial Accounting Standards Board issued a standard requiring certain large publicly held firms to make supplementary disclosures concerning the effects of inflation on their operations. A more detailed discussion of the problem will be given in Chapter 13.

EFFECT OF TRANSACTIONS ON THE BALANCE SHEET

An **accounting transaction** is a business activity or event that requires accounting recognition. Therefore, an event that affects any of the elements in the accounting equation (assets, liabilities, or owners' equity) must be recorded. Some activities—for example, ordering supplies, bidding for an engagement or contract, and negotiating for the acquisition of assets—may represent business activities, but an accounting transaction does not occur until such activities result in a change in the firm's assets, liabilities, or owners' equity.

Earlier, we observed that the balance sheet of a business indicates the firm's financial position at a particular point in time. We emphasized that the total assets should always equal the sum of the creditors' and owners' equities. If a balance sheet were prepared after each accounting transaction was completed, this equality of assets and equities would always hold true. Obviously, no one would care to do this, since the statements are required only periodically. However, keep in mind that although each transaction changes the complexion of the balance sheet, equality of assets and equities is always maintained.

Transactions Not Affecting Owners' Equity

Certain transactions may change the character and amounts of assets or liabilities, or both, but have no effect on owners' equity. For example, if George Taylor of Star Photolab (see Exhibit 1–2) purchases additional equipment for $1,000 cash, the asset Equipment will increase by $1,000, but the asset Cash will decrease by $1,000. Obviously, this transaction causes only a shift in assets on the balance sheet. In the same way, collection of accounts receivable causes a shift of assets. Collection of $500 of Accounts Receivable would result in a decrease in this asset and an increase in Cash of $500.

If the $1,000 worth of equipment had been purchased on credit rather than for cash, the result would have been a $1,000 increase in Equipment and an equal increase in the liability Accounts Payable. On the other hand, payment of liabilities reduces both assets and liabilities. If Taylor paid $500 to his creditors, both Cash and Accounts Payable would decrease by $500.

Transactions Affecting Owners' Equity

The following four types of transactions change the amount of owners' equity:

	Effect on Owners' Equity
(1) Owner contributions	Increase
(2) Owner withdrawals	Decrease
(3) Revenue	Increase
(4) Expenses	Decrease

When an owner contributes cash or other assets to a business firm, the firm's balance sheet shows an increase in assets and an increase in owners' equity. Conversely, when an owner withdraws assets from the firm, both assets and owners' equity decrease. The primary goal of any business, however, is to increase the owners' equity by earning profits, or **net income.** The net income of a firm is determined by subtracting *expenses incurred* from *revenue earned.* Owners' equity is increased by revenue and decreased by expenses. Let us examine the nature of revenue and expenses.

Revenue

A business firm earns **revenue** by providing goods or services for its customers. The revenue earned is measured by the *assets received* in exchange, usually in the form of cash or an account receivable. It is important to recognize that *revenue is earned and reflected in the accounting process at the time that goods or services are provided.* Receipt of cash by a business does not necessarily indicate that revenue has been earned. In a cash sale, revenue is earned at the time that cash is received. Revenue is also reflected when services are rendered on *credit;* assets are increased when Accounts Receivable is increased. Subsequent collection of an account does not increase revenue—it merely results in a shift in assets from Accounts Receivable to Cash. Neither is revenue earned when a business borrows money or when the owners contribute assets. Such increases in assets are not earned, because the business firm has provided no goods or services.

Expenses

Expenses are costs incurred by the firm in the process of earning revenue. Generally, expenses are measured by the costs of *assets consumed* or *services used* during an accounting period. Depreciation on equipment, rent, employees' salaries, and costs of heat, light, and other utilities are examples of expenses incurred in producing revenue.

Because expenses are deducted from revenue to determine net income, the accounting process must relate expenses in a period to the revenue of that same period. For example, January rent—no matter when it is paid—should be related to January revenue in determining that month's net income. If an annual rent of $6,000 is prepaid on January 1, only $\frac{1}{12}$ of the $6,000, or $500, is considered expense for January. At the end of January, the remaining prepayment of $5,500 constitutes an asset (called Prepaid Rent) to be apportioned over the remaining 11 months. Other examples of assets that are used up over a period of time are Prepaid Insurance and Prepaid Advertising.

Cash expenditures made to acquire assets do not represent expenses and do not affect owners' equity. Cash expenditures made to pay liabilities, such as the payment of an account payable, also do not represent expenses and do not affect owners' equity. Similarly, owners' withdrawals, although they reduce owners' equity, do not represent expenses. Expenses are directly related to the earning of revenue. They are determined by measuring the amount of assets or services consumed (or expired) during an accounting period.

Accrual Basis

The foregoing concepts of revenue and expenses apply to firms that employ an **accrual basis** accounting system. In accrual accounting, expenses incurred are matched with related revenue earned to determine a meaningful net income figure for a particular period. As we mentioned earlier, the revenue and expenses for determining net income do not depend on when cash is actually received or expended.

Certain businesses, principally service enterprises (such as law, architecture, or hairdressing), often use a **cash basis** mode of accounting. In contrast to accrual basis accounting, the cash basis system recognizes revenue when money is received and expenses when money is paid. Cash basis accounting is used primarily because it can provide certain income tax benefits and because it is simple. Cash basis financial statements, however, may distort the portrayal of financial position and operating results of a business. Consequently, most business firms use accrual basis accounting.

TRANSACTIONS AND THE BALANCE SHEET: AN ILLUSTRATION

Now that we have described the basic concepts underlying the preparation of financial statements, let us illustrate their application with an example.

Experienced driver education instructor James Hill established a private driving school called Capital Driving School. Hill intends to buy a lot for vehicle storage and driver instruction, but to lease training vehicles. The transactions for June, the first month of operations, are analyzed below. A balance sheet is presented after each transaction so that the effect on the balance sheet may be examined.[2]

Initial Investment in Firm

TRANSACTION (1):   On June 1, Hill invested $50,000 of his personal funds in the school. This first business transaction increased the asset Cash and increased Hill's equity (Capital) on the school's balance sheet.

Balance Sheet

Assets		Liabilities	
Cash	$50,000	(none)	
		Owner's Equity	
	———	J. Hill, Capital	$50,000
		Total Liabilities and	
Total Assets	$50,000	Owner's Equity	$50,000

Purchase of Land

TRANSACTION (2):   On June 2, Hill paid $18,000 cash for a lot to be used for storing vehicles and for some driving instruction. This transaction reduced the asset Cash and created another asset, Land, for an equivalent amount. This transaction was merely the conversion of one asset to another.

Balance Sheet

Assets		Liabilities	
Cash	$32,000	(none)	
Land	18,000		
		Owner's Equity	
	———	J. Hill, Capital	$50,000
		Total Liabilities and	
Total Assets	$50,000	Owner's Equity	$50,000

Payment of Rent

TRANSACTION (3):   On June 3, Hill paid $600 to rent a furnished office near the parking lot for June, and $4,000 to lease training vehicles. These items are June expenses, the cost of services received (use of office and vehicles) for the month. The transaction reduced assets (Cash) and owner's equity (J. Hill, Capital) by $4,600.

---

[2]Note that the totals in the various financial statements shown in this chapter have been double ruled. Accountants do this principally to signify that all necessary calculations have been performed and to emphasize final amounts for the benefit of readers. We shall also employ double rulings in various other accounting records and forms illustrated in this text for these reasons and also to separate certain recorded data by time periods.

Balance Sheet

Assets		Liabilities	
Cash	$27,400	(none)	
Land	18,000		
		Owner's Equity	
	————	J. Hill, Capital	**$45,400**
		Total Liabilities and	
Total Assets	$45,400	Owner's Equity	$45,400

Prepayment of Insurance

TRANSACTION (4): On June 4, Hill paid vehicle insurance premiums of $3,600 for three years. This payment for future coverage created a new asset, Prepaid Insurance, and reduced Cash. As each month passes, $\frac{1}{36}$ of the amount, or $100, will appear on the income statement as Insurance Expense, the cost of that month's insurance coverage.

Balance Sheet

Assets		Liabilities	
Cash	$23,800	(none)	
Prepaid Insurance	3,600		
Land	18,000		
		Owner's Equity	
	————	J. Hill, Capital	$45,400
		Total Liabilities and	
Total Assets	$45,400	Owner's Equity	$45,400

Purchase of Supplies on Account

TRANSACTION (5): On June 5, Hill purchased fuel and other supplies on account for $2,200. This transaction increased assets (Supplies on Hand) by $2,200 and resulted in a liability (Accounts Payable) of $2,200. The increase in assets did not change owner's equity; it merely created a liability on the balance sheet. Because Hill could not anticipate the amount of supplies that would be *used* (become expense) in June, he classified the entire $2,200 as an asset. Later, when the amount of supplies *used* is determined, an expense will be reflected.

Balance Sheet

Assets		Liabilities	
Cash	$23,800	Accounts Payable	$ 2,200
Prepaid Insurance	3,600		
Supplies on Hand	2,200	**Owner's Equity**	
Land	18,000	J. Hill, Capital	45,400
		Total Liabilities and	
Total Assets	$47,600	Owner's Equity	$47,600

**Billing for
Fee Revenue**

TRANSACTION (6):   On June 26, students were billed $18,500 for June instructional fees. Providing instruction during the month generated an asset, Accounts Receivable, and revenue, which increased owner's equity (J. Hill, Capital), even though payment may not be received until a later period.

Balance Sheet

Assets		Liabilities	
Cash	$23,800	Accounts Payable	$ 2,200
Accounts Receivable	18,500		
Prepaid Insurance	3,600		
Supplies on Hand	2,200	**Owner's Equity**	
Land	18,000	J. Hill, Capital	63,900
		Total Liabilities and	
Total Assets	$66,100	Owner's Equity	$66,100

**Payment
of Salaries**

TRANSACTION (7):   On June 30, Hill paid instructors' salaries of $8,000 for June. This amount was June expense, because it represented the cost of employees' services used during June. Therefore, the Cash account and J. Hill, Capital were both reduced by $8,000.

Balance Sheet

Assets		Liabilities	
Cash	$15,800	Accounts Payable	$ 2,200
Accounts Receivable	18,500		
Prepaid Insurance	3,600		
Supplies on Hand	2,200	**Owner's Equity**	
Land	18,000	J. Hill, Capital	55,900
		Total Liabilities and	
Total Assets	$58,100	Owner's Equity	$58,100

**Collection
of Accounts
Receivable**

TRANSACTION (8):   On June 30, the school collected $14,000 on account from students billed in transaction (6). This transaction increased Cash and decreased Accounts Receivable—merely a shift in assets. Note that the revenue, which increased owner's equity, had already been reflected when the month's billings were made on June 26.

Balance Sheet

Assets		Liabilities	
Cash	$29,800	Accounts Payable	$ 2,200
Accounts Receivable	4,500		
Prepaid Insurance	3,600		
Supplies on Hand	2,200	**Owner's Equity**	
Land	18,000	J. Hill, Capital	55,900
		Total Liabilities and	
Total Assets	$58,100	Owner's Equity	$58,100

Payment on Accounts Payable

TRANSACTION (9):   On June 30, the school paid $1,200 on account for the fuel and supplies purchased in transaction (5). Paying $1,200 of the $2,200 owed reduced both Cash and Accounts Payable, therefore reducing both assets and liabilities. This payment was the partial settlement of a previously recorded obligation—not an expense.

Balance Sheet

Assets		Liabilities	
Cash	$28,600	Accounts Payable	$ 1,000
Accounts Receivable	4,500		
Prepaid Insurance	3,600		
Supplies on Hand	2,200	**Owner's Equity**	
Land	18,000	J. Hill, Capital	55,900
		Total Liabilities and	
Total Assets	$56,900	Owner's Equity	$56,900

Payment of Utilities

TRANSACTION (10):   On June 30, Hill paid $150 for office utilities (electricity and telephone). This amount was a June expense decreasing both assets and owner's equity because the amount represented the cost of utility services used during the month. Cash and J. Hill, Capital were reduced by $150.

Balance Sheet

Assets		Liabilities	
Cash	$28,450	Accounts Payable	$ 1,000
Accounts Receivable	4,500		
Prepaid Insurance	3,600		
Supplies on Hand	2,200	**Owner's Equity**	
Land	18,000	J. Hill, Capital	55,750
		Total Liabilities and	
Total Assets	$56,750	Owner's Equity	$56,750

Withdrawal by Owner

TRANSACTION (11):   On June 30, Hill withdrew $1,000 from the firm for personal use. This withdrawal reduced Cash and J. Hill, Capital by $1,000. Note that the effect of this transaction was the reverse of transaction (1), in which Hill invested personal funds in the school.

Balance Sheet

Assets		Liabilities	
Cash	$27,450	Accounts Payable	$ 1,000
Accounts Receivable	4,500		
Prepaid Insurance	3,600		
Supplies on Hand	2,200	**Owner's Equity**	
Land	18,000	J. Hill, Capital	54,750
		Total Liabilities and	
Total Assets	$55,750	Owner's Equity	$55,750

Recording Insurance Expense

TRANSACTION (12):   On June 30, $\frac{1}{36}$ (one month) of the prepaid insurance, or $100, had expired and no longer represented an asset; it became insurance expense for June. [Recall that in transaction (4) on June 4, the firm paid $3,600 for a 36-month policy.] Therefore, both the asset, Prepaid Insurance, and J. Hill, Capital were reduced by $100.

Balance Sheet

Assets		Liabilities	
Cash	$27,450	Accounts Payable	$ 1,000
Accounts Receivable	4,500		
Prepaid Insurance	3,500		
Supplies on Hand	2,200	**Owner's Equity**	
Land	18,000	J. Hill, Capital	54,650
		Total Liabilities and	
Total Assets	$55,650	Owner's Equity	$55,650

Recording Supplies Expense

TRANSACTION (13):   On June 30, supplies were counted, and only $550 worth of supplies remained on hand. Because supplies purchased for $2,200 in transaction (5) on June 5 were reflected as an asset, that portion of the purchase no longer on hand, $1,650, represented supplies used, or the supplies expense for the month. The result was a $1,650 decrease in both Supplies on Hand and J. Hill, Capital.

Balance Sheet

Assets		Liabilities	
Cash	$27,450	Accounts Payable	$ 1,000
Accounts Receivable	4,500		
Prepaid Insurance	3,500		
Supplies on Hand	550	**Owner's Equity**	
Land	18,000	J. Hill, Capital	53,000
		Total Liabilities and	
Total Assets	$54,000	Owner's Equity	$54,000

Transactions (12) and (13) are reflected on the balance sheet to ensure that the items on that statement reflect the current end-of-period amounts. Because $100 of prepaid insurance has expired and $1,650 of supplies on hand are used during June, the related assets are reduced, and the amounts, representing June expenses, must be subtracted from the owner's capital account. These transactions are referred to as *adjustments*. A thorough discussion of adjustments is given in Chapter 3.

Exhibit 1–3 summarizes the June activities of the Capital Driving School and shows their effect on the balance sheet equation. The final results are, of course,

EXHIBIT 1–3
Summary of June Activities
and Their Effect on the Balance Sheet Equation

Transactions		Cash	+	Accounts Receivable	+	Prepaid Insurance	+	Supplies on Hand	+	Land	=	Accounts Payable	+	J. Hill, Capital
						Assets					=	Liabilities	+	Owner's Equity
(1)	+	$50,000											+	$50,000
(2)	−	18,000								+	$18,000				
(3)	−	4,600												−	4,600
(4)	−	3,600				+	$3,600								
(5)								+	$2,200				+ $2,200		
(6)			+	$18,500										+	18,500
(7)	−	8,000												−	8,000
(8)	+	14,000	−	14,000											
(9)	−	1,200											− 1,200		
(10)	−	150												−	150
(11)	−	1,000												−	1,000
(12)						−	100							−	100
(13)								−	1,650					−	1,650
		$27,450	+	$ 4,500	+	$3,500	+	$ 550	+	$18,000	=	$1,000	+	$53,000

$54,000 $54,000

identical with those given on the balance sheet prepared after transaction (13). The June 30 balance sheet is the only one that the Capital Driving School would actually prepare, because June 30 is the end of the accounting period.

As a result of the driving school's June activities, James Hill's capital increased from his original investment of $50,000 to $53,000, an increase of $3,000. Had Hill not withdrawn $1,000 for personal use, the increase would have been $4,000, which represents the net income, or net earnings, for June.

THE INCOME STATEMENT

Although it is important to know the amount of net income, it is equally important to know how it was earned. To show the results of operations for a period, we prepare an income statement, which lists the revenue and expenses. When total revenue exceeds total expenses, the resulting amount is net income; when expenses exceed revenue, the resulting amount is a net loss. To prepare a June income statement for the Capital Driving School, we must identify the revenue and expenses by analyzing the changes in owner's equity for the period. The changes in James Hill's capital, taken from Exhibit 1–3, are shown below, with an explanation of each change:

(1)	Capital contribution	+	$50,000
(3)	Rent expense	−	4,600
(6)	Billings to students	+	18,500
(7)	Salaries expense	−	8,000
(10)	Utilities expense	−	150
(11)	Withdrawal by Hill	−	1,000
(12)	Insurance expense	−	100
(13)	Supplies expense	−	1,650
	Ending Capital Balance		$53,000

From this list of transactions and adjustments, we see that revenue, or instructional fees, equals $18,500, the June billings to students in transaction (6). The expenses are derived from transactions (3), (7), (10), (12), and (13) for rent, salaries, utilities, insurance, and supplies. Items (1) and (11), representing contributions and withdrawals by Hill, are ignored in preparing the income statement.

Capital Driving School's formal income statement for the month of June, which would be prepared to accompany the June 30 balance sheet, appears in Exhibit 1–4.

EXHIBIT 1–4

Capital Driving School
Income Statement
For the Month of June, 19XX

Revenue		
Instructional Fees		$18,500
Expenses		
Rent Expense	$4,600	
Salaries Expense	8,000	
Utilities Expense	150	
Insurance Expense	100	
Supplies Expense	1,650	
Total Expenses		14,500
Net Income		$ 4,000

RELATIONSHIP OF BALANCE SHEET AND INCOME STATEMENT

We have seen that the balance sheet and the income statement complement each other. The income statement summarizes a firm's operating results for the accounting period, and these results are reflected in the owners' equity on the balance sheet. For yearly statements, this complementary relationship might be shown graphically as follows:

STATEMENT OF OWNER'S EQUITY

Frequently at the end of an accounting period, a statement of owner's equity is prepared to accompany the balance sheet and income statement. This is simply a summary of the changes in the owner's capital balance during the period. Exhibit 1–5 shows this type of statement for the Capital Driving School. Note that the ending balance on this statement agrees with the owner's capital balance on the balance sheet at June 30, 19XX.

EXHIBIT 1–5

Capital Driving School
Statement of Owner's Equity
For the Month of June, 19XX

J. Hill, Capital, June 1, 19XX	$ –0–
Add: Capital Contributed in June	50,000
Net Income for June	4,000
	$54,000
Less: Capital Withdrawn in June	1,000
J. Hill, Capital, June 30, 19XX	$53,000

This statement further demonstrates the relationship between the income statement and the balance sheet. The net income (or net loss) for a period is an input into the statement of owner's equity, while the ending owner's equity balance on the statement is an input into the balance sheet at the end of the period. When financial statements are prepared, the sequence suggested by this relationship is customarily followed; that is, the income statement is prepared first, then the statement of owner's equity (when such a statement is prepared to accompany the income statement and balance sheet), and then the balance sheet.

DEMONSTRATION PROBLEM FOR REVIEW

L.D. Ford operates the Ford Courier Service, a single proprietorship. The firm utilizes leased vehicles, and specializes in delivery services to banks, computer centers, film dealers, pharmacies, and various small businesses. On January 1 of the current year, the assets and liabilities of the business were as follows: Cash, $8,000; Accounts Receivable, $4,200; Supplies on Hand, $1,200; Prepaid Insurance, $1,800; and Accounts Payable, $1,400. The January business activities were as follows:

(1) Paid $600 on Accounts Payable.
(2) Paid January rent, $3,600.
(3) Received $2,000 on account from customers.
(4) Purchased supplies on account, $500.
(5) Billed customers for delivery services performed on account, $11,500.
(6) Paid employees' wages, $2,400.
(7) Received $2,000 for delivery services performed for cash customers.
(8) Paid utilities expense, $180.
(9) Withdrew $900 cash for Ford's personal use.
(10) Counted supplies on hand at the end of January, $980.
(11) Determined that $150 insurance premiums had expired during January.

REQUIRED

(a) From the data in the first paragraph, prepare a balance sheet for Ford Courier Service as of January 1 of the current year. Use the horizontal form illustrated in Exhibit 1–3 and place the amounts on the first line of the form.

(b) Following the form of Exhibit 1–3, show how transactions (1)–(11) affect the beginning balance sheet, and total the columns to prove that total assets equal liabilities plus owner's equity at January 31.

(c) Prepare an income statement for January.

SOLUTION TO DEMONSTRATION PROBLEM

		Cash	+	Accounts Receivable	+	Supplies on Hand	+	Prepaid Insurance	=	Accounts Payable	+	L. Ford, Capital
(a)		$8,000 +		$ 4,200 +		$1,200 +		$1,800 =		$1,400 +		$13,800
(b)	(1) −	600								− 600		
	(2) −	3,600									−	3,600
	(3) +	2,000 −		2,000								
	(4)				+	500				+ 500		
	(5)		+	11,500							+	11,500
	(6) −	2,400									−	2,400
	(7) +	2,000									+	2,000
	(8) −	180									−	180
	(9) −	900									−	900
	(10)				−	720					−	720
	(11)						−	150			−	150
		$4,320 +		$13,700 +		$ 980 +		$1,650 =		$1,300 +		$19,350

$20,650 $20,650

(c)

Ford Courier Service
Income Statement
For the Month of January, 19XX

Revenue		
Delivery Fees		$13,500
Expenses		
Rent Expense	$3,600	
Wages Expense	2,400	
Utilities Expense	180	
Supplies Expense	720	
Insurance Expense	150	
Total Expenses		7,050
Net Income		$ 6,450

KEY POINTS TO REMEMBER

(1) Although a balance sheet and an income statement are usually prepared at the same time, a balance sheet presents financial position at a *point in time*, while the income statement presents operating results for a *period of time*.

(2) The accounting equation, Assets = Liabilities + Owners' Equity, represents the basic structure of the balance sheet and holds true after each accounting transaction.

(3) In determining net income (Revenue − Expenses) on the *accrual* basis, *revenue* is recognized *when earned* rather than when cash is collected, and *expenses* are recognized when goods and services are *used* rather than when they are paid for.

(4) Owners' equity can be increased by contributions from owners and by revenue. It can be decreased by withdrawals and expenses. Only revenue and expenses are used in determining net income.

(5) Certain fundamental concepts underlying the accounting process include the following:

Accounting entity—each business venture is a separate unit, accounted for separately.

Historical cost—assets are reported at acquisition price and are not adjusted upward.

Objectivity—where possible, recording of transactions should be supported by verifiable evidence.

Going concern—the assumption is made in accounting that a business will continue indefinitely.

Measuring unit—conventional accounting statements are not adjusted for changes in the value of the dollar.

QUESTIONS

1–1 Distinguish between *financial* and *managerial* accounting.

1–2 Name some outside groups that may be interested in a company's financial data and state their particular interests.

1–3 What factors are important in determining a firm's need for electronic data processing?

1–4 Since financial accounting data are primarily historical, how are they useful for control purposes?

1–5 What are *generally accepted accounting principles*, and by whom are they established?

1–6 Why do business firms frequently keep more than one set of records on certain aspects of their financial activities?

1–7 How do the functions of private accountants and public accountants differ?

1–8 What is the purpose of a balance sheet? An income statement?

1–9 Define *assets*, *liabilities*, and *owners' equity*.

1–10 Explain how the presentation of owners' equity in the balance sheet of a corporation differs from that of a single proprietorship.

1–11 State the effect on a corporation's balance sheet of
(a) The declaration of a dividend.
(b) The payment of a dividend.

1–12 What is meant by the *accounting entity*?

1–13 Explain the concepts of *historical cost, objectivity,* and *going concern.* How are they related?

1–14 When the owners of a business withdraw cash, do the withdrawals appear as expenses on the income statement? Explain.

1–15 The owner's capital on a particular balance sheet is $30,000. Without seeing the rest of this financial statement, can you say that the owner should be able to withdraw $30,000 cash from the business? Justify your answer.

1–16 How do the accrual basis and the cash basis of accounting differ?

1–17 Describe a transaction that would
(a) Increase one asset but not change the amount of total assets.
(b) Decrease an asset and a liability.
(c) Decrease an asset and owners' equity.
(d) Increase an asset and a liability.

1–18 Indicate whether each of the following would increase, decrease, or have no effect on owners' equity:
(a) Purchased supplies for cash.
(b) Withdrew supplies for personal use.
(c) Paid salaries.
(d) Purchased equipment for cash.
(e) Invested cash in business.
(f) Rendered service to customers, on account.
(g) Rendered service to customers, for cash.

1–19 On December 31 of the current year, the Parker Company had $400,000 in total assets and owed $160,000 to creditors. If this corporation's capital stock amounted to $200,000, what amount of retained earnings should appear on a December 31 balance sheet?

1–20 During 19XX, the owners' equity of the Benson Bicycle Shop increased from $50,000 to $65,000 even though the owners withdrew $20,000 for personal use. What was the net income (or loss) during 19XX if capital contributions were $5,000?

1–21 A business had total liabilities of $60,000 at the beginning of the year and $45,000 at year-end. At year-end, net assets were $80,000 and total assets were $25,000 greater than at the beginning of the year. If capital contributed exceeded capital withdrawn by $18,000, what was the net income for the year?

EXERCISES

1–22 Following the example shown in (a) below, indicate the effects of the listed transactions on the assets, liabilities, and owner's equity of the balance sheet of Elizabeth Daniels, certified public accountant, a sole proprietorship.
(a) Purchased, for cash, a typewriter for use in office.
  ANSWER: Increase assets (Office Equipment)
          Decrease assets (Cash)
(b) Rendered accounting services and billed customer.
(c) Paid rent for month.
(d) Rendered tax services to customer for cash.

(e) Received amount due from customer in (b).

(f) Purchased, on account, supplies estimated to last two years.

(g) Paid employees' salaries for month.

(h) Paid for supplies purchased in (f).

(i) Withdrew cash for personal use.

1–23 At the beginning of the current year, Blaney Painters had the following balance sheet:

Assets		Liabilities	
Cash	$ 7,200	Accounts Payable	$ 3,000
Accounts Receivable	4,800		
Equipment (Less		**Owner's Equity**	
Accumulated		Blaney, Capital	18,000
Depreciation)	9,000		
		Total Liabilities and	
Total Assets	$21,000	Owner's Equity	$21,000

(a) At the end of the current year, Blaney had the following assets and liabilities: Cash, $12,000; Accounts Receivable, $6,500; Equipment (less Accumulated Depreciation), $8,500; and Accounts Payable, $500. Prepare a year-end balance sheet for Blaney Painters.

(b) Assuming that Blaney did not invest any money in the business during the year, but withdrew $17,000 for personal use, what was the net income or net loss for the current year?

(c) Assuming that Blaney invested an additional $4,000 early in the year, but withdrew $17,000 before the end of the year, what was the net income or net loss for the current year?

1–24 The balance sheet of M. Ryan, attorney, at the beginning of an accounting period is given in equation form below, followed by seven transactions whose effects on the equation are shown.

(a) For each numbered item, describe the transaction that occurred. Of all the transactions affecting M. Ryan, Capital, only transaction (5) had no effect on net income for the period.

(b) What is the amount of net income for the period?

	Cash	+	Accounts Receivable	+	Supplies on Hand	+	Prepaid Rent	=	Accounts Payable	+	M. Ryan, Capital
Balance	$7,000	+	$ 9,000	+	$400	+	$3,600	=	$300	+	$19,700
(1)	+ 2,500	–	2,500								
(2)				+	200				+ 200		
(3)		+	4,800							+	4,800
(4)	– 300								– 300		
(5)	– 1,200									–	1,200
(6)				–	350					–	350
(7)						–	300			–	300
	$8,000	+	$11,300	+	$250	+	$3,300	=	$200	+	$22,650

1–25 The following income statement and balance sheet information is available for Winston Appraisers at the end of the current month:

Supplies on Hand	$3,000	Cash	$ 7,000
Accounts Receivable	8,500	Accounts Payable	1,500
Utilities Expense	400	Salaries Expense	14,000
Supplies Expense	800	Appraisal Service Fees	20,000
Rent Expense	1,600	R. Winston, Capital (at	
		beginning of month)	15,000

(a) Without preparing a formal income statement, calculate the net income or net loss for the month.

(b) If R. Winston made no additional investment during the month, but withdrew $1,200, what is the amount of her capital at the end of the month?

1–26 For the four unrelated situations below, compute the unknown amounts indicated by the letters appearing in each column.

	A	B	C	D
Beginning:				
Assets	$5,000	$8,000	$20,000	$ (d)
Liabilities	2,200	2,000	7,500	6,000
Ending:				
Assets	6,000	10,000	24,000	22,000
Liabilities	2,000	(b)	8,000	5,000
During year:				
Capital Contributed	600	1,500	(c)	3,500
Revenue	(a)	5,200	6,000	15,000
Capital Withdrawn	400	500	1,200	1,500
Expenses	3,200	3,600	3,800	10,000

1–27 The following information appears in the records of Barnes Corporation at the end of the current year:

Accounts Receivable	$ 45,000	Retained Earnings	$?
Accounts Payable	30,000	Supplies on Hand	5,000
Cash	20,000	Equipment	
Capital Stock	100,000	(Less Accumulated	
		Depreciation)	120,000

(a) Without preparing a formal balance sheet, calculate the amount of retained earnings at the end of the current year.

(b) If the amount of the retained earnings at the beginning of the current year was $40,000, and $5,000 in dividends were declared and paid this year, what was the net income for the year?

PROBLEMS

1–28 R.A. Bartlett Appraisal Service is a sole proprietorship providing commercial and industrial appraisals and feasibility studies. On January 1 of the current year, the assets and liabilities of the business were the following: Cash, $3,200; Accounts Receivable, $4,800; Supplies on Hand, $600; and Accounts Payable, $500. The following business transactions occurred during January:

(1) Paid rent for three months, $900.
(2) Received $2,600 on customers' accounts.
(3) Paid $350 on accounts payable.
(4) Received $1,500 for services performed for cash customers.
(5) Purchased $200 worth of supplies on account.
(6) Billed the city for a feasibility study performed, $3,200, and various other credit customers, $4,300.
(7) Paid salary of assistant, $1,500.
(8) Paid utilities expense, $150.
(9) Withdrew $800 cash for personal use of R.A. Bartlett.
(10) Supplies on hand at the end of January amounted to $320.
(11) Determined that rent expense for the month was $300 [see transaction (1)].

REQUIRED
(a) From the data in the first paragraph, prepare a balance sheet equation for R.A. Bartlett Appraisal Service as of January 1 of the current year. Use the horizontal form illustrated in Exhibit 1–3 and place the amounts on the first line of the form. The headings should be as follows: Cash, Accounts Receivable, Supplies on Hand, Prepaid Rent, Accounts Payable, and R.A. Bartlett, Capital.
(b) Following the form of Exhibit 1–3, show the effects of transactions (1)–(11) on the beginning balance sheet amounts, and total the columns to prove that assets equal liabilities plus owner's equity at January 31.
(c) Prepare an income statement for January.
(d) Prepare a statement of owner's equity for January.

1–29 An analysis (similar to Exhibit 1–3) of the transactions of Travis Detective Agency for the month of May appears below. Line (1) summarizes Travis' balance sheet data on May 1; lines (2)–(10) represent the business transactions for May.

	Cash	+	Accounts Receivable	+	Supplies on Hand	+	Prepaid Insur- ance	=	Notes Payable	+	Accounts Payable	+	Travis, Capital
(1)	$2,800	+	$8,000	+	$720	+	$240	=	$1,000	+	$520	+	$10,240
(2)	+ 500								+ 500				
(3)	+ 2,600	–	2,600										
(4)				+	250					+	250		
(5)		+	7,200									+	7,200
(6)	– 900											–	900
(7)	+ 1,500											+	1,500
(8)				–	550							–	550
(9)						–	20					–	20
(10)	– 1,000								– 1,000				

REQUIRED

(a) Prove that assets equal liabilities plus owner's equity at May 1.

(b) Describe the apparent transaction indicated by each line. [For example, line (2): Borrowed $500, giving a note payable.] If any line could reasonably represent more than one type of transaction, describe each type of transaction.

1–30 On March 1, Jean Carter began the Sunshine Delivery Service, which provides delivery of bulk mailings to the post office, neighborhood delivery of weekly papers, data delivery to computer service centers, and various other delivery services via leased vans. On March 1, Carter invested $25,000 of her own funds in the firm and borrowed $10,000 from her father on a six-month, non-interest-bearing note payable. The following information is available at March 31:

Accounts Receivable	$21,300	Delivery Fees	$16,200
Rent Expense	1,800	Cash	14,600
Advertising Expense	300	Supplies on Hand, March 31	6,500
Supplies Expense	2,700	Notes Payable	10,000
Accounts Payable	4,000	Prepaid Insurance, March 31	1,100
Salaries Expense	5,600	Insurance Expense	100
Miscellaneous Expense	200	J. Carter, Capital, March 1	25,000

Carter made no additional investments during March, but withdrew $1,000 during the month.

REQUIRED

(a) Prepare an income statement for the month of March.

(b) Prepare a statement of owner's equity for the month of March.

(c) Prepare a balance sheet at March 31.

1–31 The following balance sheet data is given for the Chez Michel Catering Service, a corporation, at May 31 of the current year:

Accounts Receivable	$ 5,800	Accounts Payable	$ 3,500
Notes Payable	18,000	Cash	6,500
Equipment		Capital Stock	25,000
(Less Accumulated		Retained Earnings	?
Depreciation)	46,000		
Supplies on Hand	4,200		

Assume that, during the next two days, only the following transactions occurred:

June 1 Purchased additional equipment costing $6,000, giving $2,000 cash and a $4,000 note payable.

2 Declared and paid a dividend, $2,000.

REQUIRED

(a) Prepare a balance sheet at May 31 of the current year.

(b) Prepare a balance sheet at June 2 of the current year.

1–32 On June 1 of the current year, a group of bush pilots in Fort Frances, Ontario, formed the Northwest Fly-In Service, Inc., by selling $50,000 capital stock for cash. The group then leased several amphibious aircraft and docking facilities, equipping them to transport fishermen and hunters to outpost camps owned by various resorts. The following transactions occurred during June of the current year:

(1) Sold capital stock for cash, $50,000.
(2) Paid June rent for aircraft, dockage, and dockside office, $3,200.
(3) Purchased fuel and other supplies on account, $1,950.
(4) Paid bill for June advertising in various sport magazines, $680.
(5) Paid insurance premiums for six months in advance, $3,600.
(6) Rendered fly-in services for various groups for cash, $14,800.
(7) Billed the Ministry of Natural Resources for transporting mapping personnel, $4,375, and also billed various firms for fly-in services, $4,275.
(8) Paid $350 on accounts payable.
(9) Received $2,725 on account from clients.
(10) Paid June wages, $7,400.
(11) Declared and paid a dividend, $2,500.
(12) Determined that supplies and fuel on hand at June 30 amounted to $520.
(13) Determined that $600 insurance premiums expired during June.

REQUIRED
(a) Using the horizontal form of the balance sheet illustrated in Exhibit 1–3, designate the following column headings: Cash, Accounts Receivable, Supplies on Hand, Prepaid Insurance, Accounts Payable, Capital Stock, and Retained Earnings.
(b) Following the form of Exhibit 1–3, show how the June transactions affect the balance sheet, and total all columns to prove that assets equal liabilities plus stockholders' equity.
(c) Prepare an income statement for June.

1–33 Balance sheet information for the Parker Packaging Service at the end of the last two years is given below.

	December 31, This Year	December 31, Last Year
Accounts Receivable	$56,000	$48,000
Accounts Payable	2,000	2,400
Cash	18,000	12,000
Equipment (Less Accumulated Depreciation)	24,000	28,000
Prepaid Insurance	600	400
Supplies on Hand	2,400	2,600
Land	10,000	10,000
Building (Less Accumulated Depreciation)	32,000	35,000
Mortgage Payable	52,000	55,000
Parker, Capital	?	?

REQUIRED
(a) Prepare balance sheets for December 31 of each year.
(b) Parker contributed $6,000 to the business early this year but withdrew $9,000 in December of this year. Calculate the net income for this year.

ALTERNATE PROBLEMS

1–28A Arlette Walker began the Walker Answering Service, a sole proprietorship, during December of last year. The firm provides services for professional people and is currently operating with leased equipment. On January 1 of this year, the assets and liabilities of the business were: Cash, $3,800; Accounts Receivable, $4,200; Supplies on Hand, $800; and Accounts Payable, $500. The following transactions occurred during January.

   (1) Paid rent on office and equipment for January through March, $1,800.
   (2) Collected $3,700 on account from clients.
   (3) Purchased supplies on account, $200.
   (4) Billed clients for work performed on account, $7,200.
   (5) Paid $400 on accounts payable.
   (6) Paid advertising expense, $150.
   (7) Paid salaries expense, $3,200.
   (8) Paid utilities expense, $120.
   (9) Withdrew $800 for Arlette Walker's personal use.
(10) Supplies on hand at the end of January amounted to $600.
(11) Determined that $600 of prepaid rent had expired [see transaction (1)].

REQUIRED
(a) From the information in the first paragraph, prepare a balance sheet equation for Walker Answering Service. Use the horizontal form illustrated in Exhibit 1–3 and place the balance sheet amounts at January 1 on the first line of the form. Column headings should include: Cash, Accounts Receivable, Supplies on Hand, Prepaid Rent, Accounts Payable, and A. Walker, Capital.
(b) Following the form of Exhibit 1–3, show the effects of the January transactions on the balance sheet amounts, and total all columns to prove that assets equal liabilities plus owner's equity.
(c) Prepare an income statement for January.
(d) Prepare a statement of owner's equity for January.

1–29A Appearing below is an analysis (similar to Exhibit 1–3) of the June transactions for Richard Bolton, consulting engineer. Line (1) summarizes Bolton's balance sheet data on June 1; lines (2)–(10) are the business transactions for June.

	Cash +	Accounts Receivable +	Supplies on Hand +	Prepaid Rent =	Accounts Payable +	Notes Payable +	R. Bolton, Capital
(1)	$1,800 +	$5,200 +	$600 +	$720 =	$520 +	0 +	$7,800
(2)			+ 300		+ 300		
(3)	+ 2,000					+ $2,000	
(4)	+ 3,800 −	3,800					
(5)		+ 4,500					+ 4,500
(6)	− 120						− 120
(7)	− 420				− 420		
(8)	− 2,000					− 2,000	
(9)		− 380					− 380
(10)				− 360			− 360

REQUIRED
(a) Prove that assets equal liabilities plus owner's equity on June 1.
(b) Describe the apparent transactions indicated by each line. For example, line (2): Purchased supplies on account, $300. If any line could reasonably represent more than one type of transaction, describe each type of transaction.

1–30A After all transactions and adjustments have been reflected for the current year, the records of J. Reynolds, interior decorator, show the following information:

Notes Payable	$ 1,500	Supplies on Hand, December 31	$ 1,600
Prepaid Insurance, December 31	300	Cash	2,600
Decorating Fees	32,000	Accounts Receivable	18,200
Supplies Expense	1,200	Advertising Expense	350
Insurance Expense	120	Salaries Expense	9,800
Miscellaneous Expense	80	Rent Expense	3,600
J. Reynolds, Capital, January 1	8,650	Accounts Payable	700

Reynolds made an additional investment of $2,000 in the business during the year and withdrew $7,000 near the end of the year.

REQUIRED
(a) Prepare an income statement for the current year.
(b) Prepare a statement of owner's equity for the current year.
(c) Prepare a balance sheet at December 31 of the current year.

1–31A The following balance sheet data is given for Burns Plumbing Contractors, Inc., at June 30 of the current year:

Accounts Payable	$ 4,200	Capital Stock	$120,000
Cash	21,600	Retained Earnings	?
Supplies on Hand	8,000	Notes Payable	6,000
Equipment		Accounts Receivable	24,000
(Less Accumulated Depreciation)	106,000	Prepaid Insurance	600

Assume that, during the next two days, only the following transactions occurred:

July 1 Paid non-interest-bearing note due today, $6,000.
    2 Purchased equipment for $8,000, paying $5,000 cash and giving a note payable for the balance.
    2 Declared and paid a dividend, $4,000.

REQUIRED
(a) Prepare a balance sheet at June 30 of the current year.
(b) Prepare a balance sheet at July 2 of the current year.

BUSINESS DECISION PROBLEM

Gary Lynch, a friend of yours, is negotiating the purchase of a firm called Niagara Car Wash, which operates two car washes in the city. Lynch has managed a car wash in another city and knows the technical side of the business. However, he knows little about accounting, so he asks for your assistance. The sole owner of the firm, J. Fisher, has provided Lynch with income statements for the past three years, which show an average net income of $42,000 per year. The latest balance sheet shows total assets of $150,000 and liabilities of $30,000. Included among the assets are buildings listed at $40,000 after accumulated depreciation and equipment listed at $70,000 after accumulated depreciation. Lynch brings the following matters to your attention:

(1) Fisher is asking $160,000 for the firm. He has told Lynch that, because the firm has been earning 35% on the owner's investment, the price should be higher than the net assets on the balance sheet.

(2) Lynch has noticed no salary for Fisher on the income statements, even though he worked half-time in the business. Fisher explained that because he had other income, he withdrew only $10,000 each year from the firm for personal use. If he purchases the firm, Lynch will hire a full-time manager for the firm at an annual salary of $18,000.

(3) Lynch wonders whether the buildings and equipment are really worth $110,000, the net amount shown on the balance sheet.

(4) Fisher's tax returns for the past three years report a lower net income for the firm than the amounts shown in the financial statements. Lynch is skeptical about the accounting principles used in preparing the financial statements.

REQUIRED

(a) How did Fisher arrive at the 35% return figure given in (1)? If Lynch accepts Fisher's average annual income figure of $42,000, what would Lynch's percentage return be, assuming that the net income remained at the same level and that the firm was purchased for $160,000?

(b) Should Fisher's withdrawals affect the net income reported in the financial statements? What will Lynch's percentage return be if he takes into consideration the $18,000 salary he plans to pay a full-time manager?

(c) What explanation would you give Lynch with respect to the value of the buildings and equipment?

(d) Could there be legitimate reasons for the difference between net income shown in the financial statements and net income reported on the tax returns, as mentioned in (4)? How might Lynch obtain additional assurance about the propriety of the financial statements?

2

The Double-entry
Accounting System

> What advantages does the Merchant derive by Book-keeping
> by double entry? It is amongst the finest inventions of the
> human mind.
>
> GOETHE

The format for analyzing and recording transactions illustrated in Chapter 1 was useful in conveying a basic understanding of how transactions affect financial statements. This approach is not effective, however, in meeting management's needs for timely financial information. The transactions of most business firms are numerous and complex, affecting many different items appearing on the financial statements. Therefore, a formal system of classification and recording is required so that data may be gathered for day-to-day management requirements and timely accounting reports. In this chapter, we will examine the classification and recording system commonly called double-entry accounting. At the same time, we will expand several of the basic ideas introduced in Chapter 1.

CATEGORIES OF DATA NEEDED

Exhibit 2–1 shows the balance sheet and the income statement forms explained in Chapter 1. To prepare both the balance sheet and the income statement, we need five categories of information from the accounting system: **assets, liabilities,**

EXHIBIT 2–1
The Basic Financial Statements

ABC Company Balance Sheet December 31, 19XX					ABC Company Income Statement For the Month of December, 19XX		
(List of assets)	$ XX	(List of liabilities)	$ XX		Revenue		$XXX
	XX		XX				
	XX				Expenses:	$XX	
	XX	Total Liabilities	$ XX			XX	
						XX	
						XX	
	____	Owners' Equity	XX		Total Expenses		XX
		Total Liabilities					
Total Assets	$XXX	and Owners' Equity	$XXX		Net Income		$ XX

owners' equity, revenue, and **expenses**. The first three relate to the balance sheet and the last two relate to the income statement.

In Chapter 1 we analyzed the effects of transactions on the balance sheet equation by starting with the three major categories: assets, liabilities, and owners' equity. When we used the basic accounting equation (Assets = Liabilities + Owners' Equity), we noted that owners' equity included increases from revenue and decreases from expenses. Specifically, owners' equity at the balance sheet date consisted of (1) the beginning balance, (2) net capital contributions (additional contributions less withdrawals), and (3) net income for the period (revenue less expenses). In preparing an income statement, we analyzed changes in owners' equity to obtain the necessary revenue and expense data.

Since in a typical business, most transactions relate to revenue and expense, it is more efficient to keep track of revenue and expense as a separate part of owners' equity. The following expanded form of the accounting equation is useful:[1]

$$\text{ASSETS} = \text{LIABILITIES} + \underbrace{\hspace{9cm}}_{\text{OWNERS' EQUITY}}$$

$$\left[\begin{matrix}\text{Beginning} \\ \text{Capital}\end{matrix} + \begin{matrix}\text{Contri-} \\ \text{butions}\end{matrix} - \text{Withdrawals}\right] + \left[\text{Revenue} - \text{Expenses}\right]$$

If we had used this expanded equation in summarizing the June transactions of the Capital Driving School (see Exhibit 1–3, page 23), the changes in owner's equity would have been shown in three columns, as follows:

	J. Hill, Capital + Contributions − Withdrawals	+ Revenue	− Expenses
(1) Capital contribution	+ $50,000		
(3) Rent expense			− $ 4,600
(6) Billings to students		+ $18,500	
(7) Salaries expense			− 8,000
(10) Utilities expense			− 150
(11) Withdrawal by Hill	− 1,000		
(12) Insurance expense			− 100
(13) Supplies expense			− 1,650
	$49,000	+ $18,500	− $14,500

$53,000

Observe that the column totals in the above illustration, when added together, amount to $53,000, exactly the amount of the ending owner's equity shown in Exhibit 1–3. Segregating revenue and expense amounts, however, permits us to

---

[1] In a corporation, beginning capital consists of both capital stock and retained earnings. Contributions would equal additional capital stock sold, whereas withdrawals would be the amount of dividends declared during the period.

prepare an income statement without first having to analyze all changes in the owner's capital for the period. The desirability of doing this is apparent even in a situation as simple as our Capital Driving School example. In more complex business situations—with many sources of revenue and possibly hundreds of different types of expenses—separate recording of revenue and expenses is imperative.

So far, our discussion of transaction analysis has been conceptual; we have tried to convey an understanding of how transactions affect the financial statements. Obviously, the system of transaction recording we have illustrated would be entirely inadequate for even relatively simple businesses, since even they will usually have a substantial number of transactions involving a variety of data to be reported in financial statements. In practice, the necessary data are accumulated in a set of records called *accounts*.

THE ACCOUNT

The basic component of the formal accounting system is the **account**, which is an individual record of increases and decreases in specific assets, liabilities, owner capital, revenue, and expenses. The Cash account for the Capital Driving School might appear as shown in Exhibit 2–2.

The amounts in the Capital Driving School Cash account consist of the additions and deductions in the cash column of Exhibit 1–3. Increases in the Cash account have been placed on the left side and the decreases on the right side. A formal system of placement for increases and decreases in various accounts is explained later in this chapter. In our example, there was no beginning amount (balance), because June was the first month of business. A beginning amount would have appeared with the increases, above the entry for $50,000.

The form illustrated in Exhibit 2–2, called a *two-column* account, is often used in a manually maintained record-keeping system. Another popular form, called a *running balance*, or *three-column* account, is illustrated later in this chapter. Most account forms facilitate recording the following information:

(1) The account title and number.

(2) Amounts reflecting increases and decreases.

(3) Cross-references to other accounting records.

(4) Dates and descriptive notations.

Each account has a short account title that describes the data being recorded in that account. Some common account titles are Cash, Accounts Receivable, Notes Payable, Professional Fees, and Rent Expense. In manually maintained records, increases and decreases are recorded in ruled columns under headings that indicate the meaning of the amounts appearing there. These amounts are referred to as **entries**. In other words, making an entry in an account consists of recording an amount in a particular place to represent either an increase or a decrease in the account. The normal balance of any account is simply the excess

EXHIBIT 2–2
Cash Account for the Capital Driving School

Cash   Account No. _____

Date	Description	Post. Ref.	Amount	Date	Description	Post. Ref.	Amount
19XX				19XX			
June 1			50,000	June 2			18,000
30	27,450		14,000	3			4,600
			64,000	4			3,600
				30			8,000
				30			1,200
				30			150
				30			1,000
							36,550

of increases over decreases that have been recorded to date. In Exhibit 2–2, we have indicated this balance, $27,450, on the left side of the account beside the last entry for an increase. This is the difference between the sum of the increases, $64,000, and the sum of the decreases, $36,550, both of which are written in pencil to provide temporary totals. Finally, most accounts contain space for presentation of other types of information—for example, the date of any entry, possibly some memoranda explaining a particular entry, and a posting reference column (indicated by Post. Ref.). The posting reference column is used for noting the records from which entries into this account may have been taken. This practice will be explained more fully in the next chapter.

The account is an extremely simple record that can be summarized in terms of four money elements:

(1) Beginning balance.

(2) Additions.

(3) Deductions.

(4) Ending balance.

Obviously, if any three elements are known, the fourth can easily be computed. Normally, after transactions have been recorded, only the ending balance needs to be computed. Accountants, however, are sometimes confronted with situations in which available data are incomplete and reconstruction of accounts is necessary. Let us demonstrate such an analysis with the following example:

	A	B	C	D
Beginning balance	$10	$70	$ 40	$ (?)
Additions	40	30	(?)	100
Deductions	20	(?)	160	120
Ending balance	(?)	10	0	40

In column A, the ending balance must be $20 greater than the beginning balance, because the additions exceed the deductions by $20. The ending balance is therefore $30. In B, the account balance decreased by $60, so the deductions must exceed the additions by $60. Therefore, total deductions are $90. Show that the unknown variable in C is $120 and in D is $60.

A simplified form often used to represent the account in accounting textbooks and in the classroom is referred to as the **T account** (because it resembles the letter T). This is merely a skeleton version of the account illustrated for actual record keeping. A T-account form with the June changes in Cash entered for the Capital Driving School follows:

Cash

(1)	50,000	(2)	18,000
(8)	14,000	(3)	4,600
	64,000	(4)	3,600
		(7)	8,000
		(9)	1,200
		(10)	150
		(11)	1,000
			36,550

Because dates and other related data are usually omitted in T accounts, it is customary to "key" the entries with a number or a letter to identify the transaction or entry. This permits a systematic review of the entries in the event that an error has been made. It also enables anyone to review a set of such accounts and match related entries. The numbers in this T account are the ones used to identify the June transactions for the Capital Driving School in our Chapter 1 example.

The printed account form in Exhibit 2–2 is appropriate for classifying accounting data in manual record-keeping systems. In accounting systems employing computers, the account form may not be obvious because the actual data might be stored on media such as magnetic tapes or discs. Every accounting system, however, whether manual or automated, must provide for the retrieval and printing out of the types of information shown in the manual form.

THE SYSTEM OF DEBITS AND CREDITS

One basic characteristic of all account forms is that entries recording increases and decreases are separated. In some accounts, such as the Cash account illustrated in Exhibit 2–2, increases are recorded on the left-hand side of the account and decreases on the right-hand side; in other accounts the reverse is true. The method used in different types of accounts is a matter of convention; that is, a simple set of rules is followed. The remainder of this chapter is devoted to the discussion and illustration of such rules.

The terms **debit** and **credit** are used to describe the left-hand and the right-hand sides of an account, as shown below.

(Any type of account)	
Debit	**Credit**
Always the left side	Always the right side

Regardless of what is recorded in an account, an entry made on the left-hand side is a debit to the account, while an entry recorded on the right-hand side is a credit to the account. Sometimes the abbreviations dr. and cr. are used.

THE ORIGINS OF RECORD KEEPING

Double-entry bookkeeping is simply a specialized form of keeping accounts. It is neither a discovery of science nor the inspiration of a happy moment, but the outcome of continued efforts to meet the changing necessities of trade.[*]

The origin of keeping accounts has been traced as far back as 8500 B.C., the date archaeologists have established for certain clay tokens—cones, disks, spheres, and pellets—found in Mesopotamia (modern Iraq). These tokens represented such commodities as sheep, jugs of oil, bread, or clothing and were used in the Middle East to keep records. The tokens were often sealed in clay balls, called *bullae*, which were broken on delivery so the shipment could be checked against the invoice; *bullae*, in effect, were the first bills of lading. Later, symbols impressed on wet clay tablets replaced the tokens. Some experts consider this stage of record keeping the beginning of the art of writing, which spread rapidly along the trade routes and took hold throughout the known civilized world.[†]

Development of more formal account keeping methods is attributed to the merchants and bankers of Florence, Venice, and Genoa during the thirteenth to fifteenth centuries. The earliest of these methods consisted of accounts kept by a Florentine banker in 1211 A.D. The system was fairly primitive; accounts were not related in any special way (in terms of equality for entries), and balancing of the accounts was lacking. Systematic bookkeeping evolved from these methods, however, and double-entry records first appeared in Genoa in 1340 A.D.[‡]

The first treatise on the art of systematic bookkeeping appeared in 1494, in Venice. "Everything About Arithmetic, Geometry, and Proportion (*Summa de Arithmetica, Geometria, Proportioni et Proportionalita*) was written by the Franciscan monk, Fra Luca Paciolo, one of the most celebrated mathematicians of his day. The work was not, in fact, intended to give instruction in bookkeeping, but to summarize the existing knowledge of mathematics. The treatise on bookkeeping appeared in the arithmetical part of the work. Although Paciolo made no claim to developing the art of bookkeeping, he has been regarded as the father of double-entry accounting. In "An Historical Defense of Bookkeeping," eminent accountant Henry Rand Hatfield referred to the system as one "sired four hundred years ago by a monk, and today damned by thousands of university students."[§]

---

[*]Richard Brown, ed., *A History of Accounting and Accountants* (New York: Augustus M. Kelly Publishers, 1968), page 93.
[†]"The Roots of Writing," *Time*, August 1, 1977, page 76.
[‡]Richard Brown, page 99.
[§]A paper read before the American Association of University Instructors in Accounting (now the American Accounting Association), December 29, 1923 and reprinted in *The Journal of Accountancy*, April 1924, page 247.

The terms *debit* and *credit* are not synonymous with the words *increase* and *decrease*. The system of debits and credits related to increases and decreases in each of the five categories of accounts—assets, liabilities, owners' equity, revenue, and expenses—is shown in Exhibit 2–3.

The system of debits and credits illustrated here is the standard **double-entry** system, so-called because at least two entries, a debit and a credit, are made for each transaction. The system of rules is analogous to the set of traffic rules whereby everyone in this country agrees to drive on the right-hand side of the road. Obviously, the system would work if we reversed everything; the important point is that we all follow the same rules.

Observe the following relationships in Exhibit 2–3:

(1) Debit always refers to the left side of any account, and credit refers to the right side.
(2) Increases in asset and expense accounts are debit entries, while increases in liability, owners' equity, and revenue accounts are credit entries.
(3) Decreases are logically recorded on the side opposite increases.
(4) The normal balance of any account is on the side on which increases are recorded—asset and expense accounts normally have debit balances, while the other three groups normally have credit balances. This result occurs because increases in an account are customarily greater than or equal to decreases.

Note that the pattern for assets is opposite that for liabilities and owners' equity. Also observe that the pattern for revenue is the same as for owners' equity.

EXHIBIT 2–3
Pattern of Increases and Decreases,
Debits and Credits, and Normal Balances

Five Major Categories of Accounts

	Assets		Liabilities		Owners' Equity		Revenue		Expenses	
	Debit	Credit	Debit	Credit	Debit	Credit	Debit	Credit	Debit	Credit
(1) Always true										
(2) Increases	+			+		+		+	+	
(3) Decreases		−	−			−		−		−
(4) Normal balance	★			★		★		★	★	

This is to be expected, because revenue increases owners' equity. Following the same logic, the pattern for expenses is opposite that of owners' equity, because expenses reduce owners' equity.

THE RUNNING BALANCE ACCOUNT

In manually maintained accounting records, the running balance, or three-column, ledger account is often used rather than the symmetrical two-column form illustrated in Exhibit 2–2. The Cash account for the Capital Driving School in running balance form is shown in Exhibit 2–4. Notice that the account contains all the information shown in the two-column account but also provides a balance after each transaction.

The major advantage of this type of account over the two-column account is that the account balance is apparent for any date during the period. Use of the running balance account also avoids the monthly ruling of accounts, which is customarily done when the two-column account is used. A slight disadvantage is that one must be careful to note whether the account has a normal balance or not. An abnormal account balance should be placed in parentheses. For example, if we overdrew our bank balance, the Cash account balance would be abnormal (a credit balance).

We shall employ the running balance account in our formal illustrations throughout the succeeding chapters. To assist you in the earlier chapters, we have

EXHIBIT 2–4
Cash Account for the Capital Driving School

Cash   Account No. _____

Date		Description	Post. Ref.	Debit*	Credit	Balance
19XX						
June	1			50,000		50,000
	2				18,000	32,000
	3				4,600	27,400
	4				3,600	23,800
	30				8,000	15,800
	30			14,000		29,800
	30				1,200	28,600
	30				150	28,450
	30				1,000	27,450

placed an asterisk (*) in the column of the account that designates its normal balance. In illustrations in which detail is not needed and concepts are emphasized, we will use T accounts.

ILLUSTRATION OF DEBIT AND CREDIT ANALYSIS

The following illustration of debit and credit analysis uses the transactions given in Chapter 1 for the first month's operations of the Capital Driving School. Each transaction is stated, analyzed, and followed by an illustration of the appropriate debit and credit entries in the various accounts, using T accounts for simplicity. We have numbered each transaction for reference as in Chapter 1. In the transaction analysis and the resulting debits and credits, each entry resulting from a particular transaction is parenthetically keyed to the transaction number.

TRANSACTION (1):   On June 1, James Hill deposited $50,000 of his personal funds in a special checking account for the Capital Driving School.

   Analysis: In the first transaction of Capital Driving School, Hill's contribution of capital increases both the assets and the equities of the firm. Specifically, Cash increases by $50,000, and the owner's equity account, J. Hill, Capital, increases by the same amount. The entries are

   Debit Cash $50,000   **Credit** J. Hill, Capital $50,000

The related accounts would appear as follows:

	Cash			J. Hill, Capital	
(1)	50,000			(1)	50,000

TRANSACTION (2):   On June 2, Hill paid $18,000 for a lot to be used for storing vehicles and for some driving instruction.

   Analysis: This transaction represents the conversion of one asset to another, resulting in an increase in the asset, Land, and a decrease in the asset, Cash. The entries are

   Debit Land $18,000   **Credit** Cash $18,000

The related accounts would appear as follows:

	Land			Cash		
(2)	18,000		(1)	50,000	(2)	18,000

TRANSACTION (3):   On June 3, Hill paid $600 to rent a furnished office and $4,000 for leasing training vehicles for June.

   Analysis: The cost of using the office and the training vehicles is a June operating expense. When financial statements are prepared at the end of June, the month's rent will appear on the income statement as an expense. The transaction reduces Cash and increases Rent Expense. The entries are

Debit Rent Expense $4,600   **Credit** Cash $4,600

The related accounts would appear as follows:

Rent Expense			Cash			
(3)	4,600		(1)	50,000	(2)	18,000
					(3)	4,600

TRANSACTION (4):   On June 4, Hill paid vehicle insurance premiums of $3,600 for three years.

   Analysis: This payment for future coverage creates an asset, Prepaid Insurance, and reduces the asset Cash. As each month passes, $\frac{1}{36}$ of the amount, or $100, will appear on the income statement as Insurance Expense, the cost of that month's coverage [see transaction (12)]. The entries are

Debit Prepaid Insurance $3,600   **Credit** Cash $3,600

The related accounts would appear as follows:

Prepaid Insurance			Cash			
(4)	3,600		(1)	50,000	(2)	18,000
					(3)	4,600
					(4)	3,600

TRANSACTION (5):   On June 5, Hill purchased fuel and other supplies on account for $2,200.

   Analysis: Hill has purchased the fuel and other supplies on credit terms rather than cash. This transaction increases both an asset, Supplies on Hand, and a liability, Accounts Payable. At the end of the month, supplies will be counted to determine the amount used during the month. The asset will then be reduced and the related expense increased [see transaction (13)]. The entries are

Debit Supplies on Hand $2,200   **Credit** Accounts Payable $2,200

The related accounts would appear as follows:

Supplies on Hand		Accounts Payable	
(5) 2,200			(5) 2,200

TRANSACTION (6):   On June 26, the school's students were billed $18,500 for June instructional fees.

   Analysis: Providing instruction during the month generates an asset, Accounts Receivable, and revenue, Instructional Fees. Note that the revenue is reflected in the month that instruction is given, even though the students may not pay the fees until a later period. The entries are

   Debit Accounts Receivable $18,500   **Credit** Instructional Fees $18,500

The related accounts would appear as follows:

Accounts Receivable		Instructional Fees	
(6) 18,500			(6) 18,500

TRANSACTION (7):   On June 30, Hill paid instructors' salaries for June of $8,000.

   Analysis: The services received from driving instructors during the month represent an expense that will be shown on the June income statement. Therefore, this transaction increases an expense, Salaries Expense, and decreases an asset, Cash. The entries are

   Debit Salaries Expense $8,000   **Credit** Cash $8,000

The related accounts would appear as follows:

Salaries Expense		Cash	
(7) 8,000		(1) 50,000	(2) 18,000
			(3) 4,600
			(4) 3,600
			(7) 8,000

TRANSACTION (8):   On June 30, the school collected $14,000 on account from students billed in transaction (6).

   Analysis: Receipt of this amount represents the collection of students' accounts, not new revenue. Recall that the related revenue was recorded in transaction (6), when the claims against students were recognized as the asset Accounts Receivable. This transaction changes one asset form (Accounts Receivable) into another asset form (Cash). Cash increases by $14,000 and Accounts Receivable decreases by the same amount. The entries are

Debit Cash $14,000   **Credit** Accounts Receivable $14,000

The related accounts would appear as follows:

Cash				Accounts Receivable			
(1)	50,000	(2)	18,000	(6)	18,500	(8)	14,000
(8)	14,000	(3)	4,600				
		(4)	3,600				
		(7)	8,000				

TRANSACTION (9):   On June 30, the school paid $1,200 on account for the supplies purchased in transaction (5).

   Analysis: Paying $1,200 of the $2,200 owed reduces both Cash and Accounts Payable by $1,200, therefore reducing both assets and liabilities. This payment is the partial settlement of a previously recorded obligation, not an expense. The entries are

Debit Accounts Payable $1,200   **Credit** Cash $1,200

The related accounts would appear as follows:

Accounts Payable				Cash			
(9)	1,200	(5)	2,200	(1)	50,000	(2)	18,000
				(8)	14,000	(3)	4,600
						(4)	3,600
						(7)	8,000
						(9)	1,200

TRANSACTION (10):   On June 30, Hill paid $150 for office utilities (electricity and telephone).

   Analysis: Since the utility services have been used in June, this amount is a June expense and will be reflected in the income statement prepared at June 30. Utilities Expense increases and Cash decreases by $150. The entries are

Debit Utilities Expense $150   **Credit** Cash $150

The related accounts would appear as follows:

Utilities Expense				Cash			
(10)	150			(1)	50,000	(2)	18,000
				(8)	14,000	(3)	4,600
						(4)	3,600
						(7)	8,000
						(9)	1,200
						(10)	150

TRANSACTION (11): On June 30, Hill withdrew $1,000 from the firm for personal use.

   Analysis: Hill has withdrawn this amount for his personal living expenses. The transaction reduces Cash and decreases Hill's equity in the Capital Driving School by $1,000.

   Although the reduction in owner's equity may be entered as a debit to the J. Hill, Capital account, Hill prefers to show all his withdrawals in a separate account. A proprietor uses a separate account, called the **drawing** account, to determine quickly the total amount withdrawn during a period without having to analyze the capital account. Drawing accounts (sometimes called *personal* accounts) are commonly used in sole proprietorships and partnerships. The account, J. Hill, Drawing, is a **contra** account because its balance represents a reduction of its related account, J. Hill, Capital. Debiting the drawing account to reflect the reduction in owner's equity has the same effect as debiting the owner's capital account directly. At the end of the period, after the net income has been added to the owner's capital account, the debit balance in the drawing account is deducted to arrive at the ending amount of owner's capital. Thus, the entries for Hill's withdrawal are

   Debit J. Hill, Drawing $1,000   **Credit** Cash $1,000

The related accounts would appear as follows:

J. Hill, Drawing				Cash			
(11)	1,000			(1)	50,000	(2)	18,000
				(8)	14,000	(3)	4,600
						(4)	3,600
						(7)	8,000
						(9)	1,200
						(10)	150
						(11)	1,000

TRANSACTION (12): On June 30, $\frac{1}{36}$ (one month) of the prepaid insurance, or $100, had expired.

Analysis: In transaction (4), the firm paid $3,600 in insurance premiums for a 36-month policy. Because this amount represented payment for future coverage, the asset Prepaid Insurance was debited. At the end of June, $\frac{1}{36}$ of the premiums has expired and no longer represents an asset. It will appear as Insurance Expense on the income statement prepared on June 30. The entries are

Debit Insurance Expense $100   **Credit** Prepaid Insurance $100

The related accounts would appear as follows:

Insurance Expense			Prepaid Insurance			
(12)	100		(4)	3,600	(12)	100

TRANSACTION (13):   On June 30, supplies were counted, and only $550 worth of supplies remained on hand.

Analysis: In transaction (5), supplies costing $2,200 were purchased and recorded as an asset. Supplies on hand now amount to only $550, and the $1,650 difference represents the supplies used during June. As we explained in the analysis of transaction (5), supplies used are a June expense. Therefore, an entry should be made to reduce Supplies on Hand by $1,650 and increase Supplies Expense by $1,650. The entries are

Debit Supplies Expense $1,650   **Credit** Supplies on Hand $1,650

The related accounts would appear as follows:

Supplies Expense			Supplies on Hand			
(13)	1,650		(5)	2,200	(13)	1,650

After the foregoing transactions have been entered properly, the account balances can be determined. The accounts of the Capital Driving School are shown in Exhibit 2–5 (see pages 54–55), together with the financial statements prepared from the balances of these accounts. Observe the following:

(1) Accounts accumulate data, especially revenue and expense accounts, which provide data for the income statement.
(2) Keying transactions permits tracing any entry to both its originating transaction and its related change in some other account.

EXHIBIT 2–5
The Accounts and Financial Statements of the Capital Driving School

Assets   =   Liabilities   +   ——————— Owner's Equity ———————

Cash

(1) 50,000	(2) 18,000
(8) 14,000	(3) 4,600
	(4) 3,600
	(7) 8,000
	(9) 1,200
	(10) 150
	(11) 1,000

Bal. 27,450

Accounts Receivable

(6) 18,500	(8) 14,000

Bal. 4,500

Prepaid Insurance

(4) 3,600	(12) 100

Bal. 3,500

Supplies on Hand

(5) 2,200	(13) 1,650

Bal. 550

Land

(2) 18,000	

Accounts Payable

(9) 1,200	(5) 2,200
	Bal. 1,000

J. Hill, Capital

	(1) 50,000

J. Hill, Drawing

(11) 1,000	

Instructional Fees

	(6) 18,500

Rent Expense

(3) 4,600	

Salaries Expense

(7) 8,000	

Utilities Expense

(10) 150	

Insurance Expense

(12) 100	

Supplies Expense

(13) 1,650	

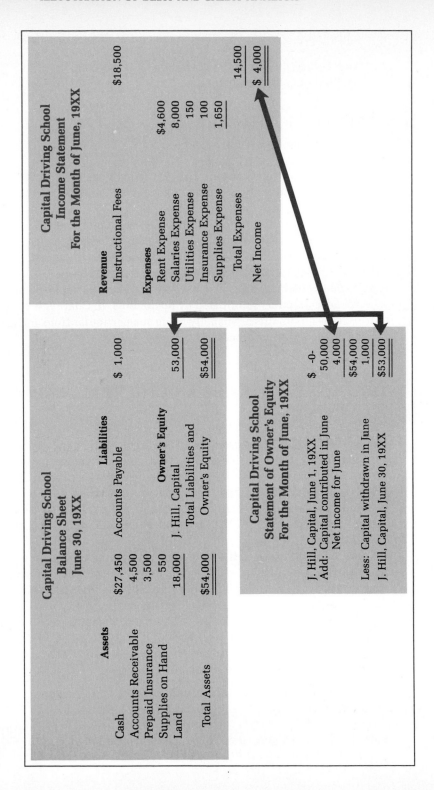

Capital Driving School
Income Statement
For the Month of June, 19XX

Revenue		
Instructional Fees		$18,500
Expenses		
Rent Expense	$4,600	
Salaries Expense	8,000	
Utilities Expense	150	
Insurance Expense	100	
Supplies Expense	1,650	
Total Expenses		14,500
Net Income		$ 4,000

Capital Driving School
Balance Sheet
June 30, 19XX

Assets		Liabilities	
Cash	$27,450	Accounts Payable	$ 1,000
Accounts Receivable	4,500		
Prepaid Insurance	3,500		
Supplies on Hand	550	**Owner's Equity**	
Land	18,000	J. Hill, Capital	53,000
		Total Liabilities and	
Total Assets	$54,000	Owner's Equity	$54,000

Capital Driving School
Statement of Owner's Equity
For the Month of June, 19XX

J. Hill, Capital, June 1, 19XX		$ -0-
Add: Capital contributed in June	50,000	
Net income for June	4,000	
		$54,000
Less: Capital withdrawn in June		1,000
J. Hill, Capital, June 30, 19XX		$53,000

(3) James Hill's equity of $53,000 at the end of June results from

(a) His original capital contribution	$50,000
(b) Plus his earnings for June	4,000
	$54,000
(c) Minus his withdrawals	1,000
Ending balance in balance sheet	$53,000

(4) Using the contra account, J. Hill, Drawing, does not change the net amount of owner's equity shown on the financial statements.

The June activities of the Capital Driving School that we have just analyzed included both transactions with individuals, for which documents such as bills or checks are usually available, and activities that are sometimes described as **internal** transactions. For example, transactions (12) and (13)—reflecting insurance expense and supplies expense—are called internal because they represent account adjustments not initiated by documents. In Chapter 3 you will learn that entries for adjustments are usually made at a particular time and are a significant part of the accounting process.

THE GENERAL LEDGER AND THE TRIAL BALANCE

The **general ledger** is the grouping of the accounts that are used to prepare financial statements for a business. The 14 accounts that we used in our example for the Capital Driving School would each constitute a page in the general ledger, which is usually maintained in a binder so that, when necessary, accounts may be added or removed. Usually, the accounts are grouped by category in the following order: (1) assets, (2) liabilities, (3) owners' equity, (4) revenue, and (5) expenses.

The **trial balance** is a list of the account titles in the ledger with their respective debit or credit balances. It is prepared at the close of an accounting period after transactions have been recorded. Exhibit 2–6 illustrates a trial balance for the Capital Driving School at the end of June.

The two main reasons for preparing a trial balance are

(1) To serve as an interim mechanical check to determine if the debits and credits in the general ledger are equal.

(2) To show all general ledger account balances on one concise record. This is often convenient when preparing financial statements.

Note that a trial balance should be dated; the trial balance of the Capital Driving School was taken at June 30, 19XX.

EXHIBIT 2–6

Capital Driving School
Trial Balance
June 30, 19XX

	Debit	Credit
Cash	$27,450	
Accounts Receivable	4,500	
Prepaid Insurance	3,500	
Supplies on Hand	550	
Land	18,000	
Accounts Payable		$ 1,000
J. Hill, Capital		50,000
J. Hill, Drawing	1,000	
Instructional Fees		18,500
Rent Expense	4,600	
Salaries Expense	8,000	
Utilities Expense	150	
Insurance Expense	100	
Supplies Expense	1,650	
	$69,500	$69,500

ERRORS IN TRANSACTION ANALYSIS

It is always reassuring when a trial balance does balance. However, even when a trial balance is in balance, the accounting records may still contain errors. A balanced trial balance simply proves that, *as recorded*, debits equal credits. The following errors may not be detected by taking a trial balance:

(1) Failing to record or enter a particular transaction.

(2) Entering a transaction more than once.

(3) Entering one or more amounts in the wrong accounts.

(4) Making an error that exactly offsets the effect of another error.

Several types of errors will cause a trial balance to be out of balance. If only one of these is present, it may be identified and located by one of the approaches suggested below. If several errors exist, however, often the only way to find them is to retrace each entry, check the arithmetic performed in balancing the accounts, and make certain that no error has occurred in transcribing amounts or in adding the trial balance. To search for errors, one should systematically follow certain procedures so that all steps are retraced only once and no steps are overlooked.

When there is a mistake in a trial balance, the first step is to determine the amount by which the total debits and credits disagree. Certain characteristics of this amount may provide a clue to identifying the type of error and finding where it was made.

DEBITS AND CREDITS INTERCHANGED   When a debit is entered as a credit (or vice versa), the trial balance totals will differ by twice the amount involved. For example, if the credits exceed the debits by $246, one should look for a $123 debit that has been treated as a credit. With this type of error, the amount of the discrepancy in the trial balance totals is divisible by two. If this is not the case, either another type of error or a number of errors are involved.

ARITHMETIC ERRORS   Single arithmetic errors frequently cause trial balance totals to differ by amounts such as $1,000, $100, $1, and so on. Multiple arithmetic errors may either combine or offset and result in discrepancies such as $990 (errors of $1,000 and $10 offsetting) and $101 (errors of $100 and $1 combining).

TRANSPOSITION OF NUMBERS   Transposing numbers means simply reversing their order. For example, transposing the first two digits in $360 would result in $630. This type of error usually occurs when amounts are transcribed from one record to another. The resulting discrepancy is easily identified because it is always divisible by nine ($630 − $360 = $270, and $270/9 = $30). Therefore, if total debits exceeded total credits by $270, one would suspect a transposition error.

AMOUNTS OMITTED   An amount can be omitted if one enters only part of an entry, fails to include an entry when balancing an account, or leaves out an account balance in a trial balance. The resulting discrepancy is equal in amount to the omitted item. Of course, the omission of a debit amount will cause an excess of credits by that amount, and vice versa.

KEY POINTS TO REMEMBER

(1) In recording changes in owners' equity, the primary reason for segregating revenue and expense items is to facilitate preparation of the income statement.

(2) The rules of debit and credit are
    (a) The left side of an account is always the debit side; the right side is always the credit side.
    (b) Increases in assets and expenses are debit entries; increases in liabilities, owners' equity, and revenue are credit entries.
    (c) The normal balance of any account appears on the side for recording increases.

(3) In transaction analysis
  (a) Each accounting transaction should be analyzed into equal debits and credits.
  (b) All accounting transactions are analyzed using one or more of the five basic account categories: (1) assets, (2) liabilities, (3) owners' equity, (4) revenue, and (5) expenses.

QUESTIONS

2–1 Why is it useful to record revenue and expenses separately from the owner's capital account?

2–2 Name the five categories of information needed to prepare the balance sheet and the income statement. Which categories are identified with the balance sheet? Which are identified with the income statement?

2–3 What information is recorded in an account?

2–4 Explain the terms *general ledger* and *trial balance*. What are the reasons for preparing a trial balance?

2–5 What general statement can be made about the *normal* side of an account?

2–6 Present three common business transactions that would not affect the amount of owners' equity.

2–7 Identify the following as asset, liability, owner's equity, revenue, or expense accounts and indicate whether a debit entry or a credit entry increases the balance of the account:

Professional Fees	Adams, Capital
Accounts Receivable	Advertising Expense
Accounts Payable	Supplies on Hand
Cash	Adams, Drawing

2–8 Indicate the normal balance (debit or credit) of each account in Question 2–7.

2–9 What are the advantages and disadvantages of the running balance, or three-column, account form compared with the two-column form?

2–10 What is the justification for using a separate owner's drawing account?

2–11 "During the year, the total owner's equity of Banton Sports Shop increased from $42,000 to $58,000. Therefore, the annual earnings must have been $16,000." Is this statement necessarily true? Explain.

2–12 Explain why purchases of supplies are usually charged to an asset account rather than to an expense account.

2–13 Describe three distinct types of errors that may be present even when a trial balance is in balance.

2–14 "A trial balance is a list showing all account titles in the general ledger and the total of debits and credits in each account." Do you agree with this statement? Why or why not?

2–15 Discuss the types of errors that may be present in each of the following independent sets of trial balance totals:

	Trial Balance Totals	
Trial Balance	Debit	Credit
A	$88,250	$89,250
B	45,820	45,640
C	26,577	26,668
D	55,668	57,392
E	34,269	34,929

2–16 The assistant bookkeeper of Star Florist prepared a trial balance that had total debits of $66,770 and total credits of $71,930. Compute the correct trial balance totals by assuming that only the following errors were involved:
(1) Accounts Payable of $4,370 was listed as a debit.
(2) During the current period, a $600 check for Salaries Expense was debited to Office Expense.
(3) Supplies on Hand of $6,300 had been omitted.
(4) Star, Drawing of $3,800 was included as a credit.

EXERCISES

2–17 Make T accounts for the following accounts that appear in the general ledger of R.L. Kinney, a veterinarian: Cash; Accounts Receivable; Supplies on Hand; Office Equipment; Accounts Payable; R.L. Kinney, Capital; R.L. Kinney, Drawing; Professional Fees; Salaries Expense; and Rent Expense. Record the following transactions in the T accounts and key all entries with the number identifying the transaction. Finally, prove equality of debits and credits by preparing a trial balance.
(1) Kinney opened a checking account on December 1 at the United Bank in the name of Animal Hospital and deposited $30,000.
(2) Paid rent for December, $500.
(3) Purchased office equipment on account, as follows: Desks, $800; typewriters, $1,250; filing cabinets, $700; and chairs, $650.
(4) Purchased supplies for cash, $700.
(5) Billed clients for services rendered, $4,800.
(6) Paid secretary's salary, $850.
(7) Paid $1,200 on account for the equipment purchased in transaction (3).
(8) Collected $2,800 from clients previously billed for services.
(9) Withdrew $1,200 for personal use.

2–18 In the five independent situations below, replace the question marks with the amounts that should appear.

	A	B	C	D	E
Owner's Equity:					
Beginning Balance	$22,000	$45,000	$34,000	$ (?)	$67,000
Capital Contributions	12,000	18,000	(?)	9,000	5,000
Net Income (Loss)	(?)	16,000	12,000	(5,000)	(?)
Capital Withdrawals	9,000	(?)	4,000	6,000	7,000
Ending Balance	$32,000	$67,000	$48,000	$19,000	$60,000

2–19 Match each of the following transactions of B. Sanchez, Printer, with the appropriate letters, indicating the debits and credits to be made. The correct answer for transaction (1) is given.

	Answer
(1) The owner contributed cash to the business.	a, f
(2) Purchased equipment on account.	_____
(3) Received and immediately paid advertising bill.	_____
(4) Purchased supplies for cash.	_____
(5) Borrowed money from bank, giving a note payable.	_____
(6) Billed customers.	_____
(7) Made partial payment on account for equipment.	_____
(8) Paid employee's salary.	_____
(9) Collected amounts due from customers billed in transaction (6).	_____

Effect of Transaction

(a) Debit an asset   (f) Credit owner's capital
(b) Credit an asset   (g) Debit revenue
(c) Debit a liability   (h) Credit revenue
(d) Credit a liability   (i) Debit an expense
(e) Debit owner's capital   (j) Credit an expense

2–20 The accounts below are from the ledger of a local accountant. For each letter given in the T accounts, describe the type of business transaction(s) or event(s) that would most probably be reflected by entries on that side of the account. For example, the answer to (a) is: The amounts of services performed for clients on account.

Accounts Receivable				Supplies on Hand	
(a)	(b)				(c)

Office Equipment			Prepaid Insurance	
(d)			(e)	

Professional Fees			Owner's Drawing	
	(f)		(g)	

Owner's Capital			Salaries Expense	
	(h)		(i)	

Accounts Payable	
(j)	(k)

2–21 Compute the unknown amount required in each of the following five independent situations. The answer to situation (a) is given as an example.

Account	Beginning Balance	Ending Balance	Other Information
(a) Cash	$ 3,200	$ 4,950	Total cash disbursed, $5,800
(b) Accounts Receivable	4,200	3,800	Services on account, $5,000
(c) Supplies on Hand	820	810	Supplies used, $420
(d) Prepaid Insurance	30	330	Premiums paid in advance, $660
(e) Owner's Equity	24,000	27,000	Withdrawals, $8,000

Unknown Amounts Required

(a) Total cash received	$7,550
(b) Total amount received from credit customers	_____
(c) Supplies purchased during the period	_____
(d) Amount of insurance expense for the period	_____
(e) Capital contributions if net income was $5,000	_____

2–22 Indicate how each of the following errors would affect the trial balance totals. For each error, specify whether the debit or credit totals would be overstated, understated, or whether both totals would be unaffected.
   (a) The Accounts Receivable balance of $41,900 was listed in the trial balance as $49,100.
   (b) A $480 payment for Advertising Expense was debited to Miscellaneous Expense during the accounting period.
   (c) The Accounts Payable balance of $36,500 was omitted from the trial balance.
   (d) Salaries Expense of $750 was listed in the trial balance as a credit.
   (e) The Owner's Drawing account, with a debit balance of $9,800, was listed as a credit in the trial balance.

PROBLEMS

2–23 Paul Gomez, electrical contractor, began business on May 1 of the current year. The following transactions occurred during May:
   (1) Gomez invested $12,000 of his personal funds in the business.
   (2) Purchased equipment on account, $1,800.
   (3) Paid the premium for a one-year liability insurance policy, $360.
   (4) Purchased supplies on account, $600.
   (5) Purchased a truck for $7,500. Gomez paid $1,500 cash and gave a note payable for the balance.
   (6) Paid rent for May, $720.
   (7) Paid fuel bill for truck, $80.
   (8) Billed customers for services rendered, $8,500.
   (9) Paid $800 on account for equipment purchased in transaction (2).
   (10) Paid utilities expense for May, $90.
   (11) Received invoice for May advertising expense, to be paid in June, $160.
   (12) Paid employees' wages, $1,250.
   (13) Collected $2,000 on accounts receivable.

(14) Withdrew $500 for personal expenses.

(15) Counted supplies on hand at May 31, $350 worth remained.

(16) Recorded the insurance expired at May 31, $30.

REQUIRED

(a) Record the above transactions in T accounts, and key entries with the numbers of the transactions. The following accounts will be needed to record the transactions for May: Cash; Accounts Receivable; Supplies on Hand; Prepaid Insurance; Equipment, Truck; Notes Payable; Accounts Payable; P. Gomez, Capital; P. Gomez, Drawing; Service Revenue; Rent Expense; Wages Expense; Utilities Expense; Truck Expense; Advertising Expense; Supplies Expense; and Insurance Expense.

(b) Prepare a trial balance of the general ledger as of May 31.

2–24 The following account balances, in alphabetical order, are from the ledger of Martin's Waterproofing Service at January 31, 19XX. The firm's accounting year began on January 1. All accounts had normal balances.

Accounts Payable	$ 1,140	Martin, Drawing	$1,500
Accounts Receivable	14,400	Prepaid Insurance	440
Advertising Expense	150	Rent Expense	560
Cash	9,200	Salaries Expense	3,000
Fee Revenue	14,100	Supplies Expense	600
Insurance Expense	40	Supplies on Hand	1,600
Martin, Capital, January 1	16,500	Utilities Expense	250

REQUIRED

(a) Prepare a trial balance in good form from the given data.

(b) Prepare an income statement for the month of January.

(c) Prepare a balance sheet at January 31.

2–25 The following T accounts contain numbered entries for the May transactions of Helen Dunbar, a market analyst, who opened her offices on May 1 of the current year:

Cash				H. Dunbar, Capital			
(1)	20,000	(2)	5,000			(1)	20,000
(9)	1,800	(4)	600				
		(6)	700				
		(8)	800				

Accounts Receivable				H. Dunbar, Drawing			
(5)	4,200	(9)	1,800	(8)	800		

Supplies on Hand				Professional Fees			
(3)	1,400	(7)	650			(5)	4,200

	Office Equipment			Rent Expense	
(2)	5,000		(4)	600	

	Accounts Payable			Supplies Expense	
(6)	700	(3) 1,400	(7)	650	

REQUIRED
(a) Give a reasonable description of each of the nine numbered transactions entered in the above accounts. Example: (1) Helen Dunbar invested $20,000 of her personal funds in her business.
(b) The following trial balance, taken for Dunbar's firm on May 31, contains several errors. Itemize the errors and indicate the correct totals for the trial balance.

Helen Dunbar, Market Analyst
Trial Balance
May 31, 19XX

	Debit	Credit
Cash	$17,400	
Accounts Receivable	4,200	
Supplies on Hand	750	
Office Equipment	5,000	
Accounts Payable		$ 700
H. Dunbar, Capital		20,000
H. Dunbar, Drawing		800
Professional Fees		4,200
Rent Expense	600	
	$27,950	$25,700

2–26 James Blake owns Art Graphics, a firm providing designs for advertisers, market analysts, and others. On July 1 of the current year, his ledger showed the following account balances:

Cash	$ 6,500	Notes Payable	$ 3,000
Accounts Receivable	16,400	Accounts Payable	2,200
Prepaid Rent	800	J. Blake, Capital	23,000
Supplies on Hand	4,500		
	$28,200		$28,200

The following transactions occurred in July:
(1) Collected $7,200 on account from customers.
(2) Paid $1,000 installment due on the $3,000 non-interest-bearing note payable to a relative.
(3) Billed customers for design services rendered on account, $14,600.
(4) Rendered design services for cash customers, $900.

(5) Purchased various art supplies on account, $1,400.

(6) Paid $1,500 to creditors on account.

(7) Collected $6,300 on account from customers.

(8) Paid a delivery service for delivery of graphics to commercial firms, $180.

(9) Paid July salaries, $2,250.

(10) Received invoice for July advertising expense, to be paid in August, $350.

(11) Paid utilities expense for July, $240.

(12) Withdrew $800 for personal use.

(13) Recorded rent expense for July, $400. (Note that on July 1, two months' rent, $800, was prepaid.)

(14) Counted supplies on hand at July 31, $2,850 worth remained.

REQUIRED

(a) Set up the appropriate T accounts for the July 1 balance sheet and enter the beginning balances. Also provide the following T accounts: J. Blake, Drawing; Service Fees; Rent Expense; Salaries Expense; Delivery Expense; Advertising Expense; Utilities Expense; and Supplies Expense. Record the listed transactions in the T accounts, and key entries with transaction numbers.

(b) Prepare a trial balance at July 31.

(c) Prepare an income statement for July.

(d) Prepare a statement of owner's equity for July.

(e) Prepare a balance sheet at July 31.

2–27 Northwest Fly-In Service, Inc. (introduced in Problem 1–32) operates leased amphibious aircraft and docking facilities, equipping the firm to transport fishermen and hunters from Fort Frances, Ontario, to outpost camps owned by various resorts in Ontario. On August 1 of the current year, the firm's trial balance was as follows:

Northwest Fly-In Service, Inc.
Trial Balance
August 1, 19XX

	Debit	Credit
Cash	$48,750	
Accounts Receivable	18,500	
Supplies on Hand	12,400	
Prepaid Insurance	2,400	
Notes Payable		$ 5,000
Accounts Payable		7,200
Capital Stock		50,000
Retained Earnings		19,850
	$82,050	$82,050

During August the following transactions occurred:

Aug. 1 Paid August rental cost for aircraft, dockage, and dockside office, $3,200.

3 Purchased fuel and other supplies on account, $4,600.

5 Paid bill for August advertising in various sports magazines, $350.

Aug. 6 Rendered fly-in services for various groups for cash, $17,250.

  8 Billed the Ministry of Natural Resources for services in transporting mapping personnel, $3,500.

 13 Received $12,300 on account from clients.

 16 Paid $4,200 on accounts payable

 18 Paid miscellaneous expenses, $120.

 24 Billed various clients for services, $6,500.

 31 Paid August wages, $7,600.

 31 Declared and paid a dividend, $2,500 (debit Retained Earnings).

 31 Determined that $600 insurance premiums expired during August.

 31 Determined that fuel and other supplies on hand at August 31 amounted to $8,100.

REQUIRED

(a) Set up running balance accounts for each item in the August 1 trial balance. Also provide similar accounts for the following items: Service Fees, Wages Expense, Advertising Expense, Rent Expense, Supplies Expense, Insurance Expense, and Miscellaneous Expense. Record the transactions for August in the accounts, using the dates given.

(b) Prepare a trial balance at August 31, 19XX.

(c) Prepare an income statement for August.

(d) Prepare a balance sheet at August 31.

2–28 The following trial balance for Fox Janitorial Service, prepared after its first month of operations on January 31 on the current year, does not balance because of a number of errors.

Fox Janitorial Service
Trial Balance
January 31, 19XX

	Debit	Credit
Cash	$ 6,840	
Accounts Receivable	8,430	
Supplies on Hand	4,850	
Prepaid Insurance	480	
Equipment	15,000	
Accounts Payable		$ 3,950
Fox, Capital		23,850
Fox, Drawing		1,200
Service Fees		16,850
Wages Expense	4,500	
Insurance Expense	120	
Advertising Expense	180	
Supplies Expense	2,270	
	$42,670	$45,850

(1) Utilities Expense, with a $200 balance, was omitted from the trial balance.

(2) Supplies Expense, listed in the trial balance as $2,270, should be $2,720.

(3) During the period, a cash payment of $650 on accounts payable was recorded as a $560 credit to Cash.

(4) A debit of $150 to Accounts Payable was erroneously recorded as a credit.

(5) In determining the Accounts Receivable balance, a credit of $180 was overlooked.

(6) The $1,200 balance of the Fox, Drawing account is listed as a credit in the trial balance.

(7) The balance of the Service Fees account was overfooted (overadded) by $100.

REQUIRED

Prepare a corrected trial balance as of January 31 of the current year.

ALTERNATE PROBLEMS

2–23A Jennifer Brown opened a tax practice on June 1 of the current year. The following accounts will be needed to record her transactions for June: Cash; Accounts Receivable; Office Supplies on Hand; Prepaid Insurance; Office Furniture and Fixtures; Notes Payable; Accounts Payable; J. Brown, Capital; J. Brown, Drawing; Professional Fees; Rent Expense; Salaries Expense; Supplies Expense; Utilities Expense; and Insurance Expense. The following transactions occurred in June:

(1) Brown opened a special checking account at the bank for the business, investing $8,000 in her practice.

(2) Purchased office furniture and fixtures for $2,500, paid $1,000 cash and gave a non-interest-bearing note payable for the balance.

(3) Paid the premium for a one-year liability insurance policy, $600.

(4) Purchased office supplies on account, $420.

(5) Paid rent for June, $500.

(6) Billed clients for professional services rendered, $4,800.

(7) Paid $250 on account to stationers for the office supplies purchased in transaction (4).

(8) Collected $2,200 on account from clients billed in transaction (6).

(9) Paid June salaries, $1,500.

(10) Withdrew $500 for personal use.

(11) Paid utilities for June, $160.

(12) Counted supplies on hand at June 30, $280 worth remained.

(13) One month's insurance premium expired during June.

REQUIRED

(a) Record the above transactions in T accounts, and key entries with the numbers of the transactions.

(b) Prepare a trial balance of the general ledger as of June 30.

2–24A The following account balances were taken (out of order) from the ledger of P. Wells, investment counselor, at January 31, 19XX. The firm's accounting year began on January 1. All accounts had normal balances.

Prepaid Insurance	$ 320	Rent Expense	$ 720
Insurance Expense	80	Supplies Expense	350
Supplies on Hand	560	Utilities Expense	140
Advertising Expense	230	Service Fees	9,420
P. Wells, Capital, January 1	21,000	Accounts Receivable	16,500
Cash	9,500	Salaries Expense	1,800
Accounts Payable	480	P. Wells, Drawing	700

REQUIRED
(a) Prepare a trial balance in good form from the given data.
(b) Prepare an income statement for the month of January.
(c) Prepare a balance sheet at January 31.

2–25A The following T accounts contain numbered entries for the May transactions of Dale Bruce, attorney, who opened his offices on May 1 of the current year:

	Cash					D. Bruce, Capital		
(1)	12,000	(2)	5,000				(1)	12,000
(10)	2,400	(4)	750					
		(6)	600					
		(8)	800					
		(9)	380					

	Accounts Receivable					D. Bruce, Drawing		
(5)	3,800	(10)	2,400		(8)	800		

	Prepaid Insurance					Professional Fees		
(6)	600	(11)	50				(5)	3,800

	Supplies on Hand					Rent Expense		
(3)	700	(7)	450		(4)	750		

	Office Equipment					Insurance Expense		
(2)	5,000				(11)	50		

	Accounts Payable					Supplies Expense		
(9)	380	(3)	700		(7)	450		

REQUIRED
(a) Give a reasonable description of each of the 11 numbered transactions entered in the above accounts. Example: (1) Dale Bruce invested $12,000 of his personal funds in his law firm.

(b) The following trial balance, taken for Bruce's firm on May 31, contains several errors. Itemize the errors, and indicate the correct totals for the trial balance.

Dale Bruce, Attorney
Trial Balance
May 31, 19XX

	Debit	Credit
Cash	$ 6,780	
Accounts Receivable	1,600	
Supplies on Hand	700	
Office Equipment	5,000	
Accounts Payable		$ 320
D. Bruce, Capital		12,000
D. Bruce, Drawing		800
Professional Fees		3,800
Rent Expense	750	
Insurance Expense	50	
Supplies Expense	450	
	$15,330	$16,920

2–26A Betty Gaylord operates the Gaylord Dance Studio. On June 1 of the current year, her ledger contained the following information:

Cash	$ 7,800	Notes Payable	$ 2,000
Accounts Receivable	3,500	Accounts Payable	330
Prepaid Insurance	300	B. Gaylord, Capital	9,730
Supplies on Hand	460		
	$12,060		$12,060

The following transactions occurred in June:

(1) Paid June rent for practice and performance studio, $850.
(2) Paid June piano rental, $50 (Rent Expense).
(3) Collected $2,500 from students on account.
(4) Paid $500 installment on non-interest-bearing note owed to a relative.
(5) Billed students for June instructional fees, $3,800.
(6) Purchased supplies (tickets, brochures, sheet music, and so on) on account, $230.
(7) Paid $120 for advertising ballet performance.
(8) Paid costume rental, $240 (Rent Expense).
(9) Collected $2,600 from performances.
(10) Paid Kleen Towel Company for June services, $40 (Miscellaneous Expense).
(11) Paid utilities expense for June, $160.
(12) Withdrew $400 for personal expenses.
(13) Counted supplies on hand at June 30, $150 worth remained.
(14) Determined that $50 insurance premiums had expired in June.

REQUIRED
(a) Set up the appropriate T accounts, and enter the beginning balances shown in the June 1 balance sheet. Also provide the following accounts: B. Gay-

lord, Drawing; Instructional Fees; Performance Revenue; Rent Expense; Supplies Expense; Insurance Expense; Utilities Expense; Advertising Expense; and Miscellaneous Expense. Record the listed transactions in the T accounts and key entries with transaction numbers.

(b) Prepare a trial balance at June 30.
(c) Prepare an income statement for June.
(d) Prepare a statement of owner's equity for June.
(e) Prepare a balance sheet as of June 30.

2–27A On December 1 of the current year, a group of individuals formed a corporation to establish the *Westside Flyer*, a neighborhood weekly newspaper featuring want ads of individuals and advertising of local firms. The paper will be mailed free to about 5,000 local residents; revenue will be generated from advertising and want ads. The December transactions are summarized below:

Dec.	1	Sold capital stock for cash, $25,000.
	2	Paid rent on office, $650.
	4	Purchased office furniture and equipment for $10,000, paying $5,000 cash and giving a $5,000 note payable for the balance.
	5	Purchased stationery and other office supplies on account, $850.
	8	Collected want ad revenue in cash, $1,600.
	12	Paid post office for bulk mailing expense, $320.
	14	Billed for advertising in first two issues of the newspaper, $4,850.
	15	Paid delivery expense to Acme Courier Service for transporting newspapers to post office, $65.
	16	Paid printing expense, $2,150.
	18	Billed firms for want ads, $1,420, and collected $980 want ad revenue in cash from various individuals.
	28	Paid utilities expenses, $115.
	31	Paid printing expense, $1,850.
	31	Paid salaries expense, $3,250.
	31	Billed for advertising in last two issues of the newspaper, $6,450.
	31	Paid post office for bulk mailing expense, $350.
	31	Paid delivery expense to Acme Courier Service for transporting newspapers to post office, $75.
	31	Collected $5,200 on accounts receivable.

REQUIRED

(a) Set up three-column running balance accounts for the following: Cash, Accounts Receivable, Supplies on Hand, Office Furniture and Equipment, Notes Payable, Accounts Payable, Capital Stock, Advertising Revenue, Want Ad Revenue, Printing Expense, Mailing Expense, Utilities Expense, Salaries Expense, Rent Expense, and Delivery Expense. Record the foregoing transactions in the accounts.
(b) Take a trial balance at December 31.
(c) Assuming that unrecorded expenses—such as supplies expense, and so on—amount to $400, calculate the net income for December.
(d) If the firm decides to declare and pay a dividend of $1,000 on January 1 of the following year, what would be the amount of stockholders' equity immediately after paying the dividend?

BUSINESS DECISION PROBLEM

Jane Meadows operates the Wildlife Picture Gallery, selling original art and signed prints received on consignment (rather than purchased) from recognized wildlife artists throughout the country. The firm receives a 30% commission on all art sold and remits 70% of the sales price to the artists. Jane began business in January of this year, but has not yet arranged for a formal set of records. She has prepared cash receipts and disbursements statements for each of the first three months of the year, but she is uneasy about relying on them to determine how well she is doing. She asks you to prepare a proper set of financial statements for the month of March.

By reviewing bank statements, check stubs, invoice files, and other data, you derive a set of balance sheets at March 1 and March 31. These are shown below, followed by a statement of cash receipts and disbursements for March.

Wildlife Picture Gallery
Balance Sheets

Assets	March 31, 19XX	March 1, 19XX
Cash	$14,600	$12,200
Accounts Receivable	3,000	2,800
Supplies on Hand	1,400	1,100
Prepaid Insurance	900	1,000
	$19,900	$17,100

Liabilities and Owner's Equity	March 31, 19XX	March 1, 19XX
Accounts Payable to Artists	$ 2,400	$ 2,600
Jane Meadows, Capital	17,500	14,500
	$19,900	$17,100

Wildlife Picture Gallery
Statement of Cash Receipts and Disbursements
For the Month of March, 19XX

Cash Receipts		
Received on account from customers	$16,800	
Cash sales	3,000	
Total cash receipts		$19,800

Cash Disbursements		
Supplies purchased for cash	$ 800	
Payments to artists on account	14,200	
Payment of salaries	1,000	
Payment for March rent	750	
Cash withdrawn for personal use	500	
Payment for utilities expense	150	
Total cash disbursements		17,400
Net increase in cash balance		$ 2,400

REQUIRED
(a) From the above information, prepare an accrual basis income statement for the month of March. To obtain the data needed, you may wish to use T accounts to reconstruct the accounts.
(b) Illustrate the apparent correctness of your net income amount by preparing a statement of owner's equity for March.

3

The Accounting Cycle

The double-entry accounting system provides a basic framework for the analysis of business activities. Now we wish to go into greater detail about the accounting procedures used to account for the operations of a business during a specific period. The accounting procedures of most businesses involve certain basic steps that are accomplished in a given order. This sequence of operations is known as the *accounting cycle*.

STEPS IN THE ACCOUNTING CYCLE

The **accounting cycle** can be divided into the following steps:

(1) Analyze transactions from source documents.

(2) Record in journals.

(3) Post to general ledger accounts.

(4) Adjust the general ledger accounts.

(5) Prepare financial statements.

(6) Close temporary accounts.

The steps in the accounting cycle enable the accountant to combine and summarize the net results of many business activities into relatively concise financial reports. Even a medium-sized business has thousands of transactions evidenced by one or more source documents (step 1); these transactions are recorded and summarized (step 2) in possibly only five or six journals. Next, data from these journals might be posted (step 3) to one general ledger having, say, 100 accounts. After certain adjustments are made (step 4), these accounts provide the balances necessary to prepare the basic financial statements (step 5). Much of the analytical usefulness of the accounting process is a result of this ability to condense and summarize business data.

The various steps in the accounting cycle do not occur with equal frequency. Usually, analyzing, journalizing, and posting (steps 1–3) take place throughout each operating period, whereas accounts are adjusted and statements are prepared (steps 4 and 5) only when management requires financial statements, usually at monthly or quarterly intervals, but at least annually. Temporary accounts are customarily closed (step 6) only at the end of the accounting year.

Business firms whose accounting year ends on December 31 are said to be on a **calendar-year** basis. Many firms prefer to have their accounting year coincide

EXHIBIT 3–1
Frequency of Accounting Cycle Steps
Required for Quarterly Financial Statements

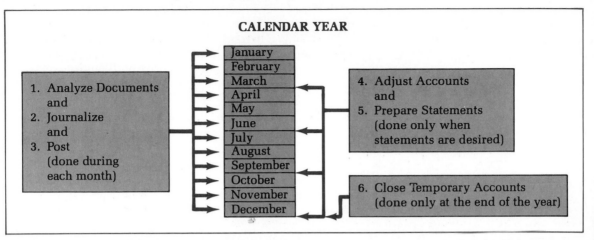

with their "natural" business year; that is, the year ends when business is slow and inventory quantities are small and easy to count. Year-end accounting procedures are most efficiently accomplished at this time. For example, most department stores choose a year ending on the last day of January or February, when their inventories are depleted from the normally heavy holiday sales and from post-holiday clearance sales. An accounting year ending with a month other than December is called a **fiscal year.**

Exhibit 3–1 illustrates the timing of steps in the accounting cycle during a calendar year for a business that prepares quarterly financial statements. In the remainder of this chapter and in Chapter 4, we shall explain the various steps in the accounting cycle. As an example, we use the first month's transactions of the Monroe TV Service, a repair business begun by Carl Monroe on December 1 of the current year.

SOURCE DOCUMENTS

Step 1: Analyze Transactions from Source Documents

Source documents are printed or written forms that are generated when the firm engages in business transactions. Even a brief source document usually specifies the dollar amounts involved, the date of the transaction, and possibly the party dealing with the firm. Some examples of source documents are (1) a sales invoice showing evidence of a purchase of supplies on account, (2) a bank check indicating payment of an obligation, (3) a deposit slip showing the amount of funds turned over to the bank, (4) a cash receipt indicating funds received from a customer, and (5) a cash register tape listing a day's over-the-counter sales to customers.

Exhibit 3–2 lists the December transactions of Monroe TV Service, together with their related source documents. Ordinarily, source documents or business papers such as those listed in Exhibit 3–2 will alert the bookkeeper to the need for an entry in the records. Usually the bookkeeper is able to analyze the transaction by examining the documents to determine the appropriate accounts to be debited and credited. For example, in transaction (2), a scrutiny of the check stub from the rent payment would reveal the need for debiting Rent Expense and

EXHIBIT 3–2
December Transactions
Monroe TV Service

Number	Date	Brief Description	Related Source Documents
(1)	Dec. 1	Carl Monroe deposited $20,000 in the firm's bank account.	Bank deposit slip
(2)	1	Paid December rent, $400.	Bank check
(3)	2	Purchased truck for $7,200 cash.	Bank check, invoice
(4)	2	Purchased test equipment for $3,000; paid $2,000 down; remainder to be paid in 60 days.	Seller's invoice, bank check
(5)	2	Signed two service contracts to perform	
		(a) Service work for a local TV dealer for four months, December–March, at $200 per month. Received $800 in advance.	Contract, dealer's check
		(b) Service work for a local hotel at a rate of $12 per hour. Settlement to be made whenever 40 hours of service has been rendered.	Contract, periodic bills
(6)	3	Purchased supplies and parts on account, $600.	Seller's invoice
(7)	7	Performed TV service for various customers during first week of December and received $550 cash.	Duplicates of customer receipt forms
(8)	14	Billed various agencies and customers for TV service rendered on account, $750.	Bills to customers
(9)	14	Paid employee's wages for first two weeks of December, $420	Bank check
(10)	14	Performed TV service for various customers during second week of December and received $480 cash.	Duplicates of customer receipt forms
(11)	17	Paid advertising bill, $50.	Invoice, bank check
(12)	19	Received $500 on account from customers.	Customers' checks
(13)	21	Performed TV service for various customers during third week of December and received $320 cash.	Duplicates of customer receipt forms
(14)	28	Paid truck expenses (gas and oil), $170.	Invoice, bank check
(15)	28	Billed various agencies and customers for TV service rendered on account, $2,400.	Bills to customers
(16)	28	Paid employee's wages for second two weeks of December, $420.	Bank check
(17)	28	Withdrew $600 for personal use.	Bank check
(18)	28	Performed TV service during fourth week in December and received $200 cash.	Duplicates of customer receipt forms

crediting Cash. In transaction (4), the seller's invoice or bill of sale would probably indicate both the cost of the equipment and the down payment. The check stub would further corroborate the amount paid, and the bookkeeper would debit Test Equipment for $3,000, credit Cash for $2,000, and credit Accounts Payable for $1,000, the amount still owing.

Some transactions can be analyzed only by making further inquiry or by referring to previously received documents and the accounting records themselves. For example, consider the two contracts signed by Carl Monroe on December 2 (transaction 5). The mere signing of the contracts would not require bookkeeping entries, since the contracts are just agreements to provide services. In transaction (5a), however, Monroe TV Service received $800 in advance, which requires a debit to Cash and a credit to Unearned Service Fees. In this case, the Unearned Service Fees of $800 represent an obligation (liability) to provide services for four months. At the end of each of these months, an entry must be made to reduce the obligation and to reflect an appropriate amount in the revenue account Service Fees. To ensure the proper entry, the bookkeeper can refer to the contract terms or review the entry made when the advance was received.

As a result of transaction (5b), the bookkeeper would record an account receivable from the hotel and credit the revenue account Service Fees at the end of each accounting period. To do this, the bookkeeper might check the contract terms to calculate the amounts of such entries. The periodic entries required to reflect properly the services rendered under these two contracts fall into the category of *adjusting entries;* we describe these in step 4 of the accounting cycle and show that such entries frequently require reference to previous accounting records.

JOURNALS

Step 2: Record in Journals

For simplicity, the entries used in Chapter 2 were made directly in the general ledger accounts. This method would not prove feasible, however, for even a modest-sized business. For instance, suppose an owner wished to investigate a $1,000 credit in the Cash account. If entries were actually recorded directly in the general ledger, the purpose of the $1,000 expenditure could be difficult to determine. The owner might be forced to search through the entire general ledger to discover the offsetting debit of $1,000. Consequently, accounting records include a set of **journals** or **records of original entry,** which show the total effect of a business transaction or adjustment in one location.

Journals are tabular records in which business activities are analyzed in terms of debits and credits and recorded in chronological order before they are entered in the general ledger. An accounting journal may be one of a group of special journals, or it may be a general journal. A special journal is designed to record a specific type of frequently occurring business transaction. For example, a business with 100 employees who are paid every two weeks would probably use a special journal for payrolls. Because two paydays would normally occur in a month, at least 200 payroll transactions would be recorded. Other types of transactions that are often kept in special journals are cash receipts, cash disbursements, merchandise sales, and merchandise purchases.

In contrast to the special journals, the general journal is a relatively simple record in which any type of business transaction or adjustment may be recorded. All adjustments are recorded in the general journal as are transactions that do not occur often enough to warrant entry in a special journal. All businesses, even those using many special journals, have a general journal. In this chapter, we shall illustrate only the use of a general journal; in Chapter 6, we will introduce the use of special journals.

Exhibit 3–3 shows the first four transactions from Exhibit 3–2 as they would be recorded in Monroe's general journal. Most journal entries are based on information appearing on a source document resulting from a transaction between the business and an outside party. The procedure for recording entries in the general journal is as follows:

(1) Indicate the year, month, and date of the entry. Usually the year and month are rewritten only at the top of each page of the journal or at the point where they change.

EXHIBIT 3–3

General Journal   Page 1

Date			Description	Post. Ref.	Debit	Credit
19XX Dec.		1	Cash		20,000	
			C. Monroe, Capital			20,000
			Opened the TV Service's bank account using personal funds.			
		1	Rent Expense		400	
			Cash			400
			Paid rent for December.			
		2	Truck		7,200	
			Cash			7,200
			Purchased truck for cash.			
		2	Test Equipment		3,000	
			Cash			2,000
			Accounts Payable			1,000
			Purchased electronic test equipment for $3,000. Terms: $2,000 down, remainder due in 60 days.			

(2) Enter titles of the accounts affected in the description column. Accounts to receive debits are entered close to the left-hand margin and are traditionally recorded first. Accounts to receive credits are then recorded, indented slightly.

(3) Place the appropriate money amounts in the left-hand (debit) and right-hand (credit) money columns.

(4) Write an explanation of the transaction or adjustment below the account titles. The explanation should be as brief as possible, disclosing all the information necessary to understand the event being recorded.

Each transaction and adjustment entered in the journal should be stated in terms of equal debits and credits. The account titles cited in the description column should correspond to those used for the related general ledger accounts. To separate clearly the various entries, we leave a line blank between entries. We explain the use of the column headed "Post. Ref." (posting reference) later in step 3 of the accounting cycle.

COMPOUND JOURNAL ENTRIES   A journal entry that involves more than just two accounts is called a **compound** journal entry. The last journal entry in Exhibit 3–3 is an example of a compound journal entry involving three accounts. The debit of $3,000 to Test Equipment is offset by credits of $2,000 to Cash and $1,000 to Accounts Payable. Any number of accounts may appear in a compound entry; but, regardless of how many accounts are used, the total of the debit amounts must always equal the total of the credit amounts.

CORRECTION OF JOURNAL ERRORS   Certain procedures should be followed when errors are found in journal entries. Errors should not be erased, because erasures completely remove the original recording. As you might imagine, the acceptance of erasures might allow someone to falsify accounting records; consequently, other procedures are used.

If an erroneous journal entry has not been transferred to the ledger, a single line is drawn through the erroneous amount or account title, and the correction is entered on the same line just above the error. Often the person correcting the entry must place his or her initials near the correction. This facilitates any subsequent inquiry about the nature of or reason for the correction. Once an erroneous journal entry has been transferred to the ledger accounts, both records contain the error. The recommended procedures for correcting this situation are discussed in step 3.

POSTING

Step 3: Post to Ledger Accounts

After transactions have been journalized, the next step in the accounting cycle is to transcribe the debits and credits in each journal entry to the appropriate general ledger accounts. This transcribing process is called **posting** to the general ledger. Thus, data from a journal that stresses the total effect of particular transactions (such as the collection of accounts receivable) are transcribed to a ledger that stresses the total effect of many business transactions on a particular business variable (such as cash, accounts receivable, and so on). This latter type of data is specifically needed for the preparation of financial statements.

When records are kept by hand, posting from the general journal may be done daily, every few days, or at the end of each month. Journalizing and posting often occur simultaneously when the record-keeping process is automated. The posting of special journals is discussed in Chapter 6.

POSTING REFERENCES It is important to be able to trace any entry appearing in a ledger account to the journal from which it was posted. Consequently, accounting records use a system of references. Both journals and accounts have posting reference columns. Entries in the posting reference columns of journals indicate the account to which the related debit or credit has been posted. Posting references appearing in ledger accounts identify the journal from which the related entry was posted.

To keep accounting records uncluttered, we make posting references simple. For example, the posting reference of the general journal might be GJ or simply J. Similarly, special journals such as Cash Receipts and Payroll might be indicated by posting references of CR and PR, respectively. Because both general and special journals usually involve many pages of entries, journal pages are numbered in sequence. Thus, a posting reference of J9 appearing on the line with a $1,000 debit entry in the Cash account means that the ninth page of the general journal contains the entire entry in which the $1,000 debit to Cash appears. Because all entries should be posted from some journal, every entry appearing in a ledger account should have a related posting reference. Posting references appearing in journals are usually the numbers that have been assigned to the general ledger accounts.

CHART OF ACCOUNTS In all but the simplest accounting systems, a number is assigned to each general ledger account. Such a numbering system permits easy reference to accounts even if the account title contains several words. For example, the account Depreciation Expense—Test Equipment might be referred to simply as account No. 57.

A **chart of accounts** is usually prepared in order to facilitate the analysis of activities and the formulation of journal entries. The chart of accounts is a list of the titles and numbers of all accounts found in the general ledger. The account titles should be grouped by, and in order of, the five major sections of the general ledger (assets, liabilities, owners' equity, revenue, and expense). Exhibit 3–4 shows a chart of accounts for the Monroe TV Service, indicating the account numbers that will now be used.

The method of assigning account numbers usually ensures that the numbers of all the accounts in a major section of the general ledger start with the same digit. In Exhibit 3–4, all asset accounts begin with 1, liabilities with 2, and so on. Complicated accounting systems may use three- or four-digit account numbers and may even employ suffixes to designate various branches, departments, or divisions.

EXHIBIT 3–4
Monroe TV Service
Chart of Accounts

Assets	Revenue
11. Cash	41. Service Fees
12. Accounts Receivable	**Expenses**
14. Supplies and Parts on Hand	51. Rent Expense
16. Test Equipment	52. Wages Expense
17. Accumulated Depreciation—Test Equipment	53. Advertising Expense
18. Truck	54. Supplies and Parts Expense
19. Accumulated Depreciation—Truck	55. Utilities Expense
Liabilities	56. Truck Expense
21. Accounts Payable	57. Depreciation Expense—Test Equipment
22. Utilities Payable	58. Depreciation Expense—Truck
23. Wages Payable	
24. Unearned Service Fees	
Owner's Equity	
31. C. Monroe, Capital	
32. C. Monroe, Drawing	
33. Income Summary	

Exhibit 3–5 diagrams the posting of Monroe TV Service's first transaction from the general journal to the ledger accounts. Each debit entry and each credit entry is posted as follows:

(1) The date (year, month, and day) is entered in the appropriate account. Note that this is the date of the journal entry, not necessarily the date of the actual posting. As with journals, the year and month are restated only at the top of a new account page or at the point where they change.

(2) The amount is entered in the account as a debit or a credit, as indicated in the journal's money columns, and the new balance is calculated.

(3) The posting reference from the journal (both symbol and page number) is placed in the posting reference column of the ledger account.

(4) The account number is placed in the posting reference column of the journal.

Regardless of the types of journals or the number of entries involved, the total debits posted should equal the total credits posted. Exhibit 3–6 (see pages 83–88) is a comprehensive illustration of the journalizing and posting of the December transactions of Monroe TV Service. You should review each transaction in the illustration for (1) the nature of the transaction, (2) the related journal entry, and (3) the subsequent postings. Bear in mind that the account numbers in the posting reference column of the journal are not entered when the journal entry is recorded; they are inserted after the entry has been posted.

EXHIBIT 3–5
Diagrams of Posting to Ledger Accounts

General Journal   Page 1

Date		Description	Post. Ref.	Debit	Credit
19XX Dec.	1	Cash	11	20,000	
		C. Monroe, Capital	31		20,000
		Opened the TV Service's bank account using personal funds.			

❶

General Ledger
Cash   Account No. 11

❸   ❷   ❹

Date		Description	Post. Ref.	Debit*	Credit	Balance
19XX Dec.	1		J1	20,000		20,000

General Journal   Page 1

Date		Description	Post. Ref.	Debit	Credit
19XX Dec.	1	Cash	11	20,000	
		C. Monroe, Capital	31		20,000
		Opened the TV Service's bank account using personal funds.			

❶

General Ledger
C. Monroe, Capital   Account No. 31

❸   ❷   ❹

Date		Description	Post. Ref.	Debit	Credit*	Balance
19XX Dec.	1		J1		20,000	20,000

*Throughout this chapter, the asterisk indicates the column that designates the normal balance.

EXHIBIT 3–6
Journalizing and Posting for Monroe TV Service

General Journal

Page 1

Date		Description	Post. Ref.	Debit	Credit
19XX					
Dec.	1	Cash	11	20,000	
		C. Monroe, Capital	31		20,000
		Opened the TV Service's bank account using personal funds.			
	1	Rent Expense	51	400	
		Cash	11		400
		Paid rent for December.			
	2	Truck	18	7,200	
		Cash	11		7,200
		Purchased truck for cash.			
	2	Test Equipment	16	3,000	
		Cash	11		2,000
		Accounts Payable	21		1,000
		Purchased electronic test equipment for $3,000. Terms: $2,000 down, remainder due in 60 days.			
	2	Cash	11	800	
		Unearned Service Fees	24		800
		Received advance on four-month contract at $200 per month.			
	3	Supplies and Parts on Hand	14	600	
		Accounts Payable	21		600
		Purchased supplies and parts on account; 60-day terms.			
	7	Cash	11	550	
		Service Fees	41		550
		Services for cash, December 1–7.			
	14	Accounts Receivable	12	750	
		Service Fees	41		750
		Services rendered on account.			
	14	Wages Expense	52	420	
		Cash	11		420
		Paid wages for first two weeks of December.			

EXHIBIT 3–6 (continued)

General Journal   Page 2

Date			Description	Post. Ref.	Debit	Credit
19XX Dec.	14		Cash	11	480	
			Service Fees	41		480
			Services for cash, December 8–14.			
	17		Advertising Expense	53	50	
			Cash	11		50
			Paid *Daily News* for December advertising.			
	19		Cash	11	500	
			Accounts Receivable	12		500
			Received $500 on account from credit customers.			
	21		Cash	11	320	
			Service Fees	41		320
			Services for cash, December 15–21.			
	28		Truck Expense	56	170	
			Cash	11		170
			Gas and oil for December.			
	28		Accounts Receivable	12	2,400	
			Service Fees	41		2,400
			Services rendered on account.			
	28		Wages Expense	52	420	
			Cash	11		420
			Paid wages for second two weeks of December.			
	28		C. Monroe, Drawing	32	600	
			Cash	11		600
			Withdrew $600 for personal use.			
	28		Cash	11	200	
			Service Fees	41		200
			Services for cash, December 22–28.			

General Ledger

Cash

Account No. 11

Date		Description	Post. Ref.	Debit*	Credit	Balance
19XX						
Dec.	1		J1	20,000		20,000
	1		J1		400	19,600
	2		J1		7,200	12,400
	2		J1		2,000	10,400
	2		J1	800		11,200
	7		J1	550		11,750
	14		J1		420	11,330
	14		J2	480		11,810
	17		J2		50	11,760
	19		J2	500		12,260
	21		J2	320		12,580
	28		J2		170	12,410
	28		J2		420	11,990
	28		J2		600	11,390
	28		J2	200		11,590

Accounts Receivable

Account No. 12

Date		Description	Post. Ref.	Debit*	Credit	Balance
19XX						
Dec.	14		J1	750		750
	19		J2		500	250
	28		J2	2,400		2,650

Supplies and Parts on Hand

Account No. 14

Date		Description	Post. Ref.	Debit*	Credit	Balance
19XX						
Dec.	3		J1	600		600

EXHIBIT 3–6 (continued)

Test Equipment   Account No. 16

Date		Description	Post. Ref.	Debit*	Credit	Balance
19XX Dec.	2		J1	3,000		3,000

Truck   Account No. 18

Date		Description	Post. Ref.	Debit*	Credit	Balance
19XX Dec.	2		J1	7,200		7,200

Accounts Payable   Account No. 21

Date		Description	Post. Ref.	Debit	Credit*	Balance
19XX Dec.	2		J1		1,000	1,000
	3		J1		600	1,600

Unearned Service Fees   Account No. 24

Date		Description	Post. Ref.	Debit	Credit*	Balance
19XX Dec.	2		J1		800	800

C. Monroe, Capital   Account No. 31

Date		Description	Post. Ref.	Debit	Credit*	Balance
19XX Dec.	1		J1		20,000	20,000

C. Monroe, Drawing
Account No. 32

Date		Description	Post. Ref.	Debit*	Credit	Balance
19XX Dec.	28		J2	600		600

Service Fees
Account No. 41

Date		Description	Post. Ref.	Debit	Credit*	Balance
19XX Dec.	7		J1		550	550
	14		J1		750	1,300
	14		J2		480	1,780
	21		J2		320	2,100
	28		J2		2,400	4,500
	28		J2		200	4,700

Rent Expense
Account No. 51

Date		Description	Post. Ref.	Debit*	Credit	Balance
19XX Dec.	1		J1	400		400

Wages Expense
Account No. 52

Date		Description	Post. Ref.	Debit*	Credit	Balance
19XX Dec.	14		J1	420		420
	28		J2	420		840

EXHIBIT 3–6 (continued)
Advertising Expense   Account No. 53

Date		Description	Post. Ref.	Debit*	Credit	Balance
19XX Dec.	17		J2	50		50

Truck Expense   Account No. 56

Date		Description	Post. Ref.	Debit*	Credit	Balance
19XX Dec.	28		J2	170		170

TAKING A TRIAL BALANCE   After the journal entries have been posted to the ledger accounts, the next step is to determine the balance of each account and take a trial balance of all the accounts. The trial balance of the Monroe TV Service at December 31 is shown in Exhibit 3–7.

EXHIBIT 3–7

Monroe TV Service
Trial Balance
December 31, 19XX

	Debit	Credit
Cash	$11,590	
Accounts Receivable	2,650	
Supplies and Parts on Hand	600	
Test Equipment	3,000	
Truck	7,200	
Accounts Payable		$ 1,600
Unearned Service Fees		800
C. Monroe, Capital		20,000
C. Monroe, Drawing	600	
Service Fees		4,700
Rent Expense	400	
Wages Expense	840	
Advertising Expense	50	
Truck Expense	170	
	$27,100	$27,100

CORRECTING ERRONEOUS POSTINGS   Even the most carefully kept accounts will occasionally contain posting errors. An error involving only the wrong amount being posted may be corrected by drawing a line through the incorrect amount, entering the correct amount above, and initialing the correction. When an amount has been posted to the wrong account, however, the correction should be made with a journal entry. Let us assume that Monroe TV Service purchased test equipment for $100 cash and that the bookkeeper erroneously debited the amount to Supplies and Parts on Hand instead of to Test Equipment. The following entry in the journal corrects the error by transferring the debit to the correct account:

Test Equipment	100	
Supplies and Parts on Hand		100
To correct entry for purchase of		
test equipment.		

ADJUSTMENTS

Step 4: Adjust the Ledger Accounts

It is important that accounts appearing in financial statements at the end of an accounting period be properly stated. Clearly, if the income statement is to portray a realistic net income figure based on accrual accounting, all revenues *earned* during the period and all expenses *incurred* must be shown. Therefore, revenues and costs must be properly aligned for the reporting period in question. This process of aligning costs and expenses with related revenue is the **matching** concept frequently mentioned in accounting literature.

Many of the transactions reflected in the accounting records through the first three steps in the accounting cycle affect the net income of more than one period. Therefore, to achieve a proper matching of costs and expenses with revenue, we must adjust the account balances at the end of each accounting period. The **adjusting** step of the accounting cycle occurs after the journals have been posted, but before financial statements are prepared.

Four general types of adjustments are made at the end of an accounting period:

(1) Aligning *recorded costs* with the appropriate accounting periods.

(2) Aligning *recorded revenue* with the appropriate accounting periods.

(3) Reflecting *unrecorded expenses* incurred during the accounting period.

(4) Reflecting *unrecorded revenue* earned during the accounting period.

Adjustments in the first two categories—aligning recorded costs and revenue with the appropriate periods—are often referred to as **deferrals.** Adjustments in the last two categories—reflecting unrecorded expenses and revenue—are often referred to as **accruals.**

ALIGNING RECORDED COSTS   Many business outlays may benefit a number of accounting periods. Some common examples are purchases of buildings, equipment, supplies, and payments of insurance premiums covering a period of years. Ordinarily, these outlays are debited to an asset account at the time of expenditure. Then, at the end of each accounting period, the estimated portion of the outlay that has expired during the period or that has benefited the period is transferred to an expense account.

The preceding chapters included two examples of adjustments aligning recorded costs with the appropriate accounting period. One example allocated part of the cost of three years' insurance coverage to insurance expense for the current month. The total cost of the insurance premium had been debited initially to the asset account Prepaid Insurance. The adjustment then allocated the cost of one month's coverage ($\frac{1}{36}$ of the premium) to insurance expense. The other example dealt with the cost of supplies. The adjustment transferred the cost of supplies used during the current month from the asset account Supplies on Hand to the expense account Supplies Expense. We shall consider another example involving supplies and parts in this chapter.

Under most circumstances, we can discover when adjustments of this type are needed by inspecting the monthly trial balance for costs that benefit several periods. By looking at the December 31 trial balance of Monroe TV Service (Exhibit 3–7), for example, we would find that adjustments are required to apportion the costs of the supplies and parts, the test equipment, and the truck between December and subsequent periods.

Supplies and parts   During December, Monroe TV Service purchased supplies and parts and recorded the outlay in an asset account, Supplies and Parts on Hand, as follows:

Dec. 3	Supplies and Parts on Hand	600	
	Accounts Payable		600
	Purchased supplies and parts on		
	account; 60-day terms.		

The firm could not conveniently keep a daily count of parts and supplies used in service work. Instead, at the end of December, it would count the items still on hand. Suppose the count shows $220 worth of supplies and parts on hand at the end of the month, indicating that $380 worth of supplies and parts have been used in service work during the month. Therefore, at the end of the period, an adjusting entry will transfer this amount to an expense account, Supplies and Parts Expense, as follows:

Dec. 31	Supplies and Parts Expense	380	
	Supplies and Parts on Hand		380
	To record expense of supplies and		
	parts used in December.		

When this adjusting entry is posted, it will properly reflect the December expense for supplies and parts and will reduce the asset account Supplies and Parts on Hand to $220, the actual amount of the asset remaining at December 31. After the entry is posted, the related ledger accounts appear as follows:

Supplies and Parts on Hand   Account No. 14

Date		Description	Post. Ref.	Debit*	Credit	Balance
19XX						
Dec.	3		J1	600		600
	31		J3		380	220

Supplies and Parts Expense   Account No. 54

Date		Description	Post. Ref.	Debit*	Credit	Balance
19XX						
Dec.	31		J3	380		380

Obviously, if financial statements were prepared without this adjustment, the December income statement would omit an important expense and would overstate net income by $380. Similarly, the balance sheet would overstate assets by $380, because the Supplies and Parts on Hand balance would remain at $600. As a result of overstating net income, owner's equity in the balance sheet would also be overstated by $380.

Depreciation   The process of allocating the costs of a firm's equipment, vehicles, and buildings to the periods benefiting from their use is called **depreciation** accounting. Because these long-lived assets help generate revenue in a company's operations, each accounting period in which the assets are used should reflect a portion of their cost as expense. This periodic expense is known as depreciation expense.

Periodic depreciation expense must be estimated by accountants. The procedure we use here estimates the annual amount of depreciation expense by dividing the cost of the asset by its estimated useful life in years. This method is called *straight-line* depreciation. (We will explore other methods in Chapter 10.)

When recording depreciation expense, the asset amount is not reduced directly. Instead, the reduction is recorded in a contra account called Accumulated Depreciation. *Contra* accounts are so named because they are used to record reductions in or offsets against a related account. The Accumulated Depreciation account will normally have a credit balance and will appear in the balance sheet as a deduction from the related asset amount. Use of the contra account Accumulated Depreciation allows the original cost of the related asset to be shown in the balance sheet, followed by the accumulated amount of depreciation.

Let us assume that the test equipment purchased by Monroe TV Service for $3,000 has an estimated life of five years and that the truck costing $7,200 is expected to last six years. Straight-line depreciation recorded on the test equipment is therefore $600 per year, or $50 per month. Similarly, the depreciation on the truck is $1,200 per year, or $100 per month. At the end of December, we would make the following adjusting entries:

Dec. 31	Depreciation Expense—Test Equipment	50	
	Accumulated Depreciation—		
	Test Equipment		50
	To record December depreciation on		
	test equipment.		
Dec. 31	Depreciation Expense—Truck	100	
	Accumulated Depreciation—Truck		100
	To record December depreciation on truck.		

When the preceding entries are posted, they will properly reflect the cost of using these assets during December, and the correct expense will appear in the December income statement. After the adjusting entries have been posted, the asset accounts, accumulated depreciation accounts, and depreciation expense accounts appear as follows:

Test Equipment   Account No. 16

Date		Description	Post. Ref.	Debit*	Credit	Balance
19XX Dec.	2		J1	3,000		3,000

Accumulated Depreciation—Test Equipment   Account No. 17

Date		Description	Post. Ref.	Debit	Credit*	Balance
19XX Dec.	31		J3		50	50

Depreciation Expense—Test Equipment   Account No. 57

Date		Description	Post. Ref.	Debit*	Credit	Balance
19XX Dec.	31		J3	50		50

Truck   Account No. 18

Date		Description	Post. Ref.	Debit*	Credit	Balance
19XX Dec.	2		J1	7,200		7,200

Accumulated Depreciation—Truck   Account No. 19

Date		Description	Post. Ref.	Debit	Credit*	Balance
19XX Dec.	31		J3		100	100

Depreciation Expense—Truck   Account No. 58

Date		Description	Post. Ref.	Debit*	Credit	Balance
19XX Dec.	31		J3	100		100

If the firm failed to record the adjusting entries for depreciation, expenses would be omitted from the income statement. In the above situation, such an omission would result in an overstatement of net income by $150. Furthermore, assets and owner's equity would be overstated by the same amount on the balance sheet.

On the balance sheet, the accumulated depreciation amounts are subtracted from the related asset amounts. The resulting balances (cost less accumulated depreciation), which are the assets' **book values,** represent the unexpired asset costs to be applied as expenses against future operating periods. For example, the December 31, 19XX, balance sheet would show test equipment with a book value of $2,950, presented as follows:

		$3,000	
Test Equipment		$3,000	
Less: Accumulated Depreciation		50	$2,950

ALIGNING RECORDED REVENUE   Sometimes a business receives fees for services before service is rendered. Such transactions are ordinarily recorded by debiting Cash and crediting a liability account. The liability account in this situation, sometimes called a **deferred credit,** shows the obligation for performing future service. For example, a monthly magazine publisher receiving $72 for a three-year subscription would debit Cash and credit Unearned Subscription Revenue for $72. Each month that magazines are supplied to the subscriber, $\frac{1}{36}$ of the publisher's obligation is fulfilled. At the end of each month, the bookkeeper would transfer $2 from the liability account Unearned Subscription Revenue to a revenue account, Subscription Revenue. This procedure reflects revenue when service is performed rather than when it is paid for.

During December, Monroe TV Service entered one transaction that requires an end-of-month adjustment to recorded revenue. On December 2, the firm signed a four-month contract to perform service for a local TV dealer at $200 per month, with the entire contract price of $800 received in advance. The entry made on December 2 was as follows:

Dec. 2	Cash	800	
	Unearned Service Fees		800
	Received advance on four-month contract at $200 per month.		

On December 31, the following adjusting entry would be made to transfer $200, the revenue earned in December, to Service Fees and reduce the liability Unearned Service Fees by the same amount:

Dec. 31	Unearned Service Fees	200	
	Service Fees		200
	To record portion of advance earned in December.		

After this entry is posted, the liability account will show a balance of $600, the amount of future services still owing, and the Service Fees account will reflect the $200 earned in December.

Unearned Service Fees   Account No. 24

Date		Description	Post. Ref.	Debit	Credit*	Balance
19XX Dec.	2		J1		800	800
	31		J3	200		600

Service Fees   Account No. 41

Date		Description	Post. Ref.	Debit	Credit*	Balance
19XX						
Dec.	7		J1		550	550
	14		J1		750	1,300
	14		J2		480	1,780
	21		J2		320	2,100
	28		J2		2,400	4,500
	28		J2		200	4,700
	31		J3		200	4,900

A similar entry would be repeated at the end of each month of the contract period; $200 in revenue would be included in Service Fees in the income statement, and the liability account in the balance sheet would be reduced by $200.

We emphasize here that if the adjusting entries are ignored, the revenue is never reflected in any income statement and the liability remains on the balance sheet after the obligation has been discharged. Therefore, it is important to make these adjustments carefully.

REFLECTING UNRECORDED EXPENSES   Often a business will use certain services before paying for them. Obligations to pay for services such as salaries, utilities, and taxes may build up, or accrue, over a period of time. Most businesses make adjusting entries for such **accrued expenses** in order to reflect the proper cost in the period when the benefit was received. The bookkeeper must realize that services received have not yet been reflected in the accounts and make appropriate adjustments. If source documents are not available, amounts may be estimated.

Accrued utilities   During December, Monroe TV Service used telephone service and utility service for heat and light. Bills from the telephone and power companies will not arrive until January. Let us assume, however, that based on inquiries to the landlord and knowledge of local rates, the firm estimates that it received $80 worth of services during the month. On December 31, the bookkeeper makes the following adjusting entry:

Dec. 31	Utilities Expense	80	
	Utilities Payable		80
	To record estimated amount of		
	December utilities expense.		

This adjustment reflects both the cost of services received during the period and the estimated amount owed for such services to be included on the balance sheet. If this adjustment were not made, net income would be overstated by $80 in the

December income statement; on the December 31 balance sheet, liabilities would be understated and owner's equity overstated by $80.

Note that the credit in the adjusting entry above could have been made to Accounts Payable. Because the amount is an estimate, however, many businesses prefer to credit a separate account such as Utilities Payable.

After the bookkeeper posts the adjusting entry for estimated utilities expense, the expense and liability accounts would appear as follows:

Utilities Expense   Account No. 55

Date		Description	Post. Ref.	Debit*	Credit	Balance
19XX Dec.	31		J3	80		80

Utilities Payable   Account No. 22

Date		Description	Post. Ref.	Debit	Credit*	Balance
19XX Dec.	31		J3		80	80

Suppose the utility bill that arrives in early January is for $84, indicating that the firm has underestimated the December expense by $4. Obviously, $84 will be credited to Cash since the full amount of the bill must be paid. But what would be debited to balance the $84 credit? The firm might remove the liability by debiting $80 to Utilities Payable and debiting the remaining $4 to Utilities Expense for January. This tactic places some of December's utilities expense in January. Such a small discrepancy as $4 is not material, however, and most persons would not be disturbed about the minor inaccuracy. Another method of handling the accrual in the subsequent period, involving reversing entries, will be explained in Chapter 4.

Accrued wages   A Monroe TV Service employee is paid every two weeks at the rate of $210 for each six-day workweek. The employee was paid $420 on December 14 and December 28. Let us assume that both these dates fell on Saturday and that Sunday is the employee's day off. If financial statements are prepared at the close of business on Tuesday, December 31, the employee will have worked two days (Monday and Tuesday) during December for which he will not be paid until January. Because the employee's wages are $35 per day ($210 ÷ 6 days), additional wages expense of $70 should be reflected in the income statement for December. The adjusting entry at the end of December would be as follows:

Dec. 31	Wages Expense	70	
	Wages Payable		70
	To record accrued wages for		
	December 30 and 31.		

After posting, the Wages Expense and Wages Payable accounts would appear as follows:

Wages Expense   Account No. 52

Date		Description	Post. Ref.	Debit*	Credit	Balance
19XX						
Dec.	14		J1	420		420
	28		J2	420		840
	31		J3	70		910

Wages Payable   Account No. 23

Date		Description	Post. Ref.	Debit	Credit*	Balance
19XX						
Dec.	31		J3		70	70

    This adjustment enables the firm to reflect as December expense all wages *earned* by the employee during the period rather than just the wages *paid*. In addition, the balance sheet will show the liability for unpaid wages at the end of the period. Omitting this adjustment would cause a $70 overstatement of net income in the December income statement, with a concurrent $70 overstatement of owner's equity and a $70 understatement of liabilities in the December 31 balance sheet.

    When the employee is paid on the next regular payday in January, the bookkeeper must make sure that the two days' pay accrued at the end of December is not again charged to expense. If we assume that the employee is paid $420 on Saturday, January 11, the following entry can be made:

Jan. 11	Wages Payable	70	
	Wages Expense	350	
	Cash		420
	To record wages paid.		

This entry eliminates the liability recorded in Wages Payable at the end of December and debits January Wages Expense for only those wages earned by the employee in January. Another method of avoiding dual charges, that of reversing entries, will be explained in Chapter 4.

REFLECTING UNRECORDED REVENUE A company may provide services during a period that are neither billed nor paid for by the end of the period. Yet the value of these services represents revenue earned by the firm and should be reflected in the firm's income statement. Such accumulated revenue is often called **accrued revenue.** For example, a firm may have loaned money on which interest has been earned that is not collected by the end of the period. The amount of the interest should be reflected in the net income of the period in which it is earned. In this situation, an adjusting entry would be made debiting Interest Receivable and crediting Interest Income for the amount of interest earned.

In the case of Monroe TV Service, the service contract with the local hotel negotiated on December 2 could result in accrued revenue. Under the terms of the contract, Monroe TV Service will bill the hotel for work at $12 per hour whenever 40 hours of work have been completed. Suppose that by December 31, Monroe has performed 15 hours of work for the hotel. Unbilled revenue of $180 (15 hours × $12) has accrued during the month and should be reflected in the accounts by the following adjusting entry:

Dec. 31	Accounts Receivable	180	
	Service Fees		180
	To record unbilled revenue earned during December.		

This entry includes in the December accounts the revenue earned by performing service but not yet billed to the hotel. It also enters the amount owed by the hotel as a receivable on the balance sheet. After the entry is posted, the related accounts would appear as follows:

Accounts Receivable   Account No. 12

Date		Description	Post. Ref.	Debit*	Credit	Balance
19XX						
Dec.	14		J1	750		750
	19		J2		500	250
	28		J2	2,400		2,650
	31		J3	180		2,830

Service Fees   Account No. 41

Date		Description	Post. Ref.	Debit	Credit*	Balance
19XX						
Dec.	7		J1		550	550
	14		J1		750	1,300
	14		J2		480	1,780
	21		J2		320	2,100
	28		J2		2,400	4,500
	28		J2		200	4,700
	31		J3		200	4,900
	31		J3		180	5,080

The bookkeeper must be careful when the regular 40-hour billing is sent to the hotel in January. Let us assume that 40 hours of work has accumulated by January 21. Because the revenue from 15 hours of work ($180) was recorded in the December 31 adjusting entry, the billing made on January 21 contains only $300 (25 hours × $12) of revenue earned during January. The following entry could be made when the hotel is billed for $480 (40 hours × $12):

Jan. 21	Accounts Receivable	300	
	Service Fees		300
	To record revenue earned during January; customer billed $480 for work performed in December and January.		

An alternative way of handling this situation, using reversing entries, is discussed in Chapter 4.

If we did not make the adjustment for accrued revenue, the December net income for Monroe TV Service would be understated by $180, and the January net income would be overstated by the same amount. On the December 31 balance sheet, assets and owner's equity would also be understated.

PREPAYMENTS RECORDED IN EXPENSE AND REVENUE ACCOUNTS Expenditures made to benefit future periods and amounts received for services yet to be performed should be recorded initially in balance sheet accounts. Then the adjusting procedure consists of transferring the expired portion of prepaid expenses to expense accounts and transferring the earned portion of unearned revenue to revenue accounts. We have essentially just described these procedures.

Occasionally, an outlay benefiting future periods may be debited to an expense account rather than to prepaid expense, or an amount received for future services may be credited to a revenue account rather than to unearned revenue. In such situations, the adjusting procedure consists of transferring the unexpired or unearned portion of the recorded amount to the appropriate balance sheet account. For example, suppose that a one-year insurance premium of $1,200 was initially debited to Insurance Expense. At the end of the first month after the outlay, the following adjusting entry is appropriate:

ADJUSTING THE ADJUSTMENTS

Estimates play a large role in determining the amounts for various adjusting entries. As circumstances change, the estimate underlying an adjusting entry may also change, and even modest estimate modifications may have significant financial effects. We illustrate this concept with two examples—(1) allocating the cost of program rights for a television network and (2) accruing the cost of redeeming trading stamps for a trading stamp company.

A television network acquires the right to televise certain program material—such as a movie or series—through a license agreement. The license agreement may permit the network to broadcast the program a specified number of times or permit unlimited broadcasts over a specified time period. The network pays a fee to acquire these program rights and reflects this cost in the asset account Program Rights. A program's cost is allocated to expense over the estimated number of future showings. This allocation process matches the programming costs with the advertising revenue received from the commercials shown during the program's broadcasts. The difficult estimate, of course, is the portion of the program's cost to expense with each showing. If the initial showing is more valuable than reruns (and this is often the case), a larger amount of cost should be expensed with the first broadcast. [*]

To match revenue and programming costs more closely, American Broadcasting Companies, Inc. (ABC) in 1980 modified its write-off rates for prime time programming. The amount expensed on the original broadcast was reduced, and the amounts expensed on subsequent broadcasts were increased. Although ABC did not disclose the specific change in write-off rates, the first time charge was estimated to have declined from 80% to 75% of the

program's cost. [†] This change increased ABC's net income by $8,928,000 in 1980 and $13,405,000 in 1981. [‡] Indeed, the 1981 effect was more than 9% of the corporation's net income.

A trading stamp company sells trading stamps to retailers who, in turn, give the stamps to their customers. Customers who accumulate enough stamps redeem them for merchandise from the trading stamp company. Many stamps may not be redeemed for a year or more, and some stamps are never redeemed. The trading stamp company records revenue when it sells the stamps. To match expenses with revenue, the company must accrue in the same period the estimated expense of redeeming the stamps (the merchandise cost and related redemption service costs) and set up a liability for stamp redemptions. The accrued amount depends on the estimate of stamps ultimately redeemed.

The Sperry and Hutchinson Company sells and redeems S & H Green Stamps. Prior to 1979, Sperry and Hutchinson based its accrued redemption expenses on an estimated 95% stamp redemption rate. In 1979, statistical evaluations revealed that the eventual stamp redemption rate had declined to 90%; the company's 1979 accrual utilized a 90% estimate. The estimate change caused 1979's net income to increase $5,187,000, [§] an amount representing almost 18% of the 1979 net income.

[*] *Statement of Financial Accounting Standards No. 63*, "Financial Reporting by Broadcasters" (Stamford, CT: Financial Accounting Standards Board, 1982), page 3.
[†] Thomas Baker, "A Question of Judgment," *Forbes*, February 16, 1981, page 52.
[‡] American Broadcasting Companies, Inc., *Annual Report*, 1981, page 57.
[§] The Sperry and Hutchinson Company, *Annual Report*, 1980, page 25.

Prepaid Insurance	1,100	
Insurance Expense		1,100
To transfer unexpired insurance cost		
to asset account.		

This entry sets up an asset of $1,100 and leaves $100 in the expense account.

Suppose also that the firm received a six-month prepayment of rent totaling $1,200 from a tenant and credited the entire amount to Rental Income (a revenue account). After the first month has elapsed, the appropriate adjusting entry is:

Rental Income	1,000	
Unearned Rental Income		1,000
To transfer unearned rental income		
to liability account.		

This adjustment records $1,000 as a liability and leaves a $200 balance in the revenue account.

It is important to note that the nature of the adjusting entry depends on how the transaction was recorded initially (a prepayment debited to either an asset or expense account and an advance receipt credited to either a liability or revenue account). *After* the adjusting entry has been made and posted, however, the balances in the affected accounts will be the same regardless of how the transaction was initially recorded.

Exhibit 3–8 summarizes our discussion about the various types of adjustments.

KEY POINTS TO REMEMBER

(1) Six major steps are in the accounting cycle:

Steps	**When Normally Done**
1. Analyze transactions	
2. Record in journals	Throughout every period
3. Post to ledgers	
4. Adjust accounts	When statements are required
5. Prepare statements	
6. Close temporary accounts	At the end of the year

(2) Accounting entries are initially recorded in a journal; the entries are in chronological order, and the journal shows the total effect of each transaction or adjustment.

(3) After journal entries are posted to the accounts, a trial balance is taken to ensure that the general ledger is in balance.

(4) Adjusting entries made to achieve the appropriate matching of expenses and revenue consist of the following four types:
(a) Aligning recorded costs with periods benefited.

Exhibit 3–8
Summary of Adjustments

Adjustment Category	Nature of Adjusting Entry	Text Page	Examples — Entry		
1. Aligning Recorded Costs					
a. Initially recorded as an asset	Increase expense Decrease asset	90	Supplies and Parts Expense Supplies and Parts on Hand	380	380
For depreciation	Increase expense Increase contra asset (which decreases asset's book value)	92	Depreciation Expense—Test Equipment Accumulated Depreciation—Test Equipment	50	50
		92	Depreciation Expense—Truck Accumulated Depreciation—Truck	100	100
b. Initially recorded as an expense	Increase asset Decrease expense	101	Prepaid Insurance Insurance Expense	1,100	1,100
2. Aligning Recorded Revenue					
a. Initially recorded as a liability	Decrease liability Increase revenue	94	Unearned Service Fees Service Fees	200	200
b. Initially recorded as revenue	Decrease revenue Increase liability	101	Rental Income Unearned Rental Income	1,000	1,000
3. Reflecting Unrecorded Expenses	Increase expense Increase liability	95	Utilities Expense Utilities Payable	80	80
		97	Wages Expense Wages Payable	70	70
4. Reflecting Unrecorded Revenue	Increase asset Increase revenue	98	Accounts Receivable Service Fees	180	180

(b) Aligning recorded revenue with periods in which it is earned.

(c) Reflecting unrecorded expenses incurred during the period.

(d) Reflecting unrecorded revenue earned during the period.

QUESTIONS

3–1 List in their proper order the steps in the accounting cycle.

3–2 If we assume that a business prepares quarterly financial statements, at what time(s) during the year is each step in the accounting cycle accomplished?

3–3 Explain the nature and purpose of a general journal.

3–4 What is a compound journal entry?

3–5 What is the appropriate procedure for correcting an erroneous general journal entry (a) before it has been posted and (b) after it has been posted?

3–6 Explain the technique of posting references. What is the justification for their use?

3–7 Describe a chart of accounts, and give an example of a coding system for identifying different types of accounts.

3–8 Why is the adjusting step of the accounting cycle necessary?

3–9 What four different types of adjustments are frequently necessary at the close of an accounting period? Give examples of each type.

3–10 On January 1, Prepaid Insurance was debited with the cost of a one-year premium, $324. What adjusting entry should be made on January 31?

3–11 Referring to Question 3–10, suppose the bookkeeper had charged the entire $324 premium to Insurance Expense when it was paid on January 1. What adjusting entry should be made on January 31 before financial statements are prepared for the month?

3–12 At the beginning of January, the first month of the accounting year, the Supplies on Hand account had a debit balance of $500. During January, purchases of $800 worth of supplies were debited to the account. Although only $600 worth of supplies were on hand at the end of January, the necessary adjusting entry was omitted. How will the omission affect (a) the income statement for January and (b) the balance sheet prepared at January 31?

3–13 *International View*, a monthly magazine, received two-year subscriptions totaling $7,800 on January 1. (a) What entry should be made to record the receipt of the $7,800? (b) What entry should be made at the end of January before financial statements are prepared for the month?

3–14 Grogan Travel Agency pays an employee $325 in wages each Friday for the five-day workweek ended on that day. The last Friday of January falls on January 25. What adjusting entry should be made on January 31?

3–15 If the Grogan Travel Agency in Question 3–14 fails to make the necessary adjusting entry on January 31, how will the omission affect (a) the income statement for January and (b) the balance sheet prepared at January 31?

3–16 Francisco Lopez earns interest amounting to $155 per month on some of his investments. He receives the interest every six months, on December 31 and June 30. What adjusting entry should he make on January 31?

EXERCISES

3–17 Design Masters, a firm providing art services for advertisers, has the following accounts in its general ledger: Cash; Accounts Receivable; Supplies on Hand; Office Equipment; Accounts Payable; F. Buhler, Capital; F. Buhler, Drawing; Fees Earned; Rent Expense; Utilities Expense; and Salaries Expense. Record the following transactions for June in a two-column general journal:

June 1 Faye Buhler invested $18,000 cash to begin the business.
　　　2 Paid rent for June, $750.
　　　3 Purchased office equipment on account, $6,300.
　　　6 Purchased art materials and other supplies costing $2,100; paid $1,000 down with the remainder due within 30 days.
　　　11 Billed clients for services, $2,800.
　　　17 Collected $1,750 from clients.
　　　19 Paid $3,150 on account to office equipment firm (see June 3).
　　　25 Faye Buhler withdrew $800 for personal use.
　　　30 Paid utilities bill for June, $140.
　　　30 Paid salaries for June, $1,600.

3–18 The following erroneous journal entries have been posted to the general ledger. Prepare the journal entries to correct the errors.
(a) A $300 cash collection of an account receivable was recorded as a debit to Cash and a credit to Service Fees.
(b) A $500 purchase of supplies on account was recorded as a debit to Supplies on Hand and a credit to Cash.
(c) A $900 billing of customers for services rendered was recorded as a debit to Accounts Payable and a credit to Service Fees.
(d) A $150 cash payment for the current month's newspaper advertising was recorded as a debit to Rent Expense and a credit to Cash.
(e) A $600 cash payment for office equipment was recorded as a debit to Cash and a credit to Office Equipment.

3–19 Selected accounts of Ideal Properties, Inc., a real estate management firm, are shown below as of January 31 of the current year, before any adjusting entries have been made.

	Debit	Credit
Prepaid Insurance	$2,880	
Supplies on Hand	950	
Office Equipment	4,320	
Unearned Rental Fees		$ 3,600
Salaries Expense	2,300	
Rental Fees		12,000

Using the following information, record in a general journal the adjusting entries necessary on January 31:
(a) Prepaid Insurance represents a two-year premium paid on January 1.
(b) Supplies of $400 were on hand January 31.
(c) Office equipment is expected to last eight years.
(d) On January 1, the firm collected six months' rent in advance from a tenant renting space for $600 per month.
(e) Accrued salaries not recorded as of January 31 are $230.

3–20 Eleanor Taylor began the Antique Refinishing Service on July 1 of the current year. Selected accounts are shown below as of July 31, before any adjusting entries have been made.

	Debit	Credit
Prepaid Rent	$3,000	
Prepaid Advertising	180	
Supplies on Hand	1,000	
Unearned Refinishing Fees		$ 500
Refinishing Fees		1,500

Using the following information, record in a general journal the adjusting entries necessary on July 31:

(a) On July 1, Taylor paid one year's rent of $3,000.

(b) On July 1, $180 was paid to the local newspaper for an advertisement to run daily for the months of July, August, and September.

(c) Supplies on hand at July 31 total $700.

(d) At July 31, refinishing services of $300 have been performed but not yet billed to customers.

(e) One customer paid $500 in advance for a refinishing project. At July 31, the project is one-fourth complete.

3–21 For each of the following unrelated situations, prepare the necessary adjusting entry in general journal form.

(a) Unrecorded depreciation expense on equipment is $900.

(b) The Supplies on Hand account has a balance of $870. Supplies on hand at the end of the period total $350.

(c) On the date for preparing financial statements, an estimated utilities expense of $95 has been incurred, but no utility bill has yet been received.

(d) On the first day of the current month, rent for three months was paid and recorded as a $900 debit to Rent Expense and a $900 credit to Cash. Monthly statements are now being prepared.

(e) Eight months ago, Solid Insurance Company sold a one-year policy to a customer and recorded the sale by debiting Cash for $660 and crediting Premium Revenue Earned for $660. No adjusting entries have been prepared during the eight-month period. Annual statements are now being prepared.

(f) At the end of the accounting period, wages expense of $740 has been incurred but not paid.

(g) At the end of the accounting period, $200 of repair services have been rendered to customers who have not yet been billed.

3–22 Ace Building Maintenance Service offers janitorial services on both a contract basis and an hourly basis. On January 1 of the current year, Ace collected $9,600 in advance on six-month contracts for work to be performed evenly during the next six months.

(a) Give the general journal entry to record the receipt of $9,600 for contract work.

(b) Give the adjusting entry to be made on January 31 for the contract work done during January.

(c) At January 31, a total of 30 hours of hourly rate janitor work was unbilled. The billing rate is $10 per hour. Give the adjusting entry needed on January 31.

3-23 Selected T-account balances for the Martin Company are shown below as of January 31 of the current year; adjusting entries have already been posted. The firm operates on a calendar year.

wed

Supplies on Hand	
Jan. 31 Bal. 400	

Supplies Expense	
Jan. 31 Bal. 660	

Prepaid Insurance	
Jan. 31 Bal. 455	

Insurance Expense	
Jan. 31 Bal. 65	

Wages Payable	
	Jan. 31 Bal. 700

Wages Expense	
Jan. 31 Bal. 4,400	

Truck	
Jan. 31 Bal. 9,300	

Accumulated Depreciation—Truck	
	Jan. 31 Bal. 2,170

(a) If the amount in Supplies Expense represents the January 31 adjustment for the supplies used in January, and $700 worth of supplies were purchased during January, what was the January 1 balance of Supplies on Hand?

(b) The amount in the Insurance Expense account represents the adjustment made at January 31 for January insurance expense. If the original premium was for one year, what was the amount of the premium and on what date did the insurance policy start?

(c) If we assume no balance existed in Wages Payable or Wages Expense on January 1, how much was paid in wages during January?

(d) If the truck has a useful life of five years, what is the monthly amount of depreciation expense and how many months has Martin owned the truck?

3-24 The Olson Repair Service shows the following trial balance at the end of its first month of operations:

	Debit	Credit
Cash	$ 4,000	
Supplies on Hand	2,600	
Equipment	12,000	
Accounts Payable		$ 1,900
Olson, Capital		14,000
Service Revenue		5,700
Wages Expense	2,150	
Utilities Expense	400	
Advertising Expense	450	
	$21,600	$21,600

The repair service's bookkeeper prepared an income statement for the month showing a net income of $2,700. She obtained this sum by deducting the $3,000 total of Wages Expense, Utilities Expense, and Advertising Expense from the Service Revenue of $5,700. However, she did not consider the following:

(a) Depreciation for the month should have been $200.

(b) Supplies on hand at the end of the month were $1,800.

(c) Accrued wages payable at the end of the month were $350.

(d) Unbilled service revenue at the end of the month was $600.

Using the preceding information, calculate the correct net income for the month.

PROBLEMS

3–25 Carl Stacey opened the Stacey Window Cleaning Service on April 1 of the current year. Transactions for April are as follows:

Apr. 1   Stacey contributed $15,000 of his personal funds to begin the business.
2   Purchased a used truck for $4,000 cash.
2   Purchased ladders, scaffolding, and other equipment for a total of $1,800; paid $1,000 cash, with the balance due in 30 days. (Classify this outlay as Equipment.)
3   Paid three-year premium on liability insurance, $720.
5   Purchased supplies on account, $550.
5   Received an advance payment of $200 from a customer for cleaning services to be rendered during April and May.
12   Billed customers for services, $1,700.
18   Collected $1,300 on account from customers.
29   Paid bill for truck fuel used in April, $60.
30   Paid April newspaper advertising, $70.
30   Paid assistants' wages, $1,100.
30   Billed customers for services, $1,500.

REQUIRED

(a) Record these transactions in general journal form.

(b) Devise a chart of accounts for the firm and set up the general ledger. Allow for accounts that may be needed when adjusting entries are made at the close of the accounting period [see part (e)].

(c) Post journal entries to the ledger accounts.

(d) Take a trial balance.

(e) Make the journal entries to adjust the books for insurance expense, supplies expense, depreciation expense on the truck, depreciation expense on the equipment, and service fees earned. Supplies on hand on April 30 amounted to $190. Depreciation for April was $100 on the truck and $40 on the equipment. One-half of the service fees received in advance were earned by April 30. Post the adjusting entries.

3–26 Davis Shade Shop ended its first month of operations on June 30 of the current year. The unadjusted account balances are as follows:

Davis Shade Shop
Trial Balance
June 30, 19XX

	Debit	Credit
Cash	$1,100	
Accounts Receivable	900	
Prepaid Rent	600	
Supplies on Hand	700	
Equipment	4,800	
Accounts Payable		$ 800
Davis, Capital		5,100
Davis, Drawing	600	
Service Fees		4,000
Wages Expense	1,200	
	$9,900	$9,900

The following information is also available:
(1) The balance in Prepaid Rent was the amount paid on June 1 for the first two months' rent.
(2) Supplies on hand at June 30 were $360.
(3) The equipment, purchased June 1, has an estimated life of eight years.
(4) Unpaid wages at June 30 were $350.
(5) Utility services used during June were estimated at $120. A bill is expected early in July.
(6) Fees earned for services performed but not yet billed on June 30 were $400.

REQUIRED
In general journal form, make the adjusting entries needed at June 30.

3–27 Pictures, Inc., a commercial photography studio, has just completed its first full year of operations on December 31 of the current year. The ledger account balances before year-end adjustments are given below. No adjusting entries have been made to the accounts at any time during the year. Assume that all balances are normal.

Cash	$1,200	Unearned Photography Fees	$ 750
Accounts Receivable	2,900	Capital Stock	11,000
Prepaid Rent	4,680	Photography Fees	13,200
Supplies on Hand	3,100	Wages Expense	3,800
Equipment	6,300	Insurance Expense	2,520
Accounts Payable	1,520	Utilities Expense	1,970

An analysis of the firm's records discloses the following items:
(1) Photography services of $700 have been rendered, but customers have not yet been billed.
(2) The equipment, purchased January 1, has an estimated life of seven years.
(3) Utilities expense for December is estimated to be $180, but the bill will not arrive until January of next year.

(4) The balance in Prepaid Rent represents the amount paid on January 1 for a two-year lease on the studio.

(5) In November, customers paid $750 in advance for pictures to be taken for the holiday season. When received, these fees were credited to Unearned Photography Fees. By December 31, all these fees are earned.

(6) A three-year insurance premium paid on January 1 was debited to Insurance Expense.

(7) Supplies on hand at December 31 are $900.

REQUIRED

(a) Set up T accounts, and enter the unadjusted balances shown above. Prove that debits equal credits by preparing a trial balance.

(b) Record adjusting entries in a general journal, and post these entries in the T accounts opened in part (a). Create any additional accounts needed.

3–28 For the *unrelated* accounts given below, the current balances and the balances they should have after adjusting entries have been posted are indicated.

Account Title	Current Balance	Adjusted Balance
(1) Supplies on Hand	$800	$560
(2) Depreciation Expense—Building	500	750
(3) Utilities Payable	—	175
(4) Insurance Expense	400	500
(5) Wages Payable	—	800
(6) Unearned Service Fees	860	420
(7) Accumulated Depreciation—Equipment	700	900
(8) Prepaid Rent	750	450
(9) Unearned Commissions Revenue	290	150
(10) Prepaid Advertising	—	400
(11) Interest Receivable	—	90

REQUIRED

For each item listed, prepare the *most probable* general journal entry (including an explanation) for each adjustment.

3–29 The Complete Catering Service had the following transactions in July, its first month of operations:

July 1 Myra Han contributed $9,000 of personal funds to the business.

     1 Purchased the following items for cash from a catering firm that was going out of business (make a compound entry): delivery van, $2,700; equipment, $1,500; and supplies, $2,000.

     2 Paid premium on a one-year liability insurance policy, $600.

     2 Entered into a contract with a local business to cater weekly luncheon meetings for one year at a fee of $200 per month. Received six months' fees in advance.

     3 Paid rent for July, August, and September, $1,800.

    12 Paid employee's two weeks' wages (five-day week), $400.

    15 Billed customers for services rendered, $2,100.

    18 Purchased supplies on account, $1,900.

July 26 Paid employee's two weeks' wages, $400.
  30 Paid July bill for gas, oil, and repairs on delivery van, $220.
  30 Collected $1,800 from customers on account.
  31 Billed customers for services rendered, $2,500.
  31 Han withdrew $500 for personal use.

REQUIRED
(a) Set up a ledger that includes the following accounts, using the account numbers shown: Cash (11); Accounts Receivable (12); Supplies on Hand (13); Prepaid Rent (14); Prepaid Insurance (15); Delivery Van (16); Accumulated Depreciation—Delivery Van (17); Equipment (18); Accumulated Depreciation—Equipment (19); Accounts Payable (21); Wages Payable (22); Unearned Catering Fees (23); M. Han, Capital (31); M. Han, Drawing (32); Catering Fees (41); Wages Expense (51); Rent Expense (52); Supplies Expense (53); Insurance Expense (54); Delivery Van Expense (55); Depreciation Expense—Delivery Van (56); and Depreciation Expense—Equipment (57).
(b) Record July transactions in general journal form and post to the ledger accounts.
(c) Take a trial balance at July 31.
(d) Record adjusting journal entries in the general journal and post to the ledger accounts. The following information is available on July 31:

    Supplies on hand, $300
    Accrued wages, $120
    Estimated life of delivery van, three years
    Estimated life of equipment, five years

Also, make any necessary adjusting entries for insurance, rent, and catering fees indicated by the July transactions.

3–30 The following information relates to December 31 adjustments for Prompt Print, a printing company:
(1) Weekly salaries for a five-day week total $800, payable on Fridays. December 31 of the current year is a Tuesday.
(2) Prompt Print received $500 during December for printing services to be performed during the following year. When received, this amount was credited to Printing Fees.
(3) During December, Prompt Print provided $250 of printing services to clients who will be billed on January 2.
(4) All maintenance work on Prompt Print's equipment is handled by Top Repair Company under an agreement whereby Prompt Print pays a fixed monthly charge of $100. Prompt Print paid three months' service charge in advance on December 1, debiting Prepaid Maintenance for $300.
(5) The firm paid $900 on December 5 for a series of radio commercials to run during December and January. One-half of the commercials have aired by December 31. The $900 payment was debited to Advertising Expense.
(6) Starting December 16, Prompt Print rented 200 square feet of storage space from a neighboring business. The monthly rent of $1.50 per square foot is due in advance on the first of each month. Nothing was paid in December,

however, because the neighbor agreed to add the rent for one-half of December to the January 1 payment.

(7) Prompt Print invested $3,000 in securities on December 1 and earned interest of $25 on these securities by December 31. No interest will be received until January.

(8) The monthly depreciation on the firm's equipment is $175.

REQUIRED

Prepare the required December 31 adjusting entries in general journal form.

ALTERNATE PROBLEMS

3−25A The Chung Karate School began business on June 1 of the current year. Transactions for June were as follows:

June   1   Jay Chung contributed $6,000 of his personal funds to begin business.
       2   Purchased equipment for $1,440, paying $440 cash, with the balance due in 30 days.
       2   Paid six months' rent, $1,500.
       3   Paid one-year premium on liability insurance, $420.
       8   Paid June newspaper advertising, $80.
       15 Billed participants for karate lessons to date, $1,100.
       20 Received $300 from a local company to conduct a special three-session class on self-defense for its employees. The three sessions will be held on June 29, July 6, and July 13, at $100 per session.
       21 Collected $1,000 on account from participants.
       25 Paid $300 to repair damage to wall caused by an errant kick.
       30 Billed participants for karate lessons to date, $1,400.
       30 Paid assistant's wages, $350.

REQUIRED

(a) Record the given transactions in a general journal.

(b) Devise a chart of accounts for the firm and set up the general ledger. Allow for accounts that may be needed when adjusting entries are made at the close of the accounting period [see part (e)].

(c) Post journal entries to the ledger accounts.

(d) Take a trial balance.

(e) Make the adjusting entries for rent expense, insurance expense, depreciation expense, utilities expense, and karate fees earned. Depreciation expense for June is $24; estimated utilities expense for June is $100. Post the adjusting entries.

3−26A Frank Fister started The Fine Align on March 1 of the current year to provide automotive wheel alignment and balancing services. On March 31, the unadjusted balances of the firm's accounts are as follows:

The Fine Align
Trial Balance
March 31, 19XX

	Debit	Credit
Cash	$ 3,200	
Accounts Receivable	2,800	
Prepaid Rent	2,700	
Supplies on Hand	1,650	
Equipment	25,200	
Accounts Payable		$ 3,400
Unearned Service Revenue		600
F. Fister, Capital		28,000
F. Fister, Drawing	850	
Service Revenue		7,400
Wages Expense	3,000	
	$39,400	$39,400

The following information is also available:
(1) The balance in Prepaid Rent was the amount paid on March 1 to cover the first three months' rent.
(2) Supplies on hand on March 31 amounted to $700.
(3) The equipment has an estimated life of seven years.
(4) Unpaid wages at March 31 were $580.
(5) Utility services used during March were estimated at $420. A bill is expected early in April.
(6) The balance in Unearned Service Revenue was the amount received on March 1 from a new car dealer to cover alignment and balancing services on all new cars sold by the dealer in March and April. Fister agreed to provide the services at a fixed fee of $300 each month.

REQUIRED
In general journal form, make the adjusting entries needed at March 31.

3–27A Deliverall, a mailing service, has just completed its first full year of operations on December 31 of the current year. The firm's ledger account balances before year-end adjustments are given below. No adjusting entries have been made to the accounts at any time during the year. Assume that all balances are normal.

Cash	$ 3,280	Logan, Drawing	$ 2,300
Accounts Receivable	5,500	Mailing Fees	50,000
Prepaid Advertising	720	Wages Expense	31,600
Equipment	24,500	Rent Expense	4,800
Accounts Payable	3,000	Utilities Expense	1,900
Logan, Capital	25,000	Supplies Expense	3,400

An analysis of the firm's records reveals the following:
(1) The balance in Prepaid Advertising represents the amount paid for newspaper advertising for one year. The agreement, which calls for the same

amount of space each month, covers the period from February 1 of the current year to January 31 next year. Deliverall did not advertise during its first month of operations.

(2) The equipment, purchased January 1, has an estimated life of 10 years.

(3) Utilities expense does not include expense for December, estimated at $260. The bill will not arrive until January of next year.

(4) At year-end, employees have earned $600 in wages that will not be paid until January.

(5) All supplies purchased during the year were debited to Supplies Expense. Supplies on hand at year-end amounted to $800.

(6) Mailing services amounting to $4,000 were rendered to customers who have not yet been billed for the services.

(7) The firm's lease calls for rent of $400 per month payable on the first of each month, plus an amount equal to $\frac{1}{2}$% of annual mailing fees earned. The rental percentage is payable within 15 days after the end of the year.

REQUIRED

(a) Set up T accounts and enter the unadjusted balances shown above. Prove that debits equal credits by preparing a trial balance.

(b) Record adjusting entries in general journal form, and post these entries in the T accounts opened in part (a). Add any accounts needed.

3–29A Market-Pulse, a market research firm, had the following transactions in June, its first month of operations.

June 1 J. Royce invested $15,000 of personal funds in the firm.

  1 The firm purchased the following from an office supply company: office equipment, $12,000; supplies, $800. Terms called for a cash payment of $4,500, with the remainder due in 60 days. (Make a compound entry.)

  2 Paid June rent, $500.

  2 Contracted for three months' advertising in a local newspaper at $100 per month and paid for the advertising in advance.

  2 Signed a six-month contract with an electronics firm to provide research consulting services at a rate of $1,500 per month. Received two months' fees in advance.

  10 Billed various customers for services rendered, $2,600.

  12 Paid two weeks' salaries (five-day week) to employees, $2,000.

  15 Paid J. Royce's travel expenses to business conference, $900.

  18 Paid post office for bulk mailing of survey research questionnaire, $350 (postage expense).

  22 Billed various customers for services rendered, $3,700.

  26 Paid two weeks' salaries to employees, $2,000.

  30 Collected $4,000 from customers on account.

  30 J. Royce withdrew $800 for personal use.

REQUIRED

(a) Set up a ledger that includes the following accounts, using the account numbers shown: Cash (11); Accounts Receivable (12); Office Supplies on Hand (14); Prepaid Advertising (15); Office Equipment (16); Accumulated Depreciation—Office Equipment (17); Accounts Payable (21); Salaries Payable (22); Unearned Service Fees (23); J. Royce, Capital (31); J. Royce, Drawing (32); Service Fees (41); Salaries Expense (51); Advertising Expense (52); Supplies Expense (53); Rent Expense (54); Travel Expense (55); Depreciation Expense—Office Equipment (56); and Postage Expense (57).

(b) Record June transactions in general journal form and post to the ledger accounts.

(c) Take a trial balance at June 30.

(d) Record adjusting journal entries in general journal form, and post to the ledger accounts. The following information is available on June 30:

> Supplies on hand, $260
> Accrued salaries, $400
> Estimated life of office equipment, eight years
> Unbilled services rendered, $1,300

Also, make any necessary adjusting entries for advertising and for service fees indicated by the June transactions.

3–30A   The following information relates to the December 31 adjustments for Keep-Dry, a firm providing waterproofing services for commercial and residential customers.

(1) The firm paid a $3,300 premium for a three-year insurance policy, coverage to begin October 1 of the current year. The entire amount of the premium was debited to Insurance Expense; no other entry concerning this premium has been recorded.

(2) Weekly wages for a five-day workweek total $1,500, payable on Fridays. December 31 of the current year is a Wednesday.

(3) Keep-Dry received $1,600 during December for services to be performed during the following year. When received, this amount was credited to Service Fees.

(4) During December, Keep-Dry provided $750 worth of services to clients who will not be billed until early January.

(5) During December, fuel oil costs of $400 were incurred to heat the firm's buildings. Because the monthly bill from the oil company has not yet arrived, no entry has been made for this amount (fuel oil costs are charged to Utilities Expense).

(6) The Supplies on Hand account has a balance of $3,800 on December 31. However, the December purchases of supplies, totaling $700, were inadvertently debited to the Supplies Expense account, which now has a balance of $700. A count of supplies on December 31 indicates that $1,800 worth of supplies are still on hand.

(7) On December 1, Keep-Dry borrowed $6,000 from the bank, giving an interest-bearing note payable. Interest is not payable until the note is due near the end of January. However, the interest expense for December is $60. No entries have been made for the interest expense or interest payable.

REQUIRED
Prepare the necessary December 31 adjusting entries in general journal form.

BUSINESS DECISION PROBLEM

Cross Analytic Services, a firm started several years ago by Roger Cross, offers consulting services for material handling and plant layout. The balance sheet prepared by the firm's bookkeeper at the close of the current year is shown below:

Cross Analytic Services
Balance Sheet
December 31, 19XX

Assets			Liabilities		
Cash		$ 3,000	Accounts Payable	$ 2,000	
Accounts Receivable		9,000	Notes Payable—Bank	20,000	
Supplies on Hand		6,500	Total Liabilities		$22,000
Equipment	$30,000				
Less: Accumulated			**Owner's Equity**		
Depreciation	7,500	22,500	R. Cross, Capital		19,000
			Total Liabilities and		
Total Assets		$41,000	Owner's Equity		$41,000

Earlier in the year, Cross obtained a bank loan of $20,000 for the firm. One of the provisions of the loan is that the year-end ratio of total liabilities to total owner's equity shall not exceed 1:1. Based on the above balance sheet, the ratio at the end of the current year is 1.16:1.

Cross is concerned about being in violation of the loan agreement and asks your assistance in reviewing the situation. Cross believes that his rather inexperienced bookkeeper may have overlooked some items at year-end.

In discussions with Cross and the bookkeeper, you learn the following:

(1) On January 1, 19XX, the firm paid a $4,200 insurance premium for three years of coverage. The full amount was debited to Insurance Expense.

(2) Depreciation on the equipment should be 10% of cost per year. The bookkeeper has recorded only one-half this amount for the current year.

(3) Interest on the bank loan has been paid through the end of the current year.

(4) The firm concluded a major consulting engagement in December, doing a plant layout analysis for a new factory. The $5,000 fee has not been billed or recorded in the accounts.

(5) On December 29, 19XX, the firm received a $900 advance payment from Steel Handlers, Inc., for consulting services to be rendered next year. This payment was credited to the Consulting Fees account.

(6) Supplies costing $5,200 were on hand on December 31. The bookkeeper filed the record of the count but made no entry in the accounts.

REQUIRED
What is the correct ratio of total liabilities to total owner's equity at December 31, 19XX? Is the firm in violation of the loan agreement? Prepare a schedule to support your computation of the correct total liabilities and total owner's equity at December 31, 19XX.

4

The Accounting Cycle Concluded

The first four major steps in the accounting cycle—analyzing and recording transactions, posting to accounts, and adjusting the accounts—are essential to the process of classifying financial data and, where necessary, aligning the data with appropriate periods. The goal of these procedures is to prepare the data so that they can be summarized in a set of meaningful financial statements.

In this chapter, we shall explain the two remaining principal steps in the accounting cycle: preparation of financial statements (other than the statement of changes in financial position) and closing procedures. Our discussion is based on the December financial data given in Chapter 3 for Monroe TV Service. We will discuss the preparation of the statement of changes in financial position in Chapter 19.

PREPARING FINANCIAL STATEMENTS

Step 5: Prepare Financial Statements

Once the appropriate adjusting entries have been made and posted to the ledger accounts, another trial balance is taken to ensure that the general ledger still balances. This **adjusted trial balance** lists the proper balances for all accounts. An income statement and a balance sheet may be prepared directly from these account balances.

In practice, however, many accountants utilize a **worksheet** in compiling the information necessary for the preparation of financial statements. The worksheet is a tool of the accountant, not part of a company's formal accounting records. The accountant prepares a worksheet at that stage of the accounting cycle when it is time to make adjustments and prepare financial statements.

The basic structure of the worksheet is presented in Exhibit 4–1, which includes an explanation of the scheme being used. A completed worksheet for Monroe TV Service appears in Exhibit 4–2. A careful study of these two illustrations shows the following advantages of the worksheet:

(1) The balances of all general ledger accounts appear in one location and may be easily reviewed to determine whether any of them need adjusting.

(2) The total effect of any adjustment—whether contemplated or actually made on the worksheet—can be readily determined. Because these adjustments are reviewed before adjusting entries are journalized and posted, the likelihood of incorrect adjustments appearing in the formal accounting records is reduced.

EXHIBIT 4–1
Basic Structure of Worksheet

❶ (Heading for worksheet)

Description	Trial Balance		Adjustments		Adjusted Trial Balance		Income Statement		Balance Sheet	
	Debit	Credit	Debit	Credit	Debit	Credit	Debit	Credit	Debit	Credit
❷ (The unadjusted trial balance)			❸ (Amounts of adjustments)		❹ (Amounts of adjusted account balances)		❺ (Extension of adjusted account balances)			
(Titles of accounts not in unadjusted trial balance, added as needed)							(Income statement accounts)		(Balance sheet accounts)	
							❻ (Balancing of columns for each statement)			

EXHIBIT 4-2

Monroe TV Service
Worksheet
For the Month Ended December 31, 19XX

Description	Trial Balance Debit	Trial Balance Credit	Adjustments Debit	Adjustments Credit	Adjusted Trial Balance Debit	Adjusted Trial Balance Credit	Income Statement Debit	Income Statement Credit	Balance Sheet Debit	Balance Sheet Credit
Cash	11,590				11,590				11,590	
Accounts Receivable	2,650		(g) 180		2,830				2,830	
Supplies and Parts on Hand	600			(a) 380	220				220	
Test Equipment	3,000				3,000				3,000	
Truck	7,200				7,200				7,200	
Accounts Payable		1,600				1,600				1,600
Unearned Service Fees		800	(d) 200			600				600
C. Monroe, Capital		20,000				20,000				20,000
C. Monroe, Drawing	600				600				600	
Service Fees		4,700		(d) 200 / (g) 180		5,080		5,080		
Rent Expense	400				400		400			
Wages Expense	840		(f) 70		910		910			
Advertising Expense	50				50		50			
Truck Expense	170				170		170			
	27,100	27,100								
Supplies and Parts Expense			(a) 380		380		380			
Depreciation Expense—Test Equipment			(b) 50		50		50			
Accumulated Depreciation—Test Equipment				(b) 50		50				50
Depreciation Expense—Truck			(c) 100		100		100			
Accumulated Depreciation—Truck				(c) 100		100				100
Utilities Expense			(e) 80		80		80			
Utilities Payable				(e) 80		80				80
Wages Payable				(f) 70		70				70
			1,060	1,060	27,580	27,580	2,140	5,080	25,440	22,500
Net Income							2,940			2,940
							5,080	5,080	25,440	25,440

(3) Once all the adjustments have been made, the adjusted account balances can be determined and separated into a group for the income statement and a group for the balance sheet, simplifying the preparation of these statements.

The worksheet is prepared in the order indicated by the circled numbers in Exhibit 4–1. Refer to Exhibits 4–1 and 4–2 when reading through the following procedures for preparing a worksheet.

(1) HEADING The worksheet heading should include (a) the name of the accounting entity involved, (b) the term "Worksheet" to indicate the type of analysis performed, and (c) a date describing the period covered. The worksheet includes both income statement data (for the period described) and balance sheet data (for the end of the period described).

The worksheet form we have illustrated has a description column and 10 amount (money) columns. A set of debit and credit columns is provided for each of the five headings, "Trial Balance," "Adjustments," "Adjusted Trial Balance," "Income Statement," and "Balance Sheet."

(2) UNADJUSTED TRIAL BALANCE The trial balance, taken in step 3 of the accounting cycle, is entered in the description column and the first pair of money columns. Because this trial balance reflects the account balances before adjustment, it is often designated the **unadjusted trial balance**. Once the trial balance is placed on the worksheet and double ruled, it reflects the state of the general ledger at the time the worksheet is prepared.

(3) ADJUSTMENTS When a worksheet is used, all adjustments are first entered on the worksheet. This procedure permits the adjustment to be reviewed for completeness and accuracy. To adjust accounts already appearing in the unadjusted trial balance, we simply enter the amounts in the appropriate side (debit or credit) of the adjustments columns on the lines containing the accounts. When accounts not appearing in the unadjusted trial balance require adjustment, their titles are listed as needed in the description column below the accounts already listed.

The adjustments recorded on the worksheet in Exhibit 4–2 are identical with those recorded in general journal form in step 4 of the accounting cycle (see Chapter 3). It is common practice to "key" the amounts of each adjusting entry with the same letter or number. Note that the letters (a) through (g) are used in Exhibit 4–2. This procedure makes it easy to check the equality of debits and credits in each entry and to identify all the amounts related to a particular adjustment.

We repeat the adjusting entries made at the end of December for Monroe TV Service and explain their placement on the worksheet (Exhibit 4–2). Remember, because we are preparing a worksheet, these adjustments are entered on the worksheet; they are not yet recorded in the general journal.

(a)	Supplies and Parts Expense	380	
	Supplies and Parts on Hand		380

Because $220 worth of supplies were on hand at December 31, we needed to reduce the asset Supplies and Parts on Hand from $600 to $220 and to record the $380 difference as expense. Note that the expense account, Supplies and Parts Expense, does not appear in the unadjusted trial balance and must be added below the accounts already listed.

(b)	Depreciation Expense—Test Equipment	50	
	Accumulated Depreciation— Test Equipment		50
(c)	Depreciation Expense—Truck	100	
	Accumulated Depreciation—Truck		100

These entries recorded the expiration of the test equipment and truck costs for December. The entries to record depreciation expense and reduce the asset accounts (via accumulated depreciation contra accounts) require accounts that do not appear in the unadjusted trial balance. Therefore, the four accounts in entries (b) and (c) must be listed in the description column below the accounts in the trial balance.

(d)	Unearned Service Fees	200	
	Service Fees		200

This adjustment was made to reflect the portion of an $800 advance earned in December. The liability account Unearned Service Fees, originally credited for the $800 advance, was reduced by a $200 debit, and a corresponding credit was made to the revenue account Service Fees. Since both accounts appear in the unadjusted trial balance, we record this adjustment on the lines already provided for these accounts.

(e)	Utilities Expense	80	
	Utilities Payable		80
(f)	Wages Expense	70	
	Wages Payable		70

These adjusting entries reflected expenses incurred in December but not paid until January. The utilities expense was the estimated cost of services consumed in December. Wages were accrued for the last two days in December. Because no utilities expense was paid in December, the expense account does not appear in the unadjusted trial balance. Both the expense account and the liability Utilities Payable must be added below the accounts already listed. Since wages were paid during December, Wages Expense appears in the trial balance, but Wages Payable must be added.

(g)	Accounts Receivable	180	
	Service Fees		180

This entry was made to reflect unbilled service fees earned in December. Since both accounts appear in the unadjusted trial balance, we record this adjustment on the lines already provided for these accounts.

After recording all the adjusting entries on the worksheet, we total the adjustments columns to prove that debits equal credits.

(4) ADJUSTED TRIAL BALANCE   The numbers in the adjusted trial balance are the account balances reflecting the impact of adjustments. These figures are determined by combining horizontally, line by line, the amounts in the first four money columns—that is, the unadjusted trial balance and the adjustments.

We review the calculations for the first three lines of Exhibit 4–2 to illustrate this process. The first line shows Cash with a debit of $11,590 in the trial balance. Because Cash is not affected by any adjustments, the $11,590 appears in the debit column of the adjusted trial balance. The second line shows a debit of $2,650 for Accounts Receivable in the trial balance and a debit of $180 in the adjustments columns. These two debit amounts are added, and the sum of $2,830 is shown in the debit column of the adjusted trial balance. On the third line, Supplies and Parts on Hand begins with a debit of $600 in the trial balance and then shows a credit of $380 in the adjustments columns. The $380 credit is subtracted from the $600 debit, and the remaining $220 is shown as a debit in the adjusted trial balance.

After computing the adjusted trial balance amounts for all the accounts on the worksheet, we total the two columns of the adjusted trial balance to confirm that they are equal and that our worksheet, therefore, still balances.

(5) EXTENSION OF ADJUSTED BALANCES   The amounts in the adjusted trial balance columns are extended into the two remaining pairs of columns as follows:

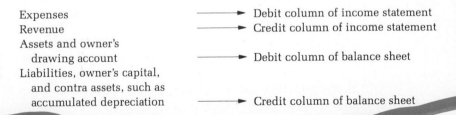

Expenses	⟶ Debit column of income statement
Revenue	⟶ Credit column of income statement
Assets and owner's drawing account	⟶ Debit column of balance sheet
Liabilities, owner's capital, and contra assets, such as accumulated depreciation	⟶ Credit column of balance sheet

Note that the positions of the adjusted balances in the worksheet correspond to the normal balances of the accounts. That is, expenses and assets are debits on the income statement and balance sheet, respectively; revenue is a credit on the income statement, and liabilities and owner's capital are credits on the balance sheet. The owner's drawing account is a debit in the balance sheet columns because it is a contra owner's equity account. The accumulated depreciation accounts are credits on the balance sheet because they are contra asset accounts. Once the proper extensions are made, the worksheet is complete except for the balancing of the two pairs of statement columns containing the adjusted balances.

(6) BALANCING THE WORKSHEET   The first step in balancing is to add each of the income statement and balance sheet columns and record their respective totals on the same line as the totals of the adjusted trial balance columns. The

EXHIBIT 4–3

Monroe TV Service
Income Statement
For the Month of December, 19XX

Revenue		
Service Fees		$5,080
Operating Expenses		
Rent Expense	$400	
Wages Expense	910	
Advertising Expense	50	
Truck Expense	170	
Supplies and Parts Expense	380	
Depreciation Expense—Test Equipment	50	
Depreciation Expense—Truck	100	
Utilities Expense	80	
Total Operating Expenses		2,140
Net Income		$2,940

difference between the total debits and total credits in the income statement columns will be the difference between total revenue and total expenses—that is, the net income for the period. The net income should also be the amount by which the debit and credit columns for the balance sheet differ. This is true because the capital account balance, as extended, does not yet reflect the net income for the current period.

When revenue exceeds expenses, we balance the two pairs of statement columns by adding the net income figure to both the debit column of the income statement and the credit column of the balance sheet. If expenses exceed revenue, we add the amount of net loss to the credit column of the income statement and to the debit column of the balance sheet. After we have added the net income (or loss) to the proper columns, we total and double rule the four columns. The worksheet is now complete and contains the account data necessary to prepare an income statement and a balance sheet. Note that Carl Monroe's equity at this point is indicated by three amounts appearing on the worksheet:

Credit balance of capital account extended	$20,000
Debit balance for drawings	(600)
Credit amount of net income to balance the balance sheet columns	2,940
Carl Monroe's equity at end of period	$22,340

Exhibits 4–3 and 4–4 illustrate an income statement and a balance sheet, respectively, for the Monroe TV Service, prepared from the worksheet.

A formal set of financial statements frequently includes a **statement of owner's equity.** This statement simply lists the beginning balance, additions, deduc-

EXHIBIT 4-4

Monroe TV Service
Balance Sheet
December 31, 19XX

Assets			Liabilities		
Cash		$11,590	Accounts Payable	$1,600	
Accounts Receivable		2,830	Utilities Payable	80	
Supplies and Parts on Hand		220	Wages Payable	70	
Test Equipment	$3,000		Unearned Service Fees	600	
Less: Accumulated Depreciation	50	2,950	Total Liabilities		$ 2,350
Truck	$7,200		**Owner's Equity**		
Less: Accumulated Depreciation	100	7,100	C. Monroe, Capital		22,340
			Total Liabilities and		
Total Assets		$24,690	Owner's Equity		$24,690

tions, and ending balance of owner's equity for the accounting period. Exhibit 4-5 illustrates such a statement for Monroe TV Service for the month of December. When capital contributions have been made during the accounting period, we cannot determine from the worksheet alone the beginning balance of owner's capital and amounts of capital contributions during a period. Consequently, in preparing a statement of owner's equity, we must examine the owner's capital account in the general ledger.

RECORDING AND POSTING WORKSHEET ADJUSTING ENTRIES   At the close of the calendar or fiscal year, the adjusting entries on the worksheet must be recorded in the general journal and posted to the ledger accounts in order to accomplish the proper closing procedures described in the next section. Although Monroe TV Service has been in business only for December, its accounting year ends on December 31. Therefore, the adjusting entries are entered in the records

EXHIBIT 4-5

Monroe TV Service
Statement of Owner's Equity
For the Month of December, 19XX

Carl Monroe, Capital, December 1, 19XX		$ -0-
Add: Capital Contributed in December	$20,000	
Net Income for December	2,940	22,940
		$22,940
Less: Capital Withdrawn in December		600
Carl Monroe, Capital, December 31, 19XX		$22,340

EXHIBIT 4–6
Adjusting Entries

General Journal

Date			Description	Post. Ref.	Debit	Credit
19XX Dec.	31		Supplies and Parts Expense	54	380	
			Supplies and Parts on Hand	14		380
			To record expense of supplies and parts used in December.			
	31		Depreciation Expense—Test Equipment	57	50	
			Accumulated Depreciation—Test Equipment	17		50
			To record December depreciation on test equipment.			
	31		Depreciation Expense—Truck	58	100	
			Accumulated Depreciation—Truck	19		100
			To record December depreciation on truck.			
	31		Unearned Service Fees	24	200	
			Service Fees	41		200
			To record portion of advance earned in December.			
	31		Utilities Expense	55	80	
			Utilities Payable	22		80
			To record estimated amount of December utilities expense.			
	31		Wages Expense	52	70	
			Wages Payable	23		70
			To record accrued wages for December 30 and 31.			
	31		Accounts Receivable	12	180	
			Service Fees	41		180
			To record unbilled revenue earned during December.			

and closing procedures are followed. The adjusting entries appear in the general journal as shown in Exhibit 4–6.

These journal entries are posted to the ledger accounts of Monroe TV Service shown in Exhibit 4–9 (pages 130–35). The entries are identified by the parenthetical notation "(adjusting)."

CLOSING PROCEDURES

Step 6: Close Temporary Accounts

Revenue, expense, and drawing accounts are temporary accounts that accumulate data related to a specific accounting year. These temporary accounts facilitate preparation of the income statement and provide additional information. At the end of each accounting year, the balances of these temporary accounts are transferred to the capital account (the Retained Earnings account for corporations). Therefore, the balance of the owner's capital account includes on a cumulative basis the net result of all revenue, expense, and drawing transactions. This final phase in the accounting cycle is referred to as **closing procedures.**

An account is said to be *closed* when an entry is made that changes its balance to zero—that is, an entry that is equal in amount to the account's balance but opposite to the balance as a debit or credit. An account that is closed is said to be closed *to* the account that receives the offsetting debit or credit. Thus, a closing entry simply transfers the balance of one account to another account. In this manner, closing procedures transfer the balances of temporary accounts to the capital account.

A summary account is traditionally used to close the temporary revenue and expense accounts. For our illustration, we shall use an account titled "Income Summary," although a variety of titles are found in practice (Revenue and Expense Summary, Income and Expense Summary, or Profit and Loss Summary, for example). The entries for opening and closing Income Summary are quite simple and occur only during the closing procedures. The entries that close the temporary accounts are as follows:

(1) Debit each revenue account in an amount equal to its balance, and credit Income Summary for the total revenue involved.

(2) Credit each expense account in an amount equal to its balance, and debit Income Summary for the total expense involved.

After these temporary accounts have been closed, the balance of the Income Summary account is equal to the net income for the period—hence the title "Income Summary." The remaining closing steps are as follows:

(3) Debit Income Summary for its balance, and credit the capital account (Retained Earnings for a corporation) for the same amount. In the case of a net loss, debit the capital account and credit Income Summary.

(4) For noncorporate businesses, credit the drawing account in an amount equal to its balance and debit the capital account for the same amount.

In Exhibit 4–7, we illustrate the entries for closing the revenue and expense accounts to the Income Summary account of Monroe TV Service as they would be recorded in the general journal. The effect of these two entries is shown using T accounts.

At this point, the balance of Income Summary is a credit equal to the net income of $2,940. The closing procedure is completed by closing the Income Summary and C. Monroe, Drawing accounts to the C. Monroe, Capital account. These two entries are recorded in the general journal as shown in Exhibit 4–8. The effect of these entries on the general ledger is also diagramed.

It is probably most convenient to take the data necessary for formulating the closing entries from the worksheet, although the information can also be derived from the ledger. After the closing entries for Monroe TV Service have been recorded and posted to the firm's general ledger, all temporary accounts have zero balances and the capital account has a balance equal to the amount shown on Monroe TV Service's balance sheet (see Exhibit 4–4). Exhibit 4–9 illustrates the general ledger of Monroe TV Service after all the closing procedures have been followed. Closing entries are identified by the parenthetical notation "(closing)."

CORPORATION ACCOUNTING   The entries involving owners' equity are different if Monroe TV Service is organized as a corporation. The persons forming the corporation receive capital stock in exchange for the $20,000 cash contribution. The transaction is recorded as a debit to Cash and a credit to Capital Stock. The $600 cash withdrawal is considered a cash dividend and is recorded as a debit to Retained Earnings and a credit to Cash.

The revenue and expense accounts of a corporation are closed to the Income Summary account exactly as they are closed in a proprietorship. Because a corporation is subject to an income tax, however, it must close an additional expense account, Income Tax Expense. Disregarding income taxes, the revenue and expense accounts are closed as shown in Exhibit 4–7. Once the revenue and expense accounts are closed to Income Summary, the closing procedures for a corporation are completed by closing the Income Summary account to Retained Earnings. We show this in the T accounts below.

Capital Stock		Retained Earnings		Income Summary	
	20,000	600	2,940 ←	2,140	5,080
				2,940	

After closing entries are posted, the Retained Earnings account reflects the $2,340 earned and retained in the business. Combined with the Capital Stock of $20,000, total owners' equity is $22,340.

EXHIBIT 4–7
Closing Revenue and Expense Accounts

General Journal   Page 4

Date		Description	Post. Ref.	Debit	Credit
19XX					
Dec.	31	Service Fees	41	5,080	
		Income Summary	33		5,080
		To close the revenue account.			
	31	Income Summary	33	2,140	
		Rent Expense	51		400
		Wages Expense	52		910
		Advertising Expense	53		50
		Truck Expense	56		170
		Supplies and Parts Expense	54		380
		Depreciation Expense—Test Equipment	57		50
		Depreciation Expense—Truck	58		100
		Utilities Expense	55		80
		To close the expense accounts.			

EXHIBIT 4 – 8
Closing the Income
Summary and Drawing Accounts

General Journal
Page 4

Date			Description	Post. Ref.	Debit	Credit
19XX						
Dec.	31		Income Summary	33	2,940	
			C. Monroe, Capital	31		2,940
			To close the Income Summary account.			
	31		C. Monroe, Capital	31	600	
			C. Monroe, Drawing	32		600
			To close the drawing account.			

C. Monroe, Drawing

600	600

C. Monroe, Capital

600	20,000
	2,940

Income Summary

2,140	5,080
2,940	2,940

EXHIBIT 4 – 9
Monroe TV Service
General Ledger

Cash

Account No. 11

Date		Description	Post. Ref.	Debit*	Credit	Balance
19XX						
Dec.	1		J1	20,000		20,000
	1		J1		400	19,600
	2		J1		7,200	12,400
	2		J1		2,000	10,400
	2		J1	800		11,200
	7		J1	550		11,750
	14		J1		420	11,330
	14		J2	480		11,810
	17		J2		50	11,760
	19		J2	500		12,260
	21		J2	320		12,580
	28		J2		170	12,410
	28		J2		420	11,990
	28		J2		600	11,390
	28		J2	200		11,590

EXHIBIT 4–9 (continued)

Accounts Receivable   Account No. 12

Date		Description	Post. Ref.	Debit*	Credit	Balance
19XX Dec.	14		J1	750		750
	19		J2		500	250
	28		J2	2,400		2,650
	31	(adjusting)	J3	180		2,830

Supplies and Parts on Hand   Account No. 14

Date		Description	Post. Ref.	Debit*	Credit	Balance
19XX Dec.	3		J1	600		600
	31	(adjusting)	J3		380	220

Test Equipment   Account No. 16

Date		Description	Post. Ref.	Debit*	Credit	Balance
19XX Dec.	2		J1	3,000		3,000

Accumulated Depreciation—Test Equipment   Account No. 17

Date		Description	Post. Ref.	Debit	Credit*	Balance
19XX Dec.	31	(adjusting)	J3		50	50

Truck   Account No. 18

Date		Description	Post. Ref.	Debit*	Credit	Balance
19XX Dec.	2		J1	7,200		7,200

EXHIBIT 4 – 9 (continued)

Accumulated Depreciation—Truck   Account No. 19

Date		Description	Post. Ref.	Debit	Credit*	Balance
19XX Dec.	31	(adjusting)	J3		100	100

Accounts Payable   Account No. 21

Date		Description	Post. Ref.	Debit	Credit*	Balance
19XX Dec.	2		J1		1,000	1,000
	3		J1		600	1,600

Utilities Payable   Account No. 22

Date		Description	Post. Ref.	Debit	Credit*	Balance
19XX Dec.	31	(adjusting)	J3		80	80

Wages Payable   Account No. 23

Date		Description	Post. Ref.	Debit	Credit*	Balance
19XX Dec.	31	(adjusting)	J3		70	70

Unearned Service Fees   Account No. 24

Date		Description	Post. Ref.	Debit	Credit*	Balance
19XX Dec.	2		J1		800	800
	31	(adjusting)	J3	200		600

C. Monroe, Capital

Account No. 31

Date		Description	Post. Ref.	Debit	Credit*	Balance
19XX						
Dec.	1		J1		20,000	20,000
	31	(closing)	J4		2,940	22,940
	31	(closing)	J4	600		22,340

C. Monroe, Drawing

Account No. 32

Date		Description	Post. Ref.	Debit*	Credit	Balance
19XX						
Dec.	28		J2	600		600
	31	(closing)	J4		600	—0—

Income Summary

Account No. 33

Date		Description	Post. Ref.	Debit	Credit*	Balance
19XX						
Dec.	31	(closing)	J4		5,080	5,080
	31	(closing)	J4	2,140		2,940
	31	(closing)	J4	2,940		—0—

Service Fees

Account No. 41

Date		Description	Post. Ref.	Debit	Credit*	Balance
19XX						
Dec.	7		J1		550	550
	14		J1		750	1,300
	14		J2		480	1,780
	21		J2		320	2,100
	28		J2		2,400	4,500
	28		J2		200	4,700
	31	(adjusting)	J3		200	4,900
	31	(adjusting)	J3		180	5,080
	31	(closing)	J4	5,080		—0—

EXHIBIT 4 – 9 (continued)

Rent Expense
Account No. 51

Date		Description	Post. Ref.	Debit*	Credit	Balance
19XX						
Dec.	1		J1	400		400
	31	(closing)	J4		400	−0−

Wages Expense
Account No. 52

Date		Description	Post. Ref.	Debit*	Credit	Balance
19XX						
Dec.	14		J1	420		420
	28		J2	420		840
	31	(adjusting)	J3	70		910
	31	(closing)	J4		910	−0−

Advertising Expense
Account No. 53

Date		Description	Post. Ref.	Debit*	Credit	Balance
19XX						
Dec.	17		J2	50		50
	31	(closing)	J4		50	−0−

Supplies and Parts Expense
Account No. 54

Date		Description	Post. Ref.	Debit*	Credit	Balance
19XX						
Dec.	31	(adjusting)	J3	380		380
	31	(closing)	J4		380	−0−

Utilities Expense

Account No. 55

Date		Description	Post. Ref.	Debit*	Credit	Balance
19XX						
Dec.	31	(adjusting)	J3	80		80
	31	(closing)	J4		80	—0—

Truck Expense

Account No. 56

Date		Description	Post. Ref.	Debit*	Credit	Balance
19XX						
Dec.	28		J2	170		170
	31	(closing)	J4		170	—0—

Depreciation Expense—Test Equipment

Account No. 57

Date		Description	Post. Ref.	Debit*	Credit	Balance
19XX						
Dec.	31	(adjusting)	J3	50		50
	31	(closing)	J4		50	—0—

Depreciation Expense—Truck

Account No. 58

Date		Description	Post. Ref.	Debit*	Credit	Balance
19XX						
Dec.	31	(adjusting)	J3	100		100
	31	(closing)	J4		100	—0—

EXHIBIT 4–10

Monroe TV Service
Post-closing Trial Balance
December 31, 19XX

	Debit	Credit
Cash	$11,590	
Accounts Receivable	2,830	
Supplies and Parts on Hand	220	
Test Equipment	3,000	
Accumulated Depreciation—Test Equipment		$ 50
Truck	7,200	
Accumulated Depreciation—Truck		100
Accounts Payable		1,600
Utilities Payable		80
Wages Payable		70
Unearned Service Fees		600
C. Monroe, Capital		22,340
	$24,840	$24,840

POST-CLOSING TRIAL BALANCE   A post-closing trial balance is usually taken after the closing process. This procedure ensures that an equality of debits and credits has been maintained throughout the adjusting and closing procedures. Obviously, since the temporary accounts have been closed, only balance sheet accounts appear in this trial balance. Exhibit 4–10 presents the post-closing trial balance for Monroe TV Service.

REVERSING ENTRIES   In our discussion of adjusting entries for accrued items in Chapter 3, we pointed out that certain precautions are necessary to avoid reflecting the same expense or revenue in two successive periods. We now review two alternative procedures for recording the settlement of accrued items in the period after their accrual. We illustrate these procedures using wages expense for Monroe TV Service.

    Wages expense in December   Recall from Chapter 3 that the Monroe TV Service employee received wages of $210 for each six-day workweek ($35 per day) and that the employee was paid every other Saturday. We assumed that the two paydays in December fell on December 14 and 28. Wages expense of $70 was accrued for December 30 and 31. We made the following adjusting entry to reflect the proper expense for December:

Dec. 31   Wages Expense   70
                Wages Payable   70
             To record accrued wages for
             December 30 and 31.

After this adjusting entry was posted, the Wages Expense account had a debit balance of $910. This consisted of two debits of $420 made on December 14 and 28 and the $70 accrual on December 31. Along with other expenses, the Wages Expense account was closed to Income Summary on December 31. After the closing procedures, the Wages Expense and Wages Payable accounts appeared in the ledger as follows:

Wages Expense   Account No. 52

Date		Description	Post. Ref.	Debit*	Credit	Balance
19XX						
Dec.	14		J1	420		420
	28		J2	420		840
	31	(adjusting)	J3	70		910
	31	(closing)	J4		910	−0−

Wages Payable   Account No. 23

Date		Description	Post. Ref.	Debit	Credit*	Balance
19XX						
Dec.	31	(adjusting)	J3		70	70

Settlement of accrued wages   On January 11, the employee will receive another $420 wage payment. Of this amount, only $350 should be reflected as January expense since only 10 days were worked in January (the other two days were worked in December and accrued as December wages expense). We may record the wage payment and the correct January wages expense by making the entry we presented in Chapter 3, as follows:

Jan. 11   Wages Payable   70
                Wages Expense   350
                   Cash   420
             To record wages paid.

This procedure, however, requires extreme vigilance in recording routine transactions on the part of the bookkeeper, who must keep in mind previously made accruals in order to record subsequent payments correctly. Many bookkeepers find this a nuisance and avoid the problem by reversing adjustments made for accruals.

As an alternative to the preceding procedure, then, a bookkeeper may use **reversing entries.** Reversing entries are made after all closing procedures have been completed, and they are dated the first day of the following period. For example, the reversing entry for the accrual of wages would be

Jan. 1	Wages Payable	70
	Wages Expense	70
	To reverse accrual made December 31.	

The entry reduces the liability Wages Payable to zero and results in a $70 abnormal credit balance in the Wages Expense account at the start of the new accounting period. On the next payday, however, the wage payment of $420 is recorded as all wage payments are recorded, as follows:

Jan. 11	Wages Expense	420
	Cash	420
	Paid wages for two weeks ended January 11.	

When this entry is posted to the Wages Expense account, the $420 debit is combined with the $70 credit balance created by the reversing entry. As a result, the account balance is the proper wages expense for January 1–11 ($350). After the January 1 reversing entry and the January 11 payment have been posted, the Wages Expense and Wages Payable accounts appear as shown below. Note the $70 abnormal balance is placed in parentheses.

Wages Expense   Account No. 52

Date		Description	Post. Ref.	Debit*	Credit	Balance
19XX						
Dec.	14		J1	420		420
	28		J2	420		840
	31	(adjusting)	J3	70		910
	31	(closing)	J4		910	–0–
19XI						
Jan.	1	(reversing)	J5		70	(70)
	11		J6	420		350

Wages Payable   Account No. 23

Date		Description	Post. Ref.	Debit	Credit*	Balance
19XX Dec.	31	(adjusting)	J3		70	70
19XI Jan.	1	(reversing)	J5	70		−0−

Both of the alternative procedures for handling the December accrued wages in January give the same result—the elimination of the $70 wages payable and the portrayal of $350 of wages expense for the first 11 days in January. By using reversals, however, the bookkeeper can record the first January payroll without having to consider the amount of wages accrued at December 31.

Other reversals A reversing entry may simplify the recording of a transaction that relates to an earlier adjusting entry. No hard and fast rule determines which adjusting entries should be reversed. Generally, though, *accruals* of revenue and expenses that relate to routine, repetitive transactions are the most appropriate adjustments to reverse. Of the adjustments made by Monroe TV Service (in addition to the accrual of wages), reversing entries would be employed for the two other accruals—the $80 estimated utilities expense and the $180 unbilled service fees. The bookkeeper would therefore make two additional reversing entries after the books are closed:

Jan. 1	Utilities Payable	80	
	Utilities Expense		80
	To reverse accrual made December 31.		

Jan. 1	Service Fees	180	
	Accounts Receivable		180
	To reverse accrual made December 31.		

These entries eliminate the accrued amounts from the liability and asset accounts and create an abnormal credit balance of $80 in Utilities Expense and an abnormal debit balance of $180 in Service Fees.

The credit balance in Utilities Expense will be eliminated when the utility bills are received and paid in January. If we assume that bills amounting to $84 arrived and were paid on January 6, the entry would be

Jan. 6	Utilities Expense	84	
	Cash		84
	To record payment of December utilities.		

After the entry for payment is posted, Utilities Expense will have a $4 debit balance to be absorbed in January. As we mentioned in Chapter 3, charging a small amount of one period's expense in another period must be tolerated when estimates are used.

The debit balance in Service Fees is eliminated when Monroe TV Service bills the local hotel after the completion of 40 hours of work (per its contract with the hotel). This billing, made on January 21, is recorded as follows:

Jan. 21	Accounts Receivable	480	
	Service Fees		480
	To record billing for 40 hours of		
	work at $12 per hour.		

This entry leaves a credit balance of $300 in the Service Fees revenue account, reflecting the proper amount of revenue for work performed in January (25 hours × $12). The $480 debit to Accounts Receivable represents the amount of cash to be collected from the hotel.

Although the use of reversing entries is optional, it does permit us to analyze routine, repetitive transactions the same way all the time. For example, if reversals are used, a bookkeeper may be instructed (or a computer programmed) to debit Wages Expense and credit Cash every time wages are paid. Similarly, every utility payment may be analyzed as a debit to Utilities Expense and a credit to Cash, and every billing of service fees may be recorded as a debit to Accounts Receivable and a credit to Service Fees. Reversals eliminate the need to remember the effects of previous accruals and, therefore, contribute to the more efficient processing of data.

Reversals normally are not appropriate for adjustments involving prepayments of expense or advance receipts of revenues. Only if a company's policy is to record expense prepayments in expense accounts and advance revenue receipts in revenue accounts might adjustments involving these items be reversed. In these cases, the reversals reestablish the remaining expense prepayments and advance revenue receipts in the appropriate expense and revenue accounts. These types of situations, however, are not common and will not be illustrated here.

Interim Financial Statements

Financial statements covering periods within a company's calendar or fiscal year—such as monthly or quarterly statements—are called **interim financial statements.** Most companies prepare interim financial statements from worksheet data because they prefer to journalize and post adjusting entries only at year-end. Interim adjustments, then, are reflected only on the worksheet. When making interim adjusting entries on the worksheet, the bookkeeper must consider the period for which the adjustments are made. Some adjustment amounts will accumulate, while others will not. For example, in writing off a $1,200 one-year prepaid insurance premium paid on January 1 and debited to the asset account, the bookkeeper would debit Insurance Expense and credit Prepaid Insurance for $100 at January 31. The amount of the adjustment would be $200 at the end of February, $300 at the end of March, and so on. Similarly, the amount of the adjusting entry for depreciation will increase each month. On the other hand, an adjusting entry to accrue salaries at the end of any month will consist only of unpaid salaries at the date of adjustment, because salaries accrued at the end of each month are ordinarily paid during the ensuing month.

REPORTS TO STOCKHOLDERS

Corporations include their financial statements in periodic reports to stockholders. The annual report to stockholders for large corporations may be quite extensive, often running 20–50 pages or more. In addition to financial statements, the annual report may include a message from the chairman of the board of directors and the chief executive officer, a review of the year's operations, a financial review, the accountants' report, and selected financial statistics for several years. Supplementing these items may be a variety of charts, graphs, and photographs of the company's products and facilities.

Reports to stockholders covering less than one year (interim reports) are much less extensive. They are intended to provide owners and potential investors with timely information on the corporation's progress and may include summarized financial information rather than a complete set of financial statements.

Comprehensive annual reports to stockholders are a relatively recent development in the United States. Before the 1900s, corporate management generally disclosed little, if any, financial information to stockholders. The first corporations were usually small and obtained much of their funding through short-term bank loans rather than from the public sale of stocks. Bankers who needed to assess the borrower's ability to repay short-term loans considered the balance sheet the primary financial statement because it revealed the total short-term obligations and the assets that would likely be converted to cash in the near future. By the late 1920s, however, corporate expansion led to increased financing through stock issuances and long-term debt. Owners and creditors used the income statement to judge earning power. Corporate reporting, then, evolved from providing balance sheets for bankers to providing income statements and balance sheets for stockholders and creditors.[*]

The first modern annual report was issued in 1902 by U.S. Steel Corporation. The report was lengthy and detailed, revealing so much about the corporation's operations that the directors were practically scandalized.[†] The extensive disclosures broke with tradition, and most corporations did not follow U.S. Steel's lead for many years.

Considerable variety exists in the length and detail of reports to stockholders. Remarks by the president of Diamond Match Company used 100 pages of the company's 1942 annual report.[‡] In contrast, a 1972 semiannual report from North American Publishing of Philadelphia was more to the point. The report was poster size (3 feet long) and featured letters 8 inches high and 6 inches wide that stated: "We Had a BIG IMPROVEMENT for the First Six Months."[§]

Many corporations view the annual report, in part, as a public relations document. Imagine the chagrin, then, at Citizens Valley Bank in Albany, Oregon several years ago. Half of the copies of the bank's 1973 annual report had been mailed before a particular omission was noted—the bank's name had been dropped from the report's cover and did not appear anywhere in the report.[‖]

[*]A.C. Littleton and V.K. Zimmerman, *Accounting Theory: Continuity and Change* (Englewood Cliffs, NJ: Prentice-Hall, Inc., 1962), pages 92–97.
[†]"Annual Reports—No Longer Dry," *Fortune*, February 1944, page 62.
[‡]*Ibid*.
[§]"The Numbers Game: A Few (Fairly) Kind Words," *Forbes*, May 1, 1973, page 36.
[‖]"Business Bulletin," *The Wall Street Journal*, February 14, 1974, page 1.

When the year-end worksheet is prepared, the adjusting data will pertain to the entire year. Therefore, the adjusting entries to be journalized and posted to the ledger accounts can be taken directly from this worksheet.

It is a simple matter to prepare income statements for portions of a year by merely subtracting data on earlier worksheets from those prepared later. For example, income statement data for February can be obtained by subtracting the relevant data on the January 31 worksheet from the same data on the February 28 worksheet, since the latter worksheet would be cumulative. Similarly, income statement data for the second quarter of the year can be found by subtracting data on the March 31 worksheet from data on the June 30 worksheet, and so on.

KEY POINTS TO REMEMBER

(1) The worksheet facilitates the preparation of financial statements.

(2) The unadjusted trial balance is recorded directly on the worksheet; adjustments usually are made only on the worksheet when interim financial statements are being prepared.

(3) Adjusted balances, which are extended into the income statement and balance sheet columns of the worksheet, provide the data for formal financial statements.

(4) Adjusting and closing entries are recorded in the journal and ledger at the end of the accounting year.

(5) *Closing the books* means closing the revenue, expense, and other temporary accounts. Revenue and expense account balances are transferred to the Income Summary account. The balances of the Income Summary account and the owners' drawing accounts are closed to the owners' capital accounts. For corporations, the Income Summary account is closed to Retained Earnings.

(6) The method of reversing adjustments made for *accrued* items permits normal recording of subsequent transactions. It safeguards against reflecting the same revenue or expense in successive periods.

QUESTIONS

4–1 Assume that a company does not use a worksheet to help prepare financial statements. On December 31, the close of the accounting year, all transactions have been analyzed, recorded, and posted, and adjusting entries have been recorded and posted to the accounts. What two major steps of the accounting cycle remain?

4–2 Assume that a company uses a worksheet to help prepare financial statements. After the worksheet is completed at the end of the accounting year, what steps remain to complete the accounting cycle?

4–3 What are the advantages of preparing a worksheet?

4–4 Identify each of the 10 amount columns of the worksheet and indicate to which columns the adjusted balances of the following accounts would be extended:

(a) Accounts Receivable
(b) Accumulated Depreciation
(c) Barker, Drawing
(d) Wages Payable
(e) Depreciation Expense

(f) Rent Receivable
(g) Prepaid Insurance
(h) Service Fees
(i) Capital Stock
(j) Retained Earnings

4–5 Suppose the total adjusted revenue of a business is $90,000 and total adjusted expense is $80,000. (a) When the worksheet is completed, in which columns would the $10,000 difference appear? (b) If total adjusted expense amounted to $105,000, in which columns of the computed worksheet would the $15,000 difference appear?

4–6 What are some reasons why the totals of the balance sheet columns of the worksheet may differ from the total asset amount on the formal balance sheet?

4–7 When adjusted balances are extended on the worksheet, Unearned Fees of $900 is extended as a credit in the income statement columns and Accounts Receivable of $600 is extended as a debit in the income statement columns. All other extensions are properly made. (a) Does the worksheet balance? (b) How do these incorrect extensions affect the calculation of net income shown on the worksheet?

4–8 Which groups of accounts are closed at the end of the accounting year?

4–9 How is the Income Summary account used in closing procedures?

4–10 How do closing entries for a corporation differ from closing entries for a proprietorship?

4–11 Which of the following accounts should not appear in the post-closing trial balance: Cash; Unearned Revenue; Jensen, Drawing; Depreciation Expense; Utilities Payable; Supplies Expense; and Retained Earnings?

4–12 Why are reversing entries made? If reversals are made, which entries would normally be reversed?

4–13 A firm accrued wages of $800 on December 31. On January 8, the next payday, the firm paid $2,000 in wages. The company does not make reversing entries. On January 8, the company debited Wages Expense and credited Cash for $2,000. How will this procedure affect January net income?

4–14 Since the firm in Question 4–13 did not make a reversing entry, what entry should it have made to record the January 8 payment of wages?

4–15 Assume that the firm in Question 4–13 did use reversing entry procedures. What reversing entry should the firm have made on January 1? How should the company have recorded the January 8 payment if a reversing entry had been made?

4–16 Define *interim financial statements*. Give an example of an interim financial statement.

4–17 When would adjusting entries be entered only on a worksheet and not in the accounts? Why?

4–18 A firm on a calendar-year basis prepares cumulative statements monthly, using a worksheet. Adjusting and closing entries are entered in journals and posted only on December 31. On January 1, the firm paid $720 for a two-year insurance policy. What worksheet adjustments for insurance should be made on (a) January 31, (b) February 28, and (c) May 31?

EXERCISES

4–19 The adjusted trial balance columns of a worksheet are as follows:

	Adjusted Trial Balance Debit	Adjusted Trial Balance Credit
Cash	4,000	
Supplies on Hand	5,300	
Equipment	35,000	
Accumulated Depreciation		7,000
Accounts Payable		2,400
W. Zulty, Capital		33,800
W. Zulty, Drawing	6,700	
Service Fees		21,200
Rent Expense	7,000	
Supplies Expense	2,900	
Depreciation Expense	3,500	
	64,400	64,400

Complete the worksheet by (a) extending these amounts to the income statement and balance sheet columns and (b) balancing the worksheet.

4–20 The income statement and balance sheet columns of a worksheet for F. Hillstrom, Consultant, are shown below. The worksheet is prepared on December 31, 19XX, for the year ended on that date.

	Income Statement Debit	Income Statement Credit	Balance Sheet Debit	Balance Sheet Credit
Cash			2,400	
Accounts Receivable			6,200	
Office Equipment			10,000	
Accumulated Depreciation				4,000
Accounts Payable				1,200
Wages Payable				400
F. Hillstrom, Capital				6,000
F. Hillstrom, Drawing			1,400	
Service Fees		26,000		
Wages Expense	8,500			
Rent Expense	4,800			
Depreciation Expense	2,000			
Advertising Expense	2,300			
	17,600	26,000	20,000	11,600
Net Income	8,400			8,400
	26,000	26,000	20,000	20,000

Prepare an income statement and a balance sheet for F. Hillstrom, Consultant.

4–21 On January 1, 19X2, the credit balance of the Jane Simon, Capital account was $17,000, and on December 31, 19X2, the credit balance before closing was $25,000. The Jane Simon, Drawing account had a debit balance of $4,800 on December 31, 19X2. After revenue and expense accounts were closed, the Income Summary account had a debit balance of $1,200. Prepare a 19X2 statement of owner's equity for Jane Simon, Architect.

4–22 The income statement columns of a worksheet prepared December 31 contain only the following:

	Debit	Credit
Service Fees		38,200
Rent Expense	5,400	
Salaries Expense	19,800	
Supplies Expense	1,500	
Depreciation Expense	2,600	

Included among the accounts in the balance sheet columns of the worksheet are Munn, Capital, $31,000 (credit), and Munn, Drawing, $3,600 (debit). Prepare entries to close the accounts, including the owner's drawing account. After these entries are made, what is the balance of the Munn, Capital account?

4–23 In the midst of closing procedures, Sunbelt Corporation's bookkeeper became ill and was hospitalized. You have volunteered to complete the closing of the books, and you find that all revenue and expense accounts have zero balances and that the Income Summary account has a single debit entry for $71,800 and a single credit entry for $96,500. The only entry in Retained Earnings this year is a debit of $4,000 for dividends, which reduced the balance to $52,000. Capital Stock has a normal balance of $120,000 and shows no entries for the year. Give the journal entries to complete the closing procedures and calculate the balance of the owners' equity.

4–24 Use the information in Exercise 4–20 to prepare the closing entries for F. Hillstrom, Consultant, on December 31, 19XX.

4–25 The following selected accounts appear in a firm's unadjusted trial balance at December 31, the end of the accounting year:

Prepaid Advertising	$ 680 (debit)	Unearned Service Fees	$ 3,800
Wages Expense	23,500 (debit)	Service Fees	39,000
Prepaid Insurance	920 (debit)	Rental Income	1,800

(a) Make the necessary adjusting entries in general journal form at December 31, assuming the following:
   (1) Prepaid advertising at December 31 is $450.
   (2) Unpaid wages earned by employees in December are $600.
   (3) Prepaid insurance at December 31 is $460.
   (4) Unearned service fees at December 31 are $1,400.
   (5) Rental income of $200 owed by a tenant is not recorded at December 31.

(b) Assume the company makes reversing entries. Which of the adjustments in part (a) should be reversed? Make the proper reversing entries on January 1.

(c) Assume reversing entries have been made. Prepare the journal entries on

January 8 to record (1) the payment of $1,400 in wages and (2) the receipt from the tenant of the $200 rental income.

(d) Assume reversing entries have not been made. Prepare the journal entries on January 8 to record (1) the payment of $1,400 in wages and (2) the receipt from the tenant of the $200 rental income.

PROBLEMS

4–26 Gard Cleaning Service will prepare financial statements on December 31 of the current year. The trial balance and adjustments columns of the firm's worksheet at December 31 are shown below.

	Trial Balance Debit	Trial Balance Credit	Adjustments Debit	Adjustments Credit
Cash	3,500			
Accounts Receivable	2,400			
Supplies on Hand	1,100			(a) 440
Prepaid Insurance	540			(b) 180
Equipment	12,000			
Accumulated Depreciation		3,000		(c) 1,500
Accounts Payable		1,600		
B. Gard, Capital		8,900		
B. Gard, Drawing	900			
Cleaning Fees		13,300		
Salaries Expense	3,400		(d) 270	
Rent Expense	2,350			
Miscellaneous Expense	610			
	26,800	26,800		
Insurance Expense			(b) 180	
Supplies Expense			(a) 440	
Depreciation Expense			(c) 1,500	
Salaries Payable				(d) 270
			2,390	2,390

REQUIRED

(a) Complete the worksheet.

(b) Prepare the closing entries at December 31 in general journal form.

4–27 The following unadjusted trial balance was taken at March 31 of the current year:

Wold Travel Agency
Trial Balance
March 31, 19XX

	Debit	Credit
Cash	$ 2,900	
Accounts Receivable	1,000	
Supplies on Hand	810	
Prepaid Insurance	600	
Equipment	9,600	
Accumulated Depreciation		$ 1,920
Accounts Payable		630
Unearned Commissions		400
L. Wold, Capital		5,500
L. Wold, Drawing	1,400	
Commissions Earned		15,170
Salaries Expense	5,350	
Rent Expense	900	
Advertising Expense	790	
Utilities Expense	270	
	$23,620	$23,620

The trial balance data are cumulative for the first three months of 19XX. No adjusting entries have been made in the accounts during this period. The following additional information is available:

(1) Depreciation for the first quarter is $240.
(2) Supplies on hand at March 31 amount to $460.
(3) During the quarter, $260 of the unearned commissions were earned.
(4) Insurance expense for the quarter is $150.
(5) Accrued salaries payable total $540 at March 31.
(6) Unbilled commissions earned during the quarter were $570.

REQUIRED
(a) Enter the trial balance on a worksheet and complete the worksheet using the adjustment data given above.
(b) Prepare an income statement for the first quarter of the year and a balance sheet at March 31.

4–28 The first six columns of a worksheet for Spohn Upholstery Service are given below. However, only the totals of the adjustments columns are given.

Spohn Upholstery Service
Worksheet
For the Year Ended December 31, 19XX

	Trial Balance Debit	Trial Balance Credit	Adjustments Debit	Adjustments Credit	Adjusted Trial Balance Debit	Adjusted Trial Balance Credit
Cash	600				600	
Accounts Receivable	1,920				2,120	
Prepaid Rent	780				520	
Supplies on Hand	1,690				840	
Equipment	3,000				3,000	
Accumulated Depreciation		750				1,050
Accounts Payable		400				400
C. Spohn, Capital		4,200				4,200
C. Spohn, Drawing	1,300				1,300	
Service Fees		11,930				12,130
Wages Expense	4,500				4,850	
Utilities Expense	630				700	
Rent Expense	2,860				3,120	
	17,280	17,280				
Supplies Expense					850	
Depreciation Expense					300	
Wages Payable						350
Utilities Payable						70
			2,030	2,030	18,200	18,200

REQUIRED
Determine the adjusting entries for Spohn Upholstery Service and prepare these entries in general journal form.

4–29 The unadjusted trial balance shown on page 149 is for Kelly Freight Service at December 31, 19X1. The following data for adjustments are also available at December 31:

(1) Supplies on hand amount to $310.
(2) Prepaid insurance is $200.
(3) Depreciation for the year is as follows: Equipment, $300; Trucks, $2,100.
(4) Accrued wages payable are $600.
(5) Estimated December utilities expense is $250; the bill has not arrived.
(6) Kelly has completed, but not yet billed, work amounting to $900.

	Debit	Credit
Cash	$ 2,500	
Accounts Receivable	1,950	
Supplies on Hand	760	
Prepaid Insurance	800	
Equipment	2,400	
Accumulated Depreciation— Equipment		$ 500
Trucks	16,800	
Accumulated Depreciation—Trucks		3,500
Notes Payable		3,000
Accounts Payable		1,200
D. Kelly, Capital		6,660
D. Kelly, Drawing	5,000	
Service Fees		65,700
Rent Expense	5,900	
Salaries and Wages Expense	33,400	
Fuel Expense	8,000	
Utilities Expense	2,820	
Interest Expense	230	
	$80,560	$80,560

REQUIRED

(a) Prepare a 10-column worksheet for the year ended December 31, 19XI. Set up any additional accounts needed.

(b) Prepare an income statement for the year and a balance sheet at December 31, 19XI.

(c) Prepare closing entries in general journal form.

4–30 V. Bailey, tax consultant, began business on December 1 of the current year. December transactions were as follows:

Dec. 1   V. Bailey invested $12,000 in the business.

     2   Paid rent for two months to Star Realty, $800.

     2   Purchased various supplies on account, $660.

     3   Purchased $5,000 of office equipment, paying $2,000 down with the balance due in 30 days.

     8   Paid $660 on account for supplies purchased December 2.

     13   Paid assistant's wages for two weeks, $575.

     20   Performed consulting services for cash, $1,500.

     27   Paid assistant's wages for two weeks, $575.

     30   Billed customers for December consulting services, $2,800.

     31   Bailey withdrew $900 from the business.

REQUIRED

(a) Open the following ledger accounts, using the account numbers shown: Cash (11); Accounts Receivable (12); Prepaid Rent (13); Supplies on Hand (14); Office Equipment (15); Accumulated Depreciation (16); Accounts Payable (21); Wages Payable (22); V. Bailey, Capital (31); V. Bailey, Drawing (32); Income Summary (33); Consulting Fees (41); Supplies Expense (51); Wages Expense (52); Rent Expense (53); and Depreciation Expense (54).

(b) Journalize the December transactions, and post to the ledger.

(c) Prepare a trial balance directly on a worksheet, and complete the worksheet using the following information:

(1) Supplies on hand at December 31 are $360.
(2) Accrued wages payable at December 31 are $115.
(3) Depreciation for December is $50.
(4) Bailey has spent 20 hours on an involved tax fraud case during December. When completed in January, his work will be billed at $40 per hour.
(5) Prepaid rent at December 31 is $400.

(d) Prepare a December income statement and a December 31 balance sheet.
(e) Journalize and post adjusting and closing entries.
(f) Prepare a post-closing trial balance.
(g) Journalize and post the appropriate reversing entries.

4–31 The last four columns of a 10-column worksheet prepared at December 31, 19XX, for Graphco, Inc. are reproduced below.

	Income Statement		Balance Sheet	
	Debit	Credit	Debit	Credit
Cash			4,100	
Accounts Receivable			6,000	
Prepaid Insurance			900	
Equipment			23,500	
Accumulated Depreciation				1,100
Accounts Payable				3,800
Capital Stock				12,000
Retained Earnings				6,300
Service Fees		27,900		
Miscellaneous Income		1,400		
Salaries Expense	10,700			
Rent Expense	3,500			
Insurance Expense	400			
Salaries Payable				300
Depreciation Expense	1,500			
Income Tax Expense	2,200			
	18,300	29,300	34,500	23,500
Net Income	11,000			11,000
	29,300	29,300	34,500	34,500

REQUIRED

(a) From the given information, prepare closing entries in general journal form.
(b) After the closing entries are posted, what is the balance in the Retained Earnings account?
(c) Which accounts in the worksheet would not appear if the company were organized as a sole proprietorship rather than a corporation?

4–32 Quality Engineering Services prepares monthly income statements and balance sheets, but makes adjusting and closing entries in its accounts only at December 31 each year. The firm's income statement for the three months ended March 31, 19XX, and its unadjusted trial balance at April 30, 19XX, are given as follows. The firm, owned by William Beck, is a sole proprietorship.

Quality Engineering Services
Income Statement
For the Three Months Ended March 31, 19XX

Revenue

Service Fees		$64,800
Expenses		
Salaries Expense	$21,050	
Depreciation Expense	5,100	
Rent Expense	2,850	
Advertising Expense	3,530	
Utilities Expense	1,270	
Supplies Expense	2,960	
Insurance Expense	480	
Legal Fees Expense	5,500	
Total Expenses		42,740
Net Income for the Quarter		$22,060

Quality Engineering Services
Trial Balance
April 30, 19XX

	Debit	Credit
Cash	$ 22,700	
Prepaid Insurance	1,440	
Supplies on Hand	10,200	
Equipment	176,000	
Accumulated Depreciation		$ 10,200
Accounts Payable		6,400
W. Beck, Capital		154,800
W. Beck, Drawing	5,000	
Service Fees		92,500
Salaries Expense	30,400	
Advertising Expense	7,000	
Rent Expense	3,800	
Utilities Expense	1,860	
Legal Fees Expense	5,500	
	$263,900	$263,900

The following data for adjustments are available at April 30, 19XX:

(1) Prepaid insurance at April 30 is $800.
(2) Supplies on hand at April 30 are $6,000.
(3) Monthly depreciation on equipment is $1,700.
(4) Accrued salaries at April 30 are $600.
(5) The firm is involved in a lawsuit with a former client. Legal fees incurred in April but not yet billed are estimated at $1,200 (credit Legal Fees Payable).

REQUIRED

(a) Record the April 30 trial balance on a 10-column worksheet. Enter the necessary adjusting entries and complete the worksheet for the four months ended April 30, 19XX.

(b) Prepare an income statement for the four months ended April 30, 19XX.

(c) Prepare an income statement for the month of April, 19XX.

ALTERNATE PROBLEMS

4–26A The trial balance and adjustments columns of the worksheet for Topp Roofing Service at December 31 of the current year are shown below.

| | Trial Balance | | Adjustments | | |
	Debit	Credit	Debit		Credit
Cash	3,600				
Accounts Receivable	5,150				
Supplies on Hand	1,700			(b)	750
Prepaid Insurance	600			(c)	300
Truck	7,500				
Accumulated Depreciation— Truck		2,700		(d)	900
Equipment	18,100				
Accumulated Depreciation— Equipment		3,400		(e)	1,150
Accounts Payable		1,200			
Unearned Service Fees		3,000	(a)	800	
F. Topp, Capital		18,800			
F. Topp, Drawing	2,050				
Service Fees		36,000		(a)	800
Salaries Expense	20,900				
Rent Expense	4,800				
Advertising Expense	700				
	65,100	65,100			
Supplies Expense			(b)	750	
Insurance Expense			(c)	300	
Depreciation Expense— Truck			(d)	900	
Depreciation Expense— Equipment			(e)	1,150	
				3,900	3,900

REQUIRED

(a) Complete the worksheet.

(b) Prepare the closing entries at December 31 in general journal form.

4–27A The July 31 unadjusted trial balance of Thurow Outfitters, a firm renting equipment and supplies to canoeists and fishermen, is shown below.

Thurow Outfitters
Trial Balance
July 31, 19XX

	Debit	Credit
Cash	$ 3,300	
Supplies on Hand	4,600	
Prepaid Insurance	2,800	
Equipment	93,500	
Accumulated Depreciation		$ 32,500
Accounts Payable		3,900
Unearned Rental Fees		2,200
B. Thurow, Capital		36,400
B. Thurow, Drawing	500	
Rental Fees		57,350
Wages Expense	21,800	
Rent Expense	2,500	
Advertising Expense	2,430	
Travel Expense	920	
	$132,350	$132,350

The trial balance data are cumulative for the first three months of the firm's fiscal year, which begins May 1. No adjusting entries have been made in the accounts during the quarter. The following additional information is available:

(1) Supplies on hand at July 31 amount to $2,900.

(2) Insurance expense for the first quarter is $700.

(3) Depreciation for the first quarter is $2,400.

(4) The unearned rental fees consist of deposits received from customers in advance when reservations are made. During the quarter, $1,650 of the unearned rental fees were earned.

(5) At July 31, unbilled revenue from rental services earned for outfitting several church groups during July amounts to $1,800.

(6) Accrued wages payable for equipment handlers and guides amounts to $750 at July 31.

REQUIRED

(a) Enter the trial balance in a worksheet and complete the worksheet using the adjustment data given above.

(b) Prepare an income statement for the first quarter and a balance sheet at July 31.

4–28A Roland Dye, owner of the Dye Refinishing Service, has completed a worksheet for his business at the end of its first year of operations. He is unsure of his accounting skills, however, and asks you to review the worksheet before he prepares financial statements from it. You have reviewed the unadjusted trial balance, the adjustments, and the compilation of the adjusted trial balance columns and have found no errors. The last six columns of the worksheet are shown below (as noted, the adjusted trial balance columns are correct).

Dye Refinishing Service
Worksheet
For the Year Ended December 31, 19XX

	Adjusted Trial Balance		Income Statement		Balance Sheet	
	Debit	Credit	Debit	Credit	Debit	Credit
Cash	600				600	
Accounts Receivable	400				400	
Prepaid Rent	270				720	
Supplies on Hand	590				590	
Equipment	3,000				3,000	
Accounts Payable		650				650
R. Dye, Capital		4,400				4,400
R. Dye, Drawing	500		500			
Service Fees		4,850		4,850		
Wages Expense	2,500		2,500			
Utilities Expense	710		170			
Rent Expense	1,080		1,080			
Supplies Expense	460		460			
Depreciation Expense	300		300			
Accumulated Depreciation		300		300		
Wages Payable		140			140	
Utilities Payable		70				70
	10,410	10,410	4,820	5,150	5,450	5,120
Net Income			330			330
			5,150	5,150	5,450	5,450

REQUIRED
(a) Identify the errors contained in this partial worksheet.
(b) Prepare a correct partial worksheet (the last six columns).

4–29A Glide and Stride, Inc. publishes magazines for skaters and hikers. The firm has the following unadjusted trial balance at December 31 of its second year of operations.

Glide and Stride, Inc.
Trial Balance
December 31, 19X2

	Debit	Credit
Cash	$ 13,200	
Accounts Receivable	6,200	
Supplies on Hand	3,750	
Prepaid Insurance	1,840	
Office Equipment	28,000	
Accumulated Depreciation—Office Equipment		$ 2,800
Building	120,000	
Accumulated Depreciation—Building		3,000
Land	60,000	
Accounts Payable		3,400
Unearned Subscription Revenue		8,200
Capital Stock		100,000
Retained Earnings		41,800
Subscription Revenue		225,200
Advertising Revenue		31,600
Salaries Expense	96,150	
Printing and Mailing Expense	50,600	
Advertising Expense	8,720	
Utilities Expense	5,340	
Income Tax Expense	22,200	
	$416,000	$416,000

The following information for adjusting the accounts is available at December 31:

(1) Supplies on hand amount to $1,700.
(2) Prepaid insurance at December 31 is $920.
(3) Accrued salaries at December 31 are $3,500.
(4) Of the unearned subscription revenue shown in the trial balance, $3,400 was earned during the year. The remainder will be earned next year.
(5) Advertising revenue earned during the period but unbilled at December 31 is $1,600.
(6) Depreciation on office equipment for the year is $2,800.
(7) Depreciation on the building for the year is $3,000.

REQUIRED
(a) Prepare a 10-column worksheet for the year ended December 31, 19X2. Set up any additional accounts needed.
(b) Prepare an income statement for the year and a balance sheet at December 31.
(c) Prepare closing entries in general journal form.

4–30A E. Keene, attorney, opened her practice on December 1 of the current year. December transactions were as follows:

Dec. 1   E. Keene invested $10,000 in the firm.
       2   Paid rent for six months to Acme Realty, $2,700.
       2   Purchased various supplies for cash, $850.
       3   Purchased office furniture and fixtures on account, $4,500.
       8   Paid $1,500 on account for furniture and fixtures purchased December 3.
      13   Paid assistant's salary for two weeks, $650.
      20   Performed legal services for cash, $2,900.
      27   Paid assistant's salary for two weeks, $650.
      30   Billed clients for legal work completed during the month, $1,100.
      31   Keene withdrew $1,000 from the business.

REQUIRED
(a) Open the following ledger accounts, using the account numbers shown: Cash (11); Accounts Receivable (12); Prepaid Rent (13); Supplies on Hand (14); Furniture and Fixtures (15); Accumulated Depreciation (16); Accounts Payable (21); Salary Payable (22); E. Keene, Capital (31); E. Keene, Drawing (32); Income Summary (33); Fees Earned (41); Supplies Expense (51); Salary Expense (52); Rent Expense (53); and Depreciation Expense (54).
(b) Journalize the December transactions, and post to the ledger.
(c) Prepare a trial balance directly on a worksheet, and complete the worksheet using the following information:
    (1) Supplies on hand at December 31 are $670.
    (2) Accrued salary payable at December 31 is $130.
    (3) Depreciation for December is $60.
    (4) Keene has spent 25 hours on an involved estate planning case during December. When completed in January, her work will be billed at $45 per hour.
    (5) Prepaid rent at December 31 is $2,250.
(d) Prepare a December income statement and a December 31 balance sheet.
(e) Journalize and post adjusting and closing entries.
(f) Prepare a post-closing trial balance.
(g) Journalize and post the appropriate reversing entries.

BUSINESS DECISION PROBLEM

As an alternative to a summer job paying $5 per hour between her junior and senior years in college, Jan Wallen accepted an opportunity to lease and operate the tennis court concession in a local city recreational complex during June, July, and August. Although she kept no accounting records, Jan was careful to handle all funds related to the tennis concession through a special bank account opened for that purpose. An analysis of those deposit slips and check stubs for the three months is summarized below:

Receipts:

Wallen's investment of personal funds	$1,800
Court rentals	6,450
Tennis lesson fees	600
Proceeds of short-term loan from bank	1,000
Total receipts	$9,850

Disbursements:

Purchase of ball-throwing machine	$ 100
Supplies purchased	500
Utilities	390
Lease payments to city	1,650
Wages to part-time assistant	800
Liability insurance premiums	135
Repayment of bank loan, including interest	1,040
Withdrawals of cash for personal expenses	600
Total disbursements	$5,215
Cash balance, August 31	$4,635

Jan confides in you, a personal friend who happens to be studying accounting, that she is pleased with her apparent profit of $4,635 for the summer. Eager to practice your newly acquired skills, you offer to review her records and prepare an income statement for the three months and a balance sheet at the end of August. In discussions with Jan, you learn that:

(1) Rental receipts include all revenue earned except for $400 due from a company that rented the entire set of courts for a weekend late in August.
(2) Some tennis lessons, paid for in advance, could not be scheduled during the summer. Jan plans to refund these fees, which total $75.
(3) A ball-throwing machine, purchased used, turned out to be quite temperamental. After a complete breakdown in July, it was junked.
(4) Supplies consisted of cans of tennis balls. Jan gave away a free can of tennis balls for each five hours of court time rented by an individual. Supplies amounting to $160 were on hand at August 31; these may be returned for a full refund. Jan estimates that each month during the summer, she took home $30 worth of supplies for personal use.
(5) The insurance premiums represent coverage for the months of June, July, and August.
(6) Repayment to the bank included $40 of interest expense on the loan.
(7) All lease payments due the city were paid except for the final amount of $300.
(8) Jan estimates that the utility bill for August, when received, will be $200.

REQUIRED
Prepare financial statements for Jan's tennis concession (a sole proprietorship). You should formulate general journal entries summarizing the cash receipts and the cash disbursements and incorporating the additional data. After posting these to T accounts, you will be able to prepare the financial statements.

In further talks with Jan, you learn that the amount she contributed had been in a savings account earning 8% interest and that she worked an average of 60 hours in each of the 13 weeks the tennis concession was operated. What observations might you offer Jan regarding the financial success of the summer venture? What nonfinancial considerations are involved?

5

Merchandising Operations

T hus far in our discussion of the accounting cycle, we have used as examples firms providing services rather than those selling products. Revenue for small service enterprises such as the driving school and the television repair service consisted of fees earned for the services performed. In these firms, net income is determined simply by deducting total expenses incurred from total fees earned during a period.

Revenue for firms that sell products consists of the total amount for which the products are sold. To determine net income for such firms, we deduct from the revenue (called *sales*) for the period not only the operating expenses incurred, but also the costs of acquiring the products sold. In this chapter we shall discuss the procedures followed in accounting for the costs of acquiring and selling products.

THE NATURE OF MERCHANDISING OPERATIONS

The total business segment of society is often classified into three broad types of enterprises: (1) service, (2) manufacturing, and (3) merchandising. Commercial airlines, physicians, lawyers, insurance companies, and banks are examples of service enterprises. Manufacturing enterprises convert raw materials into finished products through the application of skilled labor and machine operations. Merchandising enterprises are characterized by the basic operations of buying and selling finished products and include both wholesalers and retailers. Exhibit 5–1 illustrates the position of merchandising enterprises in the manufacturing and distribution process.

The accounting records of a merchandising firm must accommodate many transactions for the purchase of products and payment of the related accounts. Moreover, the accounting reports should indicate whether the difference between the acquisition price and the sales price to customers covers the costs of storing, displaying, advertising, selling, delivering, and collecting for the merchandise. Finally, the accounting records must reflect not only cash sales but also individual accounts receivable for a large number of customers.

EXHIBIT 5–1
The Manufacturing and Distribution Process

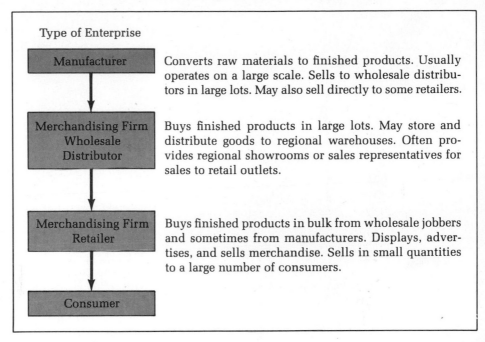

Type of Enterprise

Manufacturer — Converts raw materials to finished products. Usually operates on a large scale. Sells to wholesale distributors in large lots. May also sell directly to some retailers.

Merchandising Firm Wholesale Distributor — Buys finished products in large lots. May store and distribute goods to regional warehouses. Often provides regional showrooms or sales representatives for sales to retail outlets.

Merchandising Firm Retailer — Buys finished products in bulk from wholesale jobbers and sometimes from manufacturers. Displays, advertises, and sells merchandise. Sells in small quantities to a large number of consumers.

Consumer

INCOME STATEMENT FOR A MERCHANDISING FIRM

Exhibit 5–2 is an income statement for a merchandising firm, Madison Electronics Company. For simplicity, we have condensed the operating expenses into two amounts—selling expenses and administrative expenses. (These classifications are explained later in the chapter.)

The major difference between the income statement of a merchandising firm and that of a service business is the inclusion of an amount for the cost of goods sold to customers in the merchandising firm's statement. Ordinarily, this amount is deducted from the revenue figure (sales) to arrive at an intermediate amount called **gross profit on sales.** The operating expenses are then deducted from the gross profit on sales to obtain net income.

The gross profit on sales amount (sometimes called *gross margin*) is highly significant to management. When divided by the sales amount, it yields a gross profit percentage (sometimes called *average mark-up percentage on sales*), which is carefully monitored by the firm. In our illustration, the gross profit is 40% of sales ($140,000/$350,000 = 0.40 = 40%). This figure means that after 60 cents is deducted from each sales dollar to cover the cost of goods sold, 40 cents remains to cover operating expenses.

EXHIBIT 5–2

Madison Electronics Company
Income Statement
For the Year Ended December 31, 19XX

Sales		$350,000
Cost of Goods Sold		210,000
Gross Profit on Sales		$140,000
Operating Expenses:		
Selling Expenses	$81,000	
Administrative Expenses	38,000	
Total Operating Expenses		119,000
Net Income		$ 21,000

Management usually compares its current gross profit percentage with similar calculations for prior periods or with industry averages. Such comparisons may alert management to a need to modify prices, purchasing policies, or merchandise control procedures. Industry averages are usually available from such sources as trade associations or credit reporting agencies that compile statistics for various industries.

Cost of Goods Sold

To calculate the cost of goods sold to customers, we must consider data from a number of special merchandise accounts. We discuss the treatment of such accounts in detail later in this chapter. To provide a perspective, however, we show in condensed form in Exhibit 5–3 how cost of goods sold was calculated for the income statement in Exhibit 5–2.

At the beginning of the year, Madison Electronics had a supply of merchandise costing $89,000. During the year, the firm purchased additional merchandise with a net cost of $212,000. The sum of these two amounts is the total cost of all

EXHIBIT 5–3
Computation of Cost of Goods Sold

Beginning Inventory, January 1	$ 89,000
Add: Net Cost of Purchases	212,000
Cost of Goods Available for Sale	$301,000
Less: Ending Inventory, December 31	91,000
Cost of Goods Sold	$210,000

goods that were available for sale to customers during the year ($301,000). At the end of the year, merchandise costing $91,000 remained unsold, so we deduct this amount to arrive at the cost of goods sold, which is $210,000.

STEPS IN A MERCHANDISE TRANSACTION

Whenever a transaction for the purchase or sale of merchandise occurs, the buyer and the seller should agree on the price of the merchandise, the terms of payment, and the party to bear the cost of transportation. Owners or managers of small merchandising firms may settle the terms of the transaction informally by telephone or by discussion with the supplier's sales representative. Most large businesses, however, fill out a purchase order when ordering merchandise. A typical sequence of events for a large firm is as follows:

(1) When certain items are needed or when quantities of certain merchandise fall below established reorder points, a request for a purchase, called a **purchase requisition,** is sent to the purchasing department by the person in charge of merchandise stock records. These requisitions may also be initiated by other authorized personnel, such as department heads.

(2) The purchasing department then prepares a **purchase order** after consulting price lists, quotations, or suppliers' catalogs. The purchase order, addressed to the selected vendor, indicates the quantity, description, and price of the merchandise ordered. It may also indicate expected terms of payment and arrangements for transportation, including payment of freight costs.

(3) After receiving the purchase order, the seller forwards an **invoice** to the purchaser upon shipment of the merchandise. The invoice—called a **sales invoice** by the seller and a **purchase invoice** by the buyer—defines the terms of the transaction. A sample invoice is shown in Exhibit 5–4.

(4) Upon receiving the shipment of merchandise, the purchaser's receiving department counts and inspects the items in the shipment and makes out a **receiving report** detailing the quantities received.

(5) Before approving the invoice for payment, the accounts payable department compares copies of the purchase order, invoice, and receiving report to ensure that quantities, descriptions, and prices are in agreement.

Although all of the above papers—purchase requisition, purchase order, invoice, and receiving report—are source documents, only the invoice provides the basis for recording the purchase. The other three documents are merely supporting documents. The purchaser makes no entries in the accounts until the invoice is approved for payment. The seller enters the transaction in the records when the invoice is prepared, usually upon shipment of the merchandise.

EXHIBIT 5–4
Invoice

MADISON ELECTRONICS COMPANY	FOR CUSTOMER'S USE ONLY

MADISON ELECTRONICS COMPANY
1400 South Park St.
Madison, Wisconsin 53705

Customer's Order No. & Date 1503 Requisition No. Contract No.	Refer to Invoice No. 12015 Invoice Date Nov. 20, 19XX Vendor's Nos.

SOLD   ABC Company
  TO   120 Weston Street
             Kenosha, Wisconsin

Shipped to
  and
Destination   Same
Date Shipped Nov. 20, 19XX   From Madison   Prepaid or Collect
Car Initials and No.
How Shipped and   F.O.B. Kenosha   Prepaid
   Route
Terms 2/10, n/30

FOR CUSTOMER'S USE ONLY

Register No.   Voucher No.

F.O.B. Checked

Terms Approved | Price Approved
                       L.N.D.

Calculations Checked
   R.S.D.

Transportation

Freight Bill No.   Amount

Material Received

Date   Signature   Title

Satisfactory and Approved

Adjustments

Accounting Distribution

Audited | Final Approval

QUANTITY	DESCRIPTION	UNIT PRICE	AMOUNT
7	Model E Voicemaster Tape Recorders	$70	$490

TERMS OF TRANSACTIONS

Merchandise may be purchased and sold either on credit terms or for cash on delivery. Most merchandise transactions today are made on account rather than on cash (sometimes referred to as *net cash*) terms. When goods are sold on account, a period of time called the **credit period** is allowed for payment. The length of the credit period varies among business firms and may even vary within a firm, depending on the type of product. A typical credit period for wholesalers is 30 days. Payment is expected within 30 days of the invoice date, after which the purchaser is considered delinquent. The credit period is frequently described as the *net* credit period, or *net terms*, and the notation commonly used to designate this period is "n/" followed by the length of the period in days; for example, n/30 indicates that the credit period is 30 days.

Cash Discounts To encourage early payment of bills, many firms designate a **discount period** that is shorter than the credit period. Purchasers who remit payment during this period are entitled to deduct a **cash discount** from the total payment. Ostensibly, this discount is for prompt payment. The discount is designated by such notation

IMPACT OF SALES TERMS ON PRICING

The concept of pricing is frequently confined to the identification of the price per unit charged to the customer on the sales invoice, or as listed on the company's price sheet or in its catalog. The terms and conditions of sale, often shown in fine print on the back of the invoice, are not always seen as having any direct bearing on price. In reality, they have a substantial impact on the actual price recovered, and in many instances serve to negate completely the effect of the pricing decision. Some of the sales terms are readily measurable as to the effect on price; others are not, being either hidden from view or misleading as to interpretation. In total they constitute an integral part of the pricing process, and the effects of each must be measured on a step-by-step basis to obtain the desired economic results.

One of the more obvious examples of pricing impact is the measurement of cash discounts allowed for early payment. Typical is the discount of "2% 10 days net 30." First, the discount is a direct reduction of 2% in the selling price, a reduction that will usually be taken by the customer, even beyond the 10-day period allowed. Second, the offer of a 2% reduction for payment 20 days early—in 10 days rather than 30—amounts to an annual interest rate of 36% per year, a payment for the use of money far in excess of the bank rate for funds even in times of double-digit inflation.

Taken together, these two points add up to the fact that cash discounts seldom work as intended, that in practice they routinely become nothing more

than a price concession. Management is not deliberately offering 36% per annum for the use of money, but an alert customer will make the calculation properly and be quick to take advantage of it. Furthermore, the fact that many accounts take the discount well after the time allowed is evidence that customers regard it more as a price concession than a reward for early payment. Some companies attempt to charge back the unearned discount, a procedure that creates undesirable friction with their own customers, a situation the sales force would prefer to avoid.

Variations of the cash discount terms, such as "2% 10th prox," further complicate the picture by encouraging customers to bunch their orders around the first of the month to get the greatest leverage on the terms offered. This, obviously, can have the undesirable effect of creating peak work loads in order entry, shipping, and billing with consequent dry periods toward month-end.

In short, cash discounts make little economic sense as payment for the use of funds and in practice become nothing more than a reduction of price. In recent years, the great majority of companies have found it to be an awkward vehicle for price adjustment and have abandoned it in favor of net terms.

as "2/10," which means that 2% may be deducted if payment is made within 10 days. For example, if a November 10 invoice for $800 carries terms of 2/10, n/30, the purchaser may deduct 2% from the invoice price if the bill is paid by November 20. The cash discount would be $16 (2% of $800), and the amount of the remittance would be $784. The full amount of the invoice, $800, would be expected if the purchaser paid between November 20 and December 10. After December 10, the amount would be overdue.

Most business firms maintain a good cash position so they can take advantage of discounts. For example, assume that a firm purchased $800 worth of merchandise on terms of 2/10, n/30. The firm has a choice of paying $784 within 10 days of the invoice date or the full amount before the end of another 20 days. Passing up the discount is essentially the same as paying 2% interest for the use of $800 for 20 days, which is equivalent to a 36% annual interest rate (360 days/ 20 days × 2%). Clearly, the firm would be wiser to borrow from a bank at an annual interest rate of 10–12% rather than lose a discount that amounts to a much higher rate.

Trade Discounts   Certain business firms furnish customers with price lists or catalogs showing suggested retail prices for their products. These firms, however, also include a schedule of **trade discounts** from the listed prices that enable a customer to determine the invoice price to be paid. Suppose that the Madison Electronics Company quoted a list price of $100 for each Model E tape recorder, less a discount of 30% if purchased in lots of 10 items or less and 40% if purchased in lots of more than 10. If the ABC Company ordered seven tape recorders, it would calculate its invoice cost as follows:

List Price ($100 × 7)	$700
Less 30%	210
Invoice Cost	$490

Trade discounts enable a supplier to vary prices for small and large purchasers and, by changing the discount schedule, to alter prices periodically without the inconvenience and expense of revising catalogs and price lists. Trade discounts are simply a means of determining invoice prices and should not be confused with cash discounts. Trade discounts and list prices are not reflected in the accounts of either the purchaser or the seller of merchandise. In the foregoing example, both the purchaser and the seller would record only the $490 invoice amount.

RECORDING MERCHANDISE SALES

After a vendor has processed a customer's purchase order and prepared the goods for shipment, a sales invoice is prepared in several copies. The original copy is usually sent to the customer; duplicate copies are retained by the seller. The duplicates may be distributed to the shipping department to support its shipping records; to the sales department so it can analyze sales by product, territory, or sales representative; and to the accounting department so that the transaction will be recorded in the accounts.

Suppose the accounting department of Madison Electronics Company receives its copy of the November 20 invoice for the sale of the tape recorders described in the previous section. The general journal entry to record the sale would be

Nov. 20	Accounts Receivable	490	
	Sales		490
	To record the sale of seven Model E		
	tape recorders to the ABC Company.		
	Terms 2/10, n/30.		

The Sales account is used by almost all manufacturing and merchandising companies to record revenue transactions. It is the same type of account as the Instructional Fees (revenue) account used by the Capital Driving School, our example in Chapter 2. The Sales account is credited whenever credit or cash sales are made, and invariably it has a credit balance at the end of the accounting period. Only sales of merchandise held for resale are recorded in the Sales account. If a merchandising firm sold one of its delivery trucks, the credit would be made to the Delivery Equipment account, not the Sales account. At the end of the accounting period, the Sales account is closed to the Income Summary account in the same way that the Instructional Fees account is closed. Sales is debited and Income Summary is credited for the accumulated credit balance in the Sales account.

As we mentioned earlier, the sales invoice is the document used to record credit sales. For cash sales, however, the procedure is different. For a large volume of cash sales, as in a retail merchandising establishment, cash sales are recorded and accumulated on a cash register tape as they are made. At the end of each day, the amount of sales shown on the tape is recorded on a summary sheet or report. The totals on these reports are usually recorded in the Sales account each week. Shorter or longer recording intervals may be used, depending on management's reporting needs. In general journal form, the entry to record a week's cash sales of $3,200 would be

Nov. 27	Cash	3,200	
	Sales		3,200
	To record cash sales for week of		
	November 23–27.		

RECORDING MERCHANDISE PURCHASES

When a business purchases merchandise for resale to customers, the amount is debited to the Purchases account. The credit is made to Accounts Payable or to Cash, depending on whether the purchase was on credit or cash terms. Assume that on November 23, the ABC Company received its shipment of seven tape recorders from the Madison Electronics Company, along with the vendor's invoice for $490. To record the credit purchase, the ABC Company makes the following entry:

Nov. 23	Purchases	490	
	Accounts Payable		490
	To record the purchase of seven Model E tape		
	recorders from Madison Electronics		
	Company. Terms 2/10, n/30.		

Only merchandise purchased for resale is recorded in the Purchases account. Acquisitions of such things as equipment, supplies, and investments are entered in the corresponding asset accounts rather than in Purchases.

The Purchases account normally has a debit balance at the end of the accounting period. The account is treated as an income statement account and, like the other temporary accounts, is closed at the end of the accounting year. The closing of the Purchases account is explained later in this chapter.

RETURNS AND ALLOWANCES

Sometimes a customer returns merchandise to the seller because of defects, damage in transit, or because the wrong merchandise was shipped. Upon returning merchandise, the customer requests an appropriate reduction in the original amount billed. Similar requests are made when an invoicing error has occurred. Upon receiving notification that the buyer has returned goods or has requested an allowance, the seller usually issues the customer a **credit memorandum** such as the one illustrated in Exhibit 5–5.

The credit memorandum (sometimes called *credit memo*) is a formal acknowledgment that the seller has reduced the amount owed by the customer.

EXHIBIT 5–5
Credit Memorandum

MADISON ELECTRONICS COMPANY **1400 South Park St.** **Madison, Wisconsin 53705**	CREDIT MEMORANDUM No. 23

TO: ABC Company   Date Nov. 25, 19XX

120 Weston Street

Kenosha, Wisconsin

We credit your account as follows:

Return of two Model E tape recorders,
our invoice No. 12015 . . . . $140.00

When the seller issues a credit memorandum, the accounting department retains a duplicate copy, which is the source document for an entry crediting the customer's account. For example, suppose two of the seven tape recorders sold to the ABC Company were returned for credit. Upon issuing a credit memo to the ABC Company, Madison Electronics Company would make the following entry:

Nov. 25	Sales Returns and Allowances	140	
	Accounts Receivable		140
	To record the issuance of credit memo		
	No. 23 for two Model E tape recorders		
	returned by the ABC Company.		

Upon receipt of the credit memo, the ABC Company would make the following entry:

Nov. 27	Accounts Payable	140	
	Purchases Returns and Allowances		140
	To record the receipt of credit memo No. 23		
	for two Model E tape recorders returned		
	to Madison Electronics Company.		

In the first entry above, Madison Electronics Company could have debited the Sales account rather than Sales Returns and Allowances. If Sales were debited, however, the account balance at the end of the accounting period would not reveal total sales made but total sales less all returns and allowances. Most companies prefer to record sales returns and allowances in a separate contra account in order to determine the aggregate amount of such items. If the amount is abnormally large, an investigation should be made to determine the reason. Returns may be caused by defective products, faulty packing or shipping, or improper billing procedures. The additional handling of goods and the additional clerical work of making adjustments can be costly, and customers may be lost in the process.

For similar reasons, the purchaser ordinarily credits the Purchases Returns and Allowances account rather than the Purchases account when a credit memorandum is received. The separate accounting permits a company to determine whether its purchasing or requisitioning procedures should be reviewed. The company may discover, for instance, that not enough care is exercised in filling out requisitions and purchase orders or in selecting reliable suppliers.

The Sales Returns and Allowances account invariably has a debit balance at the end of the accounting period. On the income statement, the amount is a deduction from the Sales amount. The Purchases Returns and Allowances account has a credit balance at the end of the accounting period, and the balance is subtracted from the Purchases amount on the income statement. Both the Sales Returns and Allowances and the Purchases Returns and Allowances accounts are closed at the end of the accounting year in a manner we shall explain shortly.

Many companies record all credit memos in the returns and allowances accounts. When the memos are issued as a result of mere clerical or arithmetical errors, however, the adjustment is best recorded in the Sales or Purchases accounts.

RECORDING RECEIPTS AND PAYMENTS

A set of merchandise transactions concludes when the seller receives the proper remittance from the purchaser and each firm makes the appropriate entries for the settlement of accounts. To illustrate let us review the entries made thus far for Madison Electronics Company's sale of the tape recorders to the ABC Company.

Seller (Madison Electronics Company)			**Buyer (ABC Company)**		
To Record Sale			**To Record Purchase**		
Nov. 20 Accounts Receivable	490		Nov. 23 Purchases	490	
Sales		490	Accounts Payable		490
To record the sale of			To record the purchase		
seven Model E tape			of seven Model E tape		
recorders to the ABC			recorders from Madison		
Company. Terms 2/10,			Electronics Company.		
n/30.			Terms 2/10, n/30.		
To Record Return of Merchandise			**To Record Return of Merchandise**		
Nov. 25 Sales Returns and			Nov. 27 Accounts Payable	140	
Allowances	140		Purchases Returns		
Accounts Receivable		140	and Allowances		140
To record the issuance			To record the receipt of		
of credit memo No. 23			credit memo No. 23 for		
for two Model E tape			two Model E tape		
recorders returned by			recorders returned to		
the ABC Company.			Madison Electronics		
			Company.		

After these transactions have been posted, the seller's Accounts Receivable account and the buyer's Accounts Payable account appear as follows:

Seller **(Madison Electronics Company)**				**Buyer** **(ABC Company)**			
Accounts Receivable				Accounts Payable			
19XX		19XX		19XX		19XX	
Nov. 20	490	Nov. 25	140	Nov. 27	140	Nov. 23	490

If the ABC Company takes advantage of the 2% discount, its remittance must be made within 10 days of the November 20 invoice date. Usually, the discount is granted if the remittance is postmarked on the last day of the discount period. The amount that the ABC Company should remit by November 30 is $343 ($350 balance owing less 2% discount of $7). Note that the discount is calculated only on the cost of the merchandise kept by the purchaser, not on the invoice price of the goods originally shipped. The entries made on the books of the seller and buyer are

Seller (Madison Electronics Company)				**Buyer (ABC Company)**		
Dec. 2	Cash	343	Nov. 30	Accounts Payable	350	
	Sales Discounts	7		Purchases Discounts		7
	Accounts Receivable	350		Cash		343
	To record remittance in			To record payment of		
	full of account.			account.		

After this entry is posted, the seller's Accounts Receivable and the purchaser's Accounts Payable appear as follows:

<table>
<tr><th colspan="3">Seller
(Madison Electronics Company)</th><th colspan="3">Buyer
(ABC Company)</th></tr>
<tr><th colspan="3">Accounts Receivable</th><th colspan="3">Accounts Payable</th></tr>
<tr><td>19XX</td><td></td><td>19XX</td><td>19XX</td><td></td><td>19XX</td></tr>
<tr><td>Nov. 20</td><td>490</td><td>Nov. 25 140</td><td>Nov. 27 140</td><td></td><td>Nov. 23 490</td></tr>
<tr><td></td><td></td><td>Dec. 2 350</td><td>30 350</td><td></td><td></td></tr>
</table>

Note that the discount taken in this transaction is not revealed in either the seller's Accounts Receivable account or the buyer's Accounts Payable account. Discounts are accumulated in Sales Discounts on the seller's books and Purchases Discounts on the buyer's books.

The other accounts relevant to the set of transactions for the tape recorders are shown below in T-account form, after the appropriate postings have been made.

Seller
(Madison Electronics Company)

Sales

		19XX	
		Nov. 20	490

Sales Returns and Allowances

19XX			
Nov. 25	140		

Sales Discounts

19XX			
Dec. 2	7		

Buyer
(ABC Company)

Purchases

19XX			
Nov. 23	490		

Purchases Returns and Allowances

		19XX	
		Nov. 27	140

Purchases Discounts

		19XX	
		Nov. 30	7

From this illustration, we see that both Sales Returns and Allowances and Sales Discounts have debit balances, and the Sales account has a credit balance. This relationship always holds true, and at the close of the accounting period, the net sales for the period can be calculated by subtracting the balances of the Sales Returns and Allowances account and the Sales Discounts account from the

Sales account. The revenue section of the income statement for the year will show this calculation as follows:

Revenue		
Sales		$357,500
Less: Sales Returns and Allowances	$1,500	
Sales Discounts	6,000	7,500
Net Sales		$350,000

Similarly, Purchases Returns and Allowances and Purchases Discounts have credit balances at the close of the accounting period. On the income statement for the period, the sum of these account balances is deducted from the Purchases account balance. However, because the concept of net cost of purchases is a net *delivered* cost, we usually add another amount, *Transportation In*, to arrive at net cost of purchases. (Transportation In will be explained later in this chapter.) The calculation of net cost of purchases for Madison Electronics Company for the year appears on its income statement as follows:

Net Cost of Purchases		
Purchases		$209,800
Less: Purchases Returns and Allowances	$1,400	
Purchases Discounts	3,800	5,200
		$204,600
Add: Transportation In		7,400
Net Cost of Purchases		$212,000

This calculation appears in the cost of goods sold section of the income statement, which we shall examine more closely later in this chapter.

NET PRICE METHOD OF RECORDING PURCHASES

Some firms anticipate the cash discounts they expect to take on merchandise purchases and initially record such purchases net of the discounts. For example, if a firm purchased merchandise for $500 on terms of 2/10, n/30, the 2% discount ($10) would be deducted from the invoice cost and the entry to record the transaction would debit Purchases and credit Accounts Payable for $490. When this amount is paid during the discount period, the debit to Accounts Payable and the credit to Cash would be for the net amount, $490. No purchase discount would be recorded. When the net price method is used, returns and allowances are also recorded net of the related discount.

If a firm delays payment beyond the discount period, the amount of the discount not taken is debited to an account called Discounts Lost when the remittance is made. If the firm in our example failed to remit within the discount period, it would record the payment as a $490 debit to Accounts Payable, $10 debit to Discounts Lost, and a $500 credit to Cash.

The Discounts Lost account balance is normally added to the cost of purchases in the cost of goods sold section of the income statement. However, some firms include it with operating expenses. The principal advantage of the net price method is that it focuses attention on discounts not taken, so that management can take immediate corrective action when the aggregate amount of lost discounts becomes significant.

TRANSPORTATION ACCOUNTS

When merchandise is forwarded by a common carrier—a railroad, a trucking company, or an airline—the carrier prepares a *freight bill* in accordance with the instructions of the party making the transportation arrangements. (As mentioned earlier, such arrangements may be specified in the purchase order.) The freight bill designates which party bears the shipping costs and whether the shipment is *prepaid* or *collect*.

Freight bills usually show whether the shipping terms are F.O.B. shipping point or F.O.B. destination (F.O.B. is an abbreviation for "free on board"). When the freight terms are F.O.B. shipping point, the purchaser bears the shipping costs; when the terms are F.O.B. destination, the seller bears the shipping costs.

The shipping costs borne by a purchaser are debited to an account called **Transportation In.** On the firm's income statement, the balance in this account is added to net cost of purchases to arrive at the net *delivered* cost of purchases. Transportation costs incurred by a seller are debited to an account called **Transportation Out.** This account—sometimes called Delivery Expense—is listed with expenses on the income statement. The primary reason for such treatment is that the seller ordinarily has a number of different types of expenses directly associated with selling merchandise. Such expenses as advertising, salespersons' salaries, and insurance are frequently grouped in the income statement under the caption "Selling Expenses"; including Transportation Out with this group is logical.

Usually, the party assuming the freight cost pays the carrier. Thus, goods are shipped *freight collect* when the terms are F.O.B. shipping point and *freight prepaid* when the terms are F.O.B. destination. Sometimes, as a matter of convenience, the firm not assuming the freight cost pays the carrier. When this situation occurs, the seller and buyer simply adjust the amount of the payment for the merchandise. To illustrate, let us assume that Madison Electronics Company sells $600 worth of merchandise on account to Chicago Supply Company on terms F.O.B. shipping point, 2/10, n/30, and shipping costs of $60 are prepaid by the seller. Madison Electronics Company adds the $60 freight charge to the invoice amount, billing Chicago Supply Company for $660. On its records, Chicago Supply Company reflects the freight cost as Transportation In.

In this situation, the buyer is not entitled to a discount on the amount of the freight. Thus, if Chicago Supply Company pays the invoice during the discount period, the amount to be remitted is calculated as follows:

Invoice amount ($600 plus $60 prepaid freight)	$660
Less: Discount (2% of $600)	12
Amount to be remitted	$648

On the other hand, if freight terms are F.O.B. destination but the buyer pays the shipping charges (freight collect), the buyer deducts the freight charges in remitting to the seller. The buyer, however, is entitled to a discount calculated on the invoice price of the merchandise. Thus, if $600 worth of merchandise is purchased and freight is $60, a 2% discount of $12 would be taken and the remittance would be $528 ($600 worth of merchandise less the $12 discount less the $60 shipping charge paid by the buyer).

WORKSHEET FOR A MERCHANDISING FIRM

We pointed out in Chapter 4 that a worksheet is prepared at the close of an accounting period to facilitate preparation of the financial statements. The structure of a worksheet for a merchandising firm is the same 10-column form used in Chapter 4 for a service firm, with pairs of columns for the trial balance, adjustments, adjusted trial balance, income statement, and balance sheet. Madison Electronics Company's worksheet in Exhibit 5–6 (pages 176–77) is prepared after all transactions for the year are recorded and posted to the accounts. The first step in preparing the worksheet is to take a trial balance to the general ledger at December 31 and record the account balances in the first two columns of the worksheet.

Adjustments in the Worksheet

The second step in preparing the worksheet is to record the year-end adjusting entries in the adjustments columns. These entries, with explanations, are as follows:

(1)	Dec. 31	Insurance Expense	240	
		Prepaid Insurance		240
		To charge one year's premium to expense. (Three-year premium, $720, paid January 1.)		
(2)	31	Supplies Expense	1,200	
		Supplies on Hand		1,200
		To charge to expense the supplies used during year. (Inventory of supplies is $1,400 on December 31.)		
(3)	31	Depreciation Expense	4,000	
		Accumulated Depreciation		4,000
		To charge to expense one year's depreciation on delivery equipment.		
(4)	31	Sales Salaries Expense	500	
		Salaries Payable		500
		To reflect the salaries earned by salespersons but not paid at December 31.		

To reflect the adjusting entries, we add the accounts not included in the trial balance to the bottom of the worksheet. After making these entries, we total the adjustments columns to confirm that debits equal credits. The trial balance amounts are combined with the adjustments to obtain the adjusted trial balance amounts; these amounts are also summed to determine the equality of the totals. We then extend the adjusted trial balance amounts into the income statement and balance sheet columns. We can see in Exhibit 5–6 that Sales, Purchases, related returns and allowances, discounts, and expense accounts are extended into the income statement columns. Assets, liabilities, and owner's equity accounts are extended into the balance sheet columns.

Inventories in the Worksheet

The inventory of a merchandising firm consists of a stock of goods that are on hand waiting to be sold to customers. The dollar amount of this stock of goods is carried in an asset account called **Merchandise Inventory,** or simply **Inventory.** A firm that records the acquisition of merchandise during the period in a Purchases account is using a *periodic* inventory system.[1] This system implies that the inventory account balance does not change during the period. Before the firm prepares year-end financial statements, it must determine the amount of unsold goods to be reported. The amount of this asset is usually calculated by counting and pricing individual items in stock, multiplying unit costs by number of items, then adding all amounts to obtain an aggregate measure.

In Exhibit 5–6, the inventory figure that appears in the unadjusted trial balance is the January 1 inventory. This amount still appears in the account because additions and deductions during the year have not been reflected in the account. The beginning inventory of $89,000 is extended as a debit in the income statement columns because it is combined with Purchases (less returns and allowances and discounts) and Transportation In to determine the cost of goods available for sale. The $91,000 ending inventory, recorded at the bottom of the worksheet, is a credit in the income statement columns because it is deducted from cost of goods available for sale in the calculation of cost of goods sold. In Exhibit 5–6, all the amounts comprising cost of goods sold appear in color to emphasize how cost of goods sold is reflected in the income statement columns of the worksheet. The ending inventory of $91,000 is also entered as a debit in the balance sheet columns because it is an asset at December 31.

The last step in completing the worksheet is to total the income statement and balance sheet columns and insert the balancing amount—the $26,250 net income for the year. A net income amount results in a debit in the income statement columns and a credit in the balance sheet columns. A net loss would result in a credit in the income statement columns and a debit in the balance sheet columns.

FINANCIAL STATEMENTS OF A MERCHANDISING FIRM

Once the worksheet is completed, preparing the formal financial statements for the period is a simple matter. Exhibits 5–7 and 5–8 present the income statement for the year and the balance sheet at the end of the year for Madison Electronics

---

[1] Under the *perpetual* inventory system described in Chapter 9, the Inventory account is adjusted throughout the accounting period for the cost of goods purchased and sold.

EXHIBIT 5-6

Madison Electronics Company
Worksheet
For the Year Ended December 31, 19XX

	Trial Balance Debit	Trial Balance Credit	Adjustments Debit	Adjustments Credit	Adjusted Trial Balance Debit	Adjusted Trial Balance Credit	Income Statement Debit	Income Statement Credit	Balance Sheet Debit	Balance Sheet Credit
Cash	20,420				20,420				20,420	
Accounts Receivable	28,000				28,000				28,000	
Inventory, January 1	89,000				89,000		89,000			
Prepaid Insurance	720			(1) 240	480				480	
Supplies on Hand	2,600			(2) 1,200	1,400				1,400	
Delivery Equipment	32,000				32,000				32,000	
Accumulated Depreciation		5,600		(3) 4,000		9,600				9,600
Accounts Payable		13,750				13,750				13,750
Long-term Notes Payable		10,000				10,000				10,000
J. Madison, Capital		118,000				118,000				118,000
J. Madison, Drawing	4,800				4,800				4,800	
Sales		357,500				357,500		357,500		
Sales Returns and Allowances	1,500				1,500		1,500			
Sales Discounts	6,000				6,000		6,000			
Purchases	209,800				209,800		209,800			

Account	Trial Balance Dr	Trial Balance Cr	Adjustments Dr	Adjustments Cr	Adjusted Trial Balance Dr	Adjusted Trial Balance Cr	Income Statement Dr	Income Statement Cr	Balance Sheet Dr	Balance Sheet Cr
Purchases Returns and Allowances		1,400				1,400		1,400		
Purchases Discounts		3,800				3,800		3,800		
Transportation In	7,400				7,400		7,400			
Sales Salaries Expense	52,000		(4) 500		52,500		52,500			
Advertising Expense	3,760				3,760		3,760			
Delivery Expense	15,250				15,250		15,250			
Office Salaries Expense	19,500				19,500		19,500			
Rent Expense	14,500				14,500		14,500			
Utilities Expense	2,800				2,800		2,800			
	510,050	510,050								
Insurance Expense			(1) 240		240		240			
Supplies Expense			(2) 1,200		1,200		1,200			
Depreciation Expense			(3) 4,000		4,000		4,000			
Salaries Payable				(4) 500		500				500
			5,940	5,940	514,550	514,550				
Inventory, December 31								91,000	91,000	
							427,450	453,700	178,100	151,850
Net Income							26,250			26,250
							453,700	453,700	178,100	178,100

Company. Both were prepared from the worksheet in Exhibit 5–6. Note that these are **classified** financial statements, meaning that accounts are separated into various categories. The income statements in previous illustrations were not classified because only a few accounts were used. A business with many accounts and transactions, however, classifies the items on the statements to facilitate analysis and interpretation of the data.

The Income Statement

The major categories of the income statement are revenue, cost of goods sold, and operating expenses. For a merchandising firm, the major revenue source is sales of goods to customers. In the revenue section, sales returns and allowances and sales discounts are deducted from gross sales to yield net sales.

We stated earlier that the cost of goods sold amount is obtained by adding the beginning inventory and net cost of purchases and deducting the ending inventory. To calculate net cost of purchases, we deduct purchases returns and allowances and purchases discounts from the purchases amount and add transportation costs of purchased goods.

A business firm's *operating expenses* relate to its primary function and appear with some regularity on the income statement. The operating expenses of a merchandising business are typically classified as selling or administrative expenses. Therefore, in our illustration, expenses resulting from sales efforts—such as salespersons' salaries, advertising, and delivery costs—are classified separately from expenses of rent, utilities, and other administrative costs. Of course, certain types of expenses may appear under both categories. For example, the insurance expense in Exhibit 5–7 is apparently on merchandise or delivery equipment, because it appears as a selling expense. Insurance on a company-owned office building, on the other hand, would appear with the administrative expenses.

Some business items affecting the final net income amount may not relate to the primary operating activity of the business. Interest income and interest expense, for example, may relate more to financing and investing activities than to merchandising efforts. For this reason, such items are often shown in a separate category called "Other Income and Expense" at the bottom of the income statement. Likewise, any extraordinary items (explained in Chapter 16), such as catastrophic loss from an earthquake, are shown in a separate "Extraordinary Items" category before the final net income amount is figured. Madison Electronics Company had no such transactions or events to list on the income statement in Exhibit 5–7.

Because the income statement is divided into the major categories just discussed and expenses are classified into selling and administrative expenses, the reader of the statement may pick out key figures at a glance. The reader might first observe the net income figure, $26,250, and perhaps relate it (as a percentage) to the net sales figure, $350,000. This result, called **return on sales,** is 7.5% for Madison Electronics Company. Next, the reader might determine the gross margin percentage by performing the calculation

$$\frac{\$140,000 \text{ (gross profit)}}{\$350,000 \text{ (net sales)}} = 40\%$$

EXHIBIT 5–7

Madison Electronics Company
Income Statement
For the Year Ended December 31, 19XX

Revenue

Sales			$357,500
Less: Sales Returns and Allowances		$ 1,500	
Sales Discounts		6,000	7,500
Net Sales			$350,000

Cost of Goods Sold

Inventory, January 1			$ 89,000	
Add: Net Cost of Purchases				
Purchases		$209,800		
Less: Purchases Returns and Allowances	$1,400			
Purchases Discounts	3,800	5,200		
		$204,600		
Add: Transportation In		7,400	212,000	
Cost of Goods Available for Sale			$301,000	
Less: Inventory, December 31			91,000	
Cost of Goods Sold				210,000
Gross Profit on Sales				$140,000

Operating Expenses

Selling Expenses			
Sales Salaries Expense	$ 52,500		
Delivery Expense	15,250		
Advertising Expense	3,760		
Depreciation Expense	4,000		
Insurance Expense	240		
Total Selling Expenses		$ 75,750	
Administrative Expenses			
Rent Expense	$ 14,500		
Office Salaries Expense	19,500		
Utilities Expense	2,800		
Supplies Expense	1,200		
Total Administrative Expenses		38,000	
Total Operating Expenses			113,750
Net Income			$ 26,250

EXHIBIT 5–8

Madison Electronics Company
Balance Sheet
December 31, 19XX

ASSETS			LIABILITIES AND OWNER'S EQUITY		
Current Assets			**Current Liabilities**		
Cash	$ 20,420		Accounts Payable	$ 13,750	
Accounts Receivable	28,000		Salaries Payable	500	
Inventory	91,000		Total Current		
Prepaid Insurance	480		Liabilities		$ 14,250
Supplies on Hand	1,400				
Total Current Assets		$141,300	**Long-term Liabilities**		
			Long-term Notes Payable		10,000
Long-term Assets			**Owner's Equity**		
Delivery Equipment	$ 32,000		J. Madison, Capital		139,450
Less: Accumulated					
Depreciation	9,600	22,400			
			Total Liabilities and		
Total Assets		$163,700	Owner's Equity		$163,700

In a similar fashion, we can relate the total expenses, expense categories, or even individual expenses to net sales. We might also compare the results with those of prior periods or industry averages to determine whether the company's progress is satisfactory. A detailed treatment of such analysis appears in Chapter 20.

The Balance Sheet

The balance sheet for Madison Electronics Company at December 31 is shown in Exhibit 5–8. Note that the company's assets have been classified into *current assets* and *long-term assets*.

CURRENT ASSETS Current assets include cash and assets that will be converted into cash or used up during the normal operating cycle of the business or one year, whichever is longer. The *normal operating cycle* of a business is the average period required for merchandise to be bought and sold and the resulting accounts receivable to be collected. For many businesses, this period is one year or less, although certain industries—such as lumbering and distilling—may have an operating cycle of several years. Examples of current assets other than those shown in Exhibit 5–8 are notes receivable and marketable securities acquired as temporary investments. Current assets are usually listed in the order of their liquidity, that is, their convertibility into cash.

Prepaid expenses such as rent, insurance, and supplies are normally consumed during the operating cycle rather than converted into cash. These items are considered current assets, however, because the prepayments make cash outlays for services unnecessary during the current period.

LONG-TERM ASSETS Long-term assets are noncurrent, relatively long-lived assets used in operating a business. When its balance sheet was prepared, Madison Electronics Company had only one long-term asset, delivery equipment, but many firms own land, buildings, machinery, and equipment. The terms *plant assets* or *plant and equipment* are often used when such assets are extensive. Depreciable assets are normally shown at their original cost, and the accumulated depreciation to date is credited to a separate account. Other examples of long-term assets held by some firms include natural resources, intangible assets, and long-term investments. These assets are explained in later chapters.

CURRENT LIABILITIES Current liabilities are amounts due within the normal operating cycle or one year, whichever is longer. Examples of current liabilities are accounts payable, accrued wages and salaries payable, income or property taxes payable, and short-term notes payable. Any amounts a firm has received from customers but has not yet earned as revenue are also customarily included in this category, for example, customers' deposits on future purchases and magazine subscriptions covering future periods.

LONG-TERM LIABILITIES After current liabilities, the balance sheet lists all **long-term liabilities**—amounts that are not due for a relatively long time, typically more than one year. Long-term notes, mortgages, and bonds payable are a few examples. Madison Electronics Company owed $10,000 on a long-term note when its balance sheet was compiled (Exhibit 5–8).

OWNER'S EQUITY The owner's interest in the assets of the firm appears in the owner's equity section of the balance sheet. J. Madison's capital balance at December 31 (Exhibit 5–8) is determined by adding the net income to the beginning capital balance and deducting withdrawals, as shown in Exhibit 5–9, the year-end Statement of Owner's Equity.

EXHIBIT 5–9

Madison Electronics Company
Statement of Owner's Equity
For the Year Ended December 31, 19XX

J. Madison, Capital, January 1	$118,000
Add: Net Income for 19XX	26,250
	$144,250
Less: Withdrawals for 19XX	4,800
J. Madison, Capital, December 31	$139,450

ADJUSTING AND CLOSING ENTRIES

As we explained in Chapter 4, a company often will prepare monthly or quarterly financial statements directly from worksheets and not record adjusting and closing entries in the general ledger until the end of the year. Let us examine year-end procedures for Madison Electronics Company.

Adjusting Entries

After financial statements have been prepared from the worksheet, the adjusting entries shown on the worksheet are recorded in the general journal and posted to the accounts. These entries, given in general journal form on page 174, will not be repeated here.

Closing Entries

The closing entries follow the adjusting entries in the general journal. The procedure consists of the following steps:

(1) Close the beginning inventory and all income statement accounts with *debit* balances, and debit the total to the Income Summary account.

(2) Record the ending inventory, close all income statement accounts with *credit* balances, and credit the total to the Income Summary account.

(3) Transfer the balance of the Income Summary account to the owner's capital account (the Retained Earnings account in a corporation).

(4) Transfer the balance of the owner's drawing account to the owner's capital account.

Closing entries for Madison Electronics Company are given below:

Dec. 31	Income Summary	427,450	
	Inventory (January 1)		89,000
	Sales Returns and Allowances		1,500
	Sales Discounts		6,000
	Purchases		209,800
	Transportation In		7,400
	Sales Salaries Expense		52,500
	Advertising Expense		3,760
	Delivery Expense		15,250
	Office Salaries Expense		19,500
	Rent Expense		14,500
	Utilities Expense		2,800
	Insurance Expense		240
	Supplies Expense		1,200
	Depreciation Expense		4,000

To close the beginning inventory and income statement accounts with debit balances.

31	Inventory (December 31)	91,000	
	Sales	357,500	
	Purchases Returns and Allowances	1,400	
	Purchases Discounts	3,800	
	Income Summary		453,700
	To record the ending inventory and to close income statement accounts with credit balances.		

31	Income Summary	26,250	
	J. Madison, Capital		26,250
	To close the Income Summary account and transfer net income to the owner's capital account.		

31	J. Madison, Capital	4,800	
	J. Madison, Drawing		4,800
	To close the owner's drawing account to the capital account.		

After the adjusting and closing entries have been recorded and posted, the Income Summary and J. Madison, Capital accounts appear as shown below. Although we have labeled these entries for illustrative purposes, they would ordinarily not be labeled in the actual accounts.

Income Summary

Beginning Inventory, Purchases, Expenses, and Other Debits	427,450	Ending Inventory, Sales, and Other Credits	453,700
Net Income	26,250		
	453,700		453,700

J. Madison, Capital

Withdrawals	4,800	Beginning Balance	118,000
Ending Balance	139,450	Net Income	26,250
	144,250		144,250
		Ending Balance	139,450

POST-CLOSING TRIAL BALANCE   As we explained in Chapter 4, another trial balance of the ledger accounts is customarily taken after the books have been

EXHIBIT 5–10

Madison Electronics Company
Post-closing Trial Balance
December 31, 19XX

	Debit	Credit
Cash	$ 20,420	
Accounts Receivable	28,000	
Inventory	91,000	
Prepaid Insurance	480	
Supplies on Hand	1,400	
Delivery Equipment	32,000	
Accumulated Depreciation		$ 9,600
Accounts Payable		13,750
Salaries Payable		500
Long-term Notes Payable		10,000
J. Madison, Capital		139,450
	$173,300	$173,300

closed to ensure that the ledger balances and is ready for recording transactions in the next period. A December 31 post-closing trial balance for Madison Electronics Company is shown in Exhibit 5–10.

REVERSING ENTRIES   If Madison Electronics Company employs reversing entries in its accounting system (see Chapter 4), it would make only one reversing entry on January 1. The only accrual made by the firm at the end of December was for salespersons' salaries; therefore, the entry to reverse this accrual would be

Jan. 1	Salaries Payable	500	
	Sales Salaries Expense		500
	To reverse accrual of salespersons' salaries made on December 31.		

DEMONSTRATION PROBLEM FOR REVIEW

Sportcraft, a wholesaler of sporting goods, had the following trial balance at December 31 of the current year:

Sportcraft
Trial Balance
December 31, 19XX

	Debit	Credit
Cash	$ 6,200	
Accounts Receivable	28,000	
Inventory, January 1	45,000	
Office Supplies on Hand	800	
Prepaid Insurance	2,100	
Land	34,000	
Building	82,000	
Accumulated Depreciation—Building		$ 16,000
Office Equipment	21,300	
Accumulated Depreciation—Office Equipment		5,300
Accounts Payable		19,000
J. Moran, Capital		161,200
J. Moran, Drawing	10,000	
Sales		252,000
Sales Discounts	3,500	
Purchases	151,000	
Purchases Returns and Allowances		2,400
Transportation In	8,200	
Sales Salaries Expense	27,600	
Transportation Out	7,800	
Advertising Expense	6,100	
Office Salaries Expense	22,300	
	$455,900	$455,900

The following information is available at December 31:

(1) Office supplies on hand at December 31 are $250.

(2) Prepaid insurance at December 31 is $1,500.

(3) Depreciation for the year is building, $2,000; office equipment, $2,400.

(4) Salaries payable at December 31 are sales salaries, $300; office salaries, $200.

(5) Inventory at December 31 is $43,500.

REQUIRED
(a) Prepare a 10-column worksheet for the year.
(b) Prepare a classified income statement for the year. Of the insurance expense and depreciation expense on the building, 75% is treated as selling expense and 25% is treated as administrative expense.
(c) Prepare a classified balance sheet at December 31.
(d) Prepare adjusting entries in general journal form.
(e) Prepare closing entries in general journal form.

SOLUTION TO DEMONSTRATION PROBLEM

(a)

Sportcraft
Worksheet
For the Year Ended December 31, 19XX

	Trial Balance Debit	Trial Balance Credit	Adjustments Debit	Adjustments Credit	Adjusted Trial Balance Debit	Adjusted Trial Balance Credit	Income Statement Debit	Income Statement Credit	Balance Sheet Debit	Balance Sheet Credit
Cash	6,200				6,200				6,200	
Accounts Receivable	28,000				28,000				28,000	
Inventory, January 1	45,000				45,000		45,000			
Office Supplies on Hand	800			(1) 550	250				250	
Prepaid Insurance	2,100			(2) 600	1,500				1,500	
Land	34,000				34,000				34,000	
Building	82,000				82,000				82,000	
Accumulated Depreciation—Building		16,000		(3) 2,000		18,000				18,000
Office Equipment	21,300				21,300				21,300	
Accumulated Depreciation—Office Equipment		5,300		(3) 2,400		7,700				7,700
Accounts Payable		19,000				19,000				19,000
J. Moran, Capital		161,200				161,200				161,200
J. Moran, Drawing	10,000				10,000				10,000	
Sales		252,000				252,000		252,000		
	252,000	252,000				252,000				

Account	Trial Balance Dr	Trial Balance Cr	Adjustments Dr	Adjustments Cr	Adjusted Trial Balance Dr	Adjusted Trial Balance Cr	Income Statement Dr	Income Statement Cr	Balance Sheet Dr	Balance Sheet Cr
Sales Discounts	3,500				3,500		3,500			
Purchases	151,000				151,000		151,000			
Purchases Returns and Allowances		2,400				2,400		2,400		
Transportation In	8,200				8,200		8,200			
Sales Salaries Expense	27,600		(4) 300		27,900		27,900			
Transportation Out	7,800				7,800		7,800			
Advertising Expense	6,100				6,100		6,100			
Office Salaries Expense	22,300		(4) 200		22,500		22,500			
	455,900	455,900								
Office Supplies Expense			(1) 550		550		550			
Insurance Expense			(2) 600		600		600			
Depreciation Expense—Building			(3) 2,000		2,000		2,000			
Depreciation Expense—Office Equipment			(3) 2,400		2,400		2,400			
Salaries Payable				(4) 500		500				500
			6,050	6,050	460,800	460,800				
Inventory, December 31								43,500	43,500	
							277,550	297,900	226,750	206,400
Net Income							20,350			20,350
							297,900	297,900	226,750	226,750

(b)

Sportcraft
Income Statement
For the Year Ended December 31, 19XX

Revenue
Sales		$252,000	
Less: Sales Discounts		3,500	
Net Sales			$248,500

Cost of Goods Sold
Inventory, January 1		$ 45,000	
Add: Net Cost of Purchases			
Purchases	$151,000		
Less: Purchases Returns and Allowances	2,400		
	$148,600		
Add: Transportation In	8,200	156,800	
Cost of Goods Available for Sale		$201,800	
Less: Inventory, December 31		43,500	
Cost of Goods Sold			158,300
Gross Profit on Sales			$ 90,200

Operating Expenses
Selling Expenses
Sales Salaries Expense	$ 27,900		
Transportation Out	7,800		
Advertising Expense	6,100		
Insurance Expense	450		
Depreciation Expense—Building	1,500		
Total Selling Expenses		$43,750	

Administrative Expenses
Office Salaries Expense	$ 22,500		
Office Supplies Expense	550		
Insurance Expense	150		
Depreciation Expense—Building	500		
Depreciation Expense—Office Equipment	2,400		
Total Administrative Expenses		26,100	
Total Operating Expenses			69,850
Net Income			$ 20,350

(c)

Sportcraft
Balance Sheet
December 31, 19XX

ASSETS

Current Assets

Cash		$ 6,200
Accounts Receivable		28,000
Inventory		43,500
Office Supplies on Hand		250
Prepaid Insurance		1,500
Total Current Assets		$ 79,450

Long-term Assets

Land		$ 34,000	
Building	$82,000		
Less: Accumulated Depreciation	18,000	64,000	
Office Equipment	$21,300		
Less: Accumulated Depreciation	7,700	13,600	
Total Long-term Assets			111,600
Total Assets			$191,050

LIABILITIES AND OWNER'S EQUITY

Current Liabilities

Accounts Payable		$ 19,000
Salaries Payable		500
Total Current Liabilities		$ 19,500

Owner's Equity

J. Moran, Capital*	171,550
Total Liabilities and Owner's Equity	$191,050

*$161,200 Beginning Balance + $20,350 Net Income − $10,000 Withdrawals = $171,550

(d) Adjusting entries:

Dec. 31	Office Supplies Expense	550	
	Office Supplies on Hand		550
	To reflect as expense supplies used		
	during the year.		
31	Insurance Expense	600	
	Prepaid Insurance		600
	To reflect as expense insurance		
	expired during the year.		
31	Depreciation Expense—Building	2,000	
	Depreciation Expense—Office Equipment	2,400	
	Accumulated Depreciation—Building		2,000
	Accumulated Depreciation—		
	Office Equipment		2,400
	To record depreciation on building		
	and office equipment.		
31	Sales Salaries Expense	300	
	Office Salaries Expense	200	
	Salaries Payable		500
	To reflect salaries earned by		
	employees but unpaid at December 31.		

(e) Closing entries:

Dec. 31	Income Summary	277,550	
	Inventory (January 1)		45,000
	Sales Discounts		3,500
	Purchases		151,000
	Transportation In		8,200
	Sales Salaries Expense		27,900
	Transportation Out		7,800
	Advertising Expense		6,100
	Office Salaries Expense		22,500
	Office Supplies Expense		550
	Insurance Expense		600
	Depreciation Expense—Building		2,000
	Depreciation Expense—		
	Office Equipment		2,400
	To close the beginning inventory		
	and income statement accounts		
	with debit balances.		

31	Inventory (December 31)	43,500	
	Sales	252,000	
	Purchases Returns and		
	Allowances	2,400	
	Income Summary		297,900
	To record the ending inventory		
	and to close income statement		
	accounts with credit balances.		
31	Income Summary	20,350	
	J. Moran, Capital		20,350
	To close the Income Summary		
	account and transfer net income		
	to the owner's capital account.		
31	J. Moran, Capital	10,000	
	J. Moran, Drawing		10,000
	To close the drawing account.		

KEY POINTS TO REMEMBER

(1) Purchase and sales invoices are the basic documents initiating entries for merchandise transactions.

(2) Cash discounts (for prompt payment during the discount period) are normally reflected in financial records, but trade discounts are not. Cash discounts are calculated on the billed price of merchandise retained in a purchase or sale— not on amounts representing returns and allowances or transportation costs.

(3) The terms prepaid and collect designate the party expected to remit to the freight company. The party who is to bear transportation costs is designated by the terms F.O.B. destination (seller) and F.O.B. shipping point (buyer).

(4) A major difference between the financial statements of service firms and merchandising firms is the inclusion of cost of goods sold in the income statement of merchandising firms. Cost of goods sold is deducted from net sales to obtain gross profit. Expenses are then deducted from gross profit to arrive at net income.

(5) A firm using a periodic inventory system determines its inventory only at the end of a period. In the closing procedures, the beginning inventory is closed to Income Summary, together with the income statement accounts having debit balances. The ending inventory is recorded in the entry to close the income statement accounts with credit balances to Income Summary.

(6) The final steps in the closing procedure are to close the Income Summary account—representing net income or net loss—to the owner's capital account (Retained Earnings in a corporation) and to close the owner's drawing account to the capital account.

QUESTIONS

5–1 What is the most significant difference between the income statement of a service firm and that of a merchandising firm?

5–2 What is meant by *gross profit on sales*, and of what significance is this item to management?

5–3 Explain the nature, purpose, and key information appearing on each of the following forms:
(a) Purchase requisition.
(b) Purchase order.
(c) Sales invoice.
(d) Receiving report.
(e) Credit memorandum.

5–4 Differentiate between (a) credit period and discount period and (b) cash discounts and trade discounts.

5–5 For the accounts titled Sales Returns and Allowances and Purchases Returns and Allowances, indicate (a) the justification for their use; (b) their normal balances (debit or credit); and (c) their position in the financial statements.

5–6 Explain the appropriate treatment in the income statement of the accounts Transportation In and Transportation Out.

5–7 Under each of the following selling terms, who (buyer or seller) would *bear* the freight cost and who would *remit* to the freight company?
(a) F.O.B. shipping point, freight collect.
(b) F.O.B. destination, freight prepaid.
(c) F.O.B. shipping point, freight prepaid.
(d) F.O.B. destination, freight collect.

5–8 On April 2, Wood Company purchased $810 worth of merchandise from Lord Company, F.O.B. shipping point, freight collect, terms 2/10, n/30. On April 4, Wood Company returned $60 of the goods for credit. On April 5, Wood paid $40 freight on the shipment. If Wood settles its account with Lord Company on April 11, how much would the company remit?

5–9 How much does Wood remit in Question 5–8 if the terms are F.O.B. destination rather than F.O.B. shipping point?

5–10 A wholesale firm's gross purchases during an accounting period totaled $40,000, and Transportation In was $1,000. If the firm returned goods amounting to $2,000 and took $500 in purchases discounts during the period, what was the net purchases cost for the period?

5–11 When an unadjusted trial balance of the general ledger is taken for a merchandising firm on a periodic inventory basis, does the beginning inventory or the ending inventory appear in the trial balance? Explain.

5–12 The beginning inventory for a merchandising firm was $52,000 and the ending inventory is $46,000. If the net cost of purchases was $90,000 and net sales was $136,000, what was the gross profit?

5–13 A portion of a worksheet for a merchandising firm is shown below. Identify the columns—A, B, C, or D—into which the balance of any of the listed accounts should be extended.

	Income Statement		Balance Sheet	
	Debit	**Credit**	**Debit**	**Credit**
	(A)	**(B)**	**(C)**	**(D)**
Inventory (Beginning)				
Sales				
Sales Returns and Allowances				
Purchases				
Purchases Returns and Allowances				
Purchases Discounts				
Transportation In				
Salaries Payable				
Inventory (Ending)				

5–14 Define (a) current assets and (b) current liabilities.

5–15 The Wilson Company had net sales of $400,000, cost of goods sold of $260,000, and net income of $24,000. Compute (a) its gross margin percentage and (b) its return on sales.

5–16 A firm using the net price method of recording merchandise purchases bought goods with a list price of $500, terms 2/10, n/30. What amount would be debited to the Purchases account?

EXERCISES

5–17 On April 1, Barr Company sold merchandise with a list price of $2,400. For each of the sales terms below, determine (a) the amount recorded as a sale and (b) the proper amount of cash received.

	Applicable Trade Discount (%)	Credit Terms	Date Paid
(1)	30	2/10, n/30	April 8
(2)	40	1/10, n/30	April 15
(3)	—	2/10, n/30	April 11
(4)	20	1/15, n/30	April 14
(5)	40	n/30	April 28

5–18 For each of the following Adams Company purchases, assume that credit terms are 2/10, n/30 and that any credit memorandum was issued and known before Adams Company made the payments.

	Amount of Sale	Shipping Terms	Prepaid Freight (by seller)	Credit Memorandum
(1)	$ 600	F.O.B. shipping point	$40	$100
(2)	1,000	F.O.B. destination	70	200
(3)	800	F.O.B. shipping point	—	50
(4)	2,000	F.O.B. shipping point	50	—

In each case, determine (a) the appropriate cash discount available and (b) the cash remitted if the payment is made within the discount period.

5–19 On June 8, Mann Company sold merchandise listing for $800 to Hall Company,
terms 2/10, n/30. On June 12, $250 worth of the merchandise was returned
because it was the wrong color. On June 18, Mann Company received a check
for the amount due.

Record the general journal entries made by Mann Company for the above
transactions.

5–20 On March 10, Chan Company purchased $4,000 worth of merchandise from
Brink Company, terms 1/10, n/30, F.O.B. shipping point. On March 12, Chan
paid $60 freight on the shipment. On March 15, Chan returned $400 worth
of the merchandise for credit. Final payment was made to Brink on March 19.
Chan Company records purchases at invoice price.
(a) Give the general journal entries that Chan should make on March 12, March
15, and March 19.
(b) Give the entries that Chan should make on these three dates if the terms
are F.O.B. destination.

5–21 The following are selected transactions of Jordan, Inc.:

April 20   Sold and shipped on account to Baker Stores merchandise listing for
$900, terms 2/10, n/30.
27   Baker Stores returned defective merchandise billed at $50 on April 20.
29   Received from Baker Stores a check for full settlement of the April 20
transaction.

Record, in general journal form, the above transactions as they would appear
on the books of (a) Jordan, Inc. and (b) Baker Stores. Baker Stores records
purchases at invoice price.

5–22 Jason, Inc., uses the net price method of recording purchases. On July 1, the
firm purchased merchandise for $650, terms 2/10, n/30. On July 5, the firm
returned $150 of the merchandise to the seller. Payment of the account occurred
on July 8.
(a) Give the general journal entries for July 1, July 5, and July 8.
(b) Assuming that the account was settled on July 14, give the entry for payment on that date.

5–23 The diagram below contains portions of five unrelated income statements,
each with certain data omitted. Fill in the lettered blanks with the appropriate
amounts.

	(1)	(2)	(3)	(4)	(5)
Net Sales	$60,000	$ (d)	$90,000	$70,000	$160,000
Beginning Inventory	10,000	20,000	(g)	25,000	(m)
Net Cost of Purchases	40,000	(e)	60,000	40,000	90,000
Cost of Goods					
Available for Sale	(a)	(f)	90,000	(j)	(n)
Ending Inventory	12,000	15,000	(h)	(k)	70,000
Cost of Goods Sold	(b)	60,000	(i)	(l)	(o)
Gross Profit	(c)	20,000	15,000	24,000	10,000

5-24 A company's operating figures for four consecutive periods are given below.

	Period			
	(1)	**(2)**	**(3)**	**(4)**
Beginning Inventory	$35,000	$ 40,000	$24,000	$18,000
Net Cost of Purchases	50,000	60,000	46,000	40,000
Cost of Goods Available for Sale	$85,000	$100,000	$70,000	$58,000
Ending Inventory	25,000	30,000	20,000	20,000
Cost of Goods Sold	$60,000	$ 70,000	$50,000	$38,000

Assuming that the following errors were made, compute the correct cost of goods sold for each period:

Period	Error in Ending Inventory
1	Overstated $3,000
2	Understated $1,000
3	Overstated $2,000

5-25 A portion of the December 31 worksheet for Link Distributors is shown below. For simplicity, all operating expenses have been combined.

	Income Statement		Balance Sheet	
	Debit	**Credit**	**Debit**	**Credit**
Inventory, January 1	20,000			
Link, Capital				80,000
Link, Drawing			3,000	
Sales		200,000		
Sales Returns and Allowances	1,500			
Sales Discounts	2,500			
Purchases	120,000			
Purchases Returns and Allowances		1,000		
Purchases Discounts		2,000		
Transportation In	3,000			
Operating Expenses	50,000			
Inventory, December 31		22,000	22,000	

Using the given information, prepare the general journal entries to close the books.

PROBLEMS

5-26 The following transactions occurred between the Lennox Company and Wisco Stores, Inc. during March of the current year.

Mar. 8 Lennox sold $3,200 worth of merchandise to Wisco Stores, terms 2/10, n/30, F.O.B. shipping point. Lennox paid freight charges of $60 and added it to the amount of the invoice for the merchandise.

Mar. 12 Wisco Stories notified Lennox of a $400 error in pricing the merchandise shipped on March 8. Lennox issued a credit memorandum for this amount.

17 Lennox received full payment for the net amount due from the March 8 sale.

20 Wisco Stores returned goods that had been billed originally at $150. Lennox issued a check.

REQUIRED

Record the above transactions in general journal form as they would appear on (a) the books of Lennox Company and (b) the books of Wisco Stores, Inc. Wisco Stores, Inc. records purchases at invoice price.

5–27 Wonder Corporation, which began business on August 1 of the current year, sells on terms of 2/10, n/30, F.O.B. shipping point. Credit terms and freight terms for its purchases vary with the supplier. Selected transactions for August are given below. Unless noted, all transactions are on account and involve merchandise held for resale. All purchases are recorded at invoice price.

Aug. 1 Purchased merchandise from Osborne, Inc., $850, terms 2/10, n/30, F.O.B. shipping point, freight collect.

4 Purchased merchandise from Oliver Company, $1,200, terms 2/10, n/30, F.O.B. destination. Freight charges of $60 were prepaid by Oliver Company.

5 Paid freight on shipment from Osborne, Inc., $60.

7 Sold merchandise to Reardon Corporation, $600.

7 Paid freight on shipment to Reardon Corporation, $35, and billed Reardon for the charges.

9 Returned $50 worth of the merchandise purchased August 1 from Osborne, Inc., because it was defective.

9 Issued a credit memorandum to Reardon Corporation for $100 worth of merchandise returned by Reardon.

10 Paid Osborne, Inc. the amount due.

14 Purchased from Randall, Inc. goods with a list price of $2,000. Wonder Corporation was entitled to a 25% trade discount; terms 1/10, n/30, F.O.B. shipping point, freight collect.

15 Paid freight on shipment from Randall, Inc., $40.

17 Received the amount due from Reardon Corporation.

18 Sold merchandise to Denton, Inc., $1,800.

19 Paid Oliver Company for the amount due on its August 4 invoice.

20 Paid freight on August 18 shipment to Denton, Inc., $65.

20 Received a credit memorandum of $200 from Randall, Inc., adjusting the price charged for merchandise purchased on August 14.

24 Paid Randall, Inc. the amount due.

28 Received the amount due from Denton, Inc.

REQUIRED

Record the transactions for Wonder Corporation in general journal form.

5–28 The unadjusted trial balance of Burton Distributors on December 31 of the current year is shown below:

Burton Distributors
Trial Balance
December 31, 19XX

	Debit	Credit
Cash	$ 7,200	
Accounts Receivable	40,500	
Inventory, January 1	69,000	
Prepaid Insurance	3,600	
Supplies on Hand	3,200	
Delivery Equipment	40,000	
Accumulated Depreciation		$ 9,500
Accounts Payable		34,800
Burton, Capital		84,000
Burton, Drawing	13,000	
Sales		406,000
Sales Returns and Allowances	5,800	
Sales Discounts	7,300	
Purchases	261,000	
Purchases Returns and Allowances		2,600
Purchases Discounts		5,100
Transportation In	6,400	
Salaries Expense	54,000	
Rent Expense	20,000	
Gas, Oil, and Repairs Expense	9,200	
Utilities Expense	1,800	
	$542,000	$542,000

The following data are available at December 31:
(1) Prepaid insurance at December 31 is $1,200.
(2) Supplies on hand at December 31 amount to $2,100.
(3) Depreciation on the delivery equipment is 20% per year.
(4) At December 31, the company owes its employees $600 in salaries.
(5) At December 31, the company has not recorded a utility bill for $140.
(6) Inventory at December 31 is $72,000.

REQUIRED
Prepare a 10-column worksheet for Burton Distributors for 19XX.

5–29 The following selected information is available for the Gardner Wholesale Company for March of the current year.

Purchases	$42,000
Sales	97,500
Transportation In	1,000
Purchases Discounts	1,200
Inventory, March 1	36,000
Inventory, March 31	21,000
Purchases Returns and Allowances	800

Sales Returns and Allowances	$ 1,700
Transportation Out	460
Rent Expense	1,650
Sales Salaries Expense	19,250
Sales Discounts	1,800
Depreciation Expense—Office Equipment	80
Office Supplies Expense	240
Office Salaries Expense	6,400
Advertising Expense	1,250
Insurance Expense (a selling expense)	170

REQUIRED

(a) Prepare the March income statement for Gardner Wholesale Company.

(b) Calculate the ratio of gross profit to net sales and express it as a percentage.

(c) Calculate the ratio of net income to net sales and express it as a percentage.

5–30 Winslow Trading Company, whose accounting year ends on December 31, had the following normal balances in its general ledger at December 31 of the current year:

Cash	$ 6,800	Sales	$300,000
Accounts Receivable	12,500	Sales Returns and	
Inventory, January 1	52,000	Allowances	2,200
Prepaid Insurance	3,000	Sales Discounts	2,800
Office Supplies on Hand	2,100	Purchases	186,000
Furniture and Fixtures	10,500	Purchases Returns and	
Accumulated Depreciation—		Allowances	1,900
Furniture and Fixtures	2,500	Purchases Discounts	2,100
Delivery Equipment	42,000	Transportation In	4,500
Accumulated Depreciation—		Sales Salaries Expense	40,000
Delivery Equipment	6,000	Delivery Expense	6,400
Accounts Payable	15,500	Advertising Expense	2,800
Notes Payable (Long-term)	20,000	Rent Expense	7,200
M. Winslow, Capital	68,000	Office Salaries Expense	28,000
M. Winslow, Drawing	4,800	Utilities Expense	2,400

Rent expense and utilities expense are administrative expenses. During the year, the accounting department prepared monthly statements using worksheets, but no adjusting entries were made in the journals and ledgers. Data for the year-end procedures are as follows:

(1) Prepaid insurance, December 31 (75% of insurance expense is classified as selling expense, and 25% is classified as administrative expense)	$ 600
(2) Office supplies on hand, December 31	950
(3) Depreciation expense on furniture and fixtures for the year (an administrative expense)	800
(4) Depreciation expense on delivery equipment for the year	6,450

(5) Sales salaries payable, December 31	$ 500
(6) Office salaries payable, December 31	400
(7) Inventory, December 31	49,500

REQUIRED

(a) Prepare a worksheet for the current year.
(b) Prepare a classified income statement for the year.
(c) Prepare a classified balance sheet at December 31.
(d) Record the necessary adjusting entries in general journal form.
(e) Record the closing entries in general journal form.
(f) Record any necessary reversing entries in general journal form.

5–31 While on her way to the bank to negotiate a loan, Sarah Kelley, the treasurer of Arrowhead, Inc., realizes that the income statement for the current year is missing from her papers. She has a December 31 balance sheet, however, and after searching through her papers, locates an unadjusted trial balance taken at December 31. She arrives at your office shortly before her appointment at the bank and asks your assistance in preparing an income statement for the year. The available data at December 31 are given below:

	Unadjusted Trial Balance Debit	Credit	Balance Sheet Data
Cash	$ 32,000		$ 32,000
Accounts Receivable	48,500		48,500
Inventory	75,000		81,000
Office Supplies on Hand	3,500		2,400
Prepaid Insurance	2,800		1,600
Delivery Equipment	54,000		54,000
Accumulated Depreciation		$ 16,500	(24,500)
			$195,000
Accounts Payable		36,000	$ 36,000
Salaries Payable			1,000
Capital Stock		100,000	100,000
Retained Earnings		32,000	58,000
Sales		250,000	
Purchases	165,000		
Rent Expense	7,200		
Salaries Expense	34,000		
Advertising Expense	4,100		
Delivery Expense	8,400		
	$434,500	$434,500	$195,000

REQUIRED

Use the given data to prepare the year's income statement for Arrowhead, Inc. for Sarah Kelley.

5–32 The first six columns of a 10-column worksheet prepared for the Viking Sport Shop are as follows:

	Trial Balance Debit	Trial Balance Credit	Adjustments Debit	Adjustments Credit	Adjusted Trial Balance Debit	Adjusted Trial Balance Credit
Cash	8,000				8,000	
Inventory, January 1	36,000				36,000	
Office Supplies on Hand	2,000			1,200	800	
Prepaid Insurance	1,200				1,200	
Equipment	30,000				30,000	
Accumulated Depreciation		6,000		2,000		8,000
Accounts Payable		9,000				9,000
J. Viking, Capital		47,000				47,000
J. Viking, Drawing	5,000				5,000	
Sales		120,000				120,000
Purchases	65,000				65,000	
Transportation In	1,800				1,800	
Rent Expense	3,000				3,000	
Salaries Expense	30,000		600		30,600	
	182,000	182,000				
Depreciation Expense			2,000		2,000	
Salaries Payable				600		600
Office Supplies Expense			1,200		1,200	
			3,800	3,800	184,600	184,600
Inventory, December 31						
Net Income						

In completing the worksheet, Viking's accountant made the following errors:
(1) The adjustment for expired insurance was omitted; premiums amounting to $800 expired during the year.
(2) The $5,000 balance of Viking's drawing account was extended as a debit in the income statement columns.
(3) The $600 credit to Salaries Payable was extended as a credit in the income statement columns.
(4) The January 1 Inventory balance of $36,000 was extended as a credit in the income statement columns.
(5) The December 31 Inventory balance of $40,000 was recorded as a debit in the income statement columns and as a credit in the balance sheet columns.

REQUIRED
(a) Which of the errors would cause the worksheet not to balance?
(b) Without completing the worksheet, calculate the net income for the year. Assume that the accountant made no other errors and that the worksheet totals, before adding net income or net loss, were:

	Debit	Credit
Income Statement	$148,600	$156,600
Balance Sheet	40,000	104,000

ALTERNATE PROBLEMS

5—26A Badger Distributing Company had the following transactions with Haley Stores, Inc.:

Nov. 10 Badger sold and shipped $3,000 worth of merchandise to Haley Stores, terms 2/10, n/30, F.O.B. shipping point. Badger paid freight charges of $180 and added the amount to the invoice for the merchandise.

14 Upon notification from Haley Stores, Inc., Badger issued a credit memo for $300 adjusting the price originally charged for the merchandise sold on November 10.

19 Badger received payment in full for the net amount due on the November 10 sale.

24 Haley Stores, Inc. returned goods that had originally been billed at $100. Badger issued a check.

REQUIRED

Record the above transactions in general journal form as they would appear (a) on the books of Badger Distributing Company and (b) on the books of Haley Stores, Inc. Haley Stores, Inc. records purchases at invoice price.

5—27A The Conway Company was established on July 1 of the current year. Its sales terms are 2/10, n/30, F.O.B. destination. Credit terms for its purchases vary with the supplier. Selected transactions for the first month of operations are given below. Unless noted, all transactions are on account and involve merchandise held for resale. All purchases are recorded at invoice price.

July 1 Purchased goods from Weston, Inc., $650; terms 1/10, n/30, F.O.B. shipping point, freight collect.

2 Purchased goods from Rider Company, $1,500, terms 2/10, n/30, F.O.B. destination. Freight charges of $60 were prepaid by Rider.

3 Paid freight on shipment from Weston, $40.

5 Sold merchandise to Ellis, Inc., $875.

5 Paid freight on shipment to Ellis, Inc., $70.

8 Returned $50 worth of the goods purchased July 1 from Weston, Inc. because some goods were damaged.

9 Issued credit memorandum to Ellis, Inc. for $75 worth of merchandise returned.

10 Paid Weston, Inc. the amount due.

10 Purchased goods from Davis Company with a list price of $750. Conway was entitled to a $33\frac{1}{3}$% trade discount; terms 2/10, n/30, F.O.B. destination, freight collect.

11 Paid freight on shipment from Davis Company, $55.

15 Received the amount due from Ellis, Inc.

15 Sold merchandise to Moore Corporation, $1,500.

16 Mailed a check to Rider Company for the net amount due on its July 2 invoice.

17 Received a notice from Moore Corporation stating that it had paid freight of $100 on the July 15 shipment.

July 18   Received a credit memorandum of $50 from Davis Company, adjusting the price charged for the merchandise purchased on July 10.

   19   Paid Davis Company the amount due.

   25   Received the amount due from Moore Corporation.

REQUIRED

Record the transactions for Conway Company in general journal form.

5–28A The unadjusted trial balance of Dane Corporation on December 31 of the current year is shown below:

Dane Corporation
Trial Balance
December 31, 19XX

	Debit	Credit
Cash	$ 20,900	
Accounts Receivable	30,600	
Inventory, January 1	48,000	
Prepaid Insurance	900	
Supplies on Hand	1,800	
Furniture and Fixtures	15,000	
Accumulated Depreciation—Furniture and Fixtures		$ 1,800
Delivery Equipment	34,000	
Accumulated Depreciation—Delivery Equipment		10,000
Accounts Payable		8,200
Capital Stock		100,000
Retained Earnings		24,000
Sales		185,000
Sales Returns and Allowances	2,400	
Sales Discounts	2,000	
Purchases	108,000	
Purchases Returns and Allowances		2,800
Purchases Discounts		1,400
Transportation In	5,600	
Salaries Expense	42,000	
Rent Expense	10,400	
Delivery Expense	7,400	
Utilities Expense	4,200	
	$333,200	$333,200

The following data are available at December 31:

(1) Prepaid insurance at December 31 is $500.

(2) Supplies on hand at December 31 amount to $1,200.

(3) Depreciation on the furniture and fixtures is 10% per year.

(4) Depreciation on the delivery equipment is 25% per year.

(5) At December 31, accrued salaries total $800.

(6) Inventory at December 31 is $56,000.

REQUIRED

Prepare a 10-column worksheet for Dane Corporation for 19XX.

5–29A The following selected information is available for the Spartan Trading Company for February of the current year.

Purchases	$ 65,000
Sales	124,000
Transportation In	1,200
Purchases Discounts	900
Inventory, February 1	24,500
Inventory, February 28	18,000
Purchases Returns and Allowances	1,500
Sales Returns and Allowances	1,800
Transportation Out	4,300
Rent Expense	5,600
Salaries Expense	20,300
Sales Discounts	2,200
Depreciation Expense	2,800

REQUIRED
(a) Prepare a February income statement for Spartan Trading Company.
(b) Calculate the ratio of gross profit to net sales and express it as a percentage.
(c) Express the ratio of net profit to net sales as a percentage.

5–30A Redstone Distributors, whose accounting year ends on December 31, had the following balances in its ledger accounts at December 31 of the current year:

Cash	$18,400	Sales	$595,000
Accounts Receivable	24,500	Sales Returns and	
Inventory, January 1	64,000	Allowances	4,800
Prepaid Insurance	3,600	Sales Discounts	8,200
Office Supplies on Hand	2,500	Purchases	398,000
Furniture and Fixtures	14,000	Purchases Returns and	
Accumulated Depreciation—		Allowances	1,600
Furniture and Fixtures	5,500	Purchases Discounts	4,200
Delivery Equipment	38,000	Transportation In	17,400
Accumulated Depreciation—		Sales Salaries Expense	51,000
Delivery Equipment	12,200	Delivery Expense	18,600
Accounts Payable	36,700	Advertising Expense	12,900
Notes Payable (Long-term)	10,000	Rent Expense	15,000
L. Redstone, Capital	70,000	Office Salaries Expense	36,000
L. Redstone, Drawing	4,000	Utilities Expense	4,300

Rent expense and utilities expense are administrative expenses. During the year, the accounting department prepared monthly statements using worksheets, but no adjusting entries were made in the journals and ledgers. Data for the year-end procedures are as follows:

(1) Prepaid insurance, December 31 (insurance expense
   is classified as a selling cost) $ 1,200
(2) Office supplies on hand, December 31   800
(3) Depreciation expense on furniture and fixtures
   for the year (an administrative expense)   1,400

(4) Depreciation expense on delivery equipment for the year	$ 6,400
(5) Sales salaries payable, December 31	700
(6) Office salaries payable, December 31	300
(7) Inventory, December 31	62,500

REQUIRED
(a) Prepare a worksheet for the current year.
(b) Prepare a classified income statement for the current year.
(c) Prepare a classified balance sheet at December 31.
(d) Make the necessary adjusting entries in general journal form.
(e) Make the closing entries in general journal form.
(f) Make any necessary reversing entries in general journal form.

BUSINESS DECISION PROBLEM

This year's income statement for Olympic Wholesalers is given below in condensed form.

Sales	$375,000
Cost of Goods Sold	250,000
Gross Profit	$125,000
Operating Expenses	88,500
Net Income	$ 36,500

Olympic allows its customers a trade discount of 25% of list price. To arrive at the list price, Olympic adds a mark-up of 100% to its cost.

Olympic's president asks you to evaluate a proposal she has received from the sales manager to improve the company's return on sales. The memo from the sales manager states, "I suggest we permit our customers a trade discount of 30% rather than 25%. My estimates show that with the higher trade discount, we will sell 30% more units next year than this year. We can achieve this increase volume with only a 10% increase in operating expenses."

REQUIRED
(a) Compute Olympic's return on sales for this year.
(b) Compute what Olympic's return on sales will be if the sales manager's proposal is accepted and his projections are correct. Support this computation with an income statement showing the effect of the sales manager's proposal.
(c) What is your recommendation with respect to the sales manager's proposal?

6

Data Processing: Manual and Electronic Systems

I in the preceding chapters, we limited our discussion of the processing of accounting transactions to recording in a general journal and posting to a general ledger. Such a system is satisfactory for introducing basic accounting procedures. However, for two reasons, this method would be inadequate for a business having even a moderate number of transactions. First, recording all transactions in the general journal would seriously curtail the number of transactions that could be processed in a day, simply because only one person at a time could make entries. Second, transactions recorded in a general journal must be posted individually, resulting in a great deal of posting labor. Therefore, even small- and moderate-sized firms employ *special journals* to make their systems flexible and to reduce the amount of posting required. The use of special journals is one of the features we consider in this chapter.

Our previous illustrations were simple and contained a single Accounts Receivable account and a single Accounts Payable account. Business firms that keep accounts with individual customers and creditors find it quite burdensome to work with a general ledger containing a large number of customer and creditor accounts. Therefore, firms often use control accounts in the general ledger and keep separate subsidiary ledgers to record accounts of individual customers and creditors.

Finally, in large businesses, the sheer volume of transactions and the need for fast processing and retrieval of information call for electronic data-processing systems. In the last section of this chapter, we introduce the principal types of equipment used in such systems.

CONTROL ACCOUNTS AND SUBSIDIARY LEDGERS

In Chapter 3, we entered all the charges to and payments from customers of Monroe TV Service in a single general ledger account. The following T account illustrates these transactions:

*R.S. Sullivan, "Good Old Days," as it appeared in *The Wall Street Journal,* May 9, 1983. Reprinted by permission of the author.

Accounts Receivable

Dec. 14	750	Dec. 19	500
28	2,400		

Monroe TV Service cannot bill or mail statements to customers, answer inquiries about individual customer balances, or make any collection efforts if the firm has only a single record showing total claims against customers. The company needs to know each customer's name and address, transaction dates, amounts charged for services, and amounts received on account for each account receivable.

We could solve this problem by maintaining in the general ledger an individual Account Receivable for each customer. The trial balance of such a general ledger might appear as follows:

	Trial Balance	
	Debit	Credit
Cash	$ 4,210	
Accounts Receivable—Customer A	50	
Accounts Receivable—Customer B	100	
Accounts Receivable—Customer C	200	
Accounts Receivable—Customer D	300	
(All other assets)	8,400	
(All liabilities)		$ 2,400
Owner's Equity		9,400
Sales		2,700
(All expenses)	1,240	
	$14,500	$14,500

We can easily see the limitations of this approach. The general ledger becomes unreasonably large when hundreds of customers' accounts are involved. With thousands of customers, it becomes absolutely unworkable. Alternatively, we might use one **control account** titled Accounts Receivable in the general ledger and maintain individual customer accounts in a **subsidiary ledger.** Under this approach, the general ledger is kept to a manageable size, and a detailed record of transactions with individual customers exists.

The accounts receivable subsidiary ledger, like the general ledger, may be simply a group of accounts in a binder, or it may be a file card arrangement.[1] In either case, the order is usually alphabetical by customer name. Exhibit 6–1 shows a typical form for an accounts receivable subsidiary ledger. When the three-column form is used, abnormal balances are enclosed in parentheses or shown in red. The information placed at the top of the account varies with the needs of the business and the type of customer. Often, such information concerns the granting of credit.

---

[1] In electronic data-processing systems (discussed in the last section of this chapter), the customers' ledger might be in the form of a magnetic tape file or stored internally in a computer.

EXHIBIT 6–1
Customer Account Form in Subsidiary Ledger

Name				
Address _____		Phone _____		
Employed at _____		Position _____		
Special terms _____		Maximum credit $ _____		

Date	Remarks	Debit	Credit	Balance

In the following diagram, we show the relationships between the Accounts Receivable control account in the general ledger and the accounts receivable subsidiary ledger.

Subsidiary Ledger				General Ledger Trial Balance	
				Debit	**Credit**
Customer A	Customer B		Cash	$ 4,210	
50	100	Accounts Receivable (control account)	Accounts Receivable	650	
			(All other assets)	8,400	
			(All liabilities)		$ 2,400
Customer C	Customer D		Owner's Equity		9,400
		650	Sales		2,700
200	300		(All expenses)	1,240	
				$14,500	$14,500

Because the total of all the balances in the accounts receivable subsidiary ledger must equal the balance in the Accounts Receivable control account in the general ledger, it follows that for every amount posted to the Accounts Receivable control account, an equal amount must be posted to one or more of the customers' accounts in the accounts receivable subsidiary ledger. We shall consider the specific posting procedures later in this chapter.

The control account–subsidiary ledger technique can be used to yield a detailed breakdown of many general ledger accounts, not just Accounts Receivable. Subsidiary ledgers are often used for Accounts Payable, Inventory, Buildings, and Equipment.

SPECIAL JOURNALS

Journals specifically designed in a tabular fashion to accommodate the recording of one type of transaction are called **special journals.** In addition to a general journal, most firms use at least the following special journals:

Special Journal	Specific Transactions Recorded
Sales journal	Sales on credit terms
Cash receipts journal	Receipt of cash
Invoice register (purchases journal)	Purchase of merchandise and other items on credit terms
Cash disbursements journal	Payment of cash

Cash sales are usually recorded in the cash receipts journal rather than the sales journal because cash is best controlled when *all* routine cash receipts are recorded in one journal. Similarly, a firm can increase control over cash disbursements by recording purchases of merchandise for cash in the cash disbursements journal rather than in the purchases journal.

Advantages of Special Journals

A major advantage of special journals is that their use permits a division of labor. When special journals are used, the recording step in the accounting cycle can be divided among several persons, each of whom is responsible for particular types of transactions. Persons making entries in special journals do not have to be highly skilled or have a thorough knowledge of the entire accounting system.

The use of special journals often reduces recording time. Special journal transactions of a given type need no routine explanations for each entry. Also, because special column headings are used, account titles need not be repeated as is necessary in the general journal.

Probably the most significant advantage of using special journals is the time saved in posting from the journals to the ledgers. When a general journal is used, each entry must be posted separately to the general ledger. The tabular arrangement of special journals however, often permits all entries to a given account to be added and posted as a single aggregate posting. For instance, if we entered 1,000 sales transactions in a general journal, we would make 1,000 separate credit postings to the Sales account. If we use a sales journal, however, the amounts of the 1,000 sales will appear in one money column. Therefore, we may easily obtain a total and post it as one credit to the Sales account. The sales journal has saved us the time necessary for 999 postings to the Sales account. Clearly, as more transactions are involved, more posting time is saved.

The advantages of special journals will be apparent in the examples we use on the following pages.

SALES JOURNAL

The **sales journal** of the Excel Company, shown in Exhibit 6–2, lists all credit sales for June. The information for each sale comes from a copy of the related sales invoice. Note that the tabular form of the journal is specifically designed to record sales on account.

If the same credit terms are extended to all customers, we need not describe them in the sales journal. We assume this case in our illustration. When credit terms vary from customer to customer, a column can be added to the sales journal to explain the terms of each sale.

As we might expect, the posting of any journal to the general ledger must result in equal debits and credits. Also, for any posting to a control account in the general ledger, the same total amount must be posted to one or more related subsidiary ledger accounts. Exhibit 6–2 illustrates how to post the amounts in Excel Company's sales journal.

Usually, as entries are recorded in the sales journal throughout each month, they are also posted to the accounts receivable subsidiary ledger. A customer's account then reflects a transaction within a day or two of its occurrence. Consequently, the credit office can check a customer's account balance at times other than a billing date. Daily postings to the accounts receivable subsidiary ledger also allow for cycle billings (for example, billing customers whose names begin with different letters at different times of the month). The advantage of cycle billings is that statements of account can be mailed throughout the month rather than in one large group at the end of the month.

A check mark is placed in the posting reference column of the sales journal to indicate that the amount has been posted to the customer's account. At the end of the month, when all sales have been recorded and the sales journal has been totaled and ruled, the total sales figure is posted to the general ledger as a debit to the Accounts Receivable control account and as a credit to the Sales account. Note the double posting reference at the bottom of the posting reference column in the illustration; this indicates that Accounts Receivable is account No. 12 in the ledger and Sales is account No. 40. Posting of the sales journal is now complete.

Sales journals may accommodate additional information. For example, columns could be included for sales by department or by product, so that a breakdown of sales is available to management. Columns may also be provided for sales tax information, where necessary.

EXHIBIT 6–2

Sales Journal   Page 1

Date		Invoice No.	Account	Post Ref.	Amount
19XX June	1	101	J. Norton	✓	$ 200 ⎫
	5	102	L. Ross	✓	100
	12	103	B. Travis	✓	1,000
	22	104	R. Douglas	✓	400
	29	105	M. Holton	✓	300
	30	106	E. Knight	✓	500 ⎭
				12/40	$2,500

General Ledger

Accounts Receivable (12)

6/30   S1 2,500

Sales   (40)

6/30   S1 2,500

Accounts Receivable Subsidiary Ledger

R. Douglas

6/22   S1   400

J. Norton

6/1   S1   200

M. Holton

6/29   S1   300

L. Ross

6/5   S1   100

E. Knight

6/30   S1   500

B. Travis

6/12   S1 1,000

CASH RECEIPTS JOURNAL

Transactions involving cash receipts are recorded in a **cash receipts journal** similar to that shown in Exhibit 6–3. Because cash sales and collections from credit customers occur most often, this journal provides special columns for recording

EXHIBIT 6–3

Cash Receipts Journal

Page 1

Date		Description	Cash Debit	Sales Discounts Debit	Accounts Receivable Post. Ref.	Accounts Receivable Credit	Sales Credit	Other Accounts Account	Other Accounts Post. Ref.	Other Accounts Debit	Other Accounts Credit
19XX June	1	Sale of capital stock	$ 5,000					Capital Stock	(31)		$5,000
	8	J. Norton	196	$ 4	✔	$ 200					
	10	United Bank loan	3,000					Notes Payable	(23)		3,000
	15	Cash sales, June 1–15	2,000				$2,000				
	21	B. Travis	490	10	✔	1,000		Notes Receivable	(15)	$500	
	29	M. Holton	294	6	✔	300					
	30	Cash sales, June 16–30	2,500				2,500				
			$13,480	$20		$1,500	$4,500			$500	$8,000
			(10)	(42)		(12)	(40)			(X)	(X)

General Ledger

Cash	(10)
6/30 CR1 13,480	

Accounts Receivable	(12)
6/30 S1 2,500	6/30 CR1 1,500

Notes Receivable	(15)
6/21 CR1 500	

Sales Discounts	(42)
6/30 CR1 20	

Sales	(40)
	6/30 S1 2,500
	6/30 CR1 4,500

Capital Stock	(31)
	6/1 CR1 5,000

Notes Payable	(23)
	6/10 CR1 3,000

Accounts Receivable Subsidiary Ledger

R. Douglas	
6/22 S1 400	

M. Holton	
6/29 S1 300	6/29 CR1 300

E. Knight	
6/30 S1 500	

J. Norton	
6/1 S1 200	6/8 CR1 200

L. Ross	
6/5 S1 100	

B. Travis	
6/12 S1 1,000	6/21 CR1 1,000

debits to Cash and to Sales Discounts and credits to Sales and Accounts Receivable. In addition, the columns on the right-hand side of the journal can be used for debits and credits to any other account.

Note that the entries on June 15 and June 30, debiting Cash and crediting Sales, record cash sales for a certain period. Actually, cash sales would be recorded daily rather than semimonthly, but we have recorded them only twice here for simplicity. The entry on June 8 records $196 received from J. Norton in payment of his June 1 purchase of $200, less the 2% cash discount taken. The entry debits Cash for $196, debits Sales Discounts for $4, and credits Accounts Receivable for $200. The entry for M. Holton on June 29 is similar. The June 21 entry illustrates the use of the Other Accounts debit column. Here, B. Travis settles her $1,000 billing of June 12 by giving a note for $500 of the debt and remitting $490 ($500 less the 2% discount) for the remainder. The debits are to Notes Receivable, $500, in the Other Accounts column; to Cash, $490; and to Sales Discounts, $10. The $1,000 credit to Accounts Receivable completes the entry. The entries on June 1 and June 10 represent cash received for the sale of capital stock and for a bank loan, respectively. In both cases, the Other Accounts credit column is used.

Before posting the cash receipts journal, we add each column and *balance* the journal to make sure that aggregate debits equal aggregate credits. (Note in our illustration, that $13,480 + $20 + $500 = $1,500 + $4,500 + $8,000.) The totals of the Cash, Sales Discounts, Accounts Receivable, and Sales columns are posted to the general ledger, as noted by the posting references below these columns. Also, the individual items in the Other Accounts columns are posted to the general ledger; the totals of the Other Accounts columns are used only to balance the journal and are not posted. Finally, the individual items in the Accounts Receivable column are posted to the customers' subsidiary ledger to keep this ledger in balance with the Accounts Receivable control account. The postings to the customers' accounts are indicated by a check mark (✔).

A **schedule** of the account balances in a subsidiary ledger is usually prepared at the end of each accounting period, to verify that the subsidiary ledger agrees with the related control account. The following schedule of Accounts Receivable for Excel Company indicates that the subsidiary ledger agrees with its control account in the general ledger.

Excel Company
Schedule of Accounts Receivable
June 30, 19XX

R. Douglas	$ 400
E. Knight	500
L. Ross	100
Total	$1,000

INVOICE REGISTER (PURCHASES JOURNAL)

To record purchases of merchandise on account, we can use a single-column journal similar to the sales journal considered earlier. (See Exhibit 6–2, page 211). Then, we would post each entry in the journal to the individual creditors' accounts in the accounts payable subsidiary ledger. At the end of the month, we would post the total of the amount column to the general ledger as a debit to the Purchases account and a credit to the Accounts Payable control account.

Most businesses, however, keep a multicolumn journal to record all acquisitions on account, including such items as supplies and equipment as well as merchandise. This journal may be called a purchases journal, but it is usually called an invoice register. Exhibit 6–4 illustrates an invoice register.

The illustration shows special columns for debits to Purchases, Office Supplies on Hand, and Store Supplies on Hand, as well as for credits to Accounts Payable. A column is also provided for debits to accounts for which no special column is available.

The amounts in the Accounts Payable column are posted to the accounts payable subsidiary ledger on a daily basis. A check mark in the posting reference column indicates that this has been done. At the end of the month, the columns of the register are totaled and the journal is balanced to ensure that total debits equal total credits. (In the example, $4,000 + $500 + $200 + $1,200 = $5,900.) The posting pattern for the invoice register is diagramed in Exhibit 6–4.

CASH DISBURSEMENTS JOURNAL

Exhibit 6–5 shows the June **cash disbursements journal** for Excel Company after the related transactions have been recorded and the journal balanced and posted. Note the special columns for credits to Cash and Purchases Discounts, and for debits to Accounts Payable. Ordinarily these accounts will have the most entries. Also observe that, as in the cash receipts journal, the Other Accounts columns are available for recording debits or credits to any other accounts.

The June 2 entry in Exhibit 6–5 recorded a check for $2,800, which provided the cash needed to pay employees for the last part of May. The entries on June 12 and June 19 paid the accounts payable balances due Able, Inc., and Barr Company, less 2% and 1% cash discounts, respectively. Note that $1,000 of equipment was purchased on June 15 by giving $500 cash and a note payable for $500; the latter amount was recorded in the Other Accounts credit column. Also observe that the cash purchase of merchandise for $150 is recorded in the cash disbursements journal rather than the purchases journal. The other entries in the journal are self-explanatory. Again, we have diagramed the posting format for the journal.

EXHIBIT 6–4

Invoice Register

Page 1

Date	Account Credited	Post. Ref.	Accounts Payable Credit	Purchases Debit	Office Supplies on Hand Debit	Store Supplies on Hand Debit	Other Debits		
							Account	Post. Ref.	Amount
19XX June									
2	Able, Inc.	✓	$ 700	$ 700					
9	Barr Company	✓	1,900	1,900					
14	Stix Supply Company	✓	1,200				Office Equipment	19	$1,200
18	Ward Company	✓	1,400	1,400					
25	Echo Distributors	✓	400		$400				
30	Holt, Inc.	✓	300		100	$200			
			$5,900	$4,000	$500	$200			$1,200
			(21)	(50)	(16)	(17)			(X)

Accounts Payable Subsidiary Ledger

Able, Inc.

| 6/2 IR1 | 700 |

Barr Company

| 6/9 IR1 | 1,900 |

Echo Distributors

| 6/25 IR1 | 400 |

Holt, Inc.

| 6/30 IR1 | 300 |

Stix Supply Company

| 6/14 IR1 | 1,200 |

Ward Company

| 6/18 IR1 | 1,400 |

General Ledger

Purchases (50)

| 6/30 IR1 | 4,000 |

Office Supplies on Hand (16)

| 6/30 IR1 | 500 |

Store Supplies on Hand (17)

| 6/30 IR1 | 200 |

Accounts Payable (21)

| | 6/30 IR1 | 5,900 |

Office Equipment (19)

| 6/14 IR1 | 1,200 |

EXHIBIT 6–5
Cash Disbursements Journal

Page 1

Date	Ck. No.	Description	Cash Credit	Purchases Discounts Credit	Accounts Payable Post. Ref.	Accounts Payable Debit	Other Accounts Account	Other Accounts Post. Ref.	Other Accounts Debit	Other Accounts Credit
19XX June										
2	101	Paid employees	$2,800				Wages Payable	27	$2,800	
3	102	Paid June rent	600				Rent Expense	56	600	
12	103	Able, Inc.	686	$14	✓	$ 700				
15	104	Purchased equipment	500				Store Equipment	18	1,000	
							Notes Payable	23		$500
19	105	Barr Company	1,881	19	✓	1,900				
28	106	Purchased merchandise	150				Purchases	50	150	
30	107	Insurance policy	120				Prepaid Insurance	14	120	
			$6,737	$33		$2,600			$4,670	$500
			(10)	(52)		(21)			(X)	(X)

General Ledger

Cash

6/30 CR1	13,480	6/30 CD1	6,737

(10)

Prepaid Insurance

6/30 CD1	120

(14)

Store Equipment

6/15 CD1	1,000

(18)

Accounts Payable

6/30 CD1	2,600	6/30 IR1	5,900

(21)

Purchases

6/28 CD1	150	
6/30 IR1	4,000	

(50)

Purchases Discounts

	6/30 CD1	33

(52)

Notes Payable

	6/10 CR1	3,000
	6/15 CD1	500

(23)

Wages Payable

6/2 CD1	2,800	5/31 Bal.	2,800

(27)

Rent Expense

6/3 CD1	600	

(56)

Accounts Payable Subsidiary Ledger

Able, Inc.

6/12 CD1	700	6/2 IR1	700

Holt, Inc.

	6/30 IR1	300

Barr Company

6/19 CD1	1,900	6/9 IR1	1,900

Stix Supply Company

	6/14 IR1	1,200

Echo Distributors

	6/25 IR1	400

Ward Company

	6/18 IR1	1,400

After both the invoice register and the cash disbursements journal have been posted, the Accounts Payable control account has a $3,300 balance ($5,900 − $2,600). This total agrees with the following schedule of creditors' accounts:

Excel Company
Schedule of Accounts Payable
June 30, 19XX

Echo Distributors	$ 400
Holt, Inc.	300
Stix Supply Company	1,200
Ward Company	1,400
	$3,300

USE OF THE GENERAL JOURNAL

When special journals are used, transactions that cannot be recorded appropriately in a special journal are recorded in the general journal. Examples include certain transactions involving notes receivable and notes payable, dispositions of fixed assets, write-offs of uncollectible accounts, and merchandise returns. A special posting pattern is followed for posting to subsidiary ledgers. For example, Exhibit 6–6 demonstrates the treatment of purchases returns and allowances and sales returns and allowances. Note that whenever a posting is made to the Accounts Receivable control account or the Accounts Payable control account from the general journal, a posting is also made to the related subsidiary ledger account. The latter posting is indicated by a check (✔) in the posting reference column.

EXHIBIT 6–6

General Journal   Page 1

Date		Description	Post. Ref.	Debit	Credit
19XX July	2	Sales Returns and Allowances	41	100	
		Accounts Receivable—R. Douglas	12/✔		100
		R. Douglas returned $100 merchandise for credit.			
	5	Accounts Payable—Ward Company	21/✔	70	
		Purchases Returns and Allowances	51		70
		Returned $70 merchandise to Ward Company for credit.			

THE VOUCHER SYSTEM

Many companies control expenditures with a method that is known as the **voucher system.** Under this system, a written authorization form, called a **voucher,** is initiated for every disbursement the firm makes. Before the designated responsible official approves the voucher for payment, different employees must perform several verification steps, including the following:

(1) Comparison of purchase requisition, purchase order, invoice, and receiving report for agreement of quantities, prices, types of goods, and credit terms.

(2) Verification of extensions and footings (additions) on invoice.

(3) Approval of account distribution (items to be debited).

Usually, each step in the verification process is listed on the face of the voucher, along with space for the signature or initials of the various employees responsible for accomplishing the procedures. The original copies of the purchase requisition, purchase order, invoice, and receiving report (if the item is merchandise) should be attached to the voucher. The voucher is then recorded in a book of original entry called the voucher register.

The Voucher Register

When a voucher system is used, the **voucher register** replaces the invoice register (or purchases journal) we discussed earlier. The voucher register provides columns for all items—merchandise, other assets, and services—for which payment must be made. Because all such items are recorded in the voucher register whether the transaction is for cash or on account, the voucher register also substitutes for part of the cash disbursements journal. Exhibit 6–7 shows one form of a simple voucher register.

Vouchers are entered in the voucher register in sequence. They should be prenumbered, of course, so they can be accounted for and referred to easily. All entries result in a credit to Vouchers Payable, which serves as the Accounts Payable control account for the company. The register has columns for those expense and asset accounts most frequently debited, such as Purchases, Transportation In, Office Supplies on Hand, and Delivery Expense. Debits to accounts for which columns are not provided are made in the Other Accounts section. A credit column also included in this section may be used for adjustments to vouchers and for recording purchases returns and allowances.

After vouchers have been entered in the voucher register, they are filed in an unpaid vouchers file in the order of required date of payment. In this way, the company will not miss discounts and its credit standing will not be impaired. When a voucher is processed, the due date is usually written on the face of the voucher for filing convenience.

On the due date, the voucher is removed from the unpaid file and forwarded to the firm's disbursing officer for final approval of payment. After signing the voucher, the disbursing officer has a check drawn and mailed to the payee. The

EXHIBIT 6-7

Voucher Register

Voucher No.	Date	Name	Date Paid	Check No.	Vouchers Payable Credit	Purchases Debit	Trans-portation In Debit	Office Supplies on Hand Debit	Delivery Expense Debit	Other Accounts Account	Post. Ref.	Other Accounts Debit	Other Accounts Credit
121	12-1	Olson Company	12-9	528	$ 350	$ 350							
122	12-3	Tempo Freight	12-5	527	30		$ 30						
123	12-5	Horder, Inc.	12-15	531	120			$120					
•	•	•											
146	12-21	Jones Company	12-31	539	1,200					Office Equipment	15	$1,200	
147	12-27	Green Company			250	250			$ 25				
148	12-30	Dee Delivery			25				$320				
					$18,500	$12,200	$850	$460				$4,670	
					(32)	(55)	(56)	(16)	(68)			(X)	

check number and payment date are recorded on the voucher, which is then returned to the accounting department. To safeguard against irregularities, the voucher should not be handled again by those who prepared it, and the underlying documents should be canceled or perforated by the disbursing officer before the voucher is returned to the accounting department.

After a voucher is paid, the check number and payment date are entered in the appropriate columns of the voucher register. The total unpaid ("open") vouchers at any time may be determined by adding the items in the Vouchers Payable column for which the date paid and check number columns contain no entries. This total should, of course, agree with the total of vouchers in the unpaid file and, at the end of the month, with the amount in the Vouchers Payable account.

After these procedures have been followed, the payment is recorded in a book of original entry called the check register. Finally, the vouchers are filed in numerical sequence in a paid vouchers file.

The Check Register

In a voucher system, the **check register** replaces the cash disbursements journal. Because debits to asset, expense, and other accounts are made in the voucher register, only a few columns are required in the check register. We can see in Exhibit 6–8 that these consist of a debit column for vouchers payable and credit columns for purchases discounts and cash in bank. In addition, the check register has columns for the check number, date, and voucher number.

The check register is a company's chronological record of all check payments. Since checks are entered in the check register in numerical sequence, this record provides a convenient reference for payments when either the date or check number is known.

EXHIBIT 6–8

Check Register

Check No.	Date	Payee	Voucher No.	Vouchers Payable Debit	Purchases Discounts Credit	Cash in Bank Credit
525	12–2	Able Corporation	120	$ 250		$ 250
526	12–4	Smith Company	119	500	$ 10	490
527	12–5	Tempo Freight	122	30		30
528	12–9	Olson Company	121	350	7	343
•						
•						
•						
539	12–31	Jones Company	146	1,200		1,200
				$16,700	$120	$16,580
				(32)	(57)	(11)

Under the voucher system, discounts may cause the amount of the check to differ from the gross amount of the voucher. For example, the entries for recording and paying the liability to the Olson Company for merchandise (voucher No. 121, dated December 1; see Exhibit 6–7) are summarized in general journal form as follows:

	Voucher Register				**Check Register**	
Dec. 1	Purchases	350		Dec. 9	Vouchers Payable	350
	Vouchers Payable		350		Purchases	
					Discounts	7
					Cash in Bank	343

Because both the gross and the net amounts of the liability are indicated on the voucher, this system should create no difficulty. Some companies, however, anticipate taking all discounts and prepare vouchers at the net amount. When this procedure is followed, only two money columns are needed in the check register—one for a debit to Vouchers Payable and one for a credit to Cash in Bank. If the company should miss a discount, an adjustment must be made in the voucher (or the original voucher must be canceled and a new one prepared). The bookkeeper must also record discounts lost in the general journal. (We explained the "net of discount" procedure and the Discounts Lost account in Chapter 5.) An alternative solution for handling lost discounts when the net price method is used is to provide a Discounts Lost column in the check register.

Recording Purchases Returns and Allowances

Companies usually handle purchases returns and allowances by canceling the original voucher and issuing a new one for the lower amount. Consider the following example.

Voucher No. 147 for $250, prepared for a merchandise purchase from the Green Company, is recorded in the voucher register on December 27. Assume that merchandise costing $50 is returned for credit and that a credit memo arrives on December 30. The original voucher for $250 is canceled and a reference made on it to a new voucher for $200. Furthermore, a note about the new voucher (No. 149) is made in the date paid column of the voucher register beside the entry for the original voucher. In recording the new voucher, the bookkeeper credits $200 in the Vouchers Payable column. In the Other Accounts columns, Vouchers Payable is debited for $250 and Purchases Returns and Allowances is credited for $50. The net effect of these recording procedures is a debit of $250 to Purchases, a credit of $200 to Vouchers Payable, and a credit of $50 to Purchases Returns and Allowances (see Exhibit 6–9).

Recording Partial Payments

When installment or other partial payments are made on invoices, a separate voucher is prepared for the amount of each check issued. If a single voucher has been prepared for an invoice and the firm later decides to pay in installments, the original voucher is canceled and new vouchers prepared. The cancellation of the original voucher and the issuance of new vouchers can be recorded in the same way that purchases returns are recorded.

EXHIBIT 6–9

Voucher Register

Voucher No.	Date	Name	Date Paid	Check No.	Vouchers Payable Credit	Purchases ⋯ Debit	Other Accounts		
							Account	Debit	Credit
147	12–27	Green Company	Canceled, see # 149		$250	$250			
⋅ ⋅ ⋅ ⋅						⋅ ⋅ ⋅			
149	12–30	Green Company			200		Vouchers Payable Purchases Returns and Allowances	$250	$50

ELECTRONIC DATA PROCESSING (EDP)

We have described the manner in which data-processing functions are accomplished in a manual record-keeping system. Source documents are prepared and entered manually; classification and sorting are accomplished through columnar arrangements such as journals and ledgers; computations are often done manually; and storage is achieved by manual filing. Storage is in the form of ledger accounts, subsidiary ledgers, and various files. Retrieval and summarization are entirely manual. This type of record keeping is suitable for small firms with a limited number of transactions.

Computer Processing

Today, all large business firms—and even many small firms—employ computers in processing accounting data. In recent years, advancing technology has reduced both the size and cost of computers, and small computers (**minicomputers** and **microcomputers**) are now used by many modest-sized firms. Computers offer the advantages of speed in processing, fast retrieval of data, and less human intervention in processing.

Computers perform essentially the same record-keeping functions that are performed in a manual system. Data from source documents—such as sales invoices, purchases invoices, and checks—are converted into an input mode that can be read by the computer. This transaction data is processed by means of a set of instructions, called a **program,** to prepare summaries (equivalent to journals), post to the general and subsidiary ledgers, determine balances, and prepare various reports, including financial statements.

Elements of an EDP System

An electronic data-processing system contains the following elements:

(1) A central processing unit (CPU), often called the computer, which performs arithmetic, logic, data storage while processing, and control.

(2) Associated peripheral equipment, including data-preparation, input, and output devices.

(3) Personnel and programs to provide instructions for the computer.

(4) Procedures that coordinate the preparation and processing of data and the reporting of results.

The computer and associated equipment are often referred to as the system's **hardware,** whereas the programs, written procedures, and other documentation for the system are called **software.** Exhibit 6–10 diagrams a typical system's hardware components, which are designed to perform input, processing, storage, and output functions.

INPUT　Input devices transmit the instructions to the computer and the data on which the various steps will be carried out. The major input media are punched cards, magnetic tape, magnetic characters, disks, and terminals. The devices that

THE VERSATILE MICROCOMPUTER

The computing and processing capabilities of a microcomputer approach those of the largest mainframe of only 20 years ago. Ever smaller, faster, cheaper, and easier to use, the microcomputer has enjoyed spectacular sales growth. Microcomputer sales are now running at a rate very close to two million units per year. And the business market—as opposed to the home or hobbyist market—is now accounting for the lion's share of sales.

The small business is an obviously large market. Long closed out from the advantages of computer processing by prohibitive cost, and the need for specially trained personnel, an increasing number of small businesses now find it feasible to use microcomputers to process their basic accounting transactions, to provide ready access to necessary operating data, and to handle correspondence.

But this use—essential as it is—is only the tip of the iceberg. Microcomputers expand the options available to businesses of all sizes. Using microcomputers, management can arrange data-processing facilities with much less concern for hardware costs. A micro might be used to automate activities that for reasons of cost or confidentiality are not suitable for processing on the company's mainframe. Typical business applications include the following:

(1) Forecasting, modeling, and financial statement consolidation are simplified by a microcomputer program known as an electronic spreadsheet. Once a model of relationships among a specific set of data has been established, an electronic spreadsheet program will automatically update all of the items affected by a change in one or more components. Some simple examples include the effect on the bottom line if sales double, if a division is sold, or if a union contract is settled at various possible levels.

(2) Data bases may be created for the use of individual executives or departments. Once a data base file has been created in a common format, the information can be retrieved, summarized, sorted, rearranged, or used to prepare special purpose reports. The publications department might use a microcomputer to keep its mailing list current. Personnel data, meeting calendars, information on contracts with potential customers, tickler files, almost any type of data an individual or department needs to file and find for later use could become the subject of a microcomputer application. Applications that may not be cost-effective on the company's mainframe computer might well be practicable on a micro.

(3) Graphics software available for microcomputers can reduce the time and cost associated with preparing illustrative charts for many types of presentations. The graphics capabilities of microcomputers are easily seen in the games run on home computers.

(4) Security portfolio analysis, trend analysis, and plotting are possible with specialized programs. Arrangements can be made to use the microcomputer as a terminal to access data bases of specialized information maintained by outsiders. The Source and CompuServe are such examples available in the United States. Prestel can be accessed in the United Kingdom, and so on.

Not so long ago corporate electronic data processing was highly centralized. The high cost of the computer carried with it the need to allocate service facilities principally to priority tasks. Relatively inexpensive machines with enough processing power were simply not available. That has changed—less expensive computers have put computer power into the hands of many individuals. The power of the computer is being dispersed throughout the business organization.

Microcomputers—ever smaller and less expensive machines—are accelerating this already widespread trend. Microcomputers will not replace the mainframe computer for large-scale applications, but microcomputers are becoming so inexpensive that it is quite reasonable to automate additional activities. Distributed data processing—the use of several different computers (and now including microcomputers) in different locations all connected by transmission facilities—is becoming more and more common.

From *Microcomputers: Their Use and Misuse in Your Business*, Price Waterhouse, 1983, pages 1–2.

EXHIBIT 6–10
Hardware Components of a Data-processing System

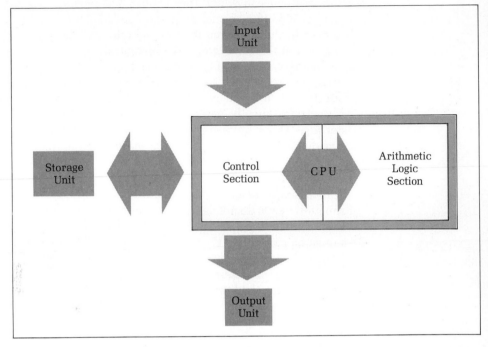

transmit data include cards readers, tape and disk drives, character recognition devices, and terminal keyboards.

In some cases, source document data are converted into machine-readable media by such data preparation devices as keypunch machines, key-to-tape devices, and key-to-disk devices. In other cases, source documents can be read directly. For example, in commercial banks, bank checks and deposit tickets with magnetic ink characters are processed directly by magnetic character readers. Data input by terminals is effected by a keyboard device. Terminal input, which is slow compared with other input devices, does not transmit large amounts of data. The use of terminals is expanding, however, because they permit direct interaction with the computer. Most terminals have a visual screen or printing capability for output. Thus, computer files can be interrogated and can print out answers in a short period of time. This aspect makes terminals useful in updating accounts when a transaction is occurring. Such processing is often referred to as **real time** processing.

PROCESSING AND STORAGE   In an EDP system, practically all of the manipulative functions of record keeping—classifying, matching, calculating, and so on—are performed automatically by the central processing unit. These functions are directed by stored instructions—a program. The control unit interprets the instructions and directs the various processing operations. If required, fairly standardized programs may be obtained from equipment vendors. In other cases, special programs are written by programmers, who usually first work out a flow-chart that shows the specific operations and decisions to be made by the computer and the sequence in which they should occur. The programmer then prepares the instructions in a special programming language, and the program is eventually stored in the computer to be called into use when needed.

All computers have temporary storage facilities that are used during processing. Permanent storage of files (such as accounts receivable master files) may be external, on media such as magnetic tapes or punched cards, when the storage capabilities of the system are limited. These files, in **off-line storage,** must be processed periodically with current transaction files in order to "update" the master files. When storage capacity within the system is adequate—most often, core or disk storage—direct access to master files is possible, and storage is **on-line.**

When storage is off-line, transaction data are usually accumulated for a period and processed in **batches** at specific intervals. Batch processing is useful when information needs do not demand the immediate processing of transactions. Data must be organized (sequenced) in a particular order, however, because all master files must be read when they are processed with a current batch of transactions. This type of processing is called **sequential** processing.

Interactive processing is possible with on-line storage. Here, master file information is available at random, and sequencing is not necessary. Transactions can be processed immediately, in any order, without batching.

OUTPUT   Output devices provide either immediately usable information or results that can be stored for further processing and analysis. Because terminals perform both input and output, they are important in providing immediately usable information. Though less immediate, printers also provide useful output information that can be analyzed and interpreted. Output often is in the form of magnetic tapes or disks when further processing is contemplated. Punched cards create a storage problem and slow down processing, so they are falling into disuse as an output medium.

The various electronic data-processing systems can be quite detailed and complex, and an elaborate discussion of such systems is beyond the scope of this book. We hope, however, that this brief introduction will help you appreciate some of the basic concepts.

KEY POINTS TO REMEMBER

(1) A single *control* account for accounts receivable and another for accounts payable are used in the general ledger, while individual customer and creditor accounts are kept in separate *subsidiary* ledgers.

(2) When the journals have been posted at the end of the accounting period, subsidiary ledger balances are totaled. These totals should agree with control account balances.

(3) The use of special journals for credit sales and purchases (sales journal and invoice register, or purchases journal) and for cash transactions (cash receipts journal and cash disbursements journal) has the following advantages: (a) It permits a division of labor and often requires fewer skilled record keepers; (b) it reduces the labor required to enter transactions; and (c) it requires fewer postings.

(4) Only sales of merchandise on account are recorded in the sales journal. Cash sales are recorded in the cash receipts journal.

(5) Purchases of any items on account are recorded in the invoice register (purchases journal). Acquisitions of any items for cash are recorded in the cash disbursements journal.

(6) Transactions that cannot be appropriately recorded in a special journal are recorded in the general journal.

(7) When master files (such as customer records) in an EDP system are stored off-line (outside the system), transactions are batched and processed *sequentially* to update records at specific time intervals.

(8) Master files that are stored on-line (within the system) can be updated at random without batching. This type of processing is sometimes called an *interactive* system.

QUESTIONS

6–1 What is a control account? What is a subsidiary ledger?

6–2 Criticize the following statement: "When a debit entry is made to a control account, one or more credit entries of the same aggregate total must be posted to the related subsidiary ledger."

6–3 Compare the benefits of using special journals with using only a general journal.

6–4 Explain why transactions should be posted to the subsidiary ledgers more frequently than to the general ledger.

6–5 How would you prove that a special journal "balances"?

6–6 Identify the type of transaction that would be entered in the following:
(a) A sales journal.   (d) A cash receipts journal.
(b) A (single-column) purchases journal. (e) A cash disbursements journal.
(c) An invoice register.

6–7 A sale made on account to Robert Ames for $400 was recorded in a single-column sales journal on April 7. On April 9, Ames returned $60 worth of merchandise for credit. Where should the seller record the entry for the sales return? What entry would be made and how would it be posted?

6–8 A $50 purchase of merchandise on account from D. Hart was properly recorded in the invoice register, but was posted as $60 to Hart's subsidiary ledger account. How might this error be discovered?

6–9 Indicate how the following errors might be discovered:
(a) The total of the Accounts Payable column of the invoice register was overstated by $50.
(b) The total of the single-column sales journal was understated by $80.

6–10 A retail merchandising firm recorded the sale of one of its delivery trucks in the sales journal. Why is this procedure incorrect?

6–11 Roy Turner keeps an invoice register and employs the net method of recording merchandise purchases. Assume that he makes an $800 purchase from Ace Company, terms 2/10, n/30. Which journal columns would he use to record the purchase, and what debits and credits would be made?

6–12 Suppose that, in Question 6–11, Turner made his remittance 20 days after the date of purchase. State the amounts involved, and describe how the payment would be recorded in a multicolumn cash disbursements journal.

6–13 Compare the advantages of electronic accounting systems with manual data processing.

6–14 What are the major elements in an EDP system?

6–15 What is meant by *hardware* in an EDP system? What is meant by *software*?

6–16 What is meant by *real time* processing in a computer processing system?

6–17 Distinguish between *sequential processing* and *interactive processing* in EDP systems.

EXERCISES

6–18 Listed below are headings for the columns into which dollar amounts are entered for four special journals and a general journal. (For the sales journal, the accounts to which the single column relates are shown.) For each column heading, show where the amounts in that column should be posted, using the space provided. Use the appropriate letter (or letters) from the following key.

Key
(a) Column total posted to general ledger
(b) Column detail posted to subsidiary ledger
(c) Column detail posted to general ledger

The correct answer for the first item is given.

Sales Journal
    (1) Accounts Receivable   a, b
    (2) Sales   _____

Invoice Register
    (3) Accounts Payable   _____
    (4) Purchases   _____
    (5) Office Supplies on Hand   _____
    (6) Store Supplies on Hand   _____
    (7) Other Debits   _____

Cash Receipts Journal
    (8) Cash   _____
    (9) Sales Discounts   _____
    (10) Accounts Receivable   _____
    (11) Sales   _____
    (12) Other Accounts—Debit   _____
    (13) Other Accounts—Credit   _____

Cash Disbursements Journal

(14) Cash   _____

(15) Purchases Discounts   _____

(16) Accounts Payable   _____

(17) Other Accounts—Debit   _____

(18) Other Accounts—Credit   _____

General Journal

(19) Debit column   _____

(20) Credit column   _____

6–19   Jordan Suppliers uses the four special journals illustrated in this chapter and a general journal. In which journal(s) would each of the following kinds of transactions be recorded?

(a) Owner's cash investment in business.

(b) Sale of merchandise for cash.

(c) Sale of merchandise on account.

(d) Return of merchandise sold on account.

(e) Owner's withdrawal of cash.

(f) Owner's withdrawal of merchandise for personal use.

(g) Collections from customers on account.

(h) Purchase of merchandise for cash.

(i) Purchase of merchandise on account.

(j) Return of merchandise purchased on account.

(k) Purchase of office supplies on account.

(l) Purchase of equipment for cash and a note payable.

6–20   John Atwood is a wholesaler of office supplies, candy products, and commercial cleaning supplies. His income statement shows sales, cost of goods sold, and gross profit amounts for each of his three product lines. He takes periodic inventories separately for each of these three departments. Design multicolumn sales and purchases journals to provide the information Atwood wants.

6–21   In recording transactions and posting from various journals, the bookkeeper made the following errors. In each case, state how the error might be discovered or whether discovery is unlikely.

(a) In the single-column sales journal, this month's total was underfooted (underadded) by $100.

(b) The total of the purchases column in the multicolumn invoice (purchases) register, correctly footed as $7,250, was posted to the Purchases account as $7,520.

(c) In the single-column sales journal, a sale to J. Webb was correctly recorded at $670, but posted to J. Weber's account as $760.

(d) A $600 remittance from R. King was correctly recorded in the cash receipts journal, but the amount was inadvertently posted to R. Kohl's account in the customers' ledger.

(e) A $260 payment to a creditor, G. Bart, was recorded in the cash disbursements journal as $160.

6–22   Describe how the following transactions would be recorded, indicating the journals used, the columns of each journal involved, and the way in which posting procedures are accomplished. Assume the four special journals illustrated in the chapter are available, together with a general journal.

(a) Purchased equipment for $2,000, giving $800 cash and a note payable for $1,200.

(b) Returned to a creditor merchandise purchased on account for $420.

(c) Owner contributed $500 cash and $6,000 in delivery equipment to the business.

(d) The business sold the delivery equipment in part (c) for $6,000 cash.

(e) Sent check for $50 to a customer, R. Wright, who had overpaid his account by this amount.

(f) Paid $80 freight to Speedy Express Company on sale to a customer, B. Young. However, terms were F.O.B. shipping point, and customer was obligated to pay freight.

PROBLEMS

Note: In the following problems, the journal forms used should correspond to those illustrated in the chapter.

6–23 The Wonder Company makes all sales on terms of 2/10, n/30. Transactions for May involving sales, related returns and allowances, and cash receipts are shown below:

May 1 Sold merchandise on account to Dunn, Inc., $500. Invoice No. 901.

      2 Collected $400 from Barker, Inc., on account.

      3 Sold merchandise for cash to S. Francis, $80.

      4 Issued credit memorandum to Dunn, Inc. for return of $100 worth of merchandise purchased May 1.

      7 Sold merchandise on account to Norton Company, $650. Invoice No. 902.

      8 Received remittance from Dunn, Inc. for the amount owed, less discount.

    11 Sold merchandise for cash to J. Martin, $120.

    16 Sold merchandise to D. Fuller, receiving a note receivable for $300. Invoice No. 903.

    21 Collected a non-interest-bearing note receivable from M. Yates, $600.

    22 Sold merchandise on account to Rudd Company, $700. Invoice No. 904.

    25 Owner C. Wonder contributed cash to the business, $3,000.

    28 Norton Company paid for merchandise purchased May 7.

    29 Issued credit memorandum to Rudd Company for $80 worth of merchandise purchased on May 22.

    30 Sold merchandise on account to Brill, Inc., $750. Invoice No. 905.

REQUIRED

(a) Record the given transactions in a single-column sales journal, a general journal, and a cash receipts journal.

(b) Open the following general ledger accounts and insert balances, when given: Cash (11) $5,000; Notes Receivable (15) $600; Accounts Receivable (16) $400; Wonder, Capital (31) $6,000; Sales (41); Sales Returns and Allowances (42); and Sales Discounts (43). Also open a subsidiary ledger with the following customer accounts: Barker, Inc., $400; Brill, Inc.; Dunn, Inc.; Norton Company; and Rudd Company. Only Barker's account had a beginning balance.

(c) Post all necessary amounts to the general and subsidiary ledger accounts.

(d) Prove that the Accounts Receivable control account agrees with the subsidiary ledger.

6–24 McCauley Company had the following transactions involving purchases, purchases returns and allowances, and cash payments during August. McCauley uses the gross price method to record purchases.

Aug. 1 Purchased merchandise on account from Mann Company, $700, terms 2/10, n/30, F.O.B. shipping point.

2 Paid Acme Trucking, Inc. freight bill for August 1 purchase, $40. Check No. 100.

5 Paid Denton, Inc. on account, $300. Check No. 101.

8 Purchased store supplies on account from Larson Supply Company, $250, terms n/30.

9 Owner J. McCauley withdrew $500 cash from the business. Check No. 102.

11 Paid Mann Company for August 1 purchase. Check No. 103.

 12 Returned $50 worth of the store supplies purchased from Larson Supply Company on August 8.

15 Purchased store supplies for cash from Gordon Wholesalers, $120. Check No. 104.

17 Purchased merchandise on account from Cable, Inc., $600, terms 1/10, n/30.

18 Paid Larson Supply Company in full of account. Check No. 105.

19 Returned $100 worth of merchandise to Cable, Inc. for credit.

22 Paid Cable, Inc. for August 17 purchase. Check No. 106.

24 Purchased office supplies on account from Denton, Inc., $80, terms n/30.

26 Purchased delivery equipment from King, Inc. $8,000, giving $1,000 cash and a note payable for $7,000. Check No. 107.

29 Purchased office equipment on account from Denton, Inc., $650, terms n/30.

31 Purchased merchandise on account from Mann Company, $750, terms 2/10, n/30, F.O.B. shipping point.

REQUIRED

(a) Record these transactions in an invoice register (purchases journal), a cash disbursements journal, and a general journal.

(b) Open the following general ledger accounts and insert balances, when given: Cash (11) $6,000, Office Supplies on Hand (15) $450; Store Supplies on Hand (16) $100; Delivery Equipment (17) $9,000; Office Equipment (18) $2,500; Notes Payable (21); Accounts Payable (22) $300; J. McCauley, Drawing (32); Purchases (51); Purchases Returns and Allowances (52); Purchases Discounts (53); and Transportation In (54). Also open a subsidiary ledger with the following creditor accounts: Cable, Inc.; Denton, Inc., $300; Larson Supply Company; and Mann Company. Only the Denton account had a beginning balance.

(c) Post all necessary amounts to the general and subsidiary ledger accounts.

(d) Prove that the Accounts Payable control account agrees with the subsidiary ledger.

6–25 Whitney Company began business on April 1. The purchases and sales made on account during April have been recorded in the sales and purchases journals below. Purchases are recorded using the gross price method.

Sales Journal   Page 1

Date		Customer	Terms	Post. Ref.	Amount
19XX					
Apr.	5	Mills, Inc.	2/10, n/30		$400
	10	White Wholesalers	2/10, n/30		700
	18	Wagner, Inc.	2/10, n/30		600
	21	White Wholesalers	2/10, n/30		300
	28	L. Taylor	2/10, n/30		800

Purchases Journal   Page 1

Date		Creditor	Terms	Post. Ref.	Amount
19XX					
Apr.	2	Thorp Company	2/15, n/30		$1,500
	4	Allen Corporation	n/30		650
	12	Lane, Inc.	2/10, n/30		800
	22	Thorp Company	2/15, n/30		750
	29	Wilson, Inc.	1/10, n/30		400

The April transactions to be recorded in the cash receipts and cash disbursements journals are the following:

Apr. 1 Whitney invested $9,000 cash and $7,000 worth of office equipment in the firm, a sole proprietorship. (Use two lines for entry.)
   2 Paid April rent, $850. Check No. 101.
   5 Received rental income for space sublet to Wood Realty, $250.
   7 Purchased office supplies for cash, $380. Check No. 102.
   14 Paid Thorp Company for April 2 purchase. Check No. 103.
   15 Received $392 from Mills, Inc. in payment of account.
   18 Received $686 from White Wholesalers in payment of account.
   21 Paid Lane, Inc. for April 12 purchase. Check No. 104.
   30 Paid office clerk's salary, $1,200. Check No. 105.

REQUIRED
(a) Record the April transactions in cash receipts and cash disbursements journals.
(b) Total and balance the cash receipts and cash disbursements journals.

6–26 Benson Distributors, which sells on terms of 2/10, n/30, had the following transactions during October, the first month of the current fiscal year.

Oct. 1 Paid October rent, $500. Check No. 200.
   2 Paid Lane, Inc. $735 for merchandise purchased September 28. A 2% discount was taken. Check No. 201.

3 Issued checks of $300 to Butler Company and $350 to Kent Suppliers, both creditors. No discount was taken on these amounts. Checks No. 202 and No. 203.

7 Sold merchandise on account to Flynn, Inc., $450. Invoice No. 470.

8 Received checks in payment of accounts as follows: Flynn, Inc., $196; Preston Company, $500; and Young Company, $98. Discounts had been taken by Flynn, Inc. and Young Company.

9 Sold merchandise on account to Preston Company, $400. Invoice No. 471.

10 Issued check for freight to Allied Freight, Inc. on Preston Company shipment, $80, terms F.O.B. destination. Check No. 204.

11 Issued credit memorandum to Preston Company for merchandise returned, $50.

14 Purchased merchandise on account from Butler Company, $700, terms 1/10, n/60.

15 Issued check for freight to Wynn Transport on purchase from Butler Company, $65, terms F.O.B. shipping point. Check No. 205.

15 Paid office salaries, $900. Checks No. 206 and No. 207 for $450 each for L. Webb and R. Baker.

16 Received check in payment of Davis Company account, $450.

17 Received check from Flynn, Inc. in payment of October 7 shipment, $441.

18 Purchased store supplies, $60; equipment, $300; and office supplies, $40, on account from Kent Suppliers, terms n/30.

21 Paid Butler Company for October 14 purchase, $693. Check No. 208.

22 Paid miscellaneous expenses, $25. Check No. 209.

24 Issued check to R. Benson for a personal withdrawal, $450. Check No. 210.

28 Purchased merchandise on account from Lane, Inc., $200, terms 2/15, n/60.

29 Returned $60 worth of merchandise to Lane, Inc. for credit.

30 Sold merchandise on account to Young Company, $275. Invoice No. 472.

31 Sold merchandise for cash to K. Mills, $100.

31 Collected miscellaneous income from Ace Advertising for use of billboard space, $200.

REQUIRED

(a) Open the following general ledger accounts, and enter the indicated October 1 balances. Number the accounts as shown.

Cash (11)	$ 3,500	Sales Discounts (43)
Accounts Receivable (12)	1,250	Miscellaneous Income (44)
Inventory (14)	18,000	Purchases (51)
Store Supplies on Hand (15)	600	Purchases Returns
Office Supplies on Hand (16)	150	and Allowances (52)
Equipment (17)	20,000	Purchases Discounts (53)
Accumulated Depreciation (18)	(4,000)	Transportation In (54)
Accounts Payable (21)	(1,400)	Rent Expense (61)
R. Benson, Capital (31)	(38,100)	Salaries Expense (62)
R. Benson, Drawing (32)		Transportation Out (63)
Sales (41)		Miscellaneous Expense (64)
Sales Returns and Allowances (42)		

(b) Open the following accounts in the subsidiary ledgers and enter the October 1 balances:

Customers		Creditors	
Davis Company	$ 450	Butler Company	$ 300
Flynn, Inc.	200	Kent Suppliers	350
Preston Company	500	Lane, Inc.	750
Young Company	100		
	$1,250		$1,400

(c) Record the October transactions in the four special journals (sales, invoice register, cash receipts, and cash disbursements) and in the general journal. Benson uses the gross price method to record purchases.

(d) Using the forms prepared in parts (a) and (b), post all necessary amounts to the general ledger and subsidiary ledgers from the journals. Postings should be made to the subsidiary ledgers throughout the month.

(e) Prepare a trial balance of the general ledger.

(f) Prepare a schedule of accounts receivable and a schedule of accounts payable to prove control account balances.

6–27 The post-closing trial balance at December 31, 19XX, for Cooper Distributors is given below:

Cooper Distributors
Post-closing Trial Balance
December 31, 19XX

	Debit	Credit
Cash	$ 6,500	
Accounts Receivable	15,600	
Inventory	42,500	
Office Supplies on Hand	420	
Store Supplies on Hand	180	
Office Equipment	8,000	
Accumulated Depreciation		$ 2,400
Accounts Payable		21,300
J. Cooper, Capital		49,500
	$73,200	$73,200

At the end of January, 19X1, the totals of the firm's special journals, before posting, are as follows:

Invoice Register:		Sales Journal	$68,400
Accounts Payable	$54,250		
Purchases	52,100	Cash Receipts Journal:	
Office Supplies on Hand	300	Cash	63,500
Store Supplies on Hand	450	Sales Discounts	1,360
Other Accounts:		Accounts Receivable	49,400
Office Equipment (Dr.)	1,400		

Sales	$10,460		
Other Accounts:			
J. Cooper, Capital (Cr.)	5,000		

Cash Disbursements Journal:			
Cash	51,750	Advertising Expense (Dr.)	$ 620
Purchases Discounts	920	Salaries Expense (Dr.)	1,800
Accounts Payable	49,050		
Other Accounts:			
Rent Expense (Dr.)	1,200		

REQUIRED

Prepare an unadjusted trial balance for Cooper Distributors at January 31. *Note:* A convenient method is to use a six-column worksheet, placing the post-closing trial balance in the first two columns and listing the account titles of the temporary accounts below. The next two columns are used to record the debits and credits from the special journals, while the last two columns are used for the unadjusted trial balance at January 31.

6–28 Fastcraft, Inc. controls its disbursements through a voucher system. The following transactions occurred during June of the current year. The firm records merchandise purchases at gross invoice price.

June 1   Recorded voucher No. 601 payable to Realty Associates for June rent, $750.

2   Recorded voucher No. 602 payable to Badger Supply, Inc. for $550 worth of merchandise purchased, terms 2/10, n/30.

3   Issued check No. 702 in payment of voucher No. 601.

5   Recorded voucher No. 603 payable to Oregon Sales, Inc. for $480 worth of office supplies, terms n/30.

7   Recorded voucher No. 604 payable to Towline Freight Company for transportation in on merchandise purchased, $60, terms F.O.B. shipping point.

10   Issued check No. 703 in payment of voucher No. 602, less discount.

12   Issued check No. 704 in payment of voucher No. 603.

15   Recorded voucher No. 605 payable to Bates, Inc. for equipment, $1,500, terms 2/20, n/60. (Make voucher for net amount.)

18   Issued check No. 705 in payment of voucher No. 604.

22   Recorded voucher No. 606 payable to Gary, Inc. for merchandise purchased, $440, terms 2/10, n/30.

26   Recorded voucher No. 607 payable to Tower Gas and Light Company for utilities expense, $128.

26   Issued check No. 706 in payment of voucher No. 607.

28   Received credit memo for $40 from Gary, Inc. for merchandise returned to it. Canceled original voucher (No. 606) and issued voucher No. 608.

28   Issued check No. 707 in payment of voucher No. 605.

30   Recorded voucher No. 609 payable to Burke, Inc. for merchandise purchased, $875, terms 2/10, n/30.

REQUIRED

(a) Record Fastcraft's transactions in a voucher register and check register.

(b) Total the voucher register and the check register amount columns, and post the appropriate amounts to the following accounts:

Cash in Bank (11)	Purchases Returns
Office Supplies	and Allowances (52)
on Hand (17)	Purchases Discounts (53)
Equipment (18)	Transportation In (54)
Vouchers Payable (21)	Rent Expense (61)
Purchases (51)	Utilities Expense (62)

(c) List the unpaid vouchers, and compare the total with the balance of the Vouchers Payable account.

6-29 The Ranger Company, which employs a voucher system, had the following transactions during July:

July 1   Recorded voucher No. 701 payable to R. Nelson for $600 worth of merchandise purchased, terms 2/10, n/30.

2   Recorded voucher No. 702 payable to Walton Rentals for July rent, $650.

3   Issued check No. 803 in payment of voucher No. 702.

9   Recorded voucher No. 703 payable to Whalen Express, Inc. for transportation in, $35, terms F.O.B. shipping point.

10   Issued check No. 804 in payment of voucher No. 701.

11   Issued check No. 805 in payment of voucher No. 703.

15   Recorded voucher No. 704 payable to Bailey Company for $800 worth of merchandise, terms n/30.

20   Received credit memo from Bailey Company for $300 worth of the merchandise recorded on voucher No. 704. Canceled voucher No. 704 and issued voucher No. 705.

REQUIRED

Prepare a voucher register and check register, and record the transactions for the Ranger Company. The firm records merchandise purchases at gross invoice price.

ALTERNATE PROBLEMS

Note: In the following problems, the journal forms used should correspond to those illustrated in the chapter.

6-23A The Arden Sales Company makes all sales on terms of 2/10, n/30. Transactions for May involving sales, related returns and allowances, and cash receipts are shown below:

May 1   Collected $500 from D. Sanders on account.

1   Sold merchandise on account to Carter, Inc., $350. Invoice No. 201.

4   Sold merchandise for cash to W. Young, $60.

5   Issued credit memorandum to Carter, Inc. for return of $50 worth of merchandise purchased May 1.

8   Sold merchandise on account to Norton Company, $400. Invoice No. 202.

10 Received remittance from Carter, Inc. for the amount owed, less discount.

12 Sold merchandise for cash to R. Johnson, $40.

15 Sold merchandise to L. Baker, receiving a note receivable for $500. Invoice No. 203.

18 Collected a non-interest-bearing note receivable from J. Ritter, $600.

20 Owner G. Arden contributed cash to the business, $1,500.

24 Sold merchandise on account to Little Company, $240. Invoice No. 204.

25 Norton Company paid for merchandise purchased on May 8.

26 Issued credit memorandum to Little Company for $40 merchandise purchased on May 24.

30 Sold merchandise on account to B. Rivers, Inc., $360. Invoice No. 205.

REQUIRED

(a) Record the given transactions in a single-column sales journal, a general journal, and a cash receipts journal.

(b) Open the following general ledger accounts and insert balances, when given: Cash (11) $2,000; Notes Receivable (15) $600; Accounts Receivable (16) $500; G. Arden, Capital (31) $5,000; Sales (41); Sales Returns and Allowances (42); Sales Discounts (43). Also open a subsidiary ledger with the following customer accounts: Carter, Inc.; Little Company; Norton Company; B. Rivers, Inc.; and D. Sanders, $500. Only D. Sanders' account had a beginning balance.

(c) Post all necessary amounts to the general ledger and subsidiary ledger accounts.

(d) Prove that the Accounts Receivable control account agrees with the subsidiary ledger.

6–24A   Eastwood Distributors had the following transactions involving purchases, purchases returns and allowances, and cash payments during June. Eastwood uses the gross price method to record purchases.

June 1   Paid Atwood, Inc. on account, $300. Check No. 100.

1   Purchased merchandise on account from Dutton Company, $250, terms 2/10, n/30, F.O.B. shipping point.

2   Paid freight bill to Acme Delivery for June 1 purchase, $20. Check No. 101.

5   Purchased store supplies on account from Burt Supply Company, $160, terms n/30.

7   Owner T. Eastwood withdrew cash from the business, $300. Check No. 102.

8   Purchased store supplies for cash from Ace Wholesalers, $70. Check No. 103.

10 Paid Dutton Company amount due for June 1 purchase. Check No. 104.

11 Returned $30 worth of the store supplies purchased from Burt Supply Company on June 5.

June 15 Purchased merchandise on account from Wales, Inc., $800, terms 1/10, n/30.

16 Paid Burt Supply Company in full of account. Check No. 105.

18 Returned $100 worth of merchandise to Wales, Inc. for credit.

20 Paid Wales, Inc. for June 15 purchase. Check No. 106.

21 Purchased office supplies on account from Atwood, Inc., $80, terms n/30.

25 Purchased delivery equipment from Atlas, Inc., $4,000, giving $1,000 cash and a note payable for $3,000. Check No. 107.

30 Purchased office equipment on account from Atwood, Inc., $480, terms n/30.

30 Purchased merchandise on account from Dutton Company, $280, terms 2/10, n/30, F.O.B. shipping point.

REQUIRED

(a) Record these transactions in an invoice register (purchases journal), a cash disbursements journal, and a general journal.

(b) Open the following general ledger accounts and insert balances, when given: Cash (11) $4,000; Office Supplies on Hand (15) $200; Store Supplies on Hand (16) $100; Delivery Equipment (17) $5,000; Office Equipment (18) $300; Notes Payable (21); Accounts Payable (22) $300; T. Eastwood, Drawing (32); Purchases (51); Purchases Returns and Allowances (52); Purchases Discounts (53); and Transportation In (54). Also open a subsidiary ledger with the following creditor accounts: Atwood, Inc. $300; Burt Supply Company; Dutton Company; and Wales, Inc. Only the Atwood, Inc. account had a beginning balance.

(c) Post all necessary amounts to the general ledger and subsidiary ledger accounts.

(d) Prove that the Accounts Payable control account agrees with the subsidiary creditors' ledger.

6–25A Travis Wholesalers began business on May 1. The purchases and sales made on account during May have been recorded in the sales and purchases journals below. Purchases are recorded using the gross price method.

Sales Journal Page 1

Date			Customer	Terms	Post. Ref.	Amount
19XX						
May		6	Holt, Inc.	2/10, n/30		$100
		9	Lyon and Company	2/10, n/30		350
		17	R.D. Ellis	2/10, n/30		200
		22	Lyon and Company	2/10, n/30		250
		25	B.L. Nash	2/10, n/30		400

Purchases Journal   Page 1

Date		Creditor	Terms	Post. Ref.	Amount
19XX					
May	3	G. Holman	2/10, n/30		$800
	5	Billings Corporation	n/30		450
	16	Swanson, Inc.	2/10, n/30		300
	25	G. Holman	n/30		150
	30	R. Dunn	1/10, n/30		200

The May transactions to be recorded in the cash receipts and cash disbursements journals are the following:

May 1 R. Travis invested $8,000 cash and $5,000 worth of office equipment in the firm, a sole proprietorship. (Use two lines for entry.)

2 Paid May rent, $300. Check No. 101.

3 Received rental income for space sublet to Jim's Shoe Repair, $50.

4 Purchased office supplies for cash, $120. Check No. 102.

10 Paid G. Holman for May 3 purchase. Check No. 103.

16 Received $98 from Holt, Inc. in payment of account.

19 Received $343 from Lyon and Company in payment of account.

26 Paid Swanson, Inc. for May 16 purchase. Check No. 104.

31 Paid office clerk's salary, $650. Check No. 105.

REQUIRED
(a) Record the May transactions in cash receipts and cash disbursements journals.
(b) Total and balance the cash receipts and cash disbursements journals.

6–26A West Wholesalers, which sells on terms of 2/10, n/30, had the following transactions during January, the first month of the current accounting year.

Jan. 2 Paid Simpson, Inc. for merchandise purchased December 28, $490. Check No. 125. West took a 2% discount.

3 Paid January rent, $500. Check No. 126.

5 Issued checks of $160 to Britton Company and $140 to Gilman Suppliers, both creditors. No discount was taken on these amounts. Checks No. 127 and No. 128.

5 Sold merchandise on account to David, Inc., $450. Invoice No. 251.

6 Received checks in payment of accounts as follows: David, Inc., $294; Foster Company, $120; and Roman Distributors, $196. Discounts had been taken by David, Inc. and Roman Distributors.

7 Sold merchandise on account to Foster Company, $350. Invoice No. 252.

8 Issued check for freight to Roadway, Inc. on Foster Company shipment, $60, terms F.O.B. destination. Check No. 129.

9 Issued credit memorandum to Foster Company for merchandise returned, $50.

Jan. 12 Purchased merchandise on account from Britton Company, $300, terms 1/10, n/60.

13 Issued check for freight to United Freightways on purchase from Britton Company, $40, terms F.O.B. shipping point. Check No. 130.

14 Received check in payment of Artway Company account, $480.

15 Received check from David, Inc. in payment of January 5 shipment, $441.

15 Paid office salaries, $900. Checks No. 131 and No. 132 for $450 each for D. George and S. Cimino.

19 Purchased store supplies, $120; equipment, $200; and office supplies, $50, on account from Gilman Suppliers, terms n/30.

20 Paid Britton Company for January 12 purchase, $297. Check No. 133.

21 Paid miscellaneous expense, $40. Check No. 134.

22 Owner J. West made a personal withdrawal, $500. Check No. 135.

26 Purchased merchandise on account from Simpson, Inc., $360, terms 2/15, n/60.

27 Returned $60 worth of merchandise to Simpson, Inc. for credit.

28 Sold merchandise on account to Roman Distributors, $950. Invoice No. 253.

30 Sold merchandise for cash to R. Adams, $80.

30 Collected miscellaneous income from Best Advertising for use of billboard space, $50.

REQUIRED

(a) Open the following general ledger accounts, and enter the indicated January 1 balances. Number the accounts as shown.

Cash (11)	$ 3,400	Sales Discounts (43)
Accounts Receivable (12)	1,100	Miscellaneous Income (44)
Inventory (14)	12,000	Purchases (51)
Store Supplies on Hand (15)	400	Purchases Returns and
Office Supplies on Hand (16)	100	Allowances (52)
Equipment (17)	18,000	Purchases Discounts (53)
Accumulated Depreciation (18)	(5,000)	Transportation In (54)
Accounts Payable (21)	(800)	Rent Expense (61)
J. West, Capital (31)	(29,200)	Salaries Expense (62)
J. West, Drawing (32)		Transportation Out (63)
Sales (41)		Miscellaneous Expense (64)
Sales Returns and		
Allowances (42)		

(b) Open the following accounts in the subsidiary ledgers and enter the January 1 balances:

Customers		Creditors	
Artway Company	$ 480	Britton Company	$160
David, Inc.	300	Gilman Suppliers	140
Foster Company	120	Simpson, Inc.	500
Roman Distributors	200		
	$1,100		$800

(c) Record the January transactions in the four special journals (sales, invoice register, cash receipts, and cash disbursements) and in the general journal. West uses the gross price method to record purchases.

(d) Using the forms prepared in parts (a) and (b), post all necessary amounts to the general ledger and subsidiary ledgers from the journals. Postings should be made to the subsidiary ledgers throughout the month.

(e) Prepare a trial balance of the general ledger.

(f) Prepare a schedule of accounts receivable and a schedule of accounts payable to prove control account balances.

6–28A   Astroline, Inc. controls its disbursements through a voucher system. The following transactions occurred during April of the current year.

Apr.   1   Recorded voucher No. 401 payable to Jordan Realty for April rent, $800.
       2   Recorded voucher No. 402 payable to Madison Service Corporation for $450 worth of merchandise purchased, terms 2/10, n/30.
       2   Issued check No. 506 in payment of voucher No. 401.
       5   Recorded voucher No. 403 payable to Verona Sales, Inc. for $300 worth of office supplies, terms n/30.
       7   Recorded voucher No. 404 payable to Intercity Freight Lines, Inc. for freight in on merchandise purchased, $45, terms F.O.B. shipping point.
      10   Issued check No. 507 in payment of voucher No. 402, less discount.
      12   Issued check No. 508 in payment of voucher No. 403.
      14   Recorded voucher No. 405 payable to Jarman Equipment Sales, Inc. for equipment, $1,200, terms 2/15, n/60. (Make voucher for net amount.)
      18   Issued check No. 509 in payment of voucher No. 404.
      21   Recorded voucher No. 406 payable to Hill, Inc. for merchandise purchased, $360, terms 2/10, n/30.
      25   Recorded voucher No. 407 payable to Consolidated Gas and Light Company for utilities expense, $72.
      26   Issued check No. 510 in payment of voucher No. 407.
      28   Received credit memo for $60 from Hill, Inc. for merchandise returned to it. Canceled original voucher (No. 406) and issued voucher No. 408.
      28   Issued check No. 511 in payment of voucher No. 405.
      30   Recorded voucher No. 409 payable to Alcan, Inc. for merchandise, $600, terms 2/10, n/30.

REQUIRED

(a) Record Astroline's transactions in a voucher register and check register.

(b) Total the voucher register and the check register amount columns, and post the appropriate amounts to the following accounts:

Cash in Bank (11)	Purchases Returns
Office Supplies	and Allowances (52)
on Hand (17)	Purchases Discounts (53)
Equipment (18)	Transportation In (54)
Vouchers Payable (21)	Rent Expense (61)
Purchases (51)	Utilities Expense (62)

(c) List the unpaid vouchers and compare the total with the balance of the Vouchers Payable account.

BUSINESS DECISION PROBLEM

Mayflower, Inc., sells a variety of office products and supplies, including typewriters, word processing equipment, desks, chairs, filing systems, and sundry office supplies. Most sales are on account; however, many small equipment items and supplies are sold over the counter for cash.

Manager T. Jensen asks you to provide special journals for the firm's accounting system. After discussing the matter with Jensen, you decide to design journals for three departments: Equipment, Furniture, and Supplies. Jensen wants the income statement to show sales, cost of goods sold, and gross profit for each of the three departments. Merchandise inventory for the three departments will be taken separately.

Practically all the firm's purchases are merchandise for resale. Most cash disbursements are payments on account to suppliers, freight on purchases (most purchases are made on terms F.O.B. shipping point), and for advertising expense. Spot advertising in local newspapers and television is paid when bills are received; no accounts payable are kept for these expenses. Employees are paid monthly.

REQUIRED
List the column headings (from left to right) that you would provide in the (a) sales journal, (b) invoice register, (c) cash receipts journal, and (d) cash disbursements journal for the three departments in Mayflower, Inc.

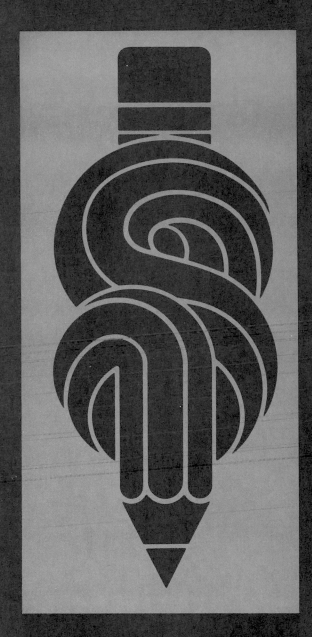

7

Internal Control, Cash, and Short-term Investments

Most people agree that accounting is the most important part of any
management information system. To assist management in planning
and controlling operations, the accounting system should be dependable and efficient and provide a measure of security for the firm's resources. A
system with these attributes provides an adequate measure of *internal control*.

The elements of control are important to all aspects of a firm's operations,
but they are particularly critical in establishing methods of handling and accounting for monetary assets. We therefore consider first the general features that are
desirable in an accounting control system and then examine certain procedures
that are especially important in accounting for and controlling cash transactions.
The latter procedures include bank reconciliations and petty cash procedures.[1]
We conclude the chapter by examining accounting for short-term investments in
stocks and bonds.

THE NATURE OF INTERNAL CONTROL

Internal control has been defined as

> the plan of organization and all of the coordinate methods and measures adopted
> within a business to safeguard its assets, check the accuracy and reliability of its
> accounting data, promote operational efficiency, and encourage adherence to prescribed managerial policies.[2]

The organization, planning, and procedures for safeguarding assets and the reliability of financial records are usually called *accounting controls*. The procedures
and methods concerned mainly with operational efficiency and managerial policies are *administrative controls*. These controls include statistical analyses, time-and-motion studies, performance reports, and quality controls.

An accountant should be conversant with both accounting controls and
administrative controls. Indeed, many controls within these two categories are
interrelated. Naturally, an accountant is more directly concerned with accounting
controls, which we now discuss.

---

[1] The voucher system discussed in Chapter 6 is a system of controls over cash disbursements.
[2] Auditing Standards Board, *Codification of Statements on Auditing Standards* (New York:
American Institute of Certified Public Accountants, 1983), Auditing Section 320.09.

244

FEATURES OF AN ACCOUNTING CONTROL SYSTEM

Good internal accounting control includes the following requirements:

(1) Competent personnel.

(2) Assignment of responsibility.

(3) Division of work.

(4) Separation of accountability from custodianship.

(5) Adequate records and equipment.

(6) Rotation of personnel.

(7) Internal auditing.

(8) Physical protection of assets.

Competent Personnel

Employees should be carefully selected and their talents used intelligently in the operation of the accounting information system. Each individual should thoroughly understand his or her function and its relationship to other functions in the system. Above all, an employee must realize the importance of following the procedures prescribed by management and should be in sympathy with the system. A well-formulated system of internal control can be destroyed by employees' lack of confidence or cooperation.

Assignment of Responsibility

The plan of organization should fix responsibility for functions and confer the authority necessary to perform them. Responsibility and authority for a given function should not be shared, because this may result in duplication of effort and in jobs going undone if individuals think that another is performing the assignment. When one person is responsible for a function, praise or blame can be clearly assigned for specific results. Thus, if a plant foreman is responsible for staying within budgeted amounts for labor costs, he or she should be given the authority to assign personnel to jobs, control overtime, and so on.

Division of Work

Division of work is one of the most important facets of a good system of controls. The duties of individuals should be defined so that no single individual has complete control over a sequence of related transactions. That is, the person who authorizes a purchase order should not also confirm receipt of the merchandise or authorize payment for the merchandise. Likewise, the person handling bank deposits and the person keeping the cash books should not receive bank statements or make bank reconciliations. Improper segregation of duties increases the possibility of fraud, carelessness, and unreliable record keeping, whereas with a proper division of duties, the work of one person or group can act as a check on work performed by another person or group. For example, when purchase orders and receiving reports are processed by different individuals, a third person can compare the order, receiving report, and vendor's invoice before approving payment. This practice reduces the likelihood of errors from carelessness as well as the possibility of fictitious purchases or fraudulent conversion of goods.

Work division is valuable not only in preventing errors and fraud, but also in providing the advantages of specialization—better performance and easier employee training.

Separation of Accountability from Custodianship

Employees who are responsible for keeping records of a firm's assets should not have custody of the assets nor access to them. Separating the custody of assets from the maintenance of records is another safeguard against fraud. An employee should not be able to convert assets for personal use and cover up the conversion by falsifying the records. When custody of assets is adequately separated from record keeping, collusion among employees is usually necessary to perpetrate fraud. If collusion does exist, embezzlement can go undetected for a long time.

The separation feature, which should be incorporated in the system to protect all assets, is especially important in handling cash and negotiable items. For example, cash remittances from customers should be listed by personnel who have no access to accounting records. These lists can then be forwarded to the accounts receivable department for posting to customer accounts in the subsidiary ledger, while the remittances themselves are sent to the cashier for deposit. A duplicate list of remittances should also be given to the person who makes the cash receipts journal entries. This method provides several cross-checks—bank deposits must agree with the recorded cash receipts, and the Accounts Receivable control account must agree with subsidiary ledger totals. Finally, the bank should send its statement to someone other than the cashier or those keeping cash-related records, so that an independent bank reconciliation can be made.

Adequate Records and Equipment

Adequate records are important not only in accounting for a company's resources but also in providing management with accurate and reliable information. One of the most important features in a satisfactory record-keeping system is a comprehensive chart of accounts that classifies information in a manner best suited to management's needs. Control accounts and subsidiary records should be used when appropriate, so that work can be subdivided, and cross-checks may be made when the two types of accounts are reconciled. Control and subsidiary accounts can be used for such areas as accounts and notes receivable, accounts and notes payable, plant assets, and the major expense classifications of manufacturing expense, selling expense, and administrative expense.

The forms used with the accounting records should promote accuracy and efficiency. If possible, individual forms should be prenumbered so that the sequence of forms used can be accounted for. Moreover, prenumbering helps a firm trace its transactions and reduces the possibility of failing to record a transaction. For example, suppose a firm issues prenumbered sales slips for each sale. A check of the number sequence would disclose any diversion of sales proceeds accomplished by destruction of the sales slip. Likewise, accounting for the sequence of prenumbered checks can detect whether unrecorded checks have been issued for unauthorized purchases.

Various types of equipment can be used with the record-keeping system to provide helpful controls. The cash registers used in retail operations, for example, have several important control features—a bell signals that the register has been opened, and a receipt allows the customer to check the transaction. Furthermore, most cash registers have a locked-in tape that accumulates and classifies transactions that have been registered. A responsible employee controlling the key can reconcile amounts shown on the tape with daily cash counts. Some registers contain separate cash drawers so that several clerks can handle the same cash register and each be accountable for his or her own operation. Another device that protects cash is the autographic register, which produces a locked-in copy of a sales invoice when the original is prepared in an over-the-counter sale. Check protectors, which perforate checks with indelible ink, are another example of a protective device for cash transactions. Checks written with such a machine cannot be altered without the change being obvious.

An electronic cash register tied in to a computer may improve control over the extension of credit to a customer using a credit card. Quick point-of-sale credit verification is possible. In a few seconds, the computer can ensure that the customer has not exceeded his or her credit limit and has been prompt with payments. The computer can also determine if the card has been reported lost or stolen. The computer either authorizes or disapproves the use of the credit card, depending on the status of the customer's account.

Bookkeeping machines, punched-card equipment, and electronic data-processing equipment all permit certain procedural controls or have built-in controls to reduce the possibility of errors and unauthorized actions. The automatic features of such equipment produce records more error-free and legible than those resulting from a manual system.

Rotation of Personnel

Some companies rotate the positions of certain operating personnel. For example, accounts receivable clerks, each responsible for a certain alphabetical segment of the accounts, might be rotated periodically to other segments. This procedure may disclose errors and irregularities caused by carelessness or dishonesty. Requiring employees to take vacations may also reveal lapses, carelessness, and dishonesty on the part of employees. Misappropriations of funds—especially in financial institutions such as banks—have often been discovered during an employee's absence, when the perpetrator could no longer control or manipulate records.

Internal Auditing

An important feature of the internal control system of large companies is the internal audit function. The internal auditing department independently appraises the firm's financial and operational activities. In addition to reviewing activities for errors and irregularities, the internal audit staff determines whether prescribed policies and procedures are being followed and attempts to uncover wasteful and inefficient situations. Internal auditing is a *staff*, or advisory, function that consists of reviewing activities and making written recommendations to management. To be effective, the internal audit staff must be independent of operating (line) functions and should report to a high-ranking executive or to the firm's board of directors.

Physical Protection of Assets

Frequently, management initiates a number of physical controls to protect company property. Although some of these controls may not be closely related to the accounting system, they are almost invariably discussed in the context of internal control.

A business must be adequately insured against losses from fire, outside theft, and similar events. In addition to insuring its physical assets, a company should obtain fidelity insurance; employees having access to cash, securities, and other easily diverted assets should be bonded. For a fee, a bonding company guarantees to make good any loss from theft or embezzlement by the bonded person, up to some specified maximum amount. The bonding company investigates employees to be bonded, and anyone with a record of questionable integrity is not likely to qualify.

Only minimal amounts of cash or negotiable assets should be kept on the company premises, and these should be stored in a vault. A firm should keep its inventory in a secure area and maintain strict controls over issuances and physical counts of inventory. Security personnel are often engaged to protect inventories and other physical property. A company may employ outside protection services to safeguard against burglary and arson and might post gatekeepers at plant entrances and exits to observe employees and others entering and leaving the plant.

CASH AND CASH CONTROLS

In accounting, the term **cash** means paper money, coins, checks, and money orders—all items that are acceptable for deposit in a bank—as well as money already on deposit with a bank. IOUs, postdated checks (checks dated in the future), and uncollected customers' checks returned by the bank stamped "NSF" (not sufficient funds) are not considered cash but are normally classified as **receivables.** Notes sent to the bank for collection remain classified as **notes receivable** until notification of collection is received from the bank.

Cash in the Balance Sheet

Various ledger accounts are used to record cash transactions; some common examples are Cash on Hand, Petty Cash, and Cash in Bank. The Cash on Hand account reflects cash receipts not yet deposited in the bank, and Petty Cash represents a fund used for small disbursements. Cash in Bank usually refers to demand deposits in a checking account.

When a business firm has several checking accounts, a separate ledger account should be maintained for each account rather than one overall Cash in Bank account. Although a balance sheet prepared for management may show all individual cash accounts, a balance sheet prepared for outsiders normally shows the combined balances of all cash accounts under a single heading, *Cash.* Management is interested in the detail because it must establish policies on balances to be maintained in various bank accounts and on hand. Most outsiders, on the other hand, are interested only in the aggregate cash balance and its relationship to other items on the financial statements.

Cash amounts subject to use or withdrawal without restriction are current assets and are normally shown first in the balance sheet listing of assets. Cash controlled by a trustee—such as sinking fund cash—and amounts in foreign banks subject to exchange restrictions are noncurrent assets in the balance sheet.

EMPLOYEE THEFT

Few people, from corporate executives on down, realize how big employee theft is. The fact is, it's a crime that amounts to 1% of the Gross National Product, or some $40 billion a year, and just about every employee this side of sainthood will commit it some time during his or her working life. Moreover, employee theft accounts for 80% of all crime against corporations.

Security experts divide internal crime into three categories—the theft of things such as raw materials, finished products, cash, and tools; the theft of information; and fraud.

The theft of raw materials occurs primarily in the manufacturing and construction businesses. For a manufacturing firm, it most often occurs in the shipping and receiving or warehouse end of the operation, where controls are notoriously lax. With hundreds of shipments going in and out of a docking area each day, keeping an eye on materials is taxing, and the opportunity for theft astounding.

At construction sites, there are often hundreds of workers performing a wide variety of tasks and trucks coming and going with materials. It is relatively easy for an employee to slip off the job to nab some lumber, plasterboard, or insulating material and stash it in a pick-up truck, or to arrange for a commercial truck to pick up material and haul it away.

The illegal siphoning off of crude and refined oil plagues the oil industry. The measurement of how much oil goes into a tank is relatively imprecise, so employees are able, undetected, either to siphon oil from a storage tank or to pump only part of the oil in a tanker truck into a tank.

When it comes to the outright theft of money, banks are where the big action is. Wells Fargo Bank was the victim of one of the biggest recent rip-offs. An employee in the operations department fiddled with customer accounts entered in the bank computers and embezzled about $21 million in a two-year period before he was caught.

Theft of information, though less prevalent than the theft of objects or services, can be disastrous. The energy industry is a frequent target of such thefts. Seismic surveys and exploration data, which cost millions of dollars to collect, have been pilfered from major oil companies and sold to small independent drillers or to foreign concerns.

Fraudulent schemes are the most costly form of employee theft. "The creation of dummy or shell companies is on the upswing, and it is not especially difficult to arrange," says Errol M. Cook, a security expert at Arthur Young. He tells of one executive who formed an "offshore" insurance company. This executive had the authority to place insurance, so he bought a policy from the dummy company and pocketed the premiums. Cook notes that "where phony insurance companies are used, the type of insurance placed is usually where claims would not be occurring—officers' and directors' liability and bonding insurance, for example."

Employees in a payroll department can easily rip off a company. At a Baltimore hospital, one worker added the names of two friends to the payroll and managed to funnel $40,000 their way before she was caught.

The most distressing thing about employee theft, security experts say, is that companies make it so easy. They leave valuable items unlocked or do not check to see that supplies actually exist. "It is just astounding the number of the top 500 corporations in America that have woefully inadequate security systems. I should know, because many of them are my clients," says August Bequai, a lawyer, author, and consultant in the area of corporate security.

From Lynn Adkins, "The High Cost of Employee Theft." Reprinted with the special permission of Dun's Business Month (formerly Dun's Review), October 1982, pages 66–73, Dun & Bradstreet Publications Corporation.

Cash Control Procedures

A firm must control the handling and recording of cash because it is so susceptible to misappropriation. An adequate system of internal control over cash would include the following features:

(1) Cash is handled separately from the recording of cash transactions.

(2) The work and responsibilities of cash handling and recording are divided in such a way that errors are readily disclosed and the possibility of irregularities is reduced.

(3) All cash receipts are deposited intact in the bank each day.

(4) All major disbursements are made by check, and an imprest (fixed amount) fund is used for petty cash disbursements.

In our earlier discussion of internal control, we described and explained the desirability of the first two features. By observing the last two—depositing all receipts intact daily at the bank and making all disbursements by check—a company establishes a double record of cash transactions. One record is generated by the firm's record-keeping procedures, and another is furnished by the bank. Comparing the two records and accounting for any differences provides control. This important procedure is called *reconciling the bank statement with the book record of cash transactions* or, simply, making a *bank reconciliation*.

The Bank Account

When a firm opens a checking account at a bank, the members of the firm who are authorized to draw checks sign signature cards that the bank files. Occasionally, bank employees may check the signatures on these cards against the signatures on the checks.

The bank submits monthly statements to the depositor showing the beginning cash balance, all additions and deductions for the month, and the ending cash balance. In addition, the bank returns the paid (or canceled) checks for the month, together with "advice" slips indicating other charges and credits made to the account. The bank may also send copies of such advice slips individually during the month to the depositor.

To reduce handling costs, some banks do not return canceled checks to the depositor, but use a procedure called *check truncation*. The bank retains the canceled checks for a period of time (typically 90 days) and a microfilm copy of the checks for a longer period (at least one year). Should the depositor need to review a canceled check within these periods, the bank provides the check or a photocopy of it for a small fee. A bank's monthly statements to a depositor usually list paid checks in numerical sequence, so check truncation does not affect the preparation of a bank reconciliation. Further, businesses generally use a check preparation system that produces a copy of each check issued.

Exhibit 7–1 is an example of a bank statement. The left-hand section of the statement lists deposits and other credits in sequence by date. The middle section lists checks paid and other charges to the account. The checks are listed in numerical sequence, and the payment date for each check is shown in the date column. Listing checks in numerical sequence helps the depositor identify checks written

EXHIBIT 7–1
Bank Statement

First National Bank · Madison (1st) STATEMENT OF ACCOUNT

EAST WASHINGTON – CAPITOL SQUARE

G.A. Shaw Company
101 Beltline Highway
Madison, Wisconsin
53718

ACCOUNT NUMBER
313111386

STATEMENT DATE: December 31, 19XX

Deposits/Credits		Checks/Charges			Balance	
Date	Amount	No.	Date	Amount	Date	Amount
12/01	300.00 √	149	12/02	125.00 √	12/01	5,940.30
12/02	750.00 √	154	12/03	56.25 √	12/02	6,565.30
12/07	560.80 √	155	12/10	135.00 √	12/03	6,509.05
12/10	480.25 √	156	12/08	441.21	12/07	6,927.30
12/14	525.00 √	157	12/07	107.15	12/08	6,486.09
12/17	270.25 √	158	12/11	27.14	12/10	6,831.34
12/21	640.20 √	159	12/18	275.00	12/11	6,804.20
12/26	200.00CM	160	12/15	315.37	12/14	7,329.20
12/26	475.00 √	161	12/17	76.40	12/15	7,013.83
12/30	440.00 √	162	12/21	325.60	12/17	7,207.68
		163	12/21	450.00	12/18	6,932.68
		164	12/23	239.00	12/21	6,731.58
		165	12/21	65.70	12/23	6,492.58
		166	12/28	482.43	12/26	7,165.58
		169	12/28	260.00	12/28	6,423.15
		170	12/31	122.50	12/30	6,493.04
		171	12/30	370.11	12/31	6,365.54
		RT	12/07	35.40		
		DM	12/26	2.00		
		SC	12/31	5.00		

Beginning Balance	Deposits/Credits		Checks/Charges		Ending Balance
11/30/XX 5,640.30	No. 10	Amount 4,641.50	No. 20	Amount 3,916.26	12/31/XX 6,365.54

Item Codes:	EC—Error Correction	DM—Debit Memo	CM—Credit Memo
	SC—Service Charge	OD—Overdraft	RT—Returned Item
	LS—List of Checks	IN—Interest	

but not yet paid by the bank. The right-hand section shows the checking account balance as of the date shown in the date column. Each time a receipt or a payment occurs, a new balance is shown.

Code letters on a bank statement identify charges and credits not related to paying checks or making deposits. A legend usually appears at the bottom of the statement explaining the code letters. Although such codes are not standard from bank to bank, they are easy to understand. As we mentioned before, the depositor also receives an advice slip from the bank explaining nonroutine entries. The statement illustrated in Exhibit 7–1 uses the following codes:

EC —Error correction   Identifies transcription, arithmetic, and similar errors and corrections made by the bank.

DM—Debit memo   Identifies collection charges, repayment of bank loans, and other special charges made by the bank against the depositor's account.

CM—Credit memo   Identifies amounts collected by the bank for the depositor, such as a note receivable left at the bank by the depositor, or a loan from the bank to the depositor which is credited to the depositor's checking account.

SC —Service charge   Identifies the amount charged by the bank for servicing the account. The amount is normally based on the average balance maintained and the number of items processed during the month. Service charges are usually made on small accounts that are not otherwise profitable for the bank to handle.

OD—Overdraft   Indicates a negative, or credit, balance in the account.

RT —Returned item   Indicates items such as postdated checks or checks without proper endorsement received from customers and deposited. Sometimes NSF (not sufficient funds) checks charged back to the account are identified with these letters in the statement. NSF checks may also be identified with the letters DM (debit memo), explained earlier.

LS —List of checks   Identifies the total of a batch of checks too numerous to list separately on the statement. An adding machine tape listing the individual check amounts usually accompanies each batch of checks listed.

IN —Interest   Indicates the amount of interest added to the account. Sole proprietorships, nonprofit organizations, and individuals may open NOW (negotiable order of withdrawal) checking accounts and earn interest monthly based on the balance maintained in the account.

The Bank Reconciliation

Almost invariably, the ending balance on the bank statement differs from the balance in the company's Cash in Bank account. Some reasons for differences are:

(1) Outstanding checks—checks written and deducted in arriving at the book balance but not yet presented to the bank for payment.

(2) Deposits not yet credited by the bank—deposits made near the end of the month and processed by the bank *after* the monthly statement has been prepared. These deposits in transit will appear on next month's statement.

(3) Charges made by the bank but not yet reflected on the depositor's books—for example, service and collection charges, NSF checks, and repayments of the depositor's bank loans.

(4) Credits made by the bank but not yet reflected on the depositor's books—for example, collections of notes and drafts by the bank for the depositor and interest earned by the depositor on the checking account balance.

(5) Accounting errors—errors may be made either by the depositor or by the bank.

The bank reconciliation is a schedule that accounts for any of the above differences between the bank statement balance and the company's book balance. Although we could reconcile either of these figures to the other, it is more convenient to reconcile both figures to an **adjusted balance,** which is the cash balance that will appear on the balance sheet. This amount could be withdrawn from the bank after all outstanding items have cleared. A convenient reconciliation form is illustrated below.

Balance per bank statement		$XXX	Balance per books		$XXX
Add: Deposits not yet credited by bank		XXX	Add: Items credited by bank, not yet entered on books (i.e., notes collected)		XXX
		$XXX			$XXX
Less: Outstanding checks: (list)	$XXX XXX XXX	XXX	Less: Items charged by bank, not yet entered on books (i.e., service and collection charges, NSF checks)		XXX
Adjusted balance		$XXX	Adjusted balance		$XXX

These final amounts should agree

After the reconciliation is prepared, the adjusted balance per bank statement should agree with the adjusted book balance. If these amounts do not agree, we should look carefully for reconciling items omitted from the schedule or for possible errors in record keeping. The bank reconciliation may not only bring to light transactions that must be recorded, but may also detect errors or irregularities.

BANK RECONCILIATION PROCEDURE   Assume that a December 31 bank reconciliation is to be prepared for the G.A. Shaw Company, whose bank statement is illustrated in Exhibit 7–1. Exhibits 7–2 and 7–3 show the company's December cash receipts and cash disbursements journals, respectively, in abbreviated form. Cash receipts journals may have a column for bank deposits, as shown in Exhibit 7–2.

EXHIBIT 7–2
G.A. Shaw Company
(Partial) Cash Receipts Journal
December 19XX

Date			Description	Cash Receipts	Bank Deposits
19XX					
Dec.		1	Jensen Brothers	$ 350.00	
		2	Cash sales	400.00	$ 750.00 ✓
		4	Denton Company	410.80	
		7	Jewel and Son	150.00	560.80 ✓
		8	Benson Company (note)	300.00	
		10	Cash sales	180.25	480.25 ✓
		14	Taylor Brothers	525.00	525.00 ✓
		17	Cash sales	270.25	270.25 ✓
		18	Johnson Company	250.15	
		21	Bates Company	390.05	640.20 ✓
		26	Jordan Brothers	475.00	475.00 ✓
		30	Cash sales	440.00	440.00 ✓
		31	Johnson Company	225.00	225.00
				$4,366.50	$4,366.50

After the cash journals have been posted, the Cash in Bank account of the G.A. Shaw Company appears as follows:

Cash in Bank (First National Bank)   Account No. 11

Date			Description	Post. Ref.	Debit	Credit	Balance
19XX							
Nov.		30	Balance				5,624.05
Dec.		31		CR	4,366.50		9,990.55
		31		CD		4,699.27	5,291.28

The procedures for reconciling the December 31 bank statement balance of $6,365.54 with the $5,291.28 balance on the company's books are:

(1) Trace outstanding items on the previous (November) bank reconciliation to this period's statement. The November reconciliation for the G.A. Shaw Company appears in Exhibit 7–4. The items identified with the ✓ mark, which were outstanding at the end of November, were all processed in December;

EXHIBIT 7–3
G.A. Shaw Company
(Partial) Cash Disbursements Journal
December 19XX

Date		Description	Check No.	Cash Payments
19XX				
Dec.	1	Jordan Company	156	$ 441.21 ✔
	2	Edson Brothers	157	107.15 ✔
	4	Rapid Transit, Transportation In	158	27.14 ✔
	7	Acme Realty, December rent	159	275.00 ✔
	8	Stanton Company	160	315.37 ✔
	10	Horder, Inc., Office supplies	161	76.40 ✔
	14	A.L. Smith Company	162	325.60 ✔
	17	J.B. Adams, Office salary	163	450.00 ✔
	17	O.L. Holmes, Office salary	164	239.00 ✔
	18	Abbot Van Lines, Transportation In	165	65.70 ✔
	21	Millston, Inc.	166	482.43 ✔
	21	Odana Corporation	167	301.66
	22	R.W. Knight, Cash purchase	168	149.50
	26	W.A. Sutton	169	260.00 ✔
	29	Border and Son, Cash purchase	170	122.50 ✔
	30	R.L. Olson	171	370.11 ✔
	31	J.B. Adams, Office salary	172	450.00
	31	O.L. Holmes, Office salary	173	240.50
				$4,699.27

EXHIBIT 7–4
G.A. Shaw Company
Bank Reconciliation
November 30, 19XX

Balance per bank statement	$5,640.30	Balance per books	$5,629.05
Add: Deposit not credited			
by bank	300.00 ⋀		
	$5,940.30		
Less: Outstanding checks:		Less: Bank service charge	5.00
No. 149	$125.00 ⋀		
No. 154	56.25 ⋀		
No. 155	135.00 ⋀ 316.25		
Adjusted balance	$5,624.05	Adjusted balance	$5,624.05

these amounts are identified by the same mark (✓) on the bank statement in Exhibit 7–1. Any checks that have still not cleared in December should appear again on the December reconciliation.

(2) Compare the record of deposits in the cash receipts journal (Exhibit 7–2) with the list of deposits on the bank statement. A check mark (✔) has been placed next to the amounts that appear in both records. Note that the $225.00 deposit made on December 31 does not appear on the bank statement. Enter this item in the December bank reconciliation as a deposit not yet credited by the bank.

(3) Arrange in numerical sequence the paid checks that have been returned by the bank. Compare the record of checks written from the cash disbursements journal (Exhibit 7–3) with the checks paid by the bank and returned with the bank statement. A check mark (✔) has been placed in the cash disbursements journal next to the amount of each check paid by the bank. Since checks numbered 167, 168, 172, and 173 have not cleared the bank, enter them in the December bank reconciliation as outstanding checks. (If paid checks are not returned with the bank statement, compare the record of checks written from the cash disbursements journal with the numerical listing of paid checks on the bank statement.)

(4) Scan the bank statement for charges and credits not yet reflected in the company's records. Note that the statement contains a charge of $35.40 for a returned item, a debit memo of $2.00, and a service charge of $5.00. Also, a credit for $200.00 appears in the deposits column on December 26. Bank advices indicate that an NSF check for $35.40 was charged against the company's account; that a $200.00 note receivable was collected on the company's behalf and a $2.00 collection charge was made; and that a $5.00 service charge was made for the month. Enter these items also in the December bank reconciliation.

EXHIBIT 7–5
G.A. Shaw Company
Bank Reconciliation
December 31, 19XX

Balance per bank statement		$6,365.54	Balance per books		$5,291.28
Add: Deposits not credited			Add: Collection of note	$200.00	
by bank		225.00	Less: Collection charge	2.00	198.00
		$6,590.54			$5,489.28
Less: Outstanding checks:					
No. 167	$301.66				
No. 168	149.50				
No. 172	450.00		Less: NSF check	$35.40	
No. 173	240.50	1,141.66	Bank service charge	5.00	40.40
Adjusted balance		$5,448.88	Adjusted balance		$5,448.88

After the preceding procedures have been completed, the December bank reconciliation for the G.A. Shaw Company appears as shown in Exhibit 7–5.

Before financial statements are prepared for the period ended December 31, journal entries should be made to bring the Cash account balance into agreement with the adjusted balance shown on the reconciliation. The entries for the G.A. Shaw Company would reflect the collection of the note receivable and the related collection expense, reclassification of the NSF check as an account receivable, and the bank service charge for the month.

Cash	198.00	
Miscellaneous Expense	2.00	
Notes Receivable		200.00
To record note collected by bank, less service charge.		
Accounts Receivable	35.40	
Cash		35.40
To reclassify NSF check as an account receivable.		
Miscellaneous Expense	5.00	
Cash		5.00
To record bank service charge for December.		

Electronic Funds Transfer

Billions of paper checks are written each year by businesses and individuals. The costs of processing this large volume of checks have motivated financial institutions to develop systems for transferring funds among parties electronically, without the need for paper checks. The exchange of cash through such a system is called **electronic funds transfer (EFT)**.

A typical example of EFT is the payment of a payroll. An employer firm obtains authorizations from its employees to deposit their payroll checks directly to their checking accounts. The firm then sends to the bank a magnetic tape coded with the appropriate payroll data. The bank's computer processes the magnetic tape, deducts the total payroll amount from the firm's checking account, and adds each employee's payroll amount to his or her checking account.

The use of EFT will increase with the development of expanded computer networks capable of handling electronic funds transfers. The specific controls over cash transactions handled through EFT, of course, may vary from the internal control procedures under a paper check system. However, adequate controls are no less important in an electronic funds transfer system.

THE PETTY CASH FUND

Most business firms find it inconvenient and expensive to write checks for small expenditures. Therefore, small amounts of cash needed for such items as postage, delivery service, and purchases of supplies and notions are most conveniently handled by establishing a **petty cash fund.**

The size of the petty cash fund depends on the number and the amounts of minor expenditures. Of course, it is unwise to have a large amount of cash on hand because of the risk of theft or misuse. Yet, too frequent replenishment can be a nuisance. Many firms maintain funds that will last three or four weeks. The size of expenditures made from the fund is also usually limited.

Although the use of a petty cash fund technically violates the control maxim of making all expenditures by check, control can be maintained by handling the fund on an **imprest** basis and by following certain well-established procedures. In accounting, an imprest fund contains a fixed amount of cash.

Although expenditures from an imprest petty cash fund are made in currency and coin, the fund is established by writing a check against the general bank account. Replenishments are also accomplished by issuing checks—after a review of expenditures. Therefore, in the final analysis, all expenditures are actually controlled by check.

Establishing the Fund

Assume that the G.A. Shaw Company establishes a petty cash fund of $100. It draws a check payable to Cash and exchanges it at the bank for currency and coin in denominations that are convenient for small expenditures. The entry reflecting establishment of the fund is:

Petty Cash	100	
Cash in Bank		100
To establish imprest petty cash fund.		

As evidence of a disbursement from the fund, the person in charge should place a prenumbered petty cash receipt in the petty cash box. At any time, the total cash on hand plus the amounts on the receipts should equal $100. Each receipt should give the date, amount, and nature of the expenditure and should be signed by the recipient of the cash. Such documents as cash register tapes and copies of invoices should be attached to the receipts.

Replenishing the Fund

When the fund must be replenished, a check is drawn to Cash in an amount that will bring the cash value of the fund back to $100. Expenditures from the fund are analyzed according to expense or other account category and recorded in the books. For example, assume that the G.A. Shaw Company's fund has been drawn down to $28 and that analysis of the $72 in receipts reveals the following expenditures: Office Expense, $40; Transportation In, $27; and Postage Expense, $5. The bookkeeper makes the following entry in the cash disbursements journal (shown in general journal form):

Office Expense	40	
Transportation In	27	
Postage Expense	5	
Cash in Bank		72
To replenish petty cash fund.		

The fund cashier cashes the replenishment check at the bank and places the cash in the petty cash box.

If the imprest amount is adequate, no further entries are made to the Petty Cash account itself. Notice that replenishment results in an entry to the Cash in Bank account. Only when the prescribed amount of the imprest fund is changed will entries be made to the Petty Cash account, increasing or decreasing the amount of the fund.

One person in the firm's office should be solely responsible for custody of the fund and expenditures made from it. The replenishment checks, however, should be written by another authorized person, after review of the petty cash receipts and the expense distribution. Furthermore, this person should stamp, perforate, or otherwise mutilate the supporting receipts and documents to prevent them from being used again as a basis for reimbursement.

Cash Short and Over

Errors in making change from cash funds result in less or more cash than can be accounted for. Usually, such shortages or overages are not material in amount. An account called **Cash Short and Over** is commonly used to record these discrepancies; shortages are debited to the account, and overages are credited. For example, suppose a $100 petty cash fund contains $80 in receipts for office expense and only $16 in currency and coins. The entry to replenish the fund and to record the $4 shortage would be:

Office Expense	80	
Cash Short and Over	4	
Cash in Bank		84
To replenish petty cash fund and		
record shortage.		

If the fund had contained $24 cash together with the $80 in expense receipts, the $4 overage would be credited to the Cash Short and Over account. The credit to Cash in Bank for replenishment would be $76.

The Cash Short and Over account may also be used to record cash short or over from sales when cash register tape totals do not agree with the count of cash receipts. Large discrepancies, particularly recurring shortages, should always be investigated to determine appropriate corrective steps.

A Cash Short and Over account with a debit balance at the close of an accounting period is classified as Miscellaneous Expense on the income statement. A credit balance can be classified as Other Income.

INTERNAL CONTROL IN OTHER AREAS

While it is vitally important to establish effective controls over the handling of and accounting for cash, control should also be provided for a firm's other activities. As with cash, most controls separate the authorization of a transaction, accounting for the transaction, and the custody of any related assets. For example, the purchase and sale of securities normally require authorization by a company's board of directors, and officers who have access to the securities should not have access to the accounting records. Other personnel should record security trans-actions and keep a record of security certificates by certificate number and amount.

Similarly, clerks handling inventory items should not have access to inven-tory records, and their duties should be separated from the receiving department and the processing of accounts payable. Similar controls should be exercised over receivables, plant assets, payroll transactions, and every other facet of business activity.

The subject of internal control is quite complex. Both external and internal auditors devote a great deal of attention to internal control when analyzing an accounting system and preparing audits. The importance of internal control was underscored by the enactment of the Foreign Corrupt Practices Act in 1977. Among other provisions, this law requires all corporations registering with the Securities and Exchange Commission to devise and maintain an adequate system of internal accounting controls.

SHORT-TERM INVESTMENTS

Corporate stocks and bonds may be acquired by a variety of investors, including individuals, partnerships, corporations, mutual funds, pension funds, founda-tions, and trusts. Shares of stock, of course, represent ownership interests in a corporation. Some corporations have more than one type of stock (discussed in Chapter 15). Investors holding a corporation's *common stock* have the most basic ownership rights. *Bonds* are long-term debt securities issued by corporations and various governmental agencies. Our discussion here focuses on short-term investments in stocks and bonds made by corporations.

A firm issuing stocks or bonds may sell directly to investors, or the securities may be sold through an underwriter. Most investments, however, do not involve original issues. In the typical investment, one investor purchases from another investor who happens to be selling at that time. Stocks and bonds are bought and sold on organized exchanges—such as the New York Stock Exchange—and through a less formal *over-the-counter market*. Both the buyer and the seller of a security normally use the services of a broker to acquire or dispose of their investments.

Many firms make temporary investments in highly marketable securities using seasonal excesses of cash. Furthermore, some firms invest in high-quality stocks and bonds as "back-up cash." Management could convert these securities to cash, if needed, without interfering with the company's normal operations. In the meantime, the investments produce dividend and interest income for the company. Both of these types of investments (investments of seasonal excesses of cash and for "back-up cash") are considered **short-term investments** and are classified as current assets on the balance sheet.

**Short-term
Investments
in Stocks**

When stock is purchased as a short-term investment, the amount initially recorded in the investment account is the stock's cost; that is, its total purchase price. The purchase price may include charges for such items as broker's commissions and transfer taxes. Suppose 100 shares of United Pride common stock are acquired as a short-term investment on October 1 at a cost of $4,290, including commissions and taxes. The investment is recorded as follows:

Oct. 1	Investment in United Pride Stock	4,290	
	Cash		4,290
	To record purchase of 100 shares of		
	common stock for $4,290.		

DIVIDENDS   A corporation's board of directors may declare a **dividend,** which is a distribution of the corporation's assets. The asset distributed is usually cash. A corporation also may distribute a **stock dividend**—shares of its own stock. For example, if a board of directors declares a 5% stock dividend, then additional shares of stock equal to 5% of the corporation's outstanding stock are distributed to the current stockholders in proportion to their current stock holdings.

Cash dividends do not accrue on shares of stock. A corporation has no legal obligation to pay a dividend until it is declared by the board of directors. A company holding stock may record the cash dividend after it has been declared by debiting Dividends Receivable and crediting Dividend Income, but ordinarily no entry is made until the dividend is received. Assuming the United Pride board of directors declares a cash dividend of $1.00 per share and dividend income is recorded when received, the entry to record the receipt of the dividend on December 29 would be:

Dec. 29	Cash	100	
	Dividend Income		100
	To record receipt of $100 dividend on		
	investment in United Pride stock.		

The receipt of a stock dividend does not constitute income, and requires no formal journal entry. A memorandum of the number of shares received, however, should be recorded in the investment account. The recipient of the stock dividend now holds more stock without further investment, so the average cost of each share held has been reduced. If United Pride declares a 10% common stock dividend, the company holding 100 shares of United Pride would make the following notation on receipt of 10 additional shares:

(Memorandum) Received 10 shares of United Pride common stock as stock dividend. Average cost per share of 110 shares held is now $39 ($4,290/110).

LOWER OF COST OR MARKET FOR PORTFOLIO   A corporation's stock **portfolio** refers to its investment in several different stocks. At the end of an accounting period, short-term stock investments are reported on the balance sheet at the lower of the aggregate cost or market value of the portfolio. Should the aggregate market value drop below total cost, an unrealized loss[3] is recorded and a contra asset account (to offset short-term stock investments) is credited. To illustrate, let us assume a company has the following portfolio of short-term stock investments at the end of its first year of operations:

Stock	Cost	Market Value
United Pride Common	$ 4,290	$ 3,800
Bayou Oil Common	17,000	17,500
Swan, Inc., Common	16,500	15,200
Total	$37,790	$36,500

Because the total market value ($36,500) is less than total cost ($37,790), the following journal entry is made:

Dec. 31	Unrealized Loss on Short-term		
	Investments	1,290	
	Allowance to Reduce Short-term		
	Investments to Market		1,290
	To record unrealized loss on portfolio		
	of short-term stock investments.		

The unrealized loss is reported in the current year's income statement. The credit to the contra asset account (1) permits original cost to remain in the various stock investment accounts and (2) reduces the total book value of the investments to market value on the balance sheet. The short-term stock investments would appear on the balance sheet as follows:

Short-term Stock Investments (cost)	$37,790	
Less: Allowance to Reduce Short-term Investments to Market	1,290	$36,500

Or, the investments may be reported in condensed form:

Short-term Stock Investments, at market (cost $37,790)	$36,500

Of course, if the portfolio's market value exceeds its total cost, the investments are reported at cost and no allowance account is created.

SALE OF SHORT-TERM STOCK INVESTMENTS

When a short-term stock investment is sold, a gain or loss is recorded equal to the difference between the proceeds of the sale and the stock's original cost (or the original cost adjusted for

[3] Unrealized losses are losses on securities still owned by the firm. For details, see Statement of Financial Accounting Standards No. 12, "Accounting for Certain Marketable Securities" (Stamford, CT: Financial Accounting Standards Board, 1975).

the effect of a stock dividend). For example, if all 110 shares of the United Pride stock discussed above were sold on February 1 of the next year for $3,800, the following entry would be made:

Feb. 1	Cash	3,800	
	Loss on Sale of Investments	490	
	Investment in United Pride Stock		4,290
	To record sale of stock for $3,800.		

RECOVERY OF UNREALIZED LOSS   The difference between the total cost and market value of a short-term stock portfolio will likely change from one year-end to the next because of changes in market values or in the portfolio's composition. Thus, the contra asset account will be increased or decreased each year-end to reflect the net unrealized portfolio loss at that time. If the net unrealized loss at year-end is smaller than the year before, the adjusting entry records a recovery of an unrealized loss. To illustrate, let us assume the company whose investments we have been analyzing has the following portfolio of short-term stock investments at the end of its second year of operations:

Stock	Cost	Market Value
Bayou Oil Common	$17,000	$17,600
Swan, Inc., Common	16,500	15,700
Total	$33,500	$33,300

The net unrealized loss is now $200 ($33,500 − $33,300); at the end of the preceding year, it had been $1,290. The following entry would adjust the allowance account:

Dec. 31	Allowance to Reduce Short-term		
	Investments to Market	1,090	
	Recovery of Unrealized Loss on		
	Short-term Investments		1,090
	To record decrease in net unrealized loss		
	on short-term stock investments.		

The recovery of the unrealized loss is included in the current year's income statement. The $200 credit balance now in the allowance account offsets the cost of short-term investments in the year-end balance sheet.

Short-term Investments in Bonds   A short-term bond investment is initially recorded at its acquisition cost, which includes any broker's commissions and transfer taxes. Because a bond is a debt security, the bondholder receives periodic interest payments from the bond issuer. Interest accrues daily on a bond and usually is paid semiannually. On an interest payment date, a bondholder receives the full amount of interest accrued since the last payment date, regardless of when the bond was purchased. As a result, the purchase price of a bond that is sold between interest payment dates includes not only the current market price but also any interest accrued since the last interest payment date. The bond seller, therefore, receives the interest income earned up to the date of sale. The bond investor debits the accrued interest purchased to a Bond Interest Receivable account. Because the accrued interest is received with the first interest payment, it is not treated as part of the initial cost of the investment.

The **face value,** or **maturity value,** of a bond is the amount of principal to be repaid at the maturity date. The annual rate of interest payable on a bond— often called the *coupon* or *nominal* rate of interest—is stated in the bond agreement. To determine the amount of interest paid semiannually on such bonds, we multiply the face value by one-half the coupon rate of interest.

Purchasing a bond at **par** means paying an amount equal to its face value. A bond purchased at a **discount** costs less than its face value, and a bond purchased at a **premium** costs more than its face value. An investor discounts a bond when the current market rate of interest exceeds the bond's coupon interest rate; a bond sells at a premium when its coupon rate exceeds the current market interest rate. Bond prices are usually stated as a percentage of face value—for example, a bond selling at 98 costs 98% of its face value, and a bond quoted at 101 sells for 101% of its face value.

Let us assume that $10,000 face value of Anko Company 12% bonds are bought on May 1 at 97 plus accrued interest. The brokerage commission is $40. Semiannual interest is paid on January 1 and July 1. The accrued interest from January 1 to May 1 is $400 ($10,000 $\times$ 0.12 $\times$ $\frac{4}{12}$), which is recorded separately in a Bond Interest Receivable account. The cost entered in the bond investment account is $9,740, including the brokerage commission. The following entry records the acquisition:

May 1	Investment in Anko Company Bonds	9,740	
	Bond Interest Receivable	400	
	Cash		10,140
	To record purchase of bonds at 97 plus commission of $40 plus four months' accrued interest.		

The entry to record the receipt of the semiannual interest payment on July 1 would be:

July 1	Cash	600	
	Bond Interest Receivable		400
	Bond Interest Income		200
	To record receipt of semiannual interest on Anko Company bonds.		

The $200 credit to interest income reflects the interest earned for the two months the bonds have been held. The other $400 is the accrued interest purchased when the bonds were acquired.

Short-term bond investments are usually sold at a gain or loss. Such gain or loss is computed by comparing the proceeds of the sale, net of any accrued interest received, to the carrying value of the investment. If the proceeds from the sale of the Anko Company bonds on October 1 were $9,800 plus accrued interest of $300 for three months, the following entry would be made:

Oct. 1	Cash	10,100	
	Investment in Anko Company Bonds		9,740
	Bond Interest Income		300
	Gain on Sale of Investments		60
	To record sale of bond investment for		
	$9,800 plus interest of $300.		

Certificates of Deposit

In addition to marketable stocks and bonds, a corporation may invest excess cash in another type of security—a **certificate of deposit (CD)**. These certificates may be purchased at banks and other financial institutions. They offer fixed rates of return on investments for specified periods (such as 90 days, six months, or one year). Generally, the fixed interest rate increases with the amount or the duration of the investment. CDs are recorded at cost and reported on the balance sheet as a current asset immediately below cash. Interest income from CDs is recorded in the period in which it is earned. These accounting guidelines apply also to short-term investments in other forms of savings certificates: The investment is recorded at its cost, and interest income is recorded in the period in which it is earned.

DEMONSTRATION PROBLEM FOR REVIEW

At December 31 of the current year, the Cash account in Tyler Company's general ledger had a debit balance of $18,434.27. The December 31 bank statement showed a balance of $19,726.40. In reconciling the two amounts, you discover the following:

(1) Bank deposits made by Tyler on December 31 amounting to $2,145.40 do not appear on the bank statement.

(2) A non-interest-bearing note receivable for $2,000, left with the bank for collection, was collected by the bank near the end of December. The bank credited the proceeds, less a $5 collection charge, on the bank statement. Tyler Company has not recorded the collection.

(3) Accompanying the bank statement is a debit memorandum indicating that John Miller's check for $450 was charged against Tyler's bank account on December 30 because of insufficient funds.

(4) Check No. 586, written for advertising expense of $869.10, was recorded as $896.10 in Tyler Company's cash disbursements journal.

(5) A comparison of the paid checks returned by the bank with the cash disbursements journal revealed the following checks still outstanding at December 31:

No. 561	$306.63	No. 591	$190.00
No. 585	440.00	No. 592	282.50
No. 588	476.40	No. 593	243.00

(6) The bank mistakenly charged Tyler Company's account for check printing costs of $30.50, which should have been charged to Taylor Company.

(7) The bank charged Tyler Company's account $42.50 for rental of a safe deposit box. No entry has been made in Tyler's records for this expense.

REQUIRED

(a) Prepare a bank reconciliation at December 31.

(b) Prepare any necessary journal entries at December 31.

SOLUTION TO DEMONSTRATION PROBLEM

(a)

Tyler Company
Bank Reconciliation
December 31, 19XX

Balance per bank statement	$19,726.50	Balance per books		$18,434.27
Add: Deposits not credited		Add: Collection		
by bank	2,145.40	of note	$2,000.00	
Error by bank (Check		Less:		
printing charge of		Collection		
Taylor Co.)	30.50	charge	5.00	1,995.00
	$21,902.30	Error in		
		recording		
		check No.		
		586		27.00
				$20,456.27
Less: Outstanding checks:		Less:		
No. 561	$306.63	NSF check	$450.00	
No. 585	440.00	Charge for		
No. 588	476.40	safe deposit		
No. 591	190.00	box	42.50	492.50
No. 592	282.50			
No. 593	243.00 1,938.53			
Adjusted balance	$19,963.77	Adjusted balance		$19,963.77

(b)

Dec. 31	Cash		1,995.00	
	Miscellaneous Expense		5.00	
	Notes Receivable			2,000.00
	To record collection of note by bank, less collection charge.			
31	Cash		27.00	
	Advertising Expense			27.00
	To correct error in recording advertising expense.			

Dec. 31	Accounts Receivable	450.00	
	Cash		450.00
	To reclassify NSF check as an account receivable.		
31	Miscellaneous Expense	42.50	
	Cash		42.50
	To record rental expense of safe deposit box.		

KEY POINTS TO REMEMBER

(1) *Internal control* consists of the measures to safeguard a firm's assets, check accuracy and reliability of accounting data, promote operational efficiency, and encourage adherence to managerial policies. *Accounting controls* are related to the protection of assets and the reliability of accounting data; *administrative controls* deal mainly with efficiency and management's policies.

(2) Depositing all receipts intact at the bank and making all cash disbursements by check are important cash controls. These procedures provide a double record of cash—the firm's record and the bank's record.

(3) Neither the book balance nor the bank statement balance of cash usually represents the cash balance shown on the balance sheet. Both amounts are reconciled to a third figure—the adjusted balance—which appears on the balance sheet and is the amount that could be withdrawn after all outstanding items have cleared.

(4) Petty Cash is debited when an imprest fund for small expenditures is established or increased. When the fund is replenished, the individual accounts for which expenditures have been made are debited.

(5) Short-term investments in stock are normally carried at the lower of cost or market value of the portfolio. Unrealized losses or recoveries of unrealized losses are included in the income statement.

(6) Short-term investments in bonds are recorded at their acquisition cost. When sold, the difference between the sales proceeds (net of accrued interest) and the bond's carrying value is shown as a gain (when proceeds exceed carrying value) or a loss (when carrying value exceeds proceeds).

QUESTIONS

7–1 Define *internal control*. Name several specific features of a good system of internal control.

7–2 What is the difference between internal accounting controls and administrative controls?

7–3 Why is work division an important feature of good internal accounting controls?

7–4 What internal control procedures are especially important in handling cash transactions?

7–5 Indicate whether the following statements relating to internal control systems are true or false:
   (a) Under the principle of separating accountability and physical custodianship, the accounts receivable bookkeeper should not make bank deposits.
   (b) When possible, the general ledger bookkeeper should also keep subsidiary records.
   (c) Rotation of personnel in record-keeping duties violates the rule that responsibility should not be shared.
   (d) Even with careful attention to good internal controls, guarding against defalcations and irregularities involving collusion among employees is difficult.
   (e) Internal auditing departments eliminate the need for audits by independent public accountants.

7–6 The owner of a medium-sized business asks you why she should be concerned with an internal control system for the firm, since all officers and employees who have access to cash and liquid assets are bonded. How should you respond to this question?

7–7 What is the purpose of a bank reconciliation?

7–8 In preparing a bank reconciliation, how should you determine (a) deposits not recorded in the bank statement and (b) outstanding checks?

7–9 Indicate whether the following bank reconciliation items should be (1) added to the bank statement balance, (2) deducted from the bank statement balance, (3) added to the ledger account balance, or (4) deducted from the ledger account balance:
   (a) Bank service charge.
   (b) NSF check.
   (c) Deposit in transit.
   (d) Outstanding check.
   (e) Bank error charging company's account with another company's check.
   (f) Difference of $270 in amount of check written for $858 but recorded in the cash disbursements journal for $588.

7–10 Which of the items listed in Question 7–9 require a journal entry on the company's books?

7–11 What is an imprest petty cash fund? How is such a fund established and replenished? Describe the accounting entries involved.

7–12 In preparing to replenish the $150 petty cash fund, the cashier discovers that the fund contains $138 in petty cash vouchers for office expenses and $7 in currency and coins. (a) What should be the amount of the replenishment check? (b) How should the $5 discrepancy be recorded?

7–13 Why do corporations make short-term investments in securities? Where should short-term investments be classified in the balance sheet?

7–14 Interest on bond investments is accrued, but dividends on stock investments are not accrued. Why?

7–15 What entry, if any, should be made when a corporation receives a stock dividend on a short-term stock investment? What entry should be made when a cash dividend is received on a short-term stock investment?

7-16 At what amount are short-term stock investments reported in the balance sheet? Where are unrealized losses on the short-term stock investments portfolio reported?

7-17 Malit Corporation purchased bonds with a face value of $60,000 and a 9% coupon rate at 102 plus four months' accrued interest. Calculate the total cash outlay for the bonds. What amount should be charged to the bond investment account?

7-18 What is a certificate of deposit? When should interest income on a certificate of deposit be recorded?

EXERCISES

7-19 The following four situations occurred in the Duel Corporation:
  (a) The mail opener converted a check payable to Duel Corporation to his personal use. The check was included in the list of remittances sent to the accounting department. He treated the missing amount as a deposit in transit while doing the bank reconciliation.
  (b) The purchasing agent used the company's purchase order to order building materials. Later, she instructed the building supply company by telephone to deliver the materials to her home and to charge Duel Corporation's account. At month-end, she approved the invoice for payment.
  (c) A vendor was paid twice for the same shipment. One payment was made on receipt of the invoice and a second payment on receipt of the monthly statement—the first remittance had arrived too late to appear on the monthly statement.
  (d) The cashier pocketed cash received over the counter from certain customers paying their accounts. He then wrote off the receivables as uncollectible.
  For each situation, indicate any violations of good internal control procedures, and describe the steps you would take to safeguard the system against this type of occurrence.

7-20 Explain how each of the following unrelated procedures strengthens internal control:
  (a) After preparing a check for a cash disbursement, Marlong Lumber Company's treasurer cancels the supporting documentation (purchase requisition, receiving report, and invoice) with a perforator.
  (b) The clerks of the Ideal Department Store give each customer a cash register receipt along with the proper change.
  (c) The ticket-taker of the Cinema II theater tears each admission ticket in half and gives each patron a stub.
  (d) The Cuisine Restaurant provides waiters and waitresses with prenumbered customers' checks. The servers are to void spoiled checks and issue new ones rather than make alterations or corrections on them. Voided checks must be given to the manager every day.

7-21 Use the following information to prepare a bank reconciliation for the Lawson Company at June 30 of the current year.
  (1) Balance per Cash account, June 30, $6,142.20.
  (2) Balance per bank statement, June 30, $8,430.15.
  (3) Deposits not reflected on bank statement, $940.

(4) Outstanding checks, June 30, $3,092.95.

(5) Service charge on bank statement not recorded in books, $15.

(6) Error by bank—Larson Company check charged on Lawson Company's bank statement, $210.

(7) Check for advertising expense, $480, incorrectly recorded in books as $840.

7–22 Record the following Parker Corporation activities in general journal form:

Apr. 1   Established a $250 petty cash fund by writing a check on the First National Bank.

     17   Replenished the petty cash fund by writing a check on the First National Bank. The fund contains the following:

Currency and coins	$ 24.00
Bills and receipts:	
Delivery Expense	91.00
Contributions Expense	50.00
Office Expense	85.00
	$250.00

     30   Replenished the petty cash fund and increased it to $350 by writing a check on the First National Bank. The fund contains:

Currency and coins	$ 23.00
Bills and receipts:	
Transportation In	135.00
Delivery Expense	60.00
Office Expense	32.00
	$250.00

7–23 During its first year of operations, Raglin, Inc., made two purchases of common stock as short-term investments. On May 20, 19X1, the firm acquired 400 shares of A Company at $38 per share plus a $100 broker's fee, and on July 16, 19X1, it purchased 300 shares of X Company at $81 per share plus a $120 broker's fee. On December 27, Raglin, Inc., received a cash dividend of $1.25 per share from A Company (Raglin records dividend income when received). The December 31 quoted market prices per share for the stock were A Company, $39, and X Company, $76. On January 26, 19X2, Raglin sold the A Company stock for $40 per share. Present journal entries to reflect (a) the stock purchases, (b) the receipt of the A Company dividend, (c) the reduction of the stock portfolio to the lower of cost or market at December 31, and (d) the sale of the A Company stock.

7–24 As a short-term investment, Ruhl Company purchased ten $1,000, 9% bonds at 96 plus three months' accrued interest on April 1, 19X2. The brokerage commission was $90. The bonds pay interest on June 30 and December 31. Present journal entries to reflect (a) the purchase of the bonds for cash on April 1, 19X2; (b) the receipt of the semiannual interest payment on June 30, 19X2; and (c) the receipt of the semiannual interest payment on December 31, 19X2.

7–25 Present a journal entry to record the sale of the bonds described in Exercise 7–24 at 99 plus accrued interest on March 1, 19X3.

PROBLEMS

7–26 The western branch of Fitness Distributors, Inc., handles a significant amount of credit sales, over-the-counter cash sales, and C.O.D. (cash on delivery) sales. The sales clerk prepares two copies of a sales ticket for all cash sales. One copy is given to the customer. The cashier keeps the other copy and stamps it "paid" when cash is received from an over-the-counter customer or from the delivery service. Because the sales tickets are not prenumbered, the cashier files them by the date of sale. At the end of each day, the cashier summarizes the over-the-counter cash sales and the amounts received from the delivery service for C.O.D. sales and sends the total to the bookkeeper for recording.

   The branch does its own billings and collects receivables from credit customers. Mail remittances from credit customers are opened in the mail-room. Mailroom personnel make one copy of a list of remittances, which they forward to the bookkeeper together with the customers' checks. The book-keeper verifies the cash discounts (credit sales are 2/10, n/30), records the remittances, and then sends the checks to the cashier. The cashier makes up the daily deposits for the bank, including both cash sales and remittances received on account. At the end of the month, the cashier receives the bank statement and makes the bank reconciliation. Also at month-end, the book-keeper mails monthly statements of account to customers with outstanding balances.

REQUIRED
(a) List the irregularities that might occur with this system.
(b) Suggest improvements in the system of internal control.
(c) What feature of internal control in the current system would likely reveal that a mail clerk has converted checks received through the mail to personal use (that is, the mail clerk keeps the check and does not record it on the list of remittances)?

7–27 Each of the lettered paragraphs (a)–(d) briefly describes an independent situation involving some aspect of internal control.

REQUIRED
Answer the questions at the end of each paragraph.
(a) As the office manager of a small business, R.L. Grey opens all incoming mail, makes bank deposits, and keeps both the general ledger and the customers' subsidiary ledger. Two assistants write up the special journals (cash, purchases, and sales) and prepare the customers' monthly statements.
   (1) If Grey pocketed Customer A's $50 remittance in full of account and made no effort to conceal his defalcation in the books, how would the misappropriation probably be discovered?
   (2) What routine accounting procedure would disclose Grey's $50 defalcation in (1), even if he destroyed Customer A's subsidiary ledger card?
   (3) What circumstances might disclose Grey's $50 defalcation if he marked Customer A's account "paid in full" and set up a $50 account for fictitious Customer B with a fictitious address?

(4) In (3) above, why might Grey be anxious to open the mail himself each morning?

(5) In (3) above, why might Grey want to have the authority to write off accounts considered uncollectible?

(b) A doughnut shop uses a cash register with a locked-in tape that accumulates registered transactions. A prominently displayed sign announces a free doughnut for every customer who is not given the cash register receipt with his or her purchase. How is this procedure an internal control device for the doughnut shop?

(c) Veri Klever, a swindler, sent several business firms invoices requesting payment for office supplies that had never been delivered to the firm. A 5% discount was offered for prompt payment. What internal control procedures should prevent this swindle from being successful?

(d) Customers of The Compleat Cafeteria encounter the cashier at the end of the food line. At this point, the cashier rings up the food costs, and the customer pays the bill. The customer line frequently backs up while the person paying searches for the correct amount of cash. To speed things up, the cashier often collects money from the next customer or two who have the correct change without ringing up their food costs. After the first customer finally pays, the cashier rings up the costs for these customers who have already paid.

(1) What is the internal control weakness in this procedure?

(2) How might the internal control over the collection of cash from the cafeteria customers be strengthened?

7–28 On July 31, Levin Company's Cash in Bank account had a balance of $6,742.15. On that date, the bank statement indicated a balance of $10,433.50. Comparison of returned checks and bank advices revealed the following:

(1) Deposits in transit July 31 amounted to $1,015.30.

(2) Outstanding checks July 31 totaled $1,522.15.

(3) The bank erroneously charged an $800 check of the Lanvin Company against the Levin bank account.

(4) A $10 bank service charge has not yet been recorded on the books.

(5) Levin neglected to record $4,500 borrowed from the bank on a 10% six-month note. The bank statement shows the $4,500 as a deposit.

(6) Included with the returned checks is a memo indicating that J. Carten's check for $514.50 had been returned NSF. Carten, a customer, had sent the check to pay an account of $525 less a 2% discount.

(7) Levin Company recorded a $734 payment for repairs as $743.

REQUIRED

(a) Prepare a bank reconciliation for Levin Company at July 31.

(b) Prepare the general journal entry or entries necessary to bring the Cash in Bank account into agreement with the adjusted balance on the bank reconciliation.

7–29 The bank reconciliation made by Hilton, Inc., on August 31 of the current year showed a deposit in transit of $570 and two outstanding checks, No. 597 for $260 and No. 603 for $180. The adjusted balance per books on August 31 was $6,980.

The following bank statement is available for September:

Bank Statement

| TO Hilton, Inc. | | | September 30, 19XX | | | |
| St. Louis, MO | | | STATE BANK | | | |
Date	Deposits	No.	Date	Charges	Date	Balance
					Aug. 31	$6,850
Sept. 1	$570	603	Sept. 1	$180	Sept. 1	7,240
2	350	607	5	450	2	7,590
5	420	608	5	325	5	7,235
9	296	609	9	192	8	6,977
15	580	610	8	258	9	7,081
17	404	611	17	410	15	7,419
25	335	612	15	242	17	7,413
30	256	614	25	153	25	7,595
		NSF	29	335	29	7,260
		SC	30	15	30	7,501

A list of deposits made and checks written during September, taken from the cash receipts journal and cash disbursements journal, respectively, is shown below:

Deposits Made		Checks Written	
Sept. 1	$ 350	No. 607	$ 450
4	420	608	325
8	296	609	192
12	580	610	285
16	404	611	410
24	335	612	242
29	256	613	214
30	430	614	153
	$3,071	615	357
		616	162
			$2,790

The Cash in Bank account balance on September 30 was $7,261. In reviewing checks returned by the bank, the bookkeeper discovered that check No. 610, written for $258 for repairs expense, was recorded in the cash disbursements journal as $285. The NSF check for $335, which Hilton deposited on September 24, was a payment on account from customer D. Lewis.

REQUIRED
(a) Prepare a bank reconciliation for Hilton, Inc., at September 30.
(b) Prepare the necessary journal entries to bring the Cash in Bank account into agreement with the adjusted balance on the bank reconciliation.

7–30 Cartise, Inc., established an imprest petty cash fund on July 1 of the current year. The following transactions took place during July:

July   1   Wrote check against United Bank account to establish the petty cash fund, $200.

    15   Replenished the fund by check against the United Bank account for $168.25. The following bills and receipts were on hand:

Freight on C.O.D. purchase of merchandise	$ 78.75
Postage	20.00
Typewriter repairs	52.50
Lunch with client (entertainment expense)	17.00
	$168.25

    29   Replenished the fund and increased it to $250 by writing a check against the United Bank account. On this date, the fund contained $15.50 in currency and coins. Bills and receipts on hand were for postage, $35; office supplies expense, $44.50; charitable contributions, $25; and freight on C.O.D. purchase of merchandise, $75.

REQUIRED
Record the July petty cash transactions for Cartise, Inc., in general journal form.

7–31 The following selected transactions relate to the Thermal Corporation during 19X1 and 19X2, its first two years of operations. The company closes its books on December 31.

19X1

Mar. 26   Purchased 3,000 common shares of Aspin, Inc., as a short-term investment at a total cost of $69,300.

July   1   Invested $10,000 in a one-year certificate of deposit at Local Bank. The annual interest rate on the certificate is 8.8%.

    1   Purchased, as a short-term investment, twenty $1,000, 10% Sable Company bonds at 101 plus $100 of commissions and taxes. The bonds pay interest on June 30 and December 31.

Sept. 7   Purchased 2,500 common shares of Bloom, Inc., as a short-term investment at a total cost of $112,500.

Dec.   2   Bloom, Inc., declared a cash dividend of 80 cents per common share, payable on December 29. Thermal Corporation records dividend income when dividends are received.

    3   Received 150 shares of Aspin, Inc., common stock as a 5% stock dividend. The stock's current market price per share was $19.

    29   Received cash dividend, declared December 2, from Bloom, Inc.

    31   Received semiannual interest payment on Sable Company bonds.

    31   Accrued interest receivable for six months on certificate of deposit. (Thermal Corporation does not use reversing entries.)

    31   Adjusted portfolio of short-term stock investments to lower of cost or market. Current market prices per share were Aspin, Inc., $20.50; and Bloom, Inc., $43.

19X2

June 30   Received $10,880 when the one-year certificate of deposit (purchased July 1, 19X1) was cashed in.

   30   Received semiannual interest payment on Sable Company bonds.

REQUIRED

(a) Record these transactions in general journal form.

(b) Assume that holdings of short-term stock investments did not change during 19X2. What entry would be made at December 31, 19X2, to adjust the portfolio to the lower of cost or market if the per share market prices at that date were Aspin, Inc., $21; and Bloom, Inc., $43.25?

7–32   The Toni Corporation began operations on January 1, 19X1. The following transactions relate to Toni Corporation's short-term investments in stocks during 19X1 and 19X2:

19X1

Feb.   15   Purchased 1,500 common shares of Brenner, Inc., at a total cost of $39,000.

April 20   Purchased 5,000 common shares of Downie Corporation at a total cost of $89,700.

June   25   Received 200 shares of Downie Corporation common stock as a 4% stock dividend. The stock's current market price per share was $18.50.

Aug.   6   Purchased 1,000 common shares of Sparklet, Inc., at a total cost of $27,000.

Sept.   3   Sold 2,000 Downie Corporation common shares at a price of $18 per share.

Dec.   15   Received a cash dividend of $1.20 per common share from Brenner, Inc. Brenner declared the dividend on November 20. Toni Corporation records dividend income when dividends are received.

   30   Received a cash dividend of $1 per common share from Sparklet, Inc.

   31   Adjusted portfolio of short-term stock investments to lower of cost or market. Current market prices per share were Brenner, Inc., $28; Downie Corporation, $15.50; and Sparklet, Inc., $26.50.

19X2

Mar.   11   Sold remaining 3,200 Downie Corporation common shares at a price of $17 per share.

Dec.   15   Received a cash dividend of $1.25 per common share from Brenner, Inc.

   30   Received a cash dividend of 60 cents per common share from Sparklet, Inc.

   31   Adjusted portfolio of short-term stock investments to lower of cost or market. Current market prices per share were Brenner, Inc., $27; and Sparklet, Inc., $24.

REQUIRED

Record these transactions in general journal form.

ALTERNATE PROBLEMS

7–26A   The Gallagher Company has three clerical employees who must perform the following functions:

(1) Maintain general ledger.
(2) Maintain accounts payable ledger.
(3) Maintain accounts receivable ledger.
(4) Prepare checks for signature.
(5) Maintain cash disbursements journal.
(6) Issue credits on returns and allowances.
(7) Reconcile the bank account.
(8) Handle and deposit cash receipts.

The office manager of the Gallagher Company wishes to assign the above functions to the three employees in the manner that achieves the highest degree of internal control.

REQUIRED
Distribute the functions among the employees in a manner compatible with good internal control.

7–28A On May 31, the Cash in Bank account of the Holden Company, a sole proprietorship, had a balance of $7,822.71. On that date, the bank statement indicated a balance of $9,602.78. Comparison of returned checks and bank advices revealed the following:

(1) Deposits in transit May 31 totaled $2,118.
(2) Outstanding checks May 31 totaled $3,240.37.
(3) The bank added to the account $42.20 of interest income earned by Holden during May.
(4) The bank collected a $2,000 note receivable for Holden and charged a $9.00 collection fee. Both items appear on the bank statement.
(5) Bank service charges in addition to the collection fee, not yet recorded on the books, were $20.
(6) Included with the returned checks is a memo indicating that L. Jensen's check for $784 had been returned NSF. Jensen, a customer, had sent the check to pay an account of $800 less a 2% discount.
(7) Holden Company recorded the payment of an account payable as $63.50; the check was for $635.

REQUIRED
(a) Prepare a bank reconciliation for Holden Company at May 31.
(b) Prepare the general journal entry or entries necessary to bring the Cash in Bank account into agreement with the adjusted balance on the bank reconciliation.

7–29A The bank reconciliation made by Northport Company, a sole proprietorship, on March 31 of the current year showed a deposit in transit of $810 and two outstanding checks, No. 707 for $345 and No. 804 for $400. The adjusted balance per books on March 31 was $8,160.

The following bank statement is available for April:

Bank Statement

To: Northport Company Fairbanks, AK				April, 19XX FAIRBANKS NATIONAL BANK		
Date	**Deposits**	**No.**	**Date**	**Charges**	**Date**	**Balance**
					March 31	$8,095
Apr. 1	$810	804	Apr. 2	$400	Apr. 1	8,905
3	540	807	3	325	2	8,505
7	900	808	7	530	3	8,720
13	270	809	7	274	7	8,816
18	630	810	16	190	13	8,700
23	350	811	13	386	16	8,510
27	390	813	27	72	18	9,020
30	480	814	23	250	23	9,120
30	40 IN	NSF	18	120	27	9,438
		SC	30	25	30	9,933

A list of deposits made and checks written during April, taken from the cash receipts journal and cash disbursements journal, respectively, is shown below:

Deposits Made		**Checks Written**	
Apr. 2	$ 540	No. 807	$ 325
6	900	808	530
10	270	809	274
17	630	810	190
22	350	811	368
24	390	812	335
29	480	813	72
30	525	814	250
	$4,085	815	110
		816	278
			$2,732

The Cash in Bank account balance on April 30 was $9,513. In reviewing checks returned by the bank, the bookkeeper discovered that check No. 811, written for $386 for delivery expense, was recorded in the cash disbursements journal as $368. The NSF check for $120 was that of customer R. Benson, deposited in April. Interest for April added to the account by the bank was $40.

REQUIRED
(a) Prepare a bank reconciliation for Northport Company at April 30.
(b) Prepare the necessary journal entries to bring the Cash in Bank account into agreement with the adjusted balance on the bank reconciliation.

7–30A Energy, Inc. established an imprest petty cash fund on May 1 of the current year. The following transactions took place during May:

May 1   Wrote check against American Bank account to establish the petty cash fund, $100.

    12   Replenished the fund by check against the American Bank account for $89.55. The following bills and receipts were on hand:

Charge for rush delivery of package across town	$15.75
Postage	30.00
Calculator repairs	25.00
Flowers sent to customer opening new office (advertising expense)	18.80
	$89.55

    25   Replenished the fund and increased it to $125 by writing a check against the American Bank account. On this date, the fund contained $4.50 in currency and coins. Bills and receipts on hand were for postage, $35; office supplies expense, $29.50; and instant printing charges (advertising expense), $25.

REQUIRED

Record the May petty cash transactions for Energy, Inc. in general journal form.

7–31A The following selected transactions relate to the Bayshore Corporation during 19X1 and 19X2, its first two years of operations. The company closes its books on December 31.

19X1

Feb. 17   Purchased 1,800 common shares of Telemark, Inc., as a short-term investment at a total cost of $55,800.

May 31   Purchased, as a short-term investment, twelve $1,000, 9% Rhone Company bonds at 95 plus five months' accrued interest. The brokerage commission was $80. The bonds pay interest on June 30 and December 31.

June 30   Received semiannual interest payment on Rhone Company bonds.

July 1   Invested $20,000 in a one-year certificate of deposit at Stable Bank. The annual interest rate on the certificate is 8.5%.

Aug. 10   Purchased 1,000 common shares of Galtech, Inc., as a short-term investment at a total cost of $58,300.

Dec. 1   Telemark, Inc., declared a cash dividend of $1.05 per common share, payable on December 28. Bayshore Corporation records dividend income when dividends are received.

     5   Received 60 shares of Galtech, Inc., common stock as a 6% stock dividend. The stock's current market price per share was $57.

    28   Received cash dividend, declared December 1, from Telemark, Inc.

    31   Received semiannual interest payment on Rhone Company bonds.

    31   Accrued interest receivable for six months on certificate of deposit. (Bayshore Corporation does not use reversing entries.)

    31   Adjusted portfolio of short-term stock investments to lower of cost or market. Current market prices per share were Telemark, Inc., $29.25; and Galtech, Inc., $54.

19X2

Feb.   1   Sold Rhone Company bonds for $11,800 plus accrued interest for one month.

June 30   Received $21,700 when the one-year certificate of deposit (purchased July 1, 19X1) was cashed in.

REQUIRED

(a) Record these transactions in general journal form.

(b) Assume that holdings of short-term stock investments did not change during 19X2. What entry would be made at December 31, 19X2, to adjust the portfolio to the lower of cost or market if the per share market prices at that date were Telemark, Inc., $30; and Galtech, Inc., $56?

7–32A   The following transactions relate to Woodstock Company's short-term investments in stocks and bonds during 19X5:

19X5

Jan.   10   Purchased 2,100 common shares of Pevonka Corporation at a total cost of $32,760.

Feb.   1   Purchased ten $1,000, 12% Sloan Company bonds at 102 plus one month's accrued interest. The brokerage commission was $50. The bonds pay interest on January 1 and July 1.

May 28   Purchased 1,400 common shares of Cook, Inc., at a total cost of $30,800.

June 30   Received a cash dividend of 50 cents per common share from Cook, Inc.

July   1   Received semiannual interest payment on Sloan Company bonds.

        1   Purchased six $1,000, 10% Rakor Company bonds at 95 plus a $45 brokerage commission. The bonds pay interest on January 1 and July 1.

Sept. 30   Received 84 shares of Pevonka Corporation common stock as a 4% stock dividend. The stock's current market price was $17.

Nov.   1   Sold the Sloan Company bonds for $9,950 plus accrued interest for four months.

       17   Sold the Pevonka Corporation common stock for $15.25 per share.

Dec.   1   Sold the Rakor Company bonds for $6,000 plus accrued interest for five months.

       14   Sold the Cook, Inc., common stock for $20.50 per share.

REQUIRED

Record these transactions in general journal form.

BUSINESS DECISION PROBLEM

On December 15 of the current year, Kyle Small, who owns the Small Scale Company, asks you to investigate the cash-handling activities in his firm. He thinks that an employee might be abstracting funds. "I have no proof," he says, "but I'm fairly certain that the November 30 undeposited receipts amounted to more than $7,500, although the November 30 bank reconciliation prepared by the cashier shows only $5,294.43. Also, the November bank reconciliation doesn't show several checks that have been outstanding for a long time. The cashier told me that these checks needn't appear on the reconciliation because he had notified the bank to stop payment on them and he had made the necessary adjustment on the books. Does that sound reasonable to you?"

At your request, Small shows you the following November 30 bank reconciliation prepared by the cashier:

Bank Reconciliation
November 30, 19XX

Balance per bank statement		$19,250.25	Balance per books		$25,446.89
Add: Deposits in transit		5,294.43			
		$25,454.68			
Less:			Less:		
Outstanding checks:			Bank service charge	$ 15	
			Unrecorded credit	800	815.00
No. 2351	$330.71				
No. 2353	256.80				
No. 2354	235.28	822.79			
Adjusted balance		$24,631.89	Adjusted Balance		$24,631.89

You discover that the $800 unrecorded bank credit represents a note collected by the bank on Small's behalf; it appears in the deposits column of the November bank statement. Your investigation also reveals that the October 31 bank reconciliation showed three checks that had been outstanding longer than 10 months: No. 1432 for $156; No. 1458 for $270; and No. 1512 for $283.50. You also discover that these items were never added back into the Cash account in the books. In confirming that the checks shown on the cashier's November 30 bank reconciliation were outstanding on that date, you discover that check No. 2353 was actually a payment of $526.80 and had been recorded on the books for that amount.

To confirm the amount of undeposited receipts at November 30, you request a bank statement for December 1–12 (called a "cut-off" bank statement). This indeed shows a December 1 deposit of $5,294.43.

REQUIRED

(a) Calculate the amount of funds abstracted by the cashier.
(b) Describe how the cashier concealed the abstraction.
(c) What sort of entry or entries should be made when a firm decides that checks outstanding for a long time should no longer be carried in the bank reconciliation?
(d) What suggestions would you make to Small about cash control procedures?

8

Trade Accounts
and Notes

Business practice today is governed by credit. Indeed, the vast daily sales of goods and services might not be made without it. In recent years, the use of credit has expanded immensely, particularly in the retail field. Millions of consumers possess and regularly use several credit cards.

The growth of credit has created a need for more elaborate and sophisticated systems for processing transactions and gathering credit information. However, the basic accounting problems of keeping track of payables and receivables have remained essentially the same.

TRADE RECEIVABLES AND PAYABLES

The terms **trade receivable** and **trade payable** usually refer to receivables and payables that arise in the regular course of a company's transactions with customers and suppliers. Payments normally are made within 30 to 60 days. Therefore, the amount of a sale of merchandise sold on account is debited to the appropriate customer's account in the subsidiary accounts receivable ledger; this amount is also debited to the Accounts Receivable control account when credit sales are posted periodically to it. The subsidiary record and the control account should reflect only trade accounts. Advances to company employees or officers should not be included here, nor should advances to affiliated companies, such as subsidiaries, be included. Such receivables should be recorded in separate accounts. In many instances, such receivables are not current, and as a result, they often appear in the balance sheet under a noncurrent heading, such as Other Assets. Advances to subsidiary companies are frequently semipermanent, and they may be found in the balance sheet under the Investments caption.

Likewise, trade accounts payable consist only of open amounts owing for the purchase of merchandise, materials, or the acquisition of services from outsiders. Separate current liability accounts contain amounts that a firm owes for salaries, wages, various types of taxes, sundry accruals, and so on.

The principal reason for separating trade accounts from other receivables and payables is to facilitate analyses by both management and outsiders. You will learn in Chapter 20 that certain techniques employed in studying a company's current accounts depend on such separation.

Occasionally, individual accounts within the accounts receivable or accounts payable subsidiary ledgers may show abnormal balances. A customer may have overpaid an account, paid an advance on goods not yet shipped, or returned goods already paid for. A substantial credit balance in a customer's account is reclassified as a current liability when a balance sheet is prepared. On the other hand, if the firm itself makes advances on purchases or overpays accounts, the resulting debit balances in accounts payable are reclassified as current assets in the balance sheet.

INSTALLMENT ACCOUNTS

Many business concerns—such as mail-order houses and appliance dealers—make many of their sales on the installment basis. Typically, a customer of such a firm purchases merchandise by signing an installment contract in which he or she agrees to a down payment plus installment payments of a fixed amount over a period such as 24 or 36 months. Normally, the total price of the merchandise sold includes an interest charge, and the contract allows the seller to repossess merchandise if the installment payments are not made. If the installment contract conforms to the firm's normal trade practices and terms, the installment receivable is classified as a current asset.

LOSSES FROM UNCOLLECTIBLE ACCOUNTS

Few firms that extend credit to customers are immune to credit losses. Indeed, most companies anticipate them. The magnitude of such losses is often directly related to the firm's credit policy. Sometimes a company deliberately liberalizes its credit policy to obtain increased sales, fully anticipating an increase in credit losses.

Most large companies have credit departments to administer management's established credit policies. Credit personnel may set credit limits, conduct investigations of credit ratings, and follow up on unpaid accounts. They may also decide, after following established collection procedures, when a debt is uncollectible.

Credit losses, considered operating expenses of the business, are debited to an appropriately titled account such as *Uncollectible Accounts Expense.* Other account titles frequently used are *Loss from Uncollectible Accounts, Loss from Doubtful Accounts,* or *Bad Debts Expense.* Normally, the expense is classified as a selling expense on the income statement, although some companies include it with administrative expenses.

Timing of Recognition

There are two methods for recognizing losses from uncollectible accounts. One is called the **direct write-off method.** The other method, which is preferable, is called the **allowance method.**

THE DIRECT WRITE-OFF METHOD   Under the direct write-off method, uncollectible accounts are charged to expense in the period when they are discovered to be uncollectible. Suppose that in December of last year, J.B. Stone purchased merchandise billed at $125, and that, after repeated collection attempts, the credit department decided on July 15 of the current year that the amount will never be collected. The following entry would record the loss:

July 15	Uncollectible Accounts Expense	125	
	Accounts Receivable—J.B. Stone		125
	To write off J.B. Stone's account.		

This entry charges the loss to the current year's expenses and reduces the asset Accounts Receivable by $125. Also, J.B. Stone's subsidiary ledger account no longer has a balance.

THE CREDIT DECISION

Applying for credit is like taking a test: It's the score that counts.

Many lenders use a computer-based scoring system to decide who will—and will not—get credit.

Credit-scoring systems are based on points; the lender assigns a fixed number of points to a variety of consumer characteristics and decides on a cut-off score. Applicants with a passing grade get credit; those with a failing grade are turned down.

The point assignments and the cut-off score are not chosen at random. They are based on computer profiles of good and bad borrowers. Here's how it works:

A lender selects, at random, a sample of past accounts—good and bad. All the available information on these accounts is fed into the computer. The computer determines which characteristics are shared by the good borrowers and which are shared by the bad ones. Each characteristic is given a point value.

The lender then can analyze the information to find out what combination of characteristics and what score are likely to produce a borrower who will repay the debt on time, with little chance of default.

Different lenders rely on different characteristics and score them differently. In general, the following things are important:

1. Stability—Creditors look for things like home ownership and length of time on the job as a guide to whether you are a stable, responsible person.
2. Occupation—Lenders often assign points to specific jobs. The key factor is the nature of the job; if it's in a field where people move about a lot, you're likely to score poorly.
3. Disposable income—Earnings alone are relatively unimportant; lenders are more concerned about the money you have left after paying existing bills. Someone with a salary of $2,000 a month who usually spends $1,800 a month and has $200 of disposable income would get a higher score than someone who earns $4,000 a month and spends it all.
4. Financial history—Lenders check credit-bureau reports for a record of how you have handled debt in the past. If your record shows a regular pattern of late payments, you will get a low score. You also may get a poor score if you've always used cash; the lack of a credit record can count against you even if you are a prompt payer.

From "Credit Often Based on Scoring Systems," Louise Cook, The Associated Press, as it appeared in the *Wisconsin State Journal*, June 22, 1982.

The major shortcoming of the direct write-off method is that credit losses are not matched with related sales. In our example, the revenue from the sale to J.B. Stone would be reflected in last year's income statement, but the loss would appear in the current year's income statement. The use of the direct write-off method also causes the consistent overstatement of Accounts Receivable on the balance sheet. Since generally accepted accounting principles prescribe that receivables be shown at the amount the firm expects to collect, most accountants disapprove of the direct write-off method.

This method would be obviously inappropriate in certain situations. Suppose a firm liberalized its credit policy in one year, realizing a large increase in sales revenue. Much of the related uncollectible accounts expense would not appear on the income statement until the next year, because collection efforts and follow-up procedures often extend over long periods of time. Most accountants and credit people believe that the credit loss occurs at the time of sale and therefore should be reflected in the same period.

THE ALLOWANCE METHOD   Most businesses employ the matching concept to determine net income. Therefore, they prefer to estimate the amount of uncollectible accounts expense that will eventually result from a period's sales in order to reflect the expense during the same period. This procedure not only matches credit losses with related revenue, but also results in an estimated realizable amount for accounts receivable in the balance sheet at the end of the period. The estimate is introduced into the accounts by an adjusting entry.

Let us assume that a firm with accounts receivable of $100,000 at the end of its first business year estimates that $4,000 of these accounts will be uncollectible. The firm makes the following adjusting entry:

Dec. 31	Uncollectible Accounts Expense	4,000	
	Allowance for Uncollectible Accounts		4,000
	To record uncollectible accounts expense.		

Note that in the adjusting entry, the credit is made to an account called *Allowance for Uncollectible Accounts* rather than to Accounts Receivable. This is done for two reasons. First, when the firm makes the adjusting entry, it does not know which accounts in the subsidiary accounts receivable ledger will be uncollectible. If the Accounts Receivable control account is credited and no entries are made in the subsidiary ledger, then the two records no longer agree in total. Second, because the amount involved is only an estimate, it is preferable not to reduce Accounts Receivable directly.

The Allowance for Uncollectible Accounts is a *contra* asset account with a normal credit balance. To present the expected realizable amount of Accounts Receivable, we deduct the Allowance for Uncollectible Accounts from Accounts Receivable in the balance sheet as follows:

Current Assets

Cash		$XXXXX
Accounts Receivable	$100,000	
Less: Allowance for Uncollectible Accounts	4,000	96,000
Inventory		XXXXX
Other Current Assets		XXXXX
Total Current Assets		$XXXXX

Writing Off Specific Accounts

The credit manager or other company official normally authorizes writing off a specific account. When the accounting department is notified of the action, it makes the following entry:

Jan. 5	Allowance for Uncollectible Accounts	250	
	Accounts Receivable—James Baker		250
	To write off James Baker's account.		

The credit in the above entry is made to James Baker's account in the subsidiary accounts receivable ledger as well as to the Accounts Receivable control account; therefore, these two records are still in agreement.

The entry to write off an account does not affect net income or total assets. By means of the adjusting entry, the expense is reflected in the period when the related revenue is recorded. Furthermore, because the Allowance for Uncollectible Accounts is deducted from Accounts Receivable in the balance sheet, the *net* realizable amount of accounts receivable is not changed by the write-off. After Baker's account has been written off, the Accounts Receivable and Allowance for Uncollectible Accounts ledger pages appear as follows:

Accounts Receivable   Account No. 12

Date		Description	Post. Ref.	Debit	Credit	Balance
19XX						
Jan.	1	Balance				100,000
	5	Write-off, James Baker			250	99,750

Allowance for Uncollectible Accounts   Account No. 13

Date		Description	Post. Ref.	Debit	Credit	Balance
19XX						
Jan.	1	Balance				4,000
	5	Write-off, James Baker		250		3,750

In these accounts, the net realizable amount of accounts receivable on January 1 is $96,000 ($100,000 − $4,000 allowance). After the January 5 write-off, the net realizable amount of accounts receivable is still $96,000 ($99,750 − $3,750 allowance). Thus, the write-off of an account does not affect the net asset balance.

Estimating Credit Losses

Estimates of credit losses are generally based on past experience, with consideration given to forecasts of sales activity, economic conditions, and planned changes in credit policy. The most commonly used calculations are related either to credit sales for the period or to the amount of accounts receivable at the close of the period.

ESTIMATES RELATED TO SALES   Through experience, many companies can determine the approximate percentage of credit sales that will be uncollectible. At the end of an accounting period, the amount of the adjusting entry is determined by multiplying the total credit sales by this percentage. Suppose that credit sales for a period amount to $200,000 and that past experience indicates a loss of $1\frac{1}{2}$%. The adjusting entry for expected losses would be:

Dec. 31	Uncollectible Accounts Expense	3,000	
	Allowance for Uncollectible Accounts		3,000
	To record uncollectible accounts expense.		

Because the periodic estimates for uncollectibles under this procedure are related to sales, a firm should review its allowance account regularly to ensure a reasonable balance. Should the allowance account balance become too large or too small, the percentage used for the periodic estimates should be revised accordingly.

A company that estimates its credit losses from sales figures customarily uses credit sales only. In some cases, however, a percentage of both credit and cash sales may be calculated, as long as the proportions of the two types of sales remain relatively constant over time. Whether sales discounts or sales returns and allowances are deducted before applying a percentage to sales figures depends on how the percentage was developed; the exercises and problems in this text assume that percentages are applied to gross credit sales.

ESTIMATES RELATED TO ACCOUNTS RECEIVABLE   A company's experience may show that a certain percentage of accounts receivable at the end of a period is likely to prove uncollectible. The credit balance in the allowance account should equal this amount. Therefore, the adjustment for uncollectibles is the amount needed to create the desired credit balance in the company's allowance account.

Suppose that a company estimates uncollectibles as 5% of accounts receivable and that the Accounts Receivable balance at the end of an accounting period is $50,000. Therefore, the desired credit balance in the allowance account is $2,500. If the allowance account already has a residual credit balance of $400, the amount of the adjustment is $2,100. The adjusting entry is a debit to Uncollectible Accounts Expense and a credit to Allowance for Uncollectible Accounts.

Instead of using a fixed percentage of the aggregate customers' balances, some companies determine the amount needed in the allowance account after analyzing the age structure of the account balances. These companies prepare an aging schedule similar to the one in Exhibit 8–1. An **aging schedule** is simply an analysis that shows how long customers' balances have remained unpaid. Assume that the firm whose aging schedule appears in Exhibit 8–1 sells on net terms of 30 days. Alton's account is current, which means that the $320 billing was made within the last 30 days. Bailey's account is 0–30 days *past due*, which means that the account is from 31 to 60 days old. Wall's balance consists of a $50 billing made from 91 to 150 days ago and a $100 billing made from 151 days to seven months ago, and so on.

Companies that analyze their bad accounts experience with the aged balances may develop percentages of each strata that are likely to prove uncollectible. At the end of each period, these percentages are applied to the totals of each age group to determine the allowance account balance. For our example, these percentages are shown below. Applying the percentages to the totals in our aging schedule, we calculate an allowance requirement of $1,560.

	Amount	Percent Doubtful	Allowance Required
Current	$42,000	2	$ 840
0–30 days past due	4,000	3	120
31–60 days past due	2,000	5	100
61–120 days past due	1,000	20	200
121 days–6 months past due	800	25	200
Over 6 months past due	200	50	100
Total Allowance Required			$1,560

EXHIBIT 8–1
Aging Schedule
of Customer Balances,
December 31, 19XX

			Past Due				
Customer	Account Balance	Current	0–30 Days	31–60 Days	61–120 Days	121 Days –6 Mos.	Over 6 Mos.
Alton, J.	$ 320	$ 320	$	$	$	$	$
Bailey, C.	400		400				
.							
.							
.							
Wall, M.	150				50	100	
Zorn, W.	210			210			
	$50,000	$42,000	$4,000	$2,000	$1,000	$800	$200

Again, if the allowance account has a residual $400 credit balance, the adjustment is for $1,160. The entry would be:

Dec. 31	Uncollectible Accounts Expense	1,160	
	Allowance for Uncollectible Accounts		1,160
	To record uncollectible accounts expense.		

The adjustment brings the credit balance in the allowance account to the required amount—$1,560.

Recoveries of Accounts Written Off

Occasionally, accounts written off against the Allowance for Uncollectible Accounts later prove to be wholly or partly collectible. In such situations, a firm should reinstate the customer's account for the amount recovered before recording the collection, so that the payment is recorded in the customer's account. The entry made for the write-off is reversed to the extent of the recovery and the receipt is recorded in the usual manner. For example, assume that a company using the allowance method wrote off James Baker's $250 account on January 5 but received payment in full on April 20. The following entries (including write-off) illustrate the recovery procedure.

To write off the account

| Jan. 5 | Allowance for Uncollectible Accounts | 250 | |
| | Accounts Receivable—James Baker | | 250 |

To reinstate the account

| Apr. 20 | Accounts Receivable—James Baker | 250 | |
| | Allowance for Uncollectible Accounts | | 250 |

To record remittance

| April 20 | Cash | 250 | |
| | Accounts Receivable—James Baker | | 250 |

These last two entries may be made even if the recovery occurs in a year after the write-off.

A business employing the direct write-off method that recovers a written-off account during the year of write-off simply reverses the entry made to write off the account to the extent of the recovery and records the remittance in the usual manner. Recoveries made in years after the write-off normally require two entries also. One entry reinstates the customer's account balance, with the credit made to an income statement account titled Recoveries of Accounts Written Off. The second entry records the remittance in the usual manner.

CREDIT CARD FEES

Many retailing businesses have their credit sales handled through banks that issue credit cards such as VISA and MasterCard. The bank incurs the costs of processing and collecting the amounts charged on its credit cards and absorbs any losses from uncollectible accounts. In exchange for these services, the bank charges the retail firm a fee, usually ranging from $\frac{1}{2}$–5% of the amount of the credit sale. The retailer makes the credit card sale and deposits the charge slip with the bank. The bank credits the retailer's bank account for the amount of the sale less the credit card fee. The retailer records the transaction by debiting Cash (for the amount of the sale less the fee), debiting a Credit Card Fee Expense account (for the amount of the fee), and crediting Sales.

Credit sales may also be made to customers who use nonbank credit cards, such as American Express and Diner's Club cards. The retailer sends the charge slip to the credit card company, then receives a check from that company for the sales amount less the credit card fee. The retailer records these sales by establishing a receivable from the credit card company (for the amount of the sale less the fee), debiting Credit Card Fee Expense (for the amount of the fee), and crediting Sales. The receivable is credited when the check is received from the credit card company.

NOTES RECEIVABLE AND PAYABLE

Promissory notes are often used in transactions when the credit period is longer than the 30 or 60 days typical for open accounts. Although promissory notes are used frequently in sales of equipment and real property, a note is sometimes exchanged for merchandise. Occasionally, a note is substituted for an open account when an extension of the usual credit period is granted. In addition, promissory notes are normally executed when loans are obtained from banks and other parties.

A **promissory note** is a written promise to pay a certain sum of money on demand or at a fixed and determinable future time. The note is signed by the **maker** and made payable to the order of either a specific **payee** or to the **bearer.** The note may be *non-interest bearing* or *interest bearing* at an annual rate specified on the note. An interest-bearing promissory note is illustrated in Exhibit 8–2.

EXHIBIT 8–2
A Promissory Note

$2,000.00	Madison, Wisconsin	May 3, 19XX
Sixty days	after date	I promise to pay to
the order of	Robert Ward	
Two Thousand and no/100————————————————————————dollars		
for value received with interest at 9%.		
payable at American Exchange Bank		
		James Stone

A note from a debtor is called a **note receivable** by the holder and a **note payable** by the debtor. A note is usually regarded as a stronger claim against a debtor than an open account because the terms of payment are specified in writing. Although open accounts can be sold (factored), a note can be converted to cash more easily by discounting it at a bank. (We treat the discounting of notes later in this chapter.)

Interest on Notes

Interest on notes is commonly paid on the maturity date of the obligation, except in certain discounting transactions. Interest incurred is debited to an Interest Expense account, and interest earned is credited to an Interest Income account. When business firms distinguish between operating and other items of income and expense in their income statements, they show interest expense and interest income under the heading Other Income and Expense.

INTEREST CALCULATION   The formula for determining simple interest is:

$$\text{Principal} \times \text{Rate} \times \text{Time} = \text{Interest}$$

Unless otherwise specified, we shall assume that interest rates on notes are annual rates. For example, interest on a one-year note for $2,000 at 9% would be calculated as follows:

$$\$2,000 \times \frac{9}{100} \times 1 = \$180$$

When a note is for a certain number of months, the time is usually expressed in twelfths of a year. Thus, the interest on a six-month note for $2,000 at 9% would be calculated as follows:

$$\$2,000 \times \frac{9}{100} \times \frac{6}{12} = \$90$$

When the note's duration is given in days, we express the time as a fraction of a year; the number of days' duration is the numerator and 360 is the denominator. (It is general business practice to use 360 days here, although federal agencies and certain lenders may use 365 days.) Interest on a 60-day note for $2,000 at 9% would be calculated as follows:

$$\$2,000 \times \frac{9}{100} \times \frac{60}{360} = \$30$$

DETERMINING MATURITY DATE   When a note's duration is expressed in days, we count the exact days in each calendar month to determine the maturity date. For example, a 90-day note dated July 21 would have an October 19 maturity date, which we determine as follows:

> 10 days in July (remainder of month—31 days minus 21 days)
> 31 days in August
> 30 days in September
> 19 days in October (number of days required to total 90)
>
> 90

If the duration of a note is expressed in months, we find the maturity date simply by counting the months from the date of issue. For example, a two-month note dated January 31 would mature on March 31, a three-month note of the same date would mature on April 30 (the last day of the month), and a four-month note would mature on May 31.

RECORDING NOTES AND INTEREST   When a note is exchanged to settle an open trade account, an entry is made to reflect the note receivable or payable and to reduce the balance of the related account receivable or payable. For example, suppose Acme Company sold $4,000 of merchandise to Bowman Company. On October 1, after the regular credit period had elapsed, Bowman Company gave Acme Company a 60-day, 12% note for $4,000. The following entries would be made by each of the parties:

Acme Company

Oct. 1	Notes Receivable	4,000	
	Accounts Receivable—Bowman Company		4,000
	Received 60-day, 12% note in payment of account.		

Bowman Company

Oct. 1	Accounts Payable—Acme Company	4,000	
	Notes Payable		4,000
	Gave 60-day, 12% note in payment of account.		

If Bowman Company pays the note on the November 30 maturity date, the following entries would be made by the parties involved:

Acme Company

Nov. 30	Cash	4,080	
	Interest Income		80
	Notes Receivable		4,000
	Collected Bowman Company note.		

Bowman Company

Nov. 30	Notes Payable	4,000	
	Interest Expense	80	
	Cash		4,080
	Paid note to Acme Company.		

Note that the interest for 60 days at 12% is reflected by the respective parties on the maturity date of the note. This would be true even if the maker defaulted on the note. If Bowman Company did not pay the note when due, Acme would debit the $4,080 to Accounts Receivable rather than to Cash. When a note receivable is dishonored at maturity, the combined principal and interest are converted to an open account. This procedure leaves only current, unmatured notes in the Notes Receivable account.

Discounting Customer Notes

Occasionally, a business may not wait until the maturity date of a note receivable to obtain cash from a customer transaction. Instead, it can endorse the note over to a bank, *discounting* the note and receiving an amount equal to the note's maturity value less the discount charged by the bank. By endorsing the note (unless it is endorsed *without recourse*), the business agrees to pay the note at the maturity date if the maker fails to pay it. Consequently, the note is the endorser's **contingent liability** (that is, the liability is contingent on the failure of the maker to pay). While the note is outstanding, the endorser discloses the contingent liability in its balance sheet. However, because a contingent liability is a potential liability rather than an actual liability, the amount is not included with the liabilities, but is disclosed in a footnote to the balance sheet. For example, the footnote may read "At December 31, 19XX, the Company was contingently liable for discounted notes receivable having a maturity value of $(amount)."

DISCOUNTING NON-INTEREST-BEARING NOTES RECEIVABLE   Assume that the $4,000, 60-day note received on October 1 by Acme Company from Bowman Company is non-interest bearing. Suppose that Acme Company discounts the note at the bank on October 31 and that the bank's discount rate is 12%.

The bank discount calculation is always based on the maturity value (Principal + Interest) of the note and the number of days that the bank must hold the note. Because the note in our example is non-interest bearing, the maturity value equals the face value, $4,000. The bank must hold the note for 30 days—October 31 to November 30. (In calculating the discount period, we ignore the discount date and count the maturity date as a full day). We calculate the proceeds as follows:

$$\text{Maturity Value} \times \text{Discount Rate} \times \text{Discount Period} = \text{Discount}$$
$$\$4,000 \quad \times \quad 12\% \quad \times \quad \tfrac{30}{360} \quad = \quad \$40$$

$$\text{Maturity Value} - \text{Discount} = \text{Proceeds}$$
$$\$4,000 \quad - \quad \$40 \quad = \quad \$3,960$$

To record the discounting transaction, Acme Company makes the following entry:

Oct. 31	Cash	3,960	
	Interest Expense	40	
	Notes Receivable		4,000
	Discounted Bowman's non-interest-bearing note.		

DISCOUNTING INTEREST-BEARING NOTES RECEIVABLE   We also use the procedure just described for interest-bearing notes. In this case, however, maturity value includes interest for the full term of the note. The discount computation and calculation of proceeds for a $4,000, 60-day, 12% note dated October 1 and discounted at 12% on October 31 by Acme Company is as follows:

$$\text{Maturity Value} \times \text{Discount Rate} \times \text{Discount Period} = \text{Discount}$$
$$\$4,080 \quad \times \quad 12\% \quad \times \quad \tfrac{30}{360} \quad = \$40.80$$

$$\text{Maturity Value} - \text{Discount} = \text{Proceeds}$$
$$\$4,080 \quad - \quad \$40.80 \ = \$4,039.20$$

Acme Company records the discounting transaction as follows:

Oct. 31	Cash	4,039.20	
	Interest Income		39.20
	Notes Receivable		4,000.00
	Discounted Bowman's 60-day, 12% note at 12%.		

Note that although Acme Company and the bank each hold a note 30 days, the bank exacts an additional amount of interest. The extra 80 cents is the interest for 30 days on $80 at the 12% bank discount rate. The bank considers the transaction a loan of $4,080, the amount that must be repaid at the end of the note's term.

Normally, a firm discounting a customer's interest-bearing note at the bank earns interest income, as shown in our illustration. However, the proceeds from discounting may be less than the note's face value when the firm's holding period is fairly short and the bank's discount rate exceeds the interest rate on the note.

Suppose that Acme Company discounts the $4,000 note after holding it only six days, and the discount rate is 16%. The discount would be $4,080 × 16% × $\tfrac{54}{360}$ = $97.92. Subtracting this amount from the $4,080 maturity value yields proceeds of $3,982.08. In this case, Acme Company would record the $17.92 difference between face value and proceeds as interest expense.

Oct. 7	Cash	3,982.08	
	Interest Expense	17.92	
	Notes Receivable		4,000
	Discounted Bowman's 60-day, 12% note at 16%.		

DISCOUNTED NOTES RECEIVABLE DISHONORED   When the maker of a note receivable fails to pay it (dishonors it) at maturity, the bank notifies the endorsing party and charges the full amount owed, including interest, to the endorser's bank account. In addition, the bank may also charge a small protest fee. Suppose that Bowman Company's $4,000, 60-day, 12% note, which Acme discounted on October 31, was dishonored by Bowman Company at maturity. Assume also that the bank notified Acme Company on November 30 that the maturity value of the note, $4,080, plus a $5 protest fee was charged against Acme Company's bank account. Acme Company's entry to record paying the maturity value of the note plus the protest fee and to charge the entire amount to Accounts Receivable—Bowman Company is as follows:

Nov. 30	Accounts Receivable—Bowman Company	4,085	
	Cash		4,085
	Paid Bowman Company's note and $5 protest fee.		

Acme Company would then endeavor to collect the $4,085 from Bowman Company. If Acme fails in its efforts, it writes off the account as uncollectible, using the procedures described earlier in this chapter.

Borrowing at a Discount

When a business borrows from a bank by giving its own note, the bank often deducts the interest in advance. With this type of transaction, a business is said to be "discounting its own note." Suppose that Acme Company discounts at 12% its own $8,000, 60-day note, dated December 16, at the bank. The calculation of discount and proceeds follows the pattern used for discounting notes receivable:

$$\text{Maturity Value} \times \text{Interest Rate} \times \text{Discount Period} = \text{Discount (Interest)}$$
$$\$8,000 \quad \times \quad 12\% \quad \times \quad \frac{60}{360} \quad = \quad \$160$$

$$\text{Maturity Value} - \text{Discount (Interest)} = \text{Proceeds}$$
$$\$8,000 \quad - \quad \$160 \quad = \$7,840$$

Acme records this transaction as follows:

Dec. 16	Cash	7,840	
	Discount on Notes Payable	160	
	Notes Payable		8,000
	Discounted our 60-day note at 12%.		

Note that the $160 is charged to Discount on Notes Payable. This *contra* account balance is subtracted from the Notes Payable amount on the balance sheet. As the period for the note elapses, the discount is reduced and charged to Interest Expense. Thus, at December 31, after 15 days have elapsed, $40 would be charged to Interest Expense and credited to Discount on Notes Payable. A complete discussion of the adjustment procedure is offered in the next section.

Because the proceeds of this type of note are less than the maturity value of the note, the *effective interest rate* for the loan is greater than the stated interest rate. The effective interest rate may be calculated by the following formula:

$$\text{Effective Interest Rate} = \frac{\text{Maturity Value of Note} \times \text{Stated Interest Rate}}{\text{Cash Proceeds from Note}}$$

Therefore, the effective interest rate on the Acme Company note is computed as follows:

$$\frac{\$8,000 \times 12\%}{\$7,840} = 12.24\%$$

Adjusting Entries for Interest

When the term of an interest-bearing note extends beyond the end of an accounting period, adjusting entries are usually necessary to reflect interest in the proper period. When material amounts are involved, year-end adjustments are normally made to accrue interest income on notes receivable and interest expense on notes payable. Often, entries are also necessary to record interest expense on a company's own discounted notes.

ACCRUED INTEREST   Assume that Acme Company received a $12,000, 60-day, 10% note from Cable Company on December 16 of the current year. By the close of the accounting period on December 31, Acme Company would have earned 15 days' interest, or $50, on the note, and Cable Company would have incurred an equal amount of interest expense. The adjusting entries made by each company on December 31 are shown below:

Acme Company

Dec. 31	Interest Receivable	50	
	Interest Income		50
	To accrue interest income on Cable		
	Company note.		

Cable Company

Dec. 31	Interest Expense	50	
	Interest Payable		50
	To accrue interest expense on note to		
	Acme Company.		

As a result of its adjusting entry, Acme Company would report the interest earned during December in its income statement for the current year and would show the interest receivable at December 31 among the current assets in its balance sheet. Likewise, Cable Company would report the interest expense incurred during December in its income statement for the current year and the interest payable as a current liability in its December 31 balance sheet.

In Chapter 4, we mentioned that some accountants prefer to make reversing entries for most accrual adjustments, after the books have been closed and statements have been prepared. If Acme Company followed this practice, the January 1 reversing entry (debit Interest Income and credit Interest Receivable for $50) would eliminate the Interest Receivable balance and reflect a debit balance of $50 in the Interest Income account (which had no balance after closing). Collection of the note and interest on the maturity date, February 14, would be recorded in the usual manner, as follows:

Feb. 14	Cash	12,200	
	Interest Income		200
	Notes Receivable		12,000
	Collected Cable Company note and		
	interest.		

After this collection entry has been posted to the accounts, the Interest Income account would show a net credit balance of $150—the proper amount of income earned on the note during the new year. The Interest Income account would appear as follows:

Interest Income   Account No. 42

Date		Description	Post. Ref.	Debit	Credit	Balance
19XX						
Jan.	1	(reversing)		50		(50)
Feb.	14	Collection of interest			200	150

Alternatively, if Acme Company had not reversed the accrual adjustment on January 1, it would record the collection of principal and interest as follows:

Feb. 14	Cash	12,200	
	Interest Receivable		50
	Interest Income		150
	Notes Receivable		12,000
	Collected Cable Company note and interest.		

When accrual adjustments are not reversed, we must analyze the subsequent related cash transaction as we did in the above entry. This procedure accomplishes the same result with fewer entries than reversing accruals, but we must be more circumspect in recording transactions during the period after adjustment.

Obviously, our remarks also apply to accrued interest on notes payable. For example, if Cable Company reversed its accruals, the entry for payment of the note and interest would be:

Feb. 14	Notes Payable	12,000	
	Interest Expense	200	
	Cash		12,200
	Paid note and interest to Acme Company.		

If Cable Company did not follow the practice of reversing accruals, the entry at maturity date would be:

Feb. 14	Notes Payable	12,000	
	Interest Payable	50	
	Interest Expense	150	
	Cash		12,200
	Paid note and interest to Acme Company.		

DISCOUNT ON NOTES PAYABLE   We pointed out earlier that when a firm discounts its own note payable, the bank deducts the interest (discount) immediately from the note's face value to obtain the proceeds. In our example, Acme Company's $8,000, 60-day note payable was discounted at 12% at the bank on December 16. Acme Company's entry is repeated below:

Dec. 16	Cash	7,840	
	Discount on Notes Payable	160	
	Notes Payable		8,000
	Discounted our 60-day note at 12%.		

At the close of the accounting period on December 31, 15 of the 60 days had elapsed, and one-fourth, or $40, of the discount was recognized as interest. Acme Company would make the following adjusting entry on December 31:

Dec. 31	Interest Expense	40	
	Discount on Notes Payable		40
	To record interest expense on our discounted note.		

In its December 31 balance sheet, Acme Company would show the remaining $120 Discount on Notes Payable as a *contra* liability account, subtracted from the Notes Payable amount.

When the note is paid, Acme Company would make the following entry:

Feb. 14	Notes Payable	8,000	
	Interest Expense	120	
	Discount on Notes Payable		120
	Cash		8,000
	Payment of discounted note at maturity.		

Current accounting principles prescribe the use of a contra account such as Discount on Notes Payable and the balance sheet treatment described in the foregoing paragraphs.[1] For many years, accountants treated the discount as a prepayment of interest—the borrower's balance sheet included prepaid interest as a current asset. Such practice is no longer considered correct, because a prepayment would actually reduce the amount borrowed and raise the effective interest rate. Discount on notes payable is still regarded as a prepayment by the Internal Revenue Service, however. For tax purposes, a cash basis taxpayer can deduct—as interest—the difference between the face value and the proceeds of a note in the period when the note is discounted.

Notes and Interest in Financial Statements

A business shows short-term trade notes receivable as current assets in the balance sheet; because they can normally be converted to cash fairly easily, these notes usually are placed above trade accounts receivable. As with accounts receivable, trade notes receivable are separated from notes from officers and employees and notes representing advances to affiliated companies. If such notes are not truly short term, they should not be classified as current assets. Interest Receivable is normally shown with Notes Receivable.

Sometimes companies with a large volume of notes receivable must provide for possible losses on notes. Frequently, the provision for credit losses also covers losses on notes as well. In such cases, the Allowance for Uncollectible Accounts is deducted from the sum of Accounts Receivable and Notes Receivable in the balance sheet.

Trade notes payable and notes payable to banks are usually shown separately in the current liabilities section of the balance sheet. Interest Payable is normally shown with Notes Payable—often as an addition, as presented in Exhibit 8–3. Discount on Notes Payable is deducted from the related Notes Payable amount. The order in which current payables appear is less important than the sequence of current assets; however, Notes Payable customarily precedes Accounts Payable.

A current section of a balance sheet is shown in Exhibit 8–3 to illustrate the presentation of items discussed in this chapter.

[1]*Opinions of the Accounting Principles Board, No. 21,* "Interest on Receivables and Payables" (New York: American Institute of Certified Public Accountants, 1971).

EXHIBIT 8-3

Huron Company
Partial Balance Sheet
December 31, 19XX

Current Assets

Cash		$ 2,000
Notes Receivable—Trade	$24,000	
Interest Receivable	300	24,300
Accounts Receivable—Trade	$50,000	
Less: Allowance for Uncollectible Accounts	1,500	48,500
Inventory		75,000
Prepaid Expenses		200
Total Current Assets		$150,000

Current Liabilities

Notes Payable—Banks	$ 8,000	
Less: Discount on Notes Payable	60	$ 7,940
Notes Payable—Trade	$20,000	
Interest Payable	400	20,400
Accounts Payable—Trade		30,000
Other Accrued Liabilities		11,660
Total Current Liabilities		$ 70,000

Because they are financial rather than operating items, we often separate Interest Expense and Interest Income from operating items in the income statement. They frequently appear under the classification *Other Income and Expense*, as shown in Exhibit 8-4. With this type of presentation, readers can make intercompany comparisons of operating results that are not influenced by financing patterns of the companies involved (such comparisons are explained more fully in Chapter 20).

KEY POINTS TO REMEMBER

Accounts Receivable

(1) When a debt is considered uncollectible, the *direct write-off* method of recording credit losses results in a debit to Uncollectible Accounts Expense and a credit to Accounts Receivable.

(2) The *allowance* method of recording credit losses can be summarized as follows:
   (a) To provide for losses, estimate them in advance, and then debit Uncollectible Accounts Expense and credit Allowance for Uncollectible Accounts. The amount of the entry may be either a percentage of the period's credit

EXHIBIT 8–4

Huron Company
Partial Income Statement
For the Year Ended December 31, 19XX

Sales		$200,000
Cost of Goods Sold		140,000
Gross Profit		$ 60,000
Operating Expenses:		
•		•
•		•
•		•
Total Operating Expenses		40,000
Net Operating Income		$ 20,000
Other Income and Expense:		
Interest Income	$1,400	
Interest Expense	800	600
Net Income		$ 20,600

sales or an amount necessary to bring the allowance account to a desired balance that is based on an analysis of the receivables.

(b) To write off accounts, debit Allowance for Uncollectible Accounts and credit Accounts Receivable when accounts are considered uncollectible.

Notes Receivable and Payable

(1) Discount is calculated on the maturity value of a note for the period the bank must hold it. Proceeds of a note are obtained by subtracting the discount from the maturity value.

(2) To record the discounting of a customer's note, we debit Cash for the proceeds, and credit Notes Receivable for the face value of the note. If proceeds exceed face value, we credit the difference to Interest Income. If proceeds are less than face value, we debit the difference to Interest Expense. When a firm discounts its *own* note, Notes Payable is credited.

(3) If the maker of a discounted note receivable fails to pay the note at maturity, the bank notifies the endorser of the default and charges the maturity value (plus any protest fee) to the endorser's bank account. The endorser then records the payment as a debit to Accounts Receivable and a credit to Cash.

(4) When a firm discounts its own note, Discount on Notes Payable is debited for the difference between face value and proceeds. This contra liability account is deducted from the related Notes Payable on the balance sheet. As the term of the note expires, adjusting entries reduce the discount by charging Interest Expense.

QUESTIONS

8–1 What events might cause credit balances in customers' accounts and debit balances in creditors' accounts? How are such items classified in the balance sheet?

8–2 A mail-order firm regularly makes a large proportion of its sales on the installment basis, requiring a 20% down payment and monthly payments over a period of six to 24 months, depending on the type of item sold. Where should the installment receivables be classified in the balance sheet of this mail-order firm?

8–3 How do the direct write-off and allowance methods of handling credit losses differ with respect to the timing of expense recognition?

8–4 When a firm provides for credit losses under the allowance method, why is the Allowance for Uncollectible Accounts credited rather than Accounts Receivable?

8–5 Describe the two most commonly used methods of estimating uncollectible accounts expense when the allowance method is employed.

8–6 The Knowles Company estimates its uncollectibles by aging its accounts and applying percentages to various strata of the aged accounts. This year, it calculated a total of $2,200 in possible losses. On December 31, the Accounts Receivable balance is $80,000 and the Allowance for Uncollectible Accounts has a credit balance of $600 before adjustment. Give the adjusting entry to provide for credit losses. Determine the net amount of Accounts Receivable added into current assets.

8–7 In June of last year, Sims, Inc. sold $750 worth of merchandise to Dodd Company. In November of last year, Sims, Inc. wrote off Dodd's account. In March of this year, Dodd Company paid the account in full. Give the entries made by Sims, Inc. for the write-off and the recovery, assuming that Sims, Inc. uses (a) the direct write-off method, and (b) the allowance method of handling credit losses.

8–8 Brand Company sold a $700 refrigerator to a customer who charged the sale with a VISA bank credit card. Brand Company's bank charges a credit card fee of 4% of sales. What entry should Brand Company make to record the sale?

8–9 Verdon, Inc. received a 60-day, 12% note for $9,000 on August 10 of this year.
(a) What is the maturity date of the note?
(b) What is the maturity value of the note?
(c) Assuming Verdon, Inc. discounted the note at 12% at the bank on August 25, calculate the proceeds of the note.

8–10 On October 15 of this year, Roger Blaine discounted at the bank his own 120-day note for $12,000 at 12%.
(a) What is the maturity date of the note?
(b) What is the maturity value of the note?
(c) What are the proceeds of the note?

8–11 Why is a discounted customer's note a contingent liability of the endorser?

8–12 The maturity value of an $8,000 customer's note discounted by Ames Company is $8,160. The customer dishonored the note, and the bank charged the

$8,160 plus an $8 protest fee to Ames' bank account. What entry should Ames make to record this event?

8–13 King Company received a 120-day, 12% note for $15,000 on December 1. What adjusting entry is needed to accrue interest on December 31?

8–14 On December 11, Mary Dunn discounted her own 90-day note for $6,000 at the bank at 12% and charged the discount to Discount on Notes Payable. What adjusting entry is necessary on December 31?

8–15 Lee Brown gave a creditor a 60-day, 10% note for $9,600 on December 16. What adjusting entry should Brown make on December 31?

EXERCISES

8–16 Ryan Company uses the allowance method of handling credit losses. It estimates losses at 1% of credit sales, which were $400,000 during the current year. On December 31 of the current year, the Accounts Receivable balance was $80,000, and the Allowance for Uncollectible Accounts had a credit balance of $600 before adjustment.
(a) Give the adjusting entry to record credit losses for the current year.
(b) Show how Accounts Receivable and the Allowance for Uncollectible Accounts would appear in the December 31 balance sheet.

8–17 Winco, Inc. analyzed its Accounts Receivable balances at December 31 and arrived at the aged balances listed below, along with the percentages of each age group that have proven uncollectible in the past.

Age	Loss (%)	Balance
Current	1	$ 90,000
30–60 days past due	2	18,000
61–120 days past due	8	9,000
121 days–six months past due	15	6,000
Over six months past due	30	4,000
		$127,000

The company handles credit losses with the allowance method. The credit balance of the Allowance for Uncollectible Accounts is $700 on December 31 before any adjustments.
(a) Prepare the adjusting entry for estimated credit losses on December 31.
(b) Give the entry to write off Leslie James' account in April of the following year, $450.

8–18 On March 10 of this year, Dillon, Inc. declared a $500 account receivable from Westgate Company uncollectible and wrote off the account. On November 18 of this year, Dillon received a $500 payment on the account from Westgate.
(a) Assume Dillon uses the allowance method of handling credit losses. Give the entries to record the write-off and the subsequent recovery of Westgate's account.
(b) Assume Dillon uses the direct write-off method of handling credit losses. Give the entries to record the write-off and the subsequent recovery of Westgate's account.

(c) Assume the payment from Westgate arrives on February 5 of next year rather than November 18 of this year. Give the entries to record the write-off and subsequent recovery of Westgate's account under the allowance method.

(d) Assume the payment from Westgate arrives on February 5 of next year rather than November 18 of this year. Give the entries to record the write-off and subsequent recovery of Westgate's account under the direct write-off method.

8–19 Determine the maturity date and compute the interest for each of the following notes:

Date of Note	Principal	Interest Rate (%)	Term
(a) March 9	$ 5,400	10	60 days
(b) May 3	6,000	12	75 days
(c) June 25	2,500	9	90 days
(d) August 16	3,200	15	120 days
(e) October 17	15,000	12	45 days

8–20 Record the following transactions on the books of both Landon Company and Neal, Inc.:

Oct. 1 Neal, Inc., gave Landon Company a $12,000, 60-day, 10% note in payment of account.

16 Landon Company discounted the note at the bank at 12%.

Nov. 30 On the maturity date of the note, Neal, Inc., paid the amount due.

8–21 Suppose that, in Exercise 8–20, Neal, Inc. dishonored its note and the bank notified Landon Company that it had charged the maturity value plus a $10 protest fee to Landon Company's bank account. What entry should Landon Company make on the maturity date?

8–22 On November 16, Lambert Company discounted its own $8,400, 60-day note at the bank at 12%.
(a) What is the maturity date of the note?
(b) What are the proceeds of the note?
(c) What amount of interest expense should be recorded as an adjustment at December 31?
(d) What will be the balance in the Discount on Notes Payable account at December 31?
(e) What is the effective interest rate on the note?

8–23 The following note transactions occurred during the current year for the Conroy Company:

Nov. 25 Conroy received a 90-day, 10% note for $6,000 from Todd Company.

Dec. 7 Conroy discounted its own 90-day, $5,000 note at the bank at 12%, charging the discount to Discount on Notes Payable.

23 Conroy gave Franklin, Inc., a $9,000, 10%, 60-day note in payment of account.

Give the general journal entries necessary to adjust the interest accounts at December 31.

8–24 Compute the interest accrued on each of the following notes receivable held by McClean, Inc., on December 31, 19X6:

Maker	Date of Note	Principal	Interest Rate (%)	Term
Carver	11/16/X6	$8,000	12	120 days
Langdon	12/10/X6	6,000	10	90 days
Powers	12/19/X6	7,500	14	60 days

PROBLEMS

8–25 Rimrock, Inc., which has been in business for three years, makes all sales on account and does not offer cash discounts. The firm's credit sales, collections from customers, and write-offs of uncollectible accounts for the three-year period are summarized below:

Year	Sales	Collections	Accounts Written Off
1	$450,000	$426,000	$2,400
2	580,000	570,000	3,800
3	650,000	638,000	4,400

REQUIRED

(a) If Rimrock, Inc. had used the direct write-off method of recognizing credit losses during the three years, what amount of Accounts Receivable would appear on the firm's balance sheet at the end of the third year? What total amount of uncollectible accounts expense would have appeared on the firm's income statement during the three-year period?

(b) If Rimrock, Inc. had used an allowance method of recognizing credit losses and had provided for such losses at the rate of 1% of sales, what amounts of Accounts Receivable and Allowance for Uncollectible Accounts would appear on the firm's balance sheet at the end of the third year? What total amount of uncollectible accounts expense would have appeared on the firm's income statement during the three-year period?

(c) Comment on the use of the 1% rate to provide for losses in part (b).

8–26 At the beginning of the current year, Spartan Company had the following accounts on its books:

Accounts Receivable	$90,000 (debit)
Allowance for Uncollectible Accounts	2,500 (credit)

During this year, credit sales were $600,000 and collections on account were $585,000. The following transactions, among others, occurred during the year:

Feb. 17 Wrote off J. Lowell's account, $800.

May 28 Wrote off B. Andrews' account, $500.

Oct. 13 B. Andrews, who is in bankruptcy proceedings, paid $200 in final settlement of the account written off on May 28. This amount is not included in the $585,000 collections.

Dec. 15 Wrote off M. Piper's account, $700.

31 In an adjusting entry, recorded the provision for uncollectible accounts at $\frac{1}{2}$% of credit sales for the year.

REQUIRED

(a) Prepare general journal entries to record the credit sales, the collections on account, and the above transactions.

(b) Show how Accounts Receivable and the Allowance for Uncollectible Accounts would appear in the December 31 balance sheet.

8–27 At December 31 of the current year, the Upton Company had a balance of $140,000 in its Accounts Receivable account and a credit balance of $1,800 in the Allowance for Uncollectible Accounts. The Accounts Receivable subsidiary ledger consisted of $142,500 in debit balances and $2,500 in credit balances. The company has aged its accounts as follows:

Current	$124,000
0–60 days past due	9,000
61–180 days past due	6,000
Over six months past due	3,500
	$142,500

In the past, the company has experienced losses as follows: 1% of current balances, 5% of balances 0–60 days past due, 15% of balances 61–180 days past due, and 40% of balances over six months past due. The company bases its provision for credit losses on the aging analysis.

REQUIRED

(a) Prepare the adjusting journal entry to record the provision for credit losses for the year.

(b) Show how Accounts Receivable (including the credit balances) and Allowance for Uncollectible Accounts would appear in the December 31 balance sheet.

8–28 Allied Products, Inc. had the following transactions for 19X1 and 19X2:

19X1

May 18   Discounted its own $20,000, 90-day note at the bank at 12%.
Aug. 16   Paid the bank the amount due from the May 18 loan.
Oct. 2   Discounted its own $8,400, 120-day note at the bank at 14%.
Dec. 31   Made the appropriate adjusting entry for interest expense.

19X2

Jan. 30   Paid the bank the amount due from the October loan.

REQUIRED

(a) Record the above transactions and adjustment in general journal form.

(b) Compute the effective interest rate on the loan of:
   (1) May 18.
   (2) October 2.

8–29 York Company had the following transactions during the current year:

Apr.   8   Received a $9,600, 75-day, 12% note from G. Hart in payment of account.
May 24   Wrote off customer D. Lewis' account against the Allowance for Uncollectible Accounts, $475.
June 22   G. Hart paid note in full.

Oct. 10 Gave a $4,800, 60-day, 14% note to R. Sharp in payment of account.
18 D. Lewis paid account written off on May 24.
Dec. 4 Discounted its own $15,000, 90-day note at the bank at 12%.
9 Paid principal and interest due on note to R. Sharp.
21 Received a $9,000, 60-day, 12% note from W. Craig on account.

REQUIRED
(a) Record the above transactions in general journal form.
(b) Make any necessary adjusting entries for interest at December 31.

8–30 Treadway, Inc. began business on January 1 of the current year. Certain transactions for the current year are given below:

May 1 Borrowed $25,000 from the bank on a six-month, 14% note, interest to be paid at maturity.
June 13 Received a $16,000, 60-day, 12% note on account from M. Cahill.
28 Discounted Cahill's note at the bank at 15%.
Aug. 12 M. Cahill paid her note, with interest.
Sept. 1 Received an $18,000, 120-day, 10% note from C. King on account.
Oct. 11 Discounted King's note at the bank at 15%.
Nov. 1 Paid May 1 note, with interest.
21 Discounted its own $15,000, 120-day note at the bank at 12%.
Dec. 16 Received a $5,400, 45-day, 12% note from T. Myer on account.
30 The bank notified Treadway, Inc., that C. King's note was dishonored. Maturity value of the note plus an $8 protest fee was charged against Treadway's checking account at the bank.
31 Wrote off King's account as uncollectible. Treadway, Inc., uses the allowance method of providing for credit losses.
31 Recorded expected credit losses for the year by an adjusting entry. Write-offs of accounts during this first year have created a debit balance in the Allowance for Uncollectible Accounts of $1,700. Analysis of aged receivables indicates that the desired balance of the allowance account is $7,500.
31 Made the appropriate adjusting entries for interest.

REQUIRED
Record the foregoing transactions and adjustments in general journal form.

8–31 At December 31, 19X0, Cascade Corporation held one note receivable and had one note payable outstanding. At December 31, 19X1, Cascade again held one note receivable and had outstanding one note payable. The notes are described below.

	Date of Note	Principal	Interest Rate (%)	Term
December 31, 19X0				
Note Receivable	11/25/X0	$16,000	12	120 days
Note Payable	12/16/X0	16,800	15	30 days
December 31, 19X1				
Note Receivable	12/11/X1	$ 8,400	12	60 days
Note Payable	12/7/X1	$18,000	14	150 days

REQUIRED

(a) Assume that the appropriate adjusting entries were made at December 31, 19X0, but that no reversing or adjusting entries were made in 19X1. Give the journal entries to record payment of the notes that were outstanding December 31, 19X0.

(b) Assume that the appropriate adjusting entries were made at December 31, 19X0. However, no reversing or adjusting entries were made in 19X1, and the bookkeeper neglected to consider the related interest receivable and interest payable when the notes were paid in 19X1. Make the necessary adjusting entries for interest at December 31, 19X1.

ALTERNATE PROBLEMS

8–26A At January 1 of the current year, Artway, Inc. had the following accounts on its books:

Accounts Receivable	$120,000 (debit)
Allowance for Uncollectible Accounts	4,200 (credit)

During this year, credit sales were $260,000 and collections on account were $248,000. The following transactions, among others, occurred during the year:

Jan. 11 Wrote off L. Jacobs' account, $1,200.

Apr. 29 Wrote off F. Ahearn's account, $750.

Nov. 15 F. Ahearn paid debt of $750, written off April 29. This amount is not included in the $248,000 collections.

Dec. 5 Wrote off B. Holmes' account, $1,600.

    31 In an adjusting entry, recorded the provision for uncollectible accounts at $1\frac{1}{2}\%$ of credit sales for the year.

REQUIRED

(a) Prepare general journal entries to record the credit sales, the collections on account, and the above transactions.

(b) Show how Accounts Receivable and the Allowance for Uncollectible Accounts would appear in the December 31 balance sheet.

8–27A At December 31 of the current year, the Argonaut Company had a balance of $90,000 in its Accounts Receivable account and a credit balance of $800 in the Allowance for Uncollectible Accounts. The Accounts Receivable subsidiary ledger consisted of $91,500 in debit balances and $1,500 in credit balances. The company has aged its accounts as follows:

Current	$80,000
0–60 days past due	6,000
61–180 days past due	3,000
Over six months past due	2,500
	$91,500

In the past, the company has experienced losses as follows: $1\frac{1}{2}$% of current balances, 6% of balances 0–60 days past due, 15% of balances 61–180 days past due, and 30% of balances more than six months past due. The company bases its provision for credit losses on the aging analysis.

REQUIRED
(a) Prepare the adjusting journal entry to record the provision for credit losses for the year.
(b) Show how Accounts Receivable (including the credit balances) and Allowance for Uncollectible Accounts would appear in the December 31 balance sheet.

8–28A The Bolt Corporation had the following transactions for 19X3 and 19X4:

19X3

Mar.   6   Sold $7,200 worth of merchandise to J. Brown and received a $7,200, 60-day, 10% note.
       26   Discounted J. Brown's note at the bank at 15%.
May   5   Brown paid the bank the amount due on the March 6 note.
Dec. 11   Received a $4,000, 60-day, 9% note from L. Owens in settlement of an open account.
       31   Made the appropriate adjusting entry for interest income.

19X4

Jan.   1   Reversed the December 31 adjustment for interest income.
Feb.   9   Received payment from L. Owens on the December 11 note.

REQUIRED
(a) Record the above transactions, adjustment, and reversal in general journal form.
(b) Assume Bolt Corporation does not make reversing entries. Give the entry to record the receipt of the note payment from L. Owens on February 9, 19X4.

8–29A The Pawnee Company had the following transactions during the current year:

July   15   Received a $7,200, 90-day, 12% note from J. Barker in payment of account.
Sept.   5   Wrote off customer G. Boyd's account against the Allowance for Uncollectible Accounts, $600.
Oct.   3   Gave a $6,600, 60-day, 10% note to L. Jacobson in payment of account.
       13   J. Barker paid note in full.
       21   G. Boyd paid account written off on September 5.
Dec.   2   Paid principal and interest due on note to L. Jacobson.
       13   Discounted its own $12,000, 90-day note at the bank at 10%.
       19   Received a $4,500, 60-day, 12% note from F. Gill on account.

REQUIRED
(a) Record the above transactions in general journal form.
(b) Make any necessary adjusting entries for interest at December 31.

8–30A Fisher, Inc. began business on January 1 of the current year. Several transactions for the current year are given below:

Mar. 1 Borrowed $20,000 from the bank on a five-month, 12% note, interest to be paid at maturity.

May 2 Received a $9,000, 60-day, 10% note on account from D. Mitchell.

22 Discounted Mitchell's note at the bank at 12%.

July 1 D. Mitchell paid his note, with interest.

1 Received a $6,000, 60-day, 10% note from Mary Taylor on account.

25 Discounted Taylor's note at the bank at 10%.

Aug. 1 Paid March 1 note, with interest.

30 The bank notified Fisher, Inc. that Mary Taylor's note was dishonored. Maturity value of the note plus a $10 protest fee was charged against Fisher's checking account at the bank.

Dec. 1 Discounted its own $7,500, 120-day note at bank at 12%.

9 Wrote off Taylor's account as uncollectible. Fisher, Inc. uses the allowance method of providing for credit losses.

11 Received a $10,000, 90-day, 9% note from J. Crane on account.

31 Recorded expected credit losses for the year by an adjusting entry. The Allowance for Uncollectible Accounts has a debit balance of $2,600 as a result of write-offs of accounts during this first year. Analysis of aged receivables indicates that the desired balance of the allowance account is $3,200.

31 Made the appropriate adjusting entries for interest.

REQUIRED
Record the foregoing transactions and adjustments in general journal form.

BUSINESS DECISION PROBLEM

The latest income statement for Viking, Inc.—a wholesaler of electronic parts and equipment—is shown below. Company president James Baldwin has been dissatisfied with the firm's rate of growth for several years. He believes that increasing sales promotion and liberalizing credit policies would raise gross sales substantially. Specifically, Baldwin is fairly confident that gross sales would increase by 30% if the firm adopted the plan shown at the top of page 310.

Viking, Inc.
Income Statement
For the Year Ended December 31, 19XX

Sales	$600,000	
Less: Sales Discounts	8,000	
Net Sales	$592,000	100%
Cost of Goods Sold	384,800	65
Gross Profit on Sales	$207,200	35%
Selling Expenses (excluding Uncollectible Accounts Expense)	$148,000	25%
Uncollectible Accounts Expense	5,920	1
Administrative Expenses	30,000	5
Total Expenses	$183,920	31%
Net Income	$ 23,280	4%

(1) Increase certain of the firm's trade discounts. This change would reduce the average selling price of merchandise somewhat, but it would increase sales volume.
(2) Extend credit to an additional number of less "select" customers.

The controller for Viking, Inc. makes the following comments after analyzing Baldwin's proposal for its likely impact on other income statement items:

(1) Gross Profit on Sales—The slight decline in average selling prices of merchandise resulting from an increase in trade discounts will reduce the gross profit rate from 35% to $33\frac{1}{3}\%$.

(2) Sales Discounts—The firm has been selling to selected retailers on terms of 2/15, n/30, with about two-thirds of total sales subject to the discount. Even with an increased number of customers, two-thirds of total sales will still be subject to the discount.

(3) Selling Expenses—Excluding uncollectible accounts expense, selling expenses will remain at 25% of net sales. Because of the expected 30% increase in sales, selling expenses, including promotion outlays, will rise accordingly.

(4) Uncollectible Accounts Expense—Uncollectible accounts expense has been about 1% of gross sales for several years. The proposed liberalization of credit policies will increase this expense to 2% of gross sales.

(5) Administrative Expenses—These expenses will remain constant even if gross sales increase.

REQUIRED
Prepare an income statement based on Baldwin's proposal and the controller's comments. Based on your results, should the firm adopt Baldwin's proposal?

9

Inventories

> **Money and goods are certainly the best of references.**
>
> CHARLES DICKENS

I nventories constitute the lifeblood of merchandising and manufacturing firms. For these firms, inventory is a significant asset, and the sale of inventory provides the major source of revenue. This chapter focuses on inventory accounting for merchandisers—firms that buy finished products to sell to their customers. Inventories of manufacturing companies are covered in a later chapter.

We have already introduced the special source documents, business transactions, and accounting techniques related to routine inventory transactions. Now we build on these facts by briefly considering the basic notions of inventories, examining and illustrating the problems of inventory determination, and comparing the consequences for periodic income determination of various inventory pricing methods.

REVIEW OF BASIC CONCEPTS

Before discussing new material, let us review some of the pertinent concepts covered earlier.

Inventory is all merchandise owned by a company and held for resale to customers in the ordinary course of business. Inventories are current assets because they typically will be sold within one year, or during a firm's normal operating cycle if it should be longer than a year. For retailing firms, inventories are often the largest or most valuable current asset.

Inventory costs are all costs necessary to acquire the merchandise and bring it to the site of sale. Inventory costs include the purchase price, plus any transportation or freight in, less purchases returns and allowances and purchases discounts.

The **cost of goods sold** is the net acquisition cost of the goods sold to customers in generating the sales revenue of an operating period. The following is a typical example of the computation of the cost of goods sold:

Beginning Inventory			$10,000
Add: Net Cost of Purchases			
Purchases		$31,000	
Less: Purchases Returns and Allowances	$2,100		
Purchases Discounts	400	2,500	
		$28,500	
Add: Transportation In		500	29,000
Cost of Goods Available for Sale			$39,000
Less: Ending Inventory			9,000
Cost of Goods Sold			$30,000

THE NEED FOR INVENTORIES

Most well-managed merchandisers find it necessary and desirable to maintain large, varied inventories. As a consumer, you have probably experienced a favorable buyer reaction to the availability of a wide assortment of colors, sizes, qualities, and types of the goods for which you shop. The prevailing affluence of our society and the related buyer habits have probably made large, varied inventories an operating necessity for most retail firms.

Other business factors can justify the existence of relatively large inventories. Clearly, a firm can sell more goods in a period than it can purchase or produce only by having beginning inventories. Beginning inventories are particularly important to seasonal industries or markets. Attractive quantity discounts may justify a firm's buying in excess of its current sales requirements and therefore creating additional inventories. Strategic purchases offer still another reason for carrying inventories. Many firms—especially those that sell in seasonal markets—buy in excess of their needs when supply prices are favorable. They store the goods and can then maintain sales during a period of unfavorable supply prices.

Progressive firms take into account customer preferences, competitors' merchandising patterns, and favorable market situations in determining inventory size and balance, but they must also consider the cost of carrying large inventories. Often, savings obtained by purchasing in large quantities or under favorable market conditions may be more than offset by increased carrying costs. Storage and handling costs for large inventories can increase substantially. In addition, the firm may suffer losses from inventory deterioration and obsolescence. Finally, inventories tie up working capital that might be used more profitably elsewhere. These latter factors often cause merchandisers to contract inventory during recessionary periods.

INCOME DETERMINATION AND INVENTORY MEASUREMENT

Proper income determination depends on the appropriate measurement of all assets; higher asset amounts result in higher reported income amounts. Because inventories are often relatively large and their sizes fluctuate, accounting correctly for inventories is important in determining net income properly. Other things being equal, **changing the dollar amount of ending inventory changes net income dollar for dollar** (ignoring any income tax effects), as Exhibit 9–1 illustrates. Note that sales, beginning inventory, and purchases are identical in all four cases. As ending inventory increases by a given amount—$1,000 from A to B, $2,000 from B to D, for example—cost of goods sold decreases and income increases by the same amount.

Accountants must be concerned with the problems of inventory measurement because of its role in the determination of reported income. We consider these problems in the remainder of this chapter.

EXHIBIT 9–1
Relationship of Inventory Measurements to Reported Income

Assumed Data	Amounts (in Thousands of Dollars)			
	A	B	C	D
Sales	$25	$25	$25	$25
Beginning inventory	$ 3	$ 3	$ 3	$ 3
Purchases	20	20	20	20
Goods available for sale	$23	$23	$23	$23
Ending inventory	4	5	6	7
Cost of goods sold	$19	$18	$17	$16
Reported income	$ 6	$ 7	$ 8	$ 9

INVENTORY MEASUREMENT

The dollar amount of an inventory depends on two variables—quantity and price. We usually express inventories as the aggregate dollar value (Quantity × Price) of the goods on hand at a specific time. "Taking" an inventory consists of (1) counting the items involved, (2) pricing each item, and (3) summing the amounts. Exhibit 9–2 illustrates these three steps.

Inventory counts can be extremely complicated and expensive. Even moderate-sized firms may have thousands of items, hundreds of types, sizes, and qualities, purchased at a variety of unit prices, and located in dozens of warehouses, stores, branches, and departments. Proper planning and coordination are imperative if all items are to be counted—only once—and properly priced. Although some firms "close" for inventory-taking, many continue operations during the count and must, of course, know if counted or uncounted merchandise is sold during the inventory period.

Another problem in inventory counts is deciding what goods should be counted. Often the proper inventory is not simply "all merchandise on site." By definition, the inventory should include—and be limited to—goods *owned* by the firm and *available* for resale. Items that the firm has purchased but has not received (often called *goods in transit*) should be included in the inventory count. We indicated in Chapter 5 that legal ownership depends on where title to the goods resides. Therefore, a firm purchasing merchandise on terms F.O.B. shipping point acquires title to the goods before it physically receives the goods.

Merchandise that has been sold to customers does not belong in the inventory count, even if it has not been removed from the store or warehouse. It is no longer owned by the firm nor available for resale. To include in the inventory count merchandise for which a sales transaction has been recorded overstates the inventory and therefore reports the firm's net income, assets, and owners' equity incorrectly. Similarly, goods held for resale on consignment from another

EXHIBIT 9–2
The Three Steps of Taking an Inventory

(1) PHYSICAL COUNT		(2) PRICING	(3) SUMMATION
Merchandise Item	Unit Count	Unit Price	Extension
A	3	$6	$18
B	4	7	28
C	5	8	40
			$86

firm are not included in the inventory count, because the goods are not owned by the firm holding them.

We see, therefore, that although a firm's ownership of merchandise often is indicated by the physical presence of goods, a firm can also own goods that it has not yet received and not own goods that it still possesses.

INVENTORY PRICING METHODS

In general, inventories are priced at their cost. Inventory pricing is quite simple when acquisition prices remain constant. When prices for like items change during the accounting period, however, it is not always apparent which price should be used to measure the ending inventory. Consequently, when cost prices fluctuate, we must either keep track of all costs for specific goods or make assumptions about which goods have been sold and which goods are on hand. The need for such assumptions has led to the commonly used methods of inventory pricing that we illustrate in this section. We illustrate a rising price pattern, which is the most prevalent in our economy.

Two terms—*goods flow* and *cost flow*—are useful in considering the problems of pricing inventories under fluctuating prices. **Goods flow** describes the actual physical movement of goods in the firm's operations. Goods flow is a result of physical events. **Cost flow** is the real or *assumed* association of unit costs with goods either sold or on hand. The assumed cost flow does not always reflect the actual goods flow. Furthermore, generally accepted accounting principles permit the use of an assumed cost flow that does *not* reflect the real goods flow. There is nothing illicit about this practice; in fact, there are often compelling reasons for adopting it.

We introduce four generally accepted methods of pricing inventories: (1) specific identification; (2) weighted average; (3) first-in, first-out; and (4) last-in, first-out. Again, the four methods illustrated use historical costs. In this section, we concentrate primarily on the computational technique of each method. A comparative evaluation is presented in the following section.

To compare more easily the four inventory methods, we illustrate all four with identical data. In each case, goods available for sale during the period are as follows:

Beginning inventory	6 units @ $10 =	$ 60
Purchases:	10 units @ 11 =	110
	10 units @ 13 =	130
	4 units @ 15 =	60
Totals	30 units	$360

Therefore, in each illustration:

(1) Beginning inventory is priced at $60.

(2) Three purchases are made during the period, as listed above.

(3) Goods available for sale during the period amount to 30 units at a total cost of $360.

In each case, 22 units are sold during the period, leaving an ending inventory of eight units. The four inventory methods differ in the way they assign costs to the units sold and to those remaining in inventory.

By assigning costs we are simply dividing the cost of goods available for sale between cost of goods sold and ending inventory. Therefore, we can compute costs by:

(1) Pricing out *either* the cost of goods sold or the ending inventory.

(2) Subtracting the amount determined in step (1) from the cost of goods available for sale.

(3) Assigning the residual to the element not priced in (1).

It will usually be advantageous to price out the ending inventory (and assign the residual amount to cost of goods sold), because the ending inventory involves fewer units than cost of goods sold. We use this approach in our illustrations.

Specific Identification

The **specific identification** method involves (1) keeping track of the purchase price of each specific unit, (2) knowing which specific units are sold, and (3) pricing the ending inventory at the actual prices of the specific units not sold. Obviously, this approach is not practical for merchandise having large unit volumes and small unit prices. Accounting students may consider specific identification the most "precise" way of evaluating inventory because the actual unit costs are attached to a given inventory. We shall see, however, that there is compelling justification for using other inventory pricing methods.

Assume that the eight unsold units consist of two units from beginning inventory, one unit from each of the first two purchases, and all four of the last units purchased. The costs assigned to the ending inventory and cost of goods sold are shown in Exhibit 9–3. Note that the full $360 cost of the goods available for sale has been assigned as either ending inventory or cost of goods sold.

EXHIBIT 9–3
Specific Identification Inventory Pricing

	Goods Available			Ending Inventory		
	Units	Cost	Total	Units	Cost	Total
Beginning inventory	6 @	$10 =	$ 60	2 @	$10 =	$ 20
Purchases:	10 @	11 =	110	1 @	11 =	11
	10 @	13 =	130	1 @	13 =	13
	4 @	15 =	60	4 @	15 =	60
	30		$360	8		$104

Cost of goods available for sale	$360
Less: Ending inventory	104
Cost of goods sold	$256

Weighted Average

The **weighted average** method spreads the total dollar cost of the goods available for sale equally among all units. In our illustration, this figure is $360/30, or $12 per unit. Exhibit 9–4 diagrams the assignment of costs under this method. Note again that the entire cost of goods available for sale has been divided between ending inventory and cost of goods sold.

It would be incorrect to use a *simple* average of the prices. The average price paid is ($10 + $11 + $13 + $15)/4 = $12.25; this figure fails to take into account the different numbers of units available at the various prices. The simple average yields the same figure as the weighted average only when the same number of units are purchased at each price.

First-in, First-out (FIFO)

First-in, first-out (FIFO) pricing assumes that the oldest goods on hand (or earliest purchased) are sold first. Thus, ending inventories are always made up of the most recent purchases. Under FIFO, goods in the beginning inventory can also

EXHIBIT 9–4
Weighted Average Inventory Pricing

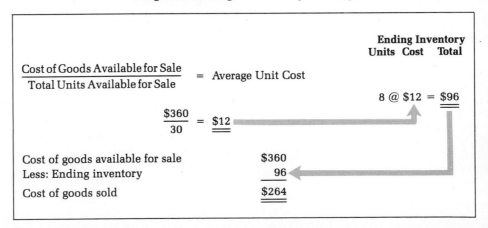

	Ending Inventory		
	Units	Cost	Total

$$\frac{\text{Cost of Goods Available for Sale}}{\text{Total Units Available for Sale}} = \text{Average Unit Cost}$$

8 @ $12 = $96

$$\frac{\$360}{30} = \$12$$

Cost of goods available for sale	$360
Less: Ending inventory	96
Cost of goods sold	$264

EXHIBIT 9–5
First-in, First-out Inventory Pricing

	Goods Available			Ending Inventory		
	Units	Cost	Total	Units	Cost	Total
Beginning inventory	6 @	$10 =	$ 60			
Purchases:	10 @	11 =	110			
	10 @	13 =	130	4 @	$13 =	$ 52
	4 @	15 =	60	4 @	15 =	60
	30		$360	8		$112

Cost of goods available for sale	$360
Less: Ending inventory	112
Cost of goods sold	$248

be in the ending inventory only when the number of units sold is less than the number of units in the beginning inventory. A FIFO approach would result in the cost allocations as shown in Exhibit 9–5. This method assumes the first 22 units acquired are sold and the last eight units purchased are still on hand.

Last-in, First-out (LIFO)

The **last-in, first-out (LIFO)** approach assumes that the most recent purchases are sold first. Thus, unless sales exceed purchases, the beginning inventory remains on hand as part of the ending inventory. Exhibit 9–6 shows how LIFO works. This method assumes the 22 units most recently purchased are sold, and the eight oldest units available for sale (six units from the beginning inventory and two units from the period's first purchase) remain on hand at the end of the period.

EXHIBIT 9–6
Last-in, First-out Inventory Pricing

	Goods Available			Ending Inventory		
	Units	Cost	Total	Units	Cost	Total
Beginning inventory	6 @	$10 =	$ 60	6 @	$10 =	$60
Purchases:	10 @	11 =	110	2 @	11 =	22
	10 @	13 =	130			
	4 @	15 =	60			
	30		$360	8		$82

Cost of goods available for sale	$360
Less: Ending inventory	82
Cost of goods sold	$278

COMPARATIVE ANALYSIS OF INVENTORY PRICING METHODS

In this section, we consider the effects of and reasons for using the various inventory pricing methods just illustrated.

Variations in Income Patterns

For comparative purposes, let us assume that the 22 units in our illustration were sold for $20 each. Exhibit 9−7 shows the differences among gross profit figures resulting from each of the inventory pricing methods. Remember that these differences in reported gross profit result from assumptions made about cost flows, not from any difference in actual goods flows. Pretax income will also reflect these differences if operating expenses are equal in each case.

Cost Flows

The specific identification method is most appropriate for operations that involve somewhat differentiated products of relatively high unit values. New automobiles and construction equipment are good examples of merchandise that would justify the cost of maintaining the price of each inventory unit and specifically identifying each sale. Specific identification is not feasible when products have low unit values and involve large volumes.

Specific identification offers limited potential for income manipulation. To the degree that like units of inventory are available at various cost figures, we can maximize reported income by "choosing" to sell the unit with the lowest cost. Income could be minimized by choosing to sell the unit with the highest cost.

The weighted average approach to inventory measurement is best suited to operations that store a large volume of undifferentiated goods in common areas. Liquid fuels, grains, and other commodities are good examples. To some degree,

EXHIBIT 9−7
Differential Gross Margins on Sales
Based on Various Inventory Pricing Methods

	Inventory Pricing Method			
	Sp. Id.	Average	FIFO	LIFO
Sales (22 units @ $20)	$440	$440	$440	$440
Beginning inventory	$ 60	$ 60	$ 60	$ 60
Total purchases	300	300	300	300
Cost of goods available for sale	$360	$360	$360	$360
Less: Ending inventory				
(See earlier computations)	104	96	112	82
Cost of goods sold	$256	$264	$248	$278
Gross profit on sales	$184	$176	$192	$162
Increased gross profit compared with LIFO	$22	$14	$30	

the weighted average cost represents all the various costs of accumulating the goods currently on hand. Consequently, weighted average costs typically fall between the extreme cost figures that can result from other methods.

As a matter of good business, most companies—especially those with perishable or style-affected goods—attempt to sell the oldest merchandise first. This is especially true of companies dealing in foods, certain chemicals, or drugs. In these cases, FIFO most nearly matches the cost flow to the probable goods flow.

Finding an example of a business operation in which LIFO represents the natural flow of goods is difficult. Purchases of coal or a similar commodity may all be dumped onto one pile from an overhead trestle, and sales may be taken from the top of the pile by a crane. If beginning inventories have been maintained or increased, we conclude that the firm's original purchases are still in inventory. In this case, LIFO represents the actual goods flow. Although LIFO is not the goods flow for most businesses, an estimated 50% or more of major businesses use LIFO to price some of their inventories. We explore the reasons for this choice later in this chapter.

In summary:

(1) In a physical sense, specific identification best presents actual cost of goods sold.

(2) Weighted average can best be associated with business operations in which like goods are commingled.

(3) FIFO probably represents most accurately the actual goods flow for most firms.

(4) Although LIFO represents the least plausible goods flow for most businesses, many major firms use it.

MATCHING COSTS AND REVENUE Because the use of FIFO and LIFO can result in extreme differences during times of changing prices (see Exhibit 9–7), we examine the effects of these two methods.

Consider the data below, taken from our earlier computations, which show that FIFO matches the older costs against current revenue and LIFO matches the most recent costs against current revenue. Under FIFO, therefore, the ending inventory is measured at relatively recent prices, whereas under LIFO, the ending inventory amount reflects older prices.

	Units	Cost	Total
Beginning inventory	6 @	$10 =	$ 60
Purchases:	10 @	11 =	110
	10 @	13 =	130
	4 @	15 =	60

FIFO	**LIFO**
Cost of goods sold: $248 (oldest 22 units)	Cost of goods sold: $278 (latest 22 units)
Ending inventory: 112 (latest 8 units)	Ending inventory: 82 (oldest 8 units)

Most accountants agree that when prices are rising, FIFO tends to overstate income because older, lower unit costs are included in cost of goods sold and matched against current sales prices. In other words, in our example, some of the units sold are charged to costs of goods sold at unit costs of $10, $11, and $13. If our latest purchases reflect current acquisition prices, the units sold must be replaced by units costing $15 (or more if prices continue to rise). Thus, we can argue that when prices rise, LIFO better matches current costs against current revenue, because the cost of the most recent purchases constitutes cost of goods sold.

However, while LIFO associates the current, most significant, unit prices with cost of goods sold, it consequently prices the ending inventory at the older, less realistic unit prices. Because of this, the LIFO inventory figure on the balance sheet is often meaningless in terms of current prices. As we noted earlier, when inventory quantities are maintained or increased, the LIFO method prevents the older prices from appearing in the cost of goods sold. No doubt, some firms still carry LIFO inventories at unit prices that prevailed more than 25 years ago.

Phantom Profits and Income Tax Advantage

A highly simplified example will illustrate how to reduce the undesirable effects of *phantom profits* that result from the use of FIFO during times of rising prices. The same computations will show a related tax advantage of using LIFO during such periods.

Assume that a firm has an opening inventory of five units costing $500 each. The firm sells the five units for $750 each and replaces its inventory by purchasing five more units costing $650 per unit. All transactions are for cash and, for simplicity, we also assume that operating expenses are zero and the applicable income tax rate is 40%. Exhibit 9–8 shows how FIFO produces a phantom profit that is

EXHIBIT 9–8
FIFO–LIFO Comparison: Phantom Profit Effect and Tax Benefit

	FIFO		LIFO	
	Income Statement	Cash In (Out)	Income Statement	Cash In (Out)
Sales (5 @ $750)	$3,750	$3,750	$3,750	$3,750
Cost of goods sold:				
Beginning inventory (5 @ $500)	$2,500		$2,500	
Purchases (5 @ $650)	3,250	(3,250)	3,250	(3,250)
Goods available (10 units)	$5,750		$5,750	
Ending inventory:				
5 @ FIFO	3,250			
5 @ LIFO			2,500	
Cost of goods sold	$2,500		$3,250	
Pretax income	$1,250		$ 500	
Income tax at 40%	500	(500)	200	(200)
Net after-tax income	$ 750		$ 300	
Net cash proceeds		$ 0		$ 300

avoided under LIFO and also shows the tax benefit of LIFO when purchase prices are rising.

Note that under FIFO, $750 of after-tax net income is reported, but the amount of cash from sales is only enough to replace the inventory sold and pay the income

THE OTHER SIDE OF LIFO

Discussions of the LIFO cost basis for inventory valuation usually focus on this method's superiority and its widespread adoption. The conventional rationale for LIFO is its consistency with the matching principle during a period of rising prices. Historically, the most significant adoption of LIFO by U.S. corporations occurred during the period from 1973 to 1974, which was characterized by rapidly rising prices and sharp increases in interest rates. However, the motivation for the widespread use of LIFO did not derive from the desire to achieve better matching of cost and revenue, but rather, from the reduced reported income that led to tax savings and increased cash flow.

Recently, another facet of LIFO, known as LIFO liquidation, has appeared in the annual reports of some companies. This process occurs during a reporting period when a company sells (withdraws) goods in greater quantity than it purchases (enters). As a result, inventories are reduced to a point at which cost layers of prior years are related to current inflated sales prices.

Possible factors causing LIFO liquidations are

(1) Decreased expected demand associated with a recessionary economy.

(2) High interest rates resulting in high inventory carrying costs. These high rates also present alternative economic opportunities for funds invested in inventories if there is a belief that the inflation rate will decrease in relation to interest rates.

(3) A sluggish economy that could lead management to minimize losses or improve reported profits.

To get a notion about the extent, if any, to which companies that recorded a LIFO liquidation increased net income, the financial reports of 17 LIFO companies for the years 1980 and 1981 were randomly selected. Nine of these companies reported an increase in pretax income (or a reduction of loss) of at least 10% for either 1980, 1981, or both, as a direct result of LIFO liquidation. What these preliminary results suggest is that other aspects of LIFO require more extensive study. The original justification for LIFO was its superiority in reflecting results consistent with the matching principle. The liquidation of LIFO layers in recent years has had the opposite effect. It mismatches current revenue and historical cost, which results in the inclusion of inventory holding gains in reported income.

Thus, we have come full circle. FIFO valuation methods, originally criticized for poor matching when compared with LIFO, may actually be superior in the sense that, compared with companies experiencing LIFO liquidations, FIFO companies match cost and revenue relatively well. Furthermore, it may be argued that the sole motivation attributed to companies for switching to LIFO—to improve cash flows—may need broadening. Since the timing of the decision to liquidate LIFO inventories is entirely up to management, it would appear that such liquidations may give rise to income smoothing. It must be stressed that the smoothing may enhance the image conveyed by financial statements, but it has a negative impact on cash flow to the extent that taxes are paid (or loss carryforwards reduced) on the incremental profit associated with the sale of the liquidated inventories.

From Allen I. Schiff, "The Other Side of LIFO," *Journal of Accountancy*, May 1983, pages 120–21. Copyright © 1983 by the American Institute of Certified Public Accountants, Inc.

tax on the $1,250 pretax income. Thus, the net income of $750 is not realized in cash that can be declared as dividends or reinvested in the business; it is considered *phantom profit* (or *inventory profit*). We can easily imagine how the phantom profit element causes problems in the planning of dividend policy and the use of net income as a source of capital investments.

When prices rise, LIFO's tax benefit is obvious. Under LIFO, inventories are measured at older (lower) prices, which causes cost of goods sold to increase and net income (and therefore income taxes payable) to decrease. Use of LIFO during times of *falling* prices, however, can have quite the opposite tax consequence.

Disclosure

A firm's financial statements should disclose its inventory pricing methods. This is often done in footnotes to the financial statements or parenthetically within the appropriate section of the statements.

DEPARTURES FROM COST

Inventories are generally measured at cost. The measurement may be reduced below cost, however, if there is evidence that the inventory's utility has fallen below cost. Such *inventory write-downs* may occur when (1) merchandise must be sold at reduced prices because it is damaged or otherwise not in normal salable condition, or (2) the cost of replacing items in the ending inventory has declined below their recorded cost.

Net Realizable Value

Damaged, physically deteriorated, or obsolete merchandise should be measured and reported at **net realizable value** when this value is less than cost. Net realizable value is the estimated selling price less the expected cost of disposal. For example, assume that an inventory item cost $300 but can be sold for only $200 because it is damaged. Related selling costs are an estimated $20. We should write down the item to $180 ($200 estimated selling price less $20 estimated disposal cost) and reflect a $120 loss for this period.

Lower of Cost or Market

The **lower of cost or market (LCM) rule** provides for the recognition of a loss when prices decline on new inventory items. Under this rule, the loss is reported in the period when the prices decline, rather than during a subsequent period of sale. *Market* is defined as the current replacement cost of the merchandise. If applicable, the LCM rule simply measures inventory at the lower (replacement) market figure. Consequently, reported income decreases by the amount that the ending inventory has been written down. When the ending inventory becomes part of the cost of goods sold in a future period of lower selling prices, its reduced carrying value helps maintain normal profit margins in the period of sale.

To illustrate, let us assume an inventory item that cost $80 has been selling for $100 during the year, yielding a gross profit of 20% on sales. At year-end, the item's replacement cost has dropped to $60—a 25% decline—and a proportionate reduction in the selling price to $75 is expected. In this case, the inventory would be written down to the $60 replacement cost, reducing the current period's net income by the $20 loss. When the item is sold in a subsequent period for $75, a normal gross profit of 20% on sales will be reported ($75 − $60 = $15 gross profit).

Because of the scale and complexity of modern markets, not all decreases in replacement prices are followed by proportionate reductions in selling prices. In these cases, the application of the LCM rule is modified as follows:

(1) If selling price is not expected to drop, inventory may be carried at cost even though it exceeds replacement cost. Using the above example, if the selling price remains at $100 even though the replacement cost drops to $60, we need not write down the inventory.

(2) If selling price is expected to drop—but less than proportionately to the decline in replacement cost—inventory is written down only to the extent necessary to maintain a normal gross profit in the period of sale. Referring again to the above example, if the selling price drops from $100 to $90 when the replacement cost declines to $60, inventory would be written down to $72. This amount maintains a 20% gross profit when the item is sold ($90 − $72 = $18 gross profit).

We may apply the LCM rule to (1) each inventory item, (2) the totals of major inventory classes or categories, or (3) the total inventory. The following simple illustration shows the application of two of these alternatives and indicates that the inventory amount obtained depends on how the rule is applied.

Inventory Item	Quantity	Unit Price Cost	Unit Price Market	Inventory Amounts Cost	Inventory Amounts Market	LCM (by Item)
A	4	$4	$3	$16	$12	$12
B	3	6	7	18	21	18
				$34	$33	$30

If we apply LCM to the total inventory, our result is $33. Applied by item, however, the LCM amount is $30. Although the item by item procedure is used most often, either way is acceptable, but one method should be used consistently. Inventory market values appear in such sources as current price catalogs, purchase contracts with suppliers, and other forms of price quotations.

ESTIMATING INVENTORIES

Several good reasons exist for estimating inventories. When taking physical inventory counts for interim financial statements is impractical, an estimate is sufficient. The adequacy of inventory insurance coverage may be determined on the basis of an inventory estimate. Finally, an estimate may be necessary to determine the loss from merchandise destroyed by fire or other disaster. Therefore, we should examine some methods for estimating inventories.

EXHIBIT 9–9
Gross Profit Method of Estimating Inventory

Beginning inventory		$20,000
Net cost of purchases		50,000
Cost of goods available for sale		$70,000
Net sales	$80,000	
Estimated gross profit (30%)	24,000	
Estimated cost of goods sold		56,000
Estimated ending inventory		$14,000

Gross Profit Method

The **gross profit method** of estimating inventories merely rearranges the cost of goods sold section of the income statement—estimated cost of goods sold is deducted from the cost of goods available for sale to derive the estimated ending inventory. Subtracting an estimated gross profit amount from sales provides the estimated cost of goods sold figure. For the gross profit method to be valid, the gross profit percentage used must be representative of the merchandising activities leading up to the date of the inventory estimate.

Suppose that over the past three years a company's gross profit averaged 30% of net sales. Assume also that the net sales for the interim period are $80,000; the inventory at the beginning of the period was $20,000; and net cost of purchases for the period are $50,000. Exhibit 9–9 shows how to estimate the ending inventory using the gross profit method.

Retail Inventory Method

Another approach to estimating inventories is widely used by retail businesses, such as department stores, that keep periodic inventory records. Such firms typically mark each item of merchandise with the retail price and record purchases at both cost and retail price. A firm can estimate its ending inventory at *retail* price merely by subtracting sales from the retail price of merchandise available for sale. To determine the inventory *cost*, the firm applies a cost-to-retail price percentage, which is the ratio of cost to retail price of merchandise available for sale. In Exhibit 9–10 this ratio is 70%, which yields a cost amount of $21,000 when applied to the $30,000 retail value of the inventory.

The cost-to-retail ratio can also be used to compute the cost of a physical inventory taken at retail prices. Thus, the firm saves the considerable effort and expense of determining cost prices for each inventory item. Suppose, for example, that sales clerks count their stock and determine that the ending inventory has an aggregate retail value of $40,000. If the cost-to-retail price ratio is 70%, management could easily obtain the estimated cost of the inventory, $28,000, that is needed to prepare financial statements.

The accuracy of the retail inventory method depends on the assumption that the ending inventory contains the same proportion of goods at the various mark-up percentages as did the original group of merchandise available for sale. To the extent that the mix of mark-up percentages does not remain constant, the accuracy of the estimate is impaired.

EXHIBIT 9–10
Retail Inventory Method

	Cost	Retail Price
Beginning inventory	$14,000	$ 22,000
Net purchases	70,000	98,000
Total merchandise available for sale	$84,000	$120,000

Cost-to-retail percentage:

$$\frac{\$84,000}{\$120,000} = 70\%$$

Less: Sales during period		90,000
Estimated ending inventory at retail prices		$ 30,000
Applicable cost percentage		× 0.70
Estimated ending inventory at cost		$ 21,000

THE EFFECT OF INVENTORY ERRORS

To determine the effect of inventory errors on income determination, we must consider the method for calculating cost of goods sold. We illustrate why in Exhibit 9–11, where we assume that the ending inventory of period 1 was overstated by $1,000.

EXHIBIT 9–11
Effect of Inventory Error on Two Operating Periods

	Amounts (in Thousands of Dollars)				
	Period 1			Period 2	
	Correct	Erroneous		Erroneous	Correct
Sales	$80	$80		$100	$100
Beginning inventory	$20	$20		$14	$13
Net cost of purchases	50	50		66	66
Goods available	$70	$70		$80	$79
Ending inventory	13	14		10	10
Cost of goods sold	57	56		70	69
Gross profit	$23	$24		$ 30	$ 31
Overstatement (or under-statement) of net income	$1			($1)	

Because the ending inventory in period 1 is overstated by $1,000, the cost of goods sold is understated by $1,000, and thus reported income is overstated by that amount. Because the ending inventory in period 1 is also the beginning inventory in period 2, the reported income for both periods will be misstated unless the error is corrected. Note, however, that the error in period 2 causes a misstatement of reported income that is equal in amount ($1,000) to the error in period 1 but opposite in direction (an understatement); thus, the errors in the two periods offset each other.

Therefore, uncorrected errors in ending inventories affect income determination for two periods. Overstating or understating ending inventory overstates or understates income, respectively. Regardless of the direction of the error, it will cause an offsetting error of like amount in the second period if it is not corrected.

PERPETUAL INVENTORY PROCEDURES

Thus far in our discussion, we have assumed that all inventory situations involve a *periodic* system. This system (1) records acquisitions of merchandise as debits to a Purchases account, (2) makes no entry at the time of sale for the cost of goods sold, and (3) only periodically (hence its name) updates the Inventory account when closing entries are made. The periodic system is most suitable for businesses that have many sales transactions of relatively small unit product costs—for example, retail grocery, drug, variety, or department stores.

Other types of business firms, notably those with fewer sales transactions but relatively high unit product costs, may use a **perpetual** inventory system. Under the perpetual inventory system (also descriptively named), the Inventory account is "perpetually," or continually (as opposed to periodically), maintained. Perpetually updating the Inventory account requires (1) that at the time of purchase, merchandise acquisitions be recorded as debits to the Inventory account and (2) that at the time of sale, the cost of goods sold be determined and recorded by a debit to a Cost of Goods Sold account and a credit to the Inventory account. With a perpetual inventory system, Cost of Goods Sold is an actual account in the general ledger rather than merely a category on the income statement as it is with a periodic inventory system.

Perpetual Inventory Entries

When a firm employs perpetual inventory procedures, the Inventory account shows the amount of inventory on hand at the end of the period—assuming that no theft, spoilage, or error has occurred. However, even if there is little chance for or suspicion of inventory discrepancy, most companies take a physical inventory count at least once a year. At that time, the account is adjusted for any inaccuracies discovered.

The following entries demonstrate the recording procedures followed under the perpetual inventory system, contrasted with the periodic system.

Journal Entries

<table>
<tr><td align="center">**Periodic**
Inventory System</td><td align="center">**Perpetual**
Inventory System</td></tr>
</table>

(1) Purchased $1,200 worth of merchandise on account, terms 2/10, n/30 (recorded at invoice price).

Purchases	1,200		Inventory	1,200	
Accounts Payable		1,200	Accounts Payable		1,200

(2) Returned $200 worth of merchandise to vendors.

Accounts Payable	200		Accounts Payable	200	
Purchases Returns and Allowances		200	Inventory		200

(3) Paid for merchandise (discount taken).

Accounts Payable	1,000		Accounts Payable	1,000	
Purchases Discounts		20	Inventory		20
Cash		980	Cash		980

(4) Sold goods costing $500 for $800 on account.

Accounts Receivable	800		Accounts Receivable	800	
Sales		800	Sales		800
			Cost of Goods Sold	500	
			Inventory		500

(5) Counted inventory at end of period, $19,800. The balance in the Inventory account under the periodic system is $25,000 (the beginning inventory). The balance in the Inventory account under the perpetual system is $20,000.

(Closing entries for periodic inventory)

Income Summary	25,000		Loss on Inventory Shrinkage	200	
Inventory		25,000	Inventory		200
Inventory	19,800				
Income Summary		19,800			

Note that under a perpetual system the Inventory account is increased by purchases and decreased by the cost of goods sold, purchases returns and allowances, and discounts. Therefore, at the end of the period, one entry brings the Inventory account balance into agreement with the amount of the physical inventory. Because we assumed the physical inventory of goods on hand amounted to $19,800, and the Inventory account had a balance of $20,000, we charged the $200 difference to Loss on Inventory Shrinkage and reduced the Inventory account balance to $19,800.

Perpetual Inventory Pricing Methods

When purchase prices for inventory items change during an accounting period, we must select a perpetual inventory pricing method so that the debit to Cost of Goods Sold for each sale may be determined. The same four methods we examined under the periodic inventory system are available—specific identification, average, FIFO, and LIFO. To illustrate these methods on a perpetual basis, we shall use the following data about an inventory item:

		Units	Unit Cost	Total Cost
January 1	Beginning inventory	5	$30.00	$150.00
January 15	Purchase	10	33.00	330.00
September 12	Sale	(9)		
September 29	Purchase	10	36.00	360.00

We must compute the cost of goods sold amount for the nine units sold on September 12.

SPECIFIC IDENTIFICATION   When specific identification is used, the actual costs of the specific items sold constitute the cost of goods sold. Assuming two of the nine units sold are from the beginning inventory and the remaining seven units are from the January 15 purchase, the cost of goods sold is $291 [(2 × $30) + (7 × $33)]. Of course, the costs remaining in inventory are the actual costs of the specific items that are unsold. Specific identification gives the same results for both perpetual and periodic systems.

MOVING AVERAGE   The average method under a perpetual inventory system is called the **moving average** method. Each time goods are purchased, a new average unit cost is computed for the goods on hand. Cost of goods sold for each sale is computed by multiplying the average unit cost at that time by the number of units sold. On September 12, the average unit cost is $32 ($480 total cost ÷ 15 units available for sale). Therefore, the cost of goods sold is $288 (9 × $32). On September 29, a new average unit cost of $34.50 is computed ($552 total cost ÷ 16 units available for sale).

Because unit average costs are recomputed each time a purchase occurs, the moving average method gives different answers from those obtained by using the weighted average method under a periodic inventory system.

FIRST-IN, FIRST-OUT   Under the perpetual FIFO method, each time a sale is made the costs of the oldest goods on hand are charged to cost of goods sold. In our illustration, the FIFO cost of goods sold on September 12 is $282 [(5 × $30) + (4 × $33)]. The FIFO method applied on a perpetual basis results in the same total cost of goods sold amount—and the same ending inventory—as that achieved under the periodic FIFO method.

LAST-IN, FIRST-OUT   When perpetual LIFO is used, each time a sale is made the costs of the most recent purchases are charged to cost of goods sold. For the

EXHIBIT 9–12
Perpetual Inventory Record—FIFO Basis

INVENTORY CONTROL

Part No. 1342

Description Flexible shaft ($\frac{3}{8}$")

Prime Supplier Ball Machinery Company

Location Small Parts Warehouse (Bin 32)

Maximum 16

Reorder Level 6

Reorder Quantity 10

Date		Received			Sold			Balance		
		Units	Cost/Unit	Total	Units	Cost/Unit	Total	Units	Cost/Unit	Total
19XX										
Jan.	1	Balance Fwd.						5	$30	$150
	15	10	$33	$330				{ 5	30	
								{ 10	33	480
Sept.	12				5	$30	$150			
					4	33	132	6	33	198
	29	10	36	360				{ 6	33	
								{ 10	36	558

September 12 sale, the most recent costs for nine units were incurred on January 15. Thus, cost of goods sold is $297 (9 × $33).

Perpetual LIFO normally gives results different from periodic LIFO for both the total cost of goods sold for a period and the period's ending inventory.

Perpetual Inventory Records

When a perpetual inventory system is used, a detailed perpetual inventory record must be maintained—manually or by computer—for each inventory item. The perpetual inventory records must provide for both the inflow and outflow of merchandise as well as disclose the quantities and prices of items at any time. Although these records are continually maintained, their accuracy should be verified at least once each year by physical counts of merchandise.

Exhibit 9–12 illustrates a perpetual inventory record for an inventory item priced on the FIFO basis. At year-end, the balances on all the perpetual inventory records are added, and their total dollar amount should agree with the amount in the Inventory account, which serves as a control account.

DEMONSTRATION PROBLEM FOR REVIEW

Mackenzie, Inc. began operations on April 1 of the current year. Sales revenue for April totaled $90,000. The company uses the periodic inventory system. Its beginning inventory was $4,000, consisting of 2,000 units at $2 per unit. A summary of April purchases appears below.

April	8	5,000 units	@	$2.50 =	$12,500
	19	10,000	@	3.00 =	30,000
	29	6,000	@	3.50 =	21,000
			Total		$63,500

At the end of April, 7,000 units were on hand.

REQUIRED

(a) How much gross profit on sales would Mackenzie, Inc. report for April under (1) first-in, first-out inventory pricing, and (2) last-in, first-out inventory pricing?

(b) Calculate Mackenzie's gross profit on sales for April under (1) first-in, first-out, and (2) last-in, first-out if the April 29 purchase had been postponed until May.

(c) Calculate Mackenzie's gross profit on sales for April under (1) first-in, first-out, and (2) last-in, first-out if the April 29 purchase had been 9,000 units instead of 6,000 units.

(d) Based on your answers to parts (a), (b), and (c), what can you conclude about the impact of the timing or amount of end-of-period purchases on the gross profit on sales computed under the (1) first-in, first-out, and (2) last-in, first-out methods of inventory pricing?

SOLUTION TO DEMONSTRATION PROBLEM
(a)

	FIFO	LIFO
Sales	$90,000	$90,000
Cost of Goods Sold:		
Beginning Inventory	$ 4,000	$ 4,000
Add: Purchases	63,500	63,500
Cost of Goods Available for Sale	$67,500	$67,500
Less: Ending Inventory		
FIFO: 6,000 × $3.50 = $21,000		
1,000 × $3.00 = 3,000	24,000	
LIFO: 2,000 × $2.00 = $ 4,000		
5,000 × $2.50 = 12,500		16,500
Cost of Goods Sold	$43,500	$51,000
Gross Profit on Sales	$46,500	$39,000

(b) If the April 29 purchase of 6,000 units was postponed until May, the April 30 inventory would have been 1,000 units and purchases for April would have totaled $42,500 ($12,500 on April 8 + $30,000 on April 19). The gross profit on sales would then be computed as follows:

	FIFO	LIFO
Sales	$90,000	$90,000
Cost of Goods Sold:		
Beginning Inventory	$ 4,000	$ 4,000
Add: Purchases	42,500	42,500
Cost of Goods Available for Sale	$46,500	$46,500
Less: Ending Inventory		
FIFO: 1,000 × $3.00	3,000	
LIFO: 1,000 × $2.00		2,000
Cost of Goods Sold	$43,500	$44,500
Gross Profit on Sales	$46,500	$45,500

(c) If 9,000 units were purchased on April 29, then the April 30 inventory would have been 10,000 units and purchases for April would have totaled $74,000 ($12,500 on April 8 + $30,000 on April 19 + $31,500 on April 29). The gross profit on sales would then be computed as follows:

	FIFO	LIFO
Sales	$90,000	$90,000
Cost of Goods Sold:		
Beginning Inventory	$ 4,000	$ 4,000
Add: Purchases	74,000	74,000
Cost of Goods Available for Sale	$78,000	$78,000
Less: Ending Inventory		
FIFO: 9,000 × $3.50 = $31,500		
1,000 × $3.00 = 3,000	34,500	
LIFO: 2,000 × $2.00 = $ 4,000		
5,000 × $2.50 = 12,500		
3,000 × $3.00 = 9,000		25,500
Cost of Goods Sold	$43,500	$52,500
Gross Profit on Sales	$46,500	$37,500

(d) Gross profit on sales under the FIFO method is the same in all three cases. The gross profit is unaffected by changes in the amount or timing of end-of-period purchases.

Gross profit on sales under the LIFO method is different in each case. Gross profit is affected by changes in the amount or timing of end-of-period purchases, because—under the periodic LIFO method—the costs of the most recently purchased goods are the first costs charged to cost of goods sold expense.

KEY POINTS TO REMEMBER

(1) Cost of goods sold under a periodic system is calculated as beginning inventory plus net cost of purchases less ending inventory.

(2) Other things being equal, changing the dollar amount of ending inventory changes reported pretax income by a like amount.

(3) Taking inventory consists of three stages: (a) counting, (b) pricing, and (c) summation.

(4) An inventory amount under a periodic system can be calculated by using any of the following methods: specific identification; weighted average; first-in, first-out (FIFO); and last-in, first-out (LIFO). Reported income can be influenced by choosing among inventory pricing methods.

(5) When prices are rising, LIFO matches current costs against revenue and results in lower reported income than FIFO does and thus may provide a related tax benefit.

(6) Inventories can be estimated by the gross profit method or the retail inventory method. The gross profit method requires the use of a representative gross profit percentage. An appropriate cost-to-retail price percentage must be computed under the retail inventory method.

(7) Uncorrected ending inventory measurement errors cause the reported income of two periods to be misstated. The errors are equal in amount, opposite in direction, and therefore offsetting.

(8) A perpetual inventory system (a) does not use a Purchases account, (b) records cost of goods sold at the time of sale, and (c) continually updates the balance in the Inventory account. Pricing methods under a perpetual system are specific identification, moving average, FIFO, and LIFO.

QUESTIONS

9–1 List six factors (or cost categories) typically included in the cost of goods sold computation under a periodic inventory system and indicate whether the amount of each normally increases or decreases the cost of goods sold figure.

9–2 Define *inventory* and identify the costs that should be included as inventory costs.

9–3 Under a periodic inventory system, why is reported income affected dollar-for-dollar (disregarding income taxes) by any change in the dollar amount of ending inventory?

9–4 For a physical inventory count, explain (a) the three steps involved, (b) why firms maintaining perpetual inventory records still take physical counts, and (c) what merchandise should be included.

9–5 What is meant by *goods flow* and *cost flow*?

9–6 Briefly describe each of the following inventory pricing methods under a periodic inventory system: (a) specific identification; (b) weighted average; (c) first-in, first-out; and (d) last-in, first-out.

9–7 Describe an appropriate operating situation (that is, goods flow corresponds with cost flow) for each of the four approaches to inventory pricing listed in Question 9–6.

9–8 Why do relatively stable purchase prices reduce the significance of the choice of an inventory pricing method?

9–9 Briefly explain the nature of *phantom profits* during periods of rising merchandise purchase prices.

9–10 If prices have been rising, which inventory pricing method—weighted average; first-in, first-out; or last-in, first-out—yields (a) the lowest inventory amount? (b) The lowest net income? (c) The largest inventory amount? (d) The largest net income?

9–11 Identify two situations in which merchandise may be inventoried at an amount less than cost.

9–12 At year-end, Britt's Appliance Shop has a refrigerator on hand that has been used as a demonstration model. The refrigerator cost $380 and sells for $570 when new. In its present condition, the refrigerator will be sold for $360. Related selling costs are an estimated $20. At what amount should the refrigerator be carried in inventory?

9–13 Even though it does not represent their goods flow, why might firms adopt last-in, first-out inventory pricing during periods when prices are consistently rising?

9–14 Discuss the effect on reported income of applying the lower of cost or market rule.

9–15 Under what circumstances might firms estimate the dollar amount of their inventories rather than actually count them?

9–16 Casten Company overstated its 19X1 ending inventory by $8,000. Assuming the error was not discovered, what was the effect on income for 19X1? For 19X2?

9–17 Contrast the accounting procedures for periodic and perpetual inventory systems.

9–18 Which inventory pricing methods give the same results (ending inventory and total cost of goods sold) when applied under a perpetual inventory system and a periodic inventory system?

EXERCISES

9–19 Gannon Stores, Inc., uses the periodic inventory system. Its accounting records include the following normal balances:

Accounts Payable (all for merchandise)	$ 6,300
Delivery Expense (to customers)	2,200
Inventory	19,000

Purchases	$71,000
Purchases Discounts	1,300
Purchases Returns and Allowances	3,100
Sales	99,000
Sales Discounts	1,600
Sales Returns and Allowances	2,000
Transportation In	2,400

(a) Assuming that the ending inventory, determined by physical count, is $21,000, compute the cost of goods sold.

(b) How would the above accounts differ if the firm used a perpetual inventory system?

9–20 The December 31, 19XX, inventory of Jenson Company was $81,000. In arriving at this amount, the following items were considered:

(1) Included in the inventory count were goods on hand costing $7,000 owned by Ward Company but on consignment to Jenson Company.

(2) Included in the inventory count were goods in transit at December 31 to Jenson Company from Tiempo, Inc. These goods, costing $9,000, were shipped F.O.B. destination and arrived on January 3.

(3) Excluded from the inventory count were goods sitting on Jenson Company's shipping dock on December 31. These goods, costing $3,000, were sold to Alden, Inc., on December 31 and were picked up by an Alden truck on January 2.

Compute the correct December 31, 19XX inventory amount for Jenson Company.

9–21 The following information is for the Becker Company for May 19XX. Becker sells just one product.

	Units	Unit Cost
Beginning inventory	50	$ 8
Purchases: May 11	90	9
18	70	11
23	30	12

During May, 170 units were sold, leaving an ending inventory of 70 units. Assume periodic inventory procedures and compute the ending inventory and the cost of goods sold using (a) first-in, first-out; (b) last-in, first-out; and (c) weighted average.

9–22 Lopez Company, which uses the periodic inventory system, has the following records for July:

	Units	Unit Cost
Beginning inventory	55	$18
Purchases: July 6	45	16
15	60	15
28	40	13

Ending inventory for July was 65 units. Compute the ending inventory and the cost of goods sold using (a) first-in, first-out; (b) weighted average; and (c) last-in, first-out.

9–23 A firm has gathered the following inventory data at the end of a period:

Commodity	Units on Hand	Unit Cost	Market Price to Replace
A	200	$ 1.60	$ 1.80
B	400	7.50	6.00
C	500	3.30	3.00
D	40	11.00	11.60

Determine the ending inventory amount by applying the lower of cost or market rule to (a) the total inventory and (b) each item of the inventory.

9–24 Over the past several years Baylor Company's gross profit has averaged 38% of net sales. During the first six months of the current year, net sales are $450,000 and net cost of purchases totals $273,000. Inventory at the beginning of the period was $46,000. The company prepares quarterly interim financial statements. Use the gross profit method to determine the estimated cost of inventory at the end of the current six-month period.

9–25 Allen Company's April 1 inventory had a cost of $39,000 and a retail value of $57,000. During April, Allen's net merchandise purchases cost $78,000 and had a net retail value of $123,000. Net sales for April totaled $130,000.
(a) Compute the estimated cost of the April 30 inventory using the retail inventory method.
(b) What key assumptions underlie the validity of this estimate of inventory cost?

9–26 The following information is available for Rusk Company during four consecutive operating periods:

| | Amounts by Period | | | |
	1	2	3	4
Beginning inventory	$16,000	$20,000	$24,000	$18,000
Net cost of purchases	80,000	52,000	60,000	43,000
Cost of goods available for sale	$96,000	$72,000	$84,000	$61,000
Ending inventory	20,000	24,000	18,000	19,000
Cost of goods sold	$76,000	$48,000	$66,000	$42,000

Assuming that the company made the following errors, compute the revised cost of goods sold figure for each period.

Period	Error in Ending Inventory	
1	Understated	$4,000
2	Overstated	2,000
3	Understated	3,000

9–27 Present journal entries to record the following transactions if (a) a periodic inventory system is used and (b) a perpetual inventory system is used.
(1) Merchandise is purchased for (and recorded at) $2,600, terms 2/10, n/30.

(2) Goods originally costing $100 (in the preceding transaction) are returned to the seller before payment is made.

(3) The remainder of the purchase in transaction (1) is paid for and the related discount is taken.

(4) Goods costing $1,500 are sold on account for $2,200.

(5) The proper balance in the Inventory account is established at the end of the period. A physical inventory at the end of the period shows goods costing $1,730 on hand. Assume that the beginning balance in this account was $800.

9–28 The following are July inventory data for Busse Company, which uses perpetual inventory procedures.

July 1 Beginning inventory, 90 units @ $40 per unit.
     10 Purchased 60 units @ $50 per unit.
     15 Sold 100 units.
     26 Purchased 110 units @ $60 per unit.

Compute the cost of goods sold for July 15 using (a) first-in, first-out; (b) last-in, first-out; and (c) moving average.

PROBLEMS

9–29 Daper Sales, Inc. had a beginning inventory for May comprising 600 units that had cost $30 per unit. A summary of purchases and sales during May follows:

	Unit Cost	Units Purchased	Units Sold
May 2			400
6	$32	1,400	
10			800
19	34	1,000	
23			1,300
30	36	500	

REQUIRED

(a) Assuming Daper uses a periodic inventory system, calculate the amount of ending inventory under each of the following pricing methods: first-in, first-out; last-in, first-out; and weighted average.

(b) Which inventory pricing method would you choose:
  (1) to reflect what is probably the physical flow of goods?
  (2) to minimize income tax for the period?
  (3) To report the largest amount of income for the period?
  Justify your answers.

(c) Assuming Daper uses a perpetual inventory system, calculate cost of goods sold amounts on May 2, May 10, and May 23 under each of the following pricing methods: first-in, first-out; last-in, first-out; and moving average.

9–30 Examine the following July data for Weaver, Inc., which prices inventory on the last-in, first-out basis and uses the periodic inventory system.

Beginning inventory: 5,000 units @ $4 each

Purchases		Sales		
July 5	10,000 @ $5	July 8	7,000 @ $ 8
19	30,000 @ 7	21	25,000 @ 10
30	6,000 @ 8	28	11,000 @ 11

REQUIRED
(a) How much gross profit on sales would Weaver, Inc. report for July?
(b) By what amount would Weaver's reported gross profit for July change if the final merchandise purchase had been postponed for several days?
(c) How would Weaver's reported gross profit differ if the final purchase had been for 20,000 units instead of 6,000 units?
(d) Assuming Weaver used the first-in, first-out method, calculate the answers to parts (a), (b), and (c).

9−31 The following is a summary of Kemp Company's inventory amounts at the end of each of its first three years of operations, assuming various inventory pricing procedures.

Year-end	First-in, First-out	Last-in, First-out	Weighted Average
1	$2,900	$2,500	$2,650
2	4,100	3,700	3,900
3	3,500	3,300	3,450

REQUIRED
Answer each of the following questions, providing supporting computations or other reasoning (disregard income tax effects).
(a) For year 1, by how much could reported income change simply by choosing among the three inventory pricing methods?
(b) For year 2, which inventory pricing method would result in the *highest* reported income?
(c) For year 3, which inventory pricing method would result in the *lowest* reported income?
(d) For year 3, by how much and in what direction would reported income differ under first-in, first-out compared with weighted average?
(e) Which inventory pricing method would result in the *highest* reported income for the *three years combined*?

9−32 The Lawler Company had the following inventory at December 31, 19X7:

		Unit Price	
	Quantity	Cost	Market
Fans			
Model X1	400	$12	$13
Model X2	100	17	15
Model X3	200	25	22
Heaters			
Model B7	150	20	18
Model B8	190	30	32
Model B9	80	35	36

REQUIRED

(a) Determine the ending inventory amount by applying the lower of cost or market rule to:

    (1) each item of inventory.

    (2) each major category of inventory.

    (3) the total inventory.

(b) Which of the LCM procedures from part (a) result in the lowest net income for 19X7? Explain.

9–33 Sales clerks for Fame Company, a retail concern, took a year-end physical inventory at retail prices and determined that the total retail value of the ending inventory was $80,000. The following information for the year is available:

	Cost	Selling Price
Beginning inventory	$ 53,900	$ 77,000
Net purchases	180,100	248,000
Sales		238,000

Management estimates its inventory loss from theft and other causes by comparing its physical ending inventory at retail prices with an estimated ending inventory at retail prices (determined by subtracting sales from goods available for sale at selling prices) and reducing this difference to cost by applying the proper cost ratio.

REQUIRED

(a) Compute the estimated cost of the ending inventory using the retail inventory method. This inventory amount will appear in the balance sheet, and the calculation should be based on the physical inventory taken at retail prices.

(b) Compute the estimated inventory loss for the year from theft and other causes.

9–34 Selected operating data follow for Kraft Sales, Inc., a franchised distributor of personal computers:

Beginning inventory	200 units @ $250 each		
Purchases:	400	@	300
	150	@	320
Sales	550	@	520
Operating expenses	$56,000		

Kraft uses the periodic inventory system priced at first-in, first-out. Assume all sales, purchases, operating expenses, and taxes are paid in cash and that a 40% income tax rate is applicable.

REQUIRED

(a) What is Kraft's after-tax net income for the period?

(b) What is the net amount of cash generated by the period's activity?

(c) Why are the amounts in parts (a) and (b) different? How would you explain this to a stockholder who expected a cash dividend equal to one-half of the reported after-tax income?

(d) What would be your answers to parts (a) and (b) if the firm used the last-in, first-out method to price its ending inventory?

(e) Briefly explain the nature of any phantom profit on inventory in part (a). Also, explain the nature of any tax advantage of the last-in, first-out inventory pricing in part (d).

(f) Contrast the inventory carrying values in parts (a) and (d). Which figure is more meaningful? Why?

(g) Contrast the reported income in parts (a) and (d). Which figure is more meaningful? Why?

9–35 Automotive Company, an automobile parts supplier, was robbed of a portion of its inventory on the night of August 16, 19X4. The company does not keep perpetual inventory records and must, therefore, estimate the theft loss. To aid in this determination, the accounting staff compiles the following information:

Inventory, August 1, 19X4	$245,000
Inventory, August 16, 19X4 (not stolen)	106,400
Purchases, August 1–16, 19X4	77,000
Purchases returns, August 1–16, 19X4	2,000
Sales, August 1–16, 19X4	155,000
Average gross profit margin	38%

REQUIRED

Use the gross profit method to estimate the amount of the inventory theft loss.

9–36 Assume that Zemke Company had a $15,000 ending inventory balance at the close of the last period. The following sales and purchase transactions occurred during the current period:

(1) Purchased merchandise on account, $7,600, terms 1/10, n/30.

(2) Returned part of the above merchandise that had an original gross purchase price of $500.

(3) Paid the balance of the purchase in time to receive the purchases discount.

(4) Sold goods costing $12,000 for $20,000. Cash of $4,600 was received, with the balance due on account.

REQUIRED

(a) Record these transactions assuming that (1) a periodic inventory system is used and (2) a perpetual inventory system is used. Assume also that accounts payable are initially recorded at the full invoice price.

(b) Suppose that a physical inventory at the end of the current period shows inventory costing $9,800 to be on hand. Present the journal entries (if any) required under each inventory system to establish the proper balance in the Inventory account.

(c) Which system would best disclose any possible inventory loss in the income statement? Why?

9–37 Bueno Company uses a perpetual inventory system. Transactions for an inventory item during April were as follows:

April 1   Beginning inventory, 60 units @ $105 per unit.
       9   Purchased 10 units @ $112 per unit.
    14   Sold 20 units @ $200 per unit.
    23   Purchased 30 units @ $114 per unit.
    29   Sold 25 units @ $205 per unit.

REQUIRED
Record the beginning inventory, purchases, cost of goods sold, and the continuous (perpetual) inventory balance for April on an inventory control record like the one illustrated in Exhibit 9–12, page 330. Use the (a) first-in, first-out method; (b) last-in, first-out method; and (c) moving average method.

ALTERNATE PROBLEMS

9–29A   Logan Sales, Inc., had a beginning inventory for July comprising 1,300 units that had cost $48 per unit. A summary of purchases and sales during July follows:

	Unit Cost	Units Purchased	Units Sold
July 3			500
8	$54	1,200	
13			1,500
19	60	1,600	
23	62	900	
28			800

REQUIRED
(a) Assuming Logan uses a periodic inventory system, calculate the amount of ending inventory under each of the following pricing methods: first-in, first-out; last-in, first-out; and weighted average.
(b) Which inventory pricing method would you choose:
   (1) to reflect what is probably the physical flow of goods?
   (2) to minimize income tax for the period?
   (3) to report the largest amount of income for the period?
   Justify your answers.
(c) Assuming Logan uses a perpetual inventory system, calculate cost of goods sold amounts on July 3, July 13, and July 28 under each of the following pricing methods: first-in, first-out; last-in, first-out; and moving average.

9–30A   Examine the April data below for Ample, Inc., which prices inventory on the last-in, first-out basis and uses the periodic inventory system.

Beginning inventory: 4,000 units @ $3 each

Purchases			Sales		
Apr. 5	5,000 @	$4	Apr. 8	3,000 @	$ 7
12	15,000 @	5	16	12,000 @	8
21	10,000 @	6	22	13,000 @	9
30	5,000 @	7	27	4,000 @	10

REQUIRED

(a) How much gross profit on sales would Ample, Inc., report for April?

(b) By what amount would Ample's reported gross profit for April change if the final merchandise purchase had been postponed for several days?

(c) How would Ample's reported gross profit differ if the final purchase had been for 10,000 units instead of 5,000 units?

(d) Assuming Ample used the first-in, first-out method, calculate the answers to parts (a), (b), and (c).

9–32A The Prince Company had the following inventory at December 31, 19X4:

		Unit Price	
	Quantity	Cost	Market
Desks			
Model 9001	80	$120	$110
Model 9002	50	170	175
Model 9003	40	250	260
Cabinets			
Model 7001	250	40	45
Model 7002	60	80	70
Model 7003	90	100	105

REQUIRED

(a) Determine the ending inventory amount by applying the lower of cost or market rule to:
(1) each item of inventory.
(2) each major category of inventory.
(3) the total inventory.

(b) Which of the LCM procedures from part (a) result in the lowest net income for 19X4? Explain.

9–33A Sales clerks for Globe Company, a retail concern, took a year-end physical inventory at retail prices and determined that the total retail value of the ending inventory was $120,000. The following information for the year is available:

	Cost	Selling Price
Beginning inventory	$ 37,000	$ 60,000
Net purchases	275,000	420,000
Sales		354,000

Management estimates its inventory loss from theft and other causes by comparing its physical ending inventory at retail prices with an estimated ending inventory at retail prices (determined by subtracting sales from goods available for sale at selling prices) and reducing this difference to cost by applying the proper cost ratio.

REQUIRED

(a) Compute the estimated cost of the ending inventory using the retail inventory method. This inventory amount will appear in the balance sheet, and the calculation should be based on the physical inventory taken at retail prices.

(b) Compute the estimated inventory loss for the year from theft and other causes.

9–36A Assume that Miller's Appliance Shop had an $8,000 ending inventory balance at the close of the last period. The following sales and purchase transactions occurred during the current period:

(1) Purchased merchandise on account, $4,700, terms 2/10, n/30.

(2) Returned part of the above merchandise that had an original gross purchase price of $600.

(3) Paid the balance of the purchase in time to receive the purchases discount.

(4) Sold goods costing $8,600 for $15,000. Cash of $11,000 was received, with the balance due on account.

REQUIRED

(a) Record these transactions assuming that (1) a periodic inventory system is used and (2) a perpetual inventory system is used. Assume also that accounts payable are initially recorded at the full invoice price.

(b) Suppose that a physical inventory at the end of the current period shows inventory costing $3,300 to be on hand. Present journal entries (if any) required under each inventory system to establish the proper balance in the Inventory account.

(c) Which system would best disclose any possible inventory loss in the income statement? Why?

9–37A Lasater Company uses a perpetual inventory system. Transactions for an inventory item during June were as follows:

June 1   Beginning inventory, 25 units @ $160 per unit.
      5   Purchased 5 units @ $190 per unit.
   13   Sold 12 units @ $350 per unit.
   25   Purchased 8 units @ $178 per unit.
   29   Sold 6 units @ $340 per unit.

REQUIRED

Record the beginning inventory, purchases, cost of goods sold, and the continuous (perpetual) inventory balance for June on an inventory control record like the one illustrated in Exhibit 9–12, page 330. Use the (a) first-in, first-out method; (b) last-in, first-out method; and (c) moving average method.

BUSINESS DECISION PROBLEM

Hart Company's entire inventory and many of its accounting records were destroyed by fire early in the morning of April 1, 19X3. Hart filed an inventory loss claim of $90,000 with Dependable Insurance Company. As Dependable's representative, you must evaluate the reasonableness of Hart's claim. You and Hart's head bookkeeper have gathered the following information from various sources:

(1) The January 1, 19X3, inventory figure of $50,000 was found on a copy of a personal property tax declaration filed with the local municipality.

(2) From a statistical summary filed with a trade association, the sales and cost of goods sold for the preceding three years were as follows:

	19X0	19X1	19X2
Net Sales	$700,000	$850,000	$900,000
Cost of goods sold	434,000	544,000	540,000

(3) Hart buys an estimated 80% of its merchandise from three wholesale suppliers. According to these three suppliers, Hart's purchases for the first three months of 19X3 were as follows:

Supplier	Purchases
Jackson Corporation	$ 75,000
Nevin Company	120,000
Ross, Inc.	65,000

(4) Hart's sales average 10% cash and the balance on credit. Adding machine tapes totaling the accounts receivable subsidiary ledger were found and showed $50,000 and $58,000, respectively, for December 31, 19X2, and March 31, 19X3. An analysis of bank deposit slips indicates that collections from credit customers deposited in the bank in 19X3 were: $90,000 for January; $170,000 for February; and $200,000 for March.

REQUIRED

Based on the preceding data, use the gross profit method to estimate Hart Company's ending inventory destroyed by fire. Is Hart's loss claim reasonable?

10

Plant Assets: Measurement and Depreciation

> **The mystery of mysteries is to view machines making machines.**
>
> BENJAMIN DISRAELI

In this chapter and Chapter 11, we discuss the accounting problems related to the acquisition, use, and disposal of assets whose benefits to a firm extend over many accounting periods. These long-term assets fall in three major balance sheet categories—**plant assets, natural resources,** and **intangible assets.** Plant assets, or *fixed assets*, refer to a firm's *property, plant,* and *equipment.*

The carrying values of these long-term assets are normally based on historical costs. As with other business assets, the costs related to the use of long-term assets must be properly calculated and matched against the revenue they help generate, so that periodic net income is determined correctly. Each period's expired portion of the asset's cost is called *depreciation, depletion,* or *amortization,* depending on the type of asset involved. All of these terms have the same meaning in accounting, that is, periodic charging to expense.

Exhibit 10–1 gives several specific examples within each asset category. The exhibit also associates the term for the periodic write-off to expense with the proper asset category. Note that site land—that is, a place on which to operate—usually has an indefinite useful life and therefore does not require any periodic write-off to expense.

EXHIBIT 10–1
Classification of Long-term Assets
and Related Write-off

Asset Category	Examples	Term for Periodic Write-off to Expense
Plant Assets	Buildings, equipment, tools, furniture, fixtures, and vehicles	Depreciation
	Land for site use	No periodic write-off; considered to have an indefinite life.
Natural Resources	Oil, timber, coal, and other mineral deposits	Depletion
Intangible Assets	Patents, copyrights, leaseholds, franchises, trademarks, and goodwill	Amortization

OVERVIEW OF PLANT ASSET PROBLEMS

We consider the problems associated with plant assets in the order shown in Exhibit 10–2. This exhibit is a graphic presentation of the typical accounting problems created by plant assets in relation to an asset's life cycle.

Measurement problems associated with plant assets include identifying the types and amounts of expenditures that make up the original recorded cost of the particular asset. During the use period of a limited-life asset, it is important to charge the appropriate amounts against yearly revenue to reflect the asset's consumption. This involves estimating the asset's useful life and its probable salvage value at disposal. Also during the use period, expenditures for simple maintenance (expense) must be properly differentiated from expenditures that increase the capacity or extend the life of the asset (added to asset costs). On disposal, the adjusted accounting cost of the asset must be compared with the net proceeds from disposal in order to determine any related gain or loss. We consider this last problem in Chapter 11.

EXHIBIT 10–2
Typical Problems of
Plant Asset Accounting

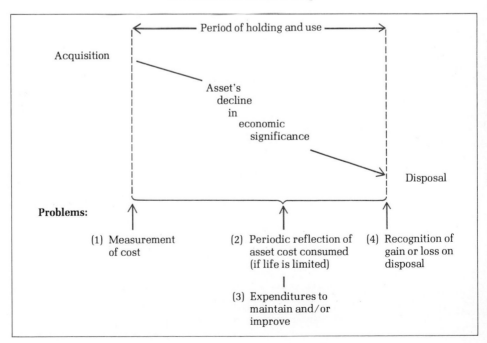

ORIGINAL MEASUREMENT OF PLANT ASSETS

Plant assets are originally recorded at their cost. These measures are also called *historical costs* because they provide the basis for accounting for the assets in subsequent periods. Usually we do not attempt to reflect subsequent changes in market values for plant assets. In general, the initial cost of a plant asset is equal to the cash and/or the cash equivalent of that which is given up in order to acquire the asset *and* to prepare it for use. In other words, initial cost includes the asset's (1) implied cash price and (2) cost of preparation for use.

The expenditures to acquire and prepare the asset for use must be reasonable and necessary to be considered part of the asset's cost. Accountants do not capitalize (charge to an asset account) wasteful or inefficient expenditures. Costs of

THOROUGH THOREAU

Henry David Thoreau lived alone on the shore of Walden Pond near Concord, Massachusetts from July 4, 1845 to September 6, 1847. Living on property owned by his friend Ralph Waldo Emerson, Thoreau maintained a record of his experiences and thoughts. *Walden*, a masterpiece of American literature, re-creates the nature and tenor of Thoreau's life at the pond.

Thoreau built a house for his stay at Walden Pond. His thoroughness in keeping records is reflected in the following passage concerning the cost of the house:

I have thus a tight shingled and plastered house, ten feet wide by fifteen long, and eight-feet posts, with a garret and a closet, a large window on each side, two trap doors, one door at the end, and a brick fireplace opposite. The exact cost of my house, paying the usual price for such materials as I used, but not counting the work, all of which was done by myself, was as follows; and I give the details because very few are able to tell exactly what their houses cost, and fewer still, if any, the separate cost of the various materials which compose them:—

Boards, ... $ 8 03½, mostly shanty
                                                    boards.
Refuse shingles for
   roof and sides, ...   4 00

Laths, ...	$ 1 25	
Two second-hand windows with glass, .	2 43	
One thousand old brick,	4 00	
Two casks of lime, ...	2 40	That was high.
Hair, ...	0 31	More than I needed.
Mantle-tree iron, ...	0 15	
Nails, ...	3 90	
Hinges and screws, ...	0 14	
Latch, ...	0 10	
Chalk, ...	0 01	
Transportation, ...	1 40	} I carried a good part on my back.
In all, ...	$28 12½	

These are all the materials excepting the timber stones and sand, which I claimed by squatter's right. I have also a small wood-shed adjoining, made chiefly of the stuff which was left after building the house.

I intend to build me a house which will surpass any on the main street in Concord in grandeur and luxury, as soon as it pleases me as much and will cost me no more than my present one.*

*Henry D. Thoreau, *Walden*, J. Lyndon Shanley, ed. (Princeton, NJ: Princeton University Press, 1971), pages 48–49.

waste and inefficiency are expensed when incurred. For example, suppose equipment is damaged while it is being installed or a firm's receiving dock is damaged while equipment is being unloaded. Expenditures made to repair these damages are not part of the cost of the equipment; they are instead charged to expense.

Cash and Noncash Purchases

Often an asset's historical cost is simply the amount of cash paid when the asset is acquired and readied for use. Consider, for example, the following expenditures for a certain piece of equipment:

Purchase price factors:		
Gross invoice price	$10,000	
Less: Cash discount (1/10, n/30)	(100)	
Sales tax	500	$10,400
Related expenditures:		
Freight charges	$ 200	
Installation costs	500	
Testing of installed machine	300	1,000
Cost of equipment		$11,400

The total initial equipment cost is $11,400, consisting of a cash purchase price of $10,400 and preparation costs of $1,000. The sales tax is a necessary component of the purchase price and should not be charged to a tax expense account. Similarly, the costs of freight, installation, and testing are expenditures necessary to get the asset in condition and location for use.

If an asset's purchase price is not immediately paid in cash, we determine the cash equivalent purchase price at the acquisition date and record that amount in the asset account. Suppose we purchased the above equipment on a financing plan requiring a $1,500 cash down payment and a non-interest-bearing note for $10,000 due in one year. The implied cash price remains $10,400, even though the financing plan is used. The difference between the $10,400 and the $11,500 total disbursement under the financing plan ($1,500 down payment plus $10,000 payment on note) represents the interest cost of the financing plan. The entry to record the purchase of the asset under the financing plan would be:

Equipment	10,400	
Discount on Notes Payable	1,100	
Cash		1,500
Notes Payable		10,000
To record purchase of equipment.		

Of course, the expenditures for freight, installation, and testing are still debited to the Equipment account when they are incurred.

Capitalization of Interest

Interest cost is part of an asset's initial cost if a period of time is required to get the asset ready for use. For example, the construction of a factory building takes time to complete. Accordingly, an appropriate portion of the actual interest cost incurred during the construction period is added to the factory building's cost. We compute the amount of interest capitalized by multiplying the periodic interest rate times the period's average accumulated construction expenditures.

To illustrate, let us assume Miller Company borrowed $500,000 at 12% to finance the construction of a factory building. Interest of $5,000 is paid monthly. During the first month, construction expenditures total $300,000. The interest cost capitalized this first month is $1,500, computed as follows:

Average accumulated construction expenditures:		
Accumulated construction expenditures, beginning of month	$ –0–	
Accumulated construction expenditures, end of month	300,000	
Average accumulated construction expenditures for the month	$300,000	÷ 2 = $150,000
Monthly interest rate (1%)		0.01
Interest capitalized for the month		$ 1,500

The entry to record the first month's interest payment is

Factory Building	1,500	
Interest Expense	3,500	
Cash		5,000
To record interest payment, of which $1,500 is capitalized to factory building.		

Interest is capitalized until the factory building is completed. Of course, in subsequent months, the average accumulated construction expenditures increase, so larger amounts of interest cost are capitalized. If the average accumulated construction expenditures exceed $500,000, then additional computations based on the company's other borrowings are needed to determine the interest cost associated with the expenditures over $500,000. These computations are covered in intermediate accounting texts.

Related Expenditures

A purchase of land often raises some interesting questions about related expenditures. Suppose a firm retains a local real estate broker at a fee of $2,000 to locate an appropriate site for its new office building. The property eventually chosen has an old residence on it, which will be razed. The terms of the sale include a payment of $40,000 to the seller, with the buyer paying off an existing mortgage of $10,000 and $300 of accrued interest. In addition, the buyer agrees to pay accrued real estate taxes of $800. Other related expenditures include legal fees of $400 and a title insurance premium of $500. A local salvage company will raze the old residence, level the lot, keep all the materials, and pay the firm $200. If we apply the general plant asset measurement rule, we compute the initial cost of the land as follows:

Payment to the seller	$40,000
Commission for finding property	2,000
Payment of mortgage and interest due at time of sale	10,300
Payment of property taxes owed by seller	800
Legal fees	400
Title insurance premium	500
	$54,000
Less: Net recovery from razing	(200)
Cost of land	$53,800

Again, expenditures for the taxes, insurance, legal fees, and interest should be capitalized as part of the land, because they were necessary for its acquisition and preparation for use. Removing the old residence prepares the land for its intended use. The $200 net recovery from razing, therefore, reduces the land's cost. A net payment to remove the old building would have increased the land's cost.

When a land site is acquired in an undeveloped area, the firm may pay special assessments to the local government for such property improvements as streets, sidewalks, and sewers. These improvements are normally maintained by the local government and, accordingly, are considered relatively permanent improvements by the firm. In these circumstances, the company capitalizes the special assessments as part of the cost of the land.

The firm may make property improvements that have limited lives. Paved parking lots, driveways, private sidewalks, and fences are examples. These expenditures are charged to a separate account, **Land Improvements,** which is depreciated over the estimated lives of the improvements.

Package Purchases

Sometimes several types of assets are purchased concurrently as a package. For example, assume that a company purchased a small freight terminal including land, a building, and some loading equipment for a total price of $90,000. For accounting purposes, the total purchase price should be divided among the three asset forms because (1) they are reported in different accounts, (2) only the building and equipment are subject to depreciation, and (3) the equipment will have an estimated useful life different from the building.

The price of package purchases is commonly allocated on the basis of relative market or appraisal values. We assume estimated market values to illustrate this approach.

Asset	Estimated Market Value	Percent of Total	Allocation of Purchase Price	Estimated Useful Life
Land	$ 40,000	40	$36,000	Indefinite
Building	50,000	50	45,000	30 years
Equipment	10,000	10	9,000	8 years
Totals	$100,000	100	$90,000	

Actually, the firm may obtain realistic market values from a knowledgeable employee, a professional appraiser, or from assessed values on related property tax bills.

Nonroutine Acquisitions

Not all asset acquisitions involve specific amounts of money. Often nonmonetary assets are traded for other nonmonetary assets, and therefore the implied cash price is not readily apparent. Generally accepted accounting principles normally provide that the transaction price should be the market value of either the asset given up or the asset received, whichever is more objectively determinable. General-purpose property and equipment (standard office or factory equipment) and widely traded securities usually have more objectively determinable market values than do highly specialized buildings or equipment and securities that are new or seldom traded. In the latter instances, the accountant must exercise professional judgment.

An exception to this guideline is the exchange of a nonmonetary productive asset for a similar asset. We consider this exception in Chapter 11 in our discussion of exchanges of similar plant assets.

THE NATURE OF DEPRECIATION

With the exception of site land, the use of plant assets to generate revenue consumes their economic potential. At some point of reduced potential—usually before they are totally worthless—these assets are disposed of and possibly replaced. We can diagram the typical pattern of plant asset utilization (indicated in Exhibit 10−2) as follows:

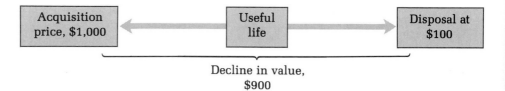

The asset is acquired for $1,000, used for several accounting periods, and then sold for $100. The $900 decline in value is, in every sense of the word, an expense of generating the revenue realized during the periods that the asset was used. Therefore, if the income figure is to be meaningful, $900 of expense must be allocated to these periods and matched against the revenue. Failure to do so would overstate income for these periods.

Note that in this process we estimate an asset's useful life and salvage value as well as properly determine its acquisition cost. **Useful life** is the expected period of economic usefulness to the current entity—the period from date of acquisition to expected date of disposal. **Salvage value** (or residual value) is the expected net recovery (Sales proceeds − Disposal costs) when the asset is sold or removed from service. When the salvage value is insignificant, it may be ignored in the depreciation process.

Because an asset's useful life typically involves several accounting periods, the $900 in our example must be divided in some way. If we assume a five-year useful life and each period receives an equal amount, then $900/5 = $180 is the periodic amount of depreciation for the asset. The basic entry to record each period's depreciation expense is:

Depreciation Expense	180	
Accumulated Depreciation—Equipment		180
To record depreciation expense for the year.		

Like other expense accounts, Depreciation Expense is deducted from revenue in determining net income and is closed at year-end to the Income Summary account. The offsetting credit is posted to the contra account, Accumulated Depreciation, which is deducted from the related asset account on the balance sheet to compute the asset's book value, or carrying value. In this manner, the original cost of an asset is maintained in the asset account, and the cumulative balance of depreciation taken is carried in the contra account as long as the asset is in service. When an asset is disposed of, the related cost and accumulated depreciation are removed from the accounts.

For our simple illustration, the table below shows account balances and the progression of certain amounts during the asset's five-year life.

			End-of-Period Balance	
Period	Balance of Asset Account	Periodic Depreciation Expense	Accumulated Depreciation Account	Asset's Book Value
1	$1,000	$180	$180	$820
2	1,000	180	360	640
3	1,000	180	540	460
4	1,000	180	720	280
5	1,000	180	900	100
	Total depreciation	$900		

Observe that (1) the asset account always shows the original cost of the asset, (2) each period reflects $180 of depreciation expense, (3) the Accumulated Depreciation account balance is cumulative and shows the portion of the original cost taken as depreciation to date, (4) the asset's book value is the original cost less total accumulated depreciation to date, and (5) the asset's book value at the end of five years equals the estimated salvage value. Thus, the book value decreases to the estimated salvage value as the asset is depreciated during its useful life.

The book value of the asset is shown on the balance sheet by deducting the Accumulated Depreciation account (normally a credit balance) from the asset account (normally a debit balance) in this manner:

Equipment (original cost)	$1,000
Less: Accumulated Depreciation	900
Equipment (book value)	$ 100

Shortly, we examine some widely used depreciation techniques that do not allocate depreciation equally to all periods of an asset's useful life.

Allocation versus Valuation

Although the idea is theoretically appealing, accountants do not specifically base depreciation on the changes in market value or the measured wear of assets—primarily because a reliable, objective, and practical source for such data rarely exists. Rather, depreciation accounting attempts to allocate in a rational and systematic manner the difference between acquisition cost and estimated salvage value over the *estimated* useful life of the asset. Depreciation accounting techniques are convenient expedients for measuring asset expirations and are therefore not precise. Though tentative, depreciation estimates and allocations clearly provide better income determination than would result from completely expensing the asset at either the date of acquisition or the date of disposal.

Several factors are naturally related to the periodic allocation of depreciation. Depreciation can be caused by wear from use, natural deterioration through interaction of the elements, and technical obsolescence. Each factor reduces the value of the asset. To some extent maintenance (lubrication, adjustments, parts replacements, and cleaning) may partially arrest or offset wear and deterioration. Quite logically, then, when useful life and salvage values are estimated, a given level of maintenance is assumed. Therefore, the cost of using plant assets tends to be the sum of periodic maintenance expenditures plus some measure of the depreciation that occurs despite the maintenance performed. Maintenance expense normally increases toward the latter stages of most assets' lives.

How to allocate depreciation expense is just one facet of the overall problem of matching revenue and expenses. The most defensible reason for choosing one allocation pattern over another is that one pattern may better portray the pattern of services received each period from using the asset. It would be only coincidence if the book value of a particular asset were exactly equal to its market value at any time during its useful life. On the other hand, the general pattern of an asset's book value may be closely related to its decline in market value. Indeed, the goal is that at the end of an asset's useful life, its book value and market value (that is, salvage value) should be the same.

COMPUTATIONS OF PERIODIC DEPRECIATION

We now illustrate four widely used methods of computing periodic depreciation. For each illustration, we assume that the asset costs $1,000 and has an estimated useful life of five years. The estimated salvage value at the end of the five-year period is $100. Our computations illustrate different ways to *allocate* the amount depreciated among each of the five accounting periods in the asset's life.

Straight Line

Straight-line depreciation is probably the simplest to compute. An equal amount of depreciation expense is allocated to each full period of the asset's useful life. Using straight-line depreciation,

$$\text{Annual Depreciation} = \frac{\text{Original Cost} - \text{Salvage Value}}{\text{Periods of Useful Life}}$$

which in our example is

$$\frac{\$1,000 - \$100}{5 \text{ years}} = \$180/\text{year}$$

For periods of less than one year, straight-line depreciation amounts are simply proportions of the annual amount. For example, if the asset had been acquired on April 1, depreciation for the period ended December 31 would be $\frac{9}{12} \times \$180 = \$135$. Assets acquired or disposed of during the first half of any month are usually treated as if the acquisition or disposal occurred on the first of the month. When either event occurs during the last half of any month, we assume it occurred on the first of the following month.

Straight-line allocation is best suited to an asset with a relatively uniform periodic usage and a low obsolescence factor. Examples include pipelines, storage tanks, fencing, and surface paving. These types of assets can provide approximately equal utility during all periods of their useful lives.

Units of Production

The **units-of-production method** allocates depreciation in proportion to the asset's use in operations. First, the depreciation per unit of production is computed by dividing the total expected depreciation (in our example, $900) by the asset's projected units-of-production capacity. Therefore,

$$\text{Depreciation per Unit} = \frac{\text{Original Cost} - \text{Salvage Value}}{\text{Estimated Total Units of Production}}$$

Units-of-production capacity may represent miles driven, tons hauled, or number of cuttings, drillings, or stampings of parts. Assume that our example is a drilling tool that will drill an estimated 45,000 parts during its useful life. The depreciation per unit of production is

$$\frac{\$1,000 - \$100}{45,000 \text{ parts}} = \$0.02 \text{ per part}$$

To find periodic depreciation expense, we multiply the depreciation per unit of production by the number of units produced during the period. If 8,000 units are produced during the first year, then $8,000 \times \$0.02 = \$160$ is the year's depreciation expense. If 12,000 parts are drilled the next year, that year's depreciation expense is $12,000 \times \$0.02 = \$240$.

The units-of-production approach is particularly appropriate when wear is the major cause of depreciation and the amount of use varies from period to period. Of course, if use is uniformly spread over the asset's life, the same allocation of depreciation would result from either the straight-line or units-of-production method. The units-of-production method may necessitate some extra record keeping to express the periodic use in terms of production capacity. However, this data may already be tabulated as part of a periodic production report.

Sum of the Years' Digits

The **sum-of-the-years'-digits (SYD) method** accelerates depreciation expense so that the amounts recognized in the early periods of an asset's useful life are greater than those recognized in the later periods. The SYD is found by estimating an asset's useful life in years, assigning consecutive numbers to each year, and totaling these numbers. For N years,

$$SYD = 1 + 2 + 3 + \ldots + N$$

In our example, the SYD for a five-year asset life is $1 + 2 + 3 + 4 + 5 = 15$.

Determining the SYD factor by simple addition can be somewhat laborious for long-lived assets. For these assets, the formula $N(N + 1)/2$, where N = the number of periods in the asset's useful life, can be applied to derive the SYD. In our example, we have

$$\frac{5(5 + 1)}{2} = \frac{30}{2} = 15$$

The yearly depreciation is then calculated by multiplying the total depreciable amount for the asset's useful life by a fraction whose numerator is the remaining useful life and whose denominator is the SYD. Thus, the formula for yearly depreciation is

$$\text{Annual Depreciation} = (\text{Original Cost} - \text{Salvage Value}) \times \frac{\text{Remaining Useful Life}}{\text{SYD}}$$

The calculations for our example are shown below:

Year of Useful Life	Fraction of Total Depreciation Taken Each Year		Original Cost Less Salvage Value		Annual Depreciation Allocation
1	$\frac{5}{15}$	×	$900	=	$300
2	$\frac{4}{15}$	×	900	=	240
3	$\frac{3}{15}$	×	900	=	180
4	$\frac{2}{15}$	×	900	=	120
5	$\frac{1}{15}$	×	900	=	60
SYD 15					Total $900

When the acquisition of an asset does not coincide with the beginning of the fiscal period, the annual depreciation amounts are allocated proportionately to the appropriate fiscal periods. For example, assume we purchased the asset on April 1. Depreciation for the period ended December 31 would be $\frac{9}{12} \times \$300 = \$225$. For the next fiscal year, a full year's depreciation would be calculated as $(\frac{3}{12} \times \$300) + (\frac{9}{12} \times \$240) = \$255$.

As an accelerated depreciation method, the SYD approach is most appropriate when the asset renders greater utility during its early life and less in its later life. Accelerated depreciation is suitable for assets with either a high technological obsolescence factor in the early life phase or a high maintenance factor in the late life phase.

**Double
Declining
Balance**

Another accelerated depreciation method is the **double declining-balance method,** which derives its name from the fact that a *constant percentage* factor of twice the straight-line rate is applied each year to the *declining balance* of the asset's book value.

The *straight-line rate* is simply the number of years in the asset's useful life divided into 100%. In our example, this would be 100%/5 = 20%. Double the straight-line rate is then 40%. In equation form,

$$\text{Double Declining-balance Rate} = \frac{100\%}{\text{Years of Useful Life}} \times 2$$

To determine the annual double declining-balance depreciation expense, we simply *multiply the asset's book value at the beginning of the period by the constant rate (or percentage)*. Remember that an asset's book value at any time is its original cost less its accumulated depreciation to date. The book value of a depreciable asset *declines* as it is depreciated. The important thing to remember is that the percentage depreciation rate remains constant; the book value—to which the percentage is applied—declines. Salvage value is not considered in the calculations, except that depreciation stops when the asset's book value equals its estimated salvage value.

Applying the general rule for double declining-balance depreciation to our example, we obtain the accelerated depreciation pattern shown in the following table (amounts to nearest dollar).

Year of Useful Life	Original Cost	Beginning Accumulated Depreciation	Beginning Book Value		Twice Straight-line Percentage		Amount of Depreciation Expense
1	$1,000	$ 0	$1,000	×	40%	=	$400
2	1,000	400	600	×	40%	=	240
3	1,000	640	360	×	40%	=	144
4	1,000	784	216	×	40%	=	86
5	1,000	870	130				30
					Total depreciation taken		$900

Observe that in the fifth year depreciation expense is only $30, the amount needed to reduce the asset's book value to the estimated salvage value of $100. Assets are not depreciated below their salvage values. If no salvage value has been estimated, the double declining-balance technique automatically provides one. When a fraction (40%, or $\frac{4}{10}$, for example) is applied to an asset's book value, the entire original cost can never be depreciated; some balance, though small, will always remain.

If an asset is purchased during the fiscal period, a pro-rata allocation of the first year's depreciation is necessary. If we acquired our asset on April 1, depreciation for the period ended December 31 would be $\frac{9}{12} \times (40\% \times \$1,000) =$ $300. In subsequent periods, the usual procedure is followed; that is, the asset's book value at the beginning of the period is multiplied by the constant rate. The next year, for example, depreciation would be 40% × ($1,000 − $300) = $280.

Because double declining-balance depreciation is also an accelerated depreciation method, it is appropriate in the same situations as the SYD method.

REVISION OF DEPRECIATION

We have stressed that depreciation allocations are based on estimates of both useful lives and salvage values. Circumstances change, however, and original estimates may be too high or too low. Erroneous estimates cause the misstatement of depreciation expense in one or more periods, which in turn, misstates reported net income, the asset's book value, and owners' equity.

In the past, revisions of depreciation expense were quite involved because of efforts to restate earlier years' accounts to reflect the corrected depreciation amounts. Currently accepted practice is simpler. It only reflects the depreciation revision in the period of change and in any subsequent periods by allocating the revised undepreciated balance of the asset over the revised remaining useful life. To illustrate this revision procedure, we use the data from our previous examples in which an asset costing $1,000 has a five-year life and an estimated salvage value of $100.

If, based on the original estimates, straight-line depreciation of $180 has been recorded for each of the first three years, the accumulated depreciation would be 3 × $180 = $540. Now suppose that just before recording the fourth year's depreciation, circumstances indicate that the asset's life will be six years instead of five and that its salvage value at the end of the sixth year will be $40. The revised depreciation expense to be taken during the revised remaining useful life is computed as follows:

Original asset cost	$1,000
Depreciation already recorded (3 years @ $180)	540
Book value at start of fourth year	$ 460
Revised salvage value	40
Revised remaining depreciation	$ 420
Revised remaining useful life	3 years
Revised periodic depreciation expense for fourth, fifth, and sixth years	$420/3 = $140 per year

This revision method does not correct the overstatement of recorded depreciation and related misstatements of other accounts in the first three years. Instead, it offsets the early overstatements with an equal amount of understatements during the later years. The justification for this approach is that (1) such errors are often immaterial, (2) errors of overstatement are often offset by errors of understatement in the same accounting period, and (3) depreciation is a relatively imprecise estimate anyway. Recording the revision of depreciation in this manner complies with the recommendations of Accounting Principles Board *Opinion No. 20.*

DEPRECIATION FOR TAX PURPOSES

Depreciation expense is deducted by a business on its federal income tax return. The depreciation amount on the tax return, however, may differ from the amount reported in the firm's income statement. Indeed, different tax depreciation guidelines apply to property acquired before 1981 than apply to property acquired after 1980.

Property acquired before 1981 is depreciated for income tax purposes over its useful life. Depreciation methods acceptable for tax purposes include straight line, units of production, sum of the years' digits, and double declining balance. The method used on the tax return, however, need not be the same method used in the financial statements. Typically, a firm uses an accelerated depreciation method for tax purposes and the straight-line method in its financial statements. In a sense, accelerated depreciation provides an interest-free loan to the firm because the accelerated methods allow the firm to pay less tax in the early phase of an asset's life and more in the later phase. During the intervening time, the firm can use the amount of funds equal to the postponed income tax payments.

The Economic Recovery Tax Act of 1981 changed significantly the system of tax depreciation by creating the **Accelerated Cost Recovery System (ACRS).** ACRS applies to property acquired after 1980 and eliminates the concept of useful life. Instead, ACRS establishes classes of property with prescribed lives—3, 5, 10, or 15 years. The type of property determines its class; most machinery and equipment, for example, is in the five-year class. When acquired, property is placed in the appropriate class (regardless of its useful life) and depreciated over the prescribed period following a specific accelerated write-off pattern. The tax law contains tables showing the percentage write-off allowed each year of the asset's prescribed life. The purpose of ACRS is to encourage more capital investment by businesses. ACRS permits a faster recovery of an asset's cost, and thus larger tax benefits during the asset's early life, than was previously possible.

The **investment tax credit** is another feature of the tax law that encourages capital investment. Businesses that invest in depreciable assets other than buildings and their structural components reduce their income taxes by a specified percentage of the assets' costs. In 1983, the percentage was 6% for assets with a three-year class life and 10% for assets with 5-, 10-, or 15-year class lives. For example, in 1983, a firm purchasing $10,000 worth of equipment with a five-year class life reduced its taxes that year by $1,000 (10% × $10,000).

Beginning in 1983, the tax law required businesses, in most instances, to reduce the depreciable base of their assets for tax purposes by one-half of the investment tax credit.[1] For example, equipment purchased for $10,000 with a $1,000 investment tax credit may only be depreciated a total of $9,500 ($10,000 − $500) under ACRS. This reduction in the total depreciation allowed for tax purposes limited the tax benefits of ACRS. However, the combination of ACRS and investment tax credits still offers a strong tax incentive to invest in depreciable property.

Change and modification characterize the history of U.S. tax law. Although amendments to the system of ACRS and investment tax credits are likely, the tax law will probably retain features that stimulate capital investment.

REVENUE EXPENDITURES

Revenue expenditures are expenditures relating to plant assets that are expensed when incurred. The following list identifies three types of revenue expenditures:

(1) Expenditures for ordinary maintenance and repairs of existing plant assets.

(2) Expenditures to acquire low-cost items that benefit the firm for several periods.

(3) Expenditures considered unnecessary or unreasonable in the circumstances.

Maintenance and Repairs

Some level of maintenance and repairs must be assumed when estimating useful lives and salvage values of property, plant, and equipment. Obviously, a plant asset that is not maintained or repaired has a shorter useful life than a similar asset that is properly maintained. Periodic upkeep—such as lubrication, cleaning, and replacement of minor parts—is necessary to maintain an asset's expected level and length of usefulness. These periodic upkeep costs are charged to expense as they are incurred.

Low-cost Items

Most businesses purchase items that provide years of service at a relatively small cost, such as paperweights, ashtrays, and wastebaskets. Because of the small dollar amounts involved, establishing these items as assets and depreciating them over their expected useful lives really serves no useful purpose. The effect on the financial statements is not significant. Consequently, expensing these expenditures at the time of purchase is more efficient. The accounting for such low-cost items is thus completed in the period they are purchased. This practice of accounting for small dollar transactions in the most expedient fashion is an example of the basic principle of *materiality*. (We discuss materiality in more detail in Chapter 13.)

Unnecessary or Unreasonable Costs

As noted earlier, costs of waste and inefficiency related to the acquisition of plant assets are expensed when incurred. Because an asset's initial cost includes only necessary and reasonable expenditures, any unnecessary or unreasonable outlays

[1] A business may retain the full depreciation base by electing to reduce its investment tax credit by two percentage points.

are expensed. An accountant may need to exercise considerable judgment, however, in determining whether a particular expenditure is necessary and reasonable. Identical expenditures may be treated differently, depending on the circumstances. For example, assume a company pays an overtime premium to have a piece of equipment delivered on a holiday. If it is essential that the equipment be available for use on the next workday, then the overtime premium should be added to the equipment's cost as a necessary and reasonable expenditure. In contrast, if the equipment could just as well be delivered on the next workday, then the overtime premium is an unnecessary and wasteful expenditure that should be expensed.

CAPITAL EXPENDITURES

Capital expenditures increase the book value of long-term assets. To *capitalize* an amount, then, means to increase an asset's book value by that amount. Typical capital expenditures related to property, plant, and equipment are as follows:

(1) Initial acquisitions and additions.

(2) Betterments.

(3) Extraordinary repairs.

Initial Acquisitions and Additions

Earlier in this chapter, we discussed the guidelines governing the initial measurement of plant assets. Expenditures equal to the asset's implied cash price plus the costs necessary to prepare the asset for use were debited to the asset account. These amounts were capital expenditures.

The same guidelines apply in accounting for additions to existing plant assets. Adding a new wing to a building or expanding the size of an asphalt parking lot are examples of additions. These capital expenditures should also be debited to an asset account. A separate account (and depreciation schedule) should be used for an addition when its estimated useful life differs from the remaining useful life of the existing plant asset.

Betterments

Betterments improve the quality of services rendered by a plant asset but do not necessarily extend its useful life. Examples include adding a power winch to a highway service truck or air conditioning to an automobile. In each instance, the vehicle's services are enhanced, but its useful life is not changed. Expenditures for betterments are debited to the appropriate asset account, and the subsequent periodic depreciation expense is increased to allocate the additional cost over the asset's remaining useful life.

To illustrate, let us assume Tray Service Station purchased a new service truck for $6,500 on January 2, 19X1. Its estimated useful life is six years with a salvage value of $500. Using the straight-line method, $1,000 of depreciation expense is recorded in 19X1 [($6,500 − $500)/6 = $1,000]. On January 2, 19X2, a power winch costing $700 is added to the truck. The truck's useful life does not change, but its estimated salvage value increases to $600. The January 2, 19X2 entry to record the new winch is

Truck	700	
Cash		700
To record cost of power winch added to truck.		

Annual depreciation expense of $1,120 for 19X2–19X6 is computed as follows:

Original truck cost	$6,500
Power winch cost	700
Total cost	$7,200
Depreciation recorded in 19X1	1,000
Book value after 19X2 betterment	$6,200
Revised salvage value	600
Revised remaining depreciation	$5,600
Remaining useful life	5 years
Revised periodic depreciation expense for 19X2–19X6	$5,600/5 = $1,120 per year

The December 31, 19X2 entry to record depreciation expense is

Depreciation Expense—Truck	1,120	
Accumulated Depreciation—Truck		1,120
To record 19X2 depreciation on truck.		

Betterments may involve replacing a significant asset component with an improved component. Again, the cost of the new asset component should be added to the asset account and depreciated over the asset's remaining useful life. Further, the cost and accumulated depreciation of the replaced asset component should be removed from the accounts. For example, if a building's gas furnace is replaced by a more efficient model, the cost of the new furnace is added to the Building account, and the cost and applicable depreciation on the old furnace are removed from the accounts. The book value of the old asset component may be difficult to determine if it is not accounted for separately, but a reasonable estimate frequently can be made.

Extraordinary Repairs

Extraordinary repairs are expenditures that extend an asset's expected useful life beyond the original estimate. These capital expenditures are debited to the asset's Accumulated Depreciation account (which increases the asset's book value). We charge Accumulated Depreciation because some of the previous years' depreciation presumably is recovered by the expenditures that extend the asset's useful life. Depreciation entries after an extraordinary repair should lead to the salvage value at the end of the revised (extended) useful life.

For example, assume $12,800 worth of equipment is purchased; it has an estimated useful life of eight years and a salvage value of $800. Annual straight-line depreciation expense is $1,500 [($12,800 − $800)/8]. At the beginning of the seventh year, the equipment is extensively overhauled at a cost of $2,200. The overhaul extends the equipment's useful life an estimated two years beyond the original eight, with no change in the expected salvage value. The entry to record the overhaul is

Accumulated Depreciation—Equipment	2,200	
Cash		2,200
To record cost of equipment overhaul.		

Beginning with the seventh year, annual depreciation expense is $1,300, computed as follows:

Original cost		$12,800
Less: Depreciation for six years	$9,000	
Less: Extraordinary repairs	2,200	6,800
Book value at start of seventh year		$ 6,000
Salvage value		800
Remaining depreciation		$ 5,200
Revised remaining useful life		4 years
Revised periodic depreciation expense for years 7–10		$5,200/4 = $1,300 per year

The entry to record depreciation expense at the end of the seventh year is

Depreciation Expense—Equipment	1,300	
Accumulated Depreciation—Equipment		1,300
To record depreciation on equipment.		

In practice, the distinctions among additions, betterments, and extraordinary repairs to plant assets often become blurred. Some expenditures, for example, may improve an asset's quality of services *and* extend its useful life. Accountants must use reasonable judgment to identify (and account for) the primary effect of the transaction.

Preparation of accurate financial statements depends on maintaining the proper distinction between capital expenditures and revenue expenditures. A misclassification of expenditures results in incorrect financial statements for several periods. For example, capitalizing a revenue expenditure overstates the current period's income and understates income in subsequent periods as the amount incorrectly capitalized is depreciated. Similarly, if a capital expenditure is immediately expensed, then the current period's income is understated and income is overstated during the subsequent periods when the incorrectly expensed amount should have been depreciated. Exercising care in analyzing expenditures, of course, will minimize these undesirable effects.

KEY POINTS TO REMEMBER

(1) The major types of long-term assets are plant assets, natural resources, and intangible assets.

(2) The cost (less salvage value) of a long-term asset is periodically charged to expense over its useful life as follows:

Plant assets: Depreciation
Natural resources: Depletion
Intangible assets: Amortization

(3) The initial cost of a plant asset is its implied cash price plus the expenditures necessary to prepare it for use.

(4) The most commonly used depreciation methods are straight line, units of production, sum of the years' digits, and double declining balance.

(5) Revisions of depreciation are accomplished by recalculating depreciation charges for current and subsequent periods.

(6) Revenue expenditures, expensed as incurred, include the performance of ordinary repairs and maintenance, the purchase of low-cost items, and the incurrence of unnecessary or unreasonable outlays.

(7) Capital expenditures, which increase a plant asset's book value, include initial acquisitions, additions, betterments, and extraordinary repairs.

QUESTIONS

10–1 List three major types of long-term assets, present examples of each, and indicate for each type the term that denotes the periodic write-off to expense.

10–2 In what way is land different from other long-term assets?

10–3 Describe the typical sequence of transactions and related problem areas associated with plant assets.

10–4 In general, what amounts constitute the initial cost of plant assets?

10–5 Lucas Company borrowed $1,000,000 to finance the purchase of a new office building, which was ready for immediate use. May Lucas add a portion of the interest cost on the $1,000,000 to the building's cost? Explain.

10–6 Doyle Company bought land with a vacant building for $850,000. Doyle will use the building in its operations. Must Doyle allocate the purchase price between the land and building? Why or why not? Would your answer be different if Doyle intends to raze the building and build a new one? Why or why not?

10–7 Explain why the recognition of depreciation expense is necessary to match revenue and expense properly.

10–8 How is the use of the contra account Accumulated Depreciation justified when recording depreciation?

10-9 How can we justify the use of accelerated depreciation?

10-10 Briefly describe an operational situation that lends itself naturally to each of the following depreciation methods: (a) straight line, (b) units of production, (c) sum of the years' digits, and (d) double declining balance.

10-11 How should we handle a revision of depreciation charges due to a change in an asset's estimated useful life or salvage value? Which periods—past, present, or future—are affected by the revision?

10-12 Explain the benefit of accelerating depreciation for income tax purposes when the total depreciation taken is no more than if straight-line depreciation is used.

10-13 Identify three types of revenue expenditures. What is the proper accounting for revenue expenditures?

10-14 "We cannot properly estimate an asset's useful life without first considering the level of maintenance employed." Do you agree? Why or why not?

10-15 West Company purchased a $15 pencil sharpener with an estimated useful life of 15 years. How should West account for this expenditure?

10-16 Identify three types of capital expenditures. What is the proper accounting for capital expenditures?

10-17 What is the difference between an ordinary repair and an extraordinary repair? What is the rationale for charging extraordinary repairs to accumulated depreciation?

EXERCISES

10-18 The following data relate to a firm's purchase of a machine used in the manufacture of its product:

Invoice price	$20,000
Applicable sales tax	980
Purchase discount taken	400
Freight paid	450
Cost of insurance coverage on machine while in transit	70
Installation costs	900
Testing and adjusting costs	250
Repair of damages to machine caused by the firm's employees	360

Compute the initial amount at which the machine should be carried in the firm's accounts.

10-19 On April 1, 19X1, Western Company borrowed $600,000 at 15% to finance the construction of a new wing on its headquarters office building. The construction will take several months. Interest of $7,500 is paid monthly. Construction begins April 1, 19X1, and accumulated construction expenditures are $260,000 at April 30, 19X1. Determine how much interest cost should be capitalized for April.

10–20 Royle Company purchased a small established plant from one of its suppliers. The $800,000 purchase price included the land, a building, and factory machinery. Royle also paid $1,000 in legal fees to negotiate the purchase of the plant. The property tax bill for the plant showed the following assessed values for the items included:

Property	Assessed Values
Land	$133,000
Building	322,000
Machinery	245,000
	$700,000

Using the assessed valuations on the property tax bill as a guide, allocate the total purchase price of the plant to the land, building, and machinery accounts in Royle Company's records.

10–21 A delivery truck costing $9,000 is expected to have a 10% salvage value at the end of its useful life of four years or 150,000 miles.

(a) Assume the truck was purchased on January 2, 19X1. Compute the depreciation expense for 19X1 using each of the following depreciation methods: (1) straight line, (2) sum of the years' digits, (3) double declining balance, and (4) units of production (assume the truck was driven 39,000 miles in 19X1).

(b) Assume the truck was purchased on March 1, 19X1. Compute the depreciation expense for 19X2 using each of the following depreciation methods: (1) straight line, (2) sum of the years' digits, (3) double declining balance, and (4) units of production (assume the truck was driven 42,000 miles in 19X2).

10–22 A machine costing $24,300 was purchased January 2, 19X2. The machine should be obsolete after three years and, therefore, no longer useful to the company. The estimated salvage value is $900. Compute the depreciation expense for each year of the machine's useful life using each of the following depreciation methods: (a) straight line, (b) sum of the years' digits, and (c) double declining balance.

10–23 Assume the machine from Exercise 10–22 was purchased May 1, 19X2. Compute each year's depreciation expense for 19X2–19X5 using each of the following depreciation methods: (a) straight line, (b) sum of the years' digits, and (c) double declining balance.

10–24 On January 2, 19X0, Schauer, Inc., purchased new equipment for $44,000. The equipment was expected to have a $2,000 salvage value at the end of its estimated seven-year useful life. Straight-line depreciation has been recorded. Before adjusting the accounts for 19X4, Schauer decided that the useful life of the equipment should be extended by two years and the salvage value decreased to $1,000.

(a) Present a general journal entry to record depreciation expense on the equipment for 19X4.

(b) What is the book value of the equipment at the end of 19X4 (that is, after recording the depreciation expense for 19X4)?

10–25 On January 3, 19X1, Opal Company purchased a warehouse for $370,000 with an estimated useful life of 30 years and a salvage value of $40,000. Opal uses straight-line depreciation on the warehouse. In early January, 19X9, Opal spent $24,000 for the installation of a fire detection and sprinkler system in the warehouse. The useful life of the warehouse was unchanged, but its estimated salvage value increased to $42,000.

(a) Prepare the general journal entry to record the cost of the fire detection and sprinkler system.

(b) Compute the 19X9 depreciation expense on the warehouse.

(c) Prepare the general journal entry to record the warehouse's 19X9 depreciation expense.

10–26 At the end of last year, the balance sheet of Mullin Company shows a building with a cost of $700,000 and accumulated depreciation of $432,000. The company uses the straight-line method to depreciate the building. When acquired, the building's useful life was an estimated 40 years, and its salvage value was $60,000. Early in January of the current year, Mullin made major structural repairs to the building costing $206,000. Although the capacity of the building was unchanged, the improvements will extend the useful life of the building to an estimated 50 years, rather than the original 40 years. The salvage value remains $60,000.

(a) By the end of last year, how many years had the company depreciated the building?

(b) Present the general journal entry to record the cost of the structural repairs.

(c) Present the general journal entry to record the building's depreciation expense for the current year.

PROBLEMS

10–27 The items below represent expenditures (or receipts) related to the construction of a new home office for the Helix Company.

Cost of land site, which included an old apartment building appraised at $50,000	$ 190,000
Legal fees, including fee for title search	1,800
Payment of mortgage and related interest due at time of sale	9,000
Payment of delinquent property taxes assumed by the purchaser	3,400
Cost of razing the apartment building	11,000
Proceeds from sale of salvaged materials	(2,900)
Grading and drainage on land site	7,000
Architect's fees on new building	90,000
Proceeds from sale of excess dirt (from basement excavation) to owner of adjoining property (dirt was used to fill in a low area on property)	(700)
Payment to building contractor	2,200,000
Interest cost incurred during construction (based on average accumulated construction expenditures)	250,000
Payment of medical bills of employee accidentally injured while inspecting building construction	500

Special assessment for paving city sidewalks (paid to city)	$10,000
Cost of paving driveway and parking lot	14,000
Cost of installing lights in parking lot	5,200
Premium for insurance on building during construction	4,000
Cost of open house party to celebrate opening of new building	3,500

REQUIRED

From the given data, compute the proper balances for the Land, Building, and Land Improvements accounts of the Helix Company.

10–28 To expand its business, Forest Company paid $475,000 for most of the property, plant, and equipment of a small trucking company that was going out of business. Before agreeing to the price, Forest hired a consultant for $5,000 to appraise the assets. The appraised values were as follows:

Land	$100,000
Building	200,000
Trucks	150,000
Equipment	50,000
	$500,000

Forest issued two checks totaling $480,000 to acquire the assets and pay the consultant on July 1, 19X3. Forest depreciated the assets using the straight-line method on the building, the double declining-balance method on the trucks, and the sum-of-the-years'-digits method on the equipment. Estimated useful lives and salvage values were as follows:

	Useful Life	Salvage Value
Building	20 years	$10,000
Trucks	4 years	8,000
Equipment	7 years	6,000

REQUIRED

(a) Compute the amounts allocated to the various types of plant assets acquired on July 1, 19X3.
(b) Prepare the July 1, 19X3 general journal entries to record the purchase of the assets and the payment of the consultant.
(c) Prepare the December 31, 19X3 general journal entries to record 19X3 depreciation expense on the building, trucks, and equipment.

10–29 On January 2, Wang, Inc. purchased a laser cutting machine to be used in the fabrication of a part for one of its key products. The machine cost $85,000, and its estimated useful life was four years or 500,000 cuttings, after which it could be sold for $7,000.

REQUIRED

Compute the depreciation expense for each year of the machine's useful life under each of the following depreciation methods:
(a) Straight line.

(b) Sum of the years' digits.

(c) Double declining balance.

(d) Units of production. (Assume annual production in cuttings of 110,000; 125,000; 175,000; and 90,000.)

10-30 During the first few days of 19X5, the Carland Company entered into the following transactions:

(1) Purchased a parcel of land with a building on it for $880,000 cash. The building, which will be used in operations, has an estimated useful life of 25 years and a residual value of $20,000. The assessed valuations for property tax purposes show the land at $90,000 and the building at $630,000.

(2) Paid $22,500 for the construction of an asphalt parking lot for customers. The parking lot is expected to last 15 years and have no salvage value.

(3) Paid $1,500 to have parking lot lines painted.

(4) Purchased store equipment, paying the invoice price (including 5% sales tax) of $21,000 in cash. The estimated useful life of the equipment is seven years, and the salvage value is $1,250.

(5) Paid $250 freight on the new store equipment.

(6) Paid $400 to repair damages to floor caused when the store equipment was accidentally dropped as it was moved into place.

(7) Paid $6,000 for three-year insurance policy on building.

REQUIRED

(a) Prepare general journal entries to record the above transactions.

(b) Prepare the December 31, 19X5 general journal entries to record the proper amounts of depreciation expense for the year. Sum-of-the-years'-digits depreciation is used for the equipment, and straight-line depreciation is used for the building and land improvements.

10-31 Flury Corporation had the following transactions related to its delivery truck:

19X1

Jan. 5 Purchased for $9,640 cash a new truck with an estimated useful life of three years and a salvage value of $1,000.

Feb. 20 Installed a new set of rear view mirrors at a cost of $40 cash.

June 9 Paid $140 for an engine tune-up, wheel balancing, and a periodic lubrication.

Aug. 2 Paid a $250 repair bill for the uninsured portion of damages to the truck caused by Flury's own driver.

Dec. 31 Recorded 19X1 depreciation on the truck.

19X2

May   1 Installed a set of parts bins in the truck at a cost of $500 cash. This expenditure was not expected to increase the salvage value of the truck.

Dec. 31 Recorded 19X2 depreciation on the truck.

19X3

July 1 Paid $1,560 for a major engine overhaul on the truck. The overhaul should extend the useful life of the truck an additional two years (to December 31, 19X5) with no change in the salvage value.

Dec. 31 Recorded 19X3 depreciation on the truck.

Flury's depreciation policies include (1) using straight-line depreciation, (2) recording depreciation to the nearest whole month, and (3) expensing all truck expenditures of $50 or less.

REQUIRED

Present general journal entries to record these transactions.

10–32 Todd Company uses straight-line depreciation in accounting for its machines. On January 3, 19X1, Todd purchased a new machine for $40,000 cash. The machine's estimated useful life was 10 years with a $4,000 salvage value. In 19X3, the company decided its original useful life estimate should be reduced by two years. Beginning in 19X3, depreciation was based on an eight-year total useful life, and no change was made in the salvage value estimate. On January 2, 19X4, Todd added an automatic guide and a safety shield to the machine at a cost of $2,000 cash. These improvements did not change the machine's useful life, but did increase the estimated salvage value to $4,400.

REQUIRED

(a) Prepare general journal entries to record (1) the purchase of the machine, (2) 19X1 depreciation expense, (3) 19X2 depreciation expense, (4) 19X3 depreciation expense, (5) the 19X4 improvements, and (6) 19X4 depreciation expense.

(b) Compute the book value of the machine at the end of 19X4 (that is, after recording the depreciation expense for 19X4).

10–33 Lira Company acquired new machinery costing $120,000 in January 19X1. The machinery has an estimated useful life of eight years and no salvage value. Lira uses straight-line depreciation for its financial reporting. For tax purposes, Lira utilizes the Accelerated Cost Recovery System and elects to depreciate the full $120,000. The machinery is placed in the five-year property class and will be depreciated over the five years according to the following schedule:

Year	Depreciation Percentage
19X1	15
19X2	22
19X3	21
19X4	21
19X5	21

REQUIRED

(a) Prepare a schedule showing the annual depreciation on the machinery for eight years under (1) the straight-line method used for financial reporting purposes and (2) the Accelerated Cost Recovery System used for tax purposes.

(b) Compute for 19X1–19X5 the annual reduction in Lira's income tax payment because it depreciates the machinery using ACRS for tax purposes rather than the straight-line depreciation. Assume an income tax rate of 45%.

(c) Compute for 19X6–19X8 the annual increase in Lira's income tax payment because it depreciates the machinery using ACRS for tax purposes rather than using straight-line depreciation. Assume an income tax rate of 45%.

ALTERNATE PROBLEMS

10–27A The items below represent expenditures (or receipts) related to the construction of a new home office for Sellers Investment Company.

Cost of land site, which included an abandoned railroad spur	$ 210,000
Legal fees relating to land purchase	2,000
Title insurance premiums on property	1,100
Cost of removing railroad tracks	5,000
Payment of delinquent property taxes assumed by the purchaser	4,800
Proceeds from sale of timber from walnut trees cut down to prepare site for construction	(8,000)
Proceeds from sale of salvaged railroad track	(1,500)
Grading and drainage on land site	9,000
Cost of basement excavation (contracted separately)	7,500
Architect's fees on new building	70,000
Payment to building contractor—original contract price	1,800,000
Cost of changes during construction to make building more energy efficient	46,000
Interest cost incurred during construction (based on average accumulated construction expenditures)	120,000
Cost of replacing windows broken by vandals	1,200
Cost of paving driveway and parking lot	15,000
Out-of-court settlement for mud slide onto adjacent property	4,000
Special assessment for paving city sidewalks (paid to city)	17,000
Cost of brick and wrought iron fence installed across front of property	6,300

REQUIRED
From the given data, compute the proper balances for the Land, Building, and Land Improvements accounts of Sellers Investment Company.

10–28A In an expansion move, Grove Company paid $914,000 for most of the property, plant, and equipment of a small manufacturing firm that was going out of business. Before agreeing to the price, Grove hired a consultant for $6,000 to appraise the assets. The appraised values were as follows:

Land	$ 160,000
Building	350,000
Equipment	450,000
Trucks	40,000
	$1,000,000

Grove issued two checks totaling $920,000 to acquire the assets and pay the consultant on April 1, 19X4. Grove depreciated the assets using the straight-line method on the building, the sum-of-the-years'-digits method on the equipment, and the double declining-balance method on the trucks. Estimated useful lives and salvage values were as follows:

	Useful Life	Salvage Value
Building	15 years	$25,000
Equipment	9 years	24,000
Trucks	5 years	4,000

REQUIRED

(a) Compute the amounts allocated to the various types of plant assets acquired on April 1, 19X4.

(b) Prepare the April 1, 19X4 general journal entries to record the purchase of the assets and the payment of the consultant.

(c) Prepare the December 31, 19X4 general journal entries to record the 19X4 depreciation expense on the building, equipment, and trucks.

10−29A On January 2, 19X1, Corgan Company purchased an electroplating machine to help manufacture a part for one of its key products. The machine cost $91,125 and was estimated to have a useful life of six years or 180,000 platings, after which it could be sold for $9,225.

REQUIRED

Compute each year's depreciation expense for 19X1–19X6 under each of the following depreciation methods:

(a) Straight line.

(b) Sum of the years' digits.

(c) Double declining balance.

(d) Units of production. (Assume annual production in platings of: 27,000; 36,000; 45,000; 32,400; 21,600; and 18,000.)

10−31A Altoc Delivery Service had the following transactions related to its delivery truck:

19X4

Mar.   1   Purchased for $11,340 cash a new delivery truck with an estimated useful life of four years and a $1,500 salvage value.

      2   Paid $240 for painting the company name and logo on the truck.

Dec. 31   Recorded 19X4 depreciation on the truck.

19X5

July   1   Installed air conditioning in the truck at a cost of $900 cash. Although the truck's estimated useful life was not affected, its estimated salvage value was increased by $100.

Sept. 7   Paid $360 for truck tune-up and safety inspection.

Dec. 31   Recorded 19X5 depreciation on the truck.

19X6

May   2   Paid $1,220 for a major overhaul of the truck. The overhaul should extend the truck's useful life one year (to February 28, 19X9), when the revised salvage value should be $1,700.

Sept. 3 Installed a set of front and rear bumper guards at a cost of $60 cash.
Dec. 31 Recorded 19X6 depreciation on the truck.

19X7
Dec. 31 Recorded 19X7 depreciation on the truck.

Altoc's depreciation policies include (1) using straight-line depreciation, (2) recording depreciation to the nearest whole month, and (3) expensing all truck expenditures of $75 or less.

REQUIRED
Present general journal entries to record these transactions.

10–32A Yoder Company uses straight-line depreciation in accounting for its machines. On January 2, 19X1, Yoder purchased a new machine for $66,000 cash. The machine's estimated useful life was eight years with a $6,600 salvage value. In 19X6, the company decided its original useful life estimate should be increased by six years. Beginning in 19X6, depreciation was based on a 14-year total useful life, and no change was made in the salvage value estimate. On January 3, 19X7, Yoder added an automatic cut-off switch and a self-sharpening blade mechanism to the machine at a cost of $4,000 cash. These improvements did not change the machine's useful life, but did increase the estimated salvage value to $7,400.

REQUIRED
(a) Prepare general journal entries to record (1) the purchase of the machine, (2) 19X1 depreciation expense, (3) 19X6 depreciation expense, (4) the 19X7 improvements, and (5) 19X7 depreciation expense.
(b) Compute the book value of the machine at the end of 19X7 (that is, after recording the depreciation expense for 19X7).

BUSINESS DECISION PROBLEM

I. Waver, president of Waver, Inc., wants you to resolve his dispute with Mia Surchum over the amount of a finder's fee due Surchum. Waver hired Surchum to locate a new plant site to expand the business. By agreement, Surchum's fee was to be 15% of the "cost of the property (excluding the finder's fee) measured according to generally accepted accounting principles."

Surchum located Site 1 and Site 2 for Waver to consider. Each site had a selling price of $150,000, and the geographic locations of both sites were equally acceptable to Waver. Waver employed an engineering firm to conduct the geological tests necessary to determine the relative quality of the two sites for construction. The tests, which cost $8,000 for each site, showed that Site 1 was superior to Site 2.

The owner of Site 1 initially gave Waver 30 days—a reasonable period—to decide whether or not to buy the property. However, Waver procrastinated in contracting the geological tests, and the results were not available by the end of the 30-day period. Waver requested a two-week extension. The Site 1 owner granted Waver the additional two weeks but charged him $5,000 for the extension (which Waver paid). Waver eventually bought Site 1.

Waver sent Surchum a fee of $23,700, which was 15% of a cost computed as follows:

Sales price, Site 1	$150,000
Geological tests, Site 1	8,000
Total	$158,000

Surchum believes she is entitled to $25,650, based on a cost computed as follows:

Sales price, Site 1	$150,000
Geological tests, Site 1	8,000
Geological tests, Site 2	8,000
Fee for time extension	5,000
Total	$171,000

REQUIRED

What fee is Surchum entitled to under the agreement? Explain.

11

Plant Asset Disposals, Natural Resources, and Intangible Assets

The preceding chapter dealt with the measurement and depreciation of plant assets. In this chapter, we examine the remaining plant asset problem area—accounting for their disposal. We then consider the accounting issues related to the acquisition and use of natural resources and intangible assets. Although plant assets, natural resources, and intangible assets are separate identifiable categories of long-term assets, the basic accounting procedures related to each category are similar.

DISPOSALS OF PLANT ASSETS

A firm may dispose of a plant asset in a variety of ways. The asset may be sold, retired, exchanged for a dissimilar asset, or traded in as partial payment for a new, similar asset. The asset's usefulness to the firm may also be ended by an unfavorable and unanticipated event—the asset may be stolen or destroyed by a natural disaster.

Depreciation must extend through an asset's total useful life to a firm. Therefore, depreciation must be recorded up to the disposal date, regardless of the manner of the asset's disposal. Should the disposal date not coincide with the end of an accounting period, a journal entry must record depreciation for a partial period (the period from the date depreciation was last recorded to the disposal date). We illustrate this partial period depreciation in two of our subsequent examples.

We use the following basic data to illustrate disposals of plant assets:

Equipment's original cost	$1,000
Estimated salvage value after five years	100
Annual straight-line depreciation	180

(Unless stated otherwise, assume that depreciation to the date of sale has been recorded.)

Sale of Plant Assets

Firms normally sell their plant assets once they are no longer efficient or useful. Generally, the asset still has some book value and some sales value in the used market.

Most sales of plant assets involve the following related factors:

(1) The sale transaction exchanges a used plant asset for cash. Because the plant asset sold is no longer on hand, the journal entry must remove from both the asset and accumulated depreciation accounts all amounts related to that asset. These amounts reflect the asset's book value.

376

(2) Because plant assets are most often sold for amounts either greater or less than their book values, gains or losses are produced. Sales proceeds in excess of book values create gains from the sales. Book values in excess of sales proceeds cause losses from the sales.

SOLD FOR MORE THAN BOOK VALUE   Assume the equipment is sold for $230 midway through its fifth year. Depreciation was last recorded at the end of the fourth year. The related entries are

Depreciation Expense	90	
Accumulated Depreciation		90
To record depreciation expense for		
six months.		

Cash	230	
Accumulated Depreciation	810	
Equipment		1,000
Gain on Sale of Plant Assets		40
To record sale of equipment for $230.		

Note that recording depreciation to the date of sale adds $90 to the Accumulated Depreciation account, which totals (4 × $180) + $90 = $810. To reflect the sale properly, we must remove this entire amount of accumulated depreciation from the books. The gain is the proceeds of $230 minus the asset's book value of $190.

SOLD FOR LESS THAN BOOK VALUE   Assume the equipment is sold for $30 at the end of the fifth year. The correct entry is

Cash	30	
Loss on Sale of Plant Assets	70	
Accumulated Depreciation	900	
Equipment		1,000
To record sale of equipment for $30.		

The loss equals the book value of $100 minus the sales proceeds of $30. The cash receipt is recorded, and balances from both accounts related to the asset—the asset account and its contra account—are removed from the books.

SOLD FOR BOOK VALUE   Assume the equipment is sold for $280 at the end of the fourth year. The proper entry is

Cash	280	
Accumulated Depreciation	720	
Equipment		1,000
To record sale of equipment for $280.		

The equipment's book value at the end of the fourth year is $280 ($1,000 cost − $720 accumulated depreciation). The $280 sales proceeds exactly equal the book value; no gain or loss is involved. Of course, we still remove from the accounts the amounts reflecting the book value of the asset sold.

Retirement of Plant Assets

When a plant asset that has no sales value in the used market is retired from productive service, we record a loss equal to the asset's book value. Assume the equipment in our example is scrapped at the end of five years. The entry to record this event is

Loss on Retirement of Plant Assets	100	
Accumulated Depreciation	900	
Equipment		1,000
To record retirement of equipment.		

Ideally, any plant asset that will be scrapped should have a zero salvage value. Then the asset's book value is zero (accumulated depreciation equals the asset's cost) at the end of its estimated useful life. If the asset is retired on that date, no loss is recorded. The asset's cost and accumulated depreciation, of course, must still be removed from the accounts. To illustrate, let us change our example and assume a zero salvage value for the equipment. Over the equipment's five-year life, we record depreciation totaling $1,000 ($200 per year). The following entry records the equipment's retirement at the end of five years:

Accumulated Depreciation	1,000	
Equipment		1,000
To record retirement of equipment.		

Note, however, that the equipment's book value reaches zero only at the end of five years. Should the equipment be retired before that date, a loss equal to the equipment's book value will be recorded.

Exchange of Dissimilar Plant Assets

A plant asset may be exchanged for a different kind of plant asset. The seller of the new asset establishes a trade-in allowance for the used asset with the balance of the selling price due in cash. The trade-in allowance is not related to the used asset's book value. When it is applied against a legitimate cash selling price, the allowance does represent the used asset's fair value. In some exchanges, the suggested selling price may be higher than the asset's cash selling price; therefore the trade-in allowance is inflated and does not indicate the used asset's fair value.

When dissimilar plant assets are exchanged, the cash equivalent (fair) value of what is given up is not always obvious. Therefore, the new asset should be recorded at the fair value of the assets given up or the fair value of the asset received, whichever is more clearly evident. The used asset's book value, of course, is removed from the accounts. We determine any gain or loss on the transaction by comparing the fair value assigned to the new asset with the total of the used asset's book value plus any cash payment. If the new asset's fair value is larger, a gain is recorded. Should the used asset's book value plus cash paid exceed the new asset's fair value, we reflect a loss.

To illustrate, assume our equipment ($1,000 cost and $100 salvage value) is exchanged for an office desk two-thirds of the way through the second year. The desk's cash selling price is $950. The equipment receives an $800 trade-in allowance, so a $150 cash payment is required. Because equipment depreciation was last recorded at the end of the first year, the correct entries are

Depreciation Expense	120	
Accumulated Depreciation		120
To record depreciation expense for eight months.		

Office Furniture	950	
Accumulated Depreciation	300	
Equipment		1,000
Cash		150
Gain on Exchange of Plant Assets		100
To record trade of equipment for office furniture.		

The $100 gain on the transaction is the excess of the desk's fair value ($950) over the equipment's book value ($700) plus cash paid ($150).

Exchange of Similar Plant Assets

When a plant asset is traded in for a similar new asset, the guidelines for analyzing the transaction differ from those that apply when the asset is sold outright or exchanged for a dissimilar asset. The Accounting Principles Board concluded that an exchange of similar productive assets is not the culmination of an earnings process, and consequently no gain should be recognized on such an exchange.[1] Instead, the new asset is recorded at an amount equal to the sum of the book value of the asset traded in plus any cash paid.

Assume that the equipment in our illustration is traded in after three years (accumulated depreciation, $540) on similar new equipment that has a $1,400 cash price. A trade-in allowance of $600 is given. The following entry records the exchange of assets and the related payment:

Equipment (new)	1,260	
Accumulated Depreciation	540	
Equipment (old)		1,000
Cash		800
To record trade of equipment.		

The new equipment is recorded at $1,260—the sum of the $460 book value of the old equipment and the $800 cash payment. This treatment departs from the general rule that newly acquired assets are recorded at their implied cash cost. The new equipment has a cash price of $1,400, but it is recorded at $1,260. Essentially, its book value has been reduced by the $140 gain that is not recognized in the exchange.

A loss in an exchange of similar productive assets is recognized. If in the preceding exchange the company's trade-in allowance was $400 (rather than $600), the entry to record the exchange would be

[1] *Opinions of the Accounting Principles Board, No. 29,* "Accounting for Nonmonetary Transactions" (New York: American Institute of Certified Public Accountants, 1973).

Equipment (new)	1,400	
Loss on Exchange of Plant Assets	60	
Accumulated Depreciation	540	
Equipment (old)		1,000
Cash		1,000
To record trade of equipment.		

In this case, the sum of the old equipment's book value and the cash payment is $1,460 ($460 book value + $1,000 cash payment). This amount exceeds the new equipment's $1,400 fair value, so a loss equal to the difference ($60) is recorded.

TRADE-IN AND TAX REGULATIONS   The Internal Revenue Code specifies that any gains or losses on trade-in transactions involving similar assets are not reported in the year of exchange. The treatment of gains parallels the analysis discussed above. Losses, however, are treated as adjustments of the carrying value of the new asset. The above trade-in illustration resulting in a loss would be recorded as follows under the income tax guidelines:

Equipment (new) ($1,400 + $60 loss)	1,460	
Accumulated Depreciation	540	
Equipment (old)		1,000
Cash		1,000
To record trade of equipment.		

This treatment does not recognize the loss in the year of exchange, but increases the depreciation available in future years. Generally accepted accounting principles require that significant losses on trade-ins be recognized rather than deferred. Some firms, however, follow the income tax method when losses are immaterial to avoid keeping a separate record for income tax purposes.

Destruction or Theft of Plant Assets

A company's plant assets may be destroyed—by fire, flood, earthquake, tornado, or other natural disaster—or they may be stolen. If an uninsured asset is destroyed or stolen, the firm suffers a loss measured by the asset's book value. Assume the equipment in our example is uninsured and after three years is destroyed by fire. Its book value when destroyed is $460 ($1,000 cost − $540 accumulated depreciation). The proper journal entry is

Fire Loss	460	
Accumulated Depreciation	540	
Equipment		1,000
To record equipment fire loss.		

Business firms normally insure their property to eliminate, or reduce, the risk of loss by destruction or theft. When an insured asset is destroyed or stolen, a claim is filed with the insurance company. The maximum amount recoverable from the insurance company is the asset's fair market value. Because the accounting records reflect a plant asset's book value—not its fair market value—the accounting analysis of the asset's theft or destruction may show a gain or loss, even when the asset is insured. The gain or loss is the difference between the insurance settlement and the asset's book value. To illustrate, assume the equipment from the preceding example is insured and has a fair market value of $500 when destroyed by fire. The $500 insurance claim exceeds the equipment's book value, so we reflect a $40 gain from the insurance settlement in the following entry:

Receivable from Insurance Company	500	
Accumulated Depreciation	540	
Equipment		1,000
Gain on Insurance Settlement		40
To record insurance claim on		
equipment destroyed by fire.		

Cash is debited and Receivable from Insurance Company is credited when the $500 check settling the claim is received from the insurance company.

CONTROL OF PLANT ASSETS

Firms with a large number of plant assets normally maintain some formal records and follow systematic inventory procedures so that specific persons can be held accountable for the assets' use and protection. Many firms assign a specific serial number to each significant asset. This is usually done by small decals, stampings, or etchings that are not easily removed or altered.

Coupled with the identification procedures is a formal record of the assets called a **plant ledger** or an **equipment ledger.** This record is often a subsidiary ledger to the various plant asset accounts. The ledger may be maintained by a manual or an electronic data-processing system. Regardless of the record's form, the following basic data are usually incorporated:

Description
Manufacturer's identification or model number
Firm's assigned serial number and accounting classification
Date purchased
Assigned physical location
Insurance coverage
Person accountable
Original cost
Major modifications and repairs
Depreciation method and data
Disposition data (date, price, remarks)

This record requires a formal notation of any purchase, transfer, or disposition of property. Also, a company should periodically verify its equipment ledger by a physical count of the items involved.

NATURAL RESOURCES

Natural resources include such items as timber, petroleum, natural gas, coal, and other mineral deposits mined by the extractive industries. These resources are also known as *wasting assets*. As with plant assets, natural resources are initially accounted for at their cost. When known deposits are purchased, the initial measurement is quite simple. When the natural resource is discovered after extensive exploration, however, determining its initial cost is more difficult. Because not all exploration activities are successful, we must determine which activities were necessary to discover the resource. Expenditures for these activities are capitalized as the cost of the resource, and the remaining amounts are expensed. The cost of developing the site so the natural resource may be extracted is another component of initial cost. Expenditures to remove land overburdens, build access roads, and construct mine entrances illustrate these development costs.

Depletion

The term **depletion** refers to the allocation of the cost of natural resources to the units extracted from the ground or, in the case of timberland, the board feet of timber cut. Accounting for the depletion of natural resources is comparable to units-of-production depreciation of plant assets. The average depletion cost per unit of natural resource is computed as follows:

$$\text{Depletion per Unit} = \frac{\text{Cost of Natural Resource} - \text{Residual Value}}{\text{Estimated Total Units of Resource}}$$

The unit measure used depends on the natural resource; the unit may be barrels, tons, board feet, cubic feet, or some other unit appropriate for the resource. Once depletion per unit is computed, periodic depletion is determined as follows:

Periodic Depletion = Depletion per Unit × Units Extracted in Current Period

For example, assume that a company acquires for $520,000 a parcel of land whose major commercial value is a soft coal mine that contains an estimated 800,000 tons of extractable coal. Development costs of $100,000 are incurred to prepare the site for mining coal. The property's estimated residual value is $20,000. The coal deposit's initial cost is $620,000 ($520,000 acquisition cost + $100,000 development costs). We calculate the depletion per ton of mined coal as follows:

$$\frac{\$620,000 - \$20,000}{800,000 \text{ tons}} = \$0.75 \text{ per ton}$$

If, during the first period, 60,000 tons are extracted, that period's depletion charge would be 60,000 × $0.75 = $45,000. We would make the following entry:

Depletion of Coal Deposit	45,000	
Accumulated Depletion		45,000
To record depletion of coal deposit.		

In the balance sheet, Accumulated Depletion is a contra account deducted from the cost of the natural resource as follows:

Coal Deposit (original cost)	$620,000
Less: Accumulated Depletion	45,000
Coal Deposit (book value)	$575,000

This treatment is similar to handling Accumulated Depreciation accounts.

The disposition of the periodic depletion charge depends on whether the extracted units are sold or on hand at the end of the period. The depletion amount of units sold is deducted in the income statement as part of the cost of the resource sold. Units on hand at year-end, however, constitute inventory items, so their depletion charge appears in the balance sheet as part of the inventory cost. In addition to the depletion charge, the costs of extracting and processing the natural resource are part of the inventory cost.

Assume, for example, that $81,000 of extracting and processing costs are incurred the first period to mine the 60,000 tons of coal. The total cost of the 60,000 mined tons is $126,000 ($45,000 depletion + $81,000 extracting and processing costs); the average cost per ton is $2.10 ($126,000/60,000 tons). If 40,000 tons are sold during the first period, $84,000 (40,000 tons × $2.10 per ton) is expensed in the income statement as the cost of coal sold. The year-end balance sheet will show a mined coal inventory of $42,000 (20,000 tons × $2.10 per ton).

Revision of Depletion

Estimating accurately the recoverable units of a natural resource is difficult. Imagine trying to estimate the barrels of oil or the ounces of silver located underground. After extracting activities begin, better information may result in revisions of such estimates. When an estimate of recoverable units changes, a revised depletion per unit is computed. The revised depletion per unit becomes effective in the period the estimate of recoverable units changes—depletion amounts computed in prior periods are not changed. The revised depletion per unit is computed as follows:

$$\text{Revised Depletion per Unit} = \frac{\text{Book Value of Natural Resource} - \text{Residual Value}}{\text{Revised Estimate of Remaining Units of Resource}}$$

To illustrate, assume that at the beginning of the second year of our coal mining example, the estimated total amount of recoverable coal is changed to 560,000 tons. Because 60,000 tons have already been mined, an estimated 500,000 tons remain underground. The coal deposit's book value at the start of the second year is $575,000 (Cost − Accumulated Depletion). Therefore, the revised depletion per ton is $1.11, determined as follows:

$$\frac{\$575,000 - \$20,000}{500,000 \text{ tons}} = \$1.11 \text{ per ton}$$

Depletion for Tax Purposes

The Internal Revenue Code permits a deduction for the depletion of natural resources sold. The depletion deduction may be based on the resource's cost, using the procedures illustrated. Companies mining certain resources, however, may use **percentage depletion** if it gives a larger deduction. Under percentage depletion, the depletion deduction is a specified percentage of the gross revenue from mining activities, with certain limitations. The depletion percentages range from 5%–22%, depending on the natural resource. Percentage depletion is not limited by the resource's cost and may, over a period of years, result in income tax depletion deductions that exceed total cost. Percentage depletion is a special income tax feature; it is not permitted under generally accepted accounting principles for financial reporting purposes.

On-site Equipment

The extraction of many natural resources requires the construction of *on-site* equipment, such as drilling and pumping devices, crushing equipment, and conveyor systems. Often in remote places, this equipment may be abandoned when the natural resource is exhausted. If the useful life of these assets expires before the resources are exhausted, ordinary depreciation techniques are appropriate. When the reverse is true—natural resources are exhausted, and the asset is abandoned before the end of its physical life—depreciation should be based on the length of the extraction period. Alternatively, we could employ the units-of-production approach based on the estimated total resource to be extracted.

For example, assume coal mining equipment was acquired at a cost of $210,000 in our preceding example. The equipment has an estimated $10,000 salvage value after the coal is mined. If the units-of-production method were used, depreciation per ton for the first year would be

$$\frac{\$210,000 - \$10,000}{800,000 \text{ tons}} = \$0.25 \text{ per ton}$$

The first year's depreciation, when 60,000 tons are mined, is $60,000 \times \$0.25 = \$15,000$.

Under the units-of-production method, depreciation per unit must be revised if the estimate of extractable resource units changes. The process is similar to the depletion per unit revision discussed earlier. We compute the revised depreciation per unit by dividing the asset's book value (less any salvage value) by the revised remaining resource units. For example, at the beginning of the second year, the coal mining equipment's book value is $195,000 ($210,000 cost − $15,000 accumulated depreciation). If the coal remaining underground is now estimated at 500,000 tons, then depreciation per ton, beginning in the second year, is $0.37, computed as follows:

$$\frac{\$195,000 - \$10,000}{500,000 \text{ tons}} = \$0.37 \text{ per ton}$$

Supplemental Disclosures

Many companies in the extractive industries—especially oil- and gas-producing companies—are holding for future operations large discovered and proven reserve fields. Most often these reserves are carried at historical cost figures that may represent only a small fraction of their current values. In such cases, the financial statements may include supplemental disclosures about reserve quantities and other data useful in estimating reserve values.[2]

---

[2]Specific disclosure requirements have been established for oil- and gas-producing companies. For details, see *Statement of Financial Accounting Standards No. 69*, "Disclosures about Oil and Gas Producing Activities" (Stamford, CT: Financial Accounting Standards Board, 1982).

INTANGIBLE ASSETS

In accounting, intangible assets include certain resources that benefit an enterprise's operations but lack physical substance. Several intangible assets are exclusive rights or privileges obtained from a governmental unit or by legal contract—such as patents, copyrights, franchises, trademarks, and leaseholds. Other intangible assets (1) arise from the creation of a business enterprise—namely, organization costs—or (2) reflect a firm's ability to generate above-normal earnings—that is, goodwill.

The term *intangible asset* is not used with precision in accounting literature. By convention, only certain assets are included in the intangible category. Some resources that lack physical substance—such as prepaid insurance, receivables, and investments—are not classified as intangible assets. Because intangible assets lack physical characteristics, the related accounting procedures may be more subjective and arbitrary than for tangible assets.

Measurement of Intangible Assets

A firm should record intangible assets acquired from outside entities initially at their cost. Similarly, some intangible assets created internally by a firm are measured at their cost. For example, the costs of forming a business are charged to an Organization Costs account, and the costs to secure a trademark—such as attorney's fees, registration fees, and design costs—are charged to a Trademarks account.

Most expenditures related to internally created intangible assets are expensed rather than capitalized. Because these intangibles are not acquired from outside entities, accountants lack an objective measure for the asset account. The accountant responds to uncertainty about an intangible asset's existence, or its proper measure, by expensing the related amounts. This situation is particularly evident in accounting for research and development costs.

RESEARCH AND DEVELOPMENT COSTS   American industry annually spends billions of dollars searching for new knowledge and translating this knowledge into new or significantly improved products or processes. These **research and development costs** are important, but usually a significant uncertainty exists about the future benefits of specific research and development efforts. Only a small portion of research and development projects culminate in a new product or process, and then, commercial success is not certain. The market failure rate is high for new products. Uncertain future benefits of research and development costs influenced the Financial Accounting Standards Board's development of the following accounting guideline: *All research and development costs related to a firm's products and its production processes must be expensed when incurred.*[3]

The preceding guideline does not apply to a firm's selling and administrative activities nor to the unique exploration and development efforts of firms in the

[3] *Statement of Financial Accounting Standards No. 2*, "Accounting for Research and Development Costs" (Stamford, CT: Financial Accounting Standards Board, 1974).

extractive industries. Also, legal costs of obtaining or defending a patent for a new product or process may be capitalized.

COMPUTER SOFTWARE   The extensive use of computers has encouraged the development of diverse types of computer software. Accountants immediately expense computer software costs when they fall within the guideline for research and development costs discussed above. Firms that sell computer software, for example, expense the costs of researching and developing new software packages. Also, costs of developing computer software included in a new or significantly improved product should be expensed immediately. Assume, for example, that a firm develops a computerized typesetting machine as a new product. The development costs for the machine's software, as well as all other research and development costs, are expensed immediately.

Accountants who question the immediate expensing of all research and development costs for computer software products believe that firms developing computer software products do not risk the high failure rate representative of most research and development projects. Much software development utilizes a proven process to create new products to predetermined specifications based on an analysis of market needs. The risk of technical failure is small compared with research and development efforts in other industries. On the other hand, rapidly changing computer technology makes the continued usefulness of new software products and the market's long-run acceptance of these products significantly uncertain. Such uncertainty supports the position that expensing software product research and development costs is appropriate. Nonetheless, accountants must constantly evaluate the appropriateness of their guidelines for research and development costs in the growing computer software industry.

Computer software—whether purchased or internally developed—that relates to selling and administrative activities may be capitalized when it clearly benefits future periods. For example, the purchase cost of a computer software package designed to serve a firm's general management information needs should be capitalized if it will be used several years. A hotel chain's internally developed software for a computerized reservation system will be used several years in the firm's selling activities; its development costs may be capitalized. Capitalized computer software costs may be classified as intangible assets, although some firms may classify software with their property, plant, and equipment.

Amortization of Intangibles   The **amortization** of an intangible asset is the periodic write-off to expense of the asset's cost over the term of its expected useful life. Because salvage values are ordinarily not involved, amortization typically entails (1) determining the asset's cost, (2) estimating the period over which it benefits the firm, and (3) allocating the cost in equal amounts to each accounting period involved. The Accounting Principles Board modified this general approach by specifying that the period of amortization for intangibles should not exceed 40 years.[4] As a result,

_____

[4]*Opinions of the Accounting Principles Board, No. 17,* "Accounting for Intangible Assets" (New York: American Institute of Certified Public Accountants, 1970).

intangibles are treated as if they have a limited life—even though some, such as trademarks, may legally have indefinite lives. Straight-line amortization must be used for intangible assets unless another method is shown to be more appropriate.

The amortization entry debits the appropriate amortization expense account. The entry's credit may go to an accumulated amortization account—a contra account to the related intangible asset. In amortizing intangibles, however, frequently the asset account is credited directly; that is, no contra account is used.

Intangible assets originally deemed to have specific useful lives should be reviewed periodically to determine if their value or their economic lives have decreased. If so, an immediate write-off or a plan of periodic amortization at an increased rate is appropriate.

Patents

A **patent** is an exclusive right, granted by the federal government for 17 years, to use a specific process or to make a specific product. Patent laws were originated to encourage inventors by protecting them from imitators who might usurp the invention for commercial gain. Just what a patentable idea is has become quite complex in the modern realm of technical knowledge. Consequently, long periods of patent "searching" and, frequently, successful defense of infringement suits may precede the validation of a patent. Even though patents have a legal life of 17 years, changes in technology or consumer tastes may shorten their economic life. Because of their uncertain value, patents should probably be accounted for conservatively. When patents are purchased some time after having been granted, the buyer enjoys the privilege at most for only the remaining legal life.

To illustrate the accounting for patents, assume that, early in January, a company pays $34,000 legal costs to obtain a patent on a new product. The journal entry is

Patents	34,000	
Cash		34,000
To record legal costs of acquiring patent.		

The company expects the patent to provide benefits for 17 years. If a contra asset account is used, the following entry records the first year's straight-line amortization:

Patent Amortization Expense	2,000	
Accumulated Amortization—Patents		2,000
To record patent amortization.		

The expense would be deducted from revenue, and the Accumulated Amortization—Patents contra account would be deducted from the related asset account on the balance sheet as follows:

Patents (original cost)	$34,000
Less: Accumulated Amortization	2,000
Patents (book value)	$32,000

If the asset account is credited directly (no contra account is used), the amortization entry would be as follows:

Patent Amortization Expense   2,000
  Patents   2,000
To record patent amortization.

When no contra account is used, the asset account reflects the asset's book value, and the balance sheet presentation would be

Patents (cost less amortization to date) $32,000

Copyrights

Copyrights protect the owner against the unauthorized reproduction of a specific written work or artwork. A copyright lasts for the life of the author plus 50 years. The purchase price of valuable copyrights can be substantial, and proper measurement and amortization are necessary for valid income determination. But even with the related legal fees, the cost of most copyrights is seldom sufficiently material to present accounting problems.

A copyright's legal life exceeds the 40-year maximum amortization period allowed for intangibles. However, copyright costs are generally amortized over periods much shorter than 40 years. Copyright costs should be amortized over the period that the copyrighted work produces revenue—for a proper matching of revenue and expense—which may be only a few years.

Franchises

Franchises most often involve exclusive rights to operate or sell a specific brand of products in a given geographical area. Franchises may be for definite or indefinite periods. Although many franchises are agreements between two private firms, various governmental units award franchises for public utility operations within their legal jurisdictions. The right to operate a Kentucky Fried Chicken restaurant or to sell Midas Mufflers in a specific area illustrates franchise agreements in the private sector.

Some franchise agreements require a substantial initial payment by the party acquiring the franchise. This amount should be debited to the intangible asset account Franchise and amortized on a straight-line basis over the franchise period or 40 years, whichever is shorter.

Trademarks and Trade Names

Trademarks and **trade names** represent the exclusive and continuing right to use certain terms, names, or symbols, usually to identify a brand or family of products. An original trademark or trade name can be registered with the federal government at nominal cost, so few accounting problems exist. On the other hand, the purchase of well-known, and thus valuable, trademarks or trade names may involve substantial amounts of funds. In such cases, the purchase cost is debited to an appropriate intangible asset account—Trademarks, for example—and amortized over the period of expected benefit (not exceeding 40 years).

Organization Costs

Expenditures incurred in launching a business (usually a corporation) are called **organization costs.** These expenditures, which may include attorney's fees, fees paid to the state, and other costs related to preparation for operations, are debited to the intangible asset account Organization Costs. Theoretically, these expenditures benefit the firm throughout its operating life, but all intangibles must be amortized over 40 years or less. Most firms amortize organization costs over a five- to 10-year period. Income tax guidelines reinforce this practice by permitting the amortization of organization costs for tax purposes over a period of at least five years.

Goodwill

Goodwill is the value derived from a firm's ability to earn more than a normal rate of return on its specific, identifiable net assets. The measurement of goodwill is complex, because it can stem from any factor that can make income rates high relative to investment. Examples of such factors include exceptional customer relations, advantageous location, operating efficiency, superior personnel relations, favorable financial sources, and even monopolistic position. Furthermore, goodwill cannot be severed from a firm and sold separately. Because measuring goodwill is difficult, a firm records it in the accounts only when another firm is purchased and the amount paid to acquire it exceeds the recognized value of the identifiable net assets involved. Determining the amount of goodwill often requires complex negotiations, but the agreed-on amount is almost always based on the anticipated above-normal earnings.

Accountants expense immediately all costs associated with the internal development or maintenance of goodwill. This means many firms that have created goodwill through their operations do not reflect it in the accounts because it was not purchased.

To illustrate the concept of goodwill, assume Carley Company is for sale. We know the following information about the company and the industry in which it operates:

Fair market value of Carley Company's identifiable net assets	$2,000,000
Normal rate of return on net assets for industry	× 11%
Normal earnings on $2,000,000 of identifiable net assets	$ 220,000
Average annual earnings for Carley Company (past four years)	286,000
Above-average earnings for Carley Company	$ 66,000

Carley's $66,000 of superior earnings suggests the presence of an asset—not specifically identifiable—that helps generate these excess earnings. That asset is goodwill—a combination of factors unique to Carley Company that generates the above-average rate of return on its identifiable net assets. The price paid for Carley will exceed $2,000,000 because the goodwill is also being purchased.

How much should be paid for goodwill? Although above-average earnings in the past are evidence of goodwill, the purchaser is interested in future earnings performance. Goodwill estimates are subject to uncertainty about how long the superior earnings may be sustained. A purchaser may use several methods to estimate a goodwill amount. We illustrate the following two methods:

(1) Goodwill may be estimated by capitalizing the superior earnings at the normal rate of return. *Capitalizing earnings* here means dividing earnings by the rate of return; this computation for Carley Company is $66,000/0.11 = $600,000. The $600,000 represents the dollar investment that, at an 11% rate of return,

will earn $66,000 each year. However, this approach implies that *every* future year will generate the $66,000 excess earnings—a tenuous assumption in a competitive environment. Sometimes excess earnings are capitalized at an above-normal rate of return in recognition of the greater risk of continued superior earnings. The higher the capitalization rate used, the lower the goodwill estimate.

(2) Goodwill may be estimated as some multiple of the superior earnings. Carley's purchaser, for example, may pay five times the above-average earnings for goodwill, or 5 × $66,000 = $330,000.

Of course, the seller also estimates goodwill in determining an overall value for the firm. When the buyer and seller agree on the firm's total purchase price, we can establish the portion assignable to goodwill. The difference between the total purchase price and the fair value of the specific, identifiable net assets is the goodwill measure. For example, if Carley Company is purchased for $2,400,000,

GOODWILL—UP AND OUT

The accounting guidelines for goodwill are straightforward: Goodwill may only be recorded when another firm is purchased. The amount assigned to goodwill is equal to the excess of the price paid for the firm purchased over the fair value of its identifiable net assets. Yet even these guidelines may cause a problem, as evidenced by the following situation.

In January 1982, Alexander & Alexander Services (A&A), an insurance brokerage house, purchased the Alexander Howden Group, a British insurance brokerage house, for $300 million. The fair value of Howden's identifiable net assets (Assets − Liabilities) was established as $120 million. Accordingly, A&A set up $180 million of goodwill, to be amortized over 40 years—so far, so good.

A postacquisition audit of Howden, however, turned up $40 million of unrecorded liabilities, a significant amount. These liabilities reduced the fair value of Howden's net assets from $120 million to $80 million. A&A therefore increased its recorded goodwill by $40 million (from $180 million to $220 million). A&A had paid $300 million for Howden, whose identifiable net assets were subsequently determined to be worth only $80 million. A&A reasoned the $220 million differ-

ence must represent goodwill, per the accounting goodwill guidelines. Stated A&A, these guidelines apply because the purchase of Howden was a normal business transaction.[*]

Not so, argued the Securities and Exchange Commission (SEC). Taking issue with A&A's accounting, the SEC believed the appropriate treatment for the $40 million debit was an immediate write-off as a current period loss. It was hardly a normal business transaction in the SEC's eyes. Given the circumstances surrounding the unrecorded liabilities, the SEC concluded A&A could not have known about the liabilities when the purchase price was set. Had A&A been aware of the $40 million net asset decrease, the SEC observed, the company would have adjusted the purchase price.[†]

The SEC prevailed, and A&A charged off a $40 million loss in 1982's third quarter. For that quarter, A&A reported an overall $36.4 million loss rather than a $3.6 million profit.

[*]Richard Greene, "Men of Goodwill, Disagreeing," *Forbes*, December 6, 1982, page 168.
[†]Stephen Piontek, "A&A Takes $40M 'Howden' Charge Against Its Third Quarter Earnings," *National Underwriter*, Property & Casualty Insurance Edition, November 19, 1982, page 2.

$2,000,000 is assigned to the identifiable net assets and $400,000 is assigned to goodwill.

Shown as an intangible asset in the financial statements, goodwill must be amortized over 40 years or less.

Leases   A firm may rent property for a specified period under a contract called a **lease.** The company acquiring the right to use the property is the **lessee;** the owner of the property is the **lessor.** The rights transferred to the lessee are called a **leasehold.** Examples of leased assets are land, buildings, trucks, factory machinery, office equipment, and automobiles. A lessee's accounting treatment depends on whether a lease is an operating lease or a capital lease.

OPERATING LEASE   The typical rental agreement illustrates an **operating lease**— the lessee pays for the use of an asset for a limited period, and the lessor retains the usual risks and rewards of owning the property. The lessee usually charges each lease payment to rent expense. Sometimes leases extending over long periods require advance payments from the lessee. The lessee debits these payments to a **Leasehold** account, then allocates the amount to rent expense over the period covered by the advance payment. For example, assume Graphic Company makes an $18,000 advance payment for the final year's rent on a 10-year lease of office space. The following entry records the advance payment:

Leasehold	18,000	
Cash		18,000
To record advance lease payment.		

The leasehold amount is an intangible asset. In this illustration, the advance payment relates specifically to year 10, so the $18,000 is classified as an intangible asset for nine years. In year 10, the $18,000 is expensed. The following entry recognizes a full year's rent expense at the end of year 10:

Office Rent Expense	18,000	
Leasehold		18,000
To record annual rent expense.		

Expenditures made by a lessee to alter or improve property leased under an operating lease are called **leasehold improvements.** For example, a company may construct a building on leased land or make improvements to a leased building. The improvements or alterations become part of the leased property and revert to the lessor at the end of the lease. Thus, the cost of leasehold improvements should be amortized over the life of the lease or the life of the improvements, whichever is shorter. The classification of leasehold improvements varies—some businesses classify them as intangible assets, whereas others include them in the property, plant, and equipment section of the balance sheet.

To illustrate, assume Graphic Company improves the office space leased for 10 years by adding new interior walls and built-in bookshelves. The improvements were made at the start of the lease, cost $40,000, and have an estimated life of 40 years. Graphic Company records the expenditures for the improvements as follows:

Leasehold Improvements	40,000	
Cash		40,000
To record office improvements.		

Leasehold Improvements is an intangible asset. Because Graphic Company benefits from these leasehold improvements only for the 10-year lease period, it should amortize the improvements over 10 years. The following entry is made in each of the 10 years (assuming a contra account is not used):

Leasehold Improvements Amortization Expense	4,000	
Leasehold Improvements		4,000
To record amortization of leasehold improvements.		

CAPITAL LEASE   A **capital lease** transfers to the lessee substantially all of the benefits and risks related to the ownership of the property. A lease meeting at least one of the following criteria is a capital lease:[5]

(1) The lease transfers ownership of the property to the lessee by the end of the lease term.

(2) The lease contains a bargain purchase option.

(3) The lease term is at least 75% of the estimated economic life of the leased property.

(4) The present value of the lease payments[6] is at least 90% of the fair value of the leased property.

The economic effect of a capital lease is similar to that of an installment purchase. The lessee accounts for a capital lease by recording the leased property as an asset and establishing a liability for the lease obligation. The present value of the future lease payments determines the dollar amount of the entry. The leased property is then depreciated over the period it benefits the lessee. Part of each lease payment made by the lessee is charged to interest expense and the remainder reduces the lease obligation.

We have identified the basic differences between operating and capital leases. Accounting for capital leases is quite complex. Similar complexities face lessors because they may treat some leases as sales or financing transactions rather than typical rental agreements. These areas, beyond the scope of this text, are covered in intermediate accounting texts.

---

[5] *Statement of Financial Accounting Standards No. 13*, "Accounting for Leases" (Stamford, CT: Financial Accounting Standards Board, 1976).
[6] Present values are discussed in Appendix A to Chapter 17.

EXHIBIT 11-1
Balance Sheet Presentation
of Plant Assets, Natural Resources, and Intangible Assets
(in Thousands of Dollars)

Plant Assets		
Fixtures	$ 90	
Less: Accumulated Depreciation	20	$ 70
Equipment	$1,400	
Less: Accumulated Depreciation	300	1,100
Buildings	$4,600	
Less: Accumulated Depreciation	1,200	3,400
Land		800
Total Plant Assets		$5,370
Natural Resources		
Timberland	$ 500	
Less: Accumulated Depletion	200	$ 300
Coal Deposit	$ 900	
Less: Accumulated Depletion	150	750
Total Natural Resources		$1,050
Intangible Assets (cost less amortization to date)		
Patents		$ 200
Goodwill		500
Organization Costs		100
Total Intangible Assets		$ 800

BALANCE SHEET PRESENTATION

Plant assets, natural resources, and intangible assets usually are presented in the balance sheet below the sections for current assets and investments. Exhibit 11-1 shows how these assets may appear on a balance sheet.

DEMONSTRATION PROBLEM FOR REVIEW

Rochelle Company has an office copier that originally cost $10,250 and that has an $800 expected salvage value at the end of an estimated seven-year useful life. Straight-line depreciation on the machine has been recorded for five years; the last depreciation entry was made at the end of the fifth year. Two months into the sixth year, Rochelle disposes of the copier.

REQUIRED

(a) Prepare the journal entry to record depreciation expense to the date of disposal.

(b) Prepare journal entries to record the machine's disposal in the following unrelated situations:

(1) Sale of the machine for cash at its book value.

(2) Sale of the machine for $3,000 cash.

(3) Sale of the machine for $5,000 cash.

(4) Exchange of the machine for a new office copier costing $13,000. The trade-in allowance received for the old copier is $4,200. The $8,800 balance is paid in cash. Follow generally accepted accounting principles in recording this transaction.

(5) Destruction of the machine by flood. Unfortunately, Rochelle does not carry flood insurance.

SOLUTION TO DEMONSTRATION PROBLEM

(a)

Depreciation Expense	225	
Accumulated Depreciation		225

To record depreciation expense for two months.

Annual depreciation: $\dfrac{\$10,250 - \$800}{7} = \$1,350$

Two months' depreciation: $\$1,350 \times \frac{2}{12} = \$225$

(b) (1)

Cash	3,275	
Accumulated Depreciation	6,975	
Office Equipment		10,250

To record sale of machine for book value.

Cost		$10,250
Accumulated depreciation:		
5 years × $1,350 = $6,750		
2 months	225	6,975
Book value		$ 3,275

(2)

Cash	3,000	
Loss on Sale of Plant Assets	275	
Accumulated Depreciation	6,975	
Office Equipment		10,250

To record sale of machine for $3,000.

(3)

Cash	5,000	
Accumulated Depreciation	6,975	
Office Equipment		10,250
Gain on Sale of Plant Assets		1,725

To record sale of machine for $5,000.

(4)	Office Equipment (new)	12,075	
	Accumulated Depreciation	6,975	
	Office Equipment (old)		10,250
	Cash		8,800
	To record trade of office copiers.		

(5)	Flood Loss	3,275	
	Accumulated Depreciation	6,975	
	Office Equipment		10,250
	To record flood loss to machine.		

KEY POINTS TO REMEMBER

(1) When a firm disposes of a plant asset, depreciation must be recorded on the asset up to the disposal date.

(2) Gains and losses on plant asset dispositions are determined by comparing the assets' book values to their sales proceeds. Gains are not recognized on exchanges of similar productive assets, although losses on such exchanges are recognized.

(3) Depletion is the allocation of a natural resource's cost to the resource units as they are mined, cut, or otherwise extracted from their source.

(4) The units-of-production depreciation method may be appropriate for equipment used exclusively in the mining and extracting of natural resources.

(5) Amortization is the periodic write-off to expense of an intangible asset's cost over the asset's useful life or 40 years, whichever is shorter.

(6) Intangible assets and natural resources are initially measured at their cost.

(7) Research and development costs related to a firm's products and its production processes are expensed as incurred.

(8) Goodwill reflects a firm's ability to generate above-normal earnings. Goodwill may be shown in the accounts only when it has been purchased.

QUESTIONS

11–1 Identify three ways that a firm may dispose of a plant asset.

11–2 What factors determine the gain or loss on the disposition of a plant asset?

11–3 Under what condition does a firm show neither a gain nor a loss from (a) the sale of a plant asset and (b) the retirement of a plant asset?

11–4 Meir Company depreciates a piece of equipment $240 per year on a straight-line basis. After the last depreciation entry on December 31, 19X4, the equipment's book value is $1,300. On July 31, 19X5, the equipment is sold for $1,500 cash. What is the gain (or loss) on the sale of the equipment?

11–5 Ascot, Inc. exchanged a used microcomputer with a $600 book value and $400 cash for office furniture having a cash selling price of $1,200. At what amount should Ascot record the office furniture? What is the gain (or loss) on the exchange of assets?

11–6 Assume a company exchanged a used microcomputer with a $600 book value and $400 cash for a new microcomputer having a cash selling price of $1,200. At what amount should the company record the new microcomputer? What is the gain (or loss) on the exchange of assets?

11–7 How is the amount of loss determined when an uninsured plant asset is destroyed by flood?

11–8 What is an equipment ledger?

11–9 Define *depletion*. The total depletion charge for a period may not all be expensed in the same period. Explain.

11–10 Taper Company installed a conveyor system that cost $24,000. The system can only be used in the excavation of gravel at a particular site. Taper expects to excavate gravel at the site for 10 years. Over how many years should the conveyor be depreciated if its physical life is estimated at (a) 8 years and (b) 12 years?

11–11 Why is computing the depletion of natural resources similar to computing units-of-production depreciation?

11–12 List and briefly explain the nature of six different types of intangible assets.

11–13 How should a firm account for research and development costs related to its products and production processes?

11–14 Input Company purchased for $3,500 computer software that is designed to process the firm's payroll, bill customers, and process customer payments. The software should be useful without significant modification for five years. What is the proper accounting for the software's cost?

11–15 What is the maximum amortization period for an intangible asset?

11–16 Briefly describe two methods for estimating the goodwill amount for a firm that is generating above-average earnings.

11–17 What is the difference between an operating lease and a capital lease?

EXERCISES

11–18 Warner Company has a machine that originally cost $38,000. Depreciation has been recorded for five years using the straight-line method, with a $2,000 estimated salvage value at the end of an expected nine-year life. After recording depreciation at the end of the fifth year, Warner sells the machine. Prepare the journal entry to record the machine's sale for
(a) $22,000 cash.
(b) $18,000 cash.
(c) $15,000 cash.

11–19 On January 2, 19X1, Soffit, Inc. purchased a floor maintenance machine costing $2,100. Soffit estimates the machine's useful life at seven years with no salvage value. Straight-line depreciation is recorded each year on December 31. Prepare the journal entry to record the machine's disposal in the following situations:

(a) The machine is scrapped on December 31, 19X7. Assume 19X7 depreciation has been recorded.

(b) The machine is scrapped on June 30, 19X6. Prepare an entry to update depreciation before recording the machine's disposal.

(c) The machine is traded in on a lawn tractor (a dissimilar asset) on December 31, 19X5. The tractor's cash selling price is $1,700. Soffit's trade-in allowance is $900, and it pays the remaining $800 in cash. Assume 19X5 depreciation has been recorded.

11–20 Refer to Exercise 11–19. Assume Soffit, Inc. had estimated a $350 salvage value for the floor maintenance machine, and all other data remain the same. Prepare the journal entry to record the machine's disposal in the three situations described in Exercise 11–19.

11–21 Brodt Company exchanges used equipment costing $60,000 (on which $50,000 of depreciation has accumulated) for similar new equipment. The new equipment's cash price, with no trade-in, is $72,000.

(a) Following generally accepted accounting principles, prepare the journal entry to record Brodt's trade-in transaction when

   (1) The equipment's trade-in allowance is $9,000, and the balance is paid in cash.

   (2) The equipment's trade-in allowance is $13,000, and the balance is paid in cash.

(b) Following income tax guidelines, prepare the journal entry to record Brodt's trade-in transaction when

   (1) The equipment's trade-in allowance is $9,000, and the balance is paid in cash.

   (2) The equipment's trade-in allowance is $13,000, and the balance is paid in cash.

11–22 Assume Shafer Company trades a used machine for a new machine with a cash price of $14,000. The old machine originally cost $11,000 and has $8,000 of accumulated depreciation. The seller allows $4,500 as a trade-in for the old machine; Shafer pays the balance in cash. Following generally accepted accounting principles, prepare the journal entry to record Shafer's trade-in transaction assuming

(a) The machines are dissimilar plant assets.

(b) The machines are similar plant assets.

11–23 A storage building owned by Stanley Company was destroyed by flood exactly eight years after its purchase. The building, purchased for $125,000, had an estimated 20-year useful life and a $5,000 salvage value. Depreciation was up to date when the building was destroyed. Prepare the journal entry to record the destruction of the building assuming

(a) The building was not insured.

(b) The building was insured, and Stanley expects an $85,000 insurance settlement.

(c) The building was insured, and Stanley expects a $75,000 insurance settlement.

11–24 Shynee Copper Company recently acquired a parcel of land containing an estimated 600,000 tons of commercial grade copper ore. Shynee paid $5,500,000 for the land and acquired extraction equipment at a cost of $990,000. Although the equipment will be worthless when the ore is depleted, Shynee estimates that the land can be sold for $400,000 after the mining operations are completed.

(a) Compute the proper depletion charge for a period during which 80,000 tons of ore are extracted and sold.

(b) Compute the proper depreciation expense on the extraction equipment, using the units-of-production method, for a period during which 80,000 tons of ore are extracted and sold.

11–25 For each of the following unrelated situations, calculate the annual amortization expense and present a general journal entry to record the expense. Assume contra accounts are not used for accumulated amortization.

(a) A two-year-old patent was purchased for $560,000. The patent will probably be commercially exploitable for another eight years.

(b) Certain sales counter fixtures, costing $97,500, were constructed and permanently installed in a building leased from another firm. The physical life of the counters was an estimated 20 years. When the counters were installed, the operating lease had 13 years to run and contained no provision for the removal of the fixtures.

(c) A trademark is carried at a cost of $84,000, which represents the out-of-court settlement paid to another firm that has agreed to refrain from using or claiming the trademark or one similar to it. The trademark has an indefinite life.

(d) A patent was acquired on a device designed by a production worker. Although the cost of the patent to date consisted of $27,200 in legal fees for handling the patent application, the patent should be commercially valuable during its entire legal life and is currently worth approximately $289,000.

(e) A franchise granting exclusive distribution rights for a new solar water heater within a four-state area for three years was obtained at a cost of $36,000. Satisfactory sales performance over the three years permits renewal of the franchise for another three years (at an additional cost determined at renewal).

11–26 Byden Company, which is for sale, has identifiable net assets with a fair value of $7,500,000 and no recorded goodwill. Byden's annual net income in recent years has averaged $900,000 in an industry which considers 10% a normal rate of return on net assets.

(a) Compute Byden's above-normal earnings.

(b) Estimate Byden's goodwill amount by capitalizing the above-normal earnings at the normal rate of return on net assets.

(c) How much will the goodwill estimate from part (b) change if the excess earnings are capitalized at 15%?

PROBLEMS

11–27 Spokane Company has a used executive charter plane that originally cost $450,000. Straight-line depreciation on the plane has been recorded for six years, with a $54,000 expected salvage value at the end of its estimated eight-year useful life. The last depreciation entry was made at the end of the sixth year. Eight months into the seventh year, Spokane disposes of the plane.

REQUIRED
Prepare journal entries to record
(a) Depreciation expense to the date of disposal.

(b) Sale of the plane for cash at its book value.

(c) Sale of the plane for $142,000 cash.

(d) Sale of the plane for $114,000 cash.

(e) Exchange of the plane for a new aircraft costing $600,000. The trade-in allowance received is $145,000, and the balance is paid in cash. Follow generally accepted accounting principles in recording this transaction.

(f) Destruction of the plane in a fire. Spokane expects a $100,000 insurance settlement.

(g) Exchange of the plane for a new yacht costing $600,000. The trade-in allowance received is $145,000, and the balance is paid in cash.

11–28 On July 1, 19X1, Edgeton Construction Company purchased a small bulldozer for $9,500. Edgeton estimates a six-year useful life and an $800 salvage value for the bulldozer. On October 1, 19X1, the company purchased a flatbed truck for $8,000. Edgeton estimates the truck's useful life at seven years and its salvage value at $300. Edgeton uses straight-line depreciation for all plant assets and records depreciation on December 31 each year.

On March 31, 19X6, Edgeton traded in the truck for a new truck. The manufacturer's "sticker" price on the new truck was $10,500, but the dealer's cash price was $10,000. After the dealer deducted the allowance for the old truck, Edgeton paid $7,400 cash for the new truck. Edgeton estimates the new truck will last five years and have a $1,000 salvage value.

On June 30, 19X6, Edgeton exchanged the bulldozer for a new bulldozer with a cash price of $12,000. Edgeton's trade-in allowance for the old bulldozer was $3,000, and the company paid $9,000 cash. The new bulldozer's estimated useful life is six years; its estimated salvage value is $750.

REQUIRED

Following generally accepted accounting principles, prepare journal entries to record the following events in 19X6:

Mar. 31   Update depreciation on the truck.

   31   Exchange of trucks.

June 30   Update depreciation on the bulldozer.

   30   Exchange of bulldozers.

Dec. 31   Depreciation for 19X6 on new truck and new bulldozer.

11–29 Quarry Gravel, Inc. has just purchased a site containing an estimated 2,200,000 tons of high-grade aggregate rock. Quarry makes the following expenditures before starting production:

Purchase price of property	$950,000
Legal fees to acquire title and secure proper zoning for operations	7,000
Removal of overburden and grading for drainage	91,000
Construction of on-site crushing, washing, and loading facilities	260,000

Once the rock deposits are no longer commercially valuable, Quarry estimates the land will sell for $80,000. Certain parts of the on-site crushing, washing, and loading facilities have an estimated salvage value of $18,000 when operations are terminated.

REQUIRED

(a) Compute the total depletion charge for the first year, during which 200,000 tons of rock are extracted from the quarry.

(b) Compute the amount of depreciation on the crushing, washing, and loading facilities during the first year, in which 200,000 tons of rock are extracted. Use the units-of-production depreciation method.

(c) Compute the cost of a 15,000-ton inventory of rock at the end of the first year for which all extraction and processing costs except depletion and depreciation of crushing, washing, and loading facilities average $0.50 per ton.

(d) At the beginning of the second year, Quarry estimates that only 1,600,000 tons of rock remain in the quarry. Compute the revised (1) depletion per ton of rock and (2) depreciation per ton of rock.

11–30 Essex Company owns several retail outlets. In 19X1, it expands operations and enters into the following transactions:

Jan. 2   Signed an eight-year operating lease for additional retail space for an annual rent of $21,600. Essex pays the first and last years' rent in advance of this date. (Hint: Debit the first year's rent to Prepaid Rent.)

     3   Paid $8,400 to contractor for installation of new oak floor in leased facility. The oak floor's life is an estimated 50 years with no salvage value.

     3   Purchased new cash register for $3,940. The cash register initially will be used in the leased outlet, but may eventually replace a cash register at another location. The cash register's estimated useful life is 14 years with a $300 salvage value.

REQUIRED

(a) Prepare general journal entries to record these transactions.

(b) Prepare the necessary adjusting entries on December 31, 19X1 for these transactions. Essex makes adjusting entries once a year. Essex uses straight-line depreciation and amortization but does not use contra accounts when amortizing intangible assets.

11–31 Selected 19X6 transactions and events for the Walkman Company are given below:

Jan.   2   Paid $13,000 for a four-year franchise to distribute a product line locally.

Mar. 31   Discovered a computer was stolen from the accountant's office. Walkman carries no theft insurance. The computer cost $9,160 when purchased on January 2, 19X3 and was being depreciated over six years with a $400 salvage value. Straight-line depreciation was last recorded on December 31, 19X5.

Apr.   1   Entered into a nine-year operating lease for additional warehouse space. Paid in advance the final month's rent of $900 when the lease was signed.

June 30   Discarded office equipment and realized no salvage value. A $400 salvage value, after a six-year useful life, had been estimated when the equipment was acquired for $4,600 on July 1, 19X0. Straight-line depreciation was last recorded on December 31, 19X5.

Aug.   1   Paid a $3,000 cash bonus to employee for designing and developing a new product.

Sept. 1   Paid a $7,500 legal services fee to obtain a new product patent, which was granted today. Walkman estimates the patent will provide effective protection from competitors for 10 years.

Oct. 1 Constructed storage bins at a cost of $5,100 in the warehouse space leased April 1. The physical life of the storage bins is an estimated 15 years. The lease contains no provision for the removal of the bins; the lessor takes control of the bins at the end of the lease.

Nov. 1 Exchanged a used forklift truck for a similar new truck. The used truck cost $5,000 and had accumulated depreciation of $4,200 (through October 31, 19X6). The new truck's cash price was $6,000. Walkman's trade-in allowance was $1,200, and the company paid $4,800 cash. Walkman estimates a 10-year useful life and a $200 salvage value for the new truck.

REQUIRED

(a) Prepare general journal entries to record these transactions.

(b) Prepare the December 31, 19X6, general journal entries to record the proper amounts of depreciation and amortization expense for assets acquired during the year. Walkman uses straight-line depreciation and amortization but does not use contra accounts when amortizing intangible assets.

11–32 Cronier Company's December 31, 19X4 post-closing trial balance contains the following normal balances:

Cash	$ 4,000
Accounts Payable	5,000
Stone Quarry	190,000
Building	100,000
Notes Payable (long term)	300,000
T. Cronier, Capital	319,000
Accumulated Depreciation—Equipment	45,000
Leasehold	3,000
Accumulated Depletion—Stone Quarry	50,000
Land	23,000
Accounts Receivable	6,000
Timberland	250,000
Accumulated Depreciation—Building	20,000
Wages Payable	7,000
Patent (net of amortization)	15,000
Accumulated Depletion—Timberland	75,000
Notes Payable (short term)	40,000
Inventory	70,000
Equipment	200,000

REQUIRED

Prepare a December 31, 19X4 classified balance sheet for Cronier Company.

ALTERNATE PROBLEMS

11–27A Carbon Company has a used delivery truck that originally cost $8,400. Straight-line depreciation on the truck has been recorded for three years, with a $600 expected salvage value at the end of its estimated six-year useful life. The last depreciation entry was made at the end of the third year. Three months into the fourth year, Carbon disposes of the truck.

REQUIRED
Prepare journal entries to record
(a) Depreciation expense to the date of disposal.
(b) Sale of the truck for cash at its book value.
(c) Sale of the truck for $6,000 cash.
(d) Sale of the truck for $3,700 cash.
(e) Exchange of the truck for a new truck costing $12,500. The trade-in allowance received is $4,000, and the balance is paid in cash. Follow generally accepted accounting principles in recording this transaction.
(f) Theft of the truck. Carbon carries no insurance for theft.
(g) Exchange of the truck for golf carts costing $12,500 for the company golf course. The trade-in allowance received is $5,000, and the balance is paid in cash.

11–28A On April 1, 19X1, Wilde Excavators, Inc. purchased a tractor for $18,500. Wilde estimates a nine-year useful life and a $500 salvage value for the tractor. On September 1, 19X1, the company paid $26,500 for a new trenching machine. Wilde estimates the machine's useful life at five years and its salvage value at $1,000. Wilde uses straight-line depreciation for all plant assets and records depreciation on December 31 each year.

On June 30, 19X6, Wilde traded in the tractor for a new tractor with a cash price of $27,000. The dealer allowed a trade-in value of $7,000 for the old tractor, and Wilde paid the remaining $20,000 in cash. Wilde estimates the new tractor will last seven years and have a $400 salvage value.

On August 31, 19X6, Wilde exchanged the trenching machine for a new trenching machine with a cash price of $31,000. Wilde's trade-in allowance for the old trenching machine was $1,700, and the company paid $29,300 cash. The new machine's estimated useful life is six years; its estimated salvage value is $1,500.

REQUIRED
Following generally accepted accounting principles, prepare journal entries to record the following events in 19X6:

June 30   Update depreciation on the tractor.
   30   Exchange of tractors.
Aug. 31   Update depreciation on the trenching machine.
   31   Exchange of trenching machines.
Dec. 31   Depreciation for 19X6 on new tractor and new trenching machine.

11–29A Western Mining Company has just purchased a site containing an estimated 1,500,000 tons of coal. Western makes the following expenditures before starting operations:

Cost of land survey	$ 32,000
Purchase price of property	1,275,000
Legal fees to acquire title and secure proper zoning for operations	18,000
Construction of on-site conveyance and loading facilities	400,000

After all the coal has been extracted, Western expects to sell the property for $125,000 and certain parts of the conveyance and loading facilities for $40,000.

REQUIRED
(a) Compute the total depletion charge for the first year, during which 150,000 tons of coal are extracted from the mine.
(b) Compute the amount of depreciation on the conveyance and loading facilities during the first year, in which 150,000 tons of coal are extracted. Use the units-of-production depreciation method.
(c) Compute the cost of a 25,000-ton inventory of coal at the end of the first year for which all extraction and processing costs except depletion and depreciation of conveyance and loading facilities average $3.10 per ton.
(d) At the beginning of the second year, Western estimates that only 1,200,000 tons of coal remain underground. Compute the revised (1) depletion per ton of coal and (2) depreciation per ton of coal.

11–31A During the first few days of 19X2, Geneva Company began business and entered into the following transactions:
(1) Paid $10,000 in attorney's fees and other costs related to the organization of the company.
(2) Purchased an existing patent on a product for $84,000. The patent's legal protection and useful life cover 12 more years.
(3) Entered into a six-year operating lease for additional office space. Paid in advance the final month's rent of $1,000 when the lease was signed.
(4) Paid $4,200 to have recessed lighting installed in the leased office space. The lighting is estimated to last 20 years with no salvage value.
(5) Paid $100,000 for a 20-year franchise to distribute a product line in a three-state region.
(6) Spent $5,000 on the initial research for a promising new product to complement the patented product.
(7) Purchased a computer software package to aid the controller's financial planning and budgeting activities. The software cost $6,000, should be useful without significant modification for four years, and has no salvage value.

REQUIRED
(a) Prepare general journal entries to record these transactions.
(b) Prepare the December 31, 19X2 general journal entries to record the proper amounts of amortization expense for the year. Organization costs are amortized over five years. Geneva uses straight-line amortization but does not use contra accounts when amortizing intangible assets.

11–32A Center Company's December 31, 19X5 post-closing trial balance contains the following normal account balances:

Interest Payable	$ 20,000
Accumulated Depreciation—Equipment	75,000
Inventory	205,000
Organization Costs (net of amortization)	60,000
Copper Deposit	650,000
Notes Payable (short term)	125,000
Cash	3,000

Accumulated Depletion—Coal Deposit	$100,000
Building	80,000
Accounts Receivable	10,000
Patent (net of amortization)	42,000
Equipment	300,000
C. Center, Capital	540,000
Accumulated Depreciation—Building	15,000
Accounts Payable	25,000
Accumulated Depletion—Copper Deposit	330,000
Land	180,000
Notes Payable (long term)	800,000
Coal Deposit	500,000

REQUIRED

Prepare a December 31, 19X5 classified balance sheet for Center Company.

BUSINESS DECISION PROBLEM

Frank Ladell wants to buy Surf Company from Julia Surf. His first offer was rejected, and he seeks your advice as he prepares another offer. Your discussions with Ladell and an analysis of related data disclose the following:

(1) Ladell's first offer of $1,500,000 was equal to the fair value of Surf Company's identifiable net assets. Ladell and Surf agree this amount represents the fair value of these net assets.

(2) Surf rejected the first offer because she believes her company has exceptionally good supplier, customer, and employee relationships. These attributes do not appear on the balance sheet, but they are a component of the company's overall value and should be reflected in the purchase price.

(3) Ladell recognizes Surf Company's favorable relationships. However, he is uncertain how long they will last when Surf leaves the company after the sale.

(4) Ladell is willing to incorporate a goodwill amount in his offer and accepts a "capitalization of excess earnings" approach to estimating goodwill. In light of his uncertainty about the long-run continuation of superior earnings, however, the capitalization rate must be twice the average rate of return for the industry.

(5) The industry's average rate of return on identifiable net assets is 13%.

(6) Over the past several years, Surf Company's net income has averaged $325,000.

REQUIRED

Estimate a goodwill amount for Surf Company, and recommend a purchase price that Frank Ladell should offer Julia Surf.

12

Current Liabilities and Payroll Accounting

L iabilities, one of the three elements in the accounting equation, generally represent a firm's obligations to nonowners. Total liabilities are divided into two subcategories—current liabilities and long-term liabilities. In this chapter, we focus on current liabilities, and because several liabilities are associated with a firm's payroll, we will examine payroll accounting procedures and requirements in some depth.

THE NATURE OF LIABILITIES

Liabilities are obligations resulting from past transactions that require the firm to pay money, provide goods, or perform services in the future. The existence of a past transaction is an important element in the definition of liabilities. For example, a purchase commitment is actually an agreement between a buyer and a seller to enter into a *future* transaction. The performance of the seller that will create the obligation on the part of the buyer is, at this point, a future transaction; hence, a purchase commitment is not a liability. Another example is a company's long-term salary contract with an executive. When the agreement is signed, each party is committed to perform in the future—the executive to render services and the company to pay for those services. The company does not record a liability when the contract is signed, because at this point the executive has not yet rendered any services.

Although they involve definite future cash payments, the foregoing examples are not reported as liabilities because they are related to future transactions. However, significant purchase commitments and executive compensation commitments should be disclosed in footnotes to the balance sheet.

In general, items shown as liabilities are often not legally due and payable on the balance sheet date. For example, the routine accrual of wages expense incurred but not paid during the period results in a credit balance account titled Wages Payable. In most cases, accrued wages are not legally due until several days after the balance sheet date. In the case of other accrued expenses—such as property taxes and executive bonuses—payment may not be legally due until months after the balance sheet date. Bonds payable, although shown as liabilities, may not be actually payable for several decades. These items are all reported as liabilities, however, because they are obligations resulting from past transactions that will be settled as the business continues to operate.

The determination of liabilities is basic to accounting properly for a firm's operations. For example, if a liability is omitted, then either an asset or an expense has been omitted also. If expense is involved, then income and owners' equity are misstated as well. Thus, the balance sheet or the income statement, or both, may be affected if liabilities are not reported correctly.

Most liabilities are satisfied by the eventual remittance of cash. Some may require a firm to furnish goods—for instance, a publisher obligated to provide issues of a magazine to customers who have subscribed in advance. Other liabilities may be obligations to provide services, for example, product warranties and maintenance contracts that accompany a new appliance or automobile.

Definition of Current Liabilities

For many years, current liabilities were considered obligations to be paid during the coming year—a simple and useful rule. The rule was subsequently made more flexible and broader in scope. The present version designates current liabilities as all obligations that will require within the coming year or the operating cycle, whichever is longer, (1) the use of existing current assets or (2) the creation of other current liabilities. We contrast the two versions of the rule by noting, for example, that a one-year note payable satisfied by the issuance of another short-term note is a current liability only under the later version of the rule. Also, the newer version has significant effects on firms in industries (for example, distilling and lumber) with operating cycles longer than one year.

Obligations that do not meet these guidelines are long-term liabilities. Two examples are mortgage notes payable and bonds payable, which we examine in Chapter 17.

Measurement of Current Liabilities

Generally speaking, current liabilities should be measured and shown in the balance sheet at the money amount necessary to satisfy the obligation. Of course, when future provision of services or goods is involved, the related dollar amount is only an estimate of the costs. The liability for product warranties, for example, may have to be estimated. Interest included in the face amount of a note payable is subtracted from the face amount when presenting the liability in the balance sheet. For example, if a company discounts its own note at the bank, the Discount on Notes Payable arising from this transaction is a contra account to the Notes Payable account.

EXAMPLES OF CURRENT LIABILITIES

In this section, we review the common types of current liabilities. Although not exhaustive, these concepts should enable you to look deeper into the accounting problems and techniques involved.

Trade Accounts and Notes Payable

In a balance sheet listing of current liabilities, amounts due to short-term creditors on open accounts or notes payable are commonly shown first. Most of the accounting procedures for accounts and notes payable are fairly routine and have been discussed in previous chapters. However, we should carefully account for transactions that occur shortly before and after the end of the accounting period. At the end of the period, recently received inventory items must be reflected as accounts payable, if unpaid, and as purchases of the period. Likewise, items that the company owns and for which a payable has been recorded must be included in inventory whether or not the items have been received. In other words, we need a proper "cut-off" of purchases, payables, and inventory for valid income determination and presentation of financial position.

Dividends Payable

Ordinary dividends are distributions of corporate earnings to stockholders. We discuss many of the accounting problems related to dividends in Chapter 16. Because the corporate board of directors determines the timing and amounts of dividends, they do not accrue as does interest expense. Instead, dividends are shown as liabilities only on formal declaration. Once declared, however, dividends are binding obligations of the corporation. Dividends are current liabilities because they are almost always paid within several weeks of the time they are declared.

Portions of Long-term Debt

The repayment of many long-term obligations is a series of installments over several years. To report liabilities involving installments properly, we should show the principal amount of the installments due within one year (or the operating cycle, if longer) as a current liability.

Sales and Excise Taxes

Many products and services are subject to sales and excise taxes. The laws governing these taxes usually require the retail (or selling) firm to collect the tax at the time of sale and to remit the collections periodically to the appropriate taxing agency. Assume that a particular product selling for $1,000 is subject to a 4% state sales tax and a 10% federal excise tax. Each tax should be figured on the basic sales price only. We record the above sale as follows:

Accounts Receivable (or Cash)	1,140	
Sales		1,000
Sales Tax Payable		40
Excise Tax Payable		100
To record sales and related taxes.		

Recording this transaction as a $1,140 sale is incorrect, because this overstates revenue and may lead to the omission of the liabilities for the taxes collected. The selling firm periodically completes a tax reporting form and remits the period's tax collections with it. The tax liability accounts are then debited and Cash is credited.

As an expedient, some firms record sales at the gross amount, including taxes collected. Then, to convert this type of revenue figure to actual sales, we divide the transaction total of $1,140 by 1.14 to yield $1,000 as the basic sales price and $140 as the total tax.

Estimated or Accrued Liabilities

Estimated or accrued liabilities are often referred to as *accrued expenses*. Generally they are the credits offsetting a series of debits to various expense accounts that are necessary for matching periodic revenue and expenses. Examples are the accrual of incurred (but unpaid) product warranty expense, various taxes, and vacation pay.

PRODUCT WARRANTIES   Many firms guarantee their products for a period of time after the sale. Proper matching of revenue and expenses requires that the estimated costs of providing these warranties be recognized as an expense of the period of sale rather than of a later period when the warranty costs may actually be paid.

Let us suppose that a firm sells a product for $300 per unit, which includes a 30-day warranty against defects. Past experience indicates that 3% of the units will prove defective and that the average repair cost is $40 per defective unit. Furthermore, during a particular month, product sales were $240,000, and 13 of the units sold in this month were defective and were repaired during the month. Using this information, we calculate the accrued liability for product warranties at the end of the month as follows:

Number of units sold ($240,000/$300)	800
Rate of defective units	× 0.03
Total units expected to fail	24
Less: Units failed in month of sale	13
Units expected to fail in the remainder of the warranty period	11
Average repair cost per unit	× $ 40
Estimated liability for product warranty provision at end of period	$440

This accrued liability would be recorded at the end of the period of sale as

Product Warranty Expense	440	
Estimated Liability for Product Warranty		440
To record estimated warranty expense.		

When a unit fails in a future period, the repair costs will be recorded by debiting the accrued liability, Estimated Liability for Product Warranty, and crediting Cash, Supplies, and so forth.

PROPERTY TAXES   Property taxes are a primary source of revenue for city and county governments. The property taxes paid by business firms are, to some extent, the price for the many governmental services from which the firms benefit. Thus, property taxes are considered an operating expense that applies pro rata to each operating period.

Although procedures vary widely, property taxes are usually assessed annually. A typical sequence involves

(1) Determination of the tax rate by relating the total revenue needed to the total value of property taxed.

(2) Assessment of specific amounts of taxes against specific property parcels— at this time, the taxes are usually liens against the property.

(3) Payment of taxes, usually in one or two installments.

Taxes may be assessed and paid after or before the tax year to which they relate. For example, if property taxes are assessed during the fiscal year to which the taxes relate, firms must accrue an estimated amount of property tax expense (and the related liability) until they know their actual tax liability. To illustrate, let us assume Willetts Company, which ends its accounting year on December 31, is located in a city whose fiscal year runs from July 1 to June 30. City taxes are assessed on October 1 (for the fiscal year started the preceding July 1) and are paid by November 15. Willetts Company estimates in July that its property taxes for the next year will be $18,000. At the end of July, August, and September, the following entry would reflect the estimated monthly property taxes ($18,000/12 = $1,500):

Property Tax Expense	1,500	
⠀Estimated Property Taxes Payable		1,500
To record estimated property tax expense.		

On October 1, Willetts Company receives a $19,008 property tax bill from the city. Willetts' estimate for July–September is too low by $252 ($19,008/12 = $1,584; $1,584 − $1,500 = $84; $84 × 3 months = $252). The $252 difference may be handled as an increase in the property taxes for October. The entry to record the October taxes would then be:

Property Tax Expense ($1,584 + $252)	1,836	
⠀Estimated Property Taxes Payable		1,836
To record estimated property tax expense.		

The Estimated Property Taxes Payable account has a balance of $6,336 after the October entry. The entry on November 15 to record the property tax payment in full is:

Estimated Property Taxes Payable	6,336	
Prepaid Property Taxes	12,672	
⠀Cash		19,008
To record payment of property taxes.		

The balance in the Prepaid Property Taxes account is amortized to Property Tax Expense from November–June—$1,584 each month.

In contrast with the preceding illustration, if property taxes are assessed and paid before the taxing agency's fiscal year begins, the entire tax payment is initially charged to Prepaid Property Taxes. No estimates are necessary; the prepayment is simply amortized over the year to which the taxes apply.

INCOME TAXES The federal government, most states, and some municipalities levy income taxes against corporations, individuals, estates, and trusts. Sole proprietorships and partnerships are not taxable entities—their owners include the businesses' income on their personal tax returns. In the United States, income is generally reported annually on one or more income tax forms, and taxpayers compute (or assess themselves) the amount of tax due. The tax due is determined in accordance with generally accepted accounting principles, modified by the various tax laws, rulings of the taxing agencies, and many applicable court decisions. Because administration of tax laws is quite complex and many honest differences exist in their interpretation, the final tax liability for certain firms may not be settled until several years after a given tax year. Thus, the liability for income taxes is often an estimated obligation for some period of time.

Because corporations are separate taxable entities, they ordinarily incur a legal obligation for income taxes whenever corporate income is earned. Therefore, corporate financial statements are routinely adjusted for income tax liabilities. This adjustment is often recorded as follows:

Income Tax Expense	XXX	
Income Tax Payable		XXX
To record estimated income tax.		

Income Tax Expense may be included among the operating expenses in the income statement. Alternatively, to highlight the impact of income taxes, some companies derive an intermediate figure in the income statement labeled "income before income taxes." All expenses except income taxes are subtracted from revenue to derive this figure. Income taxes are then subtracted last in the income statement. Income taxes are discussed more fully in Chapter 28.

VACATION PAY   Most employees enjoy vacation privileges—typically, at least two weeks per year with regular pay. Depending on the particular agreement, an employee may earn some fraction of his or her annual vacation each payroll period. Other contracts may require a full year's employment before any vacation is given. In the latter case, the proportion of employees who earn annual vacations depends on the employee turnover rate.

Generally, an employer accrues vacation benefit expense if the employees' vacation benefits relate to service already rendered and they vest over time, as long as payment is probable and can be estimated.[1] Assume that a firm provides an annual two-week vacation for employees who have worked 50 weeks and that with the employee turnover rate, 80% of the staff will, in fact, receive vacation benefits. These employees earn the two weeks' vacation pay during the 50 weeks worked each year, or at the rate of 4% (2 weeks vacation/50 weeks worked). The proper accrual of vacation benefits expense for a $10,000 payroll would be

$$\$10,000 \times 0.04 \times 0.8 = \$320$$

The appropriate journal entry would be

Vacation Benefits Expense	320	
Estimated Liability for Vacation Benefits		320
To record estimated vacation benefits.		

---

[1]*Statement of Financial Accounting Standards No. 43*, "Accounting for Compensated Absences" (Stamford, CT: Financial Accounting Standards Board, 1980).

VACATION LIABILITIES

The Financial Accounting Standards Board has come up with a recent ruling that will force companies to recognize a new set of liabilities. The ruling, number 43, requires all employers to accrue a liability for future vacation benefits and those sick leave benefits used for extra time off. For firms with a large number of employees, such liabilities can be substantial, not least because employees often bank their benefits just like additional pay.

What's curious is that the FASB—along with the rest of the accounting world—has left the problem unresolved for municipalities. That's where the *real* vacation and sick leave liabilities are stocked away, since city leaders have for years sated employees with sick leave and vacation benefits in lieu of cash.

The origins of the corporate ruling date back to 1973, when the Civil Aeronautics Board ordered domestic airlines to accrue vacation benefits as a liability on their balance sheets instead of paying them out of expenses as they occurred. Eastern Air Lines had problems with the ruling. It was putting out $30 million a year in vacation pay, yet that liability didn't appear anywhere on the books. The CAB backed down in Eastern's case, and things were rosy until March 1977, when the company registered a $50 million debt offering with the SEC. The SEC blew the whistle: Record that liability on your balance sheet, it said, or forget about your debt issue. Eastern needed financing, so it was forced to comply, plopping a $35 million net loss onto its restated 1975 accounts. The result was a record $96 million loss for that year.

Now, with the FASB ruling, *all* companies have been ordered to record vacation and some sick leave benefits as a liability on their balance sheets. Of course, the blow to most companies' earnings will not be nearly as great as it was in the case of Eastern, because the FASB allows companies to assume the liability over previous years and restate earnings.

While that's the kind of liability an investor wants to know about, it's not a matter of life or death, of course, and often is so small it won't even show up as a separate line item. But with cities, these liabilities could be nearly enough to push them over the brink. According to a study of 100 cities published by Ernst & Whinney in 1979, 59% did not provide any information whatsoever on vacation and sick leave liabilities. Often, if cities don't disclose the information, they don't have it internally either.

Take the case of a Brookline, MA, assistant superintendent of schools who worked for around 20 years and rarely took a vacation or sick day. A month or so before she retired, the city discovered that she was due nearly $30,000 in accrued benefits. Yet that liability was never on the city's books. The retiring school official settled for somewhat less, and Brookline soon changed its vacation accrual policy.

In New York City, vacation and sick leave liabilities were first reported in the annual report in 1978. That year they amounted to $590 million. Last year, they hit $670 million but were still listed as long-term obligations. If they were shown as short-term liabilities, they could conceivably increase New York's $3.2 billion net general fund deficit to nearly $4 billion.

In 1979, the city of Dallas disclosed vacation liabilities of $8.6 million and a potential $33 million of sick pay liabilities. Contrast that with a mere $3.5 million in the general fund for that year.

Back in 1977, the SEC wouldn't allow Eastern Air Lines to go to the market until it cleaned up its vacation and sick leave liabilities. Why don't Standard & Poor's and Moody's—which have been acting as if they were going to impose good accounting on municipalities—make the same kind of threat?

From *Forbes*, May 11, 1981, page 211. "Off-the-Book Time Bombs," by Alyssa Lappen. Copyright Forbes Inc., 1981.

When the vacation benefits are paid, the amount would be recorded as follows:

Estimated Liability for Vacation Benefits	XXX	
Cash		XXX
To record payment of vacation benefits.		

This treatment reflects the annual vacation expense in the appropriate periods and recognizes throughout the year the accrued liability for vacation benefits.

CONTINGENT LIABILITIES

A contingent liability is an obligation that *may* develop out of an existing situation. Whether or not the obligation develops depends on the occurrence of a future event.

If the future event will probably occur and the amount of the liability can be reasonably estimated, the liability should be recorded in the accounts.[2] The estimated liability for product warranty discussed earlier in the chapter is an example of this situation. Our analysis assumed that customers were likely to make claims under warranties for goods they had purchased and that a reasonable estimate of the amount of warranty obligation could be made.

When the future event will likely not occur or the amount of the liability cannot be reasonably estimated, contingent liabilities are not recorded in the accounts. They should, when significant, be disclosed in the financial statements either in a parenthetical note in the body of the statements or as a footnote to the balance sheet. Some common examples of contingent liabilities are given below.

Notes receivable discounted   As explained in Chapter 8, firms that discount (sell to others) notes receivable with recourse are contingently liable for their payment should the original maker fail to honor the note. We noted that this contingent liability is usually disclosed in a footnote to the balance sheet.

Credit guarantees   To accommodate important but less financially secure suppliers or customers, a firm may guarantee the other company's debt by cosigning a note. Until the original debtor satisfies the obligation, the cosigning firm is contingently liable for the debt.

Lawsuits   In the course of its operations, a firm may be the defendant in a lawsuit involving potential damage awards. During the time a lawsuit is pending, the firm should disclose in its financial statements the nature of the suit and any potential liability.

Additional income tax assessments   Earlier in this chapter, we explained that many aspects of income tax laws and rulings are subject to a significant degree of interpretation. Consequently, many firms do not know their final income

[2]*Statement of Financial Accounting Standards No. 5*, "Accounting for Contingencies" (Stamford, CT: Financial Accounting Standards Board, 1975).

tax liability for a given tax period until the related return has been audited or until the applicable statute of limitations becomes effective. The federal statute of limitations for income taxes is three years. No statute of limitations exists in cases of fraud or failure to file returns. Proposed assessments for additional taxes often are contested in court for extended periods. During this time, the taxpaying firm is contingently liable for the proposed additional tax.

PAYROLL ACCOUNTING

Wages and salaries represent a major element in the cost structure of most businesses. Indeed, the largest single expense incurred by some service businesses may be the compensation paid to employees. As we examine the procedures and requirements associated with accounting for salaries and wages, we see that several different current liabilities are related to a company's payroll expense.

IMPACT OF LEGISLATION ON PAYROLL PROCEDURES

Payroll accounting procedures are influenced significantly by legislation enacted by the federal and state governments. These laws levy taxes based on payroll amounts, establish remittance and reporting requirements for employers, and set up certain minimium standards for wages and hours.

Levy of Taxes

FEDERAL INSURANCE CONTRIBUTIONS ACT   In the mid-1930s, the federal government enacted a national Social Security program to provide workers with a continuing source of income during retirement. The program has been expanded several times since then, one example being the 1965 enactment of the Medicare program of hospital and medical insurance for persons 65 years of age and older. Today, in addition to health insurance benefits for eligible people, Social Security provides monthly payments to workers and their dependents when a worker retires, is disabled, or dies.

Monthly benefit payments and hospital insurance protection under Medicare are financed by taxes levied on employees, their employers, and self-employed people. Approximately 9 out of 10 employed persons in the United States currently earn Social Security protection through this process. Medical insurance under Medicare is financed by premiums paid by persons who enroll for this protection and from the general revenue of the federal government. Because we focus on payroll accounting in this chapter, we consider in more detail the financing provided by a tax on employees and their employers.

The Federal Insurance Contributions Act (FICA) establishes the tax levied on *both* employee and employer. A schedule of tax rates and the amount of earnings subject to the tax are amended at intervals. At this writing, the future solvency of the Social Security program is of serious concern, and increases in the tax rates are being considered, along with other measures. A National Commission on Social Security Reform has made certain recommendations, one of which is the following rate schedule for the next few years:

Calendar Year	FICA Rate
1984	7.0 %
1985	7.05
1986–1987	7.15

The FICA tax applies to wages paid to employees during a calendar year, up to a certain amount per employee. For example, in 1984 the tax is applied to the first $35,700 of an employee's wages. At a 7% rate, the maximum tax on any one employee in a year would be 7% × $35,700 = $2,499. The amount of earnings subject to the FICA tax may be revised from time to time.

The employee's tax is deducted from each paycheck by the employer. The amount of tax levied on the employer and the employee is the same. At a 7% rate, the employer's total tax for a year would equal 0.07 times the total amount of employees' wages subject to FICA tax during the year. We use the 7% rate in our illustrations and problems.

FEDERAL UNEMPLOYMENT TAX ACT   The Federal Unemployment Tax Act (FUTA) is also part of the federal Social Security program. The states and the national Social Security Administration work together in a joint unemployment insurance program. FUTA raises funds to help finance the administration of the unemployment compensation programs operated by the states. Generally, funds collected under this act are not paid out as unemployment compensation benefits, but are used to pay administrative costs at the federal and state levels. In times of high unemployment, however, the federal government may appropriate funds from its general revenue to provide extended unemployment benefits.

FUTA generates funds by a payroll tax levied only on the employer. For 1983 and 1984, the rate is 3.5% of the first $7,000 of an employee's wages. However, the employer is entitled to a credit against this tax for unemployment taxes paid to the state. The maximum credit allowed is 2.7% of the first $7,000 of each employee's wages. Because states typically set their basic unemployment tax rates at this maximum credit, the effective FUTA rate on the employer is generally 0.8% (3.5% − 2.7%) of the first $7,000 of each employee's wages.

On January 1, 1985, the tax rate increases to 6.2%, with employers eligible for a credit up to 5.4% for state unemployment taxes paid. However, in our illustrations and problems, we use the 1984 rate of 3.5% of the first $7,000 of wages and assume that the employer receives a 2.7% credit, giving an effective rate of 0.8%.

STATE UNEMPLOYMENT COMPENSATION TAXES   Benefit payments to compensate individuals for wages lost during unemployment are handled through unemployment compensation programs administered by each state. Generally, a worker who becomes unemployed through no fault of his or her own, is able to work, and is available for work is eligible for unemployment benefits. The duration and amount of benefits typically depend on the worker's length of employment and average wage during a previous base period.

The funds for unemployment benefits are generated in most states by a payroll tax levied exclusively on *employers*. In a few states, the employee must also contribute. Because of the credit allowed against the FUTA tax, states usually establish their unemployment tax rate for new employers at 2.7% of the first $7,000 of wages paid each employee. However, the rate may vary over time according to an employer's experience rating. Employers with records of stable employment may pay less than the basic rate, while employers with irregular employment records may pay more than the basic rate. An employer with a favorable experience rating who pays less than the basic rate is still entitled to the maximum 2.7% credit against the federal unemployment tax.

We should remember that FICA, FUTA, and state unemployment taxes are levied on certain maximum amounts of payroll. Throughout the calendar year, employers must be alert to the fact that a greater amount of each period's wages may no longer be subject to one or more of these taxes. The following schedule indicates the possible divergence between the total payroll for a period and the payroll subject to the FICA and unemployment taxes.

Total payroll	$205,000
Wages subject to FICA tax (In 1984, for example, excludes any wages in excess of $35,700 per employee.)	176,000
Wages subject to FUTA and state unemployment taxes (Excludes any wages in excess of $7,000 per employee.)	59,000

FEDERAL INCOME TAX WITHHOLDING   Employers are required to withhold federal income taxes from wages and salaries paid to employees. Current withholding of income taxes facilitates the government's collection of the tax and also eliminates the possible burden on the employee of having to pay a tax on income after the income has been used for other purposes.

The amount of income tax withheld from each employee is based on the amount of the employee's wage or salary, the employee's marital status, and the number of withholding allowances to which the employee is entitled. When first employed, each employee reports his or her marital status, Social Security number, and number of withholding allowances to the employer on an *Employee's Withholding Allowance Certificate*, also known as *Form W-4*. Employees file new W-4s if withholding allowances or marital status change. Employees are entitled to each of the withholding allowances for which they qualify, including one for the employee, one for his or her spouse, and one for each dependent. Additional allowances may be claimed if the employee is (1) 65 or older, or (2) blind, or if the employee's spouse is (3) 65 or older, or (4) blind. An employee may also claim one or more additional allowances based on expected excessive itemized deductions on his or her annual income tax return.

Employers usually use the government's wage-bracket tables to determine the amount of federal income taxes to withhold from each employee. These tables indicate the amounts to withhold at different wage levels for different numbers of withholding allowances. Exhibit 12–1 illustrates a few lines from a 1983 wage-bracket table.

Alternatively, employers may use the percentage method, which is especially useful when no wage-bracket tables pertain to the length of the payroll period in question. Both the wage-bracket tables and the percentage method incorporate a

EXHIBIT 12–1
Wage-bracket Table

WEEKLY Payroll Period—Employee MARRIED											
And the wages are—		And the number of withholding allowances claimed is—										
At least	But less than	0	1	2	3	4	5	6	7	8	9	10 or more
		The amount of income tax to be withheld shall be—										
$300	$310	$40.80	$37.20	$33.50	$29.90	$26.30	$23.20	$20.10	$17.10	$14.00	$10.90	$ 8.00
310	320	42.70	39.10	35.40	31.80	28.10	24.80	21.70	18.70	15.60	12.50	9.40
320	330	44.60	41.00	37.30	33.70	30.00	26.40	23.30	20.30	17.20	14.10	11.00
330	340	46.50	42.90	39.20	35.60	31.90	28.30	24.90	21.90	18.80	15.70	12.60
340	350	48.40	44.80	41.10	37.50	33.80	30.20	26.50	23.50	20.40	17.30	14.20
350	360	50.30	46.70	43.00	39.40	35.70	32.10	28.40	25.10	22.00	18.90	15.80

graduated system of withholding. That is, the withholding rates increase as the earnings subject to withholding increase.

STATE INCOME TAX WITHHOLDING   Most states now have an income tax that is withheld by employers. Payroll procedures for withholding state income taxes are similar to those for withholding federal income taxes.

INCIDENCE OF PAYROLL TAXES   Taxes related to payroll amounts may be levied on the employee, the employer, or both. Exhibit 12–2 summarizes the incidence of the various payroll taxes we have just discussed.

Employee versus Independent Contractor

Salaries and wages paid to employees provide the basis for withholding taxes from employees and levying payroll taxes on the employer. Independent contractors are not subject to withholding and are therefore distinguished from employees. In general, an *employee* performs services subject to the supervision and control of another party known as the employer. The following variables

EXHIBIT 12–2
Incidence of Taxes Related to Payroll Amounts

Tax	Employer	Employee
Federal Insurance Contributions Act	X	X
Federal Unemployment Tax Act	X	
State Unemployment Compensation Taxes	X	In a few states
Federal Income Tax Withholding		X
State Income Tax Withholding		X

establish the existence of an employer–employee relationship: (1) the employer has the power to discharge the individual worker, (2) the employer sets the work hours for the individual worker, and (3) the employer furnishes a place to work. An *independent contractor*, on the other hand, may also perform services for a business firm, but that firm does not have the legal right to direct and control the methods used by this person. Independent contractors are in business for themselves; examples are certified public accountants, lawyers, and physicians.

Wages are the earnings of employees who are paid on an hourly or piecework basis. *A salary* is the compensation of employees paid on a monthly or annual basis. In practice, however, these terms are used more or less synonymously. Amounts paid to independent contractors are identified as *fees*. For example, the expense account Audit Fees may be charged for the amounts paid to a certified public accountant for audit work, and Legal Fees may be charged for payments to a lawyer for legal work.

Remittance and Reporting Requirements

The legislation levying various taxes on payroll amounts also specifies the procedures for remitting these taxes to the government and establishes the reports an employer must file. A sound system of payroll accounting ensures that these payments are made and reports are filed on time.

FICA TAXES AND FEDERAL INCOME TAXES WITHHELD   Employer remittance and reporting requirements are the same for both employer's and employees' FICA taxes and federal income taxes withheld, because these taxes are combined for payment and reporting purposes. Generally, remittances are deposited in a Federal Reserve bank or authorized commercial bank. The specific remittance requirements vary depending on the combined dollar amount of the taxes. An employer has three banking days to make a deposit if the unpaid taxes are at least $3,000 by the 3rd, 7th, 11th, 15th, 19th, 22nd, 25th, or last day of the month. At the end of any month, undeposited taxes of $500–$3,000 must be deposited within 15 days. If the undeposited taxes are less than $500 at the end of a calendar quarter, the amount must be deposited within one month (or paid with the employer's quarterly tax return).

Each quarter, employers file an Employer's Quarterly Federal Tax Return, Form 941, with the Internal Revenue Service. On this form, the employer schedules a record of its liability for FICA taxes and withheld income taxes throughout the quarter and reports its deposits of these taxes.

By January 31, an employer must give each employee two copies of *Form W-2, Wage and Tax Statement*, which specifies the employee's total wages paid, the federal income taxes withheld, the wages subject to FICA tax, and the FICA tax withheld for the preceding calendar year. The worker attaches one copy of Form W-2 to his or her federal income tax return. The employer sends a copy of each employee's Form W-2 to the Social Security Administration, which, in turn, provides the Internal Revenue Service with the income tax data that it needs from these forms.

FEDERAL UNEMPLOYMENT INSURANCE TAXES   The amount due on federal unemployment insurance taxes must be reviewed quarterly. If undeposited taxes exceed $100 at the end of any of the first three quarters of a year, a deposit must be made in a Federal Reserve bank or authorized commercial bank during the first month after the quarter. If the amount due is $100 or less, no deposit is necessary. By January 31, each employer must file a Form 940, Employer's Annual Federal Unemployment Tax Return, for the preceding year. If the annual tax reported on Form 940, less deposits made, exceeds $100, the entire amount due must be deposited by January 31. If this amount is $100 or less, it may be either deposited or remitted with Form 940.

STATE UNEMPLOYMENT COMPENSATION TAXES The filing and payment requirements for unemployment compensation taxes vary among the states. Often, however, employers must pay the taxes when they file quarterly reports. Some states require payments more frequently, sometimes monthly, if the taxes owed by an employer exceed a preestablished level.

Wages and Hours

FAIR LABOR STANDARDS ACT The Fair Labor Standards Act establishes minimum wage, overtime pay, and equal pay standards for employees covered by the act and sets record-keeping requirements for their employers. The act's coverage has been amended several times since its passage in 1938. Its provisions now extend, with certain exemptions, to employees directly or indirectly engaged in interstate commerce and to domestic service workers. Executive, administrative, and professional employees are exempt from the act's minimum wage and overtime provisions.

At this writing, for example, the minimum wage that an employee must receive in 1983 is $3.35 per hour. Of course, employers and employees may agree to higher wages. Employers often operate under contracts negotiated with their employees' unions that provide more favorable terms to employees than the standards provided by the Fair Labor Standards Act.

A covered employee must be paid an amount equal to at least $1\frac{1}{2}$ times that employee's regular pay rate for every hour beyond 40 that he or she works in a week. The following are some examples of overtime pay computations under this standard; the examples differ by the basic method of compensating the employee.

(1) Jody Green receives $5.10 per hour as her regular rate of pay. Her overtime rate of pay is $7.65 ($5.10 + $2.55) per hour. This week she worked 44 hours. Her gross earnings this week are $234.60, computed as (40 hours × $5.10/hour) + (4 hours × $7.65/hour).

(2) Jack Tyler is paid on a piece rate basis. His earnings this week, before any overtime compensation, are $206.40 for 43 hours of work. For overtime pay computations, his regular hourly rate of pay is determined by dividing his weekly earnings on a piece rate basis by the number of hours worked in that week, or $206.40/43 = $4.80. For each hour worked over 40 in the week, Tyler is entitled to an overtime premium of $2.40 ($\frac{1}{2}$ of $4.80). Therefore, his total earnings this week are $206.40 + $7.20 (3 hours × $2.40) = $213.60.

The act permits an alternative way to compute overtime for piece rate workers, if agreed upon in advance of the work. This method pays $1\frac{1}{2}$ times the piece rate for each piece produced during overtime hours.

(3) Bill Jantz receives a salary of \$240 for a 40-hour workweek. This week he worked 46 hours. Bill's regular rate of pay is computed at \$6 per hour (\$240/ 40); his overtime rate of pay is \$6 $\times$ $1\frac{1}{2}$, or \$9 per hour. Bill's gross earnings for the current 46-hour week are \$240 + (6 $\times$ \$9), or \$294.

Again, we note that employees may negotiate overtime pay rates in excess of the minimum standard illustrated in the preceding discussion. A union contract, for example, may require double the regular pay rate for hours worked on Sundays and holidays.

Under the Fair Labor Standards Act, employers may not discriminate on the basis of sex in the rates paid to men and women employees performing equal work on jobs demanding equal skill, effort, and responsibility and having similar working conditions. The equal pay provisions also provide that employers must eliminate illegal pay differentials by a means other than reducing employee pay rates. The law does permit wage differentials between men and women when due to a job-related factor other than sex, such as a difference based on a bona fide seniority or merit system.

Employers are required under the law to maintain a detailed record of each employee's wage and hours, including the hour and day the employee's workweek begins, the regular hourly rate of pay, the total overtime pay for any week in which more than 40 hours are worked, the deductions from and additions to wages, and the employee's total wages paid each period. The law does not prescribe any particular form for these records. The payroll records maintained in a typical payroll accounting system contain much of this information, which is also needed to comply with other laws and regulations.

OTHER PAYROLL DEDUCTIONS

In addition to FICA taxes, federal income taxes, and perhaps state and local income taxes, other items may be deducted from an employee's gross earnings in arriving at the net *take-home* pay for the period. Each additional deduction must be authorized by the employee; often this is done individually, although in some instances the union contract provides the authorization needed by the employer. Examples of these items are payments for

(1) Union dues.

(2) Premiums on life, accident, hospital, surgical care, or major medical insurance.

(3) Installment loan from employees' credit union.

(4) Advance from employer.

(5) U.S. savings bonds.

(6) Contributions to charitable organizations.

(7) Retirement plan.

NET PAY COMPUTATION FOR INDIVIDUAL EMPLOYEE

To illustrate the computation of an individual employee's net pay for a payroll period, let us assume Donald Bork's regular salary is $320 for a 40-hour work-week. He is married and claims three withholding allowances on Form W-4. He has authorized his employer to deduct $3 per week from his earnings for group hospital insurance and $2 per week as a contribution to the United Way Charity. During the current week, he works 42 hours. Prior to the current week, his gross earnings for the year are $1,328. The applicable FICA tax rate is 7%. The amount paid to Donald Bork is shown in the following summary:

Gross earnings		$344.00
Deductions:		
FICA tax (@ 7%)	$24.08	
Federal income tax withheld	37.50	
Group hospital insurance	3.00	
United Way Charity contribution	2.00	
Total deductions		66.58
Net earnings		$277.42

An explanation of these amounts follows:

(1) Gross earnings—Bork's regular hourly pay rate is $320 ÷ 40 hours, or $8. His overtime pay rate is $1\frac{1}{2} \times$ $8, or $12 per hour. Because Bork worked two hours overtime, his overtime pay is 2 × $12 = $24. His gross pay equals his regular salary plus his overtime pay ($320 + $24 = $344).

(2) FICA tax—Bork's gross earnings to date for the year ($1,672) have not yet exceeded the maximum to which the FICA tax applies. Therefore, the FICA tax on Bork's earnings is 7% × $344 = $24.08.

(3) Federal income tax withheld—We apply the wage-bracket table of Exhibit 12–1 to this illustration. From this table, we see that the income tax withheld from a married employee with three withholding allowances earning wages of at least $340 but less than $350 per week is $37.50.

(4) Group hospital insurance and charitable contribution—Bork has specifically authorized his employer to make these deductions.

PAYROLL RECORDS

The precise nature of an enterprise's payroll records and procedures depends to a great extent on the size of the work force and the degree to which the record keeping is automated. In some form, however, two records are basic to most payroll systems—the payroll register and individual employee earnings records.

The Payroll Register

The **payroll register,** prepared each pay period, lists the company's complete payroll in detail. Each employee's earnings and deductions for the period are contained in the payroll register. Exhibit 12–3 (page 423) illustrates a typical payroll register for a firm with a small number of employees. The pay period covered by this payroll register is one week.

In Exhibit 12–3, the column immediately after each employee's name shows the total hours worked by that employee during the week. Data on the hours worked are taken from time cards or similar documents maintained for each employee. In this illustration, each employee is paid a regular salary for a 40-hour workweek. The regular salary is shown in the first column of the earnings section of the register. Overtime pay, computed at $1\frac{1}{2}$ times the regular hourly rate (Regular weekly salary ÷ 40), is presented in the next column. The employees' gross earnings appear in the final column in the earnings section.

The 7% FICA tax is deducted from each employee's gross earnings. Because the payroll illustrated is early in the calendar year (the week ended February 4), no employee's earnings have exceeded the maximum amount of wages subject to the FICA tax. As discussed earlier, the federal income tax withheld is based on an employee's earnings, marital status, and number of withholding allowances. In Exhibit 12–3, for example, David Plank's relatively high federal income tax withheld is due to the fact that he is single and claims only one withholding allowance. The deductions for hospital insurance, contributions to charity, and purchases of U.S. savings bonds are specifically authorized by each employee affected by the deductions. The hospital insurance premiums vary with the number of persons covered by the plan.

An employee receives an amount equal to gross earnings less total deductions for the pay period. These net earnings are shown in the payment section of the payroll register, along with the number of the check issued by the company in payment of the wages.

In the last two columns of the payroll register, gross earnings are distributed between the office salaries and sales salaries categories. This division permits the total salaries for the period to be recorded in the proper expense accounts.

Recording the Payroll and Related Taxes

For some businesses, the payroll register is a special journal; in these cases the pertinent payroll register information is posted directly to the general ledger. Often, however, the payroll register is the basis for a general journal entry that is then posted to the general ledger. The journal entry to record the weekly payroll shown in Exhibit 12–3 would be

Office Salaries Expense	724.00	
Sales Salaries Expense	1,062.00	
FICA Tax Payable		125.02
Federal Income Tax Withholding Payable		197.80
Hospital Insurance Premiums Payable		18.50
United Way Contributions Payable		3.50
U.S. Savings Bond Deductions Payable		10.00
Payroll Payable		1,431.18
To record payroll for week ended February 4.		

EXHIBIT 12–3
Payroll Register
For the Week Ended February 4, 19X1

Employee	Total Hours	Earnings Regular	Earnings Overtime	Earnings Gross	FICA Tax	Federal Income Tax	Hospital Insurance	Other (see key)		Total Deductions	Net Earnings	Check No.	Office Salaries	Sales Salaries
Donald Bork	42	320	24	344	24.08	37.50	3.00	(A)	2.00	66.58	277.42	566	344	
Jane Latt	40	210		210	14.70	22.80	2.50	(B)	5.00	45.00	165.00	567		210
Raul Lopez	44	200	30	230	16.10	16.50	3.00			35.60	194.40	568		230
David Plank	40	300		300	21.00	46.40	2.00	(B)	5.00	74.40	225.60	569		300
Myra Smiken	44	280	42	322	22.54	42.00	3.00			67.54	254.46	570		322
Fred Wells	40	180		180	12.60	14.70	2.50	(A)	1.50	31.30	148.70	571	180	
Beth White	40	200		200	14.00	17.90	2.50			34.40	165.60	572	200	
Totals		1,690	96	1,786	125.02	197.80	18.50		13.50	354.82	1,431.18		724	1,062

Key: A—United Way Charity
B—U.S. Savings Bonds

The employer company may, when recording each payroll, also record its payroll tax liabilities. The year-to-date gross earnings for the employees in Exhibit 12–3 have not exceeded the maximum limits for either the FICA or unemployment taxes. The entry to record the employer's taxes for the week's payroll follows:

Payroll Tax Expense	187.53	
FICA Tax Payable (7% × $1,786)		125.02
Federal Unemployment Tax Payable		
(0.8% × $1,786)		14.29
State Unemployment Tax Payable		
(2.7% × $1,786)		48.22
To record payroll tax expense for week		
ended February 4.		

Payment of the Liabilities

The various liabilities established in the entries recording the payroll and the employer's payroll taxes are settled when the employer makes payments to the appropriate parties. The issuance of the employees' payroll checks results in the following entry:

Payroll Payable	1,431.18	
Cash		1,431.18
To pay net payroll for week ended		
February 4.		

The FICA taxes, federal income taxes withheld, and federal unemployment insurance taxes are remitted to a depository bank in accordance with the remittance requirements discussed earlier. The state unemployment compensation taxes are remitted to the appropriate state agency, according to the state's requirements. The hospital insurance premiums are sent to the company providing the coverage, the United Way contributions are paid to that charitable organization, and the deductions for the purchase of U.S. savings bonds are remitted to the financial institution handling the acquisition of the bonds. If any of these liabilities remain unpaid when financial statements are prepared, they are classified as current liabilities in the balance sheet.

Accrual of Employer Payroll Taxes

Employer payroll taxes are based on employees' salaries and wages. A company that accrues wages and salaries with a year-end adjusting entry should also record the related employer payroll taxes as year-end adjustments. Payroll taxes are properly an expense of the period during which the related salaries and wages were earned, although the employer is *legally* obligated for these taxes in the period the salaries and wages are actually paid. This circumstance, coupled with a possibly immaterial amount of payroll taxes, leads some companies to an alternative procedure: They record the total amount of payroll taxes only in the year the payroll is paid.

Individual Employee Earnings Record

Employers maintain an **individual earnings record** for each employee. This record contains much of the information needed for the employer to comply with the various taxation and reporting requirements established by law. Exhibit 12–4 illustrates Donald Bork's individual earnings record, for the first five weeks of 19X1.

EXHIBIT 12-4
Individual Employee Earnings Record

Employee's Name _____ Donald Bork _____   Social Security No. _____ 719-23-4866 _____   Employee No. _____ 6

Address _____ 510 Many Lane _____   Male __X__   Single _____   Weekly Pay Rate _____ $320.00

_____ Archer, Florida 32600 _____   Female _____   Married __X__   Hourly Equivalent _____ $8.00

Date of Birth _____ May 6, 1946   Withholding Allowances _____ 3

Position _____ Clerk-Analyst   Date of Employment _____ June 1, 19X0

   Date Employment Ended _____

| 19X1 | | Earnings | | | Deductions | | | | | Payment | | Cumulative |
Period Ended	Total Hours	Regular	Overtime	Gross	FICA Tax	Federal Income Tax	Hospital Insurance	Other: A—United Way B—Savings Bonds	Total Deductions	Net Earnings	Check No.	Gross Earnings
Jan. 7	40	320.00		320.00	22.40	33.70	3.00	A2.00	61.10	258.90	412	320.00
Jan. 14	44	320.00	48.00	368.00	25.76	41.30	3.00	A2.00	72.06	295.94	447	688.00
Jan. 21	40	320.00		320.00	22.40	33.70	3.00	A2.00	61.10	258.90	480	1,008.00
Jan. 28	40	320.00		320.00	22.40	33.70	3.00	A2.00	61.10	258.90	525	1,328.00
Feb. 4	42	320.00	24.00	344.00	24.08	37.50	3.00	A2.00	66.58	277.42	566	1,672.00

The individual earnings record contains the details on earnings and deductions shown earlier in the payroll register. In addition, the cumulative gross earnings column alerts the employer when an employee's yearly earnings have exceeded the maximum amounts to which the FICA and unemployment taxes apply.

Employers prepare Form W-2—the Wage and Tax Statement sent to every employee each year—from the individual employee earnings records. Although Form W-2 is sent only once and covers an entire year, employers typically provide employees with an earnings statement each pay period, detailing the earnings and deductions for that period. These earnings statements may be a detachable portion of the employee's paycheck or may be enclosed as a separate document with the paycheck.

PAYMENT TO EMPLOYEES

A company with a small number of employees may pay them with checks drawn on the firm's regular bank account. A company with a large number of employees usually establishes a separate bank account to pay the payroll.

Payroll Bank Account

A company with a separate payroll bank account draws a check on its regular bank account each pay period in an amount equal to the total net earnings of the employees. This check is deposited in the payroll bank account. Individual payroll checks are then drawn on this account and delivered to the employees. The issuance of the payroll checks reduces to zero the book balance in the payroll bank account.

One advantage of maintaining a separate payroll bank account is that it divides the work between the preparation and issuance of regular company checks and payroll checks. A related advantage is that it simplifies the monthly reconciliation of the regular bank account. The large number of payroll checks, many of which may be outstanding at month-end, are not run through the regular bank account. Of course, the payroll bank account must also be reconciled, but the only reconciling items for this bank account are payroll checks outstanding.

Payment in Cash

Sometimes employees are paid in currency and coin rather than by check. This may happen, for example, if the employees work in a location where it may not be convenient for them to deposit or cash checks. The company prepares and cashes its own checks for the payroll amount. Each employee's pay is delivered to the employee in an envelope. For internal control, and to have evidence of the payment, an employee signs a receipt for the payroll envelope. Often the outside of the envelope contains an itemization of the employee's gross earnings and deductions for the period.

KEY POINTS TO REMEMBER

(1) Liabilities are obligations resulting from past transactions to pay money, provide goods, or perform services in the future.

(2) Current liabilities must be satisfied within the coming year or the operating cycle, whichever is longer. To meet these obligations, a firm must use existing current assets or create other current liabilities.

(3) Failure to accrue liabilities properly will cause a misstatement of financial position and reported income.

(4) A contingent liability is an obligation that depends on the occurrence of a future event. A contingent liability is recorded in the accounts if the future event will probably occur and if the amount of the liability can be reasonably estimated.

(5) Payroll accounting is influenced significantly by several legislative acts. Payroll transactions involve a series of withholdings from the employee's wages and a series of payroll taxes levied against the employer.

(6) A payroll register lists information on the gross earnings and deductions of all employees for each payroll period. Individual employee earnings records contain information on gross earnings and deductions for each employee for all payroll periods during the year.

QUESTIONS

12–1 For accounting purposes, how are *liabilities* defined?

12–2 Present a general rule for measuring current liabilities on the balance sheet.

12–3 Define *current liabilities*.

12–4 "Because they are a matter of governmental discretion, property taxes should be recognized as expense in the period in which the assessment becomes a lien against the property involved." Comment on this statement.

12–5 Under what conditions should an employer accrue employees' vacation benefits?

12–6 Define *contingent liabilities*. List three examples of contingent liabilities. When should contingent liabilities be recorded in the accounts?

12–7 On whom is the FICA tax levied? What does the FICA tax finance?

12–8 On whom are the federal and state unemployment insurance taxes levied? What do these taxes finance?

12–9 Why does an employee file a Form W-4, Employee's Withholding Allowance Certificate, with his or her employer?

12–10 What is the difference between an employee and an independent contractor?

12–11 What does Form W-2, Wage and Tax Statement, report? Who receives copies of this form?

12–12 Michael Burns is employed at $7.50 per hour. Under the Fair Labor Standards Act, how many hours in a week must he work before he is entitled to overtime pay? What is the minimum overtime rate of pay he must receive?

12–13 List at least five examples of deductions from an employee's gross earnings other than FICA taxes and federal income taxes withheld.

12–14 What is a payroll register? How does it differ from an individual employee earnings record?

12–15 If earned but unpaid wages are accrued at year-end, should employer payroll taxes on these wages be accrued at the same time? Explain.

12–16 List two advantages of maintaining a special payroll bank account for the payment of a net payroll.

EXERCISES

12–17 For each of the following situations, indicate the amount shown as a liability on the balance sheet of Fields, Inc. at December 31, 19X2.
  (a) Fields has trade accounts payable of $60,000 for merchandise included in the 19X2 ending inventory.
  (b) Fields has agreed to purchase a $12,000 drill press in January 19X3.
  (c) During November and December of 19X2, Fields sold products to a firm and guaranteed them against product failure for 90 days. Estimated costs of honoring this provision during 19X3 are $800.
  (d) On December 15, 19X2, Fields declared a $40,000 cash dividend payable on January 15, 19X3, to stockholders of record on December 31, 19X2.
  (e) Fields provides a profit-sharing bonus for its executives equal to 5% of the reported before-tax income for the current year. The estimated income (as defined above) for 19X2 is $240,000.

12–18 Allen Company has just billed a customer for $603.20, an amount that includes a 10% excise tax and a 6% state sales tax.
  (a) What amount of revenue is recorded?
  (b) Present a general journal entry to record the transaction on the books of Allen Company.

12–19 Kendall, Inc.'s current vacation policy for its production workers provides four weeks paid vacation at the end of a full year's employment. An analysis of the company's employee turnover rates indicates that approximately 10% of the employees will forfeit their vacation benefits.
  (a) Compute the proper provision for estimated vacation benefits for a four-week period in which the total pay earned by the employee group was $157,500.
  (b) Present a general journal entry to recognize the above vacation benefits.

12–20 Graybar Company sells an electric timer that carries a 60-day unconditional warranty against product failure. Based on a reliable statistical analysis, Graybar knows that between the sale and lapse of the product warranty, 2% of the units sold will require repair at an average cost of $20 per unit. The following data reflect Graybar's recent experience.

	October	November	December
Units sold	16,000	14,000	20,000
Known product failures from sales of:			
October	80	160	80
November		40	140
December			90

Calculate and prepare a general journal entry to record properly the estimated liability for product warranties at December 31. Assume that warranty costs of known failures have already been reflected in the records.

12–21 James Bell is an employee subject to the Fair Labor Standards Act. His regular pay rate is $8 per hour, and he is paid overtime at $1\frac{1}{2}$ times his regular pay rate. He worked 43 hours in the current week. His gross earnings prior to the current week are $9,600. He is married and claims four withholding allowances on Form W-4. No deductions other than FICA and federal income taxes are subtracted from his paycheck. Compute the following amounts related to Bell's current week's wages:

(a) Regular earnings.
(b) Overtime earnings.
(c) FICA taxes (assume 7% rate).
(d) Federal income tax withheld (use wage-bracket table in Exhibit 12–1).
(e) Net earnings.

12–22 Regent Company's August payroll register shows total gross earnings of $156,000. Of this amount, $11,000 is not subject to FICA taxes, and $148,000 is above the maximum amount subject to federal and state unemployment taxes. Regent Company has a favorable employment record, so its state unemployment tax rate is 2%. It is subject to a 7% FICA tax and a 0.8% federal unemployment tax. Prepare the general journal entry to record Regent Company's payroll tax expense for August.

12–23 Amy Winslow is an employee subject to the Fair Labor Standards Act who is paid on a piece rate basis. Her earnings for the current week, before any overtime compensation, are $294.40 for 46 hours of work. For each hour over 40 worked in a week, she receives an overtime premium of one-half her regular hourly pay rate based on the total hours worked in that week. Her gross earnings prior to the current week were $6,600. She is married and claims one withholding allowance on Form W-4. No deductions other than FICA and federal income taxes are subtracted from her paycheck. Compute the following amounts related to Winslow's current week's wages:

(a) Regular hourly pay rate.
(b) Gross earnings.
(c) FICA taxes (assume 7% rate).
(d) Federal income tax withheld (use wage-bracket table in Exhibit 12–1).
(e) Net earnings.

PROBLEMS

12–24 Sloan Company prepares monthly financial statements and ends its accounting year on December 31. Its headquarters building is located in the city of Freeport. City taxes are assessed on September 1 each year, are paid by October 15, and relate to the city's fiscal year which ends the next June 30 (10 months after assessment). For the city tax year 19X5–19X6, Sloan paid $40,000 in property taxes on its headquarters building.

REQUIRED
(a) What amount of property tax expense should be accrued on the financial statements for July 19X6, if property taxes for 19X6–19X7 are an estimated 5% higher than the preceding year?
(b) Assume that the 19X6–19X7 tax bill received on September 1, 19X6, was for $43,800 and that the estimate in part (a) was used through August.

What is the proper monthly property tax expense for September 19X6, if the deficiencies in the monthly property tax estimates through August are handled as an increase in the property tax expense for September 19X6?

(c) How does the payment of the tax bill on October 15, 19X6, affect the amount of property tax expense recognized for October?

12–25 Grant Corporation had the following payroll for February 19X1:

Officers' salaries	$30,000
Sales salaries	84,000
Income taxes withheld	23,500
FICA taxes withheld	7,980
Hospital insurance premiums deducted	1,200
United Way contributions deducted	750
Salaries (included above) subject to unemployment taxes	90,000

REQUIRED

Present general journal entries to record:

(a) Accrual of the payroll.

(b) Payment of the net payroll.

(c) Accrual of employer's payroll taxes. (Assume that the FICA tax matches the amount withheld, the federal unemployment tax is 0.8%, and the state unemployment tax is 2.7%.)

(d) Payment of all liabilities related to this payroll. (Assume all are settled at the same time.)

12–26 Sierra Corporation initially records its sales at amounts that include any related excise and sales taxes. During June 19XX, Sierra recorded total sales of $150,640. An analysis of June sales indicated the following:

(1) Four-tenths of sales were subject to both a 10% excise tax and a 4% sales tax.

(2) One-half of sales were subject only to the sales tax.

(3) The balance of sales were for labor charges not subject to either excise or sales tax.

REQUIRED

Calculate the amount of sales revenue for June 19XX, and the related liabilities for excise and sales taxes.

12–27 The following data are taken from Deerfield Wholesale Company's July 19X5 payroll:

Administrative salaries	$32,000
Sales salaries	48,000
Custodial salaries	6,000
Total payroll	$86,000
Wages subject to FICA tax	$72,000
Wages subject to FUTA and state unemployment taxes	9,000
Income taxes withheld from all salaries	17,600

Assume that (1) FICA taxes are 7% each for the employee and the employer and (2) the company is subject to a 2% state unemployment tax (due to a favorable experience rating) and a 0.8% federal unemployment tax on the first $7,000 paid to each employee.

REQUIRED

Record the following in general journal form:
(a) Accrual of the payroll.
(b) Payment of the net payroll.
(c) Accrual of the employer's payroll taxes.
(d) Payment of the above payroll-related liabilities. (Assume all are settled at the same time.)

12-28 The Chapman Company employs five persons, one of whom receives a $500 salary for a 40-hour week; the other four are paid an hourly rate. All employees receive overtime pay at $1\frac{1}{2}$ times their regular pay rate. Data relating to the payroll for the week ended March 31 are given below:

Employee	Hours Worked	Pay Rate	Gross Earnings to End of Prior Week
Lee Arden	46	$7.00 per hour	$3,860
Ellen Dunn	40	$500 per week	6,720
Walter Mann	44	$8.00 per hour	4,140
Luis Sanchez	40	$8.00 per hour	3,650
James Topp	40	$6.00 per hour	2,980

Additional Data:
(1) Ellen Dunn's salary is charged to Office Salaries Expense; the gross earnings of the other employees are charged to Sales Salaries Expense.
(2) The FICA tax is 7% of the first $35,700 of salaries and wages.
(3) The federal unemployment tax is 0.8%, and the state unemployment tax is 2.7% of the first $7,000 of salaries and wages.
(4) Each employee has a $3.60 per week deduction for group medical insurance.
(5) Assume the federal income tax withheld the last week in March is:

Arden	$63.60
Dunn	91.90
Mann	44.20
Sanchez	31.80
Topp	36.80

REQUIRED

(a) Prepare the payroll register for the week ended March 31, using the following column headings:

	Earnings			Deductions				Net Earnings
Employee	Regular	Overtime	Gross	FICA Tax	Federal Income Tax	Medical Insurance	Total	

(b) Prepare the general journal entry to record:
   (1) The week's payroll.
   (2) The employer's payroll taxes for the week.
   (3) The payment of the net payroll.
(c) Chapman Company remits the group medical insurance premiums to the Puritan Insurance Company monthly. Total premiums withheld in March were $76. Prepare the general journal entry to record the monthly remittance of these premiums.
(d) The March 31 balances in the FICA Tax Payable and Federal Income Tax Withholding Payable accounts—after posting the entries from part (b)— are $1,025 and $1,140, respectively. Prepare the general journal entry to record the monthly remittance of these taxes to an authorized commercial bank.
(e) Chapman Company's total federal unemployment tax for the quarter ended March 31 is $142.80—after posting the entries from part (b). Chapman Company deposits the taxes quarterly in an authorized commercial bank. Prepare the general journal entry to record this remittance.
(f) The total state unemployment tax for the quarter ended March 31 is $503.20— after posting the entries from part (b). Prepare the general journal entry to record the quarterly remittance of this tax.

ALTERNATE PROBLEMS

12–24A Clayton Company prepares monthly financial statements and ends its accounting year on December 31. The company owns a factory in the city of Verona, where city taxes are assessed on March 1 each year, are paid by May 1, and relate to the city's fiscal year which ends the next June 30 (four months after assessment). For the city tax year 19X1–19X2, Clayton paid $24,000 in property taxes on its factory.

REQUIRED
(a) What amount of property tax expense should be accrued on the financial statements for July 19X2, if property taxes for 19X2–19X3 are an estimated 9% higher than the preceding year?
(b) Assume that the 19X2–19X3 tax bill received on March 1, 19X3, was for $26,400 and that the estimate in part (a) was used through February. What is the proper monthly property tax expense for March 19X3, if the deficiencies in the monthly property tax estimates through February are handled as an increase in the property tax expense for March 19X3?
(c) How does the payment of the tax bill on May 1, 19X3, affect the amount of property tax expense recognized for May?

12–25A Glover, Inc. had the following payroll for March 19X8:

Officers' salaries	$24,000
Sales salaries	46,000
Income taxes withheld	15,200
FICA taxes withheld	4,900
Hospital insurance premiums deducted	1,400
Salaries (included above) subject to unemployment taxes	58,000

REQUIRED

Present general journal entries to record:

(a) Accrual of the payroll.

(b) Payment of the net payroll.

(c) Accrual of employer's payroll taxes. (Assume that the FICA tax matches the amount withheld, the federal unemployment tax is 0.8%, and the state unemployment tax is 2.7%.)

(d) Payment of all liabilities related to this payroll. (Assume all are settled at the same time.)

12–26A Union Corporation initially records its sales at amounts that include any related excise and sales taxes. During May 19XX, Union recorded total sales of $235,840. An analysis of May sales indicated the following:

(1) Three-tenths of sales were subject to both a 10% excise tax and a 6% sales tax.

(2) Four-tenths of sales were subject only to the sales tax.

(3) The balance of sales were for labor charges not subject to either excise or sales tax.

REQUIRED

Calculate the amount of sales revenue for May 19XX, and the related liabilities for excise and sales taxes.

12–27A The following data are taken from Shaw Plumbing Company's March 19X4 payroll:

Administrative salaries	$15,000
Sales salaries	32,000
Custodial salaries	4,000
Total payroll	$51,000
Wages subject to FICA tax	$51,000
Wages subject to FUTA and state unemployment taxes	36,000
Income taxes withheld from all salaries	12,400

Assume that (1) FICA taxes are 7% each for the employee and the employer and (2) the company is subject to a 2.7% state unemployment tax and an 0.8% federal unemployment tax on the first $7,000 paid to each employee.

REQUIRED

Record the following in general journal form:

(a) Accrual of the payroll.

(b) Payment of the net payroll.

(c) Accrual of the employer's payroll taxes.

(d) Payment of the above payroll-related liabilities. (Assume all are settled at the same time.)

12–28A The Hilldale Company employs five persons, one of whom receives a $400 salary for a 40-hour week; the other four are paid an hourly rate. All employees receive overtime pay at $1\frac{1}{2}$ times their regular pay rate. Data relating to the payroll for the week ended June 30 are given below:

Employee	Hours Worked	Pay Rate	Gross Earnings to End of Prior Week
Ann Brady	42	$6.00 per hour	$6,240
Pat Ford	40	$400 per week	8,400
Tony Hill	46	$6.40 per hour	6,656
Mark Rudd	44	$6.40 per hour	6,460
Tim Ward	40	$5.60 per hour	5,820

Additional Data:

(1) Pat Ford's salary is charged to Office Salaries Expense; the gross earnings of the other employees are charged to Sales Salaries Expense.

(2) The FICA tax is 7% of the first $35,700 of salaries and wages.

(3) The federal unemployment tax is 0.8%, and the state unemployment tax is 2.7% of the first $7,000 of salaries and wages.

(4) Each employee has a $3.00 per week deduction for group medical insurance.

(5) Assume the federal income tax withheld the last week in June is:

Brady	$25.50
Ford	54.20
Hill	41.40
Rudd	39.40
Ward	32.00

REQUIRED

(a) Prepare the payroll register for the week ended June 30, using the following column headings:

Employee	Earnings			Deductions				Net Earnings
	Regular	Overtime	Gross	FICA Tax	Federal Income Tax	Medical Insurance	Total	

(b) Prepare the general journal entry to record:
 (1) The week's payroll.
 (2) The employer's payroll taxes for the week.
 (3) The payment of the net payroll.

(c) Hilldale Company remits the group medical insurance premiums to the Badger Insurance Company monthly. Total premiums withheld in June were $60. Prepare the general journal entry to record the monthly remittance of these premiums.

(d) The June 30 balances in the FICA Tax Payable and Federal Income Tax Withholding Payable accounts—after posting the entries from part (b)—are $830 and $754, respectively. Prepare the general journal entry to record the monthly remittance of these taxes to an authorized commercial bank.

(e) Hilldale Company's total federal unemployment tax for the quarter ended June 30 is $99.39—after posting the entries from part (b). Although a deposit is not required (since the balance is under $100), Hilldale Company deposits the taxes quarterly in an authorized commercial bank. Prepare the general journal entry to record this remittance.

(f) The total state unemployment tax for the quarter ended June 30 is $306.21—after posting the entries from part (b). Prepare the general journal entry to record the quarterly remittance of this tax.

BUSINESS DECISION PROBLEM

Brandon Enterprises manages office buildings in several Midwestern cities. The firm maintains its own janitorial staff for all buildings managed. The firm manages 10 buildings in Rainbow City, where it maintains a staff of 40 people, with a total annual payroll of $590,000. Of this staff, only two supervisors earn more than $35,700 per year; each receives $38,000 annually. All of the staff earn more than $7,000 per year. The annual nonpayroll costs of the janitorial service are:

Supplies	$45,000
Depreciation on Equipment	28,000
Insurance	20,000
Miscellaneous	5,000
	$98,000

Brandon pays a 7% FICA tax on its payroll and is subject to a 2.7% state unemployment tax. Its federal unemployment compensation tax rate is 0.8%. The firm also pays part of the employees' health insurance costs, averaging $48 per employee.

The firm has a high employee turnover rate and has not always kept tenants happy with the janitorial service. President Dorothy Brandon has been approached by Many Hands, Inc., a commercial janitorial service chain, which has submitted a bid of $725,000 annually to provide janitorial service for the 10 buildings in Rainbow City. This firm is noted for efficiency and satisfactory service. Brandon estimates that hiring an outside firm would save $8,000 annually in bookkeeping costs and costs of contracting with other commercial firms for substitutes for regular help. These costs are not included in the above list of nonpayroll costs.

REQUIRED

Prepare a cost analysis for Brandon to help her decide whether to accept the bid of Many Hands, Inc. Assume the FICA tax applies to the first $35,700 paid to each employee and the unemployment taxes apply to the first $7,000 paid to each employee.

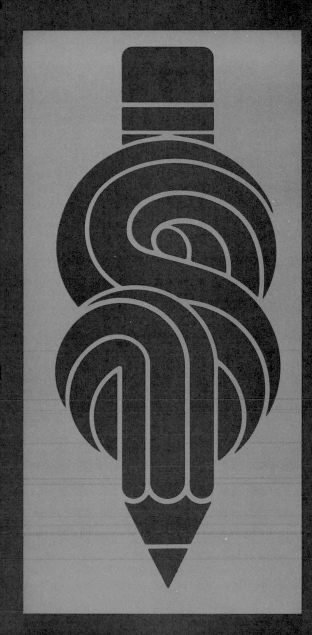

13

Accounting Principles;
Accounting for
Inflation

I in Chapter 1, we touched briefly on the role of generally accepted accounting principles as the rules by which financial accounting statements are prepared. The phrase *generally accepted accounting principles* encompasses a wide spectrum of accounting guidelines, ranging from basic concepts and standards to detailed methods and procedures. There are principles covering almost every aspect of financial accounting and reporting. We have already discussed many of the methods and procedures within the domain of generally accepted accounting principles, such as inventory pricing methods and depreciation methods. In this chapter, we focus on the fundamental and pervasive principles of accounting, an understanding of which is indispensable to anyone who uses financial accounting data. We also consider the topic of accounting for inflation.

HISTORICAL DEVELOPMENT

In contrast to the physical sciences, accounting has no immutable or natural laws, such as the law of gravity. The closest approximation to a law in accounting is probably the use of arithmetic functions and logic. Because no basic natural accounting law exists, accounting principles have developed on the basis of their *usefulness*. Consequently, the growth of accounting is more closely related to experience and practice than to the foundation provided by ultimate law. As such, accounting principles tend to evolve rather than be discovered, to be flexible rather than precise, and to be subject to relative evaluation rather than being ultimate or final.

Conventional accounting comprises a relatively recent body of knowledge. Although the origin of double-entry bookkeeping has been traced back to the fourteenth century, most important accounting developments have occurred in the last century.

The recent rapid development of accounting as an information system is largely explained by the economic history of the last eight to ten decades. This period included (1) the development of giant industrial firms, (2) the existence of large stockholders' groups, (3) the pronounced separation of ownership and management of large corporate firms, (4) the rapid growth of industrial and economic activity, and (5) the expansion of government regulation of industry. These factors helped create the large groups of interested parties who require a constant stream of reliable financial information concerning the economic entities they own, manage, or regulate. This information is meaningful only when prepared according to some agreed-on standards and procedures.

Accounting principles—like common law—originate from problem situations such as changes in the law, tax regulations, new business organizational arrangements, or new financing or ownership techniques. In response to the effect such problems have on financial reports, certain accounting techniques or procedures are tried. Through comparative use and analysis, one or more of these techniques are judged most suitable, obtain substantial authoritative support, and are then considered a generally accepted accounting principle. Organizations such as the Financial Accounting Standards Board (FASB), the American Institute of Certified Public Accountants (AICPA), the Securities and Exchange Commission (SEC), the Internal Revenue Service, and the American Accounting Association—and the literature each publishes—are instrumental in the development of most accounting principles.

The general acceptance of accounting principles is not determined by a formal vote or survey of practicing accountants. An accounting principle must have substantial authoritative support to qualify as generally accepted. References to a particular accounting principle in authoritative accounting literature constitute substantive evidence of its general acceptance.

Pronouncements by the FASB are the most direct evidence of whether or not a specific accounting principle is generally accepted. Organized in 1973, the FASB issued more than 70 statements dealing with generally accepted accounting principles during its first 10 years. Before the creation of the FASB, pronouncements by the AICPA—many of which are still in effect—represented the most authoritative indicators of general acceptance.

During the two decades ending in 1959, the AICPA issued 51 *Accounting Research Bulletins*. These bulletins dealt with a variety of problems and, although they lacked formal legal status, they considerably influenced generally accepted practice. In 1959, the AICPA established the Accounting Principles Board (APB) to issue authoritative *opinions* on problems related to generally accepted accounting principles. Many of the 31 opinions issued during its existence were preceded by considerable research, wide circulation of *exposure drafts*, and partial revisions based on the resulting feedback. These opinions increased in importance in 1964 when the AICPA required that any departure from an opinion be disclosed in a footnote to the financial statements or in the accompanying auditor's report. When the FASB succeeded the APB in 1973, this requirement was extended to cover FASB pronouncements.

CONCEPTUAL FRAMEWORK

A major FASB project is the development of an overall **conceptual framework** to guide the formulation of accounting principles. When complete, the conceptual framework will be a cohesive set of interrelated objectives and fundamentals for external financial reporting by business enterprises. Consequently, accounting principles based on this framework should form a consistent and coherent set of guidelines for financial reporting.

The first components of the conceptual framework confirm the role of usefulness in financial reporting. The framework begins with an identification of financial reporting objectives.[1] The objectives focus primarily on information useful to investors and creditors, who share a common interest in assessing a firm's ability to generate favorable future cash flows. Financial reports should help an investor or creditor predict a firm's future performance or evaluate earlier expectations, or both. Accordingly, financial reports should contain information about a firm's economic resources, obligations, owners' equity, and periodic financial performance.

The conceptual framework also identifies the qualities of accounting information that contribute to decision usefulness.[2] The two primary qualities are **relevance** and **reliability.** Relevant information, of course, contributes to the predictive and evaluative decisions made by investors and creditors. Reliable information contains no error or bias, and faithfully portrays what it intends to represent.

Until the conceptual framework is completed, its impact on existing accounting principles is difficult to assess. Beyond this potential impact on existing principles, however, the framework should simplify the determination of appropriate principles for future accounting problem situations.

BASIC PRINCIPLES

The accounting principles we consider in this section are among the most important ideas in accounting theory. Though less than exhaustive, the treatment here should provide sufficient background for further accounting studies. The discussion of each principle begins with a brief description.

Accounting Entity

Each entity should be accounted for separately.

The most fundamental concept in accounting is the entity. An accounting entity is an economic unit with identifiable boundaries for which accountants accumulate and report financial information. Before accountants can analyze and report activities, they must identify the particular entity (and its boundaries) for which they are accounting. Every financial report specifies the entity in its heading.

Each proprietorship, partnership, and corporation is a separate entity, and separate accounting records should be kept for each unit. In accumulating financial information, we must separate the activities of an accounting entity from the other economic and personal activities of its owners. For example, Matt and Lisa Cook own the Good Cook Inn restaurant as partners. The Good Cook Inn partnership is an accounting entity. Matt Cook is also an attorney whose activities

[1] *Statement of Financial Accounting Concepts No. 1,* "Objectives of Financial Reporting by Business Enterprises" (Stamford, CT: Financial Accounting Standards Board, 1978).
[2] *Statement of Financial Accounting Concepts No. 2,* "Qualitative Characteristics of Accounting Information" (Stamford, CT: Financial Accounting Standards Board, 1980).

constitute a proprietorship. Therefore, he keeps a set of accounting records for his legal activities separate from Good Cook Inn's records of its business activities. Lisa Cook's activities as a realtor also constitute a proprietorship. She keeps a set of accounting records for her realty activities separate from both the records of Good Cook Inn and of Matt Cook, attorney.

An accounting entity may be a unit other than a proprietorship, partnership, or corporation. Data for two or more corporations may be combined to provide financial reports for a larger economic entity. For example, a parent corporation and its wholly owned subsidiaries (corporations in their own right) may consolidate their individual financial reports into a set of consolidated statements covering the group of corporations. (This process is a topic of Chapter 18.) In contrast, internal reports to corporate management may contain financial data concerning the activities of units as small as a division, a department, a profit center, or a plant. In this type of financial reporting, the entity is the division, the department, the profit center, or the plant.

The entity concept does not negate the legal fact that an all-inclusive legal liability exists in proprietorships and partnerships. In other words, business assets are available to personal creditors, and business creditors may have legal access to both business and personal assets in these noncorporate business organizations.

Accounting Period

Accounting reports relate to specific periods—typically, one year.

The operations of most businesses are virtually continuous except for some changes associated with cyclical time periods, seasons, or dates. Thus, any division of the total life of a business into segments based on annual periods is somewhat artificial. However, the idea of accounting periods is useful. Many taxes are assessed on an annual basis, and comprehensive reports to corporation stockholders are made annually. In addition, many other noneconomic factors tend to consider the year a natural division of time.

For special purposes, accounting reports may cover other periods. For instance, many companies prepare *interim* financial reports for time spans of less than one year, such as quarterly (three months) or even monthly periods. To compare data for periods of more than one year, many firms prepare five- or 10-year summaries, which are usually statistical and tabular abstracts of related financial statements.

The combined effect of the entity and periodicity concepts is illustrated in Exhibit 13–1, which uses the Good Cook Inn and its two owners as an example. The shaded box isolates Good Cook Inn's activities for 19X2. Proper accounting requires that both the entity and the period be identified in financial reports.

As useful as it is, the idea of artificially "cutting off" the business at the end of a certain period presents many problems. Transactions incurred and consummated entirely within one accounting period present few problems. However, many transactions bridge two or more periods, and their total effect on the entity must often be properly allocated among these periods. Problems of *periodicity* are closely related to the concept of matching revenue and expense, which is developed later in the chapter.

EXHIBIT 13–1

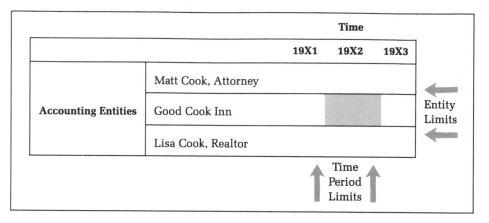

Materiality

Accounting transactions so insignificant that they would not affect the actions of financial statement users are recorded as is most expedient.

Sound accounting procedures require effort and cost money. When the amounts involved are too small to affect the overall picture significantly, the application of theoretically correct accounting procedures is hardly worth its cost. For example, accounting theory asserts that assets acquired and used over several accounting periods should first be recorded as assets, with systematic amounts of depreciation expense recognized in each of the periods in which the assets are used (directly or indirectly) to earn revenue. The principle of *materiality*, however, permits a firm to expense the costs of such items as small tools, pencil sharpeners, and waste paper baskets when acquired because they are "immaterial" in amount. Many firms set dollar limits—such as $25 or $100—below which the costs of all items are expensed.

The concept of materiality is relative—an immaterial amount for General Motors Corporation may be material for smaller companies. Also, the nature of the transaction should be considered. A difference of $1,000 in depreciation expense might be immaterial, but the same discrepancy in cash could be material.

The materiality of an item in a financial statement is usually judged in comparison to a related amount. For example, to determine the effect of the inclusion or omission of an income statement item, we express it as a percentage of net income; a current asset item might be expressed as a percentage of total current assets, and so on. Accounting literature is not precise about what quantitative proportions are deemed material. In specific instances, 5–15% of related amounts have been considered material, but this matter is best subject to judgment. Always remember, however, that although a given series of transactions might *each* be considered immaterial in amount, their aggregate effect could be material in certain circumstances.

Conservatism

Accounting measurements take place in a context of significant uncertainties, and possible errors in measurement of net assets and income should tend toward understatement rather than overstatement.

Accounting determinations are often based on estimates of future events and are therefore subject to a range of optimistic or pessimistic interpretations. In the early 1900s, many abuses were perpetrated on financial statement users who were given overly optimistic measurements of assets and estimates of income. Consequently, the investor was reassured when a company used the "most conservative" accounting procedures. In some instances, banks would write down handsome multistory office buildings, showing them on the balance sheet at a nominal value of $1. The intention was to emphasize the understatement of assets as evidence of conservative accounting and financial strength.

More recently, accountants have recognized that intentional understatement of net assets and income can be as misleading as overly optimistic accounting treatments. For example, stockholders might erroneously decide to sell their stock in a company that grossly understates its income through overly conservative accounting procedures. Also, a conservative treatment in one accounting period may cause the overstatement of reported income for many other periods. For example, the bank that writes its building down to $1 is, in a sense, "overdepreciating" and therefore understating both assets and income for that period. During the building's remaining useful life, the bank's income is overstated because the related building depreciation expense is omitted from the income statements of those periods.

Today, *conservatism* is the accountant's reaction to situations in which significant uncertainties exist about the outcomes of transactions still in progress. In contrast to the intentional understatements of net assets and income, accountants follow conservative accounting procedures when they are unsure of the proper measure to use. Possible errors in measuring net assets and income should tend toward understatement rather than overstatement. From the range of possible accounting determinations applied in these cases, we should use the one that results in the lowest current statement of net assets and income.

Consistency

Unless otherwise disclosed, accounting reports are prepared on a basis consistent with the preceding period.

In many instances, more than one method of applying a generally accepted accounting principle is possible. In other words, two firms that have identical operating situations might each choose a different—but equally acceptable— accounting method and report different amounts for the same types of transactions.

Changes in accounting procedures that lead to different reported values may affect the amount of reported income. Under certain circumstances, a firm could, by design, increase or decrease its reported earnings simply by changing from one generally accepted accounting principle to another that yields different values. This situation justifies the *consistency* principle. Financial statement users should know when and to what extent reported earnings result in some part from changes in accounting techniques. In Chapter 16, we discuss how to report the effects of changes in accounting principles.

Full Disclosure

All facts necessary for the users' understanding of the financial statements must be disclosed.

Often facts or conditions exist that, although not specifically part of the financial statement data for the period reported, have considerable influence on the firm's financial status. Such conditions may pertain to the period covered by the statements or to the period immediately afterward. To inform users properly, the firm should disclose this additional information. Certain provisions of leases, significant amounts of purchases commitments, and notices of pending lawsuits or settlements are examples of items that should be disclosed in footnotes to the financial statements. Likewise, if the company issues a large amount of securities or suffers a casualty loss after the balance sheet date, this information and any other factors that may significantly affect the firm's operations should be reported to the reader, even though the situation arose subsequent to the balance sheet date. Firms are responsible for disclosing such events that occur between the balance sheet date and the date of their report. If a report is submitted to the SEC as part of a registration statement for the sale of securities, the period extends to the effective date of registration.

A company should also disclose a summary of the accounting principles it follows in preparing its financial statements. This disclosure requirement recognizes that different firms may use different accounting procedures for similar transactions and that therefore the usefulness of the financial statements is enhanced if users are aware of the accounting procedures used. Items disclosed in a summary of accounting principles would include, among others, depreciation methods, inventory pricing methods, methods of accounting for intangibles, and consolidation procedures.

Objectivity

Whenever possible, accounting entries must be based on objectively determined evidence.

The concept of *objectivity* requires bias-free and verifiable accounting data. Users want accounting data that are not subject to the capricious whim of either management or the accountant who prepares or audits the statements. Consequently, whenever possible, accounting determinations are based on actual invoices, documents, bank statements, and physical counts of items involved.

Not all accounting determinations can be totally objective. Periodic depreciation and estimates of the eventual collectibility of credit sales are examples of relatively subjective factors routinely incorporated into accounting reports. Several accountants required to determine independently the depreciation expense for a given period on an item of special-purpose equipment would probably come up with a range of suggested amounts. We might expect the range to be in some proportion to the degree of subjectivity involved.

Obviously, variations in accounting measurements lead to variations in reported income. Thus, the more subjective accounting records are, the greater variety there may be in reported income. Because highly subjective determinations are not readily verifiable, a user of a subjectively derived accounting report does not know where this particular statement falls in the range of reportable income figures. An even greater disadvantage is that the user has no way of knowing the motives of the individual preparing the statements. Was he or she trying to be "fair" or attempting to minimize or maximize reported income? We have no reliable source of answers to this question. For this reason, accountants—particularly independent auditors—look for objective evidence to support the accounting data in financial reports.

Going Concern   **In the absence of evidence to the contrary, a business is assumed to have an indefinite life.**

With few exceptions, business organizations have no anticipated termination date. Most firms operate profitably for indefinite periods and are, in fact, *going concerns*. Firms that do not succeed usually have indications of impending termination for some time before operations actually cease.

The going concern assumption has important implications for accounting procedures. It allows firms to defer costs—such as ending inventories, prepaid expenses and undepreciated asset balances—that will be charged against the revenue of future periods. Furthermore, the going concern concept assumes the use of cost-based accounting measures rather than market-based liquidation values. Firms that expect to continue profitable operations do not ordinarily sell their operating assets; therefore, potential liquidation prices for these assets at the end of an accounting period may not be especially relevant. In this sense, the going concern assumption justifies the use of historical cost as the primary basis for accounting entries.

Measuring Unit   **The unit of measure in accounting is the base money unit of the most relevant currency.**

Although other descriptive information is often relevant, money is the common measure for recording accounting transactions. By expressing all assets and equities in terms of money, the accountant creates a common denominator that permits addition and subtraction of all forms of assets and equities and makes possible the preparation of financial statements. Expressing all statement items in money terms also permits the comparison of (1) various elements in the financial statements of a firm, (2) different sets of statements for the same firm, and (3) the statements of two or more firms. This principle also assumes the unit of measure is stable; that is, changes in its general purchasing power are not considered sufficiently important to require adjustments to the basic financial statements.

Historical Cost   **Accounting measures are primarily based on historical costs.**

The dollar amounts in account balances represent the accounting measures of the items about which information is collected. Possible sources of these measures are opinions of management, professional appraisals, various market prices, and historical costs. Accountants have experimented with all of these sources at various times, but with few exceptions, they have used historical cost whenever it is available. Most practicing accountants feel that other sources are so subjective that their use should be seriously limited.

We can describe *historical cost* as the money equivalent of the object given up (and/or obligations assumed) in an exchange transaction. Most accountants agree that no asset has a single ultimate value and that for the millions of exchanges that occur daily, the exchange price probably best indicates the value of an item at the time of the transaction.

Historical costs tend to be highly objective because under classical assumptions they are derived in the marketplace by informed, rational, and independent parties. Also, the details of the original transaction can easily be verified by consulting the documents that are customarily executed at the time of exchange (deeds, bills of sale, checks, and mortgages). An overlooked advantage of historical cost measurement is that the data are a natural byproduct of the exchange transaction itself and are therefore available at little additional cost or effort. Relative objectivity may be the primary justification for historical cost-based accounting measures, but their natural availability at negligible cost is also an important factor—especially when the historical cost method is compared with more expensive sources of values such as professional appraisals.

Matching Expenses with Revenue

To the extent feasible, all expenses related to given revenue are matched with and deducted from that revenue for the determination of periodic income.

The income determination process relates, or matches, expenses and revenue in the following ways:

(1) Costs that relate to specific revenue are recognized as expenses whenever the related revenue is recognized. For example, cost of goods sold relates to the specific revenue from the sale of goods. Cost of goods sold is recorded, therefore, in the same accounting period as the sales revenue.

(2) Costs that relate to the revenue of several accounting periods are expensed in a systematic and rational manner throughout these periods. The impact of some assets benefiting several periods cannot be traced to any specific revenue amounts. Instead, the asset's cost is matched with each period's overall revenue through appropriate depreciation and amortization procedures. The depreciation of office equipment illustrates this category of matching.

(3) Costs that relate only to the current period's overall revenue are expensed immediately. Expenditures that benefit only the current accounting period, such as office salaries expense, fit this category.

The proper matching of expenses and revenue is accomplished primarily through the accrual accounting techniques illustrated throughout the text.

EXHIBIT 13-2
Typical Operating Cycle for a Firm

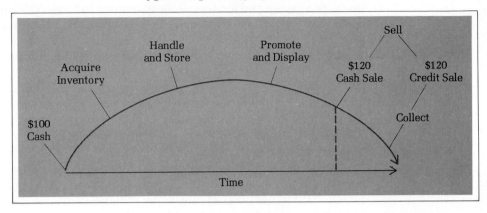

Revenue Recognition at Point of Sale

With limited exceptions, revenue is recognized at the point of sale.

At first, this principle may seem obvious. However, modern business operations are often so complicated and so extended that practical questions arise concerning the point at which revenue should be recognized. With the exceptions discussed later in this section, generally accepted accounting principles require the recognition of revenue in the accounting period in which the sale is deemed to have occurred. Moreover, the matching principle (explained above) dictates that we match any related expenses with this revenue in that period. Thus, the combined effect of the two principles requires the recognition of revenue and related expenses in the period of sale.

For services, the sale is deemed to occur when the service is performed. When merchandise is involved, the sale takes place when title to the goods transfers from seller to buyer.[3] In many situations this coincides with the delivery of the merchandise. As a result, accountants usually record revenue when goods are delivered.

To understand the logic of and the exceptions to the principle of recognizing revenue at point of sale, we must consider some underlying factors. Most firms have some sort of cash-to-cash operating cycle, which is diagramed in Exhibit 13-2. In reality, most firms are engaged in many partially overlapping operating cycles represented by the following diagram:

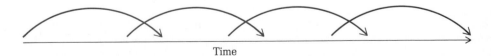

[3] The *Uniform Commercial Code*, which establishes when title transfers to the buyer, is a codification of many statutes and common law related to commerce. It has widely replaced often varying state laws.

For our purposes, it is sufficient to consider the isolated cycle. In Exhibit 13–2, the firm starts with $100 cash and then uses the cash to acquire, handle, store, promote, display, and finally sell the inventory. In a cash sale, inventory is immediately converted to $120 cash. If the sale is made on credit terms, the collection process must be accomplished. The $20 difference between the cash at the cycle's beginning and at its end, reduced by any applicable noncash expenses, is the income generated by the operating cycle.

Throughout the cycle, the firm works toward the eventual sale of the goods and collection of the sales price. From a purely theoretical view, accountants would like to recognize some part of the income for each phase of the cycle. Because all allocation methods are arbitrary and based on estimates, however, the income is not recognized until the point of sale. At the point of sale, we know (1) the basic cost, (2) that a sale has occurred, (3) the selling price, and (4) that the seller either has received cash or has an enforceable claim against the customer. Prior to the point of sale, some of these items may be unknown. Hence, the sale is reasonably considered the critical event in the operating cycle.

Other Bases for Revenue Recognition

COLLECTION BASES   For selected exceptions, revenue recognition occurs at times other than the point of sale. Methods that delay recognition until cash is collected are **collection basis methods.** These methods usually relate to installment credit sales. A conservative method, known as the **cost recovery method,** considers all cash collections a return of costs until all costs are recovered; the remaining collections are considered gross profit.

A more widely used collection basis method is the **installment method.** The installment method takes its name from the popular sales term for purchases of moderate to large dollar amounts. In effect, the installment method treats each dollar received as part return of cost and part gross profit. The specific proportion of each is determined by the relationship between the cost and the sales price of the merchandise involved. For example, assume that on October 1, 19X7, a refrigerator costing $450 is sold for $600, with installment terms consisting of a 20% down payment and the balance due in 24 equal payments of $20 on the last day of each month. Under the installment basis, because the cost was 75% of the selling price ($450/$600), each dollar collected will be considered 75% return of cost and 25% gross profit. The resulting gross profit during the three years would be recognized as follows:

	19X7 Down Payment	19X7 Three $20 Payments	19X8 Twelve $20 Payments	19X9 Nine $20 Payments	Totals
Total received (100%)	$120	$60	$240	$180	$600
Considered return of cost (75%)	90	45	180	135	450
Considered gross profit (25%)	30	15	60	45	150

The installment method of revenue recognition should be used when firms cannot reasonably estimate the extent of collectibility of the installment receivables. Companies that can reasonably predict and make accruals for future losses should not employ the installment method. Instead, they should recognize revenue at point of sale and match with it an appropriate estimate of uncollectible accounts. These companies may, however, still use the installment method for income tax purposes, because it may be advantageous to delay gross profit recognition until the cash is collected.

PERCENTAGE OF COMPLETION Some operations—such as the construction of roads, dams, and large office buildings—take a long time and therefore cover several accounting periods. In such situations, the point-of-sale recognition method does not work very well, because the earnings from several years of construction work may be reported as the income of only the period in which the project was completed and sold. Consequently, another method of revenue recognition, **percentage of completion (POC),** may be used.

The POC method simply allocates the estimated total gross profit on a contract among the several accounting periods involved, in proportion to the estimated percentage of the contract completed each period. To use this method, we must have a reasonably accurate and reliable procedure for estimating periodic progress on the contract. Most often, estimates of the percentage of contract completion are tied to the proportion of total costs incurred.

For example, assume that a dam is to be constructed during a two-year period beginning July 1, 19X1. The contract price is $3 million, and estimated total costs are $2.4 million; thus, estimated gross profit is $600,000. If the total cost incurred in 19X1 is $720,000 (that is, 30% of the estimated total), then $180,000 (or 30% of the estimated total gross profit) is recognized in 19X1. Similarly, if another 50% of the total estimated costs is incurred in 19X2, then 50% of the estimated total gross profit (or $300,000) is recognized in 19X2. Under the POC method, the gross profit is reflected among the three calendar years as follows:

(Dollars in Thousands)

	19X1	19X2	19X3	Total
Cost incurred	$720	$1,200	$480	$2,400
Percent of total costs	30%	50%	20%	100%
Gross profit recognized	$180	$ 300	$120	$ 600

Clearly, in long-term construction, the POC method of revenue recognition more reasonably reflects reported income as an indicator of productive effort than the point-of-sale basis.

ACCOUNTING FOR INFLATION

Inflation has an impact on virtually every aspect of economic affairs, including investment decisions, pricing policies, marketing strategies, and salary and wage negotiations. Persons making economic decisions utilize financial data prepared by accountants. Conventional financial statements, however, contain no explicit adjustments for the impact of inflation on the financial data. The usefulness of financial statements would likely increase if they contained supplementary information about the effects of inflation and changing prices on the enterprise.

Exactly what type of supplementary information to report during inflationary periods is an unresolved issue for accountants. The following two approaches have been proposed:

(1) Adjust conventional financial data for changes in the general purchasing power of the dollar, a process called **constant dollar accounting.**

(2) Incorporate current value measurements of the goods and services used or held by an enterprise.

We now examine these two approaches.

Constant Dollar Accounting   The general purchasing power of the dollar is a measure of its ability to buy goods and services. **Price-level changes** are changes in the prevailing exchange ratio between money and goods or services. Whenever a rise in the general level of prices for goods and services occurs, the general purchasing power of the dollar declines; this is **inflation.** In contrast, **deflation** is an increase in the dollar's general purchasing power as the general level of prices declines. Our discussion is in the context of inflation, the prevailing price-level movement of the last two decades. In a significant period of deflation, most of the problems we consider would occur in a reversed form.

21-DIGIT INFLATION

If you find double-digit inflation painful, imagine living with the triple-digit rates plaguing Israel (130% inflation) and Brazil (119%). In Argentina, the perennial champion of modern world inflation, residents are happy now with an 82% inflationary rate—half their 1979 level, and a mere fraction of the 347% peak of five years ago. But even these levels of inflation pale before the world's all-time record.

No, the famous hyper-inflation of the German mark in 1923 is not the world's record. That distinction is held by Hungary, whose inflation in 1946 was a *thousand* times worse. In 1939, just before World War II, one American dollar bought 3.38 Hungarian pengös. In July 1946, the same dollar was worth 500,000,000,000,000,000,000 (500 million trillion) pengös. Never before—or since—has so much been worth so little.

After the war, rural Hungarians quickly abandoned money in favor of primitive barter, but people in Budapest had to cope with the monetary system. Wages were raised daily, but prices rose by the hour. Shoppers carried their money in large bags, as high-speed presses raced to turn out currency notes in ever larger denominations. Savings evaporated and the moneyed classes were wiped out. The $100,000 worth of pengös one had banked in 1939 weren't worth the trouble it took to withdraw them in 1946. Not when a haircut cost 800 trillion pengös in Budapest, and the average annual income there would buy only $50 worth of merchandise on the black market—the only place where consumer goods could be purchased.

From "21-Digit Inflation," Irving Wallace, David Wallechinsky, and Amy Wallace, in "Significa," *Parade* Magazine, October 18, 1981, page 20.

PRICE INDEXES   Price indexes measure price-level changes. A **price index** represents a series of measurements, stated as percentages, indicating the relationship between (a) the weighted average price of a sample of goods and services at various points in time and (b) the weighted average price of a similar sample of goods and services at a common, or base, date.

For example, assume we wish to construct a price index for a single commodity that was priced at $1.60 in December 19X2, $2 in December 19X3, and $3 in December 19X4. If we select December 19X3 as our base date, our price index expresses the price of this commodity in December of 19X2, 19X3, and 19X4 as a percentage of its price in December 19X3. The 19X2 price is 80% ($1.60/$2) of the 19X3 price, and the 19X4 price is 150% ($3/$2) of the 19X3 price. The percentage relationship on the base date is, of course, always 100%. The price index for each date is as follows (the percent sign is understood and usually not shown with index numbers):

December 19X2	80
December 19X3	100
December 19X4	150

Prominent examples of price indexes are the Consumer Price Index for All Urban Consumers and the Gross National Product Implicit Price Deflator. The FASB recommends the use of the Consumer Price Index for any general purchasing power adjustments.[4] The monthly calculation of the Consumer Price Index is one advantage it has over the GNP Implicit Price Deflator, which is calculated quarterly.

CONVERSION FACTORS   With index numbers, amounts stated in terms of dollars of general purchasing power at a particular time may be restated in terms of dollars of different purchasing power at another time. We simply multiply the amount to be restated by the following conversion factor:

$$\frac{\text{Index You Are Converting TO}}{\text{Index You Are Converting FROM}}$$

For example, suppose we acquired a parcel of land for $5,000 in December 19X3, when the general price index was 100. Suppose also that the general price indexes for various times were as follows:

December 19X2	80
December 19X3	100
December 19X4	150
Average for 19X4	125

We restate the cost of the land in terms of the December 19X4 dollar by multiplying the $5,000 by the conversion factor 150/100 (December 19X4 index/December 19X3 index). The resulting measure is $7,500, the cost of the land stated in dollars

[4]*Statement of Financial Accounting Standards No. 33*, "Financial Reporting and Changing Prices" (Stamford, CT: Financial Accounting Standards Board, 1979).

of December 19X4 general purchasing power. The conversion process works in the other direction as well. The cost of the land in terms of the December 19X2 dollar is $5,000 × 80/100 = $4,000. The amounts $5,000, $7,500, and $4,000 each represent the cost of the land, but the cost is expressed in a different unit of measure in each case. Usually, amounts stated in "old" dollars are converted to current dollars because the latter figure is more relevant to the overall economic situation.

Events that occur fairly evenly throughout the year, such as sales, are assumed to be originally stated in dollars of the average purchasing power for the year. Consider a firm with sales of $50,000 in 19X4. We assume these sales are made at the average price index for 19X4. The calculation $50,000 × 150/125 = $60,000 converts these sales into dollars of December 19X4 general purchasing power.

ADJUSTMENT PROCEDURES   Basically, constant dollar adjustments cause all items in the financial statements to be stated in dollars with a common purchasing power content. Conversion factors are used to make the adjustments. Our illustrations in this section state the converted data in terms of the dollar's purchasing power at the latest balance sheet date.

Balance sheet conversion   Before a balance sheet conversion, we must separate **monetary** assets and liabilities from nonmonetary items. Monetary assets include cash and other assets—such as receivables—that represent the right to receive a fixed number of dollars in the future, regardless of price-level changes. Monetary liabilities are obligations to disburse a fixed number of dollars in the future, regardless of price-level changes. Most liabilities are monetary.

By their nature, monetary items in a balance sheet are stated in dollars of current purchasing power at the balance sheet date and therefore do not require adjustment. All other balance sheet accounts comprise the **nonmonetary** items, which are adjusted by conversion factors.

Holding monetary items during a period of rising prices creates purchasing power gains and losses on these items. For example, suppose you hold $1,000 cash during a period when the general price level increases from 100 to 150. Obviously, at the end of the period, your $1,000 will buy fewer goods and services than it would at the beginning of the period. This decrease in your ability to buy goods and services as a result of inflation is a *purchasing power loss on cash*. The amount of the loss is $500, calculated by multiplying the percentage increase in prices, 50%, by the $1,000 cash you held.

Assume you also had a note payable of $800 outstanding during the time the general price index increased from 100 to 150. As a result of inflation, you owe dollars whose general purchasing power at the end of the period is less than it was at the beginning of the period. The decrease in the general purchasing power of the dollars with which you will settle the liability represents a *purchasing power gain on the note payable*. The amount of the gain is $400 (50% × $800). Purchasing power gains and losses on monetary items are included in constant dollar statements.

To illustrate a simple balance sheet conversion, we assume Amaya Corporation organized on January 1, 19X4, when the general price index was 100. Its opening balance sheet was as follows:

Amaya Corporation
Balance Sheet
January 1, 19X4

Assets		Stockholders' Equity	
Cash	$ 5,000	Common Stock	$75,000
Inventory	30,000		
Land	40,000		
Total Assets	$75,000	Total Stockholders' Equity	$75,000

Assume no further transactions occurred during 19X4, but the general price index increased to 150. Amaya Corporation's balance sheet at the end of 19X4, in conventional terms, would be the same as the one shown above. The price-level adjusted balance sheet at December 31, 19X4, would be as follows (the conversion computations are in parentheses):

Amaya Corporation
Constant Dollar Balance Sheet
December 31, 19X4
(End-of-year Dollars)

Assets		
Cash	$ 5,000	(Monetary asset, no adjustment needed)
Inventory	45,000	[$30,000 × (150/100)]
Land	60,000	[$40,000 × (150/100)]
Total Assets	$110,000	
Stockholders' Equity		
Common Stock	$112,500	[$75,000 × (150/100)]
Deficit	(2,500)	(Purchasing power loss on cash, 50% × $5,000)
Total Stockholders' Equity	$110,000	

Income statement conversion   We use the following income statement and related data of the Banon Company to convert an income statement into a constant dollar income statement.

Banon Company
Income Statement
For the Year Ended December 31, 19X4

Sales	$60,000	(Sales made uniformly throughout the year)
Cost of Goods Sold	$30,000	(Goods purchased when price index was 100)
Depreciation Expense	5,000	(Related asset bought when price index was 80)
Other Expenses	7,000	(Expenses incurred uniformly throughout the year)
Total Expenses	$42,000	
Net Income	$18,000	

The average price index for the year was 125, and the price index at year-end was 150. Banon Company's constant dollar income statement appears below (the conversion computations are in parentheses):

Banon Company
Constant Dollar Income Statement
For the Year Ended December 31, 19X4
(End-of-year Dollars)

Sales	$72,000	[$60,000 × (150/125)]
Cost of Goods Sold	$45,000	[$30,000 × (150/100)]
Depreciation Expense	9,375	[$5,000 × (150/80)]
Other Expenses	8,400	[$7,000 × (150/125)]
Total Expenses	$62,775	
Net Income	$ 9,225	

Of course, any purchasing power gains or losses on monetary items held by Banon Company are also included in the company's constant dollar income statement.

ADVANTAGES OF ADJUSTED DATA   Generally accepted accounting principles use the dollar as a measuring unit and assume it is stable (that is, that no significant price-level changes occur); therefore, all dollars are considered economically equal. Obviously, some single-year levels of inflation have strained the stable dollar assumption, and certainly, some multiyear periods have invalidated it. Some of the benefits of adjusting for changes in the general purchasing power of the dollar are (1) better comparisons of financial data through time, (2) improved additivity of financial data, and (3) increased disclosure of information through calculation of purchasing power gains and losses on monetary items.

   Comparability of data through time   Assume that the average price-level indexes and Company A's sales revenue for 19X2–19X4 are as shown:

	Average Price-level Index	Unadjusted Sales
19X2	75	$1,000,000
19X3	90	1,170,000
19X4	125	1,380,000

Further assume that the price-level index at the end of 19X4 is 150.

The unadjusted sales figures indicate a healthy increase in sales. However, if we convert the dollars stated in the average price-level index for 19X2, 19X3, and 19X4 to the dollar as of the end of 19X4 (the latest balance sheet date), we discover the following sales levels:

	Average Price-level Index	Unadjusted Sales	Conversion Factor	Restated Sales
19X2	75	$1,000,000	150/75	$2,000,000
19X3	90	1,170,000	150/90	1,950,000
19X4	125	1,380,000	150/125	1,656,000

Adjusting the data to a common dollar indicates a decrease in sales activity rather than an increase. We can easily imagine the erroneous operating decisions that could result from similar data distortions.

Additivity of financial data The basic mathematical law of additivity asserts that only like units can be added or subtracted. Supporters of general price-level adjustments claim that addition and subtraction of dollars of different purchasing power violate the law of additivity. Suppose Company A (from above) purchased a building in 19X1 for $5,400,000 when the price-level index was 60, and the building is depreciated $270,000 per year. Company A's other expenses for 19X4—totaling $900,000—were incurred and paid uniformly throughout the year. The conventional income statement for 19X4 and the data restated in terms of the 19X4 year-end dollar appear as follows:

	Historical		Conversion Factor	Restated	
Sales		$1,380,000	150/125		$1,656,000
Depreciation Expense	$270,000		150/60	$ 675,000	
Other Expenses	900,000		150/125	1,080,000	
Total Expenses		1,170,000			1,755,000
Net Income (Loss)		$ 210,000			$ (99,000)

In the historical cost income statement, depreciation expense, expressed in 19X1 dollars, is added to other expenses, expressed in average 19X4 dollars, and then subtracted from sales, also expressed in average 19X4 dollars. In the restated income statement, all items are stated in dollars of a common general purchasing power. The restated amounts for 19X4 are decidedly different from the unadjusted amounts. Company A's board of directors may declare a dividend for 19X4 based on the net earnings calculated in the historical income statement. The restated numbers show that the dividend is not supported by 19X4 earnings.

The problem of nonadditivity also affects the balance sheet. Company A, for example, purchased a building in 19X1. Other assets held at the end of 19X4 were acquired at different times, some in 19X4 and others in other years. Yet the measures of these resources, expressed in dollars of varying purchasing power, are added together in the balance sheet. Applying constant dollar conversion factors restates the dollar measures in a common dollar.

Purchasing power gains and losses on monetary items   Purchasing power gains and losses on monetary items have no counterpart in conventional financial statements. These gains and losses are computed and reported only through constant dollar adjustments. Because they indicate how well management has handled monetary items during periods of inflation or deflation, their disclosure should increase the usefulness of the income statement as a performance report.

Current Value Accounting

The current value approach receiving the most attention from accountants is **current cost** accounting. The current cost of an asset is the estimated cost to acquire a similar asset at current prices. Under a system of current cost accounting, current operating income is determined by subtracting from revenue the current cost of assets used in the earning process. Assets are reported in the balance sheet at their current costs. Changes in the current cost of an asset are recorded in the period the change in value occurs. Holding gains and losses are therefore reflected in the financial statements.

A simple example illustrates the basic concepts of a current cost system. Assume Densmore, Inc., started business on January 1, 19X1, by issuing $100,000 of common stock and acquiring the following assets:

Cash	$10,000
Inventory (7,500 units @ $10)	75,000
Land	15,000

During 19X1, Densmore, Inc., sold 5,000 inventory units at $16 each and incurred cash operating expenses of $18,000. Densmore's 19X1 historical cost income statement follows:

Densmore, Inc.
Income Statement
For the Year Ended December 31, 19X1

Sales	$80,000	(5,000 units @ $16)
Cost of Goods Sold	$50,000	(5,000 units @ $10)
Operating Expenses	18,000	
Total Expenses	$68,000	
Net Income	$12,000	

Further, assume that before any inventory was sold in 19X1, its replacement cost increased to $11 per unit and remained there until year-end. Also assume the current cost of land increased to $19,000 by year-end. We now illustrate the various components of a current cost system—current operating income, realized holding gains and losses, unrealized holding gains and losses—and the change in the balance sheet content.

CURRENT OPERATING INCOME Current operating income shows earnings after first providing for the replacement of assets used in operations. Expenses are measured at their current costs. Current operating income, therefore, indicates the profitability of operations at the company's current level of operating costs. It also represents the maximum dividend the company could pay and still maintain its present level of operations. Densmore's current operating income is $7,000, as follows:

Sales	$80,000	
Cost of Goods Sold	$55,000	(5,000 units @ $11)
Operating Expenses	18,000	
Total Expenses	$73,000	
Current Operating Income	$ 7,000	

REALIZED HOLDING GAINS AND LOSSES A holding gain is an increase, and a holding loss is a decrease, in the current cost of an asset while it is held by a company. A holding gain or loss is realized when an asset is sold or used in operations (and its cost is therefore charged to expense). A realized holding gain (or loss) is the difference between the current cost expense amount and the historical cost expense amount. Realized holding gains less realized holding losses plus current operating income equals the historical cost net income amount. Densmore, Inc., realizes a $5,000 holding gain on inventory in 19X1, computed as the difference between the current cost of goods sold ($55,000) and the historical cost of goods sold ($50,000).

UNREALIZED HOLDING GAINS AND LOSSES Increases in the current costs of assets still on hand at year-end are unrealized holding gains. Assets on hand at year-end whose current costs have fallen below their acquisition costs create unrealized holding losses. Densmore, Inc., has unrealized holding gains on its 2,500 units of ending inventory and its land. The current cost of inventory increased by $1 per unit, and the land increased in value from $15,000 to $19,000.

Unrealized Holding Gains:	Inventory	$2,500
	Land	4,000
	Total	$6,500

A current cost system separates holding gains and losses from current operating income. Financial statement readers may use holding gains and losses to evaluate management's effectiveness in timing its asset acquisitions. One of many unresolved questions in current cost accounting is how best to report holding gains and losses (for example, as part of net income or in a new and separate statement). Accountants agree, however, that such gains and losses are items that affect owners' equity.

BALANCE SHEET CONTENT   A comparison of Densmore, Inc.'s, assets at December 31, 19X1, under current cost accounting and under historical cost accounting follows:

Assets	Current Cost	Historical Cost
Cash	$ 72,000	$ 72,000
Inventory	27,500	25,000
Land	19,000	15,000
Total Assets	$118,500	$112,000

The $6,500 difference between the asset totals represents Densmore's unrealized holding gains at December 31, 19X1. Under current cost accounting, Densmore's assets increased $18,500 during 19X1 ($118,500 − $100,000). The stockholders' equity also increased $18,500 ($7,000 current operating income + $5,000 realized holding gain + $6,500 unrealized holding gain).

     Proponents of current cost accounting contend that the use of current costs would introduce more economic reality into financial reports during inflationary periods than constant dollar adjustments would. On the other hand, the determination of current costs would also introduce more subjectivity into the accounting measurement process. Current cost accounting, along with constant dollar adjustments, is now being evaluated by the FASB as explained below.

Financial Accounting Standards Board

In 1979, the FASB issued a standard dealing with financial reporting in an inflationary environment.[5] The standard applies to publicly held companies with more than $1 billion in assets or more than $125 million in inventories and gross property, plant, and equipment. These companies must supplement their basic, historical cost financial statements with selected information, including some data calculated using constant dollar adjustments[6] and other data computed using current cost procedures. These disclosures permit the FASB to assess the financial reporting experience under both approaches. With this experience, the FASB will determine which information best reflects the impact of changing prices on corporate performance.

[5] *Statement of Financial Accounting Standards No. 33,* "Financial Reporting and Changing Prices" (Stamford, CT: Financial Accounting Standards Board, 1979).

[6] Beginning in 1982, constant dollar disclosures were not required for companies with significant operations measured in foreign functional currencies. About one-half the companies making supplementary disclosures were affected by this change, caused by changed guidelines for translating foreign currency financial statements into U.S. dollars for purposes of preparing consolidated financial statements. *Statement of Financial Accounting Standards No. 70,* "Financial Reporting and Changing Prices: Foreign Currency Translation" (Stamford, CT: Financial Accounting Standards Board, 1982).

CURRENT YEAR DISCLOSURES Each company required to make these supplemental disclosures reports the following information for the current year:

(1) Net income[7] computed using constant dollar accounting procedures.

(2) Net income computed using current cost accounting procedures.

(3) The purchasing power gain or loss on net monetary items. The FASB does not include this item in the computation of net income.

(4) The increase (or decrease) in the current cost of inventory and property, plant, and equipment, both before and after eliminating the effects of inflation.

(5) The current cost of inventory and property, plant, and equipment at the end of the current year.

FIVE-YEAR SUMMARY In addition to the current year disclosures, a five-year summary of selected data must be reported. The five-year summary presents the following three items computed using constant dollar adjustments and also using current cost procedures: (1) net income, (2) net income per common share, and (3) net assets at year-end. The summary also contains (1) net sales and other operating revenue; (2) increases or decreases in current cost amounts of inventory and property, plant, and equipment, net of the effects of inflation; (3) purchasing power gain or loss on net monetary items; (4) cash dividends declared per common share; (5) market price per common share at year-end; and (6) the Consumer Price Index for each year. All financial data in the five-year summary must be reported in dollars of the same general purchasing power.

The FASB intends to review, and possibly amend, these disclosure requirements. The 1982 financial statements of the Whirlpool Corporation, shown on pages 1029–1042, illustrate these initial disclosure requirements.

DEMONSTRATION PROBLEM FOR REVIEW

Norgaard Corporation prepared the following income statement for 19XX:

Sales		$625,000
Cost of Goods Sold	$320,000	
Depreciation Expense	80,000	
Other Operating Expenses	100,000	
Income Tax Expense	38,000	
Total Expenses		538,000
Net Income		$ 87,000

[7]If a company reports extraordinary items or discontinued operations, then income from continuing operations rather than net income is reported on a constant dollar and current cost basis. We discuss extraordinary items, discontinued operations, and income from continuing operations in Chapter 16.

Additional data:

(1) The average general price index for 19XX was 200, and the price index at December 31, 19XX was 210.

(2) The goods sold were purchased when the general price index was 192. The current cost of goods sold expense is an estimated $352,000.

(3) The plant assets being depreciated were acquired when the general price index was 140. The current cost depreciation expense is an estimated $132,000.

(4) Sales were made uniformly throughout 19XX; other operating expenses and income taxes were incurred uniformly throughout the year.

REQUIRED

(a) Prepare a constant dollar income statement for 19XX, stated in terms of the dollar at December 31, 19XX. Ignore the calculation of any purchasing power gain or loss on monetary items.

(b) Using current cost accounting procedures, (1) prepare a schedule showing Norgaard's current operating income for 19XX, and (2) compute Norgaard's realized holding gains or losses for 19XX.

SOLUTION TO DEMONSTRATION PROBLEM

(a)

Norgaard Corporation
Constant Dollar Income Statement
For the Year Ended December 31, 19XX
(End-of-year Dollars)

Sales		$656,250	[$625,000 × (210/200)]
Cost of Goods Sold	$350,000		[$320,000 × (210/192)]
Depreciation Expense	120,000		[$80,000 × (210/140)]
Other Operating Expenses	105,000		[$100,000 × (210/200)]
Income Tax Expense	39,900		[$38,000 × (210/200)]
Total Expenses		614,900	
Net Income		$ 41,350	

(b)(1) Current Operating Income for 19XX

Sales		$625,000
Cost of Goods Sold	$352,000	
Depreciation Expense	132,000	
Other Operating Expenses	100,000	
Income Tax Expense	38,000	
Total Expenses		622,000
Current Operating Income		$ 3,000

(2) Realized Holding Gains for 19XX
       Inventory

Current cost of goods sold	$352,000
Historical cost of goods sold	320,000
Realized holding gain, inventory	$ 32,000

Plant assets

Current depreciation expense	$132,000
Historical depreciation expense	80,000
Realized holding gain, plant assets	$ 52,000

KEY POINTS TO REMEMBER

(1) Each of the following is an important basic accounting principle:

accounting entity	objectivity
accounting period	going concern
materiality	measuring unit
conservatism	historical cost
consistency	matching expenses with revenue
full disclosure	point-of-sale revenue recognition

(2) The installment method of revenue recognition treats each dollar received as part return of cost and part gross profit.

(3) The percentage-of-completion method recognizes gross profit in proportion to the amount of the total contract completed in each period.

(4) Two possible responses to inflation are (a) adjusting financial statements for changes in the general purchasing power of the dollar, and (b) using a system of current value accounting.

(5) Constant dollar adjustments restate financial data in dollars of the same general purchasing power.

(6) Current cost accounting reflects operating expenses at their current costs and shows current costs in the balance sheet.

QUESTIONS

13–1 How would you determine whether a particular accounting technique is a generally accepted accounting procedure?

13–2 Discuss the origin of accounting principles.

13–3 Identify two primary qualities of accounting information that contribute to decision usefulness.

13–4 In one sentence of your own words, describe each of the following accounting principles:

accounting entity	objectivity
accounting period	going concern
materiality	measuring unit
conservatism	historical cost
consistency	matching expenses with revenue
full disclosure	point-of-sale revenue recognition

13–5 Why do accounting principles emphasize historical cost as a basis for measuring assets?

13–6 How do accountants justify using the point of sale for revenue recognition when revenue recognition at some earlier point has so much theoretical appeal?

13–7 Explain the procedures and justification for using the following methods of revenue recognition: (a) the installment method and (b) the percentage-of-completion method.

13–8 Identify and briefly explain two proposed approaches to improving financial data during inflationary periods.

13–9 Explain how price-level indexes can be used to convert the dollars of one year to those of another year.

13–10 Define *inflation*. What difficulty does inflation cause for financial accounting?

13–11 Define *monetary assets* and *monetary liabilities*. Give examples of each.

13–12 Rex Company makes sales uniformly during a year. Last year's sales were $120,000, and the current year's sales were $140,000. The average general price index last year was 220 and this year 240. At the current year-end it is 264. Restate the sales for the two years in terms of the current year-end dollar.

13–13 How is current operating income computed in a current cost accounting system? What is the significance of the current operating income amount?

13–14 Define *holding gain* and *holding loss*. When is a holding gain realized?

13–15 Using a current cost accounting approach, Eckle Company determined that its 19X1 current operating income was $39,000, total realized holding gains were $15,000, and total unrealized holding gains were $8,000. What is Eckle Company's 19X1 historical cost net income?

13–16 Are the disclosures required for large, publicly held corporations on the effects of changing prices replacing historical cost financial statements? Explain.

EXERCISES

13–17 Indicate the basic principle or principles of accounting that underlie each of the following independent situations:

(a) Dr. Burns is a practicing radiologist. Over the years, she has accumulated a personal investment portfolio of securities, virtually all of which have been purchased from her earnings as a radiologist. The investment portfolio is not reflected in the accounting records of her medical practice.

(b) A company purchases a stapler for use by the office secretary. The stapler cost $9 and has an estimated useful life of 10 years. The purchase is debited to the Office Supplies Expense account.

(c) A company sells a product that has a two-year warranty covering parts and labor. In the same period that sales are recorded, an estimate of future warranty costs is debited to the Product Warranty Expense account.

(d) A company pays $16,000 for a patent that has an estimated useful life of 14 years and no salvage value. The amount, debited to the Patent account, is amortized over a 14-year period.

(e) A company purchased a parcel of land several years ago for $26,000. The land's estimated current market value is $40,000. The Land account balance is not increased, but remains at $26,000.

(f) A company has a calendar-year accounting period. On January 8, 19X2, a tornado destroyed its largest warehouse, causing a $500,000 loss. This information is reported in a footnote to the 19X1 financial statements.

13–18 For each of the following independent situations, determine how much revenue should be reported in the current period and how much should be deferred to a future period. If either the installment method or percentage-of-completion method applies, determine the appropriate gross profit amounts rather than revenue amounts.

(a) Purchased merchandise for $18,000 that will be sold early in the next period for $26,000.

(b) Took a special order for merchandise that is both acquired and delivered to the customer during the next period. The merchandise costs $4,200 and sells for $6,000.

(c) Began work on a long-term construction contract with a price of $800,000. Expected costs total $640,000, of which $80,000 were incurred this period.

(d) Sold undeveloped real estate lots for $90,000 on installment terms. Of the $90,000, 15% was collected during this period. No reasonable estimate of the collectibility of the remaining balances is possible. The cost of the property sold is $54,000.

(e) Accomplished approximately 25% of the work on an order of machinery that will be completed during the first month of the next period and sold for $62,000. Total estimated cost for the machinery when completed is $42,000.

13–19 On October 1, 19X2, Power Appliance Company sold a combination refrigerator–freezer for $1,000 on terms of 20% down on the purchase date, and 20 equal monthly payments beginning November 1, 19X2. The appliance cost $600. Compute the amount of gross profit shown in each calendar year involved using the following revenue recognition methods:

(a) The cost recovery method.

(b) The installment method.

(c) The point-of-sale method.

13–20 The Mandel Company purchased a parcel of land for $50,000 several years ago when the general price index was 120. The year-end index for each of the four most recent years follows:

19X1	132
19X2	150
19X3	156
19X4	180

Compute the restated amount for land that would appear in a constant dollar balance sheet at December 31, (a) 19X1; (b) 19X2; (c) 19X3; and (d) 19X4. State balance sheet data in terms of the general purchasing power of the dollar as of the balance sheet date.

13–21 Towell Corporation has reported sales revenue for the past three years as follows:

19X5	$6,400,000
19X6	7,200,000
19X7	8,200,000

The average price-level indexes for these three years are as follows: 19X5, 200; 19X6, 220; and 19X7, 250. The price-level index at the end of 19X7 is 275. Prepare a schedule of sales revenue for 19X5–19X7 stated in the purchasing power of the dollar at the end of 19X7.

13–22 Flores, Inc., organized on January 1 of the current year by issuing common stock in exchange for $4,000 cash and land valued at $4,000. Its balance sheet at this point was

Cash	$4,000	Common Stock	$8,000
Land	4,000		
	$8,000		$8,000

The company engaged in no further transactions during the year. The general price index was 220 on January 1 and 253 on December 31. Prepare the constant dollar balance sheet at December 31, stated in terms of the December 31 dollar.

13–23 On January 2, 19X5, Cheng Company bought 4,000 inventory items at $60 each. On January 4, the unit purchase price increased to $63 and remained there until year-end. During 19X5, Cheng sold 2,400 of these items. If Cheng followed current cost accounting procedures, what would be the amount of (a) 19X5 cost of goods sold expense, (b) 19X5 realized holding gain on inventory, and (c) the unrealized holding gain on inventory at December 31, 19X5?

PROBLEMS

13–24 The following are certain unrelated accounting situations and the accounting treatment, in general journal form, that has been followed in each firm's records.
   (1) Lucky Company mounts a $300,000, year-long advertising campaign on a new national cable television network. The television network required full payment in December at the beginning of the campaign. Accounting treatment is

Advertising Expense	300,000	
Cash		300,000

   (2) Because of a local bankruptcy, machinery worth $80,000 was acquired at a "bargain" purchase price of $72,000. Accounting treatment is

Machinery	72,000	
Cash		72,000

(3) Luis Aparicio, a consultant operating a sole proprietorship, withdrew $5,000 from the business and purchased securities as a gift to his wife. Accounting treatment is

Investments	5,000	
Cash		5,000

(4) The Stable State Bank, by action of the board of directors, wrote down the book value of its home office building to a nominal amount of $100. The objective was to bolster its customers' confidence in the bank's financial strength by obviously understating bank assets. Accounting treatment is

Retained Earnings	899,900	
Buildings		899,900

(5) Templar, Inc., ends its fiscal year on June 30. Financial statements for the year just ended are prepared on July 10. During the July 4 holiday weekend, a fire destroyed most of the inventories of the company. Because the company may have violated local fire regulations, the loss may not be covered by insurance. This possible loss is reflected in the financial statements for the year just ended. Accounting treatment is

Fire Loss	175,000	
Merchandise Inventory		175,000

(6) Brick Company received a firm offer of $90,000 for a parcel of land it owns which cost $63,000 two years ago. The offer was refused, but the indicated gain was recorded in the accounts. Accounting treatment is

Land	27,000	
Income from Increase in Value of Land		27,000

(7) Because of an increase in the general level of prices, Guardian, Inc., determined that the recorded depreciation expense of its store building was understated by approximately $6,200. The company reflects this in its accounts. Accounting treatment is

Depreciation Expense	6,200	
Accumulated Depreciation		6,200

REQUIRED
(a) In each of the given situations, indicate which generally accepted accounting principles apply and whether they have been used appropriately.
(b) If you decide the accounting treatment is not generally accepted, discuss the effect of the departure on the balance sheet and the income statement.

13–25 The following events relate to the sale of a machine by Houston Equipment Company in April 19X1:

March   Houston received a sales order accompanied by a $750 deposit from the customer, as is usual when special devices are custom ordered for the machine. The machine was acquired on account from a local supplier for $4,800. Purchase terms required net cash payment in May.

April   The machine was modified at an additional cash cost of $600 to Houston. The machine was sold for a total price of $7,500 (including the deposit)

on terms that required the customer to pay an additional $4,000 at the time of sale and the balance before the end of May.

May   Houston paid its supplier for the machine. The customer made the final payment on the machine.

REQUIRED

(a) Calculate the amount of gross profit (or loss) that would be reported each month if a cash basis accounting treatment (cash receipts less cash disbursements) were used.

(b) Prepare journal entries to reflect properly the accrual accounting treatment of these transactions. (*Hint:* For the first March transaction, credit the liability account Customer Deposit.) What is each month's reported gross profit? Assume a perpetual inventory method.

(c) Comment briefly on the usefulness of each method in parts (a) and (b) to a manager concerned with evaluating the effect of these transactions on the firm's operations.

13–26 On December 1, 19X7, Century Company initiated a policy of permitting customers to buy goods on an installment basis. Sales of $120,000 were made during December on an installment basis. Terms were 25% down on the date of purchase, and 18 equal monthly payments beginning January 2, 19X8. The cost of goods sold on the installment basis was $72,000. Century Company elects the installment method to report the gross profit from these sales on its income tax return. On its books, the company recognizes the revenue and related cost of goods sold when the sale is made.

REQUIRED

(a) Comment on why Century Company would elect the installment method to report the gross profit on its income tax return.

(b) Assuming all installment payments are collected as scheduled, how much gross profit from these December installment sales will Century Company report on its income tax return for (1) 19X7, (2) 19X8, and (3) 19X9?

(c) Assuming all installment payments are collected as scheduled, how much gross profit from these December installment sales will Century Company report on its books for (1) 19X7, (2) 19X8, and (3) 19X9?

13–27 On December 1, 19X1, Transtar, Inc., signed a contract to build a communications satellite. Completion and sale of the satellite were scheduled for November 19X3. The total contract price for the satellite was $50,000,000, and total estimated cost was $40,000,000. The contract specified the following cash payments by the buyer:

$5,000,000 on signing the contract;
$20,000,000 when the satellite is considered one-half completed;
$20,000,000 when the satellite is completed; and
$5,000,000 90 days after completion.

The degree of completion is considered equal to the proportion of estimated total cost incurred by the builder. Transtar accounts for operations on a calendar-year basis. Costs for the satellite were incurred and paid as follows:

December 19X1	$ 4,800,000
19X2	23,200,000
19X3	12,000,000

The satellite was finished and the sale was consummated November 8, 19X3.

REQUIRED

(a) Calculate the gross profit (or loss) that would be reported each year if a cash basis of accounting (cash receipts less cash disbursements) were used.

(b) Calculate the gross profit that would be reported each year on an accrual basis of accounting using (1) the point-of-sale method of revenue recognition; and (2) the percentage-of-completion method of revenue recognition.

(c) Comment on the relative usefulness of these approaches to periodic income determination.

13–28 Borg, Inc., reported the following conventional income statement for 19X2:

Borg, Inc.
Income Statement
For the Year Ended December 31, 19X2

Sales		$500,000
Cost of Goods Sold		280,000
Gross Profit on Sales		$220,000
Operating Expenses:		
Depreciation Expense—Equipment	$20,000	
Depreciation Expense—Building	60,000	
Selling Expenses	48,000	
Administrative Expenses	18,000	
Income Tax Expense	16,000	162,000
Net Income		$ 58,000

Additional Data:

(1) Sales, selling expenses, and administrative expenses have taken place evenly throughout the year, and income taxes have accrued ratably throughout the year.

(2) The goods sold were acquired at a general price index of 240.

(3) Equipment depreciation of $8,000 relates to equipment purchased when the general price index was 160. The rest of the equipment was purchased when the index was 176.

(4) The building was constructed when the general price index was 132.

(5) The general price index averaged 220 for 19X2 and was 264 at December 31, 19X2.

REQUIRED

Prepare a constant dollar income statement for 19X2, stated in terms of the dollar at December 31, 19X2. Ignore the calculation of any purchasing power gain or loss on monetary items.

13-29 Appearing below is a list of accounts for Bablitch Company, their year-end balances, and the general price-level index on the date each account was established.

	Balance	Price-level Index
Cash	$ 80,000	125
Notes Receivable	30,000	100
Buildings	900,000	60
Supplies on Hand	8,000	120
Patent (less amortization of $50,000)	60,000	80
Mortgage Payable	500,000	75

REQUIRED

Assume the current price-level index is 150.

(a) For each item, compute the amount that would appear in a constant dollar balance sheet stated in dollars of current purchasing power.

(b) Identify each monetary item. Assume the balance of each monetary item has not changed since it was established by the company, and compute the purchasing power gain or loss on each monetary item.

(c) Comment on the effect that omission of general price-level adjustments tends to have on the balance sheet and on the income statement.

13-30 Assume you have just started a summer internship in the controller's office of Dolphin, Inc., a large merchandising firm. For your first project, you must familiarize the controller, Mr. Botumlyne, with developments in the area of inflation accounting. He knows that accountants have been experimenting with adjusting data for general price-level changes and compiling data under current cost accounting procedures. For your first meeting with him, you should be prepared to discuss the following items:

(1) What is the basic difference between adjusting financial data for general price-level changes and employing current cost accounting procedures?

(2) What are the benefits of adjusting financial data for general price-level changes?

(3) What is a purchasing power gain or loss on monetary items? Will the fact that Dolphin, Inc., has large inventory balances adversely affect the calculation of its purchasing power gain or loss on monetary items?

(4) What are the benefits of employing current cost accounting procedures?

(5) Are any significant disadvantages associated with current cost accounting?

(6) What is the difference between a realized holding gain and an unrealized holding gain?

(7) How does current operating income under current cost accounting differ from net income under historical cost accounting?

(8) What does the current operating income amount under current cost accounting disclose?

(9) What is the position of the Financial Accounting Standards Board on inflation accounting?

REQUIRED

In preparation for your meeting with Mr. Botumlyne, write out brief answers to each of these items.

13-31 Haven Corporation began operations on January 2, 19X2, by issuing $300,000 of common stock in exchange for the following assets:

Cash	$ 40,000
Inventory (10,000 units @ $14)	140,000
Land	120,000

During 19X2, Haven sold 4,000 inventory units at $28 each and incurred cash operating expenses of $30,000. Haven's historical cost income statement for 19X2 was as follows:

Sales		$112,000
Cost of Goods Sold	$56,000	
Operating Expenses	30,000	
Total Expenses		86,000
Net Income		$ 26,000

Haven did not purchase any inventory units after January 2, 19X2. If the goods sold had been replaced, their current cost per unit would have averaged $17. By the end of 19X2, the current cost of inventory was $18 per unit. The current cost of the land at December 31, 19X2, was $134,000.

REQUIRED
Using current cost accounting procedures:
(a) Prepare a schedule showing Haven's 19X2 current operating income.
(b) Compute Haven's 19X2 realized holding gains or losses.
(c) Compute the unrealized holding gains or losses that exist at December 31, 19X2, for Haven Corporation.

ALTERNATE PROBLEMS

13–24A The following are several unrelated accounting practices:
(1) A recession has caused slow business and low profits for Roller Company. Consequently, the firm takes no depreciation on its plant assets this year.
(2) Lyle Rote, a consultant operating a sole proprietorship, used his business car for a personal, month-long vacation. A full year's depreciation on the car is charged to the firm's depreciation expense account.
(3) Damon Company purchased a new $12 snow shovel that is expected to last six years. The shovel is used to clear the firm's front steps during the winter months. The shovel's cost is debited to the Snow Shovel asset account and will be depreciated over six years.
(4) Mira Corporation has been named as the defendant in a $10,000,000 pollution lawsuit. Because the lawsuit will take several years to resolve and the outcome is uncertain, Mira's management decides not to mention the lawsuit in the current year financial statements.
(5) Legend Corporation's portfolio of short-term stock investments has an aggregate market value below cost. Management believes that stock prices will rise soon and, therefore, does not write down the portfolio at year-end to its lower market value amount.
(6) The management of Hoya Corporation prefers the financial results in a set of constant dollar financial statements and issues these statements (rather than the conventional statements) to stockholders.

REQUIRED

(a) For each of the given practices, indicate which generally accepted account-ing principles apply and whether they have been used appropriately.
(b) For each inappropriate accounting practice, indicate the proper accounting procedure.

13–27A On November 1, 19X2, Wellbilt, Inc. signed a contract to build a large sea-going oil tanker. Completion and sale of the ship were scheduled for October 19X4. The total contract price for the ship was $18,000,000 and the total estimated cost was $13,000,000. The contract specified the following cash payments by the buyer:

$1,000,000 on signing the contract;
$10,000,000 when the ship is considered one-half completed;
$5,000,000 when the ship is completed;
$2,000,000 90 days after completion.

The degree of completion is considered equal to the proportion of estimated total cost incurred by the builder. Wellbilt accounts for operations on a cal-endar-year basis. Costs for the ship were incurred and paid as follows:

November and December, 19X2	$1,300,000
19X3	7,150,000
19X4	4,550,000

The ship was finished and the sale was consummated October 20, 19X4.

REQUIRED

(a) Calculate the gross profit (or loss) that would be reported each year if a cash basis of accounting (cash receipts less cash disbursements) were used.
(b) Calculate the gross profit that would be reported each year on an accrual basis of accounting using (1) the point-of-sale method of revenue recog-nition; and (2) the percentage-of-completion method of revenue recognition.
(c) Comment on the relative usefulness of these approaches to periodic income determination.

13–28A Sage Company reported the following conventional income statement for 19X3:

Sage Company
Income Statement
For the Year Ended December 31, 19X3

Sales		$800,000
Cost of Goods Sold		460,000
Gross Profit on Sales		$340,000
Operating Expenses:		
Depreciation Expense—Equipment	$16,000	
Patent Amortization Expense	12,000	
Selling Expenses	60,000	
Administrative Expenses	90,000	
Income Tax Expense	55,000	
Total Operating Expenses		233,000
Net Income		$107,000

Additional Data:
(1) Sales, selling expenses, and administrative expenses have taken place evenly throughout the year, and income taxes have accrued ratably throughout the year.
(2) The goods sold were acquired at a general price index of 150.
(3) The equipment being depreciated was purchased when the general price index was 100.
(4) Sage Company acquired a patent for $120,000 at a general price index of 120. The patent is being written off over 10 years.
(5) The general price index averaged 160 for 19X3 and was 180 at December 31, 19X3.

REQUIRED
Prepare a constant dollar income statement for 19X3, stated in terms of the dollar at December 31, 19X3. Ignore the calculation of any purchasing power gain or loss on monetary items.

13–29A Appearing below is a list of accounts for Byrd Company, their year-end balances, and the general price-level index on the date each account was established.

	Balance	Price-level Index
Cash	$ 10,000	250
Accounts Receivable	20,000	240
Land	200,000	150
Inventory	45,000	180
Timberland (less depletion of $70,000)	180,000	160
Bonds Payable	100,000	200

REQUIRED
Assume the current price-level index is 270.
(a) For each item, compute the amount that would appear in a constant dollar balance sheet stated in dollars of current purchasing power.
(b) Identify each monetary item. Assume the balance of each monetary item has not changed since it was established by the company and compute the purchasing power gain or loss on each monetary item.
(c) Comment on the effect that omission of general price-level adjustments tends to have on the balance sheet and on the income statement.

13–31A Key Corporation began operations on January 2, 19X5, by issuing $200,000 of common stock in exchange for the following assets:

Cash	$ 30,000
Inventory (5,000 units @ $20)	100,000
Land	70,000

During 19X5, Key sold 2,000 inventory units at $30 each and incurred cash operating expenses of $8,000. Key's historical cost income statement for 19X5 was as follows:

Sales		$60,000
Cost of Goods Sold	$40,000	
Operating Expenses	8,000	
Total Expenses		48,000
Net Income		$12,000

Key did not purchase any inventory units after January 2, 19X5. If the goods sold had been replaced, their current cost per unit would have averaged $22. By the end of 19X5, the current cost of inventory was $24 per unit. The current cost of the land at December 31, 19X5, was $76,000.

REQUIRED

Using current cost accounting procedures:
(a) Prepare a schedule showing Key's 19X5 current operating income.
(b) Compute Key's 19X5 realized holding gains or losses.
(c) Compute the unrealized holding gains or losses that exist at December 31, 19X5, for Key Corporation.

BUSINESS DECISION PROBLEM

Flitepath, Inc., started operations on January 1, 19X1. Its primary asset is a helicopter, which is used in the following ways:

(1) For carrying passengers between a major air terminal and a downtown heliport. As a new business promotion, the company sold 400 booklets of one-way tickets. Each booklet contained 10 tickets and was priced at $200. During 19X1, purchasers of the booklets used 2,100 tickets.

(2) For passenger charter flights. A local corporation charters the helicopter to transport executives to and from an island conference facility. A deposit of 25% of the charter fee is required when a charter flight is booked. On December 31, 19X1, the company had deposits of $8,000 for scheduled charter flights. The company received a total of $46,000 for charter flights flown during 19X1.

(3) For construction material and equipment transportation. Building contractors rent the helicopter for $120 per hour for moving material and equipment to and from construction sites. Contractors used the helicopter a total of 200 hours during 19X1. Of this total, 20 hours occurred in December, for which the company has not yet received payment.

(4) For "Save A Life" efforts during holidays. The state rents the helicopter for $80 per hour on holiday weekends to carry a medical team to accident locations. The state used the helicopter a total of 60 hours in 19X1. The company has not yet collected for 12 hours of use in December.

Flitepath's bookkeeper has prepared the following schedule of revenue for 19X1:

One-way ticket booklets (400 @ $200)	$ 80,000
Charter flights made	46,000
Deposits on charter flights scheduled	8,000
Contractors (180 hours @ $120)	21,600
"Save A Life" program (48 hours @ $80)	3,840
Total Revenue	$159,440

The president of Flitepath, Inc., has asked you to evaluate whether the bookkeeper has correctly determined the 19X1 revenue in accordance with generally accepted accounting principles.

REQUIRED

Has the bookkeeper correctly determined the 19X1 revenue? If not, prepare a revised 19X1 revenue schedule. Give reasons for any changes you make from the bookkeeper's schedule.

14

Partnership Accounting

We are made for cooperation, like feet, like hands, like eyelids, like the rows of upper and lower teeth—

MARCUS AURELIUS

The essence of the partnership form of business organization is captured by the proverb, "Two heads are better than one." A **partnership** is a voluntary association of two or more persons for the purpose of conducting a business for profit. The Uniform Partnership Act governs the formation and operation of partnerships in many states. A partnership is easily formed—the parties need only agree to the partnership. The ease of formation makes the partnership an attractive form of organization for a business that requires more capital than a single proprietor can provide or for persons who want to combine specialized talents. Professional people, such as physicians, attorneys, and public accountants, as well as many small business concerns, often operate as partnerships.

Partnership agreements may be oral, but sound business practice demands a written agreement to avoid misunderstandings. A written partnership agreement constitutes the **articles of co-partnership.** The articles of co-partnership should detail the important provisions of the partnership arrangement, including the name and location of the partnership, the nature and duration of the business, the duties of partners, the capital contribution of each partner, the procedure for sharing profits and losses, permitted withdrawals of assets, the manner of keeping the books, the procedure for withdrawals of partners, and the procedure for dissolving the business.

CHARACTERISTICS OF A PARTNERSHIP

Although a partnership is an accounting entity, it is not a legal entity separate from its owners. Several characteristics—in addition to ease of formation—relate to this aspect of partnerships.

Mutual Agency

Mutual agency means that every partner is an agent for the firm, with the authority to bind the partnership to contracts. This authority applies to all acts typical of a partner engaging in the usual activities of the firm. Although the partners may limit the authority of one or more partners to act on customary matters, a partner acting in contravention of a restriction may still contractually bind the partnership if the other party to the contract is unaware of the limitation. The partnership would not be bound, however, if the other party knew of the restriction.

Unlimited Liability

Each partner in a **general partnership** is individually liable for the firm's obligations regardless of the amount of personal investment. Thus, creditors of a general partnership unable to pay its debts may obtain payment from the personal assets of individual partners. In addition to at least one general partner, a **limited**

partnership has one or more limited partners. The liability of a limited partner is restricted to his or her capital investment. A limited partner who becomes active in the control of the firm, however, assumes the status—and unlimited liability—of a general partner, as provided in the Uniform Limited Partnership Act.

Limited Life

Because a partnership is a voluntary association of persons, many events may cause its dissolution. These events include the expiration of the agreed-on partnership term; the accomplishment of the business objective; the admission of a new partner; the withdrawal, death, or bankruptcy of an existing partner; and the issuance of a court decree because of a partner's incapacity or misconduct. Even though a change in membership dissolves a partnership, business continuity is often unaffected. A new partnership continues the operations of the former partnership without interruption.

Co-ownership of Property

Assets contributed by partners become partnership property jointly owned by all partners. Individual partners no longer separately own the specific resources invested in the firm. Unless an agreement to the contrary exists, each partner has an equal right to the firm's property for partnership purposes.

Nontaxable Entity

Although a partnership must file an information return for federal income tax purposes, the organization itself is not a taxable entity. The information return shows the distributive shares of the partnership's net income that the partners include on their individual tax returns. The individual members must pay income taxes on their respective shares of partnership earnings whether or not these amounts have been withdrawn from the firm.

ADVANTAGES AND DISADVANTAGES OF A PARTNERSHIP

In contrast with a corporation, a partnership is easier and less expensive to organize and is subject to less government regulation and fewer reporting requirements. Certain corporate actions require the approval of stockholders or directors; partners have fewer constraints on their actions. Businesses of modest size or of planned short duration may find these features advantageous. The same may be true for new businesses hesitant to incur the cost of incorporation until their ventures prove successful.

Disadvantages of the partnership form of organization are mutual agency, unlimited liability, and limited life. The first two in particular underscore the importance of selecting partners with great care and are no doubt partially responsible for the rule that no person may be admitted to a partnership without the consent of all existing partners. A corporation, which offers limited liability to investors, is better able than a partnership to raise large amounts of capital.

The impact of taxes varies from one circumstance to the next. A partnership is a nontaxable entity; a corporation is a taxable entity. Partners' earnings are taxable whether distributed or not; corporate income is taxable a second time, but only when distributed as dividends. The tax rate on individuals in high tax brackets exceeds the corporate tax rate. To determine the most advantageous form of organization for tax purposes requires careful analysis of existing tax laws and the tax status of the persons going into business.

THE UBIQUITOUS, VERSATILE PARTNERSHIP

Ubiquitous means existing everywhere; versatile means having many uses. No terms could better describe the modern business partnership. Traditionally, the *general* partnership was an extension of the proprietorship. Its main advantage stemmed from the possibility of more than a single owner contributing capital and working in concert towards a business's objectives. Probably its most significant limitation is that all partners are individually liable for the obligations of the partnership not only to the extent of their partnership investments, but of their personal assets as well.

In spite of its limitations, the most recent U.S. Department of Commerce statistics* indicate that during the 1970s the number of partnerships increased almost 40% to 1.3 million and their total reported receipts grew almost 180% to $258 billion. More than 275,000 partnerships each had receipts of $100,000–$500,000, and 78,000 partnerships each had receipts exceeding $500,000. Included in this last group are the so-called "Big Eight" accounting firms—each having as many as several hundred partners.

A relatively recent phenomenon contributing to the popularity of partnerships is the use of limited partnerships in business ventures designed to serve as "tax shelters." Limited partnerships must have at least one general partner who manages the partnership and who incurs the unlimited liability associated with general partnerships. They may also have limited partners who, as long as they are not active in managing the partnership, enjoy a partnership liability limited to their partnership investments. Tax shelters are investments designed to produce, early in their lives, "book" or "paper" losses that can be combined with—and thus shelter from income taxes—other sources of taxable income. Since partnerships are not taxable enti-

ties, such losses are channeled directly to and reported on each partner's personal tax return. Thus, tax shelters organized as limited partnerships avoid the organizational complexities and legal regulation of corporations, provide limited liability to limited partners, avoid the double taxation inherent in corporations, and automatically channel each partner's share of losses to his or her personal tax return. Quite a bag of tricks!

The variety of tax shelter ventures employing limited partnership organizations is indicated by a sampling of headlines in the financial press: "Partnerships Still Popular Despite Slump in Real Estate,"[†] "'R&D' [Research and Development] Tax Shelters Catching Fire, but Potential Abuses Cause Concern,"[‡] "Wall Street Serving Up Fast-food Tie-in for Investors,"[§] "If You Have Always Wanted to Be in [Motion] Pictures, Partnerships Offer the Chance, but With Risks,"[‖] and "Low-rollers Can Now Own Racehorses."[#] Further testimony is offered by the realization that, as there are the "Big Three" in autos and the "Big Eight" in accounting, there is now the "Big Six" in the public syndication of limited partnerships for property investments. Collectively, these firms raised $1.33 billion in investment capital in 1982.[**]

Indeed, the partnership is a highly versatile, ubiquitous form of business organization!

*Statistical Abstract of the U.S. (103 ed.), 1982–83, U.S. Department of Commerce, Bureau of Census, Washington D.C.
†Robert Guenther, The Wall Street Journal, December 22, 1982, page 17.
‡Hal Lancaster, The Wall Street Journal, September 14, 1981, page 33.
§Ron Scherer, The Christian Science Monitor, March 29, 1982, page 10.
‖Laura Landro, The Wall Street Journal, May 23, 1983, page 60.
#Jan Juffer, The Wall Street Journal, September 8, 1982, page 35.
**James P. Meagher, "A Newcomer to Syndication's Big Six," Barron's, February 14, 1983, page 55.

CAPITAL, DRAWING, AND LOAN ACCOUNTS

Accounting for partnerships is similar in most respects to accounting for sole proprietorships. Each partner has a capital account and a drawing account that serve the same functions as the related accounts for a sole proprietor. A partner's capital account is credited for his or her investments, and each individual drawing account is debited to reflect assets withdrawn from the partnership. At the end of each accounting period, the balances in the drawing accounts are closed to the related capital accounts.

Occasionally a partner may advance amounts to the partnership beyond the intended permanent investment. These advances should be credited to the partner's loan account and classified among the liabilities, separate from liabilities to outsiders. By the same token, if a partner withdraws money with the intention of repaying, the debit should go to the partner's advance (or loan receivable) account and be classified separately among the partnership's receivables.

The formation of partnerships, the division of profits and losses, the admission and retirement of partners, and the liquidation of partnerships represent areas of particular interest in accounting for these entities. We focus on these issues in the remainder of the chapter.

FORMATION OF A PARTNERSHIP

A partnership's books are opened with an entry reflecting the net contribution of each partner to the firm. Asset accounts are debited for assets invested in the partnership, liability accounts are credited for any liabilities assumed by the partnership, and a separate capital account is credited for the amount of each partner's net investment (Assets − Liabilities).

Assume that Earl Ames, a sole proprietor, and John Baker form a partnership. Ames invests $8,000 cash, office equipment with a current fair value of $25,000, and office supplies worth $2,000. The partnership agrees to assume the $5,000 balance on a note issued by Ames when he acquired the equipment. Baker invests $10,000 cash. The following opening entries on the books of the partnership record the investments of Ames and Baker:

Cash	8,000	
Office Equipment	25,000	
Office Supplies on Hand	2,000	
Notes Payable		5,000
E. Ames, Capital		30,000
To record Ames' investment in the partnership of Ames and Baker.		
Cash	10,000	
J. Baker, Capital		10,000
To record Baker's investment in the partnership of Ames and Baker.		

Assets invested in the partnership should be recorded at their current fair values. These assets (less any liabilities assumed by the partnership) determine the opening capital balances for each partner. If the assets are not recorded initially at their fair values, inequities develop among the partners in terms of their respective capital balances.

For example, assume the office equipment invested by Ames was recorded incorrectly at $22,000 (its book value from his proprietorship records). If the partnership immediately sold the equipment for its current fair value of $25,000, the resulting $3,000 gain, on closing, would increase the capital balances of both Ames and Baker. This is not equitable. The $3,000 "gain" was not added to the asset by the operations of the partnership. Baker should not be credited with any part of this amount. A similar inequity develops if the equipment is used in operations rather than sold. Owing to a lower total depreciation over the life of the equipment, income would be $3,000 greater over the same period. To avoid such inequities, the partnership records the office equipment initially at $25,000. The values assigned to assets invested in a partnership are important and should be agreeable to all partners.

DIVISION OF PARTNERSHIP PROFITS AND LOSSES

In the absence of a profit and loss sharing agreement, partnership profits and losses are divided equally. Partners who do not wish to share profits equally must specify, preferably in a formal written agreement, the manner in which profit and loss distributions are made. Such arrangements may specify a fixed ratio (such as $\frac{2}{3}$ to $\frac{1}{3}$, 60% to 40%, or 5:3) or a sharing formula of some kind based on the relative financial participation of the partners, the services performed by the partners, or both. Any arrangement can be made, and losses may be shared differently from profits. If an agreement specifies the manner of sharing profits but is silent on the sharing of losses, losses will be divided in the same fashion as profits. In the following sections, we discuss several common arrangements.

Capital Ratios   When the services performed or skills provided by the various partners are considered equal, profits and losses may be divided according to the partners' relative investments in the firm. Assume that the Ames and Baker partnership had a profit of $18,000 for the year and that the partners' capital balances before any profit distribution at year-end were as follows:

E. Ames, Capital			J. Baker, Capital		
	19XX			19XX	
	Jan. 1	30,000		Jan. 1	10,000
				July 1	10,000

The $18,000 profit might be divided according to the beginning capital investment ratio or the average capital investment ratio for the year.

BEGINNING CAPITAL RATIO   At the beginning of the year, the total capital investment in the firm was $40,000—$30,000 for Ames and $10,000 for Baker. If they shared according to the ratio of beginning capital balances, the profit distribution would be 3 to 1, or $13,500 for Ames and $4,500 for Baker, computed as follows:

	Beginning Capital	Percent of Total	Division of Profit
Ames	$30,000	75	$13,500
Baker	10,000	25	4,500
	$40,000	100	$18,000

The following entry would be made to distribute the balance in the Income Summary account:

Income Summary	18,000	
E. Ames, Capital		13,500
J. Baker, Capital		4,500
To close the Income Summary account.		

AVERAGE CAPITAL RATIO   Because partners' investments may change during the year, the partners may decide that using *average* capital balances rather than beginning capital balances provides a more equitable division of profits. Under this scheme, investment balances are *weighted* by multiplying the amount of the investment by the portion of the year that these funds were invested. Because Baker invested an additional $10,000 on July 1, his average capital would be based on a $10,000 investment for the first six months and a $20,000 investment for the last six months. The computation might be as follows:

		Dollars × Months		Average Investment
Ames				
$30,000 × 12 months		$360,000	÷ 12	$30,000
Baker				
$10,000 × 6 months	$ 60,000			
$20,000 × 6 months	120,000	180,000	÷ 12	15,000
		$540,000		$45,000

Profit Distribution

$$\text{Ames: } \frac{\$30,000}{\$45,000} \times \$18,000 = \$12,000$$

$$\text{Baker: } \frac{\$15,000}{\$45,000} \times \$18,000 = \underline{\quad 6,000}$$

$$\$18,000$$

The entry to close the Income Summary account would credit E. Ames, Capital with $12,000 and J. Baker, Capital with $6,000.

Salary and Interest Allowances

A sharing agreement may provide for variations in the personal services contributed by partners and in their relative investments. **Salary allowances** provide for differences in personal services; **allowances for interest** on capital balances provide for differences in the financial participation of partners.

The terms *salary allowances* and *allowances for interest* describe only the process of dividing net income among partners. These terms should not be confused with any salary expense and interest expense appearing in the firm's records or with any cash withdrawals the partners make. For example, the partnership agreement may provide that partners may make withdrawals equal to their salary allowances. These withdrawals would be debited to each partner's drawing account, which is eventually closed to his or her capital account. The cash withdrawals in no way affect the division of net income among partners—the division of net income is governed by the sharing agreement.

SALARY ALLOWANCE Suppose Ames and Baker render different degrees of personal services and therefore specify a salary allowance in their sharing agreement—$6,000 for Ames and $4,000 for Baker. The remainder of net income is divided equally. The division of the $18,000 net income is as follows:

	Ames	Baker	Total
Earnings to be divided			$18,000
Salary allowances:			
Ames	$ 6,000		
Baker		$4,000	10,000
Remainder			$ 8,000
Remainder ($8,000) divided equally	4,000	4,000	
Partners' shares	$10,000	$8,000	

The $18,000 balance in the Income Summary account would be closed by crediting E. Ames, Capital for $10,000 and J. Baker, Capital for $8,000.

SALARY AND INTEREST ALLOWANCES Next, assume that Ames and Baker wish to acknowledge the differences in their financial involvement as well as their personal services. They have the following sharing agreement: salaries of $6,000 to Ames and $4,000 to Baker; 8% interest on *average* capital balances; and the remainder divided equally. We computed average investments for Ames and Baker earlier at $30,000 and $15,000, respectively. The $18,000 net income would therefore be divided as follows:

	Ames	Baker	Total
Earnings to be divided			$18,000
Salary allowances:			
Ames	$ 6,000		
Baker		$4,000	10,000
			$ 8,000
Allowance for interest on average capital:			
Ames ($30,000 × 0.08)	2,400		
Baker ($15,000 × 0.08)		1,200	3,600
Remainder			$ 4,400
Remainder ($4,400) divided equally	2,200	2,200	
Partners' shares	$10,600	$7,400	

The entry closing the $18,000 net income to the Income Summary account would credit E. Ames, Capital for $10,600 and J. Baker, Capital for $7,400.

If Ames and Baker had withdrawn cash equal to their salary allowances, their drawing accounts at the end of the year would contain debit balances of $6,000 and $4,000, respectively. The entry to close the drawing accounts would be

E. Ames, Capital	6,000	
J. Baker, Capital	4,000	
E. Ames, Drawing		6,000
J. Baker, Drawing		4,000
To close the partners' drawing accounts.		

ALLOWANCES EXCEED EARNINGS   Unless a special provision is included in the sharing agreement, the same allocation procedures apply in the event of a loss or of earnings insufficient to cover allowances for salary and interest. For example, assume that net income for the year was only $8,000. After salary and interest allowances are allocated, a *sharing agreement loss* of $5,600 would be divided equally between the partners to fulfill their agreement. The computations are shown below:

	Ames	Baker	Total
Earnings to be divided			$ 8,000
Salary allowances	$6,000	$4,000	
Interest allowances	2,400	1,200	
Total salary and interest	$8,400	$5,200	13,600
Remainder (sharing agreement loss)			($ 5,600)
Remainder divided equally	(2,800)	(2,800)	
Partners' shares	$5,600	$2,400	

The entry closing the $8,000 net income to the Income Summary account would credit E. Ames, Capital with $5,600 and J. Baker, Capital with $2,400.

PARTNERSHIP FINANCIAL STATEMENTS

A few unique features of partnership financial statements arise because a partnership consists of co-owners. The partnership income statement may show, at the bottom, how the net income is divided among the partners. A capital account for each partner appears in the owners' equity section of the balance sheet. The statement of partners' (or owners') capital portrays the changes in the capital balances of each partner, as shown in Exhibit 14–1.

ADMISSION OF A PARTNER

New partners may be admitted to a partnership either by purchasing an interest from current members or by investing in the firm. When a person buys an interest from one or more of the current partners, the assets of the firm are not affected. Payment is made personally to the member or members from whom the interest is obtained, resulting in merely a transfer among capital accounts. When an investment is made in the firm, however, total assets increase by the amount contributed.

Economic circumstances usually dictate a new partner's mode of entry. A firm with sufficient capital may seek the skills and services of a particular new partner. Or, current partners may wish to liquidate part of their interests and scale down their individual investments. In these situations, the firm may sell

EXHIBIT 14–1

Ames and Baker **Statement of Partners' Capital** **For the Year Ended December 31, 19XX**			
	Ames	**Baker**	**Total**
Capital Balances, January 1, 19XX	$30,000	$10,000	$40,000
Add: Additional Contributions		10,000	10,000
Net Income for 19XX	10,600	7,400	18,000
Totals	$40,600	$27,400	$68,000
Less: Withdrawals	6,000	4,000	10,000
Capital Balances, December 31, 19XX	$34,600	$23,400	$58,000

an interest in the current partnership. On the other hand, if additional capital is needed, adding a partner who will contribute assets may be a proper solution.

For the benefit of the existing partners, the net assets of the current partnership should reflect their current fair values when a new partner is admitted. This may require a revaluation of certain assets. The resultant gain or loss would be apportioned to the current partners in their profit and loss sharing ratio. If the net assets do not reflect their fair values, the new partner may share in gains and losses that developed before admission to the firm. In the following examples of new partner admissions, we assume that the recorded book values of the current partnership's assets do not require restatement.

Purchase of an Interest

Suppose that Ames and Baker have capital balances of $30,000 and $10,000, respectively, and that Ames sells one-half of his interest to Susan Carter. For Carter to become a partner, both Ames and Baker must consent to the sale. The entry to record Carter's admission would be

E. Ames, Capital	15,000	
S. Carter, Capital		15,000
To record admission of Carter.		

The actual cash amount paid to Ames is entirely a personal matter between the two persons and is not relevant in recording Carter's admission. Whether an interest is purchased from one partner or several, a transfer of capital is made only for the amounts of the interests purchased without regard to the payment made. Suppose that Carter purchased a one-fourth interest in the firm by obtaining one-fourth of each partner's current share. One-fourth interest would amount to $10,000 (one-fourth of $40,000 present capital). The entry for Carter's admission would be

E. Ames, Capital	7,500	
J. Baker, Capital	2,500	
S. Carter, Capital		10,000
To record admission of Carter.		

Clearly, if an incoming partner contributes assets to the firm, total capital increases. If the current partners' capital balances are realistically stated, the new partner simply contributes assets equal to the desired proportionate interest in the total capital of the new firm. In our example, present capital is $40,000—$30,000 for Ames and $10,000 for Baker. Carter wants to contribute enough cash to obtain one-third interest in the new firm. The current partners' capital of $40,000 represents two-thirds of the new firm's capital; therefore, Carter should contribute $20,000. The entry for admission would be

Cash	20,000	
S. Carter, Capital		20,000
To record admission of Carter.		

BONUS TO CURRENT PARTNERS   If a partnership interest is especially attractive because of a superior earnings record or the promise of exceptional future earnings, the current partners may require the new partner to pay an additional amount as a "bonus" for admission. Suppose that Ames and Baker required a $35,000 payment for a one-third interest in the new firm. The total capital of the new firm would then be $75,000, of which a one-third interest would be $25,000, as shown below:

E. Ames, Capital	$30,000
J. Baker, Capital	10,000
Present Capital	$40,000
Contribution of Carter	35,000
Capital of New Firm	$75,000
One-third Interest	$25,000

The $10,000 difference between Carter's payment of $35,000 and her interest of $25,000 is a bonus to the former partners, to be divided according to their profit and loss sharing ratio. If the agreement provides for equal sharing, the entry to admit Carter is

Cash	35,000	
E. Ames, Capital		5,000
J. Baker, Capital		5,000
S. Carter, Capital		25,000
To record admission of Carter.		

BONUS TO NEW PARTNER   A firm eager to add a partner who has ready cash or unique skills, management potential, or other desirable characteristics may award the new partner a larger interest than would be warranted by his or her contribution. Because the capital of the new partner will be greater than his or her asset contribution, the current partners must make up the difference (bonus to new partner) by reducing their capital balances. Assume that Carter receives a one-third interest by contributing only $14,000 to the new firm. The capital of the new firm increases to $54,000 ($40,000 + $14,000), of which a one-third interest is $18,000, as shown below:

E. Ames, Capital	$30,000
J. Baker, Capital	10,000
Present Capital	$40,000
Contribution of Carter	14,000
Capital of New Firm	$54,000
One-third Interest	$18,000

The $4,000 difference between Carter's $14,000 contribution and her $18,000 interest is a bonus to Carter. Ames and Baker reduce their capital balances accordingly, with amounts based on the profit and loss sharing ratio. With equal sharing, the entry to admit Carter as a partner in the firm is

Cash	14,000	
E. Ames, Capital	2,000	
J. Baker, Capital	2,000	
S. Carter, Capital		18,000
To record admission of Carter.		

RETIREMENT OF A PARTNER

A retiring partner may (1) sell his or her interest to an outsider, (2) sell that interest to one or more of the remaining partners, or (3) receive payment for the interest from partnership funds.

Sale of Partnership Interest

INTEREST SOLD TO NEW PARTNER The procedure for recording the sale of a retiring partner's interest to an outsider is similar to that illustrated earlier for the purchase of an interest. Suppose that retiring partner Baker, with the firm's approval, sells his $10,000 interest to Stan Dodge. Regardless of the personally determined amount of Dodge's actual payment to Baker, the entry to record Dodge's admission and Baker's departure is

J. Baker, Capital	10,000	
S. Dodge, Capital		10,000
To record Dodge's purchase of Baker's interest.		

INTEREST SOLD TO REMAINING PARTNERS This transaction is a personal one between Baker and his partners. If Baker sells his interest to remaining partners Ames and Carter, Baker's interest is merely transferred to their capital accounts, regardless of the actual amount of the payments. If Baker sells equal portions of his interest to the remaining partners, the entry is

J. Baker, Capital	10,000	
E. Ames, Capital		5,000
S. Carter, Capital		5,000
To record sale of Baker's interest to Ames and Carter.		

Payment from Partnership Funds

SETTLEMENT EXCEEDS CAPITAL BALANCE A partner's retirement may be an occasion for reviewing partners' capital balances. Because of such factors as appreciation of assets or an exceptional partnership performance record, the capital balances may not provide a realistic basis for determining the value of partnership interests. In such situations, the partners may recognize any amount by which the current fair value of the retiring partner's partnership interest exceeds his or her capital balance by paying a bonus to the retiring partner.

If the retiring partner receives funds from the partnership for his or her interest, any difference between the amount of this interest and the sum paid affects the capital balances of the remaining partners. For example, assume that the capital balances of Ames, Baker, and Carter are $35,000, $15,000, and $25,000, respectively, when Baker retires and that the firm pays $20,000 for Baker's interest. Baker's $5,000 bonus is divided by the other partners according to their profit and loss sharing ratio (assumed here to be equal). The entry would be:

E. Ames, Capital	2,500	
S. Carter, Capital	2,500	
J. Baker, Capital	15,000	
Cash		20,000
To record Baker's withdrawal		
from the partnership.		

When the fair value of a retiring partner's interest exceeds his or her related capital balance, the remaining partners might revalue total partnership assets proportionately upward, distribute the increase to all partners in their profit and loss sharing ratio, and then pay the retiring partner an amount equal to his or her new capital balance. Such an approach, however, obviously departs from the principle of historical cost. Although the increased value of the partnership interest is properly considered in settling with the retiring partner, revaluing total partnership assets above their historical cost is not acceptable.

CAPITAL BALANCE EXCEEDS SETTLEMENT   In certain circumstances, a retiring partner may accept a settlement less than his or her capital balance. Examples include a history of poor partnership earnings or recognition of operating disadvantages resulting from the partner's retirement. In such cases, the excess of the retiring partner's capital balance over the settlement constitutes a bonus to the remaining partners. Assume that Baker, who has a capital balance of $15,000, accepts $11,000 rather than $20,000 for his interest. The $4,000 bonus is allocated to the remaining partners in their profit and loss sharing ratio (assumed here to be equal). The entry to record this bonus is

J. Baker, Capital	15,000	
E. Ames, Capital		2,000
S. Carter, Capital		2,000
Cash		11,000
To record Baker's withdrawal from the		
partnership.		

LIQUIDATION OF A PARTNERSHIP

The situations that arise during partnership liquidations can be quite complex. Because liquidations are treated comprehensively in advanced accounting texts, we shall provide only a basic approach to them here. When a business partnership is discontinued, the assets are sold, liabilities are paid, and the remaining cash is distributed to the partners. Essentially, gains and losses realized in selling assets are carried to the partners' capital accounts (in the established profit and loss sharing ratio), and each partner eventually receives the balance remaining in his or her capital account.

Let us suppose that Ames, Baker, and Carter share profits and losses in the ratio of 40%, 40%, and 20%, respectively, and that before liquidation the partnership's balance sheet can be summarized as follows (assume that for the final operating period, the partnership books have been adjusted and closed and the profit or loss allocated to each partner):

Cash	$ 15,000	Liabilities	$ 40,000
Other Assets (net)	100,000	E. Ames, Capital	35,000
		J. Baker, Capital	15,000
		S. Carter, Capital	25,000
	$115,000		$115,000

Capital Balances Exceed Losses

If the noncash assets in the balance sheet in our example are sold for $80,000, the firm sustains a $20,000 loss. Because the partners share the loss, their capital balances are ultimately reduced by the following amounts: Ames, $8,000; Baker, $8,000; and Carter, $4,000. The appropriate entries might be as follows:

Cash	80,000	
Loss on Realization of Assets	20,000	
Other Assets (net)		100,000
To record loss on sale of other assets.		
E. Ames, Capital	8,000	
J. Baker, Capital	8,000	
S. Carter, Capital	4,000	
Loss on Realization of Assets		20,000
To distribute loss on sale of other assets.		

After these entries have been recorded, the firm's balance sheet accounts would be as follows:

Cash	$95,000	Liabilities	$40,000
		E. Ames, Capital	27,000
		J. Baker, Capital	7,000
		S. Carter, Capital	21,000
	$95,000		$95,000

Finally, the entries to pay the liabilities and distribute the remaining cash to the partners would be:

Liabilities	40,000	
Cash		40,000
To record payment of liabilities.		

E. Ames, Capital	27,000	
J. Baker, Capital	7,000	
S. Carter, Capital	21,000	
Cash		55,000
To record cash distribution to partners.		

Observe that *only gains* and *losses* on liquidation are shared in the profit and loss sharing ratio—not the residual cash. Remaining funds are distributed to partners *in the amounts of their capital balances* after all gains and losses have been shared.

Losses Exceed Partner's Capital

When liquidation losses occur, a partner's share of losses may exceed his or her capital balance. That partner will be expected to contribute cash to the partnership to offset the capital account debit balance. For example, suppose that in our illustration the $100,000 of other assets are sold for only $60,000. The resulting $40,000 loss on realization of assets is recorded and then distributed in the 40%:40%:20% sharing ratio, reducing partners' capital accounts as follows: Ames, $16,000; Baker, $16,000; and Carter, $8,000. Entries to record and distribute the loss and to pay the liabilities are

Cash	60,000	
Loss on Realization of Assets	40,000	
Other Assets (net)		100,000
To record loss on sale of other assets.		

E. Ames, Capital	16,000	
J. Baker, Capital	16,000	
S. Carter, Capital	8,000	
Loss on Realization of Assets		40,000
To distribute loss on sale of other assets.		

Liabilities	40,000	
Cash		40,000
To record payment of liabilities.		

After recording and distributing the loss on the sale of other assets and payment of the liabilities, the following account balances remain:

Cash	$35,000	E. Ames, Capital	$19,000
		J. Baker, Capital	
		(debit)	(1,000)
		S. Carter, Capital	17,000
	$35,000		$35,000

Note that Baker's $16,000 share of the loss on realization of the other assets absorbs his $15,000 capital balance and leaves a $1,000 capital deficit (debit balance) in his capital account.

If Baker pays the firm $1,000 to make up his deficit, the resulting $36,000 cash balance is the amount distributed to Ames ($19,000) and Carter ($17,000). If Baker cannot make the contribution, the $1,000 is treated as a loss distributed to Ames and Carter in their profit and loss sharing ratio. Because the ratio of their respective shares is 40:20, Ames sustains 40/60, or two-thirds, of the $1,000 loss and Carter, 20/60, or one-third. The entry to redistribute Baker's debit balance would be

E. Ames, Capital	667	
S. Carter, Capital	333	
J. Baker, Capital		1,000
To record distribution of Baker's capital deficit to Ames and Carter.		

The $35,000 cash is then paid to Ames and Carter in the amounts of their final capital balances.

E. Ames, Capital	18,333	
S. Carter, Capital	16,667	
Cash		35,000
To record cash distribution to partners.		

Sometimes a partner with a capital account deficit may be uncertain about making up the deficit. At the same time, the other partners may want to distribute whatever cash is available after creditors have been paid. In our illustration, if Ames and Carter had doubts about receiving $1,000 from Baker, cash might be distributed as shown in the last entry—$18,333 to Ames and $16,667 to Carter. This would leave sufficient amounts in their capital accounts—$667 for Ames and $333 for Carter—to absorb a $1,000 loss in the sharing ratio if Baker defaults on payment. If he does contribute the amount needed, the other partners will be paid the balances of their capital accounts.

Statement of Partnership Liquidation

Liquidation of a partnership can continue over an extended period. To provide interested parties with a comprehensive report of the initial assets and liabilities, the sale of noncash assets, the payment of liabilities, and the final distribution of cash to the partners, the partnership may prepare a statement of partnership liquidation. Using data from our illustration, Exhibit 14–2 presents a statement of liquidation for the Ames, Baker, and Carter partnership. We assume that non-cash assets are sold for $60,000 and that Baker does not cover his $1,000 capital deficit.

Observe the following about the statement of partnership liquidation:

(1) The statement is dated to reflect the period during which the liquidation took place.

EXHIBIT 14-2

Ames, Baker, and Carter (Partnership)
Statement of Partnership Liquidation
From January 1 to March 31, 19XX

	Cash	Noncash Assets	Liabilities	E. Ames, Capital (40%)	J. Baker, Capital (40%)	S. Carter, Capital (20%)	Realization Gain (Loss)
Beginning Balances	$15,000	$100,000	$40,000	$35,000	$15,000	$25,000	
Sale of Noncash Assets	60,000	(100,000)					($40,000)
	$75,000	$ -0-	$40,000	$35,000	$15,000	$25,000	($40,000)
Allocation of Loss to Partners				(16,000)	(16,000)	(8,000)	40,000
	$75,000		$40,000	$19,000	$ (1,000)	$17,000	$ -0-
Payment of Liabilities	(40,000)		(40,000)				
	$35,000		$ -0-	$19,000	$ (1,000)	$17,000	
Allocation of Baker's Capital Deficit				(667)	1,000	(333)	
	$35,000			$18,333	$ -0-	$16,667	
Final Distribution of Cash	(35,000)			(18,333)		(16,667)	
	$ -0-			$ -0-		$ -0-	

(2) The initial numbers on the statement reflect the partnership balance sheet at the beginning of the liquidation (see page 487 in our illustration).

(3) Each line that reflects a step in the liquidation (sale of noncash assets, allocation of loss, payment of liabilities, allocation of partner's capital deficit, and final cash distribution) matches related journal entries in the illustration (see pages 488–89).

(4) The statement shows how each step affects the liquidation and is therefore an excellent vehicle for analysis.

DEMONSTRATION PROBLEM FOR REVIEW

J. Porter and M. Kantor have been partners for several years, operating Fast Moves, a moving business. The business has had its ups and downs, but overall has been quite successful. In recognition of Porter's administrative responsibilities, the profit and loss sharing agreement allows him a salary of $5,000, with the remainder shared equally.

On January 1, 19X1, Porter and Kantor had capital balances of $14,000 and $9,000, respectively. During 19X1, Porter withdrew $4,000 cash from the partnership, and 19X1 net income was $11,000. On December 31, 19X1, the partnership had the following assets and liabilities: Cash, $4,000; Other Assets, $29,000; and Accounts Payable, $3,000.

Porter and Kantor liquidate the partnership on January 1, 19X2. On that date, other assets are sold for $35,000, creditors are paid, and the partners receive the remaining cash.

REQUIRED

(a) Prepare a schedule showing how the $11,000 net income for 19X1 should be divided between Porter and Kantor.

(b) Prepare a statement of partners' capital for 19X1.

(c) Prepare a balance sheet at December 31, 19X1.

(d) Give the January 1, 19X2 journal entries to record the sale of other assets and recognition of any related gain or loss, the distribution of any gain or loss to partners' capital accounts, the payment of liabilities, and the distribution of cash to the partners.

SOLUTION TO DEMONSTRATION PROBLEM

(a)

	Porter	Kantor	Total
Earnings to be divided			$11,000
Salary allowance	$5,000		5,000
Remainder			$ 6,000
Remainder divided equally	3,000	$3,000	
Partners' shares	$8,000	$3,000	

(b)

Fast Moves
Statement of Partners' Capital
For the Year 19X1

	Porter	Kantor	Total
Capital Balances, January 1, 19X1	$14,000	$ 9,000	$23,000
Add: Net Income for 19X1	8,000	3,000	11,000
Totals	$22,000	$12,000	$34,000
Less: Withdrawals	4,000		4,000
Capital Balances, December 31, 19X1	$18,000	$12,000	$30,000

(c)

Fast Moves
Balance Sheet
December 31, 19X1

Assets		Liabilities		
Cash	$ 4,000	Accounts Payable		$ 3,000
Other Assets	29,000			
		Owners' Equity		
		J. Porter, Capital	$18,000	
		M. Kantor, Capital	12,000	30,000
		Total Liabilities and		
Total Assets	$33,000	Owners' Equity		$33,000

(d)

19X2				
Jan. 1	Cash		35,000	
	Other Assets			29,000
	Gain on Realization of Assets			6,000
	To record sale of other assets.			
Jan. 1	Gain on Realization of Assets		6,000	
	J. Porter, Capital			3,000
	M. Kantor, Capital			3,000
	To distribute gain on sale of			
	other assets.			
Jan. 1	Accounts Payable		3,000	
	Cash			3,000
	To record payment of liabilities.			
Jan. 1	J. Porter, Capital		21,000	
	M. Kantor, Capital		15,000	
	Cash			36,000
	To record cash distribution to partners.			

KEY POINTS TO REMEMBER

(1) A partnership is a voluntary association of persons who agree to become joint owners of a business. Each general partner is an agent for the partnership, has unlimited liability for partnership obligations, and co-owns firm property with all partners. A partnership is a nontaxable entity and may be dissolved by any membership change or by court decree.

(2) Partnership assets should be recorded initially at their current fair values, which precludes future inequities in partners' capital balances resulting from the use of these assets.

(3) Partnership profits and losses are divided among partners according to their sharing agreement. If no sharing agreement exists, profits and losses are divided equally.

(4) New partners may be admitted to a partnership either by purchasing an interest or by investing assets. Because the purchase of an interest is a personal transaction between the incoming partner and one or more current partners, the firm's assets do not change. Admission of a partner through an investment increases the assets of the partnership.

(5) A retiring partner may sell his or her interest to an outsider, to one or more of the remaining partners, or receive payment for the interest from partnership funds.

(6) The liquidation of a partnership involves conversion of assets to cash, recognition and distribution of any related gain or loss, payment of creditors, and distribution of any remaining cash to partners. The final distribution of cash to partners is based on their capital balances.

QUESTIONS

14–1 What is meant by *mutual agency?* By *unlimited liability?*

14–2 A corporation is said to have continuity of existence, whereas a partnership is characterized by a limited life. Name several events that may cause the dissolution of a partnership.

14–3 Sayers understands that a partnership is a nontaxable entity and believes that if she does not withdraw any assets from the firm this year, she will not have any taxable income from her partnership activities. Is Sayers correct? Why or why not?

14–4 Boone invests in his partnership a machine that originally cost him $12,000. At the time of the investment, his personal records carry it at a book value of $8,000. Its current market value is $9,000. At what amount should the partnership record the machine? Why?

14–5 What factors should persons going into partnership consider in deciding how to share profits and losses?

14–6 If a partnership agreement is silent on the sharing of profits and losses, how will they be divided? What if the agreement indicates the method of sharing profits, but states nothing about the sharing of losses?

14–7 What are salary allowances? What is the difference between a salary allowance and salary expense?

14–8 In what ways do the financial statements of a partnership differ from those of a sole proprietorship? What is the purpose of a statement of partners' capital?

14–9 Distinguish between the admission of a partner by the purchase of an interest and by investment in the firm.

14–10 What circumstances might cause (a) current partners to receive a bonus when admitting a new partner and (b) an incoming partner to receive a bonus?

14–11 Frank and Barns, who share profits and losses equally, admit Patt as a new partner. Patt contributes $40,000 for a one-fourth interest in the new firm. The entry to admit Patt shows a $5,000 bonus each to Frank and Barns. What is the apparent total capital of the new partnership?

14–12 When a partner retires, are the assets and capital of the partnership reduced? Explain.

14–13 When a partnership liquidates, how do accountants handle the gains and losses realized in selling the assets?

14–14 In a partnership liquidation, the residual cash is distributed to partners in the amounts of their capital balances just prior to the distribution. Why is this the proper distribution procedure?

14–15 Assume that during liquidation a debit balance arises in a partner's capital account and the partner is unable to contribute any more assets to the partnership. How does the partnership dispose of the debit balance in the capital account?

14–16 How is a statement of partnership liquidation dated and what accounting information does this statement contain?

EXERCISES

14–17 Cook and Lang form a partnership on May 1. Cook contributes $50,000 cash and Lang contributes the following items from a separate business:

> Marketable securities—cost of $9,000; current fair value of $15,000
> Equipment—cost of $35,000; accumulated depreciation of $12,000; current fair value of $25,000
> Land—cost of $30,000; current fair value of $43,000
> Note payable (secured by equipment)—$8,000 assumed by partnership

Give the opening general journal entries of the partnership to record the investments of Cook and Lang.

14–18 Keller and Evees are partners whose profit and loss sharing agreement gives salary allowances of $12,000 to Keller and $8,000 to Evees, with the remainder divided equally.
(a) Net income for the year is $38,000. Give the general journal entry to distribute the income to Keller and Evees.
(b) Assume a $12,000 net loss for the year. Give the general journal entry to distribute the loss to Keller and Evees.

14–19 Use the following data to prepare a 19XX statement of partners' capital for Dann and Post, who share profits and losses in the ratio of 60% to Dann and 40% to Post.

Dann, Capital, January 1, 19XX	$72,000
Post, Capital, January 1, 19XX	35,000
Dann, Drawing	45,000
Post, Drawing	10,000
Additional investments by Dann	18,000
Net income for 19XX	50,000

14–20 Estes and Robin are partners with capital balances of $60,000 and $40,000, respectively. They share profits and losses in the ratio of 70% to Estes and 30%

to Robin. Moon receives a one-fourth interest in the firm by investing $40,000 cash on May 4.

(a) Give the general journal entry to record Moon's admission assuming a bonus is allowed Estes and Robin.

(b) Briefly explain circumstances that might cause existing partners to receive a bonus when admitting a new partner.

14–21 Avon, Bass, and Cook are partners sharing profits and losses in the ratio 5:3:2, respectively. Their capital balances are Avon, $45,000; Bass, $30,000; and Cook, $20,000. Avon retires from the firm on June 30 and is paid $50,000 from partnership funds.

(a) Give the general journal entry to record Avon's retirement, assuming that Bass and Cook absorb the bonus paid Avon.

(b) Briefly explain circumstances that might cause a retiring partner to receive a bonus.

14–22 In the liquidation of the ABC Partnership, noncash assets were sold for $11,000 and the related gain or loss on realization resulted in debits to the capital accounts of partners A, B, and C for $2,500, $1,500, and $1,000, respectively.

(a) Were the noncash assets sold at a gain or a loss? How do you know? How much was the gain or the loss?

(b) What is the partners' apparent profit and loss sharing ratio?

(c) What was the apparent book value of the noncash assets sold?

14–23 Just before liquidation, the balance sheet of Don and Wallis, who share profits and losses equally, appeared as follows:

Cash	$13,000	Liabilities	$ 5,000
Other Assets	22,000	Don, Capital	20,000
		Wallis, Capital	10,000
	$35,000		$35,000

(a) If other assets are sold for $20,000, what amounts will Don and Wallis receive as the final cash distribution?

(b) If other assets are sold for $25,000, what amounts will Don and Wallis receive as the final cash distribution?

(c) If Don receives $14,000 and Wallis receives $4,000 as the final (and only) cash distribution, what amount was received from the sale of the other assets?

14–24 Dunn, Ned, Potts, and Roan are liquidating their partnership. All assets have been converted to cash, and all liabilities have been paid. At this point, the capital accounts show the following: Dunn, $9,000 credit balance; Ned, $6,000 credit balance; Potts, $12,000 debit balance; and Roan, $8,000 credit balance. Profits and losses are shared equally.

(a) How much cash is available to distribute to partners?

(b) If there is doubt concerning Potts' ability to make up the $12,000 deficit, how should the available cash be distributed?

14–25 The following is a summary of a statement of partnership liquidation. Each numbered line represents some aspect of the liquidation in the order in which it normally occurs. Amounts in parentheses represent decreases or losses. Briefly describe the implications of each numbered line, indicating the apparent partners' sharing ratio when appropriate.

	Cash	Noncash Assets	Liabilities	A, Capital	B, Capital	Gain or Loss on Realization
(1)	$10,000	$30,000	$12,000	$20,000	$8,000	
(2)	25,000	($30,000)				($5,000)
(3)	(12,000)		($12,000)			
(4)				(3,000)	(2,000)	$5,000
(5)	($23,000)			($17,000)	($6,000)	

PROBLEMS

14–26 Hall and Mills form a partnership and invest $60,000 and $20,000, respectively. During its first year, the partnership earned a $12,000 net income.

REQUIRED
(a) Give the entry to close the Income Summary account and distribute the $12,000 net income under each of the following independent assumptions:
  (1) The partnership agreement is silent on the sharing of profits and losses.
  (2) Profits and losses are shared in the ratio of beginning capital investments.
  (3) Profits and losses are shared by allowing 10% interest on beginning capital investments, with the remainder divided equally.
(b) Assume the partnership had an $8,000 loss in its first year. Give the entry to close the Income Summary account and distribute the $8,000 loss under each of the foregoing assumptions.

14–27 The capital accounts and the Income Summary account of the Moss, Todd, and Hall partnership appear below. None of the partners withdrew capital during the year.

Moss, Capital		
	19XX	
	Jan. 1	6,000
	July 1	8,000

Todd, Capital		
	19XX	
	Jan. 1	8,000
	Oct. 1	8,000

Hall, Capital		
	19XX	
	Jan. 1	20,000

Income Summary		
	19XX	
	Dec. 31	15,000

REQUIRED
(a) Give the entry to distribute the $15,000 net income if Moss, Todd, and Hall share profits and losses:
  (1) Equally.
  (2) In the ratio 5:3:2, respectively.
  (3) In the ratio of *average* capital balances for the year.
  (4) Under an agreement allowing $8,000 salary to Hall, 10% interest on *beginning* investments, with the remainder shared equally.

(b) Assume that net income was $7,200 rather than $15,000. Give the entry to distribute the $7,200 earnings if the agreement allows $8,000 salary to Hall, 10% interest on beginning investments, with the remainder shared equally.

14–28 Dorth and Nunn are partners with capital balances of $30,000 and $12,000, respectively. Profits and losses are shared equally.

REQUIRED

Give the entries to record the admission of a new partner, Boen, under each of the following separate circumstances:

(a) Boen purchases one-half of Nunn's interest, paying Nunn $11,000 personally.
(b) Boen invests sufficient funds to receive exactly a one-fourth interest in the new partnership. (No bonuses are recorded.)
(c) Boen invests $18,000 for a one-fifth interest, with any bonus distributed to the capital accounts of Dorth and Nunn.
(d) Boen invests $12,000 for a one-fourth interest, with any bonus credited to Boen's capital account.
(e) In parts (c) and (d) above, what do the terms of admission imply regarding the relative negotiating positions of the new partner versus the old partners?

14–29 Stedd, Dobbs, and Victor are partners with capital balances of $60,000, $35,000, and $40,000, respectively. Profits and losses are shared equally. Victor retires from the firm.

REQUIRED

Record the entries for Victor's retirement in each of the following separate circumstances:

(a) Victor's interest is sold to Bailey, a new partner, for $48,000.
(b) One-half of Victor's interest is sold to each of the remaining partners for $24,000 apiece.
(c) Victor receives $46,000 of partnership funds for his interest. The remaining partners absorb the bonus paid Victor.
(d) The partners agree that Victor's abrupt retirement presents operating disadvantages and therefore Victor should receive only $36,000 for his interest. Payment is from partnership funds, with any bonuses going to Stedd and Dobbs.

14–30 Goss and Carr formed a partnership on January 1, 19X1, with capital investments of $20,000 and $32,000, respectively. The profit and loss sharing agreement allowed Goss a salary of $12,000, with the remainder divided equally. During the year, Carr made withdrawals of $6,000; no other investments or withdrawals were made in 19X1. The partnership incurred a net loss of $16,000 in 19X1.

On January 1, 19X2, Lomar was admitted to the partnership. Lomar purchased one-third of Goss's interest, paying $8,000 directly to Goss. Goss, Carr, and Lomar agreed to share profits and losses in the ratio 3:5:2, respectively. No provision was made for salaries. The partnership earned a net income of $20,000 in 19X2.

On January 1, 19X3, Carr withdrew from the partnership. Carr received $24,000 of partnership funds for her interest. Goss and Lomar absorbed the bonus paid Carr.

REQUIRED

(a) Give the December 31, 19X1 entry to close the Income Summary account and distribute the $16,000 loss for 19X1.

(b) Compute the capital balances of Goss and Carr at December 31, 19X1.

(c) Give the entry to record the admission of Lomar on January 1, 19X2.

(d) Give the December 31, 19X2 entry to close the Income Summary account and distribute the $20,000 income for 19X2.

(e) Compute the December 31, 19X2 capital balances of Goss, Carr, and Lomar.

(f) Give the January 1, 19X3 entry to record Carr's withdrawal.

14–31 Anson and Ford formed a partnership in 19X1, agreeing to share profits and losses equally. On December 31, 19X1, their capital balances were Anson, $30,000; Ford, $18,000.

On January 1, 19X2, Pratt was admitted to a one-fourth interest in the firm by investing $24,000 cash. Pratt's admission was recorded by according bonuses to Anson and Ford. The profit and loss sharing agreement of the new partnership allowed salaries of $6,000 to Anson and $8,000 to Pratt, with the remainder divided in the ratio 3:3:2 among Anson, Ford, and Pratt, respectively.

Net income for 19X2 was $38,000. Anson and Pratt withdrew cash during the year equal to their salary allowances. Immediately after the net income had been closed to the partners' capital accounts, Pratt retired from the firm. Pratt received $34,000 of partnership funds for his interest, and the remaining partners absorbed the bonus paid Pratt.

REQUIRED

Prepare a statement of partners' capital for 19X2.

14–32 Foe, Gahn, and Hoxx are partners who share profits and losses in the ratio of 5:3:2, respectively. Just before the partnership's liquidation, its balance sheet accounts appear as follows:

Cash	$15,000	Accounts Payable	$20,000
Other Assets	80,000	Foe, Capital	15,000
		Gahn, Capital	40,000
		Hoxx, Capital	20,000
	$95,000		$95,000

REQUIRED

(a) Assuming that other assets are sold for $70,000, give the entries to record the sale of the other assets and distribute the related loss, pay liabilities, and distribute the remaining cash to the partners.

(b) Assuming that other assets are sold for $40,000, give the entries to record the sale of the other assets and distribute the related loss, pay liabilities, apportion any partner's deficit among the other partners (assuming any such deficit is not made up by the partner involved), and distribute the remaining cash to the appropriate partners.

(c) Assuming that liquidation procedures occurred between January 1 and February 15, 19X4, prepare a statement of partnership liquidation using the data in part (b).

14–33 Ale, Boa, Cass, and Domm are partners who share profits and losses in the ratio of 4:3:2:1, respectively. Their partnership agreement provides for annual interest at 20% on partners' average capital balances and annual salaries of $15,000 and $5,000 to Ale and Boa, respectively.

Due to a history of modest earnings, they liquidate their partnership at December 31, 19X4. Just prior to completing the closing of the partnership books for 19X4, the trial balance is summarized as follows:

Cash	$ 30,000	Liabilities	$ 40,000
Noncash Assets (net)	90,000	Ale, Capital	20,000
Ale, Drawings	15,000	Boa, Capital	60,000
Boa, Drawings	5,000	Cass, Capital	15,000
Income Summary	10,000	Domm, Capital	15,000
	$150,000		$150,000

REQUIRED
(a) Assuming that the only partners' capital transaction during the year was Boa's $20,000 contribution on July 1, prepare journal entries to complete the closing of the books at December 31, 19X4.
(b) Starting with the partnership closing trial balance at December 31, 19X4, prepare a statement of partnership liquidation assuming that
   (1) Noncash assets were sold for $50,000 cash.
   (2) All liabilities were paid in cash.
   (3) Any partner experiencing a capital deficit would be able to pay only one-half of such amount (in cash) to the partnership.
   (4) The final distribution of cash to partners was made on February 20, 19X5.

ALTERNATE PROBLEMS

14–26A Barr and Mason form a partnership and invest $60,000 and $30,000, respectively. During its first year, the partnership earned a $12,000 net income.

REQUIRED
(a) Give the entry to close the Income Summary account and distribute the $12,000 net income under each of the following independent assumptions:
   (1) The partnership agreement is silent on the sharing of profits and losses.
   (2) Profits and losses are shared in the ratio of beginning capital investments.
   (3) Profits and losses are shared by allowing 10% interest on beginning capital investments with the remainder divided equally.
(b) Assume the partnership had a $6,000 loss in its first year. Give the entry to close the Income Summary account and distribute the $6,000 loss under each of the foregoing assumptions.

14–27A The capital accounts and the Income Summary account of the Maus, Taylor, and Hamm partnership appear below. None of the partners withdrew capital during the year.

Maus, Capital			Taylor, Capital		
	19XX			19XX	
	Jan. 1	24,000		Jan. 1	30,000
	July 1	12,000		Oct. 1	60,000

Hamm, Capital			Income Summary		
	19XX			19XX	
	Jan. 1	15,000		Dec. 31	54,000

REQUIRED

(a) Give the entry to distribute the $54,000 net income if Maus, Taylor, and Hamm share profits and losses:
  (1) Equally.
  (2) In the ratio 4:3:2, respectively.
  (3) In the ratio of *average* capital balances for the year.
  (4) Under an agreement allowing $21,000 salary to Hamm, 10% interest on *beginning* investments, with the remainder shared equally.
(b) Assume that net income was $25,200 rather than $54,000. Give the entry to distribute the $25,200 earnings if the agreement allows $21,000 salary to Hamm, 10% interest on beginning investments, with the remainder shared equally.

14–28A Davis and Noonan are partners with capital balances of $66,000 and $36,000, respectively. Profits and losses are shared equally.

REQUIRED

Give the entries to record the admission of a new partner, Beecham, under each of the following separate circumstances:

(a) Beecham purchases one-half of Noonan's interest, paying Noonan $20,000 personally.
(b) Beecham invests sufficient funds to receive exactly a one-fourth interest in the new partnership. (No bonuses are recorded.)
(c) Beecham invests $38,000 for a one-fifth interest, with any bonus distributed to the capital accounts of Davis and Noonan.
(d) Beecham invests $26,000 for a one-fourth interest, with any bonus credited to Beecham's capital account.
(e) In parts (c) and (d) above, what do the terms of admission imply regarding the relative negotiating positions of the new partner versus the old partners?

14–29A Stans, Dubbs, and Vasser are partners with capital balances of $90,000, $70,000, and $60,000, respectively. Profits and losses are shared equally. Vasser retires from the firm.

REQUIRED

Record the entries for Vasser's retirement in each of the following separate circumstances:

(a) Vasser's interest is sold to Brown, a new partner, for $62,000.
(b) One-half of Vasser's interest is sold to each of the remaining partners for $31,000 apiece.

(c) Vasser receives $76,000 of partnership funds for his interest. The remaining partners absorb the bonus paid to Vasser.

(d) The partners agree that Vasser's abrupt retirement presents operating disadvantages and therefore Vasser should receive only $54,000 for his interest. Payment is from partnership funds, with any bonuses going to Stans and Dubbs.

14-32A Faley, Goode, and Hill are partners who share profits and losses in the ratio of 5:3:2, respectively. Just before the partnership's liquidation, its balance sheet appears as follows:

Cash	$15,000	Accounts Payable	$13,000
Other Assets (net)	80,000	Faley, Capital	12,000
		Goode, Capital	20,000
		Hill, Capital	50,000
	$95,000		$95,000

REQUIRED

(a) Assuming that other assets are sold for $65,000, give the entries to record the sale of the other assets and distribute the related loss, pay liabilities, and distribute the remaining cash to the partners.

(b) Assuming that others assets are sold for $50,000, give the entries to record the sale of the other assets and distribute the related loss, pay liabilities, apportion any partner's deficit among the other partners (assuming any such deficit is not made up by the partner involved), and distribute the remaining cash to the appropriate partners.

(c) Assuming that liquidation procedures occurred between January 1 and February 8, 19X5, prepare a statement of partnership liquidation using the data in part (b).

14-33A Mann, Neeley, Oscar, and Poe are partners who share profits and losses in the ratio of 5:3:1:1, respectively. Their partnership agreement provides for annual interest at 20% on partners' average capital balances and annual salaries of $10,000 and $20,000 to Mann and Neeley, respectively.

Due to a history of modest earnings, they liquidate their partnership on December 31, 19X5. Just prior to completing the closing of the partnership books for 19X5, the trial balance is summarized as follows:

Cash	$ 30,000	Liabilities	$ 17,000
Noncash Assets (net)	80,000	Mann, Capital	25,000
Mann, Drawings	10,000	Neeley, Capital	20,000
Neeley, Drawings	20,000	Oscar, Capital	50,000
Income Summary	7,000	Poe, Capital	35,000
	$147,000		$147,000

REQUIRED

(a) Assuming that the only partners' capital transaction during the year was Poe's $20,000 contribution on October 1, prepare journal entries to complete the closing of the books at December 31, 19X5.

(b) Starting with the partnership closing trial balance at December 31, 19X5, prepare a statement of partnership liquidation assuming the following:

(1) Noncash assets were sold for $60,000 cash.
(2) All liabilities were paid in cash.
(3) Any partner experiencing a capital deficit would be able to pay only one-half of such amount (in cash) to the partnership.
(4) The final distribution of cash to partners was made on January 31, 19X6.

BUSINESS DECISION PROBLEM

Holt and Ivan were in business for several years, sharing profits and losses equally. Because of Ivan's poor health, they liquidate the partnership. Holt managed the liquidation because Ivan was in the hospital. Just before liquidation, the partnership balance sheet contained the following information:

Cash	$ 40,000	Liabilities	$ 30,000
Other Assets	140,000	Holt, Capital	60,000
		Ivan, Capital	90,000
	$180,000		$180,000

Holt (1) sold the other assets at the best prices obtainable, (2) paid off all the creditors, and (3) divided the remaining cash between Ivan and himself equally, according to their profit and loss sharing ratio.

Ivan received a note from Holt that read "Good news—sold other assets for $180,000. Have $95,000 check waiting for you. Get well soon." Because he will not be released from the hospital for several days, Ivan asks you to review Holt's liquidation and cash distribution procedures.

REQUIRED

Do you approve of Holt's liquidation and cash distribution procedures? Explain. If you believe Holt erred, what amount of final cash settlement should Ivan receive?

15

Corporations:
Organization and
Capital Stock

> The genius of the industrial system lies in
> its organized use of capital and technology.
>
> JOHN KENNETH GALBRAITH

❝It was once said that the sun never set on the British Empire. Today the sun does set on the British Empire, but not on the scores of corporate empires. . . ."[1] Without a doubt, the modern corporation dominates the national and international economic landscape. In the United States, corporations generate well over three-fourths of the combined business receipts of corporations, partnerships, and proprietorships, even though fewer than one of every five businesses is organized as a corporation. The corporate form of organization is used for a variety of business efforts—from the large, multinational corporation with more than a million owners operating in countries all over the world to the small, family-owned business in a single community.

In this and the next three chapters, we consider various aspects of accounting for the corporation. In this chapter, we emphasize the organization of the corporation and the accounting procedures for its capital stock transactions.

NATURE AND FORMATION OF A CORPORATION

A corporation is a legal entity—an artificial legal "person"—created on the approval of the appropriate governmental authority. The right to conduct business as a corporation is a privilege granted by the state in which the corporation is formed. All states have laws specifying the requirements for creating a corporation. In some instances—such as the formation of a national bank—the federal government must approve the creation of a corporation.

To form a corporation, the incorporators (often at least three are required) must apply for a charter. The incorporators prepare and file the **articles of incorporation,** which delineate the basic structure of the corporation, including the purposes for which it is formed, the amount of capital stock to be authorized, and the number of shares into which the stock is to be divided. If the incorporators meet the requirements of the law, the government issues a charter or certificate of incorporation. After the charter has been granted, the incorporators (or, in some states, the subscribers to the corporation's capital stock) hold an organization meeting to elect the first board of directors and adopt the corporation's bylaws.

Because assets are essential to corporate operations, the corporation issues **certificates of capital stock** to obtain the necessary funds. As owners of the corporation, **stockholders,** or **shareholders,** are entitled to a voice in the control and management of the company. Stockholders with voting stock may vote at the annual meeting and participate in the election of the board of directors. The board of directors is responsible for the overall management of the corporation. Nor-

[1]Lester R. Brown, "How Big Are the Multinationals?" *The Saturday Evening Post,* March 1974.

mally, the board selects such corporate officers as a president, one or more vice-presidents, a controller, a treasurer, and a secretary. The officers implement the policies of the board of directors and actively manage the day-to-day affairs of the corporation.

Creating a corporation is more costly than organizing a proprietorship or partnership. The expenditures incurred to organize a corporation are charged to Organization Costs, an intangible asset account. These costs include attorney's fees, fees paid to the state, and costs of promoting the enterprise. As we discussed in Chapter 11, organization costs typically are amortized over a period of five to 10 years.

CHARACTERISTICS OF CORPORATIONS

Separate Legal Entity

A business with a corporate charter is empowered to conduct business affairs apart from its owners. The corporation, as a legal entity, may acquire assets, incur debt, enter into contracts, sue, and be sued—all in its own name. The owners, or stockholders, of the corporation receive stock certificates as evidence of their ownership interests; the stockholders, however, are separate and distinct from the corporation. This characteristic contrasts with proprietorships and partnerships, which are accounting entities but not legal entities apart from their owners. Owners of proprietorships and partnerships can be held responsible separately and collectively for unsatisfied obligations of the business.

Limited Liability

The liability of shareholders with respect to company affairs is usually limited to their equity in the corporation. Because of this limited liability, state laws restrict distributions to shareholders. Most of these laws have fairly elaborate provisions that define the various forms of owners' equity and describe distribution conditions. To protect creditors, the state controls the distribution of contributed capital. Distributions of retained earnings (undistributed profits) are not legal unless the board of directors formally declares a dividend. Because of the legal delineation of owner capital available for distribution, corporations must maintain careful distinctions in the accounts to identify the different elements of stockholders' equity.

Transferability of Ownership

Shares in a corporation may be routinely transferred without affecting the company's operations. The corporation merely notes such transfers of ownership in the stockholder records (ledger). Although a corporation must have stockholder records to notify shareholders of meetings and to pay dividends, the price at which shares transfer between owners is not recognized in the corporation's accounts.

Continuity of Existence

Because routine transfers of ownership do not affect a corporation's affairs, the corporation is said to have continuity of existence. In this respect, a corporation is completely different from a partnership. In a partnership, any change in ownership technically results in discontinuance of the old partnership and formation of a new one. (Many large professional service partnerships, however, follow procedures that provide for continuity with changes in ownership.)

In a partnership, the individual partners' capital accounts indicate their relative interests in the business. The stockholders' equity section of a corporate balance sheet does not present individual stockholder accounts. A shareholder, however, can easily compute his or her interest in the corporation by calculating the proportion of the total shares outstanding that his or her shares represent. For example, if only one class of stock is outstanding and it totals 1,000 shares, an individual owning 200 shares has a 20% interest in the corporation's total stockholders' equity, which includes all contributed capital and retained earnings. The dollar amount of this interest, however, is a book amount, rarely coinciding with the market value. A stockholder who liquidates his or her investment would sell it at a price negotiated with a buyer or, if the stock is traded on a stock exchange, at the exchange's quoted market price.

Capital-raising Capability

The limited liability of stockholders and the ease with which shares of stock may be transferred from one investor to another are attractive features to potential stockholders. These characteristics enhance the ability of the corporation to raise large amounts of capital by issuing shares of stock. Because both large and small investors may acquire ownership interests in a corporation, a wide spectrum of potential investors exists. Corporations with thousands of stockholders are not uncommon. The ability to accumulate and use tremendous amounts of capital makes the corporation the dominant form of business organization in the U.S. economy.

Taxation

As legal entities, corporations are subject to federal income taxes on their earnings, whether distributed or not. In addition, shareholders must pay income taxes on earnings received as dividends. In many small corporations in which the shareholders themselves manage the business affairs, large salaries may reduce earnings to a point where the double taxation feature is not onerous. However, the firm may have to justify the reasonableness of such salaries to the Internal Revenue Service. Under certain circumstances, a corporation with 35 shareholders or fewer may elect partnership treatment for tax purposes. Although partnerships must submit "information" tax returns, an income tax is not imposed on their earnings. Instead, the partners report their respective shares of partnership earnings on their individual income tax returns.

Usually, corporations are subject to state income taxes in the states in which they are incorporated or are doing business. They may also be subject to real estate, personal property, and franchise taxes.

Regulation and Supervision

Corporations are subject to greater degrees of regulation and supervision than are proprietorships and partnerships. Each state has the right to regulate the corporations it charters. State laws limit the powers a corporation may exercise, identify reports that must be filed, and define the rights and liabilities of stockholders. If stock is issued to the public, the corporation must comply with the laws governing the sale of corporate securities. Furthermore, corporations whose stock is listed and traded on organized security exchanges—such as the New York Stock Exchange—are subject to the various reporting and disclosure requirements of these exchanges.

OWNERS' EQUITY AND ORGANIZATIONAL FORMS

Differences arise between accounting for the owners' equity of a corporation and that of a sole proprietorship or partnership. In a sole proprietorship, only a single owner's capital account is needed to reflect increases from capital contributions and net earnings as well as decreases from withdrawals and net losses. In practice, as explained in Chapter 2, many sole proprietors keep a separate drawing account to record withdrawals of cash and other business assets. This separate record is kept only for convenience, however; no subdivision of the owner's capital account is required either by law or by accounting principles.

A similar situation exists in most partnerships, which customarily maintain capital and drawing accounts for each partner. A partnership is simply an association of two or more persons who agree to become joint owners of a business. Because more than one individual is involved in the business, a written agreement should govern the financial participation and business responsibilities of the partners. However, no legal or accounting requirement demands that a distinction be maintained between contributed capital and undistributed earnings.

A corporation, on the other hand, is subject to certain legal restrictions imposed by the government approving its creation. These restrictions focus on the distinction between contributed capital and retained earnings and make accounting for the owners' equity somewhat more complex for corporations than for other types of business organizations. Note that much of the accounting for corporate owners' equity is actually a polyglot of legal prescription and accounting convention. The detailed reporting of stockholders' equity transactions, however, provides analytical information that is often useful and, in many instances, required by law.

TYPES OF STOCK

The amounts and kinds of stock that a corporation may issue are enumerated in the company's charter. Providing for several classes of stock permits the company to raise capital from different types of investors. The charter also specifies the corporation's **authorized stock**—the maximum number of shares of each class of stock that may be issued. A corporation that wishes to issue more shares than its authorized number must first amend its charter. Shares that have been sold and issued to stockholders constitute the **issued stock** of the corporation. Some of this stock may be repurchased by the corporation. Shares actually held by stockholders are called **outstanding stock,** whereas those reacquired by the corporation are **treasury stock.** We discuss treasury stock later in the chapter.

Common Stock

When only one class of stock is issued, it is called **common stock.** Common shareholders compose the basic ownership class. They have rights to vote, to share in earnings, to participate in additional issues of stock, and—in the case of liquidation—to share in assets after prior claims on the corporation have been settled. We now consider each of these rights.

As the owners of a corporation, the common shareholders elect the board of directors and vote on other matters requiring the approval of owners. Common shareholders are entitled to one vote for each share of stock they own. Owners who do not attend the annual stockholders' meetings may vote by proxy (this may be the case for most stockholders in large corporations).

A common stockholder has the right to a proportionate share of the corporation's earnings that are distributed as dividends. All earnings belong to the corporation, however, until the board of directors formally declares a dividend.

Each shareholder of a corporation has a **preemptive right** to maintain his or her proportionate interest in the corporation. If the company issues additional shares of stock, current owners of that type of stock receive the first opportunity to acquire, on a pro-rata basis, the new shares. In certain situations, management may request shareholders to waive their preemptive rights. For example, the corporation may wish to issue additional stock to acquire another company. Further, stockholders of firms incorporated in some states do not receive preemptive rights.

A liquidating corporation converts its assets to a form suitable for distribution, usually cash, which it then distributes to parties having claims on the corporate assets. Any assets remaining after all claims have been satisfied belong to the residual ownership interest in the corporation—the common stockholders. These owners are entitled to the final distribution of the balance of the assets.

A company may occasionally use **classified** common stock; that is, it may issue more than one class of common stock. Two classes of common stock issued are identified as Class A and Class B. The two classes usually differ in either their respective dividend rights or their respective voting powers. Usually, classified common stock is issued when the organizers of the corporation wish to acquire funds from the public while retaining voting control. To illustrate, let us assume 10,000 shares of Class A stock are issued to the public at $40 per share, while 20,000 shares of Class B stock are issued to the organizers at $5 per share. If each shareholder receives one vote per share of stock, the Class B stockholders have twice as many votes as the Class A stockholders. Yet the total investment of Class B stockholders is significantly less than that of the Class A stockholders. To offset the difference in the voting power per dollar of investment, the Class A stockholders may have better dividend rights, such as being entitled to dividends in early years, while the Class B stockholders may not receive dividends until a certain level of earning power is reached.

Preferred Stock

Preferred stock is a class of stock with various characteristics that distinguish it from common stock. To determine the features of a particular issue, we must examine the stock contract. The majority of preferred issues, however, have certain typical features, which we discuss below. Obviously, among a stock's most important features is its specified rights to dividends.

DIVIDEND FEATURES When the board of directors declares a distribution of earnings, preferred stockholders are entitled to a certain annual amount of dividends before common stockholders receive any distribution. The amount is usually specified in the preferred stock contract as a percentage of the face value (called par value) of the stock or in dollars per share if the stock does not have a par value. (Par value and no-par value stock are discussed later in this chapter.) Thus, if the preferred stock has a $100 par value and a 6% dividend rate, the preferred shareholders receive $6 per share in dividends. However, the amount is owed to the stockholders only if declared.

Preferred dividends are usually **cumulative**—that is, regular dividends to preferred stockholders omitted in past years must be paid in addition to the current year's dividend before any distribution is made to common shareholders. For example, a dividend may not be declared in an unprofitable year. If the $6 preferred stock dividend mentioned above is one year in arrears and a dividend is declared in the current year, preferred shareholders would receive $12 per share before common shareholders received anything. If a preferred stock is noncumulative, omitted dividends do not carry forward. Because investors normally consider the noncumulative feature unattractive, noncumulative preferred stock is rarely issued.

Dividends in arrears (that is, omitted in past years) on cumulative preferred stock are not an accounting liability and do not appear in the liability section of the balance sheet. They do not become an obligation of the corporation until the board of directors formally declares such dividends. Any arrearages are typically disclosed to investors in a footnote to the balance sheet.

Ordinarily, preferred stockholders receive a fixed amount and do not participate further in distributions made by the corporation. In rare circumstances, however, the stock contract may make the preferred a **participating** stock. To illustrate the participating feature, let us assume that a company had outstanding 1,000 shares of $100 par value, 6% *fully participating* cumulative preferred stock and 2,000 shares of $100 par value common stock. Assume also that the company declared total dividends of $27,000 and that no preferred dividends were in arrears. The distribution would be made as follows:

	Preferred	Common	Total
Outstanding stock (total par value)	$100,000	$200,000	$300,000
Preferred dividends in arrears	$–0–		$ –0–
Regular dividend (6%) and matching rate to common (6%)	6,000	$12,000	18,000
Remainder of $9,000 ($27,000 − $18,000) divided to give each class the same rate: $9,000/$300,000 = 3%	3,000	6,000	9,000
Total distribution	$9,000	$18,000	$27,000
Rate of distribution (based on total par value)	9%	9%	

Note that, after the preferred stock is accorded its regular 6% dividend, a like rate of 6% ($12,000) is allocated to the common stock. The remaining $9,000 is then apportioned so both classes of stock receive the same *rate* of distribution. This rate is determined by dividing the remainder to be distributed by the total par value of both classes of stock ($300,000). It is important to note that the preferred stock does not participate until the common stock is accorded an amount corresponding to the regular preferred dividend rate.

Preferred stock may also be *partially* participating. For example, suppose that the preferred shares participate to 8%. They would then be entitled only to an additional 2% over their regular 6% dividend, and any remaining amount would be accorded to the common shares.

Any arrearage on cumulative preferred stock must first be awarded to the preferred shareholders. Therefore, had there been one year's arrearage on the fully participating stock in the foregoing example, $12,000 ($6,000 dividends in arrears and $6,000 current dividends) would have been allocated to the preferred stock and then the normal 6%, or $12,000, to the common stock. Of the remaining $3,000, $1,000 would be assigned to the preferred stock and $2,000 to the common stock.

Of course, if either the common stock or the preferred stock is no-par value stock, preferred stock participation is determined on some basis other than total par values. For example, the participation may be achieved by allocating dividends of equal dollar amounts per share to each class of stock.

VOTING RIGHTS   Although preferred shareholders do not ordinarily have the right to vote in the election of directors, this right can be accorded by contract. Some state laws require that all stock issued by a corporation be given voting rights. Sometimes, a preferred stock contract confers full or partial voting rights under certain conditions—for example, when dividends have not been paid for a specified period.

OTHER FEATURES   Preferred stock contracts may contain features that cause the stock to resemble the common stock equity at one end of a spectrum or a debt obligation at the other end. The stock may, for example, be **convertible** into common stock at some specified rate. With this feature, the market price of the preferred often moves with that of the common. When the price of the common stock rises, the value of the conversion feature is enhanced. Preferred stock may also be convertible into long-term debt securities (bonds). Furthermore, when a corporation is liquidated, preferred shareholders normally have a liquidation preference, that is, a prior claim to assets after creditor claims are satisfied.

Preferred stock may be **callable,** which means the corporation can redeem the stock after a length of time and at a price specified in the contract. The call feature makes the stock similar to a bond, which frequently is callable or has a limited life. Most preferred stocks are callable, with the call or redemption price set slightly above the original issuance price.

To be successful in selling its preferred stock, a corporation often must cater to current market vogues. Features are added or omitted, depending on market conditions and the desires of the investor group the corporation wishes to attract. Management must balance market requirements with its own goals. Sometimes management must compromise and issue securities that it hopes to change over time, perhaps through conversion or refinancing, to arrive at the desired financial plan.

Preferred stocks appeal to investors who want a steady rate of return that is normally somewhat higher than that on bonds. These investors often feel that preferred stock entails less risk than common stock, although the common will pay off more if the company does well.

PREFERRED STOCK FEATURES

Dividends paid on preferred and common stocks are distributions of earnings and, as such, are not deductible on a corporation's tax return. Interest paid on bonds is tax deductible. Therefore, when corporations decide whether to issue stocks or bonds to raise new capital, they usually consider the nondeductible tax status of dividends a disadvantage of issuing stock. The disadvantage disappears, however, when a corporation is unprofitable and pays no taxes. This situation, which existed for many corporations during the economic recession in the early 1980s, contributed to the creation of two new forms of preferred stock—adjustable-rate preferred stock and convertible exchangeable preferred stock.

The unique feature of *adjustable-rate preferred stock* is the dividend rate, which changes each quarter. The rate is tied to a U.S. Treasury index within an upper and a lower limit—for example, a 15% maximum rate and a $7\frac{1}{2}$% minimum rate. These stocks were immediately popular when first sold in 1982. During a three-month period in 1982, for example, $1.3 billion of adjustable-rate preferred stocks were issued, primarily by banks. Banks were having profit problems then, and their common stock prices were depressed. Indeed, some proceeds from the preferred stock issuances were used to buy up the bank's own common stock.[*]

Profitable corporations are the major purchasers of these preferred stocks because the stocks can generate extraordinarily high returns. The tax law creates this outcome by permitting a corporation to exclude from its taxable income 85% of the dividend income it receives. This means, for example, that an adjustable-rate preferred stock paying a 13% dividend yields about the same return after taxes as a taxable investment paying 22.5% interest.[†]

As its name suggests, *convertible exchangeable preferred stock* has two distinguishing features. The convertible feature permits the owner to convert the preferred stock into common stock at any time. The exchangeable feature—added because of the issuing company's tax status—gives the issuer the option, after two years, to call in the preferred stock and exchange it for convertible bonds (which may be converted into common stock).

When the preferred stock is sold, the issuing company expects little, if any, taxable income within the next two years. Because taxes during this period are negligible, the tax deduction for bond interest is not important. While the company works to regain its profitable status, the preferred stock issued adds equity (rather than debt) to the company's balance sheet. After two years, though, the corporation plans to be operating profitably. The deduction for bond interest is then significant, and the issuing company wants to replace the preferred stock with bonds.[‡]

Martin Marietta Corporation issued the first convertible exchangeable preferred stock in December 1982. Within a few months, several corporations—such as Boise Cascade and Crown Zellerbach—had followed suit with their own convertible exchangeable preferred stocks.[§]

[*]"Companies Love the New Preferreds," *Business Week*, August 23, 1982, page 92.
[†]Ibid.
[‡]Arlene Hershman, "New Strategies in Equity Financing," *Dun's Business Month*, June 1983, page 40.
[§]Ibid.

From both the legal and the accounting standpoint, all types of preferred stock, whatever their features, are part of stockholders' equity. Dividends are distributions of earnings and, unlike interest on bonds, are not shown as expenses on the income statement. Also, because of the legal classification of preferred stock as stockholders' equity, the company cannot deduct dividends as expenses for income tax purposes, whereas interest on debt can be deducted as an expense.

PAR AND NO-PAR VALUE STOCK

The corporate charter may specify a face value, or **par value,** for each share of stock of any class. Although this face value may relate to the initial price of the stock, it is often arbitrary and has no connotation of value once operations begin. Par value may have legal implications, however, because it invariably is used to determine the *legal capital* of the business. State laws normally define this term and restrict the distribution of legal capital. For this reason, accountants carefully segregate and record the par value amount of stock transactions in an appropriate capital stock account.

Because investors may confuse par value with realistic values, many states have permitted **no-par** stock since the early 1900s. Most states, however, permit a company's directors to set a **stated value** on the shares (some states insist on this). Again, this figure is arbitrary, but in contrast to par value, the stated value is not printed on the stock certificates. For accounting purposes, stated value amounts are treated in a fashion similar to par value amounts.

A **premium** is the amount in excess of par value paid for a corporation's stock. The excess of par value over the amount paid may be called **discount.** In some states, persons purchasing stock for less than par value may have a liability for the discount should creditor claims remain unsatisfied after the company's liquidation. Stocks are rarely sold at a discount—in certain states this practice is even forbidden. When no-par stock with a stated value is sold, the price paid invariably exceeds the stated value. In accounting, the difference is called *excess of amount paid over stated value;* the terms *premium* and *discount* are not used with no-par stock.

To record differences between amounts paid for shares and par value, the accountant uses appropriately descriptive accounts. When an amount greater than par value is received, we may use the account Paid-in Capital in Excess of Par Value, or simply Premium on Stock. The account Excess of Par Value over Amount Paid, or simply Discount on Stock, can be used when a discount is involved. For no-par stock with a stated value, accounts have titles such as Paid-in Capital in Excess of Stated Value.

To illustrate how the stockholders' equity accounts present the amounts paid in for stock, let us assume that in its first year of operations, a corporation had the following transactions:

(1) Sold 1,000 shares of $100 par value, 9% preferred stock at $107 per share.

(2) Sold 1,000 shares of $100 par value, 6% preferred stock at $98 per share.

(3) Sold 5,000 shares of no-par common stock at $30 per share. Stated value is $20 per share.

(4) The company earned $50,000 during the year. After paying dividends of $9,000 on the 9% preferred stock, $6,000 on the 6% preferred stock, and $10,000 to the common shareholders, the company had $25,000 in retained earnings.

The stockholders' equity section of the company's December 31 balance sheet appears in Exhibit 15–1.

In the illustration, we assume that all authorized amounts of both classes of preferred stock and half of the 10,000 shares of common stock authorized have been issued. Note that both the premium on the 9% preferred stock and the excess received over stated value of the no-par common stock are added to the par and stated values, respectively. On the other hand, the $2,000 discount on the 6% preferred stock is deducted from par value to show the amount paid for this class. All the accounts in the illustration have credit balances in the general ledger, except Excess of Par Value over Amount Paid on the 6% preferred stock, which has a $2,000 debit balance.

Corporate owners' equity accounts are presented in a variety of ways in published reports. One popular format groups the par and stated values of the three classes of stock together under the heading Capital Stock—a total of $300,000 in our example. The remainder of the paid-in capital items are placed under a heading such as Paid-in Capital. In our example, the paid-in amounts in excess of par and stated values less the excess of par value over amount paid on the 6% preferred stock total $55,000. This type of presentation is not as clear as Exhibit 15–1, because the capital stock of a firm is really part of total paid-in capital.

EXHIBIT 15–1
Stockholders' Equity

Paid-in Capital:		
9% Preferred Stock, $100 Par Value, 1,000 shares authorized, issued, and outstanding	$100,000	
Paid-in Capital in Excess of Par Value	7,000	$107,000
6% Preferred Stock, $100 Par Value, 1,000 shares authorized, issued, and outstanding	$100,000	
Excess of Par Value over Amount Paid	(2,000)	98,000
No-par Common Stock, Stated Value $20, 10,000 shares authorized; 5,000 shares issued and outstanding	$100,000	
Paid-in Capital in Excess of Stated Value	50,000	150,000
Total Paid-in Capital		$355,000
Retained Earnings		25,000
Total Stockholders' Equity		$380,000

STOCK ISSUANCES FOR CASH

In issuing its stock, a corporation may use the services of an investment banker, a specialist in marketing securities to investors. The investment banker may *underwrite* a stock issue—that is, the banker buys the stock from the corporation and resells it to investors. The corporation does not risk being unable to sell its stock. The underwriter bears this risk in return for the profits generated by selling the stock to investors at a price higher than that paid the corporation. An investment banker who is unwilling to underwrite a stock issue may handle it on a *best efforts* basis. In this case, the investment banker agrees to sell as many shares as possible at a set price, but the corporation bears the risk of unsold stock.

The stock issues in Exhibit 15–1, which were all for cash, would have been entered in the corporation's books by the following entries:

(1) Sale of 1,000 shares of $100 par value, 9% preferred stock at $107 per share.

Cash	107,000	
9% Preferred Stock		100,000
Paid-in Capital in Excess of Par Value		7,000

(2) Sale of 1,000 shares of $100 par value, 6% preferred stock at $98 per share.

Cash	98,000	
Excess of Par Value over Amount Paid	2,000	
6% Preferred Stock		100,000

(3) Sale of 5,000 shares of no-par common stock, stated value $20, at $30 per share.

Cash	150,000	
Common Stock		100,000
Paid-in Capital in Excess of Stated Value		50,000

The appropriate capital stock account is always credited with the par value of shares, or if the stock is no-par, with its stated value, if any. Cash received is debited, and any difference is placed in an appropriately named account. The $7,000 premium on the 9% preferred stock may be credited to an account called Premium on Preferred Stock. Similarly, the $2,000 discount on the 6% preferred stock may be debited to an account called Discount on Preferred Stock. The account titles we have used in the illustration, however, are most common.

When no-par stock has a stated value, as in entry (3), the stated value of the total shares issued is credited to the proper capital stock account and any additional amount received is credited to an account called Paid-in Capital in Excess of Stated Value. This amount, though treated similarly to a stock premium, should not be regarded as a premium—the stated value is arbitrarily set by the board of directors. If no stated value for no-par stock exists, the entire proceeds should be credited to the appropriate capital stock account. In entry (3), if the common stock had no stated value, the entire $150,000 amount would have been credited to the Common Stock account.

STOCK SUBSCRIPTIONS

Sometimes a corporation sells stock directly to investors rather than through an investment banker. The corporation may obtain signatures of prospective purchasers on *subscription contracts* prior to issuing shares. Frequently, such contracts provide for installment payments. When subscriptions are obtained, the corporation debits a receivable account, Stock Subscriptions Receivable. Instead of crediting the regular Common Stock account, the firm credits a temporary paid-in capital account called Common Stock Subscribed. The use of a temporary account signifies that the shares have not yet been paid for or issued. Until the shares are paid for, the account is shown separately in the stockholders' equity section of the balance sheet. Stock Subscriptions Receivable appears with the current assets. After all payments have been received and the stock is issued, the corporation debits the temporary account, Common Stock Subscribed, and credits the regular account, Common Stock.

To illustrate the journal entries for stock subscription transactions, let us assume that 500 shares of $100 par value stock were sold on subscription for $120 a share, paid in installments of $40 and $80. The entries would be

To record receipt of subscriptions

Stock Subscriptions Receivable—Common	60,000	
Common Stock Subscribed		50,000
Paid-in Capital in Excess of Par Value		10,000
Received subscriptions for 500 shares at $120 per share.		

To record collection of first installment

Cash	20,000	
Stock Subscriptions Receivable—Common		20,000
Collected first installment of $40 per share.		

To record collection of final installment and issuance of shares

Cash	40,000	
Stock Subscriptions Receivable—Common		40,000
Collected final installment of $80 per share.		

Common Stock Subscribed	50,000	
Common Stock		50,000
To record issuance of 500 shares.		

STOCK ISSUANCES FOR ASSETS OTHER THAN CASH

When stock is issued for property other than cash or for services, the accountant must determine the amount recorded with care. We should not assume that the par or stated value of the shares issued automatically sets a value for the property or services received. In the early years of U.S. corporations, such an assumption frequently resulted in the recording and reporting of excessive asset valuations.

Property or services acquired should be recorded at their current fair value or the fair value of the stock issued, whichever is more clearly determinable. If the stock is actively traded on a securities exchange, the market price of the stock issued may indicate an appropriate value. For example, if the current market price is $140 per share and 500 shares are issued for a parcel of land, this land may be valued, in the absence of other price indicators, at $70,000. An effort should be made, however, to determine a fair value for the property. Certainly, all aspects of the transaction should be carefully scrutinized to ascertain that the number of shares issued was objectively determined. Obviously, if no market value for the stock is available, we would seek an independently determined value for the property or services received.

Let us suppose the stock issued for the land is $100 par value common stock and its market value is the best indicator of the property's fair value. The entry to record the transaction would be

Land	70,000	
Common Stock		50,000
Paid-in Capital in Excess of Par Value		20,000
To record issuance of 500 shares of common stock for land valued at $70,000.		

TREASURY STOCK

When a corporation reacquires its own outstanding shares for a purpose other than retiring them, the reacquired shares are called *treasury stock*. Treasury stock may be purchased for a variety of reasons, which include reissuing them to officers and employees in profit-sharing schemes or stock-option plans. Whatever the purpose, the corporation is reducing owner capital for a period of time. Consequently, treasury stock is not regarded as an asset. The shares do not carry voting privileges or preemptive rights, are not paid dividends, and do not receive assets on the corporation's liquidation.

Accountants commonly record treasury stock at cost, debiting a Treasury Stock account. The aggregate cost is deducted from total stockholders' equity in the balance sheet. Suppose a corporation had outstanding 2,000 shares of $100 par value common stock and then repurchased 100 shares at $120 per share. The entry for the repurchase would be

Treasury Stock	12,000	
Cash		12,000

To record purchase of 100 shares of
treasury stock at $120 per share.

The corporation may accept any price for the reissue of treasury stock. Treasury stock transactions are not part of a firm's normal operating activities, and any additional capital obtained from reissuing such shares at more than cost is not regarded as earnings and is not added to retained earnings. The corporation should regard any additional amounts paid by subsequent purchasers as paid-in capital. Therefore, increases in capital from reissue of treasury shares are credited to a paid-in capital account such as Paid-in Capital from Treasury Stock. Decreases on reissue of treasury stock at less than cost offset previously recorded paid-in capital from treasury stock transactions or, if that is not possible, retained earnings.

Let us assume that 50 shares of the treasury stock reacquired are resold by the corporation at $130 per share. The entry to record the reissue would be

Cash	6,500	
Treasury Stock		6,000
Paid-in Capital from Treasury Stock		500

To record sale of 50 shares of treasury
stock at $130 per share.

Observe that Treasury Stock is credited at the cost price of $120 per share, a basis consistent with the original debit to the account. The excess over cost is credited to Paid-in Capital from Treasury Stock. If a balance sheet is prepared after this transaction, the stockholders' equity section would appear as shown below (assuming retained earnings of $40,000):

Stockholders' Equity

Paid-in Capital:	
Common Stock, $100 Par Value, authorized and issued 2,000 shares; 50 shares in treasury, 1,950 shares outstanding	$200,000
Paid-in Capital from Treasury Stock	500
Retained Earnings	40,000
	$240,500
Less: Treasury Stock (50 shares) at Cost	6,000
Total Stockholders' Equity	$234,500

Note that the $200,000 par value of all *issued* stock is shown, although 50 shares are no longer outstanding. The total cost of the 50 shares, however, is later deducted from total stockholders' equity.

In the above owners' equity situation, the corporation apparently has $40,000 retained earnings unfettered by any legal restrictions; the entire amount might be distributed as dividends if the corporation's cash position permits. In some states, however, the corporation must restrict (reduce) the retained earnings available for declaration of dividends by the cost of any treasury stock held. Then, in our illustration, only $34,000 in retained earnings would be available for dividends, and the reason would be disclosed in the stockholders' equity section. Methods of disclosing retained earnings restrictions are discussed in Chapter 16. The statutory restriction exists because a corporation that reduces its paid-in capital by repurchasing shares must protect creditors by "buffering" the reduced capital with its retained earnings in an amount equal to resources expended.

DONATED CAPITAL

Occasionally, a shareholder may donate shares to the corporation. Perhaps the donor received the shares for a process or patent and now wishes the corporation to raise additional capital to promote and market it. Because treasury shares represent stock that has been issued once, they can be reissued at any price. Thus, the corporation may find it easier to market these shares than to sell unissued shares, especially if investors have shown little interest in the venture and the unissued shares could be sold only at a discount. (As we mentioned earlier, a liability may attach to discounted shares in some states, whereas other states do not permit issuance at a discount.)

    The reacquisition of treasury shares by donation, whatever the reason, is usually not recorded—except for a memorandum entry—at the time of reacquisition. When such shares are subsequently sold, the amount received is credited to Donated Capital, a form of paid-in capital. To illustrate, suppose a stockholder donates 100 shares of common stock to a corporation, which then resells the shares at $125 per share. The entries for these transactions would be

To record receipt of donated treasury shares

(Memorandum) Received 100 shares of donated common stock.

To record sale of donated treasury shares

Cash	12,500	
Donated Capital		12,500

To record sale of 100 donated shares
at $125 per share.

    The Donated Capital account may also be credited for the fair market value of any property donated to the corporation, assuming that a value can be determined objectively. For example, communities wanting to attract industry have donated land sites to corporations. If fair values can be established by appraisal or by study of prices for similar local property, the amount may be recorded. In any event, amounts acquired through donation should never be credited to Retained Earnings, because this account is used solely for accumulating earnings from operations.

    Assume that a city donates a plant site to a corporation. An independent appraiser values the land at $26,000, which is accepted by the board of directors as an appropriate valuation. The entry to record the donation would be

Land	26,000	
Donated Capital		26,000
To record receipt of donated land		
valued at $26,000.		

REDEMPTION OF PREFERRED STOCK

Corporations often retain the right to call or redeem their outstanding preferred stock by paying the preferred stockholders the par value of the stock plus a premium. For example, assume that a company has issued 1,000 shares of $100 par value preferred stock at $105 per share. After such issue, the stockholders' equity would include the following accounts:

Preferred Stock, $100 Par Value,	
1,000 shares issued and outstanding	100,000
Paid-in Capital in Excess of Par Value	5,000

Suppose that 500 shares are then redeemed at $102 per share. When the redemption is recorded, the amounts in the above accounts related to the 500 redeemed shares must be eliminated. In other words, half of the preferred stock ($50,000) and half of the original premium ($2,500) must be removed from the accounts. Because the shares were redeemed for $3 less per share than the issue price, a $1,500 premium is realized on redemption. This **redemption premium** is a form of paid-in capital. The entry to record the redemption is as follows:

Preferred Stock	50,000	
Paid-in Capital in Excess of Par Value	2,500	
Redemption Premium on Preferred Stock		1,500
Cash		51,000
To record redemption of 500 shares		
of preferred stock at $102 per share.		

When preferred stock is redeemed at a price higher than the issue price, the excess is debited to Retained Earnings, inasmuch as it represents a distribution of earnings to stockholders. If the redemption price in the above situation had been $106 per share, the appropriate entry would have been

Preferred Stock	50,000	
Paid-in Capital in Excess of Par Value	2,500	
Retained Earnings	500	
Cash		53,000
To record redemption of 500 shares		
of preferred stock at $106 per share.		

BOOK VALUE PER SHARE

Book value per share is often calculated for a class of stock, particularly common stock. **Book value per share,** which is the dollar amount of net assets represented by one share of stock, is computed by dividing the amount of stockholders' equity associated with a class of stock by the number of outstanding shares in that class. The computation uses stockholders' equity, because a corporation's net assets (Assets − Liabilities) equals its stockholders' equity. The measure is based on amounts recorded in the books and presented in the balance sheet—hence, the term *book* value per share.

For example, assume the following stockholders' equity section of a balance sheet:

Stockholders' Equity

Paid-in Capital:	
Common Stock, $50 Par Value, 5,000 shares authorized, issued, and outstanding	$250,000
Paid-in Capital in Excess of Par Value	100,000
Retained Earnings	80,000
Total Stockholders' Equity	$430,000

Because this corporation has only one class of stock, the book value per share is the total stockholders' equity divided by the shares outstanding, that is, $430,000/5,000 = $86. Note that the divisor is shares outstanding; it does not include shares of unissued common stock or treasury stock.

To compute book values per share when more than one class of stock is outstanding, we must determine the portion of stockholders' equity attributable to each class of stock. Preferred stocks are assigned the amounts their owners would receive if the corporation liquidated—that is, the liquidation preference of preferred stock plus any dividend arrearages on cumulative stock. The common shares receive the remainder of the stockholders' equity. For example, assume the following stockholders' equity section:

Stockholders' Equity

Paid-in Capital:	
9% Preferred Stock, $100 Par Value, 1,000 shares authorized, issued, and outstanding	$100,000
Paid-in Capital in Excess of Par Value—Preferred Stock	5,000
No-par Common Stock, Stated Value $40, 3,000 shares authorized, issued, and outstanding	120,000
Paid-in Capital in Excess of Stated Value—Common Stock	6,000
Retained Earnings	73,000
Total Stockholders' Equity	$304,000

If the stated liquidation preference is $103 per share for the preferred stock (with no dividends in arrears), then the book value per share for the preferred stock is also $103. The computation for the common stock follows:

Total Stockholders' Equity	$304,000
Less: Equity Applicable to Preferred Stock	103,000
Equity Allocated to Common Stock	$201,000
Shares of Common Stock Outstanding	3,000
Book Value per Share of Common Stock ($201,000/3,000)	$67

The book value per share of common stock may be used in many ways. Management may include the book value per share—and any changes in it for the year—in the annual report to stockholders. Two corporations negotiating a merger through an exchange of stock may find their respective book values per share to be one of several factors influencing the final exchange ratio. Or an individual may acquire an option to buy stock in the future, with the purchase price related to the future book value of the stock.

MARKET VALUE AND LIQUIDATION VALUE

The book value of common stock is different from its market value and its liquidation value. The **market value per share** is the current price at which the stock may be bought or sold. This price reflects such things as the earnings potential of the company, dividends, book values, capital structure, and general economic conditions. Because book value is only one of several variables influencing market price (and usually not the most significant one at that), market values and book values rarely coincide.

The **liquidation value per share** of common stock is the amount that would be received if the corporation liquidated. The amounts recorded in the books do not portray liquidation proceeds, so no correlation exists between liquidation values and book values of common stocks. Liquidation values may not be easy to determine, but corporate managements must be alert to the relationship between the market value and the approximate liquidation value of their common stock. A corporation whose liquidation value exceeds its market value may be the object of a "raid." A raider acquires control of a corporation (by buying stock at market values) and then liquidates the business (at liquidation values), keeping the difference as a gain.

KEY POINTS TO REMEMBER

(1) A corporation is a separate legal entity chartered by the state in which it is formed or, in some cases, by the federal government.

(2) The liability of corporate shareholders is usually limited to their ownership investment, whereas claims against partners and sole proprietors may extend to their personal resources.

(3) Unlike proprietorships and partnerships, corporations must report paid-in equity capital separately from the accumulated balance of retained earnings. Distributions to shareholders are limited by the amount of retained earnings and other capital as specified by state law.

(4) Common stock represents a corporation's basic ownership class of stock. Preferred stocks may differ from common stock in any of several characteristics. Typically, preferred stocks have some type of dividend preference and a prior claim to assets in liquidation.

(5) In financial statements, the par values or stated values of different forms of stock (preferred, common) are shown separately, along with any excess or deficiency received for the shares. These differences are called premium and discount, respectively, for par value stock. For no-par stock with a stated value, an appropriate title (for example, paid-in capital in excess of stated value) describes the difference.

(6) Treasury stock represents repurchased shares of the firm's own stock. It is commonly recorded at cost and deducted from total stockholders' equity in the balance sheet.

(7) Donated capital results from gifts to the corporation which, if feasible, should be recorded at fair market value.

(8) The book value per share of common stock indicates the net assets, based on recorded amounts, associated with a share of common stock. Common stock book values are different from market values or liquidation values.

QUESTIONS

15–1 Explain the meaning of each of the following terms and, when appropriate, how they interrelate: articles of incorporation, corporate charter, board of directors, corporate officers, and organization costs.

15–2 What is meant by the limited liability of a shareholder? Does this characteristic enhance or reduce a corporation's ability to raise capital?

15–3 Contrast the federal income taxation of corporations with that of sole proprietorships and partnerships. Which of the three types of organizations must file a federal income tax return?

15–4 What is the preemptive right of a shareholder?

15–5 What are the basic differences between preferred stock and common stock? What are the typical features of preferred stock?

15–6 What features make preferred stock similar to debt? Similar to common stock?

15–7 What is meant by dividend arrearage on preferred stock? If dividends are two years in arrears on $300,000 of 8% preferred stock and dividends are declared this year, what amount of total dividends must preferred shareholders receive before any distributions can be made to common shareholders?

15–8 What is fully participating preferred stock? Partially participating preferred stock?

15–9 Distinguish between authorized stock and issued stock. Why might the number of shares issued be greater than the number of shares outstanding?

15-10 Distinguish between premium and discount on stock. Where do such amounts appear in the balance sheet?

15-11 What is no-par stock? How is the stated value, if any, of no-par stock determined?

15-12 A company acquired machines with a fair market value of $90,000 in exchange for 700 shares of $100 par value common stock. How should this transaction be recorded in the accounts?

15-13 Define *treasury stock*. Why might a corporation acquire treasury stock? How is treasury stock shown in the balance sheet?

15-14 If a corporation purchases 600 shares of its own common stock at $15 per share and resells it at $20 per share, where would the $3,000 increase in capital appear in the financial statements? Why is no gain reported?

15-15 A corporation has total stockholders' equity of $121,500 and one class of $50 par value common stock. The company has issued 3,000 shares and currently holds 300 shares as treasury stock. What is the book value per share?

15-16 A corporation has total stockholders' equity of $2,100,000 and one class of $60 par value common stock. The corporation has 50,000 shares authorized; 30,000 shares issued; 28,000 shares outstanding; and 2,000 shares as treasury stock. What is the book value per share?

EXERCISES

15-17 On June 1, Laker, Inc., issued 5,000 shares of $40 par value preferred stock at $62 per share and 6,000 shares of no-par common stock at $35 per share. The common stock had no stated value. All issuances were for cash.
(a) Give the general journal entries to record the issuances.
(b) Give the entry for the issuance of the common stock, assuming it had a stated value of $30 per share.
(c) Give the entry for the issuance of the common stock, assuming it had a par value of $25 per share.

15-18 On May 1, the Rydal Company received subscriptions for 6,000 shares of $30 par value common stock at $34 per share, paid as follows: 50% with subscription, 25% on June 15, and 25% on July 1. All payments were received on schedule, and the shares were issued on July 1. Give the general journal entries made on May 1, June 15, and July 1.

15-19 Panda Corporation was organized in 19X4. The company's charter authorizes 100,000 shares of $10 par value common stock. The attorney who helped organize the corporation billed Panda $3,500 for services rendered. On August 1, 19X4, the attorney accepted 250 shares of Panda common stock in settlement of the bill. On October 15, 19X4, Panda issued 1,000 common shares to acquire a vacant land site appraised at $15,000. Give the general journal entries to record the stock issuances on August 1 and October 15.

15-20 The Dome Company had 8,000 shares outstanding of $50 par value, 9% cumulative preferred stock and 20,000 shares of $10 par value common stock. The company declared cash dividends amounting to $120,000.
(a) If no arrearage on the preferred stock exists, how much in total dividends, and in dividends per share, is paid to each class of stock?
(b) If one year's dividend arrearage on the preferred stock exists, how much

in total dividends, and in dividends per share, is paid to each class of stock?

(c) Assume that no arrearage on the preferred stock exists but that the stock is fully participating. How much in total dividends, and in dividends per share, is paid to each class of stock?

15–21 Case Corporation issued 15,000 shares of $30 par value common stock at $34 per share and 8,000 shares of $40 par value, 8% preferred stock at $45 per share. The company then repurchased 2,000 shares of common stock at $38 per share.

(a) Give the general journal entries to record the stock issuances and the repurchase of the common shares.

(b) Assume that Case resold 1,200 shares of the treasury stock at $40 per share. Give the general journal entry to record the resale of this treasury stock.

(c) Assume that Case resold the remaining 800 shares of treasury stock at $37 per share. Give the general journal entry to record the resale of this treasury stock.

15–22 Speaker, Inc., recorded certain capital stock transactions shown in the following respective journal entries: (1) issuance of common stock for $23 cash per share; (2) subsequent repurchase of some shares at $27 per share; and (3) reissuance of some of the reacquired shares.

(1) Cash	276,000	
Common Stock		180,000
Paid-in Capital in Excess of Par Value		96,000
(2) Treasury Stock	13,500	
Cash		13,500
(3) Cash	5,800	
Treasury Stock		5,400
Paid-in Capital from Treasury Stock		400

(a) How many shares were originally issued?
(b) What was the par value of the shares issued?
(c) How many shares of treasury stock were reacquired?
(d) How many shares of treasury stock were reissued?
(e) At what price per share was the treasury stock reissued?

15–23 Clipper Company has 9,000 shares of $20 par value common stock outstanding. Prepare the general journal entries (if required) to record the following transactions:

Aug. 12   The community in which Clipper Company is building a new plant donated the land site to the company. The appraised value of the land is $85,000.

Oct.   7   Shareholders donated 450 shares to the corporation.
     22   The company sold the donated shares for $32 cash per share.

15–24 Ferris Corporation has 8,000 shares outstanding of 7%, $50 par value preferred stock that were originally issued at par. The company redeemed all of the stock at $54 per share.

(a) Prepare the journal entry to record the redemption of the stock.

(b) Assume that the original issue price was $59 per share; prepare the journal entry to record the redemption.

15–25 The stockholders' equity section of the Jersey Company appears as follows:

Paid-in Capital:		
8% Cumulative Preferred Stock, $100 Par Value, 5,000 shares authorized, issued, and outstanding	$500,000	
Paid-in Capital in Excess of Par Value—Preferred Stock	6,000	$506,000
No-par Common Stock, $25 Stated Value, 10,000 shares authorized, issued, and outstanding	$250,000	
Paid-in Capital in Excess of Stated Value—Common Stock	60,000	310,000
Paid-in Capital from Treasury Stock		23,000
Total Paid-in Capital		$839,000
Retained Earnings		110,000
Total Stockholders' Equity		$949,000

The preferred stock has a liquidation preference of $102 per share, and no dividends are in arrears. Compute the book value per share of the common stock.

PROBLEMS

15–26 The Jackson Corporation was organized on April 1 of the current year with an authorization of 5,000 shares of 8%, $50 par value preferred stock and 60,000 shares of $25 par value common stock. During April, the following transactions affecting stockholders' equity occurred:

Apr. 1 Issued 4,000 shares of preferred stock for $60 cash per share and 30,000 shares of common stock at $29 cash per share.

3 Issued 500 shares of common stock to attorneys and promoters in exchange for their services in organizing the corporation. The services were valued at $15,000.

8 Issued 800 shares of preferred stock in exchange for equipment with a fair market value of $48,000.

17 Received land valued at $100,000 as a donation from the city to attract Jackson to its present location. The land will allow Jackson to have adequate parking for its operations.

20 Issued 5,000 shares of common stock for cash at $31 per share.

30 Closed the $20,000 net income for April from the Income Summary account to Retained Earnings.

REQUIRED

(a) Prepare general journal entries to record the foregoing transactions.

(b) Prepare the stockholders' equity section of the balance sheet at April 30.

15–27 The Vilas Corporation has outstanding 10,000 shares of $30 par value, 7%, cumulative preferred stock and 50,000 shares of $10 par value common stock. The company has declared cash dividends of $136,000.

REQUIRED
(a) Calculate the total dividends and the dividends per share paid to each class of stock. There are no dividend arrearages.
(b) Assuming that one year's dividend arrearage exists on the preferred stock, calculate the total dividends and the dividends per share paid to each class of stock.
(c) Assuming that the 7% preferred stock is participating only to 8% (and no dividend arrearages exist), calculate the total dividends and the dividends per share paid to each class of stock.
(d) Assuming that the 7% preferred stock is fully participating (and no dividend arrearages exist), calculate the total dividends and the dividends per share paid to each class of stock.

15–28 The stockholders' equity of the Cardinal Corporation at January 1 of the current year appears below:

8% Preferred Stock, $50 Par Value, 8,000 shares authorized;	
6,000 shares issued and outstanding	$300,000
Paid-in Capital in Excess of Par Value—Preferred Stock	42,000
Common Stock, $20 Par Value, 100,000 shares authorized;	
40,000 shares issued and outstanding	800,000
Retained Earnings	320,000

During the current year, the following transactions occurred:

Jan.	10	Issued 9,000 shares of common stock for $22 cash per share.
	23	Repurchased 4,000 shares of common stock for the treasury at $23 per share.
Mar.	2	Shareholders donated 1,800 shares of common stock to the corporation.
	14	Sold one-half of the treasury shares acquired January 23 for $25 per share.
	14	Sold the donated shares at $25 per share.
July	15	Issued 1,000 shares of preferred stock to acquire special equipment with a fair market value of $62,000.
Sept.	15	Received subscriptions to 5,000 shares of common stock at $30 per share. One-third of the subscription price was received in cash.
Nov.	15	Received the balance due on the September 15 stock subscriptions in cash, and issued the stock certificates.
Dec.	31	Closed the net income of $82,000 from the Income Summary account to Retained Earnings.

REQUIRED
(a) Set up T accounts for the stockholders' equity accounts at the beginning of the year, and enter January 1 balances.
(b) Prepare general journal entries to record the foregoing transactions, and post to T accounts (set up any additional T accounts needed).
(c) Prepare the December 31 stockholders' equity section of the balance sheet.

(d) Assume the preferred stock has a liquidation preference of $53 per share. No dividends are in arrears. Compute the book value per share of common stock at December 31.

15–29 Comparative stockholders' equity sections from two successive years' balance sheets of Springer, Inc., are as follows:

	Dec. 31, 19X2	Dec. 31, 19X1
Paid-in Capital:		
8% Preferred Stock, $100 Par Value, authorized 6,000 shares; issued and outstanding, 19X1: 6,000 shares; 19X2: 4,500 shares	$ 450,000	$ 600,000
Paid-in Capital in Excess of Par Value—Preferred Stock	63,000	84,000
Common Stock, No-par Value, $10 Stated Value, authorized 70,000 shares; outstanding, 19X1: 34,000 shares; 19X2: 44,000 shares	440,000	380,000
Paid-in Capital in Excess of Stated Value—Common Stock	75,000	57,000
Redemption Premium on Preferred Stock	15,000	
Paid-in Capital from Treasury Stock	12,000	
Donated Capital	95,000	
Retained Earnings	297,000	226,000
		$1,347,000
Less: Treasury Stock (4,000 shares common) at Cost		44,000
Total Stockholders' Equity	$1,447,000	$1,303,000

No dividends were declared or paid during 19X2. The company received a donated parcel of land from the city in 19X2.

REQUIRED
(a) What was the redemption price in 19X2 per share of preferred stock?
(b) For what price per share was the treasury stock sold in 19X2?
(c) Prepare the general journal entries for the transactions affecting stockholders' equity that evidently occurred during 19X2.

15–30 Ruth Corporation has the following stockholders' equity section in its balance sheet:

Paid-in Capital:		
7% Preferred Stock, $100 Par Value, 3,000 shares authorized, issued, and outstanding	$300,000	
Paid-in Capital in Excess of Par Value—Preferred Stock	12,000	
Common Stock, $20 Par Value, 40,000 shares authorized; 20,000 shares issued and outstanding	400,000	
Paid-in Capital in Excess of Par Value— Common Stock	30,000	
Paid-in Capital from Treasury Stock	10,000	$752,000
Retained Earnings		100,000
Total Stockholders' Equity		$852,000

REQUIRED

For each of the following independent cases, compute the book value per share for the preferred stock and the common stock.

(a) The preferred stock is noncumulative, nonparticipating, and has a liquidation preference of $103 per share.

(b) The preferred stock is cumulative, nonparticipating, and has a liquidation preference per share equal to par value plus dividends in arrears. No dividends are in arrears.

(c) The preferred stock is cumulative, nonparticipating, and has a liquidation preference of $105 per share plus dividends in arrears. Dividends are three years in arrears.

15–31   The stockholders' equity section of Badger Corporation's balance sheet at January 1 of the current year is shown below:

8% Preferred Stock, $50 Par Value, 5,000 shares authorized; 3,000 shares issued and outstanding	$ 150,000
Paid-in Capital in Excess of Par Value—Preferred Stock	9,000
Common Stock, $10 Par Value, 50,000 shares authorized; 35,000 shares issued and outstanding	350,000
Paid-in Capital in Excess of Par Value—Common Stock	140,000
Retained Earnings	362,000
Total Stockholders' Equity	$1,011,000

The following transactions, among others, occurred during the year:

Jan. 12   Redeemed all the preferred stock at $55 per share (and retired the shares).
      20   Received subscriptions for the sale of 5,000 shares of common stock at $16 per share. Received one-half of the subscription price in cash.
Feb.   9   Received the remainder of payment for the shares subscribed on January 20 in cash, and issued the stock certificates.
Apr. 14   Received a plant site valued at $175,000 as a gift from the city.
June   1   Acquired equipment with a fair market value of $72,000 in exchange for 4,000 shares of common stock.
Sept. 1   Reacquired 1,500 shares of common stock for cash at $20 per share.
Oct. 12   Resold 300 treasury shares at $21 per share.
Nov. 30   Received subscriptions for the sale of 2,000 shares of common stock at $18 per share. Received one-third of the subscription price in cash.
Dec. 28   Resold one-half of the remaining treasury shares at $17 per share.
      31   Closed the Income Summary account, with net earnings of $80,000, to Retained Earnings.

REQUIRED

(a) Set up T accounts for all stockholders' equity accounts needed. Enter the balances as of January 1 of the current year.

(b) Prepare general journal entries for the given transactions, and post them to the T accounts (set up any additional T accounts needed).

(c) Prepare the stockholders' equity section of the balance sheet at December 31 of the current year.

15–32 The T accounts below contain keyed entries representing seven transactions involving the stockholders' equity of Graphic, Inc.

	Cash		
(1)	37,200	(4)	2,400
(2)	50,000	(7)	4,060
(6)	1,040		

	Land	
(3)	77,000	
(5)	65,000	

Preferred Stock, $50 Par

(7)	3,500	(1)	30,000

Paid-in Capital in Excess of Par Value—Preferred Stock

(7)	840	(1)	7,200

Common Stock, $20 Par

		(2)	50,000
		(3)	70,000

Paid-in Capital in Excess of Par Value—Common Stock

		(3)	7,000

Treasury Stock

(4) (100 shares of common)	2,400	(6)	960

Paid-in Capital from Treasury Stock

		(6)	80

Donated Capital

		(5)	65,000

Redemption Premium on Preferred Stock

		(7)	280

REQUIRED

Using this information, give detailed descriptions, including number of shares and price per share when applicable, for each of the seven transactions.

ALTERNATE PROBLEMS

15–26A The Lanox Corporation was organized on July 1 of the current year with an authorization of 10,000 shares of $5 no-par value preferred stock ($5 is the annual dividend) and 40,000 shares of $10 par value common stock. During July, the following transactions affecting stockholders' equity occurred:

July 1 Issued 7,000 shares of preferred stock for $51 cash per share and 12,000 shares of common stock at $16 cash per share.

5   The local municipality donated a vacant building to the corporation as an inducement to operate the business in the community. The fair market value of the building was $250,000.

12   Issued 1,500 shares of common stock in exchange for equipment with a fair market value of $27,000.

15   Issued 2,000 shares of preferred stock for cash at $50 per share.

23   Received subscriptions for 4,000 shares of common stock at $20 per share. A 25% cash down payment accompanied the subscriptions. The balance of the subscription price is due on August 31.

31   Closed the $39,000 net income for July from the Income Summary account to Retained Earnings.

REQUIRED
(a) Prepare general journal entries to record the foregoing transactions.
(b) Prepare the stockholders' equity section of the balance sheet at July 31.

15–27A   Seahawk Corporation has outstanding 5,000 shares of $100 par value, 9%, cumulative preferred stock and 40,000 shares of $25 par value common stock. The company has declared cash dividends of $225,000.

REQUIRED
(a) Calculate the total dividends and the dividends per share paid to each class of stock. There are no dividend arrearages.
(b) Assuming that two years' dividend arrearages exist on the preferred stock, calculate the total dividends and the dividends per share paid to each class of stock.
(c) Assuming that the 9% preferred stock is participating only to 11% (and no dividend arrearages exist), calculate the total dividends and the dividends per share paid to each class of stock.
(d) Assuming that the 9% preferred stock is fully participating (and no dividend arrearages exist), calculate the total dividends and the dividends per share paid to each class of stock.

15–28A   The stockholders' equity of the Bantam Corporation at January 1 of the current year appears below:

Common Stock, $40 Par Value, 50,000 shares authorized;	
22,000 shares issued and outstanding	$880,000
Paid-in Capital in Excess of Par Value—Common Stock	55,000
Retained Earnings	376,000

During the current year, the following transactions occurred:

Jan.   5   Issued 5,000 shares of common stock for $47 cash per share.

18   Repurchased 2,000 shares of common stock for the treasury at $45 per share.

Mar.   10   Shareholders donated 750 shares to the corporation.

12   Sold one-half of the treasury shares acquired January 18 for $48 per share.

12   Sold the donated shares at $48 per share.

July 17 Sold one-half of the remaining treasury stock for $43 per share.

Sept. 20 Received subscriptions to 4,000 shares of common stock at $46 per share. Received one-fourth of the subscription price in cash.

Nov. 25 Received the balance due on the September 20 stock subscription in cash, and issued the stock certificates.

Dec. 31 Closed the net income of $54,000 from the Income Summary account to Retained Earnings.

REQUIRED

(a) Set up T accounts for the stockholders' equity accounts at the beginning of the year, and enter January 1 balances.

(b) Prepare general journal entries to record the foregoing transactions, and post to T accounts (set up any additional T accounts needed).

(c) Prepare the December 31 stockholders' equity section of the balance sheet.

(d) Compute the book value per share of common stock at December 31.

15–30A Endle, Inc., has the following stockholders' equity section in its balance sheet:

Paid-in Capital:

8% Preferred Stock, $50 Par Value, 7,500 shares authorized, issued, and outstanding	$375,000	
Paid-in Capital in Excess of Par Value—Preferred Stock	18,000	
Common Stock, $10 Par Value, 80,000 shares authorized; 30,000 shares issued and outstanding	300,000	
Paid-in Capital in Excess of Par Value—Common Stock	45,000	
Donated Capital	17,000	$755,000
Retained Earnings		208,000
Total Stockholders' Equity		$963,000

REQUIRED

For each of the following independent cases, compute the book value per share for the preferred stock and the common stock.

(a) The preferred stock is noncumulative, nonparticipating, and has a liquidation preference of $52 per share.

(b) The preferred stock is cumulative, nonparticipating, and has a liquidation preference per share equal to par value plus dividends in arrears. No dividends are in arrears.

(c) The preferred stock is cumulative, nonparticipating, and has a liquidation preference of $54 per share plus dividends in arrears. Dividends are two years in arrears.

15–31A The stockholders' equity section of Sabre Corporation's balance sheet at January 1 of the current year is shown on the following page.

9% Preferred Stock, $100 Par Value, 3,000 shares authorized;	
2,000 shares issued and outstanding	$ 200,000
Paid-in Capital in Excess of Par Value—Preferred Stock	30,000
Common Stock, $25 Par Value, 40,000 shares authorized;	
25,000 shares issued and outstanding	625,000
Paid-in Capital in Excess of Par Value—Common Stock	85,000
Retained Earnings	280,000
Total Stockholders' Equity	$1,220,000

The following transactions, among others, occurred during the year:

Jan. 12   Issued 500 shares of preferred stock for $120 cash per share.

20   Received subscriptions for the sale of 2,000 shares of common stock at $32 per share. Received one-half of the subscription price in cash.

Feb.   9   Received the remainder of payment for the shares subscribed on January 20 in cash, and issued the stock certificates.

Apr. 14   Received a vacant school building valued at $315,000 as a gift from the city. The company plans to remodel the building for additional office space.

May 18   Redeemed all the preferred stock at $108 per share (and retired the shares).

June   1   Acquired equipment with a fair market value of $105,000 in exchange for 3,000 shares of common stock.

Sept. 1   Reacquired 2,400 shares of common stock for cash at $37 per share.

Oct. 12   Resold 600 treasury shares at $39 per share.

Nov. 30   Received subscriptions for the sale of 4,000 shares of common stock at $38 per share. Received one-fifth of the subscription price in cash.

Dec. 28   Resold one-half of the remaining treasury shares at $34 per share.

31   Closed the Income Summary account, with net earnings of $71,000, to Retained Earnings.

REQUIRED

(a) Set up T accounts for all stockholders' equity accounts needed. Enter the balances as of January 1 of the current year.

(b) Prepare general journal entries for the given transactions, and post them to the T accounts (set up any additional T accounts needed).

(c) Prepare the stockholders' equity section of the balance sheet at December 31 of the current year.

BUSINESS DECISION PROBLEM

Howard Strong has operated Strong's Variety very successfully as a sole proprietorship. He feels that the continued growth and success of his business depends on increasing its scale of operations, which requires additional working capital. He also wishes to relocate his store from its rented quarters to a new shopping center. After exploring several opportunities that would result in large personal debts, Strong incorporates his business, taking in as stockholders Dr. Burns, who invests cash, and Ms. Hanby, a real estate developer who owns a suitable vacant building in the desired shopping area.

As an initial step, Strong and his attorney secure a corporate charter for Towne Varieties, Inc., authorizing it to issue 15,000 shares of $25 per value common stock. Other details of the agreement follow:

(1) On June 1 of the current year, the date of incorporation, the post-closing trial balance of Strong's Variety is as follows:

	Debit	Credit
Cash	$ 3,500	
Accounts Receivable	8,700	
Allowance for Uncollectible Accounts		$ 300
Merchandise Inventory	97,000	
Store Equipment	36,000	
Accumulated Depreciation—Store Equipment		9,000
Accounts Payable		12,400
Note Payable (due two years hence)		25,000
H. Strong, Capital		98,500
	$145,200	$145,200

(2) After a detailed review of the accounts of Strong's Variety, the new stockholders agree that:

(a) The allowance for uncollectible accounts should increase by $200.

(b) Because of damaged and shopworn goods, the merchandise inventory should be written down by $5,000.

(c) The store equipment will be recorded in the corporate accounts at its fair market value of $30,000.

(d) The new corporation assumes at face value the recorded liabilities of the proprietorship.

Strong has agreed to accept shares in the new corporation at par value in exchange for his adjusted equity in the assets of the proprietorship. He will purchase for cash at par value any additional shares necessary to bring his total holdings to the next even 100 shares.

(3) The total value of Hanby's building and land is agreed to be $98,000, of which $18,000 is associated with the land. Hanby has agreed to accept stock at $28 per share for her land and building.

(4) In an effort to stimulate local business, the Business Development Commission of the local city government has deeded to the corporation, for a token fee of $600, a small strip of land that will provide better delivery access to the rear of Hanby's building. The fair value of the parcel is $6,000.

(5) Burns has agreed to purchase for cash 2,000 shares at $28 per share. He will subscribe to an additional 1,000 shares at $30 per share, paying 20% of the issue price on subscription and the balance in two equal installments, 90 and 180 days later.

(6) Legal and accounting costs of $3,000 associated with acquiring the corporate charter and issuing the stock are paid from corporate funds. (Treat these as the asset, Organization Costs.)

REQUIRED

(a) As Strong's accountant, you must prepare a balance sheet for the new corporation reflecting the shares issued, the stock subscription received, the parcel of land received from the city, and payment of legal and accounting costs. (*Hint:* You may wish to prepare a worksheet with the following headings:

Accounts	Strong's Variety Trial Balance		Adjustments and Organizational Transactions		Towne Varieties, Inc. Trial Balance	
	Dr.	Cr.	Dr.	Cr.	Dr.	Cr.

Properly combining and extending the amounts in the first two pairs of columns provide amounts for the trial balance of Towne Varieties, Inc. When recording the Strong's Variety trial balance, leave extra lines for the several transactions that will affect the Cash, H. Strong, Capital, and Common Stock accounts. Also, for purposes of review, you may wish to key your adjustments and transactions to the letters and numbers used in the problem data.)

(b) In contrast to what they contributed to the corporation, what specifically do Strong and Hanby "own" after the incorporation?

(c) From Strong's viewpoint, what are the advantages and disadvantages of incorporating the variety store?

16
Corporations:
Earnings Disclosure,
Dividends, and
Retained Earnings

> **All things have their place, knew we how to place them.**
>
> GEORGE HERBERT

Profits play a significant role in the organization and functioning of economic activity in the United States. A corporation's profitability is vitally important both to its owners and to potential investors. For this reason, earnings data are usually considered the most important financial information presented by corporate entities. Earnings data encompass not only the net income or loss for the period, but also any prior period adjustments and earnings per share amounts.

As explained earlier, the balance of the Retained Earnings account represents the stockholders' equity arising from the corporation's retention of assets generated from profit-directed activities. At the end of an accounting period, the Retained Earnings account is credited with the corporation's net income (when the Income Summary account is closed to it) or debited with a net loss. A debit balance in the Retained Earnings account resulting from accumulated losses is called a **deficit.** In certain instances, Retained Earnings is charged or credited directly to correct errors made in past periods; these items do not appear in the income statement.

The board of directors may decide, based on the income performance of the corporation, to distribute assets to stockholders, in which case they declare a *dividend*. The board of directors may also decide to retain some of the assets resulting from profitable operations for an identifiable purpose, such as expansion of operations or as a buffer for possible losses. They may then appropriate or restrict a portion of retained earnings.

Because of the importance of income data, accountants have developed several guidelines for their disclosure. In this chapter, we discuss the procedures for reporting earnings data and accounting for dividends and appropriations of retained earnings.

INCOME STATEMENT SECTIONS

Accountants believe that the usefulness of the income statement is enhanced if certain types of transactions and events are reported in separate sections. For this reason, information about extraordinary items, discontinued operations, and effects of changes in accounting principles are disclosed separately in an income statement. Segregating these categories of information from the results of ordinary, continuing operations should make it easier for financial statement users to estimate the future earnings performance of the company.

The creation of several sections in the income statement, however, complicates the reporting of income tax expense. Items affecting the overall amount of income tax expense may appear in more than one section. If this is the case, accountants allocate the income tax expense among those sections of the statement in which the items affecting the tax expense appear.

We now examine these areas in more detail.

EXTRAORDINARY ITEMS

Extraordinary items are transactions and events that are *unusual in nature* and *occur infrequently.*[1] An item that is unusual in nature is highly abnormal and significantly different from the firm's ordinary and typical activities. To determine a firm's ordinary and typical activities, we must consider such things as the type of operations, lines of business, operating policies, and the environment in which the firm operates. The operating environment includes the characteristics of the industry, the geographic location of the firm's facilities, and the type of government regulations imposed. A transaction or event is considered to occur infrequently if the firm does not expect it to recur in the foreseeable future.

The two criteria—unusual nature and infrequent occurrence—considerably restrict the events and transactions that qualify as extraordinary items. For example, suppose a tobacco grower suffers crop loss from a flood, which normally happens every few years in this area. The history of floods creates a reasonable expectation that another flood will occur in the foreseeable future. The loss, therefore, does not meet the criteria for an extraordinary item. Now consider a different tobacco grower who suffers flood damage to his crop for the first time from a broken dam. The dam is repaired and is not expected to fail in the foreseeable future. The flood loss in this circumstance is an extraordinary item.

Other events that may generate extraordinary losses are earthquakes, expropriation of property, and prohibitions under newly enacted laws (such as a government ban on a product currently marketed). An extraordinary gain may result from a nonrecurring sale of an asset never used in operations. Assume a manufacturing company acquired land several years ago for future use but then changed its plans and held the land for appreciation. If this is the only land the company owns and it will not speculate in land in the foreseeable future, any gain from the sale of the land is considered extraordinary.

One exception to the criteria defining extraordinary items relates to gains and losses incurred when a company extinguishes its own debt. These gains and losses are aggregated and, if material, classified as extraordinary items.[2] An example of a debt extinguishment loss is presented in Chapter 17.

---

[1] *Opinions of the Accounting Principles Board, No. 30,* "Reporting the Results of Operations—Reporting the Effects of Disposal of a Segment of a Business, and Extraordinary, Unusual and Infrequently Occurring Events and Transactions" (New York: American Institute of Certified Public Accountants, 1973).

[2] Unless the gains or losses result from cash purchases of debt made to satisfy sinking-fund requirements. See *Statement of Financial Accounting Standards No. 4,* "Reporting Gains and Losses from Extinguishment of Debt" (Stamford, CT: Financial Accounting Standards Board, 1975).

EXHIBIT 16–1

Pacific Corporation
Income Statement
For the Year Ended December 31, 19XX

Sales		$700,000
Cost of Goods Sold		360,000
Gross Profit on Sales		$340,000
Less: Selling Expenses	$90,000	
Administrative Expenses	80,000	
Loss from Plant Strike	45,000	215,000
Income before Taxes and Extraordinary Item		$125,000
Less: Income Taxes		50,000
Income before Extraordinary Item		$ 75,000
Extraordinary Item:		
Gain from Sale of Z Company Stock	$80,000	
Less: Income Taxes	22,400	57,600
Net Income		$132,600

Exhibit 16–1 is an income statement for a corporation with an extraordinary item. During 19XX, the Pacific Corporation, a manufacturing concern, sold a block of common stock of Z Company, a publicly traded company, at a gain of $80,000. The shares of stock were the only security investment the company had ever owned, and it does not plan to acquire other stocks in the foreseeable future. For Pacific Corporation, this gain is unusual, infrequent, and properly considered an extraordinary item. The gain, taxed at 28%, is reported net of $22,400 income taxes, as shown in Exhibit 16–1.

UNUSUAL OR NONRECURRING ITEMS

Events and transactions that are unusual or nonrecurring, but not both, are not extraordinary items. *Accounting Principles Board Opinion No. 30* notes several examples of gains and losses that are not extraordinary either because they are typical or because they may recur as a result of continuing business activities. Examples of such items are gains and losses from (a) the write-down or write-off of receivables, inventories, and intangible assets; (b) the exchange or translation of foreign currencies; (c) the sale or abandonment of property, plant, or equipment used in the business; (d) the effects of a strike; and (e) the adjustments of long-term contract accruals. An unusual or infrequently occurring item of a material amount should be reported as a separate component of income before extraordinary items.

Assume that during 19XX the Pacific Corporation incurred a $45,000 loss because of a labor strike at one of its plants. The strike was not part of the company's ordinary activities, but Pacific Corporation has a history of labor difficulties. Therefore, even though the strike loss was unusual, it was not infrequent because it will likely happen again in the foreseeable future. Because it did not qualify as an extraordinary item, the before-tax amount of the strike loss was reported as a separate item among the ordinary expenses, as shown in Exhibit 16–1.

TAX ALLOCATION WITHIN A PERIOD

Note that the extraordinary gain in Exhibit 16–1 is shown net of applicable income taxes. Pacific Corporation's total income tax expense of $72,400 has been allocated to two parts of the income statement: $50,000 deducted in deriving income before extraordinary items, and $22,400 deducted in the extraordinary items section. This process, known as **tax allocation within a period**, reports the tax effect of an extraordinary item in the same section of the income statement as the item itself. By the same token, the income taxes deducted in the income before extraordinary items section relate only to the revenue and expenses disclosed in that section. Thus, tax allocation within a period portrays normal relationships within the income statement between income taxes and the items affecting their calculation.

A tax reduction due to an extraordinary loss would be deducted from the loss in the extraordinary items section. Suppose that instead of the $80,000 gain, Pacific Corporation incurred an extraordinary flood loss of $30,000, which reduced income subject to a 40% tax rate. The lower portion of the company's income statement, after tax allocation, would appear as follows:

Income before Taxes and Extraordinary Item		$125,000
Less: Income Taxes		50,000
Income before Extraordinary Item		$ 75,000
Extraordinary Item:		
Flood Loss	$30,000	
Less: Tax Reduction from Flood Loss	12,000	18,000
Net Income		$ 57,000

An alternative way of reporting the tax effects of extraordinary items is to disclose them parenthetically. Using this procedure, the extraordinary gain would be shown as

Gain from Sale of Z Company Stock (net of $22,400 of income taxes)	$57,600

The extraordinary loss would be reported as follows:

Flood Loss (net of $12,000 reduction of income taxes)	$18,000

DISCONTINUED OPERATIONS

When a company sells, abandons, or otherwise disposes of a segment of its operations, a **discontinued operations** section of the income statement reports information about the discontinued segment. The discontinued operations section presents two categories of information:

(1) The income or loss from the segment's operations for the portion of the year before its discontinuance.

(2) The gain or loss from the disposal of the segment.

The section is placed after information about ordinary, continuing operations and before any extraordinary items.

A **segment** of a business is a unit—such as a department or a division—whose activities constitute a separate major line of business or serve a particular class of customer. The assets and operating results of the segment must be clearly distinguishable from the rest of the company. For example, a furniture manufacturing division of a diversified manufacturing company is a segment of the business.

To illustrate the reporting of discontinued operations, we assume that on July 1 of the current year, Atlantic Corporation sold its Division Y. From January 1 through June 30, Division Y had operated at a loss, net of taxes, of $15,000 ($25,000 operating loss less a $10,000 reduction in income taxes caused by the operating loss). The loss, net of taxes, from the sale of the division was $42,000 ($70,000 loss on the sale less a $28,000 reduction in income taxes caused by the loss). Exhibit 16–2 illustrates the income statement for Atlantic Corporation, including the information about Division Y in the discontinued operations section. Note that when there is a discontinued operations section, the difference between the ordinary revenue and expenses is labeled "income from continuing operations."

CHANGES IN ACCOUNTING PRINCIPLES

Occasionally a company may change an accounting principle, that is, switch from one generally accepted principle to another. Examples include a change in inventory pricing method—such as from FIFO to weighted average—or a change in depreciation method—such as from double declining balance to straight line. Because the comparability of financial data through time is enhanced by the consistent use of accounting principles, a company should change principles only when it can demonstrate that the new principle is preferable.

Almost all changes in accounting principles introduce a new item into the income statement—the **cumulative effect of a change in principle.** This item represents the total difference in the cumulative income for all prior years had the new principle been used in those years. It is equal to the difference between (a) the retained earnings at the beginning of the year and (b) the retained earnings

EXHIBIT 16–2

Atlantic Corporation
Income Statement
For the Year Ended December 31, 19XX

Sales		$1,900,000
Expenses:		
Cost of Goods Sold	$1,100,000	
Selling Expenses	200,000	
Administrative Expenses	180,000	
Interest Expense	20,000	
Income Tax Expense	160,000	
Total Expenses		1,660,000
Income from Continuing Operations		$ 240,000
Discontinued Operations:		
Loss from Operations of Discontinued Division Y (net of $10,000 reduction of income taxes)	$ 15,000	
Loss on Disposal of Division Y (net of $28,000 reduction of income taxes)	42,000	57,000
Income before Extraordinary Item and Cumulative Effect of a Change in Accounting Principle		$ 183,000
Extraordinary Item:		
Earthquake Loss (net of $16,000 reduction of income taxes)		(24,000)
Cumulative Effect on Prior Years of Changing to a Different Depreciation Method (net of $8,000 income taxes)		12,000
Net Income		$ 171,000

amount at the beginning of the year had the new principle been used in all years in which the previous principle was followed for the items in question. The cumulative effect is disclosed between the extraordinary items section and the net income figure.

To illustrate the reporting of the cumulative effect of a change in principle, we assume the Atlantic Corporation in Exhibit 16–2 changed its method of depreciating plant equipment in 19XX, switching from an accelerated method to the straight-line method. Cumulative income before income taxes for years prior to 19XX would have been $20,000 greater if the straight-line method had been used to depreciate the plant equipment in those years. If we assume an income tax rate of 40%, the $12,000 after-tax amount of the effect of the change in principle would be reported on Atlantic Corporation's income statement as shown in Exhibit 16–2.

In addition to reporting the cumulative effect, the company should, in a note to the financial statements, justify the change and disclose the effect of the change on the current year's income exclusive of the cumulative adjustment. The effect of the change on earnings per share should also be reported.

Annual financial reports often include financial statements for prior periods for comparative purposes. These prior period statements are not revised to reflect the new principle adopted this period. For each period reported, however, the income before extraordinary items, net income, and the related earnings per share amounts are recomputed as if the new principle had been in effect in that period. Each period's income statement will disclose these recomputed amounts.

The above disclosure requirements accommodate two conflicting positions on the appropriate method of disclosing a change in accounting principle. One position stresses the possible dilution of public confidence in financial statements if previously reported statements are revised to reflect a new principle— hence, the inclusion of a cumulative effect on prior years' income in the current year's income statement with no revision of prior period statements. The other position emphasizes the importance of consistency in the use of accounting principles for comparative analysis of data—hence, the disclosure of selected, significant pieces of information, recomputed using the new principle, for all periods presented in the financial statements.

SINGLE-STEP AND MULTIPLE-STEP INCOME STATEMENTS

Exhibit 16–2 (page 541) illustrates a **single-step** income statement, in which the ordinary, continuing income of the business is derived in one step—by subtracting total expenses from total revenue. In Exhibit 16–2, all the expenses, totaling $1,660,000, are combined and then subtracted from the total revenue of $1,900,000. The single-step statement is a popular reporting format.

Exhibit 16–1 (page 538) is an example of a **multiple-step** income statement, in which one or more intermediate amounts are derived before the ordinary, continuing income is reported. In Exhibit 16–1, "gross profit on sales" and "income before taxes and extraordinary item" are intermediate amounts presented before the "income before extraordinary item" figure. Both the multiple-step and the single-step formats are acceptable procedures.

PRIOR PERIOD ADJUSTMENTS

Essentially, **prior period adjustments** correct errors made in financial statements of prior periods.[3] Errors may result from mathematical mistakes, oversights, incorrect applications of accounting principles, or improper analyses of existing facts when the financial statements are prepared.

---

[3] *Statement of Financial Accounting Standards No. 16,* "Prior Period Adjustments" (Stamford, CT: Financial Accounting Standards Board, 1977).

Prior period adjustments are not included in the current year's income statement. Instead, corrections of material errors of past periods are charged or credited directly to Retained Earnings and are reported as adjustments to the beginning balance of Retained Earnings in the current year's retained earnings statement. For example, in 19X2, a company discovered that several mathematical errors caused its December 31, 19X1, inventory to be understated by $30,000, a material amount. Assuming an applicable income tax rate of 30%, the company reports the $21,000 prior period adjustment on the retained earnings statement. A partial statement showing this disclosure follows (beginning balance assumed):

Retained Earnings Balance, January 1, 19X2	$43,000
Add: Correction of Prior Period Inventory Error (net of $9,000 income taxes)	21,000
Retained Earnings Adjusted Balance, January 1, 19X2	$64,000

Exhibit 16–4 (page 554) contains this prior period adjustment.

Of course, a current period error does not require a prior period adjustment. The correction of current period errors was discussed in Chapter 3. As noted there, a journal entry posted to the wrong account is most easily corrected by making a new journal entry that transfers the amount to the proper account. An error that involves the right accounts but the wrong amounts may be corrected by drawing a line through the wrong amounts, entering the correct amounts above, and initialing the correction. Because the errors and corrections occur in the same period, the financial statements reflect the correct data.

CHANGES IN ACCOUNTING ESTIMATES

Estimates play an integral part in accounting. In preparing periodic financial statements, we estimate the effects of transactions continuing in the future. For example, we must estimate uncollectible accounts, useful lives of plant and intangible assets, salvage values of plant assets, and product warranty costs. As a normal consequence of such estimates, new information, changed conditions, or more experience may require the revision of previous estimates.

The effect of a change in an estimate should be reflected in the income statements of current and future periods to the extent appropriate in each case. The effect may not be treated as a prior period adjustment and bypass the income statement.

The total impact of some changes in estimates is included in the current year's income statement. A revision of an estimated liability recorded in prior periods is one example. Assume that unanticipated cost increases have caused a company to underestimate its liability for product warranty carried into the current year by $900. The estimated liability is revised as follows:

Product Warranty Expense	900	
Estimated Liability for Product Warranty		900
To record estimated warranty expense.		

An estimate revision may affect both the period of change and future periods. If so, the effect of the revision should be accounted for over the current and future periods. The revision of depreciation discussed on page 358 illustrates this type of change.

The Accounting Principles Board concluded in its *Opinion No. 20,* "Accounting Changes," that the restatement of amounts reported in prior period financial statements is an inappropriate way to account for changes in estimates. Presumably, the previous estimates were the best possible, given the information then available. Thus, amounts reported for those periods should not be changed.

SUMMARY OF REPORTING FORMAT

Reporting the income of a corporation with the variety of items discussed in this chapter can be complex. Exhibit 16–3 summarizes these items and indicates their placement on the income or retained earnings statement, the order in which they are normally reported, and whether each is reported before or net of its income tax effect. Each of these items on the financial statements is keyed with the number of its related explanation.

Note that all items except prior period adjustments are reported on the income statement. Changes in accounting estimates and unusual or nonrecurring items are reported without any related income tax amounts because they are included in the computation of income from continuing operations. Income tax expense in this section relates to all preceding items of revenue and expense. All items below income from continuing operations are reported at amounts net of their income tax effects. The income statement in Exhibit 16–3 is a single-step income statement. Income from continuing operations is computed in one step, subtracting total expenses from sales. Of course, a single-step statement may include sections other than income from continuing operations.

EARNINGS PER SHARE

A financial statistic of great interest to corporation shareholders and potential investors is the earnings per share of common stock. Consequently, earnings per share data are widely disseminated, reaching interested persons through such channels as annual stockholder reports, financial newspapers, and financial statistical services. Because this financial information is so important, the Accounting Principles Board requires the disclosure of earnings per share data on the income statement.[4]

In determining the presentation of earnings per share data, the Accounting Principles Board has distinguished between corporations with simple capital

[4]*Opinions of the Accounting Principles Board, No. 15,* "Earnings Per Share" (New York: American Institute of Certified Public Accountants, 1969).

EXHIBIT 16–3
Summary of Reporting Format

EXPLANATIONS

1. Changes in Accounting Estimates
Before-tax amounts are reported as part of related ordinary expenses.

2. Unusual or Nonrecurring Items
Before-tax amounts are separate items listed among the ordinary expenses.

3. Income Tax Expense
The initial allocation of income taxes applies to the net of all preceding revenue and expense items. All items appearing below income from continuing operations are reported net of income taxes.

4. Discontinued Operations
Involves reporting separately for the discontinued segment:
(a) Gain or loss from operations net of income taxes.
(b) Gain or loss on disposal net of income taxes.

5. Extraordinary Items
Reported net of income taxes.

6. Cumulative Effect of Change in Accounting Principle
Reported net of income taxes as the last item before net income on the income statement.

7. Prior Period Adjustments
Reported net of income taxes as a separate item leading to an adjusted beginning balance of retained earnings.

ABC Corporation
Income Statement
For the Year Ended December 31, 19XX

Sales			$XXX
Expenses:			
1 Ordinary Expenses (including effects of changes in accounting estimates)		$XX	
2 Unusual or Nonrecurring Items		XX	
3 Income Tax Expense		XX	
Total Expenses			XXX
Income from Continuing Operations			$XXX
4 Discontinued Operations:			
Gain or Loss from Operations (net of income taxes)		$XX	
Gain or Loss on Disposal (net of income taxes)		XX	XX
Income before Extraordinary Items and Cumulative Effect of a Change in Accounting Principle			$XXX
5 Extraordinary Items (net of income taxes)			XX
6 Cumulative Effect on Prior Years of Change in Accounting Principle (net of income taxes)			XX
Net Income			$XXX

ABC Corporation
Retained Earnings Statement
For the Year Ended December 31, 19XX

Balance, January 1, 19XX	$XXX
7 Add (Less): Prior Period Adjustments (net of income taxes)	XX
Adjusted Balance, January 1, 19XX	$XXX
Add (Less): Net Income (Loss)	XXX
	$XXX
Less: Dividends Declared	XX
Balance, December 31, 19XX	$XXX

structures and those with complex capital structures. A **simple capital structure** contains no securities that, if exercised or converted, reduce (dilute) earnings per share of common stock. Convertible debt, convertible preferred stock, stock options, and stock warrants are examples of potentially dilutive securities, because if they are exercised or converted, the number of outstanding shares of common stock increases. A **complex capital structure** contains one or more potentially dilutive securities. Corporations with simple capital structures make a single presentation of earnings per share, while corporations with complex capital structures make a dual presentation.

Simple Capital Structure

Corporations with simple capital structures calculate earnings per share by dividing net income by a weighted average of the shares of common stock outstanding during the year. If preferred stock also is outstanding, its dividend requirements are first subtracted from net income to derive earnings available to common stockholders.

Suppose that the Owens Corporation has a net income of $39,000 for 19XX. On January 1, 19XX, 10,000 shares of common stock were outstanding. An additional 6,000 shares were issued on July 1. The company has no preferred stock. The weighted average of the shares of common stock outstanding during the year is computed as follows:

Shares		Months Outstanding		Share Months
10,000	×	6	=	60,000
16,000	×	6	=	96,000
		12		156,000

$$\text{Weighted Average of Common Shares Outstanding} = \frac{156,000}{12} = 13,000$$

$$\text{Earnings per Share} = \frac{\text{Net Income}}{\text{Weighted Average of Common Shares Outstanding}}$$

$$= \frac{\$39,000}{13,000} = \$3.00$$

Complex Capital Structure

The dual presentation for corporations with complex capital structures consists of primary earnings per share and fully diluted earnings per share data. The computation of **primary earnings per share** considers the common stock outstanding during the year plus any potentially dilutive securities that are equivalent to common stock. (The Accounting Principles Board has established criteria for determining when a potentially dilutive security is a common stock equivalent.) The calculation of **fully diluted earnings per share** is based on the *assumption* that all dilutive securities are converted into common stock. The difference between the two per-share amounts shows the maximum possible dilution in earnings per share from any outstanding dilutive securities that are not common stock equivalents.

To illustrate the computation of primary and fully diluted earnings per share, let us suppose the Bodeen Company had a net income of $90,000 for the current year. All year the company had 40,000 shares of common stock and 5,000 shares of convertible preferred stock outstanding. The annual dividend on the convertible preferred stock is 80 cents per share, and each share is convertible into one share of common stock. The convertible preferred stock is a potentially dilutive security; we assume it is not a common stock equivalent.

Primary Earnings per Share

Net Income	$90,000
Less: Preferred Stock Dividend Requirement	
(5,000 shares × $0.80)	4,000
Earnings Available to Common Stockholders	$86,000
Weighted Average of Common Shares Outstanding	40,000

$$\text{Primary Earnings per Share} = \frac{\$86,000}{40,000} = \$2.15$$

Fully Diluted Earnings per Share*

Net Income (under the assumption of preferred stock conversion, there is no deduction for a preferred stock dividend requirement)	$90,000
Weighted Average of Common Shares Outstanding (40,000 shares of common stock + 5,000 shares from assumed conversion of preferred stock)	45,000

$$\text{Fully Diluted Earnings per Share} = \frac{\$90,000}{45,000} = \$2.00$$

*Assumes all preferred stock was converted into common stock at the beginning of the year.

Additional per-Share Disclosures

The form in which earnings per share data are disclosed should correspond with the income statement contents. Thus, if a firm reports extraordinary gains or losses, an earnings per share amount should be disclosed for income before extraordinary items as well as for net income. Companies may also disclose the per-share effect of each extraordinary item. Similar disclosures should be made if the income statement contains an adjustment for the cumulative effect of a change in accounting principle. The following hypothetical data from a comparative income statement for a company with 10,000 outstanding shares of common stock illustrate the proper disclosure:

	19X2	19X1
Income before Extraordinary Items	$50,000	$60,000
Extraordinary Gain (net of tax)	18,000	
Net Income	$68,000	$60,000
Earnings per Share of Common Stock:		
Income before Extraordinary Items	$5.00	$6.00
Extraordinary Gain (net of tax)	1.80	
Net Income	$6.80	$6.00

This form of disclosure precludes drawing misleading inferences from comparative earnings per share data. Note that although the earnings per share for net income increase from 19X1 to 19X2, the data for 19X2 are influenced by an extraordinary (and therefore unusual and nonrecurring) gain. A per-share comparison of income before extraordinary items shows a decrease from 19X1 to 19X2.

The variety of potentially dilutive securities and of events that affect outstanding common stock can make the computations of earnings per share quite complex. The analysis required for such computations is covered in advanced courses.

DIVIDENDS

A corporation can distribute dividends to shareholders only after its board of directors has formally declared a distribution. Dividends are usually paid in cash but may also be property or additional shares of stock in the firm. Legally, declared dividends are an obligation of the firm, and an entry to record the dividends payable is made on the **declaration date.** Cash and property dividends payable are carried as liabilities, and stock dividends to be distributed are shown in the stockholders' equity section of the balance sheet. At the declaration, a **record date** and **payment date** are established. For example, on April 25 (declaration date), the board of directors might declare a dividend payable June 1 (payment date) to those who own stock on May 15 (record date). Stockholders owning stock on the record date receive the dividend even if they dispose of their shares before the payment date. Therefore, shares sold between the record date and payment date are sold **ex-dividend** (without right to the dividend).

Most dividend declarations reduce the balance of Retained Earnings; under certain conditions, however, state laws may permit distributions from paid-in capital. Shareholders should be informed of the source of such dividends, because, in a sense, they are a return of capital rather than a distribution of earnings.

Cash Dividends   The majority of dividends distributed by corporations are paid in cash. Although companies may pay such dividends annually, many large firms pay quarterly dividends. Some companies occasionally pay an extra dividend at year-end. Usually this is done when the company wishes to increase the total annual distribution without departing from a standard quarterly amount that was established by custom or announced in advance.

In declaring cash dividends, a company must have both an appropriate amount of retained earnings and the necessary amount of cash. Uninformed investors often believe that a large Retained Earnings balance automatically permits generous dividend distributions. A company, however, may successfully accumulate earnings and at the same time not be sufficiently liquid to pay large dividends. Many companies, especially new firms in the so-called growth industries, use retained earnings for expansion and pay out only a small portion, or perhaps none, of their earnings.

Cash dividends are based on the number of shares of stock outstanding. When a company's directors declare a cash dividend, an entry is made debiting Retained Earnings and crediting Dividends Payable, a current liability account. Assume, for example, that a company has outstanding 1,000 shares of $100 par value, 6% preferred stock and 3,000 shares of $50 par value common stock. If

DIVIDEND REINVESTMENT PLANS

As a means of attracting capital and promoting goodwill among shareholders, dividend reinvestment plans (DRPs) were devised. Originally begun by Allegheny Power Company, these plans became increasingly popular during the 1970s. There are currently over 1,000 companies offering DRPs, and about 200 of them use the plan to issue new common stock.

The DRPs allow participants to reinvest automatically any cash dividends in common shares of the company. The shareholder notifies the company of a willingness to participate in the plan, and then instead of receiving cash dividends, the shareholder receives an equivalent value of stock. This provides a simple, convenient, systematic method for the investor to increase equity investment in the company. Because the expenses for the new issue plans are absorbed by the company, the new issue DRPs are also an inexpensive method of investment.

Many companies have added other features to their plans. Some companies issue shares of stock through DRPs at a discount from the market price (typically 5%). In addition, many plans permit the investor to contribute limited amounts of additional cash to the plan, ranging from $1,000 to $25,000 per quarter.

DRPS are a popular investment vehicle. It is estimated that over $2 billion of new equity capital was raised through them in 1979. This represents about 25% of all new common stock sold in public offerings. Based on historical evidence, the importance of DRPs in raising new equity capital is expected to grow significantly in the future.

This investment method has had special appeal to the small shareholder. Surveys conducted by several companies have indicated that over 75% of the participants in DRPs hold fewer than 200 shares of the company's stock.

The benefits of DRPs to the individual shareholder are numerous. They allow the shareholder to decide whether to be paid dividends in the form of cash or stock. By selecting the stock alternative, the shareholder has access to a simple, systematic investment vehicle, which provides the advantages of dollar cost averaging of the investments as well as the benefits of compounding. The plans also allow the investor to invest small amounts without incurring transaction costs.

DRPs also have important advantages for the issuing companies. The relatively low issuance costs of the DRP stock make the plans an inexpensive means of raising common equity capital.

Because the plans provide a relatively stable, assured, and continuous flow of new equity capital, companies are able to reduce the number and size of public equity offerings and the associated downward pressure on the market price. The market has demonstrated an ability to accept a small steady stream of new common stock without a significant impact on the market price, while an equivalent number of new shares issued at one time in a public offering could result in a significant decrease in the stock price.

By strengthening the equity base of companies, DRPs provide a means of improving their competitive capabilities. The benefits of an improved capital base have been noted by several credit rating agencies, including Moody's and Duff and Phelps, who have stated that the use of DRPs could lead to improved credit ratings for firms.

From Brent Wilson, "Reinvesting Dividends: A Way To Revitalize Your Company," *Financial Executive*, December 1982, pages 42–43. Reprinted by permission of Financial Executives Institute.

the company declares the regular $6 dividend on the preferred stock and a $4 dividend on the common stock, the dividend payment totals $18,000. The following entry is made at the declaration date:

Retained Earnings	18,000	
Dividends Payable—Preferred Stock		6,000
Dividends Payable—Common Stock		12,000
To record declaration of $6 dividend		
on preferred stock and $4 dividend on		
common stock.		

Unpaid cash dividends are carried as a current liability on the balance sheet. On the payment date, the following entry is made:

Dividends Payable—Preferred Stock	6,000	
Dividends Payable—Common Stock	12,000	
Cash		18,000
To record payment of dividends on		
preferred and common stocks.		

Some companies, especially those paying quarterly dividends, debit an account called Dividends on the declaration date. Dividends is a contra account to Retained Earnings until it is closed by a debit to Retained Earnings at year-end.

Stock Dividends

Companies frequently distribute shares of their own stock as dividends to shareholders in lieu of, or in addition to, cash dividends. A company may issue **stock dividends** when it does not wish to deplete its working capital by paying a cash dividend. Distribution of a stock dividend may also signify management's desire to "plough back" earnings. The distribution transfers a portion of retained earnings to the paid-in capital accounts. The so-called permanent capital is thereby increased although no new assets are acquired. Young and growing companies often issue stock dividends, inasmuch as earnings are needed to acquire new facilities and to expand. The use of stock dividends is by no means confined to such companies, however.

Although stock dividends may take a number of forms, usually common shares are distributed to common shareholders. We limit our discussion to this type of distribution.

For small stock dividends—additional shares issued are fewer than 20–25% of the number previously outstanding—an amount equal to the market value of the shares issued is transferred from Retained Earnings to Paid-in Capital. In some respects, the issuance of new shares in the form of a dividend can be viewed as a transaction that avoids the test of the marketplace. If the shareholders receive cash and immediately purchase additional shares of the firm's stock, the purchases are made at market value. Thus, the number of shares issued in exchange for a given amount of retained earnings should be related to the market value of the shares.

To illustrate the entries reflecting a declaration of a stock dividend, we assume that the stockholders' equity of a company is as follows before declaration of a 10% stock dividend:

Common Stock, $50 Par Value, 2,000 shares issued and outstanding	$100,000
Paid-in Capital in Excess of Par Value	5,000
Retained Earnings	80,000
Total Stockholders' Equity	$185,000

With 2,000 shares outstanding, declaration of a 10% stock dividend requires the issuance of an additional 200 shares. Let us assume that the market price per share is $70. The amount transferred from Retained Earnings is $14,000, of which $10,000 (par value of the shares) is credited to the Stock Dividend to Be Issued account. The premium of $20 per share, or $4,000, is credited to Paid-in Capital in Excess of Par Value.

Retained Earnings	14,000	
Stock Dividend to Be Issued		10,000
Paid-in Capital in Excess of Par Value		4,000
To record declaration of 10% stock		
dividend on common shares.		

When the stock is distributed, the following entry is made:

Stock Dividend to Be Issued	10,000	
Common Stock		10,000
To record issuance of stock dividend		
on common shares.		

After the stock dividend is distributed, the stockholders' equity appears as follows:

Common Stock, $50 Par Value, 2,200 shares issued and outstanding	$110,000
Paid-in Capital in Excess of Par Value	9,000
Retained Earnings	66,000
Total Stockholders' Equity	$185,000

If a balance sheet is prepared between the declaration date and distribution date of a stock dividend, the Stock Dividend to Be Issued account is shown as a separate item added to the Common Stock account.

The relative position of a common shareholder is not altered by the receipt of a common stock dividend. If a 10% stock dividend is distributed, all shareholders increase their proportionate holdings by 10%, while the total stock outstanding is increased in the same proportion. No income is realized by the shareholders. If the stock dividend distributed is not large in relation to the outstanding shares, little or no change may occur in the market value of the stock. If the market value does not decrease and the company continues the same cash dividends per share, shareholders have benefited by the distribution.

When the number of shares issued as a stock dividend is large enough to reduce materially the per-share market value, the shareholders may not perceive the same benefits as they do for small stock dividends. The transaction is analogous to a stock split, whereby a company increases the number of outstanding shares and proportionately reduces the par or stated value of its stock. For this reason, the accounting analysis is different for large stock dividends (in excess of 20–25%). The amount transferred from Retained Earnings to Paid-in Capital is the minimum required by law (that is, the legal capital). Usually this amount is the par or stated value of the stock.

STOCK SPLITS

Occasionally, a corporation reduces the par or stated value of its common stock and issues additional shares to its stockholders. This type of transaction, called a **stock split,** does not change the balances of the stockholders' equity accounts—only a memorandum entry is made in the records to show the altered par or stated value of the stock. For example, if a company that has 1,000 shares outstanding of $100 par value common stock announced a 2 for 1 stock split, it would simply reduce the par value of its stock to $50 per share. After the stock split, each shareholder would have twice the number of shares held before the split.

Note the difference between accounting for a stock split, which requires a memorandum entry, and accounting for a large stock dividend, which requires a transfer equal to the legal capital from Retained Earnings to Paid-in Capital. A stock split reduces the par or stated value of the stock and therefore does not change the total par or stated value of shares outstanding. In a stock dividend, no change occurs in the par or stated value per share, so an entry must reflect the increased legal capital associated with the additional shares issued.

The major reason for a stock split is to reduce the market price of the stock. Some companies like their stock to sell within a certain price range. They may feel that higher prices narrow the breadth of their market, because investors often prefer to buy 100-share lots (purchases of fewer shares are odd-lot purchases and may be subject to higher brokers' fees), and obviously, many small investors cannot purchase high-priced stocks in 100-share lots.

When shares are selling below the desired price, a *reverse split* can be accomplished by increasing the par value of the shares and reducing the number outstanding. Such transactions are encountered less frequently than stock splits.

APPROPRIATIONS OF RETAINED EARNINGS

Portions of the Retained Earnings balance are often restricted so that these amounts cannot be paid out as dividends. The amounts so segregated are called **retained earnings appropriations,** or *retained earnings reserves.*

In some instances, appropriations of retained earnings may be entirely *voluntary*—the board of directors may restrict dividends to use corporate funds for a specific internal purpose. For example, the company may want to enlarge its plant or establish a buffer against possible adversity. By appropriating retained earnings, the directors inform the shareholders of the need to restrict dividend payments.

Other types of retained earnings appropriations may be *statutory* or *contractual*. In Chapter 15, we mentioned a statutory appropriation in connection with treasury stock purchases—some states require that retained earnings be restricted in an amount equal to the cost of treasury stock purchased by the corporation.

A contractual appropriation sometimes results from agreements made when the company issues bonds or preferred stock. At one time, bond contracts commonly required the company to restrict retained earnings during the life of the contract in an amount equal to the debt. In most cases, a pro-rata amount was set aside each year until the accumulated appropriation equaled the total amount of bonds outstanding, usually at the maturity date of the bonds. This type of arrangement is no longer common; contemporary bond contracts usually dictate that the company maintain a specified working capital position to avoid restrictions on dividend payments.

Retained earnings may be appropriated by making an entry in the company's records. For example, if the board of directors appropriates $60,000 for plant expansion, the following entry is made:

Retained Earnings	60,000	
Retained Earnings Appropriated for		
Plant Expansion		60,000
To record retained earnings		
appropriation for plant expansion.		

The appropriated amount is presented in the balance sheet as follows:

Retained Earnings

Appropriated for Plant Expansion	$ 60,000
Unappropriated	90,000
Total Retained Earnings	$150,000

Note that this company has total retained earnings of $150,000, of which only $90,000 is available for the declaration of dividends.

Certain points should be emphasized regarding the appropriation of retained earnings. First, segregating retained earnings for a particular objective only restricts dividend amounts. The procedure does not ensure that funds will be available for the avowed objective, because a company may have a large Retained Earnings balance without having an ample amount of liquid assets. When a company appropriates earnings for plant expansion, for example, management may also *fund* the appropriation. This is accomplished by setting aside funds, as they become available, in a special asset account to permit eventual *spending* for plant expansion.

Second, expenditures are never charged against retained earnings appropriations. When the purpose is accomplished or the event transpires for which the appropriation was made, the restricted amount is returned, intact, to unappropriated retained earnings. For example, suppose that the company in our preceding illustration implemented its expansion plans, spending $55,000 for new facilities. After recording the purchase by debiting plant assets and crediting Cash for the amount spent, the company reverses the entry made to appropriate retained earnings:

Retained Earnings Appropriated for		
Plant Expansion	60,000	
Retained Earnings		60,000
To return appropriation to Retained		
Earnings.		

As an alternative to segregating retained earnings formally, a note to the balance sheet may inform shareholders of restrictions on retained earnings. The note should indicate the nature and amount of the restrictions and the amount of retained earnings free from restrictions.

EXHIBIT 16–4

Holmes Corporation
Retained Earnings Statement
For the Year Ended December 31, 19X2

Appropriated

Appropriated for Plant Expansion, Balance, January 1, 19X2	$40,000	
Appropriated in 19X2	10,000	$ 50,000

Unappropriated

Balance, January 1, 19X2		$43,000	
Add: Correction of Prior Period Inventory Error (net of $9,000 income taxes)		21,000	
Adjusted Balance, January 1, 19X2		$64,000	
Add: Net Income		35,000	
		$99,000	
Less: Dividends Declared	$15,000		
Appropriation for Plant Expansion (see above)	10,000	25,000	74,000
Total Retained Earnings, December 31, 19X2			$124,000

RETAINED EARNINGS STATEMENT

A **retained earnings statement** is an analysis of the Retained Earnings accounts (both appropriated and unappropriated) for the accounting period and is usually presented with the other corporate financial statements. The form of the statement is not standardized, and sometimes it is combined with the income statement. An example of a retained earnings statement is shown in Exhibit 16–4.

DEMONSTRATION PROBLEM FOR REVIEW

Information related to the income and retained earnings of Alpha, Inc., for 19X1 is listed below. For simplicity, amounts are limited to three digits. Using these data, prepare a single-step income statement and a retained earnings statement for Alpha, Inc., for 19X1. Assume that all changes in income are subject to a 30% income tax rate. Use the format in Exhibit 16–3 and disregard earnings per share disclosures.

Additional uncollectible accounts expense due to revised estimate of percentage of anticipated uncollectible accounts (considered a selling expense)	$ 20	Increase in prior years' reported income before income taxes due to change in depreciation method	$ 20
Cost of goods sold	420	Loss from labor strike (considered unusual but recurring)	40
Dividends declared	70	Loss from operations of discontinued Beta Division	50
Overstatement of 19X0 ending inventory (caused by error)	10	Other operating expenses	230
Gain on condemnation of property (considered unusual and infrequent)	40	Retained earnings balance at end of 19X0	454
		Sales	980
Gain on disposal of discontinued Beta Division	80	Selling and administrative expenses (before revised estimate of uncollectible accounts)	170

SOLUTION TO DEMONSTRATION PROBLEM   (Selected computations appear as notes to the financial statements.)

Alpha, Inc.
Income Statement
For the Year Ended December 31, 19X1

Sales		$980
Expenses:		
Cost of Goods Sold	$420	
Other Operating Expenses	230	
Selling and Administrative Expenses (Note A)	190	

Loss from Labor Strike	40	
Income Tax Expense (Note B)	30	
Total Expenses		910
Income from Continuing Operations		$ 70

Discontinued Operations:

Loss from Operations of Discontinued Beta Division (net of $15 reduction of income taxes) (Note C)	($ 35)	
Gain on Disposal of Discontinued Beta Division (net of $24 income taxes) (Note D)	56	21
Income before Extraordinary Item and Cumulative Effect of a Change in Accounting Principle		$ 91

Extraordinary Item:

Gain on Condemnation of Property (net of $12 income taxes) (Note E)	28
Cumulative Effect on Prior Years of Changing to a Different Depreciation Method (net of $6 income taxes) (Note F)	14
Net Income	$133

Alpha, Inc.
Retained Earnings Statement
For the Year Ended December 31, 19X1

Balance, January 1, 19X1	$454
Less: Correction of Prior Period Inventory Error (net of $3 reduction of income taxes) (Note G)	7
Adjusted Balance, January 1, 19X1	$447
Add: Net Income	133
	$580
Less: Dividends Declared	70
Balance, December 31, 19X1	$510

Notes to financial statements:
- (A) $170 + $20 = $190
- (B) 30% [$980 − ($420 + $230 + $190 + $40)] = $30
- (C) $50 − [0.3 ($50)] = $35
- (D) $80 − [0.3 ($80)] = $56
- (E) $40 − [0.3 ($40)] = $28
- (F) $20 − [0.3 ($20)] = $14
- (G) $10 − [0.3 ($10)] = $7

KEY POINTS TO REMEMBER

(1) Special sections of the income statement report
   (a) Gains and losses from discontinued operations.
   (b) Extraordinary items, that is, items that are both unusual and unlikely to recur.
   (c) The cumulative effects of most changes in accounting principles.

(2) Tax allocation within a period improves the reporting of income taxes by disclosing both the tax effect and the items causing that effect in the same location in financial statements.

(3) Corrections of material errors made in previous periods are charged or credited directly to Retained Earnings.

(4) The effects of changes in accounting estimates are spread over the appropriate current and future periods.

(5) Corporations with complex capital structures present data on both primary earnings per share and fully diluted earnings per share. A single presentation of earnings per share is appropriate for a corporation with a simple capital structure.

(6) Some of the major transactions related to retained earnings are
  (a) Cash dividends, which reduce retained earnings and are a current liability when declared.
  (b) Stock dividends, which represent a transfer of retained earnings to the appropriate stock and paid-in capital accounts at the market value of the shares for small stock dividends and at the legal minimum for large stock dividends.
  (c) Appropriations, which are segregations of retained earnings. The appropriated amount reduces the retained earnings available for dividends.

(7) Stock splits change the par or stated value of stock and affect the number of shares outstanding. Only a memorandum notation records stock splits.

QUESTIONS

16–1 Define *extraordinary items*. How are extraordinary items shown in the income statement?

16–2 A manufacturing plant of the Parke Corporation was destroyed by an earthquake, which is rare in the region where the plant was located. Where should this loss be classified in the income statement?

16–3 A Florida citrus grower incurs substantial frost damage to crops. Frost damage typically is experienced every few years. How should the loss on the crops be shown in the income statement?

16–4 What is meant by *tax allocation within a period*? What is the purpose of this type of tax allocation?

16–5 Define a business *segment*. Why are gains and losses from a discontinued segment reported in a separate section of the income statement?

16–6 This year, the Kaper Company switched from the FIFO method of inventory pricing to the weighted average method. Cumulative income before income taxes for previous years would have been $50,000 lower if the weighted average method had been used.
  (a) Assuming a 40% income tax rate, how should the effect of this inventory pricing change be shown in the income statement?
  (b) If a comparative income statement is presented in the annual report, should Kaper revise last year's income statement using the weighted average method?

16–7 What is the difference between a single-step income statement and a multiple-step income statement?

16–8 Which one of the following amounts would appear only in a multiple-step income statement?

Income from Continuing Operations
Income before Extraordinary Item
Gross Profit on Sales
Net Income

16–9 The Madira Company discovered this year that a significant portion of its inventory was overlooked during its inventory count at the end of last year. How should the correction of this error be disclosed in the financial statements?

16–10 Distinguish between an error and a change in an estimate. How is reporting corrections of errors different from reporting changes in accounting estimates?

16–11 Distinguish between corporations with simple capital structures and those with complex capital structures. What does the type of capital structure imply regarding the presentation of earnings per share data?

16–12 In 19XX, Tiger Company earned a net income of $87,000. The company, which has a simple capital structure, started the year with 8,000 shares of common stock outstanding and issued an additional 6,000 shares on September 1. What is Tiger Company's 19XX earnings per share?

16–13 What assumption underlies the computation of fully diluted earnings per share? What does the difference between the amounts of primary earnings per share and fully diluted earnings per share reveal?

16–14 What is a stock dividend? How does a common stock dividend paid to common shareholders affect their respective ownership interests?

16–15 Distinguish between a stock dividend and a stock split by indicating (a) the effect of each on shareholders' individual interests, (b) the possible effect of each on the market price of stock, and (c) the entries necessary to record these events in the accounting records.

16–16 What is an *appropriation* of retained earnings? Why and by whom are such appropriations made?

16–17 Where do the following accounts (and their balances) appear in the balance sheet?
(a) Dividends Payable—Common Stock
(b) Stock Dividend to Be Issued
(c) Retained Earnings Appropriated for Contingencies

EXERCISES

16–18 During the current year, Dane Corporation incurred an extraordinary tornado loss of $160,000 and sold a segment of its business at a gain of $70,000. Until it was sold, the segment had a current period operating loss of $55,000. Also, the company discovered that an error caused last year's ending inventory to be understated by $25,000 (a material amount). The company had $480,000 income from continuing operations for the current year. Prepare the lower part of the income statement, beginning with the $480,000 income from continuing operations. Follow tax allocation procedures, assuming all changes in income are subject to a 40% income tax rate. Disregard earnings per share disclosures.

16–19 For each of the following current year events for Boulder, Inc., (1) identify the type of accounting change or other category of event involved; (2) indicate where each would be reported on the current year's income or retained earnings statement; and (3) illustrate how each would be disclosed including the relevant dollar amounts. Assume all changes in income are subject to a 30% income tax rate.

(a) The company changed from the sum-of-the-years'-digits to the straight-line method of depreciating its equipment. Cumulative income before income taxes for prior years would have been $30,000 higher under the straight-line method.

(b) The company discovered that, because of a new employee's oversight, depreciation of $20,000 on an addition to the plant had been omitted last year. The amount is material.

(c) A patent acquired at a cost of $49,000 four years ago (including the current year) has been amortized under the straight-line method using an estimated useful life of 14 years. In reviewing accounts for the year-end adjustments, the company revised its estimate of the total useful life to 10 years.

16–20 The Li Corporation began the year with a simple capital structure consisting of 14,000 shares of common stock outstanding. On March 1, 9,000 additional shares were issued, and another 6,000 shares were issued on August 1. The company had a net income for the year of $90,000.

(a) Compute the earnings per share of common stock.

(b) Assume that the company also had 3,000 shares of.8%, $50 par value cumulative preferred stock outstanding throughout the year. Compute the earnings per share of common stock.

16–21 During 19X3, the Baylor Corporation had 15,000 shares of $50 par value common stock and 3,000 shares of 7%, $100 par value convertible preferred stock outstanding. The preferred stock is not a common stock equivalent. Each share of preferred stock may be converted into two shares of common stock. Baylor Corporation's 19X3 net income was $94,500.

(a) Compute the primary earnings per share for 19X3.

(b) Compute the fully diluted earnings per share of 19X3.

16–22 Lowe, Inc., discloses earnings per share amounts for extraordinary items. Use the following summarized income data for the current year to prepare earnings per share disclosures for the company, assuming that a 40% income tax rate is applicable and that 12,000 shares of common stock were outstanding during the year.

Sales	$720,000
Total operating expenses (excluding income taxes)	540,000
Extraordinary flood loss	40,000

16–23 Illini Corporation has 5,000 shares of $10 par value common stock outstanding and retained earnings of $97,000. The company declares a cash dividend of $2 per share and an 8% stock dividend. The market price of the stock at the declaration date is $24 per share.

(a) Give the general journal entries for (1) the declaration of dividends and (2) the payment (or issuance) of the dividends.

(b) Assume that the company declares a 30% stock dividend rather than an 8% stock dividend. Give the general journal entries for (1) the declaration of the stock dividend and (2) the issuance of the stock dividend.

16–24 In both 19X3 and 19X4, the Levine Construction Company appropriated $45,000 of retained earnings for a future truck crane acquisition. In 19X5, the company acquired the truck crane for $94,000 cash. Prepare general journal entries to record the appropriations of retained earnings in 19X3 and 19X4, the purchase of the truck crane in 19X5, and the disposition of the balance in the appropriated retained earnings account after the purchase

16–25 Use the following data to prepare the stockholders' equity section of Rotor Corporation's balance sheet.

Unappropriated Retained Earnings	$248,000
Paid-in Capital in Excess of Par Value—Common Stock	60,000
Paid-in Capital in Excess of Par Value—Preferred Stock	20,000
Retained Earnings Appropriated—Treasury Stock Purchases	16,000
8% Preferred Stock, $40 Par Value, 5,000 shares outstanding	200,000
Common Stock, $20 Par Value, 25,000 shares issued	500,000
Treasury Stock (Common), 500 shares (at cost)	16,000
Retained Earnings Appropriated—Plant Expansion	180,000

16–26 Use the following data to prepare a retained earnings statement for the Kyler Corporation for 19X2. Assume a 30% tax rate.

Total retained earnings originally reported at December 31, 19X1, of which $90,000 is appropriated for future plant expansion	$250,000
Cash dividends declared in 19X2	40,000
Net income reported for 19X2	135,000
Additional appropriation of retained earnings in 19X2 for future plant expansion	25,000
Understatement of 19X1 ending inventory discovered late in 19X2 (caused by arithmetic errors)	20,000

PROBLEMS

16–27 The following information from Century Company's 19X1 operations is available:

Administrative expenses	$ 60,000
Cost of goods sold	720,000
Sales	990,000
Flood loss (considered unusual and infrequent)	30,000
Selling expenses	105,000
Interest expense	15,000
Loss from operations of discontinued segment	40,000

Gain on disposal of discontinued segment	$ 20,000
Income taxes:	
Amount applicable to ordinary operations	27,000
Reduction applicable to flood loss	9,000
Reduction applicable to loss from	
operations of discontinued segment	12,000
Amount applicable to gain on disposal of	
discontinued segment	6,000

REQUIRED

(a) Prepare a multiple-step income statement for the Century Company for 19X1.

(b) Prepare a single-step income statement for the Century Company for 19X1.

16–28 The Matrix Corporation began 19XX with 14,000 shares of common stock and 2,000 shares of convertible preferred stock outstanding. On February 1 an additional 5,000 shares of common stock were issued. On August 1, another 3,000 shares of common stock were issued. On November 1, 2,000 shares of common stock were reacquired for the treasury. The preferred stock has a $2.25 per-share dividend rate, and each share may be converted into one share of common. The preferred stock is not a common stock equivalent. Matrix Corporation's 19XX net income is $90,300.

REQUIRED

(a) Compute primary earnings per share for 19XX.

(b) Compute fully diluted earnings per share for 19XX.

(c) If the preferred stock were not convertible, Matrix Corporation would have a simple capital structure. What would be its earnings per share for 19XX?

16–29 Verona Corporation discloses earnings per share amounts for extraordinary items. The following summarized data are related to the company's 19X3 operations:

Sales	$760,000
Cost of goods sold	400,000
Selling expenses	70,000
Administrative expenses	75,000
Loss from earthquake damages (considered unusual and infrequent)	50,000
Loss on sale of equipment	15,000
Shares of common stock:	
Outstanding at January 1, 19X3	14,000 shares
Additional issued at May 1, 19X3	7,000 shares
Additional issued at November 1, 19X3	8,000 shares

REQUIRED

Prepare a multiple-step income statement for Verona Corporation for 19X3. Assume a 40% income tax rate. Include earnings per share disclosures for 19X3 at the bottom of the income statement.

16–30 Searson Company presented the following earnings per share data:

Earnings per Share of Common Stock:

Income before Extraordinary Items	$6.70
Extraordinary Gain (net of tax)	.85
Net Income	$7.55

The company, which has a simple capital structure, began the year with 26,000 shares of $20 par value common stock and 5,000 shares of 7%, $40 par value preferred stock outstanding. On October 1, an additional 8,000 shares of common stock were issued. Cash dividends were distributed to both preferred and common stockholders.

REQUIRED
(a) What is the annual preferred stock dividend requirement?
(b) What was the net income for the current year for Searson Company?
(c) What was the amount of the extraordinary gain, net of the tax effect? What was the amount of the gain before the tax effect, assuming a 30% tax rate on the gain?
(d) If the tax rate on ordinary income is 40%, what amount of income tax expense was reported in the income before extraordinary items section of the income statement?

16–31 The stockholders' equity of the Esposito Corporation at January 1, 19X2, appears below:

Common Stock, $30 Par Value, 40,000 shares authorized; 25,000 shares issued and outstanding	$750,000
Paid-in Capital in Excess of Par Value—Common Stock	175,000
Unappropriated Retained Earnings	315,000

During 19X2, the following transactions occurred:

June 7   The board of directors appropriated $75,000 of retained earnings for future land acquisition.
Dec. 10   Declared a cash dividend of $1.80 per share and a 4% stock dividend. Market value of the common stock was $39 per share.
31   Closed the net income of $133,000 from the Income Summary account to Retained Earnings.

REQUIRED
(a) Prepare general journal entries to record the foregoing transactions.
(b) Prepare a retained earnings statement for 19X2.
(c) The cash dividend was paid and the stock dividend was issued on January 17, 19X3. Make the necessary journal entries.
(d) The board of directors dropped its plan to acquire land in the future and on January 25, 19X3, eliminated the appropriation for future land acquisition. Make the necessary journal entry.

16–32 The stockholders' equity of the Target Corporation at January 1, 19X4, appears at the top of the next page.

5% Preferred Stock, $40 Par Value, 6,000 shares	
authorized; 4,000 shares issued and outstanding	$ 160,000
Common Stock, $15 Par Value, 50,000 shares	
authorized; 35,000 shares issued and outstanding	525,000
Paid-in Capital in Excess of Par Value—Common Stock	210,000
Retained Earnings Appropriated for Plant Expansion	200,000
Unappropriated Retained Earnings	270,000
Total Stockholders' Equity	$1,365,000

The following transactions, among others, occurred during 19X4:

Feb. 10   Discovered the bookkeeper overlooked a 19X3 adjusting entry for $15,000 of goodwill amortization. Goodwill amortization is not deductible for tax purposes, so this error has no income tax effect. Target Corporation does not use a contra account when recording goodwill amortization.

June 18   Declared a 6% stock dividend on all outstanding shares of common stock. The market value of the stock was $22 per share.

July 1   Issued the stock dividend declared on June 18.

Sept. 8   The board of directors appropriated an additional $50,000 of retained earnings for plant expansion.

Dec. 20   Declared the annual cash dividend on the preferred stock and a cash dividend of $1.60 per share of common stock, payable on January 20 to stockholders of record on December 28.

   31   Closed the Income Summary account, with net earnings of $154,000, to Retained Earnings.

REQUIRED
(a) Prepare general journal entries to record the foregoing transactions.
(b) Prepare a retained earnings statement for 19X4.

16–33   The stockholders' equity of the Doyle Corporation at January 1, 19X2, is shown below:

8% Preferred Stock, $75 Par Value, 8,000 shares authorized;	
6,000 shares issued and outstanding	$ 450,000
Paid-in Capital in Excess of Par Value—Preferred Stock	36,000
Common Stock, $40 Par Value, 30,000 shares authorized;	
24,000 shares issued and outstanding	960,000
Paid-in Capital in Excess of Par Value—Common Stock	54,000
Unappropriated Retained Earnings	347,000
Total Stockholders' Equity	$1,847,000

The following transactions, among others, occurred during 19X2:

Jan. 15   Doyle Corporation carries life insurance on its key officers (with the corporation as beneficiary), and in 19X1 it paid insurance premiums of $6,000 covering 19X1 and 19X2. Today the company discovered that the full $6,000 had been charged to Insurance Expense in 19X1. These premiums are not deductible for tax purposes, so this error has no tax effect.

May	1	Announced a 2 for 1 stock split, reducing the par value of the common stock to $20 per share. The authorization was increased to 60,000 shares.
Sept.	1	Reacquired 3,000 shares of common stock for cash at $24 per share.
	2	Appropriated an amount of retained earnings equal to the cost of the treasury shares acquired September 1.
Dec.	5	Declared a 5% stock dividend on all outstanding shares of common stock. The market value of the stock was $26 per share.
	15	Issued the stock dividend declared on December 5.
	16	Declared the annual cash dividend on the preferred stock and a cash dividend of $1.50 per common share, payable on January 10 to stockholders of record on December 30.
	31	Recorded the annual patent amortization expense. In reviewing the accounts for year-end adjustments, management revised the estimated total useful life of the patent from 17 years to 9 years. The patent cost $61,200 when acquired at the beginning of last year. The company uses the straight-line method for amortization and does not use a contra account.
	31	Closed the Income Summary account, with net earnings of $280,000, to Retained Earnings.

REQUIRED

(a) Prepare general journal entries to record the foregoing transactions.
(b) Prepare a retained earnings statement for 19X2.
(c) Prepare the stockholders' equity section of the balance sheet at December 31, 19X2.

ALTERNATE PROBLEMS

16–27A The information listed below is related to Charter Corporation's 19X3 income and retained earnings.

Administrative expenses	$ 35,000
Appropriation of retained earnings in 19X3 for plant expansion	100,000
Cash dividends declared	50,000
Cost of goods sold	510,000
Understatement of 19X2 depreciation expense (caused by an error)	10,000
Increase in prior years' income before income taxes due to change in inventory pricing method (from weighted average to FIFO)	60,000
Loss from uninsured portion of brushfire damages (considered unusual but recurring)	15,000
Loss from expropriation of property by foreign government (considered unusual and infrequent)	75,000
Retained earnings appropriated for plant expansion (balance at December 31, 19X2)	200,000
Unappropriated retained earnings (balance at December 31, 19X2)	420,000
Sales	980,000
Selling expenses	90,000
Income taxes:	
Amount applicable to ordinary operations	132,000

Reduction applicable to loss from expropriation of property	$ 30,000
Amount applicable to increase in prior years' income before income taxes due to change in inventory pricing method	24,000
Reduction applicable to 19X2 depreciation expense error	4,000

REQUIRED

(a) Prepare a single-step income statement for the Charter Corporation for 19X3.

(b) Prepare a retained earnings statement for the Charter Corporation for 19X3.

16–28A The Valley Corporation began the year 19XX with 7,000 shares of common stock and 1,500 shares of convertible preferred stock outstanding. On May 1, an additional 7,000 shares of common stock were issued. On July 1, 4,000 shares of common stock were reacquired for the treasury. On September 1, the 4,000 treasury shares of common stock were reissued. The preferred stock has a $2 per-share dividend rate, and each share may be converted into two shares of common. The preferred stock is not a common stock equivalent. Valley Corporation's 19XX net income is $91,000.

REQUIRED

(a) Compute primary earnings per share for 19XX.

(b) Compute fully diluted earnings per share for 19XX.

(c) If the preferred stock were not convertible, Valley Corporation would have a simple capital structure. What would be its earnings per share for 19XX?

16–29A Wiley Corporation discloses earnings per share amounts for extraordinary items. The following summarized data are related to the company's 19X2 operations:

Sales	$1,200,000
Cost of goods sold	700,000
Selling expenses	120,000
Administrative expenses	80,000
Gain from expropriation of property by foreign government (considered unusual and infrequent)	65,000
Loss from plant strike	25,000
Shares of common stock:	
Outstanding at January 1, 19X2	25,000 shares
Additional issued at April 1, 19X2	5,000 shares
Additional issued at August 1, 19X2	3,000 shares

REQUIRED

Prepare a multiple-step income statement for Wiley Corporation for 19X2. Assume a 40% income tax rate. Include earnings per share disclosures for 19X2 at the bottom of the income statement.

16–31A The stockholders' equity of the Laird Corporation at January 1, 19X9, appears below:

Common Stock, $10 Par Value, 60,000 shares authorized; 50,000 shares issued and outstanding	$500,000
Paid-in Capital in Excess of Par Value—Common Stock	75,000
Unappropriated Retained Earnings	184,000

During 19X9, the following transactions occurred:

May 12   Fearing a strike early next year, the board of directors appropriated $40,000 of retained earnings for contingencies.

Dec. 5   Declared a cash dividend of 60 cents per share and a 7% stock dividend. Market value of the common stock was $13 per share on this date.

     31   Closed the net income of $105,000 from the Income Summary account to Retained Earnings.

REQUIRED
(a) Prepare general journal entries to record the foregoing transactions.
(b) Prepare a retained earnings statement for 19X9.
(c) The cash dividend was paid and the stock dividend was issued on January 20 of the following year. Make the necessary journal entries.
(d) The expected employee strike did not materialize, and the board of directors on January 22 eliminated the appropriation for contingencies. Make the necessary journal entry.

16–32A   The stockholders' equity of the Cliffside Corporation at January 1, 19X5, appears below:

6% Preferred Stock, $50 Par Value, 8,000 shares authorized; 3,000 shares issued and outstanding	$ 150,000
Common Stock, $30 Par Value, 40,000 shares authorized; 20,000 shares issued and outstanding	600,000
Paid-in Capital in Excess of Par Value—Common Stock	100,000
Retained Earnings Appropriated for Future Litigation	80,000
Unappropriated Retained Earnings	345,000
Total Stockholders' Equity	$1,275,000

The following transactions, among others, occurred during 19X5:

Jan. 22   Discovered the bookkeeper made an arithmetic error in 19X4 causing a $16,000 overstatement of goodwill amortization for that year. Goodwill amortization is not deductible for tax purposes, so this error has no income tax effect. Cliffside Corporation does not use a contra account when recording goodwill amortization.

Aug. 10   Declared a 9% stock dividend on all outstanding shares of common stock. The market value of the stock was $38 per share.

     26   The board of directors appropriated an additional $25,000 of retained earnings for possible future litigation.

Sept. 5   Issued the stock dividend declared on August 10.

Dec. 5   Declared the annual cash dividend on the preferred stock and a cash dividend of $1.75 per share of common stock, payable on January 25 to stockholders of record on December 27.

     30   Appropriated $45,000 of retained earnings for general contingencies.

     31   Closed the Income Summary account, with net earnings of $185,000, to Retained Earnings.

REQUIRED

(a) Prepare general journal entries to record the foregoing transactions.

(b) Prepare a retained earnings statement for 19X5.

16–33A The stockholders' equity of the Odana Corporation at January 1, 19X4, is shown below:

5% Preferred Stock, $80 Par Value, 8,000 shares authorized;	
4,000 shares issued and outstanding	$ 320,000
Paid-in Capital in Excess of Par Value—Preferred Stock	16,000
Common Stock, $75 Par Value, 20,000 shares authorized;	
15,000 shares issued and outstanding	1,125,000
Paid-in Capital in Excess of Par Value—Common Stock	45,000
Unappropriated Retained Earnings	416,000
Total Stockholders' Equity	$1,922,000

The following transactions, among others, occurred during 19X4:

Feb. 12   Odana Corporation carries life insurance on its key officers (with the corporation as beneficiary), and in 19X3 it paid insurance premiums of $7,500 covering the three-year period 19X3–19X5. Today the company discovered that none of the $7,500 had been charged to Insurance Expense in 19X3 (it all remained in Prepaid Insurance). These premiums are not deductible for tax purposes, so this error has no tax effect.

Apr.   1   Announced a 3 for 1 stock split, reducing the par value of the common stock to $25 per share. The authorization was increased to 60,000 shares.

Aug. 11   Reacquired 5,000 shares of common stock for cash at $27 per share.

      12   Appropriated an amount of retained earnings equal to the cost of the treasury shares acquired August 11.

Dec.   7   Declared a 3% stock dividend on all outstanding shares of common stock. The market value of the stock was $30 per share.

      17   Issued the stock dividend declared on December 7.

      20   Declared the annual cash dividend on the preferred stock and a cash dividend of $1.20 per common share, payable on January 15 to stockholders of record on December 31.

      31   Recorded the annual patent amortization expense. In reviewing the accounts for year-end adjustments, management revised the estimated total useful life of the patent from 8 years to 13 years. The patent cost $38,400 when acquired at the beginning of last year. The company uses the straight-line method for amortization and does not use a contra account.

      31   Closed the Income Summary account, with net earnings of $198,000, to Retained Earnings.

REQUIRED

(a) Prepare general journal entries to record the foregoing transactions.

(b) Prepare a retained earnings statement for 19X4.

(c) Prepare the stockholders' equity section of the balance sheet at December 31, 19X4.

BUSINESS DECISION PROBLEM

The stockholders' equity section of Spectrum Corporation's comparative balance sheet at the end of 19X7 and 19X8—part of the financial data just reviewed at a stockholders' meeting—is presented below:

	December 31, 19X8	December 31, 19X7
Common Stock, $25 Par Value, 300,000 shares authorized; issued at December 31, 19X8, 207,000 shares; 19X7, 180,000 shares	$5,175,000	$4,500,000
Paid-in Capital in Excess of Par Value	1,305,000	900,000
Retained Earnings:		
Appropriated for Plant Expansion	600,000	500,000
Unappropriated	1,407,000	2,380,000
Total Stockholders' Equity	$8,487,000	$8,280,000

The following items were also disclosed at the stockholders' meeting: Net income for 19X8 was $621,000; a 15% stock dividend was issued December 14, 19X8, when the market value was $40 per share; the market value per share at December 31, 19X8, was $36; management plans to borrow $200,000 to help finance a new plant addition, which is expected to cost a total of $700,000; and the customary $2.30 per-share cash dividend has been revised to $2.

As part of their stockholders' goodwill program, during the stockholders' meeting management asked stockholders to write any questions they might have concerning the firm's operations or finances. As assistant controller, you are given the stockholders' questions.

REQUIRED

Prepare brief but reasonably complete answers to the following questions:

(a) What did Spectrum do with the cash proceeds from the stock dividend issued in December?
(b) What was my book value per share at the end of 19X7 and 19X8?
(c) I owned 4,500 shares of Spectrum in 19X7 and have not sold any shares. How much more or less of the corporation do I own at December 31, 19X8, and what happened to the market value of my interest in the company?
(d) I heard someone say that stock dividends don't give me anything I didn't already have. Why did you issue one? Are you trying to fool us?
(e) Instead of a stock dividend, why didn't you declare a cash dividend and let us buy the new shares that were issued?
(f) Why are you cutting back on the dividends I receive?
(g) If you have $600,000 put aside for the new plant addition, which will cost $700,000, why are you borrowing $200,000 instead of just the $100,000 needed?

17

Long-term Liabilities and Bond Investments

Some of the most frequently encountered long-term liabilities of business firms are mortgage notes payable, bonds payable, deferred income taxes payable, and capital lease liabilities. We discuss the accounting treatment of the first three of these long-term liabilities in this chapter; accounting for capital leases, a direct method of financing plant and equipment, was discussed in Chapter 11. Because accounting for long-term bond investments is similar to that for bonds payable, this chapter also includes a discussion of such investments.

MORTGAGE NOTES AND BONDS PAYABLE

At various times in the course of business operations, particularly during phases of expansion, firms must secure additional long-term funds. Often they choose long-term borrowing, rather than issuing additional capital stock, to avoid diluting the ownership interests or because the borrowed funds may have a lower net cost to current stockholders.[1] The interest cost of long-term debt has identifiable limits; that is, creditors do not receive an increased return on investment if profits grow. Furthermore, the borrowing firm may deduct interest payments on debt for tax purposes, but it may not deduct dividend distributions to owners.

Not all aspects of long-term debt are necessarily desirable for the borrowing company. In contrast with dividends on common stock, interest on debt represents a fixed periodic expenditure that the firm is contractually obligated to make. Fixed interest charges can be a financial burden when operations do not develop as favorably as expected. Because long-term debt normally has a definite maturity date, the firm must also provide for repayment of the obligation. Finally, a long-term borrowing agreement may restrict the company's financial policies while the debt is outstanding.

Mortgage Notes Payable

A firm may borrow long-term funds by issuing a **mortgage note,** which is actually two related agreements. The note is an agreement to repay the principal and to pay specified interest amounts on certain dates; the mortgage is a legal agreement pledging certain property of the borrower as security for repayment of the note. Usually, a mortgage note is used when all the funds are borrowed from one lender. Sometimes a firm finds it more strategic or even necessary to borrow large amounts of funds from several lenders. In these latter cases, issuing bonds is more practical.

Bonds Payable

Bonds are, in essence, notes payable. Their special characteristics are dictated by the specific objectives of a given borrowing situation. Because a complete dis-

---

[1] The concept of investment leverage is explained in Chapter 20.

cussion of the wide variety of bonds is beyond the scope of this text, only the more significant characteristics of bonds are described below.

Bonds are used most often when a borrower receives funds from a large number of lenders contributing various amounts. Consequently, bonds are usually drawn up to be negotiable. Because many parties are involved, the borrower should select a **trustee**—often a large bank—to represent the group of bondholders. As a third party to the transaction, the trustee may take security title to any pledged property and is likely to initiate any action necessitated by failure to meet the terms of the bond agreement.

If the borrower fails to meet the provisions of the bond agreement, the bondholders, represented by the trustee, may institute a variety of actions. Examples of less significant actions are enforcing agreements restricting dividend payments, prescribing minimum cash balances or financial operating ratios, placing restrictions on additional financing, and electing new members to the board of directors. The ultimate action, of course, is to bring foreclosure proceedings. The trustee may also maintain a record of current bond owners and may act as disbursing agent for the interest and principal payments.

CHARACTERISTICS OF BONDS   Bond agreements may be formulated to capitalize on certain lending situations, appeal to special investor groups, or provide special repayment patterns. We now list some common bond characteristics.

Secured bonds pledge some specific property as security for meeting the terms of the bond agreement. The specific title of the bonds may indicate the type of property pledged—for example, real estate mortgage bonds (land and/or buildings), chattel mortgage bonds (machinery or equipment), and collateral trust bonds (negotiable securities). If property is subject to two or more mortgages, the relative priority of each mortgage is denoted by its identification as a "first," "second," or even "third" mortgage.

Bonds that have no specific property pledged as security for their repayment are **debenture bonds.** Holders of such bonds rely on the borrower's general credit reputation. Because the lender's risk is usually greater than with secured bonds, the sale of unsecured bonds may require offering a higher interest rate.

The maturity dates of **serial bonds** are staggered over a series of years. For example, a serial bond issue of $15 million may provide for $1 million of the bonds to mature each year for 15 years. An advantage of serial bonds is that lenders can choose bonds with maturity dates that correspond with their desired length of investment.

The issuing corporation (or its trustee) maintains a record of the owners of **registered bonds.** At appropriate times, interest payments are mailed to the registered owners. Interest on **coupon bonds** is paid in a different manner. A coupon for interest payable to the bearer is attached to the bond for each interest period. Whenever interest is due, the bondholder detaches a coupon and deposits it with his or her bank for collection.

Callable bonds allow the borrower to *call in* (retire) the bonds and pay them off after a stated date. Usually, an extra amount or premium must be paid to the holders of the called bonds. Callable bonds offer borrowers an additional flexibility that may be significant if funds become available at interest rates substantially lower than those being paid on the bonds. To some degree, borrowers can in effect "call" any of their bonds by buying them in the open market.

Convertible bonds grant the holder the right to convert them to capital stock at some specific exchange ratio. This provision gives an investor the security of a creditor during a certain stage of a firm's life, with the option of becoming a stockholder if the firm becomes sufficiently profitable.

BOND PRICES   Most bonds are sold in units of $1,000 face (maturity) value, and the market price is expressed as a percentage of face value. For example, a bond quoted at 98 sells for $980, and a bond quoted at 103 sells for $1,030. Generally, bond prices fluctuate in response to changes in market interest rates, which are determined by government monetary policies (managing the demand and supply of money) and economic expectations. Obviously, they are also affected by the outlook for the issuing firm. Market prices are quoted in the financial news at the nearest $\frac{1}{8}$% of the true market price.

RECORDING BOND ISSUES   Firms often authorize more bonds than they actually anticipate issuing at one time. Authorization of bonds usually includes (1) formal action by the board of directors, (2) application to and approval of some government agency, (3) retention of a trustee, and (4) all the attendant negotiations and legalities. For secured bonds, the total value of the bonds authorized is typically some fraction of the value of the property pledged. The difference between the dollar amount of the bonds issued and the value of the pledged property represents a margin of safety to bondholders.

Because individual bond issues may have widely varying characteristics, separate accounts with reasonably descriptive titles should be used for each bond issue. When the bonds are authorized, an account is opened in the general ledger, and a memorandum entry may be made in the account stating the total amount of bonds authorized.

The *face value* of a bond is the amount of principal to be repaid at the maturity date. Interest on bonds is usually paid semiannually, with the payments six months apart (such as January 1 and July 1). The annual rate of interest—also called the *coupon* or *nominal* rate of interest—payable on a bond is stated in the bond agreement. The amount of interest paid semiannually on such bonds is the face value multiplied by one-half the nominal rate of interest. If financial statements are prepared between interest payment dates, the periodic interest expense and the related liability for interest payable are accrued to the date of the statements.

To provide a simple illustration, we use informal account titles and an unrealistically short bond life. Assume that on January 1, Reid, Inc. issues at face value ten $10,000, 10% bonds that mature in four years with interest paid on June 30 and December 31. The following entry records the bond issue:

Jan. 1	Cash	100,000	
	Bonds Payable		100,000
	To record issuance of bonds.		

Interest of \$5,000 (\$100,000 $\times$ 0.10 $\times$ $\frac{6}{12}$) will be paid on each of the eight payment dates (four years, semiannual payments). For example, the entry on June 30, the first interest payment date, is

June 30	Bond Interest Expense	5,000	
	Cash		5,000
	To record payment of semiannual interest on bonds payable.		

When the bonds mature, Reid, Inc. records their retirement in the following manner:

(final year)			
Dec. 31	Bonds Payable	100,000	
	Cash		100,000
	To record retirement of bonds.		

Issuance between interest dates   Not all bonds are sold on the exact day on which their interest begins to accumulate. For example, issuance may be delayed in anticipation of a more favorable bond market. Investors who buy bonds after the interest begins to accrue are expected to "buy" the accrued interest. Such bonds are said to be sold at some price "plus accrued interest." If Reid, Inc. had sold its bonds on April 1 instead of January 1, the entry would have been

Apr. 1	Cash	102,500	
	Bonds Payable		100,000
	Bond Interest Payable		2,500
	To record bond issuance at face value plus three months' accrued interest.		

The interest accrued on the bonds on the April 1 issue date is \$2,500 (\$100,000 $\times$ 0.10 $\times$ $\frac{3}{12}$). On the first interest payment date, June 30, Reid, Inc. makes the following entry:

June 30	Bond Interest Payable	2,500	
	Bond Interest Expense	2,500	
	Cash		5,000
	To record payment of semiannual interest on bonds payable.		

This entry records interest expense at \$2,500, the appropriate amount for the three months the bonds have been outstanding. The other \$2,500 represents the return of the accrued interest collected from the bond purchasers on April 1.

BOND PRICES AND INTEREST RATES   In our illustration, we assume that the Reid, Inc. bonds are issued at par or face value. Often, the issue price differs from the face value because the market rate of interest for the bonds differs from the **nominal** or **contract** rate on the bond certificate. The nominal rate dictates the amount of interest paid each period, whereas the **market** rate—sometimes called the **effective** rate—is the rate of return investors expect on their investment. Market rates of interest fluctuate constantly.

When the market rate of interest on the bonds exceeds the nominal rate, investors expect the bonds to sell at a *discount* (Face Value − Price). When the market rate falls below the nominal rate, investors expect to pay a *premium* (Price − Face Value).

Since bonds are usually printed and sold at different times, the two interest rates often differ. Also, a firm may desire a nominal rate expressed in even percents or in easily recognized fractions of a percent (that is, 10% or $9\frac{1}{2}$%), whereas the market rate for a particular bond issue may be expressed in a more complex fraction or decimal amount.

Bonds issued at a discount   If the nominal rate of interest on the bonds issued is less than the current market rate of interest for the type and quality of the bonds, they can be sold only at a price less than their face value. In such cases, investors "discount" the bonds to earn the amount of interest reflected in the current money market. For example, assume that Reid, Inc.'s $100,000 issue of 10%, four-year bonds are sold on January 1 at 98—98% of their face value—because the applicable market rate exceeds the 10% nominal rate. The following entry records the issue of these bonds:

Jan. 1	Cash	98,000	
	Bond Discount	2,000	
	Bonds Payable		100,000
	To record issuance of bonds at 98.		

The $2,000 discount is not an immediate loss or expense to Reid, Inc. Rather, it represents an adjustment of interest expense over the life of the bonds. We illustrate this by comparing the funds Reid, Inc. receives with the funds it must pay to the bondholders. Regardless of their selling price, the bonds are an agreement to pay $140,000 to the bondholders ($100,000 principal plus eight semiannual interest payments of $5,000 each).

Total funds paid to bondholders	$140,000
Total funds received from bond sale	98,000
Difference equals total interest paid	$ 42,000
Average expense per year ($42,000/4)	$ 10,500

Although Reid, Inc. makes only two $5,000 interest payments—a total of $10,000—each year, its full annual interest expense on the bonds exceeds that amount. To reflect the larger periodic interest expense, the bond discount is *amortized*. Amortization of bond discount means that periodically an amount is transferred from bond discount to interest expense.

Basically, there are two methods of amortization—the straight-line method and the effective interest method. Under the *straight-line method*, equal amounts are transferred from bond discount to interest expense for equal periods of time. For Reid, Inc., this amount is $250 every six months ($2,000 total bond discount ÷ 8 semiannual interest periods). Some companies may amortize the discount annually rather than semiannually; the annual amortization for Reid, Inc. is $500. The more complex *effective interest method* reflects a constant rate of interest over the life of the bonds. The effective interest method is discussed later in this chapter.

Assuming the straight-line method of amortization, the journal entries each year to record interest expense for Reid, Inc. are as follows. (We assume that the bond sale is already recorded as illustrated above and that the bonds were issued on the day they are dated.)

June 30	Bond Interest Expense	5,000	
	Cash		5,000
	To record first semiannual interest payment.		
30	Bond Interest Expense	250	
	Bond Discount		250
	To record semiannual amortization of bond discount.		
Dec. 31	Bond Interest Expense	5,000	
	Cash		5,000
	To record second semiannual interest payment.		
31	Bond Interest Expense	250	
	Bond Discount		250
	To record semiannual amortization of bond discount.		

These entries result in four debits to the Bond Interest Expense account each year, a total of $10,500 annual interest expense. Amortizing the bond discount over the four-year life of the bonds at $250 every six months leaves a zero balance in the Bond Discount account at the maturity date of the bonds. The retirement of the bonds is then recorded by debiting Bonds Payable and crediting Cash for $100,000, the amount of their face value.

Bonds issued at a premium   If the market rate of interest had been below the 10% offered by Reid, Inc.'s bonds, investors would have been willing to pay a premium for them. Like a bond discount, a bond premium is considered an adjustment of interest expense over the life of the bonds. We just saw that bond discount increases interest expense; now we see that bond premium reduces interest expense. The following entries illustrate the sale of Reid, Inc. bonds at 104 (104% of face value), the payments of interest, the amortization of bond premium, and the retirement of the bonds at maturity:

Jan. 1	Cash	104,000	
	Bonds Payable		100,000
	Bond Premium		4,000
	To record sale of bonds at a premium.		
June 30	Bond Interest Expense	5,000	
	Cash		5,000
	To record first semiannual interest payment.		
	Bond Premium	500	
	Bond Interest Expense		500
	To record semiannual amortization of bond premium.		
Dec. 31	Bond Interest Expense	5,000	
	Cash		5,000
	To record second semiannual interest payment.		
31	Bond Premium	500	
	Bond Interest Expense		500
	To record semiannual amortization of bond premium.		
(final year)			
Dec. 31	Bonds Payable	100,000	
	Cash		100,000
	To retire bonds at maturity.		

The eight semiannual $500 debit entries to the Bond Premium account leave it with a zero balance when the bonds mature. We can verify the $9,000 total annual interest expense reflected by the above entries as follows:

Total funds paid to bondholders	$140,000
Total funds received from bondholders	104,000
Difference equals total interest paid	$ 36,000
Average interest expense per year ($36,000/4)	$ 9,000

The related interest expense account would have a balance of $9,000, shown in the following T account:

Bond Interest Expense

| First semiannual interest payment | 5,000 | First semiannual amortization of bond premium | 500 |
| Second semiannual interest payment | 5,000 | Second semiannual amortization of bond premium | 500 |

Year-end or interim adjustments   When a periodic interest payment date does not correspond with year-end, adjustment of the general ledger accounts should include an entry reflecting the amount of interest expense incurred but not paid and an entry reflecting a pro-rata amortization of bond discount or bond premium for the portion of the year involved. Similar adjustments are appropriate when interim financial statements are prepared and the interim date does not correspond with an interest payment date.

Assume the bonds issued by Reid, Inc. at 98 were issued on April 1 and had interest payment dates on April 1 and October 1. At December 31 of each year, the following entries would be made:

Dec. 31	Bond Interest Expense	2,500	
	Bond Interest Payable		2,500
	To accrue interest expense for three months		
	($100,000 × 0.10 × $\frac{3}{12}$).		
31	Bond Interest Expense	125	
	Bond Discount		125
	To amortize bond discount for three months		
	($500 annual amortization/4).		

If the bonds were issued at a premium rather than at a discount, an entry would amortize the bond premium for three months. The Bond Interest Payable account is classified as a current liability in the balance sheet.

BONDS PAYABLE ON THE BALANCE SHEET   In this section, we use the data relating to Reid, Inc. bonds with interest payment dates of June 30 and December 31 and straight-line amortization. Exhibit 17–1 shows that regardless of whether bond premium or bond discount is involved, the book value of bonds progresses toward and equals their face value at the time of maturity.

EXHIBIT 17–1
Amortization Schedule

	Reid, Inc. Bonds Sold at 104 (Premium) (Straight-line Amortization)			Reid, Inc. Bonds Sold at 98 (Discount) (Straight-line Amortization)		
	Balances			Balances		
At Year-end	Bonds Payable (Credit)	Bond Premium (Credit)	Book Value	Bonds Payable (Credit)	Bond Discount (Debit)	Book Value
At issue	$100,000	$4,000	$104,000	$100,000	$2,000	$ 98,000
19X1	100,000	3,000	103,000	100,000	1,500	98,500
19X2	100,000	2,000	102,000	100,000	1,000	99,000
19X3	100,000	1,000	101,000	100,000	500	99,500
19X4	100,000	0	100,000	100,000	0	100,000

Assume that Reid, Inc. issued bonds at the end of 19X0 corresponding to each of the examples above. At the end of the second year, the firm's trial balance would include the following accounts:

	Debit	Credit
Bond Discount, Second Mortgage Series	$1,000	
Bonds Payable, 10%, 19X4, First Mortgage Series		$100,000
Bonds Payable, 10%, 19X4, Second Mortgage Series		100,000
Bond Premium, First Mortgage Series		2,000

The Bond Premium and Bond Discount accounts are classified properly as an addition to and as a deduction from, respectively, the face value of the bonds in the balance sheet, as follows:

Long-term Liabilities:

Bonds Payable, 10%, 19X4, First Mortgage Series	$100,000	
Add: Unamortized Premium	2,000	$102,000
Bonds Payable, 10%, 19X4, Second Mortgage Series	$100,000	
Less: Unamortized Discount	1,000	99,000

Bonds payable maturing within the next year should be classified as a current liability. An exception to this guideline arises when a bond sinking fund, a non-current asset, is used to retire the bonds. In that case, because a current asset is not utilized to retire the bonds, the bonds payable may be classified as long-term liabilities.

EFFECTIVE INTEREST METHOD OF AMORTIZATION   Many business firms use the straight-line method of amortizing bond discount and premium because of its simplicity. This method recognizes equal amounts of interest expense each year. However, because the **book value** (**carrying value**) of the bonds changes each year (see Exhibit 17–1), the interest, expressed as a percentage of the book value, changes over the life of the bonds. Theoretically, this percentage should be constant; otherwise, the firm's borrowing cost appears to change constantly. The **effective interest method** of amortization corrects this deficiency. With this method, a constant percentage of the book value of the bonds is recognized as interest expense each year, resulting in unequal recorded amounts of interest expense. In *APB Opinion No. 21*, the Accounting Principles Board recommends the use of the effective interest method whenever the two methods yield materially different results.

To obtain a period's interest expense under the effective interest method, we multiply the bonds' book value at the beginning of each period by the effective interest rate. The difference between this amount and the amount of interest paid (Nominal Interest Rate × Face Value of Bonds) is the amount of discount or premium amortized. When using the effective interest method of amortization, accountants often prepare an amortization schedule similar to Exhibit 17–2, explained in the following example.

EXHIBIT 17–2
Bonds Sold at a Discount:
Periodic Interest Expense, Amortization,
and Book Value of Bonds

Year	Interest Period	(A) Interest Paid (4% of face value)	(B) Interest Expense (5% of bond book value)	(C) Periodic Amortization (B − A)	(D) Balance of Unamortized Discount (D − C)	(E) Book Value of Bonds, End of Period ($100,000 − D)
(at issue)					$6,448	$ 93,552
1	1	$4,000	$4,678	$678	5,770	94,230
	2	4,000	4,712	712	5,058	94,942
2	3	4,000	4,747	747	4,311	95,689
	4	4,000	4,784	784	3,527	96,473
3	5	4,000	4,824	824	2,703	97,297
	6	4,000	4,865	865	1,838	98,162
4	7	4,000	4,908	908	930	99,070
	8	4,000	4,930*	930	0	100,000

*Adjusted for cumulative rounding error of $24.

Bonds issued at a discount Assume that, on April 1, 19X1, a firm issues four-year bonds of $100,000 face value with an 8% annual interest rate and interest dates of April 1 and October 1. The selling price is $93,552, which provides an effective interest rate of 10%.[2] Exhibit 17–2 gives an amortization schedule for the life of the bonds, with amounts rounded to the nearest dollar.

The schedule shows six-month interest periods; therefore, the interest rates shown in columns (A) and (B) are one-half the annual rates. Column (A) lists the constant amounts of interest paid each six months, that is, the nominal interest rate times face value (4% × $100,000). The amounts in column (B) are obtained by multiplying the book value at the beginning of each period [column (E)] by the 5% effective interest rate. For example, the $4,678 interest expense for the first period is 5% of $93,552; for the second period, it is 5% of $94,230, or $4,712, and so on. Note that the amount changes each period. For discounted bonds, the amount increases each period because the book value increases over the life of the bonds until it reaches face value at the maturity date. The amount of discount amortization for each period, given in column (C), is the difference between the corresponding amounts in columns (A) and (B). Column (D) lists the amount of unamortized discount at the end of each period.

The amounts recorded for the issuance of the bonds and each interest payment can be read directly from the amortization schedule. The following entry records the issuance:

---

[2] See Appendix A for a discussion of effective interest rates and the determination of issue prices.

Apr. 1	Cash	93,552	
	Bond Discount	6,448	
	Bonds Payable		100,000
	To record issuance of bonds.		

The following entry records interest expense and discount amortization on October 1, 19X1:

Oct. 1	Bond Interest Expense	4,678	
	Bond Discount		678
	Cash		4,000
	To record semiannual interest expense and discount amortization.		

Bonds issued at a premium Suppose that the bonds in our illustration carried an 8% nominal interest rate but that the effective interest rate was 6%. These bonds would be issued at $106,980 (for computations, see Appendix A). The amortization schedule for the bond issue is given in Exhibit 17–3. The nominal interest rate of 4% in column (A) and the effective interest rate of 3% in column (B) are one-half the annual rates for the bonds, because the calculations are for six-month periods. The issuance of the bonds is recorded as follows:

Apr. 1	Cash	106,980	
	Bond Premium		6,980
	Bonds Payable		100,000
	To record issuance of bonds.		

EXHIBIT 17–3
Bonds Sold at a Premium:
Periodic Interest Expense, Amortization, and Book Value of Bonds

Year	Interest Period	(A) Interest Paid (4% of face value)	(B) Interest Expense (3% of bond book value)	(C) Periodic Amortization (A − B)	(D) Balance of Unamortized Premium (D − C)	(E) Book Value of Bonds, End of Period ($100,000 + D)
(at issue)					$6,980	$106,980
1	1	$4,000	$3,209	$791	6,189	106,189
	2	4,000	3,186	814	5,375	105,375
2	3	4,000	3,161	839	4,536	104,536
	4	4,000	3,136	864	3,672	103,672
3	5	4,000	3,110	890	2,782	102,782
	6	4,000	3,083	917	1,865	101,865
4	7	4,000	3,056	944	921	100,921
	8	4,000	3,079*	921	0	100,000

*Adjusted for cumulative rounding error of $51.

The entry to record interest expense and premium amortization on October 1, 19X1 is

Oct. 1	Bond Interest Expense	3,209	
	Bond Premium	791	
	Cash		4,000
	To record semiannual interest		
	expense and premium amortization.		

Year-end adjusting entries   We record interest and premium amortization for the bonds in our example on April 1 and October 1. Therefore, at December 31, three months' interest should be accrued.

The amounts recorded can be computed from those shown for the second interest period in the amortization schedule in Exhibit 17–3. One-half of the amount in column (A) [($4,000/2) = $2,000] is the interest payable. Similarly, [($3,186/2) = $1,593] is the interest expense, and [($814/2) = $407] is the premium amortization. The year-end adjusting entry is

Dec. 31	Bond Interest Expense	1,593	
	Bond Premium	407	
	Bond Interest Payable		2,000
	To accrue interest for three		
	months and amortize one-half of the		
	premium for the interest period.		

Retirement of Bonds before Maturity   Bonds are usually retired at their maturity dates with an entry debiting Bonds Payable and crediting Cash for the amount of the face value of the bonds. However, bonds may be retired before maturity—for example, to take advantage of more attractive financing terms.

In accounting for the retirement of bonds before maturity, the following factors should be considered:

(1) Amortization of any related premium or discount as of the retirement date.

(2) Removal of both the bond liability account and any related Bond Premium or Bond Discount accounts.

(3) Recognition of any gain or loss on the retirement of the bonds.

For this example, assume that the Reid, Inc. bonds issued at 104 were called for retirement at 105 plus accrued interest on April 1 of their fourth and final year. Exhibit 17–1 shows that the related account balances at the end of their third year are

| Bonds Payable | $100,000 |
| Bond Premium | 1,000 |

If interest is paid semiannually on June 30 and December 31, and financial statements are prepared annually, no premium amortization entry has been made since the end of the third year. Thus, the following entries properly reflect the retirement of the bonds on April 1:

Apr. 1	Bond Premium	250	
	Bond Interest Expense		250
	To amortize bond premium for three		
	months ($1000/4).		
1	Bonds Payable	100,000	
	Bond Premium	750	
	Bond Interest Expense	2,500	
	Loss on Bond Retirement	4,250	
	Cash		107,500
	To retire bonds at 105 plus interest and		
	record the loss on retirement.		

The loss on retirement is the difference between the retirement amount ($105,000) and the book value of the bonds at retirement ($100,750). The amount of interest paid at retirement ($2,500) does not affect the gain or loss on retirement. The gain or loss, if material, should be classified as an extraordinary item on the income statement.

Conversion of Bonds

Few convertible bonds are redeemed for cash, since at some point, these bonds are usually converted into common stock. Because, as noted earlier, the conversion feature is attractive to potential investors, a company may issue convertible bonds at a lower interest rate than it would pay without the conversion feature.

A company may also issue convertible bonds to reduce the dilutive effect that a common stock issue would have on earnings per share. This occurs because the conversion price is higher than the current market price of the stock when the convertible bonds are issued. For example, suppose a company that needs $100,000 of funds could issue additional common stock at $20 per share. The company needs to issue 5,000 shares to obtain $100,000. Alternatively, the firm may issue $100,000 of convertible bonds and establish a conversion price of $25 per share. When the bonds are converted into stock (and the company expects this to happen), the number of common shares issued will be 4,000 ($100,000/ $25). The fewer number of common shares associated with the convertible bonds produces higher earnings per share than if common stock had been issued initially.

Convertible bonds include a call feature. When the market value of the stock to be received on conversion is significantly higher than the call price on the bond, a company may force conversion by calling in the bonds. Of course, one of the risks of issuing convertible bonds is that the market price of the stock may not increase in the future. Bondholders may then decide it is not to their advantage to convert the bonds, and the company cannot force conversion by exercising the call feature.

The entry to record a bond conversion transfers the book value of the bonds to the common stock acccounts. For example, assume that the Reid, Inc. bonds issued at 98 were convertible into 2,000 shares of $40 par value common stock. All the bonds were converted into stock on January 1 of the third year. Exhibit 17–1 shows that the book value of the bonds at the end of the second year is $99,000. The following entry records the conversion:

Jan. 1	Bonds Payable	100,000	
	Bond Discount		1,000
	Common Stock		80,000
	Paid-in Capital in Excess of Par Value		19,000

To record conversion of bonds into 2,000 shares of $40 par value common stock.

BOND SINKING FUNDS

As additional security to bondholders, some bond agreements require the borrower to make periodic cash deposits to a **bond sinking fund,** which is used to retire the bonds. The fund is often controlled by a trustee—usually a bank or a trust company. The trustee invests the cash deposited periodically in the sinking fund in income-producing securities. The objective is to accumulate investments and investment income sufficient to retire the bonds at their maturity.

We now illustrate typical transactions for a simple bond sinking fund managed by a trustee. Assume that Reid, Inc. establishes such a fund to retire its $100,000 bond issue, which matures in four years. Reid, Inc. makes equal annual deposits to the sinking fund at the end of each of the four years.

PERIODIC DEPOSIT OF CASH TO THE FUND The amount of the equal periodic contributions is determined by compound interest tables and assumes an average annual rate of net investment income. If the trustee estimates that the sinking-fund securities will earn 8% annually, Reid, Inc.'s annual cash payment to the trustee should be $22,192. Earning 8% annually, the fund will grow to $100,000 after four years, as follows:

Year	Annual Cash Deposit	8% Annual Interest	Fund Balance at Year-end
1	$22,192	—	$ 22,192
2	22,192	$1,775	46,159
3	22,192	3,693	72,044
4	22,192	5,764	100,000

The entry to record the annual cash deposit is

Bond Sinking Fund	22,192	
Cash		22,192

INCOME REPORTED ON SINKING-FUND SECURITIES Reid, Inc. records on its books the trustee's periodic reports on the earnings of the sinking-fund securities. For example, if the fund earned $1,775 during the second year, Reid, Inc. makes the following journal entry:

Bond Sinking Fund	1,775	
Bond Sinking-fund Income		1,775

RETIREMENT OF BONDS   Usually, the trustee sells the sinking-fund securities and pays the bondholders with the proceeds. Reid, Inc. then records the retirement of the bonds as follows:

Bonds Payable	100,000	
Bond Sinking Fund		100,000

Any deficit in the sinking fund needed to retire the bonds requires an additional cash payment from Reid, Inc. Any surplus is transferred to the Cash account in closing out the sinking fund.

The Bond Sinking Fund is classified in the balance sheet as an investment. Bond Sinking-fund Income is reported under Other Income and Expenses in the income statement.

LONG-TERM BOND INVESTMENTS

Corporate bonds may be acquired by a variety of investors, including individuals, partnerships, corporations, mutual funds, pension funds, foundations, and trusts. Our discussion focuses on bond investments by corporations.

Bonds may be purchased when they are originally issued or at some time thereafter from an investor. Bond investments are recorded by the purchaser at cost plus any brokerage commission. Because bonds acquired as a long-term investment may be held for extended periods, the related premium or discount is usually amortized to interest income. The straight-line method of amortization is commonly used; however, as we mentioned earlier, the effective interest method should be used when the two methods yield materially different results. In our example, we use the straight-line method.

Assume that a firm purchases 10 National Telephone $10,000, 8% bonds at 98 on a semiannual interest date (January 1) 10 years prior to maturity. Brokerage commission is $200. Because the bonds will have a maturity value of $100,000 in 10 years, the bond discount is $1,800, which is amortized (using the straight-line method) at a rate of $90 at the end of each of the 20 remaining semiannual interest periods ($1,800/20 = $90). The following entry records the purchase:

Jan. 1	National Telephone Bonds	98,200	
	Cash		98,200
	To record purchase of 10 bonds at 98 on		
	interest date plus commission of $200.		

Note that although the bond discount is amortized, no Bond Discount account is established. The investment is initially recorded at cost, and the discount amortization entry is made directly to the asset account. For example, on the next interest date, the following entries record the receipt of interest and amortization of discount:

July 1	Cash	4,000	
	Bond Interest Income		4,000
	To record receipt of semiannual interest on		
	National Telephone bonds.		
1	National Telephone Bonds	90	
	Bond Interest Income		90
	To record semiannual amortization of		
	discount on National Telephone bonds.		

As in the case of Bonds Payable on the books of borrowers, the carrying value of the bonds increases until they reach their maturity value on their maturity date.

When the purchase price of a bond exceeds its maturity value, the bond is still recorded at cost and the related premium amortization entry is a debit to Bond Interest Income and a credit to the Investment account. Thus, the carrying value of bonds acquired at a premium progresses downward toward maturity value. Also, the net amount of interest income reported is less (by the amount of premium amortized) than the cash received as interest income each period.

Bonds may be sold before they reach maturity. Assume that on January 1, five years after they were purchased, the National Telephone bonds were sold at $99\frac{1}{2}$ less a $150 commission. Discount amortization over the 10 semiannual interest periods during which the bonds were held would have raised their carrying value to $99,100 [$98,200 + (10 × $90) = $99,100]. Again, we figure the accounting gain by comparing the book value of the asset to the net proceeds from the sale. The sale is recorded as follows:

Jan. 1	Cash	99,350	
	National Telephone Bonds		99,100
	Gain on Sale of Investments		250
	To record sale of bond investment at $99\frac{1}{2}$		
	less a commission of $150.		

DEFERRED INCOME TAXES

Business firms often adopt income tax methods of determining taxable net income that differ from the methods of determining accounting net income. Almost invariably, the firms adopt tax accounting methods that defer tax payments; ordinarily, these methods defer revenue recognition or accelerate expense recognition for tax purposes. Accounting for such timing differences of revenue or expense recognition often results in *deferred tax credits*, which are classified as long-term liabilities.

Timing Differences   When **timing differences** exist, the revenue and expense items that affect pretax accounting income in one period enter into the calculation of taxable income in a different period. Eventually, however, the total amount of revenue or expense reported in both sets of records over a period of time will be the same. Timing differences arise because tax laws either (1) require recognition of certain revenue and expense items in different periods than do generally accepted accounting principles or (2) permit the use of a different method of accounting for revenue or expenses on the tax return than is used in determining pretax accounting income. In the latter case, businesses normally select a tax accounting method that minimizes their current tax liability.

A typical example of a timing difference concerns depreciation methods. A company may use an accelerated depreciation method in the tax return and straight-line depreciation in arriving at accounting income. As another example, a firm that has long-term construction contracts may recognize revenue on the percentage of completion basis in determining accounting income but use the completed contract method of revenue recognition for tax purposes.

Whenever timing differences cause pretax accounting income to differ from taxable income, the income tax expense included in the income statement should be based on the revenue and expense amounts reported in the income statement (that is, the tax expense should be based on the pretax accounting income). To do otherwise presents distorted information in the income statement.

The process of apportioning income tax expense to the income statement over the periods affected by timing differences is known as **interperiod income tax allocation.** To illustrate this process and the distortions that result if it is not employed, assume the following data: On January 1, 19X1, the Cascade Company entered a long-term construction contract with an estimated gross profit of $120,000. The percentages of work completed in 19X1, 19X2, and 19X3 were 25%, 50%, and 25% respectively. (These percentages were determined by dividing each year's costs incurred by the total estimated cost of the contract, as explained in Chapter 13.) The firm uses the percentage of completion method of recognizing gross profit on its books but selects the completed contract basis of recognition for tax purposes. Therefore, the reported income on the books for the three years is $30,000, $60,000, and $30,000, respectively, whereas the entire gross profit of $120,000 is reported in 19X3 for tax purposes. This represents Cascade Company's only timing difference between information collected in the accounts and the tax return. For simplicity, we assume that the firm generates $100,000 of income before construction contract income and taxes and that its income tax rate is 40%.

Cascade Company's taxable income and income tax payable to the Internal Revenue Service for 19X1–19X3 are as follows:

	19X1	19X2	19X3
Income before construction contract income and taxes	$100,000	$100,000	$100,000
Construction contract income	—	—	120,000
Taxable income	$100,000	$100,000	$220,000
Income tax liability (40% of taxable income)	$ 40,000	$ 40,000	$ 88,000

The pretax accounting income for each of the three years differs from the taxable income because of the timing difference in recognizing income (gross profit) on the construction contract.

	19X1	19X2	19X3
Income before construction contract income and taxes	$100,000	$100,000	$100,000
Construction contract income (25%, 50%, and 25% of $120,000)	30,000	60,000	30,000
Pretax accounting income	$130,000	$160,000	$130,000

The reporting of taxes in the income statement without income tax allocation (that is, income tax expense equals the actual tax liability for the year) is shown in part A of the following schedule. Part B shows how income tax allocation affects income tax expense and net income.

	19X1	19X2	19X3
A. Without Income Tax Allocation			
Pretax Accounting Income	$130,000	$160,000	$130,000
Income Tax Expense	40,000	40,000	88,000
Net Income	$ 90,000	$120,000	$ 42,000
B. With Income Tax Allocation			
Pretax Accounting Income	$130,000	$160,000	$130,000
Income Tax Expense	52,000	64,000	52,000
Net Income	$ 78,000	$ 96,000	$ 78,000

Accountants consider the presentation in A distorted because the relationship between pretax accounting income and income tax expense is not normal (in this example, 40%). Based on the amounts reported in the three years, the percentage relationship is 30.8%, 25%, and 67.7%, respectively. A related distortion occurs in the net income figure. In this illustration, pretax accounting income is the same ($130,000) in 19X1 and 19X3, yet the net income for 19X3 is $42,000, less than one-half of the 19X1 net income of $90,000. The reason, of course, is the timing difference, with income tax expense in part A based on taxable income, not on pretax accounting income.

In part B, income tax expense is allocated to each year according to the pretax accounting income. This income tax allocation procedure produces a normal annual relationship between pretax accounting income and income tax expense. Also, net income moves in harmony with pretax accounting income.

Deferred Tax Accounts

Under income tax allocation, the annual charge to Income Tax Expense does not equal the income tax liability for the period. **Deferred tax** accounts are needed to balance the analysis. The journal entries recording income tax expense for Cascade Company for 19X1–19X3 illustrate this point.

19X1	Income Tax Expense	52,000	
	Income Tax Payable		40,000
	Deferred Tax Credits		12,000
	To record 19X1 income tax.		
19X2	Income Tax Expense	64,000	
	Income Tax Payable		40,000
	Deferred Tax Credits		24,000
	To record 19X2 income tax.		

ROLLOVER

The liability side of Anheuser-Busch's 1980 balance sheet shows "deferred income taxes, $267.7 million." That's no small sum—equal to 19% of total liabilities and 26% of stockholders' equity. Anheuser is not an isolated case. But are deferred taxes really a *liability*?

That's a question many accountants are asking themselves these days. Says Harvey D. Moskowitz, national director of accounting and auditing for Seidman & Seidman, "The deferred taxes on the balance sheet bear no relationship to what is actually going to be owed. So the current method of income tax accounting makes it impossible for the investor to evaluate a company's liquidity, solvency, or cash flow."

Here's the explanation for this curious state of affairs: Anheuser-Busch had pretax income of $271.5 million, so, using standard corporate tax rates (less credits), it owed $99.7 million to Uncle Sam. That's what it set aside as "provision for income taxes" on its income statement. But it's not what the company actually paid. Like most businesses Anheuser keeps two sets of books, one for tax purposes, one for stock owners. It uses accelerated depreciation for taxes but straight line for reporting to investors. It expenses interest for tax purposes but often capitalizes it on the books. So, out-of-pocket, it really had to pay only $31.9 million in taxes in 1980—the line marked "current" on the income statement. The other $67.8 million, called "deferred," represents cash that's squirreled away in liabilities on the balance sheet, under the assumption that the company will pay those taxes *eventually*—when accelerated depreciation runs out, for example.

That assumption is probably wrong, though.

As long as the company keeps growing—in real terms or because of inflation—it will keep adding new assets and new interest costs to replace the ones that are running out. That means those deferred taxes, instead of getting paid, will simply roll over. And over and over and over. It could almost make you dizzy.

Dennis Beresford, national head of accounting standards for Ernst & Whinney, recently took a look at the 1980 annuals of the 250 largest industrial companies in America. He found 26 that had deferred taxes in excess of 20% of stockholders' equity, with the average for those companies being 27%. That's up sharply from 1971, when the same group of companies' deferred taxes were only 10% of equity. Clearly, these folks aren't just staying even in the rollover game—they're getting ahead of themselves. It's like the Sorcerer's Apprentice sequence in Disney's *Fantasia*, where the enchanted broomsticks dump ten buckets of water on the cellar floor for every one bucket Mickey Mouse manages to bail out. Only in this case it's cash.

In a sense then, both profits and net worth are seriously understated. "Many of these large companies say this is unrealistic reporting," says Beresford. "'We'll never pay those amounts,' they say, 'so why do we have to set them up as liabilities? They should really be considered part of our income and stockholders' equity.'"

From *Forbes*, January 18, 1982, page 75, "Rollover," by Jane Carmichael.

Authors' note: The Financial Accounting Standards Board is being pressured to reconsider the problem of tax accounting. The AICPA Accounting Standards Executive Committee has already voted—twice—unanimously to recommend that the FASB take another look at the problem.

19X3	Income Tax Expense	52,000	
	Deferred Tax Credits	36,000	
	Income Tax Payable		88,000
	To record 19X3 income tax.		

The balance in the Deferred Tax Credits account represents the tax effect of timing differences. For example, the $12,000 balance at the end of 19X1 equals the tax rate, 40%, times the timing difference in 19X1 of $30,000. The balance in the account is deferred for allocation to income tax expense (as a reduction of the expense) in the future. Once the timing differences have completely worked themselves out, the Deferred Tax Credits account has a zero balance. This occurs at the end of 19X3 for the Cascade Company, as shown in the following T account:

Deferred Tax Credits

19X3	36,000	19X1	12,000
		19X2	24,000

The balance in the Deferred Tax Credits account should be classified in the balance sheet as a liability. The amounts disclosed are frequently quite large; deferred tax credits reported by major corporations often run into millions of dollars. Because firms continually engage in transactions causing timing differences, large deferred tax liabilities persist over time. (See boxed insert, "Rollover.")

Some timing differences will first cause pretax accounting income to be less than taxable income. Initially, then, the income tax payable exceeds the charge to income tax expense, and a Deferred Tax Charges account is debited to balance the analysis. This account balance reflects the amount of tax payments allocated to income tax expense (as an increase in the expense) in the future. As with the Deferred Tax Credits account, the Deferred Tax Charges account has a zero balance after the timing differences have completely worked themselves out. Deferred tax charges should be classified in the balance sheet as an asset.

CORPORATION BALANCE SHEET

Exhibit 17–4 is a comprehensive illustration of a corporation's balance sheet that contains many of the items discussed in this chapter and in Chapters 15 and 16.

KEY POINTS TO REMEMBER

(1) To sell bonds payable is to borrow money for which interest expense is incurred.

(2) The amount of bond discount or premium (a) is determined by the difference between the nominal interest rate on the bonds and the applicable market

EXHIBIT 17–4

Superior Corporation
Balance Sheet
December 31, 19XX

ASSETS

Current Assets

Cash		$ 20,000
Short-term Investments (at lower of cost or market)		10,000
Accounts Receivable	$65,000	
Less: Allowance for Uncollectible Accounts	5,000	60,000
Inventories (at lower of cost or market)		120,000
Prepaid Expenses		10,000
Total Current Assets		$220,000

Investments

Sinking Fund for Bond Retirement		$ 20,400
Long-term Bond Investments		29,600
Total Investments		50,000

Plant Assets

	Cost	Accumulated Depreciation	Book Value	
Machinery and Equipment	$170,000	$30,000	$140,000	
Buildings	100,000	20,000	80,000	
Land	30,000	—	30,000	
Total Plant Assets				250,000

Intangible Assets (cost less amortization to date)

Goodwill		$ 28,000
Patents		12,000
Total Intangible Assets		40,000
Total Assets		$560,000

rate of interest, and (b) should be considered a long-term adjustment of interest expense.

(3) Bonds payable should be presented in the balance sheet at their face value plus any related premium or less any related discount.

(4) Premium or discount on bonds payable is usually amortized to interest expense over the life of the bonds using the straight-line method of amortization. However, the effective interest method should be used when the two methods yield materially different results.

(5) When convertible bonds are converted, the book value of the bonds is transferred to the common stock accounts.

(6) Investments in bonds are recorded at cost plus any brokerage fee, and related

EXHIBIT 17–4 (continued)

Superior Corporation
Balance Sheet
December 31, 19XX (continued)

LIABILITIES

Current Liabilities

Accounts Payable	$ 45,000	
Income Tax Payable	18,000	
Dividends Payable	15,000	
Accrued Payables	2,000	
Total Current Liabilities		$ 80,000

Long-term Liabilities

First Mortgage, 9% Bonds Payable (due 1990)	$100,000	
Premium on First Mortgage Bonds	6,000	
	$106,000	
Deferred Income Tax Credits	30,000	
Total Long-term Liabilities		136,000
Total Liabilities		$216,000

STOCKHOLDERS' EQUITY

Paid-in Capital

Common Stock, $100 Par Value, authorized and issued 2,000 shares; 50 shares in treasury	$200,000	
Paid-in Capital in Excess of Par Value	20,000	
Total Paid-in Capital		$220,000

Retained Earnings

Appropriated for Plant Expansion	$ 44,000	
Appropriated for Treasury Stock	6,000	
Unappropriated	80,000	
Total Retained Earnings		130,000
		$350,000
Less: Treasury Stock (50 shares) at Cost		6,000
Total Stockholders' Equity		$344,000
Total Liabilities and Stockholders' Equity		$560,000

interest income is accrued. Bond premium and discount are normally amortized on long-term investments.

(7) When timing differences exist in recognizing revenue and expense items per books and per tax return, income tax expense per books should be allocated based on the firm's income tax rate. This procedure often results in the appearance of deferred tax credits, which are classified as a long-term liability.

QUESTIONS

17–1 Define the following terms:
(a) mortgage notes   (g) convertible bonds
(b) bonds payable   (h) face value
(c) trustee   (i) nominal interest rate
(d) secured bonds   (j) bond discount
(e) serial bonds   (k) bond premium
(f) callable bonds   (l) amortization of bond premium
                             or discount

17–2 Explain how issuing bonds at a premium or discount "adjusts the nominal rate to the applicable market rate of interest."

17–3 A $2,000,000 issue of 10-year, 10% bonds was sold at 98 plus accrued interest three months after the bonds were dated. What net amount of cash is received?

17–4 Regardless of whether premium or discount is involved, what generalization can be made about the change in the book value of bonds payable during the period in which they are outstanding?

17–5 How should premium and discount on bonds payable be presented in the balance sheet?

17–6 On April 30, 19X5, eight months before maturity, the Beltline Company retired $20,000 of 12% bonds payable at 101 plus accrued interest. The book value of the bonds on April 30 was $18,600. Bond interest was last paid on December 31, 19X4. What is the gain or loss on the retirement of the bonds?

17–7 Give reasons why a convertible bond may be attractive to both an investor and the issuing company. Why do corporations typically include a call feature in a convertible bond?

17–8 What is the purpose of a bond sinking fund? Where is the bond sinking fund classified in the balance sheet?

17–9 Under what conditions should the effective interest method be used to amortize discount or premium on bonds payable and on long-term bond investments?

17–10 If the effective interest amortization method is used for bonds payable, how does the periodic interest expense change over the life of the bonds when they are issued (a) at a discount and (b) at a premium?

17–11 The Reynolds Company invested in bonds at a premium on a long-term basis. Should the bond premium be amortized? Where should the bond investment be classified in the balance sheet?

17–12 What are timing differences between pretax accounting income and taxable income? Give an example of a timing difference.

17–13 What is meant by *interperiod tax allocation*? Why do accountants employ interperiod tax allocation?

17–14 What does the balance in the Deferred Tax Credits account reflect? Where should the account be classified in the financial statements?

17–15 How does interperiod tax allocation differ from tax allocation within a period (discussed in Chapter 16)?

EXERCISES

17–16 On January 1, the Baxter Company issued $200,000 of 10-year, 9% convertible bonds at 102. Interest is payable semiannually on June 30 and December 31. Each $1,000 bond may be converted into 20 shares of $50 par value common stock. Present journal entries to reflect (a) the issuance of the bonds, (b) the payment of interest for the first six months, (c) the premium amortization for the first six months (straight-line), and (d) the conversion of $100,000 face amount of bonds into stock exactly five years after the issuance of the bonds.

17–17 The Lynn Company issued $500,000 of 10-year, 8% bonds at 97. The bonds were issued on March 1, 19X1, with interest payable semiannually on March 1 and September 1. Present journal entries to reflect (a) the issuance of the bonds, (b) the payment of interest for the first six months, (c) the discount amortization for the first six months (straight-line), and (d) the retirement of the bonds at 101 plus accrued interest on June 1, 19X5.

17–18 The adjusted trial balance for the Cardex Corporation at the end of the current year contains the following accounts:

Bond Interest Payable	$ 47,000
9% Bonds Payable	600,000
10% Bonds Payable	400,000
Discount on 9% Bonds Payable	5,000
Premium on 10% Bonds Payable	6,000
Sinking Fund for Bond Retirement	110,000
Long-term Bond Investment	60,500

Prepare the long-term liabilities section of the balance sheet. Indicate the proper balance sheet classification for accounts listed above that do not belong in the long-term liabilities section.

17–19 Conroy, Inc. issued $500,000 of 10-year, 8% bonds payable on January 1, 19X1. The bonds were sold for $437,740, yielding an effective interest rate of 10%. Semiannual interest is payable on January 1 and July 1, and the effective interest method is used to amortize the discount.
(a) Prepare an amortization schedule showing the necessary information for the first two interest periods.
(b) Give the entries to record interest expense and discount amortization on July 1 and December 31.

17–20 Refer to Exhibit 17–3 on page 580 of the chapter. The $100,000, 8% bonds in the example were issued on April 1, 19X1, and sold at a premium. Interest payment dates were April 1 and October 1. Give the adjusting entry to record interest expense and premium amortization on December 31, 19X2.

17–21 As a long-term investment, eight 10-year, $1,000, 10% bonds were purchased at 105 on the first day of their first semiannual interest period. Present journal entries to record (a) their purchase for cash, (b) the receipt of the first two semiannual interest payments, (c) the semiannual amortizations of bond premium for the first year (straight-line), and (d) the sale of the bonds at 102 two years after they were purchased.

17–22 Assume that the bonds in Exercise 17–21 were purchased at 96 on the first day of their first semiannual interest period. Present journal entries to record (a) their purchase for cash, (b) the receipt of the first two semiannual interest payments, (c) the semiannual amortizations of bond discount for the first year (straight-line), and (d) the sale of the bonds at 98 two years after they were purchased.

17–23 The bottom portion of Stafford, Inc. income statements for 19X1 and 19X2 is as follows:

	19X2	19X1
Income before Income Taxes	$58,000	$42,000
Income Tax Expense	20,000	20,000
Net Income	$38,000	$22,000

In 19X1, Stafford, Inc. received an advance payment of $8,000, which was subject to income tax in 19X1, but not reported in accounting income until 19X2. The income tax rate is 40%. Stafford did not employ interperiod income tax allocation.
(a) Identify the distortions in Stafford's income statements that arise from the failure to use interperiod income tax allocation.
(b) Redo the bottom portion of Stafford's income statements, using interperiod income tax allocation.

PROBLEMS

17–24 On January 1, 19X4, Rowan, Inc. sold at 97 a $400,000 issue of 9% bonds that mature in 10 years. Bond interest is payable on June 30 and December 31. Rowan's accounting year ends on December 31. The firm uses the straight-line method of amortization.

REQUIRED
(a) Show all entries pertaining to the bonds for 19X4.
(b) Present the entries necessary to record properly the retirement of one-half the bonds at 99 plus accrued interest on March 1, 19X7.

17–25 Drew, Inc., which closes its books on December 31, is authorized to issue $600,000 of 10%, 12-year bonds dated April 1, 19X1, with interest payments on October 1 and April 1.

REQUIRED
Present general journal entries to record the following events, assuming the bonds were (a) sold at 98 on April 1, 19X1; and (b) sold at $103\frac{1}{2}$ plus accrued interest on August 1, 19X1.
(1) The bond issue.
(2) Payment of the first semiannual period's interest and amortization on that date of any related bond premium or discount (straight-line).
(3) Accrual of bond interest expense and any related bond premium or discount amortization at December 31, 19X1.
(4) Retirement of $100,000 of the bonds at 102 on April 1, 19X7.

17–26 On January 1, 19X5, Rockford, Inc. issued $1,000,000 face value, 10%, 10-year bonds for $885,500, yielding an effective interest rate of 12%. Semiannual interest is payable on January 1 and July 1 each year. The firm uses the effective interest method to amortize the discount.

REQUIRED
(a) Prepare an amortization schedule showing the necessary information for the first two interest periods.
(b) Prepare the journal entry for the bond issuance on January 1, 19X5.
(c) Prepare the entry to record bond interest expense and discount amortization at July 1, 19X5.
(d) Prepare the adjusting entry to record interest expense and discount amortization at December 31, the close of the firm's accounting year.

17–27 On April 1, 19X5, Jensen, Inc. issued $2,000,000 face value 10%, 10-year bonds for $2,271,000, yielding an effective interest rate of 8%. Semiannual interest is payable on April 1 and October 1 each year. The firm uses the effective interest method to amortize the premium.

REQUIRED
(a) Prepare an amortization schedule showing the necessary information for the first two interest periods.
(b) Prepare the journal entry for the bond issuance on April 1, 19X5.
(c) Prepare the entry to record bond interest expense and premium amortization at October 1, 19X5.
(d) Prepare the adjusting entry to record interest expense and premium amortization at December 31, the close of the firm's accounting year.

17–28 Dayton, Inc. issued $80,000 of bonds and is required by its bond agreement to maintain a bond sinking fund managed by a trustee. The following transactions relate to the fund at various times in its life.
(1) The fund receives a periodic cash deposit of $6,450.
(2) The trustee reports sinking fund earnings of $2,345 during the period.
(3) The trustee reports the sale of sinking-fund securities and the retirement of the $80,000 of outstanding bonds. Just before this report, the Bond Sinking Fund account for Dayton, Inc. showed a balance of $80,000. The trustee also reports the sale of the securities generated an unexpected gain of $3,500, and a check for this amount accompanies the trustee's report (credit to Bond Sinking-fund Income).

REQUIRED
Present general journal entries for these sinking-fund transactions.

17–29 The following are selected transactions of the Moore Corporation for 19X1 and 19X2. The company closes its books on December 31.

19X1
Jan. 1 Issued $200,000 of 9%, 10-year convertible bonds at 98. Interest is payable on January 1 and July 1. The holder of each $1,000 bond may convert it into 18 shares of $50 par value Moore Corporation common stock.
July 1 Paid semiannual interest and recorded semiannual discount amortization (straight-line) on convertible bonds.

July 1 Purchased, as a long-term investment, thirty $1,000, 8% Rowe Company bonds at 103. The bonds pay interest on July 1 and January 1 and mature in 10 years.

Dec. 31 Recorded accrued interest payable and semiannual discount amortization on convertible bonds and accrued interest receivable and semiannual premium amortization on Rowe Company bonds. (Moore Corporation does not use reversing entries.) Straight-line amortization is used both for bonds payable and bond investments.

19X2

Jan. 1 Paid semiannual interest on convertible bonds and received semiannual interest on Rowe Company bonds.

2 Converted $20,000 of convertible bonds to common stock.

May 1 Sold one-half the Rowe Company bonds at 102 plus accrued interest.

REQUIRED

Record these transactions in general journal form.

17–30 The following transactions relate to certain bonds acquired by Bolton Corporation as a long-term investment.

19X2

Mar. 1 Purchased $500,000 face value of Harper, Inc. 20-year, 9% bonds dated January 1, 19X2, directly from the issuing company for $507,140 plus accrued interest. Interest is paid January 1 and July 1.

July 1 Received semiannual interest on Harper, Inc. bonds and amortized the related bond premium. The straight-line method of amortization is used.

Dec. 31 Accrued interest receivable on Harper, Inc. bonds and amortized the related bond premium. (Bolton Corporation does not use reversing entries.)

19X4

Jan. 2 Received semiannual interest on Harper, Inc. bonds

May 1 Sold the Harper, Inc. bonds at 101 plus accrued interest. A selling commission of $800 was deducted from the proceeds. Amortized bond premium to date of sale.

REQUIRED

Record these transactions in general journal form.

17–31 On January 1, 19X1, Benson Company entered a three-year construction contract that had an estimated gross profit of $80,000. The percentages of work completed in 19X1, 19X2, and 19X3 were 20%, 40%, and 40%, respectively (determined by dividing each year's costs by the estimated cost of the contract). The firm uses the percentage of completion method of recognizing gross profit on its books, but selects the completed contract basis of recognizing gross profit for tax purposes. This is the only difference between pretax accounting income and taxable income. The firm had income before construction contract income and taxes of $100,000, $140,000, and $120,000, respectively, for 19X1, 19X2, and 19X3. The applicable tax rate is 40%.

REQUIRED

(a) Prepare a schedule deriving taxable income and income tax liability for 19X1–19X3.

(b) Prepare a schedule deriving pretax accounting income for 19X1–19X3.

(c) Prepare journal entries to record (1) income taxes for 19X1–19X3, using interperiod income tax allocation, and (2) the payment of taxes. Assume that Benson Company pays its tax liability in full in the year following its recognition in the accounts.

ALTERNATE PROBLEMS

17–24A On January 1, 19X6, Woods, Inc. sold at 103 a $600,000 issue of 9% bonds that mature in 20 years. Bond interest is payable on June 30 and December 31. Woods' accounting year ends on December 31. The firm uses the straight-line method of amortization.

REQUIRED
(a) Show all entries pertaining to the bonds for 19X6.
(b) Present the entries necessary to record properly the retirement of one-third of the bonds at 102 plus accrued interest on April 1, 19X9.

17–25A Atlas, Inc., which closes its books on December 31, is authorized to issue $400,000 of 9%, 15-year bonds dated March 1, 1984, with interest payments on March 1 and September 1.

REQUIRED
Present general journal entries to record the following events, assuming the bonds were (a) sold at 96 on March 1, 1984; and (b) sold at 102 plus accrued interest on July 1, 1984.
(1) The bond issue.
(2) Payment of the first semiannual period's interest and amortization on that date of any related bond premium or discount (straight-line).
(3) Accrual of bond interest expense and any related bond premium or discount amortization at December 31, 1984 (compute to the nearest dollar).
(4) Retirement of $200,000 of the bonds at 101 on March 1, 1994.

17–26A On April 1, 19X6, Haley, Inc. issued $600,000 face value, 9%, 10-year bonds for $562,674, yielding an effective interest rate of 10%. Semiannual interest is payable on April 1 and October 1 each year. The firm uses the effective interest method to amortize the discount.

REQUIRED
(a) Prepare an amortization schedule showing the necessary information for the first two interest periods.
(b) Prepare the journal entry for the bond issuance on April 1, 19X6.
(c) Prepare the entry to record bond interest expense and discount amortization at October 1, 19X6.
(d) Prepare the adjusting entry to record interest expense and discount amortization at December 31, the close of the firm's accounting year.

17–27A Complete the requirements of Problem 17–26A assuming that the bonds were issued for $640,530, yielding an effective interest rate of 8%. The firm uses the effective interest method to amortize the premium.

17–29A The following are selected transactions of the Allison Corporation for 19X7 and 19X8. The company closes its books on December 31.

19X7

Jan. 1   Issued $800,000 of 10%, 20-year bonds payable at 102. Interest is payable on January 1 and July 1.

June 30   Purchased, as a long-term investment, twenty $1,000, 9% Artway Company bonds at 97. The bonds pay interest on June 30 and December 31 and mature in 10 years.

July 1   Paid semiannual interest and recorded semiannual discount amortization (straight-line) on bonds payable.

Dec. 31   Received semiannual interest on Artway Company bonds.

     31   Recorded accrued interest payable and semiannual premium amortization on bonds payable and discount amortization on Artway Company bonds. (Allison Corporation does not use reversing entries.) Straight-line amortization is used both for bonds payable and bond investments.

19X8

Jan. 1   Paid semiannual interest on bonds payable.

      2   Retired $80,000 of bonds payable at 101.

Feb. 1   Sold Artway Company bonds at 99 plus accrued interest.

REQUIRED

Record these transactions in general journal form.

17–30A The following transactions relate to certain bonds acquired by Dover Corporation as a long-term investment.

19X4

Feb. 1   Purchased $1,000,000 face value of Dunn, Inc. 20-year, 9% bonds dated January 1, 19X4, directly from the issuing company for $988,050, plus accrued interest. Interest is paid January 1 and July 1.

July 1   Received semiannual interest on Dunn, Inc. bonds and amortized the related bond discount. The straight-line method of amortization is used.

Dec. 31   Accrued interest receivable on Dunn, Inc. bonds and amortized the related bond discount. (Dover Corporation does not use reversing entries.)

19X6

Jan. 2   Received semiannual interest on Dunn, Inc. bonds.

May   1   Sold the Dunn, Inc. bonds at 99 plus accrued interest. A selling commission of $1,000 was deducted from the proceeds. Amortized bond discount to date of sale.

REQUIRED

Record these transactions in general journal form.

17–31A In 19X1, Ridge Company made an expenditure of $20,000, which was deductible for income taxes in 19X1 but was reported in the firm's income statement as an expense in 19X2. The firm's pretax accounting income was $80,000 in 19X1 and $75,000 in 19X2 (after the $20,000 expense item). The applicable income tax rate is 40%.

REQUIRED

(a) Prepare a schedule deriving taxable income and income tax liability for 19X1 and 19X2.

(b) Prepare a schedule deriving pretax accounting income for 19X1 and 19X2.
(c) Prepare journal entries to record (1) income taxes for 19X1 and 19X2, using interperiod income tax allocation, and (2) the payment of taxes. Assume that Ridge Company pays its tax liability in full in the year following its recognition in the accounts.

BUSINESS DECISION PROBLEM

On January 1, 19X1, Ray Parker, president of Appliance Parts & Service, Inc., tells you that the firm plans to expand its business by adding an appliance sales department. Most of the appliances will be sold on 36-month installment plans. Parker is concerned about the income tax and accounting implications of the expansion. He has furnished you with the following projected data for the next three years:

	19X1	19X2	19X3
Pretax accounting income, excluding gross profit on installment sales	$30,000	$36,000	$42,000
Gross profit on installment sales for year of sale	60,000	70,000	80,000
Gross profit on installment basis:			
19X1 installment sales	24,000	18,000	18,000
19X2 installment sales		28,000	21,000
19X3 installment sales			32,000

You suggest that the firm record gross profit from installment sales in the year of sale for accounting purposes but use the installment method of reporting for tax purposes. You also explain how the firm would employ interperiod income tax allocation.

REQUIRED
Answer Parker's questions, shown below, based on the given data. Assume an income tax rate of 40%.
(a) What will the income tax liability be for each of the three years?
(b) What amount of income tax expense will appear on the firm's income statements for each of the three years?
(c) What will the accounting net income be for each of the three years?
(d) What balance for Deferred Tax Credits will appear in the balance sheet for each of the three years, and how will this amount be classified?
(e) What is the nature of any tax advantage in adopting the installment sales method of gross profit recognition for tax purposes?

PRESENT VALUES AND EFFECTIVE INTEREST AMORTIZATION

I n this appendix, we explain the concept of present value and the techniques of bond valuation to expand on the subject of effective interest amortization, which was introduced in Chapter 17.

PRESENT VALUES

Concept of Present Value

Would you rather receive a dollar now or a dollar one year from now? Most persons would answer, "a dollar now." Intuition tells us that a dollar received now is more valuable than the same amount received sometime in the future. Sound reasons exist for choosing the earlier dollar, the most obvious of which concerns risk. Because the future is always uncertain, some event may prevent us from receiving the dollar at the later date. To avoid this risk, we choose the earlier date.

A second reason for choosing the earlier date is that the dollar received now could be invested; one year from now, we could have not only the dollar, but also the interest income for the period. Using these risk and interest factors, we can generalize that (1) the right to receive an amount of money now—its *present value*—is normally worth more than the right to receive the same amount later—its future value; (2) the longer we must wait to receive an amount, the less attractive the receipt is; and (3) the difference between the present value of an amount and its future value is a function of interest (Principal × Interest Rate × Time). The more risk associated with any situation, the higher the appropriate interest rate.

We support these generalizations with an illustration. What amount could we accept now that would be as valuable as receiving $100 one year from now if the appropriate interest rate is 10%? We recognize intuitively that with a 10% interest rate, we should accept less than $100, or approximately $91. We base this estimate on the realization that the $100 received in the future must equal the present value (100%) plus 10% interest on the present value. Thus, in our example, the $100 future receipt must be 1.10 times the present value. Dividing ($100/

1.10), we obtain a present value of $90.90. In other words, under the given conditions we would do as well to accept $90.90 now as to wait one year and receive $100. To confirm the equality of a $90.90 receipt now to a $100 receipt one year later, we calculate the future value of $90.90 at 10% for one year as follows:

$$\$90.90 \times 1.10 \times 1 \text{ year} = \$100 \text{ (rounded)}$$

Thus, we compute the present value of a future receipt by discounting (deducting an interest factor) the future receipt back to the present at an appropriate interest rate. We present this schematically below:

Present value, ⟵ Discounted for ⟵ Future value,
$90.90   one year at 10% $100

If either the time period or the interest rate were increased, the resulting present value would decrease. If more than one time period is involved, compound interest computations are appropriate.

Use of Present Value Tables

Because present value tables, such as Table I on page 993, are widely available, we need not present here the various formulas for interest computations. Table I can be used to compute the present value amounts in the illustrations and problem materials that follow. Simply stated, present value tables provide a multiplier for many combinations of time periods and interest rates, that when applied to the dollar amount of a future receipt determines its present value.

Present value tables are used as follows. First, determine the number of interest compounding periods involved (three years compounded annually is three periods, three years compounded semiannually is six periods, three years compounded quarterly is 12 periods, and so on). The extreme left-hand column indicates the number of periods covered in the table.

Next, determine the interest rate per compounding period. Note that interest rates are usually quoted on a *per year* basis. Therefore, only in the case of annual compoundings is the quoted interest rate the interest rate per compounding period. In other cases, the rate per compounding period is the annual rate divided by the number of compounding periods in a year. For example, an interest rate of 10% per year would be 10% for one compounding period if compounded annually, 5% for two compounding periods if compounded semiannually, and $2\frac{1}{2}$% for four compounding periods if compounded quarterly.

Locate the factor that is to the right of the appropriate number of compounding periods and beneath the appropriate interest rate per compounding period. Multiply this factor by the number of dollars involved.

Note the logical progressions among multipliers in Table I. All values are less than 1.0 because the present value is always smaller than the future amount if the interest rate is greater than zero. Also, as the interest rate increases (moving from left to right in the table) or the number of periods increases (moving from top to bottom), the multipliers become smaller.

EXAMPLE 1 Compute the present value of $100 one year hence, at 10% interest compounded annually.

Number of periods (one year, annually) = 1
Rate per period (10%/1) = 10%
Multiplier = 0.909
Present value = $100.00 × 0.909 = $90.90
(Note that this agrees with our earlier illustration.)

EXAMPLE 2   Compute the present value of $116.99 two years hence, at 8% compounded semiannually.

Number of periods (two years, semiannually) = 4
Rate per period (8%/2) = 4%
Multiplier = 0.855
Present value = $116.99 × 0.855 = $100 (rounded)

Annuity Form of Cash Flows

Using present value tables, we can compute the present value of any single future receipt or series of future receipts. One frequent pattern of cash receipts, however, is subject to a more convenient treatment. This pattern, known as the **annuity form,** can be described as *equal amounts equally spaced over a period.*

For example, $100 is to be received at the end of each of the next three years as an annuity. As shown below, the present value of this annuity can be computed from Table I by computing the present value of each of the three individual receipts and summing them (assuming 5% annual interest).

Future Receipts (annuity)			PV Multiplier (Table I)		Present Value
Yr. 1	Yr. 2	Yr. 3			
$100			× 0.952	=	$ 95.20
	$100		× 0.907	=	90.70
		$100	× 0.864	=	86.40
			Total present value		$272.30

Table II (page 994) provides a single multiplier for computing the present value of a series of future cash receipts in the annuity form. Referring to Table II in the "3 periods" row and the 5% column, we see that the multiplier is 2.723. When applied to the $100 annuity amount, the multiplier gives a present value of $272.30. Of course, the same present value is derived from the several multipliers of Table I. For annuities of 5, 10, or 20 years, the computations avoided by using annuity tables are considerable.

Bond Valuations

In Chapter 17, we explained that (1) the essence of a bond investment is lending money; (2) the amount received by the lender consists of a series (usually semi-annual) of interest income amounts and a single lump-sum repayment of the bond principal; and (3) bonds are sold at premiums or discounts to adjust their effective interest rates to the prevailing market rate when they are issued.

Because of the role of interest in bond investments, the selling price (or valuation) of a bond that is necessary to yield a specific rate can be determined as follows:

EXHIBIT A–1
Valuation of a Bond Issue
Using Present Value Tables

Future Cash Receipts	Multiplier (Table I)	Multiplier (Table II)	Present Values
Principal repayment, $100,000 (a single amount received eight semiannual periods hence)	0.731		$ 73,100
Interest receipts, $4,000 at end of each of eight semiannual interest periods		6.733	26,900 (rounded)
Total present value (or issue price) of bond			$100,000

(1) Use Table I to compute the present value of the future principal repayment at the desired (or effective) rate of interest.

(2) Use Table II to compute the present value of the future series of interest receipts at the desired (or effective) rate of interest.

(3) Add the present values obtained in (1) and (2).

We illustrate in Exhibit A–1 the valuation of a $100,000 issue of 8%, four-year bonds paying interest semiannually and sold on the date of issue to yield 8%.

We use the 4% column in both tables because the interest rate is 8% compounded semiannually (8%/2 = 4% per compounding period), and we use the eight periods hence line, because there are eight semiannual periods in four years. The multiplier from Table I is applied to the $100,000 because the principal repayment is a single sum. Because the eight semiannual interest receipts are in the annuity form, we use the multiplier from Table II to compute their present value. Note that the computation in Exhibit A–1 confirms the observation that the price of 8% bonds sold to yield 8% should be face (or par) value.

EFFECTIVE INTEREST AMORTIZATION

Most bonds sell at more or less than their face value, and therefore accounting for them involves amortizing bond premium or bond discount. For the remainder of this illustration, we show (1) how the $100,000, 8% bond issue used earlier would be valued if it were sold to yield either 6% or 10% compounded semiannually, and (2) how the bond discount and premium amounts would be determined under the effective interest method of amortization.

We calculate the amount of discount and premium in our illustration as follows:

	Bonds Sold at Discount (to yield 10%)		Bonds Sold at Premium (to yield 6%)	
	Present Value Multiplier	Present Value	Present Value Multiplier	Present Value
Principal receipt of $100,000 (eight semiannual periods hence, factors from Table I)	0.677	$67,700	0.789	$ 78,900
Interest receipts of $4,000 each (a series of eight in annuity form, factors from Table II)	6.463	25,852	7.020	28,080
Selling price of bond issues		$93,552		$106,980
Amount of bond discount or premium		$ 6,448		$ 6,980

According to these results, an investor wishing to earn 10%, compounded semiannually, must discount the bond by $6,448 (that is, pay only $93,552 for them). An investor paying as much as a $6,980 premium for the bonds would still earn 6%, compounded semiannually, on the investment.

As we explained in Chapter 17, the book value of bonds consists of their face value plus any unamortized premium or less any unamortized discount. Thus, at issuance, the book value of the bonds is equal to their selling price. To calculate the periodic amount of amortization using the effective interest method:

(1) Determine the period's interest expense by multiplying the bonds' book value at the beginning of the period involved by the desired (or effective) interest rate.

(2) Determine the period's amortization by comparing the period's interest expense [step (1) above] to the amount of interest actually paid. If the interest expense is greater than the amount of interest paid, the difference is discount amortization; if the expense is less than the interest paid, the difference is premium amortization.

Face value of bonds	$100,000
Less: Discount	6,448
Book value of bonds at beginning of period	$ 93,552
Multiply by the interest rate per interest period (10%/2 = 5%)	× 0.05
Interest expense for first period (rounded)	$ 4,678
Actual interest paid ($100,000 × 0.08 × $\frac{6}{12}$)	4,000
First period's discount amortization	$ 678

Exhibits A–2 and A–3 summarize the calculations, related account balances, and the general progressions involved in the other periods of our illustration. These amortization schedules also appear in Chapter 17 and are explained there. We repeat them here for your convenience.

The effective interest method of amortization is often justified as being more precise than the straight-line method. This contention probably rests on the fact that, by incorporating a changing amount of total interest expense, the effective interest method results in a uniform interest rate throughout the life of the bonds. Obviously, this increased precision is offset by the added complexity and the fact that the difference between the two methods is often considered immaterial.

EXHIBIT A–2
Bonds Sold at a Discount:
Periodic Interest Expense, Amortization,
and Book Value of Bonds

Year	Interest Period	(A) Interest Paid (4% of face value)	(B) Interest Expense (5% of bond book value)	(C) Periodic Amortization (B – A)	(D) Balance of Unamortized Discount (D – C)	(E) Book Value of Bonds, End of Period ($100,000 – D)
(at issue)					$6,448	$ 93,552
1	1	$4,000	$4,678	$678	5,770	94,230
	2	4,000	4,712	712	5,058	94,942
2	3	4,000	4,747	747	4,311	95,689
	4	4,000	4,784	784	3,527	96,473
3	5	4,000	4,824	824	2,703	97,297
	6	4,000	4,865	865	1,838	98,162
4	7	4,000	4,908	908	930	99,070
	8	4,000	4,930*	930	0	100,000

*Adjusted for cumulative rounding error of $24.

EXHIBIT A–3
Bonds Sold at a Premium:
Periodic Interest Expense, Amortization,
and Book Value of Bonds

Year	Interest Period	(A) Interest Paid (4% of face value)	(B) Interest Expense (3% of bond book value)	(C) Periodic Amortization (A – B)	(D) Balance of Unamortized Premium (D – C)	(E) Book Value of Bonds, End of Period ($100,000 + D)
(at issue)					$6,980	$106,980
1	1	$4,000	$3,209	$791	6,189	106,189
	2	4,000	3,186	814	5,375	105,375
2	3	4,000	3,161	839	4,536	104,536
	4	4,000	3,136	864	3,672	103,672
3	5	4,000	3,110	890	2,782	102,782
	6	4,000	3,083	917	1,865	101,865
4	7	4,000	3,056	944	921	100,921
	8	4,000	3,079*	921	0	100,000

*Adjusted for cumulative rounding error of $51.

PROBLEMS

Note: Use Tables I and II (pages 993 and 994, respectively) to solve the following problems.

A–1 Compute the present value of each of the following:
(a) $80,000 10 years hence if the annual interest rate is:
   (1) 12% compounded annually.
   (2) 12% compounded semiannually.
   (3) 12% compounded quarterly.
(b) $500 received at the end of each year for the next eight years if money is worth 12% per year compounded annually.
(c) $100 received at the end of each six months for the next eight years if the interest rate is 10% per year compounded semiannually.
(d) $200,000 inheritance 20 years hence if money is worth 10% per year compounded annually.
(e) $800 received each half-year for the next eight years plus a single sum of $20,000 at the end of eight years if the interest rate is 8% per year compounded semiannually.

A–2 Using Table II, calculate the present value of a five-year, $4,000 annuity if the interest rate is 8% per year compounded annually. Verify your answer by using Table I. Briefly explain how these tables are related.

A–3 You have an opportunity to purchase a bond issued by a local hospital. The bond has a face value of $10,000, will pay 8% interest per year in semiannual payments, and will mature in five years. How much should you pay for the bond if you want to earn 10% interest per year compounded semiannually on your investment?

A–4 Varden, Inc. plans to issue $100,000 of 10% bonds that will pay interest semiannually and mature in five years. Assume that the effective interest rate is 12% per year compounded semiannually.
(a) Compute the selling price of the bonds.
(b) Construct a table similar to Exhibit A–2 for the first two years of the bonds' life.

A–5 Complete the requirements of Problem A–4 assuming the effective interest rate is 8% per year compounded semiannually. For requirement (b), construct a table similar to Exhibit A–3.

A–6 A $200,000, ten-year, 8% bond issue (with interest paid semiannually) is sold when the effective interest rate is 10% per year compounded semiannually.
(a) Compute the selling price of the bonds.
(b) Prepare a schedule similar to Exhibit A–2 for the first five years of the bonds' life.
(c) Compute the amount of bond premium or discount amortized each year (1) under the straight-line method and (2) under the effective interest method.
(d) Compare the differences in reported income *each year* under the two methods in part (c). Do you consider these differences material? Why?
(e) What arguments might we advance for (or against) each of the approaches to bond premium and discount amortization in part (c)?

18
Long-term Stock Investments and Consolidated Financial Statements

> **Look beneath the surface; let not the several quality of a thing nor its worth escape thee.**
>
> MARCUS AURELIUS

I n previous chapters, we have discussed the nature and accounting treatment of short-term investments and long-term bond investments. Now we examine the nature and accounting treatment of long-term stock investments.

Firms purchase the shares of other companies on a long-term basis for a variety of reasons. Sometimes modest investments are made simply because the shares promise a good yield or an increase in value over time. Sizable long-term stock investments—particularly controlling interests in other firms—are more often made for such economic reasons as growth, product diversification, market penetration, assurance of raw material supplies, and tax savings. Most business combinations today are achieved by stock acquisitions. Practically all of the corporations listed on the organized stock exchanges own all or a majority of the voting stock of other companies. Accounting for such business combinations is treated later in this chapter.

TYPES OF OWNERSHIP INTEREST

Although all long-term investments in stock are first entered in the accounts at cost, the subsequent accounting procedures differ according to the circumstances. Basically, the accounting treatment employed depends on whether the ownership interest acquired is a controlling interest—that is, an interest that permits the investor company to exercise significant influence over the company whose stock is held—or an interest that is neither controlling nor influential.

Noncontrolling and Noninfluential Interest

Long-term investments of less than 20% of a corporation's voting stock are considered small enough to preclude the investor company from significantly influencing the policies of the company whose stock is acquired. Such investments are initially recorded at cost, and, depending on company policy, cash dividends are recorded as income either when declared or received. These procedures are known as the **cost method** of accounting for investments. On the balance sheet, however, these investments are carried at the lower of cost or market value of the portfolio, determined at the balance sheet date. Thus, like temporary stock investments, their carrying value may increase or decrease from period to period (but never above cost). Unlike temporary stock investments, however, any unrealized losses or recoveries of unrealized losses are not shown in the income statement; instead, the net unrealized loss on the portfolio of long-term stock investments is reported separately as a contra stockholders' equity account in the balance sheet.

The journal entries for noncontrolling and noninfluential investments are similar to those for temporary stock investments, shown in Chapter 7. For convenience, we review certain typical entries here.

Suppose 100 shares of Hytex, Inc. common stock are acquired on October 1 at a cost of $6,600, including commissions and taxes. The investment is recorded as follows:

Oct. 1	Investment in Hytex Stock	6,600	
	Cash		6,600
	To record purchase of 100 shares		
	of common stock for $6,600.		

DIVIDENDS As in the case of temporary investments, cash dividends received are credited to a Dividend Income account, whereas a memorandum entry records any stock dividends received, since they do not constitute income. The entry for the stock dividend reveals the new average cost of the stock held. Assume that on December 10, Hytex, Inc. paid a cash dividend of $2 per share and a stock dividend of 10%. The following entries record the cash and stock dividends:

Dec. 10	Cash	200	
	Dividend Income		200
	To record receipt of $200		
	dividend on Hytex, Inc. stock.		

(Memorandum) Received 10 shares of Hytex, Inc. common stock as stock dividend. Average cost per share of 110 shares held is now $60 ($6,600/110).

LOWER OF COST OR MARKET FOR PORTFOLIO All of a company's noncontrolling and noninfluential investments in long-term stocks constitute a portfolio. At the end of the accounting period, they are reported on the balance sheet at the aggregate cost or market value of the portfolio. Should the aggregate market value drop below total cost, an unrealized loss is recorded and a contra asset account (to offset long-term stock investments) is credited. To illustrate, assume a company has the following portfolio of long-term stock investments at the end of its first year of operations:

Stock	Cost	Market Value
Hytex, Inc. Common	$ 6,600	$ 4,800
Intersouth, Inc. Common	20,000	21,500
Wade Corporation Common	15,400	12,000
Total	$42,000	$38,300

Because the total market value ($38,300) is less than total cost ($42,000), the company makes the following journal entry:

Dec. 31	Unrealized Loss on Long-term Investments	3,700	
	Allowance to Reduce Long-term Investments to Market		3,700
	To record unrealized losses on portfolio of long-term stock investments.		

The unrealized loss on long-term investments is considered temporary and is therefore reported separately as a contra stockholders' equity account in the balance sheet (subtracted from total stockholders' equity). On the balance sheet, the Allowance to Reduce Long-term Investments to Market account balance is deducted from the cost of long-term investments or the investment is shown in the following condensed form:

Long-term Stock Investments, at market (cost $42,000)	$38,300

If the portfolio's market value exceeds its total cost, the investments are reported at cost and no allowance is created.

SALE OF LONG-TERM INVESTMENTS   When a long-term stock investment is sold, a gain or loss is recorded equal to the difference between the sale proceeds and the stock's original cost (or the original cost adjusted for the effect of a stock dividend). For example, if all 110 shares of Hytex, Inc. stock discussed above were sold on March 1 of the next year for $4,800, the following entry would be made:

Mar. 1	Cash	4,800	
	Loss on Sale of Investments	1,800	
	Investment in Hytex Stock		6,600
	To record sale of stock for $4,800.		

RECOVERY OF UNREALIZED LOSS   The difference between the total cost and market value of a stock portfolio will likely change from one year-end to the next because of changes in market values or in the portfolio's composition. Thus, the contra asset account increases or decreases each year-end to reflect the net unrealized portfolio loss at that time. If the net unrealized loss at year-end is smaller than the year before, the adjusting entry records a recovery of an unrealized loss. Assume the company whose investments we have been analyzing has the following portfolio of long-term stock investments at the end of its second year of operations:

Stock	Cost	Market Value
Intersouth, Inc. Common	$20,000	$22,100
Wade Corporation Common	15,400	12,800
Total	$35,400	$34,900

The net unrealized loss is now $500 ($35,400 − $34,900); at the end of the preceding year, it had been $3,700. The following entry would adjust the allowance account:

Dec. 31	Allowance to Reduce Long-term		
	Investments to Market	3,200	
	Unrealized Loss on Long-term		
	Investments		3,200
	To record decrease in net unrealized		
	loss on long-term stock investments.		

On the year-end balance sheet, the contra amount to stockholders' equity is only $500, and the long-term investments would be shown at market value ($35,400 cost − $500).

Influential but Noncontrolling Interest

A corporation that owns 20% or more of another corporation's voting stock may exert a significant influence on the operating or financial decisions of that company. However, if 50% or less of the total voting stock is owned, the investment will not usually represent a controlling interest. Investments in the 20−50% ownership range may therefore be considered influential but noncontrolling interests. The **equity method** of accounting is appropriate for investments in this category.

Under the equity method, the investor company records as income or loss each period its proportionate share of the income or loss reported for that period by the company whose stock is held. For example, if Warner Company owns 30% of Rose Corporation's voting stock and Rose Corporation reports earnings of $20,000 for the current year, Warner Company makes the following entry:

Investment in Rose Corporation Stock	6,000	
Income from Investment in		
Rose Corporation		6,000
To record as income 30% of Rose Corporation's		
current year earnings of $20,000.		

As this entry shows, when the investor company records its share of the other corporation's income, the investment amount also increases. When cash dividends are received, however, the investor company reports no income. The receipt of a dividend is treated as a reduction of the investment balance. To illustrate, assume Rose Corporation declared and paid a $7,000 dividend for the current year. Warner Company's entry on receipt of its share of the dividend is

Cash	2,100	
Investment in Rose Corporation Stock		2,100
To record receipt of $2,100 dividend		
from Rose Corporation.		

Controlling Interest

A company holding more than 50% of another corporation's stock owns a controlling interest. In some cases—such as by agreement with other stockholders—control may exist with a lesser percentage of stock ownership. The financial data of controlled corporations are usually consolidated (combined) with the data of the investor company in **consolidated financial statements**. Either the cost or equity method may be used for investments in these controlled corporations; in either case, the application of consolidation procedures yields the same result. The equity method should be used for controlling-interest investments in corporations whose data is not consolidated.

PARENT–SUBSIDIARY RELATIONSHIP

A corporation that controls the policies and operations of other corporations through ownership of their stock commonly presents financial statements of the combined group in published reports. Such consolidated statements portray the financial position and operating results of affiliated companies as a single economic unit. The company holding all or a majority of the stock of the others is the **parent company,** and the wholly owned or majority-held companies are **subsidiaries.** It is important to observe that the individual companies of a group are *legal entities*, each with separate financial statements. When the financial data of these legal entities are combined, the resulting statements portray the group as an *economic entity*, as shown in Exhibit 18–1.

Consolidated financial statements present both the total resources controlled by a parent company and the aggregate results of the group's operations that are difficult to perceive when viewing only the separate reports of the individual companies. Consolidated statements are particularly valuable to the managers and stockholders of the parent company. In addition, creditors, government agencies, and the general public are informed of the magnitude and scope of an economic enterprise through consolidated statements.

Most companies prepare consolidated statements when they hold more than 50% of the subsidiary's stock. With this kind of control, the parent can usually direct the policies and activities of the subsidiary. On the other hand, the accounts of some wholly or majority owned subsidiaries may be excluded from consoli-

EXHIBIT 18–1

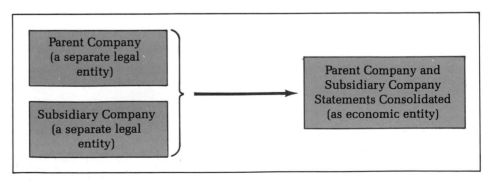

dated statements. For example, subsidiaries engaged in activities completely unrelated to those of the parent and other affiliates are normally excluded from consolidated statements. Sears, Roebuck and Company does not include its insurance firm, Allstate, in its consolidated statements, because the economic operations of an insurance company (and its accounts) are not compatible with the merchandising and manufacturing activities of the companies in Sears' consolidated statements. For similar reasons, Ford, General Motors, and FMC Corporation exclude the accounts of their wholly owned finance and insurance companies when they prepare consolidated financial statements.

Sometimes wholly or majority owned subsidiaries are located in foreign countries that restrict the parent's control of assets and operations; when the restrictions are severe, the subsidiaries' accounts may be excluded from the consolidated statements.

Whenever a subsidiary firm's accounts are not included in the consolidated statements, the parent company's investment is shown in the consolidated balance sheet as Investment in Unconsolidated Subsidiary.[1] As we mentioned earlier, the investment is accounted for under the equity method.

ACQUISITION OF SUBSIDIARIES

A corporation may obtain a subsidiary either by establishing a new firm and holding more than 50% of its voting stock or by acquiring more than 50% of the voting stock of an existing firm. Both methods have been extensively used. When an existing firm is acquired, however, the method of acquisition may play an important role in the manner of accounting for the subsidiary.

One common method of acquiring an existing firm is to give up cash, other assets, notes, or debt securities. Generally, this is a *purchase* of a subsidiary, and the **purchase method** of reporting is used in consolidated financial statements. We discuss this method of acquisition first. Another method, called *pooling of interests*, involves exchanging stock of the acquiring company for substantially all of the shares of another firm. We discuss the **pooling method** of accounting and reporting later in the chapter.

CONSOLIDATED BALANCE SHEETS AT ACQUISITION DATE

Creating a Subsidiary Company

Let us assume that, on January 1, 19XX, P Company established a new, wholly owned subsidiary, S Company, to market P Company's products. P Company acquired all of S. Company's common stock for $100,000 cash. To record this

---

[1] Often firms report condensed financial statements of unconsolidated subsidiaries in footnotes to the consolidated balance sheet.

EXHIBIT 18–2

Before Creating S Company	After Creating S Company	
P Company **Balance Sheet** **January 1, 19XX**	**P Company** **Balance Sheet** **January 1, 19XX**	**S Company** **Balance Sheet** **January 1, 19XX**
Cash and Other Assets $750,000	Cash and Other Assets $650,000	Cash $100,000
	Investment in S Company 100,000	
$750,000	$750,000	$100,000
Liabilities $200,000	Liabilities $200,000	Liabilities $ —
Common Stock 400,000	Common Stock 400,000	Common Stock 100,000
Retained Earnings 150,000	Retained Earnings 150,000	Retained Earnings —
$750,000	$750,000	$100,000

Reciprocal Items

transaction, P Company debits Investment in S Company and credits Cash for $100,000. In its records, S Company debits Cash and credits Common Stock for $100,000. Condensed balance sheets before and after the creation of the subsidiary are given in Exhibit 18–2.

Notice that the only change in P Company's balance sheet is a shift of $100,000 from Cash and Other Assets to Investment in S Company. The latter represents the 100% ownership of S Company common stock, giving P Company control over the resources of S Company ($100,000 cash). Thus, the $100,000 Investment in S Company on P Company's balance sheet and the $100,000 stockholders' equity (Common Stock) on the subsidiary's balance sheet are reciprocal items. If we combine (consolidate) the accounts on the balance sheets of the two companies at January 1, the reciprocal items must be eliminated. Otherwise, assets and stockholders' equity would be "double-counted." The eliminating entry made in a consolidated worksheet debits Common Stock (S Company) for $100,000 and credits Investment in S Company for $100,000. Exhibit 18–3 is the worksheet showing how the balance sheets are consolidated. Note that after eliminating the reciprocal elements, the consolidated balance sheet (the right-hand column in Exhibit 18–3) is identical with that of P Company before the creation of the subsidiary. This is logical because P Company commands no more resources than it did formerly. Also, observe that the stockholders' equity on the consolidated balance sheet is the parent company's—that is, *outside* shareholders. *The intercompany equity existing on the balance sheets is always eliminated.*

Acquisition of an Existing Firm

The general concept of consolidating affiliated companies is always the same, whether a subsidiary is created or an existing firm is acquired. Intercompany items—such as intercompany stockholders' equity—are eliminated so that the

EXHIBIT 18–3

P and S Companies
Consolidated Balance Sheet Worksheet
January 1, 19XX

	P Company	S Company	Eliminations Debit	Eliminations Credit	Consolidated Balance Sheet
Cash and Other Assets	650,000	100,000			750,000
Investment in S Company	100,000	—		100,000	—
	750,000	100,000			750,000
Liabilities	200,000	—			200,000
Common Stock					
P Company	400,000				400,000
S Company		100,000	100,000		—
Retained Earnings					
P Company	150,000				150,000
	750,000	100,000	100,000	100,000	750,000

consolidated statements show only the interests of outsiders. (Later we discuss the elimination of other intercompany items.)

Suppose that P Company, instead of creating a new firm, purchased 100% of the common stock of an existing firm, Z Company, for $100,000. In this case, we assume that Z Company *already has* $100,000 in Cash and Other Assets and no liabilities. The only dfference from our previous example is that Z Company's $100,000 of stockholders' equity is composed of $80,000 of Common Stock and $20,000 of Retained Earnings.

EXHIBIT 18–4

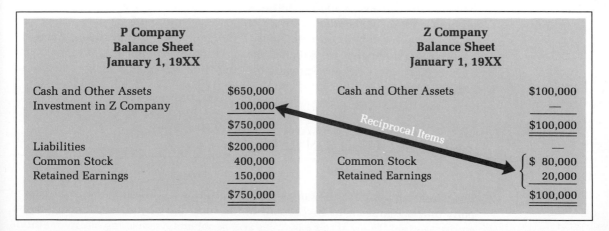

P Company Balance Sheet January 1, 19XX		Z Company Balance Sheet January 1, 19XX	
Cash and Other Assets	$650,000	Cash and Other Assets	$100,000
Investment in Z Company	100,000		—
	$750,000		$100,000
Liabilities	$200,000		—
Common Stock	400,000	Common Stock	$ 80,000
Retained Earnings	150,000	Retained Earnings	20,000
	$750,000		$100,000

Reciprocal Items

EXHIBIT 18–5

P and Z Companies
Consolidated Balance Sheet Worksheet
January 1, 19XX

	P Company	Z Company	Eliminations Debit	Eliminations Credit	Consolidated Balance Sheet
Cash and Other Assets	650,000	100,000			750,000
Investment in Z Company	100,000	—		100,000	—
	750,000	100,000			750,000
Liabilities	200,000	—			200,000
Common Stock					
P Company	400,000				400,000
Z Company		80,000	80,000		—
Retained Earnings					
P Company	150,000				150,000
Z Company		20,000	20,000		—
	750,000	100,000	100,000	100,000	750,000

The entry on P Company's books to record the acquisition debits Investment in Z Company for $100,000 and credits Cash for $100,000. Z Company makes no entry because payment is made directly to current shareholders of Z Company. Therefore, the balance sheets of the two companies *immediately after the acquisition* are as shown in Exhibit 18–4.

The only significant difference between the balance sheets in Exhibit 18–4 and the balance sheets after acquisition in Exhibit 18–2 is that the stockholders' equity of Z Company consists of $80,000 Common Stock and $20,000 Retained Earnings rather than $100,000 Common Stock. In this case, the reciprocal items are the $100,000 Investment in Z Company on P Company's balance sheet and the Common Stock and Retained Earnings ($80,000 + $20,000) on Z Company's balance sheet. To avoid double-counting assets and stockholders' equity, we must eliminate these items when consolidating the accounts of the two firms. The worksheet entry debits Common Stock (Z Company) for $80,000, debits Retained Earnings (Z Company) for $20,000, and credits Investment in Z Company for $100,000. The worksheet to prepare the consolidated balance sheet is shown in Exhibit 18–5.

CONSOLIDATED BALANCE SHEETS AFTER ACQUISITION DATE

In accounting periods following a parent–subsidiary affiliation, the parent company may account for its investment in the subsidiary by either the cost or the equity method. In all of our examples and problems, we use the equity method, because it is easier to understand.[2] Recall that under this method, the parent periodically reflects on its own records its share (100% in our example) of the subsidiary's earnings by debiting the Investment in Subsidiary account and crediting Income from Investment in Subsidiary. The latter item eventually increases the parent company's retained earnings. (If the subsidiary has a loss, the entry would be a debit to Loss from Investment in Subsidiary and a credit to Investment in Subsidiary, the debit eventually reducing the parent's retained earnings.) Whenever the subsidiary pays dividends, the parent company debits Cash and credits the Investment in Subsidiary account for the amount received.

To illustrate, let us return to the example (Exhibit 18–2) in which P Company created a subsidiary by purchasing 100% of S Company's stock for $100,000 cash. We assume that during the year following acquisition, P Company earned $40,000 *before* adding its earnings from S Company and paid no dividends. We also assume that S Company earned $20,000, paying $10,000 in dividends.

To record its share of S Company's earnings and to record the dividends received, P Company makes the following entries *in its own records:*

Investment in S Company	20,000	
Income from Investment in S Company		
(Retained Earnings)		20,000
To record 100% of S Company's earnings for the current year.		
Cash	10,000	
Investment in S Company		10,000
To record dividends received from S Company.		

The balance sheets of P Company at December 31, 19XX, are given in Exhibit 18–6.

[2] As we mentioned earlier in this chapter, both methods yield the same results when appropriate procedures are used. Consolidation procedures for both methods are taught in advanced accounting courses.

EXHIBIT 18–6

P Company Balance Sheet December 31, 19XX		S Company Balance Sheet December 31, 19XX	
Cash and Other Assets	$700,000	Cash and Other Assets	$115,000
Investment in S Company	110,000		—
	$810,000		$115,000
Liabilities	$200,000	Liabilities	$ 5,000
Common Stock	400,000	Common Stock	100,000
Retained Earnings	210,000	Retained Earnings	10,000
	$810,000		$115,000

Let us review the changes that have occurred in these two balance sheets since the date of acquisition. P Company's Cash and Other Assets has increased $50,000. This increase consists of P Company's own net income of $40,000 plus $10,000 in dividends received from S Company. (For simplicity, we assume that all of P Company's net income increases Cash and Other Assets, with liabilities remaining unchanged.) The Investment in S Company has increased $10,000 ($20,000 S Company earnings less $10,000 dividends received). P Company's Retained Earnings has increased $60,000 ($40,000 of its own net income plus $20,000 S Company net income).

For S Company, Cash and Other Assets has increased $15,000, along with a $5,000 increase in liabilities. Thus, net assets have increased $10,000. The corresponding $10,000 increase in Retained Earnings resulted from $20,000 net income less $10,000 dividends declared and paid. Exhibit 18–7 shows a worksheet to prepare a consolidated balance sheet at December 31, 19XX.

Whenever consolidated statements are prepared after the acquisition date, the worksheet entries eliminate the intercompany equity existing *at the date of the consolidated statements.* P Company's 100% interest in S Company includes all of the subsidiary's common stock and retained earnings. Therefore, the eliminating entry on the worksheet debits Common Stock (S Company) for $100,000, debits Retained Earnings (S Company) for $10,000, and credits Investment in S Company for $110,000.

A formal consolidated balance sheet is given in Exhibit 18–8. Note that the Cash and Other Assets of both firms have been combined, as well as the liabilities. The intercompany equity—100% of S Company stockholders' equity—has been eliminated; therefore, the stockholders' equity is that of the parent company.

EXHIBIT 18–7

P and S Companies
Consolidated Balance Sheet Worksheet
December 31, 19XX

	P Company	S Company	Eliminations Debit	Eliminations Credit	Consolidated Balance Sheet
Cash and Other Assets	700,000	115,000			815,000
Investment in S Company	110,000	—		110,000	—
	810,000	115,000			815,000
Liabilities	200,000	5,000			205,000
Common Stock					
P Company	400,000				400,000
S Company		100,000	100,000		—
Retained Earnings					
P Company	210,000				210,000
S Company		10,000	10,000		—
	810,000	115,000	110,000	110,000	815,000

EXHIBIT 18–8

P and S Companies
Consolidated Balance Sheet
December 31, 19XX

Cash and Other Assets	$815,000	Liabilities	$205,000
		Common Stock	400,000
		Retained Earnings	210,000
	$815,000		$815,000

MAJORITY-HELD SUBSIDIARIES

When a firm owns more than a 50% but less than a 100% interest in another firm, the parent company's interest is a **majority interest.** The interest of the other (outside) stockholders of the subsidiary company is called the **minority interest.** In preparing a consolidated balance sheet for a parent company and a majority-held subsidiary, the assets and liabilities of the affiliated companies are combined in the usual way to show their total resources and liabilities. The parent company's equity in the subsidiary at the date of the consolidated statements is eliminated as before, but in this case, the equity represents less than 100% of the subsidiary's common stock and retained earnings. The amount of the subsidiary's common stock and retained earnings not eliminated, which represents the minority interest in the subsidiary, will appear on the consolidated balance sheet.

For example, assume that P Company purchased 80% of Q Company's voting stock on January 1, 19XX, for $160,000. After the acquisition, the separate balance sheets of the two firms appeared as shown in Exhibit 18–9.

EXHIBIT 18–9

P and Q Companies
Balance Sheets
January 1, 19XX

	P Company	Q Company
Cash and Other Assets	$590,000	$220,000
Investment in Q Company	160,000	—
	$750,000	$220,000
Liabilities	$200,000	$ 20,000
Common Stock	400,000	150,000
Retained Earnings	150,000	50,000
	$750,000	$220,000

Note that Q Company's stockholders' equity is $200,000 ($150,000 Common Stock and $50,000 Retained Earnings). The equity acquired by P Company is therefore $160,000 (80% of $200,000), which is the amount P Company paid for its interest. This intercompany equity at the date of the consolidated statements is eliminated. The remaining 20% minority interest, however, must be shown in the consolidated balance sheet. In other words, the minority, or outside, shareholders have a $40,000 interest in the stockholders' equity of Q Company (20% of $200,000). The worksheet entry to eliminate the intercompany equity and to reflect the minority interest debits Common Stock (Q Company) for $150,000, debits Retained Earnings (Q Company) for $50,000, credits Investment in Q Company for $160,000, and credits Minority Interest for $40,000. The worksheet to prepare the consolidated balance sheet is given in Exhibit 18–10.

A formal consolidated balance sheet for the two companies, prepared from the right-hand column of the worksheet, is given in Exhibit 18–11. Note that the total consolidated stockholders' equity of $590,000 consists of the parent company's common stock and retained earnings (totaling $550,000) and the $40,000 minority interest. Thus, the interests of outside shareholders (the parent firm's shareholders and the subsidiary's minority shareholders) are portrayed in the consolidated balance sheet. Sometimes, in formal consolidated balance sheets, the minority interest amount is shown between the liabilities and the stockholders' equity. Most financial analysts, however, consider the minority interest part of stockholders' equity, and it is probably a better practice to classify it with the stockholders' equity.

EXHIBIT 18–10

P and Q Companies
Consolidated Balance Sheet Worksheet
January 1, 19XX

	P Company	Q Company	Eliminations Debit	Eliminations Credit	Consolidated Balance Sheet
Cash and Other Assets	590,000	220,000			810,000
Investment in Q Company	160,000	—		160,000	—
	750,000	220,000			810,000
Liabilities	200,000	20,000			220,000
Minority Interest				40,000	40,000
Common Stock					
P Company	400,000				400,000
Q Company		150,000	150,000		—
Retained Earnings					
P Company	150,000				150,000
Q Company		50,000	50,000		—
	750,000	220,000	200,000	200,000	810,000

DIFFERENCES BETWEEN ACQUISITION COST AND BOOK VALUE

So far in our examples, we have assumed that the amount paid by the parent company to acquire a particular interest in a subsidiary exactly equals the book value of the interest acquired. In the real world this rarely happens. In fact, the parent firm almost always pays more for its interest than the book values shown on the subsidiary's balance sheet. This occurs for one of two reasons, or a combination of them. First, the recorded values of the subsidiary's assets are often understated in terms of current fair market values, a common situation with the inflation of recent years. Second, the parent firm may be willing to pay an additional amount for an unrecorded asset of the subsidiary—goodwill—if the subsidiary's earning power or its potential earning power is higher than normal for similar firms.

Suppose that P Company acquires a 100% interest in Y Company's voting stock for $125,000 when Y Company has the balance sheet depicted in Exhibit 18–12. Obviously, P Company is paying $125,000 for a 100% interest in a firm with a net book value of $100,000. Negotiations for the purchase, however, reveal that Y Company's plant and equipment are undervalued by $15,000 and that its potential for future superior earnings is valued at an additional $10,000.

In preparing a consolidated balance sheet, we make a worksheet entry that eliminates the intercompany equity and reflects the additional asset values established by the acquisition. The entry includes the following debits: Common Stock (Y Company), $80,000; Retained Earnings (Y Company), $20,000; Plant and Equipment, $15,000; and Goodwill from Consolidation, $10,000. A credit of $125,000 would be made to Investment in Y Company. Thus, the intercompany equity in the recorded book values of the subsidiary is eliminated, and an additional amount of assets, $25,000, is reflected in the consolidated balance sheet.

EXHIBIT 18–11

P and Q Companies Consolidated Balance Sheet January 1, 19XX				
Cash and Other Assets	$810,000	Liabilities		$220,000
		Stockholders' Equity:		
		Minority Interest	$ 40,000	
		Common Stock	400,000	
		Retained Earnings	150,000	590,000
	$810,000			$810,000

The goodwill from consolidation[3] appears as an intangible asset on the consolidated balance sheet. In the consolidated statements of subsequent years, the amount paid in excess of the equity acquired in the subsidiary is amortized over

[3] Often this is called Excess of Cost over Book Value of Investment in Subsidiary. Many accountants and financial analysts, however, prefer to call it Goodwill from Consolidation.

GHOSTS OF ACQUISITIONS PAST

Nobody ever denied that takeovers like U.S. Steel's merger with Marathon Oil or Occidental Petroleum's gobbling up of Cities Service are expensive. But a recent Supreme Court opinion could make some of these giant acquisitions far pricier than stockholders or corporate officers ever expected. The decision sides squarely with the IRS on the tax benefit rule—an issue that has divided appellate courts for years and could cost several corporations millions in additional taxes.

When one company purchases another company using cash or notes instead of swapping stock, for example, it usually writes up the value of its new property's assets and then starts to expense them again. After all, the acquiring company pays a premium because it sees more value in its acquisition target than the balance sheet reveals. The bottom line: one asset, two tax savings.

Sadly, however, those days may soon be over. The IRS has been trying to stop this so-called double dipping for years, and the Supreme Court has just lent authority to the service's argument. "We could look at any transaction and apply the tax benefit rule to it," says one high-ranking IRS source who requested anonymity. "I can't give you a number because I have no statistics, but it will affect everyone that has stepped up the value of the assets they bought." Since company books are open to the IRS for three years and often longer, even old transactions will be subject to scrutiny.

"There have been almost no major acquisitions for cash or notes in the last several years in which the companies don't have some exposure to the IRS," says Robert Willens, Peat Marwick Mitchell's widely respected tax partner. "If a corporate taxpayer took an aggressive position—and

there is no doubt that many did—they don't have any argument to make anymore. The IRS rule applies."

Particularly vulnerable are companies that paid a premium for intangible assets such as patents or acquired large quantities of short-lived assets such as tools and supplies. These are items that often have little value on an acquired company's books, though they often contribute a great deal to the worth of an acquisition. "If an acquiring company put a value on a patent, the government may now say, 'Well, you will have to pay taxes on the R&D expense that went into that patent,'" explains Richard Berkowitz, a tax partner in Arthur Andersen's mergers and acquisitions group.

Take a look a the potential impact on a company like Warner-Lambert, which bought IMED, a designer of electronic medical instruments, for $468 million last August. IMED had expensed over $4 million in research and development costs during 1982 alone. If Warner elected to write up the value of assets associated with IMED's research, it could suddenly wind up owing the IRS taxes on at least that amount.

Naturally, much of the potential liability here still depends on how aggressively the IRS takes advantage of its newfound clout. But companies that have rejoiced over winning nasty takeover battles in the last several years have good reason to worry. Their success may become a lot more expensive. And for companies interested in takeovers of the future, acquisition costs have just gone up.

From *Forbes*, May 23, 1983, page 122, "Ghosts of Acquisitions Past," by Ellyn Spragins.

EXHIBIT 18–12

P Company Balance Sheet January 1, 19XX		Y Company Balance Sheet January 1, 19XX	
Cash and Other Assets	$XXX,XXX	Current Assets	$ 40,000
Investment in Y Company	125,000	Plant and Equipment	60,000
	$XXX,XXX		$100,000
Liabilities	$XXX,XXX	Liabilities	$ —
Common Stock	XXX,XXX	Common Stock	80,000
Retained Earnings	XXX,XXX	Retained Earnings	20,000
	$XXX,XXX		$100,000

the life of the assets to which the amount has been assigned. In the case of goodwill, the period cannot exceed 40 years.

We rarely encounter a situation in which the parent company pays less than the equity acquired for a particular interest in a subsidiary company. If this situation occurs, an analogous treatment is used to prepare a consolidated balance sheet. If the difference is attributed to an overvaluation of subsidiary assets, the eliminating entry on the worksheet credits such assets. On the other hand, if the difference is attributed to the subsidiary's poor earnings record, an account called Excess of Book Value of Investment in Subsidiary over Cost of Equity Acquired is credited. In a consolidated balance sheet, such an amount is probably best subtracted from total consolidated assets.

CONSOLIDATED INCOME STATEMENT

So far we have dealt only with consolidated balance sheets. Now we look at the problem of consolidating the income statements of affiliated firms. If we wish to show the scope of operations of affiliated companies as an entity, combining the revenue, cost of goods sold, and expenses of the several companies is logical. In preparing a consolidated income statement, however, we should present only the results of transactions with firms and individuals *outside* the entity. Any intercompany transactions—such as intercompany sales and purchases—should be eliminated. Likewise, revenue and expense amounts representing services rendered by one firm to an affiliated firm should be eliminated. Otherwise, the consolidated income statement would distort the extent of the group's operations.

For example, if a single company has two divisions—one manufacturing products and another marketing them—transfers of products from the manufacturing division to the marketing division are not regarded as sales transactions. Only sales by the marketing division are reflected in the firm's income statement.

EXHIBIT 18-13

P Company Income Statement For the Year Ended December 31, 19XX	
Sales	$500,000
Cost of Goods Sold (including $30,000 of purchases from S Company)	300,000
Gross Profit	$200,000
Operating Expenses (including income taxes)	160,000
Net Income	$ 40,000

S Company Income Statement For the Year Ended December 31, 19XX	
Sales (including $30,000 sold to P Company)	$200,000
Cost of Goods Sold	140,000
Gross Profit	$ 60,000
Operating Expenses (including income taxes)	40,000
Net Income	$ 20,000

The same situation exists when two separate firms make up one consolidated entity.

To illustrate the procedures for preparing a consolidated income statement, we use Exhibit 18–13, the separate income statements of P Company and its 75%-held subsidiary, S Company. For simplicity, we assume that P Company has not yet reflected its 75% share of S Company's net income in its own income statement.[4]

We have indicated in the income statements that $30,000 of S Company's sales were to P Company. Assume that P Company, in turn, sold all of this merchandise to outsiders. In preparing a consolidated income statement, we must eliminate $30,000 from the sales reported by S Company and from the purchases (in cost of goods sold) reported by P Company. The worksheet to prepare a consolidated income statement for the two firms is given in Exhibit 18–14.

In Exhibit 18–14, the $30,000 in S Company's sales and the reciprocal amount in P Company's cost of goods sold have been eliminated so that only sales to outsiders are reflected in the consolidated income statement. Notice that this elimination does not affect consolidated net income, because the same amount is excluded from both sales and cost of goods sold. It does, however, avoid distorting the sales volume and costs of the group. Of the $60,000 aggregate net income of the two firms, the $5,000 minority interest (25% of S Company's net income) is deducted, so the consolidated net income of the affiliated firms is $55,000. Thus, the $55,000 consolidated net income consists of $40,000 (the parent's net income from its own operations) plus $15,000 (the parent's 75% interest in the $20,000 subsidiary net income). The consolidated net income statement, shown in Exhibit 18–15, is prepared directly from the last column of the worksheet.

[4]If P Company had already included its share of S Company's earnings in its own income statement, this amount would have to be eliminated to avoid double-counting when the revenue and expenses of the two firms are consolidated.

EXHIBIT 18–14

P and S Companies
Consolidated Income Statement Worksheet
For the Year Ended December 31, 19XX

	P Company	S Company	Eliminations Debit	Eliminations Credit	Consolidated Income Statement
Sales	500,000	200,000	30,000		670,000
Cost of Goods Sold	300,000	140,000		30,000	410,000
Gross Profit	200,000	60,000			260,000
Expenses (including income taxes)	160,000	40,000			200,000
Net Income	40,000	20,000			60,000
Minority Interest in Net Income of S Company (25% of $20,000)					(5,000)
Consolidated Net Income					55,000

EXHIBIT 18–15

P and S Companies
Consolidated Income Statement
For the Year Ended December 31, 19XX

Sales	$670,000
Cost of Goods Sold	410,000
Gross Profit	$260,000
Expenses (including income taxes)	200,000
Net Income before Minority Interest	$ 60,000
Less: Minority Interest in Net Income of S Company	5,000
Consolidated Net Income	$ 55,000

CONSOLIDATED RETAINED EARNINGS STATEMENT

Preparation of a consolidated retained earnings statement for affiliated firms is a relatively simple task, and worksheets are rarely required. Using our previous example, assume that the January 1, 19XX, balance of consolidated retained earnings for P and S companies amounted to $260,000 and that P Company declared cash dividends of $25,000 during 19XX. The 19XX consolidated retained earnings statement for the two companies is given in Exhibit 18–16.

EXHIBIT 18–16

P and S Companies
Consolidated Retained Earnings Statement
For the Year Ended December 31, 19XX

Consolidated Retained Earnings, January 1	$260,000
Add: Consolidated Net Income for the Year	55,000
	$315,000
Less: Dividends Declared (by P Company)	25,000
Consolidated Retained Earnings, December 31	$290,000

Observe that the consolidated retained earnings balance is increased by consolidated net income, which consisted of P Company's earnings plus its 75% share of S Company's earnings ($40,000 + $15,000 = $55,000). P Company enters the $15,000 income from S Company on its books by increasing the Investment in S Company account. Only dividends declared by the parent company appear in the consolidated retained earnings statement. We pointed out earlier that dividends received by the parent company from the subsidiary are credited to the Investment in Subsidiary account. Dividends paid by the subsidiary to the minority shareholders reduce the minority interest in the consolidated balance sheet.

OTHER INTERCOMPANY ACCOUNTS

Because affiliated companies often engage in a variety of intercompany transactions, treating the resulting amounts in consolidated statements can be fairly complex. For example, transactions may include intercompany loans, intercompany bond and preferred stockholdings, or plant and equipment transfers. Because this chapter is only an introduction to consolidated statements, we discuss here only some of the most commonly encountered relationships—intercompany receivables and payables and intercompany profit in assets.

Intercompany Receivables and Payables In our example of the preparation of a consolidated income statement (Exhibit 18–14), S Company, a 75%-held subsidiary, sold merchandise to P Company for $30,000 during the year. Suppose that at year-end, P Company still owed $15,000 to S Company for some of the merchandise. P Company therefore had an account payable to S Company for $15,000 in its balance sheet at year-end, and S Company showed a receivable from P Company for the same amount. The consolidated balance sheet should show receivables and payables only with *outsiders*; otherwise both total receivables and payables of the consolidated entity are overstated. Therefore, the reciprocal receivable and payable of $15,000 must be eliminated in preparing the consolidated balance sheet, as shown in the following partial worksheet:

	P Company	S Company	Eliminations Debit	Eliminations Credit	Consolidated Balance Sheet
Assets					
Accounts Receivable	80,000	60,000		15,000	125,000
.					
.					
.					
Liabilities					
Accounts Payable	45,000	40,000	15,000		70,000
.					
.					
.					

Unrealized Intercompany Profit in Assets

In the above example, when S Company sold P Company $30,000 worth of merchandise, we assumed that P Company in turn sold all of it to outside parties. As far as the entity is concerned, a profit was *realized* on *all* of the merchandise. If the merchandise had cost S Company $22,000, and P Company eventually sold all of it to outsiders for $36,000, the entity would have made a profit of $14,000 on the merchandise. Remember that the only elimination necessary to avoid double-counting was excluding $30,000 from S Company sales and $30,000 from P Company's cost of goods sold.

Suppose, however, that P Company still had $10,000 worth of the merchandise in its inventory at year-end. Also assume that S Company's cost for the remaining $10,000 worth of merchandise had been $8,000. In this situation, the $2,000 of S Company profit residing in P Company's inventory is *unrealized* from the standpoint of the entity. In a consolidated balance sheet, the $2,000 is eliminated from P Company's inventory amount and from S Company's retained earnings. This elimination is made in addition to the $30,000 elimination from S Company's sales and P Company's cost of goods sold.

In addition to merchandise, a firm may sell an affiliate such assets as securities, plant, and equipment. Following our general rule, any intercompany profit residing in the assets of the entity must be eliminated in preparing consolidated financial statements; only profits earned in dealing with outsiders can be reflected in consolidated net income and in consolidated retained earnings statements.

The technical procedures for handling these detailed adjustments in preparing consolidated financial statements are somewhat complex; they are explored in detail in advanced accounting courses.

CONSOLIDATED STATEMENTS—POOLING METHOD

In all of the foregoing examples, we assumed that an acquiring company *purchased* a controlling interest in the shares of another firm by issuing cash, other assets, or debt. Thus, a purchase and sale transaction occurred, and we used the *purchase method* to prepare consolidated statements.

On the other hand, if the acquiring company obtains substantially all (90% or more) of a subsidiary company's shares by *issuing its own shares* (and by meeting certain other criteria[5]), a **pooling of interests** has occurred. In a pooling of interests, stockholders of the subsidiary company become stockholders of the parent company. Basically, two sets of interests "unite" rather than a purchase and sale transaction taking place.

If a combination is a pooling of interests, the parent's investment and the consolidated financial statements are prepared according to the pooling method of accounting. In a consolidated balance sheet prepared under the pooling method, the *book values* of the affiliated companies are combined. Of course, the market values of each firm's stock play an important part in determining the number of shares exchanged for the subsidiary's shares. However, once the negotiations are completed, the market values of the shares play no role in recording the parent's investment or in preparing consolidated financial statements.

Because the consolidated statements reflect the book values of the subsidiary's assets, we do not revalue these assets, nor does any goodwill (excess of cost over equity acquired) emerge from the consolidation. However, under the purchase method, the subsidiary's assets are revalued (almost invariably upward during periods of rising prices), and goodwill often appears in the consolidated balance sheet. Also, the increase in tangible assets and any goodwill are amortized over future periods. Consequently, future yearly consolidated earnings are less under the purchase method than under the pooling method.

Another facet of the pooling method is that the subsidiary's and the parent's net incomes for the entire period of the acquisition year can be combined regardless of the date of acquisition. For example, suppose a parent company earned $500,000 net income in the year that it used the pooling method to acquire a 100% interest in a subsidiary that earned $400,000. The acquisition occurred October 1, and the subsidiary's earnings for the last quarter were $100,000. The pooling method combines the subsidiary's entire $400,000 with the parent's earnings, for a total consolidated net income of $900,000. With the purchase method, only the last quarter's earnings of the subsidiary ($100,000) are combined with the parent's $500,000 earnings, for a net income of $600,000.

We summarize the pooling method as follows:

(1) With the pooling method, total consolidated assets do not increase, because book values of each firm are combined. With the purchase method, asset revaluation and goodwill (excess of cost over equity acquired) often increase total consolidated assets.

(2) Without amortization of revaluation increases or goodwill, the pooling method results in higher future earnings than the purchase method.

---

[5] The criteria for determining whether a pooling has occurred are set forth in *Opinions of the Accounting Principles Board, No. 16*, "Business Combinations" (New York: American Institute of Certified Public Accountants, 1970), page 297.

(3) When pooling is used, parent company and subsidiary earnings for the entire year are combined in the year of acquisition. With the purchase method, only the subsidiary's earnings after the acquisition date are included with parent company earnings.

Combination by pooling was widely used in the 1960s, because this method enabled companies to show an immediate (often synthetic) improvement in their earnings records *purely as a result of the combination* rather than through improved operations. Combining firms were allowed wide latitude in their methods of recording and consolidation, regardless of the nature of the exchange, with the result that the pooling method was selected for most combinations. In 1970, however, the Accounting Principles Board issued *Opinion No. 16*, "Business Combinations," which curtailed certain abuses by specifying more restrictive criteria that combining firms must meet to use the pooling method of accounting.

USEFULNESS OF CONSOLIDATED STATEMENTS

Consolidated statements present an integrated report of an economic unit comprising a number of business enterprises related through stock ownership. In fact, no other way can depict, fairly concisely, the extent of resources and scope of operations of many companies subject to common control.

The statements do have certain limitations, however. The status or performance of weak constituents in a group can be "masked" through consolidation with successful units. Rates of return, ratios, and trend percentages calculated from consolidated statements may sometimes prove deceptive because they are really composite calculations. Shareholders and creditors of controlled companies who are interested in their legal rights and prerogatives should examine the separate financial statements of the relevant constituent companies.

In recent years, supplemental disclosures have improved the quality of consolidated statements, particularly those of *conglomerates*—entities with diversified lines of business. Both the Financial Accounting Standards Board and the Securities and Exchange Commission have stipulated that certain firms disclose information regarding revenue, income from operations, and identifiable assets for various business segments.

DEMONSTRATION PROBLEM FOR REVIEW

On January 1, 19XX, the Montana Company purchased 75% of the common stock of the Utah Company for $180,000. On that date, the stockholders' equity of Utah Company consisted of $200,000 of common stock and $40,000 in retained earnings. Separate balance sheets of the two firms at December 31, 19XX are given on the next page.

Montana and Utah Companies
Balance Sheets
December 31, 19XX

Assets	Montana	Utah
Investment in Utah	$195,000	—
Other Assets	305,000	$300,000
	$500,000	$300,000
Liabilities and Stockholders' Equity		
Liabilities	$100,000	$ 40,000
Common Stock	300,000	200,000
Retained Earnings	100,000	60,000
	$500,000	$300,000

Neither firm declared or paid dividends during the year. At year-end, Utah Company owed $7,000 to Montana Company on a loan made during the year.

REQUIRED
Prepare a consolidated balance sheet worksheet at December 31, 19XX.

SOLUTION TO DEMONSTRATION PROBLEM

Montana and Utah Companies
Consolidated Balance Sheet Worksheet
December 31, 19XX

	Montana	Utah	Eliminations Debit		Eliminations Credit		Consolidated Balance Sheet
Investment in Utah	195,000	—			(a)	195,000	—
Other Assets	305,000	300,000			(b)	7,000	598,000
	500,000	300,000					598,000
Liabilities	100,000	40,000	(b)	7,000			133,000
Minority Interest					(a)	65,000	65,000
Common Stock							
Montana Company	300,000						300,000
Utah Company		200,000	(a)	200,000			—
Retained Earnings							
Montana Company	100,000						100,000
Utah Company		60,000	(a)	60,000			—
	500,000	300,000		267,000		267,000	598,000

Utah Company had earnings of $20,000 during the year, because its retained earnings increased from $40,000 to $60,000 and no dividends were declared. At December 31, Montana Company's $195,000 investment consisted of the $180,000 originally paid plus $15,000—its 75% share of Utah Company's earnings. At December 31, the minority interest is $65,000—25% of the total stockholders' equity of Utah Company (25% of $260,000).

KEY POINTS TO REMEMBER

(1) Long-term stock investments are of three types:
  (a) Noncontrolling and noninfluential interest, that is, amounting to less than 20% of the investee's voting stock. Such investments are recorded at cost, and the portfolio is valued at the lower of total cost or market at each year-end. Unrealized losses are shown contra to stockholders' equity.
  (b) Influential but noncontrolling interest, that is, amounting to 20–50% of the investee's voting stock. Such investments are recorded at cost, then adjusted periodically according to the equity method. The firm's share of the investee's earnings is added to and dividends are deducted from carrying value.
  (c) Controlling interest, that is, amounting to over 50% of the investee's voting stock. The investment may be carried on either the cost or equity basis; the application of consolidation procedures results in the same consolidated statements under either method.

(2) When a firm acquires another company's stock by exchanging cash, assets, notes, or debt securities, the acquisition is a purchase. If less than 90% of another firm's stock is acquired, the acquisition is a purchase, regardless of the media of exchange. However, if the acquiring firm obtains 90% or more of the other firm's shares by issuing its own shares, the transaction is usually regarded as a pooling of interests.

(3) In a purchase combination, the acquiring company initially records its investment at cost. Any amount in excess of the book value of the acquired firm's net assets is allocated among specific assets when possible. Any unallocated amount is goodwill, which must be amortized over a period of years.

(4) In a pooling combination, the parent firm records its investment in accordance with the book value of the acquired firm's net assets. Cost (as measured by the market value of shares exchanged) is ignored. The acquired firm's retained earnings at acquisition date are added to those of the acquiring company. Earnings of both companies for the period when the acquisition occurred are likewise combined.

(5) A parent company that carries its investment in a subsidiary under the equity method—as illustrated in this chapter—uses the following accounting procedures:
  (a) The parent periodically debits Investment in Subsidiary and credits Income from Subsidiary for its share of subsidiary earnings. Dividends received from the subsidiary are debited to Cash and credited to Investment in Subsidiary.
  (b) The parent eliminates its equity in the subsidiary existing when the consolidated balance sheet is prepared.

QUESTIONS

18–1 What is a noncontrolling and noninfluential long-term stock investment?

18–2 How are noncontrolling and noninfluential long-term stock investments reported in the balance sheet? Where are unrealized losses on the portfolio of such investments reported?

18–3 Describe the accounting procedures used when a stock investment represents from 20–50% of the voting stock.

18–4 Describe the accounting procedures used when a stock investment represents over 50% of the voting stock.

18–5 What is the purpose of consolidated financial statements?

18–6 In a recent annual report, FMC Corporation's consolidated financial statements showed an amount under Investments that included a 100% interest in FMC Finance Corporation and a 50% interest in Ketchikan Pulp Corporation and its subsidiaries. The latter investment represents a 50–50 joint venture with Louisiana–Pacific Corporation. Explain why the accounts of these firms are not consolidated with the accounts of FMC and its other subsidiaries. On what accounting basis are the investments in these unconsolidated subsidiaries carried?

18–7 What is the difference between a *purchase* acquisition and a *pooling of interests?*

18–8 P Company purchases all of the common stock of S Company for $250,000 when S Company has $200,000 of common stock and $50,000 of retained earnings. If a consolidated balance sheet is prepared immediately after the acquisition, what amounts are eliminated in preparing it?

18–9 Suppose, in Question 18–8, that P Company acquires only 80% of S Company's common stock by paying $200,000. If a consolidated balance sheet is prepared immediately after the acquisition, what amounts are eliminated in preparing this statement? What amount of minority interest appears in the consolidated balance sheet?

18–10 Explain the entries made in a parent company's records under the equity method of accounting to (a) reflect its share of the subsidiary's net income for the period and (b) record the receipt of dividends from the subsidiary.

18–11 On January 1 of the current year, P Company purchased 70% of the common stock of S Company for $400,000. During the year, S Company had $60,000 of net income and paid $20,000 in cash dividends. At year-end, what amount appears in P Company's balance sheet as Investment in S Company under the equity method?

18–12 Cable Company purchased an interest in Dunn Company for $230,000 when Dunn Company had $180,000 of common stock and $40,000 of retained earnings.
(a) If Cable Company had acquired a 100% interest in Dunn Company, what amount of Goodwill from Consolidation would appear on the consolidated balance sheet? (Assume that Dunn's assets are fairly valued.)
(b) If Cable had acquired only a 90% interest in Dunn Company, what amount of Goodwill from Consolidation would appear?

18–13 Pilgrim Company purchased a 75% interest in Alden Company on January 1 of the current year. Pilgrim Company had $350,000 net income for the current year before reflecting its share of Alden Company's net income. If Alden Company had net income of $60,000 for the year, what is the consolidated net income for the year?

18–14 Bryce Company, which owns 80% of Crown Company, sold merchandise during the year to Crown Company for $50,000. The merchandise cost Bryce Company $40,000. If Crown Company in turn sold all of the merchandise to outsiders for $60,000, what eliminating entry related to these transactions does Bryce make in preparing a consolidated income statement for the year?

18–15 Suppose, in Question 18–14, that Crown Company still owed Bryce Company $28,000 for the merchandise acquired during the year. What eliminating entry is made for this item in preparing a consolidated balance sheet at year-end?

18–16 P Company acquired 100% of S Company on September 1 of the current year. Explain why the consolidated earnings of the two firms for the current year might be greater if the transaction is treated as a pooling of interests rather than a purchase.

18–17 What are the inherent limitations of consolidated financial statements?

EXERCISES

18–18 As a long-term investment, 1,500 shares of Vulcan Company common stock were acquired on March 10, 19X1, at a total cost of $70,540. The investment represented 15% of the company's voting stock. On December 28, 19X1, Vulcan Company declared a cash dividend of $1.20 per share, which was received on January 15, 19X2. Dividend income is recorded when received. Present the necessary journal entries to reflect (a) the purchase of the stock and (b) the receipt of the cash dividend.

18–19 Assume the 1,500 shares purchased in Exercise 18–18 represent 25% of Vulcan Company's voting stock. Vulcan Company's 19X1 net income was $40,000. Using the equity method, present the journal entries to reflect (a) the purchase of the stock, (b) the proportionate share of Vulcan Company's 19X1 net income (dated December 31, 19X1), and (c) the receipt of the cash dividend.

18–20 During its first year of operations, a firm purchased the following noncontrolling and noninfluential long-term investments:

> 1,000 shares of A Company stock at $30 per share
> 2,000 shares of B Company stock at $40 per share

At year-end, the market value of the A Company stock was $26 per share, and the market value of the B Company stock was $41 per share. What was the unrealized loss at year-end, and where does it appear in the firm's financial statements?

18–21 On January 1 of the current year, Briggs Company purchased all of the common shares of Reed Company for $180,000 cash. On this date, the stockholders' equity of Briggs Company consisted of $500,000 in common stock and $120,000 in retained earnings. Reed Company had $150,000 in common stock and $30,000 in retained earnings.

(a) Give the worksheet eliminating entry to prepare a consolidated balance sheet on the acquisition date.

(b) What amount of total stockholders' equity appears on the consolidated balance sheet?

18–22 Price Company purchased 80% of the common stock of Vale Company for $240,000 in cash and notes when the stockholders' equity of Vale Company consisted of $250,000 in common stock and $50,000 in retained earnings. On the acquisition date, the stockholders' equity of Price Company consisted of $600,000 in common stock and $120,000 in retained earnings. Present the stockholders' equity section in the consolidated balance sheet prepared on the acquisition date.

18–23 On January 1 of the current year, Davis Company purchased all of the common shares of Holton Company for $400,000 cash and notes. Balance sheets of the two firms immediately after the acquisition were as follows:

	Davis	Holton
Current Assets	$1,600,000	$ 80,000
Investment in Holton Company	400,000	—
Plant and Equipment	3,000,000	320,000
	$5,000,000	$400,000
Liabilities	$1,000,000	$ 40,000
Common Stock	3,500,000	300,000
Retained Earnings	500,000	60,000
	$5,000,000	$400,000

During the negotiations for the purchase, Holton's plant and equipment were appraised at $345,000. Furthermore, Davis concluded that an additional $15,000 demanded by Holton's shareholders was warranted because Holton's earning power was somewhat better than the industry average. Give the worksheet eliminating entry to prepare a consolidated balance sheet on the acquisition date.

18–24 Gordon Company purchased a 70% interest in Howe Company for $520,000 cash on January 1 of the current year. During the year, Howe Company earned $60,000 net income and declared and paid half its earnings in dividends. Gordon Company carries its investment in Howe Company on the equity method. What is the carrying value of Gordon Company's Investment in Howe Company account at year-end?

18–25 Arizona Company has an 80% interest in Nevada Company. During the current year, Nevada Company sold merchandise costing $36,000 to the Arizona Company for $50,000. Assuming Arizona Company sold all of the merchandise to outsiders, what worksheet eliminating entry should be made in preparing a consolidated income statement for the period?

18–26 On January 1, 19XX, Butler Company purchased for $210,000 cash a 90% stock interest in Clipper, Inc., which then had common stock of $180,000 and retained earnings of $40,000. On December 31, 19XX, after Butler had taken up its share of Clipper's earnings, the balance sheets of the two companies were as follows:

	Butler	Clipper, Inc.
Investment in Clipper, Inc. (at equity)	$228,000	—
Other Assets	572,000	$280,000
	$800,000	$280,000
Liabilities	$180,000	$ 40,000
Common Stock	500,000	180,000
Retained Earnings	120,000	60,000
	$800,000	$280,000

Clipper, Inc. did not declare or pay dividends during the year.

(a) What was the net income of Clipper, Inc., for the year?

(b) The consolidated balance sheet prepared December 31, 19XX would show
  (1) What amount of common stock?
  (2) What amount of retained earnings?
  (3) What amount of minority interest?

(c) Assuming that Clipper, Inc., assets are properly stated, what amount of goodwill from consolidation is reported?

PROBLEMS

18–27 The following selected transactions and information are for the Melville Corporation for 19X1 and 19X2.

19X1

July 1   Purchased, as a long-term investment, 1,000 shares of Dow-Jones, Inc. common stock at a total cost of $46,200. This interest is noninfluential and noncontrolling.

Oct. 1   Purchased, as a long-term investment, 2,000 shares of Yarmouth, Inc. common stock at a total cost of $68,400, and 2,000 shares of Brixton, Inc. common stock at a total cost of $80,000. Both investments are noninfluential and noncontrolling interests.

Nov. 9   Received a cash dividend of 80 cents per share on the Yarmouth, Inc. stock.

Dec. 31   The Dow-Jones, Inc. shares have a market value of $48 per share; the Yarmouth, Inc. shares have a market value of $28 per share; and the Brixton, Inc. shares have a market value of $41 per share. (An entry should be made to adjust the carrying value of the portfolio to the lower of cost or market.)

19X2

Feb. 1   Sold the Yarmouth, Inc. stock for $30 per share less an $80 commission fee.

Dec. 31   The market value of the long-term stock investment portfolio is as follows: Dow-Jones, Inc., $49 per share; Brixton, Inc., $38 per share. (An entry should be made to adjust the carrying value of the investments and the unrealized loss account.)

REQUIRED

Give the journal entries to record these transactions and adjustments.

18–28 On January 2, 19X1, Gardner Corporation purchased, as a long-term invest-ment, 8,000 shares of Regent Company common stock for $24 per share, including commissions and taxes. On December 31, 19X1, Regent Company announced a net income of $160,000 for the year and a dividend of $1.80 per share, payable January 20, 19X2, to stockholders of record on January 10, 19X2. Gardner Corporation received its dividend on January 23, 19X2.

REQUIRED

(a) Assume the stock acquired by Gardner Corporation represents 14% of Regent Company's voting stock. Prepare all journal entries appropriate for this investment, beginning with the purchase on January 2, 19X1, and ending with the receipt of the dividend on January 23, 19X2. (Gardner Corporation recognizes dividend income when received.)

(b) Assume the stock acquired by Gardner Corporation represents 25% of Regent Company's voting stock. Prepare all journal entries appropriate for this investment, beginning with the purchase on January 2, 19X1, and ending with the receipt of the dividend on January 23, 19X2.

18–29 Sigma Company purchased all of York Company's common stock for cash on January 1, 19XX, after which the separate balance sheets of the two corpora-tions appeared as follows:

Sigma and York Companies
Balance Sheets
January 1, 19XX

	Sigma	York
Investment in York Company	$ 420,000	—
Other Assets	1,080,000	$500,000
	$1,500,000	$500,000
Liabilities	$ 500,000	$120,000
Common Stock	750,000	300,000
Retained Earnings	250,000	80,000
	$1,500,000	$500,000

During the negotiations for the purchase, Sigma Company determined that the appraised value of York Company's Other Assets amounted to $530,000.

REQUIRED

(a) Give the worksheet entry to eliminate the intercompany equity and to reflect the appraised value of York Company's assets.

(b) What amount of total assets should appear on a January 1 consolidated balance sheet?

(c) What amount of total stockholders' equity should appear on a January 1 consolidated balance sheet?

18–30 On January 1, 19XX, Denver Company purchased all of the common stock of

Billings Company for $300,000 cash. The stockholders' equity of Billings consisted of $250,000 in common stock and $50,000 in retained earnings. On December 31, 19XX, the separate balance sheets of the two firms were as follows:

Denver and Billings Companies
Balance Sheets
December 31, 19XX

	Denver	Billings
Cash	$ 40,000	$ 30,000
Accounts Receivable	80,000	70,000
Investment in Billings Company (at equity)	310,000	—
Other Assets	370,000	250,000
	$800,000	$350,000
Accounts Payable	$ 50,000	$ 40,000
Common Stock	650,000	250,000
Retained Earnings	100,000	60,000
	$800,000	$350,000

During the year, Billings Company had net income of $25,000. At December 31, Billings owed Denver $10,000 on account for merchandise.

REQUIRED
(a) What amount of dividends did Billings Company declare and pay during the year?
(b) Give Denver Company's journal entries that affect the Investment in Billings Company account.
(c) What amount of total assets would appear in a December 31, 19XX consolidated balance sheet?

18–31 On January 1, 19XX, Canyon Company purchased 75% of the common stock of Racine Company for $380,000 cash, after which the separate balance sheets of the two firms were as follows:

Canyon and Racine Companies
Balance Sheets
January 1, 19XX

	Canyon	Racine
Investment in Racine Company	$ 380,000	—
Other Assets	1,020,000	$550,000
	$1,400,000	$550,000
Liabilities	$ 300,000	$ 70,000
Common Stock	950,000	400,000
Retained Earnings	150,000	80,000
	$1,400,000	$550,000

REQUIRED

Prepare a consolidated balance sheet worksheet at January 1, 19XX. Assume that any amount paid by Canyon Company in excess of the equity acquired in Racine Company's net assets is attributable to goodwill.

18–32 Clayton Company owns 70% of the common stock of Globe Company. The income statements of the two companies for the current year are shown below. In its income statement, Clayton Company has not recorded its share of Globe Company's net income.

Clayton and Globe Companies
Income Statements
For the Current Year

	Clayton	Globe
Sales	$540,000	$360,000
Cost of Goods Sold	380,000	252,000
Gross Profit	$160,000	$108,000
Expenses (including income taxes)	92,000	66,000
Net Income	$ 68,000	$ 42,000

During the year, Clayton Company sold Globe Company merchandise for $70,000, which had cost Clayton $50,000. Globe Company sold all of this merchandise to outsiders.

REQUIRED

Prepare a consolidated income statement worksheet for the current year.

18–33 On January 1, 19XX, Austin Company acquired an interest in Troy Company for $250,000, consisting of $100,000 cash and $150,000 in notes payable. The following information is available about the two companies at December 31, 19XX:

	Austin	Troy	Consolidated
Assets			
Cash	$ 40,000	$ 26,000	$ 66,000
Accounts Receivable	75,000	34,000	94,000
Inventory	140,000	80,000	220,000
Investment in Troy (at equity)	260,000	—	
Other Assets	235,000	170,000	405,000
Excess of Cost over Equity Acquired in Troy			30,000
Total Assets	$750,000	$310,000	$815,000
Liabilities and Stockholders' Equity			
Accounts Payable	$ 55,000	$ 50,000	$ 90,000
Notes Payable	75,000	30,000	105,000
Common Stock	500,000	200,000	500,000
Retained Earnings	120,000	30,000	120,000
Total Liabilities and Stockholders' Equity	$750,000	$310,000	$815,000

REQUIRED

(a) Is the acquisition of Troy Company by Austin Company a purchase or a pooling of interests? Explain.

(b) What ownership percentage of Troy Company did Austin Company acquire?

(c) What were Troy Company's 19XX earnings? Troy declared and paid $10,000 in dividends in 19XX.

(d) How much of Troy Company's retained earnings is included in the consolidated retained earnings?

(e) What were the amounts of intercompany receivables and payables at December 31?

18–34 On January 1, 19XX, Dayton Company purchased 80% of the common shares of Flint Company for $525,000 cash. At that time, the stockholders' equity of Flint Company consisted of $500,000 of common stock and $100,000 of retained earnings. At December 31, 19XX, the separate balance sheets of the two firms were as follows:

Dayton and Flint Companies
Balance Sheets
December 31, 19XX

	Dayton	Flint
Investment in Flint (at equity)	$ 549,000	—
Other Assets	2,451,000	$730,000
	$3,000,000	$730,000
Liabilities	$ 400,000	$100,000
Common Stock	2,000,000	500,000
Retained Earnings	600,000	130,000
	$3,000,000	$730,000

REQUIRED

(a) Give Dayton Company's general journal entry to record the purchase of Flint Company's shares on January 1, 19XX.

(b) Flint Company's 19XX net income was $50,000. Flint declared and paid $20,000 in dividends near the end of 19XX.

    (1) Give Dayton Company's general journal entry to record its share of Flint's net income for the year.

    (2) Give Dayton Company's general journal entry to record the receipt of dividends from Flint Company.

(c) Prepare a consolidated balance sheet for the two firms at December 31, 19XX. Assume that two-thirds of any amount paid by Dayton Company in excess of the equity acquired in Flint's net assets at January 1 is goodwill. The remaining one-third represents an appraisal increase of Flint's Other Assets. At December 31, Flint Company owed $25,000 to Dayton Company for a loan made during the year.

ALTERNATE PROBLEMS

18–27A The following selected transactions and information are for the Spanner Corporation for 19X1 and 19X2.

19X1

Aug. 1 Purchased, as a long-term investment, 1,500 shares of Reed, Inc. common stock at a total cost of $67,500. This interest is noninfluential and noncontrolling.

Nov. 3 Purchased, as a long-term investment, 3,000 shares of Darwin, Inc. common stock at a total cost of $156,000, and 1,000 shares of Sterling, Inc. common stock at a total cost of $28,000. Both investments are noninfluential and noncontrolling interests.

   21 Received a cash dividend of $1 per share on the Darwin, Inc. stock.

Dec. 31 The Reed, Inc. shares have a market value of $46 per share; the Darwin, Inc. shares have a market value of $48 per share; and the Sterling, Inc. shares have a market value of $26 per share. (An entry should be made to adjust the carrying value of the portfolio to the lower of cost or market.)

19X2

Jan. 15 Sold the Darwin, Inc. stock for $50 per share less a $60 commission fee.

Dec. 31 The market value of the long-term investment portfolio is as follows: Reed, Inc., $47 per share; Sterling, Inc., $27 per share. (An entry should be made to adjust the carrying value of the investments and the unrealized loss account.)

REQUIRED

Give the journal entries to record these transactions and adjustments.

18–28A On January 2, 19X1, Jarvis, Inc. purchased, as a long-term investment, 15,000 shares of Lowell, Inc. common stock for $32 per share, including commissions and taxes. On December 31, 19X1, Lowell, Inc. announced a net income of $180,000 for the year and a dividend of 90 cents per share, payable January 15, 19X2, to stockholders of record on January 5, 19X2. Jarvis, Inc. received its dividend on January 18, 19X2.

REQUIRED

(a) Assume the stock acquired by Jarvis, Inc. represents 18% of Lowell, Inc.'s voting stock. Prepare all journal entries appropriate for this investment, beginning with the purchase on January 2, 19X1, and ending with the receipt of the dividend on January 18, 19X2. (Jarvis, Inc. recognizes dividend income when received.)

(b) Assume the stock acquired by Jarvis, Inc. represents 30% of Lowell, Inc.'s voting stock. Prepare all journal entries appropriate for this investment, beginning with the purchase on January 2, 19X1, and ending with the receipt of the dividend on January 18, 19X2.

18–29A Tower Company purchased 70% of Dana Company's voting stock on January 1, 19XX, after which the separate balance sheets of the two companies appeared as follows:

Tower and Dana Companies
Balance Sheets
January 1, 19XX

	Tower	Dana
Investment in Dana Company	$ 385,000	—
Other Assets	815,000	$600,000
	$1,200,000	$600,000
Liabilities	$ 250,000	$ 80,000
Common Stock	700,000	400,000
Retained Earnings	250,000	120,000
	$1,200,000	$600,000

In purchasing Dana Company's shares, Tower Company attributed the excess of the amount paid over the equity acquired in Dana entirely to that company's superior earning potential.

REQUIRED
(a) Give the worksheet entry to eliminate the intercompany equity and to reflect the goodwill.
(b) What amount of total assets should appear on a January 1 consolidated balance sheet?
(c) What amount of total stockholders' equity should appear on a January 1 consolidated balance sheet?

18–30A On January 1, 19XX, Carthage Company purchased all of the common stock of Valley Company for $285,000 cash. The stockholders' equity of Valley Company consisted of $200,000 of common stock and $60,000 of retained earnings. On December 31, 19XX, the separate balance sheets of the two firms were as follows:

Carthage and Valley Companies
Balance Sheets
December 31, 19XX

	Carthage	Valley
Cash	$ 75,000	$ 50,000
Accounts Receivable	120,000	90,000
Investment in Valley Company (at equity)	305,000	—
Other Assets	375,000	180,000
	$875,000	$320,000
Accounts Payable	$100,000	$ 40,000
Common Stock	650,000	200,000
Retained Earnings	125,000	80,000
	$875,000	$320,000

During the year, Valley Company had net income of $30,000. At December 31, Valley owed Carthage $12,000 on account for merchandise.

REQUIRED

(a) What amount of dividends did Valley Company declare and pay during the year?

(b) Give Carthage Company's journal entries that affect the Investment in Valley Company account.

(c) What amount of total assets would appear in a December 31, 19XX consolidated balance sheet?

18–31A On January 1, 19XX, Delta, Inc. purchased 70% of the voting stock of Harper, Inc. for $347,000. At that date, Harper had $300,000 in common stock outstanding and $100,000 in retained earnings. On December 31, 19XX, the separate balance sheets of the two companies were as follows:

Delta, Inc. and Harper, Inc.
Balance Sheets
December 31, 19XX

	Delta	Harper
Investment in Harper, Inc. (at equity)	$ 361,000	—
Other Assets	789,000	$490,000
	$1,150,000	$490,000
Liabilities	$ 220,000	$ 70,000
Common Stock	750,000	300,000
Retained Earnings	180,000	120,000
	$1,150,000	$490,000

During the year, Harper, Inc. paid $30,000 in dividends.

REQUIRED

Prepare a consolidated balance sheet worksheet at December 31, 19XX. Assume that any amount paid by Delta in excess of the equity acquired in Harper is attributable to goodwill.

18–32A Belmont Company purchased a 60% interest in Wales Company on January 1, 19XX. The income statements for the two companies for 19XX are given below. Belmont Company has not yet recorded its share of Wales Company's net income.

Belmont and Wales Companies
Income Statements
For the Year Ended December 31, 19XX

	Belmont	Wales
Sales	$720,000	$540,000
Cost of Goods Sold	510,000	380,000
Gross Profit	$210,000	$160,000
Operating Expenses (including taxes)	145,000	112,000
Net Income	$ 65,000	$ 48,000

Wales Company did not pay any dividends in 19XX. During the year, Belmont sold merchandise costing $75,000 to Wales for $90,000, all of which Wales sold to outsiders.

REQUIRED
Prepare a consolidated income statement worksheet for 19XX.

BUSINESS DECISION PROBLEM

Culhane, Inc., manufactures water heaters, water softeners, and filter systems. It has a 75% interest in Eversoft Company, which manufactures water softeners. It also has a 100% interest in Culhane Finance Company, created by the parent company to finance sales of its products to consumers. The parent company's only other investment is a 10% interest in the common stock of Verity, Inc., which manufactures controls for both Culhane, Inc., and Eversoft Company. A condensed consolidated balance sheet for the entity for the current year is given below:

Culhane, Inc., and Subsidiaries
Consolidated Balance Sheet
December 31, 19XX

Assets

Current Assets	$28,600,000
Investment in Stock of Culhane Finance Company (100%) at Underlying Equity	12,500,000
Investment in Stock of Verity, Inc. (10%) at Cost	3,200,000
Other Assets	37,900,000
Excess of Cost over Equity Acquired in Net Assets of Eversoft Company	1,800,000
Total Assets	$84,000,000

Liabilities and Stockholders' Equity

Current Liabilities		$11,500,000
Long-term Liabilities		8,000,000
Stockholders' Equity:		
Minority Interest	$ 3,500,000	
Common Stock	50,000,000	
Retained Earnings	11,000,000	64,500,000
Total Liabilities and Stockholders' Equity		$84,000,000

This balance sheet, along with other financial statements, was furnished to shareholders before their annual meeting, and all shareholders were invited to submit questions to be answered at the meeting. As chief financial officer of Culhane, Inc., you have been appointed to respond to the questions at the meeting.

REQUIRED

Answer the following stockholder questions:

(a) What is meant by *consolidated financial statements*?

(b) Why are investments in Verity, Inc., and Culhane Finance Company shown on the balance sheet, while the investment in Eversoft Company is omitted?

(c) What is meant by the carrying value *underlying equity* for the investment in Culhane Finance Company?

(d) Why is the investment in Verity, Inc., shown at cost, while the investment in Culhane Finance Company is shown at underlying equity?

(e) Explain the meaning of the asset Excess of Cost over Equity Acquired in Net Assets of Eversoft Company.

(f) What is meant by *minority interest* and to what company is this account related?

ACCOUNTING FOR BRANCHES

Many business firms expand by opening new outlets, or **branches,** at different locations. The development of suburban shopping centers has provided the impetus for branch marketing of goods and services by many firms, especially retail stores, banks, and savings and loan companies. Both wholesale and retail merchandising companies have expanded their marketing territories through widespread branch operations.

Typically, the various branches offer the same goods or services and follow fairly standardized operations. A manager appointed for each branch normally is responsible for that outlet's profitability. From a managerial viewpoint, each branch is an accounting entity, even though branches are usually segments of a single legal entity—a corporation, partnership, or sole proprietorship. The principal outlet, from which the firm's activities are normally directed, is often referred to as the **home office.**

Generally, merchandising policies, advertising, and promotion are directed or heavily influenced by the home office. Although branches may be given some latitude in acquiring merchandise, often the major portion of goods is purchased centrally.

The accounting system for branch operations should furnish management with complete and timely information to measure branch profitability. The size and complexity of branch operations, geographic location, and degree of autonomy, among other things, may influence the type of accounting system adopted. Most systems, however, are variations of two basic schemes—centralized accounting by the home office and decentralized accounting by the branch.

CENTRALIZED BRANCH RECORDS

Under a **centralized** accounting system, the home office maintains most of the records needed to account for branch operations. Thus, separate asset, liability, revenue, and expense records for each branch are maintained at the home office. Typically, cash is transferred to the branch to establish a working fund for small disbursements. This fund is ordinarily kept on an imprest basis (like a petty cash fund) and replenished regularly by the home office on the basis of expense vouchers or summaries submitted by the branch. A branch that collects any amounts in its operations must often deposit such amounts in a home office bank account and transmit deposit slips and lists of the remittances to the home office for recording. The branch also transmits other documents such as copies of sales invoices and credit memos to the home office for recording. The data needed to record branch transactions may be transmitted by a telecommunication or similar device, with the documents forwarded periodically. In some cases, the documents may be filed at the branch, with periodic audits by either home office auditors or independent accountants.

DECENTRALIZED BRANCH RECORDS

Under a **decentralized** accounting system, each branch ordinarily maintains a comprehensive set of accounting records for its operations and forwards periodic financial statements to the home office. Normally, the forms of the records and statements are standardized for all branches, so that they may be conveniently analyzed by the home office and integrated into the financial reports of the whole organization. Emphasis is often placed on the operating, or income statement, accounts. For example, the branch may keep accounts for current assets—such as cash, accounts receivable, and inventory—but the home office may retain the accounts for equipment, fixtures, and accumulated depreciation.

In place of owners' equity accounts, the branch has an account called **Home Office,** which represents amounts of advances or assets received from the home office plus accumulated branch earnings not transferred to the home office. A reciprocal account called **Branch Office** is maintained in the ledger of the home office. When both accounts are posted and up to date, the dollar balances should be identical.

From the branch's viewpoint, the Home Office account may be regarded as either a capital account or a liability. Likewise, the Branch Office balance on the books of the home office may be viewed either as an investment or as a receivable. The classification of these accounts is not especially important; the branch is only an accounting segment, and when its accounts are combined with those of the home office, the balances of these two accounts offset each other and do not appear in the combined financial statements.

ILLUSTRATION OF DECENTRALIZED ACCOUNTING

Assume that on May 1 of the current year the Foto-Art Company, retailer of photographic equipment, opened its Western Branch in another city, leasing the store facilities and fixtures. The home office transferred $20,000 cash and $40,000 in merchandise to the branch to begin operations. The following entries record the transfer establishing the branch:

Home Office Records		
Western Branch	60,000	
Cash		20,000
Shipments to Western Branch		40,000

Western Branch Records		
Cash	20,000	
Shipments from Home Office	40,000	
Home Office		60,000

This entry establishes the investment in the branch (or receivable from the branch) for the amount of cash and merchandise advanced to the new outlet. The $60,000 amount shown in Western Branch's reciprocal account equals the amount of capital received from the home office.

Generally, merchandise shipped from the home office to the branch should be differentiated from branch acquisitions purchased from outsiders. Therefore, a Shipments to Branch account is credited on the home office records, and a Shipments from Home Office account is debited on the branch records whenever the home office transfers merchandise to the branch. On the home office records, the Shipments to Branch account can be considered a contra account to the Purchases account. On the branch records, the Shipments from Home Office debit balance can be considered a purchases amount. When the branch closes its books, it closes the Shipments from Home Office account to the Income Summary account. Likewise, the home office closes the Shipments to Branch balance to its own Income Summary account.

The following transactions, including the asset transfer establishing the branch, are shown in summary form:

Summary of May Transactions	Home Office Records			Western Branch Records		

(1) Home office opened Western Branch, transferring $20,000 cash and $40,000 merchandise.	Western Branch
	Cash
	Shipments to
	   Western Branch
		60,000	20,000
			
			40,000
				Cash
				Shipments from Home
				   Office
				Home Office
					20,000
					
					40,000
						
						60,000

(2) Purchased $15,000 merchandise from outsiders.				Purchases Accounts Payable	15,000	 15,000
(3) Sold merchandise on account for $30,000				Accounts Receivable Sales	30,000	 30,000

(4) Incurred $5,000 selling expenses and $3,000 general expenses; of the total, $2,000 was on account.				Selling Expenses
				General Expenses
				   Cash
				   Accounts Payable
					5,000
					3,000
						
						6,000
						2,000

(5) Collected $24,000 on account from customers.				Cash Accounts Receivable	24,000	 24,000

EXHIBIT B–1

Foto-Art Company
Western Branch
Trial Balance
May 31, 19XX

	Debit	Credit
Cash	$16,000	
Accounts Receivable	6,000	
Home Office		$51,000
Accounts Payable		5,000
Sales		30,000
Purchases	15,000	
Shipments from Home Office	40,000	
Selling Expenses	5,000	
General Expenses	4,000	
	$86,000	$86,000

(6) Paid $12,000 to creditors on account.

Accounts Payable	12,000	
Cash		12,000

(7) Sent $10,000 cash to home office.

Cash	10,000	
Western Branch		10,000

Home Office	10,000	
Cash		10,000

(8) Attributed $1,000 home office general expenses to Western Branch.

Western Branch	1,000	
General Expenses		1,000

General Expenses	1,000	
Home Office		1,000

After the foregoing entries have been posted to Western Branch's ledger, the trial balance for the branch would appear as shown in Exhibit B–1.

Western Branch next records any necessary end-of-period adjustments in the usual fashion. For the sake of simplicity, we assume that none are needed.

BRANCH FINANCIAL STATEMENTS

After the branch has recorded any necessary adjusting entries, financial statements can be prepared. Exhibits B–2 and B–3 show the May income statement and the May 31 balance sheet for Western Branch. Note in the balance sheet that the net income for the period is added to the balance of the Home Office account. Actually, the branch's net income would be closed to the Home Office account at the end of the accounting period, as shown later in the closing entries.

EXHIBIT B–2

Foto-Art Company
Western Branch
Income Statement
For the Month of May, 19XX

Sales		$30,000
Cost of Goods Sold:		
Beginning Inventory	—	
Purchases	$15,000	
Shipments from Home Office	40,000	
Goods Available for Sale	$55,000	
Less: Ending Inventory	37,000	
Cost of Goods Sold		18,000
Gross Profit on Sales		$12,000
Operating Expenses:		
Selling Expenses	$ 5,000	
General Expenses	4,000	
Total Operating Expenses		9,000
Net Income		$ 3,000

EXHIBIT B–3

Foto-Art Company
Western Branch
Balance Sheet
May 31, 19XX

Assets			Liabilities and Home Office Equity		
Cash	$16,000		Accounts Payable		$ 5,000
Accounts Receivable	6,000		Home Office	$51,000	
Inventory	37,000		Net Income	3,000	54,000
	$59,000				$59,000

COMBINED FINANCIAL STATEMENTS

At the end of the accounting period, the various branches submit their financial statements (or alternatively, adjusted trial balances) to the home office, which combines the data into a single set of statements for the whole enterprise. The worksheets in Exhibit B–4 provide a convenient vehicle for compiling and inte-

Foto-Art Company
Home Office and Western Branch
Income Statement Worksheet
For the Month of May, 19XX

	Home Office	Western Branch	Eliminations	Combined Income Statement
Sales	$65,000	$30,000		$ 95,000
Cost of Goods Sold:				
Inventory, May 1	$38,000	—		$ 38,000
Purchases	70,000	$15,000		85,000
Shipments to Branch	(40,000)		$40,000	
Shipments from Home Office		40,000	(40,000)	
Goods Available for Sale	$68,000	$55,000		$123,000
Less: Inventory, May 31	28,000	37,000		65,000
Cost of Goods Sold	$40,000	$18,000		$ 58,000
Gross Profit on Sales	$25,000	$12,000		$ 37,000
Operating Expenses:				
Selling Expenses	$ 9,000	$ 5,000		$ 14,000
General Expenses	7,000	4,000		11,000
Total Operating Expenses	$16,000	$ 9,000		$ 25,000
Net Income	$ 9,000	$ 3,000		$ 12,000

Foto-Art Company
Home Office and Western Branch
Balance Sheet Worksheet
May 31, 19XX

	Home Office	Western Branch	Eliminations	Combined Balance Sheet
Assets				
Cash	$ 20,000	$16,000		$ 36,000
Accounts Receivable	36,000	6,000		42,000
Inventory	28,000	37,000		65,000
Western Branch	54,000		($54,000)	
Fixed Assets, Net of Accumulated Depreciation	80,000			80,000
Total Assets	$218,000	$59,000	($54,000)	$223,000
Liabilities and Stockholders' Equity				
Accounts Payable	$ 18,000	$ 5,000		$ 23,000
Accrued Liabilities	2,000			2,000
Home Office		54,000	($54,000)	
Common Stock	150,000			150,000
Retained Earnings	48,000			48,000
Total Liabilities and Stockholders' Equity	$218,000	$59,000	($54,000)	$223,000

grating the data for the company. In the illustration, the data for home office operations are assumed. Note that the reciprocal amounts of $40,000 representing shipments from the home office to the branch are eliminated and the accounts do not appear in the combined income statement. Likewise, the home office and branch office accounts, with $54,000 balances, are eliminated when the combined balance sheet is prepared.

CLOSING ENTRIES

After financial statements are prepared, the following closing entries are recorded by the branch:

May 31	Inventory	37,000	
	Income Summary		37,000
	To record the ending inventory.		
31	Sales	30,000	
	Income Summary		30,000
	To close the Sales account to the Income Summary account.		
31	Income Summary	55,000	
	Purchases		15,000
	Shipments from Home Office		40,000
	To close the Purchases and Shipments from Home Office accounts.		
31	Income Summary	9,000	
	Selling Expenses		5,000
	General Expenses		4,000
	To close the operating expense accounts.		
31	Income Summary	3,000	
	Home Office		3,000
	To close the Income Summary to the Home Office account.		

On May 31, the home office reflects the branch net income by making a corollary entry to the last entry shown above:

May 31	Western Branch	3,000	
	Net Income—Western Branch		3,000
	To reflect net income of Western Branch.		

In closing its records, the home office closes the Net Income—Western Branch account to its Income Summary account.

PROBLEMS

B–1 Central Branch had a beginning balance of $36,000 in its Home Office account. During the current month, Central received $48,000 in merchandise shipments from the home office. At month-end, the branch's share of home office general expenses was $4,600. After closing its records, Central Branch determined its net income as $18,500. The branch then sent $9,000 cash to the home office.

REQUIRED
(a) Give the branch's journal entry made on receiving the $48,000 in merchandise from the home office.
(b) What amount would be in the Home Office account after all entries were posted for the current month?

B–2 Westtown Branch of Fuller Tax Service, which has decentralized accounting records, opened on July 1 of the current year and had the following July transactions:

July 1   The home office transferred $8,000 cash and $15,000 in equipment to the branch.
  15   The branch collected $6,000 service fees.
  20   The branch paid $3,800 in operating expenses.
  30   The home office allocated $1,500 of home office general expenses to the branch.
  31   The branch collected $7,500 service fees and sent $5,000 cash to the home office.
  31   The branch recorded depreciation on equipment, $200. (Debit Operating Expenses.)
  31   The branch closed its revenue and expense accounts, debiting Fee Revenue $13,500, crediting Operating Expenses $5,500, and crediting Income Summary $8,000.
  31   The branch reported its net income of $8,000 to the home office.

REQUIRED
Journalize the foregoing entries on the branch books and on the home office books.

B–3 Bradford, Inc., which operates a large music store in St. Louis, arranged in May of the current year to open a branch in Columbia. Record keeping for the branch is decentralized. A summary of the branch's transactions for May is given below:

May 1   The St. Louis store transferred $20,000 cash and $35,000 in merchandise to the Columbia branch.
   3   Purchased $28,000 in merchandise on account from various dealers.
  10   Paid $7,000 on accounts payable.
  15   Sales to date: cash, $9,000; on account, $16,000.
  18   Collected $6,300 on account from customers.
  20   Selling expenses for the branch were $4,000 and general expenses were

$2,500; of the total, $1,700 was on account and the remainder paid in cash.

May 25   Sent $8,000 cash to St. Louis store.

    30   Sales during the last half of the month: cash, $9,000; on account, $14,000.

REQUIRED

(a) Journalize the May transactions on the books of the Columbia branch.

(b) Make the necessary closing entries on the Columbia branch records, assuming that the May 31 inventory is $24,000.

(c) Journalize the May transactions requiring entries on the books of the St. Louis home office, including the entry to record the branch's net income.

(d) State the May 31 Home Office account balance in the Columbia branch's ledger.

B–4 The reciprocal accounts of the home office and branch operations of Dorn Specialty Stores as they appear near the end of the accounting year are shown below.

Branch Account (Home Office Records)

Date		Description	Debit	Credit	Balance
Nov.	30	Balance			48,500
Dec.	5	Merchandise shipped	16,700		65,200
	28	Equipment sent	700		65,900

Home Office (Branch Records)

Date		Description	Debit	Credit	Balance
Nov.	30	Balance			48,500
Dec.	5	Merchandise received		17,600	66,100
	31	Net income		9,800	75,900
	31	Cash remitted	8,000		66,900

REQUIRED

(a) Review these accounts in terms of any needed updating and the appropriateness of their ending balances. If you discover any apparent bookkeeping errors, assume that the home office records are correct. Prepare any needed adjusting journal entries.

(b) Prepare a brief analysis leading to what you consider the correct year-end balances for these accounts.

(c) What eliminating entry would be appropriate on a worksheet used to prepare combined balance sheets for the home office and the branch?

B–5 Clyde, Inc. operates a store selling men's shoes, hosiery, and other men's furnishings in Detroit. The firm opened a branch in Lansing on June 1 of the current year. A summary of the branch's June transactions follows:

June   1   Received $30,000 cash and $90,000 merchandise from the home office in Detroit.

     12   Purchased $18,000 merchandise on account from various dealers.

     15   Sales to date: cash, $14,000; on account, $10,000.

     19   Collected $7,200 on account from customers.

     21   Paid $9,000 on accounts payable.

     25   Selling expenses for the branch were $12,500 and general expenses were $2,200; of the total, $4,500 was on account and the remainder paid in cash.

     26   The home office informed the Lansing branch that $3,000 home office general expense was allocated to the branch.

     30   Sales during the last half of the month: cash, $16,000; on account, $20,000.

REQUIRED

(a) Journalize the June transactions on the Lansing branch's books.

(b) Make the necessary closing entries on the Lansing branch's records, assuming that the June 30 inventory is $68,000.

(c) Journalize the June transactions requiring entries on the home office's books, including the entry to record the branch's net income.

(d) Prepare an analysis of the June 30 balance in the Home Office account in the Lansing branch's ledger.

19

Statement of Changes in Financial Position: Analysis of Funds and Cash Flows

The **statement of changes in financial position** is a basic financial statement because it contains useful information for a variety of external users who make economic decisions about an enterprise.[1] This statement provides information that is unavailable in the balance sheet and the income statement (or that is provided only indirectly) about the flow of funds and changes in financial position during the period. The statement of changes in financial position is often called a *funds statement* because it focuses on the sources and uses of funds.

We begin our discussion with the concept of funds flow and then move through the necessary steps to prepare the statement of changes in financial position. Finally, we describe an approach to cash flow analysis and the preparation of cash flow statements.

DEFINITION OF FUNDS

To most people, the term *funds* denotes cash. Business executives and financial analysts, however, think of the net circulating capital of a business as the firm's funds. Therefore, the most common definition of funds is **working capital—** *current assets less current liabilities.*

Consider the logic of this definition. A company acquires inventory on credit, converts it into receivables, then into cash, pays its short-term creditors, and then repeats the cycle over and over again. For profitable companies, the process itself generates additional working capital. Working capital is also injected into the system by other means, among the most important of which are sales of noncurrent assets, long-term borrowing, and issuances of capital stock. On the other hand, working capital is continually depleted by such activities as purchases of noncurrent assets, repayment of long-term debt, declarations of cash dividends, and retirement of capital stock. The effects of all these activities can be seen in the diagram at the top of the next page.

Because circulating capital is the lifeblood of an enterprise, financial analysts are vitally interested in it when examining a particular firm. Even a profitable company can be anemic with respect to working capital, and a poor working

---

[1] The Accounting Principles Board designated the statement of changes in financial position as a basic financial statement in 1971. *Opinions of the Accounting Principles Board, No. 19,* "Reporting Changes in Financial Position" (New York: American Institute of Certified Public Accountants, 1971).

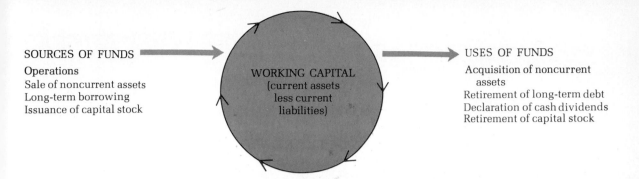

SOURCES OF FUNDS

Operations
Sale of noncurrent assets
Long-term borrowing
Issuance of capital stock

WORKING CAPITAL
(current assets
less current
liabilities)

USES OF FUNDS

Acquisition of noncurrent
assets
Retirement of long-term debt
Declaration of cash dividends
Retirement of capital stock

capital position can lead to financial and operating difficulties. The liquid, or net current, resources of a firm are important to its operations, and this broader concept of funds provides a most useful perspective.

USEFULNESS OF STATEMENT OF CHANGES IN FINANCIAL POSITION

The statement of changes in financial position discloses all important changes in financial position during an accounting period. It details the sources and uses of funds. Working capital increases when funds provided by various activities exceed the funds used. Working capital decreases when funds used exceed funds provided.

Knowing the sources of a company's working capital and the ways that capital is used, an analyst can tell a great deal about the strengths and weaknesses of the firm and about the policies of its management. One advantage of the statement of changes in financial position is that it summarizes the firm's major asset acquisitions and financing activities during the accounting period. Over time, the analyst can observe management's spending and borrowing habits. In addition, the statement of changes in financial position may reveal: (1) clues to the firm's ability to pay dividends and its dividend policy and (2) whether future financing is needed. Finally, analysts find the information on these statements extremely useful when comparing companies.

THE EFFECT OF TRANSACTIONS ON WORKING CAPITAL

When preparing a statement of changes in financial position, we should keep in mind the effects of various transactions on working capital. Let us use a simple example to illustrate how transactions may be analyzed. Exhibit 19–1 presents the XYZ Company's balance sheet at the end of year 2 and year 1. Exhibit 19–2 is the company's income statement for year 2.

EXHIBIT 19–1

XYZ Company
Balance Sheets

Assets	Dec. 31, Year 2	Dec. 31, Year 1
Cash	$ 16,000	$ 5,000
Accounts Receivable	10,000	15,000
Inventory	30,000	30,000
Plant Assets	55,000	55,000
Accumulated Depreciation	(10,000)	(5,000)
Total Assets	$101,000	$100,000
Liabilities and Stockholders' Equity		
Accounts Payable	$ 20,000	$ 25,000
Dividends Payable	3,000	—
Common Stock	50,000	50,000
Retained Earnings	28,000	25,000
Total Liabilities and Stockholders' Equity	$101,000	$100,000

Now, suppose that XYZ Company engaged in the following transactions during year 2:

(1) Sold $20,000 inventory for $35,000 on account.

(2) Paid $4,000 cash for operating expenses and income taxes.

(3) Recorded annual depreciation, $5,000.

(4) Collected $40,000 of accounts receivable.

EXHIBIT 19–2

XYZ Company
Income Statement
For the Year Ended December 31, Year 2

Sales	$35,000	
Cost of Goods Sold	20,000	(1)
Gross Profit	$15,000	
Operating Expenses and Income Taxes (excluding depreciation)	4,000	(2)
	$11,000	
Depreciation Expense	5,000	(3)
Net Income	$ 6,000	

(5) Replenished the inventory by purchasing $20,000 merchandise **on account.**

(6) Paid $25,000 on accounts payable.

(7) Declared dividends to be paid in year 3, $3,000.

We have keyed the income statement in Exhibit 19–2 with the relevant transaction numbers.

Now we can determine the change in the working capital, or funds, of the XYZ Company during year 2, as follows:

	Dec. 31, Year 2	Dec. 31, Year 1	Increase (Decrease)
Current Assets			
Cash	$16,000	$ 5,000	$11,000
Accounts Receivable	10,000	15,000	(5,000)
Inventory	30,000	30,000	—
Total Current Assets	$56,000	$50,000	$ 6,000
Current Liabilities			
Accounts Payable	$20,000	$25,000	($ 5,000)
Dividends Payable	3,000	—	3,000
Total Current Liabilities	$23,000	$25,000	($ 2,000)
Working Capital	$33,000	$25,000	$ 8,000

The $8,000 increase in working capital results from a $6,000 increase in current assets and a $2,000 decrease in current liabilities. Working capital is a net concept—current assets less current liabilities. It is increased by increases in current assets and by decreases in current liabilities; conversely, it is decreased by decreases in current assets and by increases in current liabilities.

One way of analyzing the factors that account for the $8,000 increase in working capital is to consider how each of the period's transactions affect XYZ Company's balance sheet.

Transaction and Effect on Balance Sheet			Effect on Working Capital
(1) Sold $20,000 inventory for $35,000 on account.			
Accounts Receivable	35,000		$35,000 increase
Retained Earnings (revenue)		35,000	
Retained Earnings (expense)	20,000		
Inventory		20,000	($20,000) decrease

Note that this transaction increased one current asset (accounts receivable) by $35,000 and decreased another (inventory) by $20,000. The net result was a $15,000 increase in working capital. Because revenue and expense accounts are summarized and closed to retained earnings, their impact on a balance sheet is reflected in the retained earnings account.

Transaction and Effect on Balance Sheet		**Effect on Working Capital**

(2) Paid $4,000 cash for operating expenses and income taxes.

Retained Earnings (expense)	4,000	
Cash	4,000	($4,000) decrease

The decrease in a current asset (cash) resulted in a decrease in working capital.

(3) Recorded annual depreciation, $5,000.

Retained Earnings (expense)	5,000	None
Accumulated Depreciation	5,000	

No current assets or current liabilities were involved in this entry; therefore, working capital was not affected.

(4) Collected $40,000 of accounts receivable.

Cash	40,000	None
Accounts Receivable	40,000	

This entry increased one current asset and decreased another by the same amount; the amount of working capital did not change.

(5) Replenished the inventory by purchasing $20,000 merchandise on account.

Inventory	20,000	None
Accounts Payable	20,000	

Both current assets and current liabilities were increased by the same amount, with no resulting effect on working capital.

(6) Paid $25,000 on accounts payable.

Accounts Payable	25,000	None
Cash	25,000	

Because both a current asset and a current liability were equally reduced, working capital was not affected.

(7) Declared dividends to be paid in year 3, $3,000.

Retained Earnings	3,000	
Dividends Payable	3,000	($3,000) decrease

The increase in a current liability resulted in a decrease in working capital.

Change in Working Capital in year 2		$8,000 increase

Obviously, for most businesses, analyzing all the year's transactions to account for the net change in working capital during the year would be a tedious job. Using several important observations about the foregoing procedure, however, we can develop a more efficient approach to the preparation of a statement of changes in financial position.

(1) Transactions involving only current assets and liabilities can be ignored, because there is no net effect on funds. Such transactions as collections on account, purchases of merchandise, and payments on account do not change working capital. Transactions (4), (5), and (6) are examples of such activities.

(2) Transactions involving both current and noncurrent accounts affect funds and may be divided into two groups:

    (a) Routine operating transactions recording the sale of goods, reduction of inventories, and most reflections of expense affect one or more current accounts and (ultimately) the Retained Earnings account. These transactions are already summarized in the net income figure, so we need not analyze them. Examples are transactions (1) and (2) in the foregoing illustration. We merely observe that funds were "provided by operations," using the net income figure. As explained below, however, some adjustments are almost always necessary.

    (b) Nonroutine transactions—such as purchase or sale of plant assets, long-term borrowing or repayment, sale or repurchase of stock, and declaration of cash dividends—affect one or more current accounts but are not included in the net income figure. These transactions must be analyzed separately. An example is transaction (7).

(3) Transactions involving only noncurrent accounts do not affect funds. Recording depreciation, as in transaction (3), affects only the Accumulated Depreciation and Retained Earnings accounts on the balance sheet and has no effect on funds. Therefore, *if the net income figure is used to summarize working capital provided by operations, depreciation must be added back to net income* to arrive at the correct amount of working capital provided by routine transactions described in 2(a) above. We see the rationale for this treatment of depreciation expense in Exhibit 19–2. Transactions (1) and (2) provide an $11,000 net increase in working capital from operations. If we start with the $6,000 net income figure, we must add to it the $5,000 depreciation expense to obtain the $11,000 funds provided by operations.

In fact, any write-offs or amortization of noncurrent items deducted on the income statement must be added back to net income to arrive at the amount of funds provided by operations. Other examples of such write-offs include amortization of patents, leaseholds, goodwill, and bond discount. An item such as amortization of bond premium on bonds payable *is deducted from the net income figure* on the statement of changes in financial position.

These observations apply only to the analysis of transactions affecting working capital. Certain transactions resulting in significant financial changes that may involve only noncurrent accounts, but that do not affect working capital, are also reported on the statement of changes in financial position. These transactions

EXHIBIT 19–3

XYZ Company
Statement of Changes in Financial Position
For the Year Ended December 31, Year 2

Sources of Working Capital
  Operations:

Net Income	$ 6,000	
Add Expenses Not Decreasing Working Capital:		
Depreciation	5,000	
Total Sources of Working Capital		$11,000

Uses of Working Capital

Declaration of Dividends		3,000
Increase in Working Capital		$ 8,000

Changes in Working Capital Components
  Increases (Decreases) in Current Assets:

Cash	$11,000	
Accounts Receivable	(5,000)	
Increase in Current Assets		$ 6,000
Increases (Decreases) in Current Liabilities:		
Accounts Payable	($ 5,000)	
Dividends Payable	3,000	
Decrease in Current Liabilities		(2,000)
Increase in Working Capital		$ 8,000

include issuance of securities for long-term assets, conversion of long-term debt or preferred stock into common stock, and donations of long-term assets. These transactions are best analyzed individually in preparing a statement of changes in financial position. We discuss them later in this chapter.

Exhibit 19–3 shows a statement of changes in financial position for the XYZ Company for year 2.

FORM OF STATEMENT OF CHANGES IN FINANCIAL POSITION

The statement of changes in financial position should be headed with the name of the company and the title of the statement. Because it is a statement of flows, it should, like the income statement, show the period covered. The first part of the statement—the events causing the change in funds—has two major sections, **Sources of Working Capital** (or Sources of Funds) and **Uses of Working Capital** (or Uses of Funds). The difference between the totals of these two sections is the net change in working capital during the period. The first item in the statement, working capital provided by operations, usually starts with net income and adds (or deducts) items included in net income that did not affect working capital. In Exhibit 19–3, working capital from operations is the only source of funds for the year.

The second part of the statement, **Changes in Working Capital Components,** details the changes in the various current asset and liability accounts for the period. Note that the working capital change detailed in this part equals the working capital change analyzed in the first part of the statement.

The statement of changes in financial position reports separately the effects of any extraordinary items and also clearly discloses the proceeds (reduced by any related expenses that consume working capital) from sales of long-term assets outside the normal course of business. The statement thus separates extraordinary, unusual, or nonrecurring items, net of taxes, from the resources provided by normal operations.

WORKSHEET ILLUSTRATION OF FUNDS FLOW ANALYSIS

Let us now analyze the year 3 activities of the XYZ Company, using a worksheet to prepare a statement of changes in financial position. Consider the comparative condensed balance sheets for years 2 and 3 in Exhibit 19–4 and the income statement for year 3 in Exhibit 19–5. Assume that during the year the following transactions took place, in addition to routine transactions:

EXHIBIT 19–4

XYZ Company Balance Sheets		
Assets	**Dec. 31, Year 3**	**Dec. 31, Year 2**
Cash	$ 21,000	$ 16,000
Accounts Receivable	19,000	10,000
Inventory	35,000	30,000
Plant Assets	56,000	55,000
Accumulated Depreciation	(12,000)	(10,000)
Total Assets	$119,000	$101,000
Liabilities and Stockholders' Equity		
Accounts Payable	$ 22,000	$ 20,000
Dividends Payable	4,000	3,000
Common Stock	60,000	50,000
Retained Earnings	33,000	28,000
Total Liabilities and Stockholders' Equity	$119,000	$101,000

EXHIBIT 19–5

XYZ Company
Income Statement
For the Year Ended December 31, Year 3

Sales	$50,000
Cost of Goods Sold	30,000
Gross Profit	$20,000
Operating Expenses and Income Taxes (excluding depreciation)	6,000
	$14,000 ← Funds provided
Depreciation Expense	5,000 by operations
Net Income	$ 9,000

(1) Sold plant assets having a book value of $4,000 ($7,000 cost − $3,000 accumulated depreciation) for $4,000 cash at the end of the year.

(2) Purchased new plant assets at the end of the year, $8,000.

(3) Sold additional common stock at par value, $10,000.

(4) Declared dividends to be paid in year 4, $4,000.

We construct the statement of changes in financial position by using the following steps:

STEP 1   Using balance sheet figures, calculate the change in working capital for the period. A detailed calculation of the working capital change for XYZ Company during year 3 follows:

	Dec. 31, Year 3	Dec. 31, Year 2	Increase (Decrease)
Current Assets			
Cash	$21,000	$16,000	$ 5,000
Accounts Receivable	19,000	10,000	9,000
Inventory	35,000	30,000	5,000
Total Current Assets	$75,000	$56,000	$19,000
Current Liabilities			
Accounts Payable	$22,000	$20,000	$ 2,000
Dividends Payable	4,000	3,000	1,000
Total Current Liabilities	$26,000	$23,000	$ 3,000
Working Capital	$49,000	$33,000	$16,000

We must account for the $16,000 net increase in working capital.

STEP 2 Prepare a worksheet to analyze the changes in the noncurrent accounts and identify sources and uses of working capital for the period. Exhibit 19–6 shows the worksheet for XYZ Company, which is prepared in the following manner.

Heading and form   The worksheet heading includes the name of the company, an identification of the statement the worksheet deals with, and the period covered by the analysis.

The worksheet form illustrated in Exhibit 19–6 has a description column and four money columns. Each of the two headings Changes in Noncurrent Accounts and Analyzing Entries has a debit and credit column.

Changes in noncurrent accounts   The content of the worksheet focuses on the company's noncurrent accounts.

(1) First, a list of the noncurrent accounts is entered in the description column. The debit or credit change in each noncurrent account balance for the period is entered in the appropriate column under the Changes in Noncurrent Accounts

EXHIBIT 19–6

	Changes in Noncurrent Accounts		Analyzing Entries	
Description	**Debit**	**Credit**	**Debit**	**Credit**
XYZ Company — Worksheet for Statement of Changes in Financial Position — For the Year Ended December 31, Year 3				
Plant Assets	1,000		(d) 8,000	(c) 7,000
Accumulated Depreciation		2,000	(c) 3,000	(b) 5,000
Common Stock		10,000		(e) 10,000
Retained Earnings		5,000	(f) 4,000	(a) 9,000
	1,000	17,000		
Increase in Working Capital	16,000			
	17,000	17,000		
Sources of Working Capital				
Net Income			(a) 9,000	
Add: Depreciation			(b) 5,000	
Sale of Plant Assets			(c) 4,000	
Sale of Common Stock			(e) 10,000	
Uses of Working Capital				
Purchase of Plant Assets				(d) 8,000
Declaration of Dividends				(f) 4,000
			43,000	43,000

heading. Plant Assets for XYZ Company increased from $55,000 at December 31, year 2, to $56,000 at December 31, year 3; the $1,000 increase is entered in the debit column. Accumulated Depreciation increased from $10,000 to $12,000; the $2,000 increase is entered in the credit column. The changes in Common Stock and Retained Earnings are handled the same way.

(2) At this point, the first two columns are totaled. The difference between the column totals equals the working capital change calculated in step 1. The working capital change is entered on the worksheet—an increase in the debit column, a decrease in the credit column—and the two columns are totaled to show their equality. Exhibit 19–6 shows the $16,000 working capital increase for XYZ Company in the debit column.

(3) After the first two amount columns are totaled and double ruled, the phrase "sources of working capital" is written in the description column. Several lines are skipped to allow for all possible sources of funds, and the phrase "uses of working capital" is written in the same column.

As noted earlier, only transactions involving *both* current and noncurrent accounts have a net effect on working capital. As a result, *the change in working capital for a period equals the net change in the noncurrent accounts.* The first two amount columns demonstrate this equality. Because fewer transactions affect noncurrent accounts than current accounts, it is efficient to review the changes in noncurrent accounts to determine the sources and uses of funds. The worksheet is designed for such an analysis.

Analyzing entries   Review the noncurrent accounts and reconstruct the entries, in summary form, to explain the changes that occurred during the period. If the transaction affected working capital, we enter the appropriate amount in the worksheet as either a source or use of working capital. A debit entry reflects an increase in working capital; a credit entry means a decrease in working capital. When all the changes in noncurrent accounts have been explained, our analysis is complete. The analyzing entries in Exhibit 19–6 are explained below.

(a) Because the first item on the statement of changes in financial position is funds provided by operations, we begin by reviewing income statement data for their impact on noncurrent accounts and working capital. Entry (a) on the worksheet shows the increase in Retained Earnings from the $9,000 net income, with the offsetting debit as a source of funds from net income.

(b) Depreciation expense does not affect working capital. Entry (b) credits Accumulated Depreciation for the $5,000 of depreciation and debits $5,000 under sources of working capital as an addition to net income, because depreciation expense must be added to net income to derive funds provided by operations (identified by the arrow as $14,000 on the income statement in Exhibit 19–5).

(c) The sale of plant assets increased working capital by $4,000, decreased Accumulated Depreciation by $3,000, and decreased Plant Assets by $7,000, as reflected in entry (c).

(d) Entry (d) reconstructs the purchase of plant assets. The entry debits Plant Assets for $8,000 and credits $8,000 as a use of working capital for the purchase of plant assets.

(e) The sale of common stock provided $10,000 of working capital and increased the Common Stock account balance. Entry (e) debits $10,000 as a source of working capital from the sale of common stock and credits $10,000 to Common Stock.

(f) The declaration of the $4,000 dividend is reconstructed in entry (f). This transaction reduced working capital and retained earnings—the entry debits Retained Earnings and credits uses of working capital for a declaration of dividends. The $3,000 dividend declared in year 2 was paid in year 3, but the payment did not affect working capital. It reduced both a current liability and a current asset (dividends payable and cash) by $3,000, with no net effect on funds. The dividend payment affects only current accounts and, thus, is not analyzed on the worksheet.

For each noncurrent account, the debit or credit balance of the analyzing entries now equals the change shown in the first two columns. Our analysis is complete, and we total and double rule the last two columns to complete the worksheet. Because the analyzing entries are for worksheet purposes only, they are not recorded in the accounts.

STEP 3   Prepare the statement of changes in financial position. Information for the sources and uses of working capital appears in the lower portion of the worksheet. The schedule prepared in step 1, if detailed enough, contains the necessary data for the changes in working capital components. The changes in working capital components may also be derived from the comparative balance sheets. The year 3 statement of changes in financial position for the XYZ Company is shown in Exhibit 19–7.

The form of the statement of changes in financial position in Exhibit 19–7 is typical of those in financial reports. If there is a net loss for the period, it appears in the same position as Net Income when depreciation and other adjustments added result in an increase in working capital. If depreciation and other adjustments are less than the net loss, however, funds have been *applied to* operations, and the amounts are shown in the Uses of Working Capital section.

SIGNIFICANT CHANGES NOT AFFECTING FUNDS

The funds statement is to include all important aspects of a firm's financing and investing activities, regardless of whether cash or other elements of working capital are actually affected. With this perspective, companies can present significant financial developments that otherwise might not be emphasized in any accounting report. Examples of transactions included are the issuance of securities for noncurrent assets, the conversion of long-term debt or preferred stock to common stock, and transactions involving donated assets. Transactions involving stock dividends and stock split-ups, however, are not reported in the funds statement.

These special types of transactions are presented in the statement of changes in financial position as both sources and uses of working capital. Suppose that a

EXHIBIT 19–7

XYZ Company
Statement of Changes in Financial Position
For the Year Ended December 31, Year 3

Sources of Working Capital
Operations:

Net Income	$9,000	
Add Expenses Not Decreasing Working Capital:		
Depreciation	5,000	
Total from Operations		$14,000
Sale of Plant Assets		4,000
Sale of Common Stock		10,000
Total Sources of Working Capital		$28,000

Uses of Working Capital

Purchase of Plant Assets	$8,000	
Declaration of Dividends	4,000	
Total Uses of Working Capital		12,000
Increase in Working Capital		$16,000

Changes in Working Capital Components
Increases (Decreases) in Current Assets:

Cash	$5,000	
Accounts Receivable	9,000	
Inventory	5,000	
Increase in Current Assets		$19,000
Increases (Decreases) in Current Liabilities:		
Accounts Payable	$2,000	
Dividends Payable	1,000	
Increase in Current Liabilities		3,000
Increase in Working Capital		$16,000

corporation acquired land having a fair market value of $80,000 by issuing 800 shares of $100 par value common stock. This transaction would appear in the statement of changes in financial position as follows:

Sources of Working Capital
Issuance of Common Stock for Land　　　　$80,000

Uses of Working Capital
Purchase of Land by Issuance of Common Stock　　　　$80,000

The analysis of this transaction in the worksheet for a statement of changes in financial position requires *two* analyzing entries. The first entry—debiting Land for $80,000 and crediting Common Stock for $80,000—reflects the impact of the transaction on the noncurrent accounts. The second entry debits $80,000 under the sources of working capital as an issuance of common stock for land and credits $80,000 under the uses of working capital as a purchase of land by issuance of common stock. With the second entry, the transaction is presented as both a source and a use of working capital.

The foregoing example illustrates the presentation of certain significant transactions that have no effect on working capital. The approach is consistent with the view that this type of transaction is both a financing and an investing transaction, although the presentation suggests the "fiction" that a working capital inflow and outflow have occurred. Note, however, that because these transactions do not affect working capital, the amounts shown as both sources and uses of working capital offset each other. Therefore, the difference between Total Sources of Working Capital and Total Uses of Working Capital still equals the change in working capital for the period.

COMPREHENSIVE ILLUSTRATION

We can use the procedures just described regardless of the size or complexity of a firm's operations. We now present a comprehensive exercise to illustrate the techniques for preparing a somewhat more complex statement of changes in financial position.

The comparative balance sheets and income statement for the Superior Corporation are presented in Exhibits 19–8 and 19–9 (pages 670 and 671), respectively. During year 2, the following transactions occurred, in addition to routine transactions:

(1) Abandoned equipment costing $6,000 with $4,000 accumulated depreciation.

(2) Sold investment in M Company stock, which originally cost $10,000, for $35,000. Because this was the only security investment Superior Corporation had ever owned, the sale was considered an extraordinary event. Taxes increased by $7,000 as a result of the gain on the sale.

(3) Purchased equipment, $5,000.

(4) Acquired a patent with a fair value of $30,000 by issuing 250 shares of common stock early in the year.

(5) Retired bonds payable of $20,000 at par value.

(6) Declared dividends, $10,000.

First, we determine the change in working capital. The calculation is shown here in abbreviated form, without listing the current items in detail:

	Dec. 31, Year 2	Dec. 31, Year 1	Increase (Decrease)
Current Assets	$182,000	$170,000	$12,000
Current Liabilities	59,000	80,000	(21,000)
Working Capital	$123,000	$ 90,000	$33,000

We must account for the increase of $33,000 in working capital.

EXHIBIT 19-8

Superior Corporation
Balance Sheets

ASSETS	Dec. 31, Year 2	Dec. 31, Year 1	Increase (Decrease)
Current Assets			
Cash	$ 25,000	$ 20,000	$ 5,000
Accounts Receivable (net)	55,000	60,000	(5,000)
Inventory	90,000	80,000	10,000
Prepaid Expenses	12,000	10,000	2,000
Total Current Assets	$182,000	$170,000	$12,000
Investments			
Investment in M Company Stock	$ —	$ 10,000	($10,000)
Long-term Assets			
Plant and Equipment	$165,000	$166,000	($ 1,000)
Accumulated Depreciation	(38,000)	(34,000)	(4,000)
Patents (net)	29,000	—	29,000
Total Long-term Assets	$156,000	$132,000	$24,000
Total Assets	$338,000	$312,000	$26,000
LIABILITIES AND STOCKHOLDERS' EQUITY			
Current Liabilities			
Accounts Payable	$ 30,000	$ 40,000	($10,000)
Dividends Payable	10,000	8,000	2,000
Accrued Liabilities	19,000	32,000	(13,000)
Total Current Liabilities	$ 59,000	$ 80,000	($21,000)
Long-term Debt			
Bonds Payable	$ 50,000	$ 70,000	($20,000)
Stockholders' Equity			
Common Stock ($100 par value)	$125,000	$100,000	$25,000
Paid-in Capital in Excess of Par Value	5,000	—	5,000
Retained Earnings	99,000	62,000	37,000
Total Stockholders' Equity	$229,000	$162,000	$67,000
Total Liabilities and Stockholders' Equity	$338,000	$312,000	$26,000

Next, we prepare a worksheet for the statement of changes in financial position. Exhibit 19-10 (page 672) shows the worksheet for Superior Corporation. The analyzing entries are explained below.

(a) The effects of extraordinary items are reported separately from the effects of normal items. Because Superior Corporation has an extraordinary item, we

EXHIBIT 19-9

Superior Corporation
Income Statement
For the Year Ended December 31, Year 2

Sales		$360,000
Cost of Goods Sold		240,000
Gross Profit		$120,000
Operating Expenses and Income Taxes		
(excluding depreciation, amortization, and loss)	$80,000	
Depreciation Expense	8,000	
Patent Amortization Expense	1,000	
Loss on Retirement of Equipment	2,000	91,000
Income before Extraordinary Item		$ 29,000
Extraordinary Item:		
Gain on Sale of M Company Stock	$25,000	
Less: Income Taxes	7,000	18,000
Net Income		$ 47,000

begin with the "income before extraordinary item" of $29,000 in determining funds provided by operations. Entry (a) debits this income amount under sources of working capital and credits Retained Earnings for the same amount.

(b), (c), and **(d)** Three expenses deducted in determining the $29,000 income before extraordinary item have no impact on working capital. In entries (b), (c), and (d), we add them back to the $29,000 to derive the effect of ordinary operations on working capital.

Entry (b) analyzes the depreciation expense by debiting $8,000 under sources of working capital as an addition to the income before extraordinary item and crediting $8,000 to Accumulated Depreciation.

Patent amortization expense is analyzed in a similar fashion in entry (c), with a $1,000 debit under sources of working capital as an addition to the income amount and a $1,000 credit to Patents (net).

Entry (d) reflects the abandonment of equipment with a book value of $2,000. The abandonment causes a $2,000 loss, but does not affect working capital. Entry (d) debits $2,000 under sources of working capital as an addition to the income before extraordinary item, debits $4,000 to Accumulated Depreciation, and credits $6,000 to Plant and Equipment.

Depreciation expense, patent amortization expense, and the loss on retirement of equipment total $11,000. Adding these expenses to the $29,000 income before extraordinary item gives us $40,000 of working capital provided by ordinary operations.

EXHIBIT 19–10

Superior Corporation
Worksheet for Statement of Changes in Financial Position
For the Year Ended December 31, Year 2

Description	Changes in Noncurrent Accounts Debit	Changes in Noncurrent Accounts Credit	Analyzing Entries Debit	Analyzing Entries Credit
Investment in M Company Stock		10,000		(e) 10,000
Plant and Equipment		1,000	(f) 5,000	(d) 6,000
Accumulated Depreciation		4,000	(d) 4,000	(b) 8,000
Patents (net)	29,000		(g) 30,000	(c) 1,000
Bonds Payable	20,000		(i) 20,000	
Common Stock		25,000		(g) 25,000
Paid-in Capital in Excess of Par Value		5,000		(g) 5,000
Retained Earnings		37,000	(j) 10,000	(a) 29,000
				(e) 18,000
	49,000	82,000		
Increase in Working Capital	33,000			
	82,000	82,000		
Sources of Working Capital				
Income before Extraordinary Item			(a) 29,000	
Add: Depreciation			(b) 8,000	
Amortization			(c) 1,000	
Loss on Retirement of Equipment			(d) 2,000	
Extraordinary Item: Sale of M Company Stock			(e) 28,000	
Issuance of Common Stock for Patent			(h) 30,000	
Uses of Working Capital				
Purchase of Equipment				(f) 5,000
Purchase of Patent by Issuing Common Stock				(h) 30,000
Retirement of Bonds Payable				(i) 20,000
Declaration of Dividends				(j) 10,000
			167,000	167,000

(e) Given the surrounding circumstances, the sale of M Company stock by Superior Corporation was considered extraordinary. The transaction increased working capital by a net amount of $28,000 (cash proceeds from the sale were $35,000, but income taxes on the gain amounted to $7,000). The transaction also eliminated the $10,000 balance in the investment account and increased net income by $18,000. Entry (e) summarizes this transaction with a $28,000 debit as a source of working capital from the sale of M Company stock and credits of $10,000 to Investment in M Company Stock and $18,000 to Retained Earnings.

(f) Entry (f) analyzes the purchase of equipment costing $5,000. The purchase increased equipment and decreased working capital. Plant and Equipment is debited for $5,000 and a use of working capital for the purchase of equipment is credited for $5,000.

(g) and **(h)** The acquisition of a patent by issuing common stock is one of the significant transactions affecting financial position that must be reported in the funds statement even though it does not affect working capital. As explained earlier, this situation requires two analyzing entries on the worksheet.

Entry (g) reconstructs the effect of the transaction on the noncurrent accounts. The entry debits $30,000 to Patents (net) and credits $25,000 to Common Stock and $5,000 to Paid-in Capital in Excess of Par Value.

Entry (h) reflects $30,000 as both a source and a use of working capital. Issuance of Common Stock for Patent is debited under sources of working capital and Purchase of Patent by Issuing Common Stock is credited under uses of working capital.

(i) The retirement of bonds payable utilized $20,000 of working capital. Entry (i) shows this transaction by debiting Bonds Payable for $20,000 and crediting $20,000 as a use of working capital for the retirement of bonds payable.

(j) The effect of the dividends declaration is portrayed in entry (j). Retained Earnings is debited for $10,000 and Declaration of Dividends under uses of working capital is credited for $10,000.

Once the worksheet is completed, we prepare the statement of changes in financial position for Superior Corporation shown in Exhibit 19–11. The worksheet provides the information on the sources and uses of working capital. The detail of the changes in working capital components is obtained from the comparative balance sheets shown in Exhibit 19–8.

CASH FLOW STATEMENTS

When preparing financial statements for external users, firms may prepare the statement of changes in financial position showing the sources and uses of cash[2] rather than working capital. The authoritative guidelines for reporting changes in financial position still apply, however. Such statements, which should also be titled "statement of changes in financial position," should include any significant financing and investing activities, even though cash is not directly affected. Because

[2]The definition of cash used for the statement of changes in financial position may vary somewhat among companies. Many companies define *cash* as the readily available discretionary resources—a concept that includes cash and short-term investments.

EXHIBIT 19–11

Superior Corporation
Statement of Changes in Financial Position
For the Year Ended December 31, Year 2

Sources of Working Capital
Operations:

Income before Extraordinary Item	$29,000	
Add Expenses Not Decreasing Working Capital:		
Depreciation	8,000	
Amortization	1,000	
Loss on Retirement of Equipment	2,000	
Total from Operations		$40,000
Extraordinary Item: Sale of M Company Stock (net of taxes)		28,000
Issuance of Common Stock for Patent		30,000
Total Sources of Working Capital		$98,000

Uses of Working Capital

Purchase of Equipment	$ 5,000	
Purchase of Patent by Issuing Common Stock	30,000	
Retirement of Bonds Payable	20,000	
Declaration of Dividends	10,000	
Total Uses of Working Capital		65,000
Increase in Working Capital		$33,000

Changes in Working Capital Components
Increases (Decreases) in Current Assets:

Cash	$ 5,000	
Accounts Receivable	(5,000)	
Inventory	10,000	
Prepaid Expenses	2,000	
Increase in Current Assets		$12,000
Increases (Decreases) in Current Liabilities:		
Accounts Payable	($10,000)	
Dividends Payable	2,000	
Accrued Liabilities	(13,000)	
Decrease in Current Liabilities		(21,000)
Increase in Working Capital		$33,000

the focus is on cash rather than on working capital, the title "statement of changes in financial position—cash basis" may be appropriate. These statements are often called **cash flow statements,** the term we use here for ease of discussion.

Cash flow statements will likely become a popular format for reporting changes in financial position. The Financial Accounting Standards Board believes one objective of financial reporting should be providing information to help external users "assess the amounts, timing, and uncertainty of prospective net cash inflows

CASH FLOWS VERSUS WORKING CAPITAL FLOWS

You can trace the history of the cash versus working capital controversy back to 1975. The problem is perspective. Busy accountants are aware of the many incidents that created support for a cash-based funds statement; they just have not had the time to put the whole picture together.

The W.T. Grant controversy

It took a major business failure to trigger serious interest in the cash-based funds statement. The 1975 W.T. Grant bankruptcy shocked investors everywhere. "With all the facts and figures churned out by Grant," declared one bitter shareholder, "where was the truth? Why couldn't we see this coming?" Analysts point an accusing finger at the working-capital-based funds statement.

W.T. Grant's operations were users, not providers, of cash from 1966–1975. In the decade preceding the bankruptcy, cash provided by operations was in the black for only two years. Until collapse was imminent, however, Grant's working capital from operations remained positive and fairly stable. Grant's funds statement hid a major liquidity problem.

W.T. Grant finally choked to death on its own inventory. Its failure served notice that there is an important difference between cash flows and working capital flows.

The General Electric experience

The W.T. Grant bankruptcy took most investors by surprise. Back in 1975, earnings per share was king; cash management was an unheard of art.

General Electric woke up to the importance of cash-flow information earlier than many other corporations did. In 1976, GE launched a massive campaign to force operating managers to pay closer attention to cash flow. The results were startling: At the beginning of the program, declining liquidity threatened GE's triple A bond rating; by the end of the program, the company had freed up over $1 billion in excess cash.

The financial analysts

General Electric showed business executives that cash-flow information offers a significant financial opportunity. When it became clear that companies that manage cash flow outperform those that do not, the financial analysts soon jumped on the bandwagon. As one analyst put it, "If cash-flow information makes good financial sense, it probably makes good financial reporting sense." The analysts embraced cash-flow analysis with a missionary zeal, and results were a rude surprise to a lot of business people.

Companies with good earnings records discovered their performance didn't measure up using the cash-flow yardstick. "Cannibalizing its capital structure to keep stock prices up," reads one report. "Neglecting plant and equipment and paying dividends with money that's not there," huffs another. "A perfect formula for earnings success if you don't mind rusting plants, inferior R&D and yesterday's technology," preaches a third.

Financial analysts found a powerful tool in cash-flow analysis. Although earnings information might tell them how much money a company was making, only cash-flow information could say whether that money was real.

From Richard S. Clark, "Statement of Changes: In Need of a Change?" *CA Magazine*, February 1983, pages 26–30. Excerpted, with permission, from *CA Magazine*, February 1983, published by the Canadian Institute of Chartered Accountants, Toronto, Canada.

to the . . . enterprise."[3] Although cash flow statements report past cash flows, these statements should be useful for assessing the prospective (or future) cash flows noted by the FASB. Cash flow statements may also aid evaluations of a firm's liquidity and solvency.

The management of cash flows is a critical function in the operation of a business enterprise. Cash flow statements may be prepared and used internally in planning and controlling cash movements. Internal cash flow statements need not adhere to the guidelines applicable to external statements, but they may be similar in format. Cash budgets—discussed in Chapter 25—are also important to the management of cash flows. Our focus here, however, is on cash flow statements prepared for users external to the business.

The cash flow statement has two major sections, one reporting the sources of cash and the other showing the uses of cash. No separate section reports changes in working capital components, because changes in most elements of working capital other than cash are disclosed as adjustments necessary to derive cash provided by operations.

Cash Flow from Operations

Cash provided by operations constitutes a major source of cash. It is determined by converting the accrual basis net income amount to a cash basis net income. Net income on a cash basis considers only cash receipts as revenue and subtracts from cash receipts only cash outlays for merchandise and expenses.

To better understand the process of converting a net income number from an accrual amount to a cash basis amount, let us first consider the procedures for converting individual revenue and expenses from an accrual to a cash basis. These procedures are diagramed in Exhibit 19–12. The adjustments diagramed here fall into two categories:

Changes in noncurrent accounts   Some expenses, such as depreciation, affect only noncurrent balance sheet accounts and do not affect cash. These expenses do not appear in a cash basis income statement and, therefore, must be eliminated when converting an accrual basis income statement to a cash basis income statement. Exhibit 19–12 shows the elimination of these items.

Changes in working capital accounts   When we focus on cash, we must also consider how changes in working capital accounts affect cash flows from operations. As Exhibit 19–12 shows, to obtain cash basis amounts, we adjust the appropriate revenue and expenses on the accrual income statement for changes in accounts receivable, inventories, prepaid expenses, accounts payable, and accrued liabilities. For example, if a period's sales were $10,000 and accounts receivable increased from $3,000 to $4,000 during the same period, we conclude that the cash collections for the period were $9,000.

[3] *Statement of Financial Accounting Concepts No. 1,* "Objectives of Financial Reporting by Business Enterprises" (Stamford, CT: Financial Accounting Standards Board, 1978), p. 18. The FASB also believes information should be reported about earnings. It notes that earnings measured by accrual accounting are a better indicator of periodic financial performance than information about current cash receipts and payments.

EXHIBIT 19–12

Accrual Basis	➤	Cash Basis
Sales	+ Beginning − Ending Receivables	= Receipts
Cost of Goods Sold	+ Ending − Beginning Inventory + Beginning − Ending Accounts Payable	= Payments for Goods
Operating Expenses and Income Taxes (except depreciation and similar write-offs)	+ Ending − Beginning Prepaids + Beginning − Ending Accruals	= Payments for Expense
Depreciation (and similar write-offs)	Eliminated	= 0

Individual revenue and expense items on a cash basis are not shown in the cash flow statement. Instead, cash provided by operations is presented by starting with the accrual net income figure and adjusting that number to a cash basis amount. The adjustments are derived from the two categories we established above to adjust individual revenue and expense items to cash basis amounts. The adjustments for expenses affecting only noncurrent accounts are handled as they were in deriving working capital from operations. Depreciation expense, for example, is added to the accrual net income amount. The other category of adjustments—the changes in various components of working capital—is handled as shown in the following schedule:

	Change in Working Capital: Adjustment of Accrual Basis Net Income to Convert to Cash Basis Net Income	
Working Capital Item	**Add**	**Deduct**
Accounts Receivable	Decrease	Increase
Inventory	Decrease	Increase
Prepaid Expenses	Decrease	Increase
Accounts Payable	Increase	Decrease
Accrued Liabilities	Increase	Decrease

For example, we add a decrease in accounts receivable during the period to accrual net income to convert to a cash basis figure. We deduct an increase in accounts receivable from accrual net income. The remainder of the schedule is interpreted in a similar fashion.

In summary, then, the procedures for converting an accrual basis net income amount to a cash basis net income figure are as follows:

> Accrual Basis Net Income
> + Depreciation and Similar Write-offs
> + or − Changes in Accounts Receivable, Inventory, Prepaid Expenses, Accounts Payable, and Accrued Liabilities
> = Cash Basis Net Income

**Illustration
of Cash Flow
Analysis**

To demonstrate the preparation of a cash flow statement, we use the statements of XYZ Company from Exhibits 19–4 and 19–5. For convenience they are repeated in Exhibit 19–13. We also repeat the nonroutine transactions that took place in year 3.

(1) Sold plant assets with a cost of $7,000 and accumulated depreciation of $3,000 for $4,000 cash.

(2) Purchased new plant assets for $8,000 cash.

(3) Sold additional common stock at par value for $10,000 cash.

(4) Declared dividends to be paid in year 4, $4,000. Dividends of $3,000 declared in year 2 were paid.

Our general approach in determining the sources and uses of working capital was to review the changes in all noncurrent accounts to identify the events affecting working capital. When dealing with a cash flow statement, our general approach is to review all balance sheet accounts (except Cash) to identify the events affecting cash flows. A worksheet may aid in the preparation of a cash flow statement. We construct the cash flow statement by using the following steps:

EXHIBIT 19–13

XYZ Company
Balance Sheets

Assets	Dec. 31, Year 3	Dec. 31, Year 2	Liabilities and Stockholders' Equity	Dec. 31, Year 3	Dec. 31, Year 2
Cash	$ 21,000	$ 16,000	Accounts Payable	$ 22,000	$ 20,000
Accounts Receivable	19,000	10,000	Dividends Payable	4,000	3,000
Inventory	35,000	30,000	Common Stock	60,000	50,000
Plant Assets	56,000	55,000	Retained Earnings	33,000	28,000
Accumulated Depreciation	(12,000)	(10,000)			
Total Assets	$119,000	$101,000	Total Liabilities and Stockholders' Equity	$119,000	$101,000

XYZ Company
Income Statement
For the Year Ended December 31, Year 3

Sales		$50,000
Cost of Goods Sold		30,000
Gross Profit		$20,000
Operating Expenses and Income Taxes (excluding depreciation)	$6,000	
Depreciation Expense	5,000	11,000
Net Income		$ 9,000

STEP 1 Determine the net increase or decrease in cash during the year by comparing the cash balances on the comparative balance sheets. XYZ Company's cash increased $5,000 (from $16,000 to $21,000) during year 3.

STEP 2 Prepare a worksheet to analyze the changes in the noncash accounts and identify the sources and uses of cash for the period. Exhibit 19–14 shows the worksheet for XYZ Company.

Heading and form The worksheet's heading and form are similar to the heading and form of the worksheet analyzing working capital changes. The focus on cash, however, causes two differences.

EXHIBIT 19–14

<table>
<tr><td colspan="5" align="center">XYZ Company
Worksheet for Statement of Changes in Financial Position—Cash Basis
For the Year Ended December 31, Year 3</td></tr>
<tr><td rowspan="2" align="center">Description</td><td colspan="2" align="center">Changes in
Noncash Accounts</td><td colspan="2" align="center">Analyzing Entries</td></tr>
<tr><td align="center">Debit</td><td align="center">Credit</td><td align="center">Debit</td><td align="center">Credit</td></tr>
<tr><td>Accounts Receivable</td><td>9,000</td><td></td><td>(c) 9,000</td><td></td></tr>
<tr><td>Inventory</td><td>5,000</td><td></td><td>(d) 5,000</td><td></td></tr>
<tr><td>Plant Assets</td><td>1,000</td><td></td><td>(g) 8,000</td><td>(f) 7,000</td></tr>
<tr><td>Accumulated Depreciation</td><td></td><td>2,000</td><td>(f) 3,000</td><td>(b) 5,000</td></tr>
<tr><td>Accounts Payable</td><td></td><td>2,000</td><td></td><td>(e) 2,000</td></tr>
<tr><td>Dividends Payable</td><td></td><td>1,000</td><td>(i) 3,000</td><td>(j) 4,000</td></tr>
<tr><td>Common Stock</td><td></td><td>10,000</td><td></td><td>(h) 10,000</td></tr>
<tr><td>Retained Earnings</td><td></td><td>5,000</td><td>(j) 4,000</td><td>(a) 9,000</td></tr>
<tr><td></td><td>15,000</td><td>20,000</td><td></td><td></td></tr>
<tr><td>Increase in Cash</td><td>5,000</td><td></td><td></td><td></td></tr>
<tr><td></td><td>20,000</td><td>20,000</td><td></td><td></td></tr>
<tr><td>Sources of Cash</td><td></td><td></td><td></td><td></td></tr>
<tr><td> Net Income</td><td></td><td></td><td>(a) 9,000</td><td></td></tr>
<tr><td>   Add: Depreciation</td><td></td><td></td><td>(b) 5,000</td><td></td></tr>
<tr><td>   Less: Accounts Receivable Increase</td><td></td><td></td><td></td><td>(c) 9,000</td></tr>
<tr><td>   Less: Inventory Increase</td><td></td><td></td><td></td><td>(d) 5,000</td></tr>
<tr><td>   Add: Accounts Payable Increase</td><td></td><td></td><td>(e) 2,000</td><td></td></tr>
<tr><td> Sale of Plant Assets</td><td></td><td></td><td>(f) 4,000</td><td></td></tr>
<tr><td> Sale of Common Stock</td><td></td><td></td><td>(h) 10,000</td><td></td></tr>
<tr><td>Uses of Cash</td><td></td><td></td><td></td><td></td></tr>
<tr><td> Purchase of Plant Assets</td><td></td><td></td><td></td><td>(g) 8,000</td></tr>
<tr><td> Payment of Dividends</td><td></td><td></td><td></td><td>(i) 3,000</td></tr>
<tr><td></td><td></td><td></td><td>62,000</td><td>62,000</td></tr>
</table>

(1) The heading specifically states that the worksheet deals with a cash basis statement of changes in financial position.

(2) The first set of debit and credit columns is labeled Changes in Noncash Accounts.

Changes in noncash accounts The content of the worksheet focuses on the company's noncash accounts.

(1) First, a list of all noncash accounts is entered in the description column. The debit or credit change in each account balance for the period is entered in the appropriate column under the Changes in Noncash Accounts heading. Accounts Receivable, for example, increased from $10,000 at December 31, year 2 to $19,000 at December 31, year 3; the $9,000 increase is entered in the debit column. The remaining accounts are handled in a similar fashion.

(2) After entering the changes for all noncash accounts, the two columns are totaled. The difference between the column totals equals the cash change calculated in step 1. The cash change is entered on the worksheet—an increase in the debit column, a decrease in the credit column—and the two columns are totaled to show their equality. Exhibit 19–14 shows the $5,000 cash increase for XYZ Company in the debit column.

(3) At this point, the phrase "sources of cash" is written in the description column. Several lines are skipped to allow for all possible cash sources and the phrase "uses of cash" is written in the same column. The worksheet is now ready for the analyzing entries.

Analyzing entries Analyzing entries explain the changes that occurred in the noncash accounts during the period. If the change affected cash, we enter the appropriate amount in the worksheet as either a source or a use of cash. Sources of cash are entered as debits, and uses of cash are entered as credits. When all changes in noncash accounts have been explained, our analysis is complete.

Essentially, the analysis consists of two sets of analyzing entries. The initial set determines cash provided from operations. The first analyzing entry establishes the starting point for computing cash provided from operations—accrual basis net income. We then reflect the additional entries needed to convert income from an accrual to a cash basis. As previously discussed, changes in most working capital accounts are either added to or deducted from accrual basis net income in this conversion process. Our analyzing entries reflect these adjustments. For example, if accounts receivable increased during the period, our analyzing entry would debit Accounts Receivable (to reflect the increase) and credit sources of cash (to deduct the accounts receivable increase from accrual basis net income in computing cash basis net income). Some entries in this initial set may affect noncurrent accounts. The entry analyzing depreciation, for example, debits sources of cash and credits Accumulated Depreciation.

The second set of analyzing entries explains the remaining changes in the noncash accounts. We review each noncash account whose change during the period has not been fully explained by the first set of analyzing entries and reconstruct the entries, in summary form, to explain these changes. Any effects of these transactions on cash are entered in the worksheet's lower portion as either a source or a use of cash. Of course, not every analyzing entry affects cash. Declaring a cash dividend, for example, does not immediately affect cash. The declaration requires an analyzing entry, though, because it causes a change in the noncash accounts and our analysis must explain all changes completely.

A significant financing or investing event that does not affect cash is handled on the worksheet the same way we analyzed such events when explaining working capital changes. *Two* analyzing entries are made—one entry reflects the transaction's impact on the noncash accounts, and the second entry presents the transaction as both a source and a use of cash.

We now explain the analyzing entries in Exhibit 19–14. Entries (a)–(e) derive cash provided from operations, and entries (f)–(j) explain the remaining changes in the noncash accounts.

(a) Entry (a) debits the $9,000 accrual basis net income to sources of cash and credits Retained Earnings.

(b) Entry (b) adds depreciation expense to the accrual basis net income as part of the conversion to a cash basis net income. The entry debits sources of cash and credits Accumulated Depreciation for $5,000.

(c) Accounts receivable increases are deducted when converting an accrual basis net income to a cash basis amount. Entry (c) debits Accounts Receivable and credits sources of cash for this $9,000 adjustment.

(d) Inventory increases are also deducted in converting from accrual to cash basis net income. Entry (d) debits Inventory and credits sources of cash for the $5,000 inventory increase.

(e) Entry (e) adds the increase in accounts payable to the accrual basis net income to complete the conversion to a cash basis amount. The entry debits sources of cash and credits Accounts Payable for $2,000.

(f) The sale of plant assets increased cash by $4,000, decreased Accumulated Depreciation by $3,000, and decreased Plant Assets by $7,000, as shown in entry (f).

(g) The purchase of plant assets used $8,000 cash. Entry (g) portrays this use of cash and the corresponding increase in Plant Assets.

(h) The issuance of common stock was a source of $10,000 cash. Entry (h) debits sources of cash and credits Common Stock for $10,000.

(i) The year 2 dividend of $3,000, paid in year 3, reduced cash. Entry (i) reconstructs the entry for the dividend payment, debiting Dividends Payable and crediting uses of cash.

(j) The $4,000 dividend declared in year 3 did not affect the year 3 cash flows. The dividend declaration, however, affects two noncash accounts, and an analyzing entry is required. Entry (j) reflects the dividend with a debit to Retained Earnings and a credit to Dividends Payable.

For each noncash account, the debit or credit balance of the analyzing entries now equals the change shown in the first two columns. Our analysis is complete,

EXHIBIT 19–15

XYZ Company
Statement of Changes in Financial Position—Cash Basis
For the Year Ended December 31, Year 3

Sources of Cash

Operations:

Net Income	$9,000	
Add (Deduct) Items to Convert Net Income to Cash Basis:		
Depreciation	5,000	
Accounts Receivable Increase	(9,000)	
Inventory Increase	(5,000)	
Accounts Payable Increase	2,000	
Total from Operations		$ 2,000
Sale of Plant Assets		4,000
Sale of Common Stock		10,000
Total Sources of Cash		$16,000

Uses of Cash

Purchase of Plant Assets	$8,000	
Payment of Dividends	3,000	
Total Uses of Cash		11,000
Net Increase in Cash		$ 5,000

and we total and double rule the last two columns to complete the worksheet. The analyzing entries help us compile information for a cash flow statement; they are not recorded in the accounts.

STEP 3 Prepare the cash flow statement from information in the worksheet on the sources and uses of cash. The difference between total sources and uses of cash should equal the change in cash calculated in step 1. The cash flow statement for XYZ Company is shown in Exhibit 19–15.

KEY POINTS TO REMEMBER

Statement of Changes in Financial Position— Working Capital Flow

(1) *Funds,* or *working capital,* is defined as current assets less current liabilities.

(2) The statement of changes in financial position explains the net increase or decrease in funds during the period.

(3) In preparing a statement of changes in financial position, we must review all changes in noncurrent assets, noncurrent liabilities, and owners' equity for effects on working capital.

(4) A worksheet may aid in the preparation of a statement of changes in financial position.

(5) Write-offs of noncurrent items (such as depreciation and amortization) do not affect funds. Any of these items reflected in the net income (or income before extraordinary items) figure must be added back to determine funds provided by operations.

(6) Changes in noncurrent balance sheet accounts that do not affect funds but that result from major financing or investing transactions should be shown on the statement of changes in financial position.

Cash Flow Statement

(7) The cash flow statement explains the net increase or decrease in cash during the period.

(8) In preparing cash flow statements, we must review all changes in balance sheet accounts other than Cash for cash flow effects.
  (a) To determine cash from operations, we must convert the accrual income figure to a cash basis amount.
  (b) Other cash inflows and outflows can be determined by analyzing all changes in balance sheet accounts other than those accounted for in (a).

(9) A worksheet may aid in the preparation of a cash flow statement.

(10) Changes in noncurrent balance sheet accounts that do not affect cash but that result from major financing or investing transactions should be shown on the cash flow statement.

QUESTIONS

19-1 Define the term *funds* as used by business executives and financial analysts.

19-2 What is the difference between a statement of changes in financial position portraying working capital flow and a cash flow statement?

19-3 What information shown on the statement of changes in financial position (working capital flow) is not readily available from the balance sheet and income statement?

19-4 Identify the two major parts of a statement of changes in financial position (working capital flow) and indicate the information that is presented in each part.

19-5 What are the major *sources* of a firm's working capital? What are the major *uses* of working capital?

19-6 In determining working capital provided by operations, why must we add depreciation back to net income? Give examples of other income statement items that are added to net income in deriving working capital provided by operations.

19-7 Glad Company sold for $29,000 cash long-term investments originally costing $14,000. Income taxes on the extraordinary gain were $4,200. Describe how this event is handled in a statement of changes in financial position (working capital flow).

19-8 King Company acquired a $700,000 building by issuing $700,000 worth of bonds payable. Describe how this transaction is reported in the statement of changes in financial position (working capital flow). How is this transaction reported in a cash flow statement?

19-9 Because of unforeseen circumstances, Wand Company abandoned a piece of equipment that was not fully depreciated. The asset had cost $9,500, and $8,300 of depreciation had accumulated at the time of abandonment. How did this abandonment affect Wand Company's working capital?

19-10 When a worksheet is prepared for the statement of changes in financial position (working capital flow), all changes in noncurrent balance sheet accounts are analyzed. Why?

19-11 If a business had a net loss for the year, under what circumstances could the statement of changes in financial position show working capital provided by operations?

19-12 During the year, Alvarez Company had $700 amortization of bond premium on bonds payable. Explain how this item would be handled in calculating working capital provided by operations.

19-13 During the current year, a company declared but did not pay a $4,000 cash dividend and a 10% stock dividend. Describe how the company treats these two items when it prepares a statement of changes in financial position (working capital flow) for the year.

19-14 During 19X2, Major Corporation's working capital increased $49,000, its long-term assets decreased $16,000, and its long-term liabilities increased $7,000. What was the change in Major Corporation's stockholders' equity during 19X2?

19-15 A merchandising company is preparing a cash flow statement. Net income for the year is $60,000. Accounts receivable total $34,000 at the beginning of the year and $27,000 at the end of the year. Explain how the change in accounts receivable for the year appears on the cash flow statement.

19-16 A merchandising firm is preparing a cash flow statement. Net income for the year is $66,000. Its beginning inventory was $19,000, and its ending inventory was $24,000. Accounts payable were $8,000 at the beginning of the year and $6,000 at the end of the year. Explain how the changes in inventory and accounts payable for the year appear on the cash flow statement.

19-17 On December 15 of the current year, Stout Company declared a $12,000 cash dividend to be paid January 15 of the following year. How would the treatment of this declaration in a statement of changes in financial position (working capital flow) differ from its treatment in a cash flow statement? Assume that both are prepared for the current year.

EXERCISES

19-18 For each of the following transactions, state whether working capital would increase, decrease, or remain unaffected. When appropriate, give the amount of the change.
(a) Paid a current note payable in cash, $3,000.
(b) Issued 900 shares of $40 par value common stock at $60 per share.
(c) Declared a cash dividend, $23,000.

(d) Sold plant assets for $18,000; the assets had an original cost of $40,000 and accumulated depreciation of $26,000.

(e) Sold short-term marketable securities, having a carrying value of $5,000, for $8,000.

(f) Paid the dividend in part (c).

(g) Purchased inventory on account, $35,000.

(h) Purchased plant assets for cash, $58,000.

(i) Sold bonds payable with a $200,000 face value at 98.

(j) Wrote off an uncollectible account receivable against the allowance for uncollectible accounts.

(k) Purchased 200 shares of treasury stock at $55 per share.

19–19 This year's income statement for the Dynan Company shows net income of $70,000. The following information is also available:

(1) Uncollectible accounts expense for year, $4,000.

(2) Depreciation expense for year, $6,000.

(3) Patent amortization expense for year, $3,000.

(4) Sales on account for year, $208,000.

(5) Purchases of merchandise on account for year, $92,000.

Calculate the amount of working capital provided from operations for this year's statement of changes in financial position.

19–20 The following information was obtained from the Canyon Company's comparative balance sheets.

	Dec. 31, 19X1	Dec. 31, 19X0
Cash	$18,000	$14,000
Accounts Receivable	34,000	29,000
Inventory	49,000	33,000
Prepaid Expenses	2,000	4,000
Plant Assets (net of accumulated depreciation)	95,000	86,000
Accounts Payable	39,000	27,000
Accrued Liabilities	13,000	10,000
Common Stock	85,000	85,000
Retained Earnings	61,000	44,000

Calculate the change in working capital for 19X1.

19–21 Refer to the balance sheet information in Exercise 19–20. Suppose you knew, by looking at the income statement, that depreciation on plant assets for 19X1 was $8,000 and that no assets had been sold during the year. How much working capital has been applied to the purchase of plant assets during the year?

19–22 Refer to the balance sheet information in Exercise 19–20 and assume that you know the following:

Net income per income statement	$24,000
Dividends declared and paid	7,000
Cost of plant assets purchased	?
Depreciation on plant assets	8,000

Prepare a statement of changes in financial position (working capital flow) for 19X1.

19–23 Refer to the balance sheet information in Exercise 19–20. Assume Canyon Company's 19X1 income statement showed depreciation expense of $8,000 and a net income of $24,000. Calculate the cash provided from operations that would appear in a cash flow statement.

19–24 The Rio Company, which owns no plant assets, had the following income statement for the current year:

Sales	$220,000
Cost of Goods Sold	150,000
Gross Profit	$ 70,000
Operating Expenses	48,000
Net Income	$ 22,000

Additional information about the company follows:

	End of Year	Beginning of Year
Accounts Receivable	$24,000	$21,000
Inventory	30,000	38,000
Accrued Liabilities	7,000	11,000
Accounts Payable	14,000	8,000

Using the preceding information, calculate the cash provided from operations that would appear in a cash flow statement.

19–25 Refer to the information in Exercise 19–24. Calculate the following amounts for the current year:
(a) Cash collected from customers.
(b) Cash payments for goods purchased.
(c) Cash payments for operating expenses.

PROBLEMS

19–26 Comparative balance sheets at December 31 of 19X0 and 19X1 for the Sanchez Company are shown below.

Sanchez Company
Balance Sheets

	Dec. 31, 19X1	Dec. 31, 19X0
Assets		
Cash	$ 8,000	$ 5,000
Accounts Receivable (net)	16,000	12,000
Inventory	31,000	22,000
Prepaid Expenses	2,000	3,000
Plant Assets	90,000	70,000
Accumulated Depreciation	(26,000)	(20,000)
Total Assets	$121,000	$92,000

Liabilities and Stockholders' Equity		
Accounts Payable	$ 10,000	$14,000
Bonds Payable	18,000	—
Common Stock	50,000	50,000
Retained Earnings	43,000	28,000
Total Liabilities and Stockholders' Equity	$121,000	$92,000

Net income per the income statement for 19X1 was $23,000. There were no extraordinary items. Dividends of $8,000 were declared and paid during 19X1. Plant assets were purchased for cash, and later in the year, bonds payable were sold for cash.

REQUIRED
(a) Calculate the change in working capital during 19X1.
(b) Prepare a worksheet for a statement of changes in financial position (working capital flow) for 19X1.
(c) Prepare a statement of changes in financial position (working capital flow) for 19X1.

19–27 The Retained Earnings account of the Birch Company for this year reveals the following:

Beginning Balance		$45,000
Add: Net Income		37,000
		$82,000
Less: Stock Dividend	$ 9,000	
Cash Dividend	19,000	28,000
Ending Balance		$54,000

Comparative balance sheets at December 31 of last year and this year are presented below.

Birch Company
Balance Sheets

	Dec. 31, This Year	Dec. 31, Last Year
Assets		
Cash	$ 17,000	$ 13,000
Accounts Receivable (net)	44,000	41,000
Inventory	80,000	85,000
Prepaid Expenses	6,000	4,000
Plant Assets	245,000	194,000
Accumulated Depreciation	(24,000)	(16,000)
Goodwill (less amortization)	26,000	29,000
Total Assets	$394,000	$350,000

Liabilities and Stockholders' Equity

Accounts Payable	$ 46,000	$ 39,000
Dividends Payable	19,000	15,000
Bonds Payable	100,000	115,000
Common Stock	175,000	136,000
Retained Earnings	54,000	45,000
Total Liabilities and Stockholders' Equity	$394,000	$350,000

During the year, the company sold for $9,000 old equipment that had cost $15,000 and had $6,000 accumulated depreciation. New equipment was purchased for cash. Amortization of goodwill amounting to $3,000 was included as an expense on the income statement. A portion of the bonds matured this year and were retired for cash. There were no extraordinary items. The cash dividend declared this year has not been paid. The cash dividend declared last year was paid this year. The stock dividend was declared and paid this year. Other than the stock dividend, stock issuances were for cash.

REQUIRED
(a) Calculate the change in working capital during this year.
(b) Prepare a worksheet for a statement of changes in financial position (working capital flow) for this year.
(c) Prepare a statement of changes in financial position (working capital flow) for this year.

19–28 The Pacific Company's comparative balance sheets at December 31 of this year and last year are shown below, together with this year's income statement and retained earnings statement.

Pacific Company
Balance Sheets

	Dec. 31, This Year	Dec. 31, Last Year
Assets		
Cash	$ 25,000	$ 16,000
Accounts Receivable (net)	47,000	42,000
Inventories	96,000	73,000
Prepaid Expenses	14,000	10,000
Long-term Investments	—	17,000
Land	185,000	150,000
Buildings	290,000	225,000
Accumulated Depreciation—Buildings	(62,000)	(45,000)
Equipment	175,000	190,000
Accumulated Depreciation—Equipment	(40,000)	(30,000)
Patents (less amortization)	64,000	28,000
Total Assets	$794,000	$676,000

Liabilities and Stockholders' Equity

Accounts Payable	$ 38,000	$ 30,000
Notes Payable (short-term)	20,000	35,000
Dividends Payable	41,000	—
Accrued Liabilities	15,000	17,000
Bonds Payable	190,000	190,000
Premium on Bonds Payable	8,000	9,000
Common Stock ($100 par value)	332,000	300,000
Paid-in Capital in Excess of Par Value	20,000	12,000
Retained Earnings	130,000	83,000
Total Liabilities and Stockholders' Equity	$794,000	$676,000

Pacific Company
Retained Earnings Statement
For the Current Year

Beginning Balance	$ 83,000
Add: Net Income	88,000
	$171,000
Less: Cash Dividend	41,000
Ending Balance	$130,000

Pacific Company
Income Statement
For the Current Year

Sales		$950,000
Cost of Goods Sold		645,000
Gross Profit		$305,000
Operating Expenses and Taxes	$152,600	
Depreciation Expense	39,000	
Patent Amortization Expense	4,000	
Interest Expense	22,000	
Loss on Retirement of Equipment	3,000	220,600
Income before Extraordinary Item		$ 84,400
Extraordinary Item:		
Gain on Sale of Long-term Investments	$ 5,000	
Less: Income Taxes	1,400	3,600
Net Income		$ 88,000

During the year, the following transactions occurred:
(1) Purchased land, $35,000.
(2) Sold long-term investments, costing $17,000, for $22,000. The circum-

stances of this sale qualified it as an extraordinary event for Pacific Company. The gain on the sale increased taxes $1,400.

(3) An expenditure of $65,000 made to improve the building was capitalized.

(4) Abandoned equipment that cost $15,000 and had $12,000 accumulated depreciation.

(5) Interest expense on the income statement consisted of $23,000 paid less amortization of $1,000 bond premium.

(6) Acquired a patent with a fair value of $40,000 by issuing 320 shares of common stock.

(7) Declared dividends, $41,000.

REQUIRED

(a) Calculate the change in working capital during this year.

(b) Prepare a worksheet for a statement of changes in financial position (working capital flow) for this year.

(c) Prepare a statement of changes in financial position (working capital flow) for this year.

19–29 Refer to the data given for the Sanchez Company in Problem 19–26.

REQUIRED

(a) Prepare a worksheet for a statement of changes in financial position—cash basis (cash flow statement) for 19X1 for the Sanchez Company.

(b) Prepare a statement of changes in financial position—cash basis (cash flow statement) for 19X1.

19–30 Refer to the data given for the Birch Company in Problem 19–27 and the income statement of the Birch Company shown below.

Birch Company
Income Statement
For the Current Year

Sales		$245,000
Cost of Goods Sold		127,000
Gross Profit		$118,000
Depreciation Expense	$14,000	
Goodwill Amortization Expense	3,000	
Other Operating Expenses and Taxes	64,000	81,000
Net Income		$ 37,000

REQUIRED

(a) Prepare a worksheet for a statement of changes in financial position—cash basis (cash flow statement) for the current year for the Birch Company.

(b) Prepare a statement of changes in financial position—cash basis (cash flow statement) for the current year.

19–31 The board of directors of Boldt Corporation was quite impressed with the firm's performance during the past year. The firm doubled its net income with only a 60% increase in sales volume, as shown by the company's income statements below:

Boldt Corporation
Income Statements

	This Year	Last Year
Sales	$4,224,000	$2,640,000
Cost of Goods Sold	2,746,000	1,768,000
Gross Profit	$1,478,000	$ 872,000
Operating Expenses	1,022,000	662,000
	$ 456,000	$ 210,000
Income Taxes	190,000	77,000
Net Income	$ 266,000	$ 133,000

The board members were somewhat dismayed by the company's financial position, however. Not only did working capital decline from the previous year, but the ratio of current assets to current liabilities dropped below 200%. Comparative balance sheets are shown below and on the next page.

The board's chairman wants you to prepare an analysis of the changes in financial position, showing what has happened to the firm's working capital during the year. Your investigation reveals that the following events occurred during the year:

(1) The firm acquired a $190,000 land site by issuing 3,800 shares of common stock at par value.
(2) Dividends were declared and paid (before the issuance of the new shares above) at $3 per share.
(3) Equipment that had cost $90,000 was sold for its book value of $50,000.
(4) The firm acquired $700,000 of new equipment by paying $350,000 cash and giving a 12% mortgage note of $350,000.

Boldt Corporation
Balance Sheets

	Dec. 31, This Year	Dec. 31, Last Year
Assets		
Cash	$ 100,000	$ 395,000
Accounts Receivable	575,000	250,000
Inventory	1,320,000	900,000
Prepaid Expenses	65,000	55,000
Total Current Assets	$2,060,000	$1,600,000
Land	440,000	250,000
Plant and Equipment	1,600,000	990,000
Accumulated Depreciation	(400,000)	(340,000)
Total Assets	$3,700,000	$2,500,000

Liabilities and Stockholders' Equity

Accounts Payable	$ 560,000	$ 315,000
Accrued Liabilities	380,000	260,000
Income Taxes Payable	190,000	77,000
Total Current Liabilities	$1,130,000	$ 652,000
12% Mortgage Note Payable	350,000	—
Common Stock ($50 par value)	1,590,000	1,400,000
Retained Earnings	630,000	448,000
Total Liabilities and Stockholders' Equity	$3,700,000	$2,500,000

REQUIRED

(a) Prepare a worksheet for a statement of changes in financial position (working capital flow) for this year.

(b) Prepare a statement of changes in financial position (working capital flow) for this year.

(c) Write a brief discussion of the major points to be brought to the attention of the board of directors.

ALTERNATE PROBLEMS

19–26A Comparative balance sheets at December 31 of 19X0 and 19X1 for the Ready Company are shown below.

Ready Company
Balance Sheets

	Dec. 31, 19X1	Dec. 31, 19X0
Assets		
Cash	$ 8,000	$ 15,000
Accounts Receivable (net)	14,000	10,000
Inventory	55,000	42,000
Prepaid Expenses	6,000	4,000
Plant Assets	89,000	65,000
Accumulated Depreciation	(38,000)	(31,000)
Total Assets	$134,000	$105,000
Liabilities and Stockholders' Equity		
Accounts Payable	$ 26,000	$ 11,000
Common Stock	65,000	57,000
Retained Earnings	43,000	37,000
Total Liabilities and Stockholders' Equity	$134,000	$105,000

Net income per the income statement for 19X1 was $17,000. There were no extraordinary items. Dividends of $11,000 were declared and paid during

19X1. Plant assets were purchased for cash, and later in the year, additional common stock was issued for cash.

REQUIRED
(a) Calculate the change in working capital during 19X1.
(b) Prepare a worksheet for a statement of changes in financial position (working capital flow) for 19X1.
(c) Prepare a statement of changes in financial position (working capital flow) for 19X1.

19–27A The Retained Earnings account of the Pine Company for this year reveals the following:

Beginning Balance		$ 57,000
Add: Net Income		45,000
		$102,000
Less: Stock Dividend	$ 5,000	
Cash Dividend	15,000	20,000
Ending Balance		$ 82,000

Comparative balance sheets at December 31 of last year and this year are presented below:

Pine Company
Balance Sheets

	Dec. 31, This Year	Dec. 31, Last Year
Assets		
Cash	$ 10,000	$ 12,000
Accounts Receivable (net)	31,000	17,000
Inventory	90,000	72,000
Prepaid Expenses	7,000	8,000
Plant Assets	350,000	326,000
Accumulated Depreciation	(70,000)	(60,000)
Total Assets	$418,000	$375,000
Liabilities and Stockholders' Equity		
Accounts Payable	$ 38,000	$ 24,000
Accrued Liabilities	16,000	9,000
Bonds Payable	100,000	100,000
Discount on Bonds Payable	(8,000)	(10,000)
Common Stock	200,000	195,000
Retained Earnings	82,000	57,000
Treasury Stock	(10,000)	—
Total Liabilities and Stockholders' Equity	$418,000	$375,000

During the year, Pine Company sold for $13,000 old equipment that had cost $30,000 and had $17,000 accumulated depreciation. New equipment was purchased for cash. Amortization of bond discount amounting to $2,000 was included in interest expense on the income statement. There were no extraordinary items. The dividends were declared and paid this year. At the end of this year, shares of treasury stock were purchased for cash.

REQUIRED
(a) Calculate the change in working capital during this year.
(b) Prepare a worksheet for a statement of changes in financial position (working capital flow) for this year.
(c) Prepare a statement of changes in financial position (working capital flow) for this year.

19–28A The King Company's comparative balance sheets at December 31 of this year and last year, together with this year's income statement and retained earnings statement, are shown below.

King Company
Balance Sheets

	Dec. 31, This Year	Dec. 31, Last Year
Assets		
Cash	$ 32,000	$ 22,000
Accounts Receivable (net)	38,000	40,000
Inventories	75,000	66,000
Prepaid Expenses	9,000	6,000
Long-term Investments	—	12,000
Land	180,000	125,000
Plant and Equipment	450,000	400,000
Accumulated Depreciation	(150,000)	(120,000)
Patents (less amortization)	25,000	30,000
Total Assets	$659,000	$581,000
Liabilities and Stockholders' Equity		
Accounts Payable	$ 24,000	$ 28,000
Notes Payable (short-term)	27,000	42,000
Dividends Payable	36,000	47,000
Accrued Liabilities	11,000	6,000
Bonds Payable	75,000	75,000
Premium on Bonds Payable	4,500	5,000
Common Stock ($100 par value)	305,000	240,000
Paid-in Capital in Excess of Par Value	29,500	23,000
Retained Earnings	147,000	115,000
Total Liabilities and Stockholders' Equity	$659,000	$581,000

King Company
Retained Earnings Statement
For the Current Year

Beginning Balance	$115,000
Add: Net Income	68,000
	$183,000
Less: Cash Dividend	36,000
Ending Balance	$147,000

King Company
Income Statement
For the Current Year

Sales		$690,000
Cost of Goods Sold		420,000
Gross Profit		$270,000
Operating Expenses and Taxes	$142,400	
Depreciation Expense	46,000	
Patent Amortization Expense	5,000	
Interest Expense	10,000	
Loss on Retirement of Equipment	4,000	207,400
Income before Extraordinary Item		$ 62,600
Extraordinary Item:		
Gain on Sale of Long-term Investments	$ 7,500	
Less: Income Taxes	2,100	5,400
Net Income		$ 68,000

During the year the following transactions occurred:
(1) Purchased land, $55,000.
(2) Sold long-term investments, costing $12,000, for $19,500. The circumstances of this sale qualified it as an extraordinary event for King Company. The gain on the sale increased taxes $2,100.
(3) An expenditure of $70,000 was made for buildings.
(4) Abandoned equipment that cost $20,000 and had $16,000 accumulated depreciation.
(5) Interest expense on the income statement consisted of $10,500 paid less amortization of $500 bond premium.
(6) Sold 650 shares of common stock at $110 per share.
(7) Declared dividends, $36,000.

REQUIRED
(a) Calculate the change in working capital during this year.

(b) Prepare a worksheet for a statement of changes in financial position (working capital flow) for this year.

(c) Prepare a statement of changes in financial position (working capital flow) for this year.

19–29A Refer to the data given for the Ready Company in Problem 19–26A.

REQUIRED

(a) Prepare a worksheet for a statement of changes in financial position—cash basis (cash flow statement) for 19X1 for the Ready Company.

(b) Prepare a statement of changes in financial position—cash basis (cash flow statement) for 19X1.

19–30A Refer to the data given for the Pine Company in Problem 19–27A and the income statement of the Pine Company shown below.

Pine Company
Income Statement
For the Current Year

Sales		$370,000
Cost of Goods Sold		200,000
Gross Profit		$170,000
Depreciation Expense	$27,000	
Other Operating Expenses and Taxes	84,000	
Interest Expense	14,000	125,000
Net Income		$ 45,000

REQUIRED

(a) Prepare a worksheet for a statement of changes in financial position—cash basis (cash flow statement) for the current year for the Pine Company.

(b) Prepare a statement of changes in financial position—cash basis (cash flow statement) for the current year.

BUSINESS DECISION PROBLEM

B. Sirtan, president of Sirtan, Inc., has hired you as a consultant. He believes his bookkeeper has made an error in this year's financial statements. The income statement shows that the company operated at a loss, but Sirtan believes the year was profitable. To support his belief, Sirtan points out that both cash and working capital are much higher this year than last year. These changes were accomplished without selling any long-term assets or issuing any bonds or common stock. Further, during the current year, the company declared and paid a $16,000 cash dividend.

This year's income statement and comparative balance sheets at December 31 of this year and last year are shown on the next page.

Sirtan, Inc.
Income Statement
For the Current Year

Sales		$500,000
Cost of Goods Sold		220,000
Gross Profit		$280,000
Operating Expenses and Taxes	$235,000	
Depreciation Expense	50,000	
Patent Amortization Expense	9,000	294,000
Net Loss		($ 14,000)

Sirtan, Inc.
Balance Sheets

	Dec. 31, This Year	Dec. 31, Last Year
Assets		
Cash	$ 39,000	$ 24,000
Accounts Receivable	116,000	80,000
Inventory	145,000	125,000
Land	160,000	160,000
Plant and Equipment	500,000	500,000
Accumulated Depreciation	(200,000)	(150,000)
Patents (net)	90,000	99,000
Total Assets	$850,000	$838,000
Liabilities and Stockholders' Equity		
Accounts Payable	$144,000	$100,000
Accrued Liabilities	26,000	28,000
Common Stock	600,000	600,000
Retained Earnings	80,000	110,000
Total Liabilities and Stockholders' Equity	$850,000	$838,000

REQUIRED

(a) Prepare a statement of changes in financial position (working capital flow) for the current year.

(b) Prepare a statement of changes in financial position—cash basis (cash flow statement) for the current year.

(c) Did the bookkeeper make an error? Explain.

20

Analysis and Interpretation of Financial Statements

> **The best prophet of the future is the past.**
>
> LORD BYRON

Many individuals and groups are interested in the data appearing in a firm's financial statements, including managers, owners, prospective investors, creditors, labor unions, governmental agencies, and the public. These parties are usually interested in the profitability and financial strength of the firm in question, although such factors as size, growth, and the firm's efforts to meet its social responsibilities may also be of interest. Managers, owners, and prospective investors may ask the following questions: How do profits compare with those of previous years? How do profits compare with other firms in the industry? Creditors may ask: Will our debt be repaid on time? Will the interest payments be met? Unions may ask: How can we show that the firm can support a particular wage increase? Regulatory agencies may ask: What rate of return should the firm be permitted? Is the firm enjoying windfall profits? These kinds of questions can be answered by interpreting the data in financial reports.

Various techniques are used to analyze and interpret financial statement data. In the following pages, we concentrate on some widely used methods of evaluation. In many cases, management may profitably use these techniques to plan and control its own operations, but in this discussion our viewpoint is primarily that of an outsider.

SOURCES OF INFORMATION

Except for closely held companies, business firms publish financial statements at least annually, and most large companies also issue them quarterly. Normally, annual statements are attested to by certified public accountants, and the careful analyst reads the accountants' opinion to determine the reliability of the given data. Companies listed on stock exchanges submit annual statements to the Securities and Exchange Commission. These statements, which are available to any interested parties, are generally more useful than annual reports because they furnish a greater amount of detail. Even more detail can be found in prospectuses submitted to the SEC by certain companies issuing large amounts of new securities.

For data not provided by the financial statements, a trained analyst has a number of sources: personal interviews with company management, contacts with research organizations, trade association data, and subscriptions to financial services that periodically publish analytical data for many firms. The analyst also can obtain useful information from financial newspapers—such as *The Wall Street Journal* and *Barron's*—and from magazines devoted to financial and economic reporting—such as *Business Week* and *Forbes*. Data on industry norms, average ratios, and other relationships are available from such agencies as Dun & Brad-

700

street and Robert Morris and Associates. The analyst may want to compare the performance of a particular firm with that of the industry. Both Dun & Bradstreet and Robert Morris and Associates compile industry statistics for a variety of manufacturers, wholesalers, and retailers. In addition, the Dun & Bradstreet statistics report not only median performance, but the performance of firms in the upper and the lower quartiles of the industry. Robert Morris and Associates reports statistics by size of organization.

ANALYTICAL TECHNIQUES

Absolute dollar amounts of profits, sales, assets, and other key data are not meaningful when studied individually. For example, knowing that a company's annual earnings are $1 million is of little value unless these earnings can be related to other data. A $1 million profit might represent excellent performance for a company with less than $10 million in invested capital. On the other hand, such earnings would be meager for a firm that has several hundred million dollars in invested capital. Thus, the most significant information derived in analysis concerns the relationships between two or more variables, such as earnings to assets, earnings to sales, and earnings to stockholders' investment. To describe these relationships clearly and to make comparisons easy, the analyst states these relationships in terms of ratios and percentages.

For example, we might express the relationship of $15,000 in earnings to $150,000 in sales as a 10% ($15,000/$150,000) rate of earnings on sales. To describe the relationship between sales of $150,000 and inventory of $20,000, we might use a ratio or a percentage; ($150,000/$20,000) may be expressed as 7.5, 7.5:1, or 750%.

Often, changes in selected items compared in successive financial statements are expressed as percentages. For example, if a firm's earnings increased from $40,000 last year to $48,000 this year, the $8,000 increase related to the base year is expressed as a 20% increase ($8,000/$40,000). To express a dollar increase or decrease as a percentage, however, the analyst must make the base year amount a positive figure. If, for example, a firm had a net loss of $4,000 in one year and earnings of $20,000 in the next, the $24,000 increase cannot be expressed as a percentage. Similarly, if a firm showed no marketable securities in last year's balance sheet but showed $15,000 of such securities in this year's statement, the $15,000 increase cannot be expressed as a percentage.

When evaluating a firm's financial statements for two or more years, analysts often use **horizontal analysis.** This type of analysis is useful in detecting improvement or deterioration in a firm's performance and in spotting trends. The term **vertical analysis** describes the study of a single year's financial statements.

Horizontal Analysis

COMPARATIVE FINANCIAL STATEMENTS   The form of horizontal analysis encountered most often is **comparative financial statements** for two or more years, showing dollar and percentage changes for important items and classification totals. Dollar increases and decreases are divided by the earliest year's data

EXHIBIT 20–1

Alliance Company
Comparative Balance Sheets
(Thousands of Dollars)

	Dec. 31, 19X5	Dec. 31, 19X4	Increase (Decrease)	Percent Change
Assets				
Current Assets:				
Cash	$ 5,500	$ 4,200	$ 1,300	31.0
Marketable Securities	1,500	2,400	(900)	(37.5)
Accounts Receivable (less allowance for uncollectible accounts of $2,400 in 19X5 and $2,000 in 19X4)	61,600	52,000	9,600	18.5
Inventory [lower of cost (first-in, first-out) or market]	76,000	63,000	13,000	20.6
Prepaid Expenses	900	600	300	50.0
Total Current Assets	$145,500	$122,200	$23,300	19.1
Long-term Assets:				
Property, Plant, and Equipment (net of accumulated depreciation)	$ 45,000	$ 40,000	$ 5,000	12.5
Investments	1,800	1,600	200	12.5
Total Long-term Assets	$ 46,800	$ 41,600	$ 5,200	12.5
Total Assets	$192,300	$163,800	$28,500	17.4
Liabilities and Stockholders' Equity				
Liabilities				
Current Liabilities:				
Notes Payable	$ 5,700	$ 3,000	$ 2,700	90.0
Accounts Payable	22,000	24,100	(2,100)	(8.7)
Accrued Liabilities	30,000	27,300	2,700	9.9
Total Current Liabilities	$ 57,700	$ 54,400	$ 3,300	6.1
Long-term Liabilities:				
12% Debenture Bonds Payable	$ 25,000	$ 20,000	$ 5,000	25.0
Total Liabilities	$ 82,700	$ 74,400	$ 8,300	11.2
Stockholders' Equity				
10% Preferred Stock, $100 Par Value	$ 8,000	$ 8,000	$ —	—
Common Stock, $5 Par Value	20,000	14,000	6,000	42.9
Paid-in Capital in Excess of Par Value	7,500	5,500	2,000	36.4
Retained Earnings	74,100	61,900	12,200	19.7
Total Stockholders' Equity	$109,600	$ 89,400	$20,200	22.6
Total Liabilities and Stockholders' Equity	$192,300	$163,800	$28,500	17.4

to obtain percentage changes. The 19X4 and 19X5 financial statements of Alliance Company, an electronic components and accessories manufacturer, are shown in Exhibits 20–1, 20–2, and 20–3. We use the data in these statements throughout this chapter to illustrate various analytical techniques.

When examining financial statements, the analyst focuses immediate attention on significant items only. Large percentage changes frequently occur in items whose dollar amounts may not be significant compared with other items on the statements. For example, although a large percentage change in Alliance Company's balance sheet occurred in Prepaid Expenses, the analyst would scarcely notice this item in an initial examination of changes. Instead, attention would be directed first to changes in totals—current assets, long-term assets, total assets, current liabilities, and so on. Next, changes in significant individual items, such as receivables and inventory, would be examined. These changes may be related to certain changes in income statement items to determine whether they are favorable.

For example, Alliance Company's total assets increased 17.4% (Exhibit 20–1), and sales increased 29.7% (Exhibit 20–2). A fairly large percentage increase in sales was supported by a much smaller rate of increase in assets. Furthermore, the 20.6% increase in inventory was also considerably less than the increase in

EXHIBIT 20–2

Alliance Company Comparative Income Statements (Thousands of Dollars)				
	Year Ended Dec. 31, 19X5	Year Ended Dec. 31, 19X4	Increase (Decrease)	Percent Change
Net Sales	$415,000	$320,000	$95,000	29.7
Cost of Goods Sold	290,000	230,000	60,000	26.1
Gross Profit	$125,000	$ 90,000	$35,000	38.9
Operating Expenses:				
Selling Expenses	$ 39,500	$ 27,300	$12,200	44.7
Administrative Expenses	49,640	32,600	17,040	52.3
Total Operating Expenses	$ 89,140	$ 59,900	$29,240	48.8
Operating Income	$ 35,860	$ 30,100	$ 5,760	19.1
Interest Expense	3,000	2,400	600	25.0
Net Income before Income Taxes	$ 32,860	$ 27,700	$ 5,160	18.6
Income Tax Expense	14,100	12,300	1,800	14.6
Net Income	$ 18,760	$ 15,400	$ 3,360	21.8
Earnings per Share	$5.28	$5.21		
Dividends per Share	1.44	0.81		

EXHIBIT 20–3

Alliance Company
Comparative Retained Earnings Statements
(Thousands of Dollars)

	Year Ended Dec. 31, 19X5	Year Ended Dec. 31, 19X4	Increase (Decrease)	Percent Change
Retained Earnings, Jan. 1	$61,900	$49,580	$12,320	24.8
Net Income	18,760	15,400	3,360	21.8
Total	$80,660	$64,980	$15,680	24.1
Dividends:				
On Preferred Stock	$ 800	$ 800	$ —	—
On Common Stock	5,760	2,280	3,480	152.6
Total	$ 6,560	$ 3,080	$ 3,480	113.0
Retained Earnings, Dec. 31	$74,100	$61,900	$12,200	19.7

sales. These results reflect quite favorably on the firm's performance. In addition, the 29.7% increase in sales was accompanied by an increase in accounts receivable of only 18.5%; on the surface, the company's sales growth was not associated with a relaxation in credit policy.

We see on the income statement that the 38.9% gross profit increase outstripped the rate of increase in sales, indicating a higher mark-up rate in the latest year. Net income, however, increased only 21.8%; therefore, expenses must have grown disproportionately. Indeed, selling and administrative expenses increased 44.7% and 52.3%, respectively.

From this limited analysis of comparative financial statements, an analyst would conclude that operating performance for the latest year appeared favorable. Further analysis using some of the techniques described later in the chapter, however, might cause the analyst to modify that opinion. The foregoing analysis has revealed one reservation—operating expenses, particularly administrative expenses, have increased at a fairly high rate. Many selling expenses—such as sales salaries, commissions, and advertising—should rise somewhat proportionately with sales, but administrative expenses should not. An investigation of the reasons for the large increase in the latter expense might be indicated.

TREND ANALYSIS   To observe percentage changes over time in selected data, analysts compute **trend percentages.** Most companies provide summaries of data for the past five or 10 years in their annual reports. With such information, the analyst may examine changes over a period longer than two years. For example, suppose you were interested in sales and earnings trends for Alliance Company for the past five years. The dollar data, taken from the company's published annual report in the fifth year (19X5) of the period, are shown below:

Alliance Company
Annual Performance (Millions of Dollars)

	Year 1	Year 2	Year 3	Year 4	Year 5
Sales	$202.0	$175.0	$243.0	$320.0	$415.0
Net Earnings	10.9	10.3	13.5	15.4	18.8

By inspecting the above data, we perceive a fairly healthy growth pattern for this company, but we can determine the pattern of change from year to year more precisely by calculating trend percentages. To do this, we select a base year and then divide the data for each of the other years by the base year data. The resultant figures are actually indexes of the changes occurring throughout the period. If we choose year 1 as the base year, all data for years 2 through 5 will be related to year 1, which is represented as 100%.

To create the following table, we divided each year's sales—from year 2 through year 5—by $202, the year 1 sales in millions of dollars. Similarly, the net earnings for years 2 through 5 were divided by $10.9, the year 1 net earnings in millions of dollars.

Annual Performance (Percentage of Base Year)

	Year 1	Year 2	Year 3	Year 4	Year 5
Sales	100	87	120	158	205
Net Earnings	100	94	124	141	172

The trend percentages reveal that the growth in earnings outstripped the growth in sales for years 2 and 3, then fell below the sales growth in the last two years. We saw in our analysis of comparative statements that a disproportionate increase in operating expenses emerged in 19X5 (year 5). We might therefore analyze the 19X4 data to determine if net income was affected for the same reason or if the reduced growth was caused by other factors.

We must exercise care in interpreting trend percentages. Remember that all index percentages are related to the *base year*. Therefore, the change between the year 2 sales index (87%) and the year 3 sales index (120%) represents a 33% increase in terms of *base year* dollars. To express the increase as a percentage of year 2 dollars, we divide the 33% increase by the 87% year 2 sales index, to obtain an increase of 38%. We must also carefully select a representative base year. For example, consider the following sales and earnings data during the identical period for a competing company (which we call Century Company):

Century Company
Annual Performance

	Year 1	Year 2	Year 3	Year 4	Year 5
Sales (millions of dollars)	$192.3	$204.4	$225.0	$299.0	$414.6
(Percentage of base year)	100	106	117	155	216
Net Earnings (millions of dollars)	$ 1.9	$ 3.0	$ 4.0	$ 6.5	$ 10.0
(Percentage of base year)	100	158	210	342	526

Note that Century Company's sales growth pattern is similar to Alliance Company's. When judged from trend percentages, however, the net earnings growth is almost twice that of Alliance Company. Using an unrepresentative base year for Century Company—when earnings were depressed—makes the earnings trend misleading. In year 1, Century Company earned less than 1% of sales ($1.9/ $192.3). But in the later years of the period, a more normal relationship between earnings and sales prevailed, and earnings were roughly 2 to $2\frac{1}{2}$% of sales. The earnings/sales relationship for Alliance Company was relatively normal in year 1.

Other data that the analyst may relate to sales and earnings over a period of years include total assets, plant investment, and expenditures for research and development.

EFFECT OF INFLATION As we saw in Chapter 13, financial information reported on a historical cost basis during a period of inflation does not portray economic reality. Not only may the true financial position and operating performance of a given year be distorted, but comparisons made for a firm over time and with other firms may be deceptive. In the foregoing analysis, for example, sales and net earnings growth for Alliance Company would be considerably less if the data were adjusted for the effects of inflation. Many other relationships would likewise be distorted unless adjusted for inflation. Relationships between income statement items—such as sales—and balance sheet items may be distorted because the sales figure is expressed in current dollars (current prices), and inventories (especially LIFO inventories) and plant and equipment include dollar amounts of earlier price levels.

The financial analyst should therefore attempt to determine the effect of inflation on the data being examined. Certain inflation-adjusted operating data are available for large public firms because the FASB now requires its disclosure in supplementary form (see Chapter 13). When analyzing the financial reports of small firms, the analyst must make the necessary inquiries and estimates of the effects of inflation on the data.

Vertical Analysis

The relative importance of various items in financial statements can be highlighted by showing them as percentages of a key figure or total. Calculation of such percentages is particularly useful in presenting income statement data. For example, each item on the income statement may be shown as a percentage of the sales figure, as illustrated in Exhibit 20–4, Alliance Company's 19X5 income statement.

COMMON-SIZE STATEMENTS **Common-size** financial statements contain the percentages of a key figure alone, without the corresponding dollar figures. Common-size income statements for Alliance Company are compared with Century Company's in Exhibit 20–5.

We see from Exhibit 20–5 that Century Company has a smaller gross profit margin percentage than does Alliance Company. The disparity might be due either to lower sales prices or to higher production costs for Century Company. Selling and administrative expenses as a percentage of sales are fairly comparable, except

EXHIBIT 20–4

Alliance Company Income Statement For the Year Ended December 31, 19X5 (Thousands of Dollars)		
Net Sales	$415,000	100.0%
Cost of Goods Sold	290,000	69.9
Gross Profit	$125,000	30.1%
Operating Expenses:		
Selling Expenses	$ 39,500	9.5%
Administrative Expenses	49,640	12.0
Total Operating Expenses	$ 89,140	21.5%
Operating Income	$ 35,860	8.6%
Interest Expense	3,000	0.7
Net Income before Income Taxes	$ 32,860	7.9%
Income Tax Expense	14,100	3.4
Net Income	$ 18,760	4.5%

EXHIBIT 20–5

Alliance and Century Companies Common-size Income Statements (Percentage of Net Sales)				
	Alliance Company		Century Company	
	Year Ended Dec. 31, 19X5	Year Ended Dec. 31, 19X4	Year Ended Dec. 31, 19X5	Year Ended Dec. 31, 19X4
Net Sales	100.0%	100.0%	100.0%	100.0%
Cost of Goods Sold	69.9	71.9	73.8	74.9
Gross Profit	30.1%	28.1%	26.2%	25.1%
Operating Expenses:				
Selling Expenses	9.5%	8.5%	8.6%	8.2%
Administrative Expenses	12.0	10.2	12.3	11.4
Total Operating Expenses	21.5%	18.7%	20.9%	19.6%
Operating Income	8.6%	9.4%	5.3%	5.5%
Interest Expense	0.7	0.8	1.0	0.8
Net Income before Income Taxes	7.9%	8.6%	4.3%	4.7%
Income Tax Expense	3.4	3.8	2.1	2.3
Net Income	4.5%	4.8%	2.2%	2.4%

that, combined, they are a higher percentage of the sales dollar for Alliance Company than for Century Company in 19X5. The interest expense as a percentage of sales in 19X4 is somewhat higher for Century Company than for Alliance Company. If we consider Century Company's low rate of net income to net sales

USE OF INFLATION-ADJUSTED DATA BY ANALYSTS

In this chapter, we point out that analysts' use of inflation-adjusted data helps them avoid certain distortions and deceptive results in analyzing financial statements. Consequently, analysts should be enthusiastically using the supplementary inflation-adjusted disclosures prescribed by FASB Statement No. 33.* However, a recent survey by Arthur Young & Company revealed no great amount of enthusiasm for this information, especially for the constant dollar data.†

The accounting firm surveyed a cross-section of members of the Financial Analysts Foundation to find out the following:

(1) How much analysts use Statement 33 information, and if they do not use it, why not.
(2) How those analysts who use the information view its usefulness.
(3) How those analysts who use the information would change the current reporting requirements.

About one-half of the respondents (94 of 190) use the information. Fewer than one in five of these users describe that use as "frequent"; the rest use it only "occasionally."

The following three major reasons account for nonuse of the data:

(1) Adjusted data are not comparable. Companies have a great deal of latitude in selecting adjusting procedures and need not disclose methods or assumptions.
(2) The intrinsic value of the data is suspect. Constant dollar data lack relevance, because they rely on general price-level indexes, which do not portray the effect of specific prices. On the

other hand, current cost information lacks reliability.
(3) The information is redundant; it is readily available elsewhere.

Another reason for nonuse by some analysts can be inferred from the data. Analysts who are highly familiar with the adjustment process are more willing to use the data than analysts who are not familiar with the process. User respondents list more sources of information for learning the adjustment process than nonusers.

User respondents regard "restated income from continuing operations" the most useful of current year adjusted data. They give the next highest usefulness rating to "current costs of inventory and fixed assets." Of the five-year data, "restated trend data" is rated most useful.

Should the FASB continue to require only one of the two bases—current cost or constant dollar data—user respondents would clearly prefer current cost data. Users who favor this type of disclosure outnumber by a margin of more than two to one those who favor only constant dollar disclosures. However, 60% of the user respondents favor continuation of the constant dollar information either by itself or combined with current cost information. Evidently, many analysts are reluctant to part with any information they now receive, whether or not they use it.

---

*We explain in Chapter 13 that these disclosures provide data with both a constant dollar basis and a current cost basis. With the constant dollar basis, the historical cost data are restated for the general price level. With the current cost basis, the historical cost data are restated for changes in specific prices of assets owned and used by a firm.
†Robert W. Berliner, "Do Analysts Use Inflation-Adjusted Information? Results of a Survey," *Financial Analysts Journal*, March–April 1983, pages 65–72.

(2.2% in 19X5), the interest percentage is significant. Yet Alliance Company's higher rate of return on sales (about double that of Century Company) is due mainly to its better gross profit margin.

We may also employ common-size percentages to analyze balance sheet data, although less successfully than with income statement data. For example, if for a period of several years we state current assets and fixed assets as a percentage of total assets, we can determine whether a company is becoming more or less liquid. By determining each current asset's percentage of total current assets, we may observe any changes in these ingredients of working capital.

The best use of common-size statements with balance sheet data is probably with the sources of capital (equities). The proportions of the total capital supplied by short-term creditors, long-term creditors, preferred stockholders, and common stockholders of Alliance Company are shown below for 19X5:

	Amount (Millions of Dollars)	Common-size Percentage
Current debt	$ 57.7	30
Long-term debt	25.0	13
Preferred stock equity	8.0	4
Common stock equity	101.6	53
	$192.3	100

These percentages reveal that 53% of Alliance Company's capital is supplied by the common shareholders and 47% by preferred stockholders and creditors. We shall discover shortly that such percentages are useful in appraising the financial structure of a firm.

ANALYSIS OF OPERATING PERFORMANCE

In evaluating the operating performance of a firm, the analyst invariably uses **rate of return** analysis. This analysis, which deals with the firm's profitability, relates either the operating income or the net income to some base, such as average total assets, average stockholders' equity, or the year's sales. The resultant percentage can be compared with similar rates for the firm in past years or to other firms. The most important relationships are

(1) Return on assets.

(2) Return on common stockholders' equity.

(3) Return on sales.

Return on Assets

The rate of return on the total assets available to a firm is probably one of the most useful measures of the firm's profitability and efficiency. It is calculated by dividing the year's operating income (income before deducting interest and income tax expense) by the average total assets employed during the year.

$$\text{Rate of Return on Assets} = \frac{\text{Operating Income}}{\text{Average Total Assets}}$$

Because the return for a year is earned on assets employed throughout the year and assets may vary during that time, we compute the return on the *average* amount of assets. We obtain the approximate average by summing the beginning and ending asset totals and dividing by two.

If the percentage is a true index of productivity and accomplishment, it should not be influenced by the manner in which the company is financed. Therefore, we use income before interest charges as a measure of the dollar return in the numerator. As a result, we may compare the return for a company having a relatively high proportion of debt with that of a company using mostly owners' equity to finance its assets.

For example, assume that Company X and Company Y each have $500,000 in average total assets and that each has income of $70,000 before interest expense and taxes. Suppose that Company X has no interest-bearing debt but Company Y has $200,000 of 10% bonds payable outstanding. The bottom portions of the income statements of these two companies (rearranged to highlight the effect of interest and taxes) are shown in Exhibit 20–6 (for simplicity, we assume a 40% effective income tax rate).

Company X and Company Y earn the same percentage return—14%—on their assets ($70,000 income before interest and taxes divided by $500,000 average total assets). Company Y, however, is financed partially by bonds. Thus, its interest expense of $20,000 less a 40% tax benefit of $8,000 makes its final net income $12,000 less than that of Company X. This difference is due solely to the manner in which the two companies are financed and is unrelated to their *operational accomplishment.* For this reason, the return on assets is normally measured before interest and income taxes. We demonstrate later that judicious use of debt in financing may benefit the owners of a business.

The return on assets, sometimes called the **productivity ratio,** is useful for comparing similar companies operating in the same industry. It also aids management in gauging the effectiveness of its asset utilization. When we consider

EXHIBIT 20–6

Partial Income Statements		
	Company X	**Company Y**
Operating Income (before interest expense and income tax expense)	$70,000	$70,000
Interest Expense (10% of $200,000)	—	20,000
	$70,000	$50,000
Income Tax Expense (40%)	28,000	20,000
Net Income	$42,000	$30,000

this ratio along with such relationships as return on stockholders' equity and return on sales (explained below), we gain much insight about a firm's operating performance.

Alliance Company's return on assets for 19X5 and 19X4 is calculated below:

	19X5	19X4
Operating Income	$ 35,860	$ 30,100
Total Assets:		
Beginning of Year	(a) $163,800	$142,500
End of Year	(b) 192,300	163,800
Average [(a + b)/2]	178,050	153,150
Rate of Return on Average Assets	20.1%	19.7%

Return on Common Stockholders' Equity

The rate of return to common shareholders is calculated using net income less preferred stock dividend requirements. This ratio measures the ultimate profitability of the investment to the common stockholders. Although the ratio can be figured before taxes, it is commonly done after taxes as follows:

$$\text{Rate of Return on Common Stockholders' Equity} = \frac{\text{Net Income} - \text{Preferred Dividend Requirements}}{\text{Average Common Stockholders' Equity}}$$

The return is earned on the stockholders' equity invested *throughout* the year. Because this amount varies during the year, we commonly approximate the average investment by summing the beginning and ending balances and dividing by two.

The rate of return for Alliance Company in 19X5 and 19X4 is calculated below:

	19X5	19X4
Net Income	$ 18,760	$15,400
Less: Preferred Dividend Requirements (10% of $8,000)	800	800
Common Stock Earnings	$ 17,960	$14,600
Common Stockholders' Equity:		
Beginning of Year	(a) $ 81,400	$63,500
End of Year	(b) 101,600	81,400
Average [(a + b)/2]	91,500	72,450
Rate of Return on Common Stockholders' Equity	19.6%	20.2%

Return on Sales

Another important measure of operating performance is the rate of return on the net sales of a firm. The most commonly used version of this ratio is **net income to net sales.** When common-size percentages, or component percentages, are available with the income statement, return on sales equals the net income percentage, calculated as follows:

$$\text{Rate of Return on Sales} = \frac{\text{Net Income}}{\text{Net Sales}}$$

The calculations for Alliance Company are given below:

	19X5	19X4
Net Income	$ 18,760	$ 15,400
Net Sales	415,000	320,000
Rate of Return on Sales	4.5%	4.8%

Net income to net sales percentages are performance indexes used solely when studying similar companies in the same industry or when comparing different periods for the same company. The rate of return on sales varies widely from industry to industry. Some industries are characterized by low profit margins and high turnover of principal assets. (The ratio of net sales to average total assets is called *asset turnover.*) For example, meat processing companies and supermarkets seldom have a net income to net sales ratio exceeding 2%. They have huge sales volumes, however, and turn over their assets (especially inventory) many times. In contrast, a company manufacturing and selling fine grand pianos might have an extremely high net income to net sales ratio. Because production capabilities of making pianos are inherently limited, turnover of assets is low. As a general rule, firms that deal in slow-moving products involving fairly long production periods require higher profit margins for a respectable rate of return on assets and on the owners' investments.

USING THE NET INCOME FIGURE

When analyzing the operating performance of a company, intelligent analysts make their own evaluations of a firm's reported net income. Because they are interested in the prospects for future income, they analyze carefully the factors influencing the net income figure. If possible, they wish to determine which segments of the business contribute the most to net income and what the future prospects are for these segments. In this respect, the analysts' inquiries frequently lead to information sources other than the financial statements. However, an analyst can usually determine from the statements themselves (1) how representative the net income figure is and (2) whether it was determined by conservative accounting principles.

The analyst scrutinizes a firm's income statement to determine whether its net income is representative of its earning capability. Often, any unusual and/or nonrecurring items included in the determination of net income are eliminated for analytical purposes. Such items as gains and losses on sales of fixed assets or securities, casualty losses, and the like, are either omitted or apportioned to a number of years' income calculations.

The analyst also examines such factors as inventory pricing techniques and depreciation methods (and rates) to determine their effect on net income. Company policies for investment tax credits (whether included in income immediately or deferred to future periods) and for recording fringe benefit costs (such as pension costs) must also be reviewed. The analyst wants to know whether the company's net income falls in the low (conservative) or high side of the spectrum of possible amounts. Once this is determined, the analyst may develop a more informed evaluation of a company's operating performance, stock values, growth potential, and so on.

Earnings per Share

Because stock market prices are quoted on a per-share basis, it is useful to calculate a firm's earnings on the same basis. *Earnings per share* for common stock are usually prominent in reports because both analysts and investors consider the relationship of prices and earnings to be quite important. An independent public accountant computing earnings per share for reporting purposes should follow procedures described in Accounting Principles Board *Opinion No. 15*, "Earnings Per Share," published by the AICPA. We discussed these procedures in Chapter 16.

Analysts may use the earnings-per-share figures that are available in annual reports—if they find such computations meaningful—or they may compute their own figures. We compute earnings per share by dividing common stock earnings (net income less any preferred dividend requirements) by the average number of shares outstanding during the year, as follows:[1]

$$\text{Earnings per Share} = \frac{\text{Net Income} - \text{Preferred Dividend Requirements}}{\text{Average Number of Common Shares Outstanding}}$$

The following calculations are made for Alliance Company:

		19X5	19X4
Net Income		$18,760	$15,400
Less: Preferred Dividend Requirements (10% of $8,000)		800	800
Common Stock Earnings		$17,960	$14,600
Common Shares Outstanding:			
Beginning of Year	(a)	2,800	2,800
End of Year	(b)	4,000	2,800
Average [(a + b)/2]		3,400	2,800
Earnings per Share		$5.28	$5.21

Alliance Company's earnings per share increased only slightly in 19X5 because a large number of additional shares were issued during the year.

Price–Earnings Ratio

The **price–earnings ratio** is the result of dividing the market price of a share of stock by the earnings per share. For many analysts and investors, this ratio is an important tool in assessing stock values. For example, after evaluating the strong and weak points of several companies in an industry, the analyst may compare price–earnings ratios to determine the "best buy."

---

[1] Analysts usually use the number of shares outstanding at year-end in this calculation. However, the average number of shares outstanding during the year is a more meaningful figure. The AICPA's Accounting Principles Board suggests the use of a weighted average that takes into account the periods during which various amounts of stock were outstanding.

When determing the price–earnings ratio, we customarily use the latest market price and the common stock earnings for the last four quarters of a company's operations. In our calculation for Alliance Company, we use 19X5 common stock earnings and the market price at year-end, $37\frac{1}{2}$.

$$\text{Price–Earnings Ratio} = \frac{\text{Market Price per Common Share}}{\text{Common Stock Earnings per Share}} = \frac{\$37.50}{\$5.28} = 7.1$$

In other words, the market price of a share of Alliance Company common stock was approximately seven times the amount that share earned for the year. By itself, this multiplier is not particularly meaningful, although price–earnings ratios well below 10 often indicate a depressed market price. A prospective investor might compare this ratio with that of Century Company or with the average for the (electronic accessories) industry. Coupled with a fair evaluation of the strengths and weaknesses of several investment prospects and some knowledge of the industry itself, the price–earnings ratio might indicate whether the stock is overvalued in the market or an attractive investment.

Yield and Dividend Payout

Investors' expectations vary a great deal with personal economic circumstances and with the overall economic outlook. Some investors are more interested in price appreciation of a stock investment than present income in the form of dividends. When shares are disposed of in the future, only part of the gains may be taxed under the capital gains provision of the income tax laws, whereas dividends are almost fully taxable. Other investors are more concerned with dividends than price appreciation. Such investors desire a high **yield**—or dividend rate of return—on their investments. Yield is normally calculated by dividing the current annual dividends per share by the current price of the stock. For Alliance Company, we use the 19X5 dividends and the year-end price per share to calculate yield, as follows:

$$\text{Dividend Yield} = \frac{\text{Common Dividends per Share}}{\text{Market Price per Share}} = \frac{\$1.44}{\$37.50} = 3.8\%$$

Investors who emphasize the yield on their investments may also be interested in a firm's **dividend payout ratio,** which is the percentage of the common stock earnings paid out in dividends. The payout ratio indicates whether a firm has a conservative or a liberal dividend policy and may also indicate whether the firm is conserving funds for internal financing of growth. For Alliance Company, we calculate the payout ratio for 19X5 as follows:

$$\text{Dividend Payout Ratio} = \frac{\text{Common Dividends per Share}}{\text{Common Stock Earnings per Share}} = \frac{\$1.44}{\$5.28} = 27.3\%$$

Both the yield and the dividend payout ratio for the common shares of Alliance Company were relatively low in 19X5. The firm has embarked on an expansion program and is conserving funds to finance acquisitions internally.

Low payout ratios can have a depressing effect on the market price of a stock, and reducing the payout ratio may have a dramatic effect on the stock price. For example, General Motors once reduced its payout ratio by cutting its year-end dividend, and within two weeks the common stock price skidded down 10%.

Payout ratios for typical, seasoned industrial corporations vary between 40% and 60%. Many corporations, however, need funds for internal financing of growth and pay out little or nothing in dividends. At the other extreme, some companies—principally utility companies—may pay out as much as 80% or 90% of their earnings. Utilities have less need of retaining funds for growth because the bulk of their financing is through long-term debt. They are said to "trade on the equity" to a large extent. We discuss this idea in greater detail in the next section.

TRADING ON THE EQUITY

The expression **trading on the equity** designates the use of borrowed funds, particularly long-term debt, in the capital structure of a firm. Trading *profitably* on the equity means that the borrowed funds generate a higher rate of return than the interest rate paid for the use of the funds. The excess, of course, accrues to the benefit of the common shareholders because it magnifies, or increases, their earnings. To illustrate, let us return to the example in Exhibit 20–6, in which both companies X and Y have assets of $500,000. Company X has its entire capital in common stockholders' equity, while Company Y has $200,000 in 10% bonds payable and $300,000 in common stockholders' equity. Both firms have $70,000 operating income (income before interest and taxes). For clarity, we repeat the net income calculation below, together with percentages earned on assets and on stockholders' equity.

	Company X	Company Y
Operating income	$70,000	$70,000
Interest expense (10% of $200,000)	—	20,000
	$70,000	$50,000
Income tax expense (40%)	28,000	20,000
Net income	$42,000	$30,000
Return on assets:		
For both companies: $70,000/$500,000 =	14%	14%
Return on stockholders' equity:		
For Company X: $42,000/$500,000 =	8.4%	
For Company Y: $30,000/$300,000 =		10%

Note that Company Y achieved a higher return on its stockholders' investment than did Company X. We account for this additional 1.6% on stockholders' equity as follows:

14% earned on $200,000 borrowed	$28,000
10% interest paid for use of funds	20,000
Trading on equity gain before income tax	$ 8,000
Less: 40% income tax	3,200
Trading on equity gain after taxes	$ 4,800
$4,800 gain ÷ $300,000 stockholders' equity =	1.6%

Because Company Y earned 14% on its assets (including the $200,000 borrowed) and paid only 10% on the money borrowed, it had an $8,000 gain before income taxes. After deducting 40% for taxes, the gain was $4,800. The after tax gain of $4,800 is a 1.6% return on the stockholders' equity of $300,000. Magnifying gains for the shareholders in this manner is sometimes referred to as the use of **leverage.**

Leverage in the capital structure must be used judiciously because some risk is involved. Leverage can also magnify losses. Suppose that operating income had been only $30,000, representing a 6% return on the assets of $500,000. The after tax return for Company Y would be only $6,000 [$30,000 − ($20,000 interest + $4,000 taxes)]. The return on stockholders' equity would then be only 2% ($6,000/$300,000) compared with a return of 3.6% for Company X ($30,000 − $12,000 taxes = $18,000; $18,000/$500,000 = 3.6%).

In general, companies with stable earnings can afford more debt in their capital structure than those with fluctuating earnings. Because of their stable earnings, utility companies may have as much as 70% of their financial structure in debt, whereas most industrial companies rarely have more than 50% debt financing.

ANALYSIS OF FINANCIAL STRENGTH

Because the ultimate source of any company's financial strength is its earning power, our discussion has stressed the operating performance and earning power of the business firm. However, certain other relationships in the financial statements give the analyst insight into the financial strength of a company. The first of these relationships concerns the company's financial structure and its fixed charges. The second relates to the company's working capital position.

Equity Ratio

To determine the manner in which a company is financed, we calculate the **equity ratio,** which is the common stockholders' equity divided by the company's total assets.

$$\text{Equity Ratio} = \frac{\text{Common Stockholders' Equity}}{\text{Total Assets}}$$

We commonly use year-end balances for the elements in this ratio rather than averages because we are interested in the capital structure at a particular point in time. The calculations for Alliance Company are as follows:

	19X5	19X4
Common Stockholders' Equity	$101,600	$ 81,400
Total Assets	$192,300	$163,800
Equity Ratio	53.0%	49.7%

The equity ratio is readily available in common-size percentages calculated from the balance sheet (see page 709). At the close of 19X5, 53% of Alliance

Company's capital was provided by common shareholders and 47% by debtors and preferred shareholders. Because the analyst's concern is whether the company may be trading on the equity too heavily, the equity ratio indicates the extent of the firm's borrowing in relation to its assets.

When we analyze a firm's leverage, we may question the treatment of any preferred stock outstanding. Remember that the dividends on ordinary preferred stock are not a fixed charge, such as bond interest, but a contingent charge— contingent on a declaration by the firm's board of directors. Despite this fact, most analysts treat regular preferred stock as debt when examining a company's long-term position. They evidently feel that preferred dividends should be treated as a fixed charge, because ordinarily such dividends must be paid before distributions are made to common shareholders. Usually, preferred stock is included with stockholders' equity *for analytical purposes* only when the preferred stock is convertible into common and is likely to be converted in the near future.

Although no explicit rules of thumb or standards exist for equity ratios, the analyst may have a general idea of what a company's financial structure should be. An equity ratio that falls outside the analyst's subjective range of percentages will be investigated further.

Bond Interest Coverage

To evaluate further the size of a company's debt, an analyst may observe the relationship of interest charges to earnings. For example, an extremely low equity ratio for a company may indicate heavy borrowing. However, if its earnings are sufficient, even in poor years, to meet the interest charges on the debt several times over, the analyst may regard the situation quite favorably.

Analysts, particularly long-term creditors, almost always calculate the **bond interest coverage,** sometimes called **times interest earned.** This ratio is determined by dividing the operating income (income before bond interest and income taxes) by the annual bond interest:

$$\text{Bond Interest Coverage} = \frac{\text{Operating Income}}{\text{Annual Bond Interest}}$$

The computations for Alliance Company are as follows:

	19X5	19X4
Operating Income	$35,860	$30,100
Annual Bond Interest (12% of Bonds Payable)	$ 3,000	$ 2,400
Times Interest Earned	12.0	12.5

In other words, Alliance Company's income available to meet interest charges each year was approximately 12 times the amount of its interest expense. Obviously, Alliance Company has an exceptionally good margin of safety. Generally speaking, a company that earns its interest several times before taxes in its poor years is regarded as a satisfactory risk by long-term creditors.

Preferred Dividend Coverage

Quite naturally, preferred stockholders would like some assurance that dividends will continue to be paid. They may therefore wish to calculate their **dividend coverage.** To compute the number of times preferred dividends are earned, we divide operating income (income before interest and income taxes) by the sum of the annual bond interest and preferred dividend requirements, as follows:

$$\frac{\text{Preferred Dividend}}{\text{Coverage}} = \frac{\text{Operating Income}}{\text{Annual Bond Interest} + \text{Preferred Dividend Requirements}}$$

The following calculations for Alliance Company show ample protection for the preferred dividends:

	19X5	19X4
Operating Income	$35,860	$30,100
Annual Bond Interest	$ 3,000	$ 2,400
Preferred Dividend Requirements	800	800
	$ 3,800	$ 3,200
Times Preferred Dividends Earned	9.4	9.4

The preferred dividend requirement is combined with the bond interest in the calculations because bond interest is a prior charge against earnings—that is, it must be paid before any preferred dividends are distributed.[2] An inexperienced analyst may calculate the preferred dividend coverage by dividing net income after income taxes by the dividend requirement. If we did this for Alliance Company in 19X5, the result would be a coverage of 23.5 times ($18,760/$800). This result is obviously absurd, since the bond interest coverage is only 12 times. Inasmuch as bond interest is a prior charge, the protection for dividends on a junior security such as preferred stock cannot be better than the protection for the bond interest.

Analysis of Working Capital Position

The analysis of a company's working capital position is sometimes called *short-term credit analysis*, because it emphasizes factors of particular importance to short-term creditors, who are principally interested in the company's ability to repay its current obligations on time. Long-term creditors and investors, however, should also be concerned about a company's current position. Shortages of working capital can sometimes force a company into disadvantageous borrowing at inopportune times and unfavorable interest rates and can also affect its ability to pay interest and dividends. Many long-term debt contracts contain provisions that require the borrowing firm to maintain an adequate current position.

From Chapter 19, we know that a firm's *working capital* is the difference between its current assets and current liabilities. For Alliance Company in 19X5, working capital (in thousands of dollars) was $87,800 ($145,500 current assets − $57,700 current liabilities).

The adequacy of a firm's working capital is indicated in its relation to sales and in the ratio between current assets and current debt. Compare the following sets of 19X5 data for Alliance Company and Century Company:

---

[2] Because bond interest is tax deductible and preferred dividends are not, some analysts place the dividends on the same basis as the interest by dividing them by (1 − tax rate). With a 40% tax rate, the dividends would be $1,333. We have ignored this technicality in our discussion.

	(Thousands of Dollars)	
	Alliance	Century
Current Assets	$145,500	$139,549
Current Liabilities	57,700	90,136
Working Capital	$ 87,800	$ 49,413
Sales	$415,000	$414,644

In this example, the ratio of sales to working capital (called **working capital turnover**) is 4.7 for Alliance ($415,000/$87,800) and 8.4 for Century ($414,644/$49,413). We might wonder about this disparity. How much working capital should support a given amount of sales? We can determine which of the two companies has a better defensive position by calculating the current ratio.

CURRENT RATIO   The current ratio is simply the current assets divided by the current liabilities.

$$\text{Current Ratio} = \frac{\text{Current Assets}}{\text{Current Liabilities}}$$

This ratio is a measure of a firm's ability to meet its current obligations on time and to have funds readily available for current operations. The calculations below show that Alliance Company improved its position in 19X5 and has a current ratio of 252%.

	19X5	19X4
Current Assets	$145,500	$122,200
Current Liabilities	$ 57,700	$ 54,400
Current Ratio	2.52	2.25

This represents a better current position than that of Century Company, which had a ratio of only 155% ($139,549/$90,136). Century Company's working capital may be too small to support its volume of sales.

For many years, some short-term creditors have relied on a rule of thumb that the current ratio for industrial companies should exceed 200%. This arbitrary guideline probably developed from the premise that, because inventories frequently amount to as much as one-half of current assets, the remaining, more liquid current assets should at least equal the current debt. The rule is not completely reliable, since many companies have operated successfully with lower current ratios. Nonetheless, the 200% can be used as a general guide. When a company's current ratio is low, the analyst should attempt to determine if the situation is temporary and if the company has access to a line of credit so that refinancing can be accomplished easily in the event of difficulty.

QUICK RATIO   Sometimes analysts calculate the ratio between the liquid, or quick, current assets and the current liabilities. **Quick current assets** are cash, marketable securities, and receivables. The main item omitted is the inventory. Prepaid items are also omitted, but they are usually not material in amount. The quick ratio may give a better picture than the current ratio of a company's ability to meet current debts and to take advantage of discounts offered by creditors. The quick ratio and the current ratio together indicate the influence of the inventory figure in the company's working capital position. For example, a company might have an acceptable current ratio, but if its quick ratio falls much below 100%, the analyst might be uneasy about the size of the inventory and analyze the inventory position more carefully. Again, the 100% rule of thumb for the quick ratio is an arbitrary standard used only to alert the analyst to the need for further scrutiny.

We calculate the quick ratio for Alliance Company as follows:

$$\text{Quick Ratio} = \frac{\text{Cash} + \text{Marketable Securities} + \text{Receivables}}{\text{Current Liabilities}}$$

	19X5	19X4
Cash, Marketable Securities, and Receivables	$68,600	$58,600
Current Liabilities	$57,700	$54,400
Quick Ratio	1.19	1.08

INVENTORY TURNOVER   An analyst concerned about a company's inventory position may compute the company's average **inventory turnover.** This figure indicates whether the inventory amount is disproportionate to the amount of sales. Excessive inventories not only tie up company funds and increase storage costs but may also lead to subsequent losses if the goods become outdated or unsalable. The computation always involves dividing some measure of sales volume by a measure of the typical inventory level. Most accountants use cost of goods sold as a measure of sales volume and the average inventory for the year as a measure of the typical inventory level, as follows:

$$\text{Inventory Turnover} = \frac{\text{Cost of Goods Sold}}{\text{Average Inventory}}$$

Using this measure for Alliance Company gives the following results:

		19X5	19X4
Cost of Goods Sold		$290,000	$230,000
Beginning Inventory	(a)	$ 63,000	$ 48,000
Ending Inventory	(b)	76,000	63,000
Average Inventory [(a + b)/2]		69,500	55,500
Inventory Turnover		4.17	4.14

We use cost of goods sold in the calculation because the inventory measure in the denominator is a *cost* figure; we should therefore use a *cost* figure in the numerator. However, many credit agencies and analysts commonly use the sales amount instead of cost of goods sold to calculate inventory turnover. Calculated in this manner, Alliance Company's turnover is 5.97 times in 19X5. Analysts who compare a firm's inventory turnover with industry averages computed in this manner should use the sales figure in the calculations.

Usually, the average inventory is obtained by adding the year's beginning and ending inventories and dividing by two. Since inventories taken at the beginning and end of the year are likely to be lower than the typical inventory, an unrealistically high turnover ratio may result. We should use a 12-month average if monthly inventory figures are available. Furthermore, we should be careful in calculating inventory turnover ratios for companies that use last-in, first-out inventory measurement methods. In calculating inventory turnover, company management may restate the inventories at current prices using price indexes or other available data. Outside analysts may not be able to make such adjustments and may have to make some subjective allowance for overstatement of turnover.

A low inventory turnover can, of course, result from an overextended inventory position or from inadequate sales volume. For this reason, appraisal of inventory turnover should be accompanied by scrutiny of the quick ratio and analysis of trends in both inventory and sales. Inventory turnover figures vary considerably from industry to industry, and analysts frequently compare a firm's experience with industry averages.

AVERAGE COLLECTION PERIOD   We can measure the average quality of a firm's trade receivables by calculating the **average collection period.** This calculation, sometimes called **day's sales outstanding,** is made as follows:

$$\text{Average Collection Period} = \frac{\text{Trade Accounts Receivable}}{\text{Year's Sales}} \times 365$$

Note that this equation results from first calculating the average day's sales (Sales/365) and then dividing this figure into the accounts receivable balance to determine how many average days' sales are uncollected. In the computation, the numerator should be the year-end receivables before deducting the allowance for uncollectible accounts, and only credit sales should be in the denominator. In the following calculations, we assume that all of Alliance Company's sales were credit sales.

		19X5	19X4
Year-end Receivables (before allowance for uncollectible accounts)	(a)	$ 64,000	$ 54,000
Net Credit Sales	(b)	415,000	320,000
Average Collection Period [(a/b) × 365]		56 days	62 days

Analysts calculate the average collection period to discover whether the accounts receivable are slow or overdue. A rough rule of thumb sometimes used by credit agencies is that the average collection period should not exceed $1\frac{1}{3}$ times the net credit period. For example, the average collection period of a firm selling on 30-day net terms should probably not exceed 40 days.

LIMITATIONS OF FINANCIAL ANALYSIS

The ratios, percentages, and other relationships we have described in this chapter are merely the result of analytical techniques. They may only isolate areas requiring further investigation. Moreover, we must interpret them with due consideration to general economic conditions, conditions of the industry in which the companies operate, and the positions of individual companies within the industry.

We should also be aware of the inherent limitations of financial statement data. Problems of comparability are frequently encountered. Companies otherwise similar may employ different accounting methods, which can cause problems in comparing certain key relationships. For instance, inventory turnover is different for a company using LIFO than for one using FIFO inventory costing. Inflation may distort certain computations, especially those resulting from horizontal analysis. For example, trend percentages calculated from unadjusted data may be deceptive. Sometimes, gains over time in sales, earnings, and other key figures disappear when the underlying data are adjusted for changes in price levels.

We must be careful even when comparing companies in a particular industry. Such factors as size, diversity of product, and mode of operations can make the firms completely dissimilar. Some firms, particularly conglomerates, are difficult to classify by industry. If segment information—particularly product-line data— is available, the analyst may compare the statistics for several industries. Often, trade associations like the American Meat Institute prepare industry statistics that are stratified by size of firm or type of product, making analysis easier.

KEY POINTS TO REMEMBER

The important ratios covered in this chapter are summarized below:

Analysis of Operating Performance

$$\text{Rate of Return on Assets} = \frac{\text{Operating Income}}{\text{Average Total Assets}}$$

$$\text{Rate of Return on Common Stockholders' Equity} = \frac{\text{Net Income} - \text{Preferred Dividend Requirements}}{\text{Average Common Stockholders' Equity}}$$

$$\text{Rate of Return on Sales} = \frac{\text{Net Income}}{\text{Net Sales}}$$

$$\text{Price–Earnings Ratio} = \frac{\text{Market Price per Common Share}}{\text{Common Stock Earnings per Share}}$$

$$\text{Dividend Yield} = \frac{\text{Common Dividends per Share}}{\text{Market Price per Share}}$$

$$\text{Dividend Payout Ratio} = \frac{\text{Common Dividends per Share}}{\text{Common Stock Earnings per Share}}$$

Analysis of Financial Strength

$$\text{Equity Ratio} = \frac{\text{Common Stockholders' Equity}}{\text{Total Assets}}$$

$$\text{Bond Interest Coverage} = \frac{\text{Operating Income}}{\text{Annual Bond Interest}}$$

$$\text{Preferred Dividend Coverage} = \frac{\text{Operating Income}}{\text{Annual Bond Interest} + \text{Preferred Dividend Requirements}}$$

$$\text{Current Ratio} = \frac{\text{Current Assets}}{\text{Current Liabilities}}$$

$$\text{Quick Ratio} = \frac{\text{Cash} + \text{Marketable Securities} + \text{Receivables}}{\text{Current Liabilities}}$$

$$\text{Inventory Turnover} = \frac{\text{Cost of Goods Sold}}{\text{Average Inventory}}$$

$$\text{Average Collection Period} = \frac{\text{Trade Accounts Receivable}}{\text{Year's Sales}} \times 365$$

QUESTIONS

20–1 What are trend percentages, and how are they calculated? What pitfalls must an analyst avoid when preparing trend percentages?

20–2 Distinguish between horizontal analysis and vertical analysis of financial statements.

20–3 The following data are taken from the income statements of the Seminole Company. Using year 1 as the base year, calculate trend percentages.

	Year 1	Year 2	Year 3	Year 4
Sales	$600,000	$672,000	$708,000	$744,000
Earnings	30,000	31,800	36,000	37,500

20–4 During the past year, Evans Company had net income of $2 million, and Knight Company had net income of $5 million. Both companies manufacture electrical components for the building trade. What additional information would you need to compare the profitability of the two companies? Discuss your answer.

20–5 Under what circumstances can return on sales be used to appraise the profitability of a company? Can this ratio be used to compare the profitability of companies from different industries? Explain.

20–6 Why do we calculate the rate of return on assets? Give reasons why the income measure used in this calculation is not reduced for interest or income taxes.

20–7 What does the rate of return on common stockholders' equity measure? Why are interest expense and income taxes deducted from the income measure in this ratio?

20–8 What are common-size percentages, and how are they used?

20–9 Technic, Inc., earned $4.50 per share of common stock in the current year and paid dividends of $2.50 per share. The most recent market price of the common stock is $42.75 per share. Calculate (a) the price–earnings ratio, (b) the dividend yield and (c) the dividend payout ratio.

20–10 Explain, by giving an example, what is meant by *trading on the equity*.

724 20 ■ ANALYSIS AND INTERPRETATION OF FINANCIAL STATEMENTS

20–11 Why is it dangerous for a company with unstable earnings to trade heavily on the equity?

20–12 Discuss the significance of the equity ratio, and explain how it is computed.

20–13 Why do we determine bond interest coverage, and how is it calculated?

20–14 List three important ratios for evaluating the current position of a firm, and state how they are used.

20–15 What is meant by the *yield* on a common stock investment? Give an example of a computation of yield.

20–16 Utility companies have a high "payout" ratio compared with industrial companies. What is meant by a *payout ratio*? Why would utility companies continue high payout ratios?

EXERCISES

In the following exercises, inventory turnover is calculated using cost of goods sold in the numerator.

20–17 Consider the following income statement data from the Collins Company for this year and last year:

	This Year	Last Year
Sales	$920,000	$750,000
Cost of Goods Sold	588,800	465,000
Selling Expenses	174,800	157,500
General Expenses	92,000	82,500
Income Tax Expense	14,000	9,000

(a) Prepare a comparative income statement, showing increases and decreases in dollars and in percentages.
(b) Prepare common-size income statements for each year.
(c) Comment briefly on the changes between the two years.

20–18 Hayes Company has a current ratio of 250% (2.5 to 1) on December 31 of the current year. On that date its current assets are as follows:

Cash		$ 30,000
Accounts Receivable	$70,000	
Less: Allowance for Uncollectible Accounts	5,000	65,000
Merchandise Inventory		125,000
Prepaid Expenses		5,000
		$225,000

(a) What is the firm's working capital on December 31?
(b) What is the quick ratio on December 31?
(c) If the company pays a current note payable of $10,000 immediately after December 31, how does the transaction affect the current ratio? Working capital?

20–19 Hayes Company, whose current assets are shown in Exercise 20–18, had net sales of $490,000 during the current year. The beginning inventory for the year was $75,000. Cost of goods sold for the year amounted to $300,000.

(a) What was the average collection period for receivables?

(b) What was the average inventory turnover for the year?

20–20 The following data are taken from a recent annual report of Dow Jones & Company, Inc., publishers of *The Wall Street Journal* and *Barron's*. Calculate the working capital and the current ratio.

Current Assets	$150,246,000
Current Liabilities:	
Current Maturities of Long-term Debt	$ 5,024,000
Accounts Payable	19,407,000
Accrued Wages, Royalties, etc.	22,321,000
Accrued Taxes	23,691,000
Profit Sharing and Retirement Contributions Payable	8,263,000
Other Payables	29,953,000
Unexpired Subscriptions	85,242,000
Total Current Liabilities	$193,901,000

Does any of this data suggest a modification of the normal way in which the working capital and the current ratio are calculated?

20–21 The Rand Corporation pays a quarterly dividend of $2.75 per share of common stock. Its earnings after taxes during the past four quarters of operation were $1,900,000. The company has 100,000 shares of $100 par value common stock and 20,000 shares of $50 par value, 10% preferred stock outstanding. The current market price of the common shares is $153.

(a) Calculate the earnings per share for the common stock.

(b) Calculate the price–earnings ratio for the common stock.

(c) What is the current dividend yield on the common stock?

20–22 The Lakeside Company has total assets of $1,200,000 and earns an average of $120,000 before income taxes. Currently, the company has no long-term debt outstanding. The company needs an additional $300,000 in funds on which it plans to earn 18% before income taxes. It can borrow the money at 12% or issue additional common stock. The effective tax rate is 40%. The company has 12,000 shares of common stock outstanding. Calculate the earnings per share expected (a) if the additional funds are borrowed and (b) if an additional 3,000 shares are sold.

20–23 The following information is available for the Dynel Company:

	Dec. 31, This Year	Dec. 31, Last Year
Total Assets	$3,000,000	$2,400,000
Current Liabilities	$ 500,000	$ 300,000
12% Bonds Payable	600,000	600,000
Common Stock ($100 Par Value)	1,500,000	1,200,000
Retained Earnings	400,000	300,000
	$3,000,000	$2,400,000

For this year, net sales amounted to $5,940,000, and income after income taxes was $237,600. The income tax rate was 40%. Calculate the following for this year:

(a) Return on assets.
(b) Return on common stockholders' equity.
(c) Return on sales.
(d) Bond interest coverage.
(e) Equity ratio.

PROBLEMS

Note: Unless otherwise indicated, inventory turnover is calculated using cost of goods sold in the numerator in the following problems.

20–24 Net sales, net income, and total asset figures for Wonderglow Paint, Inc., for five consecutive years are given below:

	Annual Amounts (Thousands of Dollars)				
	Year 1	Year 2	Year 3	Year 4	Year 5
Net Sales	$65,200	$72,500	$80,400	$86,700	$98,600
Net Income	2,930	3,120	3,780	4,250	4,930
Total Assets	38,500	40,250	42,750	45,100	48,500

REQUIRED
(a) Calculate trend percentages, using year 1 as the base year.
(b) Calculate the return on sales for each year. (Rates above 3% are considered good for paint and varnish companies; rates above 4.8% are considered very good.)
(c) Comment on the results of your analysis.

20–25 Selected information follows for the Electra Company, taken from the current year's and last year's financial statements:

	This Year	Last Year
Net Sales	$800,000	$500,000
Cost of Goods Sold	480,000	370,000
Bond Interest Expense	15,000	15,000
Income Tax Expense	18,000	12,000
Net Income (after income taxes)	40,000	30,000
Accounts Receivable, December 31 (before allowance for uncollectible accounts)	100,000	75,000
Inventory, December 31	200,000	140,000
Common Stockholders' Equity	320,000	300,000
Total Assets	600,000	450,000

REQUIRED
(a) Calculate the following ratios and relationships for this year. Last year's results are given for comparative purposes.

	Last Year
(1) Return on assets.	12.8%
(2) Return on sales.	5.0%
(3) Return on common stockholders' equity.	10.5%
(4) Average collection period.	54 days

(5) Inventory turnover.   2.7 times

(6) Bond interest coverage.   3.8 times

(b) Comment on the changes between the two years.

20–26 Consider the following financial statements for the Polychrome Company for the past two years.

During the year just ended, management obtained additional bond financing to enlarge its production facilities. The company faced higher costs during the year for such things as fuel, materials, and freight. Because of temporary government price controls, a planned price increase on products was delayed several months.

As a holder of both common and preferred stock, you analyze the financial statements for the past two years.

Polychrome Company
Balance Sheets
(Thousands of Dollars)

	Dec. 31, This Year	Dec. 31, Last Year
Assets:		
Cash	$ 15,000	$ 9,000
Accounts Receivable (net of allowance for uncollectible accounts)	34,000	30,000
Inventory	72,000	68,000
Prepaid Expenses	11,000	7,000
Plant and Other Assets (net)	320,000	270,000
	$452,000	$384,000
Liabilities and Stockholders' Equity:		
Current Liabilities	$ 52,000	$ 48,000
12% Bonds Payable	150,000	100,000
9% Preferred Stock, $50 Par Value	50,000	50,000
Common Stock, $10 Par Value	150,000	150,000
Retained Earnings	50,000	36,000
	$452,000	$384,000

Polychrome Company
Income Statements
(Thousands of Dollars)

	This Year	Last Year
Sales	$520,000	$460,000
Cost of Goods Sold	348,400	299,000
Gross Profit	$171,600	$161,000
Operating Expenses	98,200	91,000
Operating Income	$ 73,400	$ 70,000
Bond Interest Expense	18,000	12,000
Income before Income Taxes	$ 55,400	$ 58,000
Income Tax Expense	15,900	17,000
Net Income	$ 39,500	$ 41,000

REQUIRED

(a) Calculate the following for each year: current ratio, quick ratio, inventory turnover (inventory was $64 million two years ago), equity ratio, times interest earned, preferred dividend coverage, return on assets (total assets were $386 million two years ago), and return on common stockholders' equity (common stock equity was $174 million two years ago).

(b) Calculate common-size percentages for each year's income statement.

(c) Calculate the apparent amount of common dividends per share paid during the year just ended. (Use number of shares at year-end.)

(d) Comment on the results of your analysis.

20–27   Because you own both preferred and common stock of the Northport Corporation, a manufacturer of motor vehicle parts and accessories, you are analyzing the firm's performance for the most recent year. The following data are taken from the firm's last annual report.

	Dec. 31, This Year	Dec. 31, Last Year
Total Assets	$4,800,000	$4,200,000
Current Liabilities	$ 600,000	$ 400,000
12% Bonds Payable	1,200,000	1,200,000
10% Preferred Stock, $100 Par Value	600,000	600,000
Common Stock, $50 Par Value	2,000,000	1,700,000
Retained Earnings	400,000	300,000
Total Liabilities and Stockholders' Equity	$4,800,000	$4,200,000

For this year, net sales amount to $9,800,000, and income after income taxes is $510,000. The income tax rate is 40%.

REQUIRED

(a) Calculate the following for this year:
   (1) Return on sales.
   (2) Return on assets.
   (3) Return on common stockholders' equity.
   (4) Equity ratio.
   (5) Bond interest coverage.
   (6) Preferred dividend coverage.

(b) Trade association statistics and information provided by credit agencies reveal the following data on industry norms:

	Median	Upper Quartile
Return on sales	4.57%	6.09%
Return on assets	16.2	21.3
Return on stockholders' equity	12.5	19.4
Equity ratio	52.0	61.0

Compare Northport Corporation's performance with industry performance.

20–28   The following are the 19X8 financial statements for Anchorage Company, with almost all dollar amounts missing.

Anchorage Company
Balance Sheet
December 31, 19X8

Cash	$?	Current Liabilities	$?
Accounts Receivable (net of		10% Bonds Payable	?
allowance for uncollec-		Common Stock	?
tible accounts)	?	Retained Earnings	34,000
Inventory	?		
Equipment (net)	?		
		Total Liabilities	
		and Stockholders'	
Total Assets	$120,000	Equity	$120,000

Anchorage Company
Income Statement
For the Year Ended December 31, 19X8

Net Sales	$?
Cost of Goods Sold	?
Gross Profit	?
Operating Expenses	?
Operating Income	?
Bond Interest Expense	?
Income before Income Taxes	?
Income Tax Expense (40%)	?
Net Income	$12,000

The following information is available about Anchorage Company's 19X8 financial statements:

(1) Quick ratio, 1.2:1.
(2) Inventory turnover (inventory at January 1, 19X8 was $30,000), 3 times.
(3) Return on sales, 8%.
(4) Average collection period, 29.2 days. Allowance balance is $1,000.
(5) Gross profit rate, 30%.
(6) Return on assets (total assets at January 1, 19X8 were $100,000), 20%.
(7) Equity ratio, 70%.
(8) The interest expense relates to the bonds payable that were outstanding all year.

REQUIRED
Compute the missing amounts, and complete the financial statements of Anchorage Company. *Hint:* Complete the income statement first.

20–29 Acryline Plastics, Inc., manufactures various plastic and synthetic products. Financial statement data for the firm are as follows:

(Thousands of Dollars)

This Year:

Net Sales	$500,000
Net Income (after income taxes)	24,000
Dividends	10,000
Interest Expense	5,000
Income Tax Expense	16,000

Acryline Plastics, Inc.
Balance Sheets
(Thousands of Dollars)

Assets	Dec. 31, This Year	Dec. 31, Last Year
Cash	$ 7,200	$ 6,000
Accounts Receivable (net of allowance for uncollectible accounts of $3,600 last year and $3,200 this year)	60,800	56,400
Inventory	128,000	109,600
Total Current Assets	$196,000	$172,000
Plant Assets (net)	99,000	64,400
Other Assets	5,000	3,600
Total Assets	$300,000	$240,000

Liabilities and Stockholders' Equity		
Notes Payable—Banks	$ 10,000	$ 8,000
Accounts Payable	39,000	29,000
Income Tax Payable	5,400	6,000
Accrued Liabilities	19,600	17,000
Total Current Liabilities	$ 74,000	$ 60,000
Long-term Debt	50,000	50,000
Total Liabilities	$124,000	$110,000
Common Stock, $100 Par Value	$120,000	$ 88,000
Retained Earnings	56,000	42,000
Total Stockholders' Equity	$176,000	$130,000
Total Liabilities and Stockholders' Equity	$300,000	$240,000

REQUIRED

(a) Using the given data, calculate items (1) through (8) for this year. Compare the performance of Acryline Plastics, Inc., with industry averages (given below), and comment on its operations.

	Median Ratios for Manufacturers of Plastic and Synthetic Products
(1) Current ratio.	3.42
(2) Quick ratio.	1.30
(3) Average collection period.	51 days
(4) Net sales to ending inventory.	5.3 times

(5) Equity ratio.	52.6%
(6) Return on assets.	19.1%
(7) Return on stockholders' equity.	11.8%
(8) Return on sales.	3.4%

(b) Calculate the dividends paid per share of common stock. (Use average number of shares outstanding during the year.) What was the payout ratio?

(c) If the most recent price per share of common stock is $152.50, what is the price–earnings ratio? The dividend yield?

ALTERNATE PROBLEMS

Note: Unless otherwise indicated, inventory turnover is calculated using cost of goods sold in the numerator in the following problems.

20–24A   Net sales, net income, and total asset figures for Willshire Meat Processing, Inc. for five consecutive years are given below:

	Annual Amounts (Thousands of Dollars)				
	Year 1	Year 2	Year 3	Year 4	Year 5
Net Sales	$275,000	$280,000	$296,000	$312,000	$370,000
Net Income	4,300	6,225	7,900	6,600	8,600
Total Assets	75,000	81,000	86,000	90,000	98,000

REQUIRED

(a) Calculate trend percentages, using year 1 as the base year.

(b) Calculate the return on sales for each year. (Rates above 1% are considered good for meat processing companies; rates above 1.5% are considered very good.)

(c) Comment on the results of your analysis.

20–25A   Selected information follows for the Toronto Company, taken from the current year's and last year's financial statements:

	This Year	Last Year
Net Sales	$720,000	$640,000
Cost of Goods Sold	432,000	416,000
Bond Interest Expense	18,000	12,000
Income Tax Expense	8,100	6,400
Net Income (after income taxes)	32,400	25,600
Accounts Receivable, December 31		
(before allowance for		
uncollectible accounts	105,000	81,000
Inventory, December 31	78,000	66,000
Common Stockholders' Equity	220,000	200,000
Total Assets	380,000	350,000

REQUIRED

Calculate the following for this year:

(a) Return on assets.

(b) Return on sales.

(c) Return on common stockholders' equity.

(d) Average collection period.

(e) Inventory turnover.

(f) Bond interest coverage.

20–26A Consider the following financial statements for the Olympic Company for the past two years.

During the year just ended, management obtained additional bond financing to enlarge its production facilities. The plant addition would produce a new high-margin product, which is supposed to improve the average rates of gross profit and return on sales.

As a holder of both common and preferred stock, you analyze the financial statements for the past two years.

Olympic Company
Balance Sheets
(Thousands of Dollars)

	Dec. 31, This Year	Dec. 31, Last Year
Assets:		
Cash	$ 23,000	$ 20,000
Accounts Receivable (net of allowance for uncollectible accounts)	28,000	32,000
Inventory	87,000	58,000
Prepaid Expenses	2,000	3,000
Plant and Other Assets (net)	380,000	347,000
	$520,000	$460,000
Liabilities and Stockholders' Equity:		
Current Liabilities	$ 76,000	$ 53,000
10% Bonds Payable	150,000	125,000
8% Preferred Stock, $50 Par Value	50,000	50,000
Common Stock, $10 Par Value	200,000	200,000
Retained Earnings	44,000	32,000
	$520,000	$460,000

Olympic Company
Income Statements
(Thousands of Dollars)

	This Year	Last Year
Sales	$720,000	$600,000
Cost of Goods Sold	468,000	408,000
Gross Profit	$252,000	$192,000
Operating Expenses	190,800	147,500
Operating Income	$ 61,200	$ 44,500
Bond Interest Expense	15,000	12,500
Income before Income Taxes	$ 46,200	$ 32,000
Income Tax Expense	18,200	12,800
Net Income	$ 28,000	$ 19,200

REQUIRED

(a) Calculate the following for each year: current ratio, quick ratio, inventory turnover (inventory was $48 million two years ago), equity ratio, times interest earned, preferred dividend coverage, return on assets (total assets were $420 million two years ago), and return on common stockholders' equity (common stock equity was $220 million two years ago).

(b) Calculate common-size percentages for each year's income statement.

(c) Calculate the apparent amount of common dividends per share paid during the year just ended.

(d) Comment on the results of your analysis.

20-28A The following are the 19X8 financial statements for Wright Company, with almost all dollar amounts missing:

Wright Company
Balance Sheet
December 31, 19X8

Cash	$?	Current Liabilities	$?
Accounts Receivable (net of		8% Bonds Payable	?
allowance for uncollectible		Common Stock	?
accounts)	?	Retained Earnings	60,000
Inventory	?		
Equipment (net)	?		
		Total Liabilities	
		and Stockholders'	
Total Assets	$300,000	Equity	$300,000

Wright Company
Income Statement
For the Year Ended December 31, 19X8

Net Sales	$?
Cost of Goods Sold	?
Gross Profit	?
Operating Expenses	?
Operating Income	?
Bond Interest Expense	?
Income before Income Taxes	?
Income Tax Expense (30%)	?
Net Income	$28,000

The following information is available about Wright Company's 19X8 financial statements:

(1) Quick ratio, 1.5:1.

(2) Inventory turnover (inventory at January 1, 19X8 was $70,000), 4.48 times.

(3) Return on sales, 5%.

(4) Average collection period, 18.25 days. Allowance balance is $2,000.

(5) Gross profit rate, 40%.
(6) Return on assets (total assets at January 1, 19X8 were $180,000), 20%.
(7) Equity ratio, 60%.
(8) The interest expense relates to the bonds payable that were outstanding all year.

REQUIRED
Compute the missing amounts, and complete the financial statements of Wright Company. *Hint:* Complete the income statement first.

BUSINESS DECISION PROBLEM

Blue Ridge, Inc., which manufactures electric lighting and wiring equipment, has been in business five years. The company has had modest profits and has experienced few operating difficulties until this year, when president John Harper discusses his company's working capital problems with you, a loan officer at Shorewood Bank. Harper explains that expanding his firm has created difficulties in meeting obligations when they come due and taking advantage of cash discounts offered by manufacturers for timely payment. He would like to borrow $40,000 from Shorewood Bank. At your request, Harper submits the following financial data for the past two years:

	This Year	Last Year
Net Sales	$1,000,000	$820,000
Net Income (after income taxes)	32,000	28,000
Dividends	16,000	12,000
Interest Expense	18,000	15,000
Income Tax Expense	8,000	6,400
Total Assets Two Years Ago		480,000
Total Stockholders' Equity Two Years Ago		230,000

Blue Ridge, Inc.
Balance Sheets

Assets	Dec. 31, This Year	Dec. 31, Last Year
Cash	$ 42,000	$ 34,000
Accounts Receivable (net of allowance for uncollectible accounts of $5,000 last year and $8,000 this year)	148,000	110,000
Inventory	280,000	210,000
Prepaid Expenses	15,000	10,000
Total Current Assets	$485,000	$364,000
Plant Assets (net)	250,000	215,000
Total Assets	$735,000	$579,000

Liabilities and Stockholders' Equity

Notes Payable—Banks	$ 35,000	$ 30,000
Accounts Payable	185,000	122,000
Income Tax Payable	7,000	5,000
Accrued Liabilities	35,000	20,000
Total Current Liabilities	$262,000	$177,000
10% Mortgage Payable	150,000	120,000
Total Liabilities	$412,000	$297,000
Common Stock	$275,000	$250,000
Retained Earnings	48,000	32,000
Total Stockholders' Equity	$323,000	$282,000
Total Liabilities and Stockholders' Equity	$735,000	$579,000

You calculate the following items for both years from the given data and compare them with the typical ratios for electric lighting and wiring equipment manufacturers provided by a commercial credit firm:

	Typical Ratios for Electric Lighting and Wiring Equipment Manufacturers
(a) Current ratio	2.66
(b) Quick ratio.	1.3
(c) Average collection period.	46 days
(d) Net sales to ending inventory.	4.8 times
(e) Equity ratio.	49%
(f) Return on assets.	13.1%
(g) Return on stockholders' equity.	11.9%
(h) Return on sales.	4.08%

REQUIRED

Based on your analysis, decide whether and under what circumstances you would grant Harper's request for a loan. Explain the reasons for your decision.

21

Accounting for Manufacturing Operations

So far, our discussion of accounting systems and procedures has related mainly to merchandising firms and service firms. Another important segment of industry comprises manufacturing firms.

Although the accounting principles and techniques described earlier apply to manufacturing firms, accounting for manufacturing operations is usually more complex because more activities are involved in producing a product than in simply purchasing a product for resale as in a merchandising firm. Because specific purchase prices are known, the cost of goods purchased for resale is relatively easy to determine. In manufacturing operations, however, the costs of all inputs must be accumulated and allocated to calculate the cost of the units produced. In addition, manufacturers must account for the buying, selling, and administrative activities that are common to other types of firms. These and other accounting problems related to manufacturing operations are considered in this and the two following chapters.

Manufacturing operations vary widely in complexity. In this chapter, our approach to accounting for manufacturing activities is a general accounting system adapted to a relatively simple manufacturing operation using the periodic inventory method. No specific product costing system is involved. The two primary cost accounting systems—*job order costing* and *process costing*—are considered in Chapters 22 and 23.

KEY CONCEPTS IN MANUFACTURING ACCOUNTING

Cost of Goods Manufactured

The primary difference between merchandising and manufacturing firms is that merchandising firms *buy* finished products to sell whereas manufacturers *make* the products they sell. This difference is apparent in the following comparative illustration of cost of goods sold for each:

Merchandising Firm		Manufacturing Firm	
Beginning Merchandise Inventory	$100	Beginning Finished Goods Inventory	$100
Add: Net Cost of Merchandise Purchases	400	Add: Cost of Goods Manufactured	400
Goods Available for Sale	$500	Goods Available for Sale	$500
Less: Ending Merchandise Inventory	200	Less: Ending Finished Goods Inventory	200
Cost of Goods Sold	$300	Cost of Goods Sold	$300

Note on the manufacturing firm's statement that cost of goods manufactured corresponds to net cost of merchandise purchases on the merchandising firm's statement. In both cases, these amounts represent costs of finished goods ready for resale. The merchandising firm bought its goods in their finished state and does not have the problem of determining their cost. The manufacturing firm, however, must account for the costs of acquiring and converting raw materials into finished products.

Product and Period Costs

Product costs are all costs necessary to bring a manufactured product to completion. Thus, all the costs of factory materials and labor, as well as such other factory costs as utilities, depreciation, insurance, and repairs, are incorporated into the total cost of the products manufactured.

THE U.S. ECONOMIC BASE: AGRICULTURE→ MANUFACTURING→?

A basic variable in a country's welfare is the industry that dominates production of its gross national product. Initially for the United States, this industry was agriculture. For the past several decades, however, manufacturing has dominated U.S. production, and less than 5% of the labor force are now employed in agriculture.

Today, observers theorize that the U.S. economy is rapidly shifting from its manufacturing base as more and more products are manufactured in foreign countries. Automobiles, textiles, high-quality optics, and even the basic commodity of steel represent product lines manufactured abroad. Although its causes are complex, the shift to foreign manufacturers is primarily explained by a pursuit of low labor rates. Many so-called developing countries have large labor forces readily available at wage rates a fraction of the U.S. minimum wage. Ironically, companies losing manufacturing jobs in the United States may be considered victims of the relatively high U.S. living standard.

Personal services was first identified as the industry base that would replace manufacturing. This theory was primarily supported by recognizing that a number of manufacturing jobs have disappeared and that the new jobs are in the personal services area—such as fast-food clerks, banking clerks, personal health and beauty care clerks, and government clerks. However, well-documented theses now argue that the new U.S. economic base will be information, not personal services. In other words, the United States will increasingly create and distribute technological information rather than manufactured products. Critical events underlying this theme are the rampant technological developments in telecommunications, space satellites, and computers and the lead the United States enjoys in these phenomena.* Probably the most widely read proponent of the technology thesis is John Naisbitt, who, in his bestseller *Megatrends*, listed the shift from an industrial society to an information society as the first of his 10 "megashifts" that are transforming our lives.†

Implications stemming from such basic economic changes are difficult to state. Certainly, the quality and emphases of public education must be reexamined. In their career choices, students should consider the possibility of significantly altered opportunities in manufacturing-based companies. Accountants, for example, play a primary role in the decisions of manufacturing operations, but as information technologists, they are assured a vital place in the new information society.

*For a fascinating review of these events, see Daniel Bell, *The Winding Passage* (Cambridge, MA: ABT Books, 1980), especially Chapter 2, titled "Teletext and Technology: New Networks of Knowledge and Information in Postindustrial Society," pages 34–65.
†John Naisbitt, *Megatrends: Ten New Directions Transforming Our Lives* (New York: Warner Books, Inc., 1980).

When accounting for service and merchandising organizations, we show amounts for such items as wages, salaries, depreciation, and utilities as expenses deducted from revenue. In manufacturing accounting, however, all such "expenses" for the factory are "capitalized" (treated as an asset) and become the cost of goods manufactured. Such costs represent additions to finished goods inventory (an asset) and are not deducted from revenue as cost of goods sold until the period in which the related products are sold to customers.

Period costs are charged to expense in the period incurred. The benefits associated with such costs are considered to expire in that period rather than relate to whatever product may have been produced in that period. Traditionally, nonfactory administrative expenses and selling expenses are considered period costs that are expensed as incurred. Distinguishing between product and period costs is not always easy. Many functions in a manufacturing firm—such as high-level administrative salaries, personnel departments, and plant security departments—may benefit both factory and nonfactory activities. The costs of such functions are often allocated partly as product cost and partly as period cost.

Based on the above concepts, income statements for manufacturing firms have the following form:

Sales		$500
Cost of Goods Sold (all factory costs)		300
Gross Profit on Sales		$200
Operating Expenses:		
Nonfactory Administrative Expenses	$50	
Selling Expenses	70	120
Net Income		$ 80

Multiple Inventory Accounts

Most manufacturing operations are continuous, so that at any time units of products are at various stages of completion. Consequently, at least three inventory accounts are usually maintained, as follows:

(1) The Raw Materials Inventory account reflects all factory materials that have been acquired but not yet placed into production. Various subunits such as bearings or other parts may be included. (Even though these items may be finished products for the supplying firm, they are raw materials for the using firm.) Raw materials are carried at their net delivered cost.

(2) The Work in Process Inventory account reflects all factory costs associated with units of product that are begun but not completed on the date the firm's financial statements are prepared.

(3) The Finished Goods Inventory account reflects all factory costs associated with the units of product completed but not yet sold.

All three inventory accounts represent current assets. Accounting for changes in these accounts and their use in the financial statements are explained later in the chapter.

Manufacturing Cost Categories

Factory costs are usually accounted for in the following three categories:

(1) Raw materials (often called *direct materials*) include all of the important raw materials or parts that physically make up the product. Examples are steel sheets, electric motors, chemicals, and paint. (Small amounts of such incidental items as glue, lubricants, and polishing compounds are often accounted for as *factory supplies* and included in factory overhead.)

(2) Direct labor includes the primary costs of employing workers who apply their skills directly to the manufacture of the product. Material cutters, assemblers, and painters are examples of such workers. (Costs of employing other workers who work indirectly on the product—such as supervisors, inspectors, material handlers, and machinery maintenance personnel—are considered *indirect labor* costs and included in factory overhead.)

(3) Factory overhead (sometimes called *manufacturing overhead* or *factory burden*) includes *all* other factory costs not included in raw materials or direct labor. Factory overhead may include

Factory supplies used
Indirect factory labor
Insurance on factory
   building and equipment
Taxes on factory building
   and equipment
Repairs and maintenance on
   factory building and
   equipment

Factory utilities (heat,
   light, power)
Depreciation on factory
   building and equipment
Small tools consumed
Factory payroll taxes and
   other fringe benefits

As noted earlier, factory overhead specifically excludes nonfactory administrative expenses and selling expenses.

ASPECTS OF FINANCIAL STATEMENTS UNIQUE TO MANUFACTURING ACCOUNTING

The aspects of financial statements unique to manufacturing accounting are concentrated in the income statement. We explain these aspects using an illustrative manufacturing situation in the following sections.

Calculating Cost of Goods Manufactured

Stated simply, the cost of goods manufactured for an operating period is the sum of all costs necessary to bring the manufactured products to completion. Specifically, these costs are associated with (amounts are assumed):

Beginning Work in Process Inventory		$ 40,000
Add: Raw Materials (placed into production)	$200,000	
Direct Labor	300,000	
Factory Overhead	100,000	600,000
Total Manufacturing Costs Incurred		$640,000
Less: Ending Work in Process Inventory		20,000
Cost of Goods Manufactured		$620,000

Notice that the $620,000 cost of goods manufactured represents this period's total incurred manufacturing cost ($640,000) adjusted for the change in work in process inventories. In other words, the cost of goods manufactured during this period is the cost of partially completed products carried forward from last period ($40,000) plus the total manufacturing cost this period ($600,000) less the cost of partially completed products this period ($20,000) that are carried forward and completed in the next period. Remember that ending inventories of one period become the beginning inventories of the subsequent period.

Calculating Cost of Goods Sold and Net Income

As indicated earlier, computing the cost of goods sold for a manufacturer differs only in terminology from the computation for a merchandising firm. The inventory is more explicitly termed finished goods, and cost of goods manufactured rather than purchases is added to finished goods. Cost of goods sold is calculated as follows:

Beginning Finished Goods Inventory	$ 80,000
Add: Cost of Goods Manufactured	620,000
Goods Available for Sale	$700,000
Less: Ending Finished Goods Inventory	100,000
Cost of Goods Sold	$600,000

Note that the $600,000 cost of goods sold figure is the cost of goods manufactured ($620,000) adjusted for the $20,000 change (increase, in this case) in finished goods inventory. Quite logically, if finished goods inventory increases by $20,000 (from $80,000 to $100,000) during the period, then we must have sold $20,000 less than we manufactured. Also note that the cost of goods sold includes only factory costs; no nonfactory administrative expenses or selling expenses are involved. Instead, the cost of goods sold is deducted from sales revenue to generate a gross profit on sales, from which nonfactory administrative expenses and selling expenses are deducted to determine the period's net income (or loss).

In Exhibit 21–1, we use a typical plant layout (schematic floor plan) to illustrate the relationships between manufacturing activities and the important aspects of accounting reports for manufacturers. All amounts are assumed. The balance sheet is not included because multiple inventories (raw materials, work in process, and finished goods) are the only important items distinguishing a balance sheet for a manufacturer.

On the left side of Exhibit 21–1, the various steps in the manufacturing process are listed in their natural order, starting with the acquisition of raw materials, through the manufacture and sale of finished goods, to the computation of net income for the period. The steps are keyed with circled numbers to the various activity areas of a hypothetical factory, which is diagramed in the center of the exhibit. The arrows associate these activity areas with the related amounts reflected in the cost of goods manufactured statement and the income statement.

Exhibit 21–1 indicates the sequence of manufacturing activities and the parallels that exist between the activity centers of a factory and the accounting reports

EXHIBIT 21–1
Relationships among Manufacturing Activities, Factory Layout, and Accounting Reports

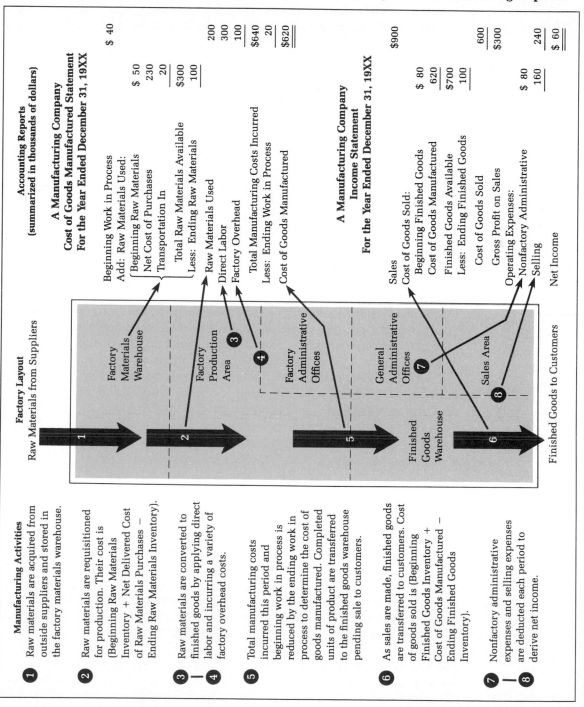

for a manufacturing operation. The exhibit also highlights the separation of product costs (the accumulation of raw materials, direct labor, and factory overhead) from period costs (nonfactory administrative and selling expenses).

Exhibit 21–2 presents a formal cost of goods manufactured statement and an income statement for a typical manufacturing firm. All amounts are assumed. Note that these statements correlate with those summarized in Exhibit 21–1 and reflect earlier generalizations regarding the accumulation of raw materials cost, direct labor, and factory overhead as the cost of goods manufactured. In turn, the cost of goods manufactured is added to finished goods to determine the cost of goods sold and gross profit on sales. Finally, nonfactory administrative expenses and selling expenses are deducted to derive net income.

The cost of goods manufactured statement presents the several cost categories in the general order in which they are incurred. In a sense, the first costs incurred are those costs carried forward from the preceding period as beginning work in process. Next, raw materials used is determined (Beginning Inventory + Net Delivered Cost of Raw Materials Purchased − Ending Raw Materials Inventory). The cost of direct labor follows, usually shown as a single figure. Factory overhead—a list of all factory costs other than raw materials and direct labor—is then added. If the list of overhead costs is extensive, only the total factory overhead may be shown with a reference to a supporting schedule of factory overhead costs. Beginning work in process, raw materials used, direct labor, and factory overhead are added to determine total manufacturing cost incurred. Finally, the ending work in process is deducted to derive cost of goods manufactured.

On the income statement of a manufacturing firm, the cost of goods sold is determined in much the same manner as for a merchandising concern—except that cost of goods manufactured, rather than merchandise purchases, is added to finished goods inventory. Gross profit on sales must absorb both nonfactory administrative expenses and selling expenses if there is to be any net income.

SPECIAL ACCOUNTS FOR MANUFACTURING

Many accounts appearing in a manufacturing firm's ledger—such as Cash, Accounts Receivable, and Sales—are similar to those of service and merchandising firms. The unique aspects of manufacturing, however, have led to the use of several special accounts, particularly Raw Materials Inventory, Raw Materials Purchases, Work in Process Inventory, Finished Goods Inventory, Factory Plant and Equipment, and Manufacturing Summary accounts. As explained later in this chapter, the Manufacturing Summary account summarizes the cost of goods manufactured during closing procedures (in much the same way as the Income Summary account summarizes periodic income for most firms).

Accounts Related to Raw Materials

When the periodic inventory method is used, accounting for the acquisition and use of raw materials is recorded in the four accounts appearing below. Each account contains an assumed normal balance amount and a brief description of the activities recorded.

EXHIBIT 21–2

A Manufacturing Company
Cost of Goods Manufactured Statement
For the Year Ended December 31, 19XX

Beginning Work in Process Inventory		$ 40,000
Raw Materials:		
Beginning Raw Materials Inventory	$ 50,000	
Net Cost of Raw Materials Purchased	230,000	
Transportation In for Raw Materials Purchased	20,000	
Cost of Raw Materials Available	$300,000	
Less: Ending Raw Materials Inventory	100,000	
Raw Materials Used		200,000
Direct Labor		300,000
Factory Overhead:		
Depreciation	$ 10,000	
Utilities	19,000	
Insurance	5,000	
Property Taxes	20,000	
Indirect Labor	30,000	
Factory Supplies Used	7,000	
Other Factory Overhead	9,000	
Total Factory Overhead		100,000
Total Manufacturing Cost Incurred		$640,000
Less: Ending Work in Process Inventory		20,000
Cost of Goods Manufactured		$620,000

A Manufacturing Company
Income Statement
For the Year Ended December 31, 19XX

Net Sales		$900,000
Cost of Goods Sold:		
Beginning Finished Goods Inventory	$ 80,000	
Cost of Goods Manufactured	620,000	
Goods Available for Sale	$700,000	
Less: Ending Finished Goods Inventory	100,000	
Cost of Goods Sold		600,000
Gross Profit on Sales		$300,000
Operating Expenses:		
Administrative Expenses	$ 80,000	
Selling Expenses	160,000	240,000
Net Income		$ 60,000
Earnings per Share of Capital Stock		$3

Raw Materials Inventory		Transportation In	
50,000		20,000	
(The cost of unused raw materials as determined by a periodic physical inventory count)		(The specific amounts paid to have raw materials transported to the factory)	

Raw Materials Purchases		Raw Materials Returns and Allowances	
240,000			10,000
(The purchase price of raw materials acquired throughout this period)			(The cost of raw materials returned to suppliers and of any related cost adjustments)

Entries in the Raw Materials Inventory account are made only when an end-of-period physical inventory count is taken. During the period, the requisition of raw materials into production is not recorded. Determining the ending raw materials inventory involves counting all units on hand, identifying an appropriate cost price per unit (perhaps from a recent purchase invoice or supply catalog), multiplying quantity by price, and combining all items for a total inventory figure.

The other three accounts are used throughout the period to record (1) purchases of raw materials, (2) related returns and adjustments, and (3) the costs of transporting raw materials purchases to the factory. In all cases, offsetting debits and credits are typically made to Accounts Payable or Cash. At the end of the accounting period, the balances of all purchases-related accounts are used to calculate the cost of goods manufactured and are closed to the Manufacturing Summary account (illustrated later in this chapter).

Work in Process Inventory Account

The Work in Process Inventory account reflects the costs of products that have been begun but are not completed at the end of the accounting period. All or some part of raw materials may have been added, but portions of direct labor and factory overhead have not. In a general accounting system using periodic inventory procedures, the amount of work in process is estimated at the end of the period, usually by a production supervisor or someone familiar with the manufacturing process. An illustrative calculation of estimated work in process inventory using assumed amounts appears on the next page.

	Estimated Cost per Finished Unit of Product	Average Proportion Applied	
Raw Materials:			
Material A (wood)	$2	100%	$ 2
Material B (paint)	4	25	1
Direct Labor	8	50	4
Factory Overhead	6	50	3
			$ 10
Number of Units in Ending Inventory			× 2,000
Estimated Cost of Ending Work in Process Inventory			$20,000

Estimating the ending work in process inventory typically involves (1) estimating the amount of each manufacturing cost element associated with a finished unit of product, (2) multiplying each cost by an appropriate estimate of the average proportion applied, (3) summing the estimated costs for the various factors, and (4) multiplying by the number of units in the ending inventory. This new work in process figure is the recorded amount of work in process for the end of the current period and the beginning of the subsequent period. Both the beginning and ending balances of work in process are used to calculate the cost of goods manufactured for the period. Procedures for recording the increase or decrease in work in process inventory are illustrated later in the chapter.

Finished Goods Inventory

The balance in the Finished Goods Inventory account represents the recorded cost of finished products awaiting sale to customers. In a periodic inventory system, the ending finished goods inventory is determined by (1) estimating the average cost per finished unit of product for each manufacturing cost element, (2) making a physical count of the unsold finished units of product on hand, (3) multiplying the units by the estimated total cost per unit, and (4) aggregating the total finished goods inventory cost. An illustrative calculation of finished goods inventory costing using assumed amounts follows:

Product	Raw Materials A	B	Direct Labor	Factory Overhead	Total Unit Cost	Units on Hand	Total Cost of Inventory
101	$3	$0	$ 4	$3	$10	2,500	$ 25,000
102	4	2	8	6	20	3,000	60,000
103	3	1	12	9	25	600	15,000
Totals						6,100	$100,000

Notice that different amounts of each manufacturing cost may be applied to various products. Entries to the Finished Goods Inventory account occur only at the end of the accounting period when a new balance is determined. Both the beginning and ending balances of Finished Goods Inventory are involved in computing the cost of goods sold for the period. Procedures for recording the change in Finished Goods Inventory are illustrated later in the chapter.

Plant and Equipment Accounts

Depending on their nature, manufacturing activities may involve extensive investments in factory buildings and production equipment. These assets are gradually consumed, and their utility is transformed into the cost of producing the firm's products. Therefore, depreciation on plant and equipment is an important element of factory overhead. Periodic computations of depreciation are similar to those illustrated for plant assets in Chapter 10. Should a firm rent or lease its productive facilities, such rental payments would be accounted for as factory overhead. When investments in productive facilities are extensive and varied, a control account titled Plant and Equipment is often used with a subsidiary ledger to reflect the detailed balances for each specific building and type of equipment.

Manufacturing Summary Account

Manufacturing firms use both a Manufacturing Summary account and an Income Summary account. As its name implies, the Manufacturing Summary account summarizes the total manufacturing costs for the period and determines the cost of goods manufactured. As is true for the Income Summary account, entries are made only during the closing procedures, after which the account itself is closed. Stated simply, the balance of the Manufacturing Summary account equals the cost of goods manufactured for the period when (1) all accounts for factory costs are closed to the Manufacturing Summary account, and (2) the Raw Materials Inventory and Work in Process Inventory accounts are closed to the Manufacturing Summary account (beginning balances debited and ending balances credited). The Manufacturing Summary and Income Summary accounts are illustrated in Exhibit 21–3 in T-account form, using the data from Exhibit 21–1 (individual entries are portrayed to emphasize cost flows).

Notice that before closing, the balances of these accounts agree with the related statement totals in Exhibit 21–1—cost of goods manufactured is $620,000 and net income is $60,000. The balance of the Manufacturing Summary account comprises a series of entries reflecting (1) debits for the manufacturing costs carried forward to this period as beginning raw materials and work in process inventories, and the other manufacturing costs incurred during this period—such as raw materials purchases, transportation in, direct labor, and factory overhead—and (2) credits representing the ending raw materials and work in process inventories. In effect, we deduct these latter amounts because they are carried forward as costs of the subsequent manufacturing period. Had raw materials returns and allowances been involved in this illustration, the debit for purchases would have included the gross amount of purchases, and an additional credit would appear in the Manufacturing Summary account for raw materials returns and allowances. In turn, the Manufacturing Summary account is closed to Income Summary, therefore becoming an important factor in determining the period's net income.

Notice that the finished goods inventory is not part of the cost of goods manufactured. Rather, the beginning and ending finished goods inventory amounts are closed to and appear, respectively, as a debit and a credit in the Income Summary account. This procedure combines the cost of goods manufactured, the beginning finished goods inventory, and the ending finished goods inventory, so that the cost of goods sold can be determined. Use of both the Manufacturing

EXHIBIT 21–3

Manufacturing Summary

19XX			19XX		
Dec. 31	Work in Process Inventory (Beginning)	40,000	Dec. 31	Work in Process Inventory (Ending)	20,000
31	Raw Materials Inventory (Beginning)	50,000	31	Raw Materials Inventory (Ending)	100,000
31	Purchases of Raw Materials (net)	230,000	31	(To close to Income Summary)	620,000
31	Transportation In	20,000			
31	Direct Labor	300,000			
31	Factory Overhead (total)	100,000			
		740,000			740,000

Income Summary

19XX			19XX		
Dec. 31	Finished Goods Inventory (Beginning)	80,000	Dec. 31	Sales	900,000
31	Cost of Goods Manufactured	620,000	31	Finished Goods Inventory (Ending)	100,000
31	Nonfactory Administrative Expenses (total)	80,000			
31	Selling Expenses (total)	160,000			
31	(To close to Retained Earnings)	60,000			
		1,000,000			1,000,000

Summary and the Income Summary accounts is illustrated in the comprehensive example of manufacturing accounting appearing later in this chapter.

END-OF-PERIOD PROCEDURES FOR A MANUFACTURING FIRM

Most end-of-period procedures for manufacturing firms are similar to those presented for other types of firms in Chapters 4 and 5. In the remainder of this chapter, we present a comprehensive illustration of these procedures for a manufacturing firm, including preparation and use of the worksheet to adjust the general ledger accounts, preparation of financial statements from worksheet data, and procedures for closing the temporary accounts at year-end. The illustration highlights the unique aspects of manufacturing accounting.

Worksheet for a Manufacturing Firm

Remember from Chapter 4 that a worksheet facilitates adjusting the general ledger accounts and preparing financial statements because

(1) It makes apparent in one location the debit and credit balances in all general ledger accounts.

(2) It makes apparent the effects of any adjustment.

(3) It groups all adjusted account balances involved in preparing each financial statement.

(4) It provides evidence of the arithmetical accuracy of the computed net income.

Worksheets for manufacturing firms differ from those presented in Chapters 4 and 5 only in that an additional set of columns is provided for the accounts contained in the cost of goods manufactured statements, and, of course, that three, rather than one, inventory accounts are involved. Also, note that the adjusted trial balance columns have been omitted. This procedural detail is considered unnecessary at this stage of your study. The following basic aspects of the worksheet are similar for all firms:

(1) The unadjusted trial balance is transcribed from the general ledger to the first set of money columns.

(2) Appropriate adjustments are formulated in the second set of money columns.

(3) Unadjusted account balances and any related adjustments are combined to derive adjusted balances for all accounts, which are then extended to the appropriate set of columns representing the cost of goods manufactured, the income statement, and the balance sheet. Special procedures are used to extend the beginning inventory balances and to record the ending inventory balances.

(4) Each set of statement columns is balanced in turn, to check the arithmetical accuracy of the worksheet.

Exhibit 21–4 presents the worksheet for Lollar Manufacturing, Inc. for an accounting year ended December 31, 19XX. Remember that in preparing monthly or quarterly financial statements, worksheet adjustments are not recorded and posted to the general ledger. When annual statements are prepared, however, both adjusting and closing entries are recorded in the general journal and posted to the general ledger.

Adjusting entry data for our year-end illustration are as follows:

(1) Unexpired insurance, $1,000.

(2) Unpaid wages and salaries at year-end (by category): direct labor, $4,000; indirect labor, $3,000; office salaries, $1,000; and sales salaries, $2,000.

(3) Depreciation on machinery and equipment, $6,000.

(4) Accrued interest payable at year-end, $1,000.

(5) Uncollectible accounts expense is an estimated 2% of sales.

(6) Factory supplies on hand, $4,000.

(7) Office supplies on hand, $2,000.

(8) Estimated income taxes, $17,000.

Because these adjustments are routine and parallel those of other firms, related journal entries with explanations are not presented here. Related amounts in the adjustments columns of the worksheet in Exhibit 21–4 are keyed to the parenthetical numbers of each data item.

MANUFACTURING INVENTORIES IN THE WORKSHEET Worksheet procedures for manufacturing inventories under the periodic method parallel those illustrated in Chapter 5 for merchandising companies. Recall that inventory amounts in a manufacturing firm's trial balance are debits representing the *beginning* balances for each inventory. Also, only raw materials and work in process inventories are involved in determining cost of goods manufactured. Finished goods inventories are involved in determining cost of goods sold (in the income statement).

The worksheet inventory procedures result in (1) beginning inventory balances being added to—and ending inventory balances being deducted from—other related net debit amounts for determining cost of goods manufactured and cost of goods sold, and (2) the ending balances of all three inventories being reflected as assets on the balance sheet. These procedures are as follows:

(1) Extend the beginning balances of raw materials and work in process inventories as debits in the cost of goods manufactured columns.

(2) Extend the beginning finished goods inventory as a debit in the income statement columns.

(3) At the bottom of the worksheet, record all three inventory account titles and record the ending balances of raw materials and work in process inventories as credits in the cost of goods manufactured columns, and the ending balance of finished goods inventory as a credit in the income statement columns.

(4) On the same respective lines used in step (3), record the ending balance of each inventory account as a debit in the balance sheet columns.

We represent these procedures schematically as follows [the parenthetical (+) and (−) signs indicate the respective effects on cost of goods manufactured, cost of goods sold, and total assets on the balance sheet].

EXHIBIT 21-4

Lollar Manufacturing, Inc.
Manufacturing Worksheet
For the Year Ended December 31, 19XX

Description	Trial Balance Debit	Trial Balance Credit	Adjustments Debit	Adjustments Credit	Cost of Goods Manufactured Debit	Cost of Goods Manufactured Credit	Income Statement Debit	Income Statement Credit	Balance Sheet Debit	Balance Sheet Credit
Cash	13,000								13,000	
Accounts Receivable	45,000								45,000	
Allowance for Uncollectible Accounts		1,000		(5) 9,000						10,000
Raw Materials Inventory	10,000				10,000					
Work in Process Inventory	6,000				6,000					
Finished Goods Inventory	20,000						20,000			
Factory Supplies on Hand	2,000		(6) 2,000						4,000	
Office Supplies on Hand	1,000		(7) 1,000						2,000	
Prepaid Insurance	4,000			(1) 3,000					1,000	
Machinery and Equipment	90,000								90,000	
Accumulated Depreciation—Machinery and Equipment		20,000		(3) 6,000						26,000
Accounts Payable		7,000								7,000
Long-term Notes Payable—9%		40,000								40,000
Common Stock—$10 Par Value		50,000								50,000
Retained Earnings		20,000								20,000
Dividends	4,000								4,000	
Sales		450,000						450,000		
Raw Materials Purchases	120,000				120,000					
Raw Materials Returns and Allowances		6,000				6,000				
Transportation In	2,000				2,000					
Direct Labor	77,000		(2) 4,000		81,000					
Indirect Labor	43,000		(2) 3,000		46,000					
Utilities	20,000				16,000		4,000			
Repairs and Maintenance	10,000				8,000		2,000			

EXHIBIT 21–4 (continued)

Description	Trial Balance Debit	Trial Balance Credit	Adjustments Debit	Adjustments Credit	Cost of Goods Manufactured Debit	Cost of Goods Manufactured Credit	Income Statement Debit	Income Statement Credit	Balance Sheet Debit	Balance Sheet Credit
Plant Facilities Rent	30,000				24,000		6,000			
Furniture and Fixtures Rent	10,000				8,000		2,000			
Factory Supplies Used	15,000			(6) 2,000	13,000					
Administrative Salaries	25,000				15,000		10,000			
Office Salaries Expense	15,000		(2) 1,000				16,000			
Office Supplies Used	4,000			(7) 1,000			3,000			
Sales Salaries Expense	16,000		(2) 2,000				18,000			
Advertising Expense	9,000						9,000			
Interest Expense	3,000		(4) 1,000				4,000			
	594,000	594,000								
Insurance			(1) 3,000		2,000		1,000			
Wages Payable				(2) 10,000						10,000
Depreciation—Machinery and Equipment			(3) 6,000		6,000					
Interest Payable				(4) 1,000						1,000
Uncollectible Accounts Expense			(5) 9,000				9,000			
Income Tax Expense			(8) 17,000				17,000			
Income Tax Payable				(8) 17,000						17,000
Ending Inventories:										
Raw Materials						18,000			18,000	
Work in Process						8,000			8,000	
Finished Goods								26,000	26,000	
			49,000	49,000	357,000	32,000				
Cost of Goods Manufactured					325,000	325,000	325,000			
					357,000	357,000	446,000	476,000	211,000	181,000
Net Income							30,000			30,000
							476,000	476,000	211,000	211,000

	Cost of Goods Manufactured		Income Statement		Balance Sheet	
	Debit	Credit	Debit	Credit	Debit	Credit
Extension of Beginning Balances:						
Raw materials inventory	(+)					
Work in process inventory	(+)					
Finished goods inventory			(+)			
Recording Ending Balances at Bottom of Worksheet:						
Raw materials inventory		(−)			(+)	
Work in process inventory		(−)			(+)	
Finished goods inventory				(−)	(+)	

Review of Exhibit 21–4 shows the effects of these procedures in the worksheet illustrated there. Note that using these procedures places all the amounts necessary to compute cost of goods manufactured and cost of goods sold in their respective sets of columns.

Later in the chapter, we show how closing entries create in the general ledger accounts the same effects that these worksheet inventory procedures create in the worksheet.

Allocation of Costs and Expenses

As mentioned earlier, the sharing of responsibilities or facilities by personnel in production, selling, and nonfactory administration often requires the allocation of certain expenses on some such rational basis as square feet of space used or number of persons involved. Our illustration assumes the following allocations:

Expense	Total	Factory	Nonfactory Administration	Selling
Utilities	$ 20,000	$16,000	$ 2,000	$ 2,000
Repairs and Maintenance	10,000	8,000	1,000	1,000
Plant Facilities Rent	30,000	24,000	3,000	3,000
Furniture and Fixtures Rent	10,000	8,000	1,000	1,000
Administrative Salaries	25,000	15,000	8,000	2,000
Office Salaries Expense	16,000	—	8,000	8,000
Insurance	3,000	2,000	—	1,000
	$114,000	$73,000	$23,000	$18,000

These allocations are reflected on the worksheet by extending the appropriate amounts to each set of columns. For example, $16,000 of the total $20,000 utilities expense would be extended to the cost of goods manufactured columns and the other $4,000 to the income statement columns. The income statement should reflect the further division of the $4,000 between nonfactory administration and selling.

TOTALING AND BALANCING THE WORKSHEET   After all other relevant amounts are extended, the cost of goods manufactured columns are added; the amount needed to balance them (a credit of $325,000) is the cost of goods manufactured figure for this period. The $325,000 credit needed to balance the cost of goods manufactured columns is then extended as a debit to the income statement columns. The $30,000 debit needed to balance these columns represents net income for the period. The $30,000 is then extended as a credit to balance the balance sheet columns. When operating losses occur, the *credit* needed to balance the income statement columns is extended as a debit to balance the balance sheet columns. This completes the worksheet.

Preparation of Financial Statements   Properly completed, the worksheet contains all the data necessary to prepare the cost of goods manufactured statement, the income statement, the retained earnings statement, and the balance sheet. Exhibit 21–5 (appearing on pages 755–758) presents those statements for Lollar Manufacturing, Inc., prepared from the

EXHIBIT 21–5
Financial Statements of Lollar Manufacturing, Inc.

Lollar Manufacturing, Inc.
Cost of Goods Manufactured Statement
For the Year Ended December 31, 19XX

Beginning Work in Process Inventory		$ 6,000
Raw Materials Used:		
Beginning Raw Materials Inventory	$ 10,000	
Raw Materials Purchased (net)	114,000	
Transportation In on Raw Materials	2,000	
Cost of Raw Materials Available	$126,000	
Less: Ending Raw Materials Inventory	18,000	
Cost of Raw Materials Used		108,000
Direct Labor		81,000
Factory Overhead:		
Indirect Labor	$ 46,000	
Utilities	16,000	
Repairs and Maintenance	8,000	
Plant Facilities Rent	24,000	
Furniture and Fixtures Rent	8,000	
Factory Supplies Used	13,000	
Administrative Salaries	15,000	
Insurance	2,000	
Depreciation—Machinery and Equipment	6,000	
Total Factory Overhead		138,000
Total Manufacturing Cost Incurred		$333,000
Less: Ending Work in Process Inventory		8,000
Cost of Goods Manufactured		$325,000

EXHIBIT 21–5 (continued)
Financial Statements of Lollar Manufacturing, Inc.

Lollar Manufacturing, Inc.
Income Statement
For the Year Ended December 31, 19XX

Net Sales			$450,000
Cost of Goods Sold:			
Beginning Finished Goods Inventory		$ 20,000	
Cost of Goods Manufactured		325,000	
Goods Available for Sale		$345,000	
Less: Ending Finished Goods Inventory		26,000	
Cost of Goods Sold			319,000
Gross Profit on Sales			$131,000
Operating Expenses:			
Nonfactory Administration:			
Utilities Expense	$ 2,000		
Repairs and Maintenance	1,000		
Plant Facilities Rent	3,000		
Furniture and Fixtures Rent	1,000		
Administrative Salaries Expense	8,000		
Office Salaries Expense	8,000		
Uncollectible Accounts Expense	9,000		
Total Nonfactory Administration		$ 32,000	
Selling:			
Utilities Expense	$ 2,000		
Repairs and Maintenance	1,000		
Plant Facilities Rent	3,000		
Furniture and Fixtures Rent	1,000		
Administrative Salaries Expense	2,000		
Office Salaries Expense	8,000		
Insurance Expense	1,000		
Office Supplies Expense	3,000		
Sales Salaries Expense	18,000		
Advertising Expense	9,000		
Total Selling Expenses		48,000	
Total Operating Expenses			80,000
Income from Operations			$ 51,000
Less: Interest Expense			4,000
Income before Income Taxes			$ 47,000
Less: Income Tax Expense			17,000
Net Income			$ 30,000
Earnings per Share of Capital Stock			$6

EXHIBIT 21–5 (continued)
Financial Statements of Lollar Manufacturing, Inc.

Lollar Manufacturing, Inc.
Balance Sheet
December 31, 19XX

ASSETS

Current Assets

Cash		$ 13,000
Accounts Receivable	$45,000	
Less: Allowance for Uncollectible Accounts	10,000	35,000
Inventories:		
Raw Materials	$18,000	
Work in Process	8,000	
Finished Goods	26,000	52,000
Prepaid Expenses:		
Factory Supplies on Hand	$ 4,000	
Office Supplies on Hand	2,000	
Prepaid Insurance	1,000	7,000
Total Current Assets		$107,000

Long-term Assets

Machinery and Equipment	$90,000	
Less: Accumulated Depreciation	26,000	64,000
Total Assets		$171,000

LIABILITIES AND STOCKHOLDERS' EQUITY

Current Liabilities

Accounts Payable		$ 7,000
Wages Payable		10,000
Interest Payable		1,000
Income Tax Payable		17,000
Total Current Liabilities		$ 35,000
Long-term Notes Payable (9%, due 5 years hence)		40,000
Total Liabilities		$ 75,000

Stockholders' Equity

Common Stock, $10 Par Value, 5,000 Shares		
Authorized and Issued	$50,000	
Retained Earnings	46,000	96,000
Total Liabilities and Stockholders' Equity		$171,000

EXHIBIT 21–5 (continued)
Financial Statements of Lollar Manufacturing, Inc.

Lollar Manufacturing, Inc. Retained Earnings Statement For the Year Ended December 31, 19XX	
Retained Earnings, January 1	$20,000
Add: Net Income for 19XX	30,000
	$50,000
Less: Dividends Declared	4,000
Retained Earnings, December 31	$46,000

data on the worksheet in Exhibit 21–4. Observe that the key income statement figures—cost of goods manufactured and net income—agree with the amounts that balance the related worksheet columns.

Closing Entries   Recall that closing procedures occur only at the end of the operating year. The worksheet provides all the data necessary to prepare closing entries for temporary manufacturing cost accounts and expense accounts and to record inventory changes at year-end. Using compound journal entries when appropriate, we use the following closing procedures:

(1) Close the beginning Raw Materials and Work in Process inventory accounts and all manufacturing cost accounts with *debit* balances and debit the total to the Manufacturing Summary account.

(2) Record (as debits) the ending raw materials and work in process inventories, close any manufacturing cost accounts with *credit* balances, and credit the total to the Manufacturing Summary account. (The balance of the Manufacturing Summary account should now equal the total cost of goods manufactured.)

(3) Close the beginning Finished Goods Inventory account, the Manufacturing Summary account, and all other income statement accounts with *debit* balances, and debit the total to the Income Summary account.

(4) Record (as a debit) the ending Finished Goods Inventory account, close any income statement account with a *credit* balance, and credit the total to the Income Summary account. (The balance of the Income Summary account should now equal net income.)

(5) Close the Income Summary account to Retained Earnings.

(6) Close the Dividends account to Retained Earnings.

The closing entries for Lollar Manufacturing, Inc., follow (entries are parenthetically numbered to indicate the related closing step involved):

(1)	Manufacturing Summary	357,000	
	Raw Materials Inventory (beginning)		10,000
	Work in Process Inventory (beginning)		6,000
	Raw Materials Purchases		120,000
	Transportation In		2,000
	Direct Labor		81,000
	Indirect Labor		46,000
	Utilities		16,000
	Repairs and Maintenance		8,000
	Plant Facilities Rent		24,000
	Furniture and Fixtures Rent		8,000
	Factory Supplies Used		13,000
	Administrative Salaries		15,000
	Insurance		2,000
	Depreciation—Machinery and Equipment		6,000

To close beginning Raw Materials
and Work in Process accounts
and temporary manufacturing cost
accounts having debit balances to the
Manufacturing Summary account.

(2)	Raw Materials Inventory (ending)	18,000	
	Work in Process Inventory (ending)	8,000	
	Raw Materials Returns and Allowances	6,000	
	Manufacturing Summary		32,000

To record the ending raw materials
and work in process inventories
and close temporary manufacturing cost
accounts having credit balances to the
Manufacturing Summary account.

(3)	Income Summary	446,000	
	Finished Goods Inventory (beginning)		20,000
	Utilities		4,000
	Repairs and Maintenance		2,000
	Plant Facilities Rent		6,000
	Furniture and Fixtures Rent		2,000
	Administrative Salaries		10,000
	Office Salaries Expense		16,000
	Office Supplies Used		3,000
	Sales Salaries Expense		18,000
	Advertising Expense		9,000
	Interest Expense		4,000
	Insurance		1,000
	Uncollectible Accounts Expense		9,000
	Income Tax Expense		17,000
	Manufacturing Summary		325,000

To close the beginning finished goods
inventory, all expense accounts,
and the Manufacturing Summary account
to the Income Summary account.

(4)	Finished Goods Inventory (ending)	26,000	
	Sales	450,000	
	Income Summary		476,000
	To record the ending finished goods		
	inventory and close Sales to the		
	Income Summary account.		

(5)	Income Summary	30,000	
	Retained Earnings		30,000
	To close the Income Summary account to		
	Retained Earnings.		

(6)	Retained Earnings	4,000	
	Dividends		4,000
	To close the Dividends account to		
	Retained Earnings.		

After the closing entries are recorded and posted, the general ledger reflects only the balances of those assets, liabilities, and stockholders' equity accounts that are carried forward as beginning balances for the subsequent year.

PROBLEMS OF COSTING MANUFACTURING INVENTORIES

Because inventories frequently constitute a significant portion of the firm's total assets, their proper costing is an important aspect of manufacturing accounting. A proper determination of periodic income depends on proper inventory costing. Inventory errors affect reported income in corresponding amounts. Further, unit cost values derived from inventory costing often play a central role in production contract negotiations, product pricing decisions, and management's overall control of production costs. Thus, an effective manufacturing operation depends on reliable accounting for product costs.

Costing the materials inventory presents no unusual problems. Routine procedures determine the physical quantity of each item on hand at the end of the period. Purchase prices, paid to or offered by suppliers, are typically available for pricing each item of the materials inventory. Thoroughness and accuracy in counting, pricing, and aggregating the total cost of the inventory are essential.

By definition, costing ending work in process inventories involves estimating the degree of completion of the specific units of product. In its simplest form, ending work in process inventory may consist of a single batch of products at a uniform stage of completion. In assembly-line operations, however, ending work in process inventory may be a group of products at varying stages of completion, ranging from those units barely started to those nearing completion. When multiple products are involved, many combinations of partially finished products are possible. A meaningful determination of work in process inventory demands informed and consistent estimation of the degree of completion of work in process.

Determining both work in process and finished goods inventories requires a knowledge of product design specifications and cost data relating to various production inputs. The cost of raw materials and direct labor, which is often related *directly* to each unit of product, is reasonably estimated as some normal or average quantity of materials or direct labor multiplied by some normal or average cost or rate for each factor. Factory overhead, however, can only be related *indirectly* to units of product. The appropriate amounts per unit of product for such costs as factory supervision, depreciation, utilities, and property taxes are not readily apparent. Most firms therefore assume that the amount of factory overhead assigned to products is in proportion to some other known and important production variable such as direct labor hours or direct labor costs. A *factory overhead rate* is determined by dividing the total overhead cost by the total of the base used to assign overhead. For example, the cost of goods manufactured statement for Lollar Manufacturing, Inc. (Exhibit 21–5) shows total direct labor costs of $81,000 and total factory overhead of $138,000. Thus, this firm might compute its factory overhead rate as:

$$\text{Factory Overhead Rate} = \frac{\text{Total Factory Overhead}}{\text{Total Direct Labor Costs}} = \frac{\$138,000}{\$81,000} = 170\% \text{ of Direct Labor Costs}$$

From this factory overhead rate, an ending work in process inventory that involved say, $5,000 of direct labor would be assigned $8,500 (1.7 × $5,000) of factory overhead. The same approach is used for ending finished goods inventory.

In manufacturing accounting, a general accounting system using the periodic inventory method may be satisfactory for small, stable, single-product firms. The limitations of this approach are critical, however, in more complex, multiproduct manufacturing operations. When periodic inventory procedures are used, the amounts of raw materials used and cost of goods sold are really residual, or plug, figures that offer little opportunity for management control. Also, periodic inventory procedures provide for income determination only at the end of the period, when ending inventories are taken, whereas management may need reliable current product cost data on a day-to-day basis. Because multiple products may involve widely varying types and amounts of materials, different production techniques, and a variety of production routines in a series of departments, product cost accounting requires a more sophisticated approach. Therefore, cost accounting systems using perpetual inventories have been developed. Cost accounting systems are discussed in Chapters 22 and 23.

KEY POINTS TO REMEMBER

(1) Product costs comprise all costs necessary to bring the manufactured product to completion.

(2) Manufacturers have three inventory accounts—Raw Materials, Work in Process, and Finished Goods.

(3) Manufacturing costs are accounted for in three categories: (1) raw materials, (2) direct labor, and (3) factory overhead, which includes all manufacturing costs other than raw materials and direct labor.

(4) In manufacturing accounting, all product costs—raw materials, direct labor, and factory overhead—are capitalized; that is, they become the cost of goods manufactured and represent additions to finished goods inventory.

(5) Cost of goods manufactured equals the total of all manufacturing costs incurred adjusted for the change in work in process inventory.

(6) Cost of goods sold equals cost of goods manufactured adjusted for the change in finished goods inventory.

(7) Neither cost of goods manufactured nor cost of goods sold includes nonfactory administrative expenses or selling expenses.

(8) Worksheets for manufacturing firms have an additional set of columns for cost of goods manufactured statement items.

(9) Closing procedures for manufacturers incorporate a Manufacturing Summary account to which beginning Raw Materials and Work in Process Inventory account balances and all temporary accounts related to the cost of goods manufactured are closed. Ending Raw Materials and Work in Process Inventory account balances are recorded as credits in the Manufacuring Summary account and as debits in the related balance sheet asset accounts. Beginning finished goods inventory, the Manufacturing Summary account, and all temporary income statement accounts are closed to the Income Summary account. Ending finished goods inventory is recorded as a credit in the Income Summary account and as a debit in the related balance sheet asset account.

QUESTIONS

21–1 In what two important ways is accounting for a manufacturing firm more complex than accounting for a merchandising firm?

21–2 How are product costs accounted for differently from period costs? Give examples of each.

21–3 What is the basic format for the income statement of a manufacturing firm?

21–4 Name the three inventory accounts maintained by manufacturing firms and briefly describe the nature of each.

21–5 Name and briefly describe the three major categories used to account for manufacturing costs.

21–6 List six examples of factory overhead costs.

21–7 In what way are total manufacturing costs incurred different from cost of goods manufactured?

21–8 If total manufacturing costs incurred are $400,000 and ending work in process inventory is $30,000, what is the amount of cost of goods manufactured?

21–9 If beginning and ending finished goods inventories are $60,000 and $80,000, respectively, and the cost of goods sold is $380,000, what is the cost of goods manufactured?

21–10 Identify and briefly describe the normal balances and typical entries in the four accounts usually maintained for the purchase and use of raw materials.

21–11 What information is necessary to estimate the ending work in process inventory? The ending finished goods inventory?

21–12 Briefly describe the nature and timing of the entries expected in the Manufacturing Summary account.

21–13 Briefly outline a typical worksheet format for a manufacturing company. What four steps are followed to prepare such a worksheet?

21–14 "Preparation of a worksheet does not specifically affect the general ledger." Do you agree or disagree with this statement? Why?

21–15 Briefly explain the year-end closing procedures for a manufacturing firm.

21–16 In what important way is the assignment of factory overhead to the work in process and finished goods inventories different from the assignment of raw materials and direct labor costs? Briefly explain the approach that is widely used to assign factory overhead.

EXERCISES

21–17 The following account balances are available from the Ervin Manufacturing Company ledger:

	Beginning of Year	End of Year
Raw Materials Inventory	$30,000	$ 20,000
Work in Process Inventory	40,000	60,000
Finished Goods Inventory	50,000	45,000
Direct Labor		125,000
Raw Materials Purchases (net)		80,000
Indirect Labor		35,000
Depreciation—Factory		12,000
Factory Supplies Used		7,000
Repairs and Maintenance—Factory		9,000
Nonfactory Administration Expenses (total)		25,000
Selling Expenses (total)		28,000

Prepare a cost of goods manufactured statement for the current year.

21–18 Ervin Manufacturing Company (see Exercise 21–17) sold 14,000 units of product for $24 each during the current year. At year-end, 5,000 shares of capital stock are outstanding. Prepare an income statement for the year.

21–19 For each of the following unrelated columns of data, compute the cost of goods manufactured and the cost of goods sold:

	A	B	C
Selling Expenses	$ 200	$ 330	$ 240
Factory Insurance	100	80	140
Nonfactory Administration Expenses	90	160	110
Ending Finished Goods Inventory	450	1,000	1,300
Factory Taxes	130	100	90
Raw Materials Inventory (beginning)	200	320	120
Direct Labor	1,000	800	2,100
Factory Maintenance	80	120	190
Raw Materials Purchased	450	650	500
Beginning Finished Goods Inventory	300	1,200	1,100
Increase (Decrease) in Work in Process	100	0	(270)
Factory Utilities	90	300	720
Depreciation—Factory	200	900	600
Indirect Labor	310	210	1,100
Factory Supplies Used	130	170	380
Raw Materials Inventory (ending)	170	250	90

21–20 During the current year, Bradley Factories, Inc. recorded the following costs and expenses:

Raw Materials Used	$ 45,000
Direct Labor	100,000
Factory Supplies Used	25,000
Indirect Labor	35,000
Sales Commissions	15,000
Factory Supervision	20,000
Nonfactory Administration Expenses	18,000
Other Factory Overhead	10,000

Assume that Bradley assigns factory overhead on the basis of direct labor costs.
(a) Compute the factory overhead rate.
(b) Indicate the total cost of the ending work in process inventory that has been assigned $5,000 of raw materials cost and $11,000 of direct labor cost.

21–21 Elgin Manufacturing Company's accounting department has estimated that each completed unit of its product involves an average of 3 pounds of raw materials costing $2 per pound and 5 hours of direct labor costing $8 per hour. Factory overhead is assigned on the basis of total direct labor cost incurred, which for the current year are $84,500 and $130,000, respectively.
(a) Determine the proper cost of an ending finished goods inventory that comprises 4,000 units.
(b) Determine the proper cost of an ending work in process inventory that involves 800 units, to which all raw materials have been added but for which only 60% of the direct labor has been assigned.

21–22 The only product of Randy Manufacturers, Inc. is produced in a continuous process. At the end of the current year, the ending inventories of work in process and finished goods were as follows:

	Estimated Amounts Assigned per Unit		
	Raw Materials	Direct Labor	Total Units
Work in Process	$ 9	$10	3,000
Finished Goods	12	22	5,000

Assuming that factory overhead is assigned at the rate of 70% of direct labor cost, compute the cost of the ending work in process and finished goods inventories.

21–23 Using the following summarized data, prepare the compound journal entries (similar to those illustrated in the chapter) to record the changes in inventories and to close the temporary manufacturing accounts at year-end to Manufacturing Summary and, in turn, to close Manufacturing Summary to Income Summary.

	Beginning of Year	End of Year
Raw Materials Inventory	$9,000	$10,000
Work in Process Inventory	4,000	8,000
Raw Materials Purchases (net)		75,000
Direct Labor		95,000
Factory Overhead (total)		70,000
Nonfactory Administration Expenses (total)		30,000
Selling Expenses (total)		14,000

21–24 The following cost of goods manufactured columns are from a James Manufacturing, Inc. worksheet at the end of the current year. For simplicity, data are summarized and in amounts of not more than three digits.

	Cost of Goods Manufactured	
	Debit	Credit
Raw Materials Inventory (beginning)	8	
Work in Process Inventory (beginning)	10	
Raw Materials Purchases	85	
Raw Materials Returns and Allowances		10
Direct Labor	55	
Transportation In—Purchases	12	
Indirect Labor	30	
Factory Supervision	18	
Factory Utilities	10	
Factory Supplies Used	7	
Depreciation—Equipment	14	
Depreciation—Factory Building	17	
Other Factory Overhead	23	
Ending Inventories:		
Raw Materials Inventory		11
Work in Process Inventory		4
	289	25
Cost of Goods Manufactured		264
	289	289

Using these data, prepare a cost of goods manufactured statement for the current year.

PROBLEMS

21–25 Selected account balances from the completed year-end worksheet of the Shaw Manufacturing Company appear below in alphabetical order:

Administrative Salaries*	$20,000	Finished Goods, Jan. 1	$20,000
Advertising and Promotion		Raw Materials, Dec. 31	5,000
Expense	13,000	Work in Process, Dec. 31	11,000
Depreciation—Machinery	8,000	Finished Goods, Dec. 31	16,000
Depreciation—Office		Maintenance—Machinery	4,000
Equipment*	10,000	Nonfactory Area Rent*	20,000
Depreciation—Sales Fixtures	5,000	Other Factory Overhead	10,000
Direct Labor	68,000	Other Selling Expenses	6,000
Factory Rent	5,000	Purchases Returns	
Factory Supervision	9,000	and Allowances	2,000
Factory Supplies Used	7,000	Raw Materials Purchases	32,000
Indirect Labor	6,000	Sales	270,000
Inventories:		Sales Salaries Expense	12,000
Raw Materials, Jan. 1	3,000	Transportation In	2,500
Work in Process, Jan. 1	4,000		

*These amounts are allocated 60% to nonfactory administration and 40% to the sales department.

REQUIRED

Using the above data, prepare a cost of goods manufactured statement and an income statement for the current year (disregard income tax and earnings per share considerations).

21–26 The following journal entries recorded the changes in inventories and closed the temporary manufacturing accounts of Jardon Factory, Inc. at year-end:

Manufacturing Summary	488,000	
Raw Materials Inventory (beginning)		18,000
Work in Process Inventory (beginning)		10,000
Direct Labor		125,000
Indirect Labor		68,000
Transportation In		6,000
Depreciation—Factory		22,000
Depreciation—Equipment		18,000
Factory Repairs and Maintenance		14,000
Factory Supplies Used		7,000
Other Factory Overhead		30,000
Raw Materials Purchases		170,000

To close the beginning raw materials and work in process inventories and the temporary manufacturing cost accounts having debit balances to the Manufacturing Summary account.

Raw Materials Inventory (ending)	23,000	
Work in Process Inventory (ending)	6,000	
Raw Materials Returns and Allowances	5,000	
Manufacturing Summary		34,000

To record the ending raw materials and work in process inventories and to close the temporary manufacturing cost accounts having credit balances to the Manufacturing Summary account.

REQUIRED

Using the above information, prepare a cost of goods manufactured statement for the current year.

21–27 The data below relate to three independent production periods of Madison Manufacturing Company. Missing data are indicated by question marks.

	A	B	C
Raw Materials:			
Beginning Inventory	$ 25	$ 75	$ 50
Purchases	?	320	225
Ending Inventory	35	45	?
Total Used	160	?	200
Direct Labor	280	440	365
Factory Overhead:			
Factory Supplies Used	45	?	55
Indirect Labor	75	70	160
Other	?	90	155
Total Factory Overhead	250	220	?
Work in Process Inventories:			
Beginning	?	40	120
Ending	30	?	45
Finished Goods Inventories:			
Beginning	?	180	35
Ending	150	50	155
Cost of Goods Manufactured	725	?	?
Cost of Goods Sold	680	920	?

REQUIRED

Using the above data, calculate the cost of goods manufactured and cost of goods sold. (You should list in order the items appearing on the cost of goods manufactured statement and the cost of goods sold computation, fill in the known data, and from those calculate the missing amounts.)

21–28 The following data relate to estimating the ending work in process and finished goods inventories of the Mendota Manufacturing Company:

	Estimated Cost of Completed Unit of Product	Estimated Proportions Assigned to Work in Process
Raw Materials: A	4 lb @ $7/lb	100%
B	2 lb @ $5/lb	40%
Direct Labor: Cutting	0.5 hr @ $10/hr	70%
Assembly	2 hr @ $8/hr	50%

For the manufacturing period, total direct labor was $200,000, and total factory overhead was $160,000. Factory overhead is assigned to products on the basis of this ratio.

REQUIRED

Using the above data, calculate the cost of (a) an ending finished goods inventory of 700 units and (b) an ending work in process inventory of 400 units.

21–29 The following balances appear in the cost of goods manufactured and the income statement columns of a December 31 worksheet for the current year's operations of the Glendale Corporation.

	Cost of Goods Manufactured		Income Statement	
	Debit	Credit	Debit	Credit
Raw Materials Inventory (beginning)	15,000			
Work in Process Inventory (beginning)	9,000			
Finished Goods Inventory (beginning)			23,000	
Sales				250,000
Raw Materials Purchases (net)	60,000			
Transportation In	2,400			
Direct Labor	70,000			
Indirect Labor	18,000			
Utilities	1,100			
Repairs and Maintenance	1,900			
Depreciation—Machinery	2,000			
Insurance	2,300			
Property Taxes	2,500			
Selling Expenses			27,000	
Administrative Expenses			21,000	
Income Tax Expense			5,600	
Ending Inventories:				
Raw Materials Inventory		12,000		
Work in Process Inventory		11,000		
Finished Goods Inventory				17,000
	184,200	23,000		
Cost of Goods Manufactured		161,200	161,200	
	184,200	184,200	237,800	267,000
Net Income			29,200	
			267,000	267,000

REQUIRED

(a) Prepare a cost of goods manufactured statement and an income statement for the Glendale Corporation. Assume that 4,000 shares of capital stock are outstanding at year-end.

(b) Prepare general journal entries to reflect the changes in inventories and to close the temporary manufacturing accounts, the Manufacturing Summary account, the revenue and expense accounts, and the Income Summary account.

21–30 Two inventors, organized as MarLee, Inc. consult you regarding a planned new product. They have fairly good estimates of the costs of materials, labor, overhead, and other expenses involved but need to know how much to charge for each unit to earn a pretax profit in the first year equal to 10% of their estimated total long-term investment of $300,000.

Their plans indicate that each unit of the new product requires:

Raw Materials
2 lb of a material costing $5/lb

Direct Labor
2 hr of a metal former's time at $8/hr
0.5 hr of an assembler's time at $8/hr

Major items of production overhead would be $36,000 annual rent on a factory building and $24,000 on machinery. Other production overhead is an estimated 50% of total direct labor costs. Nonfactory administrative expenses and selling expenses are an estimated 20% and 30%, respectively, of total sales revenue.

The consensus at MarLee is that during the first year 9,000 units of product should be produced for selling and another 1,000 units for the next year's beginning inventory. Also, an extra 2,000 pounds of materials will be purchased as beginning inventory for the next year. Because of the nature of the manufacturing process, all units started must be completed, so work in process inventories are negligible.

REQUIRED

(a) Incorporate the above data into a projected cost of goods manufactured statement and compute the unit production cost.

(b) Prepare a projected income statement (filling in the sales amount as the last item) that would provide the target amount of profit.

(c) Rounded to the nearest dollar, what unit sales price should the inventors charge for the new product?

21–31 The trial balance for the Jackson Manufacturing Corporation at the end of the current year follows:

	Debit	Credit
Cash	$ 7,000	
Accounts Receivable	44,500	
Allowance for Uncollectible Accounts		$ 1,000
Raw Materials Inventory, January 1	29,000	
Work in Process Inventory, January 1	13,000	
Finished Goods Inventory, January 1	16,000	
Factory Machinery	140,000	
Accumulated Depreciation—Factory Machinery		33,000
Factory Buildings	125,000	
Accumulated Depreciation—Factory Buildings		12,000
Land	25,000	
Accounts Payable		26,000
Long-term Notes Payable—8%		40,000
Common Stock, $200 Par Value (all outstanding)		200,000
Retained Earnings		36,200
Sales		300,000
Raw Materials Purchases	70,000	
Purchases Returns and Allowances		3,000
Direct Labor	90,000	
Indirect Labor	22,000	
Utilities	3,500	
Repairs and Maintenance	3,000	
Property Taxes	3,200	
Selling Expenses (control account)	35,000	
Nonfactory Administrative Expenses (control account)	25,000	
	$651,200	$651,200

The following information is available for adjusting and closing the accounts:
(1) December 31 inventories are: raw materials, $24,500; work in process, $14,000; and finished goods, $12,000.
(2) Accrued wage and salaries at December 31 are: direct labor, $1,500; indirect labor, $500; and sales salaries, $2,000.
(3) Annual amounts of depreciation are: factory buildings, $5,000; factory machinery, $8,000.
(4) Accrued utilities payable at December 31, $300.
(5) Uncollectible accounts expense, $\frac{1}{2}$% of sales. (Debit this expense to the Selling Expenses control account.)
(6) Assume an income tax rate of 30%.

REQUIRED
(a) Prepare a manufacturing worksheet for the year. Assume that the utilities and property taxes apply entirely to manufacturing activities.
(b) Prepare a cost of goods manufactured statement and an income statement.
(c) Prepare a balance sheet.
(d) Prepare closing entries similar to those illustrated in this chapter.

21–32 The trial balance of the Mayer Company at December 31 of the current year is given below, together with the worksheet adjustments.

	Trial Balance		Adjustments	
	Debit	Credit	Debit	Credit
Cash	8,000			
Raw Materials Inventory, Jan. 1	10,500			
Work in Process Inventory, Jan. 1	8,200			
Finished Goods Inventory, Jan. 1	12,300			
Prepaid Insurance	800			(1) 400
Factory Machinery	70,000			
Accumulated Depreciation— Factory Machinery		14,700		(2) 5,000
Unamortized Cost of Patents	12,000			(3) 900
Accounts Payable		18,000		
Common Stock, $100 Par Value		50,000		
Retained Earnings		14,800		
Dividends	6,000			
Sales		182,000		
Raw Materials Purchases (net)	42,000			
Direct Labor	52,000		(4) 1,200	
Indirect Labor	18,000		(4) 300	
Utilities	2,400			
Repairs and Maintenance— Factory	1,300			
Buildings Rent	5,000			
Sales Salaries Expense	15,000			
Advertising Expense	4,000			
Nonfactory Administrative Expenses	12,000			
	279,500	279,500		
Insurance—Factory			(1) 400	
Depreciation—Factory Machinery			(2) 5,000	
Amortization of Patents			(3) 900	
Wages Payable				(4) 1,500
Income Tax Expense			(5) 6,000	
Income Tax Payable				(5) 6,000
			13,800	13,800

Additional information:

(1) Of the total rent on buildings, $4,500 is for the factory; the remainder is nonfactory administrative expense.

(2) Of the total utilities paid, $2,000 is for the factory; the remainder is nonfactory administrative expense.

(3) December 31 inventories are: raw materials, $15,000; work in process, $9,000; and finished goods, $12,000.

(4) Patent amortization applies to factory operations.

REQUIRED
(a) Complete the manufacturing worksheet.
(b) Prepare a cost of goods manufactured statement and an income statement.
(c) Prepare closing entries similar to those illustrated in this chapter.

ALTERNATE PROBLEMS

21–25A Selected account balances from the completed year-end worksheet of the Speer
Manufacturing Company appear below in alphabetical order:

Administrative Salaries*	$20,000	Finished Goods, Jan. 1	$ 28,000
Advertising and Promotion		Raw Materials, Dec. 31	16,000
Expense	21,000	Work in Process, Dec. 31	12,000
Depreciation—Machinery	13,000	Finished Goods, Dec. 31	15,000
Depreciation—Office Equipment*	10,000	Maintenance—Machinery	8,000
Depreciation—Sales Fixtures	6,000	Nonfactory Area Rent*	12,000
Direct Labor	89,000	Other Factory Overhead	6,000
Factory Rent	15,000	Other Selling Expenses	7,000
Factory Supervision	9,000	Purchases Returns	
Factory Supplies Used	4,000	and Allowances	2,000
Indirect Labor	11,000	Raw Materials Purchases	60,000
Inventories:		Sales	300,000
Raw Materials, Jan. 1	6,000	Sales Salaries Expense	16,000
Work in Process, Jan. 1	8,000	Transportation In	2,000

*These amounts are allocated 50% to nonfactory administration and 50% to the sales department.

REQUIRED
Using the above data, prepare a cost of goods manufactured statement and an
income statement for the current year (disregard income tax and earnings per
share considerations).

21–28A The following data relate to estimating the ending work in process and finished
goods inventories of the Monona Manufacturing Company:

	Estimated Cost of Completed Unit of Product	Estimated Proportions Assigned to Work in Process
Raw Materials:		
A	3 lb @ $3/lb	100%
B	2 lb @ $5/lb	70%
Direct Labor:		
Cutting	3 hr @ $8/hr	50%
Assembly	2 hr @ $6/hr	25%

For the manufacturing period, total direct labor was $250,000 and total factory
overhead was $312,500. Factory overhead is assigned to products on the basis
of this ratio.

REQUIRED
Using the above data, calculate the cost of (a) an ending finished goods inventory of 900 units and (b) an ending work in process inventory of 600 units.

21–29A The following balances appear in the cost of goods manufactured and the
income statement columns of a December 31 worksheet for the current year's
operations of the Golden Corporation.

	Cost of Goods Manufactured		Income Statement	
	Debit	Credit	Debit	Credit
Raw Materials Inventory (beginning)	10,000			
Work in Process Inventory (beginning)	7,000			
Finished Goods Inventory (beginning)			27,000	
Sales				365,000
Raw Materials Purchases (net)	105,000			
Transportation In	7,000			
Direct Labor	65,000			
Indirect Labor	29,000			
Utilities	4,000			
Repairs and Maintenance	5,000			
Depreciation—Machinery	2,000			
Insurance	1,300			
Property Taxes	3,200			
Selling Expenses			23,000	
Administrative Expenses			16,000	
Income Tax Expense			28,000	
Ending Inventories:				
Raw Materials Inventory		14,000		
Work in Process Inventory		5,000		
Finished Goods Inventory				16,000
	238,500	19,000		
Cost of Goods Manufactured		219,500	219,500	
	238,500	238,500	313,500	381,000
Net Income			67,500	
			381,000	381,000

REQUIRED

(a) Prepare a cost of goods manufactured statement and an income statement for the Golden Corporation. Assume that 10,000 shares of capital stock are outstanding at year-end.

(b) Prepare general journal entries to reflect the changes in inventories and to close the temporary manufacturing accounts, the Manufacturing Summary account, the revenue and expense accounts, and the Income Summary account.

21–30A You are consulted by BetDan, Inc., a group of investors planning a new product. They have fairly good estimates of the costs of materials, labor, overhead, and other expenses involved but need to know how much to charge for each unit of the new product to earn a pretax profit in the first year equal to 10% of their estimated total long-term investment of $200,000.

Their plans indicate that each unit of the new product requires:

Raw Materials
3 lb of a material costing $5/lb

Direct Labor
   3 hr of a die cutter's time at $8/hr
   2 hr of an assembler's time at $7/hr

Major items of production overhead would be $60,000 annual rent on a factory building and $23,000 on machinery. Other production overhead is an estimated 80% of total direct labor costs. Nonfactory administrative expenses and selling expenses are an estimated 10% and 20%, respectively, of total sales revenue.

The consensus at BetDan is that during the first year 4,000 units of product should be produced for selling and another 1,000 units for the next year's beginning inventory. Also, an extra 6,000 pounds of materials will be purchased as beginning inventory for the next year. Because of the nature of the manufacturing process, all units started must be completed, so work in process inventories are negligible.

REQUIRED

(a) Incorporate the above data into a projected cost of goods manufactured statement and compute the unit production cost.
(b) Prepare a projected income statement (filling in the sales amount as the last item) that would provide the target amount of profit.
(c) Rounded to the nearest dollar, what unit sales price should the investors charge for the new product?

21–31A The trial balance for the Johnson Boatbuilders Corporation at the end of the current year follows:

	Debit	Credit
Cash	$ 11,000	
Accounts Receivable	42,000	
Allowance for Uncollectible Accounts		$ 2,000
Raw Materials Inventory, January 1	18,000	
Work in Process Inventory, January 1	9,000	
Finished Goods Inventory, January 1	22,000	
Factory Machinery	153,000	
Accumulated Depreciation—Factory Machinery		41,000
Factory Buildings	205,000	
Accumulated Depreciation—Factory Buildings		30,000
Land	28,000	
Accounts Payable		32,000
Long-term Notes Payable—9%		60,000
Common Stock, $50 Par Value (all outstanding)		100,000
Retained Earnings		141,000
Sales		410,000
Raw Materials Purchases	118,000	
Purchases Returns and Allowances		2,000
Direct Labor	82,000	
Indirect Labor	30,000	
Utilities	8,000	
Repairs and Maintenance	5,000	
Property Taxes	7,000	
Selling Expenses (control account)	48,000	
Nonfactory Administrative Expenses (control account)	32,000	
	$818,000	$818,000

The following information is available for adjusting and closing the accounts:
(1) December 31 inventories are: raw materials, $14,000; work in process, $12,000; and finished goods, $15,000.
(2) Accrued wages and salaries at December 31 are: direct labor, $1,700; indirect labor, $300; and sales salaries, $1,000.
(3) Annual amounts of depreciation are: factory buildings, $7,000; factory machinery, $9,000.
(4) Accrued utilities payable at December 31, $500.
(5) Uncollectible accounts expense, 1% of sales. (Debit this expense to the Selling Expenses control account.)
(6) Assume an income tax rate of 40%.

REQUIRED
(a) Prepare a manufacturing worksheet for the year. Assume that the utilities and property taxes apply entirely to manufacturing activities.
(b) Prepare a cost of goods manufactured statement and an income statement.
(c) Prepare a balance sheet.
(d) Prepare closing entries similar to those illustrated in this chapter.

21–32A The trial balance of the Maryland Company at December 31 of the current year is given below, together with the worksheet adjustments.

| | Trial Balance | | Adjustments | | |
	Debit	Credit	Debit		Credit
Cash	6,000				
Raw Materials Inventory, Jan. 1	12,000				
Work in Process Inventory, Jan. 1	9,000				
Finished Goods Inventory, Jan. 1	15,000				
Prepaid Insurance	1,800			(1)	900
Factory Machinery	102,000				
Accumulated Depreciation—Factory Machinery		8,400		(2)	4,000
Unamortized Cost of Patents	17,500			(3)	1,000
Accounts Payable		24,000			
Common Stock, $200 Par Value		40,000			
Retained Earnings		33,300			
Dividends	6,000				
Sales		340,000			
Raw Materials Purchases (net)	90,000				
Direct Labor	85,000		(4)	2,?00	
Indirect Labor	32,000		(4)	1,000	
Utilities	4,500				
Repairs and Maintenance—Factory	1,900				

	Trial Balance		Adjustments	
	Debit	Credit	Debit	Credit
Buildings Rent	8,000			
Sales Salaries Expense	24,000			
Advertising Expense	11,000			
Nonfactory Administrative Expenses	20,000			
	445,700	445,700		
Insurance—Factory			(1) 900	
Depreciation—Machinery			(2) 4,000	
Amortization of Patents			(3) 1,000	
Wages Payable				(4) 3,500
Income Tax Expense			(5) 19,000	
Income Tax Payable				(5) 19,000
			28,400	28,400

Additional information:
(1) Of the total rent on buildings, $6,000 is for the factory; the remainder is nonfactory administrative expense.
(2) Of the utilities paid, $3,000 is for the factory; the remainder is nonfactory administrative expense.
(3) December 31 inventories are: raw materials, $14,000; work in process, $6,000; and finished goods, $12,000.
(4) Patent amortization applies to factory operations.

REQUIRED
(a) Complete the manufacturing worksheet.
(b) Prepare a cost of goods manufactured statement and an income statement.
(c) Prepare closing entries similar to those illustrated in this chapter.

BUSINESS DECISION PROBLEM

Raymond Kane, an engineer, needs some accounting advice. In their spare time during the past year, Kane and his college-aged son, Greg, have manufactured a small weed-trimming sickle in a rented building near their home. Greg, who has had one accounting course in college, keeps the books.

Kane is pleased about the results of their first year's operations. He asks you to look over the following income report prepared by Greg before they leave on a well-deserved vacation to the Bahamas, after which they plan to expand their business significantly.

Sales (9,200 units at $17 each)		$156,400
Expenses of producing 10,000 units:		
Raw materials:		
Precasted blades at $3 each	$ 33,000	
Preturned handles at $2 each	21,000	
Labor costs of hired assembler	12,000	
Labor costs of hired painter	15,000	
Rent on building	7,000	
Rent on machinery	3,000	
Utilities	3,500	
Other production costs	4,000	
Advertising expense	13,000	
Sales commissions	18,000	
Delivery of products to customers	4,500	
Total expenses	$134,000	
Less: Ending inventory of 800 units at average production costs of $13.40 (or $134,000/10,000 units)	10,720	
Cost of sales		123,280
Net Income		$ 33,120

After you examine the income report, Kane responds to your questions and assures you that (1) no theft or spoilage of materials has occurred, (2) no partially completed units are involved, and (3) he and his son have averaged about 30 hours each per week in the business, and (4) he is in approximately the 40% income tax bracket (before considering the sickle venture).

REQUIRED
(a) Identify any apparent discrepancy in the income report in the cost of raw materials used.
(b) Recalculate the cost of goods manufactured, the average cost per unit produced, and the net income for the year, including a provision for estimated income taxes on the earnings.
(c) What factors should Kane consider regarding the profitability of his venture as a basis for deciding to expand it significantly?

22

Cost Accounting Systems:
Job Order Costing

> **We might as reasonably dispute whether it is the upper or the under blade of a pair of scissors that cuts a piece of paper, as whether value is governed by utility or cost of production.**
>
> ALFRED MARSHALL

In Chapter 21, we introduced the concepts of multiple manufacturing inventories, cost of goods manufactured, and financial statements for a manufacturing concern. Our approach adapted a general accounting system to a relatively simple manufacturing operation using periodic inventory procedures. The significant limitations of that approach justify the development of specialized cost accounting systems and the use of perpetual inventories to provide more meaningful cost data. In this and the following chapter, we introduce important aspects of cost accounting and illustrate two important types of cost accounting systems for manufacturing firms.

LIMITATIONS OF COST DETERMINATIONS

In studying cost accounting, we should first review the inherent limitations of most cost determinations. Misconceptions prevail that accounting cost figures are minutely exact and that a precise cost can be assigned to any asset, product, or unit of activity. Although an exhaustive consideration of these issues is beyond the scope of this chapter, a review of several examples should provide a realistic perspective.

We determine cost basically by accumulating the total costs incurred in doing something and then allocating these costs among the various units of accomplishment during a given period. Any unit of activity, service rendered, or product manufactured may be involved. Accounting procedures for both the accumulation and the allocation of costs may necessarily involve somewhat arbitrary choices. Often no single cost measurement or allocation scheme is demonstrably better than any other. Therefore, the accountant must choose—rationally but nonetheless arbitrarily—from among a group of equally defensible approaches to cost measurement and allocation. Following are several examples, the first two of which were mentioned in previous chapters.

Assumed cost flows The purchase prices of raw materials often vary throughout the year. Assigning costs to cost of goods sold and ending inventories may involve arbitrarily assuming a cost flow such as FIFO, LIFO, or some form of average cost.

Depreciation estimates The service potential of plant assets contributes to many operating periods. No method can determine the precise amount of the asset's cost for a given period. Instead, periodic depreciation expense is based on tentative estimates of useful life and salvage value as well as an often arbitrary choice between straight-line and one of several accelerated depreciation methods.

Allocated joint costs   Joint costs are common to two or more products or manufacturing processes. Costs of raw materials, supervisors' salaries, and service department costs are often joint costs. In a lumbering mill operation, for example, no single precise method can allocate the cost of a whole log to the several wood products that result—prime clear boards used for furniture, rough construction-grade boards, the bark sold as mulching to landscapers, and the sawdust used for paper. Joint product costs are often allocated arbitrarily on the basis of the relative sales value, weights, or volumes of each joint product. In Chapter 23, we illustrate accepted allocation techniques for joint products and service departments.

Realistically then, what we consider *the* cost of something is actually *a* recorded cost of that thing, often determined by our choices from among a series of perhaps equally valid assumptions.

Another aspect of the limitations of cost determination is that the concept of cost varies and different versions may be most useful for different purposes. Ordinarily, cost systems provide *full average cost*, or the total of all costs divided by all output. For example, if costs of $100,000 are incurred in producing 80,000 units of product, the average unit cost is $1.25 ($100,000/80,000). Suppose that in evaluating the opportunity to accept an additional overseas order for 10,000 units, production engineers advise that producing the additional 10,000 units would raise total costs to $108,000. In its decision to accept or reject the offer, management could consider a new full average unit cost of $1.20 ($108,000/ 90,000 units) or the incremental unit cost of 80 cents (the $80,000 increase in cost divided by the 10,000 unit increase in production). If the contemplated selling price is $1 per unit, using the $1.20 average cost results in a loss of 20 cents per unit, whereas using the incremental unit cost of 80 cents results in a profit of 20 cents per unit. Neither of these resulting costs is wrong, nor the other right. Rather, depending on certain management decision situations, either one may be defended as more appropriate. This and other instances of management's use of "different cost for different purposes" are illustrated in subsequent chapters.

It is important to realize that, as necessary and useful as cost data are, they are complex and have inherent limitations. Users of cost data must be aware of the specific assumptions made, the costing procedures used, and the proper application of the variations of needed cost data.

THE NATURE AND ADVANTAGES OF COST ACCOUNTING SYSTEMS

Any orderly method of developing cost information constitutes cost accounting. Typically, some amount of cost is accumulated and related to some unit of activity or accomplishment. Examples include accumulating the costs of cutting or forming materials, assembling parts, and the painting and finishing that might result in a completed unit of product such as a lawnmower, a piece of furniture, a computer, or a custom-designed executive jet aircraft. Although a cost system could be maintained independently of a firm's formal accounting records, most comprehensive cost systems are integrated into the general ledger accounts of the firm.

We illustrate cost accounting systems in the context of a manufacturing situation involving unit product costs. Remember, however, that reliable cost-per-unit-of-accomplishment data are vital to decision makers in all economic endeavors. For example, a municipality may need to know the cost per ton of snow

KEEPING COST SYSTEMS CURRENT

Manufacturing costing systems should be "number or data" reflections of the real world company activities they represent. Every important aspect of a company's operations—quantities and prices of materials; hours and rates of labor; and all classification, price, and quantity dimensions of overhead—should be mirrored in its cost system. Even the basic production processes—product types, production paths, process centers, organizational structure, and even the dynamics of a company's operating volume changes and economic success—are captured to some degree in its cost system. We could no doubt learn more about a company by looking at its cost records than by looking at its buildings, equipment, and its employees at work.

Many reasons explain why cost systems lose their ability to reflect accurately a company's operations.* For a costing system to portray operations realistically, any significant change in operations requires a corresponding change in the costing system. Therefore, operations–cost system disparities can simply evolve over a number of years during which many relatively small changes in operations occur without related cost systems changes. These changes can originate with such things as revisions in materials specifications or labor procedures, the substitution of machines for labor processes, and variations in product mix. Even management's (or the accounting department's) temptation to include new or significantly increased

costs in overhead, rather than accounting for them as direct costs, can lead to operations–cost data disparities. Eventually, accumulated changes result in a critical difference between operations and cost system data.

Easily recognized signals indicate an obsolete or "tired" cost system. Common signs include significant delays in getting routine cost data, the frequent need for special cost analyses, failure of plant personnel to understand all aspects of the cost system, ballooning factory overhead rates, large year-end amounts of underapplied overhead, significant adjustments to book inventories when physical inventories are taken, and a general failure on management's part to participate in and rely on routine budgeting and cost analyses.

The far-reaching implications of deficient costing systems are difficult to overstate. Cost systems are the basis for operating budgets and forecasts, materials control systems, and key aspects of financial reporting. They also provide data that are incorporated into many special areas of management decisions and performance evaluations. All important aspects of cost systems should be reviewed regularly to confirm that the cost data being generated continues to reflect the company's operations.

*For an interesting extension of these concerns, see R. Eiler, W. Goletz, and D. Keegan, "Is Your Cost Accounting Up to Date?" *Harvard Business Review* (July–August, 1982), pages 133–39.

removal or of solid waste collection; a hospital, the cost of providing various surgical or diagnostic services; a railroad, the cost per ton-mile of hauling freight; and an insurance company, the cost of providing various combinations of home-owner protection to specific groups of policyholders. Many of the costing concepts and techniques used in manufacturing costing systems apply to nonmanufacturing situations.

Use of Perpetual Inventories

The inherent weaknesses of using periodic inventory procedures for manufacturing operations were discussed in Chapter 21. Cost of raw materials used and cost of goods sold tend to be residual (or plug) figures. Also, relatively current cost data are available only at end-of-period intervals, and many significant departmental cost details are not readily apparent. For these reasons, cost accounting systems incorporate perpetual inventory procedures. That is, additions to and deductions from all inventory accounts—raw materials, work in process, and finished goods—are recorded as they occur. The more current cost information and greater cost controls justify the additional bookkeeping costs of perpetually maintaining the inventory accounts. Perpetual inventory records are customarily verified by physical inventory at least once a year. Necessary adjustments for errors and unrecorded inventory shrinkages can then be made. The flow of product costs—raw materials, direct labor, and factory overhead—through the various perpetual inventory accounts of a cost accounting system is apparent in both the simple and more comprehensive illustrations appearing in this chapter.

Timely Product Costing

A cost accounting system for a manufacturing concern must provide for the timely determination of product costs. Product costs are needed to arrive at inventory amounts for work in process and for finished goods; these amounts are required in the preparation of financial statements. Obviously, to determine income properly, we must have some method of identifying costs with the products sold and the products that remain on hand in a finished or unfinished state.

Efficiency and profitability provide equally compelling reasons for knowing product costs. Management uses engineering studies and cost analyses to establish standards and budgets for efficient performance. Only by knowing product costs can management compare actual costs with established norms and take necessary remedial action.

Management also needs product cost data to establish price lists and to submit bids on special orders for its products. Although many factors, including marketing and legal constraints, may affect pricing decisions, unit product costs are often an important determinant. Furthermore, once prices are established, knowledge of costs enables management to determine profit margins and to direct its efforts intelligently to the promotion of its more profitable items. We should mention, however, that management should consider the possibility that some cost figures may be out of date. Because cost figures are historical, they may not be currently relevant. When used for pricing purposes, costs should be updated as much as possible.

To identify costs with a product or a group of products, a manufacturer must trace factory costs—raw materials, direct labor, and factory overhead—to lots or batches of product. Tracing raw materials and labor costs to products is fairly routine. To account for the raw materials used, a firm may keep track of the costs of materials requisitioned for production of readily identifiable groups of products. Labor costs can similarly be accounted for by time-keeping methods or by identifying the product with the payroll costs of personnel in those operations or departments that produce the product. Tracing factory overhead costs to a product or to groups of products is not as simple. Obviously, a firm cannot directly determine the amount of depreciation, utilities, supervisory salaries, and so on that should be identified with different products or groups of products. Consequently, a firm assigns overhead costs throughout the production period using an estimation procedure with a predetermined overhead rate.

Use of Predetermined Overhead Rates

Many of the concepts and procedures underlying the use of **predetermined overhead rates** are extensive and complex. In this chapter, we give only a basic treatment, sufficient to convey a general understanding of the use of these rates in product costing.

Before the beginning of an accounting period, management normally prepares budgets; it translates sales forecasts into production budgets, which in turn permit estimates of plant utilization and activity. Such activity can be measured in a number of ways—direct labor hours, direct labor costs, machine hours, and so on. Using historical data and projected activity levels, management can estimate the total factory overhead to be incurred. The overhead rate is computed by dividing the estimated total factory overhead by the selected measure of activity. Calculations of predetermined overhead rates are usually based on year-long production periods.

Assume that the number of direct labor hours used is the most appropriate measure of activity for applying overhead in a given situation. If the projected number of direct labor hours is 100,000 and the estimated total factory overhead is $150,000, the overhead rate may be calculated

$$\text{Overhead Rate} = \frac{\text{Estimated Factory Overhead}}{\text{Estimated Direct Labor Hours}}$$

$$= \frac{\$150,000}{100,000 \text{ hours}}$$

$$= \$1.50/\text{direct labor hour}$$

If, during the accounting period, a particular group of products requires 50 direct labor hours of production time, $75 of overhead (50 × $1.50) is charged to this group of products.

Before selecting the basis for applying overhead to products, a firm should carefully analyze the relationship between overhead incurred and various alternative measures of activity. Probably the most common bases are related to direct labor hours or to direct labor costs. In situations with a high degree of equipment use relative to manual labor, machine-hours may be a more appropriate base.

Using a predetermined overhead rate, management can estimate the overhead costs of any job at any stage of production, computing "costs to date" both for control purposes and for inventory costing. This method also eliminates wide fluctuations in unit costs that might result if actual recorded overhead costs were assigned to products during short interim periods when production departed markedly from average levels. For example, assume that normal production is 100,000 direct labor hours per year and that production fluctuates seasonally throughout the year. Suppose also that a large share of actual factory overhead cost is spread fairly evenly over the year. (Such costs as depreciation, maintenance, utilities, and supervisory costs remain fairly constant from month to month.) If a particular month's production fell far below the monthly average of 8,333 direct labor hours (100,000 direct labor hours ÷ 12 months), and *actual* factory overhead costs were assigned to units of product, unit costs would increase abruptly because the factory overhead would be assigned to fewer units of product than usual. Similarly, in months of increased production, unit costs would decrease.

Exhibit 22–1 illustrates the possible differences between assigned overhead costs based on actual monthly overhead rates and those based on an annual overhead rate. The estimated annual rate in this example is $1.50 per direct labor hour ($150,000/100,000 direct labor hours). The actual monthly rates vary from $3.10 in February to $1.10 in July, with only the months of April, September, and October even approaching the annual average of $1.50 per direct labor hour. Using actual rates and assuming that a particular unit of product requires three direct labor hours, a unit produced in July when production activity was highest would be assigned overhead costs of $3.30 (3 × $1.10). In contrast, a unit produced in February when production activity was lowest would be assigned overhead costs of $9.30 (3 × $3.10). The $6 difference is hardly defensible, especially when the

EXHIBIT 22–1
**Comparison of Actual Monthly
and Estimated Annual Overhead Rates**

Factory Overhead Costs Incurred Each Month*		Direct Labor Hours Worked Each Month	Overhead Rates Based on Actual Monthly Costs	Estimated Annual Overhead Rate	Range in Actual Overhead Rate per Direct Labor Hour
January	$ 9,900	4,000	$2.48	$1.50	
February	9,300	3,000	3.10	1.50	$3.10 (highest)
March	10,500	5,000	2.10	1.50	
April	12,300	8,000	1.54	1.50	**
May	14,100	11,000	1.28	1.50	
June	14,700	12,000	1.23	1.50	
July	16,500	15,000	1.10	1.50	$1.10 (lowest)
August	15,300	13,000	1.18	1.50	
September	13,500	10,000	1.35	1.50	**
October	12,300	8,000	1.54	1.50	**
November	11,100	6,000	1.85	1.50	
December	10,500	5,000	2.10	1.50	
Annual Amounts	$150,000	100,000	—	$1.50	

*Assumed to be $7,500 each month plus 60 cents per direct labor hour.
**These are the only months in which actual monthly rates approach the annual rate.

two units of product may be virtually indistinguishable physically. Clearly, basing product costs on allocations of actual monthly overhead amounts is unrealistic. The use of a predetermined overhead rate employing a yearly average produces more meaningful unit cost figures.

The accumulation of actual factory overhead and the application of a predetermined overhead rate involves special accounting procedures. These procedures are introduced in the following section on flow of product costs and are explained further in the comprehensive illustration of job order costing later in this chapter.

Flow of Product Costs

To introduce the basic ideas of cost accounting systems, we present a simple illustration in the next few pages. The final part of this chapter presents a more detailed example incorporating a widely used technique for assigning costs to manufactured products. The beginning illustration involves a first phase of accumulating product costs and a second phase of tracing these costs as they sequentially become (1) work in process, during manufacturing operations; (2) finished goods, when completed; and (3) costs of goods sold, when sold. Remember in this illustration that the cumulative debit amounts of all product costs are capitalized (treated as assets) and eventually become debits to a Finished Goods Inventory account.

ACCUMULATING PRODUCT COSTS   The basic relationships in this illustration underlie all cost accounting systems, although the account titles used here vary in practice. For simplicity in presenting these basic concepts, we assume no beginning inventory and use convenient money amounts in all entries. Each entry is explained and its effect keyed to related accounts shown here in T-account form.

Acquisition of Materials

The perpetual inventory procedures for purchasing merchandise explained in Chapter 9 are used to derive the amount of this entry. Because all factory materials are being accounted for, this transaction includes both raw materials and factory supplies.

Recording Factory Payroll

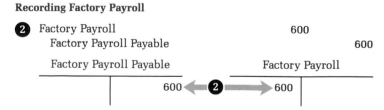

Here, the total factory payroll includes both direct and indirect labor. Later, these two items will be handled separately. Data for this entry would come from a detailed analysis of factory payroll records.

Recording Other Factory Costs as Overhead

3 Factory Overhead	1,000	
Accumulated Depreciation		400
Utilities Payable		300
Prepaid Insurance		200
Property Tax Payable		100

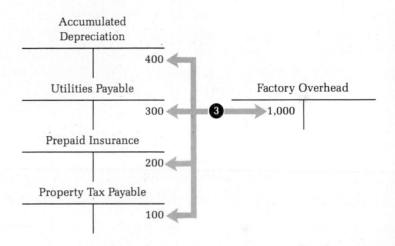

Realistically, factory overhead includes many more items than are shown here. We chose these particular items to illustrate depreciation, accruals, and the write-off of prepaid items.

At this point, all product costs have been accumulated into debit balances in the Materials Inventory, Factory Payroll, and Factory Overhead accounts. We now trace these costs through to Finished Goods Inventory and Cost of Goods Sold.

TRACING PRODUCT COSTS   In this phase of our illustration, we show how the product costs accumulated earlier as debit balances in the accounts are transferred sequentially through the Work in Process and Finished Goods Inventory accounts to the Cost of Goods Sold account. Descriptions, journal entries, and explanations for each step are keyed to the cost flow diagram in Exhibit 22–2 (page 789). As you read the material, trace each entry in the cost flow diagram.

Recording Requisitions of Raw Materials and Factory Supplies

4 Work in Process	600	
Factory Overhead	200	
Materials Inventory		800

This entry reflects the requisition of all materials used in production by the various parties. Raw materials (or direct materials) are charged directly to the Work in Process account. Costs of factory supplies (or indirect materials) are part of factory overhead. We assume here (as is often the case in practice) that the Materials Inventory account is the control account for both raw materials and factory supplies. Note that the balance in the Materials Inventory account indicates the unused portion of materials in this accounting period.

Recording Distribution of Factory Payroll

5 Work in Process 500
    Factory Overhead 100
        Factory Payroll 600

Work in Process is debited for the $500 of direct labor, and Factory Overhead is debited for the $100 of indirect labor. Observe that the total factory payroll is distributed, leaving a zero balance in the Factory Payroll account. The division of total factory payroll into direct and indirect labor is based on a detailed analysis of each employee's job description, wage rates, and hours worked.

Recording Application of Factory Overhead

6 Work in Process 1,200
    Factory Overhead 1,200

This entry adds the third and final category of factory costs to work in process. Note that the amount of this entry is not equal to the $1,300 of actual factory overhead incurred to date. As explained earlier, most firms do *not* apply the actual amount of overhead incurred each period to the goods manufactured during that period. Instead, they apply average overhead rates that reflect estimates of total annual production volume and total annual overhead costs.

Recording Completed Production

7 Finished Goods Inventory 2,000
    Work in Process 2,000

This entry assigns costs to completed production and transfers those costs from Work in Process to Finished Goods Inventory. As explained later, the amount of this entry is derived from production records, the details of which vary with the firm's particular product costing system. The balance remaining in the Work in Process account represents the costs assigned to the ending work-in-process inventory.

Recording Cost of Goods Sold

8 Cost of Goods Sold 1,400
    Finished Goods Inventory 1,400

This entry transfers the cost of finished products sold to the Cost of Goods Sold account. The balance remaining in the Finished Goods Inventory account reflects costs assigned to the ending inventory of finished goods.

Exhibit 22–2 below diagrams the results of the foregoing entries as the various product costs move through the manufacturing accounts. The following list summarizes these entries:

(1) Entries 1–3 accumulate factory costs into three accounts—Materials Inventory, Factory Payroll, and Factory Overhead.

(2) Entry 4 reflects the requisition of both raw materials and factory supplies.

(3) Entry 5 distributes the total factory payroll, including direct and indirect labor. At this point, debits in the Factory Overhead account reflect the actual factory overhead incurred.

(4) Entry 6 applies an amount of factory overhead based on predetermined estimates of total annual overhead costs and production levels. The $100 balance in the Factory Overhead account represents an amount of actual overhead incurred but not yet applied to work in process, the nature and disposition of which are explained later in the chapter. After entry 6, the Work in Process account has been charged for all three categories of product costs—raw materials, direct labor, and applied factory overhead.

(5) Entry 7 transfers to Finished Goods Inventory the costs assigned to completed production. The $300 balance in the Work in Process account is the cost assigned to the goods that are only partially completed at this point.

(6) Entry 8 transfers to Cost of Goods Sold the costs of the finished goods sold. The balance in the Finished Goods Inventory account represents the cost assigned to the goods that are finished but not yet sold.

EXHIBIT 22–2
Tracing Product Costs
through a Cost Accounting System

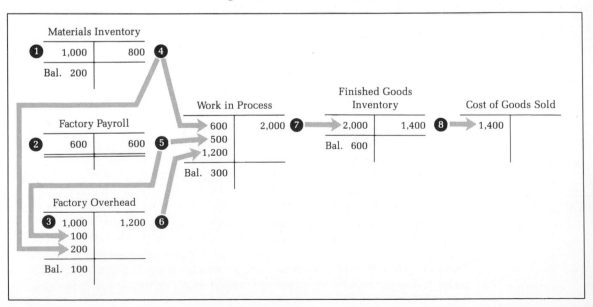

So far, we have presented the important aspects of cost accounting systems including the use of perpetual inventory procedures, the provision of timely product costs, the use of predetermined overhead rates, and an illustration of the flow of product costs through a cost accounting system. We now turn to an illustration of the widely used *job order* cost accounting system.

JOB ORDER COSTING SYSTEMS

The two basic types of cost accounting systems are job order cost accounting and process cost accounting. **Job order cost accounting** (sometimes called **job lot** or **specific order** costing) is appropriate when production is characterized by a discontinuous series of products or jobs undertaken either to fill specific orders from customers or to produce a general stock of products from which future orders are filled. This type of costing is widely used in construction, printing, and machine shop operations. Often the products or batches of products vary in their material components and manner of production. In contrast, **process cost accounting** lends itself most readily to the production of a large volume of undifferentiated products manufactured in a "continuous flow" operation, such as distillation of fuels or manufacture of paint, chemicals, wire, and similar items. Essentially the same ingredients and operations are involved during each period of manufacture.

Either system primarily allocates manufacturing costs to products to determine unit costs. In a job order system, costs are identified with specific jobs to determine the cost of products manufactured. In a process system, costs are identified with production processes and averaged over the products made during the period. Here, we illustrate a job order costing system; the basic concepts of process costing are presented in Chapter 23.

Exhibits 22–3 through 22–7 show some of the important accounting forms used in job order costing as they might appear during use. In a job order costing system, each of the three inventory accounts—Materials Inventory, Work in Process, and Finished Goods Inventory—has a subsidiary ledger in which unit costs are accounted for. **Materials ledger cards** (Exhibit 22–3) for each type of material or factory supply used make up the subsidiary record for the Materials Inventory account; the cards show quantities received, issued, and on hand, unit costs, and total amounts. **Materials requisition forms** (Exhibit 22–4) contain the initial recording of issuances of raw materials for various jobs or of factory supplies for general factory use. **Time tickets** (Exhibit 22–5) initially record the amount of time spent and the individual employee labor cost incurred for each individual job or as a part of factory overhead. **Job cost sheets** (Exhibit 22–6) are the subsidiary records for the Work in Process account. For each job in process, the sheets indicate the costs of raw materials, direct labor, and applied overhead identified with the job. When a job is completed, the total cost is divided by the number of units in the lot to obtain a unit cost. Also at this time, the job's cost sheet is removed from the Work in Process ledger and an entry is made in the **finished goods ledger,** which is the subsidiary record for Finished Goods Inventory. The

EXHIBIT 22–3
Materials Ledger Card

Materials Ledger Card

Stock No. _32_

Description _1/8 Steel Wire_

Supplier _Steel Supply Corp._

Reorder Quantity _4,000 ft._

Minimum Quantity _1,000 ft._

Date	Received				Issued				Balance		
	Rec'g. Report No.	Units	Price	Total Price	Mat'l. Req'n. No.	Units	Price	Total Price	Units	Price	Total Price
19XX											
8/1	320	4,000	0.20	800.00					4,000	0.20	800.00
8/5					567	700	0.20	140.00	3,300	0.20	660.00
8/9	332	4,000	0.21	840.00					3,300	0.20	660.00
									4,000	0.21	840.00

EXHIBIT 22–4
Materials Requisition Form

Materials Requisition

Date _8/5_   Job. No. _372_   Requisition No. _567_

Item	Quantity		Unit Price	Amount
	Authorized	Issued		
Stock No. 32 (1/8" wire)	700 ft.	700 ft.	0.20	$140
Total				$140

Authorized by: _G.E.K._   Issued by: _J.A.P._   Received by: _F.W.E._

EXHIBIT 22–5
Time Ticket

Time Ticket

Employee Name James L. Kitt   Employee No. 42

Skill Specification Wire Former   Payroll Period Ending 8/16/XX

Time Started	Time Stopped	Total Time	Hourly Labor Rate	Department	Job No.	Total Cost
8:00	12:00	4.0	$4.00	A	372	$16.00
1:00	2:00	1.0	4.00	A	372	4.00
Totals		5.0				$20.00

Approved by *R.L.J.*

EXHIBIT 22–6
Job Cost Sheet

Job Cost Sheet

Customer Ace Fabricators, Inc.   Job No. 372

Product Bracket-H3   Date Promised 9/1/XX

Quantity 200   Dates: Started 8/1   Completed 8/20

Raw Materials		Direct Labor			Cost Summary	
Mat'l. Req'n. No.	Amount	Payroll Summary Dated	Dept.	Amount		
567	140.00	8/2	A	70.00	Raw Materials	700.00
573	180.00	8/9	A	240.00	Direct Labor	600.00
591	200.00	8/16	B	190.00	Factory Overhead (applied at):	
603	180.00	8/23	B	100.00		
					150% of direct labor cost	900.00
					Total Cost	2,200.00
Totals	700.00			600.00	Units Finished 200 Unit Cost	11.00

EXHIBIT 22-7
Finished Goods Ledger Card

Finished Goods Ledger Card									

Stock No. ___H3___

Item ___Bracket-H3___   Minimum Quantity ___50___

Manufactured			Sales			Balance			
Job No.	Quantity	Total Cost	Invoice No.	Quantity	Total Cost	Date	Quantity	Unit Cost	Total Cost
372	200	2,200.00				8/20	200	11.00	2,200.00
			123	100	1,100.00	8/25	100	11.00	1,100.00

cards in this ledger (Exhibit 22–7) identify the stock number and name of the product and show quantities, unit costs, and total costs of the various lots of product awaiting sale. We now turn to the comprehensive illustration of job order costing, which shows how to use these forms.

To illustrate job order cost accounting, we make the following three assumptions:

(1) Condor Company uses raw materials A and B to produce products Y and Z.

(2) The company also uses raw material C, which is classified as factory supplies because it is employed in all parts of the factory and is not incorporated directly into products Y and Z.

(3) Condor uses a predetermined overhead rate based on direct labor hours to assign factory overhead to products.

Accounting for Materials

A materials clerk records the amounts of raw materials or factory supplies received in the materials ledger as additions to the balances on the appropriate ledger cards. At the end of the accounting period, the total purchases for the period are posted from the voucher register or invoice register to Materials Inventory. The amount added to the control account equals the sum of the amounts added to the materials ledger cards during the period.

When raw materials (A and B, in this case) are requisitioned for specific orders or jobs, the materials clerk records the reductions on the appropriate materials ledger cards. Cost clerks then enter these amounts in the materials section of the job cost sheets for the specific jobs in which the material is used. Amounts on requisitions representing general factory supplies (material C) are handled by the materials clerk in the same fashion as amounts for raw materials. The amounts, however, are charged to the Factory Overhead account, because they cannot be identified feasibly with particular jobs.

For example, assume the following:

(1) The Condor Company purchased $2,500 of material A, $1,500 of material B, and $500 of material C during its first month of operations.

(2) The following materials were requisitioned: $1,000 of material A for job 1; $500 of material B for job 2; and $200 of material C for general factory use.

The effect of these transactions is shown in Exhibit 22–8. Notice that in each subsidiary ledger, *matching* postings (debits for debits and credits for credits) totaling each entry are made to the related general ledger control account.

Accounting for Labor

To identify labor costs with specific jobs, firms use time tickets to accumulate the hours spent on various jobs by each employee. Hourly wage rates can then be used to compute the labor costs for the various jobs. Periodically, these records are sorted and the direct labor amounts posted to the job cost sheets.

We can use a number of accounts to record payroll costs. Our simple illustration shows how direct and indirect labor costs can be recorded in the accounts. To continue our example, we assume the following:

(3) Total direct labor hours used and charges incurred during the period:
Job 1—200 hours, $800 total direct labor
Job 2—100 hours, $400 total direct labor

(4) Indirect labor payroll for the period, $500.

The effect of these transactions is shown in Exhibit 22–9, where we use the Work in Process account, its subsidiary ledger (the job cost sheets), the Factory Overhead account, and the Factory Payroll account. We do not show the Factory Payroll account debit entry that would be part of the entry to record accrual of the factory payroll liability.

Accounting for Overhead

Exhibits 22–8 and 22–9 demonstrate how factory supplies used and indirect labor costs for the period are introduced into the accounts. In our example, the cost of the factory supplies amounted to $200 and the indirect labor costs were $500. Other overhead costs are charged to the Factory Overhead account as incurred or through adjusting entries at the end of the accounting period. For instance, assume that in addition to the factory supplies used and indirect labor costs, the following overhead costs were incurred during the period: utilities, $50; repairs, $60; depreciation, $80; and insurance, $40. The general journal entries to record these items are given below:

(5)	Factory Overhead—Utilities	50	
	Factory Overhead—Repairs	60	
	Factory Overhead—Depreciation	80	
	Factory Overhead—Insurance	40	
	Cash (or Accounts Payable)		110
	Accumulated Depreciation		80
	Prepaid Insurance		40

EXHIBIT 22–8

Entries for Purchase and Requisition of Raw Materials and Factory Supplies

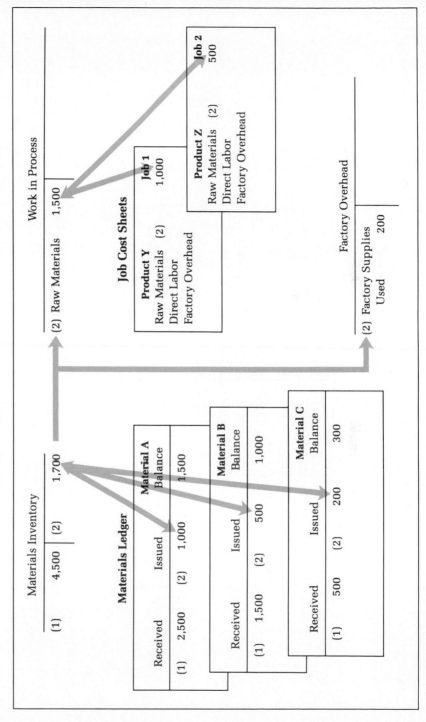

EXHIBIT 22–9
Entries for Assignment of Factory Payroll

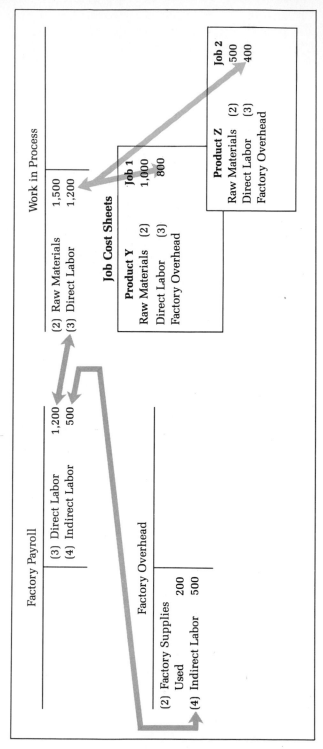

The debits in entry (5) are shown as they would appear in the Factory Overhead account (see Exhibit 22–10). The accounts credited in the entry—Cash, Accumulated Depreciation, and Prepaid Insurance—are omitted from the exhibit, because they are only indirectly involved in the example.

As explained earlier, actual overhead is not identified directly with specific jobs. Instead, through the use of a predetermined overhead rate, the Work in Process account is charged with estimated overhead applied. We assume that the Condor Company charges overhead to jobs on the basis of direct labor hours. Its forecasting and budgeting process has determined an overhead rate of $3 per direct labor hour. Because job 1 accumulated 200 hours, Condor applies $600 of overhead cost to this job, while job 2, requiring 100 hours, receives $300 of overhead cost. The general journal entry to charge the Work in Process account with estimated overhead would be

(6)	Work in Process	900	
	Factory Overhead		900
	(Job 1, $600; job 2, $300)		

Exhibit 22–10 (page 798) shows how the accounts reflect overhead items.

After overhead cost has been entered on the job cost sheets, all elements of cost to date—raw materials, direct labor, and factory overhead—can be totaled. This sum represents the cost of the job from its inception to its present stage of production. In our example, we see that $2,400 ($1,000 + $800 + $600) has been accumulated on job 1 by the end of the accounting period. Frequently, management compares the calculated cost for a job not yet completed with the costs of similar jobs in the past. Knowing such costs, management may take any necessary steps to control costs. In addition, accumulating cost by jobs permits an evaluation of the work in process inventory.

In Exhibit 22–10, the $900 overhead cost applied to jobs was credited to the Factory Overhead account. Some accountants prefer to credit a separate Applied Factory Overhead account, but this mere bookkeeping nicety is not essential to our conceptual discussion.

Note that the amount of overhead applied to jobs during the period is $30 less than the actual overhead incurred ($930). In fact, it would be unusual in any month for the amount applied to equal the actual overhead cost. There are several reasons for this. First, estimates of the total annual overhead cost and the activity in labor hours were used to calculate the overhead rate. Second, production activity normally fluctuates from month to month. Finally, the actual pattern of incurring overhead cost may also vary from month to month. Therefore, we can expect either debit or credit balances monthly in the Factory Overhead account. A debit balance in the account is called **underapplied** (or **underabsorbed**) overhead. A credit balance would be **overapplied** (or **overabsorbed**) overhead. On interim financial statements, the Factory Overhead account balance can be shown on the balance sheet as a deferred debit or a deferred credit. An existing balance at year-end is usually closed to the Cost of Goods Sold account. For example, if the

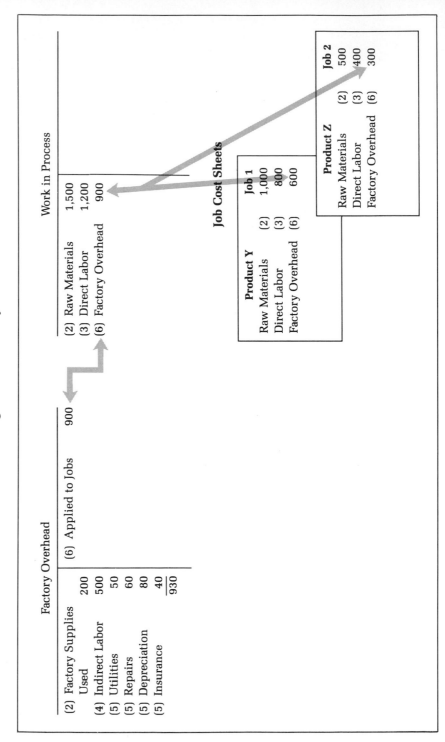

EXHIBIT 22–10
Entries for Assignment of Factory Overhead

Factory Overhead had a $30 debit balance at year-end, the following entry might be made:

Cost of Goods Sold	30	
Factory Overhead		30
To close the Factory Overhead account.		

Actually, any residual balance in the overhead account at the end of any period pertains to unfinished goods, finished goods, and goods that have been sold. We could analyze the labor hours (or other overhead application base) involved in each of these categories and apportion the residual amount in the overhead account to each category on the basis of relative labor hours. However, such a procedure is justified only when the residual balance is a material amount.

Accounting for Finished Goods

When job orders are completed, the unit cost of items is obtained by dividing the total accumulated cost by the number of units produced. The job cost sheets can then be removed from the work in process ledger and filed. At the same time, entries are made in the finished goods ledger, showing quantities, unit cost, and total cost of the items entered. At the end of the period, a journal entry credits Work in Process and debits Finished Goods Inventory for the total cost of the jobs completed during the period. When units of product are sold, the cost of those units is removed from the finished goods ledger cards; at the end of the accounting period, an entry made in the general ledger credits Finished Goods Inventory and debits Cost of Goods Sold.

To illustrate the entries made in accounting for finished goods, assume that job 1, costing $2,400, was completed during the current period, resulting in 1,000 units of product Y, and that 400 units of product Y were sold for $4 each. Job 2 was still in process at the end of the period. The following entries record the transfer of the units of product Y to finished goods and reflect the sale of 400 units:

(7)	Finished Goods Inventory	2,400	
	Work in Process		2,400
	Job 1 completed, producing 1,000 units of product Y at $2.40 per unit.		
(8)	Cost of Goods Sold	960	
	Finished Goods Inventory		960
	Cost of 400 units of product Y at $2.40 each.		
(9)	Accounts Receivable	1,600	
	Sales		1,600
	Sold 400 units of product Y at $4 per unit.		

After transactions (7)–(9) are entered, the relevant accounts and **subsidiary rec-** ords would appear as shown in Exhibit 22–11. Note three points: An obvious parallel exists between the physical flow of goods and the related accounting entries; the various subsidiary ledgers contain a detailed analysis of the aggregate balances in their related general ledger control accounts; and the sale of finished goods involves entries at both the selling price and the related cost amount.

EXHIBIT 22–11
Entries for Completion and Sale of Product

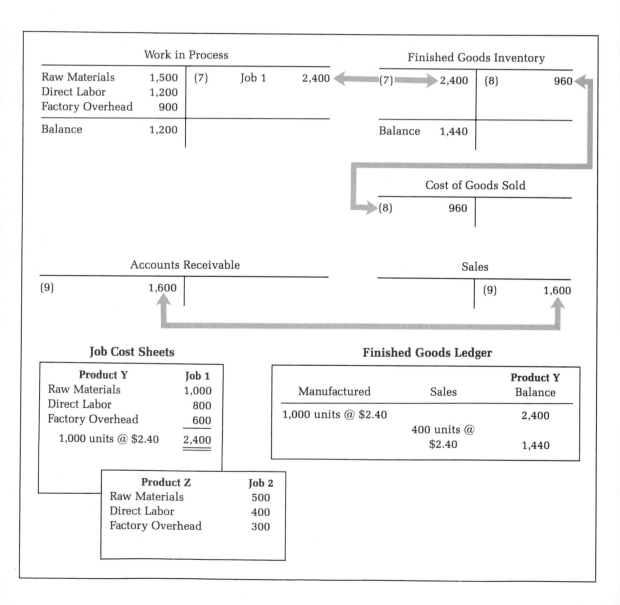

COST ACCOUNTING SYSTEMS
AND FINANCIAL STATEMENTS

When perpetual inventory procedures are used in cost accounting systems, the ending balances of all three inventory accounts reflect the period's routine transactions that increase and decrease inventories. These ending balances are adjusted only if a discrepancy appears in a year-end physical inventory. Note also that the cost of goods sold figure has been accumulated throughout the year in a general ledger account and can be placed directly on the income statement. Detailed information is available in the related accounts for preparing analyses of cost of goods manufactured and cost of goods sold. The format of financial statements for firms using cost accounting systems is similar to that illustrated in Chapter 21.

KEY POINTS TO REMEMBER

(1) The basic concept of cost accounting is the accumulation and allocation of cost to some unit of activity or accomplishment.

(2) Virtually all cost data are based on assumptions about—and relatively arbitrary choices among—equally defensible accounting procedures. Users of cost data should be aware of the variations inherent in cost data and any resulting limitations to the data used.

(3) Cost accounting systems provide timely unit product costs through the use of perpetual inventory procedures and predetermined factory overhead rates.

(4) Predetermined overhead rates are computed by dividing an estimate of the coming year's total factory overhead cost by an estimate of some unit of activity (such as direct labor hours, direct labor costs, or factory machine hours).

(5) A cost accounting system is basically a method of accumulating the costs of raw materials, direct labor, and factory overhead and allocating them sequentially to work in process, finished goods, and cost of goods sold.

(6) Job order costing lends itself to the production of a discontinuous series of jobs or products that may vary in their component materials and mode of manufacture. Process costing is most useful for undifferentiated products made in a continuous flow operation.

(7) Detailed inventory records and requisitions must differentiate between raw materials and factory supplies and accumulate the cost of raw materials by job number.

(8) Detailed payroll records and time tickets must differentiate among direct labor, indirect labor, and nonfactory labor costs and accumulate direct labor costs by job number.

(9) When all related postings are complete, the raw materials ledger cards, job cost sheets, and finished goods ledger should present a detailed analysis of the balances in the Materials Inventory, Work in Process, and Finished Goods Inventory accounts, respectively.

(10) Under- or overapplied overhead, which is expected at the end of interim accounting periods, is shown as deferred debits or credits on interim balance sheets. An immaterial amount is closed to Cost of Goods Sold at year-end; if material, it may be allocated among the Work in Process, Finished Goods Inventory, and Cost of Goods Sold accounts.

QUESTIONS

22–1 What are the two primary objectives of cost accounting systems?

22–2 What are the limitations of most cost determinations?

22–3 In a manufacturing operation, what important advantages do perpetual inventory procedures have over periodic inventory procedures?

22–4 Identify several important uses of unit product costs. Why might management need unit product costs before the operating year-end?

22–5 What is a predetermined factory overhead rate, and how, in general, is it determined?

22–6 Briefly justify the use of a predetermined annual factory overhead rate as opposed to actual monthly factory overhead.

22–7 A manufacturing company employs an overhead rate of 150% of direct labor cost. The job 301 cost sheet shows that $3,000 in raw materials has been used and that $8,000 in direct labor has been incurred. If 1,000 units of product have been produced on job 301, what is the unit cost of the product?

22–8 Briefly explain the sequential flow of product costs through a cost accounting system.

22–9 For what types of manufacturing activities are job order costing systems most appropriate? For what types are process costing systems most appropriate?

22–10 What type of records would be used or maintained for the following manufacturing activities?
(a) Determining the amount of a specific material on hand.
(b) Issuing raw materials for production.
(c) Assigning the direct labor costs for a particular worker.
(d) Accumulating the cost of a particular product or batch of products.
(e) Determining the amounts and cost of completed products on hand.

22–11 Explain the general format and give examples of the data that would appear on (a) a materials ledger card, (b) a job cost sheet, and (c) a finished goods ledger card.

22–12 Briefly explain (a) the concept of a control account and a subsidiary ledger, (b) the three inventory accounts in a manufacturing cost system that are often control accounts, (c) the name of the subsidiary ledger record for each account in part (b), and (d) how to determine that a control account and subsidiary ledger agree.

22–13 Why can we say that the sale of a manufactured product is recorded at two different amounts?

22–14 The Rogers Company records both actual overhead and applied overhead in a single Factory Overhead account. On January 31, the account has a credit balance. Has overhead been underapplied or overapplied during January? What is the significance of this balance, and how should it be treated in the January financial statements?

22–15 Outline the disposition of an amount of underapplied overhead, assuming it exists either at the end of an interim accounting period or at year-end. In the latter case, how would materiality affect the treatment?

22–16 Hanson Manufacturing Company applies factory overhead at the rate of 140% of direct labor cost. During the current period, Hanson incurred $80,000 of direct labor costs and $107,000 of factory overhead costs. What is the amount of over- or underapplied factory overhead? What disposition should be made of the Factory Overhead account balance?

EXERCISES

22–17 Selected data for the Fabrication Department of the Allied Manufacturing company are presented below:

Estimated factory overhead cost for the year	$168,000
Estimated direct labor cost for the year (@ $8/hr)	120,000
Actual factory overhead cost for January	13,500
Actual direct labor cost for January (1,200 hours)	9,780

Assuming that direct labor cost is the basis for applying factory overhead:
(a) Calculate the predetermined overhead rate.
(b) Present a journal entry that applies factory overhead for January.
(c) By what amount is factory overhead over- or underapplied in January?
(d) How would the amount in part (c) be reflected in January's financial statements?

22–18 Using the data in Exercise 22–17, but assuming that the basis for applying factory overhead is direct labor *hours*, complete requirements (a) through (d).

22–19 During the coming accounting year, Offshore, Inc. anticipates the following costs, expenses, and operating data:

Raw Materials (8,000 lb)	$18,000
Direct Labor (@ $9/hr)	36,000
Factory Supplies Used	3,000
Indirect Labor	6,000
Sales Commissions	13,500
Factory Administration	3,000
Nonfactory Administration Expenses	4,500
Other Factory Overhead*	15,000

*Provides for operating 36,000 machine hours.

(a) Calculate the predetermined overhead rate for the coming year for each of the following application bases: (1) direct labor hours, (2) direct labor costs, and (3) machine hours.

(b) For each case in part (a), determine the proper application of factory overhead to job No. 63, to which 6 direct labor hours, $40 of direct labor cost, and 70 machine hours have been charged.

22–20 Madison Manufacturing Corporation applies factory overhead on the basis of 80% of direct labor cost. An analysis of the related accounts and job cost sheets indicates that during the year total factory overhead incurred was $102,000 and that at year-end Work in Process, Finished Goods Inventory, and Cost of Goods Sold included $7,000, $28,000, and $83,000, respectively, of direct labor charges.

(a) Determine the amount of over- or underapplied overhead at year-end.

(b) Present a journal entry that closes the Factory Overhead account at year-end assuming (1) the amount was not considered material, and (2) the amount was considered material (round answers to nearest dollar).

22–21 Assuming a routine manufacturing activity, present journal entries (account titles only) for each of the following transactions:

(a) Purchased raw materials on account.

(b) Recorded factory payroll earned but not paid.

(c) Requisitioned both raw materials and factory supplies.

(d) Assigned direct and indirect factory payroll costs.

(e) Recorded factory depreciation, property tax expense, and insurance expense.

(f) Applied factory overhead to production.

(g) Completed monthly production.

(h) Sold finished goods.

22–22 The following is a cost flow diagram similar to Exhibit 22–2 in which all or part of typical manufacturing transactions (or account entries) are indicated by parenthetical letters on the debit or credit side of each account.

Materials
Inventory

(a)	(c)

Factory Payroll		Work in Process Inventory		Finished Goods Inventory		Cost of Goods Sold	
(b)	(d)	(c) (d) (f)	(g)	(g)	(h)	(h)	

Factory
Overhead

(c) (d) (e)	(f)

For each parenthetical letter, present a general journal entry indicating the apparent transaction or procedure that has occurred (disregard amounts).

22–23 For each of the manufacturing transactions or activities indicated by the parenthetical letters in the cost flow diagram in Exercise 22–22, briefly identify the detailed forms, records, or documents (if any) that would probably underlie each journal entry.

22–24 The following summary data are from the job cost sheets of the McGinley Company:

Job No.	Dates Started	Dates Finished	Shipped	Total Costs Assigned at April 30	Total Production Costs Added in May
1	4/10	4/20	5/9	$3,000	
2	4/18	4/30	5/20	2,200	
3	4/24	5/10	5/25	1,100	$2,400
4	4/28	5/20	6/3	1,500	1,900
5	5/15	6/10	6/20		1,000
6	5/22	6/18	6/28		1,700

Using the above data, compute (a) the finished goods inventory at May 1 and May 31, (b) the work in process inventory at May 1 and May 31, and (c) the cost of goods sold for May.

22–25 Before the completed production for June is recorded, the Work in Process account for Benton Company appears as follows:

Work in Process

Balance, June 1	5,000		
Raw Materials	15,000		
Direct Labor	12,000		
Factory Overhead	9,000		

Assume that completed production for June includes jobs 107, 108, and 109 with total costs of $8,000, $16,000, and $10,000, respectively.
(a) Determine the cost of unfinished jobs at June 30 and prepare a journal entry recording completed production.
(b) Using general journal entries, record the sale of job 107 for $13,000 on account.

22–26 A manufacturing company has the following account in its cost records:

Work in Process

Raw Materials	30,000	To Finished Goods	58,600
Direct Labor	20,000		
Factory Overhead	16,000		

The company applies overhead to production at a predetermined rate based on direct labor costs. Assume that the company uses a job order costing system and that job 110, the only job in process at the end of the period, has been charged with raw materials of $2,000. Complete the following cost sheet for job 110.

Cost Sheet—Job 110 (in process)

Raw Materials	————
Direct Labor	————
Factory Overhead	————
Total Cost	————

PROBLEMS

Note: In all problems, assume perpetual inventory procedures, a single Factory Overhead account, first-in, first-out costing of inventories, and that the Materials Inventory account is the control account for both raw (direct) materials and factory supplies.

22–27 Oakbrook Manufacturing, Inc. expects the following costs and expenses during the coming year:

Raw Materials	$20,000
Direct Labor (@ $6/hr)	72,000
Sales Commissions	15,000
Factory Supervision	18,000
Indirect Labor	36,000
Factory Depreciation*	20,000
Factory Taxes*	6,000
Factory Insurance*	5,000
Factory Supplies Used	10,000
Factory Utilities*	9,000

*The factory building contains a sales showroom that occupies about 20% of the floor space involved.

REQUIRED

(a) Compute a predetermined factory overhead rate applied on the basis of direct labor hours.

(b) Present a general journal entry to apply factory overhead during an interim period when 1,400 direct labor hours were worked.

(c) What amount of overhead would be assigned to job 466, to which $42 in direct labor had been charged?

22–28 The following selected ledger accounts of the James Company are for February (the second month of its accounting year):

Materials Inventory

Feb. 1 Bal.	12,000	February Credits	44,000
February Debits	40,000		

Factory Overhead

February Debits	54,000	Feb. 1 Bal.	4,000
		February Credits	48,000

Work in Process Inventory		
Feb. 1 Bal.	8,000	February
February Debits:		Credits 136,000
Raw Materials	36,000	
Direct Labor	60,000	
Factory		
Overhead	48,000	

Factory Payroll Payable		
February Debits 76,000	Feb. 1 Bal.	18,000
	February Credits 70,000

Finished Goods Inventory		
Feb. 1 Bal.	30,000	February
		Credits 150,000
February Debits 136,000		

REQUIRED

(a) Determine the amount of factory supplies requisitioned for production during February.

(b) How much indirect labor cost was apparently incurred during February?

(c) Calculate the factory overhead rate based on direct labor cost.

(d) Was factory overhead for February under- or overapplied, and by what amount?

(e) Was factory overhead for the first two months of the year under- or over-applied, and by what amount?

(f) What is the cost of production completed in February?

(g) What is the cost of goods sold in February?

22–29 Alpha Manufacturing had the following inventories at the end of its last fiscal year:

Materials Inventory	$10,000
Work in Process	4,000
Finished Goods Inventory	8,000

During the first month of the current year, the following transactions occurred:

(1) Purchased materials on account, $18,000.

(2) Incurred factory payroll, $36,000.

(3) Requisitioned raw materials of $17,000 and factory supplies of $7,000.

(4) Assigned total factory payroll, of which $6,000 was considered indirect labor.

(5) Incurred other factory overhead, $14,000. (Credit Accounts Payable.)

(6) Applied factory overhead on the basis of 80% of direct labor costs.

(7) Determined completed production, $56,000.

(8) Determined cost of goods sold, $48,000.

REQUIRED

(a) Prepare general journal entries to record these transactions.

(b) If the above transactions covered a full year's operations and the over- or underapplied overhead was considered material, present a journal entry to allocate the overhead account balance to the appropriate accounts in proportion to their ending balances. Round computations to the nearest dollar.

22–30 At the beginning of the current year, the Martin Company estimated that it would incur $48,000 of factory overhead cost during the year, using 12,000 direct labor hours to produce the desired volume of goods. On January 1 of the current year, beginning balances of Materials Inventory, Work in Process Inventory, and Finished Goods Inventory were $9,000, $–0–, and $14,000, respectively.

REQUIRED
Prepare general journal entries to record the following transactions for the current year:
(a) Purchased materials on account, $13,000.
(b) Of the total dollar value of materials used, $10,000 represented raw materials and $4,000 were factory supplies used.
(c) Determined total factory labor, $55,000 (11,000 hr at $5/hr).
(d) Of the factory labor, 80% was direct and 20% indirect.
(e) Applied factory overhead based on direct labor hours to work in process.
(f) Determined actual factory overhead other than those items already recorded, $18,000. (Credit Accounts Payable.)
(g) Ending inventories of work in process and finished goods were $10,000 and $19,000, respectively. (Make separate entries.)
(h) Closed the balance in Factory Overhead to Cost of Goods Sold.

22–31 Following are certain operating data for Carson Manufacturing Company during its first month of the current year's operations.

	Materials Inventory	Work in Process Inventory	Finished Goods Inventory
Beginning Inventory	$7,000	$3,000	$28,000
Ending Inventory	4,000	5,000	6,000

Total sales were $220,000, on which the company earned a 40% gross profit. Carson uses a predetermined factory overhead rate of 110% of direct labor costs. Factory overhead applied was $44,000. Exclusive of factory supplies used, total factory overhead incurred was $30,000; it was overapplied by $3,000.

REQUIRED
Compute the following items. (Set up the T accounts involved in the manufacturing cost flows as shown in Exhibit 22–2, fill in the known amounts, and then use the normal relationships among the various accounts to compute the unknown amounts.)
(a) Cost of goods sold.
(b) Cost of goods manufactured.
(c) Direct labor incurred.
(d) Raw materials used.
(e) Factory supplies used.
(f) Total materials purchased.

22–32 The following summary of job cost sheets relates to the production of Lester Manufacturing, Inc. during the first month of the current operating year. Lester uses the same overhead rate for all jobs.

Job No.	Raw Materials	Direct Labor	Factory Overhead
109	$ 420	$ 320	$ 240
110	600	400	300
111	1,200	1,400	1,050
112	1,000	800	600
113	620	520	390

Job 109 was in process at the end of the preceding year, when it had incurred direct labor charges of $200 and total charges of $650. Job 113 is the current month's ending work in process.

REQUIRED
(a) What is the apparent factory overhead rate?
(b) Determine the total of raw materials requisitioned in the current month.
(c) What is the total direct labor incurred in the current month?
(d) If factory overhead is underapplied by $280 at the end of the current month, what is the total factory overhead incurred during the month?
(e) If finished goods inventory decreased during the month by $700, what is the cost of goods sold for the month?

22–33 Summarized data for the first month's operations of Ajax Welding Foundry are presented below. A job order costing system is used.
(1) Materials purchased on account, $24,000.
(2) Amounts of materials requisitioned and foundry labor used:

Job No.	Materials	Foundry Labor
1	$1,500	$ 900
2	2,400	1,800
3	1,100	800
4	4,200	1,500
5	1,600	1,000
6	500	400
Foundry supplies used	2,200	
Indirect labor		1,200

(3) Foundry overhead is applied at the rate of 200% of direct labor costs.
(4) Miscellaneous foundry overhead incurred:

Prepaid foundry insurance written off	$ 500
Property taxes on foundry building accrued	800
Foundry utilities payable accrued	1,800
Depreciation on foundry equipment	2,600
Other costs incurred on account	3,600

(5) Ending work in process consisted of jobs 4 and 6.
(6) Jobs 1 and 3 and one-half of job 2 were sold on account for $7,000, $6,000, and $5,000, respectively.

REQUIRED
(a) Open general ledger T accounts for Materials Inventory, Foundry Payroll, Foundry Overhead, Work in Process Inventory, Finished Goods Inventory, and Cost of Goods Sold. Also set up subsidiary T accounts as job cost sheets for each job.
(b) Prepare general journal entries to record the summarized transactions for the month, and post appropriate entries to any accounts listed in part (a). Key each entry to the related parenthetical letter in the problem data.
(c) Determine the balances of any accounts necessary and prepare schedules of jobs in ending work in process and jobs in ending finished goods to confirm that they agree with the related control accounts.

22–34 During June, its first month of operations, Vilas Manufacturing Company completed the transactions listed below. Vilas uses a simple job order costing system. Materials requisitions and the factory payroll summary are analyzed on the fifteenth and the last day of each month, and charges for raw materials and direct labor are entered directly on specific job cost sheets. Factory overhead at the rate of 140% of direct labor costs is recorded on individual job cost sheets when a job is completed and at month-end for any job then in process. At month-end, entries to the general ledger accounts summarize materials requisitions, distribution of factory payroll costs, and the application of factory overhead for the month. All other general ledger entries are made as they occur.
(1) Purchased materials on account, $30,000.
(2) Paid miscellaneous factory overhead costs, $7,500.
(3) Paid the semimonthly factory payroll, $22,900.
(4) An analysis of materials requisitions and the factory payroll summary for June 1–15 indicates the following cost distribution:

Job No.	Materials	Factory Labor
1	$ 5,000	$ 8,500
2	2,400	3,700
3	1,000	2,500
Factory supplies used	1,800	
Indirect labor		8,200
	$10,200	$22,900

(5) Jobs 1 and 2 were completed on June 15 and transferred to Finished Goods Inventory on the next day. (Enter the appropriate factory overhead amounts on the job cost sheets, mark them completed, and make a general journal entry transferring the appropriate amount of cost to the Finished Goods Inventory account.)
(6) Paid miscellaneous factory overhead costs, $5,400.
(7) Sold job 1 on account, $43,000 (recognized its cost of sales in the general ledger).

(8) Paid the semimonthly factory payroll, $22,200.

(9) An analysis of materials requisitions and factory payroll summary for June 16–30 indicates the following cost distribution:

Job No.	Materials	Factory Labor
3	$ 5,300	$ 3,900
4	4,200	7,500
5	1,800	3,000
6	700	1,000
Factory supplies used	1,600	
Indirect labor		6,800
	$13,600	$22,200

(10) Jobs 3 and 4 were completed on June 30 and transferred to Finished Goods Inventory on the same day. [See instruction (5).]

(11) Sold job 3 on account, $36,000 (recognized its cost of sales in the general ledger).

(12) Recorded the following additional factory overhead:

Depreciation on factory building	$ 6,000
Depreciation on factory equipment	3,500
Expiration of factory insurance	1,000
Accrual of factory taxes payable	1,600
	$12,100

(13) Recorded monthly general ledger entries for the costs of all materials used.

(14) Recorded monthly general ledger entries for the distribution of factory payroll costs.

(15) Recorded factory overhead on the job cost sheets for jobs in ending work in process and in the general ledger for all factory overhead applied during the month.

REQUIRED

(a) Set up the following general ledger T accounts: Materials Inventory, Factory Payroll Summary, Factory Overhead, Work in Process Inventory, Finished Goods Inventory, Cost of Goods Sold, and Sales.

(b) Set up subsidiary ledger T accounts for each of jobs 1–6 as job cost sheets.

(c) Noting the accounting procedures described in the first paragraph of the problem, do the following:

   (1) Record general ledger entries for all transactions. Note that general ledger entries are *not* required in transactions (4) and (9). Post only those portions of these entries affecting the general ledger accounts set up in part (a).

   (2) Enter the applicable amounts directly on the appropriate job cost sheets for transactions (4), (5), (9), (10), and (15). Note parenthetically the nature of each amount entered.

(d) Present a brief analysis showing that the general ledger accounts for Work in Process Inventory and for Finished Goods Inventory agree with the related job cost sheets.

(e) Explain in one sentence each what the balance of each general ledger account established in part (a) represents.

ALTERNATE PROBLEMS

22–27A Woodfield Manufacturing, Inc. expects the following costs and expenses during the coming year:

Raw Materials	$26,000
Direct Labor (@ $6/hr)	96,000
Sales Commissions	15,000
Factory Supervision	27,000
Indirect Labor	54,000
Factory Depreciation*	30,000
Factory Taxes*	8,000
Factory Insurance*	7,000
Factory Supplies Used	15,100
Factory Utilities*	12,000

*The factory building contains a sales showroom that occupies about 30% of the floor space involved.

REQUIRED

(a) Compute a predetermined factory overhead rate applied on the basis of direct labor hours.

(b) Present a general journal entry to apply factory overhead during an interim period when 1,500 direct labor hours were worked.

(c) What amount of overhead would be assigned to job 325, to which $54 in direct labor had been charged?

22–29A Delta Manufacturing had the following inventories at the end of its last fiscal year:

Materials Inventory	$6,000
Work in Process Inventory	5,000
Finished Goods Inventory	9,000

During the first month of the current year, the following transactions occurred:

(1) Purchased materials on account, $20,000.

(2) Incurred factory payroll, $32,000.

(3) Requisitioned total materials of $18,000, of which $3,000 was considered factory supplies.

(4) Assigned total factory payroll, of which $5,000 was considered indirect labor.

(5) Incurred other factory overhead, $12,000. (Credit Accounts Payable.)

(6) Applied factory overhead on the basis of 80% of direct labor costs.

(7) Determined ending work in process, $9,000.
(8) Determined ending finished goods, $16,000.

REQUIRED
(a) Prepare general journal entries to record these transactions.
(b) If the above transactions covered a full year's operations and the over- or underapplied overhead was considered material, present a journal entry to allocate the overhead account balance to the appropriate accounts in proportion to their ending balances. Round computations to the nearest dollar.

22–30A At the beginning of the current year, the Porter Company estimated that it would incur $30,000 of factory overhead cost during the year, using 10,000 direct labor hours to produce the desired volume of goods. On January 1 of the current year, beginning balances of Materials Inventory, Work in Process, and Finished Goods Inventory were $10,000, $–0–, and $17,000, respectively.

REQUIRED
Prepare general journal entries to record the following transactions for the current year:
(a) Purchased materials on account, $24,000.
(b) Of the total dollar value of materials used, $20,000 represented raw materials and $5,000 were factory supplies used.
(c) Determined total factory labor, $72,000 (12,000 hr @ $6/hr).
(d) Of the factory labor, 75% was direct and 25% indirect.
(e) Applied factory overhead based on direct labor hours to work in process.
(f) Determined actual factory overhead other than those items already recorded, $5,500. (Credit Accounts Payable.)
(g) Ending inventories of work in process and finished goods were $11,000 and $23,000, respectively. (Make separate entries.)
(h) Closed the balance in Factory Overhead to Cost of Goods Sold.

22–32A The following summary of job cost sheets relates to the production of Norton Manufacturing, Inc. during the first month of the current operating year. Norton uses the same overhead rate for all jobs.

Job No.	Raw Materials	Direct Labor	Factory Overhead
109	$ 400	$ 500	$ 350
110	700	350	245
111	1,800	1,500	1,050
112	1,200	900	630
113	500	400	280

Job 109 was in process at the end of the preceding year, when it had incurred direct labor charges of $140 and total charges of $448. Job 113 is the current month's ending work in process.

REQUIRED
(a) What is the apparent factory overhead rate?
(b) Determine the total of raw materials requisitioned in the current month.

(c) What is the total direct labor incurred in the current month?
(d) If factory overhead is overapplied by $400 at the end of the current month, what is the total factory overhead incurred during the month?
(e) If finished goods inventory increased during the month by $600, what is the cost of goods sold for the month?

22–33A Summarized data for the first month's operations of Castle Casting Foundry are presented below. A job order costing system is used.
(1) Materials purchased on account, $32,000.
(2) Amounts of materials requisitioned and foundry labor used:

Job No.	Materials	Foundry Labor
1	$1,700	$1,300
2	1,900	2,200
3	1,400	3,300
4	5,100	4,500
5	2,400	2,600
6	1,400	700
Foundry supplies used	4,200	
Indirect labor		6,200

(3) Foundry overhead is applied at the rate of 150% of direct labor costs.
(4) Miscellaneous foundry overhead incurred:

Prepaid foundry insurance written off	$ 700
Property taxes on foundry building accrued	1,400
Foundry utilities payable accrued	1,600
Depreciation on foundry equipment	3,100
Other costs incurred on account	5,400

(5) Ending work in process consisted of jobs 4 and 6.
(6) Jobs 1 and 3 and one-half of job 2 were sold on account for $9,000, $12,000, and $7,000, respectively.

REQUIRED
(a) Open general ledger T accounts for Materials Inventory, Foundry Payroll, Foundry Overhead, Work in Process Inventory, Finished Goods Inventory, and Cost of Goods Sold. Also set up subsidiary T accounts as job cost sheets for each job.
(b) Prepare general journal entries to record the summarized transactions for the month, and post appropriate entries to any accounts listed in part (a). Key each entry to the related parenthetical letter in the problem data.
(c) Determine the balances of any accounts necessary and prepare schedules of jobs in ending work in process and jobs in ending finished goods to confirm that they agree with the related control accounts.

BUSINESS DECISION PROBLEM

Douglas Manufacturing Company plans to make and sell a newly designed fuel director valve for use in small aircraft manufactured by other companies. If made with traditional materials, the valve would require the following raw materials and labor:

Materials
A   5 lb @ $2.50 each
B   6 lb @ $3.50 each
C   4 lb @ $6.50 each
Labor
Casting   3 hr @ $5/hr
Finishing   3 hr @ $6/hr
Assembling   2 hr @ $7/hr

Overhead costs in these departments should be $10 per direct labor hour.

Management may also use a new synthetic material, D, perfected in space technology. Making the body of the valve out of material D would alter the cost and manufacturing procedures as follows: Eight pounds of D, costing $5.50 per pound, would replace both materials A and B. Casting and finishing labor time would be reduced by 50%. However, each valve would require four hours of machining labor costing $10 per hour and performed on a highly specialized, partially automated machine. Factory overhead in the machining department is applied at the rate of $6 per machine hour.

Douglas' marketing department advises management that the valve made of traditional materials would sell for 50% over the company's cost and that aircraft manufacturers would pay an additional 20% for the valve made of the new lightweight material D.

REQUIRED
Based on the relative gross profit per unit, present an analysis showing the relative advantage of the manufacturing alternative you recommend regarding use of the new material.

23

Cost Accounting Systems:
Process Costing

Value is the life giving power of everything: cost, the quantity of labor required to produce it; price, the quantity of labor which its possessor will take in exchange for it.

MUNERA PULVERIS

This chapter explains and illustrates the concepts and procedures typical of a process costing system that involves more than one processing department. The concluding sections deal with the related concerns of accounting for the costs of service departments, joint products, and byproducts.

In Chapter 22, we explained that a process costing system is appropriate in accounting for costs in the production of a large volume of relatively homogeneous products manufactured in a "continuous flow" operation. Producers of fuel, chemicals, cement, paint, and similar goods find this system useful.

In job order costing—when production is discontinuous or when materials and operations performed vary with products—costs must be identified with the specific job or order being produced before unit costs can be determined. In contrast, costs in a process system are identified with a **cost center** (a processing or production department) *during a period of time*—usually a month. Monthly costs are accumulated in separate Work in Process accounts for each processing or production department. At month-end, costs are summarized for each cost center in a **cost of production report.** This report provides the unit cost information that can be used to determine costs of goods transferred from process to process and finally into the finished goods inventory. Therefore, a job order system has one Work in Process account supported by a number of job order cost sheets, and a process system has several Work in Process accounts, each supported by a monthly cost of production report.

Exhibit 23–1 illustrates process cost flows for a liquid product, the production of which involves only two successive processes—mixing and bottling. To simplify the illustration, we assume no incomplete production in process at the beginning or end of the period. Note the following in the exhibit (the various costs are accumulated as debit balances in the Materials Inventory, Factory Payroll, and Factory Overhead accounts in much the same manner as in Chapter 22):

(1) Except that more than one Work in Process account exists, process cost flows are parallel to those illustrated for job order costing systems.

(2) Each work-in-process department may incur varying amounts of raw material, direct labor, and factory overhead costs.

(3) In sequential processes, the costs of prior departments are transferred to and become part of the total cost incurred by the subsequent department.

(4) The cumulative cost of completed production is transferred to Finished Goods Inventory and, on sale, is transferred to Cost of Goods Sold.

Let us now examine how to account for these costs.

EXHIBIT 23–1
Illustration of Cost Flows and Process Costing System

Materials Inventory			Work in Process— Mixing Department		
	(Materials requisitions) 3,000	Raw materials 1,400 Direct labor 2,000 Factory overhead 800	(Cost of completed goods to Bottling) 4,200	
			4,200	4,200	

Factory Payroll	
	(Factory labor distribution) 3,700

Factory Overhead			Work in Process— Bottling Department			Finished Goods Inventory	
	(Factory overhead allocations) 2,600	(Cost from Mixing) 4,200 Raw materials 1,600 Direct labor 1,700 Factory overhead 1,800	(Cost of completed goods to Finished Goods Inventory) 9,300	(Cost from Bottling) 9,300	(When sold, to Cost of Goods Sold)
		9,300	9,300		

DETERMINING UNIT COSTS

To trace the cost of products transferred from one processing department to another and eventually into finished goods, we must calculate unit costs. If unit costs are calculated on a monthly basis, a firm can compare its current costs with those of prior periods and determine when cost control measures are needed.

Unit cost determination is basically an averaging process. For example, assume that during January of the current year, the Mixing Department incurred $1,400 of raw materials cost, $2,000 of direct labor cost, and $800 of overhead cost in processing 800 gallons of product. The unit cost for each gallon would be

$$\frac{\text{Total Costs for January}}{\text{Total Work Accomplished}} = \frac{\$4,200}{800 \text{ gallons}} = \$5.25 \text{ per gallon}$$

Equivalent Units

In the above computation, we assumed that the 800 gallons were begun and completed during the month. Suppose, however, that unfinished units were in process at the beginning and end of the period. Assume that, of the 800 gallons handled during January, 200 were 25% complete in December and 100 were 50% complete at the end of January. Clearly, determining the January unit cost by treating all 800 gallons as if they had been started and finished in January is incorrect. Instead, we should convert the processing done on 800 gallons into a smaller number of **equivalent units** of completed product. For example, 100 gallons 50% completed during the period are equivalent to 50 gallons begun and completed; 200 gallons 75% completed are equivalent to 150 gallons begun and completed, and so on. In our example, we would calculate the equivalent units of work for January as follows:

	Total Units Involved (gallons)		Proportion Completed This Month		Equivalent Units
From beginning inventory	200	×	75%	=	150
Begun and finished in January	500	×	100%	=	500
Begun but not finished in January	100	×	50%	=	50
	800				700

If we assume that materials, labor, and overhead are added gradually throughout processing, the correct unit cost for January would be

$$\frac{\text{Total Costs for January}}{\text{Equivalent Units Processed}} = \frac{\$4,200}{700 \text{ gallons}} = \$6 \text{ per gallon}$$

Unit cost calculations may be complicated by the fact that in many manufacturing operations materials are added at a different rate or at a different time than are labor and overhead (which together are called *conversion costs*). For example, materials may be added at the beginning of the process, while conversion costs are added evenly throughout the process. In this case, the number of equivalent units used to calculate the unit cost of materials in a batch of product is different from the number used to compute the unit cost of conversion.

Exhibit 23–2 graphically presents the revised computation of equivalent units when all materials are added initially and conversion costs are incurred evenly throughout the process. Because all materials for beginning work in process were added during the previous period (when these units were started), this batch has no equivalent units for materials in this period. However, any unit of product begun this period has all materials added this period, so the 500 units begun and completed and the 100 units only begun (ending work in process) are assigned full equivalent units for materials. For conversion costs, (1) the 200 units in beginning work in process represent only 150 (75% × 200) equivalent units because only the final 75% of processing occurred this period; (2) each of the 500 units of product begun and completed this period equals one equivalent unit because all conversion was accomplished this period; and (3) the 100 units in ending work in process equal only 50 (50% × 100) equivalent units because only one-half of their processing was accomplished this period. Under these assumptions, the number of equivalent units completed for the period is not the same for materials as for conversion costs. Consequently, the computation of cost per

EXHIBIT 23–2
Graphic Illustration of Equivalent Units:
Raw Materials Added Initially; Conversion Incurred Evenly Throughout Period

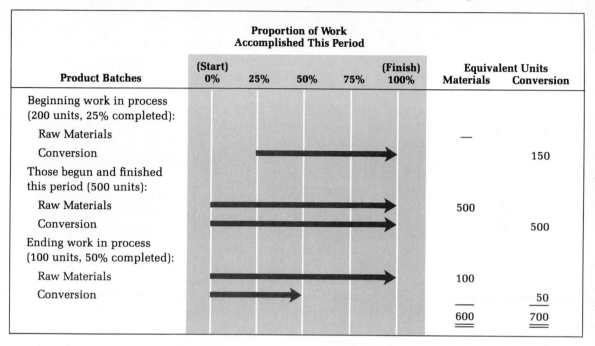

Product Batches	Proportion of Work Accomplished This Period					Equivalent Units	
	(Start) 0%	25%	50%	75%	(Finish) 100%	Materials	Conversion
Beginning work in process (200 units, 25% completed):							
Raw Materials						—	
Conversion							150
Those begun and finished this period (500 units):							
Raw Materials						500	
Conversion							500
Ending work in process (100 units, 50% completed):							
Raw Materials						100	
Conversion							50
						600	700

equivalent unit requires separate calculations for the two cost components, which are then totaled. In our illustration, these are:

$$\frac{\text{Raw Materials Cost}}{\text{Equivalent Units}} = \frac{\$1,400}{600} = \$2.333 \text{ for materials}$$

$$\frac{\text{Conversion Costs}}{\text{Equivalent Units}} = \frac{\$2,000 + \$800}{700} = \$4.000 \text{ for conversion}$$

Total cost for a unit processed this period $\underline{\$6.333}$

Note again that equivalent unit costs are average costs for a specfic period and are derived by dividing the total costs for the period by the related amount of work accomplished during that period.

COST FLOWS ILLUSTRATED

For an example of the operation of a process costing system, assume that the Kleenup Company produces an industrial cleanser called Kleeno, which it markets in one-gallon bottles. Kleeno's production involves two processing departments—the Mixing Department and the Bottling Department. In the Mixing

Department, various ingredients are added at the start of the process, and conversion costs are incurred evenly throughout processing. In the Bottling Department, where the cleanser is bottled, labeled, and placed in cartons, both raw materials and conversion costs are assumed to occur evenly throughout the process. The company uses a predetermined overhead rate of 50% of direct labor costs in both departments. On June 1, the Mixing Department had 6,000 gallons, one-third complete with respect to conversion costs; this inventory cost $8,400. No inventory was in the Bottling Department on June 1.

Materials

On June 1, the firm had a $15,000 balance in the Materials Inventory account, and during June it purchased $20,000 worth of materials on account. A summary entry for June purchases would be

Materials Inventory	20,000	
Accounts Payable		20,000
To record June materials purchased.		

The raw materials requisitioned during June for each processing department and the supplies for general factory use are shown in the following summary entry:

Work in Process—Mixing Department	26,000	
Work in Process—Bottling Department	2,100	
Factory Overhead	3,000	
Materials Inventory		31,100
To record materials and supplies		
used in June.		

Labor

The factory payroll for June indicated that direct labor costs were $28,000 in the Mixing Department, and $8,400 in the Bottling Department. Indirect labor costs of supervisors amounted to $7,000. The following summary entry distributes these costs:

Work in Process—Mixing Department	28,000	
Work in Process—Bottling Department	8,400	
Factory Overhead	7,000	
Factory Payroll		43,400
To distribute June payroll.		

In recording the payroll, the accountant would have made an earlier debit to the Factory Payroll account for the $43,400 and credited various liabilities for amounts withheld and net wages. We ignore this entry here to keep our illustration simple.

Factory Overhead

So far, we have charged $3,000 of factory supplies and $7,000 of indirect labor to the Factory Overhead account. Assume that other overhead costs (maintenance, power, depreciation, and so on) total $8,300. In recording these amounts, we credit various accounts such as Accumulated Depreciation, Accounts Payable, and Prepaid Expenses. For simplicity, we credit Other Accounts in the following summary entry:

Factory Overhead	8,300	
Other Accounts		8,300
To record various factory expenses.		

The Kleenup Company allocates factory overhead to each department at a rate of 50% of direct labor costs. (As explained in Chapter 22, a firm determines this rate at the beginning of the year by estimating factory overhead and direct labor costs.) The following entry charges the Mixing and Bottling Departments with factory overhead:

Work in Process—Mixing Department		
(50% of $28,000)	14,000	
Work in Process—Bottling Department		
(50% of $8,400)	4,200	
Factory Overhead		18,200
To charge estimated overhead to		
processing departments.		

NEAR WORKERLESS FACTORIES

The clean, brightly colored building contains rows of large, complex machining centers, each serviced by a series of robot arms and remotely guided conveyor belts and carts. Through closed-circuit television, a supervisor monitors perhaps 10 or 12 machining centers that turn out high-quality, precision-machined metal parts. During the day, a skeleton crew of supervisors and maintenance personnel work with the machines; the machines work virtually alone during the night. Such is the scenario in modern automated factories utilizing "flexible manufacturing systems" (FMS). Some of these factories exist in the United States, but most can be found in Japan.*

FMS is the latest stage in the evolution of automated machines that began about 30 years ago when a machine's operation was guided through relatively crude digital-based taped instructions. Intervening years have seen first computer-aided design and then computer-aided manufacturing. A major advantage of FMS is the capacity to be quickly and easily reprogrammed to produce different products. Hence, relatively small batches of many different products may now be manufactured. Because fixed manufacturing systems require extensive down-time and expense to retool and realign for changes in products, only large batches of identical products are feasible. In contrast, FMS can be applied to a wide array of products and production volumes.

As expected, FMS installations are comparatively costly. However, the relative productivity of FMS easily passes cost effectiveness criteria. In some cases, the FMS approach requires only 10% of the labor and production time and perhaps only one-fourth the number of machines required by traditional manufacturing procedures. Potential profits to be generated by FMS are just as spectacular.

FMS installations are more widely used for machining than for assembling processes. Apparently, all but the more routine assembly of a small number of components are still best done by human hands. As technology improves, the capacity of FMS to handle complex assembly processes will improve.

Development of FMS rests heavily on computer technology, other microcircuitry technology, the availability of highly skilled labor, and sufficient capital to fund purchase and installation. Companies—and nations—dominating the FMS phenomenon will certainly be tough competitors. Most people living today will probably have their standards of living affected by the technological revolution known as FMS.

*For an interesting version of these and related events, see Gene Bylinsky, "The Race to the Automated Factory," *Fortune*, February 21, 1983, pages 52–64.

Actual costs charged to the Factory Overhead account total $18,300, but the foregoing entry allocates only $18,200 to the processing departments, resulting in $100 of underapplied overhead. Recall that accumulated amounts of under- or overapplied overhead can be carried as deferred balance sheet charges or credits until year-end and then either closed to Cost of Goods Sold or allocated among the inventories and Cost of Goods Sold (see Chapter 22, page 797). At this point, the two Work in Process accounts contain the following amounts as debit entries:

	Mixing Department	Bottling Department
Beginning Balance	$ 8,400	$ –0–
Raw Materials	26,000	2,100
Direct Labor	28,000	8,400
Factory Overhead	14,000	4,200
	$76,400	$14,700

In accounting for the operations of each department, we account for the total amounts of these charges either as the costs attached to goods transferred out or as the cost of ending work-in-process inventory.

COST OF GOODS TRANSFERRED OUT AND INVENTORIES

We have explained how raw materials, labor, and overhead costs are charged to the Work in Process accounts for each processing department. Now we determine cost of goods transferred out and goods remaining uncompleted.[1] Exhibit 23–3 shows the June production report for the two processing departments. Note the following key observations regarding the production report:

(1) All unit figures are in whole gallons rather than equivalent units.

(2) The beginning work in process (6,000) plus units started (26,000) constitute the total number of units to be accounted for (32,000). The 32,000 units are accounted for as units transferred out (24,000) plus units in ending work in process (8,000).

(3) Units started (26,000) minus units in ending work-in-process inventory (8,000) constitute the units started *and* completed (18,000) in that period.

(4) As the arrow indicates, the number of units transferred out of the Mixing Department (24,000) is equal to the number of units transferred into the Bottling Department (24,000).

We now examine how costs are allocated to the various units, beginning with the Mixing Department.

---

[1] Calculations can be performed on either the first-in, first-out (FIFO) or weighted average basis. We illustrate the FIFO basis in this chapter.

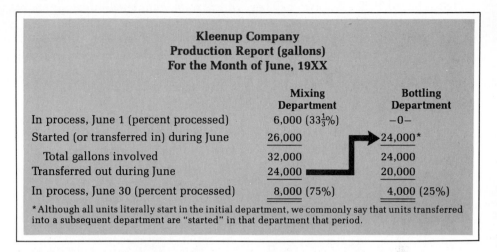

EXHIBIT 23-3

Kleenup Company
Production Report (gallons)
For the Month of June, 19XX

	Mixing Department	Bottling Department
In process, June 1 (percent processed)	6,000 (33⅓%)	-0-
Started (or transferred in) during June	26,000	24,000*
Total gallons involved	32,000	24,000
Transferred out during June	24,000	20,000
In process, June 30 (percent processed)	8,000 (75%)	4,000 (25%)

*Although all units literally start in the initial department, we commonly say that units transferred into a subsequent department are "started" in that department that period.

Mixing Department

Remember that in the Mixing Department, raw materials are added at the start of the mixing process, but conversion costs are incurred evenly throughout the process. Therefore, we must calculate equivalent units and cost per equivalent unit separately for raw materials and conversion costs. For the Mixing Department, these are as follows:

	Total Units Involved	Conversion Completed This Month	Equivalent Units Raw Materials (added initially)	Conversion (added throughout)
Transferred Out:				
From June 1 inventory	6,000	⅔	-0-	4,000
Started and completed	18,000	1	18,000	18,000
Total transferred out	24,000			
June 30 Inventory:	8,000	¾	8,000	6,000
Total units involved	32,000			
Total equivalent units			26,000	28,000
Related Costs:				
Raw materials			$26,000	
Direct labor and overhead				$42,000
Equivalent Unit Costs:				
Raw materials ($26,000/26,000)			$1.00	
Conversion ($42,000/28,000)				$1.50

In allocating costs to various units of product, three batches of Kleeno are considered: (1) units completed from the June 1 inventory, (2) units begun and completed in June, and (3) units begun but not completed in June. The cost of the first two batches, which were completed during June, are transferred to the Bottling Department in June, whereas the cost of the third batch is assigned to the Mixing Department's ending inventory. The cost allocation is shown in the Mixing Department's June cost of production report in Exhibit 23–4.

The composition of costs for the three batches of product handled by the Mixing Department can be explained as follows:

(1) Beginning inventory The 6,000 gallons in the beginning inventory had all the raw materials and one-third of the required work added in May, for an $8,400 total cost in that month. The remaining two-thirds of the work was completed in June. We multiply the conversion cost of a full unit ($1.50) by

EXHIBIT 23–4

Kleenup Company
Mixing Department
Cost of Production Report
For the Month of June, 19XX

Costs to Be Accounted for:			Current Equivalent Units	Unit Cost
Beginning work in process		$ 8,400		
Raw materials		26,000	26,000	$1.00
Conversion costs:				
Direct labor	$28,000			
Factory overhead	14,000	42,000	28,000	1.50
Total costs to account for		$76,400		

Total Units Involved	Allocation of Costs		Total Cost	Unit Cost
6,000	Beginning Inventory (33⅓% processed):			
	Cost from previous month	$ 8,400		
	Raw materials (all added last month)	–0–		
	Conversion (6,000 × 66⅔% × $1.50)	6,000	$14,400	$2.40
18,000	Units Started and Completed:			
	Raw materials (18,000 × $1.00)	$18,000		
	Conversion (18,000 × $1.50)	27,000	45,000	2.50
24,000	Total Units Transferred Out		$59,400	2.475*
8,000	Ending Inventory (75% processed):			
	Raw materials (8,000 × $1.00)	$ 8,000		
	Conversion (8,000 × 75% × $1.50)	9,000	17,000	
32,000	Totals Accounted for		$76,400	

*To avoid carrying forward multiple unit cost figures (some at $2.40 and some at $2.50), we carry forward all units completed in a period at a combined average unit cost figure ($2.475).

the equivalent units (4,000 gallons) to obtain the $6,000 cost to complete this batch. Thus, this batch cost $14,400, or $2.40 per unit.

(2) Started and completed in June During June, all required raw materials and work were applied to the 18,000 gallons started and completed. The materials added this month at $1.00 per gallon and a full unit conversion cost of $1.50 are applied to each of the 18,000 units, resulting in a cost of $45,000, or $2.50 per unit. The total cost of the 24,000 gallons in the two batches transferred to the Bottling Department amounts to $59,400, and the average cost of the two batches is $2.475 per gallon ($59,400/24,000).

(3) Ending inventory The 8,000 units begun but not completed in June contain all required raw materials but only three-fourths of the needed work. Therefore, we multiply the per-unit raw materials cost of $1.00 by 8,000 gallons to obtain the $8,000 materials cost. However, we multiply the $1.50 conversion cost by the equivalent units of work performed (8,000 × $\frac{3}{4}$ = 6,000) to obtain the $9,000 conversion cost.

Notice that the cost of production report fully accounts for the 32,000 units of product involved and the total costs of $76,400 charged to the Mixing Department for June.

The following entry transfers the cost of the work completed in the Mixing Department during June:

Work in Process—Bottling Department	59,400	
Work in Process—Mixing Department		59,400
To transfer cost of completed work		
from Mixing to Bottling		

The Work in Process account for the Mixing Department would now appear as follows:

Work in Process—Mixing Department

June 1 (beginning balance)	8,400	Transferred to Bottling	
Raw Materials	26,000	Department	59,400
Direct Labor	28,000		
Factory Overhead	14,000		
June 30 (ending balance)	17,000		

Note that all costs charged to this account have been accounted for as either transferred out or ending inventory.

Bottling Department Because this department had no beginning inventory, the units handled during June consisted only of the 24,000 gallons received from the Mixing Department. These units cost $2.475 per gallon, for a total cost of $59,400. We assume that the costs of the added raw materials, labor, and overhead are incurred evenly throughout the bottling process. These costs, totaling $14,700, cannot be averaged over the units handled, because not all of the 24,000 units were completed. Therefore, we must convert the work performed into equivalent units and obtain an equivalent unit cost, as follows:

	Total Units Handled		Conversion Completed This Month		Equivalent Units
Transferred out (all units started and completed in June)	20,000	×	1	=	20,000
June 30 inventory	4,000	×	$\frac{1}{4}$	=	1,000
	24,000				21,000

Total added costs
($2,100 Raw Materials + $8,400 Labor + $4,200 Overhead) $14,700

Equivalent unit cost per gallon ($14,700/21,000) $0.70

The cost allocation for the two batches handled is shown in the Bottling Department's June cost of production report, Exhibit 23–5. The composition of costs for the two batches processed by the Bottling Department can be explained as follows:

(1) Started and completed in June Each of the 20,000 units started and completed during June has a full unit of raw materials, labor, and overhead cost. This 70-cent per unit cost incurred in the Bottling Department can simply be added to the Mixing Department's $2.475 per-gallon cost to obtain the completed unit cost of $3.175 per gallon. Multiplying this amount by 20,000 gallons, we obtain $63,500 as the cost of the goods transferred to the finished goods inventory.

(2) Ending inventory The 4,000 units begun but not completed in June contain a full unit of the Mixing Department's cost ($2.475 per gallon), but are only one-fourth complete in the Bottling Department. Therefore, the Mixing Department unit cost of $2.475 is multiplied by 4,000 gallons to obtain the $9,900 total cost from that department. However, the 70-cent equivalent unit cost of bottling is multiplied by 1,000 gallons (4,000 × $\frac{1}{4}$) to obtain the $700 total bottling cost in the ending inventory.

Observe that the cost allocations in the cost of production report are reflected in the journal entry transferring the cost of completed units ($63,500) to Finished Goods Inventory and as the ending balance of Work in Process—Bottling Department ($10,600).

The following entry transfers the cost of completed work in the Bottling Department during June:

Finished Goods Inventory	63,500	
Work in Process—Bottling Department		63,500
To transfer cost of completed work		
to Finished Goods Inventory.		

EXHIBIT 23-5

Kleenup Company
Bottling Department
Cost of Production Report
For the Month of June, 19XX

			Current Equivalent Units	Unit Cost
Costs to Be Accounted for:				
Beginning work in process		$ –0–		
Transferred from Mixing Department		59,400		
Raw materials	$2,100			
Direct labor	8,400			
Factory overhead	4,200	14,700	21,000	$0.70
Total costs to account for		$74,100		

Total Units Involved	Allocation of Costs		Total Cost	Unit Cost
20,000	Units Started and Completed:			
	Mixing Department costs (20,000 × $2.475)	$49,500		
	Raw materials and conversion			
	(20,000 × $0.70)		14,000 $63,500	$3.175
4,000	Ending Inventory (25% processed):			
	Mixing Department costs (4,000 × $2.475)	$ 9,900		
	Raw materials and conversion			
	(4,000 × 25% × $0.70)		700 10,600	
24,000	Totals Accounted for		$74,100	

The Work in Process account for the Bottling Department would now appear as follows:

Work in Process—Bottling Department

June 1 (beginning balance)	–0–	Transferred to	
Transferred in from		Finished Goods	63,500
Mixing Department	59,400		
Raw Materials	2,100		
Direct Labor	8,400		
Factory Overhead	4,200		
June 30 (ending balance)	10,600		

Again, note that all costs accumulated to this point have been accounted for.

Finished Goods and Cost of Goods Sold

In the cost flows for a process costing system, the journal entries to record sales are similar to those made in a job order system. We assume that during June the Kleenup Company sold goods costing $45,000 for $60,000. In summary form, the following entries reflect the sales:

Accounts Receivable	60,000	
Sales		60,000
To record June sales.		
Cost of Goods Sold	45,000	
Finished Goods Inventory		45,000
To record cost of goods sold in June.		

An Overview of Process Costing

As you review the Kleenup Company example, note these basic patterns and relationships in process costing.

(1) Product costs are accumulated in three pools: raw materials, direct labor, and factory overhead; the latter two are often called conversion costs.

(2) Physical units to be accounted for include any beginning work in process and any units started (or transferred in). Physical units are accounted for by transferring them out or retaining them as ending work in process.

(3) All cost factors, including any beginning inventory costs, are combined as work in process and must be accounted for.

(4) Through equivalent unit computations, the production accomplished in a period is measured in whole units and divided into the related total cost amounts to determine the period's equivalent unit cost.

(5) In addition to any beginning inventory costs, equivalent unit costs for the current period are assigned to units transferred out and ending work in process, the total of which should equal the cost to be accounted for in (3).

ACCOUNTING FOR SERVICE DEPARTMENTS

Most factories are so large and so complex that a high degree of organizational specialization naturally exists in their operations. Production usually involves a series of specialized departments, which may include such finely focused departments as cutting, preshaping, dressing (grinding), subassembly, final assembly, painting, and packaging. In addition to these production departments, a typical factory has a series of highly specialized *service* departments, which may engage in purchasing, materials handling, personnel, warehousing, inspection, power, maintenance, and even factory dispensaries and cafeterias. Whereas production departments work directly on products, service departments provide production departments with support services that contribute indirectly to the completion of products.

Service Departments as Cost Centers

Service departments are often viewed by management as cost centers. As such, the costs of each service department are accumulated so that management can identify the total cost of such services as repairs, building maintenance, and factory power. Also, unit costs for each service—such as maintenance cost per square foot of floor space—can be derived for comparison with other operating periods and/or other sources of the service such as outside contractors. A well-designed accounting system accounts for service departments as cost centers.

Service Department Costs as Product Costs

Although service departments do not perform actual work on specific products, they do provide essential services to the production departments. Thus, service department costs are appropriately considered among the related production department's costs and are included in final product costs. This section explains how service costs are accumulated and assigned to individual products.

By their nature, service departments do not use raw materials or direct labor. Their costs are part of factory overhead. However, these departments do not work directly on a product, so overhead rates, in the strict sense, are not computed for them. Instead, service department costs are usually allocated to various production departments according to the approximate benefits received by each production department. In other words, service department costs become part of product costs by being allocated among several production departments, using the most appropriate allocation base for each, and becoming part of each production department's overhead to be applied to work in process.

The T-account diagram (with typical titles and amounts) in Exhibit 23–6 illustrates how service department costs: (1) are accumulated on a cost center basis, (2) are allocated to one or more production departments, and (3) become part of the product costs when factory overhead is applied for each production department. To simplify this illustration, we assume these amounts result in no over- or underapplied overhead.

Note that $4,000 is accumulated as the total cost for the Maintenance Department, then $1,000 and $3,000 are allocated to the Mixing and Bottling departments, respectively. The allocated service department costs are in turn included in the totals of $18,000 and $12,000 of overhead costs applied from the respective production departments. Similar observations can be made for the Power Department.

Method of Cost Allocation

Costs are allocated among various departments on a base that reflects the proportion of the service or activity that benefits each department. Some examples of allocated costs and their possible allocation bases are listed below:

Service Cost	Possible Allocation Base
Personnel salaries	Number of employees in each department
Building depreciation	Square feet of floor space used
Power	Machine hours used
Building maintenance	Square feet of floor space used
Machine maintenance	Machine hours used
Heat and light	Cubic feet of building space used

EXHIBIT 23–6
Allocation of Service Department Costs
to Production Departments' Overhead Accounts

Maintenance Department (a service department)				Power Department (a service department)			
(Various costs either identifiable with or allocated to this service department)	4,000	Allocated to: Mixing Bottling	1,000 3,000	(Various costs either identifiable with or allocated to this service department)	6,000	Allocated to: Mixing Bottling	4,000 2,000
	4,000		4,000		6,000		6,000

Factory Overhead—Mixing Department				Factory Overhead—Bottling Department			
(Various overhead costs either identifiable with or allocated to this production department) Allocations from:	13,000	Applied to Work in Process	18,000	(Various overhead costs either identifiable with or allocated to this production department) Allocations from:	7,000	Applied to Work in Process	12,000
Maintenance Department	1,000			Maintenance Department	3,000		
Power Department	4,000			Power Department	2,000		
	18,000		18,000		12,000		12,000

Work in Process—Mixing Department			Work in Process—Bottling Department	
Raw Materials	XX		Raw Materials	XX
Direct Labor	XX		Direct Labor	XX
Factory Overhead	18,000		Factory Overhead	12,000

Of course, the concern for cost control may justify the use of elaborate devices and schemes to measure service benefits. Some examples are departmental electric meters, vouchers or tickets reflecting actual hours of services requested and used, and elaborate weighting techniques in which requests for rush or peak hour services are assigned higher costs than requests honored at the convenience of the service department.

To allocate a particular cost, we simply divide the total cost among a series of departments in proportion to departmental shares of the appropriate base activity. For example, suppose that $8,000 of personnel department cost is allocated between a mixing department with 15 employees and a bottling department with 25 employees. The number of production employees is the allocation base. The two distinct steps involved and illustrative calculations follow:

(1)
$$\frac{\text{Total Cost to Be Allocated}}{\text{Total Allocation Base}} = \text{Allocation Rate}$$

$$\frac{\$8,000}{40\,\text{employees}} = \$200\,\text{per employee}$$

(2)
$$\frac{\text{Allocation}}{\text{Rate}} \times \frac{\text{Amount of Allocation Base}}{\text{Related to Department}} = \frac{\text{Specific Amount}}{\text{Allocated}}$$

$$\$200 \times 15\,\text{employees} = \$3,000\,\text{(for mixing)}$$
$$\$200 \times 25\,\text{employees} = \$5,000\,\text{(for bottling)}$$

As a final step, we should check allocations and verify that the sum of allocated amounts equals the total amount allocated.

Exhibit 23–7 illustrates a worksheet often used to accumulate and allocate factory overhead in a multidepartment factory operation that includes service departments. Note the following:

(1) Three categories of costs are involved:
  (a) Those directly identifiable with departments.
  (b) Those requiring allocations to departments.
  (c) Service department costs allocated to production departments.

(2) A total overhead amount is first accumulated for each service department and each production department.

(3) After service department costs are allocated, the total overhead is assigned to the production departments only.

(4) The final amounts assigned to each production department are used to calculate departmental overhead rates. (See the footnotes to Exhibit 23–7).

The amounts, proportions, and variety of costs shown in Exhibit 23–7 have been chosen for simplicity of presentation to stress the basic concepts.

Obviously, we might ask why service department costs are not allocated to other service departments. More sophisticated allocation techniques may involve allocations of some service department costs to other service departments and even mutual assignment of all of one or more service departments' costs to all other service departments. In many instances, these refinements do not result in materially different allocations; such detailed discussions are beyond our present objectives.

EXHIBIT 23–7

Overhead Distribution Worksheet For the Year Ended December 31, 19XX						
		Service Departments		Production Departments		Accounting Record or Allocation Base
	Totals	Building Maintenance	Machine Repairs	Mixing	Bottling	
Directly Identifiable with Departments						
Indirect labor	85,000	8,000	20,000	38,500	18,500	Factory payroll analysis
Factory supplies used	24,000	3,000	2,000	9,000	10,000	Requisition forms
Allocated to Departments						
Building depreciation	6,000	600	1,200	3,000	1,200	Square feet of floor space
Personal property taxes	4,000	400	800	1,500	1,300	Assessed value of equipment used
Total Manufacturing Overhead	119,000	12,000	24,000	52,000	31,000	
Allocation of Service Departments						
Building maintenance (assumed as $\frac{2}{3}$ for mixing and $\frac{1}{3}$ for bottling)		(12,000)		8,000	4,000	Square feet of factory area used .
Machinery repairs (assumed as $\frac{1}{6}$ for mixing and $\frac{5}{6}$ for bottling)			(24,000)	4,000	20,000	Machine hours
Totals	119,000			64,000*	55,000**	

*Assuming a factory overhead allocation base of 20,000 machine hours, the overhead rate for the Mixing Department is $3.20 per machine hour ($64,000/20,000 machine hours).
**Assuming a factory overhead allocation base of $110,000 direct labor, the overhead rate for the Bottling Department is 50 cents per direct labor dollar (or $55,000/$110,000 direct labor).

JOINT PRODUCTS

Often, the processing of raw materials results in two or more products of significant commercial value. Such products derived from a common input are **joint products,** and the related cost of the raw materials is a **joint cost.** An obvious example of a raw material whose processing results in joint products is crude oil, from which a variety of fuels, solvents, lubricants, and residual petrochemical pitches are derived. Cattle, from which the meat packer obtains many cuts and grades of meat, hides, and other products, are another example.

It is impossible to allocate a joint cost among joint products in such a way that management can decide whether to continue production or what price to charge for a joint product. To decide to produce one joint product is to decide to produce all related joint products, even if some are discarded. Therefore, to make informed decisions about joint products, management must compare the total revenue generated by all joint products with their total production costs.

The primary reason for allocating a joint cost among two or more products is to price the ending inventories of joint products when determining periodic income. The most popular method of allocating joint costs for inventory pricing purposes is the **relative sales value** method. Like the cost allocations explained earlier, this approach uses arithmetic proportions. The total joint cost is allocated to the several joint products in the proportions of their individual sales values to the total sales value of all joint products at the split-off point—that is, where physical separation is possible. For example, assume that 50,000 55-gallon barrels of crude oil costing $1,200,000 are processed into 800,000 gallons of fuel selling for 75 cents per gallon; 400,000 gallons of lubricants selling for $2 per gallon; and 1,000,000 gallons of petrochemical residues selling for 20 cents per gallon. The following calculations illustrate the joint cost allocation using the relative sales value approach:

Joint Products	Quantity Produced (gallons)	Unit Sales Value	Product Sales Value	Proportion of Total Sales Value
Fuel	800,000	$0.75	$ 600,000	6/16
Lubricants	400,000	2.00	800,000	8/16
Residues	1,000,000	0.20	200,000	2/16
Total sales value			$1,600,000	16/16

Allocations of total and per-unit joint costs would be

	Proportion of Materials Cost	Allocated Cost	Quantity Produced	Cost per Unit
Fuel	6/16 × $1,200,000	$ 450,000 ÷	800,000 =	$0.5625 per gallon
Lubricants	8/16 × $1,200,000	600,000 ÷	400,000 =	$1.50 per gallon
Residues	2/16 × $1,200,000	150,000 ÷	1,000,000 =	$0.15 per gallon
		$1,200,000		

Note that the relative sales value approach results in assigned unit costs that are the same percentage of the selling price for each product. In our illustration, the cost per unit equals 75% of the sales value per unit.

BYPRODUCTS

Byproducts have relatively little sales value compared with the other products derived from a particular process. Byproducts are considered incidental to the manufacture of the more important products. For example, the sawdust and shavings generated in a lumber planing mill or in a furniture factory's cutting department are byproducts.

We may account for byproducts by assigning them a cost equal to their sales value less any disposal costs. This net amount is charged to an inventory account for the byproduct and credited to the work in process account that was charged with the original materials. For example, consider a furniture factory in which walnut boards are processed through a cutting and shaping department. In processing $40,000 worth of lumber, 800 bushels of sawdust and shavings are generated, which, after treatment costing $80, can be sold for $1 per bushel. The following accounts illustrate the amounts and entries involved:

Work in Process— Cutting and Shaping Department		Inventory of Walnut Sawdust and Shavings	
Raw Materials	Byproduct	720	
40,000	Recovery 720		

This procedure reduces the costs of the main products by the net amount recovered from byproducts.

DEMONSTRATION PROBLEM FOR REVIEW

Luster, Inc. produces a liquid furniture polish in two sequential processes organized as the Mixing Department and the Bottling Department. Raw materials are added initially in the Mixing Department; all other costs in both departments are incurred evenly throughout the processes. The following are cost data for May:

	Mixing Department	Bottling Department
Beginning work in process inventory	$ 588	$–0–
May's operating costs:		
Raw materials	2,400	650
Direct labor	3,500	2,600
Factory overhead	1,400	1,950
	$7,888	$5,200

Beginning work in process consisted of 800 gallons, 50% processed; 8,000 gallons were started in the Mixing Department. Ending work-in-process inventories were 2,000 gallons, 30% processed, in the Mixing Department and 400 gallons, 25% processed, in the Bottling Department.

REQUIRED

(a) Prepare a production report for May reflecting the activities of both departments.

(b) For each department: (1) calculate the equivalent units accomplished and the equivalent unit costs for May, (2) prepare a cost of production report for May, and (3) prepare journal entries to record the transfer of completed units.

SOLUTION TO DEMONSTRATION PROBLEM

(a)

Luster, Inc.
Production Report (gallons)
For the Month of May, 19XX

	Mixing Department		Bottling Department	
In process, May 1 (percent processed)	800	(50%)	(–0–)	
Started (or transferred in) during May	8,000		6,800	
Total gallons involved	8,800		6,800	
Transferred out during May	6,800		6,400	
In process, May 31 (percent processed)	2,000	(30%)	400	(25%)

(b) (1) (Mixing Department)

	Total Units Involved	Conversion Completed This Month	Equivalent Units Materials (added initially)	Conversion (added throughout)
Transferred Out:				
From May 1 inventory	800	50%	–0–	400
Started and completed	6,000	100%	6,000	6,000
Total transferred out	6,800			
May 31 Inventory:	2,000	30%	2,000	600
Total units involved	8,800			
Total equivalent units			8,000	7,000
Total Related Costs:				
Raw materials			$2,400	
Direct labor and overhead				$4,900
Equivalent Unit Costs:				
Raw materials ($2,400/8,000)			$0.30	
Conversion ($4,900/7,000)				$0.70

(2) (Mixing Department)

Luster, Inc.
Mixing Department
Cost of Production Report
For the Month of May, 19XX

			Current Equivalent	
			Units	Unit Cost
Costs to Be Accounted for:				
Beginning work in process		$ 588		
Raw materials		2,400	8,000	$0.30
Conversion costs:				
Direct labor	$3,500			
Factory overhead	1,400	4,900	7,000	0.70
Total costs to account for		$7,888		

Total Units Involved	Allocation of Costs	Total Cost		Unit Cost
800	Beginning Inventory (50% processed):			
	Cost from previous month	$ 588		
	Raw materials (all added last month)	−0−		
	Conversion (800 × 50% × $0.70)	280	$ 868	$1.085
6,000	Units Started and Completed:			
	Raw materials (6,000 × $0.30)	$1,800		
	Conversion (6,000 × $0.70)	4,200	6,000	1.00
6,800	Total Units Transferred Out		$6,868	1.01
2,000	Ending Inventory (30% processed):			
	Raw materials (2,000 × $0.30)	$ 600		
	Conversion (2,000 × 30% × $0.70)	420	1,020	
8,800	Totals Accounted for		$7,888	

(3) (Mixing Department)

Work in Process—Bottling Department	6,868	
Work in Process—Mixing Department		6,868

To record completion of 6,800 units at a
cost of $1.01 per unit and their transfer to
the Bottling Department.

(b) (1) (Bottling Department)

	Total Units Involved	Conversion Completed This Month	Equivalent Units (all costs added evenly)
Transferred out (all units started and completed in May)	6,400	100%	6,400
May 31 inventory	400	25%	100
Total units involved	6,800		
Total equivalent units			6,500
Total related costs (raw materials, $650; direct labor, $2,600; overhead, $1,950)			$5,200
Equivalent unit cost ($5,200/6,500)			$ 0.80

(2) (Bottling Department)

Luster, Inc.
Bottling Department
Cost of Production Report
For the Month of May, 19XX

			Current Equivalent Units	Unit Cost
Costs to Be Accounted for:				
Beginning work in process		$ –0–		
Transferred from Mixing Department		6,868		
Raw materials	$ 650			
Direct labor	2,600			
Factory overhead	1,950	5,200	6,500	$0.80
Total costs to account for		$12,068		

Total Units Involved	Allocation of Costs	Total Cost		Unit Cost
6,400	Units Started and Completed:			
	Mixing Department costs (6,400 × $1.01)	$6,464		
	Raw materials and conversion (6,400 × $0.80)	5,120	$11,584	$1.81
400	Ending Inventory (25% processed):			
	Mixing Department costs (400 × $1.01)	$ 404		
	Raw materials and conversion (400 × 25% × $0.80)	80	484	
6,800	Totals Accounted for		$12,068	

(3) (Bottling Department)

Finished Goods Inventory	11,584	
Work in Process—Bottling Department		11,584
To record completion of 6,400 units at a		
cost of $1.81 per unit and their transfer to		
Finished Goods Inventory.		

KEY POINTS TO REMEMBER

(1) Process cost accounting averages the total process costs for a period over the related amount of production accomplished during that period.

(2) When ending work-in-process inventory exists, the measurement of work acomplished in a period requires that partially completed units be converted to a smaller number of equivalent units.

(3) When materials are added and conversion is accomplished at different rates (or unevenly), equivalent units must be computed separately for each cost factor.

(4) The manufacturing cost flows and related journal entries are similar for process and job order costing systems.

(5) The total of all costs in beginning inventories and all costs charged to work in process must be accounted for as cost of ending work in process plus cost of goods transferred out.

(6) In assigning manufacturing costs, we consider three batches of products: units transferred out from beginning work-in-process inventories, units both begun and completed this period, and units remaining in ending work-in-process inventories.

(7) The total cost accounted for in a department includes any cost associated with units transferred in from another department.

(8) Service department costs are overhead costs that are allocated to production departments and eventually assigned to products as part of the production departments' overhead.

(9) Joint products are products of significant value originating from a common raw material or process. Joint product costs are allocated among joint products primarily for inventory costing purposes.

(10) Byproducts have relatively insignificant sales values and are assigned costs equal to their net recoverable value, which is removed from the related Work in Process account and charged to an appropriate inventory account.

QUESTIONS

23–1 What are the important differences between job order and process costing systems? Give two examples of industries that might use each system.

23-2 How are all manufacturing costs for a series of processing departments accumulated as finished goods inventory?

23-3 Why do unit cost computations in a manufacturing process require equivalent unit computations?

23-4 Why do we say that process cost accounting is basically an averaging computation?

23-5 What is meant by the term *equivalent unit*?

23-6 Why must we sometimes compute equivalent units separately for raw materials and for conversion costs?

23-7 Describe the three batches of products that are typically involved in a period's production under the FIFO inventory method. In what special situation are there only two batches?

23-8 What is meant by the expression that in each department's Work in Process account all charges must be accounted for either as being transferred out or as ending work-in-process inventory?

23-9 How can the finished products of one department be the raw materials for another department? Give an example.

23-10 Contrast service departments with production departments. Give three examples of service departments.

23-11 Why might service departments be treated as cost centers?

23-12 Explain what each of the following statements means:
(a) Service departments do not work directly on products.
(b) Service department costs are factory overhead costs.
(c) Overhead rates are not used for service departments.
(d) In spite of part (c), service department costs become part of product costs.

23-13 How do we choose a base for allocating a cost to several departments?

23-14 How is an allocation rate calculated? How is the specific amount allocated to a department calculated?

23-15 Briefly describe the general format, data, and calculations that would appear on an overhead distribution worksheet for a company with a number of production and service departments.

23-16 Define *joint product*, and give two examples of industries that have joint products because of the nature of their raw materials.

23-17 If allocated joint costs are irrelevant for management decisions, how do we justify allocating joint costs among joint products?

23-18 Define *byproduct*, and briefly describe an accepted procedure in accounting for them.

EXERCISES

23-19 Scott Corporation makes a powdered rug shampoo concentrate in two sequential departments, Compounding and Drying. The raw materials are added initially in the Compounding Department. All other costs are added evenly throughout each process. In the Compounding Department, beginning work in process was 3,000 pounds (70% processed), 20,000 pounds were started in process, 18,000 pounds transferred out, and ending work in process was 60%

processed. In the Drying Department, there was no beginning work in process, 16,000 pounds were transferred out, and the ending work in process was 40% processed. Prepare a production report for the current month, and calculate the relevant amounts of equivalent units for each department.

23–20 The Mixing Department performs the last of a series of processes in which a fluid chemical is emulsified. Records indicate that the Mixing Department has been charged with $35,000 of transfer-in costs from the Compounding Department and $12,000 of direct labor costs. The factory overhead rate is 150% of direct labor costs. Beginning work in process was $8,200, and ending work in process totaled $5,500. One-half of this period's completed product is sold on account at a price equal to 160% of its cost. Prepare journal entries to record: (1) various costs charged to the Mixing Department this period, (2) transfer of this period's completed product, and (3) sale of one-half of this period's production.

23–21 The following are selected operating data for the Blending Department for April. Tinting and packaging operations are carried out subsequently in other departments.

Beginning inventory	8,000 units, 60% complete
Units both begun and completed	30,000 units
Ending inventory	9,000 units, 30% complete

Calculate the equivalent units accomplished, assuming that
(a) all raw materials are added and conversion accomplished evenly throughout the process;
(b) all raw materials are added initially and conversion costs are incurred evenly throughout.

23–22 In its first month's operation, Department No. 1 incurred charges for raw materials (6,000 units) of $60,000, direct labor of $19,200, and factory overhead of $9,600. At month-end, 4,400 units had been completed and transferred out; those remaining were completed with respect to raw materials but only 25% complete with respect to conversion. Assuming materials are added initially and conversion occurs evenly, compute
(a) The equivalent units for raw materials and conversion.
(b) The equivalent unit costs for raw materials, direct labor, and factory overhead.
(c) The total cost assigned to the units transferred out.
(d) The total cost assigned to the ending inventory. Prove that your solutions to parts (c) and (d) account for the total cost involved.

23–23 Following is the Work in Process account (and certain annotations) for the first of four departments in which Apache Company makes its only product.

Work in Process—Department 1

Beginning Balance (600 units, 70% complete)	8,400	Transferred to Department 2: Beginning Inventory (600 units)	——— (a)
Raw Materials (4,800 units @ $5)	24,000	Current Period's Production (3,600 units)	——— (b)
Direct Labor	27,300		
Factory Overhead	9,420		
Ending Balance [(c) ——— units, 25% complete]	(d) ———		

Assuming that raw materials are added initially and conversion costs are incurred evenly throughout, compute the amounts necessary to fill in the four blanks.

23–24 Following are the June charges (and certain annotations) appearing in the Work in Process account for the Dakota Company's final processing department:

Beginning inventory, (700 units, 40% complete)	$ 4,620
Transferred in from preceding department (5,000 units)	20,000
Direct labor	20,600
Factory overhead applied	10,300

Assuming that conversion costs are incurred evenly throughout and that ending work in process totals 900 units, 70% complete, compute the unit costs for
(a) Goods transferred out from June's beginning inventory.
(b) Goods transferred out from current production.
(c) Ending work-in-process inventory.

23–25 Presented below are certain operating data for the four departments in Joseph Manufacturing Company.

	Service		Production	
	1	2	1	2
Total overhead costs either identifiable with or allocated to each department	$15,000	$24,000	$26,500	$36,000
Square feet of factory floor space			25,000	50,000
Number of factory workers			20	60
Planned direct labor hours for the year			30,000	80,000

Allocate to the two production departments the costs of Service Departments 1 and 2 using as bases, factory floor space and number of workers, respectively. What is the apparent overhead rate for each production department if planned direct labor hours is the overhead application base?

23–26 Nelson, Inc. produces joint products A, B, and C from a common raw material, a batch of which costs $600,000. At the point at which each product is separated, the following quantities and unit sales prices are available.

Product	Quantity (pounds)	Selling Price/Pound
A	36,000	$10.00
B	30,000	24.00
C	120,000	1.00

Using the relative sales value approach, calculate the amount of joint cost assigned to a pound of each product.

PROBLEMS

Note: The firms in all of the following problems use the first-in, first-out method (as illustrated in the chapter) to compute equivalent units and costing inventories.

23–27 Magic Mats, Inc. manufactures quality placemats in three consecutive processing departments: Cutting, Printing, and Packaging. The following information is taken from July's unit product reports:

	Units in Beginning Inventory	Percent Complete	Units Started in July	Units in Ending Inventory	Percent Complete
Cutting Department	3,000	70	17,000	5,000	40
Printing Department	4,000	40	?	6,000	70
Packaging Department	3,000	30	?	4,000	50

Raw materials are added at the start of the process in the Cutting Department and evenly throughout processing in the Packaging Department. No raw materials are used in the Printing Department. Conversion costs are incurred evenly in all processing departments.

REQUIRED
(a) Calculate the number of units started or transferred in during July in the Printing and Packaging Departments.
(b) Calculate the equivalent units of work relating to (1) raw materials and (2) conversion costs in each department.

23–28 Chemex, Inc. produces a film developer in two sequential processes designated Phase I and Phase II. Chemex shut down during June, when all employees took their annual vacations. Production began on July 1. The following operating data apply to July:

	Phase I	Phase II
Units started in process	144,000	
Units transferred in from Phase I		120,000
Units in ending work in process (on the average, 40% processed)	24,000	30,000
Costs charged to departments:		
Raw materials	$258,000	$205,000
Direct labor	74,200	145,000
Factory overhead	56,600	160,000

Assume all manufacturing costs are incurred evenly throughout each process and that three-fourths of July's production was sold on account at a price equal to 160% of its cost.

REQUIRED
(a) Briefly explain the July 31 status of the units started in process during July.
(b) For each department, calculate the equivalent units of production and the equivalent unit costs for July.
(c) Prepare journal entries to record the completion and transfer of products from each department and the sale of three-fourths of July's production.

23–29 The Ranch Restaurant operates a plant that produces its own regionally marketed Super Steak Sauce. The sauce is produced in two processes, blending and bottling. In the Blending Department, all raw materials are added at the start of the process, and labor and overhead are incurred evenly throughout the process. An incomplete Work in Process—Blending Department account for January follows:

Work in Process—Blending Department

January 1 Inventory (3,000 gallons, 60% processed)	16,000	Transferred to Bottling Department (21,000 gallons)	———
January charges:			
Raw Materials (20,000 gallons)	40,000		
Direct Labor	18,300		
Factory Overhead	12,600		
January 31 Inventory (——— gallons, 70% processed)	———		

REQUIRED

Calculate the following amounts:

(a) Number of units in the January 31 inventory.

(b) Equivalent units for calculating unit materials cost and unit conversion cost.

(c) Unit conversion cost for January.

(d) Cost of the units transferred to the Bottling Department.

(e) Cost of the incomplete units in the January 31 inventory.

23–30 The Baker Company processes a food seasoning powder through a Compounding Department and a Packaging Department. In the Packaging Department, costs of raw materials, labor, and overhead are incurred evenly throughout the process. Costs charged to the Packaging Department in August were

Inventory, August 1 (6,000 units, 50% complete)	$ 14,800
Transferred in from Compounding Department (29,000 units)	58,000
Raw materials	6,960
Direct labor	28,020
Factory overhead	13,800
	$121,580

At August 31, 7,000 units were in process, 30% completed.

REQUIRED

Calculate the following for the Packaging Department:

(a) Equivalent units for determining unit processing cost during August.

(b) Equivalent unit processing cost.

(c) Total cost of units transferred to Finished Goods Inventory.

(d) Inventory cost at August 31.

23-31 Winston Laboratories, Inc. produces one of its products in two successive departments. All raw materials are added at the beginning of the process in Department 1; no raw materials are used in Department 2. Conversion costs are incurred evenly in both departments. January 1 inventories are as follows:

Raw Materials	$10,000
Work in Process—Department 1 (2,000 units, 35% complete)	5,400
Work in Process—Department 2	–0–
Finished Goods Inventory (2,000 units @ $6.80)	13,600

During January, the following transactions occurred:
(1) Purchased raw materials on account, $20,000.
(2) Placed 20,000 units of raw materials at $1.10 per unit into process in Department 1.
(3) Distributed total payroll costs—$50,400 of direct labor to Department 1, $21,600 of direct labor to Department 2, and $16,000 of indirect labor to Factory Overhead.
(4) Incurred other actual factory overhead costs, $15,000. (Credit Other Accounts.)
(5) Applied overhead to the two processing departments—$25,200 to Department 1 and $12,600 to Department 2.
(6) Transferred 19,000 completed units from Department 1 to Department 2. The 3,000 units remaining in Department 1 were 20% completed with respect to conversion costs.
(7) Transferred 15,000 completed units from Department 2 to Finished Goods Inventory. The 4,000 units remaining in Department 2 were 75% completed with respect to conversion costs.
(8) Sold 6,000 units on account at $9 per unit. The company uses FIFO inventory costing.

REQUIRED
(a) Record the January transactions in general journal form.
(b) State the balances remaining in the Raw Materials account, in each Work in Process account, and in Finished Goods Inventory.

23-32 Rose Company produces a cosmetic product in three consecutive processes. The costs of Department 2 for May were as follows:

Cost from Department 1		$165,600
Costs added in Department 2:		
Raw materials	$18,900	
Direct labor	27,000	
Factory overhead	10,800	56,700

Department 2 had no May 1 inventory, but it handled the following units during May:

Units transferred in from Department 1	23,000
Units transferred to Department 3	18,000
Units in process, May 31	5,000

Of the units in process on May 31, one-half were 80% complete and one-half 40% complete. Both raw materials and conversion costs occur evenly throughout the process in Department 2.

REQUIRED
Prepare the cost of production report for Department 2 for May.

23–33 The following are selected operating data for the production and service departments of Gossett Company for the current operating period.

| | Departments | | | |
| | Service | | Production | |
	1	2	1	2
Overhead costs (identified by department)				
Factory supplies used	$16,000	$26,800	$ 84,800	$172,000
Indirect labor	$32,400	$48,000	$108,000	$480,000
Square feet of building floor space used	4,800	7,200	12,000	24,000
Assessed value of equipment used	$14,000	$42,000	$ 84,000	$140,000
Cubic yards of factory spaced used			88,000	132,000
Machine hours			51,200	204,800
Direct labor			$125,000	$250,000

Building depreciation of $64,000 is allocated on the basis of square feet of floor space. Personal property taxes of $24,000 are allocated on the basis of assessed values of equipment used. Service Departments 1 and 2 costs are allocated to production departments on the basis of cubic yards of factory space and machine hours, respectively.

REQUIRED
(a) Prepare an overhead distribution worksheet similar to Exhibit 23–7.
(b) Compute the factory overhead rates for Production Departments 1 and 2 using machine hours and direct labor costs, respectively, for allocation bases.

23–34 The Smith Company produces joint products A and B and byproduct B-1 from a common raw material and manufacturing process involving sequential processing departments for blending and distilling. After distilling, the three products are separable and considered finished goods.

Because of the nature of the operation, no beginning or ending work in process inventories exist. For the current period, charges to Work in Process—Distilling Department were

Transferred in from Blending Department	$43,700
Direct labor	11,200
Factory overhead	17,700

REQUIRED
Assume that the following quantities and sales prices are available when the products are separable:

Product	Quantity (pounds)	Unit Price
A	4,000	$ 5.00
B	6,000	10.00
B-1	1,000	1.00*

*Special freight charges of $200 are incurred in selling product B-1 for this price.

(a) Allocate the joint costs to each joint product on the basis of relative sales value.
(b) Prepare journal entries to record the current period's product completion in and transfer from the Distilling Department to Finished Goods Inventory.

ALTERNATE PROBLEMS

23–28A Thomas Corporation produces a shoe polish in two sequential processes designated Phase I and Phase II. Thomas shut down during August, when all employees took their annual vacations. Production began on September 1. The following operating data apply to September:

	Phase I	Phase II
Units started in process	36,000	
Unit transferred in from Phase I		32,000
Unit in ending work in process (on the average, 30% processed)	4,000	8,000
Costs charged to departments:		
Raw materials	$12,100	$22,600
Direct labor	34,600	38,700
Factory overhead	19,700	17,900

Assume all manufacturing costs are incurred evenly throughout each process and that three-fourths of September production was sold on account at a price equal to 140% of its cost.

REQUIRED
(a) Briefly explain the September 30 status of the units started in process during September.
(b) For each department, calculate the equivalent units of production and the equivalent unit costs for September.
(c) Prepare journal entries to record the completion and transfer of products from each department and the sale of three-fourths of September's production.

23–29A Johnson House Restaurant operates a plant that produces its own regionally marketed Johnson Salad Dressing. The dressing is produced in two processes, blending and bottling. In the Blending Department, all raw materials are added at the start of the process, and labor and overhead are incurred evenly throughout the process. An incomplete Work in Process—Blending Department account for January follows:

Work in Process—Blending Department

January 1 Inventory (2,000		Transferred to Bottling	
gallons, 75% complete)	11,000	Department (27,000 gallons)	————
January charges:			
Raw materials (30,000 gallons)	120,000		
Direct labor	33,400		
Factory overhead	29,300		
January 31 Inventory			
(——— gallons, 60% complete)	———		

REQUIRED

Calculate the following amounts:

(a) Number of units in the January 31 inventory.

(b) Equivalent units for calculating unit raw materials cost and unit conversion cost.

(c) Unit conversion cost for January.

(d) Cost of the units transferred to the Bottling Department.

(e) Cost of the incomplete units in the January 31 inventory.

23–30A The Bonilla Company processes a scouring powder through a Compounding Department and a Packaging Department. In the Packaging Department, costs of raw materials, labor, and overhead are incurred evenly throughout the process. Costs charged to the Packaging Department in October were

Inventory, October 1 (4,000 units, 25% complete)	$ 7,800
Transferred in from Compounding Department	
(38,000 units)	64,600
Raw materials	10,600
Direct labor	14,000
Factory overhead	9,600
	$106,600

At October 31, 6,000 units were in process, 50% completed.

REQUIRED

Calculate the following for the Packaging Department:

(a) Equivalent units for determining unit processing cost during October.

(b) Equivalent unit processing cost.

(c) Total cost of units transferred to Finished Goods Inventory.

(d) Inventory cost at October 31.

23–31A Denton Laboratories, Inc. produces one of its products in two successive departments. All raw materials are added at the beginning of the process in Department 1; no raw materials are used in Department 2. Conversion costs are incurred evenly in both departments. August 1 inventories are as follows:

Raw Materials	$ 5,000
Work in Process—Department 1 (6,000 units, 25% complete)	6,125
Work in Process—Department 2	–0–
Finished Goods Inventory (4,000 units @ $3.30)	13,200

During August, the following transactions occurred:

(1) Purchased raw materials on account, $17,000.

(2) Placed 16,000 units of raw materials at $1.25 per unit into process in Department 1.

(3) Distributed total payroll costs—$28,275 of direct labor to Department 1, $14,960 of direct labor to Department 2, and $6,700 of indirect labor to Factory Overhead.

(4) Incurred other actual factory overhead costs, $9,700. (Credit Other Accounts.)

(5) Applied overhead to the two processing departments: Department 1, $5,850; Department 2, $3,740.

(6) Transferred 20,000 completed units from Department 1 to Department 2. The 2,000 units remaining in Department 1 were 50% completed with respect to conversion costs.

(7) Transferred 15,000 completed units from Department 2 to Finished Goods Inventory. The 5,000 units remaining in Department 2 were 40% completed with respect to conversion costs.

(8) Sold 9,000 units on account at $7 per unit. The company uses FIFO inventory costing.

REQUIRED

(a) Record the August transactions in general journal form.

(b) State the balances remaining in the Raw Materials account, in each Work in Process account, and in Finished Goods Inventory.

23–32A Brilliance Corporation produces a dandruff shampoo in three consecutive processes. The costs of Department 2 for June were as follows:

Cost from Department 1		$14,400
Costs added in Department 2:		
Raw materials	$ 4,920	
Direct labor	12,800	
Factory overhead	3,700	21,420

Department 2 had no June 1 inventory, but it handled the following units during June:

Units transferred in from Department 1	12,000
Units transferred to Department 3	8,000
Units in process, June 30	4,000

Of the units in process on June 30, one-half were 75% complete, one-fourth 50% complete, and one-fourth 20% complete. Both raw materials and conversion costs occur evenly throughout the process in Department 2.

REQUIRED
Prepare the cost of production report for Department 2 for June.

BUSINESS DECISION PROBLEM

Anchor Corporation makes a new "space-age" adhesive in a single process that blends and bottles the product, which currently sells for $8 per gallon. Market demand for the product seems good, but management is not satisfied with the product's seemingly low profit margin and has sought your advice.

Because of its concern, management has allocated a $15,000 fund for a program of product promotion or cost reduction, or both. Members of the firm's controller's office and marketing staff have identified the following three possible plans:

(1) Plan A—Devote all funds to product promotion, which allows all costs and the sales volume to remain the same, but permits a $1 per gallon sales price increase.

(2) Plan B—Spend $10,000 on product promotion and $5,000 on cost reduction techniques, which maintains sales volume, permits a price increase of 50 cents per gallon, and reduces direct labor costs by 20% per gallon.

(3) Plan C—Devote all funds to cost reduction efforts. Sales volume and price do not change. For each gallon produced, however, raw materials cost decreases 5%, direct labor cost decreases 30%, and factory overhead decreases 15%.

The controller's office also provides you with the following operating data for a typical period (all raw materials are added initially; conversion costs occur evenly throughout the process):

Beginning work in process (3,000 gallons, 60% processed)	$ 16,800
Units started in process (22,000 gallons)	
Ending work in process (5,000 gallons, 60% processed)	
Costs charged to the department:	
Raw materials	71,500
Direct labor	58,088
Factory overhead	28,832
	$175,220

Using the data from this representative production period, analyze the apparent relative benefits derived from each plan and make a recommendation supported by relevant calculations. Assume sales will equal units completed.

24

Cost–Volume–Profit
Relationships

Most of this text has been devoted to financial accounting, which deals primarily with historical data. We have seen that financial accounting primarily provides reports on the economic unit in the aggregate or on major segments of the unit. Because a firm's financial reports are used by outsiders as well as by management, the information included must be accumulated and reported in accordance with generally accepted accounting principles. Because outsiders measure the success of a firm and its management with such reports, a high degree of objectivity and standardization must be employed in their preparation.

Managerial accounting, on the other hand, concerns the development and analysis of data for the purpose of *internal planning* and *decision making*. Both historical and estimated data may be used, and, although managerial accounting uses concepts from economics, engineering, cost accounting, and finance, no rigid approaches or constraints regulate its application. A firm may use any concept, approach, or method that yields satisfactory and beneficial data for management's needs in current operations or in planning future operations. Probably the most basic technique used by management in its internal planning and decision making is **cost behavior analysis.**

Costs are monetary expressions of the sacrifices a firm makes in generating revenue sufficient for profitable operations. Costs are usually incurred before revenue is received and are generally subject to greater managerial control than revenue. Because of their significant influence on potential profit, management is extremely interested in comparing costs that may be expected from various operating alternatives with one another and with past costs.

COST BEHAVIOR ANALYSIS

Cost behavior analysis is *the study of how specific costs respond to changes in the volume of business activity.* In other words, as the volume of business activity changes, does a total cost factor increase or decrease, change proportionately, or not respond at all? Costs may change in response to other factors, of course. An increase in total property taxes may be due to an increased assessment rate, and an increase in total wages expense may be the result of higher wage rates. Presumably, neither of these increases is related to changes in the volume of business activity.

Cost behavior analysis is one of a business firm's most important elements in planning, control, and decision making. Manufacturing firms use it for planning production levels, budgeting factory costs, estimating costs for particular orders, and directing promotional efforts. It can also be used for such purposes as evaluating a product's relative profitability and determining a company's break-even activity level.

Although cost behavior analysis is most commonly applied to manufacturing costs, it can be just as useful in service businesses. Whenever management is concerned about the likely amount of costs for a particular operation, it may use the analyses presented here in one form or another.

The Activity Base

For meaningful analysis, costs must be related to some measure of business activity. In a factory operation, such measures include units of product, direct labor hours, machine hours, and percent of capacity (although the latter must first be expressed in terms of time or amount of product). The cost analyst must consider the use of the analysis when selecting the most relevant and useful activity base to which costs can be related. For example, if management uses the analysis for control purposes and for establishing reponsibility for costs, the analyst selects measures that are meaningful to those responsible for incurring costs. We may, of course, use several bases, depending on the objectives of the analysis.

Cost–Volume Graphs

One of the most useful tools for relating cost changes to volume changes is the cost–volume graph. In Exhibit 24–1, costs in dollars are measured along the vertical axis of the graph, and some measure of business volume is presented along the horizontal axis. With costs in thousands of dollars and volume in thousands of units of production, for example, point A in Exhibit 24–1 shows the production of 30,000 units with an associated cost of $20,000, and point B represents a cost of $30,000 for 50,000 units.

Cost–volume graphs are particularly valuable when available cost–volume data are plotted on the same graph and other cost–volume relationships are estimated by fitting a line to the known points. In Exhibit 24–2, for example, we use three known data points. (In reality, a graph plotted with so few points is probably

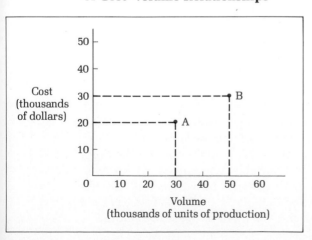

EXHIBIT 24–1
Graphic Presentation
of Cost–Volume Relationships

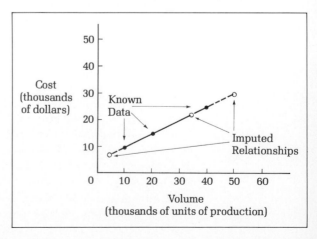

EXHIBIT 24–2
Estimation of Cost–Volume Relationships
from Known Data

not reliable.) The following data are represented by the solid points in the graph in Exhibit 24–2:

Volume (units)	Cost (dollars)
10,000	10,000
20,000	15,000
40,000	25,000

By connecting the known data points with a straight line, we may impute the costs associated with any other production volume. For example, the open points indicate that for volumes of 5,000, 35,000, and 50,000 units, the related costs would be $7,500, $22,500, and $30,000, respectively. Some important limitations to the validity of imputed cost–volume relationships are discussed later in the chapter.

Classifications of Cost Behavior Patterns

For purposes of analyzing their behavior patterns, factory costs are usually classified as *variable, fixed,* or *semivariable.* However, the classification of factory costs into these distinct groups is seldom a simple matter. Costs are frequently erratic and inconsistent, and the cost analyst must analyze their behavior carefully.

Despite the difficulties of classification, the study of approximate cost behavior patterns can aid in planning and analyzing operations. Let us examine the ways in which cost–volume graphs vary among the three cost classifcations.

Variable costs change proportionately with changes in the volume of activity. Raw (or direct) materials cost and direct labor cost, for example, are variable.

Exhibit 24–3 is a typical variable cost graph. As illustrated here, a purely variable cost pattern always passes through the origin, because zero cost is associated with zero volume. Also, because variable costs respond in direct proportion to changes in volume, a variable cost line always slopes upward to the right. The steepness of the slope depends on the amount of cost associated with each unit of volume; the greater the unit cost the steeper the slope. (Remember that the slopes of two graphs can be compared visually only when the axis scales are identical. To see this, draw a few graphs with the same data and different scales or with the same scales and different data.)

In Exhibit 24–3, volume is measured in direct labor hours, and the total variable dollar cost is twice as great at 40,000 hours as at 20,000 hours, as expected.

Fixed costs—sometimes called *nonvariable costs*—usually relate to a time period and do not change when the volume of activity changes. Examples are depreciation on buildings and property taxes.

By definition, fixed costs do not respond to changes in volume and are therefore represented by horizontal lines on a cost–volume graph. In Exhibit 24–4, fixed costs are $80,000 regardless of the volume level considered.

Semivariable costs—sometimes called *mixed costs*—can be described analytically as having both fixed and variable components. A semivariable cost increases or decreases linearly with changes in activity, but is some positive amount at zero activity, as shown in Exhibit 24–5. Changes in total semivariable costs are therefore not proportional to changes in operating volume.

EXHIBIT 24–3
Variable Cost Pattern

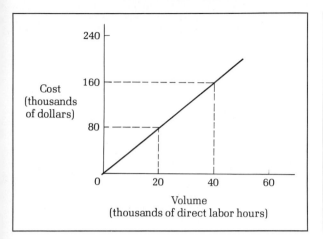

EXHIBIT 24–4
Fixed Cost Pattern

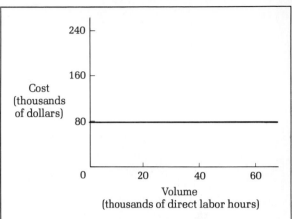

As an example of a semivariable cost, consider a firm's utility expense. Even if the firm shuts down production for one period, it must pay a minimum amount for utilities. When production resumes, the costs of heat, light, and power increase as production increases. Total production costs, in fact, are virtually always semivariable.

For purposes of cost analysis, we might divide a semivariable cost into its fixed and variable components. We accomplish this by any one of several approaches that vary in their degree of sophistication. One simple method entails plotting on a graph the amount of cost experienced at several levels of volume. If cost behavior in actual situations were perfectly correlated, the observations (points) would form a straight line. More realistically, however, we expect only a discernible pattern as shown in Exhibit 24–6.

The line in Exhibit 24–6 has been subjectively determined to approximate the pattern of data points. Extending this line to the vertical axis indicates a $1,000 fixed portion. We subtract this $1,000 fixed cost from the total $4,000 cost at 60,000 direct labor hours to find a total variable portion of $3,000. Therefore, the rate of variation is $3,000/60,000, or 5 cents, per direct labor hour. Hence, we could describe this semivariable cost as $1,000 plus 5 cents per direct labor hour.

We can obtain a better approximation by fitting the line to the cost observation pattern (data points) by the method of least squares. That technique, which is beyond the scope of this text, is illustrated in most introductory statistics texts.

When too few cost observations are available to plot a graph or when the analyst wishes to avoid fitting lines to data, the **high–low** method is sometimes used to approximate the position and slope of the cost line. This relatively simple method compares costs at the highest and lowest levels of activity for which representative cost data are available. The variable cost per activity unit (here, per direct labor hour) is determined by dividing the difference in costs at these

EXHIBIT 24–5
Semivariable Cost Pattern

EXHIBIT 24–6
Analysis of Semivariable Cost

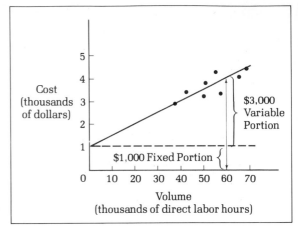

two levels by the difference in activity. The fixed element of cost is then isolated by multiplying the variable cost per unit by either the top or bottom level of activity and then subtracting the resulting product from the total cost at the selected activity level. For example, assume that the lowest and highest levels of activity are 40,000 and 60,000 direct labor hours, respectively, and that total costs for these two levels are shown below:

	Level of Activity	Total Cost
High	60,000 direct labor hours	$4,200
Low	40,000 direct labor hours	3,000
(Difference)	20,000 (increase)	$1,200 (increase)

Because an increase of 20,000 direct labor hours causes a $1,200 increase in total cost (and only the variable portion of the cost could increase), the variable portion of the total semivariable cost must be $1,200/20,000 direct labor hours, or 6 cents per direct labor hour. Subtracting the total variable portion from the total semivariable cost at each activity level gives us the fixed portion of total cost as follows:

	Volume Levels	
	Low	High
Total semivariable cost	$3,000	$4,200
Less variable portions:		
$0.06 × 40,000 direct labor hours	2,400	
$0.06 × 60,000 direct labor hours		3,600
Fixed portion of total cost	$ 600	$ 600

The high–low analysis tells us that any volume level has $600 of fixed cost plus a variable portion of 6 cents per direct labor hour, which can be formulated as

$$\text{Total Cost} = \$600 + (\$0.06 \times \text{Direct Labor Hours})$$

In other words, we can now easily compute the total cost for varying numbers of direct labor hours. Obviously, if either the high or low value used in this method is not representative of the actual cost behavior, the resulting cost formula is inexact.

The semivariable cost pattern is significant because it best represents the pattern of total cost for the firm. This relationship is developed further later in this chapter.

Relevant Range   The foregoing illustrations of cost behavior are oversimplified because they portray linear cost behavior over the entire range of possible activity. Actually, plotting costs against volume may not always produce a single straight line. For example, certain costs may increase abruptly at intervals in a "step" pattern; others may exhibit a curvilinear pattern when plotted over a wide range of activity. Examples of these cost patterns are shown graphically in Exhibit 24–7.

Clearly, an assumption of linear costs over the entire scale on either axis in these two cases causes some degree of error. The significance of this error is often mitigated by the fact that many of the firm's decisions involve relatively small changes in volume around some midrange amount (the relevant ranges in Exhibit 24–7). The actual cost pattern at extremely low or high volume levels is not relevant to the firm's decisions. The cost pattern need only be reasonably linear within the relevant range of volume.

Although we can only approximate relevant ranges for many cost factors, we must often consider these ranges for the practical application of cost behavior analysis. Throughout this chapter, unless specifically qualified, references to fixed cost assume that a relevant range has been determined.

EXHIBIT 24–7
Illustration of Relevant Ranges

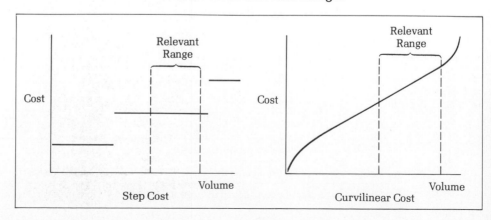

Total Versus Per-unit Costs

Thus far our discussion has been concerned with behavior patterns of total costs. We should also compare per-unit cost and total cost patterns so that the differences are apparent and we are less inclined to confuse the two.

Consider the following cost–volume data for activity levels of 0–1,000 units.

Activity Volume (units)	Variable Cost ($1/unit)		Fixed Cost ($1,000/period)		Semivariable Cost ($500 + $0.50/unit)	
	Total	Per Unit	Total	Per Unit	Total	Per Unit
0	$ 0	$0	$1,000	$0	$ 500	$0
200	200	1	1,000	5	600	3
500	500	1	1,000	2	750	1.50
1,000	1,000	1	1,000	1	1,000	1

Note that a constant cost per unit causes a variable total cost pattern; in fact, it is necessary if total cost is to vary in proportion to volume (and agree with our definition of variable costs). With a fixed cost, the cost per unit decreases proportionately with an increase in volume because the same total amount is spread over larger amounts of production as volume increases. Finally, the semivariable per-unit pattern occurs when the variable portion per unit remains constant, and the fixed portion decreases proportionately as volume increases. The net result is a less than proportionate decrease. These patterns are summarized in Exhibit 24–8.

Total fixed costs and per-unit variable costs are *stable* cost expressions, because they remain constant as volume is changed. Per-unit fixed costs and total variable costs are *unstable* cost expressions because they are valid at only one volume level. In the following section, we show how the stable forms of cost expressions—*total* fixed cost and *per-unit* variable cost—are incorporated in a general formula for total cost that is valid over a wide range of operating volumes.

Planning Total Costs

Budgeting for a business firm, which is treated in detail in Chapter 26, is usually a financial plan that reflects anticipated or planned amounts of such items as revenue, costs, cash balances, and net income. Underlying most aspects of budgeting is some assumed volume of activity or sales, as well as an analysis of the total cost incurred for that level of operation. Obviously, cost behavior analysis is a vital aspect of most budgets.

EXHIBIT 24–8
Patterns of Total and Per-unit Costs
as Volume Increases

Cost Category	Total Costs	Per-unit Costs
Variable	Increase proportionately	Remain constant
Fixed	Remain constant	Decrease proportionately
Semivariable	Increase less than proportionately	Decrease less than proportionately

FIXED PLANS   A relatively simple approach to estimating total cost is the **fixed** or **static plan.** This method attempts to determine what costs should be at a given level of activity, such as normal capacity. Fixed plans list various costs and the anticipated amounts at some specific level of operation. One of the major defects of fixed plans is that actual levels of activity and planned levels of activity are seldom the same. For this reason, with fixed plans actual cost at one level of volume must often be compared with planned costs at another level of volume. This comparison is less meaningful, if not erroneous, because any variable cost elements involved will reflect the actual—not the planned—activity levels.

FLEXIBLE PLANS   The recognized limits of fixed plans have led to the development of flexible plans. **Flexible plans** are based on a formula for total costs like that used earlier (page 859) to describe total semivariable cost: [Total Cost = Fixed Cost + (Variable Cost per Unit × Volume)]. This parallel is explained as follows.

During any operating period, most firms incur costs that fit each of the three cost behavior patterns—variable, semivariable, and fixed. Logically, the pattern representing a firm's total cost is the sum of all three patterns. As shown in Exhibit 24–9, when all three patterns are added by "stacking" them on a single graph, the result is a semivariable cost pattern.

We assume that total fixed cost is $10,000, semivariable cost has a fixed portion of $5,000 and a variable portion of $2 per unit, and that variable costs are $4 per unit. When we stack all cost factors on one graph, the top line—the total cost line—indicates a semivariable pattern. By combining the stable expressions of each cost pattern (*total* for fixed cost and *per unit* for variable cost), we can state a general formula for total cost that applies to a wide range of operating volumes.

EXHIBIT 24–9
A Firm's Total Cost as a
Semivariable Pattern

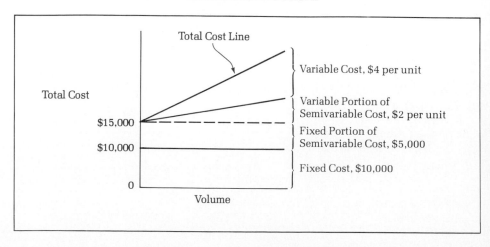

$$\text{Total Cost} = \text{Total Fixed Cost} + \left(\begin{array}{c} \text{Variable} \\ \text{Cost} \\ \text{per Unit} \end{array} \times \text{Volume} \right)$$

In our example

$$\text{Total cost} = \$15,000 + (\$6 \times \text{Volume})$$

Therefore, at zero volume, total cost is $15,000, or the total of all fixed costs. At 5,000 units of volume, total cost is $45,000, or [$15,000 + ($6 × 5,000)]. At 10,000 units of volume, total cost is $75,000, or [$15,000 + ($6 × 10,000)]. Notice that when volume doubles from 5,000 to 10,000 units, total cost responds, but less than proportionately—reflecting our definition of total semivariable cost.

By using a flexible plan, a firm can forecast costs at different levels of activity. In Exhibit 24–10, each type of cost behavior pattern is considered in the flexible plan formula. For simplicity, only a single item is shown for raw materials and for direct labor, only three items make up overhead, and selling and administrative costs are shown as a single amount. The dollar amounts have been chosen for ease of manipulation, and the 10,000-unit activity level is incorporated for illustrative purposes.

We see from Exhibit 24–10 that by combining the various cost factors into the aggregate flexible plan formula, we determine expected costs not only at the 10,000-unit level but also at other levels simply by inserting the appropriate volume figure in the final formula. For example, total planned cost at 8,000 units is [$15,000 + ($6 × 8,000) = $63,000]; at 12,000 units, it is [$15,000 + ($6 × 12,000) = $87,000].

EXHIBIT 24–10
Cost Factors in a Flexible Plan Formula
for Total Cost at 10,000 Units of Volume

Type of Cost	Total Cost	=	Total Fixed Cost	+	(Variable Cost per Unit	×	Volume)
Raw Materials (variable)	$20,000	=			($2.00	×	10,000 units)
Direct Labor (variable)	25,000	=			(2.50	×	10,000 units)
Factory Overhead:							
Factory Supplies (variable)	10,000	=			(1.00	×	10,000 units)
Property Taxes (fixed)	4,000	=	$ 4,000				
Maintenance (semivariable)	7,000	=	5,000	+	(0.20	×	10,000 units)
Selling and Administrative Expense (semivariable)	9,000	=	6,000	+	(0.30	×	10,000 units)
Total Cost	$75,000	=	$15,000	+	($6.00	×	10,000 units)
Aggregate Flexible Plan Formula:	Total Cost	=	$15,000	+	($6.00	×	10,000 units)

A word of caution is appropriate here. Because flexible planning relies so heavily on cost behavior analysis, all the limitations of the latter (assumed linearity, relevant ranges, and so on) apply. Also, we repeat, analyzing many costs into fixed and variable components is often quite complex and inexact. All these limitations to some degree affect the potential contribution of managerial accounting. In many cases, the analytical approach presented here is the best available.

COST–VOLUME–PROFIT ANALYSIS

Cost analysis is so basic to the management process that entire books are devoted to the subject. In our discussion, we survey some basic applications related to cost–volume–profit relationships and profit planning.

For purposes of illustration, we use the following data for Muzzillo Company throughout the next several sections.

Muzzillo Company
Condensed Income Statement

Sales (10,000 units @ $20)		$200,000
Costs:		
Variable Cost (10,000 units @ $12)	$120,000	
Total Fixed Cost	60,000	
Total Cost		180,000
Net Income		$ 20,000

This information assumes that any semivariable costs have been divided into their fixed and variable portions and combined with the purely fixed and purely variable cost elements. We now examine some of the uses of this information.

Break-even Analysis

Management frequently wants to know the level of revenue or number of units of sales at which there is no net income or loss. The level at which total revenue equals total cost is the **break-even point.** Sometimes it is expressed as a percent of capacity, but more frequently it is given in dollars or in units of sales. Let us calculate Muzzillo Company's break-even point, using the above condensed income statement data.

THE BREAK-EVEN CHART   For the break-even chart we use the same basic graph employed earlier to explain and portray cost behavior patterns. In this case, however, the vertical axis measures both total revenue and total cost. We demonstrate the construction of a break-even chart with the Muzzillo Company data.

As before, volume is measured along the horizontal axis. For the Muzzillo Company, the activity base is units of product, and for convenience we choose the scale shown in Exhibit 24–11. Total revenue and total cost are measured in

EXHIBIT 24–11
Break-even Chart

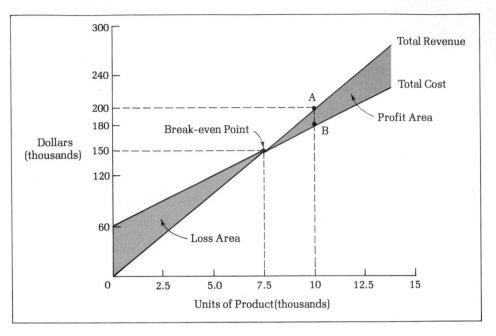

thousands of dollars along the vertical axis. Let us first determine the total revenue line.

With zero revenue for zero sales, the graph of total revenue always passes through the origin, which is one point on the line. In general, then, we draw the total revenue line by connecting the origin with any other point that represents total revenue for some volume amount. For example, for Muzzillo Company, total revenue for 10,000 units is $200,000—point A in Exhibit 24–11. To construct the total revenue line, we simply connect point A and the origin and extend the line to the right.

We now construct the total cost line in the same manner. With fixed costs of $60,000, the total cost line must intersect the dollar axis at $60,000. We locate another point by calculating the total cost at some volume as $60,000 plus the number of units times the variable cost per unit. For Muzzillo Company, we are given total cost of $180,000 for 10,000 units. From this we can plot point B and draw the total cost line for Muzzillo Company as shown in Exhibit 24–11.

Extending the dashed lines as indicated from the point of intersection of the two graphed lines to the two axes, we find Muzzillo Company's break-even point (where total revenue equals total cost) to be 7,500 units of production or $150,000 of total sales revenue. Note that all points lying below the break-even point indicate a loss, and points above the break-even level represent profit. The profit and loss areas are shaded on our graph. The amount of profit or loss at any volume level is determined by measuring the vertical distance between the total cost and total revenue lines. Clearly, a profit is indicated when the total revenue line is above the total cost line, and a loss is indicated when the reverse is true.

ASSUMPTIONS IN BREAK-EVEN ANALYSIS In our construction of a break-even chart, we assumed linear relationships over a wide range of activity. This method implies that total fixed cost and variable cost per unit are constant over the entire range and that selling price per unit remains the same regardless of the sales volume. It also implies that when more than one product is involved, as sales volume varies, each product's percent of the total sales (*sales mix*) does not change.

Break-even charts represent a type of *static analysis*, because they are drawn with the assumption that certain existing relationships among sales prices, costs, and volume remain the same and that sales mix is unvarying. Although this limits their usefulness to some degree, break-even charts are a convenient reference for measuring how an expected change in certain factors affects a company's profit and loss picture. For example, changes in selling prices or variable costs result in changes in the *slope* of both the total revenue line and the total cost line, whereas changes in fixed cost result in vertical shifts of the total cost line.

BREAK-EVEN FORMULAS By definition, the break-even point is the volume level at which total revenue equals total cost (and thus profit is zero). To calculate the break-even point, we restate this basic equality as an equation in either of the following forms:

$$\text{Total Revenue} = \text{Total Cost}$$

$$\frac{\text{Unit}}{\text{Sales Price}} \times \text{Volume} = \frac{\text{Total}}{\text{Fixed Cost}} + \left(\frac{\text{Variable Cost}}{\text{per Unit}} \times \text{Volume} \right)$$

Using the data for Muzzillo Company and letting X be the unknown volume, TFC, total fixed cost, and VCU, variable cost per unit, we have

$$\text{Break-even Sales} = \text{TFC} + (\text{VCU} \times \text{Volume})$$
$$\$20(X) = \$60,000 + \$12(X)$$
$$\$8(X) = \$60,000$$
$$X = 7,500 \text{ units}$$

Multiplying 7,500 units by the sales price of $20 yields break-even sales revenue of $150,000. Of course, the answers derived by formula should—and do—agree with the graphic solutions.

CONTRIBUTION MARGIN **Contribution margin** equals revenue minus variable costs. Either total or per-unit contribution margin is significant because it is the amount available to absorb fixed costs first and then possibly provide net income. Thus, at the break-even point, total contribution margin equals total fixed cost.

Using the data for Muzzillo Company, we see that

(1) Contribution margin per unit (CMU) equals $8 (the unit sales price of $20 less unit variable cost of $12).

(2) Total contribution margin at 7,500 units equals $60,000 ($8 × 7,500 units), which is the amount of fixed costs and therefore the break-even point.

(3) At 10,000 units, $80,000 of total contribution margin is generated, which fully absorbs the fixed costs of $60,000 and also provides $20,000 of net income (see the original data on page 863).

Two fairly common analyses related to contribution margin are widely used to compute break-even points. The first is

$$\text{Break-even Sales (in units)} = \frac{\text{Total Fixed Cost}}{\text{Unit Contribution Margin}}$$

$$= \frac{\$60,000}{\$8}$$

$$= 7,500 \text{ units}$$

The second method involves the **contribution margin ratio,** which is defined as

$$\frac{\text{Unit Sales Price} - \text{Unit Variable Cost}}{\text{Unit Sales Price}}$$

For Muzzillo Company, this ratio would be ($20 − $12)/$20, or 0.4. The contribution margin ratio, then, is simply the fractional expression of that portion of the sales price that is contribution margin. It is used in the following equation:

$$\text{Break-even Sales (in dollars)} = \frac{\text{Total Fixed Cost}}{\text{Contribution Margin Ratio}}$$

$$= \frac{\$60,000}{0.4}$$

$$= \$150,000$$

This alternate solution can be verified by dividing by the unit sales price

$$\$150,000/\$20 = 7,500 \text{ units}$$

which is indeed the break-even volume. Of course, any break-even computation may be verified by preparing a related income statement that should show zero net income.

Planning Net Income

A business firm may wish to estimate how contemplated changes in selling prices or costs affect net income, or it may wish to determine the increase in sales volume needed for a desired net income. With a careful study of cost behavior, the analytical framework we have just discussed is helpful in planning net income. Both the formula and the contribution margin approaches to break-even analysis can be slightly modified to determine target amounts of sales revenue that produce planned amounts of net income. The modification converts break-even sales to desired sales and adds the amount of net income to the other amounts that

COST–VOLUME–PROFIT ANALYSIS IN ACTION

In the mid-1970s, Founder and Chairman Sam M. Walton of Bentonville, Arkansas' Wal-Mart Stores, Inc., a chain of bare-bones discount stores, saw some disturbing patterns in the company's monthly sales charts. Not only were new units failing to achieve expected sales volume, but Wal-Mart's profit margins, once the envy of the industry, were edging downward. To make matters worse, a few aggressive competitors were starting to underprice Wal-Mart, raising the specter of a serious decline in market share.

In a bold bid to head off that possibility, Walton initiated a fundamental revision of Wal-Mart's marketing strategy. Betting that the chain could broaden its appeal without alienating its existing customer base, he launched a major capital improvement program and replaced cheap private-label merchandise with higher quality name-brand goods.

The gamble paid off. Customers flocked to the "new" Wal-Mart, triggering one of the most ambitious expansion programs in retailing history.

Along the way, Wal-Mart has put on the most impressive financial performance in the retailing industry. Over the past five years, it has increased revenue and earnings per share at an annual compounded rate of 37.8% and 37%, respectively.

Wall Street is equally impressed by Wal-Mart's 3.4% profit margin, one of the highest in the discount field, and its 25% return on equity, about 2½ times the retailing average.

Company executives are quick to point out that Wal-Mart's tireless dedication to cost control is one of its greatest strengths. "Quite simply, our philosophy from the beginning has been to price as low as we can; and the lower our costs, the less we have to charge," says Jack Shewmaker, Wal-Mart's president and chief operating officer.

The heart of Wal-Mart's cost-control effort is a monthly financial statement prepared for each store that lists every expenditure charged against the store's account, from rent and taxes to paper clips and telephone tolls. District managers review these statements line by line with store managers, discussing ways to reduce controllable expenses. "These may be minor individually, but collectively they become major," Shewmaker explains. "This is a business of attending to details."

Another important cost advantage that separates Wal-Mart from the competition is in the purchase and distribution of merchandise. Instead of using outside jobbers and contract distributors, as do most discounters, Wal-Mart orders in bulk directly from suppliers and uses its own warehouses and fleet of delivery trucks. By ordering in bulk, Wal-Mart is able to negotiate lower prices than its competitors, and it is able to deliver the merchandise to stores at a much lower cost.

Not even senior executives are exempt from the cost-cutting pressures. Corporate offices are spartan and cramped. Such frugality allows Wal-Mart to spend only 2% of sales for general administrative expenses, less than most retailers can manage.

Wal-Mart gets the payoff from these low costs where it counts—low prices, which in turn generate customer loyalty.

Customer loyalty, Walton and Shewmaker believe, reduces the peaks and valleys in volume that drive labor costs through the roof. So to make sure that Wal-Mart maintains a consistent low-price image, they eschew the kind of rapid-fire promotional techniques common to the industry. While most discounters feature sales on selected merchandise once or twice a week to generate traffic, promotions are restricted to 13 per year at Wal-Mart stores.

From "Wal-Mart: The Model Discounter," *Dun's Business Month*, December 1982, pages 60–61. Reprinted with the special permission of *Dun's Business Month* (formerly *Dun's Review*), December 1982. Copyright 1982, Dun & Bradstreet Publications Corporation.

total revenue must cover. For example, suppose Muzzillo Company wants to estimate the sales volume required to earn $24,000 income before taxes. We proceed as follows:

$$\begin{array}{c} \text{Desired Sales} \\ \text{(in units)} \end{array} = \begin{array}{c} \text{Total} \\ \text{Fixed Cost} \end{array} + \begin{array}{c} \text{Total} \\ \text{Variable Cost} \end{array} + \begin{array}{c} \text{Target Income} \\ \text{before Taxes} \end{array}$$

$$\$20(X) = \$60,000 \quad + \$12(X) \quad + \$24,000$$

$$\$8(X) = \$84,000$$

$$X = 10,500 \text{ units}$$

A brief income computation verifies the analysis.

Sales (10,500 units @ $20)		$210,000
Variable Cost (10,500 units @ $12)	$126,000	
Total Fixed Cost	60,000	
Total Cost		186,000
Income before Taxes		$ 24,000

The contribution margin approaches provide the same results. First we have

$$\begin{array}{c} \text{Desired Volume} \\ \text{(in units)} \end{array} = \frac{\text{Total Fixed Cost} + \text{Target Income before Taxes}}{\text{Unit Contribution Margin}}$$

$$= \frac{\$60,000 + \$24,000}{\$8}$$

$$= 10,500 \text{ units}$$

Alternatively, we may use

$$\begin{array}{c} \text{Desired Volume} \\ \text{(in dollars)} \end{array} = \frac{\text{Total Fixed Cost} + \text{Target Income before Taxes}}{\text{Contribution Margin Ratio}}$$

$$= \frac{\$60,000 + \$24,000}{0.4}$$

$$= \$210,000$$

The two formulas simply express the same volume in different ways, because $210,000/$20 = 10,500 units.

If we want to express the target net income as a percentage of sales rather than as a dollar amount, we can easily use a net income planning formula. Assuming we want a profit of 20% of sales,

$$\begin{array}{c} \text{Desired Sales} \\ \text{(in units)} \end{array} = \begin{array}{c} \text{Total} \\ \text{Fixed Cost} \end{array} + \begin{array}{c} \text{Total} \\ \text{Variable Cost} \end{array} + \begin{array}{c} \text{Target Income} \\ \text{before Taxes} \end{array}$$

$$\$20(X) = \$60,000 \quad + \$12(X) \quad + 0.20[\$20(X)]$$

$$\$20(X) = \$60,000 \quad + \$12(X) \quad + \$4(X)$$

$$\$4(X) = \$60,000$$

$$X = 15,000 \text{ units}$$

In this situation, desired sales are 15,000 units—or $300,000—of which $60,000 is the desired 20% profit.

Effect of Income Taxes

Suppose that Muzzillo Company's management wishes to determine the sales level needed to produce a desired net income *after income taxes*. Assume that the target net income after taxes is $14,000 and the income tax rate is 30%. We adjust the equations by dividing after-tax net income by $(1 - 0.30)$, that is, by 1 minus the tax rate. This converts the net income amount in the equation to a before-tax figure.

$$\text{Desired Sales (in dollars)} = \frac{\$60,000 + \$14,000/(1 - 0.30)}{0.40}$$

$$= \frac{\$60,000 + \$14,000/0.70}{0.40}$$

$$= \frac{\$80,000}{0.40} = \$200,000$$

This answer is confirmed by realizing that $200,000 of sales at a 40% contribution margin ratio equals $80,000 of total contribution margin, which would absorb the $60,000 of fixed costs and leave $20,000 of pretax income. Income taxes at 30% are $6,000, resulting in $14,000 of after-tax income.

Break-even Analysis and Multiple Products

As indicated earlier, we must assume in break-even analysis that only one product is involved or that the product mix (the ratio of each product to the total number of products sold) is constant. Break-even sales can be computed for a mix of two or more products by calculating the *weighted average contribution margin*. Assume that a company sells products A and B at the unit sales prices and variable costs indicated below. The company has $60,000 total fixed costs, and its product mix is two units of A for each unit of B.

	A	B
Unit selling price	$12	$5
Unit variable costs	6	2
Unit contribution margin	$ 6	$3

With two units of A providing $6 each and one unit of B providing $3, the total contribution margin generated by each group of three product units is $15. Because three units of product are involved, the weighted average unit contribution margin is $15/3, or $5. Our break-even calculation is

$$\text{Break-even Volume} = \frac{\text{Total Fixed Cost}}{\text{Weighted Average Unit Contribution Margin}}$$

$$= \frac{\$60,000}{\$5}$$

$$= 12,000 \text{ units}$$

We verify this calculation by noting that if the product mix is two units of A to one unit of B and a total of 12,000 units are sold, then the total contribution margin generated equals the total fixed cost, as shown below:

Product	Product Mix	Volume Sold	Unit Contribution Margin	Total Contribution Margin
A	2/3	8,000	$6	$48,000
B	1/3	4,000	3	12,000
		12,000		$60,000

The concepts explained here could be applied to any product mix or number of products.

A Perspective on Cost Analysis

Managing costs is a prevailing concern of management. The concepts introduced in this chapter underlie most efforts to analyze and project cost in a variety of decision situations. In practice, because projections of future costs are subject to many complicating factors, for most companies they are *estimates* of *probable* costs rather than precise determinations. Properly used—with full recognition of their limitations—cost behavior analyses can be highly useful to management.

KEY POINTS TO REMEMBER

(1) Unlike financial accounting, managerial accounting is not limited to historical cost data, nor is it constrained by generally accepted accounting principles; its only criterion is usefulness to management.

(2) Behavior of total cost in response to volume changes are divided into three basic categories within a relevant range:
  (a) Variable, which responds proportionately, with zero cost at zero volume.
  (b) Fixed, which is constant.
  (c) Semivariable, which responds, but less than proportionately, owing to a fixed component.

(3) Total cost for most firms is best represented by the semivariable cost pattern.

(4) Semivariable costs may be divided into fixed and variable subelements using either graphic plottings or the high–low method.

(5) We can often assume linearity of cost because it is approximately true within the range of volume relevant to the analysis.

(6) Per-unit costs behave as follows when volume is increased:
  (a) Variable costs remain constant.
  (b) Fixed costs decrease proportionately.
  (c) Semivariable costs decrease less than proportionately.

(7) A general formula for planning total cost is

Total Cost = Total Fixed Cost + (Variable Cost per Unit × Volume)

(8) The break-even point (Revenue = Costs) can be derived by graph, formula, or contribution margin analysis.

(9) Contribution Margin = Revenue − Variable Costs.

(10) Break-even and contribution margin formulas can be restated to provide estimates of target sales for planning net income.

(11) Break-even computations involving multiple products incorporate the concept of a weighted average contribution margin.

QUESTIONS

24–1 In what important ways do the objectives and constraints of financial and managerial accounting differ?

24–2 Define the terms *cost behavior* and *relevant range*.

24–3 Identify some common activity bases in terms of which the volume of a manufacturing operation might be stated. What general criterion might be used in choosing a base?

24–4 Name, define, and plot on a graph the three most widely recognized cost behavior patterns. Plot activity horizontally and cost vertically.

24–5 Explain (a) how a semivariable cost can be considered "partly fixed and partly variable," and (b) why a firm's total cost is best represented by the semivariable cost pattern.

24–6 Briefly describe two techniques for dividing a semivariable cost into its fixed and variable subelements.

24–7 "Actual costs often behave in a nonlinear fashion. Therefore, assumptions of linearity invalidate most cost behavior analyses." Do you agree or disagree with this statement? Briefly defend your position.

24–8 Describe how per-unit proportions of the three basic cost patterns respond to volume increases.

24–9 Present a formula for planning total costs, and explain how semivariable costs are incorporated into the formula.

24–10 Define and briefly explain three approaches to break-even analysis.

24–11 The Tasty Donut Shop has fixed costs per month of $800, and variable costs are 60% of sales. What amount of monthly sales allows the shop to break even?

24–12 The Swift Car Wash has fixed costs per month of $2,800, and variable costs are 30% of sales. The average amount collected per car serviced during the past year has been $5. How many cars must be serviced per month to break even?

24–13 You have graphed the cost–volume–profit relationships for a company on a break-even chart, after being informed of certain assumptions. Explain how the lines on the chart would change (a) if fixed costs increased over the entire range of activity, (b) if selling price per unit decreased, and (c) if variable costs per unit increased.

24–14 Define *contribution margin*. Is it best expressed as a total amount or as a per-unit amount? In what way is the term descriptive of the concept?

24–15 Explain the approach to break-even analysis that is used for a mix of two or more products.

24–16 Explain how break-even formulas can provide income-planning analyses.

24–17 In planning net income, how can after-tax net income be incorporated into the planning formula?

EXERCISES

24–18 Set up a cost–volume graph similar to those presented in the chapter with proportional sales from 0–12,000 (in 2,000-unit increments) for cost and volume. Plot each of the following groups of cost data using different marks for each group. After completing the graph, indicate the type of cost behavior exhibited by each group.

Volume (applicable to each group)	Group A Costs	Group B Costs	Group C Costs
1,000	$ 3,300	$ 1,200	$4,000
3,000	4,900	3,600	4,000
5,000	6,500	6,000	4,000
10,000	10,500	12,000	4,000

24–19 Apply the high–low method of cost analysis to the three cost data groups in Exercise 24–18. What cost behavior patterns are apparent? Express each as a cost formula.

24–20 The highest and lowest levels of activity for the Chamberlain Company were 40,000 direct labor hours and 24,000 direct labor hours, respectively. If maintenance costs were $120,000 at the 40,000-hour level and $80,000 at the 24,000-hour level, what cost might we expect at an operating level of 30,000 direct labor hours?

24–21 During the past year, Horton, Inc. operated within the relevant range of its fixed costs. Monthly production volume during the year ranged from 40,000 to 60,000 units of product and corresponding average manufacturing costs ranged from $2.20 to $2.40 per unit. Determine the total cost behavior pattern experienced by Horton, Inc.

24–22 The selected data on the next page relate to the major cost categories experienced by Monarch Company at varying levels of operating volumes. Assuming that all operating volumes are within the relevant range, calculate the appropriate costs in each column where blanks appear.

	Total Cost (at 3,000 units)	Total Cost (at 4,000 units)	Per-unit Cost (at 4,000 units)	Total Cost (at 5,000 units)	Per-unit Cost (at 5,000 units)
Direct labor (variable)	$4,500	$6,000	____	____	____
Factory supervision (semivariable)	3,700	4,700	____	____	____
Factory depreciation (fixed)	2,000	2,000	____	____	____

24–23 The Walters Company has analyzed its overhead costs and derived a general formula for their behavior: $21,000 + $5 per direct labor hour employed. The company expects to utilize 50,000 direct labor hours during the next accounting period. What overhead rate per direct labor hour should be applied to jobs worked during the period?

24–24 The following amounts of various cost categories are experienced by Olin Factories in producing and selling its only product:

Raw materials	$5 per unit of product
Direct labor	$7 per direct labor hour*
Factory overhead	$9,000 + $6 per direct labor hour
Selling expenses	$12,000 + $2 per unit of product
Administrative expenses	$7,000 + $0.25 per unit of product

*Each unit of product requires one-half direct labor hour.

Combine the various cost factors into a general total cost formula for Olin Factories, and determine the total cost for producing and selling 12,000 units.

24–25 Set up a break-even chart similar to Exhibit 24–11 with proportional scales from 0–$72,000 (in $6,000 increments) on the vertical axis and from 0–12,000 units of production (in 2,000-unit increments) on the horizontal axis. Prepare a break-even chart for O'Malley Company, assuming total fixed costs of $18,000 and unit selling price and unit variable cost for the company's one product of $6 and $4, respectively.

24–26 Compute the break-even point in units of production for each of the following independent situations. Confirm each answer using contribution margin ratio analysis.

	Unit Selling Price	Unit Variable Cost	Total Fixed Cost
(a)	$ 9	$6	$30,000
(b)	12	8	48,000
(c)	8	6	18,000

24–27 In each of the three situations presented in Exercise 24–26, what unit sales volume is necessary to earn the following related amounts of net income before income taxes? (a) $6,000; (b) $8,000; and (c) equal to 20% of sales revenue.

24–28 The Philips Company sells a single product for $17 per unit. Variable costs are $9 per unit and fixed costs are $5 per unit at an operating level of 10,000 units.

(a) What is the Philips Company's break-even point in units?
(b) How many units must be sold to earn $35,200 before income taxes?
(c) How many units must be sold to earn $35,200 after income taxes, assuming a 50% tax rate?

24–29 Matson Company has $92,400 total fixed costs and sells products A and B with a product mix of two units of A to three of B. Selling prices and variable costs for A and B result in contribution margins per unit of $6 and $3, respectively. Compute the break-even point.

24–30 Dexter Corporation made a net profit last year of $150,000 after income taxes. Fixed costs were $450,000. The selling price per unit of its product was $80, of which $20 was a contribution to fixed cost and net income. The income tax rate was 40%.
(a) How many units of product were sold last year?
(b) What was the break-even point in units?
(c) The company wishes to increase its after-tax net income by 20% this year. If selling prices and the income tax rate remain unchanged, how many units must be sold?

PROBLEMS

24–31 The following graph depicts cost–volume relations for the Harris Company:

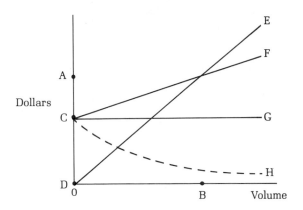

REQUIRED
Choose a labeled point or line on the graph that *best* represents the behavior of each of the following items as operating volume is increased. Answers may be the same for more than one item. Answer each item independently.
(a) Total sales revenue
(b) Total cost for the firm
(c) Variable cost per unit
(d) Total variable cost
(e) Total fixed cost
(f) Fixed cost per unit
(g) Total semivariable cost
(h) Break-even point

24–32 Selected operating data for the Austin Company in four independent situations are shown below:

	A	B	C	D
Sales	$120,000	$_____	$_____	$100,000
Variable expense	$_____	$30,000	$_____	$_____
Fixed expense	$_____	$15,000	$18,000	$ 52,000
Net income (loss)	$ 10,000	$10,000	$12,000	($ 12,000)
Units sold	20,000	_____		
Unit contribution margin	$2.00	$2.50		
Contribution margin ratio			0.40	_____

REQUIRED
Fill in the blanks for each independent situation. Show your calculations.

24–33 During a recent six-month period, Nelson Corporation has the following monthly volume of production and total monthly maintenance expenses:

	Units Produced	Maintenance Expense
Mar.	21,000	$ 70,400
Apr.	15,000	56,000
May	30,000	92,000
June	27,500	86,000
July	35,000	104,000
Aug.	25,000	80,000

REQUIRED
Assume all volumes are in the relevant range.
(a) Explain why the data indicate that the maintenance expense is neither a fixed nor a variable expense.
(b) Construct a graph similar to Exhibit 24–6 and plot the above cost observations.
(c) Fit a line (by sight) to the cost observation dots, and estimate the cost formula.
(d) Confirm your answer in part (c) with high–low analysis.

24–34 Shepherd Manufacturing produces a single product requiring the following raw materials and direct labor:

Description	Cost per Unit of Input	Required Amount per Unit of Product
Material A	$ 8/lb	10 oz
Material B	6/lb	8 oz
Material C	15/gal	0.4 gal
Cutting labor	8/hr	15 min
Shaping labor	10 hr	30 min
Finishing labor	12/hr	45 min

Factory overhead consists of factory supplies, 50 cents per unit of product; indirect labor, $600 per month plus 70 cents per unit of product; factory maintenance, $12,000 per year plus 50 cents per unit of product; factory depreciation, $15,000 per year; and annual factory property taxes, $9,000. Selling and administrative expenses include the salaries of a sales manager, $24,000 per year; an office manager, $18,000 per year; and two salespersons, each of whom is paid a base salary of $7,000 per year and a commission of $3 per unit sold. Advertising and promotion of the product are done through a year-round media package program costing $1,000 per week.

REQUIRED
(a) Analyze all cost and expense factors to determine a general formula (based on units of production) for total cost.
(b) Assuming a relevant range of 10,000 to 20,000 units, what is the estimated unit cost for producing and selling 10,000 units? 20,000 units? Explain the variation in unit cost at the two levels of production.
(c) If 15,000 units are produced and sold in a year, what selling price results in a net income of $30,000 before income taxes?

24–35 The Arnold Company has accumulated the following total factory overhead costs for two levels of activity (within the relevant range):

	Low	High
Activity (direct labor hours)	40,000	60,000
Total factory overhead	$67,000	$85,000

The total overhead costs include variable, fixed, and semivariable (mixed) costs. At 60,000 direct labor hours, the total cost breakdown is as follows:

Variable costs	$30,000
Fixed costs	25,000
Semivariable costs	30,000

REQUIRED
(a) Using the high–low method of cost analysis, determine the variable portion of the semivariable costs per direct labor hour. Determine the total fixed cost component of the semivariable cost.
(b) What should the total planned overhead cost be at 50,000 direct labor hours?

24–36 The following total cost data are for Clancy Manufacturing Company, which has a normal capacity per period of 25,000 units of product that sell for $15 each. For the foreseeable future, sales volume should continue at normal capacity of production.

Raw materials	$ 90,750
Direct labor	62,000
Variable overhead	28,500
Fixed overhead (Note 1)	50,000
Selling expense (Note 2)	31,250
Administrative expense (fixed)	20,000
	$282,500

(1) Beyond normal capacity, fixed overhead costs increase $3,000 for each 1,000 units *or fraction thereof* until a maximum capacity of 30,000 units is reached.

(2) Selling expenses are a 5% sales commission plus shipping costs of 50 cents per unit.

REQUIRED

(a) Using the information available, prepare a flexible plan formula to estimate Clancy's total costs at various production volumes up to normal capacity.

(b) Prove your answer in part (a) against the above total cost figure at 25,000 units.

(c) Calculate the planned total cost at 20,000 units, and explain why total cost did not decrease in proportion to the reduced volume.

(d) If Clancy were operating at normal capacity and accepted an order for 500 more units, what would it have to charge for the order to make a $5 profit per unit on the new sale?

24–37 Center Corporation sells a single product for $50 per unit, of which $20 is contribution margin. Total fixed costs are $40,000 and before-tax net income is $16,000.

REQUIRED

Determine the following (show key computations):

(a) The present sales volume in dollars.

(b) The break-even point in units.

(c) The sales volume necessary to earn a profit of $30,000 before taxes.

(d) The sales volume necessary to earn a before-tax income equal to 20% of sales revenue.

(e) The sales volume necessary to earn an after-tax income of $30,000 if the tax rate is 40%.

24–38 The controller of the Anderson Company is preparing data for a conference concerning certain *independent* aspects of its operations.

REQUIRED

Prepare answers to the following questions for the controller:

(a) Total fixed costs are $500,000 and a unit of product is sold for $4 in excess of its unit variable cost. What is break-even unit sales volume?

(b) The company will sell 60,000 units of product—each having a unit variable cost of $9—at a price that will enable the product to absorb $240,000 of fixed costs. What minimum unit sales price must be charged to break even?

(c) Net income before taxes of $120,000 is desired after covering $600,000 of fixed costs. What minimum contribution margin ratio must be maintained if total sales revenue is to be $1,800,000?

(d) Net income before taxes is 10% of sales revenue, the contribution margin is 30%, and the break-even dollar sales volume is $300,000. What is the amount of total revenue?

(e) Total fixed costs are $240,000, variable cost per unit is $6, and unit sales price is $20. What dollar sales volume will generate a profit of $24,000 after paying income taxes of 40%?

24–39 Taylor Company has recently leased facilities for the manufacture of a new product. Based on studies made by its accounting personnel, the following data are available:

Estimated annual sales: 3,000 units

Estimated Costs	Amount	Unit Cost
Raw materials	$18,000	$ 6.00
Direct labor	12,000	4.00
Factory overhead	9,000	3.00
Administrative expenses	4,800	1.60
	$43,800	$14.60

Selling expenses are expected to be 10% of sales, and the selling price is $20 per unit. Ignore income taxes in this problem.

REQUIRED
(a) Compute a break-even point in dollars and in units. Assume that factory overhead and administrative expenses are fixed but that other costs are fully variable.
(b) What would the total profit be if 2,500 units were sold?
(c) How many units must be sold to make a profit of 10% of sales?

24–40 Benson Company manufactures and sells the three products below:

	Economy	Standard	Deluxe
Unit sales	10,000	6,000	4,000
Unit sales price	$15	$24	$36
Unit variable cost	$10	$18	$20

REQUIRED
Assume that total fixed costs are $105,000.
(a) Compute the net income based on the sales volumes shown above.
(b) Compute the break-even point in total dollars of revenue and in specific unit sales volume for each product.
(c) Prove your break-even calculations by computing the total contribution margin related to your answer in part (b).

ALTERNATE PROBLEMS

24–32A Selected operating data for the Thomas Company in four independent situations are shown below:

	A	B	C	D
Sales	$160,000	$_____	$_____	$140,000
Variable expense	$_____	$24,000	$_____	_____
Fixed expense	$_____	$28,000	$60,000	$ 60,000
Net income (loss)	$ 20,000	$ 8,000	$24,000	($ 4,000)
Units sold	7,000	_____		
Unit contribution margin	$10.00	$4.50		
Contribution margin ratio			0.70	_____

REQUIRED

Fill in the blanks for each independent situation. Show your calculations.

24–33A During the past operating year, Amco, Inc. had the following monthly volume of production and total monthly maintenance expenses:

	Units Produced	Maintenance Expense		Units Produced	Maintenance Expense
Jan.	120,000	$11,200	July	124,000	$11,400
Feb.	144,000	12,700	Aug.	154,000	13,300
Mar.	156,000	13,400	Sept.	128,000	11,700
Apr.	130,000	11,600	Oct.	160,000	13,600
May	140,000	12,500	Nov.	152,000	13,200
June	150,000	13,200	Dec.	156,000	13,400

REQUIRED

Assume all volumes are in the relevant range.

(a) Explain why the data indicate that the maintenance expense is neither a fixed nor a variable expense.

(b) Construct a graph similar to Exhibit 24–6 and plot the above cost observations.

(c) Fit a line (by sight) to the cost observation dots, and estimate the cost formula.

(d) Confirm your answer in part (c) with high–low analysis.

24–34A Jacobs Manufacturing produces a single product requiring the following raw materials and direct labor:

Description	Cost per Unit of Input	Required Amount per Unit of Product
Material A	$ 8/lb	24 oz
Material B	6/lb	12 oz
Material C	10/gal	0.5 gal
Cutting labor	12/hr	45 min
Shaping labor	16/hr	15 min
Finishing labor	10/hr	30 min

Factory overhead consists of factory supplies, 75 cents per unit of product; indirect labor, $8,000 per year plus $1.20 per unit of product; factory maintenance, $1,000 per month plus 60 cents per unit of product; factory depreciation, $25,000 per year; and annual factory property taxes, $20,000. Selling and administrative expenses include the salaries of a sales manager, $21,000 per year, an office manager, $16,000 per year, and two salespersons, each of whom is paid a base salary of $8,000 per year and a commission of $4 per unit sold. Advertising and promotion of the product are done through a year-round media package program costing $500 per week.

REQUIRED

(a) Analyze all cost and expense factors to determine a general formula (based on units of production) for total cost.

(b) Assuming a relevant range of 20,000 to 40,000 units, what is the estimated unit cost for producing and selling 20,000 units? 40,000 units? Explain the variation in unit cost at the two levels of production.

(c) If 35,000 units are produced and sold in a year, what selling price results in a net income of $50,000 before income taxes?

24–35A The Gilbert Company has accumulated the following total factory overhead costs for two levels of activity (within the relevant range):

	Low	High
Activity (direct labor hours)	30,000	50,000
Total factory overhead	$98,000	$134,000

The total overhead costs include variable, fixed, and semivariable (mixed) costs. At 50,000 direct labor hours, the total cost breakdown is as follows:

Variable costs	$80,000
Fixed costs	30,000
Semivariable costs	24,000

REQUIRED

(a) Using the high–low method of cost analysis, determine the variable portion of the semivariable costs per direct labor hour. Determine the total fixed cost component of the semivariable cost.

(b) What should the total planned overhead cost be at 40,000 direct labor hours?

24–37A Whitehall, Inc. sells a single product for $80 per unit, of which $50 is contribution margin. Total fixed costs are $90,000 and before-tax net income is $20,000.

REQUIRED

Determine the following (show key computations):

(a) The present sales volume in dollars.

(b) The break-even point in units.

(c) The sales volume necessary to earn a profit of $30,000 before taxes.

(d) The sales volume necessary to earn a before-tax income equal to 20% of sales revenue.

(e) The sales volume necessary to earn an after-tax income of $36,000 if the tax rate is 40%.

24–38A The controller of the Larson Company is preparing data for a conference concerning certain *independent* aspects of its operations.

REQUIRED

Prepare answers to the following questions for the controller:

(a) Total fixed costs are $202,500, and a unit of product is sold for $4.50 in excess of its unit variable cost. What is break-even unit sales volume?

(b) The company will sell 20,000 units of product—each having a unit variable cost of $8—at a price that will enable the product to absorb $120,000 of fixed costs. What minimum unit sales price must be charged to break even?

(c) Net income before taxes of $55,000 is desired after covering $190,000 of fixed costs. What minimum contribution margin ratio must be maintained if total sales revenue is to be $700,000?

(d) Net income before taxes is 20% of sales revenue, the contribution margin ratio is 60%, and the break-even dollar sales volume is $80,000. What is the amount of total revenue?

(e) Total fixed costs are $200,000, variable cost per unit is $20, and unit sales price is $36. What dollar sales volume will generate a profit of $14,400 after paying income taxes of 40%?

24–40A Bauer Company manufactures and sells the three products below:

	Race	Shaft	Bearing
Unit sales	20,000	30,000	50,000
Unit sales price	$12	$28	$4
Unit variable cost	$ 5	$18	$2

REQUIRED

Assume that total fixed costs are $135,000.

(a) Compute the net income based on the sales volumes shown above.

(b) Compute the break-even point in total dollars of revenue and in specific unit sales volume for each product.

(c) Prove your break-even calculations by computing the total contribution margin related to your answer in part (b).

BUSINESS DECISION PROBLEM

The following total cost data are for Jenison Manufacturing Company, which has a normal capacity per period of 10,000 units of product that sell for $30 each. For the foreseeable future, sales volume should continue at normal capacity of production.

Raw materials	$ 72,000
Direct labor	48,000
Variable overhead	24,000
Fixed overhead (Note 1)	36,000
Selling expense (Note 2)	30,000
Administrative expense (fixed)	9,000
	$219,000

(1) Beyond normal capacity, fixed overhead costs increase $1,000 for each 500 units or *fraction thereof* until a maximum capacity of 14,000 units is reached.

(2) Selling expenses are a 10% sales commission plus shipping costs of 50 cents per unit. Jenison pays only one-half of the regular sales commission rate on any sale of 500 or more units.

Jenison's sales manager has received an order for 1,200 units from a large discount chain at a special price of $27 each, F.O.B. factory. The controller's office has furnished the following additional cost data related to the special order:

(1) Changes in the product's construction will reduce raw materials $3 per unit.
(2) Special processing will add 25% to the per-unit direct labor costs.
(3) Variable overhead will continue at the same proportion of direct labor costs.
(4) Other costs should not be affected.

REQUIRED
(a) Present an analysis supporting a decision to accept or reject the special order. Assume Jenison's regular sales are not affected by this special order.
(b) What is the lowest unit sales price Jenison could receive and still make a before-tax profit of $2,000 on the special order?

25

Special Analyses
for Management

One of the most important justifications for a well-developed accounting system is its role as a continuing source of operational information for management. A high correlation exists between the quality of information available to management and the overall success of the operating decisions based on that information. In this chapter, we consider briefly the management decision-making process and some cost concepts that are used in managerial analyses. How accounting information is used in such analyses is then illustrated in a series of examples.

MANAGEMENT AND THE DECISION-MAKING PROCESS

There are many definitions of *management*. In the broad sense, anyone who directs the activities of others is a manager. For a typical manufacturing firm, this includes shop supervisors, department heads, plant supervisors, division managers, and the company president. A large, complex firm has many management levels in addition to these.

The specific nature of a manager's activities varies with the level of management. As depicted in Exhibit 25–1, top management is responsible for establishing long-range goals and policies, including major financial arrangements, expansion into foreign operations, and mergers with other firms. Middle-level management may deal with the strategies and tactics related to the automation of a department, the establishment of new product lines, and perhaps the direction of the merchandising emphases among various products. Such matters as daily production quotas, compliance with planned costs, and other fairly detailed day-to-day operating concerns are the responsibility of lower-level management. To varying degrees, therefore, all levels of management are involved in decision making.

Decision making requires that a choice be made among alternatives, although the decision-making process as a whole covers a much more comprehensive spectrum of activities. Probably the finest analogy of the business decision process is the play of a well-organized football team. Virtually all the elements of decision making are present in football—the awareness of the objectives and goals that lead to winning; the balancing of such short-run goals as first downs with the long-run goals of winning games and conference championships; the presence of organization, strategy, and tactics in a "hostile" environment where inaction and poor performance result in losses; the development of plays with the hope

EXHIBIT 25–1

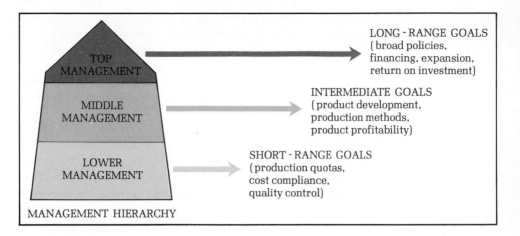

LONG - RANGE GOALS
(broad policies,
financing, expansion,
return on investment)

INTERMEDIATE GOALS
(product development,
production methods,
product profitability)

SHORT - RANGE GOALS
(production quotas,
cost compliance,
quality control)

TOP MANAGEMENT

MIDDLE MANAGEMENT

LOWER MANAGEMENT

MANAGEMENT HIERARCHY

of achieving particular results; the moment of commitment in the huddle, immediately followed by the period of execution; and finally, the informal evaluation of performance on the field followed by a formal evaluation when game films are analyzed.

Of course, not all decision making is so well organized and patterned nor, possibly, so scientific. To some degree, good managers rely on what may be called intuition but is more accurately recognized as the subtle insights gained through previous related experiences. Also, many decision situations contain qualitative factors, whose effects are not easily quantifiable or subject to scientific analysis. Some examples of common qualitative considerations are the possible reactions of competitors, employees, regulatory agencies, and consumer groups. Most decision situations, however, involve quantifiable factors and lend themselves to numerical analysis.

Phases of Decision Making

Decision making may be divided roughly into a planning phase, an execution phase, and an evaluation phase incorporating some form of adaptive or remedial feedback. The following diagram illustrates the sequential nature of the elements of most decision processes:

Planning → Execution → Evaluation | Planned | Actual

— Remedial Feedback —

The **planning phase** begins with *goal identification*, the specification of objectives to be sought or accomplished. One of the most common business goals is the long-run optimization of net income. Other goals include target growth rates in sales revenue or total assets and target shares in various markets. Still other goals—such as leadership in product research, innovation, and quality—are difficult to measure. Probably the most widely recognized goal is a specified return on assets. In Chapter 20, we described one measure of this return as the ratio of income before interest and taxes to assets employed to earn that income. The calculation of return on assets can be modified in a number of ways, depending on the preferences of management. One variation uses after-tax income to calculate the ratio.

The next steps in planning are identifying feasible alternative courses of action for achieving desired goals and estimating their qualitative and quantitative effects on the specified goals. Accounting plays an important role here because the quantifiable aspects of analysis rely heavily on accounting data.

Because all planning involves the future, it must be done with less than perfect information and therefore an element of uncertainty. Advanced treatments of decision theory weigh the value of additional information that reduces the uncertainty of decision situations against the cost of obtaining the information. Also, recognition of the uncertainties of decision analyses has led to the use of probabilistic determinations of the results expected from various courses of action. These subjects, however, are beyond the scope of this text.

The **execution phase** begins with the actual moment of decision—management's commitment to a specific plan of action. Because of the complexity of modern industry, in which an individual corporation may manufacture tens of thousands of products and sell them in worldwide markets, some elaborate plans may need lead times of several years. Poor planning, or the absence of planning, may lead to operating crises that carry significant penalties for the firm in terms of extra costs, lost opportunities, and—in extreme cases—bankruptcy.

Once a decision has been made, the plan is implemented, which usually involves the acquisition and commitment of materials, labor skills, and long-lived assets such as machinery and buildings. Management is kept informed through periodic accounting reports on the acquisition and use of these facilities during the execution phase.

In the **evaluation phase,** steps are taken to *control* the outcome of a specific plan of action. Virtually every important aspect of business—costs, product quality, inventory levels, and sales revenue—must be reasonably well controlled if a firm is to operate successfully. Measuring performance is an essential element of control; to exercise control, management must be able to compare current operations with desired operations and take remedial action when significant unfavorable variations exist. Accounting data and reports play a key role in informing management about performance in various areas during the evaluation phase of decision making. The discussions of budgeting and standard costs in Chapter 26 provide examples of accounting's contributions to management control.

Decision processes do not, of course, fall into three neatly divided phases. The sheer multiplicity of goals and related options for their implementation often generate complex decision environments. Changes in competition, technology, and customer demand must be considered. Furthermore, most management teams are engaged in all decision-making phases at any given time. They may be planning decisions in one area, executing them in a second, and evaluating them in a third.

MANAGEMENT ANALYSES AND REPORTS

Management analyses and reports are the schedules, computations, or reports requested by management as an aid in carrying out its duties. They may include comprehensive summaries of past operating data, elaborate projections of future operating data, and highly specific analyses of how certain operating procedures have affected or may affect particular cost or revenue factors. Generally speaking, top managers need broad, highly summarized reports, and lower-level managers require specialized reports containing greater detail. Management reports often relate to specific departments or operations and reflect particular operating responsibilities.

Exhibit 25–2 illustrates the sequential incorporation of accounting cost data into the performance reports prepared for successively higher echelons of management. Such a system of reports tends to ensure a continuity of cost accountability from the lowest operating units to the highest management levels. The preparation and use of performance reports is developed further in Chapter 26.

Remember that these reports are intended for management's use and are not constrained by generally accepted accounting principles. Although much of the financial data that appear on published financial statements may also be used, management reports may contain any sort of estimate of costs, revenue, or values deemed relevant to the analysis. The quality of management analyses and reports depends more on their timeliness, clarity, conciseness, and relevance to a particular problem than on their dollar-and-cents accuracy. Any type of data that is useful to management may be included in management reports.

COST CONCEPTS

Because of the variety of managerial problems and the flexibility allowable in management reports and analyses, many important cost concepts and terms are in general use. After reviewing the cost categories discussed in earlier chapters, we discuss some others that are frequently encountered. These categories, of course, are not always mutually exclusive—some costs fall into more than one category.

First let us quickly review some terms. **Product costs,** the costs of producing a product, are capitalized as inventory until the product is sold. **Period costs** are identified with and recognized as expenses of the period in which they are incurred. Whereas **direct costs** can be readily identified with a product, department, or activity, **indirect costs** are not readily identified with products or activities and

EXHIBIT 25-2

Performance Report—Vice-president of Production
For the Month of August, 19XX

	Budgeted Cost	Actual Cost	Over (Under)
Administration	$ 14,700	$ 19,100	$ 4,400
Machining	122,300	120,000	(2,300)
Fabricating	118,600	122,300	3,700
Assembly	118,400	118,600	200
	$374,000	$380,000	$ 6,000

Performance Report—Manager of Machining Operations
For the Month of August, 19XX

	Budgeted Cost	Actual Cost	Over (Under)
Lathe Department	$ 56,200	$ 51,000	$(5,200)
Drilling Department	40,200	39,000	(1,200)
Finishing Department	25,900	30,000	4,100
	$122,300	$120,000	$(2,300)

Performance Report—Supervisor of Drilling Department
For the Month of August, 19XX

	Budgeted Cost	Actual Cost	Over (Under)
Raw Materials	$16,000	$15,800	$(200)
Direct Labor	18,000	16,700	(1,300)
Factory Overhead: (listed in detail)	6,200	6,500	300
	$40,200	$39,000	$(1,200)

STANDARDS OF ETHICAL CONDUCT
FOR MANAGEMENT ACCOUNTANTS

Management accountants have an obligation to the organizations they serve, their profession, the public, and themselves to maintain the highest standards of ethical conduct. In recognition of this obligation, the National Association of Accountants has promulgated the following standards of ethical conduct for management accountants. Adherence to these standards is integral to achieving the *Objectives of Management Accounting.** Management accountants shall not commit acts contrary to these standards nor shall they condone the commission of such acts by others within their organizations.

(1) *Competence* Management accountants have a responsibility to:
 (a) Maintain an appropriate level of professional competence by ongoing development of their knowledge and skills.
 (b) Perform their professional duties in accordance with relevant laws, regulations, and technical standards.
 (c) Prepare complete and clear reports and recommendations after appropriate analyses of relevant and reliable information.

(2) *Confidentiality* Management accountants have a responsibility to:
 (a) Refrain from dislosing confidential information acquired in the course of their work except when authorized, unless legally obligated to do so.
 (b) Inform subordinates as appropriate regarding the confidentiality of information acquired in the course of their work and monitor their activities to assure the maintenance of that confidentiality.
 (c) Refrain from using or appearing to use confidential information acquired in the course of their work for unethical or illegal advantage either personally or through third parties.

(3) *Integrity* Management accountants have a responsibility to:
 (a) Avoid actual or apparent conflicts of interest and advise all appropriate parties of any potential conflict.
 (b) Refrain from engaging in any activity that would prejudice their ability to carry out their duties ethically.
 (c) Refuse any gift, favor, or hospitality that would influence or would appear to influence their actions.
 (d) Refrain from either actively or passively subverting the attainment of the organization's legitimate and ethical objectives.
 (e) Recognize and communicate professional limitations or other constraints that would preclude responsible judgment or successful performance of an activity.
 (f) Communicate unfavorable as well as favorable information and professional judgments or opinions.
 (g) Refrain from engaging in or supporting any activity that would discredit the profession.

(4) *Objectivity* Management accountants have a responsibility to:
 (a) Communicate information fairly and objectively.
 (b) Disclose fully all relevant information that could reasonably be expected to influence an intended user's understanding of the reports, comments, and recommendations presented.

*National Association of Accountants, *Statements on Management Accounting: Objectives of Management Accounting*, Statement No. 1B, New York, June 17, 1982.

are usually allocated by some arbitrary formula to various products and activities. **Variable costs** respond proportionately to changes in production volume, but **fixed costs** remain constant as volume changes. **Semivariable costs** respond to volume changes, but less than proportionately. **Joint costs** are common to two or more products or activities.

We now discuss some other important cost concepts and associated terminology. **Historical cost**—often called *actual* cost—is the money or other valuable consideration paid (and/or the cash equivalent of any obligations assumed) to acquire goods or services. With some exceptions, financial accounting records are based on historical costs adjusted for depreciation when applicable. Historical costs are appropriate for reporting net income and financial position under generally accepted accounting principles, but they may not be the best basis for, nor even relevant to, certain management analyses and reports.

Replacement cost is the current cash equivalent necessary to duplicate a particular asset. Replacement costs typically are more relevant than historical costs to managerial decisions. For example, in setting the selling price for a refrigerator that had cost $200 to acquire but would cost $400 to replace, an appliance store manager would probably rely more on replacement cost than on historical cost. Note that the replacement cost of many unique assets can only be estimated.

Out-of-pocket costs require expenditures in the current period. Wages and utilities expenses are examples of out-of-pocket costs. Current depreciation on equipment purchased in earlier periods is not an out-of-pocket cost because no current funds are spent.

Sunk costs are incurred in the past and cannot be recovered. For example, if materials purchased for a particular project remain unused and cannot be returned, any portion of their acquisition cost that cannot be recovered is properly termed a sunk cost.

Avoidable costs can be avoided, and **unavoidable costs** cannot be avoided, in following a specific course of action. For example, in closing down a regional warehouse, many operating expenses such as utilities would probably be avoidable. Other operating costs, however, such as depreciation and property taxes would be unavoidable, unless of course, we not only closed the warehouse but also sold it. If the warehouse were sold, both the depreciation and taxes would properly be considered avoidable costs.

Opportunity costs are measurable sacrifices associated with forgoing some alternative. For example, the decision to attend college for a particular term may necessitate forgoing the opportunity to earn income. Thus, one opportunity cost of attending college would be the wage income that could have been earned. Determining opportunity costs involves many "what if" questions and is often quite difficult. Although omitted from financial statements, opportunity costs are often relevant to management decisions.

Marginal cost is associated with completing one more unit of production or activity. The concept of marginal cost is useful in theoretical economics, but the amount is not easily determined in many real world situations. In recognition of this impracticality, the closely related concept of incremental or differential cost is frequently used in decision-making situations.

Incremental or **differential costs** are the increases or decreases in various costs that result from pursuing one course of action rather than another. We cannot assume that variable costs are always differential and that fixed costs are never differential, although this is often the case. For example, in a decision concerning whether to use one truck for 10 trips or five trucks for two trips to haul 10 loads, the cost of truck fuel is a variable cost but not a differential cost. If a special permit is required for each truck used, the difference in the cost of permits is a differential cost. Many costs that are fixed within the relevant range are incremental or differential costs for decisions concerning activity beyond the relevant range.

DIFFERENTIAL ANALYSIS

One of the most useful tools for decision making, **differential analysis** is based on the widely accepted decision rule that *only the aspects of a choice that differ among alternatives are relevant to a decision*. A major step in differential analysis is the identification of differential costs, which we have just discussed, and any differential revenue among the alternatives. The differences in such key variables as revenue and costs often determine the attractiveness of each alternative.

For example, when you are deciding which theater to attend, the admission price is irrelevant (has no effect) if both theaters charge the same price. However, if the taxi fare is $4 to one and $3 to the other, then the $1 differential cost is relevant to (has an effect on) the choice. The decision process is simplified by concentrating only on the factors that are different; this is the basis of differential analysis. For example, suppose a firm may use certain facilities to produce and sell either product A or product B. The decision is to be in favor of the product promising the most net income based on the following estimated operating data:

	Alternatives	
	Product A	Product B
Units that can be sold	12,000	18,000
Unit selling price	$8	$6
Manufacturing costs:		
Variable (per unit)	$3	$2
Fixed (total)	$32,000	$32,000
Selling and administrative expenses:		
Variable (per unit)	$1	$1
Fixed (total)	$6,000	$6,000

We may compare the alternatives by preparing conventional income statements for each. In this example, comparative income statements would appear as follows:

| | Alternatives | | |
	Product A	Product B	Difference
Revenue			
(12,000 units @ $8)	$96,000		
(18,000 units @ $6)		$108,000	$12,000
Cost of goods sold (manufacturing costs):			
Variable (12,000 @ $3 per unit)	$36,000		
(18,000 @ $2 per unit)		$ 36,000	$ –0–
Fixed (total)	32,000	32,000	–0–
Selling and administrative expenses:			
Variable (@ $1 per unit)	12,000	18,000	6,000
Fixed (total)	6,000	6,000	–0–
Total expenses	$86,000	$ 92,000	$ 6,000
Net income	$10,000	$ 16,000	$ 6,000

This analysis shows a $6,000 increase in net income associated with alternative B as a result of a $12,000 increase in total revenue that is partially offset by a $6,000 increase in variable selling and administrative expenses.

Differential analysis of the same situation is illustrated below, where consideration is limited to the revenue and expense factors that differ if product B is produced rather than product A.

Differential revenue:	
Revenue forgone on first 12,000 units, ($8 − $6) × 12,000	($24,000)
Additional revenue from increased sales volume, $6 × 6,000 units	36,000
Net additional revenue	$12,000
Differential costs:	
Increase in variable selling and administrative expenses, 6,000 units at $1	6,000
Net differential income in favor of product B	$ 6,000

Clearly, the differential approach shows the same net advantage for alternative B as the income statements, but does so more concisely. For this reason, management often uses differential analysis in decision making. The format of differential analysis computations varies, of course, but incremental revenue and costs must be properly calculated. In our illustration, some analysts would identify the revenue forgone by selecting alternative B instead of alternative A as an opportunity cost and list it with differential costs. The net result, however, would be the same.

Intuition might at first suggest that favorable alternatives have the greatest revenue, increased revenue, smallest costs, or decreased costs. However, these generalizations are not always true. Even decreased revenue can lead to increased profit if related costs are sufficiently reduced at the same time. On the other hand, even though revenue may hold constant or increase, the differential income may be negative if related costs increase sufficiently.

Differential analysis is useful in a variety of decision situations. In the following sections of this chapter, we illustrate a number of them, such as whether to (1) accept an order at a special price, (2) make or buy needed items, (3) discontinue an unprofitable department, (4) sell or process further, and (5) emphasize production of one product or another.

ILLUSTRATIONS OF DECISION ANALYSIS

The Special Order

Frequently, business firms receive special orders from purchasers who wish a price concession. The prospective purchaser may suggest a price or ask for a bid. Sometimes the order may be for a particularly large quantity, permitting certain cost reductions for the manufacturer. Often the buyer may request that the firm produce a special version of a product to be identified with the buyer's private brand. As long as no overriding qualitative considerations exist, management should evaluate such propositions fully and be receptive to their profit potential.

Assume that Company A makes a nationally advertised automobile accessory, which it sells to distributors for $16. A discount firm has asked the company to supply 2,000 units of the accessory for $14 per unit. The accessory would carry the brand name of the discount firm. If Company A were to accept the order, a special machine attachment would be needed to differentiate the product and imprint the private brand. This attachment, which costs $1,500, would be discarded after the order was processed. Also assume that Company A has unused production capacity, and thus anticipates no change in fixed costs. The following unit cost data are available for the regular production of the item:

Raw materials	$ 5
Direct labor	4
Variable factory overhead	2
Fixed factory overhead (allocated)	3
Total cost per accessory	$14

At first glance, the proposition seems unprofitable because the unit cost figure shown here is $14, the same as the buyer's offered price, and an additional cost of $1,500 must be incurred to process the order. However, the fixed overhead of $3 included in the $14 total unit cost is not relevant to the decision and should not be considered, because Company A's total fixed costs will be incurred whether the special order is accepted or not. The following differential cost and revenue analysis reveals that the special order should be accepted:

Increase in revenue (2,000 units × $14)			$28,000
Increase in costs:			
Raw materials	$ 5 per unit		
Direct labor	4 per unit		
Variable factory overhead	2 per unit		
	$11 × 2,000 units	$22,000	
Cost of special attachment		1,500	
Total differential cost			23,500
Net advantage in accepting special order			$ 4,500

The differential costs of accepting the order consist of the variable production costs and the additional cost of the attachment needed to differentiate the product. Actually, with any price higher than $11.75 ($23,500 total differential costs ÷ 2,000 units), the company would earn a profit on the order.

Note that excess production capacity is significant to the special order decision. Without sufficient excess capacity, the additional production would probably cause additional amounts of fixed costs to be incurred. Also observe that although the $1,500 special attachment in this example is a fixed cost (because it does not respond to volume over the 2,000 unit range), it is relevant to this decision.

Specific qualitative factors considered here include ascertaining (1) that the special price does not constitute unfair price discrimination prohibited under the Robinson–Patman Act, (2) that regular sales at regular prices are not unfavorably affected by the sales of the discount store, and (3) that the long-run price structure for the product is not adversely affected by the special order. Significant concern in any of these areas might be a basis for rejecting the special order despite the potential $4,500 profit.

Make or Buy? Many manufacturing situations require the assembly of large numbers of specially designed subparts or subassemblies. Usually, the manufacturer must choose between making these components and buying them from outside suppliers. In each situation, management should evaluate the relative costs of the two choices. Because making a component uses some portion of the firm's manufacturing capacity, we assume that no more attractive use of that capacity is available.

To illustrate the make-or-buy decision, we assume that a company has made 10,000 units of a necessary component at the following costs:

Raw materials	$ 9,000
Direct labor	12,000
Variable factory overhead	5,000
Fixed factory overhead	24,000
Total costs	$50,000
Cost per unit ($50,000/10,000)	$5

Investigations by the purchasing department indicate that a comparable component can be purchased in sufficient quantities at a unit price of $4.50, an indicated savings of 50 cents per unit. At first glance, the opportunity to purchase seems most attractive. The analysis of differential costs, however, shows quite the contrary.

An analysis of operations indicates that by purchasing the component, the firm avoids only 80% of the variable overhead and 75% of the fixed overhead associated with producing the component. A differential analysis follows:

	Make Part	Buy Part	Differential if Part Is Bought*
Cost of 10,000 units:			
Raw materials	$ 9,000		($ 9,000)
Direct labor	12,000		(12,000)
Variable factory overhead	5,000	$ 1,000	(4,000)
Fixed factory overhead	24,000	6,000	(18,000)
Purchase price of components		45,000	45,000
	$50,000	$52,000	$ 2,000

*Parentheses indicate decrease.

The following approach to this analysis confirms the more comprehensive one above.

Cost to purchase component (10,000 × $4.50)		$45,000
Less costs avoided by purchasing:		
Raw materials	$ 9,000	
Direct labor	12,000	
Variable factory overhead	4,000	
Fixed factory overhead	18,000	43,000
Increase in acquisition cost by purchasing		$ 2,000

These analyses assume that the manufacturing capacity released by the decision to purchase would not be used. However, should an opportunity arise to use this capacity to generate more than $2,000 of contribution margin, then the opportunity to purchase the components would be attractive. Management should also consider such qualitative factors as any important effects on employee relations and the probability that the levels of quality and supply remain acceptable.

Dropping Unprofitable Segments

The operations of most firms are carried out within organizational segments divided along product lines, departments, branches, or sales territories. A well-designed accounting system identifies the performance of each segment of the firm so that management can make informed decisions concerning its operations. The basic question often concerns whether to discontinue unprofitable segments of a business.

Assume that the condensed income statement in Exhibit 25–3 reflects last year's operations of Santee Company, which is made up of Departments A, B, and C. It might seem at first that the firm's total income could be raised to $125,000 by discontinuing Department C and avoiding that segment's $25,000 operating loss. The following differential analysis, however, indicates that the firm's overall income would decrease, rather than increase, by discontinuing Department C:

Decrease in revenue		$300,000
Decrease in costs and expenses:		
Variable cost of goods sold	$175,000	
Variable operating expenses	70,000	245,000
Decrease in total contribution margin (and net income) from discontinuing Department C		$ 55,000

EXHIBIT 25-3

		Departments		
Santee Company				
Condensed Income Statement				
For the Year Ended June 30, 19XX				
(Thousands of Dollars)				
	Totals	A	B	C
Sales	$1,400	$700	$400	$300
Cost of Goods Sold:				
Variable Costs	$ 600	$300	$125	$175
Fixed Costs	400	200	150	50
Total Cost of Goods Sold	$1,000	$500	$275	$225
Gross Profit on Sales	$ 400	$200	$125	$ 75
Operating Expenses:				
Variable Expenses	$ 130	$ 40	$ 20	$ 70
Fixed Expenses	170	80	60	30
Total Operating Expenses	$ 300	$120	$ 80	$100
Net Income (Loss)	$ 100	$ 80	$ 45	($ 25)

Thus, even though Department C reports a $25,000 annual loss, it does generate a contribution margin of $55,000 toward the absorption of fixed costs and expenses. Consequently, discontinuing Department C would not increase the firm's income to $125,000 but would decrease it to $45,000. The $80,000 difference represents fixed costs that have been allocated to Department C, which presumably the company would not avoid.

To highlight the central issue, this illustration did not introduce several other factors that management must often consider in decisions of this type. Among these are (1) the potential termination of employees and subsequent effects on employee morale; (2) the possible effects on patronage (for example, customers of Departments A and B may go to other firms for all their purchases if Department C's products are no longer available from the same source); and (3) the question of whether the capacity currently used in Department C could be used in other ways to generate contribution margin for the firm.

Sell or Process Further?

Most firms face the decision of either selling products at one point in the production sequence or processing them further and selling them at a higher price. Examples are finished versus unfinished furniture, regular versus high-test gasoline, and unassembled kits versus assembled units of product. These process-further decision situations present another opportunity to apply differential analysis.

Assume that Company B makes and sells 50,000 unfinished telephone stands with the following operating figures per unit:

Current sales price		$12.00
Costs:		
Raw materials	$4.00	
Direct labor	2.00	
Variable factory overhead	1.50	
Fixed factory overhead*	1.00	8.50
Gross margin per unit		$ 3.50

*Applied at 50% of direct labor costs (total fixed factory overhead is $60,000).

The company now has excess productive capacity, which should remain available in the foreseeable future. Consequently, management believes that part of this excess capacity could be used to paint and decorate the telephone stands and sell them at $15 per unit in the finished furniture market. A study carried out by the company's production department indicates that the additional processing will add $1.30 to the raw materials costs and 80 cents to the direct labor costs of each unit and that variable overhead will continue to be incurred at 75% of direct labor costs.

This decision situation illustrates how failure to consider cost behavior factors properly can lead to an erroneous decision. The following analysis, using average total unit costs, indicates that the telephone stand should not be processed further—an erroneous decision, as we shall see.

New sales price per unit		$15.00
Costs:		
Raw materials ($4 + $1.30)	$5.30	
Direct labor ($2 + $0.80)	2.80	
Variable factory overhead (75% of direct labor costs)	2.10	
Fixed factory overhead (applied at 50% of direct labor costs)	1.40	
Total costs		11.60
Gross margin per unit if processed further		$ 3.40

Because this analysis shows that the prospective gross margin after processing further would be 10 cents smaller than at the earlier stages, the decision to process further would be rejected.

The foregoing analysis contains two defects. First, it includes amounts of costs that are common to both alternatives. The manufacturing costs to bring the product to the original point of sale (as unfinished furniture) are the same for either choice and are therefore irrelevant. Second, the fixed factory overhead is erroneously treated in the analysis as though it will increase in proportion to direct labor costs. With excess capacity, fixed overhead should not increase and is therefore not a relevant cost factor. In other words, the analysis is unnecessarily complicated and contains a cost analysis error.

In contrast, the strict differential analysis shown below supports the proposal to process further.

	Per Unit	Totals for 50,000 Units
Differential revenue ($15 − $12)	$3.00	$150,000
Differential costs:		
Raw materials	$1.30	$ 65,000
Direct labor	0.80	40,000
Variable factory overhead	0.60	30,000
Fixed factory overhead	0	0
Total differential costs	2.70	$135,000
Excess of differential revenue over differential costs	$0.30	$ 15,000

Both the per-unit and total differential analyses indicate the advantage of process-ing further.

Product Emphasis

Because most firms produce several products, management must continually examine operating data and decide which combination of products offers the greatest total long-run profit potential. The decisions related to product emphasis are seldom as simple as determining the most profitable product and confining production to that one product. Typically, management faces such operational constraints as limited demand for the most profitable products, the competitive necessity of offering a line of products with a variety of qualities and capacities, and, in seeking better utilization of existing capacity, the need to produce other, less profitable products.

In product emphasis analysis, an important and widely accepted generali-zation is that *the firm optimizes its income when it maximizes the contribution margin earned per unit of constraining resource*. The concept of constraining resource stems from the realization that as a firm increases its volume, some resource is eventually exhausted and thus constrains, or limits, the continued expansion of the firm. Which resources are constraining depends on the firm, the operating conditions, and even the products under consideration. Typical exam-ples are key raw materials, labor skills, machine capacities, and factory floor space or storage space. Simply stated, management has optimized the firm's product mix when it maximizes the contribution margin earned on each unit of the par-ticular resource that limits increased production.

To illustrate product emphasis decisions, assume that Beta Company pro-duces products X, Y, and Z, and that factory machine capacity is its constraining resource. Beta Company operates at 90% capacity, and management wants to devote the unused capacity to one of the products. The following data represent Beta Company's current operations:

	Products		
	X	Y	Z
Per-unit data:			
Sales price	$20	$22	$6
Variable costs	8	16	2
Contribution margin	$12	$ 6	$4
Fixed costs*	6	2	1
Net income	$ 6	$ 4	$3

*Allocated on basis of machine hours at $1 per hour.

Intuition suggests that the extra capacity should be devoted either to product Y, which has the highest sales price, or to product X, which has the highest per-unit contribution margin and net income. However, an analysis of the *contribution margin of each product per unit of constraining factor* reveals that product Z should receive the added capacity.

Note that fixed costs are allocated among products on the basis of machine hours—the constraining resource in our example. Furthermore, the unit allocations of fixed costs, above, indicate that product X requires three times as many machine hours as product Y and six times as many as product Z. The contribution per unit of machine capacity for each product follows:

	Products		
	X	Y	Z
Contribution margin per unit	$12	$6	$4
Units of machine capacity required			
(as indicated by the allocation of fixed costs)	6	2	1
Contribution margin per unit of			
machine capacity (the constraining resource)	$ 2	$3	$4

Use of the remaining capacity generates a greater contribution margin if devoted to product Z. As this simple example illustrates, in deciding product emphasis management should use contribution margin per unit of constraining resource, rather than the relative sales prices, unit contribution margins, or even unit profit of various products.

Acquisition of Plant Assets

Because of the large amount of funds and the long-term commitments that may be involved, management decisions related to the acquisition of plant assets are often complex. These capital budgeting decisions are considered in Chapter 27.

VARIABLE COSTING

In Chapter 21, we defined product costs as all factory costs—raw (or direct) materials, direct labor, and factory overhead. These costs were capitalized as inventory during the production period and recognized as expense (cost of goods sold) only when the related merchandise was sold. This method of attaching all factory costs to the product is often descriptively termed **full** or **absorption costing.**

In contrast, some firms use **variable costing** to determine the cost of their manufactured products.[1] Under variable costing, only variable manufacturing costs are capitalized as inventory. Any fixed manufacturing costs are expensed in the period incurred. Exhibit 25–4 contrasts the two approaches to costing. The only difference between absorption and variable costing is that fixed factory overhead is capitalized under absorption costing and expensed under variable costing.

---

[1]Variable costing is widely referred to as *direct costing.* The latter is a misnomer, however, because *variable* costs—not *direct* costs—are capitalized under *direct* costing. This distinction is readily apparent in Exhibit 25–4.

EXHIBIT 25–4
Comparison of Absorption
and Variable Costing

Typical Manufacturing Cost (or Expense)	Typical Behavior Pattern	Absorption Costing Product Cost	Absorption Costing Period Cost	Variable Costing Product Cost	Variable Costing Period Cost
Direct Costs:					
Raw Materials	Variable	X		X	
Labor	Variable	X		X	
Indirect Costs:					
Factory Overhead	Variable	X		X	
Factory Overhead	Fixed	X			X
Other Expenses:					
Nonfactory Administration	(may vary)		X		X
Selling	(may vary)		X		X

In general, variable costing (carrying only variable costs in the inventory accounts listed under the current assets of the balance sheet) is considered a departure from orthodox financial accounting. The AICPA has insisted that published financial reports attested to by CPAs be prepared on an absorption costing basis. It believes that all factory costs should be attributed to products and that inventories of work in process and finished goods should contain their allocable shares of factory costs, both fixed and variable. Likewise, the Internal Revenue Service has generally insisted on the use of absorption costing in determining net income for tax purposes.

Although variable costing should not be used to prepare financial statements for external use, management may use variable costing statements for analytical purposes. A principal benefit is that variable costing usually causes net income figures to move in the same direction as sales. With absorption costing, net income may increase in periods when production volume outstrips sales and decrease when the company outsells production and thus reduces inventory levels. Because management feels that sales and net income should vary directly with each other, variable costing statements may be preferable for managerial purposes.

In Exhibit 25–5, a comparison of condensed, partial income statements for the Elway Company for four periods, using both absorption costing and variable costing, demonstrates the effects just discussed. For this simple illustration, we assume that a single item sold for $5 per unit, that variable product costs are $1 per unit, and that fixed product costs are $300 per period. The following sales and production figures, in units, are given for the four periods:

	Period 1	Period 2	Period 3	Period 4	Total
Sales (in units)	100	100	100	100	400
Production (in units)	100	150	50	100	400

EXHIBIT 25–5

The Elway Company
Partial Income Statements

ABSORPTION COSTING

	Period 1	Period 2	Period 3	Period 4
Sales (100 units @ $5)	$500	$500	$500	$500
Cost of Goods Sold:				
Beginning Inventory	$ 0	$ 0	$150	$ 0
Cost of Goods Manufactured	400	450	350	400
Available for Sale	$400	$450	$500	$400
Ending Inventory	0	150	0	0
Cost of Goods Sold	400	300	500	400
Gross Profit	$100	$200	$ 0	$100

VARIABLE COSTING

	Period 1	Period 2	Period 3	Period 4
Sales (100 units @ $5)	$500	$500	$500	$500
Cost of Goods Sold:				
Beginning Inventory	$ 0	$ 0	$ 50	$ 0
Variable Cost of Goods Manufactured	100	150	50	100
	$100	$150	$100	$100
Ending Inventory	0	50	0	0
Variable Cost of Sales	100	100	100	100
Contribution Margin	$400	$400	$400	$400
Fixed Costs	300	300	300	300
Gross Profit	$100	$100	$100	$100

The Elway Company normally produces and sells 100 units per period. Note, however, that in period 2 the company produced an additional 50 units for inventory that are sold in period 3 together with the 50 units produced in period 3.

In the absorption costing statement shown in the top half of Exhibit 25–5, the cost of goods manufactured includes fixed product costs of $300 per period and variable product costs of $1 per unit produced. The $150 inventory shown at the end of period 2 consists of $50 variable costs (50 units × $1) and $100 fixed costs. (Because one-third of the units produced remain in inventory, one-third of the $300 fixed costs is assigned to the inventory.)

In the variable costing statement shown in the lower half of Exhibit 25–5, the cost of goods manufactured includes only variable product costs at $1 per unit produced. Likewise, the inventory at the end of period 2 consists only of $1 variable product cost times the 50 units in the inventory. The $300 fixed costs are deducted from contribution margin each period.

A total of $400 gross profit is reported for the four periods under both methods. However, the variable costing method shows the same gross profit figures each period, which are correlated with the constant sales volume over the four periods. On the other hand, under the absorption costing method, gross profit moves up and down with production. The reason, of course, is that the fixed costs are added to the inventory when production outstrips sales and released when the company sells its entire inventory. Sometimes management can be quite perturbed with results from absorption costing statements—especially when profits do not improve despite an appreciable increase in sales volume. The company's controller, however, can always prepare income statements under both approaches and explain their differences, provided that the proper analysis has segregated variable and fixed costs.

To highlight the effect of variable costing on inventories and income in the foregoing illustration, we considered only manufacturing (or product) costs. When detailed income statements are prepared under the variable costing method, fixed and variable costs of all types—including selling and administrative expenses—must be properly segregated. An example of a detailed income statement prepared in accordance with the variable costing concept is shown in Exhibit 25–6.

The term **manufacturing margin,** which appears in Exhibit 25–6, sometimes describes the difference between revenue and variable cost of goods sold. Then contribution margin is obtained by deducting variable selling and administrative expenses from the manufacturing margin. Finally, all types of fixed costs and expenses—manufacturing, selling, and administrative—are deducted to arrive at net income.

We may make the following generalizations about the differences in reported income under absorption and variable costing:

(1) When sales are balanced to production (with inventories unchanged), both costing systems result in the same reported income. See periods 1 and 4 in Exhibit 25–5.

(2) When production exceeds sales (inventory increases), absorption costing reports the higher income. See period 2 in Exhibit 25–5.

(3) When sales exceed production (inventory decreases), variable costing reports the higher income. See period 3 in Exhibit 25–5.

(4) The difference in reported income is equal to the fixed overhead per unit of inventory multiplied by the change in inventory units. See periods 2 and 3 in Exhibit 25–5.

(5) Over the long run, both costing systems report the same income, because in the long run, production and sales for most firms must be balanced.

The following advantages and disadvantages of using variable costing originate in the fact that under variable costing no fixed overhead costs are assigned to inventory carrying values.

EXHIBIT 25–6

Cawley Company
Variable Costing Income Statement
For the Year Ended December 31, 19XX

Sales (20,000 units @ $5)			$100,000
Variable Cost of Goods Sold:			
Beginning Inventory (12,000 units @ $3)		$36,000	
Cost of Goods Manufactured (18,000 units @ $3)		54,000	
Goods Available for Sale		$90,000	
Ending Inventory (10,000 units @ $3)		30,000	60,000
Manufacturing Margin			$ 40,000
Variable Selling and Administrative Expenses:			
Variable Selling Expense		$ 8,000	
Variable Administrative Expense		4,000	12,000
Contribution Margin			$ 28,000
Fixed Costs and Expenses:			
Fixed Manufacturing Cost		$12,000	
Fixed Selling Expense		5,000	
Fixed Administrative Expense		3,000	20,000
Net Income			$ 8,000

Advantages of Variable Costing

(1) Management may be more aware of cost behavior factors in the firm's operations and be likely to use this information in short-term decision situations in which contribution margin analysis is most appropriate.

(2) Reported net income tends to follow sales volume. (This may not be true under absorption costing.)

(3) Cost–volume–profit relationships are more easily discerned from variable costing income statements than from conventional absorption costing statements.

Disadvantages of Variable Costing

(1) It is often difficult to classify a number of cost factors into their fixed and variable components as required with this method, and results are only tentative.

(2) Accounting measures derived under variable costing are not in accord with generally accepted accounting principles, nor are they acceptable for reporting purposes under the Internal Revenue Code.

(3) Inventories (and therefore working capital and owners' equity) tend to be understated.

(4) Carrying inventories at only their variable costs may lead to long-run pricing decisions that provide for recovery of variable cost only rather than total cost and thus does not produce net income in the long run.

KEY POINTS TO REMEMBER

(1) Decision making, which is essentially choosing among alternatives, usually comprises three phases: planning, execution, and evaluation.

(2) Managerial analyses and reports may contain not only the traditional accounting data found in financial statements but also other data useful to management such as replacement costs and opportunity costs.

(3) The general concept of cost can be used with the following specific meanings:

product cost	semivariable cost	sunk cost
period cost	fixed cost	avoidable cost
direct cost	historical cost	marginal cost
indirect cost	replacement cost	differential cost
variable cost	out-of-pocket cost	opportunity cost

(4) Differential analysis is the study of those amounts that are expected to differ among alternatives.

(5) In a decision situation, differential analysis is favorable whenever revenue increases more than costs increase or decreases less than costs decrease.

(6) Differential analysis may be applied in the following decision situations:
  (a) Whether to accept orders at special prices.
  (b) Whether to make or buy needed components.
  (c) Whether to drop unprofitable segments.
  (d) Whether to sell or process further.
  (e) Which products to emphasize.

(7) Variable costing differs from absorption costing in that it does not assign fixed factory overhead as a product cost, but expenses it in the period incurred.

QUESTIONS

25–1 In what key ways do management reports differ from financial statements?

25–2 Define *goal identification*. Identify four fairly common examples of general managerial goals or objectives.

25–3 Briefly explain each of the following terms as they relate to decision making, and indicate how accounting methods can be employed in each.
  (a) Planning phase.
  (b) Execution phase.
  (c) Evaluation phase.

25–4   Briefly define the following:
(a) Historical cost.   (e) Avoidable cost.
(b) Replacement cost.   (f) Marginal cost.
(c) Out-of-pocket cost.   (g) Differential cost.
(d) Sunk cost.   (h) Opportunity cost.

25–5   "The higher the management level receiving reports, the more detailed the reports should be." Comment.

25–6   Although separate phases of decision making are identifiable, management is usually involved in all phases at the same time. Explain.

25–7   List several common aspects of decision making that are often not subject to quantification.

25–8   Explain what is meant by the term *differential analysis*.

25–9   Explain how differential analysis can be applied to the following types of decisions:
(a) Accepting special orders.
(b) Making or buying product components.
(c) Dropping unprofitable segments of the firm.
(d) Selling or processing further.
(e) Product emphasis.

25–10 Operating at 80% capacity, Kapp Company produces and sells 16,000 units of its only product for $22. Per-unit costs are raw materials, $5; direct labor, $7; variable factory overhead, $2; and fixed factory overhead, $3. A special order is received for 1,000 units. Based on this information, what price should Kapp charge to make a $2,000 gross profit on the special order?

25–11 Frame-All Company produces unassembled picture frames at the following average per-unit costs: raw materials, $X; direct labor, $Y; and factory overhead, $Z. The company can assemble the frames at a unit cost of 80 cents and raise the selling price from $5.25 to $6.50. Could you advise management whether or not to assemble the frames without knowing the specific amounts of manufacturing costs? How? What is the apparent advantage or disadvantage of assembling the frames?

25–12 Explain the concept of *constraining resource*, and present a general rule for optimizing product mixes.

25–13 "In differential analysis, we can generally count on variable cost being relevant and fixed cost being irrelevant." Comment.

25–14 If both approaches to a decision lead to the same conclusion, why might differential analysis be considered superior to a comprehensive analysis that reflects all revenue and costs?

25–15 What is variable costing? List its advantages and disadvantages.

25–16 What generalizations can be made about the difference in income reported under variable and absorption costing?

25–17 Assume the data in Question 25–10 (disregarding the special order opportunity) represents the first year's operations of Kapp Company, except that fixed and variable selling and administrative expenses per unit produced are $2 and $1, respectively, and 14,000 of the 16,000 units produced are sold. How does reported income for the year differ under absorption costing and under variable costing?

EXERCISES

25–18 Describe the type of cost data or information represented by each of the cost amounts identified below by a letter in parentheses. In some instances, more than one description may be appropriate.

Dean Company needs a certain production task performed on one of its products. The operation can be accomplished by a machine that was purchased for $120,000 (a) and used for a period but is now stored. Although it has been "depreciated down" to $72,000 (b) on the books, it can be sold now for only $5,000 (c). To be used, the machine must be cleaned and adjusted, which costs $2,000 (d). For $4,000 (e) per year, another firm could perform the operation in question and Dean could rent its own machine to a competitor for $3,000 (f) per year. If the machine is sold before the next personal property assessment date, the company would not have to pay $1,000 (g) in personal property taxes.

25–19 In each of four independent cases, the amount of differential revenue or differential cost is as follows (parentheses indicate decreases):

	(1)	(2)	(3)	(4)
Increases (decreases) in:				
Revenue	$15,000	$–0–	?	?
Costs	?	?	($9,000)	$–0–

For each case, determine the missing amount that would be necessary for differential revenue and costs to be:
(a) $9,000 favorable.
(b) $5,000 unfavorable.

Indicate whether your answer reflects increases or decreases.

25–20 The Georgia Company sells a single product for $16 per unit. At an operating level of 8,000 units, variable costs are $7 per unit and fixed costs $4 per unit.

The Georgia Company has been offered a price of $8 per unit on a special order of 2,000 units by Lanton Discount Stores, which would use its own brand name on the item. If Georgia Company accepts the order, raw materials cost will be $1 less per unit than for regular production. However, special stamping equipment costing $3,500 would be needed to process the order; it would then be discarded.

Assuming that volume remains within the relevant range, prepare an analysis of differential revenue and costs to determine whether Georgia Company should accept the special order.

25–21 Richards Company regularly sells its only product for $80 per unit and has a 25% profit on each sale. The company has accepted a special order for a number of units, the production of which would absorb part of its unused capacity. The special order sales price is 50% of the normal price, but the profit margin is only 20% of the regular dollar profit. What, apparently, is
(a) Richards' profit per unit on the special order?
(b) Richards' total variable cost per unit?
(c) Richards' average fixed cost per unit on regular sales?

25–22 Superior Company incurs a total cost of $81,000 in producing 9,000 units of a component needed in the assembly of its major product. The component can be purchased from an outside supplier for $8 per unit. A related cost study indicates that the total cost of the component includes fixed costs equal to 50% of the variable costs involved.

(a) Should Superior buy the component if it cannot otherwise use the released capacity? Present your answer in the form of differential analysis.

(b) What would be your answer to part (a) if the released capacity could be used in a project that would generate $20,000 of contribution margin?

25–23 Walker Manufacturing Company produces a line of electric food mixers consisting of a deluxe model, a custom model, and an economy model. Last year's sales of the deluxe model incurred a net loss of $30,000; sales were $200,000, cost of goods sold $170,000, and operating expenses $60,000. Because of the indicated loss of $30,000, management may discontinue the deluxe model. A cost study indicates that 20% of the cost of goods sold and 40% of operating expenses are fixed and that elimination of the deluxe model would not materially affect the total fixed cost incurred. Prepare a differential analysis of the effects of dropping the deluxe model, and recommend whether it should be dropped. What related qualitative factors should be considered?

25–24 JCH Machine Company makes a partially completed assembly unit that it sells for $26 per unit. Normally, 42,000 units are sold each year. Variable unit cost data on the assembly are as follows:

Raw materials	$9
Direct labor	8
Variable factory overhead	3

The company is now using only 70% of its normal capacity; it could fully use its normal capacity by processing the assembly further and selling it for $32 per unit. If the company does this, materials and labor costs will each increase by $2 per unit and variable overhead will go up by 50 cents per unit. Fixed costs will increase from the current level of $160,000 to $195,000.

Prepare an analysis showing whether the company should process the assemblies further.

25–25 The following analysis of selected data is for each of the two products Barish Company produces.

	Product A	Product B
Per-unit Data		
Sales price	$20	$14
Production costs:		
Variable	6	4
Fixed	5	2
Selling and administrative expenses:		
Variable	4	2
Fixed	3	3

In Barish's operation, machine capacity is the company's constraining resource, and machine hours is the base for allocating fixed production costs. Assuming that all production can be sold at a normal price, prepare an analysis showing which of the two products should be produced with any unused productive capacity that Barish might have.

25–26 Smythe Company sells its product for $24 per unit. Variable manufacturing costs per unit are $9, and fixed manufacturing costs per unit at the normal operating level of 12,000 units are $5. Variable selling expenses are $4 per unit sold. Fixed selling and administrative expenses total $24,000. Smythe Company had no beginning inventory in 19X1. During 19X1, the company produced 12,000 units and sold 9,000. Would net income before taxes for Smythe Company in 19X1 be higher if calculated using variable costing or using absorption costing? Indicate reported income using each method.

25–27 During its first year, Taylor, Inc. showed a $5 per unit profit under absorption costing but would have reported a total profit $4,200 less under variable costing. If production exceeded sales by 600 units and an average contribution margin of 60% was maintained, what is the apparent
(a) Fixed cost per unit?
(b) Variable cost per unit?
(c) Sales price per unit?
(d) Unit sales volume if total profit under absorption costing was $36,000?

PROBLEMS

25–28 Total cost data follow for Mead Manufacturing Company, which has a normal capacity per period of 8,000 units of product that sell for $20 each. For the foreseeable future, sales volume should continue to equal normal capacity.

Raw materials	$28,000
Direct labor	19,600
Variable factory overhead	14,700
Fixed factory overhead (Note 1)	12,600
Selling expense (Note 2)	11,200
Administrative expense (fixed)	4,900
	$91,000

(1) Beyond normal capacity, fixed overhead costs increase $600 for each 500 units or *fraction thereof* until a maximum capacity of 10,000 units is reached.
(2) Selling expenses consist of a 6% sales commission and shipping costs of 25 cents per unit. Mead pays only three-fourths of the regular sales commission rate on sales totaling 501 to 1,000 units and only two-thirds the regular commssion on sales totaling 1,000 units or more.

Mead's sales manager has received a special order for 1,200 units from a large discount chain at a price of $11 each, F.O.B. factory. The controller's office has furnished the following additional cost data related to the special order:

(1) Changes in the product's design will reduce raw materials costs 40 cents per unit.

(2) Special processing will add 20% to the per-unit direct labor costs.

(3) Variable overhead will continue at the same proportion of direct labor costs.

(4) Other costs should not be affected.

REQUIRED

(a) Present an analysis supporting a decision to accept or reject the special order. (Round computations to nearest cent.)

(b) What is the lowest price Mead could receive and still make a $1,200 profit before income taxes on the special order?

(c) What general qualitative factors should Mead consider?

25–29 Michael Corporation currently makes the nylon convertible top for its main product, a fiberglass boat designed especially for water skiing. The costs of producing the 1,500 tops needed each year are:

Nylon fabric	$67,500
Aluminum tubing	24,000
Frame fittings	6,000
Direct labor	40,500
Variable factory overhead	7,500
Fixed factory overhead	38,000

Dupre Company, a specialty fabricator of synthetic materials, can make the needed tops of comparable quality for $96 each, F.O.B. shipping point. Michael would furnish its own trademark insignia at a unit cost of $3.50. Transportation in would be $6 per unit, paid by Michael Corporation.

  Michael's chief accountant has prepared a cost analysis, which shows that only 20% of fixed overhead could be avoided if the tops are purchased. The tops have been made in a remote section of Michael's factory building, using equipment for which no alternate use is apparent in the foreseeable future.

REQUIRED

(a) Prepare a differential analysis showing whether or not you would recommend that the convertible tops be purchased from Dupre Company.

(b) Assuming that the production capacity released by purchasing the tops could be devoted to a subcontracting job for another company that netted a contribution margin of $3,650, what maximum purchase price could Michael Corporation pay for the tops?

(c) Identify two important qualitative factors that Michael Corporation should consider in deciding whether to purchase the needed tops.

25–30 Based on the following analysis of last year's operations of Bourne, Inc., a financial vice-president of the company believes that the firm's total net income could be increased by $30,000 if the Soft Goods Division were discontinued. (Amounts are given in thousands of dollars.)

	Totals	All Other Divisions	Soft Goods Division
Sales	$2,620	$1,900	$720
Cost of Goods Sold:			
Variable	(900)	(600)	(300)
Fixed	(480)	(320)	(160)
Gross Profit	$1,240	$ 980	$260
Operating Expenses:			
Variable	(670)	(450)	(220)
Fixed	(290)	(220)	(70)
Net Income (Loss)	$ 280	$ 310	($ 30)

REQUIRED

Provide answers for each of the following independent situations:

(a) Assuming that fixed costs and expenses would not be affected by discontinuing the Soft Goods Division, prepare an analysis showing why you agree or disagree with the vice-president.

(b) Assume that discontinuance of the Soft Goods Division will enable the company to avoid 20% of the fixed portion of cost of goods sold and 25% of the fixed operating expenses allocated to the Soft Goods Division. Calculate the resulting effect on net income.

(c) Assume that in addition to the cost avoidance in part (b), the production capacity released by discontinuance of the Soft Goods Division can be used to produce 6,000 units of a new product that would have a variable cost per unit of $9 and would require additional fixed costs totaling $17,500. At what unit price must the new product be sold if the company is to increase its total net income by $30,000?

25–31 Review the operating data for Mead Manufacturing Company presented in Problem 25–28. Disregard the special order opportunity.

    Mead is considering whether to improve its profit by continuing to produce 8,000 units of product but processing each unit further and selling it at a higher price. In addition to the information presented in Problem 25–28, consider the following:

(1) Raw materials cost would increase by $3 per unit.

(2) Direct labor would increase 40%.

(3) Variable overhead should continue at the same proportion of direct labor costs.

(4) The further processing will require an amount of additional fixed factory capacity equal to that required for making an additional 1,500 units of product.

REQUIRED

Assuming all orders are for fewer than 500 units each:

(a) Determine the effect on Mead's profit of processing further and raising the unit selling price to $26.

(b) What is the smallest increase in per-unit selling price that Mead could accept and still decide to process further?

25–32 American Blender, Inc. manufactures both a deluxe and a standard model of a household food blender. Because of limited demand, for several years production has been at 80% of estimated capacity, which is thought to be limited by the number of machine hours available. At current operation levels, a profit analysis for each product line shows the following:

Per-unit Data	Deluxe		Standard	
Sales price		$144		$56
Production costs:				
Raw materials	$63		$ 8	
Direct labor	24		16	
Variable factory overhead	10		7	
Fixed factory overhead*	15	$112	6	$37
Variable operating expenses		12		8
Fixed operating expenses		5		3
Total costs		$129		$48
Operating income		$ 15		$ 8

*Assigned on the basis of machine hours at normal capacity.

Management wants to utilize the company's current excess capacity by increasing production.

REQUIRED
(a) What general decision guideline applies in this situation?
(b) Assuming that sufficient units of either product can be sold at current prices to use existing capacity fully and that fixed costs will not be affected, prepare an analysis showing which product line should be emphasized if net income for the firm is the decision basis.

25–33 Lakeland Corporation makes a product with total unit manufacturing costs of $9, of which $6 is variable. No units were on hand at the beginning of 19X0. During 19X0 and 19X1, the only product manufactured was sold for $14 per unit, and the cost structure did not change. The company uses the first-in, first-out inventory method and has the following production and sales for 19X0 and 19X1:

	Units Manufactured	Units Sold
19X0	120,000	90,000
19X1	120,000	130,000

REQUIRED
(a) Prepare gross profit computations for 19X0 and 19X1 using absorption costing.
(b) Prepare gross profit computations for 19X0 and 19X1 using variable costing.
(c) Explain how your answers illustrate the related generalizations presented in the chapter regarding the differences between reported income (or gross profit) under absorption and variable costing.

25–34 Summarized data for the first year's operations of Madison Manufacturing, Inc. are as follows:

Sales (75,000 units)	$7,500,000
Production costs (80,000 units):	
Raw materials	2,200,000
Direct labor	1,800,000
Factory overhead:	
Variable	1,360,000
Fixed	800,000
Selling and administrative expenses:	
Variable	420,000
Fixed	600,000

REQUIRED

(a) Prepare an income statement based on full absorption costing.

(b) Prepare an income statement based on variable costing.

(c) Assume you must decide quickly whether to accept a special one-time order for 1,000 units for $75 per unit. Which income statement presents the most relevant data? Determine the apparent profit or loss on the special order based solely on this data.

(d) If the ending inventory is destroyed by fire, which income statement would you use as a basis for filing an insurance claim for the fire loss? Why?

ALTERNATE PROBLEMS

25–28A Total cost data follows for Hardy Manufacturing Company, which has a normal capacity per period of 20,000 units of product that sell for $30 each. For the foreseeable future, regular sales volume should continue to equal normal capacity.

Raw materials	$150,000
Direct labor	120,000
Variable factory overhead	70,000
Fixed factory overhead (Note 1)	66,000
Selling expense (Note 2)	70,000
Administrative expense (fixed)	30,000
	$506,000

(1) Beyond normal capacity, fixed overhead costs increase $4,500 for each 1,000 units or *fraction thereof* until a maximum capacity of 24,000 units is reached.

(2) Selling expenses consist of a 10% sales commission and shipping costs of $1 per unit. Hardy pays only one-half of the regular sales commission rate on any sale amounting to $2,000 or more.

Hardy's sales manager has received a special order for 2,500 units from a large discount chain at a price of $24 each, F.O.B. factory. The controller's office has furnished the following additional cost data related to the special order:

(1) Changes in the product's design will reduce raw materials $2.25 per unit.

(2) Special processing will add 10% to the per-unit direct labor costs.

(3) Variable overhead will continue at the same proportion of direct labor costs.

(4) Other costs should not be affected.

REQUIRED

(a) Present an analysis supporting a decision to accept or reject the special order.

(b) What is the lowest price Hardy could receive and still make a profit of $5,000 before income taxes on the special order?

(c) What general qualitative factors should Hardy consider?

25–29A Heather Corporation currently makes the nylon mooring cover for its main product, a fiberglass boat designed for tournament bass fishing. The costs of producing the 2,000 covers needed each year are:

Nylon fabric	$80,000
Wood battens	16,000
Brass fittings	8,000
Direct labor	32,000
Variable factory overhead	24,000
Fixed factory overhead	40,000

Cohen Company, a specialty fabricator of synthetic materials, can make the needed covers of comparable quality for $78 each, F.O.B. shipping point. Heather would furnish its own trademark insignia at a unit cost of $5. Transportation in would be $4 per unit, paid by Heather Corporation.

Heather's chief accountant has prepared a cost analysis, which shows that only 30% of fixed overhead could be avoided if the covers are purchased. The covers have been made in a remote section of Heather's factory building, using equipment for which no alternate use is apparent in the foreseeable future.

REQUIRED

(a) Prepare a differential analysis showing whether or not you would recommend that the mooring covers be purchased from Cohen Company.

(b) Assuming that the production capacity released by purchasing the covers could be devoted to a subcontracting job for another company that netted a contribution margin of $10,000, what maximum purchase price could Heather pay for the covers?

(c) Identify two important qualitative factors that Heather Corporation should consider in deciding whether to purchase the needed covers.

25–30A Based on the following analysis of last year's operations of Dykman, Inc., a financial vice-president of the company believes that the firm's total net income could be increased by $25,000 if the Soft Goods Division were discontinued. (Amounts are given in thousands of dollars.)

	Totals	All Other Divisions	Soft Goods Division
Sales	$3,640	$2,800	$840
Cost of Goods Sold:			
Variable	(1,485)	(1,100)	(385)
Fixed	(970)	(800)	(170)
Gross Profit	$1,185	$ 900	$285
Operating Expenses:			
Variable	(545)	(330)	(215)
Fixed	(385)	(290)	(95)
Net Income (Loss)	$ 255	$ 280	($ 25)

REQUIRED

Provide answers for each of the following independent situations:

(a) Assuming that fixed costs and expenses would not be affected by discontinuing the Soft Goods Division, prepare an analysis showing why you agree or disagree with the vice-president.

(b) Assume that discontinuance of the Soft Goods Division will enable the company to avoid 30% of the fixed portion of cost of goods sold and 40% of the fixed operating expenses allocated to the Soft Goods Division. Calculate the resulting effect on net income.

(c) Assume that in addition to the cost avoidance in part (b), the production capacity released by discontinuance of the Soft Goods Division can be used to produce 6,000 units of a new product that would have a variable cost per unit of $15 and require additional fixed costs totaling $14,000. At what unit price must the new product be sold if the company is to increase its total net income by $45,000?

25–31A Review the operating data for Hardy Manufacturing Company presented in Problem 25–28A. Disregard the special order opportunity.

Hardy is considering whether to improve its profit by continuing to produce 20,000 units of product but processing each unit further and selling it at a higher price. In addition to the information presented in Problem 25–28A, consider the following:

(1) Raw materials cost should increase by $2.70 per unit.
(2) Direct labor should increase 20%.
(3) Variable overhead should continue at the same proportion of direct labor costs.
(4) Further processing would require additional fixed factory capacity equal to that required for making an additional 1,500 units of product.

REQUIRED

Assuming all sales orders are for $2,000 or less:

(a) Determine the effect on Hardy's profit of processing further and raising the unit selling price to $37.50.

(b) What is the smallest per-unit selling price that Hardy could accept and still make an incremental profit of $40,000?

25–32A Wolff Corporation manufactures both automatic and manual residential water softeners. Because of limited demand, for several years production has been at 90% of estimated capacity, which is thought to be limited by the number of machine hours available. At current operation levels, a profit analysis for each product line shows the following:

Per-unit Data		Automatic		Manual
Sales price		$410		$220
Production costs:				
Raw materials	$72		$42	
Direct labor	60		36	
Variable factory overhead	36		18	
Fixed factory overhead*	72	$240	36	$132
Variable operating expenses		48		12
Fixed operating expenses		84		48
Total costs		$372		$192
Operating income		$ 38		$ 28

*Assigned on the basis of machine hours at normal capacity.

Management wants to utilize the company's current excess capacity by increasing production.

REQUIRED
(a) What general decision guideline applies in this situation?
(b) Assuming that sufficient units of either product can be sold at current prices to use existing capacity fully and that fixed costs will not be affected, prepare an analysis showing which product line should be emphasized if net income for the firm is the decision basis.

25–33A The Butte Company makes a product with total unit manufacturing costs of $16, of which $9 is variable. No units were on hand at the beginning of 19X0. During 19X0 and 19X1, the only product manufactured was sold for $24 per unit, and the cost structure did not change. The company uses the first-in, first-out inventory method and has the following production and sales for 19X0 and 19X1:

	Units Manufactured	Units Sold
19X0	100,000	70,000
19X1	100,000	120,000

REQUIRED
(a) Prepare gross profit computations for 19X0 and 19X1 using absorption costing.
(b) Prepare gross profit computations for 19X0 and 19X1 using variable costing.
(c) Explain how your answers illustrate the related generalizations presented in the chapter regarding the differences between reported income (or gross profit) under absorption and variable costing.

BUSINESS DECISION PROBLEM

Champion Corporation manufactures both an automatic and a manual household dehumidifier. Because of limited demand, for several years production has been at 80% of estimated capacity, which is thought to be limited by the number of machine hours available. At current operation levels, a profit analysis for each product line shows the following:

Per-unit Data	Automatic		Manual	
Sales price		$300		$110
Production costs:				
Raw materials	$60		$16	
Direct labor	36		18	
Variable factory overhead	54		12	
Fixed factory overhead*	35	$185	14	$ 60
Variable operating expenses		42		15
Fixed operating expenses		25		11
Total costs		$252		$ 86
Operating income		$ 48		$ 24

*Assigned on the basis of machine hours at normal capacity.

Management wants to utilize the company's current excess capacity by increasing production.

REQUIRED

Present answers for the following questions in each independent situation:

(a) Assume that sufficient units of either product can be sold at current prices to utilize existing capacity fully and that fixed costs will not be affected.
   (1) To which product should the excess capacity be devoted if the decision basis is maximization of sales revenue?
   (2) What would be your answer to part (1) if the decision were based on contribution margin per unit of product?
   (3) Prepare an analysis showing which product line should be emphasized if the firm's net income is the decision basis.
   (4) What general decision guideline applies in this situation?
(b) Suppose the excess capacity represents 10,000 machine hours, which can be used to make 4,000 automatic units or 10,000 manual units or any proportionate combination. The only market available for these extra units is a foreign market in which the sales prices must be reduced by 20% and in which no more than 6,000 units of either model can be sold. All costs will remain the same except that the selling commission of 10% (included in variable operating expenses) will be avoided. Prepare an analysis showing which product should be emphasized and the effect on the firm's net income.
(c) Assume that the excess capacity can be used as indicated in part (b), and that the firm's market research department believes that the production available from using the excess capacity exclusively on either model can be sold in the domestic market at regular prices if a promotion campaign costing $150,000 is undertaken for the automatic model or $200,000 for the manual model. Prepare an analysis indicating for which product the campaign should be undertaken.

26

Standard Costs
and Budgeting

> **Fortune is the arbiter of half our actions,**
> **but she still leaves the control of the other half to us.**
>
> MACHIAVELLI

In our discussions of job order and process costing, we demonstrated that accounting provides management with the actual costs of a firm's activities and products. In Chapter 25 we showed that, if it is to carry out its planning, control, decision-making, and performance measurement functions, *management must not only know actual costs but must also have some reasonable idea of what costs should be.* To plan operations, management must plan costs, and to exercise cost control, it must compare actual costs with planned costs. To measure performance and make rational decisions, management must know whether given cost amounts are favorable (actual less than planned) or unfavorable (actual greater than planned). The need to plan costs and to know what costs should be has led to the development of standard costs and budgeting.

The processes of determining standard costs and developing budgets both involve planning what costs and cost-related aspects of operations ought to be. **Standard product costs** are derived through a detailed determination of what quantities should be used and what prices should be paid for production inputs—raw materials, direct labor, and factory overhead. **Budgeting** uses standard costs to formulate a comprehensive financial plan for a wide array of operational activities such as sales, production, operating expenses, and cash flows. The major objectives of standard costing and the broader area of budgeting are identifying the differences between planned and actual costs and taking appropriate corrective action. In this chapter, we illustrate the determination and use of standard costs and conclude with a discussion of budgeting procedures.

STANDARD COSTS

Standard costs are amounts that analysis has shown should under ideal circumstances be incurred for raw materials, direct labor, and factory overhead. Standard costs are developed prior to the applicable operating periods and remain in effect until circumstances require their revision. Management's routine comparison of actual costs with standard costs reveals the differences, or *cost variances* (often simply called *variances*). Cost variances are *unfavorable* when actual costs exceed standard costs and *favorable* when standard costs exceed actual costs. With known variances, management can operate on the principle of **management by exception,** in which it concentrates efforts on those aspects of operations that deviate from standards, as indicated by the related variances.

The concept of standard cost can be used informally in special periodic management reports comparing actual costs with what costs should have been, according to plans. However, standard costs are most effectively used when they—and related variances—are recorded in the accounts. Under such standard cost procedures, work in process, finished goods, and cost of goods sold are recorded at the standard costs for raw materials, direct labor, and factory overhead. Differences between the standard costs of goods produced and actual costs incurred are recorded as either favorable or unfavorable variances in appropriately titled accounts. Determining and accounting for standard costs and variances is explained later in the chapter.

DETERMINATION OF STANDARD COSTS

Establishing standard costs can be a complex task. For example, determining standard materials costs requires decisions concerning optimum types, combinations, qualities, quantities, and prices for all materials. Deriving standard labor costs often involves time-and-motion studies and choices among various combinations of labor skills and machine operations. Determining standard overhead costs requires an analysis of plant layout, equipment capacities, specific production techniques, and cost behavior patterns. People from a number of areas—accounting, production, product engineering, purchasing, personnel, management, and even labor unions—may all contribute to the development of cost standards.

Most companies establish cost standards on the basis of some reasonably attainable (rather than theoretically perfect) level of efficiency. Determined standards that are too seldom or too easily attained tend to lose their motivating force as a standard of performance against which actual performance can be meaningfully measured. Standards should be updated when significant changes occur in prices, materials used, production technology, labor rates or contracts, or product design. In the final analysis, variances determined with the aid of standard costs can be meaningful only if the standards used represent a potentially attainable level of efficiency under current operating conditions.

Ordinarily, a manufacturing firm establishes standard cost specfications for each of its products. Each standard cost consists of a standard raw materials cost, a standard direct labor cost, and a standard factory overhead cost.

Raw Materials Standards

The standard cost of raw materials used to make a finished unit is the product of two factors—**standard usage** and **standard price.** Usually, to determine the quantities of the raw materials used to make a unit of product, production personnel first determine the needed quality, production runs, normal spoilage, and other factors. Standard prices are often calculated by purchasing department and accounting personnel after specifications, price quotations from suppliers, possible discounts, and related factors have been considered.

To begin our illustration, assume that the Costello Manufacturing Company makes only one simple product, A, which requires one type of raw material, X.

If the standard usage is two pounds of X to make one unit of A, and the standard price of X is $1 per pound, the standard materials cost for a unit of product A is $2.

Direct Labor Standards

The standard cost of direct labor used to make a finished unit is also the product of two factors—**standard time** and **standard rate.** Using time-and-motion studies or other analyses, job analysts and other production personnel set the standard time alloted to each labor operation. Union representatives may also considerably influence the time standards. Standard rates are usually set by contracts negotiated between management and labor unions. If, for Costello Manufacturing Company, the standard direct labor time to make a unit of product A was set at one hour and the standard labor rate was $6 per hour, the standard cost for direct labor would be $6 per unit of product A.

Factory Overhead Standards

Many of the difficulties of accounting for factory overhead were discussed in earlier chapters. The inherent complexities of overhead costs—variety, indirect association with production, and the presence of both fixed and variable cost elements—require a different approach to determining factory overhead standards.

Typically, some form of flexible budgeting is used to estimate the amount of factory overhead costs at the anticipated level of production that the firm considers its normal capacity. Standard rates for factory overhead are determined by dividing the total amount of standard overhead by the units of normal production capacity. Production capacity is usually expressed in direct labor hours, direct labor costs, or perhaps machine hours. Often, a separate rate is calculated for **fixed overhead** and for **variable overhead.** A columnar flexible budget for the only production department of the Costello Manufacturing Company appears in Exhibit 26–1. The budget indicates that factory overhead is applied on the basis of direct labor hours and that normal capacity is 10,000 standard direct labor hours per month. The standard amounts of factory overhead at various levels of operation are shown.

Note that factory overhead is separated into variable and fixed cost elements, that variable overhead increases proportionately with production levels, and that fixed overhead does not respond to changes in production levels. At Costello Manufacturing Company's normal capacity of 10,000 standard direct labor hours, the budget indicates a standard variable overhead rate of $1 per direct labor hour ($10,000/10,000 direct labor hours) and a standard fixed factory overhead rate of $3 per direct labor hour ($30,000/10,000 direct labor hours).

The columnar approach to flexible budgeting shown in Exhibit 26–1 provides standard cost amounts only for the operating levels indicated at the head of each column. Thus, some interpolation would be required to determine the standard factory overhead cost at, say, 93% or 97% of normal capacity. We solve this problem easily by restating the factory overhead cost budget as a cost formula, as was illustrated in Chapter 24.

EXHIBIT 26–1

Costello Manufacturing Company
Flexible Factory Overhead Cost Budget
For the Month of June, 19XX

	Production Levels			
	80%	90%	100%	110%
Percent of Normal Capacity				
Standard Direct Labor Hours	8,000	9,000	10,000	11,000
Budgeted Factory Overhead:				
Variable costs:				
Factory supplies used	$ 800	$ 900	$ 1,000	$ 1,100
Indirect labor	1,600	1,800	2,000	2,200
Power	2,400	2,700	3,000	3,300
Other	3,200	3,600	4,000	4,400
Total variable overhead	$ 8,000	$ 9,000	$10,000	$11,000
Fixed costs:				
Supervisory salaries	$12,000	$12,000	$12,000	$12,000
Depreciation	8,000	8,000	8,000	8,000
Other	10,000	10,000	10,000	10,000
Total fixed overhead	$30,000	$30,000	$30,000	$30,000
Total Budgeted Factory Overhad	$38,000	$39,000	$40,000	$41,000

$$\begin{array}{ccc} \text{Total} & \text{Total} & \\ \text{Factory} = \text{Fixed} + \left(\begin{array}{c} \text{Variable} \\ \text{Overhead} \times \begin{array}{c} \text{Production} \\ \text{Volume} \end{array} \\ \text{per Unit} \end{array} \right) \\ \text{Overhead} & \text{Overhead} & \end{array}$$

$$\$40{,}000 = \$30{,}000 + \left(\$1 \times \begin{array}{c} 10{,}000 \text{ standard direct} \\ \text{labor hours} \end{array} \right)$$

By incorporating the appropriate number of standard direct labor hours, the cost formula can provide the standard factory overhead cost amount for any number of direct labor hours. We use this formula version of the flexible budget throughout our illustration of determining standard factory overhead costs.

Total Standard Costs

Most firms prepare for each product a document summarizing the standard costs for raw materials, direct labor, and factory overhead. Based on the preceding concepts, Costello Manufacturing Company's standard cost summary for product A would appear as in Exhibit 26–2. Thus, under normal conditions and operating at normal capacity, product A should be produced for a total cost of $12 per unit. We use these standard costs in our illustration of cost variance determination.

EXHIBIT 26-2

Costello Manufacturing Company Standard Cost Summary—Product A		
Raw Materials (2 lb @ $1/lb)		$ 2
Direct Labor (1 hr @ $6/hr)		6
Factory Overhead (applied on basis of direct labor hours):		
Variable (1 hr @ rate of $1/direct labor hour)	$1	
Fixed (1 hr @ rate of $3/direct labor hour)	3	4
Total standard cost per unit of product A		$12

Cost Variances

Even in well-managed companies with carefully established and currently maintained cost standards, actual costs often differ from standard costs. Differences may result from either short, isolated lapses or long-term general fluctuations in efficiency, or perhaps from a change in production methods that invalidates previous standards. Existing variances should be analyzed for indications of their cause so that appropriate action may be taken.

Suppose that during June, Costello Manufacturing Company produced 9,800 units of product A, for which it incurred the following actual costs (assume no work in process inventories):

Raw Materials (20,600 lb @ $1.05/lb)		$ 21,630
Direct Labor (9,700 hr @ $6.10/hr)		59,170
Factory Overhead:		
Variable	$ 8,700	
Fixed	30,000	38,700
Total actual production costs incurred in June		$119,500

In Exhibit 26-3 the actual costs are compared with standard costs for 9,800 units of product, and the differences, or variances, for each cost category are calculated. The standard costs are from our standard cost summary for product A multiplied by the actual quantity of 9,800 units produced in June. Note that both favorable and unfavorable variances exist and that the overall net variance of $1,900 is unfavorable. To initiate remedial action, management must analyze the variance for each manufacturing cost element to determine the underlying causal factors related to prices paid, quantities used, and productive capacity utilized. The following paragraphs present these analyses and the related general journal entries (in summary form) for recording variances.

Raw Materials Variances

Variances for raw materials stem primarily from paying more or less than the standard price for raw materials and from using more or less than the standard quantity of raw materials. Costello Manufacturing Company's raw materials variances for June are computed and recorded as follows:

EXHIBIT 26–3
Comparison of Actual and Standard Costs of Product A
For the Month of June, 19XX

	Actual Costs (9,800 units)	Standard Costs (9,800 units)	Variances Favorable	Unfavorable
Raw Materials	$ 21,630	$ 19,600		$2,030
Direct Labor	59,170	58,800		370
Factory Overhead:				
Variable	8,700	9,800	$1,100	
Fixed	30,000	29,400		600
	$119,500	$117,600	$1,100	$3,000
Net total variance (unfavorable)			$1,900	

$$\text{Price Variance} = \text{Price Differential} \times \text{Actual Quantity}$$
$$(\$1.05 - \$1.00) \times 20,600 \text{ pounds} = \$1,030 \text{ Unfavorable}$$

$$\text{Usage Variance} = \text{Usage Differential} \times \text{Standard Price}$$
$$(20,600 - 19,600) \times \$1 = \underline{1,000} \text{ Unfavorable}$$

Total Variance $\qquad\qquad\qquad\qquad\qquad\qquad$ $\underline{\$2,030}$ Unfavorable

The total raw materials variance is the sum of two unfavorable factors—a $1,030 unfavorable price variance caused by paying 5 cents per pound above the standard price for 20,600 pounds of materials and a $1,000 unfavorable usage variance resulting from using 1,000 pounds more than the standard amount of materials at a standard cost of $1 per pound. Notice that the total $2,030 variance accounts for the difference between total actual and total standard raw materials costs as indicated in Exhibit 26–3. The unfavorable price variance may have been caused by a lapse on the part of purchasing personnel, the improper substitution of more expensive materials than those specified, or an increase in supplier prices. The excess usage might be traced to poor handling by inexperienced workers, inattention to specifications, or even theft.

The following general journal entry records these costs and variances:

Work in Process (standard price and quantities)	19,600	
Raw Materials Usage Variance	1,000	
Raw Materials Price Variance	1,030	
Raw Materials Inventory (actual price and quantities)		21,630
To record raw materials used in June and related cost variances.		

Note that the journal entry debits Work in Process for standard costs, records the two unfavorable variances as debits (analogous to losses or expenses), and records the actual costs of raw materials requisitioned during June.[1]

Direct Labor Variances

Variances for direct labor result from paying more or less than the standard wage rates for direct labor and from using more or less than the standard amount of direct labor hours. Costello Manufacturing Company's direct labor variances are computed and recorded as shown below. Note that the basic calculations are the same as for raw materials, but the term *rate* is used instead of *price* and the term *efficiency* instead of *usage*.

Rate Variance   = Rate Differential   × Actual Hours
                         ($6.10 − $6.00)   ×   9,700   = $970 Unfavorable

Efficiency Variance = Efficiency Differential × Standard Rate
                         (9,800 − 9,700)   × $6   = $\underline{\quad 600 \quad}$ Favorable

Total Variance $\underline{\underline{\$370}}$ Unfavorable

The $970 unfavorable direct labor rate variance results from paying 10 cents per hour above standard for 9,700 direct labor hours actually worked. The $600 favorable direct labor efficiency variance is a result of producing June's output in 100 direct labor hours less than the standard allowed, in which each hour has a standard rate of $6. Again, the $370 total unfavorable variance fully explains the difference between total actual and total standard direct labor costs indicated in Exhibit 26–3.

The favorable direct labor efficiency variance might be credited to the production supervisor, who presumably oversees the production teams. The unfavorable labor rate variance could have resulted from assigning more highly paid employees than specified, paying overtime, or paying increased labor rates because of recently negotiated wage contracts.

The following journal entry records these costs and variances:

Work in Process (standard rate and hours)	58,800	
Direct Labor Rate Variance	970	
Direct Labor Efficiency Variance		600
Factory Payroll Payable (actual costs)		59,170
To record direct labor costs and related cost variances.		

The journal entry shown charges Work in Process with standard direct labor costs, records the unfavorable labor rate variance as a debit and the favorable labor efficiency variance as a credit (analogous to a gain), and records the liability for direct labor at the amount owed, which is determined by actual hours worked and actual rates paid.

---

[1] In our illustration, we recognize and record the raw materials price variance when the materials start into production. Some firms recognize and record the price variance when materials purchases are recorded.

Factory Overhead Variances

Variances for factory overhead are often identified with two major sources. Incurring more or less total overhead costs than the amount budgeted for the production level achieved results in a *controllable* variance. Operating at a production level above or below the normal capacity results in a *volume* variance.[2] The total factory overhead variance is the sum of these two variances or the difference between total actual factory overhead costs incurred and the total factory overhead applied at standard rates to the actual units produced. Costello Manufacturing Company's total factory overhead variance for June is (see original data on page 923):

Total overhead applied at standard rates	
(9,800 units produced × $4 standard overhead rate)	$39,200
Actual factory overhead ($8,700 variable + $30,000 fixed)	38,700
Total overhead variance (favorable)	$ 500

Because the actual factory overhead cost incurred is less than the standard overhead amount, the $500 difference is a favorable variance. Computation of the factory overhead variances follows:

Controllable Variance

Budgeted overhead for actual production attained		
[$30,000 fixed + (9,800 × $1 variable)]	$39,800	
Actual overhead	38,700	
Controllable variance		$1,100 Favorable

Volume Variance

Normal capacity in direct labor hours	10,000	
Standard direct labor hours for actual production		
attained (9,800 units × 1 hour)	9,800	
Production capacity not used (hours)	200	
Standard fixed overhead rate per hour	× $3	
Volume variance		600 Unfavorable

Total Overhead Variance $ 500 Favorable

The following journal entry records these costs and variances:

Work in Process (at standard overhead		
rates)	39,200	
Overhead Volume Variance	600	
Controllable Overhead Variance		1,100
Factory Overhead (actual overhead costs)		38,700
To record standard factory overhead and		
related variances.		

[2] Appendix C to this chapter presents an alternate three-variance analysis for factory overhead that isolates variances for spending, efficiency, and volume.

CONTROLLABLE OVERHEAD VARIANCE   The $1,100 favorable controllable overhead variance measures how well the actual factory overhead costs have been kept within the budget limits. Controllable overhead variances typically originate with variable overhead costs; fixed overhead costs tend to be routinely estimated and relatively stable. A small portion of Costello's favorable controllable variance—$100—resulted from the 9,800 units being produced in only 9,700 hours. This "savings" of 100 hours multiplied by the $1 standard variable overhead rate is the overhead cost avoided by producing 9,800 units of product in 100 hours less than the overhead budget allows. The remaining $1,000 of favorable controllable variance results from spending less than the budget allows for various overhead items. Costello's overhead budget indicates that total overhead for June should be $39,700 ($30,000 fixed overhead + $1 variable overhead for each of the 9,700 direct labor hours actually worked). Because actual overhead incurred was only $38,700, the $1,000 difference represents a savings of overhead costs. A detailed analysis of actual and budgeted overhead costs would indicate to what extent each overhead cost (such as factory supplies and indirect labor) contributed to the favorable variance. Department supervisors are usually responsible for controllable overhead variances.

OVERHEAD VOLUME VARIANCE   The overhead volume variance reflects the costs associated with using factory facilities at more or less than normal capacity. Volume variances are the differences between normal capacity and the standard hours allowed for actual units produced times the standard fixed overhead rate. Because Costello's capacity was 10,000 standard direct labor hours and only 9,800 hours were allowed for June's production of 9,800 units of product, 200 hours of capacity were not utilized.[3] Each of these hours has an implied cost equal to the fixed overhead rate of $3 per direct labor hour, resulting in a total unfavorable overhead volume variance of $600 ($3 × 200). When utilization exceeds normal capacity, the favorable overhead volume variance represents the amount of fixed overhead "saved" by employing the factory facilities beyond normal capacity.

Note that variable overhead costs play no role in volume variances. Because variable overhead costs respond to the level of production, failure to produce means that related variable costs are not incurred and therefore cannot contribute to volume variances. In contrast, fixed overhead does not respond (within the relevant range) to changes in production levels. Failure to produce does not avoid any portion of fixed overhead. Nor does producing beyond normal capacity increase fixed overhead (within the relevant range). Therefore, only fixed factory overhead can cause volume variances.

Volume variances result when the factory facilities are used at more or less than normal capacity. Common examples of such factors are idle time because of machine breakdowns, uneven job scheduling, and sales orders insufficient to justify production at normal capacity. Production supervisors can often influence

---

[3] Although in our example only 9,700 hours were worked, 100 of these hours were avoided by better-than-standard production efficiency (the favorable controllable overhead variance). The other 200 hours, therefore, represent an appropriate measure of plant underutilization.

volume variances caused by machine breakdowns and uneven scheduling. When the cause is insufficient sales, general management is responsible for increasing sales through product advertising and sales promotion and seeking other ways to utilize factory facilities more fully.

The summary journal entry for overhead costs (page 925) charges Work in Process with the standard overhead for the actual production attained, records each of the overhead variances in an appropriately titled variance account, and credits Factory Overhead for the actual overhead costs incurred.

STANDARD COSTS IN FINANCIAL STATEMENTS

When the standard costs and related variances for direct materials, direct labor, and factory overhead are recorded as illustrated here, the Work in Process account is debited for each in amounts representing standard quantities and standard prices. All variances—favorable or unfavorable—are carried in separate accounts with appropriate titles. Costello Manufacturing Company records completed production for June in the following entry:

Finished Goods Inventory		
(at standard cost)	117,600	
Work in Process (at standard cost)		117,600
To record completion of June's production		
of 9,800 units at a standard unit cost of $12.		

As each month's production is sold, the related amounts of standard costs are transferred from Finished Goods Inventory to Cost of Goods Sold.

Standard costs and related variances are usually reported only in financial reports intended for management's use. The following partial income statement illustrates how variances often appear on interim financial statements for internal use (amounts are assumed).

Costello Manufacturing Company
Income Statement
For the Month Ended June 30, 19XX

Sales	$166,000
Cost of Goods Sold at Standard Cost	126,000
Gross Profit at Standard Cost	$ 40,000
Less: Net Unfavorable Cost Variance	1,300
Gross Profit	$ 38,700

The total net variance could be broken down into subvariances or possibly detailed in a schedule of variances accompanying the financial statements.

At year-end, firms commonly close the variance accounts by transferring their balances to Cost of Goods Sold. In effect, this transfer converts the Cost of Goods Sold account from standard costs to actual costs. If large variances exist at year-end and there is evidence that the standards may not apply, a firm may be justified in allocating all or part of the variances to Work in Process, Finished Goods Inventory, and Cost of Goods Sold.

BUDGETING

For the typical business entity, a **budget** is a formal plan setting forth *management's intended actions and their anticipated effects on key business variables* such as sales, production, expenses, and cash flows. Formulated in quantitative terms, budgets rely heavily on accounting concepts and procedures. In fact, a comprehensive budgeting effort enables us to prepare projected financial statements for the budget period. Thus, in a sense, budgeting is the act of accounting now for the activities of future operating periods.

ADVANTAGES OF BUDGETING

A Plan for Accomplishing Objectives

Budgeting—often called *profit planning*—requires the formulation of a thorough plan of operations for the budget period. In constructing the budget, management must obtain and analyze data relating to such aspects of future operations as the anticipated demand for finished goods; the prices, quantities, types, and availability of production inputs; and the availability of financing sources. Consideration must be given to the coordination required among operating departments, outside suppliers, creditors, and other parties involved in the operations of the business. The budget must be in harmony with the company's long-run goals as well as with short-run objectives such as target amounts of costs and income. There is a significant truth in the observation that, even if they were destroyed as soon as they were completed, budgets would be justified in terms of the communication and coordination that occur during their preparation.

Without planning, most complex ventures are prone to develop crises. Without coordination, a "fine" wheelbarrow can be produced at "reasonable" costs and sold in "impressive" quantities at "competitive" prices and still result in an unbearable operating loss. Only when a comprehensively prepared budget shows that planned activities are expected to lead to an acceptable net income has management done what it can to plan successful operations. In a real sense, then, budgeting provides management with a view of the future that is an early warning system for those contemplated actions that might lead to unacceptable results.

Control of Operations

Because it is a highly detailed statement of intended operating results, a budget provides a wide array of target conditions with which management can compare actual results to test whether remedial action is necessary. Reasonably frequent comparisons of budgeted and actual operating data are sound operating procedures. This, of course, provides a natural base for the application of management by exception principles.

A Basis of Performance Measurement

A firm is successful because its key personnel do their jobs efficiently, reliably, and with general adherence to plans. For all major aspects of a firm's operation, a well-developed budget includes criteria for a high level of performance. Therefore, *properly used*, a budget can be a significant motivational force because managers at various levels know that their actual performance is evaluated by comparison with a desired level of performance.

BUDGET PREPARATION

Even though specific budgeting procedures vary widely among firms, all business enterprises engaged in comprehensive budgeting must consider certain elements of budget preparation—the budget committee, the budget period, and the master budget.

The Budget Committee

A budget committee generally consists of representatives from all major areas of a firm—such as sales, production, and finance—and is headed by the firm's controller. The committee must coordinate preparation of the budget, initiate budget procedures, collect and integrate data from various organizational units, supervise the review and modification of original estimates, and direct the implementation of the budget. When all departments participate in formulating the budget, it will more likely be accepted as a reasonable standard of performance. In the absence of such participation, the budget may be viewed as an unreasonable goal imposed by outsiders who do not fully understand the department's operations.

The Budget Period

The period covered by a budget varies according to the nature of the specific activity involved. Cash budgets may cover a week or a month, production budgets a month or a calendar quarter, general operating budgets a calendar quarter or year, and budgets for acquisition of plant assets (or, capital expenditures budgets) may cover several years. Generally, the longer the budget period, the more likely it is that the budget will be reviewed and subsequently revised with the latest information available. In **continuous budgeting,** an interesting refinement of period-by-period budgeting, the coming year is dealt with in terms of quarterly periods. At any given time, the firm has four sequential quarterly budgets, and it adds a new quarterly budget as each quarter expires. With this system, regardless of the time of the year, the current budget always covers the current calendar quarter plus the next three quarters. Continuous budgeting is also carried out in monthly periods.

The Master Budget

A **master budget** is a comprehensive planning document that integrates all the detailed budgets for the firm's various specialized activities. As indicated earlier, if sufficiently comprehensive, a master budget contains the data necessary to formulate projected (sometimes called *pro forma*) financial statements for the budget period.

The details of a master budget vary according to whether the firm's operations are manufacturing, merchandising, or service oriented. In this chapter, we illustrate budgeting for a small manufacturing operation, Woodward Company. The following key components constitute Woodward Company's master budget:

ZERO-BASE BUDGETING

Traditional budgeting procedures often start with the preceding year's budget or the preceding year's actual expenditures. In many instances, the budgeting process simply results in last year's figures plus a percentage. Although some obvious adjustments may be made, too often this approach automatically justifies the amounts budgeted or expended last year and limits thorough analysis and justification procedures to the "new money," or the incremental portion of the total budget. The obvious defect in this approach is that portions of last year's expenditures may not deserve continued justification. The firm may want to take funds from existing projects and devote them to more attractive new projects.

Zero-base budgeting (ZBB) avoids the problem in traditional budgeting described above. In general, ZBB requires each of the firm's budgetary units to justify *all* of its expenditures as if the unit's operations were just starting. Hence, the label *zero-base* budgeting.

ZBB may take different forms, but the prevailing procedure is the following:*

(1) The firm is divided into *decision units* (cost or service centers), to which budget decisions naturally relate.
(2) Decision units request funds by preparing *decision packages*, which set forth a statement of goals, a program for achieving them, benefits expected, related alternatives, consequences of not being funded, and required

expenditures. Decision packages are often grouped as they relate to continuing a minimum level of operations, increasing the level of continuing operations, and initiating new operations.
(3) Various levels of management participate in combining and ranking all departments' decision packages.
(4) Decision packages ranked higher than management's cutoff point constitute the plans for the firm's master budget.

A major drawback to ZBB is that it is time consuming—and thus costly—for all departments to justify in detail each year all aspects of their operations. Consequently, some firms use traditional budgeting procedures and have what is termed a *zero-based review* of departments every two or three years. ZBB is much more useful in budgeting for support functions—such as research and development or the power department—than it is for budgeting direct costs for materials and labor.

ZBB was a hallmark of former President Jimmy Carter. As governor of Georgia, he was credited with the broad implementation of ZBB in state government. After Carter promised to do the same in the federal government, a book on ZBB made Washington, D.C.'s nonfiction best-seller list.†

*For a comprehensive treatment of the subject, see P.A. Pyhrr, *Zero-Base Budgeting* (New York: John Wiley & Sons, Inc., 1975).
†L.H. Clark, Jr., "Zero-Base Budgeting, Advocated by Carter, Used by Many Firms," *The Wall Street Journal*, March 4, 1977, page 1.

Sales budget
Production budget
Raw materials budget   } Provide a basis for
Direct labor budget   projected income statement
Factory overhead budget
Operating expense budget

Capital expenditures budget } Provide a basis for
Cash budget   projected balance sheet

The major steps in preparing the master budget are as follows (assuming the prior development of long-run goals and plans):

(1) Prepare sales forecast.

(2) Determine production volume.

(3) Estimate manufacturing costs and operating expenses.

(4) Determine cash flows and other financial effects.

(5) Formulate projected financial statements.

Estimating sales volume is usually the initial step in constructing a master budget. Once sales are forecast, production volume can be set for the desired changes, if any, in finished goods inventories. When production volume is known, reliable estimates can be made for raw materials, direct labor, factory overhead, and operating expenses. When available, standard costs should be incorporated. With estimates of these costs and expenses, cash flows and the related effects on other accounts can be projected. Then, with proper consideration for capital expenditures and related financing, projected financial statements can be prepared. Aspects of the detailed budgets may indicate unacceptable situations such as excessive costs, exceeded capacities, or cash shortages for which revisions must be made. Of course, early identification of potential operating crises is a key advantage of budgeting.

ILLUSTRATIONS OF BUDGETS

We illustrate the preparation of a relatively simple master budget for Woodward Company. Budgeted financial statements are not illustrated because they would be virtually identical with the financial statements studied earlier throughout the text. The amounts used, unless correlated with other aspects of the illustration, are chosen for convenience.

Sales Budget   Because estimated sales volume influences items appearing in several other budgets, the sales budget is prepared first. The anticipated unit sales volume is based on a sales forecast that reflects prior periods' sales, expected general economic conditions, related market research, and specific industry trends. A reasonably reliable sales forecast is an important determination that affects such variables as the quantities produced, operating expenses, and cash requirements. Overestimating sales volume can lead to large unwanted inventories, which in turn result in extra storage costs and possibly sales price reductions when liquidating the excess inventory. Underestimating sales can lead to loss of sales revenue and perhaps lasting customer ill-will stemming from unfilled orders.

The estimated unit sales volume of each product is multiplied by planned unit sales prices to derive an estimate of total sales revenue. The calculations may be classified by sales territory or salesperson or both. A sales budget is illustrated in Exhibit 26–4. To use the sales budget to full advantage, a firm should classify data on actual sales in the same manner as budgeted sales so that it can compare budgeted sales with actual sales on the basis of sales area or salesperson.

Production Budget

The production budget reflects the quantity of each product to be produced during the budget period. Scheduled production should specifically provide for anticipated sales and desired ending inventories and, of course, consider the beginning inventories of each product. Assume Woodward Company wants to increase its inventory of product A and decrease its inventory of product B by 20%. Woodward's production budget appears in Exhibit 26–5. The firm wants scheduled production to approach full utilization of plant capacity. If not, management should investigate ways to use the excess capacity. Note that the desired change in inventory of each product is accomplished by scheduling the appropriate production volumes.

EXHIBIT 26–4

Woodward Company
Sales Budget
For the Quarter Ended June 30, 19XX

	Estimated Unit Sales Volume	Unit Selling Price	Total Sales
Product A: East Area	40,000	$10	$ 400,000
West Area	28,000	10	280,000
Total product A	68,000	10	$ 680,000
Product B: East Area	20,000	$13	$ 260,000
West Area	11,000	13	143,000
Total product B	31,000	13	$ 403,000
Total sales revenue			$1,083,000

EXHIBIT 26–5

Woodward Company		
Production Budget (in Units)		
For the Quarter Ended June 30, 19XX		
	Products	
	A	**B**
Estimated units to be sold	68,000	31,000
Desired ending inventories	12,000	4,000
Amounts to be available	80,000	35,000
Less: Beginning inventories	10,000	5,000
Total production to be scheduled	70,000	30,000

Raw Materials Budget

The quantities of raw materials acquired to meet scheduled production and desired ending inventory requirements are presented in the raw materials budget. Any beginning inventories of raw materials must be considered in estimating acquisitions for the budget period. The quantities to be acquired are multiplied by the anticipated unit cost prices to calculate the total dollar amounts of raw materials purchases. In the raw materials budget illustrated in Exhibit 26–6, we assume that Woodward Company uses only two raw materials, X and Y, in producing products A and B. Even though the quarterly totals of raw materials purchases

EXHIBIT 26–6

Woodward Company		
Raw Materials Budget		
For the Quarter Ended June 30, 19XX		
	Units of Raw Materials	
	X	**Y**
Production requirements:		
Product A (2 units per finished product)	140,000	60,000
Product B (1 unit per finished product)	70,000	30,000
Total units required for production	210,000	90,000
Desired ending inventories	30,000	20,000
Total units to be available	240,000	110,000
Less: Beginning inventories	40,000	30,000
Total units to be purchased	200,000	80,000
Unit purchase prices	× $0.60	× $0.80
Total raw materials purchases	$120,000	$64,000

may be coordinated well with quarterly production requirements, the day-to-day management of inventories should avoid having excess inventories or items out of stock.

Direct Labor Budget

The direct labor budget presents the number of direct labor hours necessary for the production volume planned for the budget period. These hours are multiplied by the applicable hourly labor rates to determine the total dollar amounts of direct labor costs to be budgeted. In the direct labor budget for Woodward Company (Exhibit 26–7), we have assumed that both products A and B require manufacturing work in the Machining and Finishing departments, as follows:

	Machining Department	Finishing Department
Product A	0.5 hours	0.3 hours
Product B	1.0 hours	0.4 hours

Factory Overhead Budget

Recall from earlier chapters that factory overhead comprises all factory costs that are not raw materials or direct labor. Examples of factory overhead are factory supplies, indirect labor and factory supervisory salaries, utilities, depreciation, maintenance, taxes, and insurance. Because of the variety of cost factors, factory overhead includes both fixed and variable cost elements.

Factory overhead can be budgeted using a fixed budget that specifies the amounts of overhead costs that should be incurred *at a specific* production volume, usually normal capacity. However, actual production volume seldom equals the budgeted production volume. Under a fixed budget, management is thus faced with comparing actual costs at one production volume with planned costs at a different volume. For many cost factors, such comparisons between actual and budgeted costs would not be meaningful. To avoid this problem, firms should budget factory overhead using a flexible budgeting approach.

EXHIBIT 26–7

Woodward Company
Direct Labor Budget
For the Quarter Ended June 30, 19XX

	Machining Department	Finishing Department
Direct labor hours required for production:		
Product A: (70,000 units × 0.5 hours)	35,000	
(70,000 units × 0.3 hours)		21,000
Product B: (30,000 units × 1.0 hours)	30,000	
(30,000 units × 0.4 hours)		12,000
Total direct labor hours	65,000	33,000
Hourly rate for direct labor	× $5.00	× $6.00
Total direct labor costs	$325,000	$198,000

A flexible factory overhead budget for the Machining Department of Woodward Company is shown in Exhibit 26–8. Note that the budget separates variable and fixed overhead cost elements and presents budgeted factory overhead costs for three different volumes of direct labor hours. A flexible budget may take the columnar form shown in Exhibit 26–8, or it may be stated as a general total cost formula as developed in Chapter 24 and used in the standard costs section of this chapter. For the Machining Department of Woodward Company for the quarter ended June 30, the overhead formula would be (assuming a planned operating volume of 65,000 direct labor hours):

$$\begin{array}{c} \text{Total} \\ \text{Factory} \\ \text{Overhead} \end{array} = \begin{array}{c} \text{Total} \\ \text{Fixed} \\ \text{Overhead} \end{array} + \left(\begin{array}{c} \text{Variable} \\ \text{Overhead} \\ \text{per unit} \end{array} \times \begin{array}{c} \text{Production} \\ \text{Volume} \end{array} \right)$$

$$\$169{,}000 = \$104{,}000 + \left(\quad \$1 \quad \times \begin{array}{c} 65{,}000\ \text{direct} \\ \text{labor hours} \end{array} \right)$$

Notice that the formula agrees with the related column for 65,000 hours in Exhibit 26–8.

EXHIBIT 26–8

Woodward Company
Machining Department
Factory Overhead Budget
For the Quarter Ended June 30, 19XX

	Variable Cost per Direct Labor Hour	Overhead Costs at		
		60,000 Direct Labor Hours	65,000 Direct Labor Hours	70,000 Direct Labor Hours
Variable costs:				
Factory supplies	$0.30	$ 18,000	$ 19,500	$ 21,000
Indirect labor	0.40	24,000	26,000	28,000
Utilities	0.20	12,000	13,000	14,000
Maintenance	0.10	6,000	6,500	7,000
Total variable overhead	$1.00	$ 60,000	$ 65,000	$ 70,000
Fixed costs:				
Supervisory salaries		$ 30,000	$ 30,000	$ 30,000
Depreciation on equipment		15,000	15,000	15,000
Utilities		20,000	20,000	20,000
Maintenance		12,000	12,000	12,000
Property taxes and insurance		27,000	27,000	27,000
Total fixed overhead		$104,000	$104,000	$104,000
Total factory overhead		$164,000	$169,000	$174,000

A flexible factory overhead budget should be prepared for each production department. Flexible departmental budgets can be adjusted for purposes of control and performance evaluation, and for changing levels of production volume. Information in the various departmental factory overhead budgets supports the total factory overhead budget included in the master budget. A particular level of production volume is usually selected for the master budget, so that a total factory overhead cost may be estimated for use in preparing the cash budget and projected financial statements. In our example, the production volume selected is derived from the direct labor budget (indicating 65,000 direct labor hours for the Machining Department), as shown in Exhibit 26–7.

Operating Expense Budgets

Operating expenses, composed of selling and general administrative expenses, are often budgeted using the flexible budget approach just illustrated for factory overhead. However, certain variable selling and administrative expenses, such as sales commissions, may vary with *sales volume* rather than production volume. As with factory overhead, for purposes of departmental cost control and performance measurement, various supplemental schedules would be prepared to relate specific portions of total selling and administrative expenses to specific departments or cost centers.

Budgeted Income Statement

With the information available from the budgets discussed above, a budgeted income statement can be prepared. Material amounts of other income or expense and estimated income taxes would be incorporated. The budgeted income statement may be supported by a schedule or statement of cost of goods sold.

The projected net income shown would be reviewed for its adequacy in relation to total sales revenue and perhaps the related amount of assets employed. If the ratio of income to sales or assets is smaller than desired, management should review each component of the master budget for possible ways to increase projected net income.

Capital Expenditures Budget

Expenditures for plant and equipment are among a firm's most important transactions. Chapter 27 considers some approaches to choosing among capital outlay proposals. Because of the large amounts involved and the relatively long lives of capital assets, such expenditures should be well planned. Even companies that are not growing must eventually replace their equipment. For expanding companies—especially those subject to high technological obsolescence—the budgeting of capital expenditures can be most challenging.

In its simplest form, a capital expenditures budget is a list of types of equipment and the amounts budgeted for their acquisition in each of a series of future operating periods, as illustrated in Exhibit 26–9. Capital outlay decisions may significantly affect aspects of other budgets, such as production capacities in production budgets, depreciation expense in factory overhead and operating expense budgets, and related cash expenditures in the cash budget. For example,

EXHIBIT 26–9

		Calendar Quarters Ending		
Woodward Company Capital Expenditures Budget For the Year Ended December 31, 19XX				
Expenditures	March 31	June 30	September 30	December 31
Machinery	$7,000	$10,000		$40,000
Delivery equipment		8,000	$ 8,000	
Conveyor system			40,000	6,000
Computer		32,000		
Totals	$7,000	$50,000	$48,000	$46,000

the $50,000 to be spent in the quarter ended June 30 appears as an April cash disbursement in Woodward Company's cash budget shown in Exhibit 26–10.

Cash Budget

The cash budget portrays the projected flows of cash during the budget period. Cash receipts are shown in terms of their sources and cash disbursements in terms of their uses. The difference between these two flows determines the net periodic change in cash balances.

Because of the characteristic time lags between many routine transactions and their related effects on cash, proper cash budgeting often requires the analysis of certain data contained in other budgets to determine their impact on cash flows. Sales precede collections from customers, purchases precede payments on account, depreciation usually does not represent current cash outlays, and, of course, several types of prepayments may call for cash outlays before the related expenses are recognized in the accounts. Generally, the shorter the budget period, the more significant may be the differences between cash flows and related aspects of the firm's operations.

For an example of one important aspect of cash budgeting, assume that Woodward Company has analyzed the collection of its total credit sales in any month as follows:

(1) In the month of sale, 30% is collected and receives a 2% cash discount. (The cash received is thus 30% of the credit sales × 0.98.)

(2) In the month following sale, 50% is collected and no discounts are involved.

(3) In the second month following sale, 18% is collected. The remaining 2% of accounts are written off as uncollectible.

Assuming estimated credit sales of $350,000 in February, $340,000 in March, and $370,000 in April, Woodward Company's cash receipts from credit customers for April could be budgeted in the following manner:

EXHIBIT 26-10

Woodward Company
Cash Budget
For the Quarter Ended June 30, 19XX

	April	May	June
Cash receipts:			
Cash sales	$ 18,000	$ 15,000	$ 17,500
Collections from customers	341,780	350,000	358,000
Sale of investments	8,000	—	—
Short-term borrowing	40,000	—	—
Other sources	3,220	6,000	6,500
Total cash receipts	$411,000	$371,000	$382,000
Cash disbursements:			
Manufacturing costs	$280,000	$290,000	$285,000
Operating expenses	60,000	61,000	58,000
Capital expenditures	50,000	—	—
Income taxes	—	—	30,000
Dividends	15,000	—	—
Other disbursements	4,000	9,000	19,000
Total cash disbursements	$409,000	$360,000	$392,000
Net cash provided (applied)	$ 2,000	$ 11,000	($ 10,000)
Beginning cash balance	20,000	22,000	33,000
Ending cash balance	$ 22,000	$ 33,000	$ 23,000

		Collections Received During		
	Monthly Credit Sales	**February**	**March**	**April**
February:	$350,000 × (30% × 0.98)	$102,900		
	350,000 × 50%		$175,000	
	350,000 × 18%			$ 63,000
March:	$340,000 × (30% × 0.98)		99,960	
	340,000 × 50%			170,000
April:	$370,000 × (30% × 0.98)			108,780
				$341,780

Woodward Company's cash budget for the quarter ended June 30, 19XX (Exhibit 26–10), reflects some of the more common examples of cash receipts and disbursements.[4] Note how virtually every other element of the master budget has affected the cash budget.

---

[4]The cash budget is an internal document that management uses to plan operations. Its format may differ from a cash flow statement, which reports actual cash flows for a past period to external users. The latter statement, discussed in Chapter 19, is subject to the guidelines set forth in *Opinions of the Accounting Principles Board, No. 19,* "Reporting Changes in Financial Position" (New York: American Institute of Certified Public Accountants, 1971).

Cash is an asset particularly crucial to the operation of a business. When a firm runs short of cash, operating crises can occur within a few days. Without sufficient cash balances, payrolls cannot be met, cash discounts are not available, credit obligations may not be met on a timely basis, and the volume of operations may be generally curtailed. Eventually the firm's credit standing suffers and further credit may be available only on less desirable terms. Although having too little cash carries the greatest potential penalties, excessively large cash balances represent unused resources. Excess cash should be placed in short-term income-producing investments or used for such strategic purposes as debt retirement.

Budgeted Balance Sheet

The budgeted balance sheet presents anticipated balances for the various balance sheet items at the end of the budget period. Assuming all other budgeting procedures have been properly coordinated, the budgeted balance sheet is extremely useful in reviewing the firm's projected financial position. Management can then identify potential financial problems—for example, by assessing the adequacy of the projected current ratio and equity ratio—and can revise plans or take other necessary corrective actions.

PERFORMANCE REPORTS

The use of budgets for cost control and performance evaluation entails the preparation of periodic performance reports. Such reports compare budgeted and actual data and show any existing variances. To facilitate their preparation, the firm should clearly define within its organizational structure the authority and responsibility for the incurrence of each cost element. In addition, the accounting system should be sufficiently detailed and coordinated to provide necessary data for reports designed for the particular use of individuals or cost centers having primary responsibility for specific costs. This detail is often maintained in subsidiary records or generated through other analyses.

Exhibit 26–11 illustrates a quarterly performance report related to Woodward Company's factory overhead for the Machining Department. Note that actual production was assumed at 60,000 direct labor hours rather than the 65,000 originally estimated, and that the budgeted amount for the corresponding volume level from the flexible budget in Exhibit 26–8 is compared with the actual costs.

Budget variances in the performance report identify aspects of the business that should be reviewed. As shown in Exhibit 26–11, variances related to individual items may require investigation even though the overall variance is immaterial. There may be justifiable reasons for any variance, including the possibility that certain conditions have made the current budget an invalid performance standard. In any event, investigation of the causes of variances should benefit the firm by controlling and evaluating current operations and assisting the budget committee in future budget preparations.

EXHIBIT 26–11

Woodward Company
Machining Department
Performance Report—Factory Overhead
For the Quarter Ended June 30, 19XX

	Budgeted at Actual Hours	Actual Overhead Costs	Variances over (under) Budget	Percent of Budget
Variable costs:				
Factory supplies	$ 18,000	$ 18,400	$400	2.2%
Indirect labor	24,000	23,280	(720)	(3.0)
Utilities	12,000	12,100	100	0.8
Maintenance	6,000	5,920	(80)	(1.3)
Total variable overhead	$ 60,000	$ 59,700	($300)	(0.5)
Fixed costs:				
Supervisory salaries	$ 30,000	$ 30,000		
Depreciation on equipment	15,000	15,000		
Utilities	20,000	20,000		
Maintenance	12,000	12,420	$420	3.5
Property taxes and insurance	27,000	26,700	(300)	(1.1)
Total fixed overhead	$104,000	$104,120	$120	0.1
Total factory overhead	$164,000	$163,820	($180)	(0.1)

DEMONSTRATION PROBLEM FOR REVIEW

The following standard per unit cost data and total actual cost data relate to producing 2,800 units of Bann, Inc.'s only product.

	Standard Unit Costs	Total Actual Costs	
Raw materials (3 lb @ $2/lb)	$ 6	(8,500 lb)	$15,300
Direct labor (0.5 hr @ $8/ hr)	4	(1,500 hr)	12,150
Factory overhead*			
Variable (0.5 hr @ $4/hr)	2		6,000
Fixed (0.5 hr @ $6/hr)	3		9,500
Total	$15		$42,950

*Normal capacity is considered 1,500 direct labor hours.

REQUIRED

(a) Calculate all variances for raw materials, direct labor, and factory overhead.
(b) Prove that the difference between total actual and total standard costs equals the total of all variances.
(c) Assume that Bann's standard unit costs will continue to be valid; that Bann

will sell 2,500 units next period; that beginning raw materials and finished goods inventories are 800 units and 1,200 units, respectively; and that Bann wants to increase both inventories 25%. Calculate for the next period (1) the units of finished goods to be produced, (2) the units of raw materials to be purchased, and (3) the budgeted direct labor cost for the period.

SOLUTION TO DEMONSTRATION PROBLEM

(a)

Price Variance = Price Differential	× Actual Quantity	
= ($2 − $1.80*)	× 8,500 lb	= $1,700 Favorable
Usage Variance = Usage Differential	× Standard Price	
= (8,500 lb − 8,400 lb†) ×	$2/lb	= 200 Unfavorable
Rate Variance = Rate Differential	× Actual Hours	
= ($8.10‡ − $8)	× 1,500 hr	= 150 Unfavorable
Efficiency Variance = Efficiency Differential × Standard Rate		
= (1,500 hr − 1,400 hr§) ×	$8	= 800 Unfavorable

Controllable Variance		
Actual factory overhead	$15,500	
Budgeted overhead for actual production attained		
[$9,000 fixed‖ + (2,800 × $2 variable)]	14,600	900 Unfavorable
Volume Variance		
Normal capacity in direct labor hours	1,500	
Standard direct labor hours for actual		
production attained (2,800 × 0.5 hr)	1,400	
Production capacity not used (hours)	100	
Standard fixed overhead rate per hour ×	$6	600 Unfavorable
Total Variances		$ 950 Unfavorable

*$15,300/8,500 lb = $1.80/lb
†2,800 units produced × 3 lb/unit = 8,400 lb
‡$12,150/1,500 hr = $8.10/hr
§2,800 units produced × 0.5 hr/unit = 1,400 hr
‖1,500 direct labor hours at normal capacity × $6 fixed overhead rate = $9,000

(b)		
Total actual costs		$42,950
Total standard costs (2,800 units × $15)		42,000
Total net variance		$ 950 Unfavorable

(c) (1) Finished goods production:

Units to be sold	2,500
Planned ending inventory (800 × 1.25)	1,000
	3,500
Less beginning inventory	800
Units to be produced	2,700

(2) Raw materials purchases:

Production requirements (2,700 × 3)	8,100
Planned ending inventory (1,200 × 1.25)	1,500
	9,600
Less beginning inventory	1,200
Units to be purchased	8,400

(3) Units to be produced (see part 1 above)	2,700
Labor requirements per unit of product	× 0.5
Labor hours required	1,350
Labor rate	× $8
Budgeted labor costs	$10,800

KEY POINTS TO REMEMBER

(1) The total net variance for each manufacturing cost element—raw materials, direct labor, and factory overhead—is the difference between total actual costs and total standard costs.

(2) You should be able to compute the amount of each of the following variances, label it favorable or unfavorable, explain its basic implications, and indicate the managerial position typically held responsible:
  (a) Raw materials price   (d) Direct labor efficiency
  (b) Raw materials usage   (e) Controllable factory overhead
  (c) Direct labor rate   (f) Factory overhead volume

(3) When standard costs are incorporated into the general ledger, work in process and finished goods inventories are carried at standard costs, with unfavorable variances recorded as debits and favorable variances recorded as credits in appropriately titled accounts.

(4) A comprehensive budget provides management with a plan for accomplishing objectives and a basis for controlling operations and measuring performance.

(5) You should know the basic format for and the key data appearing in each of the following budgets:
  (a) Sales budget   (e) Factory overhead budget
  (b) Production budget   (f) Capital expenditures budget
  (c) Raw materials budget   (g) Cash budget
  (d) Direct labor budget

(6) Flexible budgeting allows management to budget amounts that can be appropriately compared with costs incurred at actual operating volumes.

(7) A performance report compares budgeted and actual amounts and shows any variances between the two amounts.

QUESTIONS

26–1 What is the difference between standard costs and budgets?

26–2 What types of skills are required of a group responsible for establishing standard costs in a manufacturing concern?

26–3 "Standard costs can be set too high or too low for motivational purposes." Comment.

26–4 Summa Company used 4,150 pounds of raw materials costing $3.82 per pound for a batch of products that should have taken 4,000 pounds costing $4 per pound. What are the raw materials variances?

26–5 Name and briefly describe two variances included in the total factory overhead variance.

26–6 How do we justify analyzing the total variance related to, say, raw materials?

26–7 "Total actual cost exactly equals total standard cost, so everything must be okay." Comment.

26–8 Actual factory overhead is $41,000, budgeted overhead for the production level attained is $39,700, the standard fixed factory overhead rate is $6 per direct labor hour, and actual production is 150 standard direct labor hours beyond normal capacity. What are the factory overhead variances?

26–9 Who in the firm might be responsible for each of the following variances?
(a) Raw materials price and usage variances.
(b) Direct labor rate and efficiency variances.
(c) Factory overhead controllable and volume variances.

26–10 Briefly explain how standard cost variances are reported on financial statements.

26–11 List and briefly explain three advantages of budgeting.

26–12 What is meant by *continuous budgeting*?

26–13 Define *master budget*.

26–14 List, in the order of preparation, the various budgets that might constitute a master budget for a small manufacturing company.

26–15 Why do most firms prepare the sales budget first?

26–16 Beginning finished goods inventory is 4,000 units, anticipated sales volume is 49,000 units, and the desired ending finished goods inventory is 13,500 units. What number of units should be produced?

26–17 Three pounds of material X (costing $4 per pound) and 5 pounds of material Y (costing $2 per pound) are required to make one unit of product Z. If management plans to increase the inventory of material X by 500 pounds and reduce the inventory of material Y by 800 pounds during a period when 3,000 units of product Z are to be produced, what are the budgeted purchases costs of material X and material Y?

26–18 What is the total cost formula used in flexible budgeting?

26–19 What defect in fixed budgets does the use of flexible budgets avoid?

26–20 What basic information would you expect to see on a performance report?

26–21 Why are projected financial statements often prepared as part of a comprehensive budgeting process?

EXERCISES

26–22 The following actual and standard cost data for raw materials and direct labor relate to the production of 2,000 units of a product:

	Actual Costs	Standard Costs
Raw materials	3,900 units @ $6.20	4,000 units @ $6
Direct labor	6,200 hours @ $7.40	6,000 hours @ $7.50

Determine the following variances:
(a) Raw materials price.
(b) Raw materials usage.
(c) Direct labor rate.
(d) Direct labor efficiency.

26–23 Boston Company considers 5,000 direct labor hours or 2,500 units of product its normal monthly capacity. Its standard variable and fixed factory overhead rates are $3 and $6, respectively, for each direct labor hour. During the current month, $45,300 of factory overhead was incurred in working 4,900 direct labor hours to produce 2,400 units of product. Determine the following variances for factory overhead, and indicate whether each is favorable or unfavorable:
(a) Controllable
(b) Volume

26–24 The following summarized manufacturing data relate to Abco, Inc.'s May operations, during which 1,800 finished units of product were produced:

	Standard Unit Costs	Total Actual Costs
Raw materials:		
Standard (3 lb @ $2/lb)	$ 6	
Actual (5,500 lb @ $2.20/lb)		$12,000
Direct labor:		
Standard (0.5 hr @ $8/hr)	4	
Actual (850 hr @ $7.50/hr)		6,375
Factory overhead:		
Standard (Variable costs of $2 per direct labor hour and $4,000 fixed costs for normal monthly capacity of 1,000 direct labor hours)	3	
Actual		6,100
Total	$13	$24,475

Determine the raw materials price and usage variances, the direct labor rate and efficiency variances, and the factory overhead controllable and volume variances, indicating whether each is favorable or unfavorable.

26–25 From the following data, determine the total actual costs incurred for raw materials, for direct labor, and for factory overhead.

	Standard Costs	Variances over (under) Standard
Raw materials	$36,000	
Price variance		$1,500
Usage variance		(300)
Direct labor	25,000	
Rate variance		700
Efficiency variance		950
Factory overhead	65,000	
Controllable variance		(1,300)
Volume variance		(800)

26–26 For producing and selling 3,500 units of its only product for the month ended April 30, 19XX, Mautz Company's records reflect the following selected data:

	Standard Unit Costs	Actual Unit Costs
Raw materials	$5.50	$5.80
Direct labor	9.00	8.60
Factory overhead	6.00	6.50

Assuming that the product sells for $28 per unit and that Mautz Company uses standard costs in its general ledger accounts, prepare a partial summary income statement (through gross profit) presenting any existing total net variances.

26–27 For each independent situation below, determine the amounts indicated by the question marks.

Number of Units	A	B	C	D
Beginning inventory	7,000	?	4,000	?
Produced	14,000	26,000	?	57,000
Available	?	?	23,000	89,000
Sold	17,000	27,000	?	?
Ending inventory	?	12,000	17,000	15,000

26–28 Norvan Company is preparing its comprehensive budget for July. Use the given estimates to determine the amounts required in each part below. (Estimates may be related to more than one part.)
(a) What should total sales revenue be if territories A and B are estimating sales of 6,000 and 9,000 units, respectively, and the unit selling price is $27.50?
(b) If the beginning finished goods inventory is an estimated 1,600 units and the desired ending inventory is 3,500 units, how many units should be produced?
(c) What dollar amount of raw materials should be purchased at $4 per pound if each unit of product requires 3 pounds and beginning and ending raw materials inventories should be 6,000 and 2,300 pounds, respectively?
(d) How much direct labor cost should be incurred if each unit produced requires 1.5 hours at an hourly rate of $8?
(e) How much factory overhead should be incurred if fixed factory overhead is $30,000 and variable factory overhead is $1.50 per direct labor hour?
(f) How much operating expense should be incurred if fixed and variable operating expenses are $28,000 and 70 cents per unit sold, respectively?

26–29 The Walden Company is preparing its comprehensive budget for May. Use the estimates provided to determine the amounts required in each part below. (Estimates may be related to more than one part.)
(a) What should total sales revenue be if territories A and B are estimating sales of 4,000 and 10,000 units, respectively, and the unit selling price is $35?
(b) If the beginning finished goods inventory is an estimated 2,000 units and the desired ending inventory is 4,500 units, how many units should be produced?
(c) What dollar amount of raw materials should be purchased at $2 per pound

if each unit of product requires 2.5 pounds and beginning and ending raw materials inventories should be 4,000 and 1,750 pounds, respectively?

(d) How much direct labor cost should be incurred if each unit produced requires 2.5 hours at an hourly rate of $5?

(e) How much factory overhead should be incurred if fixed factory overhead is $15,000 and variable factory overhead is 80 cents per direct labor hour?

(f) How much operating expense should be incurred if fixed and variable operating expenses are $12,000 and $1.20 per unit sold, respectively?

26–30 The following summary data are from a performance report for the Moore Company for June, during which 9,600 units were produced. The budget reflects the company's normal capacity of 10,000 units.

	Budget (10,000 units)	Actual Costs (9,600 units)	Variances over (under) Budget
Raw materials	$ 35,000	$ 34,200	($800)
Direct labor	70,000	69,300	(700)
Factory overhead: variable	24,000	24,600	600
fixed	18,000	18,100	100
Total	$147,000	$146,200	($800)

(a) What is the general implication of the performance report? Why might Moore question the significance of the report?

(b) Revise the performance report using flexible budgeting, and comment on the general implication of the revised report.

26–31 Ball Company, which sells on terms 2/10, n/30, has had gross credit sales for May and June of $40,000 and $60,000, respectively. Analysis of Ball's operations indicates that the pattern of customers' payments on account is as follows (percentages are of total monthly credit sales):

	Receiving Discount	Beyond Discount Period	Totals
In month of sale	50%	15%	65%
In month following sale	20%	10%	30%
Uncollectible accounts, returns, and allowances			5%
			100%

Determine the estimated cash collected on customers' accounts in June.

26–32 The following various elements relate to Aztec, Inc.'s cash budget for April of the current year. For each item, determine the amount of cash that Aztec should receive or pay in April.

(a) At $15 each, unit sales are 5,000 and 6,000 for March and April, respectively. Total sales are typically 40% for cash and 60% on credit. One-third of credit sales are collected in the month of sale, with the balance collected in the following month. Uncollectible accounts are negligible.

(b) Merchandise purchases were $38,000 and $62,000 for March and April, respectively. Typically, 20% of total purchases are paid for in the month of purchase and a 5% cash discount is received. The balance of purchases are paid for (without discount) in the following month.

(c) Fixed operating expenses, which total $8,000 per month, are paid in the month incurred. Variable operating expenses amount to 20% of total monthly sales revenue, one-half of which is paid in the month incurred, with the balance paid in the following month.

(d) Fixed selling expenses, which total $3,000 per month, are paid in the month incurred. Variable selling expenses, which are 5% of total sales revenue, are paid in the month following their incurrence.

(e) A plant asset originally costing $6,000, on which $5,000 depreciation has been taken, is sold for cash at a loss of $200.

PROBLEMS

26-33 The following summary data relate to the operations of Murray Company for April, during which 9,000 finished units were produced:

	Standard Unit Costs	Total Actual Costs
Raw materials:		
Standard (4 lb @ $1.25/lb)	$ 5	
Actual (38,000 lb @ $1.10/lb)		$ 41,800
Direct labor:		
Standard (2 hr @ $6/hr)	12	
Actual (18,500 hr @ $6.30/hr)		116,550
Factory overhead:		
Standard (Variable costs of $1.50 per direct labor hour and $40,000 fixed costs for normal monthly capacity of 20,000 direct labor hours)	7	
Actual		67,800
Total	$24	$226,150

REQUIRED

Determine the following variances and indicate whether each is favorable or unfavorable:

(a) Raw materials price variance and usage variance.

(b) Direct labor rate variance and efficiency variance.

(c) Factory overhead controllable variance and volume variance.

26-34 A summary of James Company's manufacturing variance report for May appears on the next page.

	Total Standard Costs (9,200 units)	Total Actual Costs (9,200 units)	Variances (favorable)
Raw materials	$ 27,600	$ 30,380	$2,780
Direct labor	110,400	109,340	(1,060)
Factory overhead:			
Variable	16,560	16,400	(160)
Fixed	6,900	7,500	600
	$161,460	$163,620	$2,160

Standard raw materials cost per unit of product is 0.5 pounds at $6 each, and standard direct labor cost is 1.5 hours at $8 per hour. The total actual raw materials cost represents 4,900 pounds purchased at $6.20 per pound; total actual direct labor cost represents 14,200 hours at $7.70 per hour. Standard variable and fixed factory overhead rates are $1.20 and 50 cents, respectively, per direct labor hour (based on a normal capacity of 15,000 direct labor hours or 10,000 units of product).

REQUIRED

(a) Calculate variances for raw materials price and usage, direct labor rate and efficiency, and controllable factory overhead and overhead volume.
(b) Prepare single compound general journal entries (as illustrated in the chapter) to record standard costs, actual costs, and related variances for raw materials, direct labor, and factory overhead.
(c) Prepare journal entries to record the transfer of all completed units to Finished Goods Inventory and the subsequent sale of 8,400 units on account at $32 each (assume no beginning finished goods inventory).
(d) Prepare a partial income statement (through gross profit on sales), showing gross profit based on standard costs, the incorporation of variances, and gross profit based on actual costs.

26–35 Randall Company manufactures a single product and uses a standard costing system. The nature of its product dictates that raw materials are used as purchased and no ending work-in-process inventories occur. Per-unit standard product costs are: raw materials, $3 (4 pounds); direct labor, $5 (one-half hour); variable factory overhead, $4 (based on direct labor hours); and fixed overhead, $6 (based on a normal monthly capacity of 8,500 direct labor hours).

Randall accounts for work in process and finished goods inventories and cost of goods sold at standard cost and records each variance in a separate account. The following data relate to May, when 16,800 finished units were produced.

REQUIRED

(a) Assuming that 67,500 pounds of raw materials purchased on account at 80 cents per pound were used in May's production, present a single compound journal entry to record actual costs, standard costs, and any raw materials variances.

(b) Assuming that 8,600 direct labor hours were worked at an average hourly rate of $9.60, present a single compound journal entry to record actual costs, standard costs, and any direct labor variances.

(c) Assuming that total factory overhead incurred was $171,000, present a single compound journal entry to record actual and standard factory overhead costs and any factory overhead variances.

(d) Set up T accounts for Work in Process, Finished Goods Inventory, and Cost of Goods Sold, and enter the amounts for parts (a), (b), and (c). Assume that no beginning inventories exist, that all production was completed, and that all but 500 units produced were sold. Present and post journal entries to (1) record production completed and (2) record costs of goods sold at standard costs.

26–36 The Alton Company has established the following standard cost summary for a unit of its only product:

Raw materials (2.5 lb @ $3/lb)	$ 7.50
Direct labor (0.8 hr @ $5/hr)	4.00
Factory overhead (applied on basis of direct labor hours):	
Variable (0.8 hours @ rate of $15 per direct labor hour)	12.00
Fixed (0.8 hours @ rate of $10 per direct labor hour)	8.00
Total	$31.50

Normal monthly capacity is 10,000 units of product. In July, Alton produced 10,400 units of product, incurring the following actual costs:

Raw materials (25,800 pounds)	$ 79,980
Direct labor (8,400 hours)	40,320
Factory overhead	206,140
Total	$326,440

REQUIRED
(a) Determine both manufacturing cost variances associated with each of the following: (1) raw materials, (2) direct labor, and (3) factory overhead. Indicate whether each is favorable or unfavorable.

(b) Prove that the sum of each set of your variances explains the differences between the related amounts of total standard costs and total actual costs.

(c) Prove that the sum of all six of your variances equals the difference between the total actual costs and the total standard costs.

26–37 Brockmum, Inc. sells on terms of 5% discount for "cash and carry" or 2/10, n/30 and estimates its total gross sales for the second calendar quarter of next year as follows: April, $90,000; May, $70,000; and June, $120,000. An analysis of operations indicates the following customer collection patterns:

	Portions of Total Sales
In month of sale:	
Cash at time of sale	25%
On account, during discount period	15%
On account, after discount period	10%
In month following sale:	
On account, during discount period	20%
On account, after discount period	10%
In second month following sale:	
On account, after discount period	15%
Average portion uncollectible	5%
	100%

REQUIRED

Prepare an estimate of the cash to be collected from customers during June.

26–38 During the first calendar quarter of 19X1, Power Enterprises, Inc. is planning to manufacture a new product and introduce it in two regions. Market research indicates that sales will be 6,000 units in the urban region at a unit price of $25 and 5,000 units in the rural region at $22 each. Since the sales manager expects the product to catch on, he has asked for production sufficient to generate a 4,000-unit ending inventory. The production manager has furnished the following estimates related to manufacturing costs and operating expenses.

	Variable (per unit)	Fixed (total)
Manufacturing Costs:		
Raw materials:		
A (4 lb @ $1.50/lb)	$6	—
B (2 lb @ $2/lb)	4	—
Direct labor (one-half hour per unit)	3	—
Factory overhead:		
Depreciation	—	$ 2,000
Factory supplies	0.40	3,000
Supervisory salaries	—	6,000
Other	0.50	11,500
Operating Expenses:		
Selling:		
Advertising	—	4,000
Sales salaries and commissions	1.00*	5,000
Other	0.50*	1,000
Administrative:		
Office salaries	—	1,500
Supplies	0.10	400
Other	0.05	950

*Varies with number of units sold.

REQUIRED

(a) Assuming that the desired ending inventories of materials A and B are 4,000 and 6,000 pounds, respectively, and that work-in-process inventories are immaterial, prepare budgets for the calendar quarter in which the new product will be introduced for each of the following operating factors:

(1) Total sales revenue.
(2) Production (in units).
(3) Raw materials purchases cost.
(4) Direct labor costs.
(5) Factory overhead costs.
(6) Operating expenses.

(b) Using data generated in part (a), prepare a projected income statement for the calendar quarter. Assume an overall effective income tax rate of 30%.

26–39 Cabbe, Inc. is a wholesaler for its only product, a deluxe wireless electric drill, which sells for $32 each and costs Cabbe $20 each. On December 1, 19X1, Cabbe's management requested a cash budget for December, and the following selected account balances at November 30 were gathered by the accounting department.

Cash	$ 50,000
Marketable Securities (at cost)	80,000
Accounts Receivable (all trade)	608,000
Inventories (15,000 units)	300,000
Operating Expenses Payable	52,000
Accounts Payable (all merchandise)	216,000
Note Payable	90,000

Actual sales for October and November were 20,000 and 30,000 units, respectively. Projected unit sales for December and January are 50,000 and 40,000, respectively. Experience indicates that 50% of sales should be collected in the month of sale, 30% in the month following sale, and the balance in the second month following sale. Uncollectibles, returns, and allowances are negligible.

Planned purchases should provide ending inventories equal to 30% of next month's unit sales volume; approximately 70% are paid for in the month of purchase and the balance in the following month.

Monthly operating expenses are budgeted at $3 per unit sold plus a fixed amount of $70,000 including depreciation of $30,000. Except for depreciation, 60% of operating expenses are paid in the month incurred and the balance in the following month.

Special anticipated year-end transactions include the following:

(1) Declaration of a $10,000 cash dividend to be paid two weeks after the December 20 date of record.
(2) Sale of one-half of the marketable securities held on November 30; a gain of $8,000 is anticipated.
(3) Payment of $22,000 monthly installment (includes interest) on the note payable.
(4) Trade-in of an old computer originally costing $300,000 and now having accumulated depreciation of $240,000 at a gain of $70,000 on a new com-

puter costing $600,000. Sufficient cash will be paid at the time of trade-in so that only 50% of the total price will have to be financed.

(5) Cabbe's treasurer has a policy of maintaining a minimum month-end cash balance of $50,000 but wants to raise this to $100,000 at December 31. He has a standing arrangement with the bank to borrow any amount up to a limit of $200,000.

REQUIRED

Prepare a cash budget for Cabbe, Inc. for December 19X1. Begin your solution by scheduling collections from customers, payments on account for merchandise, and payments for operating expenses. Pattern your solution after Exhibit 26–10 on page 938.

26–40 The Polishing Department of the Mason Manufacturing Company operated during April 19X1 with the following factory overhead cost budget based on 5,000 hours of monthly productive capacity:

Mason Manufacturing Company
Polishing Department
Factory Overhead Budget
For the Month of April, 19X1

Variable costs:		
Factory supplies	$12,500	
Indirect labor	19,000	
Utilities (Usage charge)	8,500	
Patent royalties on secret process	37,000	
Total variable overhead		$77,000
Fixed costs:		
Supervisory salaries	$20,000	
Depreciation on factory equipment	18,000	
Factory taxes	6,000	
Factory insurance	4,000	
Utilities (Base charge)	10,000	
Total fixed overhead		58,000
Total factory overhead		$135,000

The Polishing Department was operated for 4,600 hours during April and incurred the following factory overhead costs:

Factory supplies	$ 12,190
Indirect labor	17,020
Utilities (usage factor)	10,350
Utilities (base factor)	12,000
Patent royalties	35,052
Supervisory salaries	21,000
Depreciation on factory equipment	18,000
Factory taxes	7,000
Factory insurance	4,000
Total factory overhead incurred	$136,612

REQUIRED

Using a flexible budgeting approach, prepare a factory overhead cost performance report for the Polishing Department for April 19X1. Pattern your solution after Exhibit 26–11 on page 940.

ALTERNATE PROBLEMS

26–33A The following summary data relate to the operations of Horner Company for April, during which 4,500 finished units were produced:

	Standard Unit Costs	Total Actual Costs
Raw Materials:		
Standard (0.6 lb @ $5/lb)	$ 3	
Actual (3,000 lb @ $5.25/lb)		$ 15,750
Direct labor:		
Standard (0.8 hr @ $7.50/hr)	6	
Actual (3,800 hr @ $7.20/hr)		27,360
Factory overhead:		
Standard (Variable costs of $5 per direct labor hour and $60,000 fixed costs for normal monthly capacity of 4,000 direct labor hours)	16	
Actual		80,400
Total	$25	$123,510

REQUIRED

Determine the following variances and indicate whether each is favorable or unfavorable:

(a) Raw materials price variance and usage variance.

(b) Direct labor rate variance and efficiency variance.

(c) Factory overhead controllable variance and volume variance.

26–34A A summary of Jensor Company's manufacturing variance report for June appears below.

	Total Standard Costs (7,600 units)	Total Actual Costs (7,600 units)	Variances (favorable)
Raw materials	$ 38,000	$ 37,200	$ (800)
Direct labor	45,600	49,200	3,600
Factory overhead:			
Variable	22,800	22,000	(800)
Fixed	68,400	72,000	3,600
	$174,800	$180,400	$5,600

Standard raw materials cost per unit of product is 4 pounds at $1.25 each and standard direct labor cost is 0.75 hours at $8 per hour. Total actual raw materials cost represents 31,000 pounds purchased at $1.20 per pound; total actual direct labor cost represents 6,000 hours at $8.20 per hour. Variable and fixed factory overhead rates are $4 and $12, respectively, per direct labor hour (based on a normal capacity of 6,000 direct labor hours or 8,000 units of product).

REQUIRED
(a) Calculate variances for raw materials price and usage, direct labor rate and efficiency, and controllable factory overhead and overhead volume.
(b) Prepare single compound general journal entries (as illustrated in the chapter) to record standard costs, actual costs, and related variances for raw materials, direct labor, and factory overhead.
(c) Prepare journal entries to record the transfer of all completed units to Finished Goods Inventory and the subsequent sale of 6,400 units on account at $35 each (assume no beginning finished goods inventory).
(d) Prepare a partial income statement (through gross profit on sales) showing gross profit based on standard costs, the incorporation of variances, and gross profit based on actual costs.

26–35A Brandiff Company manufactures a single product and uses a standard costing system. The nature of its product dictates that raw materials are used as purchased and no ending work-in-process inventories occur. Per-unit standard product costs are: raw materials, $2 (one-half pound); direct labor, $9 (1.5 hours); variable factory overhead, $3 (based on direct labor hours); and fixed overhead, $12 (based on a normal monthly capacity of 12,000 direct labor hours or 8,000 units of product).

Brandiff Company accounts for work in process and finished goods inventories and cost of goods sold at standard cost and records each variance in a separate account. The following data relate to June, when 7,800 finished units were produced.

REQUIRED
(a) Assuming that 4,200 pounds of raw materials purchased on account at $3.60 per pound were used in June's production, present a single compound journal entry to record actual costs, standard costs, and any raw materials variances.
(b) Assuming that 12,000 direct labor hours were worked at an average hourly rate of $6.20, present a single compound journal entry to record actual costs, standard costs, and any direct labor variances.
(c) Assuming that total factory overhead incurred was $120,500, present a single compound journal entry to record actual and standard factory overhead costs and any factory overhead variances.
(d) Set up T accounts for Work in Process, Finished Goods Inventory, and Cost of Goods Sold, and enter the amounts for parts (a), (b), and (c). Assume that no beginning inventories exist, that all production was completed, and that all but 900 units were sold. Present and post journal entries to (1) record production completed and (2) record cost of goods sold at standard costs.

26–38A During the first calendar quarter of 19X1, Radd Enterprises, Inc. is planning to manufacture a new product and introduce it in two regions. Market research indicates that sales will be 8,000 units in the urban region at a unit price of $29 and 6,000 units in the rural region at $24 each. Since the sales manager expects the product to catch on, he has asked for production sufficient to generate a 4,000-unit ending inventory. The production manager has furnished the following estimates related to manufacturing costs and operating expenses.

	Variable (per unit)	Fixed (total)
Manufacturing Costs:		
Raw materials:		
A (2 lb @ $1.40/lb)	$ 2.80	—
B (5 lb @ $0.60/lb)	3.00	—
Direct labor (two hours per unit)	10.00	—
Factory overhead:		
Depreciation	—	$13,000
Factory supplies	0.30	2,000
Supervisory salaries	—	7,500
Other	0.50	2,700
Operating Expenses:		
Selling:		
Advertising	—	5,000
Sales salaries and commissions	1.00*	8,000
Other	0.40*	2,000
Administrative:		
Office salaries	—	3,000
Supplies	0.10	1,000
Other	0.20	1,500

*Varies with number of units sold.

REQUIRED

(a) Assuming that the desired ending inventories of materials A and B are 4,000 and 20,000 pounds, respectively, and that work-in-process inventories are immaterial, prepare budgets for the calendar quarter in which the new product will be introduced for each of the following operating factors:
(1) Total sales revenue.
(2) Production (in units).
(3) Raw materials purchases cost.
(4) Direct labor costs.
(5) Factory overhead costs.
(6) Operating expenses.

(b) Using data generated in part (a), prepare a projected income statement for the calendar quarter. Assume an overall effective income tax rate of 40%.

26–39A Kiton, Inc. is a wholesaler for its only product, a deluxe wireless rechargeable electric shaver, which sells for $22 each and costs Kiton $14 each. On June 1, 19X1, Kiton's management requested a cash budget for June, and the following selected account balances at May 31 were gathered by the accounting department.

Cash	$ 14,000
Marketable Securities (at cost)	50,000
Accounts Receivable (all trade)	682,000
Inventories (12,000 units)	168,000
Operating Expenses Payable	61,500
Accounts Payable (all merchandise)	263,200
Note Payable	180,000

Actual sales for April and May were 30,000 and 50,000 units, respectively. Projected unit sales for June and July are 40,000 and 20,000, respectively. Experience indicates that 50% of sales should be collected in the month of sale, 30% in the month following sale, and the balance in the second month following sale. Uncollectibles, returns, and allowances are negligible.

Planned purchases should provide ending inventories equal to 30% of next month's sales volume; approximately 60% are paid for in the month of purchase and the balance in the following month.

Monthly operating expenses are budgeted at $3 per unit sold plus a fixed amount of $90,000 including depreciation of $35,000. Except for depreciation, 70% of operating expenses are paid in the month incurred and the balance in the following month.

Special anticipated June transactions include:

(1) Declaration of a $15,000 cash dividend to be paid two weeks after the June 20 date of record.
(2) Sale of all but $10,000 of the marketable securities held on May 31; a gain of $6,000 is anticipated.
(3) Payment of $60,000 installment (includes interest) on the note payable.
(4) Trade-in of an old company plane originally costing $90,000 and now having accumulated depreciation of $60,000 at a gain of $50,000 on a new plane costing $600,000. Sufficient cash will be paid at the time of trade-in so that only 50% of the total purchase price will have to be financed.
(5) Kiton's treasurer has a policy of maintaining a minimum month-end cash balance of $10,000 and has a standing arrangement with the bank to borrow any amount up to a limit of $100,000.

REQUIRED

Prepare a cash budget for Kiton, Inc. for June 19X1. Begin your solution by scheduling collections from customers, payments on account for merchandise, and payments for operating expenses. Pattern your solution after Exhibit 26–10 on page 938.

BUSINESS DECISION PROBLEM

Boomtime, Inc. has just hired Roddy Ledger as its new controller. Although Roddy has had little formal accounting training, he professes to be highly experienced, having learned accounting "the hard way" in the field. At the end of his first month's work, Roddy prepared the following cost variance report:

Boomtime, Inc.
Cost Variance Analysis
For the Month of June, 19XX

	Total Actual Costs	Total Budgeted Costs	Variances (favorable)
Raw materials	$ 71,712	$ 79,200	$ (7,488)
Direct labor	79,560	88,000	(8,440)
Factory overhead	161,000	176,000	(15,000)
	$312,272	$343,200	$(30,928)

In his presentation at Boomtime's month-end management meeting, Roddy indicated that things were going "fantastically." "The figures indicate," he said, "that the firm is beating its budget in all cost categories." Roddy's good news made everyone at the meeting happy and furthered his acceptance as a member of the management team.

After the management meeting, Kate Bonn, Boomtime's general manager, asked you as an independent consultant to review Roddy's report. Kate's concern stemmed from the fact that Boomtime has never operated as favorably as Roddy's report seems to imply, and Kate cannot explain the apparent significant improvement.

While reviewing Roddy's report, you are provided the following cost and operating data for June: Boomtime has a monthly normal capacity of 11,000 direct labor hours or 8,800 units of product. Standard costs per unit for its only product are: raw materials, 3 pounds at $3 each; direct labor, 1.25 hours at $8 each; and variable and fixed overhead rates per direct labor hour of $4 and $12, respectively. During June, Boomtime produced 8,000 units of product using 24,900 pounds of raw materials costing $2.88 each, 10,200 direct labor hours at an average rate of $7.80 each, and incurred $161,000 of total factory overhead costs.

After reviewing Boomtime's June cost data, you tell Roddy that his cost report contains a classic budgeting error, and you explain how he can remedy it. In response to your suggestion, Roddy revises his report as follows:

	Total Actual Costs	Total Budgeted Costs	Variances (favorable)
Raw materials	$ 71,712	$ 72,000	$ (288)
Direct labor	79,560	80,000	(440)
Factory overhead	161,000	160,000	1,000
	$312,272	$312,000	$ 272

Roddy's revised report is accompanied by remarks expressing regret at the oversight in the original report, but reassuring management that in view of the small variances in the revised report, the company has met its budget in all cost categories and has no basis for concern.

REQUIRED
In your role as consultant:
(a) Verify that Roddy's actual cost figures are correct.
(b) Explain how the proportions of Roddy's original variances question the validity of the budgeted cost figures.

(c) Identify and explain the classic budgeting error that Roddy apparently incorporated into his original cost report.
(d) Verify the apparent correctness of Roddy's revised budget figures.
(e) Explain why Roddy's revised figures could be considered deficient, even though substantially correct.
(f) Further analyze Roddy's revised variances, isolating underlying potential causal factors. How do your analyses indicate bases for concern to management? Briefly suggest initial areas of inquiry that management might take regarding any apparent problem area

THREE-VARIANCE ANALYSIS FOR FACTORY OVERHEAD

Chapter 26 illustrates the analysis of total factory overhead variance into a controllable variance and a volume variance. A refinement to this approach involves dividing the total factory overhead variance into the following three variances: (1) a *spending* variance, (2) an *efficiency* variance, and (3) a *volume* variance. Because volume variances are the same under either approach, the only difference is the further division of the controllable variance into a spending variance and an efficiency variance. Of course, the total overhead variance is the same, regardless of the number of variances determined. For convenience, the overhead data for Costello Manufacturing Company from Exhibit 26–3 are repeated here.

	Actual Costs (9,800 units)	Standard Costs (9,800 units)	Variances (favorable)
Factory Overhead:			
Variable	$ 8,700	$ 9,800	($1,100)
Fixed	30,000	29,400	600
Total	$38,700	$39,200	($ 500)

At its normal capacity of 10,000 direct labor hours, Costello's standard factory overhead rates per direct labor hour are $1 variable and $3 fixed, and 9,700 direct labor hours are used to produce 9,800 units of product.

The three overhead variances for Costello Manufacturing Company for June are calculated as follows:

Spending Variance

Budgeted overhead for the actual hours worked		
[$30,000 fixed + (9,700 × $1 variable)]	$39,700	
Actual overhead	38,700	
Spending variance		$1,000 Favorable

Efficiency Variance

Budgeted overhead for actual production attained		
[$30,000 fixed + (9,800 × $1 variable)]	$39,800	
Budgeted overhead for actual hours worked		
[$30,000 fixed + (9,700 units × $1 variable)]	39,700	
Efficiency variance		100 Favorable

Volume Variance

Normal capacity in direct labor hours	10,000	
Standard direct labor hours for actual production		
attained (9,800 units × 1 hour)	9,800	
Production capacity not used (hours)	200	
Standard fixed overhead rate per hour	× $3	
Volume variance		600 Unfavorable

Total Overhead Variance $ 500 Favorable

The following journal entry records these costs and variances:

Work in Process (at standard rates)	39,200	
Overhead Volume Variance	600	
Overhead Efficiency Variance		100
Overhead Spending Variance		1,000
Factory Overhead (actual overhead costs)		38,700
To record standard factory overhead and		
related variances.		

OVERHEAD SPENDING VARIANCE

The overhead spending variance reflects how much more (unfavorable) or less (favorable) was spent on factory overhead than the budget allowed for the actual hours worked. Costello's overhead budget indicated that overhead costs should be $30,000 plus $1 for each hour actually worked. Therefore, the budget allowed a total of $39,700 for the 9,700 direct labor hours worked in June. Because total actual overhead incurred was only $38,700, the $1,000 difference is a favorable overhead spending variance; thus, the company has avoided $1,000 of overhead costs.

A review of detailed spending records would show how the $1,000 savings were accumulated from savings in the many types of costs making up factory overhead—such as factory supplies, indirect labor, factory utilities, and factory repairs. Although exceptions exist, control of spending for factory overhead is usually the responsibility of production department supervisors. As a general rule, the variable portions of overhead costs account for most of the spending variance. Fixed costs, however, can also vary from the budgeted amount because of price changes occurring after the budget has been prepared and put into use. For example, supervisors' salaries are normally classified as fixed costs; if they increase after the budget has been prepared, actual fixed costs will vary from those budgeted.

OVERHEAD EFFICIENCY VARIANCE

The overhead efficiency variance shows how much overhead cost was either added or saved by operating above or below the standard level of labor efficiency. In June, Costello's employees worked 9,700 direct labor hours but produced 9,800 units of product, for which the overhead standards would have allowed 9,800 hours. We can say that June's operations have resulted in a savings of 100 direct labor hours, each of which avoided the standard variable overhead rate of $1, giving us a total favorable efficiency variance of $100. Note that fixed factory overhead does not enter into the efficiency variance; no part of a fixed cost is avoided by operating fewer hours nor is any extra amount of fixed overhead incurred (within the relevant range) by operating more than the normal number of hours for a given amount of production. In other words, a difference in direct labor hours affects only the total variable overhead; fixed overhead remains constant, at least within the relevant range. Since it is so closely tied to the efficiency of production, the overhead efficiency variance is usually the responsibility of the production supervisor.

OVERHEAD VOLUME VARIANCE

The computation and analyses for overhead volume variances are the same for either the two- or the three-variance approach to factory overhead variances; therefore, they are not repeated here. (See page 926 for this material.)

The journal entry for overhead costs (page 960) charges Work in Process with the standard overhead for the actual production attained, records each of the three variances in an appropriately titled variance account, and credits Factory Overhead for the actual overhead costs incurred.

Determining three variances for factory overhead is often justified because of the clear separation of the controllable variance into a spending element and an efficiency element. This distinction is even more significant when we realize that a controllable variance might approach zero simply because an unfavorable spending variance is virtually offset by a favorable efficiency variance (or vice versa). This potential for offsetting favorable and unfavorable cost elements could "hide" important operating data from management.

PROBLEMS

C–1 Using the following data for Astro, Inc., calculate overhead spending, efficiency, and volume variances for each independent situation:

	A	B	C
Total actual overhead	$65,700	$59,500	$133,500
Normal capacity (in direct labor hours)	5,000	8,000	20,000
Standard overhead rates:			
Variable (per direct labor hour)	$3.00	$2.50	$4.00
Fixed (per direct labor hour)	$10.00	$5.00	$2.50
Actual direct labor hours worked	4,800	8,400	19,800
Standard direct labor hours allowed for			
actual production	4,600	7,700	20,100

C–2 Zesta Company uses a standard cost system, has a monthly normal production capacity of 10,000 direct labor hours or 5,000 units of product, and has standard variable and fixed overhead rates per direct labor hour of $3 and $5, respectively. During July, Zesta incurred $78,300 of total overhead, working 9,700 direct labor hours to produce 4,700 units of product.

REQUIRED
(a) Compute overhead variances for spending, efficiency, and volume.
(b) Briefly explain the meaning of each variance in terms of operating and budgeting variables.

C–3 Using the data in Problem 26–33 (page 947), compute overhead variances for spending, efficiency, and volume.

C–4 Using the data in Problem 26–34 (page 947), compute overhead variances for spending, efficiency, and volume.

C–5 Using the data in Problem 26–33A (page 953), compute overhead variances for spending, efficiency, and volume.

C–6 Using the data in Problem 26–34A (page 953), compute overhead variances for spending, efficiency, and volume.

C–7 Able, Inc. uses a standard cost system, has a monthly normal production capacity of 5,000 direct labor hours or 10,000 units of product, and has standard variable and fixed overhead rates per direct labor hour of $4 and $5, respectively. During May, Able incurred $45,400 of total overhead costs, working 4,900 direct labor hours to produce 10,200 units of product.

REQUIRED
(a) Compute a controllable overhead variance and an overhead volume variance. Briefly describe the operating implications of the variances.
(b) Compute overhead variances for spending, efficiency, and volume. Briefly describe the operating implications of the variances.
(c) In what significant way does this situation justify a three-variance analysis of factory overhead?

27
Capital Budgeting

> **Capital is that part of wealth which is devoted to obtaining further wealth.**
>
> ALFRED MARSHALL

Using accounting data in planning long-term investments in plant and equipment is known as **capital budgeting.** The term reflects the fact that for most firms the total costs of all attractive investment opportunities exceed the available investment capital. Thus, management must ration, or budget, investment capital among competing investment proposals. In deciding which new long-term assets to acquire, management must seek investments that promise to optimize return on the funds employed.

Capital budgeting is most valuable for organizations in which managers are responsible for the long-run profitability of their area of concern and are therefore encouraged to develop new products and more efficient production processes. Firms often make their most capable employees responsible for capital budgeting decisions, because such decisions determine how large sums of money are invested and commit the firm for extended future periods, during which many important factors can only be estimated. Furthermore, investment decision errors are often difficult and costly to remedy or abandon.

Managers as well as accountants should be familiar with the special analytical techniques that evaluate the relative attractiveness of alternative uses of available capital. In this chapter, we first discuss the nature and procedures of capital budgeting, how required investment earning rates are determined, the time value of money, and the effect of income taxes on capital expenditure decisions. We conclude by illustrating three approaches to capital expenditure analysis—the *net present value method, payback analysis,* and the *average rate of* return.

ELEMENTS OF CAPITAL BUDGETING

Many firms have a capital budgeting calendar calling for consideration of capital expenditure proposals at regular intervals—for example, every six months or a year. Proposals are usually examined with respect to (1) compliance with capital budget policies and procedures; (2) aspects of operational urgency, such as the need to replace critical equipment; (3) established criteria for minimum return on capital investments; and (4) consistency with the firm's operating policies and long-run goals. Proposals for relatively small cash outlays may require the approval of low-level management only, whereas comprehensive proposals are subject to approval at high management levels, perhaps including the board of directors.

These comprehensive proposals and the decisions based on them profoundly affect a firm's long-run success.

Once approved, capital expenditures should be monitored to ensure that amounts and purposes are consistent with the original proposal. At appropriate intervals, the actual rates of return earned on important expenditures should be compared with projected rates. These periodic reviews encourage those responsible to formulate thorough and realistic proposals, and often provide an incentive for improving overall capital budgeting procedures.

CAPITAL EXPENDITURE ANALYSIS

The scope of capital expenditures varies widely, ranging from the routine replacement of production equipment to the construction of entire factory complexes. Whatever their size, most production projects have the following three recognizable stages:

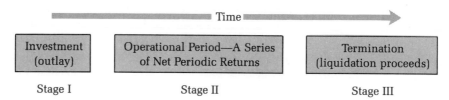

Investment (outlay)	Operational Period—A Series of Net Periodic Returns	Termination (liquidation proceeds)
Stage I	Stage II	Stage III

Investment (stage I) consists of the net cash outlay for a project or an asset. Net periodic returns during the life of the project (stage II) may result from either an excess of periodic revenue over related expenses or a periodic saving in some expense. Finally, because most efficient firms replace capital equipment before it becomes worthless, the termination of a project (stage III) often results in some amount of liquidation proceeds.

The attractiveness of a particular investment is determined in large part by the quantitative relationship between the investment in stage I and the receipts expected in stages II and III. This relationship is usually expressed as a ratio known as the *rate of return*:

$$\text{Rate of Return} = \frac{\text{Returns}}{\text{Investment}}$$

All other things being equal, the greater the expected rate of return, the more attractive the investment opportunity. Proposed investments can be ranked according to their expected rates of return, and capital outlays can be allocated among the most attractive investments. In its simplest terms, capital expenditure analysis consists of judging the adequacy or attractiveness of income-producing or cost-saving opportunities in relation to required investments. The results of this analysis are among the most important input data in capital budgeting decisions.

Three questions of considerable concern in capital budgeting are:

(1) How do we determine an acceptable rate of return for a given project?

(2) How can we meaningfully compare investments made now with returns to be received in the future?

(3) In what terms should investments and returns be measured?

These challenging problems are considered in the following sections of this chapter.

REQUIRED RATES OF RETURN

In determining an acceptable rate of return for a given project, we must consider not only the required capital outlay, but the costs associated with the acquisition of that capital. The parties providing the funds expect to be reasonably compensated for their use. When the money is borrowed (usually through a bond issue), the interest paid by the firm is obviously a cost of using the funds. When stockholder funds are used, we assume that some combination of dividend payments and increase in the value of the capital stock compensates stockholders for furnishing the investment capital. The cost to the firm of acquiring the funds used in capital investment projects—typically expressed as an annual percentage rate—is called the **cost of capital.**

Determining the actual cost of capital for a firm may require complex calculations, and even well-informed authorities in finance disagree about certain aspects of these calculations. Many firms use an approach that distinguishes among the various sources of financing.

A firm may acquire capital by issuing preferred or common stock, using retained earnings, borrowing, or some combination of these. Consequently, the overall cost of capital for a given project may reflect the cost rates of the several sources of funds in proportion to the amounts obtained from each source. This situation has led to the concept of the **weighted average** cost of capital, illustrated as follows.

Assume that a particular company had acquired capital through all four sources, in the proportions indicated below and with the cost percentages as shown.

Source of Capital	Percentage of Total	Capital Cost Percentage	Weighted Cost Percentage
Debt	40	8	3.2
Preferred stock	10	9	0.9
Common stock	20	12	2.4
Retained earnings	30	12	3.6
	Weighted average cost of capital		10.1

Multiplying the percentage of each capital source by its cost percentage provides weighted cost factors whose sum is the weighted average cost of capital. This percentage (in this case, 10.1%) can then be used to compare the attractiveness of proposed investments.

Logically, for a capital investment to be considered favorably by a firm, its expected rate of return must be *at least as great* as the cost of capital. Therefore, *the cost of capital represents a minimum required rate of return.* In other words, a firm whose cost of capital is 10% will ordinarily want to invest only in an asset or project whose expected rate of return is greater than 10%. An investment whose return is less than the cost of capital would be economically detrimental, although firms sometimes disregard their cost of capital if qualitative considerations override the quantitative aspects of the decision. Qualitative considerations might include the desire to operate a large computer, the desire to maintain research leadership in the field, and the need to maintain full employment of the work force during a business slowdown.

Some firms only consider investments whose rates of return are at least a certain number of percentage points higher than the cost of capital. This **buffer margin** acts as a safety factor, because proposals, which rely heavily on estimates of costs and future returns, may involve what will prove to be an erroneous estimated rate of return. Of course, even proposals whose expected rate of return is higher than the **cutoff** or **hurdle rate** (Cost of Capital + Buffer Margin) may be rejected if other investment opportunities offer still higher returns.

THE TIME VALUE OF MONEY

We have seen that in determining the desirability of a proposed capital investment, management compares the amount of investment required at the beginning of a project with its expected returns—typically a series of returns extending several years into the future. This comparison, which is so important in capital outlay decisions, cannot be made properly using the absolute amounts of the future returns because *money has a time value.* As discussed in Appendix A to Chapter 17, the time value of money means that the right to receive an amount of money today is worth more than the right to receive the same amount at some future date, because a current receipt can be invested to earn interest over the intervening period. Thus, if 10% annual interest can be obtained on investments, $100 received today is equal in value to $110 received one year from now. Today's $100 has a **future value** of $110 one year from now; conversely, the **present value** of a $110 receipt expected one year from today is $100. Appendix A (page 600) contains a detailed presentation of present values and techniques for their determination. Students not familiar with these two aspects of capital budgeting should review these materials.

Obviously, the difference between present and future values is a function of principal amounts, interest rates, and time periods. The greater the principal amount, interest rate, or time period involved, the greater the amount by which a future value is reduced, or *discounted*, in deriving its present value. For example, Exhibit 27–1 shows just how significant the time value of money can be at various interest rates and time periods. As the table indicates, $100 five years from now has a present value of $78, $62, or $40 if the applicable interest rates

KNOWN CUTOFF RATES: YES OR NO?

At least once a year, the senior executives and directors of many corporations address the problem of establishing a capital spending budget and selecting the projects that will be undertaken during the following year. The usual practice is for proposals to be submitted up through the organization; top management selects the most promising proposals, and the directors approve the selection. Some projects are selected for economic reasons; other selections are largely based on nonfinancial considerations such as environmental compliance.

Regardless of the common threads of this process, considerable controversy surrounds the appropriate methodology to be applied to the selection. One of the focal points of this controversy is the determination of capital spending hurdle rates: Should they even be used, and if so, how should they be calculated?

A survey of 136 companies by The Conference Board showed that 62 companies (46%) do not specify minimum cutoff rates for their capital investments. These proportions correspond with my own experience. Many companies do not establish capital spending hurdle rates for three reasons:

(1) Management wishes to reserve the prerogative of determining which proposals should be accepted and which should be turned down or referred. They do not wish to discourage the submission of any capital proposals. However, all proposals should be ranked in the order of their desirability.

(2) It is difficult to determine what "cutoff" or "hurdle rate" should apply, as risks, capital costs, and strategic considerations vary among projects. Moreover, some projects should be considered on a noneconomic basis.

(3) If a hurdle rate is made known to operating management, the figures used in proposals may be "massaged" to pass this rate rather than present the project on an objective basis.

There is merit to the point of view of not using hurdle rates. Good proposals should indeed not be discouraged, particularly those that cannot be supported on a strictly financial basis. It *is* difficult to determine the cost of capital and the impact of risks. Simplistic, arbitrary rates are not a solution either, and operating management *will* tend to play games with capital proposals if hurdle rates are know.

However, not establishing cutoff rates imposes some important disadvantages. Operating managers are not informed about the basic economics of the business. The absence of information encourages the submission of proposals that do not support these economics. It is akin to asking managers to prepare budgets without budget guidelines or objectives, or marketing managers to set selling prices without cost information. Each individual is left to his own devices without any common focus or sense of direction. Unofficial yardsticks as to "what will fly" often emerge from this vacuum. Such yardsticks are communicated through the grapevine and are as apt to provide misinformation as they are to constructively assist with the capital spending proposal and selection process.

From Allen H. Seed, III, "Structuring Capital Spending Hurdle Rates," *Financial Executive*, February 1982, pages 20–21. Reprinted by permission of Financial Executives Institute.

EXHIBIT 27–1
Present Value of $100 Discounted for Years and Interest Rates Shown (rounded to nearest dollar)

Years Discounted	Interest Rates		
	5%	10%	20%
1	$95	$91	$83
2	91	83	69
3	86	75	58
4	82	68	48
5	78	62	40
10	61	39	16
20	38	15	3
30	23	6	—
40	14	2	—
50	9	1	—

are 5%, 10%, and 20%, respectively. Note also that the greater the time period or the interest rate, the greater the difference between the future value of $100 and its current value. Comparing a current investment with its future returns without discounting the returns to their present value would substantially overstate the economic significance of the returns. Obviously, then, we must recognize the time value of money in capital budgeting procedures.

We should also recognize that techniques for discounting future cash flows to their present values apply to both cash receipts and cash outlays. In other words, the current value of the *right to receive*—or the current value of the *obligation to pay*—a sum in the future is its present value computed at an appropriate interest rate. Of course, we maximize our economic position by arranging to receive amounts as early as possible and postponing amounts to be paid as long as possible. The intrinsic role of these generalizations is apparent in the capital budgeting illustrations later in the chapter.

USING PRESENT VALUE TABLES

Although discount formulas are easily understood in theory, the associated calculations can be tedious. Widely available present value tables simplify our work considerably. Tables I and II on pages 993 and 994 give the present values of $1 for a number of rates and time periods. The amounts in these tables are called **present value factors,** or **discount factors,** because we convert any given cash flow to its present value by multiplying the amount of the cash flow by the appropriate factor.

EXHIBIT 27–2
Present Value of $1 Received
in the Future
(Excerpted from Table I)

Periods Hence	Rate per Compounding Period						
	2%	3%	4%	5%	6%	8%	10%
1	0.980	0.971	0.962	0.952	0.943	0.926	0.909
2	0.961	0.943	0.925	0.907	0.890	0.857	0.826
3	0.942	0.915	0.889	0.864	0.840	0.794	0.751
4	0.924	0.888	0.855	0.823	0.792	0.735	0.683
5	0.906	0.863	0.822	0.784	0.747	0.681	0.621
10	0.821	0.744	0.676	0.614	0.558	0.463	0.386
20	0.673	0.554	0.456	0.377	0.312	0.215	0.149
30	0.552	0.412	0.308	0.231	0.174	0.099	0.057

Single Sum Flows

Table I gives present value factors for amounts received in a single sum at the end of a specified number of periods. We use Table I to determine the present value of sporadic cash flows—when the returns expected on an investment, or the expenditures it requires, are unequal amounts or are expected at irregular intervals during or at the end of the life of the investment. An excerpt from Table I is presented in Exhibit 27–2.

To illustrate the use of Table I, we assume that an investment project promises a return of $2,000 at the end of two years and another $1,000 at the end of five years. The desired rate of return is 10%. The factor in the 10% column of the table for two periods from now is 0.826; the factor for five periods from now is 0.621. The total present value of the combined flows is $2,273, calculated as follows:

Future Receipts		PV Factor		Present Value
2 years from now	$2,000 ×	0.826	=	$1,652
5 years from now	1,000 ×	0.621	=	621
				$2,273

Annuity Flows

We can compute the present value of a single sum of cash flows—or any combinations of single sums—using Table I. Cash flows that are the same each period over two or more periods are an annuity, and using an annuity table is more convenient. Generally, annuity tables are cumulative versions of single sum tables. Table II, for example, is an annuity table based on present value factors from Table I. Exhibit 27–3 is excerpted from Table II.

To illustrate, we assume a project has expected cash inflows of $1,000 at the end of each of the next three periods, and 8% is the appropriate interest rate.

EXHIBIT 27–3
Present Value of $1 Annuity Received at the End of Each Period
(Excerpted from Table II)

Periods Hence	Rate per Compounding Period						
	2%	3%	4%	5%	6%	8%	10%
1	0.980	0.971	0.962	0.952	0.943	0.926	0.909
2	1.942	1.914	1.886	1.859	1.833	1.783	1.736
3	2.884	2.829	2.775	2.723	2.673	2.577	2.487
4	3.808	3.717	3.630	3.546	3.465	3.312	3.170
5	4.714	4.580	4.452	4.330	4.212	3.993	3.791
10	8.983	8.530	8.111	7.722	7.360	6.710	6.145
20	16.351	14.878	13.590	12.462	11.470	9.818	8.514
30	22.397	19.600	17.292	15.373	13.765	11.258	9.427

Using Table I, we compute the total present value as the sum of three individual amounts, as shown below:

Periods Hence	Cash Inflows		PV Factor (Table I @ 8%)		Present Value
1	$1,000	×	0.926	=	$ 926
2	1,000	×	0.857	=	857
3	1,000	×	0.794	=	794
					$2,577

Alternatively, using Table II, we need only multiply the periodic cash flow by a single present value factor for three periods at 8%.

Periods Hence (in annuity)	Periodic Cash Inflow		PV Factor (Table II @ 8%)		Present Value
3	$1,000	×	2.577	=	$2,577

Note that the present value factor for Table II is applied to the periodic cash flow of $1,000, not the $3,000 total amount of cash flows in the annuity.

The advantage of Table II is that a single present value factor is provided for two or more equal amounts occurring evenly throughout a series of periods. When analyzing investments involving extended series of equal cash flows, the savings in computational effort can be significant.

Tables I and II both assume that all cash flows occur at the end of the periods shown. This assumption is somewhat simplistic, because cash receipts or cost savings from most industrial investments occur in a steady stream throughout the operating period. Nevertheless, businesses use such tables principally because of their availability and ease of use. Obviously, these tables understate present values of flows that are gradual throughout the period, because the present values of cash flows early in the period are greater than similar inflows or outlays at the end of the period. The difference in the factors, however, is normally not material.

MEASUREMENT OF INVESTMENTS AND RETURNS

When present value analysis is used to make investment decisions, investments and returns must be stated in the form of *cash* flows. Present value determinations are basically interest calculations, and therefore, only money amounts—cash flows—are properly used in interest calculations. Furthermore, only the **incremental cash flows** that will occur if the project is accepted should be considered in the analysis. Often, accounting data used to make decisions are not stated in cash because accrual methods are used for accounts receivable, accounts payable, and accrued revenue or expenses. Such data must be restated in terms of their cash amounts.

For example, apportioning the cost of an asset over its life through depreciation accounting is an important feature of accrual accounting. When present value analysis is used, the cost of an asset is considered a cash outlay when the asset is paid for. In measuring future returns related to the asset, depreciation expense is irrelevant because it does not represent a cash outlay. However, depreciation provisions affect cash flows indirectly by reducing cash outlays for income tax payments.

Likewise, earnings from projects should not be influenced by the accrual process. The timing of collections is important, however, because the essence of present value analysis is that cash received can be reinvested. If accruals at the beginning and end of a period are roughly the same or are not material in amount, they are often ignored in restating accounting data as cash flows.

After-tax Cash Flows

Both federal and state income taxes are important to investment decisions; for many large companies, the combined federal and state income tax rate may exceed 50%. Generally, income taxes reduce the economic significance of taxable receipts and deductible outlays. For example, assuming a 40% tax rate, a $40,000 before-tax gain would increase taxable income by $40,000 and income taxes by $16,000 (40% × $40,000), resulting in a $24,000 after-tax gain. A $15,000 before-tax expense would reduce taxable income by $15,000 and income taxes by $6,000 (40% of $15,000), resulting in a $9,000 after-tax expense. Because income tax rates can be substantial, management has a continuing responsibility to minimize the firm's income tax. After-tax cash flows are more relevant than before-tax cash flows because they represent the amounts available to retire debt, finance expansions, or pay dividends. For these reasons, investment decision analyses must be formulated in terms of after-tax cash flows.

EXHIBIT 27–4
Illustration of Determining After-tax Cash Flows

	(A) Traditional Income Statement	(B) Income Statement Cash Inflows (Outflows)	(C) Individual After-tax Cash Inflow (Outflow) Effects
Cash revenue (Sales)	$100,000	$100,000	$60,000
Cash expenses $60,000		(60,000)	(36,000)
Depreciation expense 20,000			8,000
Total expenses	80,000		
Before-tax net income	$ 20,000		
Income tax expense at 40%	8,000	(8,000)	
After-tax net income	$ 12,000		
Add back depreciation	20,000		
After-tax cash flows	$ 32,000	$ 32,000	$32,000

Illustration of After-tax Cash Flows

Thinking in terms of after-tax cash flows represents a significant departure from the accrual-based accounting for revenue and expenses that dominates much of our earlier study of accounting. Exhibit 27–4 builds on the traditional income statement to illustrate (1) the conversion of after-tax net income to after-tax cash flows, (2) the confirmation of that amount as actual cash flows, and (3) the determination of the individual after-tax cash flow effects of receiving revenue, incurring cash expenses, and recording depreciation. An understanding of Exhibit 27–4 provides a basis for studying the comprehensive illustrations of capital budgeting later in the chapter.

The area in Exhibit 27–4 set off in color is the traditional income statement, showing that revenue minus expenses and income taxes results in an after-tax net income of $12,000. For simplicity, we assume revenue and cash expenses involve no significant accruals. Ordinarily, after-tax net income does not represent after-tax cash flows because depreciation expense—a noncash expense—is deducted to derive taxable income. As indicated in column A of Exhibit 27–4, to convert the $12,000 after-tax net income to after-tax cash flows, we must add back the depreciation of $20,000, resulting in $32,000 of after-tax cash flows.[1] Present value computations are properly applied to this amount.

Column B of Exhibit 27–4 confirms the $32,000 amount of after-tax cash flows determined in column A. This is accomplished by simply listing the amounts in column A that constitute cash inflows (revenue of $100,000) and cash outflows (cash expenses of $60,000 and income tax payments of $8,000). Depreciation is excluded because it does not represent a cash payment.

---

[1] If present, other amounts of noncash expenses—such as amortization of intangible assets and discount on bonds—are also added back.

Column C in Exhibit 27–4 illustrates the determination of the individual amounts of after-tax cash flows for each item on the income statement. We use this approach in the comprehensive illustrations of capital budgeting appearing later in the chapter. Amounts in column C are determined as follows (again, a 40% income tax rate is assumed):

Receipt of $100,000 cash revenue Receipt of $100,000 cash revenue would, by itself, increase taxable income by $100,000, adding $40,000 ($100,000 × 40%) to income taxes. The $60,000 after-tax cash inflow is the difference between the $100,000 cash revenue received and the related $40,000 increase in income taxes (a cash outflow).

Payment of $60,000 in cash expenses Payment of $60,000 in cash expenses represents a deductible cash outflow that reduces taxable income by $60,000 and thus reduces income taxes by $24,000 ($60,000 × 40%). The $36,000 net cash outflow is the difference between the $60,000 actually paid out for expenses and the $24,000 of income tax payments avoided by virtue of their tax deductibility.

Notice that *avoiding a cash outflow* has the same effect on net cash flows as a cash inflow. In other words, total net cash inflows can be increased by adding to cash inflows or by avoiding cash outflows.

Recording $20,000 of depreciation expense Although depreciation expense is tax deductible, no related cash expenditure occurs during the period. The $20,000 deduction reduces taxable income $20,000 and income taxes $8,000 ($20,000 × 40%). Because the depreciation deduction results in avoidance of an outflow, its after-tax cash flow effect is that of a cash inflow. Depreciation expense and similar noncash expense deductions are often referred to as *tax shields* because they shield an equal amount of income from whatever income tax rate is applicable.

Combining the after-tax cash flow effect of each individual amount in column C again confirms that net cash inflows total $32,000. It is helpful to realize that the after-tax cash flow effect of cash receipts and cash expenses is derived by multiplying the before-tax amounts by (1 − the tax rate). In contrast, the after-tax cash flow effect of depreciation deductions is derived by multiplying the before-tax amounts by the tax rate. In our example

Cash revenue $100,000 × (1 − 0.4) =	$60,000
Cash expenses $60,000 × (1 − 0.4) =	(36,000)
Depreciation expense $20,000 × 0.4 =	8,000
Net cash flows	$32,000

SUMMARY OF CONCERNS
UNDERLYING CAPITAL BUDGETING

(1) The typical investment pattern involves a present investment of funds resulting in anticipated returns, often extending years into the future.

(2) The basic question in capital budgeting is whether present investments are justified by related future returns.

(3) Because money has a time value, returns that occur in the future must be discounted to their present values for a proper comparison with present investments.

(4) To use discounting (interest) calculations properly, we must state amounts in capital budgeting analyses in terms of cash flows.

(5) Because income tax rates are substantial, capital budgeting analyses should be formulated in terms of after-tax cash flows.

In this chapter, we have presented a number of important aspects of capital budgeting as background for the review of several approaches to capital expenditure analysis. These background materials have focused on the analytical concept known as *net present value*. Accountants generally concede that the net present value approach is conceptually and analytically superior to the other two approaches that we illustrate—*cash payback* and *average rate of return*.

NET PRESENT VALUE ANALYSIS

The basic considerations of **net present value** analysis are shown schematically in Exhibit 27–5. Referring to the items in the diagram, we can explain the steps in the net present value approach as follows:

(1) Determine in terms of incremental after-tax cash flows the amount of the investment outlay required.

(2) Estimate in terms of incremental after-tax cash flows the amounts and timing of future operating receipts or cost savings.

EXHIBIT 27–5
Schematic Diagram of Net Present Value Analysis

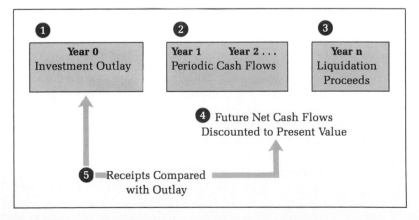

27 ■ CAPITAL BUDGETING

(3) Estimate any incremental after-tax liquidation proceeds to be received on termination of the project.

(4) Discount all future cash flows to their present value at an appropriate interest rate, usually the minimum desired rate of return on capital.

(5) Subtract the investment outlay from the total present value of future cash flows to determine *net* present value. If net present value is zero or positive (returns equal or exceed investment), then the project's rate of return equals or exceeds the minimum desired rate and should be accepted. Negative net present values indicate that the project's return is less than desired and the project should be rejected.

To illustrate net present value analysis, assume that, with a minimum desired return of 10%, management is considering the purchase of a $12,000 machine that will save $5,000 annually in cash operating expenses, have a useful life of three years, be depreciated $3,500 per year, and be sold for $2,000 at the end of the third year. Also, assume that all income and gains are taxed at 40%.

Exhibit 27–6 presents a net present value analysis of the machine as an investment project. Note how the format follows the schematic analysis presented in Exhibit 27–5: Future returns are stated in terms of after-tax cash flows; then, from Tables I and II, the present values of future cash flows are determined and compared with the investment. The computations shown in Exhibit 27–6 are explained below.

Annual cash expense savings   Cash savings or expense reductions have the same effects as cash revenue, income, or gains. Of course, they also have the same consequence of increasing income taxes. In our example, saving $5,000 in expenses each year raises taxable income by $5,000, which leads to a $2,000 ($5,000 × 40%) increase in taxes. Thus, the annual after-tax cash flow is $3,000—the $5,000 savings less the $2,000 tax increase. The $3,000 saved each year for three years can be treated as an annuity. Its present value factor of 2.487 is taken from Table II on the line for three periods and the column for 10% (the minimum return desired). The analysis shows that, with desired return at 10% and income taxes at 40%, saving $5,000 annually for the next three years has a present value of $7,461.

Annual depreciation tax shield   Recording depreciation does not in itself involve cash flows. When plant assets are purchased and used in business, however, depreciation may be deducted in the calculation of taxable income. Therefore, the depreciation deduction has a cash flow *effect* because related amounts of income tax payments are avoided. The avoided taxes are equal to the depreciation deduction multiplied by the applicable tax rate. In our illustration, the annual $3,500 depreciation deduction and the 40% tax rate result in an annual tax shield of $1,400 ($3,500 × 40%). Because they cause cash tax payments to be avoided, tax shields have the same effect as cash *inflows*. Being of equal amounts equally spaced in time—like the annual savings in expense—the tax shield in

EXHIBIT 27–6
Illustration of Net Present Value Analysis—After-tax Cash Flows
(rounded to nearest dollar)

Analysis of After-tax Cash Flows		Present Value Factors at 10% (Table I or II)	Total Present Value	Projected After-tax Cash Flows			
				Year 0	Year 1	Year 2	Year 3
Annual Cash Expense Savings:							
Annual cash expense savings	$5,000						
Less income tax @ 40%	2,000						
After-tax expense savings	$3,000	(II) 2.487	$ 7,461		$3,000	$3,000	$3,000
Annual Depreciation Tax Shield:							
Annual depreciation deduction	$3,500						
Applicable income tax rate	0.40						
Annual tax shield provided	$1,400	(II) 2.487	3,482		1,400	1,400	1,400
Liquidation Proceeds:							
Sales price of machine	$2,000						
Net book value (original cost of $12,000 less accumulated depreciation of $10,500)	1,500						
Gain on sale	$ 500						
Income tax on gain @ 40%	$ 200						
After-tax proceeds of sale:							
Sales price	$2,000						
Less tax on gain	200						
	$1,800	(I) 0.751	1,352				1,800
Total present value of future cash flows			$12,295				
Investment required in machine			(12,000)	($12,000)*			
Net positive present value			$ 295				

*Outflow.

our example can also be treated as an annuity. Its present value is $3,482, cal-
culated with the same present value factor of 2.487 from Table II.

 We discover an interesting aspect of tax planning when the present values
of the tax shields provided by the same total depreciation deduction under the
straight-line method are compared with those under an accelerated depreciation
plan such as sum of the years' digits. The straight-line depreciation deduction in
Exhibit 27–6 is $3,500 per year for three years—a total of $10,500—which results

in a tax shield with a total present value of $3,482. The present value of the tax shield provided by the same total depreciation deduction taken under the sum-of-the-years'-digits method (where the fractional denominator is 3 + 2 + 1 = 6) is computed as follows:

Year	Yearly Fraction of $10,500	Depreciation Deduction	Tax Shield at 40%	Present Value Factor (Table I)	Total Present Value
1	$\frac{3}{6}$	$ 5,250	$2,100	0.909	$1,909
2	$\frac{2}{6}$	3,500	1,400	0.826	1,156
3	$\frac{1}{6}$	1,750	700	0.751	526
		$10,500			$3,591

Therefore, in our illustration, taking the same total $10,500 depreciation deduction under sum of the years' digits increases the present value of the total tax shield from $3,482 to $3,591—a total of $109. The significance of this simple tax planning example is obvious. In terms of present value analysis, a firm's advantage in choosing the accelerated depreciation method could well be measured in thousands or millions of dollars.

Liquidation proceeds   The amount realized when an asset is liquidated contributes to the relative attractiveness of an investment in capital equipment. Liquidation proceeds on long-lived assets are sometimes disregarded because their occurrence is so far in the future that the amounts are difficult to predict, and their present values tend to be small. When useful lives are short, however, liquidation proceeds may be a deciding factor in the analysis. In our illustration, the machine originally costing $12,000 is depreciated over three years to a book value of $1,500 and then sold for $2,000 cash. The resulting $500 gain increases income taxes by $200, which is deducted from the sales price of $2,000 to produce a net after-tax cash flow of $1,800. Because the $1,800 is a single sum received at the end of year 3, its present value of $1,352 is derived by multiplying the $1,800 by the 0.751 factor from Table I (three periods hence at 10%).

To illustrate the calculations related to loss on a sale, assume that the machine was sold for only $500. The present value of the after-tax cash flow is computed as follows:

Net book value of machine ($12,000 original cost − $10,500 accumulated depreciation)	$1,500
Less sales price of machine	500
Loss on sale of machine	$1,000
Income tax benefit of loss ($1,000 loss × 40% income tax rate)	$ 400
Net cash inflow ($500 sales proceeds + $400 income tax benefit)	$ 900

Like the net cash flows from gains, the $900 is a single sum cash inflow occurring in year 3. Its $676 present value is determined by multiplying $900 by 0.751, the present value factor from Table I for three periods hence at 10%.

Required investment Proper consideration of the required investment involves neither an income tax nor a present value calculation. The $12,000 investment itself is not tax deductible; the related depreciation deductions are tax deductible, and are, of course, incorporated earlier into our analysis. Since the investment expenditure is immediate, no deferral, and therefore no discounting for present value, is required. Thus, $12,000 represents the after-tax present value of the required investment outflow.

Decision rule With its savings of cash expense, depreciation tax shield, and liquidation proceeds, the $12,000 investment results in future cash flows with a total present value of $12,295 and therefore a net present value of $295. This return on the capital invested, adjusted for the time value of money, exceeds the 10% return rate sought, and the investment is acceptable.

Another interpretation of our anaylsis is that as much as $12,295 could be paid for the machine and still retain the desired 10% rate of return. Paying more than $12,295 for the machine results in a return of less than 10%.

Excess Present Value Index

Alternative capital expenditure proposals may be compared in terms of their **excess present value index,** defined as

$$\text{Excess Present Value Index} = \frac{\text{Total Present Value of Net Future Cash Flows}}{\text{Initial Cash Investment}}$$

For the investment presented in Exhibit 27–6, the excess present value index would be

$$\frac{\$12,295}{\$12,000} = 1.0245$$

The higher the ratio of return on investment, the more attractive the proposal. Although the excess present value index may be a convenient measure for ranking various proposals, it does not reflect the amount of the investment. Two proposals, requiring initial cash investments of $5,000 and $5,000,000, respectively, could have identical excess present value indexes but could hardly be considered equal investment opportunities.

CASH PAYBACK ANALYSIS

Cash payback analysis is a form of capital expenditure analysis that is considered less sophisticated than net present value analysis. The **cash payback period** is *the time in years that it takes net future after-tax cash inflows to equal the original investment.*

Assume that a firm is considering purchasing either machine A or machine B, for which the following data are given:

Machine	Investment Required	Estimated Annual Savings in After-tax Cash Expenses	Useful Life
A	$10,000	$2,500	8 years
B	15,000	5,000	3 years

Cash payback is computed as

$$\frac{\text{Original Investment}}{\text{Annual Net Cash Inflows}} = \text{Cash Payback in Years}$$

Thus, for the two machines, we obtain

$$\text{(A)} \quad \frac{\$10,000}{\$2,500} = 4\text{-year cash payback}$$

$$\text{(B)} \quad \frac{\$15,000}{\$5,000} = 3\text{-year cash payback}$$

This analysis shows that machine A will pay back its required investment in four years, and machine B will take only three years. Because the decision rule in cash payback analysis states that *the shorter the payback period the better*, machine B would be considered the better investment.

Concern for the payback of investments is quite natural because the shorter a project's payback period, the more quickly the funds invested in that project are recovered and available for other investments. In high-risk investments, the payback period indicates how soon a firm is "bailed out" of an investment should it prove unattractive.

A primary limitation to cash payback analysis is that the *relative profitability of various investments is not specifically considered*. Note, for example, that in the foregoing illustration, machine B has the better (shorter) cash payback period. However, its useful life, which is ignored in cash payback analysis, indicates that machine B will stop generating cash inflows just when payback is completed. Consequently, there will be no opportunity to generate profit. In contrast, although machine A has the longer payback period, it will generate future cash inflows for four years beyond its payback and therefore promises to be profitable.

Regardless of its failure to consider profitability, cash payback analysis is widely used in industry, probably because of its relative simplicity. It can be useful in conjunction with other analyses or as a preliminary screening device for investment projects under consideration.

AVERAGE RATE OF RETURN

Another approach to capital outlay analysis, **average rate of return** relies heavily on accounting determinations of net income. This measure is calculated as

$$\text{Average Rate of Return} = \frac{\text{Expected Average Annual Net Income}}{\text{Average Investment}}$$

Note that here the variables are not after-tax cash flows but traditional accounting net income (with depreciation deducted) and accounting measurements for assets (based primarily on historical costs).

In the preceding illustration, machine A required an initial investment of $10,000; provided $2,500 annual cash inflows from operations; and had a useful life of eight years. Assuming no salvage value, annual straight-line depreciation on machine A would be ($10,000/8), or $1,250, so that average annual net income would be $1,250 (the operating cash inflows of $2,500 less depreciation of $1,250).

We may calculate average investment simply by adding the beginning and ending investments and dividing by 2. In our illustration, machine A has no salvage value, so the ending investment is zero. Average investment is therefore ($10,000 + $0)/2 = $5,000.

The average rate of return on machine A is

$$\frac{\$1,250}{\$5,000} = 25\%$$

The decision rule for average rate of return analyses states that *the higher the return, the more attractive the investment.*

As an approach to capital expenditure analysis, the average rate of return is often defended as being most easily understood by management personnel who are accustomed to thinking in accounting terms and concepts. It has two major limitations, however. First, the calculations rely heavily on accounting computations of net income, depreciation, and asset measures, and are thus subject to arbitrary choices, such as straight-line versus accelerated depreciation and historical cost versus current valuations. Second, average rate of return calculations do not consider the time value of money. Future cash flows are treated the same as current cash flows. Our discussion of net present value analysis amply illustrates the often substantial differences between future values and related current values discounted by even moderate interest rates.

As an example of how deceptive the average annual income figures used in average rate of return computations can be, consider three investment proposals that each require a $40,000 initial investment and promise the annual cash inflows shown in Exhibit 27–7. Note that cash flows are concentrated in year 1 in proposal A, are uniform in proposal B, and are concentrated in year 5 in proposal C. Because average rate of return calculations fail to consider the timing of cash flows from operations, these three proposals would have identical 10% average rates of return and therefore would be considered equally attractive. Such an implication is hardly defensible in view of the substantial differences in the relative net present values of the operating cash flows. In our illustration, the difference between the present values of A and C is $12,960, an amount equal to 41% of C's present value.

EXHIBIT 27–7
Present Value Comparison of Equal Annual Average Incomes

	Proposals		
	A	B	C
Annual net cash inflows			
Year 1	$46,000	$10,000	$ 1,000
2	1,000	10,000	1,000
3	1,000	10,000	1,000
4	1,000	10,000	1,000
5	1,000	10,000	46,000
Aggregate net cash inflows	$50,000	$50,000	$50,000
Average annual net cash inflows	$10,000	$10,000	$10,000
Less depreciation ($40,000/5)	8,000	8,000	8,000
Average annual net income	$ 2,000	$ 2,000	$ 2,000
Average rate of return on investment			
$2,000/($40,000/2)	10%	10%	10%

Present value of net cash inflows at 10%:

(A) One year hence, $45,000 × 0.909	$40,905		
5-year annuity of $1,000 × 3.791	3,791		
	$44,696		
(B) 5-year annuity of $10,000 × 3.791		$37,910	
(C) 5-year annuity of $1,000 × 3.791			$ 3,791
5 years hence, $45,000 × 0.621			27,945
			$31,736

CAPITAL BUDGETING—A PERSPECTIVE

Because it incorporates aspects of such fields as economics, finance, business management, and accounting, the subject of capital budgeting is too complex to treat comprehensively in an introductory accounting book. In this chapter, we have simply provided some insight into problem-solving techniques in capital budgeting by stating decision rules in their simplest form, showing the relevance of present value concepts and after-tax cash flows, and creating an awareness of the potentials and limitations of several widely used approaches to capital expenditure analysis. The illustrations have highlighted key relationships, and operational realism has been considered secondary. The rudiments presented here should serve as a basis for further study and an understanding of related subject areas.

KEY POINTS TO REMEMBER

(1) Capital budgeting is the planning of long-lived asset investments; capital expenditure analysis basically examines how well prospective future returns justify related present investments.

(2) Cost of capital is a measure of the firm's cost for investment capital; it usually represents the minimum acceptable return for investment opportunities.

(3) The time value of money concept recognizes that the farther into the future cash flows occur, the less current economic worth they have. Present value tables enable us to convert future cash flows conveniently to their present values at appropriate interest rates.

(4) After-tax cash flows probably represent the most relevant measure of the prospective returns of proposed investments.

(5) We convert cash flows from revenue and expenses into after-tax amounts by multiplying them by the factor $(1 - r)$, where r is the income tax rate. We convert depreciation deductions into their after-tax cash flow effect by multiplying the deduction by the applicable income tax rate.

(6) Net present value analysis compares the present value of net future cash flow returns with the investment. Projects having zero or positive net present values are acceptable.

(7) Cash payback analysis measures the time in years necessary for the net future after-tax cash flows to equal the original investment. In this type of analysis, the shorter the payback period, the more attractive the investment.

(8) Average rate of return analysis compares the annual average net income with the average investment. The higher this ratio, the more attractive the investment.

(9) Cash payback analysis fails to consider the relative profitability of alternative projects. Average rate of return analysis fails to consider the time value of money.

QUESTIONS

27–1 What is the nature of capital budgeting?

27–2 List three reasons why capital budgeting decisions are often important.

27–3 What are the three stages typical of most investments?

27–4 Briefly describe the concept of *weighted average cost of capital.*

27–5 In what sense does the cost of capital limit a firm's investment considerations?

27–6 Briefly describe the concept of the *time value of money.*

27–7 In which percent columns and periods hence lines in present value Table I would you expect the smallest conversion factors? Why?

27–8 In which percent columns and periods hence lines in present value Table II would you expect the largest conversion factors? Why?

27–9 Where in Table II will you find the factor equal to the sum of the factors for periods 1, 2, and 3 at 12% in Table I? Explain their equivalence.

27–10 Explain how to convert before-tax cash operating expenses and depreciation deductions into after-tax amounts.

27–11 What amounts are compared in net present value analysis? State the related decision rule.

27–12 Briefly explain how sum-of-the-years'-digits depreciation might be of greater benefit to a firm than straight-line depreciation even though the total depreciation is the same.

27–13 Define *cash payback*, state the related decision rule, and specify an important limitation of this analysis.

27–14 Define *average rate of return*, state the related decision rule, and specify an important limitation of this analysis.

27–15 You have the right to receive $15,000 at the end of each of the next three years, and money is worth 6%. Using Table II, compute the present value involved. Illustrate how Table I can be used to confirm your answer.

27–16 A company plans to accumulate 70% of its needed investment capital by issuing bonds having a capital cost percentage of 10%; the balance will be raised by issuing stock having a capital cost percentage of 12%. What would be the weighted average cost of capital for the total amount of capital?

27–17 A rich uncle allows you to stipulate which of two ways you receive your inheritance: (a) $600,000 one year after his death or (b) $150,000 on his death and $160,000 each year at the end of the first, second, and third years following his death. If money is worth 10%, what is the relative advantage of the more attractive alternative?

27–18 You can settle a debt with either a single payment now of $70,000 or with payments of $20,000 at the end of each of the next five years. If money is worth 12%, what is the relative advantage of the most attractive alternative? If money is worth 15%, would your answer change? Why?

EXERCISES

27–19 (a) Assuming money is worth 12%, compute the present value of:
   (1) $2,500 received 15 years from today.
   (2) The right to inherit $2,000,000 fifty years from now.
   (3) The right to receive $600 at the end of each of the next six years.
   (4) The obligation to pay $700 at the end of each of the next 12 years.
   (5) The right to receive $4,000 at the end of the seventh, eighth, ninth, and tenth years from today.
(b) Confirm your answer to part (a)(5) by using Table II and subtracting the present value of a six-year annuity from a 10-year annuity (isolating the four relevant years).

27–20 For each of the following independent situations, compute the after-tax income and convert it to an after-tax cash flow amount that could be properly incorporated into net present value analyses.

	A	B	C
Cash revenue received	$70,000	$180,000	$130,000
Cash expenses paid	50,000	110,000	120,000
Depreciation expense	10,000	30,000	20,000
Income tax rate	30%	40%	20%

27–21 Using the data in Exercise 27–20, (a) calculate—as shown in column C of Exhibit 27–4—the individual after-tax cash flow effect of each relevant item in each independent situation, and (b) confirm that the sum of the individual after-tax cash flows in each situation equals the after-tax income converted to after-tax cash flows.

27–22 Mason, Inc. plans to finance its expansion by raising the needed investment capital from the following sources in the indicated proportions and respective capital cost percentages:

Source	Proportion	Capital Cost Percentage
Bonds	40%	15%
Preferred stock	20	10
Common stock	10	6
Retained earnings	30	8
	100%	

Calculate the weighted average cost of capital.

27–23 Using the following data and rounding to the nearest dollar, compute the cash payback, average rate of return, net present value, and excess present value index:

Investment, $20,000
Expected annual cash savings, $6,000
Depreciation: straight-line, five years, no salvage value
Applicable income tax rate, 40%
Minimum desired rate of return, 8%

27–24 Assuming a desired annual return of 12%, use the appropriate present value table to make informed decisions in each of the following unrelated situations:
(a) You will inherit $3,000,000 in 15 years. What is the smallest amount that you would sell your inheritance for now? (Assume no taxes are applicable.)
(b) Your firm can settle a debt by either of two payment plans, which require the following after-tax cash outlays:

Outlays at end of:	Plan A	Plan B
Year 1	$ –0–	$ 1,000
Year 2	8,000	9,000
Year 3	7,000	5,000
Totals	$15,000	$15,000

Which alternative is more attractive? By how much?

(c) How much should you be willing to pay for an investment that will provide after-tax cash income of $8,000 at the end of each of the next 10 years and that at the end of the tenth year will provide a nontaxable refund of $6,000 of your original investment?

27–25 A machine costing $30,000 will be depreciated over a five-year useful life with no salvage value. Assuming a 40% income tax rate and a 10% desired annual return, compute the total present value of the tax shields provided by straight-line depreciation and by sum-of-the-years'-digits depreciation. Which would be most attractive to an investor? Why?

27–26 A special-purpose machine costing $25,000 will save Coster Company $5,000 per year in cash operating expenses for the next 10 years. Straight-line depreciation with a $5,000 salvage value will be used, and the minimum desired rate of return is 8%. Assuming a 40% income tax rate and rounding amounts to the nearest dollar, compute the following:
(a) Cash payback period.
(b) Average rate of return.
(c) Net present value (assume disposal sale at book value).

27–27 Considering the time value of money, we can generalize that the higher the appropriate interest rate and the longer we must wait to receive funds, the closer the present values of such future receipts approach zero. Illustrate the validity of this generalization by using Table I to identify for each percentage rate (per compounding period) that point at which the present value of funds received in the future falls below 50 cents on the dollar.

PROBLEMS

27–28 At a cash cost of $25,000, Boman Company can acquire a special machine that will save $8,000 in annual cash operating expenses. No salvage value is expected at the end of its five-year useful life. Assume an income tax rate of 40% and a 10% after-tax minimum desired rate of return.

REQUIRED
Assuming straight-line depreciation and rounding amounts to the nearest dollar, calculate the following:
(a) The cash payback period.
(b) The average rate of return.
(c) The net present value and the excess present value index.

27–29 Alton Company may purchase for $22,000 cash a machine that should save $8,000 in cash operating expenses each year. Straight-line depreciation will be used, and although the machine can be sold for only an estimated $2,000 at the end of its three-year useful life, the Internal Revenue Service has insisted on an estimated salvage value of $4,000.

REQUIRED
Assuming an income tax rate of 30% and a desired annual return of 12%, compute the net present value of this investment and its excess present value index (round amounts to the nearest dollar).

27–30 Below is a numbered list of various *independent* investment aspects that the capital budgeting team of Capital Investments, Inc. has incorporated into its net present value analyses during the past year. All situations assume a 40% income tax rate and a 12% minimum desired rate of return.

(1) Pretax savings of $3,000 in cash expenses will occur in each of the next three years.

(2) A machine is purchased now for $60,000 cash.

(3) Equipment costing $36,000 is depreciated using the straight-line method and an assumed salvage value of $6,000 at the end of its five-year estimated useful life.

(4) Assume the data in (3), except that sum-of-the-years'-digits depreciation is used.

(5) Pretax savings of $2,500 in cash expenses will occur in the third, fourth, and fifth years from now.

(6) Pretax savings of $2,000 in cash expenses will occur in the first, third, and fifth years from now.

(7) The equipment described in (3) is sold at the end of its useful life for $7,500 cash.

(8) The equipment described in (3) is sold at the end of its useful life for $4,000 cash.

REQUIRED

Set up an answer form with the four column headings as shown below. Answer each investment aspect separately. Prepare your calculations on a separate paper and key them to each item. The answer to investment aspect (1) is presented as an example.

Investment Aspect	(A) After-tax Cash Flow Effect(s) (Outflows)	(B) Year(s) of Cash Flow	(C) Applicable Present Value Multiple
(1)	$1,800	1, 2, 3	(II) 2.402

Calculations:

(1)	Pretax cash savings	$3,000
	Less income tax at 40%	1,200
	After-tax cash inflow	$1,800

(a) Calculate and record in column A the related after-tax cash flow effect(s). Place parentheses around outflows.

(b) Indicate in column B the timing of each cash flow shown in column A. Use 0 to indicate immediately and 1, 2, 3, 4, and so on for each year involved.

(c) When relevant, record in column C the present value multiple from Table I or II that you would apply to the cash flow amount shown in column A.

27–31 You have an opportunity to invest in a concession at a world exposition. To exploit the building and exhibits more fully, the venture is expected to cover a four-year period consisting of a preliminary year, the two years of formal exposition, and a one-year period of reduced operation primarily for tourists.

The terms of the concession agreement specify that:

(1) At inception, a $20,000 deposit is paid to World Expo, Inc., the promoting organization. This amount is returned in full at the end of the four years if the operator maintains the concession in order and keeps it open during scheduled hours. The deposit is not tax deductible, nor is its return subject to income taxes.

(2) The operator must install certain fixtures, that will cost $60,000, be depreciated using the straight-line method, and become the property of World Expo, Inc. at the end of the four years.

After careful investigation and consultation with local experts, you conclude that the following schedule reflects the pretax operating income of the concession (amounts in thousands of dollars):

	Year 1	Year 2	Year 3	Year 4
Sales (all cash)	$160	$640	$800	$220
Total operating expenses (all cash except depreciation on fixtures)	130	520	670	180
Projected pretax income	$ 30	$120	$130	$ 40

REQUIRED

Assuming an income tax rate of 40%, a desired annual return of 12%, and that term (1) is complied with, what would be the net present value of this investment opportunity at the beginning of the four years? (Round amounts to nearest dollar.)

27–32 Rasher, Inc. uses net present value analysis to budget its major capital outlays. Its capital projects analysis team—Bob Able, Nancy Baker, and Chris Charley—has just completed an analysis for the purchase of a new comprehensive computer system. The computer will provide automatic processing controls in a series of production departments, accommodate the firm's entire accounting system, and store a comprehensive data bank on Rasher's approximately 10,000 customers.

The team has assumed the computer would cost $2,000,000 now, be depreciated on a straight-line basis with a zero salvage value at the end of its 30-year estimated useful life, the desired minimum rate of return is 20%, and that the income tax rate is 40%. An analysis based on these assumptions results in an excess present value index of 1.05 for the project.

Team members agree on all aspects of the analysis except the assumed salvage value. Bob thinks it will be zero, and Nancy thinks the computer can be sold for $200,000 cash. Chris believes that, because of its total integration into the production process, accounting system, and the customers' data bank, the firm will incur a $300,000 cash "disinstallation" expense before it can install a replacement computer.

REQUIRED

Assume that a zero salvage value is used for income tax purposes regardless of the final assumption of the actual salvage value and that a 40% income tax rate applies to any related gains, losses, or expenses.

(a) Determine the effect on the original analysis of Nancy's assumption regarding the actual salvage value. Present relevant calculations.
(b) Determine the effect on the original analysis of Chris' assumption regarding the "disinstallation" expense. Present relevant calculations.
(c) What aspect of the original analysis might be questioned on an intuitive basis?

ALTERNATE PROBLEMS

27–28A At a cost of $30,000, Delco Company can acquire a special machine that will save $12,000 in annual cash operating expenses. No salvage value is expected at the end of its six-year useful life. Assume an income tax rate of 40% and a 15% minimum desired rate of return.

REQUIRED
Assuming straight-line depreciation and rounding amounts to the nearest dollar, calculate the following:
(a) The cash payback period.
(b) The average rate of return.
(c) The net present value.

27–29A Omarr Company may purchase for $24,000 cash a machine that should save $13,000 in cash operating expenses each year. Straight-line depreciation will be used, and although the machine can be sold for only an estimated $2,000 at the end of its three-year useful life, the Internal Revenue Service has insisted on an estimated salvage value of $3,000.

REQUIRED
Assuming an income tax rate of 40% and a desired annual return of 12%, compute the net present value of this investment and its excess present value index. (Round amounts to the nearest dollar.)

27–30A Below is a numbered list of various *independent* investment aspects that the capital budgeting team of Cosmos Ventures, Inc. has incorporated into its net present value analyses during the past year. All situations assume a 20% income tax rate and a 20% minimum desired rate of return.
(1) Pretax savings of $5,000 in cash expenses will occur in each of the next three years.
(2) A machine is purchased now for $90,000 cash.
(3) Equipment costing $40,000 is depreciated using the straight-line method and an assumed salvage value of $4,000 at the end of its four-year estimated useful life.
(4) Assume the data in (3), except that sum-of-the-years'-digits depreciation is used.
(5) Pretax savings of $3,000 in cash expenses will occur in the third, fourth, and fifth years from now.
(6) Pretax savings of $4,000 in cash expenses will occur in the first, third, and fifth years from now.
(7) The equipment described in (3) is sold at the end of its useful life for $7,000 cash.
(8) The equipment described in (3) is sold at the end of its usful life for $2,500 cash.

REQUIRED

Set up an answer form with the four column headings as shown below. Answer each investment aspect separately. Prepare your calculations on a separate paper and key them to each item. The answer to investment aspect (1) is presented as an example.

Investment Aspect	(A) After-tax Cash Flow Effect(s) (Outflows)	(B) Year(s) of Cash Flow	(C) Applicable Present Value Multiple
(1)	$3,500	1, 2, 3	(II) 2.106

Calculations:

(1) Pretax cash savings	$5,000
Less income tax at 30%	1,500
After-tax cash inflow	$3,500

(a) Calculate and record in column A the related after-tax cash flow effect(s). Place parentheses around outflows.

(b) Indicate in column B the timing of each cash flow shown in column A. Use 0 to indicate immediately and 1, 2, 3, 4, and so on for each year involved.

(c) When relevant, record in column C the present value multiple from Table I or II that you would apply to the cash flow amount shown in column A.

27–31A You have an opportunity to invest in a concession at a world exposition. To exploit the building and exhibits more fully, the venture is expected to cover a five-year period consisting of a preliminary year, the two years of formal exposition, and a two-year period of reduced operation primarily for tourists.

The terms of the concession agreement specify that:

(1) At inception, a $20,000 deposit is paid to Geo Expo, Inc., the promoting organization. This amount is returned in full at the end of the five years if the operator maintains the concession in order and keeps it open during scheduled hours. The deposit is not tax deductible, nor is its return subject to income taxes.

(2) The operator must install certain fixtures that will cost $85,000, be depreciated using the straight-line method, and become the property of Geo Expo, Inc. at the end of the five years.

After careful investigation and consultation with local experts, you conclude that the following schedule reflects the pretax operating income of the concession (amounts in thousands of dollars):

	Year 1	Year 2	Year 3	Year 4	Year 5
Sales (all cash)	$120	$750	$840	$230	$160
Total operating expenses (all cash except depreciation on fixtures)	90	580	690	170	120
Projected pretax income	$ 30	$170	$150	$ 60	$ 40

REQUIRED

Assuming an income tax rate of 30%, a desired annual return of 15%, and that term (1) is complied with, what would be the net present value of this investment opportunity at the beginning of the five years? (Round amounts to nearest dollar.)

BUSINESS DECISION PROBLEM

Kells Corporation, a small limited-venture investment firm, recently identified an investment opportunity involving a five-year franchise for acquiring and operating a route of vending machines. However, after preparing the investment analysis below, Kells' treasurer has recommended to Kells' investment committee that the investment be rejected. Glenda Jason, chairperson of the investment committee, finds it difficult to accept the treasurer's analysis because she "feels intuitively" that the investment is attractive. For this reason, she has retained you as an independent consultant to review the treasurer's analysis and recommendation. You are provided with the following data and summary of the treasurer's analysis:

(1) Required investment: $150,000 cash for a group of vending machines depreciated on a straight-line basis, five-year useful life, with a zero salvage value.

(2) Projected cash revenue and expenses:

Year	Cash Revenue	Cash Expenses
1	$180,000	$100,000
2	150,000	80,000
3	110,000	50,000
4	90,000	40,000
5	70,000	30,000
	$600,000	$300,000

(3) Source of capital: Kells plans to raise 50% of the needed capital by issuing bonds, 30% by issuing stock, and the balance from retained earnings. For these sources, the capital cost percentages are 6%, 12%, and 12%, respectively. Kells has a policy of seeking a return equal to the weighted average cost of capital plus three percentage points as a "buffer margin" for the uncertainties involved.

(4) Income taxes: Kells assumes an overall income tax rate of 30%.

(5) Treasurer's analysis:

Average cost of capital (6% + 12% + 12%) ÷ 3 = 10%

Total cash revenue		$600,000
Total cash expenses	$300,000	
Total depreciation	150,000	
Total expenses		450,000
Projected net income over five years		$150,000

Average annual income ($150,000 ÷ 5)	$ 30,000
Present value factor of five-year annuity at 10%	× 3.791
Present value of future returns	$113,730
Required investment	150,000
Negative net present value	$ 36,270

Recommendation: Reject investment because of insufficient net present value.

REQUIRED
(a) Review the treasurer's analysis, identifying any questionable aspects and briefly commenting on the apparent effect of each such item on the treasurer's analysis.
(b) Prepare your own analysis of the investment, including a calculation of the proper cost of capital and discount rates, a net present value analysis of the project, and a brief recommendation to Jason regarding the investment.
(c) Because of her concern for the uncertainties of the vending machine business, Jason also has asked you to provide analyses supporting whether or not your recommendation would change:
(1) If estimates of projected cash revenue were reduced by 10%.
(2) If the "buffer margin" were doubled from 3% to 6%.

PRESENT VALUE TABLES

TABLE I
Present Value of $1
Received in the Future

Periods Hence	Rate per Compounding Period									
	2%	3%	4%	5%	6%	8%	10%	12%	15%	20%
1	0.980	0.971	0.962	0.952	0.943	0.926	0.909	0.893	0.870	0.833
2	0.961	0.943	0.925	0.907	0.890	0.857	0.826	0.797	0.756	0.694
3	0.942	0.915	0.889	0.864	0.840	0.794	0.751	0.712	0.658	0.579
4	0.924	0.889	0.855	0.823	0.792	0.735	0.683	0.636	0.572	0.482
5	0.906	0.863	0.822	0.784	0.747	0.681	0.621	0.567	0.497	0.402
6	0.888	0.838	0.790	0.746	0.705	0.630	0.564	0.507	0.432	0.335
7	0.871	0.813	0.760	0.711	0.665	0.583	0.513	0.452	0.376	0.279
8	0.854	0.789	0.731	0.677	0.627	0.540	0.467	0.404	0.327	0.233
9	0.837	0.766	0.703	0.645	0.592	0.500	0.424	0.361	0.284	0.194
10	0.821	0.744	0.676	0.614	0.558	0.463	0.386	0.322	0.247	0.162
11	0.804	0.722	0.650	0.585	0.527	0.429	0.350	0.287	0.215	0.135
12	0.789	0.701	0.625	0.557	0.497	0.397	0.319	0.257	0.187	0.112
13	0.773	0.681	0.601	0.530	0.469	0.368	0.290	0.229	0.163	0.093
14	0.758	0.661	0.577	0.505	0.442	0.340	0.263	0.205	0.141	0.078
15	0.743	0.642	0.555	0.481	0.417	0.315	0.239	0.183	0.123	0.065
16	0.728	0.623	0.534	0.458	0.394	0.292	0.218	0.163	0.107	0.054
17	0.714	0.605	0.513	0.436	0.371	0.270	0.198	0.146	0.093	0.045
18	0.700	0.587	0.494	0.416	0.350	0.250	0.180	0.130	0.081	0.038
19	0.686	0.570	0.475	0.396	0.331	0.232	0.164	0.116	0.070	0.031
20	0.673	0.554	0.456	0.377	0.312	0.215	0.149	0.104	0.061	0.026
30	0.552	0.412	0.308	0.231	0.174	0.099	0.057	0.033	0.015	0.004
40	0.453	0.307	0.208	0.142	0.097	0.046	0.022	0.011	0.004	0.001
50	0.372	0.228	0.141	0.087	0.054	0.021	0.009	0.003	0.001	—

TABLE II
Present Value of $1 Annuity
Received at End of Each Period

Periods Hence	\multicolumn{10}{c}{Rate per Compounding Period}
	2%	3%	4%	5%	6%	8%	10%	12%	15%	20%
1	0.980	0.971	0.962	0.952	0.943	0.926	0.909	0.893	0.870	0.833
2	1.942	1.914	1.886	1.859	1.833	1.783	1.736	1.690	1.626	1.528
3	2.884	2.829	2.775	2.723	2.673	2.577	2.487	2.402	2.283	2.106
4	3.808	3.717	3.630	3.546	3.465	3.312	3.170	3.037	2.855	2.589
5	4.714	4.580	4.452	4.330	4.212	3.993	3.791	3.605	3.352	2.991
6	5.601	5.417	5.242	5.076	4.917	4.623	4.355	4.111	3.784	3.326
7	6.472	6.230	6.002	5.786	5.582	5.206	4.868	4.564	4.160	3.605
8	7.326	7.020	6.733	6.463	6.210	5.747	5.335	4.968	4.487	3.837
9	8.162	7.786	7.435	7.108	6.802	6.247	5.760	5.328	4.772	4.031
10	8.983	8.530	8.111	7.722	7.360	6.710	6.145	5.650	5.019	4.192
11	9.787	9.253	8.761	8.306	7.887	7.139	6.495	5.988	5.234	4.327
12	10.575	9.954	9.385	8.863	8.384	7.536	6.814	6.194	5.421	4.439
13	11.348	10.635	9.986	9.394	8.853	7.904	7.103	6.424	5.583	4.533
14	12.106	11.296	10.563	9.899	9.295	8.244	7.367	6.628	5.724	4.611
15	12.849	11.938	11.118	10.380	9.712	8.560	7.606	6.811	5.847	4.675
16	13.578	12.561	11.652	10.838	10.106	8.851	7.824	6.974	5.954	4.730
17	14.292	13.166	12.166	11.274	10.477	9.122	8.022	7.120	6.047	4.775
18	14.992	13.754	12.659	11.690	10.828	9.372	8.201	7.250	6.128	4.812
19	15.679	14.324	13.134	12.085	11.158	9.604	8.365	7.366	6.198	4.844
20	16.351	14.878	13.590	12.462	11.470	9.818	8.514	7.469	6.259	4.870
30	22.397	19.600	17.292	15.373	13.765	11.258	9.427	8.055	6.566	4.979
40	27.356	23.115	19.793	17.159	15.046	11.925	9.779	8.244	6.642	4.997
50	31.424	25.730	21.482	18.256	15.762	12.234	9.915	8.304	6.661	4.999

28

Income Taxes and Their Effect on Business Decisions

Except for a brief period during the Civil War, the United States had no federal income tax until 1913, when its constitutionality was confirmed by ratification of the Sixteenth Amendment. The federal income tax system is administered by the Internal Revenue Service, an agency of the Treasury Department. The numerous revenue acts passed since 1913 were first codified in 1939 and then recodified as the Internal Revenue Code of 1954. Regulations interpreting the code are published from time to time by the IRS, but the ultimate interpretive authority lies with the federal court system, which adjudicates conflicts between the IRS and taxpayers.

The IRS has verified that the collection rate of federal income taxes is well over 90%. Such success is surely impressive, considering that the system depends on a high degree of voluntary compliance with complex tax laws and regulations. Whereas certain taxes are withheld at the source and employers, financial institutions, and other agencies must report individuals' earnings, the system still relies to a great extent on taxpayers assessing and reporting their own obligations.

As tax rates have increased and regulations have become more complex, a large proportion of the nation's taxpayers have turned to accountants, attorneys, and others for assistance in preparing their tax returns. These professional consultants may also help to arrange business and personal affairs to minimize tax liability. Few business decisions are made without first considering which possible alternatives judged consistent with the business objective have the most desirable tax effect. Indeed, when large amounts of money are involved, this factor is so important that many accountants and attorneys confine their practices to such special areas as estate planning, pension plans, wage and stock option plans, and reorganizations and mergers. Whether they call on professionals for assistance or not, taxpayers generally benefit from a basic understanding of the tax system structure and the options it provides.

PURPOSES OF THE TAX LAW

The primary purpose for the federal income tax laws is raising revenue to pay for the operations of the government. In addition to the primary revenue-producing purpose, many amendments to the Internal Revenue Code of 1954 have been enacted for other purposes. Federal taxation has changed since 1913 in both purpose and magnitude. The income tax system has become an instrument of the federal government for economic and social policy.

Through its taxing powers, the government can attempt to distribute income more equitably, stimulate economic growth, combat inflation and unemployment, and finance projects it considers socially desirable. In addition, a number of changes in the tax laws are the result of political influences on Congress, which formulates tax laws. Thus multidimensional influences have contributed to the complexity of rapidly changing income tax laws. Because of these factors, the business manager must be keenly aware of the changing effect of income taxes on the business decision process.

INCOME TAX REFORM

At one time, the U.S. income tax system was considered a model system. As a self-assessment system, taxpayers declared their income, computed their tax liability, and with few exceptions routinely paid their income taxes.

Today the income tax system is under attack, and demands for tax reform are widely reported in the national media. This dissatisfaction has several important causes. A major taxpayer concern is the often bewilderingly complex tax law stemming from a multitude of esoteric provisions and frequent major rewritings. Increased complexity, of course, increases the cost of complying with tax regulations because taxpayers must retain expensive professional advice to take advantage of all provisions of the income tax law.

Another taxpayer concern is "bracket creep," the result of the combination of progressive tax rates and inflation. In this situation, even though nominal tax rates remain unchanged, taxpayers with constant (or even reduced) purchasing power may pay higher marginal tax rates. Bracket creep has been described as automatic tax increases for which Congress never has to vote.

A third basic taxpayer concern is the combined burden of all taxes. The Tax Foundation reported that in 1983, a moderate-income family of four earning $25,000 in wages incurred a mean total tax bite of $6,323, almost $2,500 of which is income taxes.[*] The Tax Foundation also announced that May 2, 1983 was Tax Freedom Day, the day when the average worker had year-to-date earnings sufficient to pay all federal, state, and local taxes.[†]

Perhaps the most critical source of ill feelings toward the income tax system is a general loss of taxpayer confidence. Many people feel that taxes are too high, that so-called loopholes enable the rich to avoid paying their share of taxes, and that an extensive underground economy exists in which tens of billions of dollars of income are unreported each year. Taxpayers also question the objectives for which certain of their tax dollars are spent.

Taxpayer resentment and loss of confidence may cause otherwise honest taxpayers to cut corners on their returns. An everybody-is-doing-it mentality often justifies ever bolder understatements of income and overstatements of deductions. This trend is unquestionably a critical long-term threat to our income tax system.

Calls for tax reform reflect appeals for simplification of regulations, increased compliance through closing of tax loopholes, and an indexing of income tax rates to inflation.[‡] Provisions for indexing tax rates are effective in 1985, but many observers believe they will be canceled because of the need for tax revenues. The "flat-rate" tax is widely advocated for its simplicity, lower overall tax rate, and increased equity.[§]

All citizens have a certain and prevailing interest in the successful implementation of tax reform. Reasonable tax rates, an equitable sharing of the tax burden, a high level of compliance, and an acceptable level of taxpayer confidence are all necessary to the long-term funding of our federal, state, and local governments.

[*]Tax Foundation statistics quoted in The Week in Review, Deloitte, Haskins & Sells, May 27, 1983, page 4.
[†]Tennessee CPA Newsletter, Tennessee Society of Certified Public Accountants, July 1983, page 2.
[‡]See L.C. Phillips and G.J. Previts, "Tax Reform: What Are the Issues?", Journal of Accountancy, May 1983, pages 64–74.
[§]See B. Crickmer, "The Flat-Rate Tax: What's Ahead," Nation's Business, August 1982, pages 22–24.

CLASSIFICATION OF TAXPAYERS

The main entities that are recognized for purposes of federal income taxation are individuals, partnerships, corporations, and estates or trusts. Here we cover individuals, partnerships, and corporations, leaving estates and trusts to an advanced course.

Although they are business entities, sole proprietorships and partnerships are not taxable entities. The owners of such firms must include their shares of business income along with income from other sources in their respective individual tax returns. The allocable shares of their business income are taxed directly to them whether or not they have withdrawn such amounts. In conjunction with this requirement, each partnership must file an **information return**showing the results of the firm's operations and the respective shares of net income accorded to each partner.

As taxable entities, corporations are taxed directly on their earnings. Shareholders receiving distributions of earnings must include these amounts as dividend income on their individual returns. Although this practice has led to the allegation that corporate earnings are subject to "double taxation," it is generally conceded that the bulk of corporate taxes are passed on to the consumer in the long run.

Under Subchapter S of the Internal Revenue Code, certain corporations generally are not taxed but pass income and losses through to their owners like partnerships. Firms meeting the Subchapter S criteria are referred to as **S corporations.**

Because of the many technical differences in the tax computations for individuals and corporations, we consider them separately. Thus, we first discuss the more salient features of individual income tax and then briefly cover some important aspects of corporate income tax. Keep in mind that the provisions of the tax laws relating to tax rates, exemption amounts, various prescribed limits, and other details have been changing rapidly and will continue to change.

TAXATION OF INDIVIDUALS

Generally, individuals who are citizens of the United States are taxed on all income from whatever source, unless it is specifically excluded by law. Thus, the gross income reported in an individual's tax return consists of total income and gains *less exclusions.* Various deductions and exemptions are permitted to convert gross income to taxable income. Deductions and exemptions must be enumerated in the individual's return (Form 1040) or in supporting schedules.

Although the manner in which this information is detailed in the return varies, a basic, logical format guides the computation of taxable income and the related tax liability. This format, illustrated in Exhibit 28–1, describes the classifications used in the tax laws and is a useful frame of reference in compiling the information needed to prepare an individual's tax return.

EXHIBIT 28–1
Format for Determining
Tax Liability of Individuals

	Steps	Explanation
Determine:	Total Income	All income from whatever source
Less:	Exclusions	Items of income excluded by law (page 1000)
Equals:	Gross Income	Income subject to tax (before deductions and exemptions)
Less:	Deductions from Gross Income	Business-related expenses, losses, and specific deductions from gross income (page 1000)
Equals:	Adjusted Gross Income	Base for computations of limitations on some personal (itemized) deductions
Less:	Excess Itemized Deductions	Itemized deductions in excess of the specified zero bracket amount (page 1001)
	Personal Exemptions	$1,000 for taxpayer, spouse, and each dependent, and an additional $1,000 for each taxpayer and spouse age 65 or over and for each taxpayer and spouse who is blind
Equals:	Taxable Income	Amount used to compute the tax from the appropriate tax rate schedule
Results in:	Income Tax	Taxable income multiplied by appropriate tax rate
Less:	Tax Credits	Specified credits against the tax (page 1007)
Equals:	Tax Liability	Amount of tax owed by the taxpayer

After the tax is computed by applying the appropriate rates to taxable income, certain credits against the tax may be allowed. We discuss these later in the chapter.

Gross Income   As mentioned above, gross income is income from all sources, less allowable exclusions. Some of the most common types of gross income are wages, salaries, bonuses, fees, tips, interest, dividends, profits or shares of profits from businesses, pensions, annuities, rents, royalties, prizes, and taxable gains on sale of property or securities. The list also includes income from gambling and even illegal income, such as from theft or embezzlement. (Racketeers and other criminals have often been more easily apprehended through income tax investigations than through regular criminal investigations).

Special rules and procedures apply to certain of these sources of gross income in determining the portion to be included. For example, gains from sale or exchange of capital assets are accorded special treatment. Because of the importance of this subject, we treat it separately later in this chapter.

Exclusions from Gross Income

Some items excluded by law from gross income include interest on certain state and municipal bonds; Social Security receipts;[1] gifts, bequests, and inheritances; worker's compensation for sickness or injury; certain disability benefits; life insurance proceeds received at the death of the insured; and scholarships not requiring services from degree candidates. The exclusions also exempt amounts of pensions and annuities that are returns of capital invested in them and the first $100 in dividend income ($200 for a married couple filing jointly).

The exclusions dealing with interest on state and municipal bonds and with gifts, bequests, and inheritances are important in tax planning for some taxpayers. For example, persons in high tax rate brackets often purchase state and municipal bonds to escape federal income tax on the interest. We explain this particular exclusion more fully later, in the discussion of tax shelters.

Deductions from Gross Income

Individual taxpayers are generally permitted two types of deductions—deductions from gross income to arrive at *adjusted gross income* and deductions from adjusted gross income. The first type is widely characterized as most business expenses and expenses incurred in the production of rents and royalties, whereas the second is generally described as allowable personal deductions.

The calculation of **adjusted gross income** is important in the taxation of individuals because it may affect the amount of certain personal deductions. Generally, we determine adjusted gross income to provide a more equitable base for certain other calculations than that provided by a gross income measure. Thus, a person who generates a large amount of gross income by incurring large amounts of business expenses or other related costs of producing such income is provided a base for determining personal deductions that is fairly comparable to the income of a wage earner or salaried taxpayer who does not have such business expenses.

Deductions permitted the individual taxpayer in arriving at adjusted gross income are as follows (remember these are subject to change):

(1) *Trade and business deductions*—Ordinary and necessary expenses attributable to a trade or business carried on by the taxpayer may be deducted, provided such activity does not consist of performance of services as an employee. Generally, these expenses offset business revenue, and the net amount is included in adjusted gross income.

(2) *Employee deductions*—For the most part, an employee may deduct travel and related expenses incurred in connection with employment (but not commuting costs) and the unreimbursed portion of employment expenses when the employer has a reimbursement plan. An outside salesperson can deduct all unreimbursed costs attributable to the employer's business. Employees may also deduct moving costs necessitated by job transfers.

(3) *Losses from sales or exchanges of property*—Losses from the sale or exchange

---

[1] However, for taxable years after 1983, taxpayers with "modified" adjusted gross incomes in excess of certain specified base amounts may have as much as 50% of their Social Security benefits included in taxable income.

of business or investment property are deductible in arriving at adjusted gross income. However, losses on the sale or exchange of "personal-use" property are not deductible.

(4) *Excess of long-term capital gains over short-term capital losses*—A taxpayer may deduct 60% of the excess of long-term capital gains over short-term losses (explained later in this chapter) in calculating adjusted gross income.

(5) *Net operating loss deduction*—Generally, a business's operating loss in a particular year, which is of no tax benefit for that year, may be carried back to the three preceding years and forward to the next 15 years to reduce the tax liability for those years. After certain adjustments, the loss is carried back to the earliest preceding year first, then successively to each succeeding period, if unused. A taxpayer may forego the carryback and only carry the loss forward 15 years.

(6) *Marriage penalty deduction*—Married couples who both earn income may deduct 10% of the lesser of $30,000 or the qualified earned income of the spouse with the lower earned income. *Qualified earned income* includes income earned from personal services such as salaries, wages, and net profits from a sole proprietorship; it does not include passive types of income such as interest or dividend income. A couple may qualify for the deduction even if they do not itemize their personal deductions, because the maximum $3,000 deduction is from gross income in arriving at adjusted gross income. The couple must file a joint tax return rather than two separate tax returns.

(7) *Other deductions*—Certain other deductions, relating to rents, royalties, pensions, profit sharing, bond purchase plans of self-employed individuals, and individual retirement accounts (IRAs) are allowed.

Excess Itemized Deductions

An individual taxpayer may deduct from adjusted gross income certain itemized personal expenses specified by the tax law, or may, in lieu of itemizing expenses, take advantage of a standard deduction called the **zero bracket amount.** The zero bracket amount is incorporated in the tax rate tables and schedules. For 1983, this amount was $3,400 for married taxpayers filing a joint return and $2,300 for single taxpayers or those qualifying as heads of households. A taxpayer not itemizing personal expenses automatically receives the benefit of the zero bracket amount when using the tax tables or schedules. On the other hand, a single taxpayer having $10,000 in itemized deductions would deduct only $7,700 (called *excess itemized deductions*) in calculating taxable income. The taxpayer automatically receives the benefit of the remaining $2,300 by using the tax schedules.

Personal expenses that may be itemized and deducted from adjusted gross income are classified as follows:

(1) *Medical expenses*—With certain limitations, a taxpayer may deduct his or her medical and dental expenses, and those for dependents, not compensated for by insurance or otherwise. The total medical and dental expenses are deductible to the extent that they exceed 5% of adjusted gross income. Prescription drugs and insulin costs are includible only to the extent that they exceed 1% of adjusted gross income.

For example, a taxpayer with an adjusted gross income of $20,000 has the following medical expenses: health insurance premiums, $400; prescription drugs, $320; and other medical expenses not compensated for by insurance, $900. The deduction for 1983 is calculated as follows:

Insurance premiums		$ 400
Other medical expenses		900
Prescription drugs	$320	
Less 1% of $20,000 adjusted gross income	200	120
		$1,420
Less 5% of $20,000 adjusted gross income		1,000
Medical deduction		$ 420

(2) *Taxes*—State and local income taxes, real estate taxes, personal property taxes, and sales taxes are deductible. Federal taxes do not qualify as itemized deductions, nor do flat fees paid for most types of licenses (auto, driver's, pet, and so on). Variable auto license fees required by some states may be deductible. State and local gasoline taxes are no longer deductible.

(3) *Interest*—With certain minor exceptions, interest paid on any form of personal indebtedness is deductible in computing income tax liability.

(4) *Charitable contributions*—The amount of gifts made to religious, scientific, educational, and other charitable organizations can be deducted but may not exceed 50% of adjusted gross income. Certain other limitations may also apply, as with noncash contributions and gifts to foundations. Gifts to individuals or labor unions, and donations to organizations whose major activity is to influence legislation are not deductible.

(5) *Casualty losses*—To the extent that they exceed $100 each plus 10% of adjusted gross income, certain casualty and theft losses are deductible unless compensated for by insurance. Casualty losses must be sudden and unexpected, however; uninsured losses from fire, accident, windstorm, and so forth qualify as deductions. Certain "gradual" losses (such as termite damage and Dutch elm disease) may not qualify.

(6) *Miscellaneous deductions*—Permissible deductions in this category include certain expenses that are often related to a taxpayer's income or to his or her profession but are not deductible in arriving at adjusted gross income. Some of the most important are the following:

Professional dues
Subscriptions to professional publications
Union dues
Cost of job-related work clothing, small tools, and safety equipment

Cost of business entertainment
Gambling losses (but only to the extent of gains, which are includible in gross income)
Employment agency fees

| Safe-deposit box rental (to store securities)
 Fees paid for income tax assistance | Educational expenses related to *present position*, incurred to improve or maintain skills or to meet employer's requirements |

Personal Exemptions

In arriving at taxable income, the individual taxpayer may deduct (at the present time) $1,000 for each **personal exemption** he or she may legally claim. Married taxpayers filing jointly are allowed an exemption each, plus one for each dependent. Additional exemptions are granted taxpayers who are (1) 65 or over or (2) blind.

To qualify for a dependency exemption under the tax laws, a person must (1) be closely related to the taxpayer or have lived in the household for the entire year as a member of the family; (2) have less than $1,000 income (this test is ignored for taxpayer's children under 19 years of age or who are full-time students); (3) have received more than one-half of his or her support from the taxpayer; and (4) if married, not be filing a joint return with a spouse. Both the amount of the exemption and the qualifications for a dependent have changed over time.

CAPITAL GAINS AND LOSSES

Many taxpayers have responded to high tax rates by arranging to have a good part of their income subject to preferential tax treatment. One of the most prominent tax preferences is the special treatment of certain gains on the sale or exchange of a capital asset as defined in the tax law.

Although they are sometimes difficult to define, **capital assets** generally include any of the taxpayer's property except receivables, inventories, real and depreciable business property, certain governmental obligations, and rights to literary and other artistic works. Under certain conditions, however, business real estate and depreciable assets may be treated as capital assets when gains from sales of such assets exceed losses.

Classification by Holding Period

Gains or losses on capital assets sold or exchanged are classified as *long term* if the assets have been held longer than one year and *short term* if the holding period is one year or less. This classification is significant in determining the effects of such gains and losses on the tax liability. To meet various tests of the law, we combine the gains and losses in the following fashion:

(1) Long-term gains and losses are "netted" to obtain *net long-term capital gain or loss.*

(2) Short-term gains and losses are "netted" to obtain *net short-term capital gain or loss.*

The amounts obtained in these two steps must be analyzed to determine their effect on adjusted gross income.

The excess of net long-term capital gains over net short-term capital losses is called **net capital gain,** 60% of which is deducted in determining adjusted gross income. (If the taxpayer does not have a net short-term loss, then he or she deducts 60% of any net long-term gain.) The following examples, each having the same net gain from capital asset transactions, illustrate how the amount of any capital gain is determined:

	A	B	C	D
Net long-term gain (loss)	$4,000	$3,000	$2,000	($4,000)
Net short-term gain (loss)	(1,000)	–0–	1,000	7,000
Net gain	$3,000	$3,000	$3,000	$3,000
Deductible in computing adjusted gross income (60% of net capital gain)	1,800	1,800	1,200	–0–
Net gain included in adjusted gross income	$1,200	$1,200	$1,800	$3,000

Taxpayers are taxed on net capital gains at only 40% of their marginal tax rate (highest rate for an increment of income). Thus, if the individual in column C is subject to a 50% marginal tax rate, he or she would pay only $400, or 20% of the $2,000 net long-term capital gain. Since the highest marginal tax rate is 50% for any taxpayer, the maximum marginal tax rate on net long-term gains is 20%.

Net Losses

If the net amount from capital asset transactions is a loss, individuals and other noncorporate taxpayers may, with certain restrictions, offset the loss against ordinary income up to $3,000 in any year. In determining the amount that may be offset, short-term losses are considered first, on a dollar-for-dollar basis; then long-term losses are considered on a 2-for-1 basis. Thus, $2 of net long-term loss offsets only $1 of ordinary gross income. The amount of losses that are not offset, called the **net capital loss,** may be carried forward indefinitely to offset capital gains or $3,000 ordinary income of each year. In carrying forward, the losses retain their long- or short-term character.

Suppose that this year a taxpayer has a net short-term loss of $2,300 and a net long-term loss of $1,800. The $3,000 capital loss deduction against ordinary income would consist first of the $2,300 net short-term loss and then of $1,400 of the net long-term loss. The remaining $400 can be carried forward and used in succeeding years. This carryforward must be used on a 2-for-1 basis when offset against ordinary income, but it can be used in full if offset against long-term gains or short-term gains in the future.

The following two other situations may be created by net losses:

(1) When a net long-term capital loss exceeds a net short-term capital gain, 50% of this net loss (up to $3,000) may offset ordinary income.

(2) When a net short-term capital loss exceeds a net long-term capital gain, 100% of this net loss (up to $3,000) may offset ordinary income.

DETERMINING INDIVIDUAL TAX LIABILITY

Applying the appropriate tax rate to taxable income results in the tax liability. Individual taxpayers who do not itemize their personal deductions must use simplified tax tables that incorporate both the zero bracket amount (in lieu of itemized deductions) and the number of claimed exemptions. If deductions are itemized, or if either the taxable income or number of exemptions claimed exceeds those shown in the tables, the taxpayer then must use tax schedules. Schedules are provided for (1) single taxpayers, (2) married taxpayers filing a joint return, (3) married taxpayers filing separately, and (4) unmarried taxpayers who qualify as heads of households. Exhibit 28–2 uses 1983 rates to illustrate the first two of these schedules.

Unmarried taxpayers who qualify as heads of households determine their tax liability from tables or schedules (not shown) whose rates fall between those of single taxpayers and married taxpayers filing jointly. Generally, the qualifications can be met by unmarried taxpayers who pay more than one-half the cost of maintaining a home in which a parent resides, if that parent qualifies as a dependent. A taxpayer who pays more than one-half the cost of maintaining his or her *own* home where a dependent relative resides or where unmarried children, adopted stepchildren, foster children, or grandchildren reside may also qualify as a head of household.

INCOME AVERAGING

Current tax law permits individual taxpayers who have annual incomes that vary a great deal to exercise an **income averaging** option. This option is especially useful to a taxpayer with an unusually large amount of income in a particular year, because it applies a lower tax rate to a certain amount of the increased income. The averaging process thus places the taxpayer on a more equitable footing with others who have the same aggregate income spread evenly over the same period.

The averaging procedure employs a formula that uses the average taxable income of the previous four years as a base with which to measure the current year's income level. Space does not permit a complete discussion of the process, but it is useful to know that a taxpayer receives no advantage from the averaging method unless the current year's taxable income is at least $3,000 more than 120% of the average of the prior four years' taxable income. In addition, the

EXHIBIT 28–2
1983 Tax Rate Schedules

Single Individuals

If Taxable Income Is Over	But Not Over	Tax Is Amount	+ % of	Excess Over
$ 0	$ 2,300	$ 0	0	$ 0
2,300	3,400	0	11	2,300
3,400	4,400	121	13	3,400
4,400	8,500	251	15	4,400
8,500	10,800	866	17	8,500
10,800	12,900	1,257	19	10,800
12,900	15,000	1,656	21	12,900
15,000	18,200	2,097	24	15,000
18,200	23,500	2,865	28	18,200
23,500	28,800	4,349	32	23,500
28,800	34,100	6,045	36	28,800
34,100	41,500	7,953	40	34,100
41,500	55,300	10,913	45	41,500
55,300	—	17,123	50	55,300

**Married Individuals Filing Joint Returns
and Surviving Spouses**

If Taxable Income Is Over	But Not Over	Tax Is Amount	+ % of	Excess Over
$ 0	$ 3,400	$ 0	0	$ 0
3,400	5,500	0	11	3,400
5,500	7,600	231	13	5,500
7,600	11,900	504	15	7,600
11,900	16,000	1,149	17	11,900
16,000	20,200	1,846	19	16,000
20,200	24,600	2,644	23	20,200
24,600	29,900	3,656	26	24,600
29,900	35,200	5,034	30	29,900
35,200	45,800	6,624	35	35,200
45,800	60,000	10,334	40	45,800
60,000	85,600	16,014	44	60,000
85,600	109,400	27,278	48	85,600
109,400	—	38,702	50	109,400

taxpayer generally must be self-supporting (that is, not someone else's dependent) during the base period to qualify for income averaging. This facet of the law often prevents recent college graduates from using the averaging option in their first few years of full-time employment.

CREDITS AGAINST THE TAX

Once the income tax has been calculated, certain credits specified in the tax law may reduce the amount owed. Some of the principal credits are the investment tax credit, earned income credit, dependent care credit, and political contributions credit.

INVESTMENT TAX CREDIT   Taxpayers are allowed a credit against the tax liability for investments in qualified business property. Generally, the credit is 10% of the cost of property that meets certain requirements and is used in a trade or business. Because the specific rules are complex, they are not detailed here. However, the investment tax credit may reduce significantly the total cost of acquiring new machinery and equipment since a percentage of the investment cost may reduce the total tax liability of the business entity. The investment tax credit is an excellent example of the government using the tax laws to influence the economy.

EARNED INCOME CREDIT   Certain low-income individuals are allowed a refundable credit against the tax equal to 10% of the first $5,000 of earned income, up to a maximum of $500. The credit is reduced $1.25 for every $10 of adjusted gross income (or earned income, if greater) above $6,000, phasing out completely at $10,000. The taxpayer must meet eligibility requirements defined in the law, however. Eligible employees may have advance payments of the earned income credit added to their paychecks each pay period.

DEPENDENT CARE CREDIT   A tax credit is available for taxpayers who maintain a household and incur expenses in caring for a dependent child under 15 years or an incapacitated dependent or spouse, if the expenses incurred permitted the taxpayer to be gainfully employed. The amount of the credit is 20% of the employment-related expenses up to a maximum of $2,400 for one qualifying individual and $4,000 for two or more qualifying individuals.

POLITICAL CONTRIBUTIONS CREDIT   Taxpayers may apply 50% of political contributions as a credit against the tax up to a maximum of $50 ($100 in a joint return).

OTHER CREDITS   Credits against the tax are also available for part of the cost of energy-conserving items and expenditures for solar energy and similar equipment. Other less significant credits are allowed, such as the foreign tax credit, credit for the elderly, and the work incentive credit.

WITHHOLDING AND ESTIMATED TAX

Ordinarily, tax returns must be filed within $3\frac{1}{2}$ months of the close of the individual's taxable year. Because most taxpayers are on a calendar year basis, they must file their returns by April 15 following the end of the taxable year. During the taxable year, employers of wage earners and salaried employees have withheld tax payments based on the employees' estimated earnings and the number of withholding allowances claimed. Taxpayers who have income not subject to withholding (beyond a certain amount) must estimate income for the current year and file a Declaration of Estimated Tax. The estimated tax, less the amounts expected to be withheld, is paid in four installments. Therefore, when the tax return is filed, the amounts paid through the withholding or declaration process are credits that offset the total tax liability.

INDIVIDUAL TAX COMPUTATION

We present an example of the common elements of an individual income tax computation in Exhibit 28–3. This example shows the relevant tax data for the joint return of Brian and Megan Fleming. Although some of this information would be shown in separate schedules that reveal more detail, we have condensed the data into a single schedule to conserve space.

Brian and Megan Fleming, both under 65 years of age, have three children who qualify as dependency exemptions. Brian operates a tax service and pays an estimated $922 of tax quarterly. Megan works part-time as a nurse and has tax withheld from her salary. During the year, Brian sold at a $4,000 gain some securities he had held over a year and also realized a $1,000 loss on securities held for less than a year. The Fleming family's medical expenses were not significant during the year. Other data in Exhibit 28–3 are self-explanatory.

PARTNERSHIPS

Partnerships are not recognized as separate taxable entities for income tax purposes. Although partnerships are separate business and legal entities, they are treated as conduits for tax purposes, as are S corporations. That is, the ordinary income of the partnership is allocated on a pro-rata basis to the partners, who report this amount on their individual income tax returns (or corporate return, if the partner is a corporation). Items of income other than ordinary income, as well as any deductions that are subject to limitations or special treatment on an individual tax return, are stated separately and flow through to the partners based on their pro-rata shares.

EXHIBIT 28–3
Brian and Megan Fleming's
19XX Joint Federal Income Tax Return Information

Net income from Fleming Tax Service:		
Fees collected	$46,000	
Ordinary and necessary expenses	18,000	$28,000
Salary (Megan's)		5,600
Interest on savings accounts		1,400
Dividend income	$ 850	
Less exclusion	200	650
Excess of net long-term capital gains over net		
short-term capital losses	$ 3,000	
Long-term capital gain deduction (60%)	1,800	1,200
Marriage penalty deduction (10% × 5,600)		(560)
Adjusted Gross Income		$36,290
Deductions from adjusted gross income:		
Taxes:		
Property tax on home	$1,600	
State income tax	1,530	
State sales tax	320	$ 3,450
Interest on home mortgage		1,500
Charitable contributions		850
Miscellaneous (professional dues, nurse's		
uniforms, etc.)		200
Total itemized deductions		$ 6,000
Less zero bracket amount		3,400
Excess itemized deductions		2,600
		$33,690
Less exemptions: 5 × $1,000		5,000
Taxable Income		$28,690
Tax: $3,656 + 26% of $4,090 (rounded)		$ 4,719
Less credit against tax:		
Political contributions $240 × 50% = $120,		
limited to $100		100
		$ 4,619
Less prepayments:		
Tax withheld from salary	$ 680	
Estimated taxes paid quarterly	3,688	
Total tax withheld or prepaid		4,368
Balance of tax due with return		$ 251

Since each partner must pay the tax on his or her pro-rata share of income, the partners must include the partnership items in adjusted gross income. The partnership pays no federal income tax, but must file an annual information return reflecting the partnership's ordinary income and each partner's individual items. In addition, each partner must include any prospective partnership income in his or her estimate of total personal taxes and pay the related tax quarterly.

TAXATION OF CORPORATIONS

The corporation is a taxable entity, separate from its shareholders, and must file an annual tax return whether or not it owes any tax. Certain corporations—such as banks, insurance companies, and cooperatives—are subject to special tax provisions. Tax regulations even for corporations that are not specially treated can be quite complex. Our discussion is limited to a few of the major distinguishing features of corporate taxation.

Corporate Tax Rates

The following schedule gives the 1983 rates applied to the taxable income of corporations:

If Taxable Income Is Over	But Not Over	Amount Plus	Tax Is % of	Excess Over
$ 0	$ 25,000	$ 0	15	$ 0
25,000	50,000	3,750	18	25,000
50,000	75,000	8,250	30	50,000
75,000	100,000	15,750	40	75,000
100,000	—	25,750	46	100,000

According to this schedule, a corporation with taxable income of $60,000 computes its tax as follows:

$$\$8,250 + 30\% \text{ of } \$10,000 = \$11,250$$

The effective tax rate in this example is 18.75% ($11,250/$60,000).

In computing the tax liability for corporate taxable income over $100,000, we can use the following shortcut calculation: (46% of taxable income) − $20,250. (The $20,250 figure is obtained by multiplying the percentage difference between 46% and the tax rate for each taxable income bracket times $25,000 and summing the amounts obtained.)

Corporate taxpayers must pay estimated taxes in quarterly installments, similar to individuals. Their final returns, however, are due within $2\frac{1}{2}$ months of the close of their calendar or fiscal years.

Corporate Tax Base

The tax base for corporations is taxable income, that is (Gross Income − All Allowable Deductions). There is no *adjusted gross income* for corporations. Corporation deductions can be classified as ordinary or special. Ordinary deductions are the usual expenses (with certain exceptions) of doing business and producing revenue. The most prominent special deduction is a credit for 85% of dividends received from other domestic corporations (100% if such other corporations are affiliates).

The deduction for dividends received is intended to reduce the effect of "triple" taxation. Without this deduction, the distributing corporation, the receiving corporation, and individual shareholders of the receiving corporation (if they subsequently received the dividends) would all pay tax on the earnings.

The net operating loss deduction, which also applies to sole proprietorships, offsets business losses of a particular year against the income of other years in calculating the ultimate tax liability for those years. Briefly, an operating loss in a particular year can offset the income of three preceding years, beginning with the earliest. Unused losses can be carried forward successively to the next 15 years and used to compute taxable income. The corporation may forego the carryback and only carry the loss forward 15 years.

The excess of a corporation's capital losses over its capital gains is not offset against ordinary gross income. It is carried back three years and forward five years and offset against capital gains in those years in the manner just described for a net operating loss. A corporate capital loss that is carried back or forward is treated as a short-term capital loss regardless of the holding period. Although the excess of long-term capital gains over short-term capital losses is fully includible in gross income—with no 60% deduction, as in the case of individual taxpayers—this amount is taxed at a maximum rate of 28%.

Charitable contributions of corporations are limited to 10% of taxable income, computed before considering the contributions and the special deduction for dividends received. Any contributions in excess of the limitation can be carried forward five years.

Corporate Tax Illustration

The effect of the foregoing items on the corporate tax computation is illustrated in Exhibit 28–4. In this example, we use the following data from the company's income statement:

Gross profit on sales	$200,000
Dividends from unaffiliated domestic corporations	20,000
Gain on sale of capital asset (long term)	10,000
	$230,000
Business expenses, including charitable contributions of $10,000	150,000
Reported income before taxes	$ 80,000

The firm also had an unused net capital loss carryforward of $3,000 from preceding years.

EXHIBIT 28–4
Corporate Tax Computation

Gross profit		$200,000
Dividends from domestic corporations		20,000
Gain on sale of capital asset	$10,000	
Less: Net capital loss carryforward	3,000	7,000
		$227,000
Less: Business expenses, less charitable		
contributions of $10,000		140,000
		$ 87,000
Charitable contributions, limited to 10% of $87,000		8,700
		$ 78,300
Dividends received deduction, 85% of $20,000		17,000
Taxable income		$ 61,300
Less: Excess of long-term gain over short-term loss,		
taxed at 28%		7,000
Taxable at regular rates		$ 54,300
Regular tax ($8,250 + 30% × $4,300)		$ 9,540
Alternative tax on excess of long-term gain		
over short-term loss (28% × $7,000)		1,960
Total tax liability		$ 11,500

BASIS OF DETERMINING TAXABLE INCOME

Many taxpayers' taxable income is determined on a **cash basis.** Taxable **earnings** from various sources are includible in gross income when received, and deductions are recognized when the allowable related expenditures are paid. Cash basis taxation has wide appeal because it is fairly simple and requires perhaps the least amount of record keeping.

Even a cash basis taxpayer should be aware of certain exceptions provided by the law. Although certain income may not be directly paid to the taxpayer, the law may consider the income a *constructive receipt* if the taxpayer effectively controls it. Thus, interest on savings accounts credited to the taxpayer constitutes taxable income whether or not it is withdrawn. Likewise, any checks received that represent taxable income are taxable whether or not they are cashed before the taxable year-end.

Generally, payments made during the taxable year are deductible in determining the year's taxable income if they meet the criteria for deductions. However, expenditures representing prepayments for a period must usually be allocated to the periods involved. For example, the cost of plant assets must be allocated to the periods of use through depreciation accounting. Likewise, prepayments of insurance, rent, and similar items must be allocated to the years involved rather than deducted totally in the year of payment. Some prepayments, however, may be deducted in the year of payment. Under certain circumstances, real estate taxes paid a year in advance may be deducted; also, in certain cases, prepaid interest has been allowed as a deduction when the prepayment period was not extremely long.

Cash basis taxpayers, particularly those in certain types of service business, sometimes can arrange their pattern of billings and disbursements near year-end to minimize tax liability. For example, an expected tax rate reduction for next year would suggest that billings should be delayed to postpone revenue recognition, but that expenditures qualifying as deductions should be made this year.

For the most part, **accrual basis** accounting must be used by trading or manufacturing firms, because inventories are a factor in determining their income. Revenue must be recognized when sales are made, and inventories must be considered in determining the cost of goods sold. Although some prepayments and accruals may be ignored, the method followed must be consistent and provide a reasonable income determination. Thus, the taxable income of an accrual basis taxpayer will likely not be substantially affected by altering the pattern of receipts or expenditures.

TAX AVOIDANCE AND BUSINESS DECISIONS

Taxpayers who deliberately misstate their taxable income, whether by omitting income or claiming fraudulently contrived deductions, are practicing **tax evasion.** This, of course, is illegal, and the penalties for such a practice can be severe. However, taxpayers are perfectly within their rights to practice **tax avoidance**—arranging their business affairs to minimize their tax liability.

Effective and Marginal Tax Rates

Often, persons who identify their *income tax bracket* by a tax rate are referring to the percentage rate appearing in the tax schedule beside the bracket in which their taxable income falls. For example, a single taxpayer with $30,000 taxable income might indicate that he or she is in "the 36% tax bracket." This **marginal,** or incremental, rate is an important tax consideration, but it does not represent the portion of taxable income that is relinquished to the government, since it applies only to the excess over $28,800. This person's tax liability, computed from the schedule in Exhibit 28–2, is actually slightly less than 22% of taxable income.

Tax on $28,800	$6,045
36% of excess over $28,800	432
Tax liability	$6,477
Effective tax rate ($6,477/$30,000)	21.59%

Thus, the **effective tax rate** in this situation is 21.59%, the tax liability divided by taxable income. This rate conveys the impact of the tax "bite" more accurately than the marginal rate.

Nonetheless, the marginal tax rate is extremely important in our tax thinking, especially in tax planning. For example, a single taxpayer who could, by expending some additional time and effort, augment personal income should probably think in terms of the marginal rate of tax. Given a taxable income of $30,000, an additional $1,000 is taxed at the 36% rate, leaving the taxpayer only $640. He or she may well feel that this additional amount does not justify relinquishing leisure time. The additional effect of any state and local income taxes should also be considered.

Timing of Transactions

Many methods of minimizing taxes center on the timing of transactions. As we have noted, deferring sales of certain property so that the holding period is over one year may qualify any resulting gain for preferential treatment under capital gain provisions of the tax laws. In certain other sales of property, a taxpayer might sell on an installment basis rather than for a lump-sum payment. The taxpayer spreads any gain over the life of the contract and thus postpones related portions of the tax.

Timing (and perhaps a degree of clairvoyance) is also important when a taxpayer's principal residence is sold at a gain. Under a long-standing IRS Code provision, the gain is not taxable if an amount at least as great as the selling price[1] is invested in a new residence during the period beginning 24 months before the sale and ending 24 months after the sale. The basis of the new residence is reduced by the gain not recognized; thus, the tax is deferred. Another Code provision, however, grants a once-in-a-lifetime exclusion of $125,000[2] of gain on the sale of a residence for a taxpayer who is at least 55 years old and has used the property as his or her principal residence for three of the five preceding years. Because this exclusion can be used only once in a taxpayer's life, he or she must decide when to use it. If a taxpayer sells a residence at a gain of less than $125,000, he or she must speculate on the possibility of a larger gain being realized on a future residence.

Earlier we mentioned the possibility that cash basis taxpayers may affect their pattern of receipts and expenditures. For example, some taxpayers can concentrate their personal deductions in a particular year. If their itemized deductions are below the zero bracket amount in the following year (because of the shifting process), they can take advantage of the zero bracket amount.

These are just a few examples in which the timing of transactions can alter the impact of income taxes. Because they often deal with the disposition of property, it is wise to investigate thoroughly the tax consequences of any contemplated property sales and the possible forms the sale may take.

---

[1] Selling price here means *adjusted selling price* as defined by the Code (selling price less expenses of fix-up and sale).

[2] $75,000 for married taxpayers filing separately.

Tax Shelters   Taxpayers who become affluent may look for **tax shelters**—investments that, by their nature, create either tax-exempt income or a probable deductible tax loss. They may, for example, invest in state or municipal securities, the interest on which is exempt from federal income tax. Interest rates on these securities are typically lower than on interest-taxable securities of the same quality because of the tax shelter feature. Their attractiveness, therefore, depends on the taxpayer's marginal tax rate. Suppose a taxpayer in a 30% marginal tax rate bracket had $20,000 to invest in either $6\frac{1}{2}$% municipal bonds or 9% industrial bonds (interest taxable) of equal merit. The municipal bonds would provide $1,300 tax-free income, whereas the industrial bonds would provide only $1,260 after-tax income ($1,800 − $540 tax). As the marginal tax rate increases, the investment in municipal bonds becomes more attractive. On the other hand, a taxpayer in the 26% tax bracket would find the 9% bonds more attractive.

A number of tax shelters permit the taxpayer a tax-free cash inflow on an investment and also a loss for tax purposes. Sometimes groups of taxpayers make a joint investment—typically in limited partnerships—in such ventures as apartment complexes and oil properties. Revenue from rents and royalties exceeds out-of-pocket (cash) operating costs, so a distributable amount of cash for investors exists; however, because of large write-offs (particularly through accelerated cost recovery, tax depreciation), a tax loss is allocable to the investors. Suppose, for example, that a particular taxpayer's $20,000 investment resulted in a $1,500 cash inflow and a $1,000 operating loss allocation. If the investor is in the 40% marginal tax bracket, the tax-free distribution of $1,500 is the equivalent of $2,500 in ordinary taxable income [$1,500/(1 − 0.40)]. Add the $1,000 loss allocation—because it can offset other income—to obtain a $3,500 return before taxes, or a pretax return of $17\frac{1}{2}$% The after-tax return is $9\frac{1}{2}$% [($1,500 + $400)/$20,000]. Taxpayers involved in these sheltering activities must carefully examine the "at risk" provisions of the tax laws that limit the amount of loss deduction.

Forms of   Most large businesses operate as corporations to have wider access to capital,
Business   limit liability, or enjoy other advantages of incorporation explained in Chapter
Organization   15. For small businesses, with perhaps a single owner or a few owners, tax considerations may well influence the form of ownership.

Let us examine some general factors in determining the relative tax effects. First, all income of single proprietorships and partnerships is taxable to the owners as earned, whether or not it is distributed. Second, corporations must pay a tax on earnings, but may deduct reasonable salaries paid to owners. Furthermore, corporations may pay only a portion of the earnings as dividends (as long as accumulations are not deemed unreasonable). Other relevant factors are the amount of the business earnings and the amount of the owners' other separate income.

For example, consider the comparative tax effects of the corporate and sole proprietorship forms of organization for a married individual whose business is expected to generate $40,000 net income annually. One-half of this amount is withdrawn each year (as a salary, if the corporate form is used). The owner's other

EXHIBIT 28–5
Comparative Tax Results
in Two Forms of Organization

	Corporation	Sole Proprietorship
Income from business	$40,000	$40,000
Less: Owner's salary	20,000	—
Taxable business income	$20,000	$40,000
Corporate tax on $20,000 at 15%	$ 3,000	
Salary $20,000		
Other income less deductions and exemptions 8,000		8,000
$28,000		$48,000
Tax on $28,000 [$3,656 + (26% × $3,400)]	4,540	
Tax on $48,000 [$10,334 + (40% of $2,200)]		$11,214
Total tax	$ 7,540	$11,214

income, less all deductions and exemptions, is about $8,000 annually. A comparison of the total tax effect of the two forms of organization is shown in Exhibit 28–5.

The example assumes no distribution of dividends by the corporation. This policy might require justification if questioned by the IRS. Generally, the IRS may impose a penalty on unreasonable retention of earnings without a genuine business purpose. Of course, the owner will be taxed on the $17,000 earnings retained ($20,000 − $3,000 tax) if distributed either currently or in the future. If earnings are distributed currently, total income from salary, dividends, and other sources would be $45,000 ($28,000 + $17,000), on which the tax would be $10,054.[3] Adding the $3,000 corporate tax to this amount results in $13,054. Thus the apparent advantage of the corporate form shown in Exhibit 28–5 would be lost. On the other hand, suppose that dividend distributions can be postponed indefinitely or for a fairly long period. Then the owner may find the corporate form of organization advantageous, especially if, through earnings retention and growth, the corporate stock increases in value. At a future date, the owner may exercise the option of selling all or part of the shares and receive preferential capital gains treatment on any gains.

Obviously, no general rule or formula can determine the most beneficial form of organization for tax purposes. The type of analysis we have illustrated may be modified in response to changes in the levels of business income, other income, reasonableness of salary levels, dividend policy, and other factors. The addition of owners and increases in the size and scope of the business may be influential. Finally, depending on the nature of the ownership, small corporations can sometimes elect to be taxed as partnerships.

[3] We have ignored the $200 dividend exclusion in this computation.

Other Business Decisions   In earlier chapters, we discussed some major areas in which a choice of acceptable accounting alternatives influences tax liability. In particular, we examined the effects of the *accelerated cost recovery system of depreciation*, which generally enables a business to postpone taxes and thereby over a period use funds otherwise unavailable in that period. We also pointed out how firms that use the LIFO method of inventory pricing can reduce the effect of taxes during a period of rising prices.

Another area relates to asset acquisitions, in which the investment tax credit may be allowed. If this credit is available to a firm, it should be considered when decisions are made about the cost of assets and the timing of their purchase.

Although these examples are among the most prominent situations in which choices or alternatives affect tax liability, many others might be mentioned. We emphasize, however, that the tax consequences of choices and the possible forms of business transactions must be *explored in advance*. Once decisions have been implemented with regard to the form of business organization, financing methods, assets acquisitions, and even accounting methods, changing the tax consequences by remedial action is often difficult—and in some cases infeasible.

KEY POINTS TO REMEMBER

(1) The four main classes of *taxpayers* are individuals, partnerships, corporations, and estates or trusts.

(2) The tax format for individual taxpayers is:

	Total Income	
Less:	Exclusions	(Items of income excluded by law)
	Gross Income	(Income subject to tax, before deductions and exemptions)
Less:	Deductions from Gross Income	(Business expenses and expenses incurred in the production of income)
Equals:	Adjusted Gross Income	
Less:	Excess Itemized Deductions	(Deductible personal expenses or, in lieu of these, a zero bracket amount incorporated in the tax tables)
	Personal Exemptions	($1,000 each for taxpayer, spouse, and each dependent; also, $1,000 for each taxpayer and spouse who is age 65 or over or blind)
Equals:	Taxable Income	

(3) The *effective* tax rate is the tax liability divided by taxable income. The *marginal* tax rate, which applies to additional increments of income, is important in determining the tax effect of proposed transactions.

(4) Gains and losses on sales or exchanges of capital assets are *long term* if the assets have been held longer than one year and *short term* if the assets have been held one year or less.

  (a) Long-term gains and losses are "netted" to obtain net long-term gain or loss, and short-term gains and losses are "netted" to obtain net short-term gain or loss.

  (b) The excess of any net long-term gains over net short-term losses is called *net capital gain*; individuals deduct 60% of this amount in computing their adjusted gross income.

  (c) Noncorporate taxpayers' net losses from capital asset transactions can offset ordinary income up to $3,000 in any year. Any unused amount, called the *net capital loss*, can be carried forward to future years and offset against capital gains or $3,000 ordinary income of each year. Long-term losses are used at the rate of $1 for each $1 of capital gains, but at the rate of $2 for each $1 of ordinary income.

(5) The tax format for corporations is:

	Gross Income	(All business revenue, gains, dividends,etc.)
Less:	Regular Deductions	(Business expenses, with exceptions, such as a limitation on charitable contributions)
	Special Deductions	(85% of dividends received from domestic corporations: 100% of affiliate dividends)
Equals:	Taxable Income	

(6) Net capital gains of corporations cannot be reduced by the 60% deduction available to individuals. Such gains, however, are taxed at a maximum rate of 28%. Net capital losses cannot offset ordinary income, but they may be carried back three years and forward five years to offset capital gains of those years.

QUESTIONS

28–1 In addition to raising revenue, what other purposes are served by the federal income tax?

28–2 Name the major entities recognized for federal income tax purposes.

28–3 How is the net income from sole proprietorships and partnerships taxed? Must either of these business entities file a federal income tax return?

28–4 Describe the general format used to determine an individual's taxable income.

28–5 Which of the following items can be *excluded* from gross income?
(1) Interest on savings accounts.

(2) Interest on municipal bonds.

(3) Social Security payments (benefits).

(4) Gambling gains.

(5) Bonuses.

(6) Life insurance proceeds paid at death of insured.

(7) Royalties.

(8) Scholarship of a degree candidate, not requiring services.

28–6 Generally describe the deductions allowable in computing an individual's adjusted gross income, and name two examples.

28–7 Why is the concept of adjusted gross income important in the calculation of an individual's taxable income?

28–8 Jane Jones, who operates a real estate agency as a sole proprietorship, had the following expenditures for the current year:

(1) Interest on office building mortgage.

(2) Interest on home mortgage.

(3) Property taxes on home.

(4) Expenses of automobile used solely in business.

(5) License on business automobile.

(6) License on personal automobile.

(7) State gasoline tax, business automobile.

(8) State gasoline tax, personal automobile.

(9) Dues to realty association.

(10) Church contributions by Jones family.

(11) Loss on sale of office building.

(12) Net short-term capital loss of $800 on personal investments.

(13) Uninsured termite damage to home.

Indicate whether each of these items is (a) deductible in obtaining adjusted gross income, (b) deductible from adjusted gross income, or (c) nondeductible.

28–9 What is meant by a *personal exemption*? How much is each personal exemption?

28–10 What are the criteria for determining whether a person qualifies as a dependent of a taxpayer?

28–11 Sue Smith, who is single, and has no dependents, has adjusted gross income of $18,000 this year. Personal expenses qualifying as itemized deductions amount to $2,200. Calculate her tax, using the appropriate schedule in Exhibit 28–2 (page 1006).

28–12 Samuel Cook, a single taxpayer, expects to have taxable income of $28,000 this year.

(a) What is his *marginal* tax rate?

(b) Explain how Cook might use his marginal tax rate in tax planning.

(c) What is the *effective* tax rate? Use the appropriate schedule in Exhibit 28–2 (page 1006).

28–13 An individual taxpayer had a net long-term capital gain of $6,000 and a net short-term capital loss of $3,000 for the current year. What amount resulting from such gains and losses will be included in adjusted gross income?

28–14 During the current year, an individual taxpayer had a net short-term capital loss of $800 and a net long-term capital loss of $5,000.

(a) How much of these losses can offset ordinary income of this year?

(b) How much can be carried forward to next year?

(c) If the taxpayer has no capital gains or losses next year, what amount can be deducted from next year's ordinary income?

28–15 What is the marriage penalty deduction? How is it computed?

28–16 Describe the basic accounting methods taxpayers may use in computing their taxable income.

28–17 What is the investment tax credit?

28–18 Explain the dividends received deduction. Why is it a special deduction for corporations?

28–19 What tax factors might be considered by the owner or owners of a small business in choosing the form of business organization?

28–20 What is the difference between *tax evasion* and *tax avoidance*?

EXERCISES

28–21 Calculate the adjusted gross income for the joint return of Carl and Donna Wilson from the following data:

Share of partnership net income	$29,500
Interest on municipal bonds	3,000
Dividend income	400
Interest income	160
Lottery prize	500
Gift from relative	1,000
Long-term capital gain on sale of securities	3,000

28–22 According to the joint return of Robert and Jill Klein, they have two dependents and their adjusted gross income is $29,500. Using the relevant data from the items shown below, calculate their taxable income.

Real estate taxes	$1,800	State gasoline taxes	$ 95
Interest on home mortgage	3,800	Health insurance premiums	300
Charitable contributions	800	Other medical expenses	1,200
Gift to relative	150	Automobile licenses	32
State income taxes	500	Tax return preparation	100
State sales taxes	200	Union dues	120

28–23 Using the appropriate schedule in Exhibit 28–2 (page 1006), calculate the amount of tax due from Janet Norris, a 24-year-old single taxpayer (with no dependents) who has given you the following information:

Gross income	$27,000
Deductions to determine adjusted gross income	1,800
Allowable itemized personal expenses	2,600
Tax withheld from salary	3,428
Payments of estimated tax	600

28–24 Ken and Barbara Green are married and file a joint return for the current tax year. Ken earned a salary of $24,000 and Barbara earned a salary of $26,500. In addition, Ken had interest income of $500 from a savings account. Calculate the marriage penalty deduction.

28–25 The following capital gains and losses are for four separate taxpayers identified as A, B, C, and D. For each taxpayer, indicate the amount included in gross income, if any, and the amount deductible from gross income, if any, to determine adjusted gross income.

	A	B	C	D
Long-term capital gains	$3,100	$1,500	$ 800	$2,000
Long-term capital losses	300	3,200	2,300	500
Short-term capital gains	100	–0–	4,000	800
Short-term capital losses	700	1,000	500	4,000

28–26 The Maloy Corporation had pretax income of $75,000 during the current year. In arriving at this amount, the corporation included $9,000 in dividends from nonaffiliated domestic corporations and an $18,000 long-term gain on the sale of property. Calculate the corporation's federal income tax for the year, using the rate schedule given on page 1010.

PROBLEMS

28–27 Robert and Susan Gray, who have three school-age children, are filing a joint federal income tax return. Robert, whose annual salary is $32,000 as an accountant for the Mize Corporation, operates a tax service in his spare time. During the current year, he had $5,200 gross income and $1,600 business expenses in his tax service. He received $90 in dividends from his investments and $400 interest on municipal bonds. Susan had $200 in dividend income on her stocks. In addition, Robert sold for $85 per share 100 shares of stock purchased five years ago for $40 per share. Income taxes withheld from Robert's salary for the year amounted to $4,650, and his payments of estimated tax were $800. Personal expenses of the Gray family for the year included the following:

Mortgage payments (of which $2,200 was interest)	$3,400
Real estate taxes	1,800
State income taxes	900
State sales taxes	360
Charitable contributions	510
Medical and dental expenses	1,950
License fees for auto, pets, etc.	50
Interest on charge accounts	300

REQUIRED
Calculate the amount of tax due (or overpayment) shown on the Grays' joint income tax return for the current year. Use the appropriate schedule in Exhibit 28–2 (page 1006). (Round computations to nearest dollar.)

28-28 The following items relate to the federal income taxes of individuals who itemize their deductions in computing their tax. Consider each item independently.

(1) Fee paid employment agency for obtaining employment.
(2) Payment of $100 repair bill for damage to pleasure automobile from skid on icy road (not compensated for by insurance).
(3) Labor union dues.
(4) Contribution to Empty Stocking Fund formed by neighbors for children of a needy family.
(5) State income tax paid.
(6) Federal cigarette tax.
(7) State gasoline tax for pleasure car.
(8) State fishing license.
(9) Gambling losses in excess of gambling gains.
(10) Fee paid by unemployed student to take the CPA examination.
(11) Fee paid to Smith & Brown, CPAs, for preparation of personal tax return.
(12) Cost of cleaning uniform paid by train conductor.
(13) Fair market value of furniture given to the Salvation Army.
(14) Entertainment expenses of an outside salesperson, not reimbursed.
(15) Life insurance premiums paid.
(16) Trade and business expenses of sole proprietorship.
(17) Net short-term loss of $1,200 on sale of securities.

REQUIRED

Indicate whether each of the above items is (a) nondeductible, (b) deductible in determining adjusted gross income, or (c) deductible from adjusted gross income.

28-29 Mark and Cheryl Wells are married and are both under 65 years of age. Their one child, Becky, is 18 years old and a full-time student at a university; they contribute over one-half of her support, Becky earned $1,800 from part-time work during the year.

Cheryl Wells operates a retail dress shop. Her records are kept on the accrual basis; however, all sales are for cash. The following information is available for the year's operations:

Cash receipts from sales	$48,400
Merchandise inventory, January 1	10,600
Merchandise purchases	34,800
Rent expense	3,600
Utilities and supplies expense	800
Salaries of part-time help	4,000
Insurance expense	750
Merchandise inventory, December 31	12,600

Mark Wells' annual salary as a purchasing agent for a local firm was $28,000, and income tax withheld was $3,400. Quarterly payments of estimated tax totaled $2,400. The following information for the year was compiled from Wells' checkbook and other sources:

Dividends received	$1,250
Interest income:	
Savings account	800
Municipal bonds	400
Real estate taxes on home	2,100
State sales taxes	300
Medical expenses	1,120
State income taxes paid	830
Contribution to United Fund	300
Accountant's services (preparing last year's income tax return)	175
Auto license on personal car	30
Safety deposit box rental (used for insurance policies)	25
Subscriptions to professional journals	75
Country club dues	360
Interest expense on home mortgage	1,600
Interest paid on personal loans	800

During the year, Mark sold the following corporate stock:

Security	Holding Period	Cost	Proceeds
Dow Chemical	five years	$1,750	$3,500
American Motors	three years	2,000	1,500
Datatron	five months	750	2,000
Apple	four months	2,250	1,750

REQUIRED

Compute the amount of tax due (or any overpayment) reported in the Wells' joint income tax return. Use the appropriate schedule in Exhibit 28–2 (page 1006). (Round computations to nearest dollar.)

28–30 The following information for the current year is from the records of the Artpro Corporation:

Sales	$300,000
Interest earned on corporate bonds	7,500
Dividends received on Exxon stock (a domestic corporation)	15,000
Dividends received on Atikokan stock (a Canadian company)	6,000
Cost of goods sold	195,000
Selling and administrative expenses (excluding charitable contributions)	46,500
Charitable contributions	3,000
Long-term capital gain on sale of property	12,000

In addition, the corporation had a net capital loss carryforward of $3,000 from prior years, and an $8,000 charitable contributions deduction carryforward.

REQUIRED

Prepare a schedule showing the computation of Artpro Corporation's total income tax liability for the year, using the rate schedule given on page 1010.

28–31 Adam Hornsby, who is married and has one dependent, is opening a business with an estimated annual pretax income of $80,000. He must decide whether the business should be operated as a corporation (with all shares owned by his wife and himself) or as a sole proprietorship. Hornsby has annual investment income of $15,000, which is fully taxable. He estimates that his annual total itemized deductions are approximately $12,000.

If the business is a corporation, Hornsby expects an annual salary of $40,000 and one-half of the after-tax corporate income in dividends. If the business is a sole proprietorship, he would withdraw $50,000 from the business each year.

REQUIRED
Prepare an analysis showing the expected tax results of the two types of business organization in this situation. Use the corporate tax rate schedule on page 1010 and the appropriate schedule in Exhibit 28−2 (page 1006).

ALTERNATE PROBLEMS

28−27A Jeff and Mary Black, who have two young children, are filing a joint federal income tax return. Jeff's annual salary as a credit manager for the Syncro Company is $33,500, from which $2,600 was withheld for federal income tax. Mary works part-time as an interior decorator; her gross receipts for the year were $2,800 and her business expenses were $1,100. The couple paid $800 estimated tax during the year. The Blacks' dividend income during the year amounted to $360. Mary also received a small bequest of $1,200 from a relative who died during the year. During the year, Jeff had a long-term capital gain of $1,600 and a short-term loss of $3,100 from the sale of securities.

The family's personal expenses for the year included the following:

Contributions to United Fund and church	$ 800
Flood damage to house (not insured)	4,000
State fishing and hunting licenses	42
Medical and dental expenses (not paid by insurance)	1,983
State sales taxes	380
Real estate taxes	1,500
Interest on home mortgage	3,800
State income taxes paid	1,746

REQUIRED
Calculate the amount of tax due (or overpayment) shown in the Blacks' joint income tax return for the current year. Use the appropriate schedule in Exhibit 28−2 (page 1006).

28−28A The following items relate to the federal income taxes of individuals who itemize their deductions in computing their tax. Consider each independently.
  (1) Purchase of Christmas seals (stamps) from tuberculosis association.
  (2) Travel expenses (overnight) of science teacher attending scientific convention.
  (3) Federal excise taxes on telephone calls.
  (4) Dog license.
  (5) Tuition for Dale Carnegie course taken by insurance salesperson to improve selling skills.
  (6) Loss of elm trees due to Dutch elm disease.

(7) Cost of spike shoes bought by professional baseball player.

(8) Cost of piano and ballet lessons for daughter.

(9) Interest paid on credit card purchases.

(10) Costs of traveling in search of employment.

(11) Net short-term capital loss of $800.

(12) Wagering losses of $500 (gains of $900 included in gross income).

(13) Advisor's fee for personal investment advice.

(14) Cost of professional magazine subscriptions paid by university professor.

(15) Transportation expenses driving to and from one's regular place of primary employment.

REQUIRED

Indicate whether each of the above items is (a) nondeductible, (b) deductible in determining adjusted gross income, or (c) deductible from adjusted gross income.

28–29A Jack and Diane Martin are both under 65 years of age and have two dependent children. Jack furnished over one-half the support for his mother-in-law, who lives with them. Her total income consists of $500 interest on a savings account. Diane has no outside employment. Jack owns an office building from which rentals for the year totaled $18,000. During the year, he had the following items related to the building:

Heat	$1,800
Janitor service	1,700
Depreciation (straight-line method was selected for tax purposes)	2,250
Interest on mortgage	2,800
Real estate taxes	2,400
Insurance premiums on three-year policy (paid January 1)	600

Jack's annual salary as sales manager for an insurance firm was $38,000, from which $5,100 was withheld for federal income taxes during the year. He also paid $800 in estimated tax during the year. The following information for the year was compiled from his checkbook and other sources:

Dividends received	$1,650
Interest income:	
Savings account	500
Municipal bonds	750
Real estate taxes on home	2,100
State sales taxes	380
Medical expenses	2,800
State income taxes paid	2,300
Contribution to United Fund	600
Accountant's services (preparing last year's income tax return)	150
Athletic club dues	720
Auto license on personal car	50
Safety deposit box rental (used for family heirlooms)	20
Subscriptions to professional journals	100
Lottery winnings	300
Interest expense on mortgage	4,100

During the year, Jack sold the following corporate stock:

Security	Holding Period	Cost	Proceeds
FMC	two years	$3,200	$5,000
Dow-Jones, Inc.	three years	2,400	1,600
American Tobacco Company	three months	2,800	1,100
IBM	five months	2,000	3,600

REQUIRED

Compute the amount of tax due (or any overpayment) reported in the Martins' joint income tax return. Use the appropriate schedule in Exhibit 28–2 (page 1006). (Round computations to nearest dollar.)

28–30A The following information for the current year is from the records of the Mountain Sports Company:

Sales	$1,600,000
Cost of goods sold	950,000
Interest expense	9,000
Selling and administrative expenses (excluding contributions)	460,000
Dividends received from wholly owned affiliate	5,000
Dividends received from Burlington Industries (a domestic corporation)	10,000
Long-term gain on sale of assets	18,000
Charitable contributions	28,000

In addition, the corporation had a net capital loss carryforward of $5,000.

REQUIRED

Prepare a schedule showing the computation of Mountain Sports Company's total income tax liability for the year using the rate schedule given on page 1010.

BUSINESS DECISION PROBLEM

At the beginning of the current year, Margie Sherman received an $80,000 inheritance from a relative. She asks your advice about the income tax treatment of the inheritance and also about several possible investment opportunities. She may invest the $80,000 in a partnership owned by two acquaintances or purchase either 14% high-grade industrial bonds or 9% tax-exempt municipal bonds.

Margie's annual share of the partnership net income would be 25% of an expected $50,000 for the next several years. If she invests in the partnership, she expects to withdraw only one-half of her share of net income annually.

Margie is unmarried and under 65 years of age. Her annual salary is $48,000, and she estimates that her total itemized deductions will amount to $10,300 for the year.

REQUIRED

(a) How is the $80,000 inheritance handled for income tax purposes?

(b) Which of the three investment alternatives should Margie choose if she is basing her decision on receiving the largest after-tax income for the current year? (Ignore the problem of risk in determining the best alternative.) Show calculations of the after-tax income to support your choice.

EXAMPLE OF FINANCIAL DATA OF A MAJOR CORPORATION

The following pages are the actual financial section of an annual report of Whirlpool Corporation, a major U.S. corporation. The financial section consists of management's analysis of the data, a management report on the financial statements, the independent accountants' report, the financial statements, supplemental information on inflation, and business segment information. Although some items in the financial section relate to matters not covered in an introductory accounting course, they are included to illustrate the comprehensive nature of the financial data. Note the Consolidated Statement of Stockholders' Equity presents data on the events causing changes in each category of stockholders' equity, including retained earnings. Used by permission of Whirlpool Corporation, Benton Harbor, Michigan 49022.

We have prepared the following questions to introduce several interesting aspects of Whirlpool Corporation's report:

(1) Note C to the consolidated financial statements mentions that inventory reductions resulted in partial liquidation of LIFO inventory quantities. The reduction resulted in increased earnings during the last three years. Explain how the inventory reductions have this effect.

(2) Note G to the consolidated financial statements analyzes the firm's long-term debt. What kind of leases does the firm have?

(3) Why do product warranty liabilities appear in both the Current Liabilities and the Other Liabilities sections of the balance sheet?

(4) Refer to Note P, the Estimated Effects of Inflation, in which Whirlpool Corporation shows a $6,830,000 purchasing power loss from holding net monetary assets in 1982. Using the information on average consumer price indexes, compute the 1982 inflation rate. Using this inflation rate, estimate the amount of net monetary assets the firm held during 1982.

(5) The firm's income statement shows a gain (and losses) from discontinued operations. Refer to Note B and for 1980, 1981, and 1982, determine how the year's gain or loss from discontinued operations is divided between (a) the gain or loss from operations of the discontinued segment, net of income taxes, and (b) the gain or loss on disposal of the discontinued segment, net of income taxes.

(6) Whirlpool Corporation has a complex capital structure because it has out-

standing stock options (see Note I). Yet the firm, correctly, does not make a dual presentation of primary earnings per share and fully diluted earnings per share. Why do you suppose this is the case? (Hint: One of the basic principles discussed in Chapter 13 applies here.)

(7) Why does the firm have deferred taxes in both the Current Assets and the Other Liabilities sections of the balance sheet?

(8) The firm has an interest in Appliance Buyers Credit Corporation. Why wasn't this interest eliminated in preparing the consolidated balance sheet? If Note A had not stated the subsidiary is wholly owned, how else can you determine this fact? (See Note D.)

(9) What concept of funds does the firm use in its Consolidated Statement of Changes in Financial Position? What is the amount of working capital at December 31, 1982? What was the change in working capital that occurred during 1982?

(10) Refer to the list of ratios in the Chapter 20 Key Points to Remember. Compute these ratios, where relevant, for Whirlpool Corporation's 1981 and 1982 data and comment on the results. At December 31, 1980, Whirlpool Corporation's total assets were, in thousands of dollars, $1,074,521, and total stockholders' equity, also in thousands of dollars, was $723,658. In calculating inventory turnover, use ending inventory rather than average inventory.

***Management's Discussion
and Analysis of Financial
Condition and Results of
Continuing Operations***

1. Liquidity

The Company has prepared its Consolidated Statement of Changes in Financial Position (set forth on page 18) on a cash flow basis for each of the three years ended December 31, 1982 to inform readers about the Company's liquidity. Liquidity, for this purpose, is defined as the ability of an enterprise to generate adequate amounts of cash to meet its needs, and for this purpose cash includes short-term investments.

The Consolidated Statement of Changes in Financial Position analyzes the Company's transactions from a cash flow perspective and classifies them into the following three fundamental business activities:

• *Operating activities*—transactions primarily related to the manufacture and sale of the Company's products and cash dividends paid.

• *Investing activities*—capital expenditures for the acquisition of properties and tooling used in the production of the Company's products, as well as investments in affiliated companies and subsidiaries.

• *Financing activities*—transactions associated with outside sources of financing such as short and long-term debt and equity capital.

Short-term liquidity

Indicators of the Company's short-term liquidity status are as follows:

• The Company has experienced a positive cash flow from its operating activities, after the payment of dividends to its stockholders, during each of the last three years as reflected in the Consolidated Statement of Changes in Financial Position.

• The Company's ability to meet its maturing short-term obligations, as measured by the so-called "quick" or "acid test" ratio (cash, short-term investments and receivables to current liabilities), has averaged 1.7 to 1 during the last three years and was 1.8 to 1 at December 31, 1982.

• At December 31, 1982 the Company had no short-term borrowings outstanding; however, the Company and its consolidated subsidiaries had line of credit agreements with banks permitting borrowings up to $62,000,000. In the Company's opinion, these credit agreements have been adequate to meet the Company's short-term borrowing needs and additional line of credit agreements are available, if desirable.

In the Company's opinion, its current financial resources and anticipated cash flow from operations are expected to be adequate to meet 1983 requirements.

Long-term liquidity

Indicators of the Company's long-term liquidity status are as follows:

• During each of the last three years the Company's cash flow from its operating activities, after the payment of dividends to its stockholders, has been adequate to meet its investing and financing activities as indicated in the Company's Consolidated Statement of Changes in Financial Position.

• No additional long-term debt has been incurred during the last three years and the percentage of long-term debt to invested capital during this period has declined from 8.3% at December 31, 1979 to 6.5% at December 31, 1982.

• The Company's ability to meet its interest commitments, as measured by the fixed-charge coverage ratio (earnings from continuing operations before income taxes and interest expense to interest expense), is 39.3 times, based on the Company's 1982 consolidated earnings from continuing operations.

• At July 1, 1982 (the latest valuation date) the net assets available for benefits under the Company's various pension plans exceeded the vested pension obligations of these plans. (See Note L of the Notes to Consolidated Financial Statements)

The Company has no present plans to acquire long-term capital funds, either by borrowings or by equity financing. It is the Company's opinion that its capital structure at December 31, 1982 could support increased levels of long-term debt, if desirable.

2. Capital Expenditures

The Company's capital expenditures during the last three years were primarily for the acquisition of tooling and equipment used in the production of major home appliances. Capital expenditures during 1982 reflected continuing efforts by the Company relating to the development and production of new or improved versions of existing products and expenditures for the construction of the new John H. Platts Educational Center at the Company's Corporate Complex.

The Company believes that its manufacturing facilities are generally adequate for current production and are capable of substantially increased production.

Capital expenditures in the last three years have been financed primarily through internally generated funds. It is anticipated that presently planned expenditures will be similarly financed.

3. Results of Continuing Operations

In 1981 Whirlpool Corporation discontinued the electronic organ business of its Thomas International Division, as more fully described in Note B of the Notes to Consolidated Financial Statements. The following discussion and analysis relates only to the continuing operations of the Company.

Sales, in terms of dollars, decreased 6.8% in 1982 compared to 1981 while 1981 dollar sales increased 9.5% over the 1980 levels. Dollar sales in both 1982 and 1981 reflected price increases made in an effort to recover cost increases for goods and services and, in 1981, reflected improved product mix in the Company's Refrigeration Products Group. The Company's unit sales in 1982 were approximately 11% less than in 1981 reflecting the recessionary environment of the national economy. Unit shipments for the entire year of 1981 were slightly above 1980 levels; however, unit shipments decreased 18.9% during the fourth quarter of 1981 compared to the corresponding 1980 period reflecting the downturn in the economy occurring in the latter part of 1981.

The Company's equity in net earnings of affiliated companies in 1982 and 1981, compared to the respective prior periods, reflected record earnings by the combined Brazilian affiliates and by Appliance Buyers Credit Corporation. The Company's equity in net earnings of the Brazilian affiliates in 1982 reflected their improved operating margins and the inclusion of their operating results for 16 months, in order to more currently reflect their operations. Adversely affecting such results, in part, were increased translation losses and a retroactive increase in Brazilian income taxes.

The Company's other income in 1982 decreased from 1981 due primarily to lower levels of interest income, resulting from lower rates of interest in 1982 offset in part by increased funds available for short-term investment. Other income increased in 1981 over 1980 due to increased interest income resulting from a greater amount of funds available for short-term investment at generally higher prevailing interest rates in 1981 than in 1980.

Cost of products sold by the Company decreased 7.7% in 1982 from 1981 reflecting the decline in unit shipments in 1982 referred to above, effective cost control efforts and a decline in the rate of inflation in 1982 compared with 1981 affecting the cost of purchased goods and services. Cost of products sold in 1981 increased approximately 9.8% over 1980, compared with a 9.5% increase in dollar sales, although unit shipments in 1981 were slightly above the 1980 level. During each of the last three years, cost of products sold also reflected partial liquidations of LIFO inventories as described in Note C of the Notes to Consolidated Financial Statements.

Selling and administrative expenses relative to dollar sales were at a slightly higher rate in 1982 than in 1981 and 1980 primarily resulting from lower unit shipments in 1982 than in the prior two years.

Income taxes for the Company, relative to its pre-tax earnings, were at slightly lesser percentages for 1982 and 1981 primarily due to greater investment tax credits applied than in the respective prior periods.

As a result of the foregoing principal factors, earnings from continuing operations for 1982 were $136,225,000 compared with $135,235,000 for 1981 or an increase of less than 1%, while 1981 earnings from continuing operations increased 28.7% over 1980 earnings from continuing operations of $105,044,000.

4. Effects of Inflation

For information regarding the effects of inflation on certain reported financial information of the Company, see Note P of the Notes to Consolidated Financial Statements.

Report by Management on the Financial Statements

The management of Whirlpool Corporation has prepared the accompanying financial statements. The financial statements have been examined by Ernst & Whinney, independent auditors, whose report, based upon their audit and the reports of other independent auditors, expresses the opinion that these financial statements present fairly the consolidated financial position and results of operations of Whirlpool Corporation and its consolidated subsidiaries (later referred to as "the Company") in accordance with generally accepted accounting principles. Their examination is conducted in accordance with generally accepted auditing standards and includes a review of internal controls and tests of transactions.

The financial statements were prepared from the Company's accounting records, books and accounts which, in reasonable detail, accurately and fairly reflect all material transactions or dispositions of assets. The Company maintains a system of internal controls designed to provide reasonable assurance that the Company's accounting records, books and accounts are accurate and that transactions are properly recorded in the Company's books and records, and the Company's assets are maintained and accounted for, in accordance with management's authorizations. The Company's accounting records, policies and internal controls are regularly reviewed by the Company's internal audit staff.

The Audit Committee of the Board of Directors of Whirlpool Corporation, which is comprised of three Directors who are not employed by the Company, considers and makes recommendations to the Board of Directors as to accounting and auditing matters concerning the Company, including recommending for appointment by the Board of Directors the firm of independent auditors who is engaged on an annual basis to audit the financial statements of Whirlpool Corporation and certain of its wholly-owned subsidiaries. The Audit Committee meets with the independent auditors at least twice yearly to review the scope of the audit, the results of the audit and such recommendations as may be made by said auditors with respect to the Company's accounting methods and system of internal controls. In addition, the Audit Committee approves in advance any material non-audit services that are expected to be performed by the independent auditors.

**Report of Ernst & Whinney,
Independent Auditors**

The Stockholders and
Board of Directors
Whirlpool Corporation
Benton Harbor, Michigan

We have examined the consolidated financial statements of Whirlpool Corporation and consolidated subsidiaries for each of the three years in the period ended December 31, 1982. Our examinations were made in accordance with generally accepted auditing standards and, accordingly, included such tests of the accounting records and such other auditing procedures as we considered necessary in the circumstances. The financial statements of Appliance Buyers Credit Corporation, used as the basis for recording the Company's equity in net earnings of that corporation, were examined by other independent auditors whose reports thereon were furnished to us. Our opinion expressed herein, insofar as it relates to amounts included for Appliance Buyers Credit Corporation, is based on the reports of the other independent auditors.

In our opinion, based upon our examinations and the reports of other independent auditors, the accompanying balance sheet and statements of operations, stockholders' equity, and changes in financial position present fairly the consolidated financial position of Whirlpool Corporation and consolidated subsidiaries at December 31, 1982 and 1981, and the consolidated results of their operations and changes in their financial position for each of the three years in the period ended December 31, 1982, in conformity with generally accepted accounting principles applied on a consistent basis.

Ernst & Whinney

Chicago, Illinois
January 26, 1983

Consolidated
Balance
Sheet

Assets	December 31	1982	1981
	thousands of dollars		
Current Assets	Cash	$ 23,312	$ 2,533
	Short-term investments	346,236	274,797
	Receivables, less allowances for doubtful accounts (1982—$1,480,000; 1981—$970,000)	166,285	156,169
	Inventories—Note C	228,270	256,546
	Prepaid expenses	7,666	5,743
	Deferred income taxes	12,951	12,708
	Total Current Assets	784,720	708,496
Investments and Other Assets	Appliance Buyers Credit Corporation—Note D	67,935	60,908
	Affiliated foreign companies—Note E	97,378	78,568
	Other assets	7,707	7,879
		173,020	147,355
Property, Plant and Equipment	Land	8,916	9,162
	Buildings	184,110	182,704
	Machinery, equipment and tools	307,362	275,507
		500,388	467,373
	Less allowances for depreciation and amortization	196,486	189,252
		303,902	278,121
		$1,261,642	$1,133,972

Liabilities and Stockholders' Equity	December 31	1982	1981
	thousands of dollars		
Current Liabilities	Accounts payable	$ 108,975	$ 74,824
	Payrolls and other compensation	64,665	64,627
	Taxes and other accrued expenses	49,043	53,829
	Income taxes	50,924	36,601
	Product warranty	17,381	17,790
	Total Current Liabilities	290,988	247,671
Other Liabilities	Long-term debt—Note G	60,848	60,848
	Product warranty	16,403	17,309
	Deferred income taxes	18,329	16,315
		95,580	94,472
Stockholders' Equity	Capital stock—Notes H and I	36,430	36,265
	Additional paid-in capital	27,489	23,484
	Retained earnings—Notes G and H	811,155	732,080
		875,074	791,829
		$1,261,642	$1,133,972

See notes to consolidated financial statements

Consolidated Statement of Stockholders' Equity

Year Ended December 31 thousands of dollars	**1982**	1981	1980
Common Stock			
Balance at beginning of year	$ 36,265	$ 36,238	$ 36,200
Par value of shares issued under stock option plans	165	27	38
Balance at end of year	36,430	36,265	36,238
Additional Paid-in Capital			
Balance at beginning of year	23,484	22,891	22,191
Stock option transactions	4,005	593	700
Balance at end of year	27,489	23,484	22,891
Retained Earnings			
Balance at beginning of year	732,080	664,529	613,538
Net earnings	139,015	125,560	101,699
	871,095	790,089	715,237
Cash dividends paid	(59,940)	(58,009)	(50,708)
Balance at end of year	811,155	732,080	664,529
Stockholders' equity at end of year	$ 875,074	$ 791,829	$ 723,658
Cash dividends per share of common stock	$1.65	$1.60	$1.40

See notes to consolidated financial statements

Consolidated Statement of Operations

Year Ended December 31 thousands of dollars	**1982**	1981	1980
Income			
Net sales—Notes B and K	$2,271,305	$2,437,091	$2,225,696
Equity in net earnings of affiliated companies—Notes D and E	25,652	22,190	12,264
Other	43,274	45,549	28,872
	2,340,231	2,504,830	2,266,832
Deductions From Income			
Cost of products sold	1,827,326	1,979,176	1,803,115
Selling and administrative expenses	271,749	280,677	263,451
Interest on long-term debt	5,497	5,497	5,661
Other interest expense	634	145	1,361
Income taxes—Note J	98,800	104,100	88,200
	2,204,006	2,369,595	2,161,788
Earnings from continuing operations	136,225	135,235	105,044
Gain (loss) from discontinued operations—Note B	2,790	(9,675)	(3,345)
Net earnings	$ 139,015	$ 125,560	$ 101,699
Per share of common stock:			
Earnings from continuing operations	$ 3.75	$ 3.73	$ 2.90
Gain (loss) from discontinued operations	0.08	(0.27)	(0.09)
Net earnings	$ 3.83	$ 3.46	$ 2.81
Average number of common shares outstanding	36,315,108	36,255,187	36,217,668

See notes to consolidated financial statements

Consolidated Statement of Changes in Financial Position

Year Ended December 31	**1982**	1981	1980
thousands of dollars			
Operating Activities			
Earnings from continuing operations	$ 136,225	$ 135,235	$ 105,044
Non cash charges (credits):			
Depreciation of plant and equipment	32,286	30,910	28,986
Amortization of tooling	21,639	20,047	18,419
Increase in noncurrent deferred income taxes	2,014	668	1,190
Equity in net earnings of affiliated companies:			
Appliance Buyers Credit Corporation	(7,027)	(6,643)	(6,058)
Affiliated foreign companies	(18,625)	(15,547)	(6,206)
Increase (decrease) in long-term product warranty	(906)	2,074	(1,402)
Dividends received from affiliated foreign companies	4,815	3,861	2,207
Changes in components of operating working capital other than cash and short-term investments	59,311	(1,622)	45,558
Cash provided by continuing operations	229,732	168,983	187,738
Cash dividends paid	(59,940)	(58,009)	(50,708)
Cash provided by continuing operations retained in the business	169,792	110,974	137,030
Gain (loss) from discontinued operations net of non cash items	2,790	(6,977)	(2,474)
Cash provided by operations retained in the business	172,582	103,997	134,556
Investing Activities			
Additions to properties	(39,646)	(48,205)	(37,704)
Additions to tooling	(41,582)	(29,794)	(32,381)
Disposals of properties	1,522	1,570	3,797
Increase in investment in and loans to affiliated foreign companies	(5,800)	(8,000)	—
Repayment of loans by affiliated foreign company	800	—	—
Decrease (increase) in other assets	172	(5,636)	318
Cash used for investing activities	(84,534)	(90,065)	(65,970)
Financing Activities			
Repayment of notes payable	—	(564)	(3,968)
Repayment of current maturities of long-term debt	—	—	(6,975)
Stock option transactions	4,170	620	738
Cash provided by (used for) financing activities	4,170	56	(10,205)
Increase in cash and short-term investments	92,218	13,988	58,381
Cash and short-term investments at beginning of year	277,330	263,342	204,961
Cash and short-term investments at end of year	$ 369,548	$ 277,330	$ 263,342
Changes in components of operating working capital other than cash and short-term investments			
Receivables	$ (10,116)	$ (15,636)	$ 11,477
Inventories	28,276	25,052	37,300
Prepaid expenses	(1,923)	205	1,424
Deferred income taxes	(243)	(345)	(1,522)
Accounts payable	34,151	(16,219)	(17,145)
Accrued liabilities	(5,157)	15,363	3,633
Income taxes	14,323	(10,042)	10,391
	$ 59,311	$ (1,622)	$ 45,558

See notes to consolidated financial statements

Notes to
Consolidated
Financial Statements

Note A
Summary of Principal Accounting Policies

Principles of Consolidation:
The consolidated financial statements include all majority-owned subsidiaries except Appliance Buyers Credit Corporation (ABCC), a wholly-owned finance company, and its subsidiaries. Investments in ABCC and in affiliated foreign companies are accounted for by the equity method.

Inventories:
Substantially all major home appliance inventories are stated at the lower of last-in, first-out (LIFO) cost or market. The remaining inventories are stated at the lower of first-in, first-out (FIFO) cost or market.

Property, Plant and Equipment:
Properties are stated at cost. Depreciation of plant and equipment and amortization of tooling are computed by the straight-line method based upon the estimated average useful lives of the various classes of assets.

Pensions:
The cost of pension plans represents normal cost and amortization of prior-service cost over periods ranging to forty years. The Companies fund such costs as accrued.

Investment Tax Credits:
Investment tax credits are accounted for by the flow-through method as a direct reduction of the current federal income tax provision.

Change in Financial Statement Presentation:
For the year ended December 31, 1982, the Company changed its presentation of the Consolidated Statement of Changes in Financial Position to a cash flow basis from a working capital basis. Prior period information for 1981 and 1980 has been restated on a comparable basis.

Note B
Discontinued Operations

In 1981, the Company discontinued the electronic organ business of its Thomas International Division. The results of operations of the electronic organ business have been presented as discontinued operations in the consolidated statement of operations.

The 1982 gain from discontinued operations of $2,790,000 (after a related tax charge of $2,300,000) resulted from adjustments to the estimated provision for loss on disposal recorded in 1981. The 1981 loss from discontinued operations includes a loss from operations of $4,071,000 (after a related tax benefit of $3,200,000) and a loss on disposal of $5,604,000 (after a related tax benefit of $5,200,000) consisting principally of a provision for expenses related to plant shutdown costs and severance pay and a write down of Thomas' net assets to estimated realizable value. The 1980 loss from discontinued operations was net of income tax benefits of $3,200,000.

Sales of the discontinued operations excluded from continuing operations were $12,997,000 in 1981 and $17,485,000 in 1980.

Note C
Inventories

Inventories at December 31, 1982 and 1981 consisted of:

	1982	1981
thousands of dollars		
Finished products	$151,831	$161,664
Work in process	30,800	39,537
Raw materials	45,639	55,345
Total	$228,270	$256,546

Replacement cost of the LIFO inventories exceeded the carrying amount by approximately $184,400,000 at December 31, 1982 and $186,400,000 at December 31, 1981. Such inventories represented approximately 84% and 79% of total inventories at December 31, 1982 and 1981, respectively.

The Company's reduction of inventories resulted in partial liquidations of LIFO inventory quantities carried at lower costs prevailing in prior years as compared with current costs of purchases. This had the effect of increasing net earnings by approximately $5,000,000 ($.14 per share) in 1982, $3,400,000 ($.09 per share) in 1981 and $2,700,000 ($.07 per share) in 1980.

Note D
Appliance Buyers Credit Corporation

ABCC provides floorplan financing services principally for dealers and distributors handling products of the Companies, RCA Corporation and The Toro Company and also finances retail sales by dealers of such products and the products of other manufacturers.

Condensed financial statements of ABCC and its consolidated subsidiaries follow:

Balance Sheet

December 31	1982	1981
thousands of dollars		
Assets		
Cash and marketable securities	$ 14,355	$ 13,594
Finance receivables— net	267,186	251,656
Other assets	7,344	8,137
	$288,885	$273,387
Liabilities and Stockholder's equity		
Notes payable and other liabilities	$209,950	$200,479
Long-term debt	11,000	12,000
Stockholder's equity	67,935	60,908
	$288,885	$273,387

Statement of Operations

Year Ended December 31	1982	1981	1980
thousands of dollars			
Finance charges earned	$ 61,950	$ 66,822	$ 52,428
Operating and other expenses	22,717	19,903	17,310
Interest expense	26,475	34,815	24,025
Federal income taxes	5,731	5,461	5,035
Net Earnings	$ 7,027	$ 6,643	$ 6,058

Note E
Affiliated Foreign Companies

The Company has equity interests, ranging from 20% to 37%, in three Brazilian companies (Brastemp S.A., Embraco S.A. and Consul S.A.) engaged in manufacturing major home appliances and related equipment.

The Company also has a 43% equity interest in Inglis Limited, a leading manufacturer of major home appliances located in Canada.

The Company's investment in affiliated foreign companies includes notes receivable of $16,200,000 at December 31, 1982 and $12,000,000 at December 31, 1981.

Certain aggregate financial information relative to the affiliated foreign companies is summarized as follows:

	1982	1981	1980
thousands of dollars			
Current assets	$ 337,317	$ 288,501	
Other assets	193,553	144,709	
	$ 530,870	$ 433,210	
Current liabilities	$ 190,468	$ 176,904	
Other liabilities	73,983	48,659	
Stockholders' equity	266,419	207,647	
	$ 530,870	$ 433,210	
Net sales	$ 906,627	$ 687,450	$ 524,906
Cost of products sold	$ 651,652	$ 523,688	$ 406,111
Net income	$ 66,842	$ 50,770	$ 20,231

The financial results of the combined Brazilian affiliates for the 1982 reporting period includes their operating results for 16 months, in order to more currently reflect their operations, and a retroactive increase in the Brazilian income taxes. The net effect was to increase the Company's equity in net earnings of the combined Brazilian affiliates approximately $1,600,000 or $.04 per share.

Foreign currency exchange losses, resulting from translation of the financial statements of the affiliated foreign companies, included in results of operations for 1982, 1981 and 1980 amounted to approximately $20,200,000, $9,500,000 and $12,200,000, respectively. The Company's adoption of Statement of Financial Accounting Standards No. 52 "Foreign Currency Translation" in 1981 did not have a significant impact on results of operations since the Company's foreign investments are principally in Brazilian companies which operate in a highly inflationary economy.

Notes to Consolidated Financial Statements Continued

Note F
Lines of Credit

At December 31, 1982 the Companies have several unused line of credit agreements which expire on various dates in 1983 permitting borrowings up to $62,000,000 at the prime interest rate. The Companies do not have formal compensating balance arrangements with their credit line banks. Generally, the banks are compensated for their credit lines by Company operating balances to the extent available, plus a fee which is paid by the Companies to the banks. Balances maintained pursuant to this arrangement during 1982 included amounts used, on occasion, to support lines of credit also available to Appliance Buyers Credit Corporation.

Note G
Long-Term Debt

Long-term debt at December 31, 1982 and 1981 consisted of:

	Interest Rate	1982	1981
thousands of dollars			
Sinking fund debentures:			
Due November 1, 1986 .....5¾%		$ 8,448	$ 8,448
Due September 15, 2000 ....9⅝		50,000	50,000
Lease obligations, due 1997 .....5½ to 5⁷⁄₁₀		2,400	2,400
Total		$ 60,848	$ 60,848

At December 31, 1982, the Company held debentures in the face amount of $5,552,000 which have been deducted from the sinking fund requirements due in 1983 through 1986.

There are no annual maturities or sinking fund requirements in the years 1983 through 1985. Annual maturities and sinking fund requirements are $11,798,000 in 1986 and $3,350,000 in 1987.

The indenture for the 5¾% debentures contains restrictions relating to payment of cash dividends and purchase of the Company's stock. At December 31, 1982, approximately $602,900,000 of retained earnings was free of such restrictions.

Note H
Stockholders' Equity

The Company has 50,000,000 authorized shares of common stock, par value $1 per share, of which 36,429,523 and 36,264,728 shares were outstanding at December 31, 1982 and 1981, respectively.

The Company has 500,000 authorized shares of cumulative preferred stock, par value $80 per share, none of which were issued at December 31, 1982 or 1981.

Consolidated retained earnings at December 31, 1982 included $56,390,000 of equity in undistributed net earnings of the affiliated foreign companies.

Note I
Stock Options

The Company's stock option plan permits the grant of stock options to key salaried employees of the Company and its subsidiaries. The plan, as amended in 1982, authorizes the grant of 1,250,000 shares as either incentive or non-statutory stock options and, further, authorizes the grant of stock appreciation rights with respect to options granted or outstanding. The stock appreciation rights allow option holders, in lieu of exercising options, to receive payments, in cash or shares of common stock or a combination thereof, in an amount equal to the excess of the market price of the common stock over the option price.

Options outstanding at December 31, 1982 have expiration dates ranging from June 19, 1983 to December 15, 1992. Stock appreciation rights are outstanding with respect to 238,880 shares under option at December 31, 1982.

A summary of certain information regarding employee stock options follows:

	1982		1981	
	Number of Shares	Average Option Price	Number of Shares	Average Option Price
Outstanding at January 1	761,096	$21.19	877,408	$21.11
Granted	382,000	44.63	—	—
Exercised	(160,871)	21.06	(21,212)	17.48
Surrendered under stock appreciation rights	(203,980)	21.61	(67,850)	20.44
Cancelled or expired	(15,800)	33.37	(27,250)	23.59
Outstanding at December 31	762,445	32.59	761,096	21.19
Exercisable at December 31	367,545	20.51	517,471	21.30
Available for future grant at December 31	411,050		792,250	

Note J
Income Taxes

The provisions for income taxes applicable to continuing operations follow:

thousands of dollars	1982	1981	1980
Current:			
Federal	$ 84,794	$ 88,454	$ 74,475
State and local	15,327	15,413	13,030
	100,121	103,867	87,505
Deferred (credit):			
Federal	(1,219)	168	715
State and local	(102)	65	(20)
	(1,321)	233	695
Total Income Tax Expense	$ 98,800	$104,100	$ 88,200

A reconciliation of the total income tax expense to the amount computed by applying the statutory federal income tax rate to earnings from continuing operations before income taxes and equity in net earnings of affiliated companies follows:

thousands of dollars	1982	1981	1980
46% of earnings, as defined above	$ 96,312	$ 99,887	$ 83,251
State and local taxes, net of federal tax benefit	8,222	8,358	7,025
Investment tax credit	(6,246)	(5,214)	(2,761)
Other items	512	1,069	685
Total Income Tax Expense	$ 98,800	$104,100	$ 88,200

Deferred income taxes result from the tax effect of transactions which are recognized in different periods for financial and tax reporting purposes including pension costs and other employee benefits, depreciation expense, warranty costs and other items.

Note K
Business Segment and Sales Information

The Company operates predominantly in the business segment classified as Major Home Appliances.

Percentages of consolidated net sales from continuing operations to Sears, Roebuck and Co. were 45% in 1982 and 46% in 1981 and 1980.

Note L
Pension Plans

The Companies have various pension plans covering substantially all employees. The approximate cost of the plans applicable to continuing operations was $34,400,000 in 1982, $31,900,000 in 1981 and $28,300,000 in 1980.

Accumulated plan benefit information and plan net assets, as of the latest valuation date, were as follows:

July 1 / thousands of dollars	1982	1981
Actuarial present value of accumulated plan benefits:		
Vested	$ 348,900	$ 321,700
Non-vested	44,800	41,100
Total	$ 393,700	$ 362,800
Net assets available for benefits	$ 354,300	$ 350,100

The assumed rate of return used in determining the actuarial present value of accumulated plan benefits was 7.5% for 1982 and 1981.

Note M
Supplementary Expense Information

Certain classes of expenses incurred and charged directly to continuing operations were as follows:

thousands of dollars	1982	1981	1980
Maintenance and repairs	$ 71,644	$ 72,533	$ 63,418
Research and development costs	36,950	34,120	32,460

Note N
Contingencies

The Company is involved in various legal actions arising in the normal course of business. Management, after taking into consideration legal counsel's evaluation of such actions, is of the opinion that the outcome thereof will not have a material adverse effect on the financial statements of the Company.

Notes to
Consolidated
Financial Statements
Continued

Note O
Quarterly Results of Operations (Unaudited)

The following is a tabulation of the unaudited quarterly results of operations for the years ended December 31, 1982 and 1981:

Three Months Ended	Mar. 31	June 30	Sept. 30	Dec. 31
thousands of dollars				
1982:				
Net sales	$ 550,086	$ 637,758	$ 589,744	$ 493,717
Cost of products sold	$ 444,542	$ 516,964	$ 475,813	$ 390,007
Earnings from continuing operations	$ 28,174	$ 36,211	$ 36,742	$ 35,098
Gain from discontinued operations	—	—	—	2,790
Net earnings	$ 28,174	$ 36,211	$ 36,742	$ 37,888
Per share of common stock:				
Earnings from continuing operations	$ 0.78	$ 1.00	$ 1.01	$ 0.96
Gain from discontinued operations	—	—	—	0.08
Net earnings	$ 0.78	$ 1.00	$ 1.01	$ 1.04
1981:				
Net sales	$ 588,039	$ 732,842	$ 649,592	$ 466,618
Cost of products sold	$ 476,225	$ 596,110	$ 525,324	$ 381,517
Earnings from continuing operations	$ 32,394	$ 39,267	$ 42,470	$ 21,104
Loss from discontinued operations	(833)	(3,160)	(1,861)	(3,821)
Net earnings	$ 31,561	$ 36,107	$ 40,609	$ 17,283
Per share of common stock:				
Earnings from continuing operations	$ 0.89	$ 1.09	$ 1.17	$ 0.58
Loss from discontinued operations	(0.02)	(0.09)	(0.05)	(0.11)
Net earnings	$ 0.87	$ 1.00	$ 1.12	$ 0.47

Note P
Estimated Effects of Inflation (Unaudited)

Statement of Financial Accounting Standards No. 33, as issued by the Financial Accounting Standards Board (FASB), requires disclosure of selected financial data on a constant dollar basis (reflecting the effects of general inflation) and on a current cost basis (reflecting specific price changes of goods and services). The FASB has provided for flexibility and encouraged experimentation within the guidelines of the statement; therefore, users should exercise discretion when considering the following information.

A summary of certain financial data for the year ended December 31, 1982 adjusted for changing prices follows:

	Adjusted for General Inflation	Adjusted for Changes in Specific Prices
thousands of dollars		
Earnings from continuing operations as reported	$ 136,225	$ 136,225
Adjustments for changing prices:		
Cost of products sold	(13,337)	(12,562)
Depreciation and amortization expense	(22,383)	(22,689)
	(35,720)	(35,251)
Earnings from continuing operations as adjusted for changing prices	$ 100,505	$ 100,974
Purchasing power loss from holding net monetary assets during the year	$ 6,830	
Increase in specific prices of inventories and property, plant and equipment held during the year		$ 32,766
Less effect of increase in the general price level		32,307
Excess of increase in specific prices over increase in the general price level		$ 459

At December 31, 1982, the current cost of inventory was $412,660,000 and the current cost of net property, plant and equipment was $427,507,000.

A comparison of selected historical financial data adjusted for changing prices and stated in thousands of average 1982 dollars follows:

	Historical Amount	Adjusted for General Inflation	Adjusted for Changes in Specific Prices
Net sales:			
1982	$2,271,305	$2,271,305	
1981	2,437,091	2,586,501	
1980	2,225,696	2,607,167	
1979	2,234,726	2,971,754	
1978	2,049,542	3,032,357	
Earnings from continuing operations:			
1982		$ 100,505	$ 100,974
1981		103,673	103,347
1980		82,085	75,332
1979		120,322	112,572
Earnings from continuing operations per share of common stock:			
1982		$2.77	$2.78
1981		2.86	2.85
1980		2.27	2.08
1979		3.32	3.11
Net assets at year-end:			
1982		$1,189,053	$1,171,034
1981		1,140,622	1,129,679
1980		1,107,846	1,144,280
1979		1,135,669	1,175,422
Loss from decline in purchasing power of net monetary assets held:			
1982		$ 6,830	
1981		11,490	
1980		9,978	
1979		4,552	
Excess of increase in the general price level over increase in specific prices:			
1982			$ (459)
1981			31,479
1980			30,536
1979			25,552
Cash dividends per share of common stock:			
1982	$1.65	$1.65	
1981	1.60	1.70	
1980	1.40	1.64	
1979	1.35	1.80	
1978	1.20	1.78	

Market price per share of common stock at year-end:		
1982	$43.75	$43.26
1981	25.38	26.07
1980	19.25	21.54
1979	18.75	23.58
1978	19.13	27.26

Average consumer price indexes used to adjust for general inflation were 289.1 in 1982, 272.4 in 1981, 246.8 in 1980, 217.4 in 1979 and 195.4 in 1978.

The following methods were used in the determination of estimated current cost amounts:

(1) The current cost of inventories has been estimated on the basis of standard costs adjusted to reflect current material, labor and overhead variances; however, it is estimated that the increases in overhead which would result by applying the current cost provisions for depreciation of plant and equipment and amortization of tooling are minor and therefore not included therein.

(2) The current cost of property, plant and equipment has been estimated on the basis of engineering studies, vendor quotes of current market prices, geographic construction costs, architectural estimates or by applying index numbers derived from published sources for the appropriate classifications of assets.

(3) The current cost of products sold for those inventories carried on the last-in, first-out (LIFO) method of inventory valuation are adjusted from historical cost amounts only for the effect of LIFO inventory liquidations. An estimate of the current cost of products sold for those inventories carried on the first-in, first-out (FIFO) method of inventory valuation was determined based on standard costs in effect at the end of the current year.

(4) The current cost of depreciation and amortization has been estimated on a straight-line basis using the same estimates of useful life and salvage value utilized in preparing the historical cost financial statements. The estimated current cost of property, plant and equipment was used in determining the basis upon which the estimated current cost of depreciation and amortization was computed.

Calculations of cost of products sold and depreciation and amortization expense are based on current cost and do not give effect to efficiencies that could be derived by replacing existing assets with technologically improved assets.

Computations of supplementary information exclude any adjustments to or allocations of the amount of income tax expense included in the historical cost financial statements. The effective tax rate for 1982 of 47.2% on a historical cost basis rises to 56.9% on a constant dollar basis and to 56.7% on a current cost basis.

Sales and Income
Information

Year Ended December 31	Percent	**1982**	1981	1980
thousands of dollars	Percent			
Contribution to Net Sales from Continuing Operations by Class of Similar Products				
Major Home Appliances:				
Home laundry appliances	37.8%	$ 859,001	$ 871,170	$ 830,273
Home refrigeration and room air conditioning equipment	40.1	911,740	1,023,836	909,988
Other home appliances	15.5	351,084	370,180	347,468
	93.4	2,121,825	2,265,186	2,087,729
Other Products and Services	6.6	149,480	171,905	137,967
	100.0%	$2,271,305	$2,437,091	$2,225,696
Contribution to Earnings (Losses) From Continuing Operations before Income Taxes				
Major Home Appliances	74.4%	$ 174,937	$ 171,510	$ 158,953
Other Products and Services	(3.7)	(8,838)	86	(6,845)
Other Income	18.4	43,274	45,549	28,872
Equity in Net Earnings of Affiliated Companies	10.9	25,652	22,190	12,264
	100.0%	$ 235,025	$ 239,335	$ 193,244

GLOSSARY

Chapter numbers at the end of each entry indicate where elaborations on the term may be found.

Absorption Costing A product costing method in which all manufacturing costs are treated as product costs. (Ch. 25)

Accelerated Cost Recovery System (ACRS) A system of accelerated depreciation for tax purposes introduced in the 1981 Economic Recovery Tax Act; it prescribes depreciation rates by asset classifications for assets acquired after 1980. (Ch. 10)

Accelerated Depreciation Any depreciation method under which the amounts of depreciation expense taken in the early years of an asset's life are larger than those amounts taken later. (Ch. 10)

Account A record of the additions, deductions, and balances of individual assets, liabilities, owners' equity, revenue and expenses. The basic component of a formal accounting system. (Ch. 2)

Accounting The process of recording, classifying, reporting, and interpreting the financial data of an organization. (Ch. 1)

Accounting Cycle Steps in the processing of accounting transactions during the accounting year: (1) analyzing transactions, (2) recording in journals, (3) posting to general ledger, (4) adjusting accounts, (5) preparing financial statements, and

(6) closing temporary accounts. (Ch. 3)

Accounting Entity Those people, assets, and activities devoted to a specific economic purpose and for which a separate accounting should be made. (Chs. 1, 13)

Accounting Equation An expression of the equivalency in dollar amounts of assets and equities in double-entry bookkeeping; often stated as Assets = Liabilities + Owners' Equity. (Ch. 1)

Accounting Period That time period, typically one year, to which accounting reports are related. (Ch. 13)

Accounting Principles See Generally Accepted Accounting Principles.

Accounting Transaction A business activity or event that requires accounting recognition. (Ch. 1)

Accrual Basis The accounting basis whereby revenue is recognized in the period earned whether actually received or not and expenses are recognized and matched with the related revenue of the period whether actually paid or not. (Ch. 1)

Accrue To accumulate or increase; also to recognize such accumulation or increase, usually during the adjustment step of the accounting cycle. (Ch. 3)

Accumulated Depreciation A contra account to the related asset account reflecting the cumu-

lative amounts recorded as depreciation for a specific asset or group of assets. (Ch. 3)

Adjusted Gross Income An income tax term denoting the amount obtained by subtracting from gross income certain business expenses and expenses incurred in producing rents and royalties. (Ch. 28)

Adjusted Trial Balance A trial balance of the general ledger accounts taken after adjustments have been made. (Ch. 4)

Adjusting Entries Those entries resulting from an attempt to reflect in the accounts various changes that may be appropriate although no source document is normally available; usually made to align recorded costs or revenue with the accounting period or to reflect unrecorded revenue and costs. (Ch. 3)

After-tax Cash Flow The net amount of any receipt or expenditure after incorporating the effects of income taxes. (Ch. 27)

AICPA The American Institute of Certified Public Accountants, the national professional organization of CPAs in the United States. (Ch. 1)

Allowance for Uncollectible Accounts A contra asset account with a normal credit balance shown on the balance sheet as a deduction from accounts receivable to reflect the expected realizable amount of accounts receivable. (Ch. 8)

Allowance Method An accounting procedure whereby in the period in which credit sales occur, the related amount of uncollectible accounts expense is estimated and recorded in the contra asset account Allowance for Uncollectible Accounts. (Ch. 8)

Amortization The periodic writing off or charging to expense of some amount of cost (usually associated with intangible assets). (Ch. 11)

APB The Accounting Principles Board, a committee of the AICPA responsible for formulating accounting principles until it was repaced in 1973 by the FASB. (Chs. 1, 13)

Appropriation of Retained Earnings Segregation or restriction of a portion of retained earnings that reduces the amount that would otherwise be available for dividends. No transfer of funds is necessarily involved, and the aggregate amount of retained earnings remains unchanged. (Ch. 16)

Articles of Co-partnership The formal written agreement among partners setting forth important aspects of the partnership such as name, nature, duration, and location of the business, capital contributions, duties, and profit and loss ratios. (Ch. 14)

Articles of Incorporation A document prepared by persons organizing a corporation in the United States that sets forth the structure and purposes of the corporation and specifics regarding stock to be issued. (Ch. 15)

Assets Those economic resources of an entity that can usefully be expressed in monetary terms; some examples are cash, accounts receivable, inventories, and plant and equipment. (Ch. 1)

Average Collection Period Trade accounts receivable divided by year's sales multiplied by 365. (Ch. 20)

Average Rate of Return A method of capital outlay analysis that focuses on the ratio of expected average annual net income to the related average investment. (Ch. 27)

Avoidable Costs Costs that may be avoided by following some course of action. (Ch. 25)

Balance Sheet A financial report showing the financial position of an entity in terms of assets, liabilities, and owners' equity at a specific date. (Ch. 1)

Balance Sheet Equation Assets = Liabilities + Owners' Equity. (Ch. 1)

Bank Reconciliation A procedure or analysis explaining the various items—such as deposits in transit, checks outstanding, bank charges, and errors— that lead to differences between the balance shown on a bank statement and the related Cash account in the general ledger. (Ch. 7)

Betterment A capital expenditure that improves the quality of services rendered by a plant asset but does not necessarily extend its useful life. (Ch. 10)

Bond A form of interest-bearing note payable, usually issued by the borrower for relatively long periods to a group of lenders. Bonds may incorporate a wide variety of special provisions relating to security for the debt involved, methods of paying the periodic interest payments, and maturity and retirement provisions. (Ch. 17)

Bond Discount Excess of the face value of a bond over its issue price. Bond discount arises when the coupon rate of the bond is below the market rate of interest for that type of bond. (Chs. 7, 17)

Bond Interest Coverage Income before interest expense and income taxes divided by bond interest. Sometimes called *times interest earned.* (Ch. 20)

Bond Premium The excess of the issue price of a bond over its face value. Bond premium arises when the coupon interest rate of the bond is greater than the market rate for that type of bond. (Chs. 7, 17)

Bond Sinking Fund A fund accumulated through required periodic contributions (and investment income thereon) to be used for the retirement of a specific bond issue. (Ch. 17)

Book Value per Share The dollar amount of net assets represented by one share of stock; computed by dividing the amount of stockholders' equity associated with a class of stock by the outstanding number of shares of that class of stock. (Ch. 15)

Branch Accounting The procedures for maintaining the financial records of various outlets of a single firm and coordinating the data with the home office records. (App. B)

Break-even Point That level of business volume at which total revenue equals total costs. (Ch. 24)

Budgeting A process of formal financial planning. (Ch. 26)

Byproducts Those products having relatively little sales value compared with other products derived from a process. An example would be the wood shavings generated in a shaping department of a furniture factory. (Ch. 23)

Calendar Year Firms are said to be on a calendar year when their accounting year ends on December 31. (Ch. 3)

Capital Budgeting Planning long-term investments in plant and equipment. (Ch. 27)

Capital Expenditure An expenditure that increases the book value of long-term assets. (Ch. 10)

Capital Gains and Losses Gains and losses from the sale or exchange of certain assets qualifying as "capital assets." Specific tax treatment of capital gains and losses depends on the length of time for which the assets are held (short term for one year or less, long term otherwise) and the net result of combining long- and short-term gains and losses. (Ch. 28)

Capital Lease A lease that transfers to the lessee substantially all of the benefits and risks related to ownership of the property. The lessee records the leased property as an asset and establishes a liability for the lease obligation. (Ch. 11)

Capital Ratios The quantitative relationship among the balances of partners' capital accounts. This factor is often reflected in the distribution of partnership profits and may be calculated using either beginning or average balances. (Ch. 14)

Capitalization of Interest A process adding interest to an asset's initial cost if a period of time is required to prepare the asset for use. (Ch. 10)

Cash Basis The accounting basis in which revenue is recognized only when money is received and expenses are recognized when money is paid. (Chs. 1, 19)

Cash Discount An amount—often 1 or 2% of the purchase price—that a buyer may deduct for paying within the discount period. (Ch. 5)

Cash Flow See After-tax Cash Flow.

Cash Flow Statement Also called Statement of Changes in Finan-

cial Position—Cash Basis. A statement of changes in financial position that shows the sources and uses of cash rather than working capital. (Ch. 19)

Cash Over and Short An account which contains the amounts by which actual daily cash collections differ from the amounts recorded as being collected. (Ch. 7)

Cash Payback Period A method of capital outlay analysis that considers the time in years that it will take the related net future cash inflows to equal the original investment. (Ch. 27)

Certificate of Deposit An investment security available at financial institutions generally offering a fixed rate of return for a specified period. (Ch. 7)

Chart of Accounts A list of all the account titles and numbers found in the general ledger. (Ch. 3)

Check Register A special journal used in place of a cash disbursements journal when the voucher system of controlling expenditures is used; a record of all checks written in payment of vouchers. (Ch. 6)

Check Truncation Canceled checks are not returned by a bank to its depositors when monthly bank statements are mailed. (Ch. 7)

Closing Procedures The final step in the accounting cycle in which the balances in all temporary accounts are transferred to the owner's capital or the Retained Earnings account, leaving the temporary accounts with zero balances. (Chs. 4, 5, 21)

Collection Bases Those procedures in which revenue recognition is delayed until related amounts of cash are collected. The cost recovery method and the installment method are examples. (Ch. 13)

Common-size Statements A form of financial statement analysis in which only the relative percentages of financial statement items, rather than their dollar amounts, are shown. (Ch. 20)

Common Stock Basic ownership class of corporate capital stock, carrying the right to vote, share in earnings, participate in future stock issues, and share in any liquidation proceeds after prior claims have been settled. (Ch. 15)

Comparative Financial Statements A form of horizontal financial analysis involving comparison of two or more periods' statements showing dollar and percentage changes. (Ch. 20)

Complex Capital Structure A corporate capital structure containing one or more potentially dilutive securities. Complex capital structures normally require a dual earnings per share presentation. (Ch. 16)

Compound Journal Entry An entry containing more than one debit and/or credit entry. (Ch. 3)

Conceptual Framework A cohesive set of interrelated objectives and fundamentals for external financial reporting being developed by the FASB. (Ch. 13)

Conservatism An accounting principle dictating that judgmental determinations in accounting should tend toward understatement rather than overstatement of assets and income. (Ch. 13)

Consistency An accounting principle dictating that, unless otherwise disclosed, accounting reports should be prepared on a basis consistent with the preceding period. (Ch. 13)

Consolidated Statements Financial statements prepared with intercompany (reciprocal) accounts eliminated to portray the financial position and operating results of two or more affiliated companies as a single economic entity. (Ch. 18).

Consolidation   A union of firms such that the existing firms exchange their properties for the securities of a new firm and the old firms dissolve. (Ch. 18)

Constant Dollar Accounting   An accounting process that adjusts conventional financial data for changes in the general purchasing power of the dollar. (Ch. 13)

Consumer Price Index   A price-level index of consumer goods and services published monthly by the Bureau of Labor Statistics of the Department of Labor. (Ch. 13)

Contingent Liability   A potential obligation, the eventual occurrence of which usually depends on some future event beyond the control of the firm. Contingent liabilities may originate with such things as lawsuits, credit guarantees, and contested income tax assessments. (Ch. 12)

Contribution Margin   The excess of revenue over variable costs; thus, the amount contributed toward the absorption of fixed cost and eventually the generation of profit. (Ch. 24)

Contribution Margin Ratio   That portion of the sales price that is contribution margin. (Ch. 24)

Control Account   A general ledger account, the balance of which reflects the aggregate balance of many related subsidiary accounts. Most firms maintain such records for credit customers and for creditors. (Ch. 6)

Controller   Usually the highest ranking accounting officer in a firm. (Ch. 1)

Convertible Bond   A bond incorporating the holder's right to convert the bond to capital stock under prescribed terms. (Ch. 17)

Corporation   A legal entity created by the granting of a charter from an appropriate governmental authority and owned by stockholders who have limited liability for corporate debt. (Ch. 15)

Cost Behavior Analysis   Study of the ways in which specific costs respond to changes in the volume of business activity. (Ch. 24)

Cost Center   Sometimes called an *expense center*. A division of a business with which specific costs can be identified. (Ch. 20)

Cost Method   A method of accounting by a parent company for investments in subsidiary companies in which the parent company maintains the investment in subsidiary account at its cost, not recognizing periodically its share of subsidiary income or loss. See *also* Equity Method. (Ch. 18)

Cost of Capital   See Weighted Average Cost of Capital.

Cost of Goods Manufactured   See Manufacturing Costs.

Costs of Goods Sold   The cost of merchandise sold to customers during the accounting period. It is calculated by adding the beginning inventory and net cost of purchases and deducting the ending inventory. (Ch. 5)

Cost of Production Report   A periodic summary of the costs associated with a processing cost center and the calculation of per unit costs for work in process and finished units transferred out. (Ch. 23)

CPA   Certified Public Accountant, a professional accountant who has passed the Uniform CPA Examination, satisfied other requirements regarding education, professional experience, and character, and been licensed to practice public accounting by a state, district, or territory. (Ch. 1)

Credit (Entry)   An entry on the right-hand side (or in the credit column) of any account. (Ch. 2)

Credit Memorandum   A form used by a seller to notify a customer of a reduction in the amount considered owed by the customer (Ch. 5)

Cumulative Preferred Stock   A type of preferred stock upon which any dividends in arrears must be paid before dividends can be paid on common stock. (Ch. 15)

Current Assets   Assets that will either be used up or converted to cash within the normal operating cycle of the business or one year, whichever is longer. (Ch. 5)

Current Cost Accounting   A system of accounting that reflects assets and expenses at their current replacement cost amounts. (Ch. 13)

Current Liabilities   Obligations that will require within the coming year or the operating cycle, whichever is longer, (1) the use of existing current assets or (2) the creation of other current liabilities. (Chs. 5, 12)

Current Ratio   Current assets divided by current liabilities. (Ch. 20)

Current Value   The market or economic value of some item at a point in time. (Ch. 13)

Debit (Entry)   An entry on the left-hand side (or in the debit column) of any account. (Ch. 2)

Declaration of Estimated Tax   Income tax procedures requiring taxpayers with minimum amounts of income not subject to income tax withholding to submit quarterly estimates and payments of related income taxes owed. (Ch. 28)

Deferred Tax Accounts   Accounts used in interperiod income tax allocation procedure, in which are recorded differences between the amounts of income taxes actually paid and amounts recognized in the accounts. Excess payments are Deferred Tax Charges; an excess of amounts recognized over taxes paid are Deferred Tax Credits. (Ch. 17)

Deficit A negative (or debit) balance in a corporation's Retained Earnings account. (Ch. 16)

Departmental Contribution The excess of departmental revenue over variable departmental expenses; contributed to the absorption of the firm's pool of fixed costs and expenses. (Ch. 25)

Depletion The allocation of the cost of natural resources to the units extracted from the ground or, in the case of timberland, the board feet of timber cut. (Ch. 11)

Depreciation The decline in economic potential of limited-life assets originating from wear, deterioration, and obsolescence. (Ch. 10)

Depreciation Expense That portion of the original utility and cost of a tangible constructed asset that is recognized as having expired and thus is an expense. (Chs. 3, 10)

Differential Analysis A concept of limiting consideration in a decision situation to only those factors that differ among alternatives. (Ch. 25)

Differential Costs Costs that differ between two courses of action. (Ch. 25)

Direct Expenses (Costs) Costs that can be readily identified with a particular department, product, or activity. (Ch. 25)

Direct Labor All labor of workers applying their skills directly to the manufacture of products. The labor of workers indirectly supporting the manufacturing process is accounted for as indirect labor, part of factory overhead. (Ch. 21)

Direct (or Raw) Materials All important raw materials or parts physically making up the product. Incidental amounts of materials are accounted for as indirect materials, part of factory overhead. (Ch. 21)

Direct Write-off Method An accounting procedure in which uncollectible accounts are charged to expense in the period they are determined to be uncollectible. (Ch. 8)

Discontinued Operations Operating segments of a company that have been sold, abandoned, or disposed of during the operating period. Related operating income (or loss) and related gains or losses on disposal are reported separately on the income statement. (Ch. 16)

Discount Period The number of days beyond the related sales invoice date during which payment entitles the buyer to deduct any cash discount offered (often 1 or 2%). (Ch. 5)

Discounts Lost An account reflecting the amount of cash discounts available but not taken. *See* Net Price Method of Recording Purchases. (Ch. 5)

Dividend A distribution to a corporation's stockholders usually in cash; sometimes in the corporation's stock (called a *stock dividend*); and much less frequently in property (called a *dividend in kind*). (Chs. 15, 16)

Dividend Payout Ratio Common stock dividends divided by common stock earnings. (Ch. 20)

Dividend Yield Common stock dividends per share divided by the market price per share. (Ch. 20)

Double Declining-balance Depreciation Method A depreciation method that allocates depreciation expense to each year in an accelerated pattern by applying a constant percentage to the declining book value of the asset. (Ch. 10)

Double-entry Accounting System A method of accounting that recognizes the duality of a transaction (source and dispo-

sition) such that any change in one account also causes a change in another account. For example, the receipt of cash would result in an increase in the Cash account but would also require the recognition of an increase in a liability, owners' equity, or revenue account or a decrease in an expense account or in some other asset account. (Ch. 2)

Earnings per Share Net income less any preferred dividend requirements divided by the number of common shares outstanding. (Chs. 16, 20)

Effective Interest Amortization A method of allocating bond premium or discount to various periods that results in a constant effective rate of interest and varying periodic amortization allocations. (Ch. 17, App. A)

Effective Tax Rate The amount of tax liability divided by related taxable income. (Ch. 28)

Electronic Data Processing (EDP) The processing of data utilizing computer hardware and software. (Ch. 6)

Electronic Funds Transfer (EFT) A system for transferring funds among parties electronically, without the need for paper checks. (Ch. 7)

Equity Method A method of accounting by parent companies for investments in subsidiaries in which the parent's share of subsidiary income or loss is periodically recorded in the parent company's accounts. *See also* Cost Method. (Ch. 18)

Equity Ratio Stockholders' equity divided by total assets. (Ch. 20)

Equivalent Units The smaller number of full measures of work accomplished that is the equivalent of a larger number of partially accomplished work units. For example, 1,000 units 60%

processed is equivalent to 600 units fully processed. (Ch. 23)

Excess Present Value Index Ratio of the total present value of net future cash flows to the related cash investment. (Ch. 27)

Expenses Expired costs incurred by a firm in the process of earning revenue. (Ch. 1)

Extraordinary Item A transaction or event that is unusual in nature and occurs infrequently. Gains and losses on such items are shown separately, net of tax effects, in the income statement. (Ch. 16)

Extraordinary Repair An expenditure that extends a plant asset's expected useful life beyond the original estimate. (Ch. 10)

Factory Overhead All manufacturing costs not considered direct materials or direct labor, including indirect materials, indirect labor, factory depreciation, taxes, and insurance. (Ch. 22)

Fair Labor Standards Act An act establishing minimum wage, overtime pay, and equal pay standards for employees and setting the necessary record-keeping requirements for employers. (Ch. 12)

FASB The Financial Accounting Standards Board of the American Institute of CPAs, a nongovernmental group organized in 1973 to replace the Accounting Principles Board and to promulgate authoritative rules for the general practice of financial accounting. (Ch. 1)

Federal Unemployment Taxes (FUTA) A federal tax levied against employers to help finance administration of the various unemployment compensation programs operated by the states. (Ch. 12)

FICA Federal Insurance Contributions Act, under which the income of an individual is taxed to support a national social security program providing retirement income, medical care, and death benefits. Employers pay a matching amount of tax on their eligible employees. (Ch. 12)

FIFO (First-in, First-out) Inventory Pricing A valuation method that assumes that the oldest (earliest purchased) goods on hand are sold first, resulting in an ending inventory priced at the most recent acquisition prices. (Ch. 9)

Financial Accounting Those accounting activities leading primarily to publishable, general-purpose financial statements such as the income statement, balance sheet, and statement of changes in financial position. (Ch. 1)

Finished Goods Inventory Units of product for which production has been completed. (Ch. 21)

Finished Goods Ledger A record of the amounts acquired, sold, and on hand, and the related costs of a specific finished product. In aggregate, finished goods ledger cards are a perpetual inventory record of finished goods and a subsidiary ledger for the Finished Goods Inventory account. (Ch. 22)

Fiscal Year Firms are said to be on a fiscal year when their accounting year ends on a date other than December 31. (Ch. 3)

Fixed Assets Sometimes called long-term assets, long-lived assets, or plant and equipment. May include land, buildings, fixtures, and equipment. (Ch. 10)

Fixed Costs Costs whose total remains constant within the relevant range even though the volume of activity may vary (Ch. 24)

Flexible Budget A financial plan formulated so that the assumed operating volume can be varied to agree with actual volume of activities attained. (Chs. 24, 26)

F.O.B. (Free on Board) Term used in conjunction with the terms factory, shipping point, or destination to indicate the point in the delivery of merchandise at which the purchaser bears freight costs. (Ch. 5)

Full Disclosure An accounting principle stipulating the disclosure of all facts necessary to make financial statements useful to readers. (Ch. 13)

Funds Defined most narrowly as cash; more widely considered the amount of working capital or current assets less current liabilities. (Ch. 19)

General Journal A record of original entry in which are recorded all transactions not recorded in the special journals maintained by the business. (Ch. 6)

General Ledger A grouping or binding of the accounts in which the activities of an entity are recorded. (Ch. 2)

Generally Accepted Accounting Principles A group of standards or guides to action in preparing financial accounting reports. Their content and usefulness have evolved over many decades. (Chs. 1, 13)

Going Concern An accounting principle dictating that, in the absence of evidence to the contrary, a business is assumed to have an indefinite life. (Chs. 1, 13)

Goodwill The value that derives from a firm's ability to earn more than a normal rate of return on its physical assets. Goodwill is recognized in the accounts only when it is acquired through specific purchase and payment (as opposed to gradual development). (Ch. 11)

Governmental Accounting A subdivision of accounting practice relating primarily to accounting for federal, state, or local governmental units. (Ch. 1)

Gross Profit The excess of sales price over the net delivered cost of the product sold (sometimes called gross margin). (Ch. 5)

Gross Profit Inventory Method A procedure for estimating the cost of ending inventories by multiplying the representative cost of goods sold percentage times sales and deducting that amount from goods available for sale. (Ch. 9)

Hardware A term that describes the computer and its associated equipment. (Ch. 6)

Historical Cost The money equivalent of the object given up (and/or obligations assumed) in an exchange transaction. (Chs. 1, 13)

Holding Gain or Loss An increase (gain) or decrease (loss) in the current cost of an asset while it is held. (Ch. 13)

Horizontal Analysis See Trend Analysis.

Income Averaging A tax regulation provision allowing taxpayers having relatively large amounts of taxable income in one year to, in effect, average that income over several years to reduce the progressive effects of the tax rates. (Ch. 28)

Income Statement A financial report showing the results of an entity's operations in terms of revenue, expenses, and net income for a period of time. (Chs. 1, 16)

Income Summary Account An account used only during clos-ing procedures and to which all temporary revenue and expense accounts are closed. At this point, the balance in the Income Summary account summarizes the firm's net income for the period. In turn, the Income Summary account is closed to the owner's capital or the Retained Earnings account. (Ch. 4)

Incremental Cost See Differential Costs.

Indirect Expenses (Costs) Costs (expenses) that are not readily identified with products or activities; usually allocated by some arbitrary formula to various products and activities. (Ch. 25)

Individual Earnings Record A detailed record maintained by an employer for each employee showing gross earnings, overtime premiums, all withholdings, payroll tax data, and net earnings paid, by calendar quarter. (Ch. 12)

Information System The coordinated efforts to record, organize, and present analyses and reports related to specific areas of activity and concern. (Ch. 1)

Installment Accounts The accounts receivable or payable for which payments or collections are routinely scheduled over extended periods, such as 24 or 36 months. (Ch. 8)

Intangible Assets A term applied by convention to a group of long-term assets that generally do not have physical existence, including patents, copyrights, franchises, trademarks, and goodwill. (Ch. 11)

Interactive Processing A type of processing in which master file information in an electronic data-processing system is available at random, and transactions may be processed in any order. (Ch. 6)

Interim Financial Statements Financial statements prepared at dates other than the firm's accounting year-end. Most monthly and quarterly financial statements are interim statements. (Ch 4)

Internal Auditing A continuing appraisal of a firm's operations accomplished by the firm's own internal audit staff to determine whether management's financial and operating policies are being properly implemented. (Chs. 1, 7)

Internal Control A plan of organization and all of the coordinate methods and measures adopted within a business to safeguard its assets, check the accuracy and reliability of its accounting data, promote operating efficiency, and encourage adherence to prescribed managerial policies. (Ch. 7)

Internal Revenue Code The codification of numerous revenue acts passed by Congress since 1913. Interpretation and application of the Code is supplemented by extensive Internal Revenue Code Regulations. (Ch. 28)

Interperiod Income Tax Allocation Apportionment of income tax expense to the income statement over the periods affected by timing differences between the recognition of revenue and expense on accounting statements and on related income tax returns. (Ch. 17)

Inventory Turnover Cost of goods sold divided by average inventory. (Ch. 20)

Investment Credit An income tax provision allowing taxpayers to deduct from what would otherwise be their tax liability in the year of acquisition certain portions of the cost of newly acquired assets. (Chs. 10, 28)

Investments A category on the balance sheet where assets consisting of securities of other companies, sinking funds, and other long-term holdings are reported. Temporary investments in marketable securities are properly shown as current assets. (Chs. 17, 18)

Invoice A document used in business transactions that sets forth the precise terms regarding date, customer, vendor, quantities, prices, and freight and credit terms of a transaction. (Ch. 5)

Invoice Register A special journal, sometimes called a purchases journal, in which all acquisitions on account are chronologically recorded. (Ch. 6)

IRS The Internal Revenue Service of the federal government, primarily responsible for applying the current tax codes and regulations and collecting income taxes for the federal government. (Ch. 28)

Job Cost Sheets A record of the specific manufacturing costs applied to a given job. When fully recorded, job cost sheets are a subsidiary ledger to the Work in Process Inventory account. (Ch. 22)

Job Order Cost Accounting A method of cost accounting—sometimes called job lot or specific order costing—in which manufacturing costs are assigned to specific jobs or batches of specialized products. (Ch. 22)

Joint Costs Costs common to two or more products or activities. (Ch. 23)

Joint Products Two or more products having significant value and derived from common inputs such as materials or processing. (Ch. 23)

Journals Tabular records in which business transactions are analyzed in terms of debits and credits and recorded in chronological order before being posted to the general ledger accounts. (Ch. 3)

Lease A contract between a lessor (owner) and lessee (tenant) for the rental of property. (Ch. 11)

Leasehold Improvements Expenditures made by the lessee to alter or improve leased property. Such improvements typically revert to the lessor on termination of the lease. (Ch. 11)

Liabilities Present obligations resulting from past transactions that require the firm to pay money, provide goods, or perform services in the future. (Ch. 12)

LIFO (Last-in, First-out) Inventory Pricing A valuation method that assumes that the most recently purchased goods are sold first, resulting in an ending inventory priced at the earliest related acquisition prices. (Ch. 9)

Long-term Assets Relatively long-lived assets employed in operating the firm. Some examples are land, buildings, equipment, natural resources, and intangible assets. (Chs. 5, 10, 11)

Long-term Liabilities Debt obligations of the firm not due within the firm's current operating cycle or one year, whichever is longer. Examples are mortgage notes payable and bonds payable. (Chs. 5, 17)

Lower of Cost or Market Rule An accounting procedure providing for inventories to be carried at their acquisition price or their replacement price at the balance sheet date, whichever is lower. A similar rule applies to stock investment portfolios. (Chs. 7, 9, 18)

Managerial Accounting The accounting procedures carried out by an organization's accounting staff primarily to furnish its management with accounting analyses and reports needed for decision making. (Chs. 1, 25)

Manufacturing Costs Those costs—comprising raw materials, direct labor, and factory overhead—necessary to bring the product to completion. Selling and nonfactory administrative costs are specifically excluded. (Ch. 21)

Manufacturing Margin The excess of revenue over variable manufacturing costs; an amount often presented on variable costing income statements. (Ch. 25)

Manufacturing Summary Account An account (used only during closing procedures) to which all temporary manufacturing costs and expenses are closed, resulting in a balance equal to the cost of goods manufactured. In turn, the Manufacturing Summary account is closed to the Income Summary account. (Ch. 21)

Marginal Cost The cost associated with completing one more unit of production or activity. (Ch. 25)

Marginal Tax Rate The tax rate applicable to additional increments of taxable income, especially relevant to considering the after-tax consequence of proposed transactions. (Ch. 28)

Mark-up Percentage The amount of gross profit expressed as a percentage of sales. (Ch. 5)

Master Budget A comprehensive plan comprising all operating budgets related to sales, production, operating expenses, and finance. May include pro forma financial statements for the budgeting period. (Ch. 26)

Matching Expenses with Revenue An accounting principle requiring that, to the extent feasible, all expenses related to given revenue be deducted from that revenue for the determination of periodic income. (Ch. 13)

Materiality The concept that

accounting transactions so small or insignificant that they do not affect one's actions may be recorded as is most expedient. (Ch. 13)

Measuring Unit The unit of measure in an accounting transaction, typically the base money unit of the most relevant currency. (Chs. 1, 13)

Merchandise Inventory An asset account in which is recorded the purchase price of merchandise held for resale. Sometimes simply termed *inventory*. (Ch. 5)

Merchandising The business activity of buying and selling goods already made, in contrast to a manufacturer or a service-oriented business. (Ch. 5)

Merger A union of firms in which one company acquires the assets of another and the latter company dissolves. (Ch. 18)

Minority Interest That portion of capital stock in a subsidiary corporation not owned by the controlling (parent) company. (Ch. 18)

Monetary Assets Cash and other assets that represent the right to receive a fixed number of dollars in the future, regardless of price-level changes. (Ch. 13)

Monetary Liabilities Obligations to disburse a fixed number of dollars in the future, regardless of price-level changes. (Ch. 13)

Moving Average Inventory Pricing A pricing method under a perpetual inventory system that recomputes an average unit cost of goods on hand each time a purchase occurs and uses that average unit cost to determine the cost of goods sold for each sale. (Ch. 9)

Multiple-step Income Statement An income statement in which one or more intermediate amounts (such as gross profit on sales) are derived before the ordinary, continuing income is reported. (Ch. 16)

Natural Resources Assets such as timber, petroleum, natural gas, coal, and other mineral deposits mined by the extractive industries. (Ch. 11)

Net Assets Total assets less total liabilities. Net assets are equal to owners' equity. (Ch. 1)

Net Income The excess of revenue earned over related expenses incurred, usually the final figure on the income statement. (Ch. 1)

Net Present Value Analysis A method of capital outlay analysis that compares a required investment amount with the present value of resulting net future cash flows discounted at the minimum desired rate of return. (Ch. 27)

Net Price Method of Recording Purchases An accounting procedure whereby purchases are recorded at amounts that anticipate the taking of any cash discounts available. When discounts are not taken, the amounts paid in excess of the recorded purchase price are charged to a Discounts Lost account. (Ch. 5)

Net Realizable Value An asset measure computed by subtracting the expected completion and disposal costs from the asset's estimated selling price. (Ch. 9)

Normal Balance The debit or credit balance of an account corresponding to the side of the account on which increases are recorded (debits for assets and expenses; credits for liabilities, owners' equity, and revenue). (Ch. 2)

Objectivity An accounting principle requiring that, whenever possible, accounting entries be based on objective (verifiable) evidence. (Chs. 1, 13)

Opportunity Cost Measurable sacrifices associated with forgoing some alternative. (Ch. 25)

Organization Costs Expenditures incurred in launching a business (usually a corporation); may include attorney's fees, various registration fees paid to state governments, and other start-up costs. (Ch. 11)

Out-of-Pocket Costs Costs requiring expenditures in the current period. (Ch. 25)

Overapplied Overhead The excess of overhead applied to production over the amount of overhead incurred. Such amounts are shown on interim balance sheets as deferred credits but are closed to cost of goods sold on year-end financial statements. (Ch 22)

Overhead Rate The amount of overhead costs for some period divided by the amount of some measure of production activity such as direct labor hours. May be calculated on an actual cost incurred basis or on an estimated or predetermined basis. (Ch. 22)

Owners' Equity The interest or claim of an entity's owners in the entity's assets; equal to the excess of assets over liabilities. (Ch. 1)

Parent Company A company holding all or a majority of the stock of another company, which is called a subsidiary. (Ch. 18)

Partnership A voluntary association of two or more persons for the purpose of conducting a business for a profit. (Ch. 14)

Par Value An amount specified in the corporate charter for each share of stock and imprinted on the face of each stock certificate. Usually determines the legal capital of the corporation. (Ch. 15)

Payroll Register A detailed list, prepared each pay period, showing each employee's earnings and deductions for the period. (Ch. 12)

Percentage Depletion A depletion deduction permitted for tax purposes that is a specified percentage of the gross revenue from mining activities, with certain limitations. (Ch. 11)

Percentage of Completion A method of revenue recognition that allocates the estimated gross profit on a long-term project among the several accounting periods involved, in proportion to the estimated percentage of the contract completed each period. (Ch. 13)

Performance Reports Documents portraying, for a given operating unit, planned amounts of cost, actual costs incurred, and any related variances. (Ch. 26)

Period Costs (Expenses) Costs (expenses) associated with the period in which they are incurred (rather than with the product being produced). (Ch. 21)

Periodic Inventory Method A method of accounting for inventories in which no record is made in the Inventory account for the purchase or sale of merchandise at the time of such transactions. (Chs. 5, 9)

Perpetual Inventory Method A method of accounting for inventories in which both purchases and sales of merchandise are reflected in the Inventory account at the time such transactions occur. (Ch. 9)

Personal Exemptions A prescribed amount that a taxpayer may deduct for himself or herself and each qualified dependent in computing taxable income. Additional exemptions are allowed for taxpayers who are 65 years of age or older and/or blind. (Ch. 28)

Petty Cash Fund A special, relatively small cash fund established for making minor cash disbursements in the operation of a business. (Ch. 7)

Plant Assets A firm's property, plant, and equipment. (Ch. 10)

Plant (or Equipment) Ledger A subsidiary ledger for long-lived assets, containing detailed data for each material asset, including description, acquisition date, location, cost, depreciation, and disposition. (Ch. 11)

Pooling of Interests Uniting the ownership interests of two or more companies through the exchange of 90% or more of the firms' voting stocks. (Ch. 18)

Post-closing Trial Balance A list of account titles and their balances after closing entries have been recorded and posted; all temporary accounts should have zero balances. (Ch. 4)

Posting The formal transcribing of amounts from the journals to the ledger(s) used in an accounting system. (Ch. 3)

Posting References A series of abbreviations used in the posting step of the accounting cycle that indicate to where or from where some entry is posted; account numbers and one- or two-letter abbreviations of journal titles are typically used. (Ch. 3)

Predetermined Overhead Rates Estimated overhead rates determined in advance for applying overhead to production during an operating period (usually one year). The rate is calculated by dividing total estimated overhead costs by the estimated amount of the activity (such as direct labor hours) used to assign factory overhead. *See also* Factory Overhead. (Ch. 22)

Preemptive Right The right of a stockholder to maintain his or her proportionate ownership in a corporation by having the right to purchase an appropriate share of any new stock issue. (Ch. 15)

Preferred Dividend Coverage Operating income divided by the sum of the annual bond interest and preferred dividend requirements. (Ch. 20)

Preferred Stock A class of corporate capital stock typically receiving priority over common stock in dividend payments and distribution of assets should the corporation be liquidated. (Ch. 15)

Present Value The estimated current worth of amounts to be received (or paid) in the future from which appropriate amounts of discount (or interest) have been deducted. (Ch. 17, App. A, Ch. 27)

Present Value Factors Sometimes called discount factors. Multipliers found in present value tables formulated to show the present value of $1 (or a $1 annuity) discounted at various interest rates and for various periods. (Ch. 17, App. A, Ch. 27, App. D)

Price–Earnings Ratio The market price of a share of stock divided by the related earnings per share. (Ch. 20).

Price Index A series of measurements, stated as percentages, indicating the relationship between the weighted average price of a sample of goods and services at various points in time and the weighted average price of a similar sample of goods and services at a common, or base, date. (Ch. 13)

Process Cost Accounting A method of assigning costs to relatively homogeneous products in an often continuous, high-volume operation. (Ch. 23)

Product Costs The costs properly associated with the product being produced (as opposed to the period in which the costs are incurred). Product costs are period costs (expenses) when the related products are sold. (Ch. 21)

Production Report A report (usually for a department)

showing the beginning inventory of units, units started, units finished and transferred out, and any ending inventory of units. (Ch. 23)

Productivity Ratio *See* Return on Assets.

Promissory Note A written promise to pay a certain sum of money on demand or at a determinable future time (Ch. 8)

Proprietorship A form of business organization in which one person owns the business; sometimes termed *sole proprietorship*. (Ch. 1)

Purchase Method A procedure that treats a business combination from the viewpoint of the acquiring company as a purchase transaction. (Ch. 18)

Purchase Order A document completed by the purchasing firm setting forth the quantities, descriptions, prices, and vendors for merchandise to be purchased. (Ch. 5)

Purchase Requisition A form used within a firm to initiate the procedures leading to the purchase of needed items. (Ch. 5)

Purchases The title of the account in which is recorded the acquisition price of merchandise held for resale by companies using the periodic inventory method. (Ch. 5)

Purchasing Power Gain or Loss on Monetary Items The gain or loss in general purchasing power that results from holding monetary assets or owing monetary liabilities during periods of inflation or deflation. (Ch. 13)

Quick Ratio The total of cash, marketable securities, and receivables divided by current liabilities. (Ch. 20)

Raw Materials A manufacturing cost consisting of all important

raw materials or parts physically making up the product. Incidental amounts of materials are accounted for as factory supplies, part of factory overhead. (Ch. 21)

Raw Materials Inventory All factory materials acquired but not yet placed in production. (Ch. 21)

Realized Holding Gain or Loss A holding gain or loss that relates to an asset that has been sold or used in operations. (Ch. 13)

Real Time Processing Updating computer records when the transactions occur. (Ch. 6)

Receivable An amount due from a customer, employee, or other party; usually further described as an account receivable or note receivable and representing an asset of the business. (Ch. 8)

Receiving Report A document used within a firm to record formally the quantities and descriptions of merchandise received. (Ch. 5)

Records of Original Entry Usually the various journals incorporated in the firm's accounting system. *See also* Journals. (Ch. 3)

Relevant Range The range of changes in the volume of activity within which the assumptions made regarding cost behavior patterns are valid. (Ch. 24)

Research and Development Costs Expenditures made in the search for new knowledge and in the translation of this knowledge into new or significantly improved products or processes. (Ch. 11)

Retail Inventory Estimation Method A procedure for estimating ending inventories by (1) maintaining detailed records of all goods acquired and on hand at both retail and cost prices (and any changes in these), (2) calculating a cost-to-retail percentage, (3) estimating ending

inventory at retail prices by subtracting sales from the retail price of merchandise available for sale, and (4) reducing the estimated inventory at retail to cost by applying the cost-to-retail percentage. (Ch. 9)

Retained Earnings Statement A statement showing the changes in retained earnings for the accounting period, including net income or loss, dividends declared, appropriations, and corrections of any errors in financial statements of prior periods. (Ch. 16)

Return on Assets Operating income divided by average total assets. (Ch. 20)

Return on Sales Net income divided by net sales. (Ch. 20)

Return on Stockholders' Equity Net income less preferred dividends divided by average common stockholders' equity. (Ch. 20)

Revenue The amount of cash received or claims established against customers stemming from the provision of goods or services by the firm. (Ch. 1)

Revenue Expenditure An expenditure related to plant assets that is expensed when incurred. (Ch. 10)

Revenue Recognition at Point of Sale An accounting principle requiring that, with few exceptions, revenue be recognized at the point of sale. (Ch. 1)

Reversing Entries A bookkeeping technique whereby adjusting entries involving subsequent receipts or payments are literally reversed on the first day of the following accounting period. This procedure permits the routine recording of subsequent related receipts and payments without having to recognize the portions that were accrued at an earlier date. (Ch. 4)

Running Balance Account An account form having columns for debit entries, credit entries, and for the account balance. Sometimes called the *three-column account form.* (Ch. 2)

Sales The title of the account in which revenue from the sale of goods held for resale is recorded for merchandising and manufacturing companies. (Ch. 5)

Sales Returns and Allowances A contra account to Sales in which is recorded the selling price of merchandise returned by customers and/or the amounts of sales price adjustments allowed customers. (Ch. 5)

S Corporations Corporations that qualify for income tax treatment as partnerships. (Ch. 28)

SEC Securities and Exchange Commission, the federal agency that regulates the sale and exchange of most securities. (Ch. 1)

Semivariable Costs Those costs, sometimes called *mixed costs,* whose total responds, but less than proportionately, to changes in the volume of activity. (Ch. 24)

Service Departments Departments or cost centers that provide special support activities to various production departments. Examples are purchasing, personnel, and maintenance departments. (Ch. 23)

Single-step Income Statement An income statement in which the ordinary, continuing income of the business is derived in one step by subtracting total expenses from total revenue. (Ch. 16)

Sinking Fund Cash and other assets accumulated and segregated for some specific purpose such as retiring debt. (Ch. 17)

Software A term that describes the programs, written procedures, and other documenta-

tion associated with use of computers. (Chs. 6, 11)

Source Document Any written document evidencing an accounting transaction, such as a bank check or deposit slip, sales invoice, or cash register tape. (Ch. 3)

Special Journals The records of original entry other than the general journal that are designed for recording specific types of transactions such as cash receipts, sales, purchases, and cash disbursements. (Ch. 6)

Specific Identification Inventory Pricing A method involving the physical identification of goods actually sold and goods remaining on hand and pricing the latter at the actual prices paid for them. (Ch. 9)

Standard Costs Those costs, usually expressed on a per-unit basis, that under ideal operating conditions should be incurred for raw materials, direct labor, and factory overhead. (Ch. 26)

State Unemployment Tax A payroll tax levied on employers by states to finance state unemployment compensation programs. (Ch. 12)

Stated Value A nominal amount that may be assigned to each share of no-par stock and accounted for much as if it were par value. (Ch. 15)

Statement of Changes in Financial Position A statement showing the resources provided and resources applied and thus explaining the change in funds during a specific period for the firm. (Ch. 19)

Statement of Financial Position An alternate title for a balance sheet, a financial statement showing an entity's financial position in terms of assets, liabilities, and owners' equity at a specific date. (Ch. 1)

Statement of Owners' Equity A financial statement reflecting the beginning balance, additions to,

deductions from, and the ending balance of owners' equity for a specified period. (Ch. 1)

Statement of Partnership Liquidation A statement summarizing the liquidation events of a partnership and the effect these events have on each partner's capital. (Ch. 14)

Stock Dividends Additional shares of its own stock issued by a corporation to its current stockholders in proportion to their ownership interests. (Ch. 16)

Stock Split Additional shares of its own stock issued by a corporation to its current stockholders in proportion to their current ownership interests without changing the balances in the related stockholders' equity accounts. A stock split increases the number of shares outstanding and reduces the per-share market value of the stock. (Ch. 16)

Stock Subscriptions Contracts for acquiring stock on a deferred payment plan, often used when shares are sold directly rather than through an investment banker. (Ch. 15)

Straight-line Depreciation Method Allocates uniform amounts of depreciation expense to each full period of an asset's useful life. (Ch. 10)

Subsidiary Company See Parent Company.

Subsidiary Ledger A group of accounts, not part of the general ledger, that explain or reflect the detail (such as individual customer balances) underlying the balance in a related control account (such as Accounts Receivable) in the general ledger. (Ch. 6)

Sum-of-the-Years'-Digits Depreciation Method An accelerated depreciation method that allocates depreciation expense to each year in a fractional proportion, the denominator of which is the sum of the years' digits in the useful life of the asset. (Ch. 10)

Sunk Costs Past costs that cannot be recovered. (Ch. 25)

T Account An abbreviated form of the formal account; use is usually limited to illustrations of accounting techniques. (Ch. 2)

Tax Allocation within a Period The apportionment of total income taxes among the various sources of income or loss shown on an income statement. (Ch. 16)

Tax Avoidance Arranging business affairs to minimize the impact of income taxes; in contrast to tax evasion, tax avoidance is legal and considered an aspect of sound management. (Ch. 28)

Tax Credit (or Income Tax Credit) An amount that may be deducted directly from what would otherwise be the tax liability disregarding the tax credit. (Ch. 28)

Tax Evasion A deliberate misstatement of factors determining taxable income. Tax evasion is illegal and subjects the taxpayer to legal prosecution. See also Tax Avoidance. (Ch. 28)

Tax Shelter An investment that by its nature or by qualifying for special tax treatment creates either tax-exempt income or anticipated deductible tax losses (which shelter other income from income taxation). (Ch. 28)

Taxable Income Gross income less deductions from gross income, excess itemized deductions, and personal exemptions. (Ch. 28)

Time Value of Money An expression of the ability of money to earn interest, the total potential for which is a function of the principal amount, the applicable interest rate, and the time period involved. (Ch. 17, App. A, Ch. 27)

Timing Difference A revenue or expense amount that is recognized in one accounting period for tax purposes and in a different accounting period for financial reporting purposes. (Ch. 17)

Trade Discounts The differences between suggested retail prices and the prices at which wholesale purchasers are able to buy merchandise. (Ch. 5)

Trade Receivables and Payables Assets and liabilities arising from the ordinary open account transactions between a business and its regular trade customers or suppliers. (Ch. 8)

Trading on the Equity The use of borrowed funds to generate a return in excess of the interest rate that must be paid for the funds. (Ch. 20)

Transaction Any event or activity of the firm leading to entries in two or more accounts. (Ch. 1)

Transporation In An account for recording the freight charges on merchandise purchased and held for resale. (Ch 5)

Transportation Out An account for recording the freight charges incurred in the delivery of merchandise sold to customers. (Ch. 5)

Treasury Stock Shares of outstanding stock that have been reacquired by the issuing corporation for purposes other than retiring the stock. Treasury stock is recorded at cost and the account is shown on the balance sheet as a deduction from total stockholders' equity. (Ch. 15)

Trend Analysis An approach to financial statement analysis involving comparison of the same item over two or more years. Often trend percentages are calculated by choosing a base year and stating the amounts of subsequent years as percentages of that base year. (Ch. 20)

Trial Balance A list of the account titles in the general ledger, their respective debit or credit balances, and the totals of all accounts having debit balances and all accounts having credit balances. (Ch. 2)

Unadjusted Trial Balance A trial balance of the general ledger accounts taken before the adjusting step of the accounting cycle. (Ch. 4)

Uncollectible Accounts Expense The expense stemming from the inability of a business to collect an amount previously recorded as a receivable. Sometimes called bad debts expense. Normally classified as a selling or administrative expense. (Ch. 8)

Underapplied Overhead The excess of actual overhead costs incurred over the amounts applied to production. On interim balance sheets such amounts appear as deferred charges but are closed to cost of goods sold on year-end statements. (Ch. 22)

Units-of-Production Depreciation Method A depreciation method that allocates depreciation expense to each operating period in proportion to the amount of the asset's expected total production capacity used each period. (Ch. 10)

Variable Costing A product costing method in which only variable manufacturing costs are associated with the product; fixed manufacturing costs are treated as period costs in the period incurred. (Ch. 25)

Variable Costs Those costs the total of which responds proportionately to changes in volume of activity. (Ch. 25)

Variances Favorable or unfavorable differences between standard costs and actual costs. Variances are usually isolated for price and usage factors for raw materials and rate and efficiency factors for direct labor. For factory overhead, variances may be isolated for factors related to spending, efficiency, and volume. (Ch. 26, App. C)

Vertical Analysis An approach to financial statement analysis highlighting the quantitative relationship between amounts in the same financial statement. (Ch. 20)

Voucher Register A special journal or record of original entry (in lieu of a purchases journal) for recording in numerical order all vouchers supporting the disbursement of funds. (Ch. 6)

Voucher System A system for controlling expenditures re-quiring the preparation and approval of individual vouchers for each contemplated expenditure. (Ch. 6)

Weighted Average Cost of Capital Expressed as a percentage, the cost to the firm of acquiring investment capital, weighted to reflect the specific cost rates associated with and proportions used from specific sources such as equity securities, debt, and internally generated funds. (Ch. 27)

Weighted Average Inventory Pricing A method that spreads the total dollar cost of all goods available for sale equally among all units. (Ch. 9)

Withdrawals (Owners') The amounts that proprietors or partners withdraw, usually in cash and for personal objectives, from the assets of the firm. (Chs. 1, 14)

Working Capital The excess of current assets over current liabilities. (Chs. 1, 19)

Work-in-Process Inventory All units of product that are in the process of being manufactured. (Ch. 21)

Worksheet An informal accounting document used to facilitate the preparation of financial statements. (Chs. 4, 5, 19, 21)

Yield See Dividend Yield.

Zero Bracket Amount A standard deduction for certain expenses incorporated into individual income tax rate tables and schedules. (Ch. 28)

INDEX